LANDS OF HOPE AND PROMISE

A History of North America

"I will give you as a light to the nations,
that my salvation may reach to the end of the earth."
—Isaiah: 49:6

LANDS OF HOPE AND PROMISE

A History of North America

General Editor and Author
Christopher Zehnder

President and Founder, CTP
Michael J. Van Hecke

Produced and developed by:
Catholic Textbook Project

Editing: Patricia Buckley Bozell

Design and Production: Hespenheide Design, Gary Hespenheide, and Randy Miyake

Acknowledgments:

Rollin A. Lasseter, Ph.D: contributor, editing and research

Ruth D. Lasseter: contributor

Clotilde M. Zehnder: "Highways and Byways"

James Burton Russell, Ph.D: manuscript review

©2018 Catholic Textbook Project
www.catholictextbookproject.com
All rights reserved
ISBN 978-1-935644-36-1
Printed in the United States
1 2 3 4 5 6 7 8 9 10 11

Cover Image

Cortez Landing © The Granger Collection New York; Francisco 'Pancho' Villa © The Granger Collection New York; Casablanca Conference © The Granger Collection New York; World War II: Pearl Harbor © The Granger Collection New York; New York Breadline, c1930 © The Granger Collection New York; Battle of Trenton, 1776 © The Granger Collection New York

Photo Credits

(t) top; (tl) top left; (tr) top right; (m) middle; (b) bottom; (bl) bottom left; (br) bottom right; Public Domain (Wikipedia—CC-BY-3.0)

p. 1 © Duarte Galvão/Public Domain; **p. 2** © Sebastiano del Piombo/Public Domain; **p. 3** © Everett Historical/Shutterstock; **p. 4** © Everett Historical/Shutterstock; **p. 5** © SreeBot/Public Domain; **p. 7** © Elena Korn/Shutterstock; **p. 9** © Danielho/iStockphoto; **p. 10** © Everett Historical/Shutterstock; **p. 11** © jorisvo/Shutterstock; **p. 11** © Irafael/Shutterstock; **p. 12** © Grigory Kubatyan/Shutterstock; **p. 13** © Morphart Creation/Shutterstock; **p. 17** © Vladislav Gurfinkel/Shutterstock; **p. 21** © Nagel Photography/Shutterstock; **p. 22** © Alfonso de Tomas/Shutterstock; **p. 25** © Everett Historical/Shutterstock; **p. 27** (t) © Everett Historical/Shutterstock; **p. 27** (b) © Álvaro Huerga/Public Domain; **p. 28** © goldhafen/iStockphoto; **p. 29** © Vadim Petrokov/Shutterstock; **p. 31** (t) © Boran Bogicevic/Shutterstock; **p. 31** (b) © Alejandro Linares Garcia/Public Domain; **p. 33** © Rolf Boskvar/Shutterstock; **p. 34** © Museo del Prado, Madrid /Public Domain; **p. 39** © Marzolino/Shutterstock; **p. 40** © Titian/Public Domain; **p. 41** © Samuel de Champlain/Public Domain; **p. 44** © U.S. National Archives and Records Administration/Public Domain; **p. 45** © Nancy Bauer/Shutterstock; **p. 47** © Everett Historical/Shutterstock; **p. 49** © Pierdelune/Shutterstock; **p. 53** © Fulcanelli/Shutterstock; **p. 54** © Everett Historical/Shutterstock; **p. 56** © Jodocus Hondius/Public Domain; **p. 57** (t) © Everett Historical/Shutterstock; (b) © Georgios Kollidas/Shutterstock; **p. 61** © Everett Historical/Shutterstock; **p. 62** (t) Everett Historical/Shutterstock; (b) © Everett Historical/Shutterstock; **p. 64** Everett Historical/Shutterstock; **p. 65** © Marzolino/Shutterstock; **p. 66** © Everett Historical/Shutterstock; **p. 67** © Jean Leon Gerome/Public Domain; **p. 71** © Public Domain; **p. 72** © Public Domain; **p. 73** © Andreas Juergensmeier/Shutterstock; **p. 74** © Steven Wright/Shutterstock; **p. 75** © Marzolino/Shutterstock; **p. 76** © Everett Historical/Shutterstock; **p. 77** © Captayne Underhill and Captayne Mason/Public Domain; **p. 79** © Everett Historical/Shutterstock; **p. 81** © Public Domain; **p. 83** (t) © Everett Historical/Shutterstock; (b) © Steven Wright/Shutterstock; **p. 86** © Public Domain; **p. 87** (t) © Marzolino/Shutterstock; (b) © Stocksnapper/Shutterstock; **p. 88** © National Portrait Gallery/Public Domain; **p. 89** © Edward Hicks/Public Domain; **p. 95** (t) © Hyacinthe Rigaud/Public Domain; (b) © Rob Wilson/Shutterstock; **p. 97** (t) © Everett Historical/Shutterstock; (b) © doma/Shutterstock; **p. 99** © Everett Historical/Shutterstock; **p. 101** © Benjamin West/Public Domain; **p. 105** © Nagel Photography/Shutterstock; **p. 106** © Public Domain; **p. 108** © Dmitry Chulov/Shutterstock; **p. 109** (t) © Public Domain; (b) © Bruce Raynor/Shutterstock; **p. 110** (t) © Everett Historical/Shutterstock; **p. 110** (b) © Everett Historical/Shutterstock; **p. 111** © Morphart Creation/Shutterstock; **p. 112** (a) © bcampbell 65/Shutterstock; (b) © nfoto/Shutterstock; (c) © Bill Perry/Shutterstock; **p. 113** © Georgios Kollidas/Shutterstock; **p. 114** © Pierce, C.C. (Charles C.)/Public Domain; **p. 115** © Paul B. Moore/Shutterstock; **p. 117** © James Mattil/Shutterstock; **p. 119** © Marzolino/Shutterstock; **p. 120** © Everett Historical/Shutterstock; **p. 122** © Paul Marcus/Shutterstock; **p. 123** © Doc Searls/Public Domain; **p. 124** © Public Domain; **p. 125** © *Provincias Internas*/Public Domain; **p. 129** © Public Domain; **p. 130** © William Williams/Public Domain; **p. 131** © Everett Historical/Shutterstock; **p. 132** © Everett Historical/Shutterstock; **p. 133** © John Filson/Public Domain; **p. 134** © Everett Historical/Shutterstock; **p. 135** (t) © Public Domain; (b) Godfrey Kneller, National Portrait Gallery/Public Domain; **p. 138** © Everett Historical/Shutterstock; **p. 139** (t) © Everett Historical/Shutterstock; (b) Everett Historical/Shutterstock; **p. 141** © Allan Ramsey/Public Domain; **p. 142** © Everett Historical/Shutterstock; **p. 143** © Everett Historical/Shutterstock; **p. 145** Everett Historical/Shutterstock; **p. 146** © James Gillray/Public Domain; **p. 147** (t) © Paul Revere/

Credits continue on page 863

CONTRIBUTORS

Christopher Zehnder earned his bachelor of arts degree from Thomas Aquinas College in Santa Paula, California, and his master's from Holy Apostles College and Seminary in Cromwell, Connecticut. He has taught history, theology, Latin, English grammar, composition, English literature, and universal literature at Catholic secondary schools in Connecticut and California. He has developed curricula in history and language arts. In addition to his work in education, Mr. Zehnder has authored two historical novels on the German Reformation, edited two monthlies, and written for various publications on historical, political, and theological subjects. He and his wife, Katherine, with their children live in Central Ohio.

Rollin A. Lasseter, the former General Editor of CSTP, retired in 2003 from the English faculty of the University of Dallas. He graduated *summa cum laude* from Vanderbilt University and took the M.A. and Ph.D. from Yale University. He was Director of the Honors Program at the University of Kentucky, where he received the Great Teacher Award twice. He was given tenure in the English Department at North Carolina State University. He did postgraduate work at the University of Notre Dame and taught at St. Mary's College, South Bend, and Indiana University at South Bend before joining the English faculty in 1992 at the University of Dallas. For several years he taught Latin, ancient history and literature, and English composition at an exemplary secondary school, Trinity School at Greenlawn, where his six children attended. He was Director of Curriculum at an independent Catholic school and continued as a consultant for curriculum. Dr. Lasseter passed away on May 12, 2008.

Ruth D. Lasseter, with her husband, CSTP's deceased general editor Dr. Rollin A. Lasseter, is one of the founders of the Catholic Textbook Project. She is the mother of six children, now adults and teachers. She was director of admissions at a private Catholic school. She was assistant editor of *Canticle*, a magazine for Catholic women, where she wrote a regular column. She has published and lectured in several Catholic forums.

PREFACE

As an educator I have often noted a serious problem in Catholic education—Catholic educators lack textbooks. Secular textbooks are attractive and rich in illustrations and maps but unsuitable for Catholic schools. These books often carry an anti-Catholic bias by presenting Catholic contributions in an unfavorable light, or by downplaying them. The alternatives to secular texts are old Catholic texts, but these also prove inadequate. Since no distinctively Catholic textbooks have been published since the 1960s, teachers are forced to use old copies of these texts or rely on photocopies. Even the original editions of such Catholic texts lack the graphic quality of the new secular texts, and thus they fail to attract students accustomed to the allures of a media culture. More importantly, old Catholic history texts do not address the intellectual and cultural needs of today's Catholic students. I am not alone in my assessment of this situation. Many other leading educators have also noted a defect common to both secular and Catholic texts: they are written in a style that fails to capture the drama of history.

History, as its name indicates, is, first and foremost, a story—a story as riveting as any fictional tale and as full of tragedy and comedy, of despair and hope, as any novel or epic. Its characters are real human beings like each one of us; some are heroes, others are villains; some are exceptional, but most are average people trying to work through the unique circumstances of their time and place. Since history has the character of a story, it must be told as a story, especially to young readers. History texts should draw us into the hopes and fears, the struggles and victories of men and women of past times. They should help us meet historical characters as real people of flesh and blood.

Catholic Textbook Project is committed to producing textbooks pleasing to the eye, accurate, interesting to read, and imbued with Catholic tradition. Our history textbooks relay to students the necessary "secular" historical knowledge, the "cultural literacy" so important to contemporary education, and give as well due place to God's providence and the role of the Catholic Church in the unfolding of history.

Without exaggeration or whitewashing, this volume tells the story of the accomplishments and failures of nations, groups, and individuals, both Catholic and non-Catholic. This text remains true to the vision of history set forth in the Second Vatican Council's guiding document, *Lumen Gentium*, "The Light to the Nations." It also fills a void in the historical education of young people today, who know little or nothing of the contributions of past ages to our civilization and Church. This vacuum of historical knowledge is not our true heritage. Ours is a culture of life and of hope, of faith, vast and deep, and rich achievements for the common good. May this textbook be one step toward the full restoration of that culture.

   —Michael J. Van Hecke, M.Ed.
    President
    The Catholic Textbook Project

TABLE OF CONTENTS

FROM THE FOUNDING GENERAL EDITOR, CTP

History is a treasure chest of riches. In its stories are the most exciting, the saddest, and the happiest moments of human life. All the great souls and heroes of the world are to be met in the pages of a good history book.

A Christian interpretation of History is the story of God's love for mankind. As a long and complex story, it can tell of tragedies as well as comedies, of famines as well as feasts, of exiles and homecomings, defeats and victories. There is among the many stories of history some story to entertain or to edify everyone. But over all, the story of history is the tale of God's acts in time and space, the story of rebellious mankind, and the Mercy of God for human folly. History is a story, a story of hope.

However, events in our own time tend to leave most people in fear of the future, despite the watchword of our culture, which remains: "Progress! Be always Optimistic!" Current secular ideologies have given "history" a god-like power, that makes sometimes wild proclamations: "Someday, History will look back and say . . . "; or "History will show the wisdom of . . . "; or "History will prove he was right . . . "; or "History will leave this 'whatever' behind in the dust of the ages." This ideological sense of the name "History" is more than a little idolatrous in its foolish optimism. The Holy Father, Pope Benedict XVI, wrote in several places about "optimism" as but a shallow mockery of hope.

The evidence of the stories that come down to us from the ancient world and the medieval era do not promise all good endings. Humanity makes costly mistakes. Great men and women pay for those mistakes with their lives. Great empires collapse. Utopias are neither realistic, nor realized.

The Hope that the Christian Faith offers is more than an optimistically happy ending. The end of history will be the return of Our Lord in Glory and the end of time. Providence does not mean every time a happy ending—only a blessed one. It is God's abiding care and love, in History and in individual lives. It is the vision of the perfection in Christ to which all people are called, not just what society and cultures—however great—have been.

May you, the readers of this book, young and old, find in its tales the traces of that Providence that keeps all of us safe in his Everlasting Arms.

—Rollin A. Lasseter, Ph.D.
Founding General Editor, CTP

1 EXPLORERS AND CONQUISTADORS

The Genovese Mariner

The year 1492 was a turning point for Spain. In January of that year, Isabel and Fernando, *los Reyes Católicos* (the "Catholic Monarchs") of Castile and Aragon, concluded a 700-year war by conquering the Moorish kingdom of Granada, the last stronghold of the Muslims in Spain. This 700-year war, or rather series of wars, had been a crusade for Spain, a holy war to retake lands lost to the Muslims in the eighth century. Yet, with the close of this war, the Spanish monarchs found themselves faced with a new and perhaps more arduous task—the conquest of a hitherto unknown world.

Even the strange sea captain, who for seven long years had been belaboring the Spanish monarchs to allow him to pursue this quest, did not understand the nature of it. This tall, long-faced mariner with the gray, dreaming eyes—this Cristóbal Colón from the Italian seafaring city of Genoa—had labored, until his red hair had turned white, to convince the monarchs that by sailing west one could reach the East—the fabled lands of China, Cipangu (Japan), and India.

Colón, better known to us as Christopher Columbus, was the son of a wool weaver. Born in 1451 in the seafaring city Genoa, he went to sea in his youth. In his early twenties, he joined an expedition against the Barbary corsairs and another to the Greek island of Chios (then under Genoese control) to defend Genoa's interests there against the Turks. In 1476, he sailed with a fleet of Genoese trading ships that was bound for Portugal, England, and Flanders. Off the southern coast of Portugal, enemy ships attacked the fleet, and Columbus was wounded. When his ship went down, he jumped into the sea, and grabbing hold of a sweep, swam the six or so miles to shore. In the Portuguese city of Lagos he found help for his wounds. When he recovered, he made his way to Lisbon, a port city and the capital of Portugal.

Lisbon in the first decade of the 16th century

For a seaman of Columbus' time, Portugal was the place to be. Since 1415, the ***infante***, Dom Henrique (Prince Henry the Navigator), had been promoting Portuguese navigation, and he had built a seaman's town at Cape St. Vincent. Under Dom Henrique's impetus, Portuguese navigators had by 1459 discovered the Azores and the Cape Verde Islands in the Atlantic. Hoping to forge an alliance against the Muslims with the legendary Christian monarch, Prester John, Dom Henrique had sent ships southward along the coast of Africa to see what lay around the continent's great western cape.

infante: the heir to the Portuguese or Spanish throne

1

After Dom Henrique's death in 1460, Portugal's quest to sail farther down the African coast was inspired by a more mercantile concern—to reach India and establish a direct spice trade with East Asia. For centuries, the only way European merchants could obtain spices from the "Indies" was by trade with Muslim middlemen. To cut out the middlemen, the Portuguese king Alfonso V sought a direct trade route with the East. In the 1470s, Portuguese mariners discovered the Gold and Ivory Coasts of Africa, and kept pushing south. The discovery of these regions of Africa proved immensely profitable. By the 1470s and 1480s, when Columbus arrived in Lisbon, Portugal was flourishing with a trade of pepper, ivory, and African slaves. Chests of gold dust from Africa filled the coffers of the Portuguese king.

The port of Lisbon, in the late 1400s, was thus an exciting place for a sailor. There, Columbus joined his brother Bartolomé, who worked as a cartographer in the city. There he married Dona Filipa Perestrelo e Moniz, and there his son, Diego, was born in 1480. In those years, Columbus sailed to the Gold Coast and, for a time, lived on Madeira Island in the Atlantic.

The Visionary

No one knows when Columbus first formulated what he called the "Enterprise of the Indies"—his conviction that one could reach the Indies by sailing west across the Atlantic. This rather bold conviction arose from a miscalculation—Columbus had underestimated the circumference of the earth. Not only did he reckon the earth's circumference to be 25 percent smaller than it actually is, he exaggerated the eastward stretch of Asia. These errors led him to conclude that the distance from the Canary Islands to Cipangu would be some 2,400 nautical miles. It is actually 10,600 nautical miles.

It was not mathematics however that inspired the Enterprise of the Indies. Columbus was a visionary, certain he was called to a special task. He saw himself as a true Christopher—*Christumferens,* the Christ-bearer—destined to carry the Catholic faith to the heathen oversea. His interests, of course, were not wholly spiritual, for he longed to find gold in the Indies both to enrich himself and the monarch he served. Yet, even Columbus' cupidity evinced religious goals, for he hoped his monarch, flush with the wealth of the Indies would finance a new crusade against the Muslims to recover the Holy Sepulcher in Jerusalem for Christendom.

In 1484 or 1485, Columbus presented his Enterprise to Dom João, who had become king of Portugal following the death of Alfonso V in 1481. The king rejected the plan, though he continued to show an interest in it. In 1485, Columbus left Portugal for Castile, where in 1486 he presented the Enterprise to Queen Isabel of Castile and León. The queen referred Columbus' Enterprise to a team of scholars and put Columbus on the royal payroll. In 1488 he returned to Portugal at Dom João's invitation to discuss the Enterprise. The Portuguese king, however, soon lost all interest in a westward route to the Indies, for in 1488 the Portuguese mariner, Bartolomeu Días, returned to Portugal after rounding the southern tip of Africa. Días called Africa's southern tip the "Cape of Good Hope," for it gave him and Portugal a very great hope—it opened a southern route to the wealth of the Indies, completely bypassing Muslim lands. Ten years later, in 1498, another Portuguese captain, Vasco da Gama, followed this route to the port of Calicut in India.

Though spurned by Dom João, Columbus did not despair. There was still Isabel. Yet, Columbus received scant attention from the queen when he returned to Spain; she was, after all, involved in the war with Granada. It was not until 1488, when at last Isabel paid

Christopher Columbus

some attention to him—by cutting him off from the royal payroll. This was no good omen; Columbus decided to look elsewhere and sent his brother Bartolomé to gauge the interest of the courts of England and France in the Enterprise. Then, in 1491, Columbus learned that Isabel's commission of scholars had rejected his Enterprise. This decided matters for him; he would leave Castile for France. And to France he would have gone had not an old friend, the Franciscan priest Fray Juan Pérez, persuaded him to remain in Castile. Moreover, Fray Juan obtained an audience for him with the queen.

Columbus met with Isabel before the walls of besieged Granada in the summer of 1491. The meeting, however, did not lead to the result Columbus wanted, for again the queen referred his Enterprise to a commission, and from the commission to the ***Audiencia Real***—which rejected it. A few days after the fall of Granada on January 2, 1492, Isabel and Fernando told Columbus that they would have nothing further to do with his Enterprise.

To be turned down after six years of waiting was too much to bear. No wonder a disgruntled Columbus packed his bags for France! But, the mariner had a powerful friend at court, Luis de Santangel, Keeper of the Privy Purse to King Fernando—and he persuaded Queen Isabel to reconsider Columbus' case. Why she changed her mind about Columbus and his Enterprise is unclear. It was the mystic in Columbus, perhaps, that appealed to the devout and mystically-inclined queen. But whatever the reason for the change, Columbus had at last achieved his desire. On April 17, 1492, the Catholic Monarchs agreed to confirm and finance Columbus' Enterprise to the Indies.

Vasco da Gama

Admiral of the Ocean Sea

With a crew of 90 men and boys and a fleet of three small ships, or caravels, Columbus set sail from Palos harbor on August 3, 1492. The largest of his ships, the *Santa María*, served as the flagship. The other two caravels, the *Pinta* and the *Niña*, were piloted by the brothers Pinzón—Martín Alonso and Vicente Yáñez.

Columbus set off for the Indies laden with proud titles and wide powers. In confirming his expedition, the Catholic Monarchs agreed to Columbus' demands, naming him Admiral of the Ocean Sea, viceroy and governor general over all the islands and parts of the mainland he should discover. These titles meant that Columbus was, under the monarchs, sole ruler of these lands. Isabel and Fernando also granted Columbus the privilege of keeping a tenth of all the wealth found in the lands he discovered.

The sea crossing, though not difficult on the outward voyage, was yet a novelty to the sailors. In those days, most sailing ships hugged the

Audiencia Real: the "Royal Audience"—the highest court of Spain

Columbus' voyages to the "Indies"

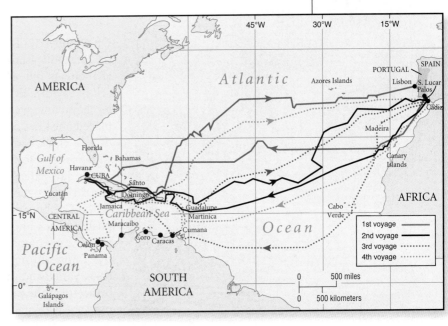

coasts, rarely venturing out onto the open sea. The sailors did not fear sailing off the end of the world, for they knew that the earth is a sphere; but they did not know how far west land actually lay and, they were worried that, so far out at sea, they would find no wind to blow them back again to Spain. To assuage their fear that they were sailing *too* far from Spain, Columbus kept two log books. In one (for himself) he marked down what he thought was the actual distance they had sailed each day; in another (for the sailors), he jotted a shorter distance.

The voyage revealed new wonders. In late September, the ships entered the Sargasso Sea in the mid-Atlantic, where their prows plowed through miles of thickly matted seaweed. On September 23, the three caravels hit calms where no wind blew and the sea was smooth as glass. The sailors bathed in the still, salt waters.

Finally on September 25, after about two months of sailing, the sea-weary sailors heard the long hoped-for cry, "*Tierra! Tierra! Señor, albricias!*" ("Land! Land! Sir, the good news!") The cry lifted the hearts of the mariners, but their spirits deflated when they discovered it was a false landfall—probably the watch had seen a bank of clouds on the horizon. It was not long before disappointment changed to resentment, and resentment to growing insubordination. For the next five days the fleet made little headway, and the crew began to grumble and contemplate mutiny. Columbus used all his powers of persuasion on his men, who only wanted to return to Spain, coaxing them with soft words and hopes of fame and riches. On October 7, the disappointed Columbus turned the fleet to follow the course of migratory birds he had seen, thinking they would surely head toward land.

By October 10, the crews had had enough. Open mutiny broke out. Columbus, hiding his own uneasiness that they had not yet reached land, again tried to encourage his men. But matters had gone too far. In the end he was forced to agree that, if after two or three days no one sighted land, the fleet would return home. As the day passed from morning, to afternoon, to night, how long the hours must have seemed to Columbus!

But, then, it came, and the history of the world changed forever. It was 2 a.m. on the second day, October 12, 1492. A moon just past full rode in the western sky. The lookout on the *Pinta* spied a dark line on the horizon. It was flanked by what looked to be white sand cliffs. Then captain and crew heard the cry—"*Tierra! Tierra!*"

This time it was no false landfall.

The Indies

On October 12, 1492, Columbus and his men went ashore on a small island called by the natives *Guanahani* (Bahamas), but which Columbus renamed San Salvador (Holy Savior). Taking the flag of Castile and León in his left hand and grasping his sword in his right, the admiral placed one knee on the sand. He then ordered the planting of the cross. San Salvador now belonged to *los Reyes Católicos* and to Christendom.

On San Salvador, Columbus and his men met a new and strange people. They were the Taino, who had come to the Caribbean islands originally from South America, pushing back and enslaving the indigenous Siboney people of Cuba, Jamaica, and the Bahamas. In Spanish eyes, the Taino did not have an advanced culture. They grew corn, yams, and other root crops, and they made cassava bread from the yucca plant. They excelled in pottery and used shells to make ornaments and utensils. Their shelters

Christopher Columbus lands on Hispaniola, 1492. An engraving from *Historia General de los Hechos de los Castellanos*, by Herrera, 1601

were simple, of wooden frame and palm leaf thatch. Their clothing was even simpler, for, much to the Spaniards' surprise, men and women both went about with no other covering than a loincloth.

Columbus noted that the Taino were a peaceful people; and they were very hospitable to the white-skinned strangers, who, they thought, were men come from heaven. The Spaniards soon learned that other natives were not so peaceful. The Taino lived in mortal terror of the Caribs, who occasionally raided them in search of slaves. The Taino related another unpleasant fact about the Caribs—that they ate human flesh.

Columbus had reached land—but was it the Indies? If it was the Indies, he was certain he would find abundant gold there. On October 14, Columbus set sail in search of fabled Cipangu (Japan), where the medieval Italian explorer Marco Polo had said were houses roofed with gold. From Cipangu, Columbus thought to visit the Great Khan in China, to present that potent monarch with letters of introduction from the monarchs of Spain.

In the course of his search for Cipangu and China, Columbus sailed along the southern coast of a long island, which he named *Juana*, for the daughter of Fernando and Isabel. This island (now called Cuba), he thought, must be part of Cipangu. On December 5, Columbus' ship caught sight of another island (Hispaniola), of which Columbus took possession on December 12. To his joy, Columbus saw that the Taino natives on Hispaniola wore ornaments made of gold—the first real sign that he had indeed reached Asia.

But on Christmas day, 1492, tragedy struck. Columbus' ship, the *Santa María*, struck a reef in a bay off the north coast of Hispaniola. Since he now had only two ships, Columbus had to leave some men on the island. Assisted by the Taino chief, Guacanagarí, Columbus and his men built a fortress from *Santa María's* salvaged planking. Since it was Christmas season, Columbus christened the fortress Navidad (Nativity)—the first Spanish settlement in the New World.

Guacanagarí told Columbus that gold could be found on Hispaniola—in a region the natives called Cibao. Encouraged by this news, Columbus prepared to return to Spain. Leaving most of the *Santa María's* crew to man Navidad, Columbus boarded the *Niña* on January 18, 1493 and, along with the *Pinta*, set sail for Spain, where they arrived after a stormy crossing, on March 15, 1493.

The Queen's Pleasure and the Pope's Precaution

The instructions Columbus received from Isabel and Fernando after his return to Spain were very clear—they wanted him to plan another voyage to the "Indies." But preparations would take several months and, in the interlude, the monarchs and all of Spain honored Columbus. News of his discovery soon spread throughout the Mediterranean basin, exciting interest and speculation. Everyone thought Columbus had reached the Indies; no one suspected that he had found a hitherto unknown land.

Portugal's king, Dom João, of course, heard the news, and he was not pleased. Because of Columbus, Spain had reached the Indies before the Portuguese had—and what did this mean for Portugal's interests in Asia?

The new pope, Alexander VI (Rodrigo Borgia), who also took an interest in Columbus' discoveries, understood Dom João's displeasure. A Spaniard, Alexander had received many favors from Fernando and Isabel, including their influence in securing the throne of Peter for him in 1492. He now came to their aid to forestall a challenge to Spain's claims in the Indies.

To appease Dom João, Pope Alexander issued, in 1493, the bull *Inter Caetera*, setting a demarcation line in the Atlantic. All lands

Pope Alexander VI coat of arms

A Line Drawn in Water

Spain and Portugal later confirmed Pope Alexander's decision in the Treaty of Tordesillas (June 7, 1494). To further appease Dom João, Isabel and Fernando agreed to place the demarcation line 370 leagues to the west of the pope's line. This treaty secured Brazil, which juts out east of the line, for Portugal.

west of the demarcation line, decreed the pope, would fall to Spain; those east of the line, to Portugal. This, Alexander thought, would forestall disputes between Spain and Portugal.

While the armada (an armed fleet) for the new voyage was making preparations, Isabel and Fernando issued instructions to Columbus. The sovereigns insisted that the expedition's first objective was the conversion of the natives to the Catholic faith. The second was the establishment of a trading colony. Columbus, the sovereigns decreed, must see that the "Indians" were treated "well and lovingly" so that friendly relations would prevail between them and the Spaniards. Columbus, the sovereigns commanded, should punish anyone who mistreated the Indians.

As events proved, Columbus would fail to carry out his sovereigns' commands.

Return to the Indies

Columbus set sail on his second voyage with an armada of 17 vessels and 1,200 to 1,500 men. Led by the Benedictine priest Bernardo Buil, twelve missionaries accompanied the expedition. The fleet transported animals, plants, seeds, and tools for settlement.

Columbus set his course for farther south, and on November 3, 1493, reached a chain of islands that he named Las Virgines (the Virgin Islands). It was here that the Spaniards made their first contact with the Caribs. All that the Taino had said of this people was confirmed. They, indeed, ate human flesh—and they were fierce warriors, as the Spanish discovered in a battle on the island of Santa Cruz on November 14, 1493.

Yet, Columbus was soon to learn that even the gentle Taino people could wax fierce and deadly, if pushed too far. After discovering an island Columbus named San Juan Bautista (now Puerto Rico), the fleet rounded the island of Hispaniola. There the Spaniards made a dreadful discovery: the village of Navidad had been burned to the ground. All the Spanish colonists had been slaughtered. Columbus soon learned the cause. The crew of the *Santa María* had maltreated the Indians, and the natives had taken a bitter revenge.

Columbus the Governor

With Navidad gone, Columbus established a new settlement farther down the coast of Hispaniola and closer to the gold-bearing region in Cibao. He named the settlement Isabela.

The story of Isabela is not a happy one. Columbus, though a great captain and navigator, proved to be a poor governor. Of course, his task was extremely difficult. The men who had accompanied him were not interested in settling Hispaniola but in exploiting the gold fields and returning rich to Spain. To his disappointment, Columbus soon learned that Cibao had no mines. Gold there was, but it needed to be extracted from the sand and the mountain streams—an arduous task, bearing little reward.

Hoping to discover the mainland of Asia, Columbus again took to sea on April 24, 1494. When he returned five months later (with no Asian discovery), he found Isabela in a dismal state. A group of malcontents had extorted food from the natives, raped their women, and enslaved their boys. Missionary work had been neglected. Gangs of Spaniards wandered the island, repeating the brutal acts of the colonists of Navidad. When the Taino responded by killing Spaniards, Columbus adopted a brutal policy; in all conflicts with natives, he said he would consider the Indians the guilty party and the Spaniards innocent. He would punish any Indian who killed a Spaniard, no matter the provocation. "Guilty" Indians were to be hunted down, punished, and enslaved.

Columbus felt a terrible burden had been laid on him. He feared that his sovereigns, disappointed at the small amount of gold found on Hispaniola, might lose interest in further exploration. Feeling that he *had to find more gold*, he commanded every native, 14 years and older, to pay him a tribute of gold dust every three months. Those who refused would be punished with death. To increase the profits of his enterprise, Columbus instituted an Indian slave trade. He thought revenues raised from this trade would please the monarchs, but he was wrong. In 1495, when five shiploads of Indian slaves arrived in Castile from Hispaniola, Isabel was livid with anger. "What power," she cried, "does the Lord Admiral have to give my subjects to another?"

The Name "America"

Amerigo Vespucci

The continents of North and South America received their name from a man who was most certainly a charlatan. In 1501, Amerigo Vespucci, a native of Florence, Italy, but living in Spain, wrote a letter in which he claimed to have been part of an expedition that had landed on the mainland of the New World in 1497—one year before Columbus had first sailed along the coast of Venezuela and eight days before the English-sponsored explorer John Cabot had touched the coast of Cape Breton Island far to the north.

Though its account was almost certainly fabricated, Vespucci's letter was published in 1504 and was widely read throughout Europe. Because Vespucci claimed to have been the first to have seen the *Mundus Novus* ("New World"), Europeans began to call the new lands after the latinized version of his Christian name, Americus. So it is that, to this day, we normally call the two great continents of the Western Hemisphere, not *Columbia* (after Columbus) but *America*.

Royal Disfavor and a Final Voyage

Columbus returned to Castile in June 1496. Two years later, he set out on another voyage and, in August 1498, discovered the South American continent. Sailing along the coast of what is today Venezuela, Columbus was so taken by its beauty that he was certain he had found the Garden of Eden.

On August 31, 1498 Columbus landed at Santo Domingo, a town on the southern coast of Hispaniola, where he had moved the island's capital from Isabela earlier that year. The colony was in rebellion. Columbus had left Hispaniola under his brother Bartolomé's governorship, but a group of discontented settlers had rebelled and withdrew to the Xarangua Peninsula in southwestern Hispaniola.

Columbus' poor showing as governor, coupled with slanders against him uttered by enemies in Spain, undermined his sovereigns' good will toward him. The revenues from the Hispaniola colony, moreover, fell below Fernando's expectations, and Isabel was angry over Columbus' enslavement of the natives and the slow progress made in their conversion.

The first sign of royal disfavor was the chartering of new expeditions under other commanders than Columbus. And Fernando and Isabel evinced their disapproval of Columbus' government by sending Francisco de Bobadilla to Hispaniola as chief justice and royal commissioner. The spectacle of rebels hanging from gibbets greeted Bobadilla when he arrived in Santo Domingo; and, suspecting misgovernment, the new chief justice clapped Columbus and his brother Bartolomé in irons, collected perjured testimony against them, and sent them back to Spain to stand trial.

Yet, despite her great disappointment in him, Queen Isabel never entirely lost confidence in Columbus. In September 1501, she dismissed the charges against him and restored his titles, though she did not allow him to exercise his powers. Instead, the Catholic sovereigns appointed Don Nicolás de Ovando as royal governor of the Indies.

On March 14, 1502, Columbus set forth on his last voyage. With four caravels, he set sail to discover a sea channel to Asia and followed southward the coastline of what are today Nicaragua and Panama. Although he did not discover a channel, Columbus learned from Indians about the Isthmus of Panama and the great ocean that lay beyond it.

After a long and dangerous voyage, and a year spent marooned on Puerto Rico, Columbus returned to Spain in 1504. After the death of Isabel on November 26, 1504, Columbus lost all favor at court, and his attempts to regain his lost privileges went unheeded. He died on May 20, 1506, fairly rich, but disappointed, at the age of 55.

Other New World Explorers

Spain sent a mixed group of adventurers to explore and colonize her "Indian" lands. Some were younger sons of nobles, left without inheritance; others were soldiers of fortune; still others were released prisoners. A desire for wealth and honor drove adventurers across the Atlantic, though there were always those whose inspiration was more spiritual and humane. One adventurer there was, however, who was drawn to exploration by a motive other than gold or God. This was Juan Ponce de León, of Valladolid in Spain.

Juan Ponce de León's motive simply was this—he had fallen in love. Already in his early fifties, this wealthy landowner had sailed with Columbus on his second voyage and had established a large plantation on the island of Hispaniola. He had founded settlements on the island of Puerto Rico and had become its governor. Now, in 1512, this 52-year old general had fallen for the beautiful and very young Beatriz de Córdoba.

Ponce de León would gladly have given all his wealth only to be young enough to win the heart of the maiden, Beatriz. In his desperation, he staked much of his wealth, his position, and his honor to follow a fable. Indians had told Ponce de León of a fountain whose waters could restore youth. This fountain, they said, could be found on an island called Bímini, to the north of Cuba.

Outfitting an expedition, Ponce de León set sail for Bímini, landing on that "island's" eastern coast on Easter Sunday, March 27, 1513. Since the Spaniards called Easter Sunday *Pascua Florida* (Flowery Sunday), Ponce de León christened the new land, Florida. Starting from what is today known as the St. John's River, he explored the eastern coast south of Cape Canaveral

Routes of Spanish explorers in the Americas

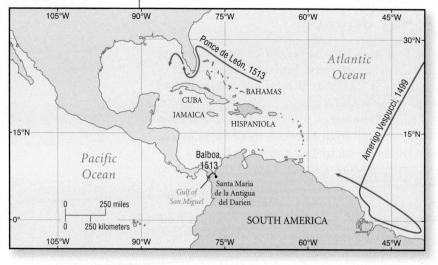

and the western coast as far north as Tampa Bay. On account of the natives' ferocity, however, the Spaniards did not attempt a settlement. Later, in 1521, with the proud title, "Captain of the Land and Sea of San Juan and Governor of Florida and Bímini," Ponce de León attempted a settlement at Charlotte Harbor on the west coast of Florida, but the Indians drove him off. They also gave him the wound from which in a short space he died.

Though other explorers did not have the amorous motives of Ponce de León, they were just as eager to find new lands. One of these explorers was Vasco Nuñez de Balboa. In 1513, Balboa, with 170 men, plunged into the interior of Darien (Panama). On September 24, from a mountaintop, Balboa sighted a new ocean. He called it the South Sea; later, men would call it the Pacific. Balboa took possession of this sea for Spain.

Balboa's discovery of the South Sea showed the Spanish that they had not reached the Indies, as they had thought. Indeed, they found that a vast ocean separated the new lands from China and Cipangu.

But the world would not know just how far the Spanish "West Indies" were from the true, "East Indies" until 1522, when Juan Sebastián Elcano sailed into a Spanish harbor after a long and arduous voyage.

Elcano had been part of the expedition under Fernando Magellan, whom in 1519 the new king of Spain, Carlos I, had commissioned to circumnavigate the globe. After crossing the Atlantic from Spain, Magellan had sailed southward along the coast of South America. Rounding Cape Horn, Magellan crossed to the Hawai'ian islands, from whence he sailed to

Vasco Nuñez de Balboa

Guam and then the Philippines. In the Philippines Magellan died from a poisoned arrow in a battle with the natives in April 1521. Elcano, taking command of the voyage, continued south and then west into the Indian Ocean. Rounding the Cape of Good Hope, he returned in triumph to Spain. Carlos I honored Elcano by placing a globe on his coat of arms, with the legend, *Primus circumdedisti me*—"you have been the first to circle me."

Magellan's expedition proved that what had come to be called "America" was not even on the outskirts of the Indies, but was itself an entirely new world. Still, Spain did not lose interest in the new lands. Even after this momentous voyage, brave explorers continued to feel their way along the coasts of North and South America in search of land and gold. These explorers included Juan de Grijalva, who landed near what is now Galveston, Texas, and Alonso Álvarez de Pineda, who discovered the mouth of the Mississippi and named that great water the Río de Espiritu Santo (River of the Holy Spirit).

The greatest discovery and conquest, however, was reserved to a young *caballero*, a native of that barren region of Spain, Estremadura—a land that gave rise to so many conquerors. His name was Hernán Cortés.

The Conqueror of Mexico

Few if any observers of his early life would have thought Hernán Cortés would ever amount to much. Sent to college to study law, Cortés just wasted his time and dropped out of school after only two years. He then returned home, where he led an idle and profitless life. Such were the unpromising beginnings of the man who was destined to carry out one of the most arduous tasks in the history of North America.

Hernán Cortés scuttles his ships

It was news of Columbus' discoveries that at last stirred the torpid spirit of the young Cortés. Leaving home, he found his way to Spain's southern ports, where, in 1504, he joined a small fleet bound for Hispaniola. When he arrived on the island, the royal governor, Don Nicolás de Ovando, granted him land and Indian slaves to work it. Seven years later, Cortés joined in the conquest of Cuba under Diego Velásquez, who became the island's governor.

At first, Cortés enjoyed Velásquez's favor; but not for long. He became the center of a group of men who were dissatisfied with Velásquez's government. Twice imprisoned by Velásquez, Cortés twice escaped. But in the end, Cortés was able to reconcile with the governor and received a grant of land in Cuba, complete with Indian slaves and a gold mine. Cortés became **alcalde** of the town of Santiago and grew to be a popular figure in Cuba.

alcalde: Spanish word for mayor

The Expedition Gets Under Way

In 1518, news reached Cuba of discoveries made by Juan de Grijalva off the coast of Yucatán and Mexico. Hungry for adventure and riches, Cortés sought and obtained from Velásquez the position of captain general of an expedition (funded by both), the sole purpose of which was to further explore and exploit the riches of the new region. But before the expedition set sail, the governor had second thoughts. Cortés had been too successful in enlisting ships and men, and Velásquez was jealous. He tried to remove Cortés from command; but getting wind of the plot, Cortés set sail with the fleet secretly by night.

Cortés' fleet of 11 ships landed off the coast of Yucatán in February 1519. His force consisted of 100 sailors, 508 soldiers, two heavy guns, four falconets (smaller guns), and 16 cavalry. Two missionaries accompanied the expedition. (One of these, the Dominican father Bartolomé de Olmedo, would in the course of the expedition temper Cortés' martial zeal to convert the natives, recommending patience and persuasion rather than force.)

Cortés and his fleet sailed for the coast of Yucatán and in March 1519 landed at Tabasco. There the Spaniards battled a force of 40,000 Indians. Following the battle, the **caciques** offered Cortés and his men 20 female slaves as a peace offering. Among these was an Aztec cacique's daughter whom her stepmother had sold into slavery. Baptized, she took the name Marina and became indispensable to Cortés as his interpreter. Later, she bore him a son, Don Martín Cortés.

cacique: a chieftain

After skirting the coast from Yucatán northward, Cortés landed on the coast of Mexico at the site of the modern city of Veracruz. It was Good Friday, April 21. Choosing a site a little farther up the coast, Cortés established a settlement there, naming it Villa Rica de Vera Cruz. Velásquez's friends who accompanied the expedition were angry. They claimed Cortés had exceeded the authority given him by the governor. He was only to explore the land, not establish settlements, they argued. Cortés defended himself, saying that in establishing a settlement he only acted "in the interests of the sovereigns" (King Carlos I of Spain and his mother, Queen Juana, the mad daughter of Fernando and Isabel). When a conspiracy to abandon Cortés and return to Cuba arose among the men, Cortés commanded the destruction of all but one of his ships. The troops were overcome with shock and dismay at this daring act. They cried out that their general had led them to Mexico only to be butchered like cattle! Cortés, however, stood before them, unflinching. He declared that at least he, like a brave man, had chosen his part:

"I will remain here," he said, "while there is one to bear me company. If there be any so craven, as to shrink from sharing the dangers of our glorious enterprise, let them go home, in God's name. There is still one vessel left. Let them take that and return to Cuba. They can tell there how they have deserted their commander and their comrades—and patiently wait until we return loaded with the spoils of the Aztecs."

Cortés had thrown down the gauntlet. He had given his men the choice between glory and riches, on the one hand, and cowardice and shame, on the other. The men, their courage rekindled by his words, cried out that they would not abandon their commander! They would go forward, not return as cravens to Cuba! One phrase alone now expressed their desire, and they shouted it with wild enthusiasm.

"To Mexico!" they cried. "To Mexico!"

The Aztecs

The burning of the ships was a wondrously daring act, for the enemy the Spaniards were about to face was formidable. In landing in this region called Anáhuac by its inhabitants, Cortés and his men had already noted that the Indians there were not primitive like the Taino. They raised buildings and temple pyramids of stone instead of dwellings of stick and thatch. They were very numerous, too, and dwelt in ordered towns surrounded by well-cultivated fields of maize, or Indian corn. They were doubtless more formidable foes than the inhabitants of the Caribbean islands.

Stained glass window in the cathedral of Brussels, Belgium, depicting an idealized Carlos I (in his office as Holy Roman Emperor Carolus or Charles V), standing, orb in hand, and his wife, Isabel of Portugal

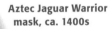

Aztec Jaguar Warrior mask, ca. 1400s

And, the Spaniards had learned, at the center of this land, in a city rising from the middle of a lake, dwelt a powerful, warlike people—the Aztecs. Since 1502, their king had been Montezuma II, who, in his 17-year reign, had conquered the tribes of Anáhuac, gathering under him more lands than his ancestors had ever ruled before. It is said that as Montezuma's power increased, so did his pride and arrogance. He ruled the subject tribes through fear, laying upon them heavy taxes and tributes.

According to their own history, the Aztecs had come from the northwest, from a region called Aztlán. In the 14th century they arrived at the shores of a lake in the high mountain valley of Mexico where they beheld, perched on the stem of a prickly pear cactus, an eagle, its wings spread to the rising sun, a serpent grasped in its talons. The Aztecs took this for a sign, and near the spot of the apparition they settled and raised their city, Tenochtitlán. In 1418, a barbaric tribe, the Tepanecs, invaded and conquered Tenochtitlán and its neighboring city, Texcuco. Later the Aztecs joined Nezahualcoyotl, king of Texcuco, and drove out the invader. As a reward, Nezahualcoyotl gave the Tepanec lands to the Aztecs.

The 15th century witnessed the growing power of Tenochtitlán and Texcuco. Until about 1500, Texcuco was predominant; however, by the time Montezuma II became king, the Aztecs were the masters of Texcuco.

The Aztecs, once a relatively primitive tribe, had learned civilization from Texcuco. By the 16th century, the Aztecs had advanced in agriculture and architecture; they planted beautiful gardens and raised a city that would elicit the praise of those Europeans who first beheld it. Aztecs excelled in metal work, especially the delicate craftsmanship of gold ornaments. The exact observation of the stars allowed the Aztecs to make a solar calendar of eighteen 20-month days. In their hieroglyphic, or picture writing, they recorded history and wrote beautiful poetry. Yet, the Aztecs never invented the wheel for transportation. No indigenous American peoples used the wheel for that purpose until the arrival of the Europeans (though they had wheeled toys for their children).

Aztec idol

The Aztecs worshiped many gods. Among the most important of their gods was Huitzilpochtli, the god of war. Another important deity was Quetzalcoatl ("feathered serpent"), god of the air. According to legend, it was Quetzalcoatl who had instructed men in agriculture, in the use of metals, and in government. Under this god a golden age had flowered. But because he had incurred the wrath of another god, he left Anáhuac, going east over the sea to the land of Tlapallan. Quetzalcoatl, who was said to have white skin, dark hair, and a flowing beard, promised his followers that, one day, he would return to Anáhuac from the east, over the sea.

It was also said that when Quetzalcoatl returned, he would abolish an integral part of Aztec worship—human sacrifice. One of the principal purposes of war for the Aztecs was the capturing of victims for sacrifice. The Aztecs solemnized every festival—and there were many festivals—with human sacrifice. It is recorded that the Aztecs sacrificed about 20,000 victims each year. On the summit of the great pyramid temple, or *teocalli*, in the center of Tenochtitlán stood a large, rounded alabaster stone. A victim was led to the stone, his back forced against it, exposing his chest. A priest, his long hair matted with human gore, then raised an obsidian knife, plunged it into the victim's chest and, cutting it open, pulled out the still beating heart. The heart alone was offered to the god. The festival spectators ate the discarded body.

March to Mexico

Apprehension filled the heart of the Aztec king, Montezuma, at the news of Cortés' landing—might this be the prophesied return of Quetzalcoatl? Reports seemed to confirm the king's fear: the strangers were white-skinned and bearded, and whatever Indian cities they entered, they freed the victims intended for sacrifice. Montezuma was uncertain what to do about the invaders. He sent embassies to Cortés. He vacillated between destroying the Spaniards and welcoming them to his capital. Through one embassy, he invited Cortés to come to Tenochtitlán by way of the ancient city of Cholula, the center of the cult of Quetzalcoatl. Cortés accepted. But, in Cholula, Marina learned of a conspiracy to destroy the Spaniards, which she relayed to Cortés. Cortés responded by brutally slaughtering thousands of Cholulans and pillaging the city.

The Cholula episode drove many of the tribes of Anáhuac into an alliance with Cortés. He had already obtained the aid of the Totonacs, a people living along the low, tropical shores of the Gulf of Mexico. As the Spaniards had ascended from the tropical plain into the colder mountain regions, they met the Tlaxcalans, the warlike enemies of the Aztecs. After Cortés defeated them in four, hard-fought battles, the Tlaxcalans joined him in an alliance against the Aztecs.

From Cholula, the Spaniards climbed to higher elevations. After passing between two great volcanoes, Popocatepetl ("the hill that smokes") and Ixtaccihuatl ("white woman"), they gained their first sight of the valley of Mexico. Below them stretched the great lake, with Tenochtitlán in its midst; and far away on the northeast bank, rose the city of Texcuco. One of the soldiers, Bernal Díaz, wrote he had never seen a sight as lordly and beautiful as Tenochtitlán. "And some of our soldiers even asked whether the things we saw were not a dream," he later wrote. So beautiful was Montezuma's city, with its great buildings and temples, that fear filled the hearts of Cortés' men. But buoyed by their commander's confident spirit, they recovered their courage and proceeded onward toward the city. Marching across the great causeways that connected Tenochtitlán with land, the 400 Spaniards with their 6,400 Indian allies beheld beautiful floating gardens and the vast population surrounding the lake and swarming on its waters in innumerable canoes. It was, as Díaz had said, a dream city, pulled into life from the romantic tales of chivalry so beloved to the stern soldiers of the Crown of Spain.

Montezuma welcomed Cortés and his men into the city and and showed them every hospitality. He allowed the Spaniards to visit the marketplace and the great *teocalli*. In the last place Cortés and his men saw signs of human sacrifice—hearts of victims, some still warm, set on the altars of the gods. Montezuma, whose religious sensibilities were more eclectic than those of the Spaniards, allowed the Spaniards to have a chapel in their quarters where Mass could be offered.

An engraving of the Great Pyramid at Cholula, as it appeared in the 1890s

A Poem from Texcuco

Banish care.
If there are bounds to pleasure,
the saddest life must also have an end.
Then weave the chaplet of flowers,
and sing thy songs in praise of the all-powerful God;
for the glory of this world soon fadeth away.
Rejoice in the green freshness of thy spring;
for the day will come when thou shalt sigh for these joys in vain;
when the scepter shall pass from thy hands,
thy servants shall wander desolate in thy courts,
thy sons, and the sons of thy nobles, shall drink the dregs of distress,
and all the pomp of thy victories and triumphs shall live only in their recollection.
Yet the remembrance of the just shall not pass away from the nations,
and the good thou hast done shall ever be held in honor.
The goods of this life, its glories and its riches are but lent to us,
its substance is but an illusory shadow, and the things of today shall change
on the coming of the morrow.
Then gather the fairest flowers from thy gardens, to bind round thy brow,
and seize the joys of the present,
ere they perish.

—translated into English from a Spanish translation by the 16th century historian, Ixtilxochitl.
Taken from the *History of the Conquest of Mexico*, by William H. Prescott

Though Montezuma appeared gracious and kind, Cortés doubted his sincerity. The Spanish general also worried that his own men and their Tlaxcalan allies might do something to provoke the Aztecs. At last, to secure his position, Cortés decided on a daring plan. He would kidnap Montezuma. Using as a pretext a report he had received from Villa Rica, where he had left a contingent of troops under Juan de Escalante, Cortés put his bold plan into action.

At an audience with Montezuma, Cortés relayed what he had learned to the king. Escalante had reported that an Aztec cacique, who had come ostensibly to give his obedience to the Spanish crown, had treacherously killed two Spanish soldiers. Subsequently, Escalante had set out with 50 Spanish soldiers and 1,000 Indians to punish the cacique. In the ensuing battle, the Spaniards were victorious, though seven or eight of them were slain, including Escalante. Indian prisoners had claimed that Montezuma was responsible for the treachery.

Why this treachery? Cortés demanded of Montezuma. The Aztec king replied that he was not responsible for the attack. Cortés refused to believe him and demanded that the king accompany the Spaniards to their quarters and punish the guilty cacique. Montezuma agreed to the demand. What else could he do, surrounded as he was by 25 to 30 armed Spaniards?

Now Cortés' captive, the humiliated Montezuma, with his nobles, swore allegiance to the Spanish crown, and he divided up his treasures among the Spanish soldiers. Montezuma allowed Cortés to take a temple on the great *teocalli* and convert it into a chapel for Christian worship.

However, a new problem soon faced Cortés. Diego Velásquez, angry over reports of Cortés' doings in Mexico, had sent against him an armada of 18 ships with 900 men and

1,000 Indians under the command of Pánfilo de Narvaez. The ships arrived at Villa Rica in the spring of 1520. Undaunted, Cortés again acted boldly. Leaving two-thirds of his force, 140 men, in Mexico, he led only 70 men to the coast to meet Narvaez. Receiving reinforcements from Juan Velásquez de León (whom Cortés had sent out earlier to found another settlement) and from Gonzalo de Sandoval, Cortés arrived at Villa Rica on a stormy night. Though outnumbered 900 to 250, Cortés and his men fell on Narvaez's troops and, in a surprise attack, defeated them. Following the battle, Cortés with soaring eloquence persuaded the defeated soldiers to abandon Narvaez and follow his standard.

Cortés would soon find he was in sore need of the reinforcements.

Disaster in Tenochtitlán

While Cortés was fighting Narvaez, disaster struck the Spanish troops in Tenochtitlán. Pedro de Alvarado, who was commander in Cortés' absence, had feared the Aztecs were plotting an attack. To forestall it, he led an assault on a large company of unarmed Aztecs gathered near the Spanish quarters to celebrate the May festival to Huitzilpochtli. Spanish swords cut down the flower of the Aztec nobility. Spurred to wrath, the Aztecs then assaulted the Spanish quarters. Only the appearance of the captured Montezuma, who addressed his people from the Spanish quarters, convinced them at last to withdraw.

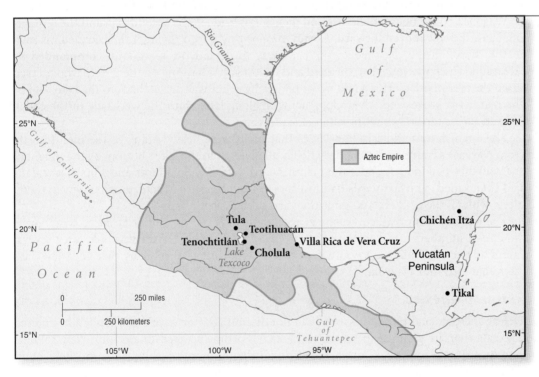

The territory of the Aztec people

Meanwhile, Cortés with a combined force of 1,000 foot soldiers, 100 horse, and 2,000 Tlaxcalan allies was marching to Mexico. He entered the city unmolested; but on all sides he saw the streets filled and the rooftops covered with armed Aztecs. Bloody fighting erupted. Once again hoping to stop the violence, Montezuma, clad in his royal robes and bearing the wand of authority, climbed to the central turret of the Spanish quarters. He pleaded with his people to withdraw and let the Spaniards depart from Tenochtitlán in peace; but this time a volley of stones from the street cut short his speech. Struck several times, Montezuma was removed to safety. Sorely wounded, shorn of his ancient glory and, it seemed, spurned by his own people, the Aztec king died shortly thereafter, on June 30, 1520.

Meanwhile, the Spaniards had not been idle. Leading a contingent of soldiers, Cortés drove the Aztecs from the great *teocalli* and there destroyed the image and temple of

Huitzilpochtli. That same night, the Spaniards burned down 300 houses adjacent to their quarters.

The Spaniards' position, however, soon proved desperate, and Cortés saw that he had no choice but to retreat from the city. The attempt, planned for the night of June 30–July 1, was perilous; the Spaniards, with their artillery and horses, along with their Indian allies, had to pass through a hostile city and over a long causeway. Flanked on two sides by water, they would be exposed to Indian assaults from the lake. Moreover, because the causeway was broken at intervals, and the bridges that normally closed the gaps had been removed, the Spaniards could easily be surrounded and slaughtered as they attempted the crossing.

The Spaniards later named this night of crossing, *la noche triste*, "the sorrowful night." Getting wind of the Spaniards' retreat, some Aztecs had alerted the city. The beating of drums and shells sounded from the great *teocalli* as the Spaniards moved onto the causeway. Soon, thousands of Aztecs set off in canoes on the lake and swarmed from the city onto the land bridge. Cortés' army passed the first gap in the causeway over a bridge they had constructed for the purpose. But when they arrived at the second gap they were in trouble —they had been unable to extricate their makeshift bridge from the mud of the first gap. Soon, they were surrounded. As the Aztecs poured onto the causeway, the Spaniards lost all order—some men and women (for some wives had accompanied their husbands) were slaughtered, while others were taken alive as sacrifices to Huitzilpochtli at the great *teocalli*.

Wagons and the bodies of horses and men at last bridged the second gap, and the remaining Spanish force moved forward. Cortés, discovering a ford through the lake, led his men to the shore, but he returned to the causeway to defend the rearguard, commanded by Alvarado, which was halted at the third and widest gap. Charging on the Aztecs who pressed upon the rearguard, Cortés could make no headway but was driven back to the lake. At last the rearguard broke, and Alvarado, placing his long lance into the wreckage in the canal, vaulted across the breach to the other side.

The Spanish and allied Indian losses that night were heavy. Many of the men (mostly from Narvaez's command) were drowned, pulled down to the lake's bottom by the weight of the gold they had hidden under their clothing. All told, 450 Spaniards and 4,000 Tlaxcalans had been killed. The Spaniards had lost most of the treasure Montezuma had given them, along with all the artillery and guns they had brought with them.

The journey from Mexico was beset with danger. Seven days after *la noche triste*, overwhelming numbers attacked the army at Otumba. Though Cortés was able after several hours to rout the Indians, it was with a broken and discouraged army that he, a few days later, marched into Tlaxcala.

Return to Mexico

Defeat and the condition of his army did not discourage Cortés. No sooner had he entered Tlaxcala than he planned to return to Mexico. Fortune seemed to aid him. New soldiers sent by Velásquez to seize Cortés ended up joining him, and a shipload from the Canary Islands, carrying guns and artillery, arrived on the coast. Another unexpected ally struck the Aztecs—the smallpox. Having no immunity against the disease, they died in great numbers. Among the dead was Montezuma's successor, Cuitlahua, the king.

Before marching on Mexico, Cortés and his generals subjugated the surrounding tribes. Then, at Tlaxcala, Cortés ordered the construction of 15 small ships, called brigantines, to assault Tenochtitlán by water while the foot soldiers advanced along the causeways. Cortés' total force numbered 818 Spaniards, including 87 cavalry, and 25,000 Indian auxiliaries.

On December 28, 1520, six months after *la noche triste*, the army began the march to Mexico. In a stirring speech, Cortés reminded his soldiers that the primary purpose of the war was the conversion of the Indians to the true God from the worship of demons; the second was to return the "rebellious" Aztecs to the service of the king of Spain. The

Spaniards considered the Aztecs rebels, since their king, Montezuma, had sworn allegiance to King Carlos.

After crossing the mountains, Cortés' army took Texcuco on December 31, 1520. From Texcuco, he sent contingents of his troops to subdue the cities surrounding the lake of Mexico. The brigantines, which had been built at Tlaxcala and carried piece-by-piece over the mountains, they reassembled at Texcuco. Finally, on April 28, 1521, after the Spaniards had confessed their sins and heard Mass, the assault on Tenochtitlán began. As they launched the brigantines, the Spaniards broke forth in a joyous *Te Deum*.

The war on Tenochtitlán proved hard and bloody. In late May, the Spaniards blockaded the city by occupying three causeways over which the three divisions of the army, led severally by Cortés, Pedro de Alvarado, and Gonzalo de Sandoval, advanced on the city. The course of the war did not always favor the Spaniards. For several nights on end, Sandoval's troops, who were camped less than a mile from the great *teocalli*, watched as the Aztecs led their captured comrades, wearing plumed headdresses and holding ceremonial fans in their hands, drums beating solemnly, to the sacrifice.

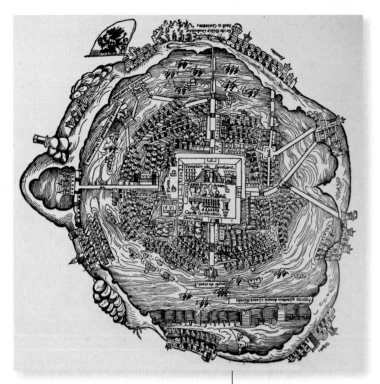

An old reproduction of a Spanish map of Mexico City

The advance into the city was hindered, too, by Aztec attacks from the roofs of buildings. To prevent these attacks, Cortés reluctantly commanded his men to destroy every building they encountered in their advance. Pushing into the city, the army saw the streets strewn with the bodies of those had died from famine. In the houses slated for destruction, they discovered starving men, women, and children. Though Cortés commanded mercy for the wretches, the Tlaxcalans took revenge on their ancient enemies: they burnt the houses over the heads of the suffering. Cortés was powerless to restrain the vengeance of his Indian allies.

When, in their slow and arduous progress, Cortés' army had reached the marketplace, seven-eighths of the city had been laid waste. Yet, despite all the destruction, and though his people suffered from famine, Guatemozin, the Aztec king, refused to surrender. On August 12, Cortés ordered a major assault on the Aztec position. The slaughter was hideous. "The piteous cries of the women and children," wrote Cortés, "were enough to break one's heart."

On August 13, 1521, the Spaniards overwhelmed what remained of the Aztec defenders. Weakened by disease and famine, the Aztecs still resisted until one of Cortés' brigantines captured Guatemozin, who, in a canoe, was seeking to escape across the lake. With Guatemozin's capture, the Aztecs laid down their arms.

"God Will Demand It of You"

The conquest of Tenochtitlán did not end Cortés' work in Mexico—and he proved that he was as much a builder as a conqueror, a governor as well as a general. From 1522 to 1524, he labored to build a new city on the ruins of Tenochtitlán, which he had destroyed. Using forced Indian labor, Cortés raised what became known as Ciudad de México, Mexico City, said to have been more beautiful and opulent than any city in Europe at the time. At Cortés' urging, many Spaniards settled in Mexico, where with Cortés' encouragement they mingled and intermarried with the Indian population.

Cortés continued to extend Spanish power in America. He himself received the submission of the cacique of Michoacán, and he personally led an expedition that discovered the Gulf of California (called the Sea of Cortés in Mexico). Hoping to find a water passage from the Atlantic to the Pacific, Cortés authorized Pedro de Alvarado to explore and conquer Guatemala and sent Cristóbal de Olid to Honduras. After Olid proved treasonous, Cortés himself went to Honduras. With him he took the Aztec king, Guatemozin, as well as the cacique of Texcuco.

It was in Guatemala, surrounded by jungle and beset with hunger, that Cortés heard the reports that Guatemozin planned treachery against him, and believed them. Though Guatemozin denied any treasonable intent, Cortés ordered his execution and that of the cacique of Texcuco. Guatemozin, who had become a Christian, berated Cortés for his treachery. "I know what it was to trust your false promises," he said. "I knew that you destined me to this fate, since I did not fall by my own hand when you entered my city of Tenochtitlán. Why do you slay me so unjustly? God will demand it of you!" The caciques received last rites and were hanged from the branches of a tree.

As it turned out, Cortés had more dangerous enemies than Guatemozin. Envious of his success, some Spaniards accused Cortés of working to establish an independent kingdom in Mexico. Returning to Spain in 1528, Cortés proved his innocence to Carlos I. However, the king removed him from governing the regions now called *Nueva España*—New Spain. Instead, Carlos made Cortés marquis of the valley of Oaxaca and military captain of New Spain, with a right to rule over any new lands he colonized.

Yet, on account of a series of unsuccessful colonizing efforts on the Gulf of California, Cortés again fell out of favor in the court of Spain. In 1540, he returned to Spain to plead his case before the king, but Carlos would not hear him. Frustrated with the rebuffs he received from Carlos (it is said he boasted to the king, "I am a man who has given you more provinces than your ancestors left you cities"), Cortés journeyed to Seville, planning to embark for Mexico. But he fell sick at Castilleja de la Cuesta, near Seville, and there died, on December 2, 1547.

Such was the inglorious end of Hernán Cortés, the "Conqueror of Mexico."

Quest for the Cities of Gold

Though he had become elaborately rich, Hernando de Soto was restless and dissatisfied. Neither his great estate in Seville, nor his status as a gentleman, nor even his beautiful wife, Isabel de Bobadilla, could content him. At the age of 35 he had become too comfortable. He longed for heroic action.

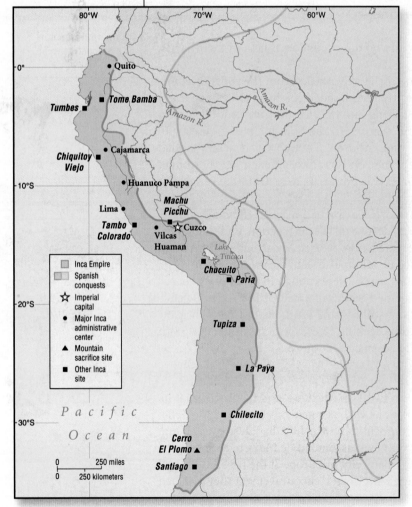

Map of the Inca's empire and the Spanish conquests in South America

Legend:
- Inca Empire
- Spanish conquests
- ☆ Imperial capital
- ● Major Inca administrative center
- ▲ Mountain sacrifice site
- ■ Other Inca site

In his 35 years, de Soto had already seen much action. He had joined Pedrarias Dávila (Pedro Arias de Ávila), his future father-in-law, who had at the ripe old age of 72 become governor of Darien, in Central America. (Pedrarias was notorious for his cruelty in subjugating the Indians of this region.) In 1516, Pedrarias made de Soto, then 16 or 20 (the records are unclear), a captain of horse. de Soto proved to be an able horseman and commander. In 1523, he joined Francisco Fernández de Cordoba in conquering the regions that are today called Nicaragua and Honduras.

In 1532, a soldier of fortune, Francisco Pizarro, with his brothers, embarked on an expedition to Peru, and de Soto joined them as second-in-command. It was de Soto who, high in the Andes, discovered the capital of the Inca, the ruler of Peru—an empire that rivaled the glory of the Aztecs. de Soto, too, was the first to meet the Inca, Atahualpa, and he participated in the bloody battle in which the Inca was captured and disgraced. De Soto became friends with Atahualpa in his captivity and was angered when the Pizarro brothers ordered him killed—even after Atahualpa had fulfilled his promise to fill a room with gold for the Spaniards. Disgusted with this treachery and Pizarro's subsequent behavior, de Soto, laden with treasure, retired to Seville in 1536.

Into Florida

De Soto had been only a year in Castile when he became interested in Florida. Believing the exaggerated account of the riches to be found there, de Soto sold all his property in Spain to outfit his own expedition. King Carlos I, who owed de Soto money, granted him the titles of *adelantado* of Florida and governor of Cuba and promised to make him marquis of any portion of the territory he might conquer.

Arriving in Cuba in 1538, de Soto settled his affairs there. Leaving his wife as governor, he set sail for Florida in May 1539 with nine ships and 1,000 men, landing at Espiritu Santo (now Tampa) Bay on May 30. De Soto explored the western Florida peninsula and subjugated Apalachee (the northwest part of Florida on the Gulf of Mexico). In February 1540, de Soto sent Diego Maldonado to Cuba to report on the progress of the expedition. He charged Maldonado to meet the army at the bay of Achusi (Pensacola) in November. But when Maldonado arrived in November at Achusi, de Soto was not there. For the next two years Maldonado sailed to Achusi but never made contact with de Soto and the army.

Where had de Soto gone?

From Florida, he had headed north in search of gold and explored what is now eastern and northern Georgia. The Indians he met were fierce, and their temper was not improved by de Soto's policy of forcing their people to carry the army's baggage. From Georgia, de Soto had turned south. At a village or fortress called Mabila, in what is now Alabama, his army fought a fierce, nine-hour battle against the Indians. At the battle's end, 70 Spaniards and 2,000 or more Indians lay dead. It was then that de Soto heard news of Maldonado's ships. But some of the soldiers had been threatening to abandon the expedition and sail to Mexico. Trying to forestall this, de Soto ordered a march to the northwest, away from Achusi.

From December 1540 to April 1541, Indians attacked de Soto's army almost every night. On May 21, 1541, the army reached the Mississippi River in what is now northern Mississippi. Crossing the river, they plunged into what is now Arkansas and wintered on the Ouachita River. There de Soto raised a large cross and preached to the Indians:

> This was he who made the sky and the earth and man in his own image. Upon this tree of the cross he suffered to save the human race and rose from the tomb on the third day . . . and having ascended into heaven, is there to receive with open arms all who would be converted to him.

adelantado: a representative of the Spanish king, holding gubernatorial powers

DeSoto's and Coronado's expeditions in North America

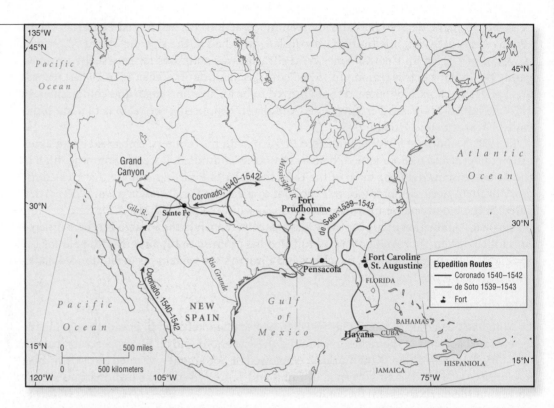

In the spring of 1542, the army returned to the Mississippi. It was on the banks of that great river that de Soto took sick with a fever and died on May 21, 1542.

The remainder of the army, now under the command of Luis de Moscoso, built makeshift brigantines and, harried by the Indians, floated down the Mississippi. Reaching the sea, the small fleet skirted the coast and arrived at Panuco in Mexico on September 10, 1542. The first thing the men did when they arrived was to hear Mass and thank God for their deliverance. Several of the adventurers later entered monasteries.

It was the faithful Maldonado who, a month later, brought Isabel the tale of her husband's death. Overwhelmed with grief at the news, she fell sick. A few days later, Isabel de Bobadilla joined her husband in death.

On the Trail of El Turco

It was a priest, Fray Marcos de Niza, who in 1539 brought reports of newly discovered riches to Mexico City. Fray Marcos had just returned from the distant north, where, he said, he had found the "Seven Cities of Cibola," filled with gold. Intrigued by Fray Marcos' stories, the viceroy of Mexico, Don Antonio de Mendoza, prepared an expedition to verify the existence of the Seven Cities.

Mendoza placed the expedition in the hands of Francisco Vásquez de Coronado, the governor of Nueva Galicia. Mendoza, it seems, not only saw the expedition as way of finding more gold but intended it as a means of ridding Mexico of undesirables and criminals. Coronado did not seem to know this; he thought it merely another expedition of conquest and settlement. Along with 436 soldiers and settlers and five Franciscans, Coronado took with him hundreds of head of livestock into the far north.

The expedition's route roughly followed the western coast of Mexico, passing through what are today the Mexican states of Sinaloa and Sonora, into what is now southeastern Arizona. At last, Coronado reached Hawikuh, the chief village (or pueblo) of the Zuñi people, and took it after a brief battle with the Indians. Hawikuh, it turned out, was one of Fray Marcos' Seven Cities of Cibola. However—Coronado found no gold there.

The People of "Cibola"

Hawikuh was one village or town among 70 or more similar towns belonging to a group of native peoples that dwelt, and still dwell, in what is now New Mexico and northeastern Arizona. We call these peoples "Pueblo," derived from the Spanish word for "town," because they dwelt in compact, permanent settlements, unlike other native peoples of the region, such as the Apache and Comanche, who led a wandering life.

A Pueblo Indian town is a congeries of rectangular structures made from adobe brick or limestone blocks. A typical Pueblo building can be up to five stories tall, with each floor set back somewhat from the floor below it to form a stair-like structure. People moved from level to level of their homes using wooden ladders. Each pueblo had one or two underground ceremonial chambers, called *kivas*, where religious rites were carried out and men could meet and carry on casual conversation.

Pueblo men were hunters, pursuing deer and antelope as their prey; men from pueblos farther to the east ventured out onto the plains to hunt buffalo. Yet, the Pueblo Indians were an agricultural people, the women farming the maize, squash, beans, and cotton (as well as gathering the wild plants) on which the life of the pueblo depended.

Traditionally, the Pueblo peoples were not politically united; each pueblo was autonomous, ruled by a council of men drawn from each of the pueblo's religious societies. The culture of the Pueblo peoples was diverse, and they spoke a number of different languages. The religion of the Pueblo peoples was a form a spirit worship. They believed that hundreds of *kachinas*, the spirits of ancestors or divinities, act as intermediaries between themselves and God. The Pueblo peoples have engaged in yearly, communal ritual cycles to ensure rainfall and the return of the Sun from his "winter house" in the spring. It was believed that if the tribe—and every member of the tribe—did not participate in the yearly rituals, the cosmos could break down and the world come to an end.

Ruins of a *kiva* (foreground) at Pueblo de Arroyo, New Mexico.

From Hawikuh, the expedition divided into three groups. One, under García Lopez de Cárdenas, went northward and discovered the Colorado River and the Grand Canyon. Another party, under Fray Juan Padilla and Hernán de Alvarado, struck to the northeast, traveling as far as northwest Texas, where they spotted a herd of "wild cows"—American buffalo. Coronado led a third group to the east, pushing all the way to the Río Grande, near the present town of Bernalillo.

It was from an Indian captured by the Pecos tribe that Coronado learned of the Quivira tribe in the plains farther east. "El Turco," as the Spaniards named the captured Indian, claimed that the Quivira had gold. Taking El Turco as guide, Coronado, with Fray Juan Padilla and a portion of their party, pushed eastward to find this "city of gold"—Quivira.

Coronado and his company advanced eastward and spent three months exploring the region around what is now Wichita, Kansas. Crossing over miles of grassland, the Spaniards saw only buffalo and nomadic Indian tribes until they came to a settlement of round wooden houses with grass roofs. This was Quivira. But, except for a bit of native copper, there was no metal, much less gold, to be found. El Turco, the Spaniards thought, had deceived them. Death was the punishment for his "crime."

Six months later, Coronado returned to his settlement in the region now named *Nuevo México*, "New Mexico." Finding the settlers discontent, Coronado and most of the expedition returned to Mexico in April 1542. However, Fray Juan Padilla with another Franciscan, two lay brothers, and a handful of soldiers remained to evangelize the Pawnee and Guia Indians.

In Mexico, Coronado received a cold reception from Mendoza—probably because the conquistador had returned with the very people the viceroy wished to be rid of. The governor thought the expedition a failure, and Coronado fell out of favor with the government.

Heroes, Villains, or Both?

Coronado was but another of the number of Columbus, Cortés, and de Soto whose lives were marked by stunning contrasts. They did extraordinary deeds, achieved glory and fame, and ended their lives in sorrow or disgrace. Not only that, but they were men of mixed character; like true Christians, they displayed zeal for souls, but, at the same time, they could be greedy, cruel, and treacherous. In many ways, as we shall see in subsequent chapters, the conquistadors revealed in their persons the contradictions of the Spanish settlement in the Americas.

The lives of the great discoverers and conquistadors, however, underline an important fact—historical characters are rarely pure heroes or mere villains. The Spanish conquistadors demonstrate how men often operate from mixed motives—the best of intentions are sullied by the basest passions: pride, lust, and greed—while all the while high ideals remain in men's hearts and inspire their deeds.

The truth of this is illustrated by a rare archaeological find. In 1886, over 300 years after Coronado's exploration of New Mexico, a sword was discovered in Kansas. It was Spanish and inscribed with the name of its owner, Juan Gallegos. An inscription found on the blade, however, is probably of more interest than the sword itself. It summarizes the ideal, if not always the reality, of Spanish chivalry. It reads: "Do not draw me without right. Do not sheathe me without honor."

Medallion of Christopher Columbus in Seville, Spain

Chapter 1 Review

Summary

- The year 1492 was an important year for Spain because Queen Isabel and King Fernando concluded the 700-year war that Christians on the Iberian Peninsula had been waging against the Muslims.

- Both Portugal and Spain desired to reach India and establish a direct spice trade with East Asia, and so they sent out explorers to find a route.

- Columbus saw himself as destined to carry the Catholic faith to the heathens overseas. He also longed to find gold, however, and it was these two things that drove him to set out for the Indies. He hoped to reach the Indies by sailing westward across the Atlantic Ocean.

- Columbus reached what he thought was the Indies on October 12, 1492. He attempted to establish colonies there. The first colony he founded on

Chapter 1 Review (continued)

Hispaniola was destroyed by the native Indians after his return to Spain.

- In 1513, by crossing the Isthmus of Panama (Darien),Vasco Balboa discovered a new ocean, thus showing the Spanish that they had not reached the Indies.

- In 1522, Juan Elcano, by circling the world, discovered how far the supposed Indies were from the real Indies.

- Hernán Cortés discovered what is now Mexico on April 21, 1519, and commenced to try to conquer the Aztecs who dwelt there.

- In 1520, while Cortés was absent from Tenochtitlán, the Aztecs rose up against the Spaniards. After Cortés' return, the Aztecs drove the Spaniards and their Indian allies from the city.

- Cortés returned with his own men and their Indian allies to Tenochtitlán. They conquered the city in August 1521.

- Hernando de Soto joined the Pizzaro brothers in their conquest of Peru. Beginning in 1539, he led an expedition in the exploration of Florida, going all the way to the Mississippi, where de Soto died.

- Hearing of cities of gold, the viceroy of New Spain sent Francisco Vásquez de Coronado on an expedition of exploration. Coronado found no cities of gold but he established the first settlement in a region to which he gave the name, New Mexico.

Key Concepts

Enterprise of the Indies: Columbus' belief that one could reach the Indies by sailing west across the Atlantic.

Treaty of Tordesillas: the treaty between Spain and Portugal in which they agreed to a decision by Pope Alexander VI to set a demarcation line in the Atlantic. Everything east of the demarcation line would fall to Portugal, while everything west of the line fell to Spain.

teocalli: a great pyramid temple of the Aztecs.

Dates to Remember

1492: King Fernando and Queen Isabel conquer Granada, thus ending the 700-year war Spanish

Christians had been waging against the Muslims.

Columbus reaches what he thought was the Indies (October 12).

1513: Vasco Nuñez de Balboa discovers the Pacific, thus showing that the New World was not the Indies.

1519: Cortés discovers Mexico (April 21).

1521: Cortés finishes the conquest of Mexico (August 13).

1522: By circumnavigating the globe, Juan Elcano discovers how far the supposed Indies are from the real Indies.

Central Characters

Isabel and Fernando: (Isabella and Ferdinand) the Catholic Monarchs of Castile and Aragon. Isabel financed Columbus' exploration of the Indies.

Christopher Columbus (1451–1506): the Italian explorer, navigator, and colonizer who discovered the New World.

Pope Alexander VI (1431–1503): the pope who set the demarcation line in the Atlantic, dividing the New World between Spain and Portugal.

Juan Ponce de León (1460–1521): Spanish explorer and conquistador who led the first European expedition to Florida.

Vasco Nuñez de Balboa (1475–1519): Spanish explorer, governor, and conquistador best known for having discovered the Pacific Ocean.

Juan Sebastian Elcano (ca. 1476–1526): Spanish explorer who completed the first circumnavigation of the world.

Hernán Cortés (1485–1547): (Hernando Cortez) Spanish conquistador who led an expedition to Mexico and conquered the Aztec Empire. He began the first phase of the Spanish colonization of North America.

Montezuma II (1466–1520): ninth ruler of Tenochtitlán, killed during the first phase of the Spanish colonization of the Americas.

Hernando de Soto (ca. 1496–1542): the first European documented to have crossed the Mississippi River.

Chapter 1 Review (continued)

Francisco Vásquez de Coronado (1510–1554):
Spanish conquistador who hoped to conquer the mythical Seven Cities of Gold and discovered New Mexico.

Questions for Review

1. What prompted Columbus to search for a route to the Indies?

2. Why was Columbus turned down so often, and what finally convinced Isabel to finance his journey to the Indies?

3. What prompted the bull, *Inter Caetera*, that led to setting a demarcation line in the Atlantic?

4. How did Columbus fail to carry out the king and queen's command to establish a trading colony? Why did he fail?

5. How did Columbus fall out of the royal favor?

6. What was Juan Ponce de León's motivation for exploration in the Indies?

7. Who discovered that the new lands were not the Indies, and how did he discover it?

8. How was it discovered how far the new lands were from the real Indies?

9. What prompted Cortés to search for new lands and so discover Mexico?

10. What is *la noche triste*? Describe the events it names.

11. Describe some of the atrocities that Cortés and his men inflicted on the Aztecs and some of the good that they accomplished in Mexico.

12. What do the lives of the discoverers and conquistadors tell us about human nature?

Ideas in Action

1. Imagine that you are a member of either Columbus' or Cortés' expeditions, and write about your first impressions of the New World. Or imagine that you are a native Indian or Aztec, and write about your impressions of the Spanish.

2. Read some historical fictional accounts of the discovery of either America or Mexico, and reflect on the complexity of the characters of the discoverers and conquistadors.

3. Read some Spanish poetry written at the time, or listen to the music of the time.

4. Read the bull *Inter Caetera* (you may find it on the internet). Do you think it permitted the conquest of the native peoples? Why or why not?

Highways and Byways

The Aztecs: the First Chocolate Lovers

Chocolate was first used in the Americas, particularly by the Aztecs. Chocolate is made from the fermented, roasted, and ground beans of the *Theobroma cacao*. These beans played a special role in the Maya and Aztec royal and religious events; they were presented as offerings to the gods, and drinks made out of the bean were drunk during the sacred ceremonies. A cocoa drink was prepared by grinding the cacao bean to powder and adding water and various spices, since sugar was unknown to these American natives. The Aztecs called this mixture *chocolatl*. The Aztecs attributed the creation of the cocoa plant to their god, Quetzalcoatl, who descended from heaven on a beam of a morning star carrying a cocoa tree stolen from paradise. The Aztecs, who also used the beans as currency, seem to have been the first chocolate addicts!

THE PROGRESS OF SPANISH AMERICA

In Search of Justice

In 1496, after exploring the coast of South America, Columbus returned to Hispaniola to find the island in revolt. Spanish colonists were discontent with the governorship of Columbus' brother, Bartolomé. Instead of crushing the rebellion, though, Columbus pacified the rebels. He gave them free land grants and Indian slaves to work them.

Columbus called these land grants *repartimientos*—"partitions." Later, when the Spanish crown regulated the *repartimientos,* they were called *encomiendas*—"complimentary land grants"—and the beneficiaries of these grants, *encomenderos.* While, strictly speaking the Indians on an *encomienda* were not slaves, their *encomendero* nevertheless could compel them to labor for him. Thus, on Hispaniola and other islands, colonists forced Indians to work in the fields and labor in the mines. Being unused to such labor, and having no immunities for European sicknesses, thousands of natives died.

As governor of New Spain, Cortés also established *encomiendas,* though he sought to regulate them justly. Under Cortés, Indians continued to live in their villages under their native chiefs, and he enacted laws regulating the number of hours an Indian should work and how much he must be paid. Cortés also required *encomenderos* to provide suitable religious instruction to their charges. Nevertheless, the Indians were often abused in Mexico, as they were elsewhere in Spanish America where the government was less benign.

Map of Spanish America, showing Cuba, Hispaniola, Florida, and New Spain

The Spanish crown recognized the Indians as the equals of the Spanish colonists and so forbade their enslavement. But because the crown had made slavery the punishment for rebellion and cannibalism, unscrupulous Spaniards found the Americas teeming with rebels and cannibals. Thus began a brisk trade in human flesh.

The Spanish government enacted laws to deal with its extraordinary position in the New World. The Laws of Burgos (1512) placed regulations on Indian labor, required that colonists work to convert the natives, and decreed that "no one may beat or whip or call an Indian *perro* [dog] or any other name, unless it is his proper name." Another document, the

Requiriemento of 1513, required the Indians to acknowledge Spanish overlordship and permit the Faith to be preached to them. The conquistadors had to read the *requiriemento* when entering an Indian village; only if the Indians resisted the *requiriemento's* demands could conquistadors subjugate them by force and enslave them as rebels. But since unscrupulous conquistadors recited the *requiriemento* in Spanish (which the Indians did not understand) and often out of earshot of the Indians, harsh conquests inevitably followed.

The Spanish crown justified the conquest of the Indians by appealing to *Inter Caetera*—Pope Alexander VI's 1493 donation of the Indies to Spain. But some questioned the character of that donation—did it give Spain the right of conquest? Some argued that it did not. The pope, they said, gave Spain the right to convert, not conquer, the natives. Among those who argued in this way was a Spanish lawyer turned priest who would gain fame as the "Defender of the Indians." His name was Bartolomé de Las Casas.

A Voice in the Wilderness

The text was the words of St. John the Baptist—"I am the voice of one crying in the wilderness" (Matthew 3:3). Commenting on the text, the Dominican friar Antonio de Montesinos declared: "Are these Indians not men? Do they not have rational souls? Are you not obliged to love them as you love yourselves?"

Bartolomé de Las Casas likely heard this sermon, preached in a straw-thatched church on the island of Hispaniola in 1511. But the appeal of Fray Antonio's "cry in the wilderness" only gradually worked its way into his heart. Las Casas had come from Spain to Hispaniola with Governor Don Nicolás de Ovando in 1502 and had participated in expeditions against the Taino, in which he witnessed atrocities. In reward for his service, Ovando gave Las Casas an *encomienda*, which he continued to hold, with its Indian workers, even after 1510, when at the age of 26 he was ordained a **secular priest**. But his own experience of the devastation the Spanish conquest wrought on the Indians of Caribbean islands along with the cries of Montesinos and others against injustice gradually worked on Las Casas' mind and heart. In 1514, he gave up his *encomienda* and a year later returned to Spain to plead for justice for the Indians.

secular priest: a diocesan priest; a priest that does not belong to a religious order

In 1517, Las Casas was a second time in Spain to complain of the *encomienda* system. His denunciations caught the attention of Cardinal Francisco Ximénes de Cisneros, the regent of Spain. Disturbed by Las Casas' reports of abuse, Ximénes sent a commission of Jeronymite Fathers to investigate and named Las Casas, "Protector General of the Indians." When he returned to America, Las Casas soon found cause to complain of the Jeronymites: he thought they compromised too much with the colonial system. With other critics of Spanish Indian policy in the New World, Las Casas suggested the importation of African slaves to replace the Indian laborers—a recommendation the government carried out. Las Casas later regretted his advocacy of black slavery. "The same law," he wrote, "applies equally to the Negro as to the Indian."

Las Casas believed that the Spanish government should place the American natives under the authority and protection of the Church. In 1519 he won approval for the establishment of a colony on *Tierra Firma* (as the mainland of Latin America was called) to be made up solely of Indians and peaceful settlers—farmers and artisans from Spain. This settlement at Cumaná on the coast of Venezuela was a failure. First, Las Casas could not attract many farmers and artisans. Then, the Indians of Cumaná rose in revolt against the violence of the Spaniards of a nearby settlement. The Indians seized supplies

The Source of the "Black Legend"

Las Casas was a stout defender of the Indians. Sometimes, though, in defending them, he exaggerated both Indian virtues and Spanish cruelty. His most famous work, *Brevíssima Relación de la Destrucción de Las Indias (A Short Account of the Destruction of the Indies)* is filled with many gross exaggerations of Spanish cruelty, recounting events Las Casas could only know by hearsay. This work was translated into several languages and became the source of the "Black Legend" used to this day by Spain's enemies to discredit her.

from the colony's storehouse, killed as many Europeans as they could find, and escaped into the interior. Discouraged at the failure of his hopes, Las Casas retired to a Dominican monastery on Hispaniola. He himself became a Dominican in 1522.

The Dominican Fray Bartolomé spent the next 40 years in the wilderness of Spanish America crying out that Indians, as human beings, had the same rights as Spaniards. The Spanish crown, he declared, had no right to conquer the Indians by force. Though he thought the crown could exercise dominion over the Indians, Las Casas insisted that it could not abolish Indian tribal governments or enslave natives. The *encomienda* system, he argued, was little better than slavery and should be abolished. Force must never be used in preaching the Gospel, he maintained, and he fought strenuously with those missionaries (most notably, the Franciscans) who baptized converts without first giving them sufficient instruction in the Faith.

Despite Fray Bartolomé's opposition to Spanish policy in the New World, King Carlos I, in 1544, appointed him bishop of Chiapas in southern Mexico. Episcopal consecration, however, did not temper Fray Bartolomé; he remained as uncompromising in his defense of the Indians as before. He provoked colonists by setting rigid standards *encomenderos* had to meet before he would absolve them from their sins—basically forbidding communion to anyone who held an *encomienda*. Though he was unpopular with the colonists, Las Casas' policy of peaceful conversion drew many natives to the Church.

Las Casas labored hard for the passage of the *Nuevas Leyes* of 1542. These "New Laws," which forbade Indian slavery and the perpetuation of the *encomienda* system, enraged the colonists. They thought the loss of their *encomiendas* a sorry return for their labors in winning such vast new territories for the king. A bloody civil struggle erupted in Peru when the Spanish governor attempted to enforce the New Laws. Fearing further civil strife, Carlos I revoked some of the New Laws in 1545. The *encomienda* system would continue as before.

The year 1547 found Las Casas again in Spain engaged in a controversy with the Spanish jurist Juan Ginés de Sepulveda. Sepulveda had never visited America; still, with all his limited knowledge of American natives, he had written a treatise that argued that Indians were "natural slaves" and as such could be conquered and reduced to servitude. Las Casas, of course, disagreed. Their controversy climaxed in a famous debate—at a conference held at Valladolid in 1550.

Spanish soldiers slaughter and enslave Native Americans. This 1595 image by Theodor de Bry helped perpetuate the "Black Legend" of Spanish cruelty.

Bartolomé de Las Casas

This debate was of intense interest to King Carlos I, for the question of the justice of the Spanish conquests troubled his conscience. He suspended all further conquests until jurists and theologians at Valladolid could discuss "how conquests may be conducted justly with sincerity of conscience." At Valladolid the king asked whether it were just to subjugate the Indians by force in order more easily to Christianize them. Sepulveda answered, yes; Las Casas insisted, no. No one, said the bishop of Chiapas, should resort to violence to win his brother to Christ.

The fruits of the Valladolid conference came 23 years later, with the enactment of the Basic Law of 1573. Though not as thoroughgoing as Las Casas would have liked, the Basic Law codified many of his demands. The Basic Law said Spaniards were not to "conquer," but to "pacify," the Indians. They were never to enslave them or exact tribute from them but to explain to them the benefits of submitting to the Spanish crown. Force could be used if the Indians refused to cooperate, but conquerors were to use as little force as possible. In preaching the Gospel, missionaries, said the law, should deal gently with the Indians' vices "so as not to scandalize them or prejudice them against Christianity." The Basic Law, however, did not abolish the *encomienda* system. Both *encomiendas* and the Basic Law would remain for as long as Spain ruled in America.

Reign of Terror

Cortés' departure for Spain in 1528 marked the beginning of a period of terror in Mexico. Suspicious of Cortés' power in Mexico, King Carlos I had sent three men—Nuño de Guzman, Juan Ortiz de Matienzo, and Diego Degadillo—as the *Audiencia Real* to investigate the conquistador's administration of New Spain. Instead, for three years, Guzman, Matienzo, and Delgadillo imposed heavy taxes on the Indians, enslaved them, branded them with hot irons, violated their women, and persecuted Cortés' Spanish supporters.

Into this hell of injustice came Juan de Zumárraga. As the newly appointed bishop of Mexico and Protector of the Indians, Zumárraga's task was immense. Though appointed bishop, he had not yet been consecrated—though even a bishop could not have influenced the cruel members of the *audiencia*. A Franciscan, Zumárraga was envied by other religious orders already in Mexico, who thus sided with the *audiencia*. When the bishop-elect tried to notify the Spanish court of what was happening in Mexico, the *audiencia* took to censoring all letters sent out from New Spain. At last, with the help of a sailor, Zumarraga placed a letter to the king in a block of wax, which was dropped into a barrel of oil. In this way, the letter escaped the scrutiny of the *Audiencia Real* and reached the king.

News of the *audiencia's* oppressions angered Carlos. In 1531, he sent a new *audiencia* to New Spain to take the place of Guzmán, Matienzo, and Delgadillo. With them

Map of New Spain, 1570

went Cortés, with the title of Captain General. The new *audiencia* imprisoned Matienzo and Degadillo, but Guzmán escaped. He had departed on an expedition to Michoacán, Jalisco, and Sinaloa to the north.

Conquistadors of the Spirit

In 1524, a small band of 12 Franciscans, clad in rugged habits, passed through Tlaxcala on foot. Hearing the Indians repeating the word, *motólinia*, the friars wondered what it meant. Learning that the word meant "poor man," one of the friars, Fray Toribio de Benavente, said, "it is the first word I have learned in this language, and that I may not forget it, it shall henceforth be my name."

Bearing wooden crosses, Motólinia and his companions continued on to Mexico City. When they arrived before the city, Cortés came out to greet them, and kneeling before them, kissed their hands. The Indians marveled, for they deemed Cortés a great being, nearly divine—and here he was honoring mere beggars! Cortés told the Indians that they, too, should reverence the holy men, who had come to teach them about the true God.

The Spanish missionaries evangelized with the zeal of conquistadors. They were conquerors, subduing the souls of men, submitting them to the rule of Christ. Their weapons were not worldly arms of iron but the more powerful weapons of the Spirit: faith, zeal for souls, and charity. Unworthy missionaries there were, who used physical force to convert the Indians; yet, most of the missionaries were noted for their holiness and charity. Like conquistadors, they undertook extremely difficult labors and suffered terrifying trials. Some even died heroically for the Faith they preached.

The Spanish government shared the missionaries' zeal for evangelization. In fact, the king was the protagonist of all missionary work in the New World. In 1508, Pope Julius II granted to the Spanish kings the *patronato real*, the "royal patronage"—the right to select all bishops and abbots in the Spanish domains, and to publish papal decrees in the New World.

La Guadalupana

Into the maelstrom of violence and tyranny over which New Spain's first *Audiencia Real* presided came an event that would change Mexico forever. On December 12, 1531, the Virgin Mary appeared to the Indian Juan Diego on Tepeyac hill—the site where an Aztec temple to the goddess Tonantzin had once stood. Appearing as an Aztec princess, the Virgin told Juan Diego to ask Bishop Zumárraga to build a church on the spot dedicated to her under the title of *Nuestra Señora de Guadalupe*. Zumárraga was at first unwilling to believe Juan Diego; however, when the Indian opened his *tilma*, or cloak, from which a flood of roses poured, the bishop believed. Not only was it wondrous that the Indian should find

Our Lady of Guadalupe

roses in the dead of winter, but upon the *tilma* appeared the image of the Lady. Zumárraga commanded that the church be built on Tepeyac hill in honor of the Virgin, under the title of Our Lady of Guadalupe.

This apparition of the Virgin brought on an amazing increase in native baptisms. The Spanish government had not been remiss in trying to convert the Indians of Mexico, but because of the brutality of the Spaniards, many Indians had remained aloof from the Church.

Our Lady of Guadalupe is to this day the patroness of Mexico and all of the Americas.

In return, the king was responsible for funding all missionary endeavors and for founding churches and monasteries.

The missionary endeavor was twofold—to evangelize and civilize. In accomplishing the first, the missionaries worked to adapt Church teaching to the native mind. They learned native tongues, and they even used drama, so eager were they to convey the message of Christ. On the sites of pagan temples, which they had ordered destroyed, they erected churches. Though they could be ruthless in stamping out paganism (and along with it, much of native culture), the missionaries preserved much of what was good in the Indians' culture and attempted to find in it a new Christian meaning. In Mexico, some missionaries translated Aztec hieroglyphics and so preserved the knowledge of Aztec institutions and history.

Though some missionaries could be harshly critical of the Indians, others saw the natives as especially suited to receive the Faith. Some missionaries viewed the conversion of the Indians as an opportunity to renew Christian civilization that, they thought, had been corrupted in Europe. Missionaries thus not only toiled to save souls; they labored to found a new Christendom.

Schools and Colleges

One way New Spain's missionaries sought to Christianize and civilize native cultures was by founding institutions of learning. In New Spain, every church and convent had its school where the children of the rich and poor learned writing, music, and Latin, as well as practical arts, such as tailoring, carpentry, and painting. At the college of Santa Cruz in Mexico City (founded 1536), students studied native American languages. Girls, too, went to school—Bishop Zumárraga himself founded eight schools for girls in Mexico. The Franciscan friar, Pedro de Gante (Peter of Ghent), a relative of Carlos I, opened a school in Mexico City for about 1,000 children where they studied religion, music, singing, and Latin. He founded a school of fine arts and practical trades, as well as a college for higher studies.

The Spaniards established the first universities in the New World, the oldest being the University of St. Thomas Aquinas in Santo Domingo, founded by the Dominicans in 1538. There students studied theology, philosophy, natural sciences, languages, and history. Other universities included Santiago de la Paz (1540) and the universities of Lima, Peru (1551), and Mexico City (1557). By the 18th century, there were 26 universities in Spanish America.

In South America, in Paraguay, the Society of Jesus (the Jesuits), carried out a more radical plan to Christianize Indian culture. In the early 17th century, the Jesuits sought and obtained permission to separate the mission field of Paraguay from the Spanish colony of Peru. In Paraguay they established Indian republics, or "reductions" (because they "reduced" or brought the natives into subjection to the Gospel), which they kept isolated from the influences of the Spanish colonists. In this way, the Jesuits hoped to preserve Indians from the influence of lax Christians and protect them from injustice and slavery.

In harmony with traditional native ways, the Indians on a reduction held and farmed their lands in common, though each family had its own house and garden. Indian leaders, elected by their communities,

Motólinia

Fray Toribio de Benavente, called Motólinia, eventually left Mexico for the regions of what are now Nicaragua and Guatemala. He became a bitter opponent of Las Casas, whose ideas on the *encomienda* he thought impractical and destructive of whatever good Spain had brought to America. Even so, the Indians loved Motólinia well, for he was most virtuous and filled with ardent charity. Of Motólinia's charity, an eyewitness wrote: "Whatever was given him he gave to the Indians, and sometimes was left without food. He wore very torn clothing and went barefoot, and the Indians loved him much, because he was a holy person."

helped the Jesuits govern the villages. To protect the villagers from raids carried out by other Indians and by Portuguese slavers from Brazil, the Jesuits oversaw the military training of the village men. The Reductions became quite prosperous between 1650 and 1720 and presented such a unique and humane way of colonization that they even earned the praise of some of the Church's enemies in Europe.

It was a treaty that Spain signed with Portugal in January 1750 that spelled the end of the Reductions. The treaty granted Portugal seven districts of Paraguay in return for the Portuguese colony of San Sacramento. Once in control of Paraguay, the Portuguese ordered the 30,000 or so Indians on the Reductions to abandon their lands. In 1759, Portugal expelled the Jesuits from its colonies.

Nuevo México

Captain Castañeda de Najera had warned him of the dangers of his plan, but it did no good. Fray Juan cared little for safety if it stood in the way of his mission.

After Coronado's return to Mexico, Castañeda had remained with a few soldiers in the *Gran Quivira* (now Kansas) as escorts to Fray Juan Padilla and his companions: Fray Luis de Ubeda and two Indian Franciscan postulants, Lucas and Sebastián.

Bell tower of the old mission church of San Geronimo, Taos Pueblo, New Mexico

A Strange Occurrence

In 1629, a group of Indians of the Jumano people from the northwest of Texas arrived in Santa Fé. They came requesting baptism. Questioning these Indians, the friars were surprised by their knowledge of Christian prayer and their grasp of Church teaching. How had they come to learn all this?

The Jumano related a strange story. Many times, they said, a beautiful lady in blue had appeared to them and instructed them in the Christian religion. It was by her command, they said, that they sought baptism. When some friars traveled the 200 miles to the Jumano settlement, a group of Indians greeted them, bearing a cross covered with wildflowers. Everyone in the tribe requested baptism.

Later, in 1631, when some of the friars returned to Spain, they found a convent of Poor Clare nuns who wore blue habits. The head of this convent, Sister María de Agreda, claimed that in an ecstasy she had several times visited the Jumanos and instructed them in the Faith. The appearance of Sister María agreed well with the Jumanos' description of a lady dressed in blue.

Blessed María de Agreda, right, displays her book, *The Mystical City of God*, while St. Francis of Assisi holds three globes, atop of which stands the Blessed Virgin. Blessed Duns Scotus, left, holds his text defending the Immaculate Conception. Fresco in the Church of the Immaculate Conception, Ozumba, Mexico.

Castañeda could see that the friars had made progress converting the Pawnee and Guia tribes. Why jeopardize this success with an imprudent foray into the eastward plains? After all, the enemies of the Pawnee and Guia lived there—how would they receive those who been the friends of their enemies? Such thoughts likely passed through the captain's mind as Fray Juan with Lucas and Sebastián, the soldier Andrés Ocampo, and a few other soldiers, set forth on their dangerous journey.

Castañeda's judgment was well founded—Fray Juan and his companions never returned to New Mexico. After traversing the wide, grass-covered plains, they met, on November 30, 1542, a band of Aciales Indians, who attacked them near the present site of Dodge City, Kansas. Pierced through with arrows, Fray Juan fell to his knees. In his hands he held a cross, "and raising it, he promised to keep it standing there for as long as it was possible to do so."

These were the words of an eyewitness of the death of the first martyr in what would one day be one of the United States of America. Fray Juan's companions, who escaped death, returned to bury Fray Juan. For several years they wandered through lands that would one day be Oklahoma, Kansas, and Texas, until, traversing hundreds of miles of desert, they returned at last to Mexico City. Years later, Fray Juan's remains were removed from his Kansas grave and buried at Isleta pueblo in New Mexico.

Fray Juan Padilla was not the sole martyr of this period. In 1542, his companion, Fray Luis de Ubeda, met his death at the hands of the Indians of the Pecos River region. That same year, natives killed Fray Juan Escalosa on the Río Grande. In 1581, the friars Agustín Rodriguez, Francisco López, and Juan de Santa Maria, were killed by the Indians of Cibola, in New Mexico.

A Successful Settlement

Juan de Oñate was one of the richest men in Mexico. A conquistador and the husband of Hernán Cortés' granddaughter, he was also one of the most well known. So the viceroy of New Spain could not doubt Oñate's competence when he promised to finance an expedition to found a settlement in New Mexico. With Oñate would go 200 soldiers and colonists, a contingent of Christian Indians from Mexico, 7,000 head of livestock, and eight Franciscan friars.

The journey to New Mexico was, as ever, long, hard, and dangerous. After crossing the harsh desert lands of northern Mexico, Oñate and the settlers forded the Río Grande at a place called El Paso ("the ford"). On Ascension Thursday, April 30, 1598, he took possession of the land in the name of the king of Spain. Continuing on to the north, Oñate established a settlement at the confluence of the Río Grande and Chama rivers. By the end of 1598, the friars who had accompanied Oñate had established three missions for the Pueblo Indians of the region.

The Pueblo Indians, however, did not submit easily to Spanish rule or the Spanish religion. In 1598, the Indians of Ácoma (a pueblo set atop a mesa of sheer cliffs) assaulted and killed a small escort led by Juan Zaldivar. To avenge his brother, Vicente Zaldivar led a Spanish force against Ácoma and for three days fought a hard battle against the Indians. Using thick ropes, the Spaniards scaled the sheer rock walls of the mesa and took the pueblo, capturing 500 Indians. The Spaniards harshly punished their captives to teach them never again to resist Spanish authority.

The Ácoma war was the last major rebellion in New Mexico for about 80 years. Still, despite the long peace, the settlers of New Mexico were unhappy. The land was poor and the task of colonization hard. When, in 1601, Oñate returned to the settlements after a five-month, 800-mile expedition across New Mexico and Kansas, the settlers' discontent was acute. They had complained to the viceroy in Mexico of the settlement and of Oñate. They wanted permission to return to Mexico. The Spanish officials would have acquiesced to this demand, but for one consideration—if there were no settlement, the Indians would be deprived of the Gospel.

Ácoma pueblo, atop a
sheer sandstone mesa

The discontent continued until, in 1608, Felipe III (who had become king of Spain in 1598) decided to withdraw the settlers. However, hearing reports of the great number of converts among the Indians in New Mexico and the growth of the missions, the king relented. Instead of abandoning New Mexico, he made it a royal province. Oñate did not fare so well. Forced to resign his governorship, he returned to Mexico, where he died in modest circumstances. He had spent his fortune on the New Mexico settlements.

In time, New Mexico began to flourish. By 1630, there were 25 missions and 90 villages of nearly 60,000 Christian Indians. Santa Fé (Holy Faith), a settlement founded in 1610 by Oñate's successor, Governor Pedro de Peralta, boasted 1,000 Spanish inhabitants.

La Florida

On August 27, 1565, sailors and passengers of a fleet sailing off the eastern coast of Florida saw "a miracle from heaven." "About nine o'clock in the evening," wrote one eyewitness, Fray Francisco López de Mendoza Grajales, "a comet appeared, which showed itself directly above us, a little eastward, giving so much light that it might have been taken for the sun." The comet traveled westward toward the coast of Florida, where the fleet was bound. The next day, August 28, the feast of St. Augustine of Hippo, the sailors sighted land. Sailing further north, the captain, Pedro Menéndez de Avilés, found a small bay and named it San Agustín in honor of the saint on whose feast he first saw the coast.

When he had learned that French Protestants called Huguenots had settled on the eastern coast of Florida, King Felipe II (Carlos I's son) sent Menéndez de Avilés to establish a settlement in Florida and to drive out the Huguenots. Menéndez founded a settlement on the

Felipe III by Juan Pantoja de la Cruz, Museo del Prado, Madrid

small bay he had discovered, naming it also San Agustín (now Saint Augustine). As for driving out the Huguenots—if it had not been for another "miracle," the Spaniards and not the French might have been the ones driven from La Florida.

It did not take long for the French at Fort Caroline, north of San Agustín, to learn of the Spanish settlement. Hoping to destroy San Agustín before the Spanish perfected its fortifications, Jean Ribault, a French naval officer, directed his fleet south on September 10, 1565. The French fleet would have made short work of the Spanish settlement, which was less than a fortnight old, had not a hurricane suddenly struck the Florida coast and driven Ribault's fleet onto the beaches south of San Agustín.

Meanwhile, learning of Ribault's foray that drew most of the men of arms from the French settlement, Menéndez surprised Fort Caroline and overwhelmed it. Then, Menéndez went after Ribault and, discovering the French force at a place called Slaughter Inlet, captured both captain and men. Unable to keep prisoners at so fledgling a settlement as San Agustín, Menéndez executed them all, sparing only the Catholics among them and some 50 women and children.

Rampage of the Polygamist

Once they had secured the eastern coast of Florida, the Spaniards began the slow work of colonizing the land and establishing missions. By the 1590s, Franciscans had set up missions in Florida, and northward into the region of the Guale people, in what is now southern Georgia. Missionary work in the region was not easy, for the Indians had to learn an entirely new culture and morality, including monogamy. Indian men had multiple wives and so found the Christian teaching on marriage difficult to embrace. Still, the Franciscans made progress in this and other areas, and many Indians became Christian.

In 1597, however, Juanillo, a converted Indian and the son of a cacique of the Guale people, took a second wife. Fearing other natives might emulate Juanillo, Fray Pedro de Campo, pastor of Juanillo's mission, Nuestra Señora de Guadalupe, privately exhorted him to give up his concubine. When, after another private exhortation, the cacique again refused, Fray Blas Rodriguez, who directed the Guale missions, publicly denounced Juanillo and removed him from the leadership of the Christian Guales.

Juanillo felt his public humiliation to be a grave affront. Seeking revenge, he gathered a group of warriors and commenced a rampage of murder. On September 13, he beheaded Fray Pedro de Campo and stuck the severed head on a pole. Juanillo and his followers then attacked several missions, killing four other missionaries, including Fray Blas Rodriguez. One priest they captured, however, they did not kill—Fray Francisco de Ávila. Instead, Fray Francisco had to spend ten months among the Guales, undergoing tortures and humiliations. Once the Indians sent a squaw to tempt Fray Francisco to violate his vow of chastity, but the priest fled into the forest.

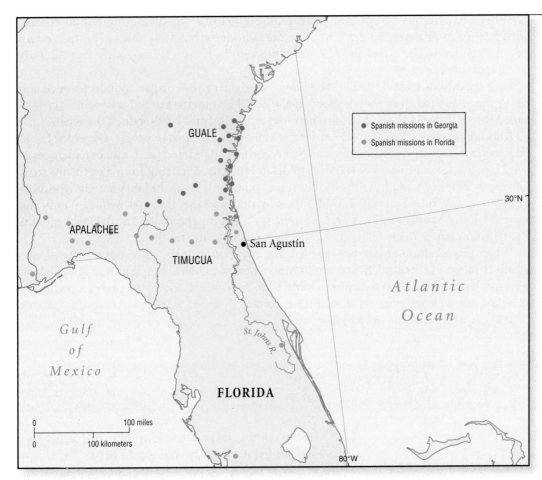

Spanish missions in 17th century Georgia and Florida.

Juanillo met his death in 1598 at the hands of a Guale cacique faithful to the missionaries. But Juanillo did not die before his rampage had destroyed the Guale missions. It would be another eight years before more friars arrived and reestablished the missions among the Guale.

Progress and More Rebellion

In 1606, the same year that saw the beginnings of the reconstruction of the Guale missions, Franciscans began establishing missions among the Timucuan people in the interior of Florida, west of San Agustín. These missionaries were so successful that, by 1612, a large number of caciques and whole villages were seeking baptism. In the 1630s, Franciscans established missions among the Apalachee Indians in western Florida, baptizing nearly half the population by 1639.

But it was not long before tension between the friars and the governors of Florida had bad effects on the missions. As representatives of the king, the Spanish governors claimed authority over all of colonial life. Outside of teaching the Faith, which they left to the friars, the governors thought they had the right to direct all Church activities in the colony. The friars disagreed. They saw the Church, not the government, as the source of their commission to go among the Indians; and so, they said, missionary activities were not subject to the royal governor.

Many of the governors imposed labor on the Indians. They forced warriors to carry baggage on long journeys—which the Indians deemed a deep insult. The government also required caciques to supply men for military and labor duty. These duties would not have been so onerous except that the Indian population was dwindling due to contact with European diseases. So great was the devastation wrought by disease on the Indian population that of the estimated 150,000 Timucuan Indians who were alive in 1492, only 3,230 remained in 1689.

Such conditions incited further rebellions. In February 1647, pagan Indians revolted and drove the Spaniards from their region, Apalachee. The Indians burned seven missions and killed three friars. By the end of March, however, the Spanish had subdued the rebels.

Another rebellion flared in 1656, this time among the Timucuan people. Governor Diego de Rebolledo, fearing a British attack on San Agustín, had ordered the Timucuan caciques to send him a large contingent of warriors to defend the city. Smarting from past insults from Governor Rebolledo and from the burdensome levies for laborers he laid on their dwindling population, the Indians revolted. Under the Christian cacique, Lucas Menéndez, Timucuan warriors killed Spanish soldiers and laborers, sparing only the friars. For the eight months the rebellion raged, many friars continued to minister to the rebels.

When the rebellion at last was quelled, the royal government investigated Rebolledo's administration of Florida. Uncovering a number of abuses, the crown removed Rebolledo as governor and brought him to Spain to stand trial. As for the Church, the years following the rebellion saw a period of expansion in the missions. By 1655, 70 friars were laboring among 26,000 Christian Indians in Florida.

Chapter 2 Review

Summary

- In 1496 Columbus pacified a revolt in Hispaniola by giving rebels free land grants and Indian slaves. This led to many problems concerning slavery and abuse of the Indians in the Spanish New World dominions.

- The Spanish government established the Laws of Burgos in 1512, which placed regulations on Indian labor in an attempt to reduce the abuse of Indians on *encomiendas*.

- In 1513 Spain established the *Requiriemento*, a document requiring Indians to acknowledge Spanish overlordship and permit the Catholic faith to be preached to them.

- After Cortés departed for Spain in 1528, the Reign of Terror began in Mexico. The *Audiencia Real*, sent to investigate the conquistador's administration of New Spain, imposed heavy taxes on the Indians and persecuted them in many violent ways.

- The Spanish priest Bartolomé de Las Casas labored hard for the passage of the *Nuevas Leyes* (New Laws) of 1542, forbidding slavery and the perpetu-

ation of *encomiendas*. These laws angered colonists and resulted in a bloody civil war in Peru.

- King Carlos I revoked the New Laws in 1545. A debate took place in which it was discussed whether Indians are natural slaves or not. This conference of Valladolid resulted in the Basic Law in 1573, which said that Spaniards were not to "conquer" but to "pacify" the Native Americans.

- The era of the Spanish missionaries began as an attempt to evangelize and civilize the Indians.

Key Concepts

repartimientos: land grants and Indian slaves given to the rebels in Hispaniola

encomiendas: complimentary land grants given to Spanish colonists in which the Indians were not slaves but were forced to labor for the colonists, who were required to civilize and evangelize them

Laws of Burgos: laws approved in 1512 that put regulations on Indian labor and required the Spaniards to convert the Indians

Requiriemento: a document of the Spanish government, written in 1513, requiring Indians to acknowl-

Chapter 2 Review (continued)

edge Spanish overlordship and permit the Catholic faith to be preached to them

Audiencia Real: the Royal Audience of Spain, which served as an appeals court

secular priest: a diocesan priest; a priest that does not belong to a religious order

Reductions: Indian republics founded by the Jesuits in Paraguay to isolate new Indian converts from Spanish settlers, many of whom were lax Christians, and to prevent injustice and slavery

Dates to Remember

1496: Columbus quells the revolts of Spanish colonists by instituting *repartimientos*.

1512: the passage of the Laws of Burgos

1513: the Spanish government issues the *Requiriemento*.

1524: Franciscan missionaries come to the New World.

1528: the Reign of Terror begins in Mexico.

1531: Our Lady of Guadalupe appears to Saint Juan Diego.

1538: the founding of the first university in the New World, St. Thomas Aquinas in Santo Domingo

1542: the passage of the New Laws

the death of Fray Juan Padilla, the first martyr in what would be the United States

1550: the Valladolid Conference

1573: the passage of the Basic Law

Central Characters

Bartolomé de Las Casas (1484–1566): Spanish lawyer turned priest who gained fame as the "Defender of the Indians"

Juan de Zumárraga (1468–1548): the first Bishop of New Spain.

Fray Juan Padilla (1500–1542): the first martyr in what would become the United States

Pedro Menéndez de Avilés (1519–1574): Spanish admiral who discovered and named the bay of San Agustín in Florida, and established a settlement there.

Questions for Review

1. What situation in the New World brought about the establishment of the *repartimientos* and the *encomiendas*?

2. What abuses arose from the establishment of the *encomiendas*, and why did so many of the Indians on the *encomiendas* die?

3. What role did Cortés' play in the establishment of *encomiendas*?

4. What were the benefits of the Laws of Burgos?

5. What were supposed to be the benefits of the *Requiriemento*, but what abuses did it lead to?

6. Why did the establishment of the New Laws result in civil war in Peru? Why were the New Laws revoked?

7. Explain the controversy that climaxed in the Conference of Valladolid. Who were the two main opponents involved?

8. Why were the missionaries so avid in their preaching and evangelizing?

9. Name two ways in which the missionaries evangelized and civilized the Indians.

10. What events led to the revival and expansion of the missions in Florida?

Ideas in Action

1. Research the lives of the early Spanish-American saints and martyrs.

2. Choose a mission church of colonial Mexico and research its founding and mission.

3. Look up the art and music of the Spanish missions. Listen to composers such as Ignacio de Jerusalem y Stella and Manuel de Zumaya. Look up the works of artists such as Sebastián López de Arteaga and Fray Alonso López de Herrera.

Chapter 2 Review (continued)

Highways and Byways

Pagan Christianity

When the Spanish came to the Americas, it was customary for their missionaries to adopt elements of the native pagan religion when converting the Indians. This made it was easier for the Indians to adapt to the Christian faith without too much resistance. For example, many of the native Indian tribes practiced human sacrifice, so they could easily accept the idea of consuming the body and blood of Christ.

The Indians had bestowed the title Tonantzin, "Our Reverend Mother," upon female deities, giving them the status of a mother figure; the idea of the Virgin Mary was thus easily introduced among the Aztecs.

The Church strove to put an end to most pagan practices, but she also made a point of assimilating pagan celebrations into Christian celebrations. All Souls Day on November 2 closely coincided with the Aztec autumn rituals in honor of departed ancestors. This assimilation gave rise to the Day of the Dead, which is still observed in Mexico today.

FRANCE SETTLES THE NEW WORLD

First Voyages

François I (Francis I), king of France, could not have been pleased with Spain's growing empire in America. Since becoming king in 1515, he had been struggling against the power of Spain's king, Carlos I. Carlos, the heir to the most powerful ruling house of Europe, the Habsburgs, was his chief enemy and the major obstacle to the expansion of France's power in Europe. From his grandfather, Maximilian, Carlos had inherited the Holy Roman Empire (where he bore the title of Emperor Karl [or Charles] V), which included all of Germany. In 1506, Carlos had succeeded his father, Philippe, in the wealthy principality of Flanders. Through his mother, Juana, the daughter of Fernando and Isabel, Carlos became king of Castile and León and Aragon—and of the West Indies with all their gold. Carlos' lands surrounded France on the northeast, the east, and the south. Carlos' wealth exceeded François' wealth. Carlos was just too powerful.

A map of North America, London, 1627

François I did everything he could to break Carlos' power. Beginning in 1520, he fought wars with this king and emperor, allying himself with Carlos' enemies, including the Muslim Turks and the Lutheran princes of Germany. François commissioned privateers (really, pirates) to prey on Spanish ships bearing gold from America to Spain and to harry Spain's New World settlements. Now, thought François, he would beat Carlos at his own game. Since Spain had not yet discovered a westward sea route to the true Indies, France would send an explorer to find it.

The man François chose for this expedition was a native of Florence, Italy—Giovanni da Verrazzano. Born ten years before Columbus' first voyage to America, Verrazzano had sailed the Mediterranean, living for brief periods in both Syria and Egypt. Coming to France, where he became known as Jean Florin, Verrazzano served King François I as a privateer against Spanish ships bound from America. Since he knew the Atlantic sea routes well, Verrazzano, it appeared, would well suit the king's purposes.

If one were to discover a passage to the Indies—the rumored "Straits of Anian"—northwest seemed the natural direction to go. Spain had already explored the sea routes to the south, and northwest waters were familiar to French fishermen, who for about 20 years had been plying their ships off the Grand Banks of Newfoundland. In January 1524, Verrazzano set sail in a ship named the *Dauphine*. From the Madeira Islands he chose a route to the north to avoid the Spanish lands.

After two months at sea, Verrazzano landed on the coast of what is now North Carolina. Thence he sailed north and became the first European to enter what would one day be called New York harbor. Still heading northward, he sailed into Narragansett Bay, and then along the coast of Maine, to Newfoundland. In July he returned to France, but without having discovered the Straits of Anian.

Though he had not found a northwest passage to the Indies, Verrazzano did not think his voyage a failure. He recommended that King François colonize the newly discovered lands. The French king, however, was too involved in a war with King Carlos to give any thought to colonies.

Ten years later, François I tried again to find a northwest passage to the Indies. This time he chose as his explorer one Jacques Cartier, a native of Saint-Malo on the coast of Brittany—a town that had long served as a haven for French privateers who raided Spanish shipping. Cartier himself was a pirate with experience of the Atlantic Ocean. In April 1534 he set sail on the king's quest in two small ships manned by 60 sailors. Following the route of the French fishermen, Cartier reached the waters off Newfoundland in 21 days, where, because of the many icebergs, he sought safety in a small harbor. There he spotted an odd and frightening beast—"as big as a calf and as white as a swan." His men killed and ate it. It was a polar bear.

From Newfoundland, Cartier sailed northward and skirted the Labrador coast. There, dense fog and barren, rocky land dampened his enthusiasm. "In all the Northland," he wrote, "I have not seen a cartload of good earth." Turning south, Cartier discovered a more pleasant land, beautifully wooded, abundant with strawberries, blackberries, and gooseberries. He had crossed the St. Lawrence waterway and landed at Prince Edward Island.

Turning northward again along the coast, Cartier eventually came upon a great channel landward, opening to the sea—could this be the Straits of Anian? Sailing into the channel, he found it to be only a bay, which he named Chaleur. Though not the fabled passage he sought, Cartier discovered on its banks what would one day become the source of France's new world wealth—furs. Cartier and his men traded knives, iron tools, glass beads, and other trinkets with the local Indians in exchange for pelts of beaver, fox, and marten.

Cartier returned to France in September 1534. Eight months later, François I sent him out again to continue his exploration. On this voyage Cartier discovered the St. Lawrence River. Using as interpreters two Indians he had captured on the previous voyage, Cartier learned from local Indians of a land of gold that purportedly lay up the river. Cartier sailed up the St. Lawrence beyond the site of what would become Montreal, but finding no land of gold, he returned to France in July 1536. Cartier gave the name "Canada" (from the native word *kanata*, which means village or settlement) to the lands he explored along the St. Lawrence.

In 1541, the French king commissioned Cartier and Jean-François de la Rocque, Sieur (Lord) de Roberval, to sail up the St. Lawrence and establish a settlement along its banks. Roberval, who was to be governor, carried with him, by the king's command, 200 settlers, many of them released prisoners. Arriving at a fort Cartier had earlier

François I, by Titian, ca. 1530

raised on the St. Lawrence, Roberval and his colonists established their settlement in the summer of 1542. Their first winter in Canada, however, was so harsh that most of the settlers died. Those who survived returned to France in 1543.

The Founding of New France

Over 60 years passed before France attempted another settlement in America. There were too many troubles at home. Civil war had broken out during the reigns of François I's successors. The teachings of the French Protestant reformer, Jean Calvin, spread rapidly through sectors of French society, and French Protestants, called Huguenots, formed a powerful core of resistance to the Catholic king. Conflict between the Huguenots and the

Map of Canada, by Samuel de Champlain

Catholic party, called the Catholic League, brought on a bitter civil feud, with each side committing acts of atrocious cruelty against the other. France was devastated. At the center of the conflict were the French kings, the Valois, who would side, now with the Catholic League, now with the Huguenots. When a monk assassinated Henri III, the last of the Valois, Henri de Bourbon, the Huguenot leader, became king as Henri IV in 1589. He established peace by himself becoming Catholic and issuing the Edict of Nantes in 1598, allowing the Huguenots religious liberty and a great deal of political and military power.

With peace achieved, Henri IV could turn his thoughts to America. In 1603, the king commissioned his viceroy, Aymar de Chastes, to explore the shores of Canada and find a site for a French settlement. As second-in-command on this expedition went the royal geographer, Samuel de Champlain. Champlain was no stranger to the New World. The son of a mariner, he had become a sailor after serving a brief stint in the military, fighting the Huguenots. He had also served for a time with the Spanish navy, battling English pirates off the coast of Puerto Rico. De Chastes's expedition however established no settlement, though Champlain took note of a place where the St. Lawrence narrows—a good spot, he thought, for a fort. The Indians called this place Québec.

In 1604, Champlain joined another expedition that explored the northeast coast of North America as far south as Cape Cod. After establishing a settlement on the coast of Nova

Scotia, the expedition returned to France. Champlain, however, convinced his patron, Pierre du Gast, Sieur de Monts, that the Saint Lawrence narrows was a far better location for a settlement; thus, in July 1608, Champlain established a dwelling and storehouse at Québec, and it became a center for fur trading and the nucleus around which a village and fortress grew up.

From Québec, Champlain explored the rivers that flow into the St. Lawrence. On one expedition he discovered a large lake that today straddles the border of New York and Vermont. In 1609, on the shores of this lake (since called Lake Champlain), near Ticonderoga, Champlain joined the Huron and Algonquin in a battle against the Iroquois nation. Defeated by this combination of Indians and French, the Iroquois became the implacable enemies of New France.

An assassin's knife ended Henri IV's life in 1610, and under his son, the child king Louis XIII, France neglected its New World colony. Once again, the Huguenots were causing trouble and, in Germany, the Protestant princes waged war against the Catholic Habsburg emperor. Yet, despite government neglect, Champlain continued his explorations down the St. Lawrence. During an expedition that he made in 1615 with the Huron against the Iroquois, Champlain, with a small band of French soldiers, crossed Lake Ontario.

Champlain found it difficult to convince anyone to settle as farmers in New France. Besides a few missionaries, the French in Canada were content to be fur traders. These traders, both the licensed ones, called *voyageurs*, and the unlicensed, called *coureurs de bois*, wandered the waters and forests of Canada in search of valuable pelts. They were a colorful lot, remaining in the wilds for months at a time, becoming as adept at woodcraft as any Indian. Often they married Indian women and "went native," living more like Indians than Frenchmen. Though some traders were unscrupulous, selling brandy to the natives and corrupting their morals by bad example, others, for their fairness and kindness, earned the Indians' trust.

Champlain however did succeed in attracting some settlers to Québec. By 1628, 400 French farmers were tilling fields on the banks of the St. Lawrence. Though not a large settlement, Québec attracted a band of English pirates, who seized the town in 1629 and imprisoned Champlain. The English released Champlain and withdrew from Québec in 1632, when the king of England returned the settlement to France. Champlain again served as governor until his death in 1635. He had spent some 40 years in New France.

The Natives of New France

The French did not find great cities like Tenochtitlán in Canada nor high, gold-rich civilizations like Mexico and Peru. The natives of Canada built no dwellings of stone but only of wood and bark. Nor they did calculate the course of the year according to precise observations of the stars nor work intricate designs in gold and silver. They were a simpler people.

That is not to say, however, that the Indians of Canada showed no signs of civilization. Though they survived by fishing and hunting and wandered far afield in search of game, the Canadian Indians practiced agriculture. In extensive fields surrounding their villages, Indian women (the men were the hunters and warriors) farmed maize, beans, squash, and tobacco. Their villages, congeries of "longhouses" formed from saplings and covered with elm bark, were more or less fixed in a location and, during war, were protected by wooden palisades.

The Canadian Indians showed their highest achievement in government. The Iroquois were really a league of five Indian nations: the Mohawk, Oneida, Onondaga, Cayuga, and Seneca. According to legend, sometime in the late 16th century, the visionary Dekanawidah advised the Mohawk chief, Hiawatha, to forsake cannibalism and form a league of tribes based on "peace, civil authority, righteousness, and the great law." Hiawatha wanted the

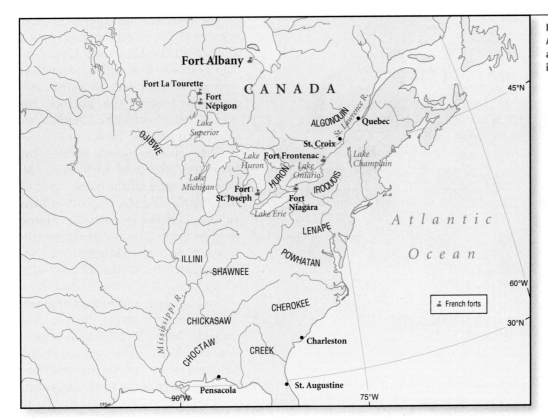

league to respect the integrity of the individual tribes that would federate under a council of leaders and by the practice of common ceremonies. The member tribes of the Iroquois League sent delegates, chosen by the clans within each tribe, to the common council. No important decisions were reached unless every delegate agreed to the proper course of action. Every tribe of the league had its own chiefs' council, made up of the leaders of the tribe. A woman's council, formed from the mothers of the tribe, had a say in all important matters affecting the tribe, including who sat on the chiefs' council.

Unlike other eastern tribes, the Iroquois were monogamous, though divorce was common among them. As the farmers and the mothers of the warriors, women had considerable say in questions of war and peace.

The Iroquois religion was polytheistic. They believed in two gods, one of winter and the other of spring, who were in continual conflict. According to one account, the gods were said to be the grandsons of Tharonyawakon, the "Sky Holder," who, out of jealousy, grew angry with his pregnant wife and cast her to the earth. Tharonyawakon's wife bore a daughter, who married a turtle in human form—the turtle being the symbol of power over earth and water. From this union came the gods of winter and spring.

The Iroquois waged bitter war on surrounding tribes. They were ruthless enemies, torturing and enslaving their captives. Some they enslaved, but others they admitted to the tribe to replace family members who had died. During the first half of the 17th century they began to wage relentless war on neighboring tribes, the Conestoga to the south and the Algonquin to the east. The Iroquois were skilled strategists, displaying a considerable talent for organization. This, coupled with guns received from the Dutch in the mid-16th century, made them nearly invincible. By 1656 they had swept over the Huron, Tionontati, the Neutrals, and the Erie. In the 18th century, the Iroquois conquered the Delaware or Lenape nation and the Illinois and harassed the English colony of Virginia. In 1715 the Tuscarora of North Carolina, who had moved north to New York, joined the Iroquois, forming what was thenceforth known as the League of Six Nations.

Algonquin village of Pomeioc in North Carolina. An 1885 drawing based on a 16th century original.

The Iroquois became implacable enemies of the French because of their alliance with the Huron and Algonquin. The Iroquois later allied themselves with the English and the Dutch, and largely because of this alliance, the French never established settlements south of upper New York.

The Huron (also called the Wyandot), who lived north of the St. Lawrence, were of the same stock as the Iroquois and shared most of their culture. Like the Iroquois, the Huron lived in longhouses, gathered in palisaded settlements. Hunting and fishing supplemented the Huron diet, which came chiefly from farming, in which both men and women engaged. The Huron, however, lacked the Iroquois' genius for political organization. Still, like the Iroquois, the Huron governed by a council or assembly, which made all-important decisions. Women selected the leaders of the tribe. The chief's role was to announce the council's decisions to the clans, though no chief had the power to enforce compliance. There was no police force or threat of punishment for anyone who refused to go along with the council; a chief had to rely on his eloquence to sway his warriors.

In fact, the power to coerce seemed entirely absent from Huron society. According to the Jesuit missionaries who worked among them, warriors did not obey their chiefs, sons did not obey their fathers. Everyone had to be persuaded before he would act. And as the Jesuit missionary Jérome Salemat wrote, since there were no punishments for crimes, "it is the community that has to atone for the misdeeds of individuals."

The Huron believed that the world is filled with good and evil spirits whose favor they sought to curry by sacrifice. The French missionaries said the Huron seemed to have some concept of a supreme being, though they offered him no worship. The missionaries deemed the Huron religion no better than demon worship.

The Iroquois eventually crushed the Huron, with their kin, the Algonquin, and their villages were scattered.

Missionaries of New France

In 1638, King Louis XIII consecrated his lands to Our Lady of the Assumption. Matters had improved in France since Louis had become king in 1610. In 1628, Louis' energetic chancellor, Cardinal Armand de Richelieu, had destroyed the power of the Huguenots at their stronghold of La Rochelle. Under Richelieu's impetus, France had then entered a war on the side of the Lutheran Swedes and the Protestant princes of Germany against the Catholic Habsburg emperor of Germany and the Catholic Habsburg king of Spain. Though at first the war had gone badly for France, by 1638 the tables had turned. France was on her way to becoming the chief power of Europe. Louis XIII thus wanted to show his gratitude to the Virgin for these dubious benefits and seek her continued protection.

Yet, New France had been dedicated to the Mother of God even before 1638—through the zeal of her missionaries. The first missionaries in New France were Jesuits sent by the

Duchesse d'Aiguillon in 1611. But their mission was short-lived. That same year, pirates from the English settlement of Jamestown destroyed the mission.

Champlain, a devout Catholic, had been as zealous for missionary work as he was for exploration. In 1614 he had brought four Franciscan Recollect missionaries to Québec. In 1625, eight Jesuits followed, among whom was a 28-year old priest, Jean de Brébeuf.

The North American Martyrs

Like other Jesuit missionaries who would come after him, Père (Father) Jean de Brébeuf not only worked among the Indians but shared their way of life, including living in a wigwam both in summer and in the dead of winter. When spring succeeded one harsh winter, he and another Jesuit, Père de Noue, traveled by canoe with a band of Huron Indians to the Georgian Bay on Lake Huron, where for two years Père Brébeuf labored among the Huron, but met with no success. In 1629, when Québec surrendered to the English, Brébeuf had to return to France.

At home in France, amid all the comforts of civilization, Père Brébeuf did not forget Canada. He returned in 1633 and set out again for the Lake Huron country. After a journey of 30 days through dense forest, beset by Indian enemies, Brébeuf and another Jesuit, Père Antoine Daniel, reached Lake Huron. There Brébeuf labored for 16 years, deprived of the French society and civilization he had always known. Then, in 1647, his Jesuit superiors transferred him to another mission near Québec.

A year earlier, 1646, war broke out between the Iroquois and the Huron, and two missionaries, trying to reach the Huron country, were captured. One of the missionaries, the Jesuit Isaac Jogues, had penetrated as far as Sault Ste. Marie, the outlet to Lake Superior (the northernmost of the Great Lakes). He had hoped to work among the Indians of the region and to carry the Gospel to the Sioux who lived at the headwaters of the Mississippi River. Instead, another task, and a greater glory, awaited him.

Lily of the Mohawk

The mission to the Iroquois was, by all worldly standards, a failure. Yet, it did produce one success—the conversion of an Indian girl, Kateri Tekakwitha. This young girl, who had at the age of four lost her mother, father, and brother to smallpox, had been raised by her uncle, the chief of the Turtle clan of the Mohawk tribe. Her face badly scored with smallpox scars, Kateri shrank from the marriages her uncle sought to arrange for her. She first learned of the Christian faith in 1667 from Jesuit missionaries. Then, only 11 years old, she embraced the Faith, but delayed her baptism.

Though surrounded by examples of immoral behavior, Kateri lived the life of a Christian virgin. When she was 18, she received baptism at the hands of Père Jacques de Lamberville. Because the Mohawk opposed her life of chastity, she had finally to flee from her home, and she escaped to an Indian village on the St. Lawrence, where she died on April 17, 1680. Shortly after her death, Kateri Tekakwitha, remembered as "Lily of the Mohawk," became an object of devotion to the Indian peoples. She was beatified by Pope John Paul II in 1980.

Kateri Tekakwitha

On August 3, 1642, the Mohawk, a tribe of the Iroquois nation, captured Père Jogues at Tres-Rívìeres on the St. Lawrence and took him a captive to their village on the Mohawk River, about 40 miles north of Fort Orange (later named Albany, New York). For a year and one month he remained in the Mohawk village, where he was treated as a slave and suffered terrible tortures, including having several of his fingers burned or chewed off. It was the Dutch Protestants from Fort Orange who finally freed Jogues. They carried him by ship down the Hudson River to New Amsterdam. From there he took ship for France.

But Père Jogues was not one to flee danger. Instead of remaining in France, he returned, in 1644, to Canada and asked to be sent as a missionary to his former captors, the Mohawk. This was not a particularly good time for a French missionary to enter Mohawk lands. Sickness had broken out among the Iroquois, and blight had struck their crops. The Indians blamed their troubles on Jogues, whom they called a sorcerer. Although knowing full well the danger that awaited him among the Mohawk, Jogues did not turn back. Abandoned by the Huron men that had accompanied him, and with only one companion, Jogues met the Iroquois. They captured him, stripped him naked, and slashed him with their knives. Finally, on October 18, 1646, the Indians felled the priest with a tomahawk stroke and cut off his head. They fixed the head on a pole and threw his body into the Mohawk River.

Père Brébeuf, meanwhile, had been working among the Huron. Though in 1642 the Iroquois made peace with the French, their war with the Huron continued. The Iroquois attacked not only Huron settlements but burned the Huron missions and slaughtered the missionaries. On March 16, 1649, they captured Jean de Brébeuf.

Père Brébeuf did not utter a groan during the tortures that followed. After beating him with clubs, the Indians tied him to posts. Kindling a fire at the missionary's feet, they slashed his body with their knives and, in mockery of baptism, poured scalding hot water over his head. Around his neck they tied a collar of red-hot tomahawk heads and thrust a hot iron rod down his throat. When Jean de Brébeuf at length expired, the Indians cut out his heart and ate it, for they wanted to partake of his courage.

Brébeuf and Jogues were not the only martyrs of this period. Among those killed by the Iroquois were Père Jean Lalende, in what is now New York, in 1646; Père Antoine Daniel in Canada, in 1648; and Brébeuf's companion, Père Gabriel Lalement in Canada, in 1649. With Brébeuf and Jogues, the Church honors these men as saints, under the title, the North American Martyrs.

New France Grows

French colonization in North America spread through the efforts of fur traders and missionaries. Though the one sought pelts and the other souls, they often accompanied each other into the wild; and the trading post of the trapper was never far from the mission post of the priest.

These adventurers went forth from a New France in Canada that was becoming more settled and regularized in its government. A governor general, appointed by the king, oversaw the French settlements of Acadia, Montreal, and Trois Rívìeres, each of which had its own local governor. Under the governor-general were an *intendant*, who looked after the colony's finances, and an administrator of justice. In 1659 the king appointed a bishop for Québec, who, together with the governor-general and the *intendant*, administered the colony. The three were aided by a council that acted like the Spanish *audiencia*.

The settlement of New France followed an almost feudal pattern. As in Europe, the farmers, called *habitants*, were organized under a local lord, called the *seigneur*. French *habitant* settlements differed from those of the English further south, in that English colonists dwelt on isolated farmsteads, while the *habitants* gathered in villages from which they went out

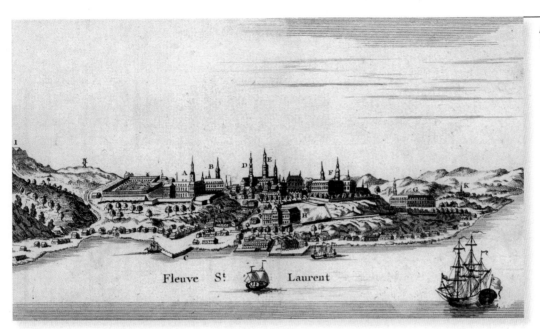

Fleuve St. Laurent

to work their fields. The *habitants* paid rent to the *seigneur* for their land and gave him six days of free labor a year.

Missionaries and fur traders went out from these more settled regions into a country that was still wild and savage. One pair, a priest and trader, would be the agents of a discovery that would add vast new territories to France.

Missionary and Explorer

King Louis XIV had grandiose plans for France. He wanted France to be the greatest power (and thus have the largest army) in Europe. He wanted France to secure her "natural boundary" in the east, the Rhine River—an ambition that would bring France into conflict with the Holy Roman Empire and anyone else who wanted to keep France down. All of this, of course, required huge expenditures of money, which is why Jean-Baptiste Colbert, Louis' finance minister, was looking for a route from New France to the silver mines of Mexico, via the Pacific. There were rumors that such a route existed—the Indians spoke of a "great water" in the west that flowed into the sea. To search for this route, the *intendant* of New France commissioned a fur trader by the name of Louis Jolliet, and Jolliet chose as his companion on this expedition an old schoolmate, now a Jesuit priest—Jacques Marquette.

Since his arrival in New France in 1666, Père Marquette had been working with refugee Ottawa and Huron at a mission in La Pointe, on the southernmost of the Apostle Islands on Lake Superior (in what is now Wisconsin). When the Sioux drove the Ottawa and the Huron out of Wisconsin, Marquette withdrew with them to Mackinac in Michigan. This mission, however, was bearing little fruit in conversions. The Indians were demoralized and much given to drinking strong liquor. It was in this discouraging position that Jolliet found his old schoolmate. With hopes of new mission fields to cultivate and greater success before him, Père Marquette joined Jolliet's expedition. On May 17, 1673, Marquette, Jolliet, and five Frenchmen set out in two birch bark canoes from Mackinac to find the "Great Water."

Paddling in their canoes across Lake Michigan, the explorers at length entered Green Bay. From Green Bay they followed the Fox River to Lake Winnebago. This was an old route, already explored and much traveled by both Jesuits and traders. However, when the party reached a swamp they grew confused about which water route to take, for there were many channels. Here Père Marquette was especially useful, for he knew many Indian languages and was able to talk with the local Indians, who directed the party through the swamp to

Jolliet and Marquette's
and La Salle's voyages
in North America

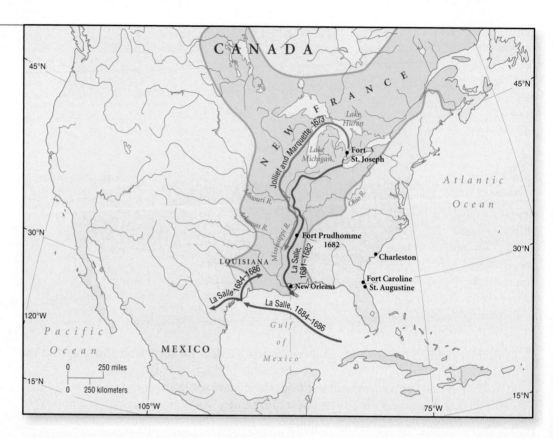

the Wisconsin River. This south-westward-flowing river, they told Marquette, led to the Great Water.

A month after they had left Mackinac, the explorers entered the Great Water—the Mississippi. Moving with the current down river, they came upon rich fields of corn—the lands of the Illini people, who treated the company with great hospitality. They asked Jolliet, Marquette, and their companions to remain among them, and Marquette promised that he would return. He greatly desired to work among these Indians, whose demeanor and culture were so superior to that of the decayed Hurons. Great progress, he thought, could be made among them.

Continuing south, the explorers eventually came upon the mouth of a great river whose swift, turbulent current carried numbers of "large and entire trees, branches, and floating islands" into the Mississippi. This new river, which the natives called the "Muddy River," was the Missouri. Marquette thought it might be the Straits of Anian—the westward channel to the Indies.

Not long after passing the mouth of the Missouri, the explorers found themselves in warmer regions where Spanish moss festooned the trees along the riverbanks. A short distance south of where the Arkansas River flows into the Mississippi, the party was welcomed and feasted by an Indian tribe. The dinner was not much to French tastes—boiled corn-meal and roasted dog—but the Indians could serve nothing better because, they explained, they feared to go out on the plains to hunt buffalo. There wandered other Indian tribes who hunted with guns they had received from white men. These white men, Jolliet and Marquette concluded, were the Spanish. If the French proceeded farther south they could be captured and then the news of the discovery of the Great Water would never reach France. Since it was clear that this southward flowing river did not run into the Pacific, but into the Gulf of Mexico, the company decided to return to Québec.

When the explorers reached the mission at Green Bay, Marquette was ill. He remained behind while Jolliet continued alone to Québec to deliver their report to the governor-general, Louis de Buade, Comte (Count) de Frontenac. When he recovered, Père Marquette returned to the Illinois Indians as he had promised. After a cold and bitter winter, he reached their village; but overcome by exhaustion and the effects of sickness, he remained only three weeks among them. Knowing he was near death, Marquette decided to return to Mackinac; but he never made it. Passing along the western shore of Michigan, Marquette asked his companions to take him ashore at the mouth of a small stream. There he died, May 19, 1675, at the age of 39.

King Louis' Land

In the winter of 1681–82, a party of 54 adventurers began a long, cold journey. So cold was the weather that their canoes had to be dragged on sleds over the frozen waters of the Chicago and Illinois Rivers. The party included French woodsmen, Indian guides, ten Indian women, and three children. Their leader was the seasoned explorer, the Sieur de La Salle, whose goal was to reach the mouth of the Mississippi and establish, both for France and for himself, a great inland empire.

René Robert-Cavelier, Sieur de La Salle, had come from France to Canada in 1666. Educated by the Jesuits in France, La Salle seems to have entered some religious order, for he had forfeited his estates in France. However, he jettisoned the religious life for the promise of adventure in the New World. When he arrived in Canada, La Salle received a large grant of land near Montreal, but the peaceful life of a farmer was not for him. He became a fur trader, exploring the Great Lakes and their tributary rivers.

Bust of King Louis XIV, Old Québec City, Quebec

With Governor Frontenac, La Salle conceived of a plan to protect the trade of New France from the inroads of the English and the Dutch. A string of forts and missions, he thought, should be built along the waterways of New France. In 1674 and 1677, La Salle went to France to convince King Louis XIV to embrace the plan. The king approved it and granted to La Salle the right to explore the Mississippi to its mouth, govern all the territory he should discover, and to own the Mississippi fur trade. La Salle had only to pay for the entire expedition himself.

So it was that La Salle's party found itself skating down the frozen Illinois River. The expedition went without mishap. Armed with a peace pipe, La Salle's party suffered no attack from Indians. By April they had reached the Mississippi Delta, and at a spot where the great river made a wide turn, La Salle dreamed of a city that would become the Paris of the New World. Reaching the mouth of the river, La Salle claimed the river and all the land on its banks and along the banks of its tributary rivers, for King Louis of France. These lands La Salle called "Louisiana" in honor of his majesty.

La Salle had taken the first step to secure his great inland empire. He next began erecting forts to defend it. His first fort, erected on Starved Rock on the Illinois River, he named St. Louis. Next, he established a trading post at the site where Chicago is today. But he was unable to do more. His trading rivals resented La Salle's monopoly over the Mississippi and poisoned the mind of the new governor (who had succeeded Frontenac) against him. The governor seized Fort St. Louis, and La Salle had to return to France to plead his case before the king.

King Louis listened to La Salle's appeal and confirmed him as governor of Louisiana. Louis agreed, as well, to La Salle's idea of a settlement in the Mississippi Delta. In 1684, La Salle sailed from France with four ships and 400 men to establish his New World Paris at the site where the Mississippi makes its wide bend.

The expedition was a disaster. The naval commander refused to heed La Salle, and the Spanish seized the main supply ship. After recovering from a long sickness that struck him in the West Indies, La Salle discovered that most of his men had deserted him. Continuing the expedition with only 180 men, La Salle missed the mouth of the Mississippi and continued eastward until he landed at Matagordo Bay in what is now Texas. Twice he and his remaining party tried to reach Canada overland. On the second attempt, the men mutinied, and one of them killed La Salle in March 1687.

The Settlement of Louisiana

Because of La Salle, France controlled what would become the most important inland waterway of North America—the Mississippi River and its tributaries, the Missouri and Ohio. King Louis XIV continued La Salle's policy in Louisiana, building forts and missions up and down the Mississippi Valley. By 1712, a number of settlements dotted the lower Mississippi Valley and, in 1717, La Salle's New Paris began to rise on the very spot he had envisioned for it. Named New Orleans, it would become a most important center for trade and French culture in the New World.

Soon Jesuits and Franciscan Capuchins began their work among the Indians of the Mississippi Valley. Their labors were extraordinary, for the territory they had to cover was immense. From Lake Pepin in Minnesota to Mobile, Alabama, these missionaries worked tirelessly. One, Père Allouez, a friend of Marquette, served two missions that were 300 miles apart. In spite of their heroic efforts, the "blackrobes" (as the Indians called the missionaries) saw few results in the Mississippi Valley. "Our life continues in the threading of thick forests," wrote one missionary, "the dragging of one's self over mountains, the crossing of lakes and rivers in a canoe, all to arrive at one poor savage who runs from us, and whom we cannot tame either by entreaty or by kindness." This father had been a missionary for 15 years!

Yet, despite the zeal of missionaries and the efforts of colonists and the king, New France could not last; the French did not settle the land in sufficient numbers to hold on to it, and too many who came to New France and Louisiana were content to lead the wandering life of the fur trader rather than the settled life of a farmer. So, even though the Indians were friendly to them (for the French, for the most part, were kind to the natives), the French had insufficient numbers of men to defend their interests in the New World. New France and, ultimately, Louisiana, were destined to become the possessions of another colonial power whose settled and thriving communities already dotted the Atlantic seaboard. New France and Louisiana would in time give way to New England and Virginia.

Chapter 3 Review

Summary

- François I, king of France, was displeased with Spain's growing empire in America, and he had been struggling against Carlos I, the king of Spain and Holy Roman Emperor. François sent out privateers to prey on Spanish ships bearing gold from America to Spain and to harass the Spanish settlements.

- François decided that, since Spain had not yet discovered a westward sea route to the true Indies, the rumored "Straits of Anian," he would send Giovanni da Verrazzano, one of his privateers, to find it. Verrazzano chose a northern route to avoid Spanish lands.

- Verrazzano first landed on the coast of what is now North Carolina and then went on to what is now New York harbor, Narragansett Bay, and then along the coast of Maine to Newfoundland. He failed to discover the Straits of Anian.

- Ten years later François sent out the pirate Jacques Cartier to find the Straits of Anian. Cartier landed on Prince Edward Island. He also discovered the St. Lawrence River and the place that would become Montreal. He gave the name "Canada" to the lands he had discovered along the St. Lawrence.

Chapter 3 Review (continued)

- In 1608, the royal geographer, Samuel de Champlain, established the first settlement at Québec, which became a center for fur trading. This brought not settlers but mostly fur traders to New France.

- The Canadian Indians were found to be farmers and showed their highest achievement in government.

- The first missionaries to New France were Jesuits, sent by the Duchesse d'Aiguillon in 1611. Jesuits and Franciscan Recollects founded and staffed missions throughout New France and, later, Louisiana. Among the Jesuit missionaries were Jean de Brébeuf, Issac Jogues, and the others whom we remember as the North American Martyrs.

- King Louis XIV, desirous of having France become the greatest power in Europe, needed a great amount of money, so he sent Louis Jolliet and Jacques Marquette to find a route from New France to the silver mines of Mexico. The two explorers discovered the "Great Water"—the Mississippi.

- Sieur de La Salle planned to protect the trade of New France from the inroads of the English and the Dutch by building a string of forts and missions along the waterways of New France. On his expedition down the Illinois River, he discovered new lands, which he called Louisiana. There he identified the site for what would become his "New Paris," later to be called New Orleans, the most important center for trade and French culture in the New World.

Key Concepts

Straits of Anian: the rumored western sea route to the Indies

fur trade: an industry dealing in the acquisition and sale of animal fur

voyageur: French name for licensed fur traders

coureurs de bois: French name for unlicensed fur traders

Iroquois or League of Six Nations: the alliance of the Mohawk, Oneida, Onondaga, Cayuga, Seneca, and Tuscarora tribes

North American Martyrs: eight men killed for the Faith during the warfare between the Iroquois and the Huron in Canada

Dates to Remember

1524: Giovanni da Verrazzano sets out to find the Straits of Anian and discovers North Carolina, New York harbor, and Newfoundland.

1534: Jacques Cartier discovers the St. Lawrence River and Montreal.

1608: Samuel de Champlain establishes the first successful settlement in Québec, which becomes a center for fur trading.

1611: the first missionaries come to Canada.

1673: Louis Jolliet and Jacques Marquette discover the Mississippi River.

1677: Sieur de La Salle sets out to explore the Mississippi and establishes forts and missions to protect New France from the English and the Dutch.

Central Characters

François (Francis) I (1494–1547): the French king who opened France's age of exploration by sending explorers to discover the Straits of Anian

Giovanni da Verrazzano (1485–1528): Italian navigator and explorer for France who was the first European to sight New York harbor and Narragansett Bay

Jacques Cartier (1491–1557): French mariner whose explorations of the Canadian coast and the St. Lawrence River claimed parts of North America for the French

Samuel de Champlain (1567–1635): French explorer who founded the city of Québec and established the fur trade in Canada

Jean de Brébeuf (1593–1649): Jesuit missionary to New France, one of the eight North American Martyrs. The patron saint of Canada.

Isaac Jogues (1607–1646): Jesuit missionary, one of the North American Martyrs, who sacrificed his life for the evangelization of the North American Indians

Chapter 3 Review (continued)

Louis Jolliet (1645–1700): French fur trader who, with his companion, Père Jacques Marquette, was the first white man to explore the Mississippi River

Père Jacques Marquette (1637–1675): French Jesuit missionary who, with Louis Jolliet, traveled down the Mississippi River and reported the first accurate data on its course

René Robert-Cavelier, Sieur de La Salle (1643–1687): French explorer in North America who led an expedition down the Illinois and Mississippi rivers and claimed all the region along that route for France, naming the region "Louisiana"

Questions for Review

1. What was François I's motivation for finding the Straits of Anian?

2. What events induced France to colonize North America?

3. What event caused the Iroquois to become the implacable enemies of New France?

4. In what ways did the Indians of Canada differ from those of Mexico and Peru?

5. In what did the Canadian Indians excel?

6. What is the League of Five Nations, or the Iroquois?

7. How did the Iroquois become the League of Six Nations?

8. Describe the government of the League of Six Nations and how it was formed.

9. Describe the government of the French settlement in Canada.

10. Why did Jolliet and Marquette set out to find a route along the "Great Water" to Mexico?

Ideas in Action

1. Look at a map of the Mississippi River and chart Jolliet and Marquette's route of exploration.

2. Read the lives of the early North American saints and martyrs, including St. Isaac Jogues and St. Kateri Tekakwitha.

3. Read some of the folktales of the American Indians of Canada and the Mississippi River region.

Highways and Byways

Folktales in North America

Like every other culture, the Indian cultures of North America have their own folk tales, which were handed down orally. While many European fairy and folk tales begin with, "once upon a time," the American Indian myth often starts with, "before the people came," or, "when Coyote was a man." American Indians use the terms *myth* and *folktale* interchangeably, for, in the Native American view, the difference between the two is a matter of time rather than content. If the incident related in the story happened at a time when the world had not yet assumed its present form, the story is regarded as a myth. If the same characters appear in the present, however, the story is called a folktale.

Storytellers would tell the tales while gathered around a fire at night, and thus transport the listeners to another world. This transportation was achieved not only through the novelty of the tale itself but also by the imaginative skill of the narrator. Narrators often added gestures and songs to the tale. Because the effect of the story depended so much on the narrator, there were many versions of each tale. The stories varied each time they were told, but they varied only within the limits of the tradition established for that plot and according to the cultural background of the narrator and the listeners.

4 ENGLAND COMES TO AMERICA

England's Columbus

About the same time Columbus was lobbying the Portuguese king for ships, another son of Genoa, Giovanni Caboto, was himself dreaming of a westward route to the Indies. Caboto had sailed the Mediterranean in the service of Venice. He had visited the Muslim holy city of Mecca where he heard talk of the spice-laden lands to the east. Like Columbus, he conceived an "Enterprise of the Indies" and sought royal help to put it into effect.

In 1484, Caboto moved to England. The Italian seafarer, whom the English called John Cabot, convinced the English merchants of the seafaring town of Bristol that they could find a passage to the Indies by sailing west. These merchants, who had long carried on a trade with Iceland, had heard legends of the "Island of Brazil" and the "Seven Cities" to the west, and Cabot's idea fired their interest. They sent out ships to find the islands, but always without success. Then, in 1493, came news of Columbus' discovery. The merchants and Cabot decided to forgo searching for the islands and, like Columbus, head directly to the Indies.

The king of England at the time was Henry VII. England had lately come out of a long civil war between two rival families who each claimed the throne. These Wars of the Roses (named from the symbols of the opposing parties, a white rose and a red) ended when Henry Tudor defeated his opponents at the Battle of Bosworth. Marrying the heiress of the opposing house, Henry became king of England in 1485.

King Henry was stingy; so, when he approved John Cabot's plan for an expedition to the Indies, he stipulated that Cabot and his sons had to finance the trip themselves. On May 20, 1497, Cabot, his sons, and 18 men set sail in the ship, the *Mathew*, bound for Asia. They sailed to the northwest and after 52 days landed on the northernmost point of Cape Breton Island. It was the feast of St. John the Baptist, June 24, when Cabot planted the colors of England and took possession of the land for King Henry. With its fertile soil and temperate climate, Cabot was certain Cape Breton must belong to the northeast coast of Asia. Sailing north again, he explored the southeast coast of Newfoundland. But finding no evidence of Asian civilization or gold (all the local Indians could offer him were furs), Cabot set sail again for England, arriving in Bristol harbor on August 6, 1497.

King Henry VII, as shown in stained glass window in Cardiff, Glamorgan, Wales

Perhaps Henry VII was displeased with Cabot for returning without evidence of having reached Asia, or maybe he was just cheap, for the only reward the explorer received from the king was ten pounds in silver (a paltry sum) and a pension of 20 pounds a year. Cabot, however, was undaunted; again he asked the king's leave to undertake another voyage, this time to Cipangu. The king approved the exploration on February 3, 1498, and even advanced money to pay the members of the expedition!

Cabot decided to set his course first to Greenland, en route to discover a northwest passage to the Indies. He set sail in May 1498 with five ships and 200 men. We know little about this expedition. One of the ships in distress sailed into an Irish port; the other four were never heard from again. Mostly likely, Cabot died in the wreck of his ship.

Cabot had failed to find a route to China or India, but he had established for England a future claim to Canada and what would become the northeast United States.

Protestantism and Piracy

King Henry VII did nothing further with Cabot's discoveries to the west. His successor, Henry VIII, also seemed indifferent. In 1520, Cardinal Wolsey, Henry VIII's lord high chancellor, did offer John Cabot's son, Sebastian, command of five ships for a voyage to Newfoundland; but when the younger Cabot decided, instead, to remove to Spain, nothing further was done. Henry VIII, too, soon had more pressing problems—he needed to convince the pope to annul his marriage to Fernando and Isabel's daughter, Catherine of Aragon, whom he had married in 1509. Henry wanted to marry Anne Boleyn, Catherine's lady-in-waiting; he claimed to feel scruples about the validity of his marriage, because Catherine had formerly been married to his deceased brother, Arthur. When Pope Clement VII refused to annul the marriage, Henry, in 1535, denied the pope's authority over the Church of England and declared himself its head. The Church of England thus went into formal schism.

The doctrines of Henry's church and its style of worship remained essentially Catholic; but under his successor, his son Edward VI, the Church of England became distinctly

Queen Elizabeth I being carried by her courtiers

Protestant. For a brief period, England was reconciled with the Catholic Church under the reign of Edward's half-sister, Mary; but under the reign of *her* half-sister, Elizabeth I, the Church of England reverted to Protestantism.

Elizabeth, who became queen in 1558, encouraged merchants to form companies to open trade with distant markets. English merchants began to trade with Russia and Poland for timber, pitch, and tar, for shipbuilding. With their growing fleet of trading ships, the English plied the waters of the Atlantic and the Mediterranean. Soon, some adventurers were carrying on a trade with the Spanish colonies in the West Indies.

Such exchange with the Spanish West Indies posed a problem, since Spain forbade any trade between her colonies and foreign nations. Also, Felipe II, the king of Spain and Queen Mary's widowed husband, was Elizabeth's most resolute enemy. To the dying Mary, Elizabeth had promised fidelity to the Catholic Church if she became queen; but as soon as she was crowned, Elizabeth led the Church of England once again into schism and Protestantism. A zealous Catholic, Felipe looked on Elizabeth as a traitor and apostate. He would grasp at any pretext to carry war into England and remove Elizabeth from the throne. Elizabeth thus had to tread carefully—she did not want to risk a war with Spain.

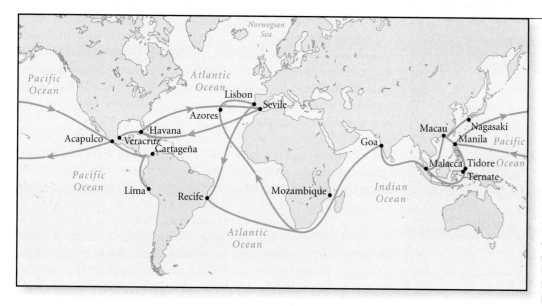

This map shows the trade routes between Europe and North and South America at the end of the 16th century. Generally, the New World provided raw materials (such as furs, lumber, and tobacco) to the European nations of England, France, Spain, and Portugal. Europe, in turn, provided manufactured goods to settlements in the New World. The trade in African slaves began with the Portuguese in the late 15th century, but it eventually included English, Spanish, and French merchants as well.

Dragon of the Spanish Main

In 1567, six English ships, anchored off the western tip of Cuba, were struck by a hurricane. The storm, which drove the fleet into the Gulf of Mexico, so badly battered the ships that the captain of the fleet, Sir John Hawkins, knew that he would need to refit his vessels before he could return to England. Sailing into the Spanish anchorage of Vera Cruz, the storm-tossed English demanded supplies.

Entering a Spanish port was an act of desperation, for Spanish law not only forbade Hawkins to ply Spanish waters, but to conduct (as he had been doing) illegal trade with Spanish colonists. The Spanish colonists had no quarrel with Hawkins; taxes on goods bought from their own countrymen were so high that they were glad to engage in a little illegal barter. The Spanish government, however, did not look kindly on such trade. Matters went from bad to worse for the English when, a day after their landing at Vera Cruz, a Spanish fleet sailed into harbor.

The Spanish ships had come to fetch the yearly gold and silver shipment; but seeing the English fleet, they mobilized. The Spanish attacked the crippled English ships, destroying four of them. Only two ships escaped—one piloted by John Hawkins and the other by his young nephew, Francis Drake. After a long and perilous voyage, Hawkins and Drake returned to England in safety, but penniless.

Although bereft of his fortune, Francis Drake's reputation did not suffer from this unfortunate affair. He had so skillfully fought off the Spanish and made the difficult voyage home across the Atlantic that he had gained the reputation for a skilled mariner and adventurer. Knowledge of his exploits even reached the court of Queen Elizabeth who, in 1570, granted Drake a commission to return to the West Indies to raid Spanish shipping.

Drake was a privateer, a "respectable pirate"; he harried ships with the queen's good pleasure. In 1572, he set sail for the West Indies in two small ships, both to serve Her Majesty and to make up for his losses. In July he arrived off the coast of Panama and made plans to attack the small Spanish settlement of Nombre de Dios. Commanding two pinnaces—shallow-draft boats that could ply the shallow waters off the coast—Drake attacked the town by night. The English took the city, where they found a supply of silver bars; but they ended up snagging little of the loot. Drake had been shot and had fainted from loss of blood; to get him to safety, and fearing a Spanish counterattack, his men fled the city.

Sir Francis Drake, a 1577 engraving by Jodocus Hondius

Despite this initial failure, Drake established a base in Darien and for the next several months conducted raids along the Spanish Main. He was able to penetrate into the interior of Panama, where, from the height of a tree, he beheld afar off the Pacific Ocean. He vowed he would one day sail its waters. In Darien, Drake received help from the Cimarroons—escaped black slaves who wandered the jungles in loose-knit tribes, raiding and plundering their former Spanish masters. With these allies and a group of French privateers, Drake captured a mule team bearing silver to Nombre de Dios for shipment to Spain. Enriched by the Spanish silver, Drake and his men sailed into Portsmouth harbor in England on August 9, 1573.

Queen Elizabeth was so pleased with Drake that she agreed to finance him in another expedition—this time, to circumnavigate the globe. Drake in his ship, the *Golden Hind*, and four other ships, set out on December 13, 1577. Four months later the fleet reached the coast of Brazil and anchored in the Río de la Plata, where Drake abandoned two of his ships. Continuing down the coast of South America, the small fleet on August 21, 1578 entered the Straits of Magellan. The passage of the straits took 16 days, during which Drake lost a ship, and another returned to England. Now with only one ship, Drake passed up the west coast of South America, seizing and plundering Spanish vessels along the way.

Drake was a terror—the Spanish called him *El Draque*, "the dragon." Though he did not murder, rape, and torture the inhabitants of Spanish settlements, as later pirates would do, he desecrated Catholic churches, stealing their precious vessels and destroying crucifixes, statues, and holy pictures.

Drake followed the Pacific coast of South and North America, finally passing into waters lying north of all Spanish settlement. Somewhere along the coast of California, Oregon, or Washington (no one is certain where) the ships anchored in a bay. (According to tradition, this bay is just south of Point Reyes in California.) On the shores of that bay, Drake and his men celebrated the first Protestant religious service in North America, and Drake laid claim to the land for Queen Elizabeth, naming it "New **Albion**." From "Drake's Bay," the *Golden Hind* continued northward until she came to the Olympic Peninsula, where, in July 1579, she launched into the open Pacific. Traversing the Pacific and Indian oceans, and rounding the Cape of Good Hope, into the Atlantic, Drake and his men arrived at

Albion: England

Plymouth, England, on September 26, 1580. At Portsmouth, Queen Elizabeth, despite her fear of Spain, publicly honored her explorer by knighting him aboard his ship, the *Golden Hind*. Thereafter he was known as *Sir Francis Drake*.

Sir Francis continued in the service of his queen. When open hostilities with Spain finally broke out a few years later, Drake commanded a fleet to the West Indies and took the cities of San Domingo, Cartagena in Colombia, and San Agustín in Florida. When in 1588 Felipe II of Spain sent an armada of ships to destroy the English fleet and invade England, Drake served as vice admiral in the small fleet that (with the help of a storm) defeated the enormous flotilla.

Drake died eight years later on an expedition in the West Indies. His body, placed in a lead casket, was cast into the waters near Nombre de Dios, the town he had plundered 16 years before.

Destruction of the Spanish fleet on Lake Maracaibo in Venezuela by the English pirate Henry Morgan, April 30, 1669

Real Estate Speculators

Sir Humphrey Gilbert had big plans for the New World: England needed to establish colonies in America, he thought, where idle subjects of the crown could go, establish themselves, and farm the land. Such colonies could enrich those who invested in them and bring glory to England.

Gilbert was able to interest his half-brother, Walter Raleigh, in his colonization plan for America. As Sir Humphrey saw it, English Catholics (who were nothing but trouble in England) could push out the natives of America and settle the new country. Raleigh did not care much for this part of Sir Humphrey's plan, but he could not pass up the opportunity to invest in what might prove a very lucrative venture. So, he funded a ship in his half-brother's fleet. It was christened *Bark Raleigh*.

The fleet set sail in 1583; but, unfortunately for Raleigh, the *Bark Raleigh,* short of supplies, returned to port only two days later. The rest of the fleet under Sir Humphrey reached St. John's in Newfoundland on August 3. Circumstances, however, did not fall out as Sir Humphrey had hoped. The men fell sick, and the flagship sank. Sir Humphrey, ignoring his men's advice to board the larger ship, the *Golden Hind*, chose to sail on a smaller ship called the *Squirrel*. On the return voyage, as they hove to near the *Squirrel*, the men on the *Golden Hind* could see Sir Humphrey on deck, reading a book, calm despite his misfortune. "We are as near to heaven by sea as by land," he told his wondering onlookers. The *Golden Hind* returned to England; the *Squirrel* never did. The ship and its captain, Sir Humphrey Gilbert, were lost at sea.

Sir Walter Raleigh, an engraving by J. Pofselwhite and published in Lodge's British Portraits encyclopedia, United Kingdom, 1823

Despite the failure of Sir Humphrey's scheme, Walter Raleigh maintained his interest in colonization. He could rely on royal support for any scheme he concocted, for Raleigh was Queen Elizabeth's darling. He had first come to her attention in 1580 when he came from Ireland, carrying dispatches from the Earl of Leicester and the Earl of Oxford, who were putting down a rebellion there. According to tradition, Raleigh once placed his cloak over a mud puddle so the Queen could pass over without dirtying her feet. It is also said that he scratched flattering verses on windows in the palace to catch the queen's eye. Whether or not these stories are true, Raleigh did get the queen's attention. Elizabeth rewarded him lavishly—far beyond what he deserved for his services in Ireland; she gave him 40,000 acres in Ireland, seized from the Irish Desmond clan, who had revolted against English rule. There, Raleigh brought English settlers and planted the first potatoes and tobacco in the British Isles. Then in 1584 Elizabeth knighted her favorite, dubbing him *Sir* Walter Raleigh.

The Lost Colony

In 1584, Queen Elizabeth gave Raleigh and his descendants the rights of possession and use of all land they explored and occupied in the New World, with the sole stipulation that they paid one-fifth of all precious metals they found there to the crown. The same year, Raleigh financed an expedition under Philip Amadas and John Barlowe. (Raleigh himself could not go; the queen would not let him leave her side.) Amadas and Barlow sailed first to Florida and then passed northward up the coast to what is now North Carolina. Landing at Roanoke Island in the region between the Pamlico and Albermarle sounds, the captains collected such items as skins and a pearl necklace to show the queen and potential investors when they returned to England. They also brought back two Indians, Manteo and Wanchese. Raleigh named the newly discovered lands "Virginia," after Queen Elizabeth—who, since she never married, was called the "Virgin Queen" by her people.

The skins, the pearl necklace, and the Indians had the desired effect: Raleigh received investment for a colony. In 1585, he sent Sir Richard Grenville and 108 settlers, all men, with Manteo the Indian, under the command of Ralph Lane to Roanoke Island. Though well-equipped with supplies, the settlement was doomed from the start. The settlers arrived at Roanoke too late in the year for planting crops, and seawater had spoiled most of their seeds. At first, relations with the local Indians were good; soon, however, Ralph Lane angered the natives by demanding supplies and labor from them. Returning from an exploring expedition into the interior, Lane and his men fell into a battle with the natives. The Indians of the region were, thereafter, hostile to the colonists.

When Sir Richard Grenville returned to England for supplies, hunger and fear of the Indians convinced the settlers that they should abandon Roanoke Island. When later Sir Francis Drake passed up the coast on a pirating expedition, he took the colonists back with him to England. A few days after Drake had embarked with the colonists, Sir Richard Grenville returned to Roanoke with supplies; but he found no colony.

The failure of the Roanoke Island colony did not discourage Raleigh. In 1587 he sent another group of colonists, this time 121 men and women, under John White. Though Raleigh's express orders were to place the colony on the Chesapeake Bay, the sailors deposited the settlers at Roanoke and refused to take them farther north. So the colonists remained on the island. There, on August 18, 1587, White's daughter Ellinor Dare gave birth to a daughter, christened Virginia Dare—the first English child born in North America.

Soon after the birth of his granddaughter, White returned to England for supplies. Because the Spanish armada threatened, the queen's government forbade White to return to America. It was not until 1590 that he finally set sail for Roanoke Island. But when he arrived at the island in March 1591, he found no trace of the colonists or their houses. All that remained was a wooden palisade the colonists had erected after White's departure. On one of the logs of the palisade was carved the word *Croatoan*—the name of Manteo's home island. Had the colonists, White's daughter Ellinor, and his granddaughter, Virginia, removed to that island? White never learned. Bad weather kept him from sailing to Croatoan, and he returned to England. Subsequent attempts to find the colonists failed. No one ever learned what happened to them.

"Sharp Medicine" from the King

After 1587, Raleigh ceased to play an active part in colonizing Virginia. He was losing influence at court—the Earl of Essex had replaced Raleigh in the queen's affections. Yet, when the queen discovered that Raleigh was having a love affair with one of her ladies-in-waiting, in a fit of jealousy she placed him in the Tower of London. Yet he did not remain there long. In 1595 he embarked on a voyage to Guiana on the northern coast of South America.

Raleigh's fortunes changed again for the worse when James I became king in 1603. Accused of plotting against the regal government, Raleigh was condemned to death after a grossly unfair trial. James, however, never carried out the sentence. Instead, he placed Raleigh in the Tower of London, where he remained for 13 years.

In 1617, an aging Raleigh led an expedition to find a gold mine in Guiana. He had received the king's permission, but only as long as the gold mine did not lie within a Spanish settlement, for James feared war with Spain. He told Raleigh that if he fought the Spanish, he would face execution upon his return to England. Raleigh fell sick when he arrived in the Caribbean and, without him, his men went on into Guiana. There they came across a Spanish settlement. A battle ensued. Raleigh's son and several Spaniards were killed.

Raleigh returned to England. King James, true to his word, had him arrested and ordered his execution. Standing at the block, Raleigh asked to see the axe that would behead him. "This is a sharp Medicine," he said, "but it is a Physician for all Diseases." He was executed on October 29, 1618.

On to Virginia

Though his colonization schemes were failures, Sir Walter Raleigh did succeed in whipping up English interest in America. By the end of the 16th century, Englishmen were determined to seize a portion of the New World for themselves. For English merchants, an American colony meant increased trade. For the government, it meant an outlet for the large number of idle soldiers lately returned from the Spanish wars. For Christian ministers, it meant an opportunity to convert the heathen.

From all sides, Englishmen were encouraged to invest in New World colonies. Two men, the navigator Bartholomew Gosnold and the geographer Richard Hakluyt, pitched the idea of a colony to the merchants of Bristol. In America are vast forests, yielding timber for ships, they told the merchants. A colony would be an investment yielding high returns!

Gosnold organized a trading company—called the Virginia Company of London, or just the London Company—and sold investments, called "bills of adventure." Soon a number of Englishmen, mostly members of the merchant class, were buying the bills. Investment received a big boost when in April 1606, King James I granted to Gosnold, Sir Thomas Gates, and others a charter to found a colony in Virginia.

A few days before Christmas 1606, three ships, the *Sarah Constant*, the *Discovery*, and the *Goodspeed* set sail from England. On board were 105 colonists under Christopher Newport and the captain, Bartholomew Gosnold. After touching off at the West Indies, the ships reached the coast of Virginia on April 26, 1607 and landed at Cape Henry at the entrance to Chesapeake Bay.

The colonists had carried with them a sealed box containing a list of the names of the colony's leaders. (The London Company had ordered them not to open the box until they reached Virginia.) At Cape Henry, the box was opened, and they discovered who were to serve on the governing council: Captain Gosnold, Edward Wingfield, Christopher Newport, John Ratliffe, John Martin, George Kendall, and John Smith.

Captain John Smith

No sooner had the name of John Smith been read than it was struck from the list. Smith's name had become an opprobrium to the other members of the governing council, who suspected him of having fomented insurrection on board ship. Though he was later cleared of the charge, the members of the governing council could perhaps be forgiven for suspecting him. John Smith was a notoriously proud, boastful, and arrogant man.

According to stories he told about himself, Smith left home in 1596, at the age of 16, and lived through a series of adventures. After serving as a soldier in France and a merchant in the Mediterranean, Smith in 1600 joined the Austrian army in a war against the Muslim Turks. For his service in Hungary, he was promoted to captain. Two years later he was wounded while fighting in Transylvania and enslaved by the Turks.

According to his own account, Smith was sold to a Turk who offered him as a present to his girlfriend in Istanbul. Naturally, his new mistress fell in love with him and sent him to her brothers to be trained in the service of the Turkish sultan. Smith killed one of these brothers and escaped. Passing into Russia and through Poland, he rejoined the Austrian army in Transylvania. From there he traveled through Europe and North Africa, returning to England in 1604 or 1605.

It was not until June 1607, after they had chosen the site for settlement, that the colonists admitted Smith to the governing council of the colony. After landing in April, the colonists had followed the path of a wide river, which they named the James in honor of the king. On a small peninsula jutting out into the river, they built a fort and established a settlement, Jamestown. The site had certain advantages—it could be easily defended from attack, and stands of large timber trees surrounded it on all sides. The area, however, was swampy, and through the hot, humid summer of 1607, swamp fever killed many of the colonists, including Captain Gosnold. Jamestown suffered from attacks by the local Algonquin Indians, who tried to drive off the settlers by raiding their camps and stealing gunpowder, pistols, and other supplies.

The colonists, however, contributed to their own hardships. Well over half of them were gentlemen and unwilling to labor. Discipline in the colony broke down; the fields were left unplowed and the crops unplanted. The ruling council was powerless to force colonists to work, for its president had no independent authority and its members wasted time in wrangling debate.

It frequently fell to Captain John Smith to go out in search of supplies for the colony, and he carried out these missions with great success. On one such expedition in December 1607, however, he was captured by the Algonquin. According to Smith's own account, warriors brought Smith to their chief, the great Powhatan, who regaled Smith with a feast "after their best barbarous manner." Then the Indians held a consultation, following which they placed two stones before Powhatan. Suddenly several braves grabbed Smith and stretched him out on one of the rocks, while other braves, with clubs, threatened to beat his head in. It was then that a young girl of about ten or 11 ran in and, taking Smith's "head in her arms . . . laid her owne upon him to save him from death." This was the chief's daughter, Matoaka, also named Pocahontas ("playful one"). The chief called off his braves. Instead of killing Smith, Powhatan proclaimed him a subchief of the tribe.

Powhatan released Smith after four weeks. But returning to Jamestown, Smith found other dangers awaiting him. In his absence, colonial leaders had ordered Smith's execution; they blamed him for causing the death of his companions on the foraging expedition. Only the arrival of supply ships under Captain Christopher Newport on January 8, 1608, spared Smith's life.

By April 1608, only 38 of the original 105 colonists were still alive at Jamestown. That month, another ship, the *Phoenix*, arrived, bringing 120 more settlers. But the influx of new settlers did not solve the colony's problems. It was John Smith who did. Having replaced John Ratliffe as president of the colonial council, Smith subjected the colonists to military discipline. He forced the lazy to work in the fields and to build new storage barns. "He who does not work shall not eat," he told the colonists, quoting St. Paul. By the spring and summer of 1609, Smith could claim he had established a solid foundation for the colony.

"Pocahontas Saving the Life of Captain John Smith," a 1939 WPA mural by Paul Cadmus, located in the Court House Annex, Richmond, Virginia.

Smith's sojourn in Powhatan's village had created good relations between the Indians and the English. The Indians frequently came to Jamestown, with game for the hungry colonists. Pocahontas accompanied the Indians on these trips to visit her friend, John Smith. The young Indian girl delighted the colonists. She played with boys of the settlement, deftly turning cartwheels in the streets. Smith described her as "a child of tenne yeares old, which not only for feature, countenance, and proportion much exceedeth any of the rest of his [Powhatan's] people but for wit and spirit [is] the only non-pariel of his countrie."

Relations with the Indians, however, began to deteriorate under Smith's administration. Faced with short supplies, Smith led foraging expeditions in which he did not shrink from force to coerce food from the Indians. Smith could be quite heavy-handed not only with the Indians but with his equals in the colony, and some of these returned to England and spread bad reports about him among members of the London Company. In 1609 a ship arrived from England bearing letters from the company, criticizing Smith for his harsh treatment of the Indians and for failing to send valuable cargoes to England. The company informed Smith that he would be replaced as president of the colony by Lord De la Warr, whose representative, Sir Thomas Gates, would soon arrive by ship.

Gates, however, was delayed by shipwreck in the Bermuda Islands, and Smith continued governing the colony. It was not a new governor, but an accident—he was badly burned with gunpowder—that forced Smith return to England in the autumn of 1609.

Smith left the colony in good condition, with the harvest newly brought in. If there had only been an able administrator to replace Smith, Jamestown might have continued to prosper.

This Colony Must Not Fail

Despite the good harvest of 1609, the harsh winter that followed was bitter for the Jamestown colonists. Starvation and cold reduced their numbers to only 60 by spring. In June, the remaining colonists buried their cannon and armor and planned to abandon the settlement. Jamestown would have shared the fate of Roanoke had not Sir Thomas Gates at last arrived with supplies. Lord De la Warr arrived soon after.

A more serious threat to Jamestown's survival was the disappointment of the London Company. It was seeing no rich returns from its investments. Virginia just didn't pay. The company had found that shipments from the colony of cedar logs, walnut boards, sassafras wood, and iron ore were not bringing in the expected profits. The company had considered turning Jamestown into a center for the manufacture of pitch, tar, glass, and soap ashes, and they sent over laborers for these projects. But manufacturing, too, did not realize the profits the company expected from the colony.

It was John Rolfe, landing in Virginia in 1610, who provided what would be Virginia's economic salvation—tobacco. Sir Walter Raleigh had popularized tobacco smoking in England; but the best tobacco came from the Caribbean islands, and the Spanish sold it to English merchants at very high prices. Though the tobacco grown by the Indians in Virginia was less expensive, it was not as good. Englishmen preferred the more fragrant Caribbean leaf.

John Rolfe had taken passage to Virginia with Sir Thomas Gates aboard the *Sea Venture,* which wrecked off the coast of the Bahamas. With Gates and about 150 passengers, Rolfe remained on the islands for ten months. In June of 1610, Rolfe arrived in Virginia with smuggled Caribbean tobacco seed. In 1612 he and others who planted the tobacco found it to be sweet, strong, and fragrant. They shipped some to England, where smokers declared that it compared favorably to Caribbean tobacco. By 1618, 20,000 pounds of Virginia leaf were being shipped to England; by 1630, 500,000 pounds had been exported.

Virginia had found its cash crop. It was Virginia tobacco, not the Virginia colony, that went up in smoke.

A depiction of John Rolfe cultivating tobacco

An Old Virginia Love Story

John Rolfe had not been long in Virginia before he fell in love. But the object of his affections troubled him greatly, for he was a pious Christian and she, an Indian and a heathen. In a letter to the governor, Rolfe spoke of his love. "It is Pocahontas," he wrote, "to whom my hearty and best thoughts are, and have been a long time so entangled, and enthralled in so intricate a labyrinth that I [could not] unwind myself thereout."

A year after Captain John Smith had departed for England, Powhatan had married his 15-year-old daughter to an Indian, Kocoum, who lived in the region of the Potomac. The Virginia colony at that time was suffering attacks from the Indians, and Powhatan kept a number of Englishmen hostage in his camp. Captain Samuel Argall, who learned of Pocahontas' whereabouts, kidnapped her and offered her to Powhatan in exchange for the English hostages and some tools and weapons the Indians had taken from the English. Seven hostages were returned, but not the tools and guns; and Pocahontas continued to live among the English at their new settlement of Henrico. There she received Christian instruction and learned English.

Portrait of Pocohontas, painted long after her death and based on a 1616 engraving by Simon van de Passe

Ætalis suæ 21. A. 1616.

Pocahontas proved of more value to the English than as a mere hostage; she became an important liaison between the English and her people. John Smith later, in 1616, wrote that she was "the instrument to pursurve this colonie from death, famine, and other confusion." It was in July 1613 that Pocahontas met John Rolfe.

In 1614 the governor of Henrico, Sir Thomas Dale, and 150 armed English went to Powhatan to demand the ransom for Pocahontas. The Indians attacked the English party, who in retaliation burned down Indian houses, destroyed villages, and killed several Indian men. More effective for peace was Dale's decision to allow Pocahontas to return to her father. Pocahontas told Powhatan that the English had treated her well and, moreover, that she wanted to marry an Englishman—John Rolfe. Powhatan agreed to the marriage.

The marriage promised peace between the English and Powhatan's people. Out of love for his country and the Indian princess, John Rolfe overcame his scruples and agreed to the marriage. Pocahontas was baptized and took on the Christian name, Rebecca. On April 5, 1614, she married John Rolfe. She was then 19 years old.

After two years, Pocahontas accompanied her husband and their infant son, Thomas, to England on a publicity tour to drum up support for the colony. There she was presented to the king and the royal family as well as the best of London society. In London, to her joy, she was reunited to John Smith, who she had thought was dead. In March 1617, the Rolfes set sail for Virginia; but before the ship was far out to sea, it became apparent that Pocahontas was very ill. She was taken ashore. As she lay on her death bed, she strove to comfort her grieving husband. "All must die," she said. "'Tis enough that the child liveth." John Rolfe buried her in the churchyard in Gravesend, England.

A New Mercantile Power

In 1609, the ten northern provinces of the Netherlands won a 14-month truce in their war with Spain. Since 1566, the provinces had been engaged in a struggle for their independence from King Felipe II of Spain, who had inherited the rule of the provinces from his father, Carlos I. Felipe had aroused the Dutch by excessive taxation; moreover, he had abolished traditional rights and tried to stamp out Protestantism in the northern provinces. The southern, Catholic provinces had at first joined in the rebellion, but by 1580 they had reconciled with Felipe. The northern provinces, joined together in the Union of Utrecht, kept up the struggle.

Dutch privateers, called "Sea Beggars," harassed Spanish shipping and became the foundation of Dutch sea power. The Sea Beggars not only fought their enemy close to home but challenged the power of Portugal (then under the rule of Spain) in the East Indies. Eventually the Dutch established their own trading colonies in the Far East.

Dutch merchants who in 1602 formed the Dutch East India Company wondered if a more direct route to India could be found by heading northeast—by finding a northeast rather than a northwest passage. They hired an English sea captain, Henry Hudson, to find out. He seemed like a good choice, for in 1608, he had sailed around the northern tip of Norway into the Arctic Circle, where the summer sun shines 24 hours a day. Hudson knew something about northern exploration.

The Voyages of Henry Hudson

Hudson sailed from Amsterdam in April 1609 with a Dutch and English crew on the ship, the *Half Moon,* and headed north. His destination was the Russian island of Novaya Zemlya in the Arctic Ocean. Spring though it was, the farther north the ship sailed, the icier grew the waters. Soon the sea became so choked with ice that Hudson, whose crew threatened mutiny if he did not change course, set his prow to the west. He would seek a northwest, instead of a northeast, passage to the Far East.

The *Half Moon* first touched North America at Newfoundland. Turning south, the ship sailed along the coasts of Nova Scotia, Maine, and Massachusetts and entered a great waterway in September 1609. Sailing up the waterway, Hudson thought that he had found the long sought-for northwest passage. He continued as far north as the present site of Albany,

"The Last Voyage of Henry Hudson," a 19th century painting by John Collier

New York, where he discovered that his northwest passage was merely a river, later named for him, the "Hudson."

Though he had found neither a northeast nor northwest passage, Hudson returned to Amsterdam with news that interested the Dutch merchants. They learned of the rich trade in furs that could be theirs in America. Though unsuccessful at finding a passage to the Far East, Hudson had opened up a new source of riches for the Netherlands.

London merchants, not the Dutch, financed Henry Hudson's second and last voyage. He set out in April 1610, again in search of a northwest passage. Sailing through a strait between Baffin Island and Newfoundland, Hudson entered a large body of water that he thought to be the Pacific Ocean. It was, however, only a great bay. He explored this bay, later named for him, until November, when the weather turned so cold his ship was icebound.

From November to June, Hudson and his men strove to survive in the arctic cold. When the seas finally thawed, Hudson's crew mutinied—their captain had suggested voyaging farther into the west! They placed Hudson; the master of the ship, John Hudson; the sick and the lame; and the ship's carpenter (who asked to remain with his captain) in a small boat. Giving them powder and shot, an iron pot, meal, and a carpenter's chest, the crew abandoned them in the waters of the far north. Hudson's ship eventually returned to port, but Hudson himself was never seen again.

A New Netherlands

In 1610, Amsterdam merchants began outfitting ships to trade for furs in the lands Henry Hudson had discovered. The business in furs was soon so lucrative that, in 1614, the Dutch government chartered a trading company, the New Netherland Company, to carry on the fur trade and establish trading posts in America. The company, in late 1614 or early 1615, established Fort Nassau on the northern Hudson River where Albany currently stands, and another post on the southern tip of Manhattan Island. In 1618, the charter for the New Netherland Company expired and it was not until 1621 that the government chartered a new company, the Dutch West India Company.

In June 1623, the government of the Netherlands formed its New World settlements into a province, called New Netherlands. In 1624, 30 families, the first permanent colonists, arrived with the first governor, Cornelius Jacobsen Mey. Some of the colonists chose to remain on Manhattan Island, while the rest followed the Hudson River north to Fort Orange (which had replaced Fort Nassau) and founded the settlement that would become Albany. By 1625, 200 or more colonists had settled along the Hudson and on Manhattan Island.

In 1626, Peter Minuit became governor of New Netherlands. Governor Minuit bought Manhattan Island from the Indians and erected Fort Amsterdam, which he made the seat of his government.

Minuit oversaw a new plan of colonial settlement, called the *patroon* system. A *patroon*, or "patron," was a man to whom the government granted land if he could fund the passage of 50 colonists to New Netherlands. The land grant, purchased from the Indians, was

16 miles on one side of a river or along the seashore, or eight miles on both sides of a river. It included as much land into the interior as the *patroon* could possibly use. The *patroon* received all rights to the plants, minerals, and springs within his land grant. He controlled rights to fishing, hunting, and the milling of grain.

The *patroon* grant was similar to the Spanish *encomienda* except that a Dutch land grant did not include Indians as laborers. Since the Dutch West India Company dealt in the West African slave trade, Indian laborers were unnecessary; the company promised "to supply the colonists with as many blacks as they possibly can." *Patroons*, however, preferred white laborers, "indentured servants," whose passage they would pay in return for a specified number of years of labor.

Governor Minuit later fell into disfavor with the company because he was said to be too partial to the *patroons*. Minuit eventually joined a Swedish trading company and oversaw the settlement of Swedes and Finns on the Delaware River. This colony, called New Sweden, remained under the control of Sweden from 1638 to 1655. In 1655, the governor of New Netherlands, Peter Stuyvesant, demanded the surrender of the Swedish Fort Christina (now Wilmington, Delaware). But under Dutch rule, New Sweden continued to attract Swedish and Finnish settlers to America.

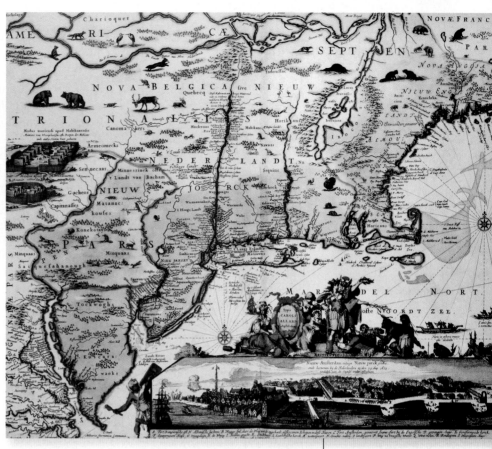

A map of New England, with inset picture depicting New Amsterdam. Amsterdam, 1700

When the "Saints" Came Marching In

In the early 16th century, a group of English men, women, and children, refugees from their own country, came to work and live in the Dutch city of Leiden. They did not come to Leiden to improve their material condition; they took the hardest and lowest paying jobs. They did not come because they disliked English ways, for they did all they could to maintain the customs of the homeland. They came to Leiden so they could worship God in the manner they saw fit.

The refugees called themselves the "Saints" because they thought they belonged to the true church of Christ, the church of the pure and holy. Their countrymen called them Separatists because, in obedience to their convictions, they had separated themselves from the Church of England. At that time, all Englishmen were required to belong to the Church of England, whose earthly head was the king. Anyone who refused to worship in the Church of England and, especially, anyone who set up a rival church, could suffer severe fines or imprisonment or, even, death. Such penalties were visited on groups like the "Saints" but especially on Catholics.

A 17th century woodcut of a Purtian family taking their meal

The Saints belonged to a larger movement in Protestantism called Puritanism. While other Puritans remained within the Church of England and tried to reform it by "purifying" it of all "papistical" (that is, Catholic) practices, the Saints believed they could only follow their pure doctrines and practices outside the established church. In Scrooby, in Nottinghamshire, England, some Puritans came together to form a church of their own. Under the leadership of William Brewster, Richard Clifton, William Bradford, and John Robinson, they made a "covenant," or solemn promise, with each other to form an independent congregation of true believers. Under this covenant, leaders were elected by the men in the community of Saints—a system in stark contrast to that of the Church of England, which was ruled by bishops. The Saints thought bishops another papistical abomination.

For fear of persecution, the Scrooby Saints could not long remain in England. In 1609 they decided to emigrate to the Netherlands, which offered religious toleration. In their first attempt, they were arrested and imprisoned. Their second attempt, however, was successful, and in 1609 they sailed into Amsterdam. Finding Amsterdam not to their liking, they received permission to remove to Leiden.

After ten years of living in Leiden, the Saints concluded that life in Holland did not suit them. Since they worked at low paying jobs (the only ones they could get as foreigners), the Saints lived under the threat of poverty. Moreover, the 12-year truce between the Netherlands and Spain was about to expire, and the Saints feared a renewal of war. Moreover, their children were adopting Dutch ways and being influenced by "corrupt" manners. The Saints wanted their children to remain English and Puritan.

Leaders of the Saints approached the Virginia Company of London to inquire into emigrating to the mouth of the Hudson River, at that time considered a part of Virginia. The company agreed to finance the Saints' expedition but required that merchant adventurers accompany them to Virginia. King James issued a charter allowing the company to establish a settlement in what was to be called New England. But when the company approached James with the Saints' request for freedom of religion, the king replied that no subject of his was free to worship outside the Church of England. If, however, the Separatists decided to remain separate, the king said he would look the other way.

On August 5, 1520, 102 passengers (whom we often remember as the "Pilgrims") set sail on the *Mayflower*, bound for Virginia. Of these passengers, the Saints numbered only 41—the greater number were merchant adventurers, indentured servants, and hired men. Frequent conflicts broke out between the prim Saints and the earthier adventurers. What would happen when they reached land and attempted a common settlement? To settle future problems beforehand, the Saints and adventurers signed a covenant, or contract, very much like the covenant the Saints made many years before in Scrooby.

"Having undertaken for the glory of God, and advancement of the Christian faith and honor of our king and country, a voyage to plant the first colony in the northern parts of Virginia," the Saints and their fellow colonists, said the covenant, did "solemnly and mutually, in the presence of God and one of another, covenant and combine ourselves together into a civil body politic, for our better ordering and preservation and furtherance of the ends aforesaid; and by virtue hereof to enact, constitute, and frame such just and equal laws, ordinances, acts, constitutions, offices from time to time as shall be thought most meet and convenient for the general good of the colony."

This, the "Mayflower Compact," thus allowed adult males, except those who were servants or hired men, to establish a government without the explicit permission of the king. This compact became the precursor of what would be characteristic of government in English America. Unlike the old European nations that were governed more by tradition and custom, English American states would be governed by written laws that were seen as covenants or contracts the people made between themselves and their government.

A Hard Winter and Thanksgiving

The *Mayflower* never made it to Virginia; instead, the ship landed on the coast of what is now Massachusetts. It was November, late in the year, and the company faced the bitter prospect of a harsh northern winter. After they established their settlement, which they named Plymouth, they hunkered down to brave a fierce cold, the likes of which they had never known in England. During the first winter, nearly one-half of the colonists died, including the first governor, John Carver. At one point, only seven of the colonists were well enough to take care of the sick.

Signing of the Mayflower Compact, 1899 painting by Jean Leon Gerome

The colonists at first had little contact with the local Indians. Then, one day in March 1521, two Indians walked into the village. One of these surprised the settlers by speaking English: "welcome, Englishmen!" he said. This was Samoset, an Abenaki from Maine, who had learned to speak English from Englishmen who had come to fish in the waters near his home. Samoset told the colonists that he would introduce them to Massasoit, the chief of the Wampanoag tribe that lived around Plymouth. Samoset arranged a meeting between the colonists and Massasoit, who signed a peace treaty with the colonists and, moreover, told his people to befriend them. The Indians taught the colonists how to farm in the new country that was now their home and enriched their larder with new crops: maize (corn), beans, squash, and Jerusalem artichokes. The natives suggested what fields to turn and how to fertilize crops.

Under the governorship of William Bradford and the military leadership of Captain Miles Standish, the future seemed more hopeful for the Plymouth colony. The autumn harvest of 1621 was good, and the colonists began a trade in beaver skin. In October 1621, the colonists, Massasoit, and some Indians joined together for a great feast, a thanksgiving to God for the harvest and for their preservation from many dangers.

Massasoit's People

Massasoit was a *sachem*, or leader, of the Wampanoag—a name meaning "eastern people," or "people of the dawn." The Wampanoag were divided into family groups that gathered together in winter to hunt and in spring to fish. In summer they would separate again so their women could cultivate corn, beans, squash, watermelon, Jerusalem artichokes, and other crops on individual plots. The men were the hunters and warriors, not the farmers.

There was no private property as we know it among the Wampanoag; rather, the entire community held their property in common and divided it among families to use. Like the Huron, Wampanoag sachems (chieftains) did not govern by force. They needed to be eloquent to convince tribesmen to follow their lead. Wise men, or *pow-waws*, also held great influence over the tribe.

Chapter 4 Review

Summary

- Like Spain, England tried to find a route to the Indies but did not succeed. When news came of Columbus' discovery, however, England abandoned the quest for the Indies and sent ships out under the direction of John Cabot and thus established for England a future claim to Canada and what would become the northeast United States.

- In 1535, King Henry VIII broke off from the Catholic Church after Pope Clement VII refused to annul his marriage to Catherine of Aragon. Henry VIII declared himself head of the Church of England and denied the pope's authority.

- Elizabeth I encouraged trade with foreign lands, and she sent the privateer Sir Francis Drake to circumnavigate the globe. In 1578 he sailed to North America, plundering and pillaging along the way. He landed on the northwestern coast and claimed the land for Elizabeth, naming it "New Albion." The first Protestant services in North America were celebrated here.

- In 1584 Elizabeth commissioned Sir Walter Raleigh to colonize North America. Raleigh sent men to Roanoke Island. He named this land "Virginia" after Queen Elizabeth, the "Virgin Queen." Raleigh did not succeed in colonizing Virginia, but he succeeded in whipping up interest in America.

- In 1606 Bartholomew Gosnold organized a trading company called the London Company, which sold investments in America. In the same year King James I granted a charter to Gosnold and others to found a colony in Virginia. This colony almost failed due to the settlers' refusal to work and the colonists' bad administration of government; but John Smith managed to pull it together, and by 1609 he had established a solid foundation for the colony.

- In 1610 John Rolfe provided what would be Virginia's economic salvation—tobacco. He brought tobacco seeds from the Caribbean and made tobacco a cash crop in Virginia. He married Pocahontas, the daughter of the chief of the Algonquin Indians, thus bringing about peace between the English and the Algonquins.

- In 1609 the Dutch became interested in finding a route to the Indies, and Henry Hudson was sent to find one. He touched North America at Newfoundland, then proceeded south to a great waterway along the coasts of Nova Scotia, Maine, and Massachusetts. He thought he had discovered the northwest passage to the Indies. He found that his passage was merely a river, however, which was later named the "Hudson" for him.

- In 1623, the Netherlands formed a province on the northern Hudson River to carry on the fur trade and establish trading posts in North America. They called this province the "New Netherlands."

- Peter Minuit became New Netherland's governor in 1626 and established a new plan of colonial settlement, called the patroon system.

- In 1609 a group of Protestants, the Puritans, left England to escape persecution. They went to Amsterdam for ten years, but finding it not to their liking, they were given a charter to establish a settlement in Virginia. They did not make it to Virginia, however, and landed on the coast of Massachusetts, establishing a settlement called Plymouth.

Key Concepts

charter: a document granting certain specified rights, powers, privileges, or functions from a sovereign state power to an individual or organized group

patroon: (patron) a man to whom the Dutch government granted land if he could fund the passage of 50 colonists to New Netherlands. The *patroon* received all rights to whatever was within his land grant, but he was not allowed Indians as laborers.

indentured servants: white laborers whose passage to America was paid in return for a specified number of years of labor

Puritanism: a sect of Protestants who tried to reform the Church of England by "purifying" it of all Catholic practices

Saints: a group of Puritans who believed they could only follow their pure doctrines and practices outside the established church

Chapter 4 Review (continued)

Dates to Remember

1497: John Cabot explores North America, thus establishing an English claim to Canada and what is now the northeast United States.

1535: Henry VIII breaks off from the Catholic Church and goes into formal schism.

1577: Sir Francis Drake claims the western coast for Elizabeth I, naming it "New Albion," and celebrates the first Protestant religious services in North America

1584: Sir Walter Raleigh claims the regions around Roanoke Island for Elizabeth I and names the new lands "Virginia."

1607: an English colony, Jamestown, is founded in Virginia.

1614: Pocahontas marries John Rolfe, thus bringing about peace between the English and the Algonquin tribe.

1620: the "Saints" land in Massachusetts and establish a settlement called Plymouth.

1623: the Netherlands establishes a province, "New Netherlands," on the northern Hudson River.

1626: Peter Minuit establishes the patroon system in New Netherlands.

Central Characters

John Cabot (1450–1499): navigator and explorer who by his voyages helped lay the groundwork for the later British claim to Canada

Henry VIII (1491–1547): king of England who began the English Reformation

Elizabeth I (1533–1603): daughter of King Henry VIII and the queen of England who authorized English settlement in North America

Francis Drake (ca. 1540–1596): English admiral and privateer who circumnavigated the globe

Walter Raleigh (1552–1618): English adventurer, a favorite of Elizabeth I, who provoked interest in America by his attempts at settlements.

John Smith (1580–1631): English explorer and early leader of the Jamestown Colony, the first permanent English settlement in North America

Pocahontas (ca. 1596–1617): Algonquin Indian woman who fostered peace between English colonists and Native Americans by befriending the settlers at the Jamestown Colony in Virginia and eventually marrying one of them

John Rolfe (1585–1622): Virginia planter and colonial official who was the husband of Pocahontas and made tobacco a cash crop in Virginia

Henry Hudson (ca. 1550–1611): English navigator and explorer who tried to discover a short route from Europe to Asia through the Arctic Ocean. A river, a strait, and a bay in North America are named for him.

Questions for Review

1. What part did John Cabot play in bringing England to America, and what did he establish there?

2. What is King Henry VIII so famous for?

3. What did Elizabeth I encourage that led to Francis Drake's exploration?

4. Name two things that Walter Raleigh accomplished.

5. What did the London Company achieve in America?

6. What happened in the Virginia Colony to bring it into danger of failing?

7. Who saved the Virginia Colony, and what did he do to save it?

8. What did the patroon system establish in America?

9. Who were the "Saints," and why did they leave England?

10. What was the "Mayflower Compact," and why is it important to law and government in America?

Chapter 4 Review (continued)

Ideas in Action

1. Look up the names of the original colonies in America. What do these names mean?
2. Read some accounts of the Pilgrims in America.

Highways and Byways

Popcorn in the New World

Popcorn is a great favorite, especially in America; but before America was discovered, popcorn was unknown to most of the world. Popcorn is native to the Western Hemisphere and is found mostly in the Americas. Thousand-year old kernels of popcorn have been found by archaeologists in Peru and Utah. The first European explorers of the New World described the toasting of popcorn by the Indians for food, for scattering in religious ceremonies, and for wearing as decoration in the hair.

There are stories about the Pilgrims first discovering popcorn. These stories tell that when the Pilgrims met with the Indians for a feast of thanksgiving, and at the end of the meal the Indians threw handfuls of dried corn into the fire. The corn exploded into fluffy white masses that were good to eat. The Pilgrims were astounded.

THE ENGLISH COLONIES

Pilgrims and Puritans

The "Saints" did not like Thomas Morton. They accused this somewhat eccentric man of various crimes, not the least of which was trading in arms and gunpowder with the Indians. Though there had been peace with the Indians, the Plymouth settlers still lived in fear of the war whoops and dreaded midnight attacks of the "savages." Still, trading arms to the Indians was only one of Morton's crimes. The Saints said he was a libertine, a corrupter of morals.

Morton was among those who settled Mount Wollaston (now Quincy, Massachusetts). In 1627 he gave the settlement its original Indian name, Ma-re Mount, which he altered to Merry Mount. To celebrate the name change the settlers and local Indians brewed beer and set up a maypole, streaming with ribbons. They danced and sang around the pole and wove brightly colored flowers into the ribbons.

Since singing and dancing about the maypole was an old English custom, dating from before the Middle Ages, Morton was merely perpetuating the folk customs of the mother country in the New World. But the Saints saw it differently. William Bradford wrote: "They also set up a Maypole, drinking and dancing about it many days together, inviting the Indian women, for their consorts, dancing and frisking together, (like so many fairies, or furies rather) and worse practices."

A German depiction of a Morris Dance

The "worse practices" were bad enough for the Saints; yet, in their minds, these were almost equaled by the blasphemy of the maypole. The dancing and singing about the maypole, wrote Bradford, "revived and celebrated the feast of the Roman goddess Flora, or the beastly practices of the mad Bacchanalians."

This last offense of the maypole was too much for the Saints. They sent Miles Standish and eight armed men to arrest "mine hoste" of Merry Mount. Morton was taken, placed in stocks, and then sent to England to stand trial; the abominable idol, the maypole, they cut down, ribbons and all. The settlers of Merry Mount dispersed.

A "City on a Hill"

The Saints despised as pagan all such folk customs as the maypole. The Catholic Church of the Middle Ages had allowed such customs taken from paganism and given them Christian meaning. The maypole, for instance, became associated with Mary, the Mother of God, whose month is May. For the puritanical Saints, such a Christianizing of pagan customs was unthinkable, and so they ended up abominating not only maypoles and Morris Dances but even Christmas and Easter as well all saints' days. The Saints recognized only three holy days: the Sabbath, the Day of Fasting and Humiliation, and the Day of Thanksgiving and Praise. The last two were not celebrated on fixed dates but only when God's wrath or his gifts were evident.

The Saints had a dour religion. Following the Calvinist, or Reformed, tradition of Protestantism, the Saints believed that man's nature is entirely corrupt—which is why they tended to condemn even innocent pleasures, or "vanities," as they called them. The Saints taught that God, according to his good pleasure, had "predestined," or chosen beforehand, that some, the "elect," would be saved and all others damned. No person could know for certain which he was. To get some assurance of his election, one needed continually to examine his life to see if he were truly virtuous; for virtue was a sign of God's good pleasure. But, according to Calvinist teaching, even the virtuous could not be sure of his election.

John Winthrop

The Saints did not see Plymouth colony primarily as a refuge from persecution but as an attempt to form a holy commonwealth, a great experiment in Christian society. They did not tolerate anyone who disagreed with them on the meaning of Scripture; only those who followed the doctrines of the Saints could abide in Plymouth. Also, since theirs was a holy commonwealth, personal transgressions were the care of the colony. This spirit was later dramatized in Nathaniel Hawthorne's novel, *The Scarlet Letter*, in which a woman named Hester Prynne is condemned to wear a scarlet letter "A" on her clothing for committing the sin of adultery—an outward sign of her interior corruption.

The Saints were determined to eradicate sin and error from their settlement, for they had made a covenant with God. One Puritan preacher, John Winthrop, in his sermon, "Christian Charitie, A Modell Hereof," aptly summarized this teaching:

> Thus stands the cause betweene God and us. We are entered into Covenant with Him for this worke. Wee have taken out a commission. The Lord hath given us leave to drawe our own articles. . . . Wee have hereupon besought Him of favour and blessing. Now if the Lord shall please to heare us, and bring us in peace to the place we desire, then hath hee ratified this covenant and sealed our Commission, and will expect a strict performance of the articles contained in it; but if wee shall neglect the observation of these articles which are the ends wee have propounded, and dissembling with our God, shall fall to embrace this present world and prosecute our carnall intentions, seeking great things for ourselves and our posterity, the Lord will surely breake out in wrathe against us; be revenged of such a people and make us knowe the price of the breache of such a covenant.

If they observed the covenant, said Winthrop, in mutual love and giving of their "superfluities" for the supply of others' necessities, their colony would become an example to all the world—a city set on a hill:

> Wee shall finde that the God of Israell is among us, when ten of us shall be able to resist a thousand of our enemies; when hee shall make us a prayse and glory that men shall

say of succeeding plantations, "the Lord make it likely that of New England." For wee must consider that wee shall be as a citty upon a hill. The eies of all people are uppon us.

When Winthrop wrote this sermon, he was not speaking of Plymouth (though he might have been) but of a new colony. By 1625, Puritans in England were looking for places where they could settle and freely practice their religion. Unlike the Saints, Puritans did not separate themselves from the Church of England but remained within it to reform it. However, when Charles I, the son of James I, came to the throne, he appointed as head of the Church of England William Laud, who began to make the Church more Catholic, at least in externals —the very opposite of what the Puritans wanted. King Charles passed laws forbidding Puritans to enter the universities of Oxford and Cambridge.

Many Puritans decided that since they could not turn old England into their model of a Puritan commonwealth, they would form such a society in New England—the Plymouth Saints had pointed the way. In 1628, Puritans led by John Endicott settled Salem. In 1629, the Massachusetts Bay Company, a commercial stock company like the Virginia Company of London, received a charter from King Charles I to settle Massachusetts Bay. This charter granted the members of the company permission to elect their own governor as head of the corporation. It said the "principall Ende of this Plantacion" was to bring the natives of New England to "the Knowledge and Obedience of the onlie true God and Sauior of Mankinde, and the Christian Fayth."

Houses at a modern reconstruction of Plymouth Plantation, Plymouth, Massachusetts

Fearing that King Charles might alter the charter, leaders of Massachusetts Bay Company agreed among themselves to take it with them to New England. There, the king could not touch it.

John Winthrop delivered his "City on a Hill" sermon on shipboard in the Atlantic. The notion that the Puritans had formed a covenant with God made them, in their own eyes, a new Israel. Just as the first Israel had fled Egypt for the promised land, Canaan, so the Puritans left England to settle New England. The Puritans took this analogy very seriously. If they were the new Israel, all others were the gentiles; if New England was Canaan, then its native inhabitants were Canaanites. Just as the Israelites once drove out the Canaanites, so, likewise, the Puritans could drive out the Indians. Indians who converted could remain; but, even then, the Puritans treated them as inferiors, and Indian converts lived apart from Puritan settlements.

The Puritans differed little if at all from the Saints in their teachings: both were Calvinist. But while the Saints were mostly farmers and artisans, the Puritans were drawn from the richer merchant classes and from the country gentlemen of England. Many were quite well educated. John Winthrop, for instance, was a lawyer, a graduate of Cambridge University, and a country gentleman who gave up much of his wealth to come to New England. The Puritans valued education highly. Though as Calvinists both they and the Saints embraced individual interpretation of Scripture and the freedom of the individual conscience, the Puritans gave the direction of society over to their learned ministers. Thus, from the beginning, the Massachusetts Bay colony was more hierarchically structured than Plymouth.

Still, these learned ministers did not keep learning to themselves. They wanted everyone to be literate so as to be able to read the Scriptures. It was Puritan New England that established the first free grammar schools in English America. In these schools, students studied Latin and Greek grammar, literature, and arithmetic. In 1636 Puritan scholars opened up a college in a small house in a cow yard outside the town of New Cambridge. This college became known as Harvard, named for the Reverend John Harvard, who bequeathed half his fortune and his library of 400 books to the college.

But in spite of the hierarchical character of Puritan society, the government of New England was rather egalitarian. Freemen (that is, everyone but slaves and indentured servants) who were members of the church elected all officials of government and members of the assembly, the body that made colonial laws. Periodically freemen flexed their independence by voting out established leaders—as they did with the colony's first governor, the highly regarded John Winthrop, who had already served multiple terms.

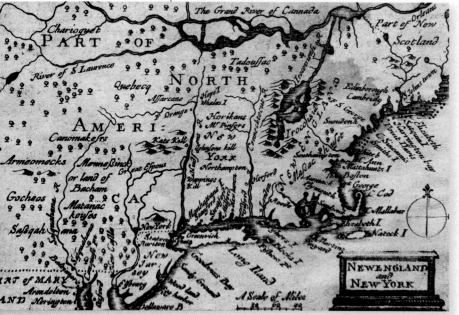

A map of New England and New York, 1675, by John Speed

In the colony's early years, elected officials such as Winthrop acted as justices, handing down decisions in the manner of the Old Testament judges. Such a system did not long endure in Massachusetts, however. The people wanted other safeguards for their freedom than the goodness and wisdom of their leaders. So, in 1641, Massachusetts adopted the "Body of Liberties," and about the same time, Plymouth established the "General Fundamentals." Both documents guaranteed the traditional safeguards of English liberty: free elections; trial by jury; the right not to be deprived of life, liberty, or property without due process of law; the right not to be taxed if not represented; and the right not to be forced to incriminate oneself in a trial.

The Puritans established the pattern of settlement that still characterizes New England. When groups began to feel too crowded in one place they, with the permission of the colonial assembly, established new townships. The townships were usually six miles square, divided into lots surrounding a "meeting house" where townsmen worshiped and conducted government business. In this way, from the original settlement at Boston, the Puritans established the towns of Charlestown, Dorchester, Medford, Watertown, Roxbury, and Lynn. To these townships migrated independent farmers and craftsman who made the Massachusetts Bay colony nearly self-sufficient in the material goods needed for living.

The doctrines of Puritanism emphasized the goodness of manual, as well as intellectual, labor. The Puritans honored industry and attached no stigma to wealth-making—in fact, material prosperity was for them a sign of God's favor. The Puritans thought idleness a sin; they frowned on all amusements that were not profitable, and so their days became mere rounds of hard labor and prayer. Though they appreciated beauty, Puritans discouraged the ornate beauty found in traditional Catholic architecture, painting, and music. While the Spanish in Mexico and South America were building glorious baroque churches and composing highly complex choral works, the Puritans crafted buildings and furniture with simple lines and composed uncomplicated church hymns.

Like the Saints, the Puritans enforced their stringent and often joyless morality through their laws, punishing, for example, those who worked on the Sabbath or used profanity.

Their colony, they believed, had a unique destiny in the plan of God. It was a city set upon a hill; the eyes of all people were upon it.

New England Heretics

Some in Massachusetts, however, objected to the way the likes of Winthrop and John Endicott were setting up their "city on a hill." One of these dissidents was Anne Hutchinson. This goodwife not only believed that it was wrong for the leaders of Massachusetts Bay to use human laws to establish the kingdom of God—she said so publicly. Hutchinson believed that individuals could have direct contact with God. Those in whom the Holy Spirit dwelt had no need of laws, she said, though laws were useful for the unsaved. Since she was attacking the very ethos of the Puritan colony, the authorities of Massachusetts tried her for heresy and exiled her from Massachusetts.

Hutchinson drew prominent followers. One of these was William Coddington, one of the richest men in the colony. He and others followed Hutchinson south to Narragansett Bay, where, on a large island, they established a settlement they named Portsmouth. This was the first settlement on what became known as Rhode Island. It was not long before dissensions arose in Hutchinson's community. After quarreling with Hutchinson, Coddington formed his own settlement on Rhode Island, calling it Newport. In time, all that was left of Hutchinson's following were her own family and household servants. In 1642, after her husband's death, Hutchinson's children, grandchildren, and household servants followed her to Long Island, where they were all slaughtered by Indians.

More threatening to Massachusetts than Hutchinson was Roger Williams. Williams, who came to Boston in 1631, criticized the Puritans for remaining in the Church of England. Like Hutchinson, Williams said it was sinful that the Puritans required everyone "to attend the religious services provided by the state or be punished." True religion, he contended, must

be freely embraced. From Boston, Williams went to Plymouth colony. There he tried to become a minister, but William Bradford put him off, thinking Williams imprudent and possibly unbalanced as well. Finally, Williams settled in Salem, where he became a minister, hurling sermons against the Puritans.

In Salem, Williams assailed the Massachusetts colony because it was "under a sin of usurpation of others' possessions"—that is, the Puritans had stolen Indian lands. This was too much for the colonial leaders, who prided themselves on their justice. After all, didn't they purchase the lands from the natives? (They did, though often for less than they were worth.) They reprimanded Williams and forced him to resign from the ministry. But this did not stop his attacks on the land-hungry colonists. Finally, when the authorities tried to arrest him, Williams fled to the Indians.

A Quaker meeting in the 18th century

Williams, who spent one winter with the Indians, greatly admired them. He learned their language and even maintained that, perhaps, their religion was as acceptable to God as the Puritans' faith. The Indians, in turn, loved and respected Williams. When he later moved to Narragansett Bay and founded the settlement of Providence, he defended the Indians there from English settlers.

In Providence, Williams established a policy of religious toleration—everyone would be allowed to worship God according to his or her own conscience. Yet Williams was never very tolerant himself. He lobbed scurrilous insults at the Quakers and spoke of the Catholic

The Salem Witch Trials

Modern folk accuse the Puritans of "superstition" whenever the subject of the Salem witch trials comes up. It is important to remember, though, that in the 17th century even the well-educated believed in witches—men or women who had made a special pact with the devil in return for certain, more often than not, pernicious powers. Persons accused as witches had been tried and executed for a long time in Europe—this was the only way, it was thought, to deal with people who trafficked with the Devil and could raise storms, blight crops, and stir up plagues.

In Salem, the trouble all began with a book and a group of mischievous girls. In 1689, the Puritan minister, Cotton Mather published a how-to-deal-with-witches book, titled *Memorable Providences, Relating to Witchcrafts and Possessions*. Some girls near Salem township read the book, and, as a prank, accused a family slave of witch-craft. When this half-black, half-Indian slave was flogged by her master, she confessed to witchcraft and accused two widows of being her associates. The girls who started the trouble continued their accusations. They were afraid of being found out if they backed down. The government of Massachusetts then established a special court to try witchcraft cases.

The Salem Witch Trials: a woman protests as one of her accusers appears to writhe on the ground in convulsions

It was an ugly spectacle. The girls accused people who, to save themselves, accused still others. Those who spoke out against the whole business were them-selves suspected of being witches. By the summer of 1692, 14 women and five men had been hanged, hun-dreds more were accused or in jail. One man, Giles Corey, was pressed to death with weights. Most were too afraid to criticize the court; but two Puritan ministers, Thomas Brattle and Increase Mather, spoke out against the frenzy. By their advice, the Massachusetts assembly dissolved the witchcraft court on October 12, 1692, and those still awaiting trial were either acquitted or simply released by the colonial government over the next two years.

Church as "the Romish wolf" gorged with "huge bowls of the blood of the saints." He refused to pray with his wife and family because they did not agree with all his opinions.

The Massachusetts Puritans were probably not pleased about the foundation of Williams' Providence, but they could not hinder it. In 1644, "Providence Plantation" received a charter from King Charles II.

Other New England "heretics" did not get on as well as Hutchinson and Williams. Massachusetts Bay passed laws against the Baptists in 1644, and, from 1656 to 1662, perse-cuted members of the Society of Friends, or "Quakers," as they were called. A Quaker could be whipped, imprisoned, branded with hot irons, or banished into the surrounding wilder-ness. During this period, Massachusetts Bay executed four Quakers.

New England Nearly Destroyed

Not all New Englanders left Massachusetts for the same reasons as Williams and Hutchinson; some merely felt cramped in the Bay Colony and wanted more room. Among these were the orthodox Puritans Thomas Hooker, Roger Ludlow, and John Haynes. These men, follow-ing the Connecticut River southwards, founded the towns of Wethersfield, Windsor, and Hartford in 1634–35—the nucleus from which grew the colony of Connecticut. Others joined John Davenport and Theophilus Eaton, who founded the colony of New Haven in 1638. The draconian policies of New Haven out-puritaned Massachusetts. Eaton and Davenport made the Scriptures, particularly the law of Moses, the supreme guide, not only in religious but in civil affairs as well. They published a series of "blue laws," as they were called, that prohibited trial by jury and commanded the observance of the Sabbath, the death penalty for adultery, and heavy fines for "concealing or entertaining Quakers or other blasphemous heretics."

Their westward expansion inevitably brought New Englanders into conflict with the Indians. Some Indians had adjusted to the European settlement; among these were the "praying Indians," who converted to the Puritan church through the efforts of John Cotton, John Eliot, and Richard Bourne. These Indians lived in self-governing settlements, separated from those of the English Puritans. Most Indians, however, remained unconverted and tried to sustain their ancient patterns of life. They did not understand European notions of land ownership, so when governments purchased land from them, they did not think that they were giving it up forever but merely lending it. The Indians suffered from contact with unscrupulous whites, who cheated them and, worse, sold them the alcohol for which the nations had no tolerance.

The first Indian conflict in New England was the short-lived Pequot uprising of 1637, wherein the Pequot, the most powerful New England tribe, were almost utterly destroyed. The stern Puritan showed no mercy in dealing with these "Canaanites." In one battle near Mystic, Connecticut, the Puritans slaughtered men, women, and children. When the survivors fled to a swamp in what is now Fairfield, Connecticut, the whites surrounded the swamp and shot anyone who tried to escape.

A far more dangerous war began because of a perceived insult. The chief sachem of the Wampanoag tribe, Metacom, whom the whites called "King Philip," was a familiar figure in the Bay Colony. He was known for his great fondness for fancy clothes, for which he paid Boston merchants with tribal land. Yet, certain things rankled with King Philip—the intrusion of Plymouth cattle into his cornfields, an annual tribute of 100 pounds the Wampanoag had to pay the colony in addition to colonists' encroachments on tribal lands, and the selling of bootleg liquor to his people. But the final insult was when he was dragged before the white man's court and fined. He had been accused of planning a revolt.

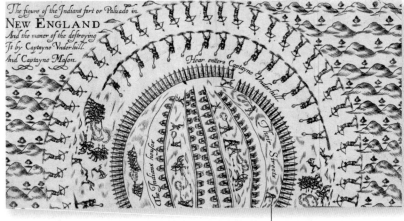

"The figure of the Indian's fort or Palizado and the maner of destroying it by Captayne Underhill and Captayne Mason," from *Nevves from America; or, A new and experimentall discoverie of New England*, London: 1638, by John Underhill

The spark that ignited Metacom's rage was the murder of John Sassamon, a Harvard educated Indian. Sassamon had been King Philip's secretary and had informed against him to Governor Winslow of Plymouth. When the Indians who murdered Sassamon had been tried and hanged, Metacom, on June 24, 1675, led an attack on the white settlement of Swansea. This was the beginning of what became known as "King Philip's War," a bloody affair that nearly destroyed the New England settlement. Metacom's people, the Nipmuk of central Massachusetts, with the Narragansett, conducted hit-and-run raids on the westernmost settlements of Massachusetts and Plymouth. Indian war cries troubled the air, as did the cries of the tortured. By the autumn of 1675, Metacom's braves had wiped out the western settlements.

The turning point in the war came with the Great Swamp Fight in December 1675, in which 1,000 men from Plymouth defeated the Narragansetts in a swamp in what is now South Kingston, Rhode Island. Later, in April 1676, the Puritans captured Metacom's ally, the Narragansett chief, Canonchet, who had burned the towns of Rehoboth and Providence. When told he was to be executed, Canonchet defied his captors."I like it well," he told them.

"I shall die before my heart is soft and I have done anything unworthy of myself." The war ended over a year after it had begun, on August 12, 1676, when Metacom himself was captured and killed. So concluded what some have called the most violent war ever fought on New England soil.

A Royal Province

Massachusetts was always something of an upstart in the eyes of Great Britain's kings. From the beginning, the colony had been left to attend to its own affairs. This was especially true after 1642, when the mother country was torn in a civil war between the forces of Parliament, led by the Puritan Oliver Cromwell, and those who supported the government of King Charles I. Massachusetts had been neutral in this war that led to the overthrow and execution of King Charles and the establishment of Parliamentary government under Cromwell's iron-willed rule.

In 1643, Massachusetts, with Plymouth, Connecticut, and New Haven, formed a loose confederation called the United Colonies of New England. Throughout the period of Cromwell and Parliament's rule, from 1649 to 1659, the United Colonies could manage their own affairs. The situation changed in 1660, when King Charles I's son, Charles II, took up the kingship of England, Scotland, Wales, and Ireland.

Devoted to the doctrine of the Divine Right of Kings, Charles II (like his father and grandfather before him) believed that the king's power had no limits, and so he had little liking for representative government whether of Parliament or the colonial assemblies in America. In 1662, King Charles II ordered the union of the colonies of Connecticut and New Haven, granting them a new charter that made no mention of royal or Parliamentary control over the new colony to be called Connecticut. Unhappy with the conclusions of a commission he had sent to New England to report on how matters stood there, Charles annulled Massachusetts' charter. In 1686, he deposed the colony's elected governor, replacing him with a royal governor, Sir Edmund Andros. Direct royal rule changed several aspects of New England government. The Stuart policies, for instance, checked the power of the Puritan church by extending the suffrage to members of other religious groups and effectively ended the persecution of Quakers.

After 1685, colonists resisted the attempts of King James II to unite all of New England into one colony. In obedience to the king's wishes, Governor Andros visited Hartford in 1687 to annul Connecticut's colonial charter of 1662. However, during a meeting between Andros and the colonial leaders, someone extinguished the candles and in the sudden darkness took the charter and hid it in an oak tree.

In 1688, by Parliament's invitation, James II was driven from the throne by his daughter Mary and her husband, William of Orange. For New England, this meant a return to old charters and liberties. New England, however, which had been a thorn-in-the-side of the Stuart kings, would prove no less troublesome to the new regime. In less than a century, Massachusetts would inspire an independence movement for England's disgruntled American colonies.

The 13 original colonies in North America

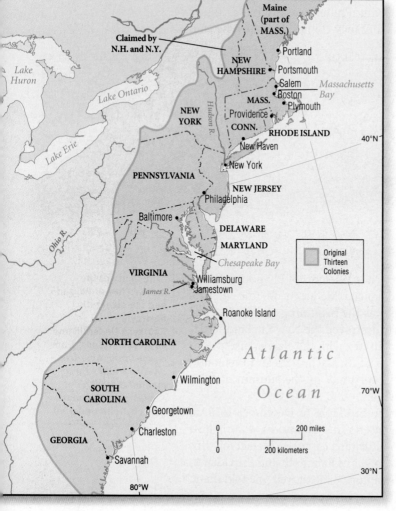

The Old Dominion

After several false starts, Virginia was flourishing. By 1622, tens of thousands of pounds of tobacco were being sold to England and making fortunes for some of the colonists. The Virginia Company, under two shrewd governors, had made what was formerly an economic outpost into a civil society. Finally, the marriage of Pocahontas and John Rolfe had brought peace between the settlers and the Indians. There was nothing more to fear from that quarter, or so it was thought.

Just when the colonists thought all was well, disaster struck. The Algonquin rose in revolt. Powhatan had died; the new chief sachem of the tribe was Opechancanough, who bitterly resented the whites' encroachments on his cornfields. He led his warriors in a secret assault that killed 347 persons, at least one-third of the colonists.

One of the victims of the unrest was the Virginia Company itself, whose charter King James I revoked two years later. The company had done much to promote Virginia's first surge into prosperity. It had introduced private landholding into the colony to give settlers an incentive to work, and in 1618 it established a representative assembly, elected by all freemen, that shared power with the colonial governor appointed by the company. This "House of Burgesses" was the first representative assembly in the New World. The company had also granted the colonists all the freedoms that they had enjoyed in England, such as the right to trial by jury and due process. This too helped advance Virginia's prosperity, for, as Captain John Smith wrote, "no man will go from hence [England] to have less freedome there [in Virginia] than here."

The Virginia Company's director, Sir Edwin Sandys, had said that in Virginia he wanted to "plant a nation, where none before hath stood." What worried him most about Virginia was that its wealth was based on tobacco alone. He wanted to introduce more varied industries that, he hoped, might make the colony more sustainable. Sir Edwin came up with a five-year plan that would make Virginia first self-sufficient, then a producer of goods for export, and finally a market for English goods. He introduced olive trees and iron works and was even planning to establish a college, when, suddenly, the Algonquin rose.

With the disbanding of the Virginia Company, King James made Virginia a crown colony, or royal province—a dominion. James appointed a governor who was to select a council to help him rule the colony. The House of Burgesses remained, whose members the freemen of the colony continued to elect. All in all, the colonists preferred the royal government to that of the Virginia Company. Soon, the colony was flourishing again, and the population began to grow. In 1624, Virginia had 1,100 colonists; by 1671 their number reached over 40,000.

A Dutch man-of-war lands 20 African slaves at Jamestown in 1619

Life in Virginia

Virginia's settlement differed markedly from New England's. While the Puritans formed tightly knit townships, the Virginians lived widely separated on farmsteads. This settlement pattern resulted from "head-right," a system whereby a settler was granted fifty acres for himself and for every person whom he brought to Virginia. Most settlers became small farmers with 100- to 200-acre holdings. Some men, however, were able to amass great estates by the head-right system and rise from middling circumstances to wealth. John Washington (George's great-grandfather) came over to Virginia as a ship's mate. Joining his brother-in-law in a partnership, John Washington was able obtain more than 5,000 acres by head-right. Another who benefited from head-right was John Carter, whose son, Robert, became so rich and influential that he was called "King" Carter. Another was William Byrd, who grew rich not only on tobacco but by exporting goods and importing slaves. After the execution of Charles I in England, some rich royalists fled to Virginia and joined the colonial aristocracy. Among them were William Randolph (from whom Thomas Jefferson was descended) and Richard Lee (the ancestor of Robert E. Lee).

In the early years of the colony, indentured white servants provided most of the labor on Virginia plantations. Before 1681, the number of black slaves in Virginia was relatively small—about 3,000 in a population of about 75,000 whites. Unlike the white servants, whose terms of service were limited to a specified number of years and who could, afterward, hope to obtain property, blacks remained slaves for life, unless their masters emancipated them. In the 17th century, emancipation was not as rare as one might expect. Some whites believed one could not hold a fellow Christian in slavery; so, when their slaves were baptized, they freed them. In Northampton County a community of freed black landowners owned hundreds of acres by head-right. These black landowners themselves imported slaves from Africa and even held indentured English servants until the House of Burgesses declared black ownership of whites illegal.

One sometimes hears that Virginia was settled by "cavaliers," members of the English aristocracy who fled England after the civil war. The Virginians, however, were not cavaliers, except insofar as they were royalists. (In England, supporters of the royal Stuart line were called "cavaliers.") Virginia's devotion to the crown was firm. During the civil war, nearly every Virginian stood behind Charles I; some even went to England to fight in his cause. When news reached Jamestown that Charles I had been executed, the House of Burgesses acknowledged the reign of his son, Charles II—treason in the eyes of Cromwell and Parliament.

Virginians were devoted as well to the Church of England. When Cromwell ordered the churches in Virginia to abandon the Anglican *Book of Common Prayer,* the royal governor, Sir William Berkeley, refused. Virginians were ardent Anglicans but with a very Puritan flavor. In their services they omitted Catholic-inspired sections of the *Book of Common Prayer,* their ministers were not ritually vested, and they received communion as a memorial (not as the Real Presence) around a table, just as the Puritans did. Their moral legislation, too, mirrored that of Plymouth and Boston. In every parish a governing body of vestrymen enforced church discipline through the offices of two churchwardens. These churchwardens meted out such punishments as whipping, the stocks, the pillory, and the **dunking stool** to those caught missing church on the Sabbath, swearing, playing cards, or throwing dice. High offenses carried harsher punishments.

dunking (or ducking) stool: a chair, attached to a long pole, on which a victim would be repeatedly ducked in a river

The moral legislation of Virginia, however, was never quite as effective as was New England's. The Virginia parishes were so large and settlements so widely separated that it was much harder to enforce regulations. In New England townships, on the other hand, neighbors were always close by and on the watch. Also, the paucity of ministers in Virginia made church life difficult—and the closest Anglican bishop was in England.

Nor did Virginia have the grammar school system that New England had developed. The colony had only two free schools—the Syms School, established 1647, and the Eaton School, founded 1659. There were "field schools" for the children of the tobacco planters, but many wealthy students were sent to private tutors for their education. It was not until 1693 that Virginia established a college—the College of William and Mary, in Williamsburg.

Though influenced by Puritanism, the Virginians were never so stern as the New Englanders. They enjoyed horse racing, drinking, and the fox chase. Theirs was not, first and foremost, a religious but an economic establishment. Their culture, with its penchant for the genteel and aristocratic, became an important counterbalance to the more egalitarian, workaday ethos of New England.

The Side of Bacon

Virginia fell on hard times during the reign of Charles II. The price of tobacco fell to less than a penny per pound. Taxes pressed heavily on the poor, while the rich, who populated the ruling council, paid no taxes at all. There were political problems as well. Sir William Berkeley, who, deposed by Cromwell, had triumphantly returned to power in 1660, controlled the workings of the colony and was bent on promoting agricultural schemes (as well as new taxes to pay for them) unpopular with most Virginians. The House of Burgesses still sat, but there had been no election for 14 years. The burgesses were all men favorable to the policies of Berkeley.

On top of all these problems, there were Indian troubles. After Opechancanough had rebelled for a second time in 1644, the dominion had settled a number of tribes on reservations; but many of the whites who had settled around the reservations wanted to drive out this dwindling population of natives. Sir William, however, saw it as his duty as royal governor to protect them. They were, after all, the king's subjects! Such a policy was not popular. Local frustration boiled over in 1675 when the Susquehannock rose and began raiding plantations on Virginia's northern frontier. When Sir William did not take immediate action against the tribe, discontented colonists gathered around a young English nobleman and rebelled.

The nobleman was Nathaniel Bacon. A cousin of the famous philosopher, Sir Francis Bacon, young Nat had attended Cambridge but was dismissed for "extravagancies." Since his family thought the only thing to do with a disgraced son was to send him off into the wilds, Nat eventually found himself in Virginia. With him went his wife and enough family money to enable him to buy two plantations. As a nobleman, Bacon was honored by Sir William, who gave the 28-year old a place on the governor's council. Life seemed to be going well for Bacon.

A 1630 map showing the Chesapeake Bay and Virginia to the Appalachian Mountains. The image to the upper left shows Powhatan in a long house, with the inscription, *Status Regis Powhatan quando praefectus Smith Captivus illi daretur* ("The condition of the king Powhatan when Captain Smith was delivered over to him.") The image of an Indian woman to the right has this inscription: *Habitus foeminarum in Provincia Sasquesahanougs* ("The clothing of women in the province of the Susquehannah.")

Then the Susquehannock attacked one of Bacon's plantations and killed his overseer. Gathering a group of colonial militiamen about him Bacon led a counterattack—not on the Susquehannock, however, but on the peaceful Occaneechee. Since, for many colonists, one Indian was just as good (or bad) as another, Bacon became a hero. Discontented poor whites, and even some discontented rich ones (like William Byrd), joined Bacon. Sir William, frightened by this show of force, agreed to call a new House of Burgesses and issue a series of reforms to improve conditions in Virginia. In particular, the governor agreed to be more aggressive with the rebellious Susquehannock. Bacon, finding this all to his taste, traveled to Jamestown and submitted to the governor.

When Bacon returned home, however, he saw that the Indians were still as free as ever. Accusing the governor of treason, Bacon again raised the standard of revolt, and it was not long before he controlled all of Virginia except the eastern shore. When he heard that Governor Berkeley had begged aid from Charles II against the rebels, Bacon grew more defiant. He said he would beat the "Red Coates" and make Virginia an independent commonwealth allied with the French and the Dutch! But this was not to be. While encamped outside Yorktown, Bacon fell ill with dysentery. He died on October 26, 1676.

Without Bacon, the revolt too died. Sir William, in a bluster of injustice, hanged 37 gentlemen who had sided with Bacon. This act, however, did not serve the governor well. When 1,100 royal troops arrived in Virginia, they carried an order from the king himself to pardon the rebels and to bring Sir William back to England to account for his government. Berkeley returned, humiliated, to England. He died before he could stand trial.

Whether one thinks of Nat Bacon as a champion of the poor or as a somewhat mad rabble-rouser, his revolt had lasting effects. Governor Berkeley's reforms did away with some of the glaring abuses that had arisen in Virginia's government. Soon, conditions improved in the Old Dominion, and Virginia took her place as one of the leaders of England's American colonies.

Mary's Land

It was difficult, and always dangerous, to be a Catholic in 17th century England. One could not practice the Faith openly, for various laws threatened him. These Penal Laws, operative since the days of Elizabeth I, placed penalties on hearing Mass (100 pounds fine and a month in prison) and for failing to attend Anglican services (20 pounds for the first month, 40 pounds for the second, and 60 pounds for the third). The law set the death penalty for those who made converts to the Faith and for priests caught in England. These laws were not always enforced but they were ever on the books, to be called up at will. The English considered Catholics dangerous subjects of a foreign prince (the pope) and potential allies of England's enemies (Spain and France). Of all who refused to submit to the state church, Catholics were thought the worst of all.

Sir George Calvert had an idea how to solve the Catholic problem in England—send English Catholics far away, to America. Calvert, the secretary of state to James I, received the king's support for a colony where Catholics could worship and not disturb the Protestant way of life in England. In 1622, Calvert sent some colonists, both Protestant and Catholic, to settle land he owned in Newfoundland. For this colony, called Avalon, Calvert decreed full religious liberty. Catholics and Protestants could worship as they saw fit and were not to argue over religion. They were even to use the same building (though at different times) for worship services.

Sir George Calvert was from Yorkshire, the most Catholic part of England. Though he and his family became Catholic in 1625, Sir George was not in much danger, for King James I was his friend. For appearance's sake, Sir George had to resign as secretary of state, but for friendship's sake, King James elevated him to the peerage as Baron Baltimore. James, like all

Stuarts, was somewhat partial to Catholics, though he could never show this openly. His mother was Mary, Queen of Scots, the last Catholic queen of Scotland.

In 1627, Calvert, his wife and children, set sail for Newfoundland to see how his colony of Avalon was getting along. He was disappointed with what he saw and decided to abandon the project. For one thing, Avalon was too near the French in Canada. For another, the Protestant colonists objected to Calvert's tolerance of "popery." From Newfoundland, Calvert sailed south, until he came to the Chesapeake Bay. The beauty of the bay, the richness of its soil, the abundance of shellfish in its waters, and its climate (more temperate than that of Newfoundland), offered better prospects for a colony, he thought.

One problem was that the Chesapeake region belonged to Virginia. When Calvert arrived in Jamestown in October 1629, he received a cold reception—there was even talk among influential Virginians of forcing him to take the **Oath of Supremacy**! Virginia, it was clear, would not welcome a colony of papists within her borders. Still, though James I had died in 1625, his son, Charles I, was friendly to Calvert. So, in 1632, Calvert received from the king a charter granting him and his descendants ownership of a portion of Virginia, including the Chesapeake Bay and lands west and north of the bay. George Calvert was made the "proprietor" of the colony, with princely powers over who should settle there and the making of laws. Under the king, Calvert held absolute sway over the new colony.

George Calvert died in April 1632, and King Charles issued the charter to Calvert's son, Cecil, the second Lord Baltimore. The king, of course, knew that both Calverts had planned the colony as a refuge for Catholics, but he could not openly tolerate such an endeavor. The charter, granted June 20, 1632, was thus so vaguely worded as to allow for a toleration of Catholics. The king granted Baron Baltimore the "Faculty of erecting and founding Churches, Chapels, and Places of Worship, in convenient and suitable Places within the Premises, and of causing the same to be dedicated and consecrated according to the Ecclesiastical Laws of our Kingdom of England . . ." The charter also named the region "Maryland"—ostensibly in honor of King Charles' Catholic wife, Queen Henrietta Maria, but secretly in honor of the Mother of God.

Sir George Calvert, First Lord Baltimore

Oath of Supremacy: a pledge that one accepted the king as head of the Church of England

A map of Maryland and Virginia by John Speed, 1675

Neither Cecil Calvert nor his father had intended that only Catholics would colonize Maryland. Such a move would have appeared suspect in England and, besides, not enough Catholics wanted to leave England for Maryland. Then, Cecil Calvert was more of a businessman than his father had been, and he wanted to make a profit off of Maryland. Only a mixed population of Catholics and Protestants could provide the numbers to make Maryland prosperous.

The Settlement of Maryland

In late fall of 1632, two ships, the *Ark* and the *Dove,* set sail for the region of the Chesapeake. The roster of passengers contained both Protestants and Catholics as well as three Jesuit priests that the ships had picked up outside of English waters. Leonard Calvert, Lord Baltimore's brother, went over as governor. In the spring of 1633, the ships arrived at the mouth of the Potomac. The colonists chose a site for a town. They called it St. Mary's.

Though it fell under Lord Baltimore's proprietorship, Maryland was to become the most self-governing of the English colonies. In addition to the governorship, Cecil Calvert established a house of burgesses. The function of the burgesses was to advise the governor and the proprietor, but it was not long before it began to vote to approve or reject laws proposed by the governor. Lord Baltimore decreed that all freemen, whether proprietors or not, had the right to vote for members of the burgesses.

In many respects, Maryland society looked a good deal like Virginia. As in Virginia, a head-right system encouraged land settlement. But in Maryland, Lord Baltimore titled "lords of manors" those who held 2,000 acres or more and gave them judicial powers to settle disputes between tenants and servants and to mete out punishments for minor offenses. This arrangement gave Maryland a somewhat feudal character.

Cecil Calvert was wise to settle workers and craftsmen in Maryland. Gentlemen, he knew, could not and would not do the work required to build a colony. Hunting and fishing were abundant in Maryland, and these workers took full advantage of them. Unlike the settlers of New England, who looked askance at such pastimes (as savoring too much of sport), the Marylanders indulged in them freely.

A good number of indentured servants came to Maryland. These at first were so numerous that there seemed to be little need for black slaves to work the tobacco plantations that became the chief source of Maryland's wealth. As the indentured servants worked themselves into freedom, however, the number of black slaves increased. Still, the number of slaves was not great in Maryland until after 1700.

While the majority of Marylanders were Protestant, the 20 richest and most influential men in the colony were Catholic. For at least the colony's first 15 years, Protestants and Catholics lived in harmony, for Lord Baltimore had decreed complete freedom of religion in Maryland. As in Avalon, so at St. Mary's—Protestants and Catholics used the same church for worship. The governor of Maryland took an oath that he would not "make any difference of persons in conferring offices, rewards or favours proceeding from the authority which his said Lordship hath conferred upon me, as his Lieutenant here, for or in respect of their said religion respectively, but merely as I shall find them faithful and well deserving of his said Lordship . . ." Lord Baltimore forbade anyone to insult another's religion under threat of a fine.

The case of one Mr. Lewis illustrates how Maryland worked. Lewis, a Catholic, was hauled into court because he rebuked a couple of his servants for reading aloud a nasty anti-Catholic sermon. The servants did it merely to annoy their master, but that did not matter—the judge, also a Catholic, fined Lewis five hundred pounds of tobacco leaf to be contributed to the building of a Protestant church.

Though a Catholic, Lord Baltimore had to oversee and promote the establishment of the Protestant Church of England in Maryland. The Jesuit priests received no such support but had to set up plantations and became farmers in order to survive. Though the priests themselves did not do much of the labor on these plantations (they had lay brothers and, later, slaves to do the work), they had to divide their time between spiritual and secular concerns.

selves did not do much of the labor on these plantations (they had lay brothers and, later, slaves to do the work), they had to divide their time between spiritual and secular concerns.

The first Jesuits did not take this state of affairs well and so came into conflict with Lord Baltimore. An Indian chief, called the "Emperor" of Piscataway, donated land to the Jesuits; but, this land fell within Lord Baltimore's proprietorship, and he would not allow the Jesuits to take it. No clergy, he said, were to be given land without his consent. The Jesuits strenuously objected. Canon law, they said, freed them from lay control. When the matter was appealed to Rome, the Jesuit general, in the interests of peace, decided in favor of Lord Baltimore and against the priests.

Maryland was the most religiously tolerant of all English colonies in the 17th century. The presence of Catholics was generally accepted, for the Catholics did not flaunt their religion but practiced it discreetly.

Toleration Threatened

William Clairborne had perhaps some claim to be discontent with Lord Baltimore's colony. Some four years before the founding of St. Mary's, he had his own settlement along the Chesapeake that had gained representation in the Virginia House of Burgesses. With news of the Maryland settlement came the assurance of the king's privy council that no private rights of Virginians living along the Chesapeake would be violated. But Clairborne's rights were violated; he was forced to pack up his settlement and move to Virginia.

In 1645, Clairborne took his revenge. In league with a Puritan pirate named Ingle, he kidnapped two Jesuit priests, Fathers Copley and White, and sent them to England. Clairborne knew that any priests found in England would face execution under the penal laws. Copley and White, in fact, came near to being executed. Their clever lawyer, however, convinced the court that the fact that the priests were forcibly brought to England was significant. The priests were released and sent out of the country.

Clairborne, as we shall see, was to cause more trouble for Maryland's Catholics. Meanwhile, many of the indentured servants, who had come to Maryland were finishing their terms of service and obtaining both land and the right to vote. Most of these were Protestant. During the English Civil War, a number of Puritans, driven from Virginia by royalist Governor Berkeley, settled in Maryland. Fearing that the growing number of Protestants boded ill for the safety of Maryland's Catholics, in 1649 Lord Baltimore directed the colonial government to approve the Toleration Act.

The opening of the Toleration Act does not sound so very tolerant; anyone, it says, who denies the Trinity "shall be punished with death and confiscation or forfeiture of all his or her lands." This would, of course, apply to Jews (who, incidentally, were never punished for this offense in Maryland). But the act continues:

> Be it Therefore . . . enacted . . . that noe person or persons whatsoever within this Province, or the Islands, Ports, Harbors, Creekes, or havens thereunto belonging professing to believe in Jesus Christ, shall from henceforth bee any waies troubled, Molested or discountenanced for or in respect of his or her religion nor in the free exercise thereof within this Province or the Islands thereunto belonging nor any way compelled to the beleife or exercise of any other Religion against his or her consent . . .

The execution of Charles I in England seemed to doom the Toleration Act. William Clairborne and another Virginian surnamed Bennett invaded Maryland under the pretext that Lord Baltimore's government was disloyal to Cromwell. Summoning a new assembly (from which all Catholics were excluded), Clairborne and Bennett repealed the Toleration Act. Catholics now stood in peril of the penal laws. Priests fled to Virginia where, according to a contemporary account, they lived "in a mean hut, sunk in the ground like a cistern or a tomb."

King William III

Strangely, it was the Puritan Oliver Cromwell himself who saved Maryland. Cecil Calvert was a very politic and shrewd man. He entered into negotiations with Cromwell and struck a political deal. Cromwell confirmed Calvert as the proprietor of Maryland, meaning that all laws confirmed under him previously, including the Toleration Act, were reinstated.

Nevertheless, Maryland's religious toleration was doomed. Catholics would remain a minority in Maryland, while the population of Protestants continually increased. After the overthrow of King James II, a former pirate-turned-Anglican-minister, John Coode, complained of the Catholics to the new king, William III. In 1692 William established the Church of England in Maryland and required everyone, except Puritans and Protestant nonconformists, to support it. Penal laws appeared on the books. It was forbidden to celebrate Mass, and parents who taught their children the Catholic faith received heavy fines. If Catholic children became Protestant, they could seize their parents' property without compensation; but someone who converted a Protestant to the Catholic Church could be killed.

Though Maryland's penal laws were not always enforced, Catholics had to be very secretive in practicing their religion—for the laws threatened. There were still priests in Maryland, but they lived as private gentlemen on their estates, to which Catholics repaired to receive the sacraments. Wealthier Catholics, of course, could send their children to receive a Catholic education in Europe; but the children of poorer Catholics often received no schooling at all.

The threatening atmosphere in which Maryland's Catholics lived is encapsulated in the words Maryland's Governor Seymour used to warn two Catholics hauled before his court in 1704. "Gentlemen," he said, "it is the unhappy temper of you and all your tribe to grow insolent under civility. . . . Yet of all people, you have the least reason for considering that if the necessary laws that are made were let loose to crush you. . . . you would need to dread. I assure you the next occasion you give me, you shall find the truth of what I say. . . . If you intend to live here let me have no more of these things, for if I do, and they are made against you, be assured I'll chastise you. . . . Pray take notice that I am an English Protestant Gentleman, and can never equivocate."

New Amsterdam Becomes New York

By the middle of the 17th century, New Amsterdam on Manhattan Island was a settlement of about 2,000 people. With its gabled houses and brick church, the town was a small portion of Holland transferred to the New World. Since it lay upon the best sea route along the Atlantic coast, the port of New Amsterdam was usually full of ships, and the town full of sailors. Here was the port of call for those engaged in the Dutch fur trade, the staple of Holland's New World wealth.

The Dutch colony had a mixed population. Here were Swedes and Finns, who introduced housing that would long be in use in North America—the log cabin. Here were also Puritan English who had come from Connecticut; the Dutch allowed these to govern themselves by their own laws. Here were black African slaves who worked farms owned by the rich *patroons*.

The Dutch West India Company imposed a series of bad governors on New Netherlands. The peg-legged Pieter Stuyvesant (he had lost the limb in a battle in the West Indies) was bad-tempered and ruled like an absolute monarch. Moreover, he alienated colonists by regulating gin shops and placing high customs on traders. Because of governors like Stuyvesant, some colonists called for direct administration by the Dutch government rather than by the Dutch West India Company. This, however, was never to be.

On August 18, 1664, during a brief war between Great Britain and Holland, Richard Nicolls, commanding four British frigates, sailed into New Amsterdam harbor and demanded the surrender of the fortress. Unable to convince the Dutch to resist the English invaders, Stuyvesant was forced to deliver his sword to Nicolls. By the end of October, the English had taken New Amsterdam, Fort Orange, and Fort Casimir on the Delaware, which they renamed respectively New York, Albany, and Newcastle. New Netherlands thus became an English possession.

A Present to the King's Brother

King Charles II held a grudge against the Dutch. Following the execution of his brother, Charles I, the Dutch had openly allied themselves with Cromwell, forcing the young prince to turn to Spain. In payment for this betrayal (as he saw it) of his father, in 1664 Charles decided to give his brother James, Duke of York, the Dutch New World possessions, plus some other lands already held by England. This was an kingly gift, since it included not only the current state of New York but all the region between the Connecticut and Delaware rivers, Long Island, Nantucket Island, Martha's Vineyard, and Maine east of the Kennebec River.

Since these lands fell to the Duke of York, they were named New York, and the city of New Amsterdam became New York City. Made sole proprietor of New York, Duke James had full command over the parceling out of lands and the making of laws in the colony. One

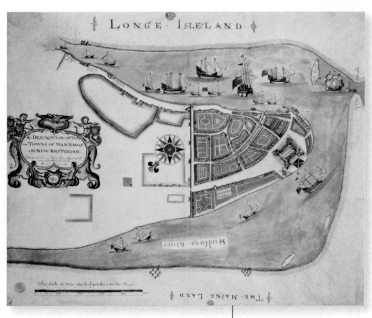

Map of New Amsterdam, 1664

Dutch Legacy in America

Though the Dutch held lands in North America for only a short time, their heritage was long-lasting. Many Dutch names have survived in the modern New York City. When the Dutch Governor Dongan built a wall to protect the settlers from wolves and Indians, the street that ran along the wall became known as "Wall Street"—now the financial center of New York. Outside this city wall lay *bouweries*, or farms for the provisioning of New Amsterdam —the origin of the word, "bowery." Names of other Dutch settlements also remain with us—Breukelen (Brooklyn) and Haarlem (Harlem). Even our word "boss" comes from Dutch workmen, who called their masters *baas*.

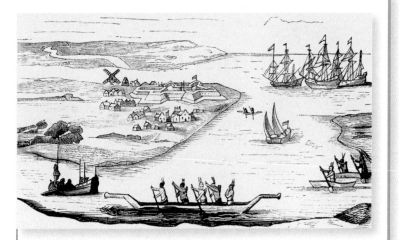

Illustration of New Amsterdam, from a Swedish book, *Nord Amerika*, published in 1880

Patroon families would give the future New York an aristocratic flavor. Dutch families have also played an important part in the history of what would be the United States of America. Martin Van Buren, the eighth president of the United States, came from a family that was tenant of the *patroon* Van Rensselaer. Presidents Theodore Roosevelt and Franklin Delano Roosevelt were descended from Dutch settlers of Breukelen and New Amsterdam.

James, Duke of York

of his first acts was to give over a portion of his lands to two friends, Sir George Carteret and Lord John Berkeley. In 1667, these two proprietors of what became New Jersey drew up a document called "Concessions and Agreements of the Proprietors of New Jersey," in which they guaranteed freedom of religion and a representative assembly to all who would settle in their colony.

James directed his deputy governor in New York, Richard Nicolls, not to harass the Dutch inhabitants of the colony, nor to force them to speak the English language; rather, he was to treat them with "humanity and gentleness." The duke, however, did not win the affection of his English colonists, for he imposed taxes on them without their consent. When he promulgated "the Duke's Laws," based on the laws of New England, the English settlers objected—not because they thought the laws were harsh but because they had had no say in their passage. James eventually allowed the New Yorkers to form an assembly, which met in 1683. This assembly enacted "The Charter of Liberties and Privileges," which declared that the assembly had the supreme legislative power in the colony and final say over any new taxes.

By the time James reviewed the New York charter he had become King James II. Facing an intransigent Parliament at home, he did not want to deal with an upstart assembly in New York; so he disallowed the charter. Meanwhile the expense of maintaining the colony as its proprietor proved too costly, and James transferred New York from his own personal possession to a possession of the crown, a royal province. In 1691, the monarchs, William and Mary, granted New York the right to have its own representative assembly.

They Followed the Inner Light

William Penn was always a nonconformist. While his father, Admiral Sir William Penn, was away at sea, young William attended schools heavily influenced by Puritanism. When he was 12 years old, he felt what he called an interior comfort, and it seemed as if his room were filled with a visible glory. He was convinced that God was present and that man is capable of enjoying union with the divine.

It was at Christ Church College, Oxford, that the younger Penn was first influenced by the Quakers. These folks, who called themselves the Society of Friends, were, except for the Catholics, the most persecuted religious group in England. Founded in 1650 by George Fox, Quakers (so named because in their meetings they would apparently "quake" or tremble with enthusiasm) believed the final authority for a believer was not the Church, nor even the Bible, but the light of the Holy Spirit's presence in the soul. Since everyone was capable of having this inner light, all were equal, and so the Friends had no clergy or hierarchy. Moreover, Quakers addressed each other as "thou" or "thee," which in the 17th century was how one addressed intimate friends and inferiors. Quakers condemned all violence and were pacifists. Though heavily persecuted, they spread all over England and into Holland, Germany, and Russia. Every English American colony, except Rhode Island, had laws against them.

Quakers believed in complete religious toleration. Penn was at Oxford when, shortly after the restoration of Charles II, statutes were passed requiring students to attend Anglican services. When Penn, with some others, resisted these statutes and refused to attend services, he was expelled from the university. His father, Admiral Penn, was not pleased with his son's behavior and sent him to France for a time to escape Quaker influences. Later, his father sent young William to Ireland to look after family possessions there. In Ireland, Penn met some Quakers and became a full convert to their beliefs.

Penn became a Quaker leader. He published many works defending Quakerism and attacking its opponents. He was arrested a few times, once for refusing to pay a fine for not removing his hat at court.

It was Penn's purpose to found a settlement in America that would provide a haven for Quakers and other persecuted religious groups. About 1675, Penn received a proprietorship in New Jersey and opened it for Quaker settlement. The following year, he and George Fox traveled through Holland and into Germany, preaching Quakerism and looking for interested settlers. It was thus that western New Jersey became heavily settled by Quakers.

Penn's Woods

King Charles II owed Penn's father money. When Admiral Penn died in 1670, the right to claim the debt passed on to his son. In 1680, the younger Penn asked the crown for a tract of land in America north of Maryland in lieu of money payment. The king agreed, and in a royal grant, dated March 1, 1681, he made Penn proprietor of the land that would extend from New Jersey westward and from the border of Maryland north to the border of New York. Penn wanted to name this grant "Sylvania" (woodland), but the king insisted on adding "Penn" to the name, in honor of the late admiral. Though Penn protested, the king's will prevailed. The new colony was named Pennsylvania.

To attract settlers to his colony, Penn, in 1682, published a tract, "Some Account of the Province of Pennsylvania." Attracted by the promise of living in a colony offering complete religious toleration, many English and continental Europeans flocked to Pennsylvania. In 1682, Penn laid out his "city of brotherly love," Philadelphia, at the confluence of the Delaware and Schuylkill Rivers. Three years later, Pennsylvania could boast nearly 9,000 inhabitants. Among these were Mennonite Germans under Franz Daniel Pastorius who, in 1683, settled Germantown. Quakers from Wales and England settled the colony in great numbers.

William Penn signs a treaty with the Indians, by Edward Hicks (1780–1849)

William Penn saw his colony as a "holy experiment" in religious toleration. This toleration extended to all groups, even Catholics, who found Pennsylvania a refuge from Maryland's penal laws. Though he did not abolish slavery in the colony, Penn insisted on laws requiring the instruction of blacks and granting them the right to marry. But the colonial assembly, which, by the time he made the recommendations, consisted of more than just Quakers, rejected the proposals.

Penn called for justice for the Indians. He wrote:

> Don't abuse them, but let them have justice, and you win them. The worst is that they are the worse for the Christians who have propagated their vices and yielded them tradition for ill, and not for good things. . . . I beseech God to incline the hearts of all that come

into these parts, to out-live the knowledge of the natives by a fixt obedience to their greater Knowledge of the will of God, for it were miserable indeed for us to fall under the just censure of the poor Indian conscience, while we make profession of things so far transcending.

Penn's kindness was reciprocated by the Pennsylvania natives, who long remained on friendly terms with the proprietor and his successors.

Penn's later life was not easy. He engaged in a boundary dispute with Lord Baltimore that was finally settled in 1764 when two surveyors named Mason and Dixon settled the boundary between Pennsylvania and Maryland—the origin of the Mason-Dixon line that became the symbolic border of North and South in Anglo America. A series of bad governors represented Penn between 1684 and 1692, when the king, for two years, removed Pennsylvania from Penn's control. In 1712, Penn's failing health induced him to surrender the colony to the crown, though it refused the offer.

After Penn's death at the age of 74 on July 30, 1718, Pennsylvania continued to prosper. Penn had been shrewd enough to attract hardworking settlers from all over Europe, and so the character of the colony became quite cosmopolitan. The German settlers in particular, who made up at least one-third of the population, were known for their well-ordered and productive farms. These were the ancestors of those whom we call the "Pennsylvania Dutch"—"dutch" being a corruption of *deutsch*, the name by which the Germans know themselves. Philadelphia, which by 1700 surpassed even New York as a cultural center, was the first colonial city after Boston to have a printing press, and it had the best hospitals and charitable institutions in the colonies.

Chapter 5 Review

Summary

- Puritans in England, deciding that they could not turn old England into their model of a Puritan commonwealth, formed such a society in New England. In 1628, under the leadership of John Endicott, they settled in Salem.

- In 1641 Massachusetts adopted the "Body of Liberties," and Plymouth established the "General Fundamentals," both of which ensured free elections; trial by jury; the right not to be deprived of life, liberty, or property without due process of law; the right not to be taxed if not represented; and the right not to be forced to incriminate oneself in trial.

- New England was nearly destroyed by two wars: the Pequot uprising of 1637 and King Phillip's War of 1675–1676.

- In 1643 Massachusetts formed a loose confederation called the United Colonies of New England with Plymouth, Connecticut, and New Haven.

- With the disbanding of the Virginia Company, King James I made Virginia a crown colony—a dominion.

- In 1675 Nathaniel Bacon started a revolt against the government of Virginia because he claimed it would not do anything about Indian attacks on settlements. Bacon soon controlled most of Virginia.

- In 1622 George Calvert, desiring to solve the problem of persecution of Catholics in England, sent English Catholics to a colony called Avalon in Newfoundland. This colony did not last long, however, and Calvert received a charter from King Charles I to found another colony in North America. When George Calvert died, the charter was confirmed to his son, Cecil. The colony became known as "Maryland."

- In 1649 Lord Baltimore directed the Maryland government to approve the Toleration Act, which said that all Trinitarian religions were to be respected in Maryland.

Chapter 5 Review (continued)

- In 1692, King William III established the Church of England in Maryland and required everyone to support it.
- King Charles II, because of a grudge he held against the Dutch, seized the Dutch New World possessions and gave them to his brother, James, duke of York. Under the duke of York, New Amsterdam became New York City.
- In 1680 William Penn received a land grant west of New Jersey as a haven for persecuted Quakers and other religious groups. King Charles II named the settlement Pennsylvania. In 1682 Penn laid out his "city of brotherly love," which he called Philadelphia.
- Following a boundary dispute between Penn and Lord Baltimore, two surveyors named Mason and Dixon settled the boundary between Pennsylvania and Maryland.

Key Concepts

General Fundamentals and Body of Liberties: two bodies of law approved respectively by the Plymouth and Massachusetts Bay colonies that ensured free elections; trial by jury; the right not to be deprived of life, liberty, or property without due process of law; the right not to be taxed if not represented; and the right not to be forced to incriminate oneself in trial

King Philip's War: a bloody war in 1675–1678 that nearly destroyed New England

Oath of Supremacy: a pledge that one acknowledged the king as head of the Church of England

Toleration Act: an act approved by Lord Baltimore and the Maryland colonial government guaranteeing the free exercise of religion for all Christian groups in Maryland

Quakers: the Society of Friends, a religious group that stresses the interior guidance of the Holy Spirit and rejects external religious rites and ordained ministry.

Dates to Remember

1628: Puritans in England form the settlement of Salem in America.

1641: Plymouth establishes the "General Fundamentals."

1643: Massachusetts, Plymouth, Connecticut, and New Haven form the United Colonies of New England.

1649: Lord Baltimore and the Maryland legislature approve the Toleration Act.

1675: King Phillip's War begins.

William Penn establishes Pennsylvania.

Nathaniel Bacon revolts against the government of Virginia.

1692: William II establishes the Church of England in America.

Central Characters

John Winthrop (1588–1649): a Puritan leader and one of the founders of Salem colony. He delivered the famous "City on a Hill" sermon.

Roger Williams (ca. 1603–1683): the founder of Providence Plantation colony, where he guaranteed complete religious toleration

Metacom (1638–1676): (also known as King Philip) an Indian leader who led one of the costliest wars in New England's history

Nathaniel Bacon (1647–1676): a Virginia planter who led a rebellion against Virginia's government

George Calvert, 1st Baron of Baltimore (ca. 1578–1632): an English statesman who founded the province of Maryland as a sanctuary for Catholics.

Cecil Calvert, 2nd Baron of Baltimore (1605–1675): George Calvert's son, who oversaw the founding of Maryland and promoted the Toleration Act

William Penn (1644–1718): an English Quaker who founded the Commonwealth of Pennsylvania as a refuge for Quakers and other persecuted Christians.

Questions for Review

1. Describe some of the beliefs of the Saints.
2. How did the Saints regard their colony of Plymouth?

Chapter 5 Review (continued)

3. Why did John Winthrop speak of Salem colony as a City on a Hill?

4. What situation prompted the founding of Salem?

5. What are some of the beliefs of the Puritans, and how do they differ from those of the Saints?

6. What two events nearly destroyed the colonies of New England?

7. What part did the "heretics" of New England play in New England's history?

8. What situation or events caused Nathaniel Bacon to revolt?

9. What effects did Bacon's revolt have on Virginia and its government?

10. What was the "Catholic problem" in England that George Calvert wanted to solve? How did he solve it?

11. Describe the situation that prompted the Toleration Act.

12. Describe the beliefs of the Quakers and their mode of church government.

Ideas in Action

1. Read Nathaniel Hawthorne's *The Scarlet Letter* and consider how it reflects Puritan ideas.

2. Write your own account of what you think it would have been like to be a Catholic in Protestant England and English America in the 17th century.

3. Find out if your family was in America in the 17th and early 18th centuries and create a family tree. See if you can discover any family stories or any accounts written about your ancestors.

Highways and Byways

"Frisking together like so many fairies"—the Maypole

The maypole dance, thought to have begun in Germany as a pagan ceremonial dance, is a folk dance that is still performed today, especially in Great Britain, Canada, and Scandinavia. The maypole dance is traditionally performed on May Day, May 1, the day that celebrates the return of spring. In pagan times the dance was performed to ensure fertility of crops. This significance became lost over the years, and May Day and the maypole dance became merely part of folk culture. The Puritans of America thought, however, that such practices were "licentious and pagan," and they forbade their observance. This may be the reason why the maypole has never been an important part of American culture.

The maypole is a long pole that is set up in the ground. A crown of flowers is placed on top of the pole, and long ribbons can be tied to the crown. There are two forms of the maypole dance: the circle dance and the ribbon dance. The circle dance involves no ribbons, and the dancers just dance in a circle around the pole. The ribbon dance involves ribbons, and the dancers hold the ends of the ribbons and weave in and out and around each other to create an intricate pattern on the pole. The maypole dance is usually danced to reels, jigs, hornpipes, or waltzes.

6 THE STRUGGLE FOR A CONTINENT

Queen Anne's War

In 1680, a band of pagan Indians attacked a Christian Indian village on St. Simon's Island in Georgia. Fortunately for the village, the Spanish governor's lieutenant at nearby mission San Buenaventura de Guadalquini was alerted in time. With a small force of Spanish soldiers and Indians, he repelled the invaders.

The attack on St. Simon's was ominous. The invading Indians were not acting on their own but were encouraged and aided by English settlers at Charles Town, 60 miles up the coast. Englishmen had settled Charles Town, or Charleston, ten years before, under a grant from King Charles II. By 1680, Protestant Huguenots and Scots, had settled in the region around Charleston. Pursuing the trade in deerskin, the settlers frequently entered Spanish territory in violation of Spanish law. The Spanish, however, could do little about such intrusions, since there were few Spanish soldiers in Florida. The Charlestonians, moreover, had made an alliance with the powerful Yamassee tribe, which gave them a buffer zone of protection against the Spanish.

One reason the inhabitants of Charleston did not respect the boundaries of Spanish Florida was that King Charles' grant to the colony of "Carolina" (named for his majesty) included all the coast south of Virginia to a point 65 miles south of San Agustín. It thus took in land already claimed by Spain. When Spain protested, the matter was resolved by the Treaty of Madrid, which placed the southern boundary of Carolina at the Savannah River, the southern boundary of the current state of South Carolina.

The inhabitants of Charleston, the principle town in the colony of South Carolina, refused to respect the Treaty of Madrid. They armed their Indian allies and led them on slaving expeditions against the tribes to the south. A short time after the attack on St. Simon's Island, Carolinians led 300 Indians against the mission Santa Catalina de Guale but were again driven off. Four years later, however, repeated Indian and pirate attacks on the Guale missions convinced the Spanish governor to evacuate all the missions on the coast north of Florida. By 1685, missions on the coast north of the St. Mary's River were no more.

Having destroyed the coastal missions, the Carolinians turned their attention to the interior. Led by Scots, some 60 Yamassee Indians attacked the mission Santa Catalina de

Queen Anne

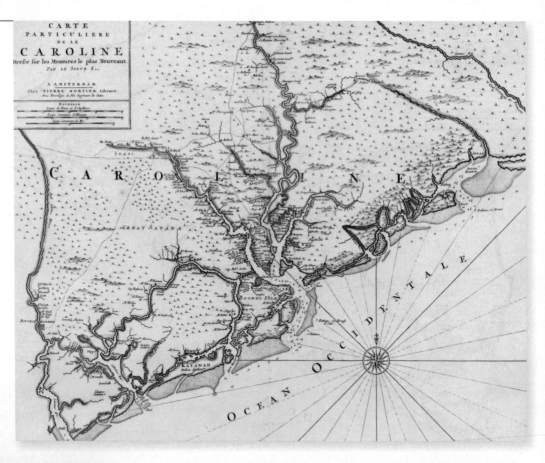

A 1690 map of South Carolina

Emperor Leopold I

Ahoica, killing 18 and enslaving 24 mission Indians, both male and female. The survivors were sent to work on plantations in both Carolina and the British West Indies.

Conditions worsened for the missions during "Queen Anne's War," which began in 1702. Queen Anne's War was the American branch of the War of the Spanish Succession. The king of Spain, Carlos II, had died, leaving his kingdom, not to Karl, the son of his Austrian Habsburg cousin, Leopold I, but to Philippe, duke of Anjou, the grandson of King Louis XIV of France. Louis XIV was the most powerful monarch of Europe, and the English and other powers feared a union of Spain and France, with all their new world wealth, under the Bourbon family. Thus a war broke out—the English (under Queen Anne, who succeeded William III in 1702), the Dutch, and the Austrians against France and Spain. The war ended when the deaths of Emperor Leopold I and his eldest son, Josef, left the claim of Spain, the empire, and other Habsburg domains to Karl, the archduke of Austria. The prospect of another Carlos I, uniting the empire and Spain, and encircling France and the Netherlands, proved more unwelcome to the European powers than a Bourbon Spain. So, with due assurances that the thrones of France and Spain would never be united, Philippe, the duke of Anjou, became Felipe V, the first Bourbon king of Spain.

With the blessing of an official war, Governor James Moore of South Carolina led 600 Carolinians and 600 Indians in an attack on San Agustín in November 1702. Destroying the coastal missions south of the St. Mary's River, the Carolinians and their Indian allies marched into San Agustín itself. Unable to resist the invasion with only 323 soldiers, the

Spanish governor, José de Zúñiga y Cerda, moved the entire population into the Castillo de San Marcos, the stone fort at San Agustín. While Zúñiga y Cerda sent for reinforcements to Havana, Governor Moore's men laid waste to San Agustín's houses, the parish church, and the Franciscan friary. By December 26, four ships from Havana had sailed into the harbor of San Agustín, forcing Moore to destroy his own small fleet and withdraw by land. He took with him 500 Christian Indians as slaves.

Ashamed that he had not taken San Agustín, James Moore resigned his governorship. Two years later, however, the South Carolina assembly chose Moore to lead a raid on the Apalachee region of western Florida. With 50 Carolinian soldiers and 1,000 Creek Indians, Moore led a surprise attack on mission Concepción de Ayubale on January 25, 1704. The Franciscan missionary, Fray Angel de Miranda, gathered a small force inside the mission church and repelled numerous attacks for as long as ammunition held out. Reinforcements from Mission San Luis de Talimali soon arrived, and 30 Spanish soldiers and 400 Apalachee braves under Captain Alonso Días Mejía twice drove the Carolinians from Ayubale plaza. But by nightfall, the Spanish and the Apalachee had run out of ammunition. They surrendered.

Felipe V, the first Bourbon king of Spain, by Hyacinthe Rigaud

Following the surrender of Ayubale, Moore and his Carolinians brutally butchered the mission's inhabitants, scalping and mutilating men, women, and children. According to the Spanish governor's report, many of the Christian Indians died heroically:

> During this cruel and barbarous martyrdom which the poor Apalachee Indians experienced, there were some of them who encouraged the others, declaring that through martyrdom they would appear before God; and to the pagans they said, "Make more fire so that our hearts may be allowed to suffer for our souls. We go to enjoy God as Christians."

Castillo de San Marcos, as it appears today, with the Spanish flag on its battlements

A Franciscan who had accompanied Mejía's force, Fray Juan de Parga Araujo, was beheaded and his body dismembered. The remaining Apalachee, about 1,000, were taken to Charleston as slaves. Moore carried out other attacks in Apalachee, no less brutal.

In July 1704, the Spanish council of war in San Agustín decided to abandon Apalachee. All inhabitants were to remove to the region around San Agustín. A representative from the French out-post at Mobile, Alabama, offered the remaining Apalachee refuge there. Eight-hundred Indians took him up on this offer. They formed a strong and devout Catholic community, whose piety the French highly praised.

Though the region around the Castillo de San Marcos was safer than their home region, the Apalachee still suffered from slaving raids throughout the remainder of Queen Anne's War. Between January and July 1704, the Apalachee region lost 4,000 native inhabitants. Its 14 prosperous missions, with the surrounding Spanish ranchos and smaller Indian settlements, were irrevocably lost.

War in the North

Though they were subject to Her Royal Majesty, Queen Anne, the English colonies could show a remarkable independence. For instance, as Queen Anne's War proved, the queen's government could not force colonists to serve in the army but were forced to ask colonial legislators to levy troops. If a colony refused, as did New York during Queen Anne's War (New York fur traders did not want war interrupting their business with Canada), it remained neutral.

New England, on the other hand, had been eager for the fight. Abenaki Indians under French officers had attacked and destroyed Maine coastal settlements (then part of Massachusetts) and laid waste to Deerfield, Massachusetts, carrying away its inhabitants. Massachusetts retaliated, attacking Port Royal in Acadia, a base for French privateers, in 1707. This first attack failed, but another campaign in 1710 succeeded. A British operation against Québec in 1711 was unsuccessful.

Queen Anne's War ended in 1713 with the Peace of Utrecht. While France and Spain gained their primary objective, the establishment of the Bourbon Felipe V as ruler of Spain, they had to make important concessions. Newfoundland, Acadia (renamed Nova Scotia—"New Scotland") in America, and Gibraltar and Minorca in the Mediterranean were ceded to the English. England also won the right to engage in the *asiento* (African slave trade with the Spanish colonies). The borders of French Canada, English America, and Spanish Florida remained unchanged.

A War for Jenkins and King George

Queen Anne's War devastated Spanish Florida. The once vibrant missions were gone. Ironically, two years did not pass after the Peace of Utrecht when Spain's former enemies, the Yamasee and other Indian tribes, sought refuge in Florida. The Carolinians had begun to enslave their former Indian allies, using other tribes against them as they once had used the Yamasee. The refugee tribes settled around San Agustín. By 1717, roughly 942 Indians lived within a ten-mile radius of the *castillo*. Six Franciscan friars labored among them.

This huddled mass of Christian Indians continued to suffer from slavers who periodically raided their settlements. More problems followed from a feud among the Franciscans themselves. Friars from America, called *criollos* or creoles, assumed control of the Florida missions and offered little support to missionaries from Spain, called *peninsulares*. The creoles did not allow the *peninsulares* to hold positions of authority and assigned them the least desirable missions. Open dissension between the groups broke out, and the king of Spain had to intervene on behalf of the *peninsulares*. The controversy grew so bad that when the second auxiliary bishop of San Agustín, Fray Francisco de San Buenaventura y Tejada, arrived in 1735, he found families in a bad state, drunkenness among the Indians, a broken-down parish church, and English traders openly preaching heresy on street corners. For the next ten years this energetic bishop worked to reform the Church in San Agustín.

The difficulties of Bishop Tejada's reform work were probably exacerbated by the outbreak of war in 1739. It all began when Spanish revenue cutters captured an English smuggler named Edward Jenkins and cropped one of his ears. It was not that the Spanish enjoyed cutting off ears—rather, they were angry that for years the English had ignored the provision of the Treaty of Utrecht that allowed them, under the *asiento*, to send only one trading ship a year to Porto Bello in the Caribbean. The unfortunate Jenkins was but one of many English smugglers engaged in illegal trade. He had the poor luck to be caught.

Members of Parliament were outraged when Jenkins, less an ear, stood before them in London. The House of Commons declared war on Spain in October 1739—a war that became popularly known as the "War of Jenkins' Ear."

Of course, illegal trade and a smuggler's ear were not the only things to stand between Spain and Great Britain. In 1733, General James Edward Oglethorpe with a group of philanthropists had established a new colony as a refuge for debtors. This colony, named Georgia after King George II, stretched from the Savannah River south to Florida—all land claimed by Spain, land where the coastal Guale missions once stood. The settlers of Georgia were not numerous. They were Germans from Salzburg, who founded Federica, a settlement up the Savannah River from Oglethorpe's town of Savannah, as well as Scots Highlanders and English debtors who wanted to start life again in a new place.

With war declared, the Spanish attacked and occupied a fort established by Oglethorpe on Amelia Island, south of the St. Mary's River—in Spanish territory. Oglethorpe responded by gathering a force of Highlanders, Indians, and a small fleet. He captured the Spanish forts at the mouth of the St. John's River and advanced on San Agustín. He laid siege to the *castillo* but could not take the strongly garrisoned fortress. After a siege of 38 days, Oglethorpe gave up and withdrew to Georgia.

James Edward Oglethorpe

Meanwhile, in November 1739, English vice-admiral Edward Vernon captured and sacked the Spanish settlement of Porto Bello in Panama. Because of this success he was given command of an expedition to conquer Cuba. Three thousand colonial volunteers, from New England to the Carolinas, eagerly joined this expedition, which left Jamaica in January of 1741. It was a failure. In an assault on Cartagena in Granada, Vernon's men caught the yellow fever, and over half of the colonial force died. Among the survivors of this expedition was George Washington's brother, Captain Lawrence Washington, who named an estate he owned in Virginia "Mount Vernon" in honor of the vice-admiral. It was during this battle that, for the first time, the English called the colonists "Americans" instead of just "provincials."

A view of Louisbourg, as it appears today

With Cuba safe, the Spanish prepared a force of 30 ships and 1,300 soldiers to assail Georgia. The expedition left Havana in May 1742 and captured a fort on St. Simon's Island on the Georgia coast south of Savannah. Oglethorpe fell back on Federica; the Spanish force pursued him. In the Battle of the Bloody Marsh on July 7, Oglethorpe's force ambushed the Spanish and threw them back to the coast. Spain's plan of (in the words of her king, Felipe V) "laying waste South Carolina and her dependencies" had failed.

In 1744, the War of Jenkins' Ear merged with another European war,

called in Europe the War of the Austrian Succession but, in America, King George's War. The war began when Louis XV of France and King Friedrich II the Great of Prussia refused to respect the succession of Maria Theresia, daughter of Emperor Karl VI, to the Austrian Habsburg territories. When Karl died, Friedrich wanted the Austrian province of Silesia; Louis XV wanted all or part of the Austrian Netherlands; and Karl, the elector of Bavaria, wanted the honor of becoming Holy Roman Emperor. The war began in December 1740, when Friedrich invaded Silesia. The European powers quickly formed up their sides. When the Spanish king, Felipe V, decided to aid his French Bourbon cousin, Louis, Great Britain allied itself with Austria.

France and Britain fought each other in Europe; their colonies fought each other in America. Governor William Shirley of Massachusetts Bay organized an expedition to capture the supposedly impregnable French fortress of Louisbourg on Cape Breton Island, in Canada. The New England militia under William Pepperell, supported by a Royal Navy squadron under Admiral Sir Peter Warren, carried on an unorthodox campaign against Fort Louisbourg. With little military discipline (and while they were not fishing), the New Englanders so befuddled the French commander that he surrendered the fort on June 16, 1745, after a siege of a little more than two weeks.

As in Queen Anne's War, the French, with their Indian allies, raided New England frontier villages and the town of Saratoga, New York, while England's allies, the Iroquois, made incursions into Canada. The French prepared an enormous fleet of one hundred ships and sent it to destroy Boston. Storms at sea ruined the fleet, an event the Bostonians ascribed to divine intervention.

The Treaty of Aix-la-Chapelle in 1748 ended King George's War. Great Britain agreed to return Louisbourg to France in return for Madras in India, which the French had captured from the British. In return for a payment of money from Spain, Great Britain renounced her part in the *asiento*. For Spain, at least, Jenkins' ear had not been shed in vain.

Between Wars

Aix-la-Chapelle did not end rivalry between the great colonial powers. Britain and France, in particular, were striving for mastery of both North America and Europe, and their struggles on the mother continent were mirrored by colonial tensions in America.

Ill feeling between French and English was exemplified by the Acadians, the French settlers of what the English now called Nova Scotia, but what the French had named l'Acadie. Since receiving l'Acadie in the Peace of Utrecht in 1713, the English had been tolerant, allowing French Acadians to keep their language, practice their Catholic religion, and even rule themselves by their own laws. The Acadians, however, remained hostile to the British. Hopes that France would one day reconquer l'Acadie kindled the fires of their resentment against British rule. The English began to worry about the French inhabitants when English settlements were established at Halifax and Annapolis Royal in Nova Scotia in 1749. After all, war with France could erupt at any time, and Britain did not want a hostile population within her colonies.

So it was that England gathered those French Acadians who lived near militarily strategic centers and deported them from Nova Scotia. Their land confiscated, some 6,000 to 7,000 Acadians were sent to various parts of British America. Families were separated; friends saw each other no more. Many years later, the American poet, William Wadsworth Longfellow, would tell in his long poem, "Evangeline," of a group of Acadians who were allowed to settle in Louisiana. Their descendants, called Cajuns (a corruption of Acadians), remain in Louisiana, speak French, and worship in the Catholic Church.

The Acadian deportation was but a minor episode in French and British relations. It was in the west, in the Ohio River Valley, that events precipitated a crisis. In 1747, some

Virginians organized what they called the Ohio Company to acquire 500,000 acres on both sides of the Ohio River to sell to English settlers. English colonists founded similar land companies to trade with the Indians and move them off their land along the Ohio.

The French saw such activities as a threat; the possession of the Ohio River Valley by the English could cut off communications between Canada and Louisiana. To forestall the English advance into the Ohio region, in 1749, the French governor of Canada sent Celeron de Bienville to take possession of the Ohio River Valley for France. Four years later, the governor erected a series of forts on the Allegheny and upper Ohio rivers. These fortresses worried Virginia, whose western boundary ran along the Ohio. Governor Robert Dinwiddie sent a 22-year old lieutenant colonel named George Washington to deliver a formal protest to the French.

The French ignored Dinwiddie's protest, and the governor again sent Washington to the Ohio Valley, this time with 150 soldiers, to keep the French from building a fort near the confluence of the Allegheny and Monongahela rivers in western Pennsylvania. Before Washington could arrive, however, the French had built their Fort Duquesne. At Great Meadows, the French and Virginians met in battle, and Washington was defeated.

The Albany Congress

News of the Virginians' defeat at Great Meadows reverberated through the colonies. The French seemed suddenly more powerful, and even the Six Nations of the Iroquois, long enemies of the French, wavered in their alliance with the English. For many English colonials, Washington's defeat was proof that the colonies needed to act in a more unified fashion if they were to defend themselves against the French. So it was that a congress of colonial representatives met at Albany, New York, in June 1754, to discuss how to maintain their alliance with the Iroquois and achieve greater colonial unity.

The Albany Congress approved a plan of union that in many respects resembles the constitution adopted by the United States over 30 years later. This plan, introduced by Benjamin Franklin of Philadelphia and Thomas Hutchinson of Boston, called for a kind of legislative assembly whose members would be appointed by the colonies, with a president appointed by the king. This quasi-government would have the powers to declare war, make peace, and conclude treaties with Indian nations in the name of all the colonies. It could raise armies, equip fleets, build forts—and raise the taxes necessary to pay for all this. The purchase of lands in the west would fall under this body, as well as the governance of the west, until the British government should decide to establish new colonies there.

Benjamin Franklin

This plan of union never became more than a proposal. Though adopted by the Albany Congress, it was rejected by every colonial legislature. The colonies were not ready—nor would they be ready for another 35 years—to unite themselves. They were jealous of their local independence and prerogatives. Moreover, even if they had adopted the plan of union, it is unlikely that the British government would have approved it, since it would have given the colonies a significant degree of independence.

Over a year after the Albany Congress met, another army set out to deal with the French. The British prime minister had sent General Braddock and two British regiments to handle what Virginia had bungled so badly—the reduction of Fort Duquesne. Unfortunately for Braddock, the British regiments were about the worst to be found in the British army, and some of the colonies refused any aid in men and money. Braddock, too, was unused to wilderness warfare.

George Washington, who marched with Braddock, wrote later of the beauty of the forests through which they passed—the sunlight streaming through the leaves of the trees, shedding a greenish luster over the combined ranks of British redcoats and the colonials, clad in blue. Though beautiful, the forests held a danger for which Braddock was ill prepared. On July 7, 1755, a combined force of 72 French officers and regulars, with 150 French Canadian militia and 637 Indian braves, surprised Braddock on the Monongahela River near Fort Duquesne. A hidden enemy assailed Braddock's forces; French and Indian gunfire tore through British and colonial ranks. Braddock's soldiers knew only how to shoot from orderly European ranks, not individually or from cover. They panicked but had nowhere to run. Braddock himself was shot through the lungs and died soon after. Of his force of 1,459 men, 977 were killed or wounded. Washington and the colonial officers were hard pressed to rally the survivors and get them home.

The effects of this British defeat were devastating for the English colonies. Braddock's successor decided to abandon the defense of the western frontier, thus putting many English settlements in mortal danger. Many Indian tribes now joined the French, and the Iroquois' fidelity to Great Britain wavered more. Suffering from repeated Indian attacks, settlers in the Shenandoah Valley fled east, abandoning all they had.

The French and Indian War

In France, Louis XV's mistress, Madame de Pompadour, was piqued. King Friedrich the Great of Prussia had written some verses about her that were not at all flattering. In retaliation, Pompadour exerted her influence over Louis in favor of Prussia's enemy, the Austrians. The Austrian ambassador, Count Wenzel Anton von Kaunitz, had come to Paris to convince the king to abandon his alliance with Prussia and join forces with Austrian empress, Maria Theresia, who wanted to regain Silesia from Friedrich II. France had much to gain from a war with Prussia, argued Kaunitz—possession of the Prussian lands on the lower Rhine, contiguous with France.

Battles and forts of the French and Indian War

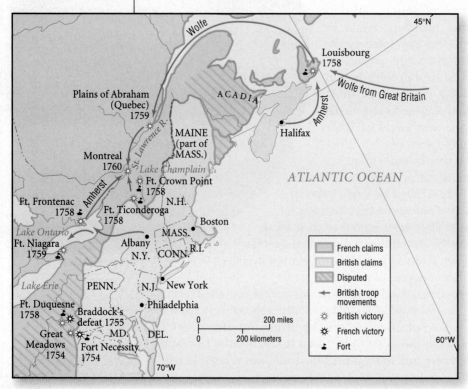

Pompadour and Kaunitz won out, and France joined an alliance with Austria. Meanwhile, Great Britain, already engaged in war with France in America, allied itself with Prussia. The resulting war, the Seven Years' War, was one of the greatest ever fought in Europe to that time. In some ways, it was a world war, since the conflict raged in Europe and in Europe's colonies in India and America.

The first three years of the war in America witnessed a series of French victories, beginning in 1755, when Massachusetts' Governor Shirley failed to take Fort Niagara. Though Shirley defeated the French at Lake George on September 8, the French were able to hold Crown Point on Lake Champlain and there raise a fortress—Fort Ticonderoga. In 1756, when this "Old French and

Indian War" became but another theater of the Seven Years' War, the British government replaced Governor Shirley with the Earl of Loudon as commander of the British forces in America. The war, however, still went badly for the British. Though George Washington and the Virginia militia were able with difficulty to hold the Shenandoah Valley, the French under the Marquis de Montcalm captured Fort Oswego on Lake Ontario and Fort William on Lake George.

The course of the war changed in 1758 when William Pitt became secretary of state and prime minister of Great Britain. Pitt saw how Britain could win the war in America. The population of the English colonies (about 1,000,000) dwarfed the population of New France (only about 60,000); thus, without reinforcements from France, New France must in the end fall to the British. To block reinforcements coming to French America, Pitt used Great Britain's greatest advantage, her navy. Great Britain had the largest navy in the world. The French navy could not vie with it.

Pitt appointed Jeffrey Amherst as commander-in-chief of the colonial forces in America. Serving as brigadier general under Amherst was the energetic James Wolfe. In July 1758, Wolfe, together with Amherst and the British fleet under Admiral Boscawan, captured Louisbourg. The same year, Colonel John

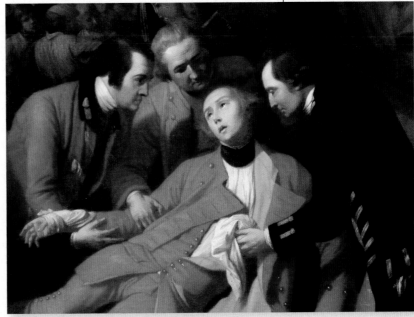

A detail from "The Death of Wolfe" by Benjamin West

Bradstreet and the New England militia took Fort Frontenac in Canada, near where the St. Lawrence flows from Lake Ontario. Fort Duquesne, too, finally fell to Brigadier General John Forbes, who renamed it Pittsburg, in honor of the prime minister.

"The paths of glory lead but to the grave." General Wolfe recited this line from Thomas Gray's "Elegy Written in a Country Churchyard" as he led his men in what would prove to be the decisive strategic move in the battle for Québec. On June 27, 1759, Admiral Saunders of the British navy had landed on Île de Orléans in the Saint Lawrence River, three miles east of Québec. The French city was well defended. The Marquis de Montcalm had concentrated 14,000 troops within the walls on the north bank of the St. Lawrence. The guns of Québec commanded the approaches of the river. The British force, under General Wolfe, numbered only 4,000 (it would later be strengthened by reinforcements). Yet, daring and strategy (and luck) secured advantages for Wolfe.

The luck came in when Wolfe discovered Montcalm's failure to secure the southern shore of the St. Lawrence. Placing a contingent of his force on the north shore to divert Montcalm's attention, Wolfe seized Point Levi on the south shore, 1,000 yards across the river from Québec. On July 19, the British opened a bombardment on Québec from Point Levi, and under cover of the bombardment, sailed 20 miles upstream from the city. The British now controlled the St. Lawrence River.

Québec, which sat perched on cliffs above the St. Lawrence, was well defended; but, the British discovered a narrow defile up the cliffs that Montcalm had not sufficiently guarded. The defile led to a plateau called the Plains of Abraham, outside the walls of the city. At 2 a.m. on September 13, Wolfe led 1,700 English up the defile and easily overcame the small French contingent guarding the approach. More boats came with reinforcements, so that, in the morning, the French saw 4,500 English deployed on the Plains of Abraham.

By 10 a.m. on September 13, Montcalm had promptly moved about 4,000 troops from the north shore and arrayed them on the Plains of Abraham. The French, clad in white, with a cry of "*Vive le Roi!*" (long live the king!) advanced on the British. Wolfe waited till the enemy was only 40 yards away before he cried out the command, "fire!" A first volley rang out, then a second. Hundreds of French fell. Then the English, bayonets fixed, charged. The enemy broke and retreated. Wolfe, himself mortally wounded, ordered the cutting off of the enemy's retreat—his last command. With the Marquis de Montcalm also wounded (he died the next day), Québec surrendered to the British. Together, both sides had lost about 650 killed and wounded; but the fortress of Québec and the Saint Lawrence, from the sea to Montreal, now belonged to the British.

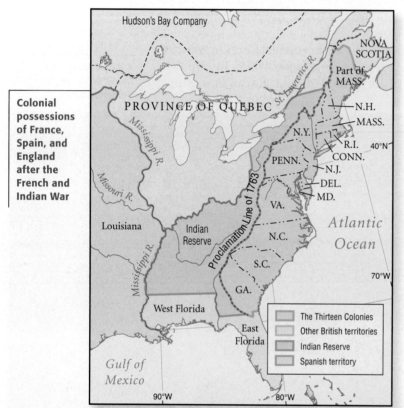

Colonial possessions of France, Spain, and England after the French and Indian War

The year 1759 saw three other British victories: the British captured the French controlled island of Guadeloupe in the West Indies, the British navy defeated the French West Indies fleet at St. Lucy in the Lesser Antilles (in the Caribbean), and Sir William Johnson and the Iroquois helped the British army capture Fort Niagara—the key to the Great Lakes. In 1760, a force of French and Canadians under the Chevalier de Lévis moved to regain Québec but failed when the British there were relieved by British warships on May 9. Lévis fell back on Montreal. By September, British generals Amherst, Haviland, and Murray had invested Montreal. On September 8, 1760, deserted by many Canadians and French regulars, the French governor, the Marquis de Vandreuil, surrendered Montreal—and all of French Canada—to the British.

Except for an Indian insurrection against the British led by Chief Pontiac in what is now Michigan, Illinois, Indiana, and Ohio, the war in North America ended with the fall of Montreal. By 1761, the British had captured all of the French West Indies, except the Island of Saint-Dominique. That year, Spain entered the war on the side of France. By a secret treaty, France ceded Louisiana to Spain to prevent it from falling to the British as a prize of war.

In 1762, King George III dismissed William Pitt as prime minister, and Britain began peace negotiations with France and Spain. The war concluded in 1763 with the Peace of Paris. According to the terms of the peace, France lost to Britain all of her North American colonies except a couple of small islands off Newfoundland, as well as Saint-Dominique and Guadeloupe in the Caribbean. The vast expanse of Louisiana passed to Spain. So ended France's adventure in America. In return for Havana, which the British had taken, King Carlos III of Spain ceded Florida to the British. On July 20, 1763, a regiment of British regulars took possession of San Agustín.

In Florida, though Catholics were promised freedom of religion, the British seized all church property because, they claimed that, under the *patronato real*, it belonged to the king of Spain, not the Church. Thus, few Catholics decided to remain in Florida. In March 1764, 3,104 people, including the 89 surviving Catholic Indians of Florida, set sail for Havana. Though Spain would again hold Florida from 1784 to 1821, the glory days of the Spanish Church and missions on the "isle" of Ponce de León would never return.

Chapter 6 Review

Summary

- Slave raids on the Spanish missions in Florida and Georgia began prior to, and continued through, Queen Anne's War. They led to the destruction of the missions along the Georgia coast and in Apalachee.

- In 1702 Queen Anne's War, the American branch of the War of Spanish Succession, began. It ended in 1713 with the Peace of Utrecht.

- In 1739 Spanish revenue cutters captured an English smuggler named Edward Jenkins and cut off his ear. When the British saw Jenkins less an ear, they declared war on Spain. This war became known as the "War of Jenkins' Ear."

- In 1744 the War of Jenkins' Ear merged with another European war, called the War of the Austrian Succession by Europeans and King George's War by Americans. King George's War ended in 1748 with the Treaty of Aix-la-Chapelle.

- The Albany Congress was founded in 1754 to discuss how to maintain the British colonies' alliance with the Iroquois and achieve greater colonial unity. Their plan of unity was never more than a proposal, however, since the colonies were not ready for it, and Great Britain was not ready to grant that much independence to the colonies.

- France joined an alliance with Austria, and Great Britain joined an alliance with Prussia. This resulted in the Seven Years' War, which raged not only in Europe but in Europe's colonies in India and America. In America this war was called the "French and Indian War."

- In 1760 the French governor, the Marquis de Vandreuil, surrendered Montreal and all of French Canada to the British. This effectively ended the French and Indian War.

- The war in Europe ended in 1763 with the Peace of Paris.

Key Concepts

Queen Anne's War: the American branch of the War of Spanish Succession

Peace of Utrecht: the peace treaty that ended Queen Anne's War

War of Jenkins' Ear: the war between Great Britain and Spain that was precipitated by the cutting off of Edward Jenkins' ear

King George's War: the merging of the War of Jenkins' Ear with the War of the Austrian Succession

Treaty of Aix-la-Chapelle: the treaty that ended King George's War

Albany Congress: a congress of colonial representatives which met in Albany, New York, and came up with a plan a colonial union

French and Indian War: the war between the British and the French in America. It ended with the surrender of Canada to Great Britain.

Peace of Paris: the treaty that ended the French and Indian War

Dates to Remember

1680: a band of pagan Indians attacks a Christian Indian village on St. Simon's Island.

1702: Queen Anne's War begins.

1713: Queen Anne's War ends.

1739: the War of Jenkins' Ear begins.

1744: the War of Jenkins' Ear merges with the War of Spanish Succession and becomes King George's War in America.

1754: the Albany Congress

1760: the French and Indian War ends in America with the surrender of French Canada to the British.

1763: the Peace of Paris concludes the Seven Years' War.

Central Characters

Queen Anne (1665–1714): the British queen under whom Queen Anne's War (the War of the Spanish Succession) was waged

James Wolfe (1727–1759): commander of the British army at the capture of Québec from the French

Questions for Review

1. Why was the attack on St. Simon's island in 1680 so ominous?

Chapter 6 Review (continued)

2. Under what conditions did Queen Anne's War begin?

3. What happened to the Catholic Indians of Georgia and Florida just before and during Queen Anne's War?

4. Why did the Spanish cut off Edward Jenkins' ear, and why did this precipitate a war?

5. What part did Georgia play in the War of Jenkins' Ear?

6. Explain what the War of the Spanish Succession was and who was involved.

7. How was America involved in the War of the Spanish Succession?

8. What was the purpose of the Albany Congress and why did it fail?

9. How did the Seven Years' War begin, and what relation did the French and Indian War have to it?

10. How did the Seven Years' War affect Florida?

Ideas in Action

1. Research the events of the counterpart wars to the wars in America mentioned in this chapter.

2. Find maps of Europe and America that refer to the time of the wars mentioned in this chapter. Mark off the territories controlled by each major power at the beginning of each war. See how the map changes over the course of each war, and mark the territorial changes in a separate color.

Highways and Byways

America's First Tourist Trap: Mount Vernon

Mount Vernon is the home and burial place of America's first president, George Washington. The estate is situated in Fairfax County, Virginia, overlooking the Potomac River. The mansion, built of wood paneled to give the appearance of cut and dressed stonework, sits on 5,000 acres. The estate, originally called Little Hunting Creek Plantation, was owned by John Washington, the first of that family to live in America. It was passed down through the family until George Washington's great-nephew was authorized to sell the property to the U.S. government.

The government, however, refused to buy Mount Vernon, and in 1853 Ann Pamela Cunningham of South Carolina organized the Mount Vernon Ladies Association of the Union. This Association raised nearly $200,000 and purchased the house and 200 acres in 1858. The Association was given a charter which bound it to restore and maintain the estate. The estate was designated a national registered historical landmark, and has been a tourist attraction ever since.

SPANISH AMERICA IN THE 17TH AND 18TH CENTURIES

Part I

New Mexico Destroyed

Though it had experienced no large-scale rebellion since the Ácoma Pueblo uprising in 1599, all was not peaceful in New Mexico. In 1632, natives attacked Fray Francisco Letrado, a missionary at Hawikuh. They riddled him with arrows as he knelt and, grasping a crucifix, prayed for his enemies. Two years later, Hopi "sorcerers" poisoned another missionary, Fray Francisco Porras, who had been working among their people.

Much progress had been made in New Mexico since 1599. Numerous missions, tens of thousands of converts, an established Spanish settlement at Santa Fé—the colony was flourishing. Though New Mexico still remained a drain on the finances of the Spanish crown, it had begun to carry on a profitable trade with Mexico City. Every two years caravans of about 32 wagons made their way from the capital to Santa Fé, carrying supplies of goods the colony could not produce itself. The arrival of a caravan occasioned rejoicing and fiesta—and all the more so because it was to return to Mexico laden with goods made and sold by the inhabitants of New Mexico.

Yet, internal and external conflicts continued. The chief internal problem was a controversy over jurisdiction between the friars and the secular governor. As in Florida, so in New Mexico—the governor claimed authority over the entire missionary enterprise, while the friars demanded complete autonomy for themselves. Raids by nomadic tribes, the Comanche and the Apache, on outlying settlements was the chief external threat throughout the 1660s. In 1669, the Comanches of Mescalero raided Christian Indian villages, taking captives, whom they sacrificed and then ate.

The natives of the outlying settlements villages were hard put to defend themselves, for they had lost many to epidemics that arose in conjunction with a terrible drought. This drought did more than endanger Christian Indian villages; it provided an opportunity for Pueblo Indians, indignant

Built probably between 1610 and 1628, the San Miguel Chapel in Santa Fé, New Mexico, is said to be the oldest church in the United States.

because the Spanish had suppressed their native gods and ceremonies. These discontents (many of whom were shamans, or medicine men) spoke to the fears of their people. Why had so many disasters befallen them? It was, the shamans said, because the people had abandoned the ceremonies and rites by which they had once appeased the gods and spirits. Only if the people returned to ancient ways would they be saved from destruction.

The shamans coaxed many natives back into pagan worship. The policies of the Spanish governors, who were wont to demand tribute and free labor from the Indians, inspired conspiracies among the natives. In 1669, Governor Juan Francisco Treviño, discovering a conspiracy among the Indians, seized and imprisoned its leaders. Forty-seven of these were sentenced to be whipped and then sold into slavery, while four others were to be hanged. But threats made by several powerful Pueblo leaders, convinced Treviño to alter the punishments. After whipping them, he released all 47 prisoners.

One of those released was Popé, a religious leader from Taos pueblo. Seething with anger over the indignity of being whipped, Popé returned home to plot his revenge. Over the next ten years he laid his plans. Popé knew that a single pueblo, or only a few, could not hope to drive out the Spanish and eradicate their hated religion; but if all the pueblos combined and acted as one, they would have a chance of ridding their land of the invader. This was no small task, for the each pueblo had always acted independently. But by appealing to the leaders, by gathering allies in every pueblo, Popé organized a force that could challenge Spanish power.

A view of Isleta Pubelo, ca. 1898

On August 10, 1680, a deluge of wrath fell upon the unsuspecting Spanish settlers and Christian natives. Everywhere the Indians rose and slaughtered Christian men, women, and children, both laymen and missionaries. None was spared. Indians once thought friends were suddenly bloodthirsty enemies. Priests and brothers died a variety of ignominious deaths. One priest, stripped naked, was bound to a hog's back and paraded before onlookers. He then was beaten by clubs until he died. Fleeing to Santa Fé, settlers and natives found refuge with the governor, Antonio de Otermín, in the presidio. There they remained until the insurgent Indians, discovering that they could cut off the the *presidio's* water supply, forced the fugitives to abandon Santa Fé. On August 21, a few soldiers surrounding 1,000 men, women, and children, marched out of the *presidio* with little opposition. They fled 70 miles south to the friendly Indians of Isleta Pueblo.

The rebel Indians had killed over 1,000 Spanish and Christian Indians, as well as 30 missionaries. From Isleta, Governor Otermín contemplated leading a force to recapture Santa Fé; but realizing that with only 146 soldiers he could accomplish little, the governor decided to retreat farther south, to El Paso. El Paso was 90 miles from Isleta, across parched and burning desert. It was summer. The fugitives suffered severely on the journey they called *jornada del muerto*, "journey of death."

With the Spanish gone, the Indians burned churches and built bonfires to destroy missals and other documents. The pagan Indians forced Christian natives to renounce the Faith and, after undergoing purification rituals, to worship their ancestral gods. Tribal leaders were so thoroughgoing in their attempt to destroy all traces of Spanish civilization that they forbade anyone to use the fruits, vegetables, and livestock the Spanish had introduced into New Mexico. The people had to be content with what they ate before the arrival of the Spanish—corn, beans, and squash.

After a time, many Pueblo Indians grew dissatisfied with the rule of Popé and other tribal leaders. For one, the tribal leaders, occupying the Spanish governor's palace, appointed a governor to rule over all the pueblos—a violation of their traditional independence. Then, without the threat of Spanish arms, the Comanche, Apache, Ute, and Navajo intensified their raids on the pueblo settlements. Discontent grew, and civil wars broke out among the pueblos. Many Indians began to long for the prosperity and stability they had under the Spanish—and some went south to El Paso to invite them back.

By 1690, the new governor of New Mexico, Diego de Vargas, thought the time was ripe to retake Santa Fé and the surrounding country. Born of a wealthy Mexican family, Vargas had decided to invest his fortune in the cause of reconquest. In August 1692, he set out with a contingent of 800 soldiers, along with colonists and Christian Indians, to New Mexico and, after a two-day battle, took Santa Fé. Over the next year, Vargas crossed the length and breadth of New Mexico, and by threats and promises, obtained the peaceful surrender of most of the pueblos. Some, however, resisted. Mesa Nueva de San Ildefonso was occupied only after a siege of eight months. The pueblos of Portrero Viejo, Peña de San Diego de Jemez, and Ácoma surrendered only after Vargas routed their defenders.

With the reconquest of Santa Fé, New Mexico entered a period of expansion. The missions were rebuilt, and 2,000 Indian children were baptized. In 1693, Vargas returned from Mexico with 100 more soldiers, seventy families, 18 Franciscans, 900 head of cattle, and 2,000 horses. The following year, 66 families under Fray Francisco Farfán and Fray Antonio Moreno founded a new village, Santa Cruz, north of Santa Fé. The same year, Vargas commissioned Fray Juan Alpuente to explore what is now southern Colorado.

On June 14, 1696, Indians in 15 Pueblo villages again rebelled. During the three months the rebellion raged, Indians killed five Franciscans and 21 Spaniards and pillaged and destroyed churches and dwellings. By September, however, Vargas had crushed the revolt and punished those responsible.

What Was Spanish America?

New Mexico was but the northern frontier of a vast new world empire that, by the end of the 18th Century, reached from Tierra del Fuego (the tip of South America) to San Francisco Bay in California. By the time of the Pueblo Rebellion, Spanish America was already a well established society. It was essentially a European society transplanted among an alien people, that was transforming those people even as they were influencing it. It was an extension of Spain in the New World.

The kings of Spain saw their New World possessions, not as colonies to be exploited for the sake of the mother country, but as new kingdoms, equal to the old kingdoms of Spain. New Spain and Peru were domains of the king no wit inferior to Castile, León, and Aragon. While the king took a portion (the royal fifth) of whatever gold or silver or other wealth was found in America, he expended great sums of money in maintaining the colonies. As noted in a previous chapter, settlements such as New Mexico and Florida were for long periods drains on the royal purse—yet, the kings of Spain continued to support them. Why?

The kings of Spain saw the free inhabitants of America, both natives and transplanted Spaniards, as equal subjects of the crown. As a Catholic king exercising the *patronato real*, the Spanish king saw it as his duty to Christianize and civilize the natives of America so that they could become full and equal subjects of his majesty, as well as of the Divine Majesty. So,

Coat of arms of the House of Austria (the Habsburg kings) with the double-headed imperial eagle on the façade of the Ozama Fortress in Santo Domingo, Dominican Republic, with the double headed, imperial eagle. The crown of Spain built the fortress between 1502 and 1510.

despite the expense, the king would maintain a colony as long as there was progress in Christianizing and civilizing the Indians. The royal intention helps us understand the *encomienda* system, which the kings of Spain at first allowed as a way of elevating the Indians to civilization. The *encomendero* was, in a sense, the king's minister responsible for the Indians' welfare.

Because the bull, *Inter Caetera*, granted much of the New World in some fashion to the king of Spain, all New World lands were called *hacienda real*, the "royal estate." All land was king's land, his exclusive possession. When a Pizarro or a Cortés fulfilled some service to the king or when settlers colonized an area, the king would grant them lands, which they would then hold under his authority as the guardian of the common good of Spain.

The Spanish government of America differed from that of the English colonies, or even from that of New France. The kings of Great Britain and France granted colonies to proprietors or companies to whom they turned over the colonial government; but the king of Spain maintained a firm control over the government of his New World possessions because each New World domain was deemed a "coordinate kingdom" of Spain. Thus, the highest authority in each "kingdom" was the king, who exercised his rule through a representative, called a "viceroy." Since the viceroy occupied the place of the king, he was forbidden to own land in his viceroyalty. This, it was thought, would keep him working in the king's interest and not his own. At the end of his six-year term of office, the viceroy's administration had to undergo a detailed review by the next viceroy.

Alongside the viceroy was the court, called the *audiencia real*. While the viceroy looked to the administration of the viceroyalty, the *audiencia* administered justice. Each province within the viceroyalty had its own *gobernador* (governor) and *audiencia*. Below the governor were a number of lesser officials. In the pueblos, or "towns," some of these officials were elected, while others were appointed—sometimes because they were rich enough to buy the office. The practice of buying political office led, naturally, to corruption. The Spanish tried to remedy this by establishing the office of the *visitador real*, the "royal visitor," who inspected the acts of officials to see that they conformed to law.

All these officials governed, and were governed, by an elaborate system of laws drawn up in Spain that attempted to cover every conceivable situation. When a situation arose not covered by the laws, one had to consult either the governor, the viceroy, or even Madrid to know what he should do. So, often one had to wait months, even years, to get an answer to a legal question. This centralized system concentrated even more power in the center under the Bourbon kings, who ruled Spain after 1700. The Habsburgs had allowed more local control, but the Bourbons, who were royal absolutists, carried centralization to sometimes ridiculous lengths. The result was that royal government was slow and inefficient, and private initiative was often thwarted.

Spanish Society in the New World

The royal policy for New Spain, from the very beginning of its New World settlement, was to break down the barriers that segregated European settlers from the American natives. To unite all Americans as equal subjects of the crown, the royal government encouraged intermarriage between Spaniards and natives. And Spaniards and Indians did intermarry. From this intermingling of the races—what the Spanish called *mestizaje*—came a new racial type, the *mestizo*, or man of mixed European and Indian blood. After a time, the *mestizos* formed the largest single class in Spanish American society.

Yet, despite *mestizaje*, Spanish American society was clearly divided into racial classes. The most influential and powerful group was the European-born Spaniards, called *peninsulares*, *chapetones*, or *gauchupines*. These controlled all the higher offices of government in Spanish America. Below the *peninsulares* were the *criollos*, or creoles, who were pure Spaniards, but born in America. The creoles were, on the whole, excluded from the highest political offices, though they occupied the less influential and powerful ones. After a time the creoles, who were often rich, were able to buy their way into higher offices and some (though not many) served as viceroys. Yet, because for the most part they could not attain to the highest offices, the creoles came to resent the power wielded by the *peninsulares*. That the *peninsulares* adopted superior airs rankled the creoles.

The creoles, however, deemed themselves superior to the *mestizos*. Even so, in population growth, the *mestizos* soon outnumbered the ruling classes and even began to occupy many of the lowest offices, such as elective offices in the pueblos.

Next in the social order after the *mestizos* were the Indians. Though considered full subjects of the king, Indians were often treated like a subject race. Among other abuses, both *encomenderos* and lower government officials charged Indians exorbitant prices for goods or forced them to buy useless items. As we showed in Chapter 2, the Spanish crown attempted to protect the Indians and to abolish the *encomienda* system. The problem was, how could the Spanish king enforce his laws across the wide expanse of the Atlantic Ocean? Much of this enforcement rested on the viceroy, and some viceroys sincerely tried to protect the Indians. Luis de Velasco, who was viceroy of New Spain from

A Spanish painting from the 18th century depicting a mixed race family—the man, a Spaniard, and the woman, an Indian

An 18th century wall mural depicting a Mexican native, sanctuary of Atotonilco, San Miguel de Allende, Mexico.

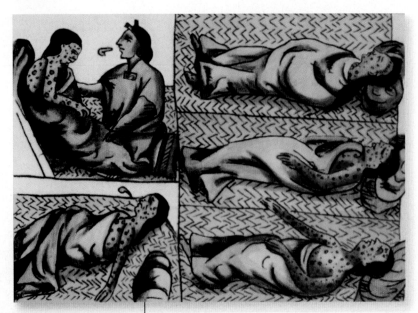

A Spanish illustration depicting Indians suffering from smallpox

Black African slaves processing sugar on Hispaniola, a 1595 engraving by Theodor de Bry with modern coloring

1550 to 1564, freed some 160,000 Indians from forced labor service. He established the *Tribunal de Santa Hermandad* (the Court of the Holy Brotherhood) to protect Indians. Among the inquiries of royal visitors, when they inspected the conduct of officials, was how they treated the Indians. Many officials were removed from office because it was discovered that they had mistreated the natives.

Transplanting Indians from their native lands or segregating them on reservations was never part of Spanish policy in America. Neither was extermination. Though thousands of Indians died under Spanish rule, this was largely because they lacked immunities to European diseases. Smallpox, measles, whooping cough, scurvy, and influenza devastated Indian tribes; in some cases, as on some Caribbean islands, disease wiped out the entire native population. On the other hand, the Spanish conquest largely obliterated one ancient source of native death—inter-tribal war.

In the 17th and 18th centuries, the crown again tried to reform the *encomienda* system. Laws passed in 1612 and 1620 decreed that all *encomiendas* that had lapsed or had terminated (for instance, if an *encomendero* had no heir) would become crown property. The Bourbon king, Felipe V (1700–1746), finally in 1720 abolished the whole system in law, though it continued to exist in practice. To remedy this, King Carlos III (1759–1788) placed an official called the *alcalde mayor* over the Indians. However, because these *alcaldes* began to behave just like the *encomenderos*, the king abolished the office in 1786 and appointed royal representatives called sub-delegates to handle Indian affairs. King Carlos III tried to abolish the selling of useless goods at high prices to Indians, and the crown encouraged Indians to become independent landowners (a policy that was disastrous, as we shall see).

Black African slaves were worse off than Indians in Spanish America. Every year, from 1600 to 1750, about 3,000 black slaves, legally, and 500, illegally, were imported to Spanish America. By 1808, black slaves numbered about 700,000 out of a population of 15 million. In many parts of Spanish America, slaves suffered cruel treatment, which inspired a number of slave revolts. A master held absolute power over a slave and could punish him with mutilation or even death for slight offenses. Such treatment, however, violated the Spanish Laws of the Indies that sought to rein in the power of slave-owners and decreed that slaves had a right to own property. The law declared the Church had to catechize black slaves and administer the sacraments to them, including sacramental marriage. Just as with Indians, Spaniards intermarried

with blacks, from which unions came another social group, the mulattos. The zambos, or sambos, came from intermarriages between blacks and Indians.

The frequent neglect of the Laws of the Indies in Spanish America caused King Carlos IV to issue another decree on May 31, 1789. The king required masters to teach their slaves the Catholic faith and give them elementary instruction in reading and mathematics. Slaves were to be worked only from sunrise to sunset and to be free from labor on holy days. The law said masters had to see that their slaves were properly fed, clothed, and sheltered and had to care for the sick, infirm, and children. Slaves were now to be tried only in civil court, and every year masters had to submit reports to the government on how their slaves were faring.

Since slaves could buy their freedom, Spanish America came to have many free blacks. Communities of free blacks could be found in Cuba, Santo Domingo, Puerto Rico, and Colombia. Some black slaves from English territory fled to Spanish lands. In 1687 six men, two women, and one infant escaped from South Carolina to San Agustín in Florida. When their masters demanded their return, the Spanish authorities refused. Having been baptized, said the Spanish, the slaves were now free. The freed slaves married, were hired by the government, and settled in a township. In 1738, Manuel de Montiano y Sopelena, the governor of Florida, proclaimed freedom for all slaves who fled from the Carolinas, and thus many Carolina blacks came to Florida. When the governor settled them in their own town, called Gracia Real de Santa Teresa de Mose ("Royal Favor of St. Teresa of Mose"), the gratitude of these former slaves expressed itself in the formation of a militia in which they pledged to "defend, to the last drop of their blood, the Crown of Spain and the holy Catholic Faith."

Life in New Spain

By the time the English arrived in North America, Spanish America—in Mexico, Central, and South America—had large, thriving cities with universities, theaters, mansions, and beautiful public buildings. These cities in some cases arose around ancient centers of Indian cultures. Others sprouted up in mining areas where the promise of gold and silver drew fortune seekers. (In mining cities many did make their fortunes—and squandered them at the gambling table: a vice dear to these colonists.) Outside the large cities were many pueblos that grew from settlements of Spanish colonists or from missions. The towns were surrounded by ranches and farms that raised cattle and crops.

At first, the colonists of Spanish America preferred mining to any other industry—for it was a quick way to wealth. However, as time passed, agriculture became increasingly more important to the economy of the Americas. The Spanish introduced a number of crops to the New World— wheat, rye, barley, oats, sugar cane, coffee, peas, onions, melons, pears, plums, peaches, grapes, and many others. They introduced plows and beasts of burden, such as oxen and horses—for the Indians had possessed no such animals. The Spanish contributed the wheel, hitherto unknown to the American natives as a means of conveyance.

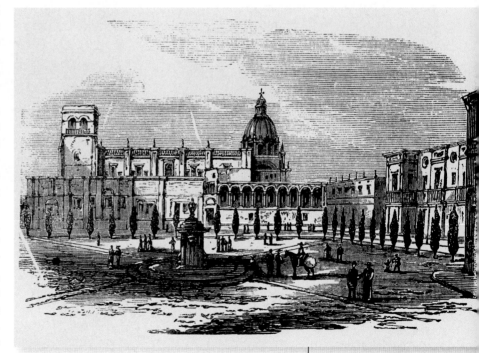

The cathedral and square in Guadalajara, Mexico; an engraving from the 1890s

Spain and, indeed, all Europe in turn benefited from American arts and agriculture. The Spanish carried back to Europe a rich storehouse of foods from the agriculture of the Americas. Native American farmers contributed to Europe's and, indeed, the world's cuisine pink and Lima beans, the potato, yellow squash and acorn squash, chili pepper, maize corn of many types, chocolate, and the tomato.

The Spanish crown strictly regulated trade between the Americas and Europe, and even between its American realms. All colonial products for foreign markets had to be shipped first to Spain, and from Spain to foreign ports. Similarly, foreign imports passed through Spain to the colonies. Trade, say, between Mexico and Peru had to go by way of Spain. These cumbersome regulations meant that colonials often resorted to illegal trade with the English, the French, the Dutch, and later the United States. Partly to curtail this smuggling, the king of Spain eventually relaxed some of the trading regulations.

The Spanish government laid burdensome taxes on all Spanish citizens whether in Europe or America. In the colonies, the crown levied about 40 different taxes. Though most of the tax money benefited America (the cost of colonization was always high for Spain), still they were hard to bear.

(a) Interior of Soccolo Cathedral, Oaxaca, Mexico, built in 1522

(a)

(b)

(b) Metropolitan cathedral in Mexico City, built between 1573 and 1813
(c) A portion of the reredos and a crucifix in the Metropolitan cathedral, Mexico City

(c)

But this expensive settlement had a rich culture. It was a Spanish, European culture, modified after a time by American influences. Throughout the land rose churches, cathedrals, monasteries, and palaces built in all the European styles—Gothic, Renaissance, and Baroque. Moorish influences were evident, too, in the design of doorways, windows, and fountains. The dark churches were filled with colorful statuary and paintings—the former often done in a realistic style, using clothes and real human hair. Artists were wont to paint crucifixes in an almost gruesomely realistic style. Behind many an altar rose an ornately carved, gilded reredos, adorned with images of Our Lord, Our Lady, and the saints.

Much of the art of Spanish America was done in service of the Church. A *mestizo* composer named Manuel de Zumaya composed beautiful church music in the Baroque style, as well as an opera, *Partenope*, in 1711. Zumaya's music compares well with the music of some of the great composers of 18th century Europe. In 1715, Zumaya became chapel master of the cathedral in Mexico City, one of the first native-born Americans to rise to this position, which gave him control over all the music performed in the liturgy of the capital. In spite of the protests of the cathedral chapel council in Mexico City, Zumaya left the capital and followed his close friend, Bishop Tomás Montaño, to Oaxaca to become chapel master of the cathedral there. Zumaya worked in Oaxaca until his death in December 1755.

Sor Juana Inés de la Cruz

Another great Mexican composer was Ignacio de Jerúsalem, who composed in the classical style popular in mid-18th century Europe. An Italian, Jerúsalem wrote music for the *coliseo* (theater) in Cadíz, Spain, until 1746, when he was recruited for the *coliseo* in Mexico City. In Mexico, Jerúsalem, a virtuoso violinist as well as a composer, wrote works for the cathedral, where he was made chapel master in 1749. He died in 1769.

Spanish America did not excel in literature, though it did produce a poet much admired today. This was Sor (sister) Juana Inés de la Cruz. Sor Juana was born in Mexico on November 12, 1648. As a young girl, the beautiful Juana learned Latin, and at the age of 16 entered a convent of Discalced (barefoot) Carmelite sisters. Because the life in that convent was hard, and her health poor, Sor Juana left the Carmelites and, a year later, in 1668, she joined the convent of San Jerónimo. There she served as doorkeeper, secretary, and accountant. Sor Juana wrote both secular and religious poetry, novels, and comedies. Collecting a library of about 4,000 books, she engaged in scientific and classical literary studies, for which she was criticized by the bishop of Puebla. In 1691, she wrote a long letter in defense of her studies. When, in 1690, Mexico was struck with famine and plagues, Sor Juana sold all her possessions (including her library) and gave all the money to the poor, hungry, and sick of Mexico. For the remaining years of her life, until 1695, she cared for the sick nuns of her convent.

The Church

One cannot properly understand New Spain without understanding the social role of the Catholic Church in Spain's New World dominions. The Church influenced all of Spanish American society. Pueblos were built around parish churches. Priests and religious worked to civilize the Indians, teaching them how to engage in civic life and how to farm. The Church opposed exploiting or enslaving the Indians. From the beginning, the Church upheld the dignity and rights of the American natives, especially since 1537, when Pope Paul III issued a bull that called the Indians "real men" and forbade enslaving them. As we have noted, one of the main goals of Spanish exploration and settlement in the New World was the conversion of the natives to the Catholic faith. Missionary work was carried out by religious orders—primarily the Dominicans, the Franciscans, and the Jesuits—under the patronage, and control, of the Spanish king.

As in Europe, so in America—it was the Church that had the care of the poor and the sick. Bishops, priests, and religious orders founded and staffed schools and hospitals, as well as missions. Endowed by the crown to carry out works of charity and social justice, the wealth of the colonial Church multiplied, making it one of the largest landholders in America. Such wealth was not always good for the Church, as some clerics became too enamored of money and possessions and so became corrupt.

One institution in Spain and Spanish America that folks today find hard to understand is the Inquisition. The Inquisition was a court that tried cases having to do with heresy and certain kinds of immorality. It was a state institution, but staffed by churchmen, mainly Dominicans. Queen Isabel and King Fernando established this court in Spain to search out and bring to justice former Jews who had converted (and thus called *conversos*) to the Church but who secretly practiced Judaism. Backsliding *conversos* were thought a threat to both Church and state in Spain. Later, the Inquisition tried heretics such as Lutherans and Calvinists, and approved or censored books.

A just treatment of the Inquisition requires more space than we can afford, here. We will only note that the king established a New World court of the Inquisition first in Lima, Peru, in 1569, and another court in Mexico two years later. These courts had jurisdiction over foreign heretics, Jews, witches, and bigamists; they had no authority over the Indians. Condemnations and executions were relatively few; more common were *autos-de-fe*, public acts of faith, in which accused heretics publicly confessed their errors.

Missions of the Pimería Alta

A Pima man and woman outside their dwelling, called a *kan*, 1900

Government bureaucracies can be hard to deal with, as Eusebio Kino came to understand all too well.

Born in the Italian Tyrolese Alps in 1645, Kino entered the Society of Jesus in 1665. It was in 1678 that he learned that his superiors were to send him to the missions in America. Three years later he was in Mexico, assigned to accompany an expedition to explore a largely unexplored region called California.

In those days mapmakers depicted California as an enormous island, separated from the mainland by a long sea channel. Since the missionization of California would help colonize the new land, Kino was an important addition to the expedition. Moreover, as a skilled cartographer, Kino could map out whatever lands the expedition discovered.

Kino accompanied an expedition to Baja California in 1682, and again in 1683. Meeting the natives there, he longed to bring them the Gospel of Christ. But returning to Mexico, he had to wait two more years while the slow machinery of the Spanish empire ground out what it would do with California. It was not until 1686 that Kino heard the news that he would shortly go to California. He was filled with joy.

But Kino traveled the long journey north only to discover that the California mission had been scrapped. The king of Spain owed the king of France a large sum of money, and the only money available was the money for the mission. Disappointed, Kino asked the *audiencia* in Guadalajara to allow him to establish two missions on the coast across the gulf from California. They agreed, even giving him the right, granted by the king, of exempting all converts from forced labor for a period of 20 years.

Once more Kino turned north, this time to consult with his Jesuit superior, Padre Manuel González, in Sonora. González, however, had other plans for Kino than coastal missions. Missionaries were needed in the Pimería Alta, a region covering what is today northern Sonora and southern Arizona. For years the Pima Indians had been asking for missionaries —and the government was now eager to send them some, for the Pimería had become economically and politically important. The Spaniards had discovered, and were exploiting, the rich silver mines in the region; but settlers there were in danger. It had been only six years since the Pueblo rebellion in nearby New Mexico. The Apaches were a continual menace, and the government feared that the Pima Indians might also revolt. If they were converted, the Pima might form an important buffer between the silver mines of Sonora and the wild nomadic tribes of the north.

Disappointed, but obedient, Padre Kino traveled north to the Pimería. At the Indian village of Corsari in modern Sonora, Kino established a mission, Nuestra Señora de los Dolores (Our Lady of Sorrows)—the first in a string of missions that eventually spread out over the southern Pimería. Aided by a number of Jesuit priests, Kino, a man of untiring energy and zeal, taught the Indians not only the Faith but the rudiments of civilization. The Pimas were already a farming folk, but the Jesuits taught them better ways of farming and introduced them to European crops and domesticated animals. The Pimería, an arid desert land, became a flourishing garden through the labor of the native Pimas and Jesuit priests and brothers. And, directing all was the untiring Padre Kino.

In 1687, Coxi, one of the most powerful Piman caciques, and his entire family accepted baptism. This encouraged many Indians of the southwest Pimería to convert. That Coxi and ever more Pimas were embracing the Church, however, provoked the *hechiceros* (medicine men). And Spanish settlers and miners of the area were chagrined. As long as the Pimas were unconverted, they were a cheap source of labor. **Neophyte** Indians were protected from all forced labor in the mines or the fields.

neophyte: a new convert

The settlers began spreading nasty rumors about Kino. The Jesuits sent visitors to investigate. Traveling the round of the missions with Padre Kino, the visitors were impressed with all they saw and returned with glowing reports. Kino became fast friends with the second visitor, Padre Juan María Salvatierra. Salvatierra learned that Kino still hoped one day to go to the "poor souls" of California. The prosperous farms of the Pimería, Kino told the visitor, could support fledgling missions on the impoverished "island."

Padre Explorer

In 1692, at the age of 47, Kino went on the first of the long explorations that would occupy him almost until his death. Kino undertook these journeys, partly to preach and seek out sites for new missions, and partly to discover if there were a land route from the Pimería to California. A land route would make it easier to supply new missions. Kino's journeys took him into what is now southern Arizona, where, near Tucson, he established missions at Guevavi, Tumacácori, and Bac. Bac was the largest Pima village in the region and later would boast a fine mission church—San Xavier del Bac. In 1694, in what is now Arizona, Kino first saw the ruins of a great building, surrounded by irrigation ditches. This was Casa Grande, the remains of a once thriving community of Indians. Kino thought it might be the remains of one of the legendary Seven Cities of Cibola, or, if tales were true, a monument of Aztlán, the Aztecs' ancient home.

Casa Grande

Filled with wonder and speculations, Padre Kino rode home—where he was soon to face the near collapse of all his efforts.

Vengeance and Revolt

Antonio, the Opata Indian overseer at mission San Pedro y San Pablo del Tubutama, had cruelly beaten a Pima. The man died of his wounds. Vowing revenge, the dead man's friends and relatives shot Antonio down with arrows as he was working in the fields. Severely wounded, Antonio ran to Padre Janusque, a mission priest, to warn him. As he crossed the priest's threshold, Antonio fell dead. Thus warned of the coming attack, Padre Janusque fled, seeking help.

It was Holy Week. Padre Francisco Xavier Saeta, a zealous missionary who tended the westernmost mission in the Pimería, Nuestra Señora de la Concepcion de Caborca, was preparing to celebrate the feast of Easter. On Holy Saturday, April 25, 1695, Saeta greeted a band of Pimas who rode up to the mission. Their angry replies were soon followed by a volley of arrows. Struck by a poisoned arrow, Padre Saeta, clutching an image of the crucified Christ that, only the previous day, had graced the ceremonies of Good Friday, fell to the ground and died. The Pimas burned down the mission. Later, Padre Saeta's half cremated remains were found among the ruins.

From Caborca, the band of Pimas went on a rampage and destroyed the mission at Oquitoa, between Tubutama and Caborca. Commanding a Spanish military unit called the Flying Company, Lieutenant Antonio de Solís set off to hunt down the murderers. Solís, believing that he had to match cruelty with cruelty, attacked several Piman **rancherías**. Alarmed at the possible destruction of the missions of the Pimería, Padre Kino arranged a meeting between the Pimas and Solís at a village site called El Tupo.

On June 9, Piman leaders, along with some of the Indians who had participated in the revolt, met with Solís at El Tupo. According to an agreement, the Pimas left their arms outside the clearing where Solís and several of his soldiers awaited them. When a cacique brought forward one of the guilty Indians, Solís, surrounded by his armed men, drew his saber. With one glittering stroke, the cavalry leader cut off the warrior's head. The Indians ran for their weapons; but before they could reach them, they were cut down, every man of them, by Solís' horsemen.

For the next three months, warfare raged through the Pimería. Bands of Pimas destroyed missions and laid waste their fields. All the while, Padre Kino worked for peace; but Solís, trusting in brute force, ranged through the country, striking terror into the natives. It soon became apparent that such harshness only prolonged the war, and at last Solís agreed to Kino's demands for a peace conference. Meeting at the scene of the El Tupo slaughter, Pima caciques and Solís signed a treaty. With peace restored, the site of the peace treaty, that had been called La Matanza (the massacre), was renamed Santa Rosa.

Hope and Disappointment

Padre Kino now faced a new difficulty. The Piman revolt had convinced officials in Mexico City that the Pimería was not so prosperous and peaceful as they had thought—perhaps, they thought, they should close down the missions. Realizing that such a course of action would place his beloved Pimas at the mercy of Spanish settlers and miners, Kino went to Mexico City. His pleadings were successful; the missions were saved. What is more, the Jesuit general in Mexico City decided to fulfill Kino's dream; he would be assigned to Baja California, along with Padre Salvatierra. Kino would spend six months in California and six months in the Pimería!

In 1697, Kino set out at last for California. But as he descended the mountains of the Pimería to the hot and arid coastal lowlands of Sonora, he met a messenger. And the message he bore brought sad news from Kino's Jesuit superior. Kino was to remain with the Pima. Padre Salvatierra and another Jesuit, Padre Juan de Uguarte, would sail to California.

ranchería: a small rural settlement

From 1697 to 1703, Kino went on a number of expeditions to the northwest to find the junction of the Gila with another great river of which he had heard. He went also to discover whether there was a land supply route to Salvatierra's missions in California. By these expeditions, Kino proved once and for all that Baja California was not an island, but a peninsula.

In October of 1700, from a range of desert mountains, Padre Kino saw for the first time the junction of the Gila with the other great river of which he had heard—the Colorado. He met a band of Yuma Indians, who begged him to come to them and preach the Gospel. Kino accompanied them to their village on the Colorado, where dwelt about a thousand Indians. Hundreds of other Yumas came from distant villages to see and hear the priest. They begged him to send them a priest when he returned to the Pimería.

Unfortunately, Kino had no priests to spare for the Yumas. Yet Kino continued to identify locations for new missions—in preparation for the missionaries he hoped would come. But even after his friend, Padre Salvatierra, became procurator for the missions of the northwest, no priests were forthcoming. Padre Kino's last few years were spent at his mission at Dolores, administering his missions and defending the rights of the Pimas. He died on March 15, 1711.

San Xavier del Bac mission church, near Tucson, Arizona. The church was built by the Franciscans in 1775, but the mission itself was established by Padre Kino.

The Pimería after Kino

Another Jesuit, Agustín de Campos, administered the Pima missions after Padre Kino's death. Like Kino, Padre Campos was an energetic missionary who explored northward into Arizona. During his time, a new contingent of German and Bohemian Jesuits began to labor in the Pimería. One of these, a Bavarian, Padre Jakob Sedelmayr, took over the missions after Campos was reassigned in 1736. Sedelmayr continued the explorations of his predecessors, journeying into western and central Arizona.

New difficulties surfaced under Padre Sedelmayr's administration. In 1736, an ambitious *alcalde mayor* with the impressive name of Baron Gabriel Prudhón de Beltran Heider y Mujica took over the administration of the northwest of New Spain. A discovery of silver in an **arroyo** near the Pima settlement of Arizonac fired the baron's ambition; he was determined to exploit the mineral wealth of the region. Soon settlers and adventurers swarmed into the Pimería. The Jesuits protested, fearing the settlement's ill effects on the Pimas, but their protests went unheeded.

Within 15 years, the settlers had so disrupted Pima life that the Pima Indian governor, Luis Oacpicogigua, was able to ignite a rebellion against the Spaniards. The Pimas assaulted both *reales* (as Spanish settlements were called) and missions, and many Spanish miners and settlers were killed. Padre Sedelmayr himself was shot with a poisoned arrow (he later recovered), and the Indians killed two missionaries, Padres Tomás Tello and Henrique Ruhen. The Spaniards eventually crushed the rebellion and restored the expelled padres to their missions.

arroyo: a deep gully cut by a stream; often dry

The revolt and its suppression, however, had dire effects on the Pimería. For one, the Spanish decided that a stronger military presence was needed there, and so the once peaceful Pimería was reduced to a military camp. Because of all the injustices they had suffered, the Pimas suffered from divisions among themselves, and long established tribal alliances were broken. Without a strong, united Piman front, the Apaches could carry their raids deep into Sonora.

In 1767, the Pimería suffered another blow when King Carlos III ordered the expulsion of the Jesuits (who numbered 5,000) from the Spanish empire. Jesuit priests and brothers were

Spanish missions in Mexico, New Mexico, Arizona and California

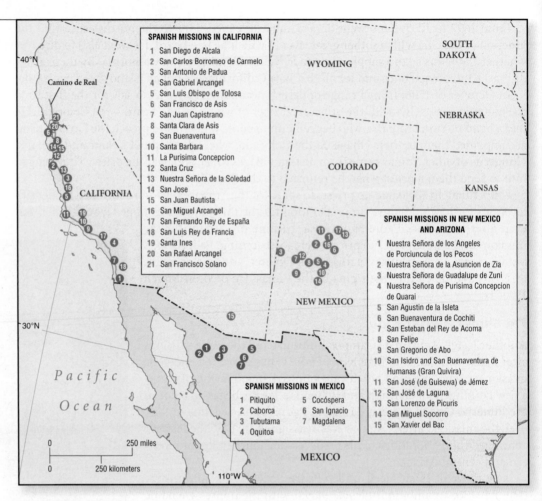

SPANISH MISSIONS IN CALIFORNIA
1. San Diego de Alcala
2. San Carlos Borromeo de Carmelo
3. San Antonio de Padua
4. San Gabriel Arcangel
5. San Luis Obispo de Tolosa
6. San Francisco de Asis
7. San Juan Capistrano
8. Santa Clara de Asis
9. San Buenaventura
10. Santa Barbara
11. La Purisima Concepcion
12. Santa Cruz
13. Nuestra Señora de la Soledad
14. San Jose
15. San Juan Bautista
16. San Miguel Arcangel
17. San Fernando Rey de España
18. San Luis Rey de Francia
19. Santa Ines
20. San Rafael Arcangel
21. San Francisco Solano

SPANISH MISSIONS IN NEW MEXICO AND ARIZONA
1. Nuestra Señora de los Angeles de Porciuncula de los Pecos
2. Nuestra Señora de la Asuncion de Zia
3. Nuestra Señora de Guadalupe de Zuni
4. Nuestra Señora de Purisima Concepcion de Quarai
5. San Agustin de la Isleta
6. San Buenaventura de Cochiti
7. San Esteban del Rey de Acoma
8. San Felipe
9. San Gregorio de Abo
10. San Isidro and San Buenaventura de Humanas (Gran Quivira)
11. San José (de Guisewa) de Jémez
12. San José de Laguna
13. San Lorenzo de Picuris
14. San Miguel Socorro
15. San Xavier del Bac

SPANISH MISSIONS IN MEXICO
1. Pitiquito
2. Caborca
3. Tubutama
4. Oquitoa
5. Cocóspera
6. San Ignacio
7. Magdalena

arrested and placed in prison to await their deportation. Many of them died from the cruel treatment they received. Why did the king do this?

For a long time, all over Europe, hatred of the Jesuits for their power and influence had been simmering. Many Jesuits had been advisers to kings and princes, and they controlled a tremendous wealth in property, which some misused. Chiefly, though, the Jesuits had been the main opponents of the Enlightenment, and they spread their "unenlightened" teachings in their far-flung schools in Europe and America. Carlos III considered himself an "enlightened monarch" and wanted to establish a more "modern" and "rational" form of government over his domains. He saw the Jesuits as an obstacle to his plans; thus, they had to go.

The "rational" governing favored by King Charles involved changing the mission system. The Indians, according to the new policy, were to take their place as equal subjects of the Spanish crown. They were no longer to be administered by missionaries but incorporated into Spanish pueblos and ruled by Spanish officials. Missionaries or, better yet, secular priests, would serve only the Indians' spiritual needs.

The mind behind both the expulsion of the Jesuits and the reform of the missions was Count José de Gálvez It was Gálvez who decided to replace the Jesuits with Franciscans because he thought they were not so worldly as the Jesuits; they were less likely to interfere in politics. Among the Franciscans who arrived in the Pimería in 1768 was Fray Francisco Hermenegildo Garcés, who took over San Xavier de Bac in Arizona. Fray Francisco flourished under the new regime, attending to purely spiritual tasks. He became an intrepid explorer. In 1775–76, Fray Francisco crossed the Colorado River into Alta California (the modern state) and pushed north into the San Joaquin Valley, the southern part of the great Central Valley of California. From the San Joaquin, Garcés passed over the Sierra Nevada through the Tehachapi Pass, crossed the Mojave Desert and, turning south again, returned to Arizona.

It soon became apparent that Gálvez's system did not work. Without missionary control over the mission lands and buildings, many churches and convents were collapsing. Finally, the government had to relent. In 1769, total control of the missions passed once again into the hands of the missionaries.

Fray Junípero and the Missions of Alta California

As it turned out, Count José de Gálvez had more to worry about than the organization of the Sonoran missions. The northern frontiers of the Spanish empire were threatened. Two powers were showing an interest in the west coast of North America. One, Russia, had by 1741 explored the Bering Strait and crossed over into Alaska. Discovering lands rich in furs, Russian adventurers were plying the waters of the northwest coast of North America and were advancing steadily southward. Great Britain, the other power, had no clear policy for the west coast; but British ships had been visiting the coast of Alta California. From what Count Gálvez could see, unless she strengthened her claim to the land by settlement, Spain might lose upper California.

Legendary Island of Amazons

It is in the narrative of Juan Rodríguez Cabrillo, the discoverer of Alta California, that we first find the name *California* given to the peninsula and the region of the modern state that both bear that name today. From whence did this name come?

The great explorers and conquistadors of Spanish America were very fond of the romances that told outlandish stories of chivalry. One such series of romances by Ordóñez de Montalvo describes the extraordinary deeds of a knight, Amadis of Gaul, and his son, Esplandián. The fifth tale in this series, *Las sergas de Esplandián* ("The Deeds of Esplandián") tells how a force of Amazons did battle with the Christians of the city of Constantinople. The leader of these warlike women was Queen Calafía, who ruled a distant island. Montalvo's romance says this of Calafía's realm:

> Know, that on the right hand of the Indies there is an island called California, very close to the side of the Terrestrial Paradise; and it is peopled by black women, without any man among them, for they live in the manner of Amazons.

In 1539, Hernán Cortés sent Francisco de Ulloa on an expedition up the coast of Mexico.

It was Ulloa who first sailed into the Sea of Cortés and discovered the Baja peninsula. It is likely that he gave the land the name of California—for Cortés had thought one might discover an island of Amazons, rich in gold and overrun by griffins, off the Pacific coast of New Spain: that is, Montalvo's realm of Queen Calafía. Though Ulloa, by sailing to the mouth of the Colorado River, found that the Baja is not an island but a peninsula, for over a hundred years mapmakers continued to depict it as an island—to which they gave the name, Calfornia.

A detail from 1678 map by Louis Hennepin showing California as an island and the region of New Mexico and the Pimería Alta

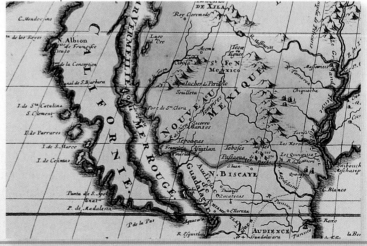

Spain's claim to Alta California dated back to 1542 when Juan Rodríguez Cabrillo explored the coasts of the North Pacific. On September 28, 1542, Cabrillo reached a large, well-sheltered bay north of the Baja California peninsula and then continued northward to discover Santa Catalina Island and the Santa Barbara Channel. Rounding Point Concepción, Cabrillo's little fleet of two ships skirted the coast of Central California but turned south again after encountering hard weather. Cabrillo himself then died and was buried on San Miguel, an island in the Santa Barbara Channel; his helmsman, Bartolomé Ferrelo, however, directed the expedition still further north, passed Cape Mendocino, and then went as far north as the 44th parallel on the coast of Oregon. Sixty years later, another explorer, Sebastián Vizcaíno, explored the same coast, landing at the first bay Cabrillo had discovered (and naming it San Diego); he then proceeded north to discover another, though less sheltered bay, which he called Monterey. At Monterey, Vizcaíno erected a stone altar where the first Mass on the Alta California coast was offered. Vizcaino's expedition continued north to Mendocino. However, perhaps because of fog, he missed a great bay (later called San Francisco.)

When he returned to Mexico, Vizcaíno encouraged the Spanish authorities to settle the coast of what became known as Alta California. But 160 years passed before the Spanish government, in the person of Count Gálvez, began to do anything about a California settlement. Gálvez conceived of colonizing California with a string of missions supported by only a skeleton force of soldiers. The man he chose to direct this endeavor had already proven himself an able administrator of missions. He was Fray Junípero Serra.

The Making of a Missionary

Junípero Serra was born on the island of Mallorca off the Mediterranean coast of Spain on November 24, 1713. At the age of 16, he decided to become a priest, and a year later he entered the Franciscan order. For the first 19 years of his life as a Franciscan, Fray Junípero lived in Mallorca, perhaps never sailing even to Spain. For many of these years he was a lecturer in philosophy in the tradition of the Franciscan philosopher and theologian, Duns Scotus—and was once investigated by the Inquisition. In those years he lectured on the works of his fellow Mallorcan and Franciscan, Ramón Lull, who argued for the peaceful conversion of the Moslems—an idea most Europeans of his day did not think practicable.

Fray Junípero Serra

In 1749, at the age of 36, Fray Junípero volunteered for the missions in Mexico. What moved him to this? "I have had no other motive," he wrote years later, "but to revive in my soul those intense longings which I have had since my novitiate when I read the lives of the saints. These longings had become deadened because of the preoccupation I had with studies."

Accompanied by his friend, Fray Francisco Palóu (who later wrote a biography of Serra), Fray Junípero sailed for America on August 30, 1749, arriving at Veracruz in December. Though offered horses (provided at the expense of the king of Spain) for the 270-mile journey from Veracruz to Mexico City, Serra and another friar who accompanied him refused. Instead, faithful to the ideals of the Rule of St. Francis, the two friars journeyed on foot to Mexico City. In the high mountains that over 200 years earlier Cortés had crossed, Fray Junípero injured his leg. "With fatigue," wrote Palóu, "the feet of the Venerable Father Junípero began to swell, so that when he arrived at an hacienda he could not stand. This swelling was attributed to mosquito bites because of the great itching he felt. Having rested there a day, unconsciously he rubbed the one leg too much while he was sleeping. In the morning it appeared all bloody so that a wound resulted which . . . lasted during all his life."

After arriving at the missionary College of San Fernando in Mexico City, Fray Junípero was sent to the missions among the pagan Pame Indians of the Sierra Gorda, a mountainous region 175 miles north of Mexico City. For eight years, he worked among the Pame and learned their language, in which he composed a catechism.

The Sierra Gorda missions were set up as large farms. The Indians were not forced onto the missions, but invited; once they came and were baptized, however, they were under the authority of the missionaries and were forbidden to leave. The missionaries taught the natives not only the Catholic faith but various crafts, as well as the arts of farming, and cattle raising. The missionaries treated the Indians as children, with the aim of educating and training them so that the mission pueblo and farms could eventually be turned over to them, and the missionaries replaced with secular priests.

Mission Indians lived a highly regimented life. Bells, rung three times a day, summoned the Indians from the fields and workshops to receive their allotments of food. The missionaries provided a special living quarters for girls older than 11 years and unmarried women. The religious life of the missions was very colorful, with processions, images, plain chant, polyphony, and Pame hymns. So beautiful and reverent was the mission liturgy that many Spaniards were drawn to the missions to celebrate holy days.

In 1758, Fray Junípero was recalled to the College of San Fernando. He spent the next nine years as choir master (he had a beautiful voice for song), novice master, and home missionary. A home missionary was a priest who traveled from parish to parish preaching missions to inspire Catholics to a deeper understanding of their faith and dedication to Christ. Fray Junípero was a zealous preacher, often going to what today we might judge extreme lengths to move his hearers to repentance. From the pulpit, he pounded his chest, scourged himself, and even once applied a lighted candle to his breast. Far from repelling his hearers, Fray Junípero's style drew many to his missions. His sermons, though long, were in great demand. Certainly the colorful and theatrical appealed to his audiences.

The year 1767 marked a new epoch in Serra's life. With the Jesuits expelled from the Spanish domains, their missions in Baja California fell to the Franciscans. At the College of San Fernando, Fray Junípero learned that he would be made *padre presidente*, or head, of the Baja California missions. He remained in Baja California, however, for only about a year before Count Gálvez chose him to found a new missionary enterprise in Alta California.

Longing to go amongst pagans who had never heard the Gospel, Fray Junípero eagerly took up his new task. At the age of 55, Fray Junípero set out on the mission for which his entire life had prepared him.

Into the Pagan North

The expedition to Alta California was to go both by land and by sea. Count Gálvez outfitted three ships for Alta California at San Blas, a port on the coast of the Mexican mainland that would serve for many years as the main supply outlet for the California missions. The first of these ships, the *San Carlos*, left harbor in January 1769 for the long voyage north. The second ship, the *San Antonio*, would follow in February. Finally, in June, the third ship, the *San José*, was to sail with additional supplies for the new colony. The land force, under the command of Don Gaspar de Portolá, marched in two parts. The first left earlier in 1769; the second, under Portolá and with Fray Junípero, departed in March. The common destination for both fleet and land forces was the bay of San Diego.

On this journey, Fray Junípero suffered such pain and swelling in his injured leg that he had to be left behind for a time. But even after catching up with the expedition in May, Serra's leg continued to trouble him. It looked as if he would have to be carried on a stretcher by Indians. Not wanting to burden anyone, Fray Junípero, after prayer, convinced a muleteer to care for his leg as he would one of his mules. The muleteer prepared a poultice for Serra's leg; the next morning the friar could continue with the expedition—on foot.

After a 650-mile journey across the barren desert wastes of Baja California, Portolá's forces reached the bay of San Diego on July 1, 1769. Leaving Serra with 40 soldiers at San Diego, Portolá with 70 men continued north to find Monterey. Portolá did not find the bay so highly praised by Vizcaíno, but further to the north he made a more important discovery —the bay of San Francisco.

Meanwhile, in San Diego, the colonists had erected some wood structures and a wooden palisade for defense. But supplies were running low; the last supply ship, the *San José*, had not arrived even by the time Portolá returned in January 1770. Fray Junípero was discouraged, for as yet he had made no converts. The natives were not merely unfriendly, they were hostile. They stole what they could from the Spanish camp—they were even bold enough to try to cut strips off the sails of the ships in the harbor. Finally, when the Spaniards resisted, the Indians attacked. Volleys of arrows fell among the weakened settlers with deadly accuracy. One pierced the neck of a young boy who, running into Fray Junípero's tent, begged absolution before falling dead at the friar's feet. But when the Spaniards began to fire off their guns, the bellicose natives withdrew.

When Portolá saw the dismal condition of the settlement, he decided to abandon San Diego and return to Mexico. Fray Junípero, who longed to remain and preach the Gospel to the natives, convinced Portolá to wait until all had prayed a novena to St. Joseph, whose feast day, March 19, was swiftly approaching. Portolá agreed but stipulated that if no supply ship arrived by that date, the expedition must return to Mexico.

On the following nine days, Fray Junípero climbed a hill that looms over San Diego harbor and looked out to sea for a ship. Every day he was disappointed. On March 19, the feast of St. Joseph, the last day of the novena, he again climbed the hill to discover—nothing. Fog had settled over the ocean, and nothing could be seen. But when the fog burned off in the afternoon, a ship under full sail appeared on the horizon; it was the *San Antonio*, returning from San Blas, laden with supplies. Saint Joseph had heard Fray Junípero. The California settlement was saved.

On to Monterey

With San Diego secure, Fray Junípero accompanied Portolá on the expedition that at last discovered the Bay of Monterey. On the feast of Pentecost 1770, near an oak tree where Mass had been celebrated for Vizcaíno and his men, the governor and the *padre presidente* took formal possession of Alta California for the king of Spain. At Monterey, now the capital of Alta California, Serra established his second mission, naming it San Carlos de Borromeo de Carmelo. With two other friars, Serra next sought a site for his third mission, to the south of Carmel. Near a river he called the San Antonio, Fray Junípero hung a bell from a great tree. Ringing it with effervescent zeal, he cried out, "Come, Gentiles! Come to the Holy Church. Come and receive the Faith of Jesus Christ!" Over the next two years Serra established this mission, San Antonio de Padua, and two others between San Diego and Monterey: San Gabriel Arcángel (in 1771), and San Luis Obispo (in 1772).

Basket made by the California Tulare people

Like the missions in the Sierra Gorda, the California missions developed into great agricultural and cattle raising concerns. The California establishment followed the pattern of the Sierra Gorda missions in other respects as well. Fray Junípero and the Franciscan missionaries did not force California natives to enter the missions; but, once baptized, they had to remain at the missions, though they were allowed visits to their native *rancherías* for up to five weeks out of the year. The friars so limited the Indians' freedom because they looked on them as children whom God had rescued from Satan. The friars feared their neophytes could easily be lured again into spirit worship and pagan immorality.

The task of converting the California Indians was slow going. California natives spoke at least 135 different languages, which the friars labored diligently to learn. Divided into small clans, the natives were highly disunited and engaged in bloody feuds with each other. The natives lived by gathering acorns, pine nuts, and wild grains. They hunted, sneaking quietly up on their prey to shoot it at close range with bow and arrow. Their weapons, though accurate, were tipped only with stone, bone, or obsidian. Their houses were small, made from reeds and branches of willow, though they did construct tight wood structures called sweat lodges. Native California arts, too, were primitive: for instance, they used stone mortars and *metates* to grind acorns and nuts. On the other hand the coastal tribes, such as the Chumash, chiseled out great urns from soft stone and built long boats in which they braved the seas, paddling out on expeditions to the Santa Barbara Channel Islands, about 15 miles offshore. Everywhere, too, the California Indians crafted exquisitely beautiful baskets with intricate designs and so tightly woven that they held water. When the Indians needed hot water, they heated stones in a fire until they grew quite hot and then cast them into the water-filled baskets.

Fray Junípero held the Alta California Indians in high esteem. Comparing the missions of Alta and Baja California, Serra wrote:

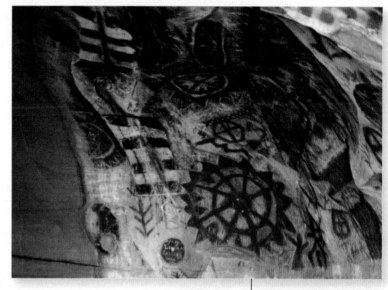

Rock art of the Chumash people, found in the mountains above Santa Barbara, California

> The missions to be founded in these parts will enjoy many advantages over the old ones [in Baja California], as the land is much better and the water supply is much more plentiful. The Indians especially of the west coast seem to me much more gifted; they are well set up, and the Governor looks upon most of them as likely Grenadier Guards because they are such stoutly built and tall fellows.

The California natives proved to be quick learners, easily mastering the crafts the friars taught. They learned to play European musical instruments, and Indian choirs and orchestras in the missions performed complex works by Ignacio de Jerúsalem and other baroque and classical composers. Visitors to California in the early 19th century commented on the precision and skill of these Indian musical ensembles. The friars trained and employed Indian artisans in adorning the mission churches. Murals painted in deep reds, blues, greens, and yellows enriched the temples with exuberant color.

The missions provided the California natives who settled in them a steady source of food, thus preserving them from the famines that periodically had affected them in their "gentile" state. But, as in the rest of America, so in California: European diseases took their toll on the Indian population. Diseases such as tuberculosis, smallpox, and syphilis (first contracted from Spanish soldiers and spread through marital and extra-marital intercourse—the friars noted that the natives found it difficult to follow Christian sexual mores) wreaked havoc on the Indian population—which numbered about 300,000 before the coming of the Spaniards. Infant mortality was high, and the conception rate was low—as it seems to have been the case before the coming of the Spaniards. The friars were puzzled at the death rate among the Indians; at San Buenaventura mission, the friars built a water purifying system, suspecting that, at least in some cases, bad water was the cause of sickness. Yet, despite the friars' efforts, the Indian population continued to decline during the mission period. By the 1820s, however, it seemed to begin to rebound as subsequent generations developed immunities to the diseases.

Along with those already mentioned, Fray Junípero established four other missions in his lifetime: in 1776, missions San Juan Capistrano and San Francisco de Asís; in 1777, Santa

Clara de Asís; and, in 1782, San Buenaventura. By 1823, Serra's successors had established 12 more missions. Generally, the California missions prospered, and in time they became self-supporting. By the late 18th century, the nine California missions boasted 5,384 head of cattle, 5,629 sheep, and 4,294 goats. In the 1820s, San Gabriel mission alone claimed 16,500 head of cattle.

California Martyrdom

In California as in Florida and other Spanish colonies, questions of jurisdiction sparked tensions between the friars and the royal governors. Fray Junípero clashed with the second governor, Pedro Fages, over the question of who commanded the soldiers at the missions. Every mission had four soldiers to guard it; and in some of the missions, soldiers were becoming a problem. Having left their wives behind in Mexico, the soldiers went after Indian women. The soldiers could be cruel. Once some soldiers hanged and mutilated a band of Indians for stealing horses.

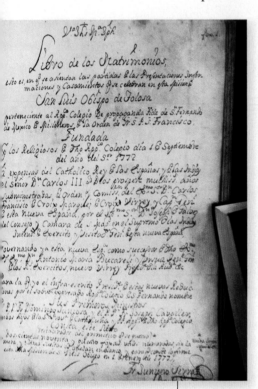

Marriage register, written in Serra's hand, from Mission San Luis Obispo de Tolosa

When Fages ignored his complaints, Fray Junípero decided to appeal to Mexico City. He undertook the long journey by sea to the capital in 1773 and there met with the viceroy, Fray Don Antonio María Bucareli y Ursua, a member of the lay Order of St. John of Jerusalem (the Knights of Malta). The viceroy listened sympathetically to Serra and asked him to write down his recommendations for California. Bucareli adopted almost all of Fray Junípero's recommendations in the regulations for California he promulgated shortly after Serra's return in 1774.

But Fray Junípero's difficulties were not over. Isolated as it was among the warlike Indians of the region, all was not well at Mission San Diego. Moreover, the mission stood some four miles from the *presidio*, too far for a quick response in case of attack; there had not been enough water to support both fortress and mission in the same location. In the autumn of 1775, two Christian Indians—Carlos, the chief of the mission Indian village, and his brother, Francisco—robbed some old pagan women of their seed and fish. Fearing punishment from the friars for their crime, Carlos and Francisco fled to the pagan villages. With six others, Carlos went from village to village, stirring up revolt. He was joined by six Indians who had been flogged for attending a pagan dance at the village of El Corral. These Indians claimed that the missionary at San Diego, Fray Vicente Fuster, had threatened to burn the village down if it were not moved away. Then on November 4, about 600 natives surrounded the mission and attacked it, setting fire to several buildings. Awakened by the crackling of flames and the smell of smoke, Fray Vicente and others ran to the guardhouse. The mission's carpenter, Urcelino, grabbed a musket but was struck with an arrow. "Ha, Indian, you have killed me," he cried. "God forgive you." The other missionary, Fray Luis Jayme, did not run to the guardhouse. Instead, he approached the attackers, with the customary greeting, *Amar a Dios, hijos* ("Love God, children"). The Indians seized Fray Luis and took him to the arroyo outside the mission compound. There they stripped him of his robes, shot him full of arrows, and pounded his head and face with stones and hunting sticks until he was unrecognizable. The war party continued their assault until daybreak, when they withdrew.

Serra rejoiced when he heard of Jayme's triumph. "Thanks be to God," said the *padre presidente*, "now indeed that land has been watered [with blood]; certainly now the conversion of the San Diego Indians will be achieved."

Yet, Fray Junípero feared for Carlos, who had led the assault on the mission. The new governor, Don Fernando Rivera y Moncada, had seized the chieftain in the church at San Diego, where he had sought sanctuary. This was a violation of the sacred right of sanctuary, or so Fray Junípero affirmed—a crime that, under Church law, brought on automatic excommunication. Serra sought mercy for Carlos, but, he knew, the governor would not heed one who had declared him excommunicated. Fray Junípero therefore, appealed to the viceroy, Antonio María Bucareli y Ursua. "As to the murderer," Serra wrote Bucareli, "let him live, in order that he should be saved—which is the very purpose of our coming here. . . . Give him to understand, after a moderate amount of punishment, that he is being pardoned in accordance with our law which commands us to forgive injuries; and let us prepare him, not for death, but for eternal life."

Carlos was not executed. Four years later, he and other Christian natives joined a larger number of pagans and attacked an Indian *ranchería*, killing 12 of the inhabitants. For this crime, the governor, despite Fray Junípero's pleas for mercy, banished Carlos to San Blas for six years.

A Passage to New Mexico

In their early days, the missions in California depended on supplies brought from Mexico by the sea route from San Blas. The supply route was long and somewhat precarious, and so it was that Fray Junípero suggested to the viceroy that a second supply route, a land route from Sonora and New Mexico, should be opened to facilitate the supplying of the missions. Fray Francisco Garcés had already explored and charted much of the Colorado River down to where it poured into the Gulf of California. Now, all that was needed was an expedition to chart a land route from New Mexico to the coast of Alta California.

The man the viceroy chose for the task was Don Juan Bautista de Anza. An intrepid explorer, a man who lived in the saddle, and moreover, a just and good friend of the Indians, Anza was a happy choice. Accompanied by Fray Francisco Garcés, who was well known and liked by the Yuma Indians on the Colorado, Anza left Tubac in what is now Arizona in January 1774. Winning the friendship of the Yumas with gifts (it was the tribe's custom so to secure treaties), Anza's men passed into the forbidding deserts of Southern California. Ascending from the barren desert into the snowy heights of the San Jacinto Mountains, Anza and Garcés entered a world of thick pine forests, streams, and lakes. From the mountains they descended into the dry, inland valleys today paved over by the sprawling suburbs of Los Angeles, but then covered, in some places, by grassland and oak woodland, in others, by dense chaparral and the spiny, succulent Spanish Bayonet plant. The expedition arrived at mission San Gabriel in March 1774.

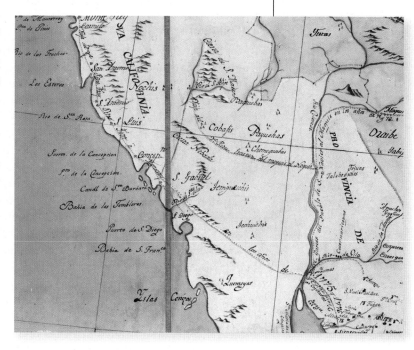

California, as it appeared in a map of the *Provincias Internas*, 1817

When Anza returned to New Mexico, he organized a second expedition—this time with Spanish settlers. On October 23, 1775, Anza with 38 families, ten soldiers, and hundreds of horses, pack mules, and beef cattle left for California. Following the route of the previous year, the party reached San Gabriel on January 4, 1776 and thence proceeded north to San Francisco Bay. There in June the settlers established a mission and *presidio*.

Fray Junípero was pleased with the new Spanish settlement of San Francisco, but not with certain political developments affecting the missions. Under King Carlos III, New Mexico, California, and Sonora were joined into one political unit, called the *Provincias Internas*. This region's first military intendant, Teodoro de Croix, wanted to apply to it the "rational" principles of government favored by the king. The new governor of California, Felipe de

Neve, shared the intendant's ideas. Both wanted to remove all political and economic control of the missions from the friars. The missions would become pueblos, with the Indians electing their own *alcalde* and *regidores* (members of the ruling council in a pueblo), while the friars (reduced to one per church) would care only for spiritual needs. This was the same system that had been put in place in the Pimería with resounding failure.

It was never tried in California, for tragedy intervened.

Intendant Croix had never been in California and New Mexico; still he thought he knew enough about the regions to plan a Spanish pueblo along the banks of the Colorado. This was not what the Yuma *cacique*, Salvador Palma, had asked from Viceroy Bucareli. Palma had wanted a mission like those Serra had founded in California; he certainly did not want a pueblo filled with Spanish settlers. But by 1781 Bucareli was dead, and Croix had other plans.

Soon, Spanish settlers from New Mexico were arriving in the Yuma lands. They did not give the customary presents the Yuma thought necessary to conclude a treaty. They began pushing the Yuma off their own land, without payment. In the oppressive heat of July, the Yuma rose in rebellion. They killed Captain Fernando Rivera from California and all the males of the Spanish settlement. They enslaved the women and children. Nor did the Franciscans escape; the Yumas cut down the priests Francisco Garcés, Juan Barreneche, and José Moreno. Though in subsequent months three military expeditions recovered 75 captives and 1,000 horses, the hostile Yumas stood athwart the trail linking New Mexico to California. No supplies would cross this trail to Serra's missions.

The Yuma massacre convinced Croix to abandon his "rational" and "enlightened" plans for the Provincias Internas. The California missions would continue under the secular and spiritual control of the friars. This was welcome news for Fray Junípero. Now the friars could continue the work they thought most beneficial to the Indians.

The Passing of the *Padre Presidente*

In the years following the Yuma massacre, Fray Junípero did not abate the strenuous life he had been living since 1767. He continued to govern his missions as *padre presidente* and to travel up and down the highway, *El Camino Real* (the Royal Highway), from San Diego to San Francisco on visits to his missionaries and beloved native neophytes. In 1778 the pope granted him the faculty of administering confirmation, a necessity when the nearest bishop was over 700 miles away.

The year 1777 saw the founding of the first Spanish pueblo in California, San José de Guadalupe, near Mission Santa Clara de Asís. The pueblo was founded to promote agriculture so that California settlers need not rely so heavily on Mexico for supplies. In 1781, 11 families under Captain Rivera founded another settlement on the coastal plain, not far from Mission San Gabriel. In this settlement, El Pueblo de Nuestra Señora Reina de Los Angeles de Porciuncula—the Pueblo of Our Lady Queen of the Angels of Porciuncula (the river adjacent to the new settlement) each family received a plot of land on which it could build a house.

In 1784 it became apparent that Fray Junípero's health was failing. He began to have strong pains in his chest, which worsened when he lay down. In August he asked his old friend and countryman, Fray Francisco Palóu, to come to him quickly at Monterey. There, Fray Francisco administered last rites to Serra and gave him *viaticum*. Fray Junipero died peacefully in his sleep, on August 28, 1784. Both Spaniards and Indians flocked to his funeral, the natives lamenting so loudly that they nearly drowned out the singing of the Office of the Dead.

Fray Junípero's body now rests in the sanctuary of the mission church of San Carlos de Borromeo in Monterey.

Chapter 7 Review

Summary

- On August 10, 1680, an Indian religious leader by the name of Popé started a large-scale rebellion in New Mexico. The Spaniards were forced to flee.

- In 1692 Diego Vargas retook Santa Fé and the surrounding countryside. With the Reconquest of Santa Fé, New Mexico entered a period of expansion.

- In the 17th and 18th centuries the Spanish crown tried to reform the *encomienda system*. In 1720 the Bourbon king, Felipe V, finally abolished the whole system in law though it continued to exist in practice.

- To address the continuing existence of the *encomienda system*, King Carlos III placed an official called the *alcalde mayor* over the Indians. This new system was abolished in 1786.

- Beginning in the late 1680s, the Jesuit priest, Eusebio Kino, began establishing missions in the Pimería Alta.

- In 1695 the Pima Indians rose in revolt. Lieutenant Antonio de Solís set off to crush the rebellion. Padre Eusabio Kino desired to keep peace, so he called the Indians to sign a treaty.

- Through a number of expeditions to the northwest to find a land supply route to missions in California, Kino proved once and for all that Baja California is not an island, but a peninsula.

- After Kino's death in 1711 and another revolt, the Pimería suffered from becoming a military camp. Division spread amongst the Pimas. The expulsion of the Jesuits from the the Spanish empire brought further suffering to the Pimería and other regions of the empire.

- As part of the Spanish king's reform of the missions, Count José de Gálvez brought in the Franciscans to attend to purely spiritual affairs. The reform did not work, however, and in 1769 the control of the missions was once again in the hands of the missionaries.

- In 1769 Fray Junípero Serra arrived at San Diego and began his work of converting the Indians and building missions all over California. He was made *padre presidente*, or head, of all the California missions.

- In 1769, Don Gaspar de Portolá found Monterey as well as the bay of San Francisco.

- In 1774 Don Juan Bautista de Anza led an expedition to find a route from California to New Mexico.

Key Concepts

hacienda real: the "royal estate": the lands in the New World claimed by the king of Spain

visitador real: the "royal visitor" in Spanish America who inspected the acts of officials in the New World

mestizaje: the result of the intermingling of Indian, black, and European races in the New World

peninsulares: European-born Spaniards, the highest social class in America

creoles: pure Spaniards, but born in America

mestizos: those in Spanish America of mixed European and Indian blood

neophyte: a new convert

Dates to Remember

1680: the opening of Popé's rebellion in New Mexico

1687: the Pima cacique, Coxi, receives baptism, thus establishing Padre Eusebio Kino's mission in the Pimería.

1692: the Spanish reconquer New Mexico

1720: Felipe V abolishes the *encomienda* system.

1749: Junípero Serra comes to America.

1769: Junípero Serra establishes his first mission at San Diego.

Don Gaspar de Portolá founds Monterey and discovers the bay of San Francisco.

1770: Portolá and Serra take formal possession of Alta California for the king of Spain.

Central Characters

Eusabio Kino (1645–1711): Jesuit missionary, cartographer, explorer, and founder of numerous missions in Spanish America

Chapter 7 Review (continued)

Junípero Serra (1713–1784): a Spanish Franciscan who founded missions in Alta California and whose work there earned him the title of Apostle of California.

Count José de Gálvez (1720–1787): the Spanish official who sought to reform and reorganize the Spanish missions in Sonora and oversaw the establishment of the missions in Alta California

Questions for Review

1. What were the conditions in New Mexico that led to the destruction of the Spanish settlement there?

2. How did the kings of Spain regard their New World possessions and the inhabitants of America?

3. In what ways did the government of Spanish America differ from that of the English colonies?

4. Name and describe the social classes of Spanish America.

5. Describe the government of Spanish America.

6. Explain how Spain and Europe benefited from America.

7. What are some of Spanish America's contributions to art and the Church?

8. What was the social role of the Catholic Church in America, and how is an understanding of the Church helpful in understanding New Spain?

9. What did Padre Kino accomplish in America?

10. What did Junípero Serra accomplish in America?

11. How did the Indians of the California and the Pimería compare to the Indians of eastern North America? What especially were the western Indians skilled in?

Ideas in Action

1. Research the missions of California and the saints they are named after.

2. Read Willa Cather's *Death Comes for the Archbishop* or a life of Junípero Serra.

3. Read some of the works of Sor Juana Inés de la Cruz.

4. Discuss whether the methods Serra used in attracting Indians to the missions and governing them were right in light of natural justice and the demands of the Gospel.

5. Compare Serra's missionary methods with those of the Jesuits in New France. Which were more effective? Why?

Highways and Byways

Willa Cather's New Mexico—Then and Now

In 1852, a young, aristocratic French bishop rides out of Santa Fe, his new diocesan seat. He is going on his first visit to the Indian pueblos. The world of the New Mexico Indians is a strange, new one to him, and he constantly marvels at the wonders of the landscape he passes through. He goes first to Isleta, "whitened with gypsum," on to Laguna "of wide pastures," and finally to "cloud-set Ácoma." Ácoma impresses the bishop the most. "From the flat red sea of sand rose great rock mesas, generally Gothic in outline, resembling vast cathedrals." Atop these vast cathedrals of stone lay the pueblos of the Ácoma people.

The story of this bishop, Jean Marie Latour, is Cather's fictionalized account of the life and work of John Baptist Lamy, bishop of New Mexico in the 19th century. Cather paints a vivid picture of life in the pueblos and the landscapes of New Mexico. Today the Ácoma and Laguna pueblos have casinos and are reached by highways, but they are still as beautiful and impressive as when Bishop Latour first set eyes on them. The Ácoma people still live in terraced dwellings made of stone and adobe atop the precipitous sandstone mesas—those same mesas that Bishop Latour and the Spaniards before him saw rising out of the flat red sea of sand.

8 THE CAUSES OF THE AMERICAN REVOLUTION

Part I: **The Colonies on the Eve of Discontent**

Colonial Growth

The French and Indian War left Great Britain the undisputed power in North America, east of the Mississippi. From Hudson's Bay in the frigid north, to the sultry swamps of Florida, Britain held masterful sway. Indeed, Great Britain had now replaced France (as once France had Spain) as the mistress of the world. British colonies, from India to North America to the South Sea islands, were linked in the world's greatest commercial empire, protected by the world's largest navy.

The British colonies were undergoing a sort of population explosion in the 18th century. Between 1660 and 1754, the colonial population grew over 17 times, from 85,000 to 1.5 million. Much of this growth, of course, came from immigration. Beginning in 1740, the

A 1759 map of the English colonies in North America

British parliament began allowing large numbers of non-British to settle in the colonies. In the colonies, one's neighbors were now not only English and Scots, but Irish, Germans, and French.

Not all the colonies grew at the same rate. New York grew slowly because the Dutch *patroons* controlled the land, and many immigrants preferred to own land, rather than be tenant farmers, if they could help it. Pennsylvania continued to grow, largely by an influx of German immigrants, who generally belonged to religious sects escaping persecution in their homeland. York and Lancaster counties became the refuge for groups like the Mennonites, the Moravians, the "Dunkers" (so named for their practice of adult immersion baptism), and the Pietists (German Lutherans who sought a

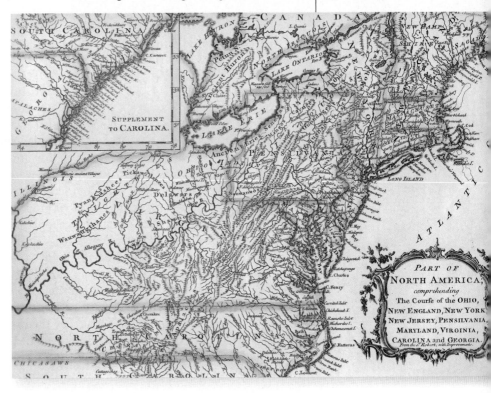

mystical and personal relationship with Christ). When Lord Culpeper and, later, Lord Fairfax, opened up the Shenandoah and Blue Ridge regions for settlement, many German Moravians and Mennonites, along with Scots Presbyterians, flowed into the western regions of Virginia. Thence they spilled over east into the Piedmont, and a large number of Moravians moved south and settled around Salem in North Carolina.

Most colonists made their living by farming. Their farms ranged from small family subsistence farms (where the bulk of the produce went to support the family, with the remainder sold on the market), to larger, more prosperous "middle-class" farms, and then to the large tobacco and rice plantations of the South. The smaller farmers tended to plant a variety of different crops, since they were feeding themselves as well as selling to markets. The large plantations, however, planted only one crop—such as tobacco or rice or wheat—that they would sell for cash. This kind of farming, called "monoculture," was damaging to farmland, since the continual planting of the same crop depleted the soil. But that was not seen as a problem in America's colonial period—there was so much new land for the taking. One could always move on.

Colonial family (the Wiley family) ca. 1771, by William Williams

After a while, some colonists pursued other avocations than farming. In Virginia, Pennsylvania, New Jersey, and Massachusetts, men set up works for smelting iron. Iron working became a thriving colonial industry—so much so that even Parliament's Iron Act in 1750 forbidding colonial iron mills from producing certain kinds of iron, didn't hurt their colonial business. The colonists, too, simply ignored Parliament. Colonists in the larger coastal towns traded with other parts of the British Empire and with Europe and non-British colonies. And, of course, they carried on an illegal trade with other European countries and their colonies. Though Parliament had laws against smuggling, the British government generally ignored it in the colonies.

Yet, despite trade and incipient industry, British colonial folk were on the whole country folk. Cities there were, but not even the three largest towns—Boston, New York, and Philadelphia—came anywhere near the population and size of London. In England, nearly half a dozen cities had populations of 30,000; there were none of such size in English America. England had over twenty cities with populations of at least 10,000; America had only three. By mid century, the colonies could boast of only about six cities of over 5,000 people; and Philadelphia, the largest colonial city, had about 20,000 people.

By the middle of the 18th century, a brisk and profitable slave trade flourished in the colonies. Every major port, from New England to the Carolinas, engaged in the African slave trade. North Carolina, in particular was the biggest importer of African slaves. The use of African slaves was increasing throughout the colonies, but particularly in the South, where the hot, humid climate and the disease-ridden cultivation of sugar and rice in the swampy coastal lowlands convinced whites that they themselves were not fit for such labor. Blacks, they argued, could take the heat and withstand disease better than they. By 1720, black slaves began to outnumber white, indentured servants in every colony south of Maryland. Not all southern whites approved of slavery, though; for instance, the Germans and the Scots Presbyterians of the Blue Ridge and Piedmont areas of North Carolina despised it.

Life in the English Colonies

Life in the English colonies in the 18th century mirrored society in England. The key words to describe English society, and consequently colonial society, are *hierarchy*, *paternalism*, and *interdependence*.

British society was *hierarchical.* At its head was the king, from whom all authority in society came. It is true that under William and Mary, Queen Anne, and the three kings George, Parliament was gaining more and more power in Britain, making the British king the weakest monarch in Europe. Nevertheless, the king was seen to be the source of Parliament's authority. The head of Parliament, the prime minister, was the king's minister; the parliamentary government was the king's government. Likewise, the king granted every colonial charter; every colonial assembly made laws by the king's grace.

In Great Britain, all power and authority were seen as coming from the top down through descending levels of authority to the lowliest member of society. British society had a defined class structure. The highest class was the aristocracy, which included the king and all the highest nobility —dukes, earls, barons, counts, and marquises.

An American gentleman, George Washington, overseeing his plantation

Then came the gentry who held no titles of aristocracy but owned large landed estates. Below the gentry were the professional classes: lawyers, doctors, lesser clergymen, farmers, merchants, mechanics, and craftsmen.

The upper and lower classes in Britain differed significantly in their mode of life. The **"gentlemen"** of the aristocracy and gentry led a life of leisure; the lower classes did not. Leisure was not necessarily idleness or mere recreation (though it often degenerated into that). Leisure signified activity carried on for reasons other than feeding and clothing oneself.

Gentry, gentleman, gentility, and *genteel,* are all words that derive from the Latin word for "family" or clan—*gens.* The gentlemen were men of a prominent family.

Leisurely activities included governing, military service, intellectual pursuits, and even the practice of medicine (as long as it was done in a leisurely fashion—that is, not for a living.) Gentlemen were not to engage in trade, in buying and selling—though they might speculate in land. Gentlemen could be farmers, though they were not to engage in the actual manual labor of farming or direct overseeing—underlings, who were not "gentle," not of an old, prominent family, did all that. Money lending at interest (especially in the colonies) was another gentlemanly activity; interest was thought to be like the rent collected from tenant farmers. Of course, one needed a certain amount of wealth to live the life of a gentleman, but wealth did not make one a gentleman. A gentleman was known by his ancestors and family connections (and his family's coat of arms), by his manners and self-control, his profession, and by his use of leisure.

A sense of honor marked the gentleman. Honor referred to one's reputation, which could be sullied by doing acts unbecoming to a gentleman or by being accused of doing such acts. A gentleman was prickly about his good name, in part because he saw himself as representing more than himself. His name was often connected with a family that represented a region (as James Stuart was called Duke of York), so to insult him would be to insult everything he represented. It was not merely to question his own personal goodness but his very position in society. So it was that a gentleman was very sensitive to insults, even to the point of at times challenging whoever insulted him to a duel to the death.

The chief distinction between gentlemen and others, then, was not wealth, but family and leisure. However wealthy they might be, those outside the aristocracy and gentry were not thought "gentle" because they did not come from a gentle family and moreover they *had* to work for a living. Their pursuits were thought honorable, because they fulfilled functions necessary to society, as did those of the gentry. Their pursuits were just different from those of the gentry. By the 18th century, however, the practical distinction between the gentry and the professional classes was often less than clear. The wealthy of the professional classes often followed the habits and dress of the aristocracy, even intermarried with them.

Paternalism characterized the attitude of gentlefolk towards those below them on the social ladder. Just as the king was thought the "father" of all British subjects, so gentlemen were to be fathers to those below them on the social ladder. Every region had its great men. If a farmer, for instance, needed money, he could ask the local gentleman, who would loan him a sum at very low interest or at no interest at all and not require payment for many years. What the gentleman asked in return was good crops, a certain respect or deference, and loyalty. The social order was thus based on an *interdependence* between all ranks of society. Common people were dependent on the nobility and gentry for leadership, loans, and land, while the nobility and gentry were dependent on the professionals, farmers and craftsmen who provided them with services, food, goods, and rental income (for many common folk did not own land, but were tenants of the gentry).

This description of British society applied to the American colonies only imperfectly. There was really no upper aristocracy, no titles (dukes, counts, marquises, etc.) in the North American colonies. Gentlemen there were, but they were never as rich or as leisurely as gentlemen in Great Britain. In England, for instance, a gentleman enjoyed a steady income from his estates, because relatively very few people below the level of gentlemen owned any land but had to rent it from gentleman landlords. In America, gentlemen did not have such a steady source of income, for America had fewer tenant farmers. Moreover, colonial gentlemen had to engage in ungentlemanly activities, such as trade or farm work, to keep up gentlemanly appearances. Some, in order to become gentlemen, had first to be tradesmen. Benjamin Franklin made his fortune as a printer in Philadelphia. Later, he sold his business and lived the life of leisure. He was, then, a gentleman.

A 1762 portrait by Mason Chamberlin of Benjamin Franklin, sitting in his study as lightening strikes outside his window

In English colonial America, interdependence not only characterized relations between superiors and inferiors, but everyone was seen as depending on every other member of society. Everybody belonged somewhere and to someone. Every village had its "warning out" laws, which required strangers to leave within a certain period of time—not because folk were inhospitable, but because they assumed that everyone belonged somewhere and should get back to where he belonged. One belonged to his family, and families took care of their own—and if they did not want to, laws and customs forced them to. One belonged to his village or locality, too, and, as in a family, people acted on trust in their relations with each other. Merchants generously extended credit for their goods in local stores because they trusted debts would be paid. If they weren't, neighborly disapproval shamed the guilty party—and as a last resort, there was debtor's prison.

In short, colonial society was a very personal society. You knew those upon whom you depended, and they knew you. Unlike today, when you go to an impersonal place like the bank to get a loan, in those days you went to your family, friends, or the local gentleman who knew your name, your face, your family, even your habits. It is easy to be anonymous now; it was nearly impossible then. Runaway indentured servants had no place to go. If they stayed home, they would be recognized. If they went elsewhere, they would be treated as strangers, and, after a time, turned out.

Someone could rise in the colonial social order, but generally he had to enlist the help of a gentleman patron to do so. It was not unusual for a gentleman to note the intelligence of a son of his tenant farmers and pay his way through school, even send him to university. Alexander Hamilton got his start this way. The illegitimate son of a bankrupt Scottish merchant in Saint Croix in the British West Indies, Hamilton was a mere merchant's clerk before influential friends discovered his talents. Through their patronage, Hamilton was able to attend King's College in New York City. Benedict Arnold, too, made his way by patronage. Arnold, whose alcoholic father, a ruined merchant, died just as his son came of age, attracted the interest of Dr. Daniel Lathrop, a wealthy apothecary of Norwich, Connecticut, and Benedict's mother's cousin. Lathrop gave Arnold 500 pounds (a very large sum in those days), the deed to the Arnold family home (whose mortgage he held), and letters of introduction to men in high places.

Some few men did make it without the help of aristocrats. John Paul Jones, whose father was a Scottish landscape gardener, went to sea at the age of 13 as an apprentice to a merchant named John Younger. When Younger's business failed, Jones served as chief mate to a slaver's ship out of Jamaica. Later, on board a ship bound for Scotland, Jones took over piloting when the first mate died in the mid-Atlantic. Having brought the ship safely into Scotland, Jones was appointed its master. He was only 21 years old. Still, Jones was an exception in the matter of patronage. Even Benjamin Franklin, whom legend calls a "self-made man," became a rich and successful printer in Philadelphia because his talents had attracted the attention of an influential patron. Even though he was bright, and his scientific accomplishments helped him along, Franklin throughout his life sought the aid of influential men in his climb up the social ladder. It was thus he became one of the premier gentlemen of the England's North American colonies.

Map of Kentucky, by John Filson, published in 1784.

A New Society in the Making

With so much open land for the taking, it was hard to be a gentleman in America. Unlike in England, it was relatively easy to obtain land in the colonies. General James Wolfe's conquest of Québec opened the wide lands west of the Appalachians for settlement. No sooner had the French surrendered than settlers began moving into the region around Lake Champlain and into central New York. Between 1760 and 1771, the population of New York colony more than doubled, from 80,000 to over 168,000.

In the 1760s, frontiersmen began pushing their way southwest over the Appalachians. The most famous of these wandering hunters and trappers was Daniel Boone. In 1769 Boone, a veteran of the French and Indian War (he had served under Braddock), began to explore the Kentucky country and opened up the Wilderness Road, from western Virginia, through Cumberland Gap in the Appalachians and into Kentucky. This road became a major route for emigrants heading west. By 1775, Kentucky boasted several new settlements, including Boonesborough, Logan's Station, and Boiling Spring. The increasing number of settlers brought new pressures on Indian tribes, who, under the French, had had little to fear from white settlement. In 1769, Captain Will, a Shawnee chief, told Daniel Boone, "Go home and stay there. Don't come here any more, for this is the Indians' hunting ground and all the animals, skins and furs are ours; and if you are so foolish as to venture here again you may be sure the wasps and yellow-jackets will sting you severely." It was not a warning Boone heeded.

The availability of land began tearing colonial society apart. Lured by the hope of ever cheaper land, men began to leave their homes; extended families dissolved as their members sought their fortunes away from the paternal hearth. Old, established families left neighborhoods and towns, and new families moved in. Since so many were changing place, it became increasingly harder to maintain that everyone had to keep to his place, that he belonged somewhere and to someone. Trust between neighbors weakened, for how could one trust someone nobody knew? Gentlemen became less paternal and more businesslike in their relations with their tenants. Because society was becoming less stable, traditional bonds, mutual trust, and friendship were disintegrating.

Due to increased trade with England and other parts of Europe, the mid-18th century was a period of waxing material prosperity in America. Everywhere people of all social groups were looking to better their circumstances. Often this took the form of buying more luxuries and comforts—silver tea sets, fancy clothes, carriages, fine linens. Common folk were trying to live more like gentlemen—a source both of disgust and amusement to gentlefolk. Farmers, small merchants, and manufacturers ran up debts to purchase more livestock or equipment to increase production and make more money. Even the family home and farm began to be seen, not as a patrimony to hand down to one's children, but as a commodity to sell for a profit. One would buy a farm, keep it a few years, and when the price of land went up, sell it, and move on.

Colonial society had enjoyed greater equality between social classes than had England; but by the mid to late 18th century, by personal initiative and hard work, a common man could further narrow the gap between himself and the rich and well born. A commentator of the period said of his fellow colonists that they participated in . . .

> . . . one continued Race, in which everyone is endeavoring to distance all behind him, and to overtake or pass by, all before him; everyone flying from his Inferiors, in Pursuit of his Superiors, who fly from him with equal alacrity. Every tradesman is a Merchant, every Merchant is a Gentleman, and every Gentleman one of the Noblesse. We are a Country of Gentry, *Populus generosorum*. We have no such thing as a common People among us: Between Vanity and Fashion, the Species is utterly destroyed.

American rural scene, 18th century

Revolutionary Ideas

It was not just the greater social mobility that was cracking the traditional order of society in America. New ideas, too, played a part with—and perhaps more than just a part than—the availability of land in the West. These ideas, "Liberalism" and "republicanism," were not American in their origin but European. These ideas enticed members of the middle class, especially in France and England; even members of the nobility bandied Liberal and republican ideas about—the very people who stood to lose most by them.

Liberalism and republicanism were not political, social, or religious philosophies alone—they were all of these. Liberalism and republicanism arose during a period called the Enlightenment. Men of the Enlightenment rejected what they considered the darkness and superstition of Europe's religious past in favor of a worldview founded solely on reason and science. What could not be proven by reasoning and logic was not to be believed; scientific experimentation and mathematical measurement and deduction should be the sole bases of human life. One had simply to discover the "natural laws" that govern and direct the world to explain the phenomena—what one saw and experienced in the world around him.

Sir Isaac Newton

The spirit of the Enlightenment was epitomized in the work of Sir Isaac Newton. In his famous work on mathematical physics, *Principia Mathematica*, Newton had laid down three "laws" of motion by which he could mathematically describe the motion of material bodies, from the dropping of stones to the movement of the planets. These "laws of motion" are familiar to all—for instance, the laws of inertia and of gravity. European thinkers waxed enthusiastic over Newton's *Principia*. Everywhere and in every subject, men began to look for "natural laws" by which they could interpret the world around them. Such laws were seen as the keys to the mysteries that had for ages baffled and confused mankind.

The belief that by identifying natural laws one could interpret all reality had an effect on religion. Some began to think that since laws governed the universe, one didn't need God as an explanation for what one did not understand. Some became atheists and agnostics and denied all religion. Others, the Deists, believed in a God who made the universe like a clockmaker builds a clock—just as the clockmaker fashions the clock, winds it, and leaves it to run by itself, so God, the Deists said, made the world to run by certain natural laws and left it to operate by itself. Deists essentially rejected the Catholic concept of God's providence—that God has created the world and remains with the world, holding it in existence.

John Locke

When men began to seek for the natural laws that govern and direct human societies, they arrived at Liberalism. Enlightenment thinkers, such as the English philosopher John Locke, said that at one time men had lived in what was called a "state of nature," a period when there was no government and each man was entirely free and unencumbered and equal to his neighbor. As Locke argued in his *Two Treatises on Government* (1689), in the state of nature, each individual possessed all rights, especially the three most important rights—life, liberty, and property. Such rights are "inalienable" because no one has the right to take away (or "alienate") another's life, or his liberty, or his property. For Liberals, the possession of rights in freedom is the foundational good of human life and the good men cherish most.

Liberals held that governments arose because of the colliding of certain "natural" forces. In the state of nature, stronger men had begun to violate the rights of weaker men—they took their wives and children, they seized their fields; at times they enslaved or killed the weak. To protect their inalienable rights, therefore, men formed governments, to which they gave up lesser, "alienable" rights so that their life, liberty, and property would be protected. So government, according to Locke and others, originally derived its right to rule from the governed; government is merely the representative and voice of the people, established by the people so they could enjoy security in the possession of their rights. This was the core conviction of republicanism.

Republicanism thus contrasted with the understanding of governmental authority that came out of Catholic medieval Europe. It is not that medieval thinkers denied that those who would rule others needed the consent of those over whom they would rule; both St. Thomas Aquinas and, later, St. Robert Bellarmine asserted a valid government needed to be rooted in popular consent. Medieval political thought, however, said the *authority* to rule is not derived from the governed but from God. A ruler's right to command obedience did not come simply from the fact that the people had chosen him but from the nature of political authority, which has been established by God. The ruler is the representative of God for his people. This does not mean (as those who proposed the Divine Right of Kings insisted) that the ruler has absolute power over his subjects; indeed, medieval thinkers said emphatically that a king's power or authority is limited to the specific tasks of promoting and protecting the common good of the whole people; he may not interfere with other rightful authority in society, whether that of lords, cities, guilds, families, or, especially, the Church. Nevertheless, his authority is not derived from men but from God.

Locke wrote his *Two Treatises* in defense of the regime that was established by the Glorious Revolution of 1688. James II, the Stuart king of England had, like his ancestors, championed the "divine right of kings"—that, since a king derives his authority from God as the father of the people, the people, in return, owe the king absolute obedience. Divine Right was dealt its death blow in England when Parliament invited William of Orange and his wife Mary (James II's daughter) to take the throne of England, forcing James to flee to France. This "Glorious Revolution," as it was called, established the principle that kings only rule by the good pleasure of Parliament—the representatives of the English people.

The Glorious Revolution raised the question, if the king's authority is not sacred, how permanent or how sacred were other authorities in society? Throughout the 17th, and into the 18th century, republican political thinkers began to doubt that anyone had a divine right to rule anyone. The Glorious Revolution confirmed in many minds the idea that the right to rule comes from those who are ruled—that political authority arises from the people. Republicanism moreover attacked kinship relationships, hierarchy, patriarchy, and dependence—the very foundations of the monarchical social order.

Republicans wreaked havoc on traditional society by denying that noble birth granted anyone a natural right to govern others. Not birth but talent, said republicans, recommends someone to political office. Why should aristocrats alone enjoy political power? There were "commoners" who were just as intelligent and talented as any noble or monarch. In fact, some men, who had risen from a humble estate and had worked their way through university or business, were more intelligent, more prudent, more virtuous than many an aristocrat, however well-born. Not birth but virtue, republicans claimed, made someone worthy of political authority. Virtue, in this connection, included not only what we call the "moral virtues"—self-control, courage, chastity, etc.—but the specific virtues required by rulers, such as prudence, insight into public affairs, a public spirit, and magnanimity—a generous and unselfish spirit.

But though they believed in the radical equality of all men, republicans were not egalitarian; they did not think the common man should direct public affairs. Mechanics, craftsmen, merchants—anyone employed by another—were not financially independent and thus unfit to govern. Though some commoners could at least be allowed the suffrage, they were, thought republicans, too bound up by their own self-interest to possess the public spirit required to look out for the good of society.

Though republicans thought wealth a necessary attribute of the public servant, they made it clear they wanted no rapprochement with the nobility. Republicans wanted to replace the hereditary gentleman with the enlightened gentlemen. Because he was enlightened, this gentleman was free from superstition; because he was wealthy, he was not distracted by workaday concerns or beholden to another. An enlightened gentleman was not absorbed in the private interest that republicans thought came from having to work for one's living; he could and would serve in government without pay and so be free from selfish motives in governing the state. Enlightened gentlemen, went the republican theory, would form a "natural aristocracy." The people, freed from traditional government and entrenchment in forms of hierarchy and family relations, would easily identify these natural aristocrats and vote them into office. Society and the state would then be ruled by only the best men.

Republicanism caught on in the English American colonies, where the distinctions between the aristocracy and the people were not so pronounced as in England. In America a number of young men had risen from more or less humble beginnings, had gone to university, had become "enlightened gentlemen." These men enjoyed more privilege but yet were not aristocrats; they saw themselves as "natural aristocrats" and resented the fact that a few families, whose only claim to rule was family connections and tradition, largely controlled the government of the colonies. They wanted a change, a *novus ordo seclorum*, a republican and enlightened society. Their names—Hamilton, Jefferson, Madison, Adams, Washington, and others—would become prominent in the coming struggle for such a society: the American Revolution.

The Great Awakening

One summer day in July 1741, a congregation listened, trembling, to a black-robed minister, lowering from the pulpit of the Enfield, Massachusetts, Congregational church. This minister, with eyes as dark as his Geneva robe, piercing, aflame with zeal, spoke of fearful things—of hell, of God's judgment, of the hopelessness of unrepentant sinners: "All you," he said, "that were never born again and made new creatures, are in the hands of an angry God . . ."

> . . . The bow of God's wrath is bent, and the arrow is made ready on the string, and justice bends the arrow at your heart, and strains the bow, and it is nothing but the mere pleasure of God, and that of an angry God, without any promise or obligation at all, that keeps the arrow one moment from being made drunk with your blood. Thus all you that never passed under a great change of heart, by the mighty power of the Spirit of God upon your souls; all you that were never born again and made new creatures, are in the hands of an angry God . . .
>
> The God that holds you over the pit of hell, much as one holds a spider or some loathsome insect over the fire, abhors you, and is dreadfully provoked; his wrath toward you burns like fire; he looks upon you as worthy of nothing else but to be cast into the fire. It is to be ascribed to nothing else that you did not go to hell the last night; that you was suffered to awake again in this world, after you closed your eyes to sleep. And there is no other reason to be given why you have not dropped into hell since you arose in the morning, but that God's hand has held you up.

The powerful words were well aimed. Many of those listening, struck with fear and remorse, with weeping and wailings, begged mercy from the terrible God whose "good pleasure" alone spared them from burning in hell. The effect was the same wherever the fiery

Jonathan Edwards

preacher, Jonathan Edwards, spoke. Since 1734, in surges of emotional enthusiasm, hundreds had chosen to renounce sin and the world and begin their long pilgrimage to heaven.

Jonathan Edwards was at the center of a great Protestant religious revival called the "Great Awakening." Since the mid 17th century, the character of New England Puritanism had undergone a slow but dramatic change. Puritans had grown lax in the practice of their religion. Striving for worldly advancement had weakened the steady, though dourly solemn, Puritan zeal for spiritual goods. Many Congregationalists had rejected the strict Calvinistic doctrines of predestination and absolute divine sovereignty and had embraced a new doctrine called "Arminianism" (named after a theologian named "Arminius"). According to Calvinist doctrines, no one could choose salvation; he had to wait on God, whose "good pleasure" and "sovereign will" alone ordained or predestined who should be saved and who damned. Arminians, on the contrary, held that man, endowed with a free will, could choose or reject salvation. Furthermore, Arminianism in New England was mutating into a new religion, Unitarianism, which denied the doctrine of the Trinity and the existence of original sin. Unitarianism emphasized man's natural goodness apart from God's grace.

Jonathan Edwards opposed both the moral laxity of his society and its backsliding from strict Calvinism. Born in 1703 in East Windsor, Connecticut, Edwards was the son of a Congregational minister and the maternal grandson of the Rev. Solomon Stoddard of Northampton, Massachusetts—a great preacher whose theology softened some of the harsher aspects of New England Puritanism. The young Edwards was a genius; at the age of ten he wrote a treatise, titled "Nature of the Soul," and at age 12 he composed another work, the "Habits of Spiders." Edwards entered Yale University in New Haven, Connecticut, at the age of 14 and graduated from there three years later.

Edwards could have gone far as a philosopher, but what he called his conversion at the age of 17 turned him in the direction of theology and the Congregationalist ministry. After studying theology in New Haven, he served a congregation in New York City, finally becoming in 1727 assistant minister for his grandfather's congregation in Northampton. At Northampton, Edwards was not known as a warm, pastoral minister. Except when there were emergencies among his congregation, he spent little time in ministering to them. His chief passion was theology, and he would spend about 14 hours a day in his study. A stout Calvinist, Edwards fought Arminianism with spoken word and pen.

Edwards called for conversion so eloquently and ardently that, from 1734 to 1735, hundreds chose to turn from sin to seek the kingdom of God. Edwards never promised his listeners an easy road to salvation. The Christian, he taught, was on a journey to heaven and so must not rest content with the pleasures of this world. The path of holiness requires extreme effort. "We should travel on in this way in a laborious manner," Edwards wrote in "The Christian Pilgrim." "Long journeys are attended with toil and fatigue, especially if through a wilderness."

By 1740, it seemed a wave of spiritual fire had descended upon the Connecticut River Valley. Edwards' "revival" meetings everywhere saw enthusiastic and emotional conversions. Edwards' 1736 work, *A Faithful Narrative of The Surprising Work of God in the Conversion of Many Hundred Souls in Northampton*, spread throughout America, England, and (translated) even into Germany and inspired others to follow Edwards' example. George Whitefield, a close associate of Methodist founder John Wesley, read the *Narrative* on a journey from Oxford to London and dedicated his life to revival preaching in both Great Britain and America.

The Great Awakening had several important effects on colonial life. For one, it revived Puritanism for a time, preserving it from decaying into a vague, this-worldly religion like Unitarianism, and gave rise to a distinctively American type of religious expression—the revival. It led to the establishment of three new universities: the College of New Jersey (Princeton), Dartmouth in New Hampshire, and Brown in Rhode Island. It fueled popular sentiment against the establishment of an Anglican bishop for the colonies. In the first half of the century, Anglican clergymen who belonged to the Church of England's Society for the Propagation of the Gospel and the Society for the Propagation of Christian Culture had been asking the royal government for a bishop for America. But with the spread of popular religion based on the notion that each individual achieved salvation through a personal relationship with God, more and more colonists became violently opposed to the idea of a bishop in America. They did not want a powerful state church directing their religious life.

The Great Awakening gave the common man a new interest in religion. Because many Congregationalist leaders in America criticized these revivals, congregations that embraced them seceded and formed "New Light" churches, which later became Baptist or Methodist. The new churches differed from the old, established Puritanism in that they emphasized personal religious experience and the ability of all men, not just learned theologians, to understand Scripture. The common man now saw himself as equal to the educated ministers of his church—and if he were equal to his superiors as regards religion, why not in other areas as well? Thus, the Great Awakening influenced the development of another strain of political thought in America, besides republicanism—democracy.

George Whitefield

Part II: **If This be Treason . . .**

Kindling the Flames of Rebellion

Only two years after the signing of the Peace of Paris, a young lawyer, Patrick Henry, addressed the Virginia House of Burgesses. "Caesar had his Brutus," Henry solemnly proclaimed as he concluded his speech, "Charles the First his Cromwell, and George the Third . . ."

"Treason!" cried the speaker of the house, interrupting Henry. Brutus had killed Caesar in the Roman Senate. Cromwell had overthrown Charles I and had him beheaded. And George III, King of Great Britain, Virginia, and all the American colonial empire—what was Henry saying of him? Others from the assembly floor took up the cry: "Treason! Treason!" But Henry finished his sentence, merely saying, ". . . may profit by their example." When the surprised hall had grown silent again, Patrick Henry cried out his defiance: "If THIS be treason, make the most of it!"

Patrick Henry

Patrick Henry had directed his speech against the Stamp Act, legislation appointed by Parliament in 1765. Henry condemned the act because it was the first internal tax ever placed on the colonies in their history. Until 1765, colonists had had to pay fees, or *duties*, on certain products brought into the American colonies. Henry and most colonists did not object to taxes on external trade, but the Stamp Act was different, for it was laid on internal commerce—transactions between people within the colonies. The Stamp Act placed tax fees on all legal documents, diplomas, licenses, newspapers, and other documents. The documents had to bear an official mark or stamp, for which the tax was paid.

Colonists such as Patrick Henry considered the stamp tax a violation of the constitutional liberties of Englishmen. In 1765, few went as far, even in thought, as Patrick Henry. Still, the Stamp Act had awakened a new sense of colonial dissatisfaction with the British government.

Prior to 1765, a working balance of imperial power and local control had been established between Britain and her colonies. Parliament controlled foreign affairs, issues involving war, and all trade between America, Britain, British dominions, and foreign countries. Colonial assemblies, like the Virginia House of Burgesses, for their part, controlled all internal affairs—the appointment of government officials and the payment of their salaries; the commissioning of military officers; the raising of troops; and the administration of schools, churches, and allotment of lands—as well as internal taxation. When Great Britain had intervened in colonial affairs, it had been only to protect minority groups against an encroaching majority and smaller colonies against larger ones.

During and after the French and Indian War, however, the British government began passing measures to bring colonial governments more into line with the wishes of king and Parliament. Prior to 1760, judges in colonial courts held their offices "during good behavior"—that is, colonial assemblies could remove judges if they thought them bad or incompetent or merely inconvenient. When George III came to the throne in 1760, however, he insisted that all colonial judges hold their offices "during the king's good pleasure"—that is, as long as the king desired that they hold it. Colonial leaders were incensed—for hadn't the Glorious Revolution of 1688 assured that, in England, judges would hold office only "during good behavior"? The colonists thought they were not being treated as full subjects of the British crown.

Another source of colonial dissatisfaction was the Archbishop of Canterbury, Thomas Secker's, suggestion that an Anglican bishop be appointed for America. Presbyterian and Congregationalist ministers, and radical political leaders like the Boston brewer, Samuel Adams, wrote pamphlets against what they saw as the establishment of a "state church," the Anglican Church, in America. Because of their protests, America received no bishop. (Later, loyalists to the king in America would say that the controversy over an American bishop was a major cause of the American Revolution.)

In 1763 the government of George III tried to strengthen the Acts of Trade and Navigation imposed by Parliament to regulate colonial trade. The government began by strengthening enforcement of the Sugar Act of 1733, which placed a heavy tax on sugar and molasses imported from the non-British West Indies. The new "Revenue Act" of 1764 lowered the duty on molasses and placed new duties on foreign sugar and some luxury items, including Madeira wine, a favorite of the colonial aristocracy. The tax on molasses hurt the New England rum manufacturers (rum is distilled from molasses); for, even though the tax was lower than it had been, the Revenue Act so stepped up trade enforcement that merchants could not evade paying the duties, as they had done in the past. Stricter enforcement of trade laws, moreover, put a crimp in all smuggling, a customary New England pursuit. According to the Revenue Act, customs officials could get a "writ of assistance"—legal permission—to search private premises for smuggled goods. Such writs, or search warrants, had always been granted for searches for specific items at specific locations; but the writs authorized by the Revenue Act gave customs officials unlimited access to a merchant's warehouse, ship,

A Proclamation for the Natives

A source of colonial discontent was a measure approved by Parliament to convince the Indians in British America "of our justice and determined resolution to remove all reasonable cause of discontent" they might feel with British rule. This measure was the Proclamation Line of 1763, which established four "distinct and separate governments" in the lands France and Spain had ceded to Britain at the end of the French and Indian War. Outside these "governments" (Quebec, East Florida, West Florida, and Grenada), all lands, west of the Appalachian Mountains were reserved ("as not being purchased by us") to the Indians "as their hunting grounds." Parliament decreed that "no private person do presume to make any purchase from the said Indians within the limits of our colonies." Any land purchases had to go through the British government, and the governor of the province in question had to issue a license before colonists could trade with the natives.

Parliament said it issued the law because "great frauds and abuses have been committed in purchasing lands of the Indians, to the great prejudice of our interests and to the great dissatisfaction of the said Indians." But this apparently humanitarian impulse did not please the colonists, who had long looked on America's natives as a threat to the existence of their settlements. Moreover, not only had colonists been settling the lands that lay beyond the Proclamation Line, but the wealthy among them had been speculating in western lands. The Proclamation Line thus threatened to cut off a lucrative source of income to the wealthy in the colonies. In a letter to a fellow land speculator, William Crawford, George Washington called the act of Parliament "a temporary expedient to quiet the Minds of the Indians [that] must fail of course in a few years especially when those Indians are consenting to our Occupying the Lands." To Washington, "any person who therefore neglects the present opportunity of hunting out good Lands and in some measure marking and distinguishing them for his own . . . will never regain it."

Indeed, speculators continued to encourage people to settle the western lands—which they did with little hindrance, because the British government did not grant sufficient funds to enforce the Parliament's act. British superintendents of the Indian reserve, though desirous of protecting the reserve, were often powerless to do so.

home—his whole property. Further, because local courts and juries (who sided with smugglers) had often thwarted customs officials, Parliament ruled that those accused of smuggling would be tried not in local courts but in an "admiralty court," located in faraway Halifax, Nova Scotia. This meant suspected smugglers would not be tried by a jury of their peers—thus denying them another right guaranteed to Englishmen. James Otis, a Boston lawyer, lost his job as the king's advocate general by arguing that the writs of assistance violated the English constitution. "An act against the Constitution is void," said Otis; "an act against natural equity is void." Otis' rhetoric inspired a young man named John Adams, who later called Otis "a flame of fire" and said of his protest that "the seeds of patriots and heroes were then and there sown."

One of the reasons the British government had begun to tighten up on the colonies was that it had incurred a large debt fighting the Seven Years War. Much of this debt arose from Britain's warring in Europe, but a respectable portion came from acquiring French Canada and Florida. Not all the colonies had contributed equally to the cost of a war that, Great Britain argued, was fought in their defense. If it had not been for British troops, the French and their savage Indian allies would have overrun the colonies—or so went the royal argument.

Thus, Parliament passed the Revenue Act to raise the needed money. Colonial response to the Revenue Act was swift. On October 18, 1764, the New York Assembly sent a peaceful protest to Parliament, arguing that freedom could not exist where a government could impose taxes

King George III in coronation robes, by Allan Ramsey

on a people without their consent. A movement began to boycott the newly taxed goods; students at Yale University in New Haven, Connecticut, it seems, initiated the boycott by refusing to buy and drink foreign liquor.

The passage of the Stamp Act in 1765, one year after the Revenue Act, showed that Parliament was not ready to heed protests from colonial assemblies. Not only Patrick Henry was upset; colonists from Halifax in Nova Scotia to the Bahaman island of Jamaica openly expressed their opposition. Even the Virginia House of Burgesses, which had shouted "treason" at Patrick Henry passed, on May 30, 1765, a set of "Resolves" or resolutions against the Stamp Act.

The burgesses' Resolves said Virginians possessed "all the liberties, privileges, franchises, and immunities, that have at any time been held, enjoyed, and possessed by the people of Great Britain." The Resolves claimed that the right to impose internal taxes belonged to the people of His Majesty's "most ancient and loyal Colony"; thus the only body that could impose such taxes on Virginians was the colonial assembly. Virginians, therefore, owed no obedience to "any law or ordinance whatever, designed to impose any taxation whatsoever upon them" other than what the colonial assembly approved. In an ominous final paragraph, the Resolves stated that anyone who maintains the contrary "shall be deemed an enemy to His Majesty's Colony."

Not all reaction to the Stamp Act was so formal or peaceful. In every colonial coastal town, middle class colonists organized themselves to take more direct action. Dressed as workmen and sailors, these "Sons of Liberty," as they were called, seized and destroyed stamp paper, forced its distributors to resign their jobs, and incited mobs to attack anyone deemed an enemy of "liberty." In New York City, a mob led by one Isaac Sears attacked the British fort at the Battery, broke into the governor's coach house, and seized and burned all the stamp paper found there. They next attacked the house of a British officer who had threatened to "cram the Stamp Act down their [the colonists'] throats." For all the officer's bragging, the mob gutted his house, burned his furniture, destroyed his garden, and drank all his liquor.

ADVERTISEMENT.

THE Members of the Affociation of the Sons of Liberty, are requefted to meet at the City-Hall, at one o'Clock, To-morrow, (being Friday) on Bufinefs of the utmoft Importance;—And every other Friend to the Liberties, and Trade of America, are hereby moft cordially invited, to meet at the fame Time and Place.   *The Committee of the Affociation.*

Thurfday, NEW-YORK, 16th December, 1773.

Broadside for a meeting of the Sons of Liberty

In the midst of all this upheaval, the Massachusetts assembly summoned the other colonies to send delegates to a meeting, a Stamp Act Congress, to be held in New York City. Nine colonies sent delegates, and in October 1765 the congress passed a series of resolutions that it sent to Parliament. While the resolutions admitted that the colonies owed "the same allegiance to the Crown of Great Britain that is owing from his subjects born within the realm, and all due subordination to that august body the Parliament of Great Britain," they insisted that the colonists were entitled to all the rights and liberties of native-born Englishmen. It was essential to such English liberties, the resolutions said, that no taxes be levied on the king's subjects without their consent; and, since the colonists "are not, and from their local circumstances cannot be, represented" in Parliament, only their own local assemblies could impose taxes on them. Against the extension of the Admiralty Courts, the congress insisted that "trial by jury is the inherent and invaluable right of every British subject in these colonies."

Seeing that it could not enforce the Stamp Act, Parliament finally backed down and repealed it in March 1766. When news reached the colonies, there was widespread celebration. Colonists saw that they could maintain their rights if they worked together. One matter they seemed to have missed, however: Parliament passed another act after repealing the Stamp Act. This was the Declaratory Act, and it stated that the king and Parliament of Great Britain could "bind the colonies in all cases whatsoever." In other words, the act said the colonists held their rights only at Parliament's pleasure. Though Parliament had repealed the Stamp Act, it had, in the Declaratory Act, reaffirmed its authority to impose such taxes, with or without the colonists' consent.

Townshend Acts and Rebellion

The Stamp Act was not enough to radicalize most American colonists. Most colonials remained loyal subjects of King George. What they wanted simply was to be recognized and treated as Englishmen, with all the rights that Englishmen possessed.

While even the radical colonists admitted that Parliament could regulate external matters such as colonial trade and relations with other countries, some, the most radical, went so far as to declare that Parliament had no authority to legislate for the colonies whatsoever. One of these most radical was Samuel Adams. Born in Boston of a middle class family, Adams had attended Harvard where he earned a master's degree. Though possessed of a university education, Adams was unsuccessful in business. He had failed both as a brewer and a tradesman; and for a time he was a very inefficient tax collector. Adams' real niche was political action. In 1765 he was elected to the Massachusetts legislature and became a prominent figure during the Stamp Act controversy.

Samuel Adams

With the repeal of the Stamp Act, it seemed that radicals like Sam Adams would quiet down. The popularity of George III was at a new high. But then, in August 1766, new leaders came to power in Parliament. One of these, Charles Townshend, became chancellor of the exchequer, which gave him the power of laying and removing taxes. Townshend was determined to tax the Americans, and he resolved to do it in such a way that no one could accuse Parliament of acting unconstitutionally. Townshend would levy external, not internal, taxes.

The "Townshend Acts," passed in June 1767, placed new duties on English manufactured items entering America—including tea imported by the British East India Company. The acts removed other taxes on colonial grain and whale oil entering England, and so encouraged colonial trade with the mother country. Bounties were placed on the production of colonial hemp, flax, and timber. Townshend strengthened the Acts of Trade and Navigation by improving customs inspection, reviving writs of assistance, and empowering the admiralty courts. The money from all this was to go to defense of the colonies and for the salaries of royal governors and judges.

The colonists could well balk at governors and judges receiving salaries from the British government (in the past, colonial legislatures themselves paid these salaries, which permitted them a certain influence over these officials); still, many were hard put to object to the Townshend Acts as a whole. Too many colonial writers had asserted that Parliament had constitutional control over external trade. And how could anyone object to customs officers simply enforcing the law? John Dickinson, a wealthy lawyer from Philadelphia, came up with an answer. In a series of newspaper articles he wrote in the guise of a simple farmer, Dickinson distinguished between Parliament regulating trade and Parliament levying taxes for the sake of raising revenue for the British government.

In one of his "Letters from a Farmer in Pennsylvania to the Inhabitants of the British Colonies," Dickinson wrote:

Parliament unquestionably possesses a legal authority to regulate the trade of Great Britain and all her colonies. Such an authority is necessary for the common good of all. Never did the British Parliament [until recently] think of imposing duties in America for the purpose of raising a revenue. This I call an innovation; and a most dangerous innovation . . . [for] if you ONCE admit that Great Britain may lay duties upon her exportations to us, for the purpose of levying money on us only, she will have nothing to do but to lay those duties on the articles which she prohibits us to manufacture—and the tragedy of American liberty is finished.

Like other colonial leaders, John Dickinson feared the renewal of the chaos and anarchy of the Stamp Act controversy. He urged that the "cause of liberty is a cause of too much dignity to be sullied by turbulence and tumult." Still, he called on the colonies to oppose firmly any parliamentary actions that would compromise their liberty.

Dickinson's calm and reasoned arguments were very influential, not only in the colonies, but in England, and even in France. Reasoned arguments alone, however, could not arouse the popular opposition necessary to the cause of colonial liberty. Sam Adams understood this. A student of the classics and an admirer of Roman virtue, Adams was a thoroughgoing republican who wrote numerous articles and tracts defending American liberty. He was also a clever politician and a true revolutionary who used pageantry, rather than argument, to inflame the masses. Gathering around the "Liberty Tree," a large elm in Boston, Adams and the Sons of Liberty threw patriotic parties and dances, complete with free rum, all funded by a wealthy, 31-year-old Boston merchant named John Hancock. From the branches of the Liberty Tree, the Sons, wearing "liberty caps" and singing liberty songs, hung effigies of their political opponents—the "enemies of liberty."

In February 1768, Adams and James Otis drafted a circular letter to the colonies that was given official sanction when it was adopted by the Massachusetts assembly. While affirming Parliament's "supreme legislative power over the whole empire," this letter, sent to every colonial legislature, denied that Parliament could take a man's property (that is, tax him) without his consent. The proper representatives of the colonists, said the letter, were their own legislatures, not Parliament. The letter noted that the Massachusetts legislature had sent "a humble, dutifull, & loyal Petition, to our most gracious Sovereign" and to "his Majesty's Ministers," seeking redress of Parliament's latest acts. Massachusetts, too, the letter pointed out, had asked the king whether a people could be free if crown-appointed judges were paid salaries by the crown without the people's consent.

Lord Hillsborough, the British secretary for the colonies, was outraged when he saw the letter. He ordered the Massachusetts assembly to rescind it; if it did not, he said, he would suspend the assembly. With a vote of 92 to 17, the Massachusetts assembly refused to rescind the letter, and Lord Hillsborough, true to his threat, suspended it. Not long after, a Boston mob attacked a crown customs official who had falsely accused John Hancock of smuggling in Madeira wine. To keep order, two regiments of British troops from Halifax occupied Boston.

These British measures gave Sam Adams and other radicals the opportunity they were looking for. At a Boston town meeting they called on Massachusetts to elect delegates to a convention. Adams himself passed through the streets of Boston, urging citizens to arm themselves against the British army. These revolutionary acts boded ill for peace. But when the convention did gather, it realized the futility of resisting the British, and no further resistance was urged.

Events in other colonies, however, injected life into the resistance movement. Not only Massachusetts had its assembly suppressed. In 1766, when two regiments of British had arrived in New York, an act of Parliament, the Quartering Act, required the New York legislature to provide lodging and supplies, including beer and rum, for the troops. When the legislature voted to provide the lodging and all the supplies, but not the beer and rum, Lord

Hillsborough suspended it. Unlike Boston, though, New York gave in. A year later, in 1769, New Yorkers elected an assembly more friendly to the British.

Unable to move Parliament on constitutional grounds, the colonies hit upon another plan. Merchants entered into voluntary agreements to boycott all British and British West Indian goods. Instead of buying English broadcloth, students, professionals, and others began wearing homespun. Instead of drinking English tea, colonists drank smuggled Dutch East India tea or tea made from local herbs, such as raspberry leaf. This Non-Importation Movement united colonists from New England to Georgia; yet, because too few merchants and colonists participated, it had no serious effect on British trade.

A cartoon by Benjamin Franklin, first published in 1754, that became a popular symbol for colonial united action in the years before and during the American Revolution

Relief from the Townshend Acts came at last from the king himself. Parliament was hard to control, and George III wanted to master it. In 1770, the king chose Frederick Lord North as his new prime minister, and on March 5 of that year, North repealed all the Townshend Acts (which were not bringing in the promised revenues anyway), except for one. He kept the tax on tea to show that Parliament still claimed the absolute right to "bind the colonies in all cases whatsoever."

The Calm Before the Storm

With the repeal of the Townshend Acts, colonial merchant societies lifted the boycott on British goods. Everywhere in the colonies, except for Boston, where merchants continued non-importation and riots troubled the peace, folks settled into a calm. The years 1770 to 1773 were prosperous for the colonies, and people were happy. Even colonial leaders who had been most outspoken against Parliament—John Adams, John Hancock, and Benjamin Franklin—counseled peace. Others, however, were worried. Thomas Jefferson said of his own colony of Virginia that the people had "seemed to fall into a state of insensibility to our situation;" after all, Jefferson noted, Parliament still claimed the right to legislate for the colonies "in all cases whatsoever." Sam Adams expressed unease for another reason—while the colonists basked in the warmth of their new-found prosperity, crown-appointed colonial governors and judges were still being placed on the royal payroll.

Sam Adams did not stint his efforts to arouse his countrymen. Ever since British troops had entered Boston, the Sons of Liberty had spread stories, some imaginary, of outrages British soldiers had perpetrated against Boston citizens. Such stories led lower-class

Tar and Feathers

Beginning in the 1760s, tarring and feathering became a common way for patriots in America to punish British loyalists. It was painful and humiliating, though rarely fatal. Typically, a mob stripped their victim of his coat and shirt, poured boiling hot tar on the bare skin, and then dumped feathers over him. So fledged, the victim was made an object of ridicule—often he was placed astraddle a wooden rail and carried in a mock procession through the streets of a town.

"Tarring and Feathering, the Patriot's Revenge," by James Gillray

Bostonians to insult the "lobster backs," as they called the red-clad soldiers, and even to assault them when they found them alone. Mobs threatened to tar and feather Bostonian citizens who befriended the soldiers.

On the evening of March 5, 1770, a mob began pelting with snowballs a soldier on sentry duty in front of the customs house on King Street (now State Street). The soldier had, shortly before, attacked a boy who had taunted him. Soon the main guard, about 20 soldiers, was called out and confronted the crowd (now grown to several hundred boys and men) with bayonets fixed. For about a half hour the soldiers merely stood there, pelted with snow and stones. Finally one soldier, hit by a club, fired against orders into the crowd. Soon other soldiers fired. When all was ended, three Bostonian men lay dead, and two others were mortally wounded.

Sam Adams and the Sons of Liberty exploited this riot for all it was worth. Calling it the "Boston Massacre," they decried it as typical of British tyranny. Thereafter, every year on March 5, the Sons led a procession in remembrance of it. The silversmith Paul Revere produced a very inaccurate engraving of the "massacre," showing British forces firing on a small group of passive, respectable Boston citizens.

Adams and the liberty boys now turned their fire on the new governor, Thomas Hutchinson. A native New Englander, Hutchinson was anything but a tyrant. Intent on preserving the liberties of the colonists, he was opposed to harsh parliamentary measures against them. Moreover, he and Benjamin Franklin had drawn up the Albany Plan of Union for the colonies in 1754. Adams engaged Hutchinson in a debate published in a series of newspaper articles. They debated constitutional questions, and Adams finally forced the governor to admit that he believed that the colonies enjoyed no freedoms except what Parliament granted them.

Then the news broke that the judges of the Massachusetts superior court were on the royal payroll. A Boston town meeting, called by Sam Adams, sent a message to Hutchinson asking him if this indeed were true? When the governor refused to answer, the meeting decided to put into effect a plan Adams had devised. They called for citizens to set up "committees of correspondence" in all Massachusetts towns. These committees would be essentially centers of revolutionary activity. Each committee would be in contact with every other so that all could act in unison over a wide area.

In June 1772 another event fed the fires of discontent in the colonies. A revenue cutter (a customs ship), the *Gaspee*, that had been successfully capturing smugglers in the Narragansett Bay, ran aground on a sandbar while chasing a smuggler craft. A group of patriots boarded the ship, beat up the crew and captain, and burned their vessel. To attack a naval ship was a serious crime in British law, and the government searched eagerly for the culprits and threatened to send them to England to stand trial.

The Boston Massacre, engraving by Paul Revere

Those who attacked the *Gaspee* were never apprehended, but the simple threat to send any colonial to England for trial aroused colonists into a fury of indignation. It was a violation of the English right to trial by jury! In response to this affront, the Virginia burgesses voted to set up a committee of correspondence for their colony and appointed Patrick Henry, Thomas Jefferson, and Richard Henry Lee as its members. And Virginia was not alone. By early 1774, 12 colonial assemblies had established committees of correspondence of their own.

Tea in Boston Harbor

Still, despite the Boston Massacre and the Gaspee Affair, the American colonists were not ready to bring matters with Great Britain to a crisis. Even in radical Boston, patriots dropped non-importation, and mob violence ended—frustrating radicals like Sam Adams. Despite all the radical propaganda, despite all the agitation, relations between America and the mother country had not essentially changed. Adams needed an issue that would spur his countrymen to act and around which he could unite their varied interests.

This issue came in the spring of 1773. In May, Parliament passed a law that allowed the British East India Company to sell its tea directly to the colonies, without it having to

An idealized view of Boston and its harbor, by Franz Xaver Haberman, ca 1770s

pass through middlemen in England. With this concession, the East India Company tea, even with the Townshend tax, could undersell even smuggled tea in the colonies. Worse yet, the East India Company was to sell its tea only to merchants (like Governor Hutchinson's sons) who had no ties to the Sons of Liberty.

Colonial agitators took up the tea issue with zeal. They accused the government of establishing an illegal monopoly on tea. When the ships bringing the tea arrived outside Philadelphia and New York, they were turned back before they entered the harbor. In Boston, however, the most radical of the port cities, the governor allowed the tea ship into harbor—with disastrous consequences.

Sam Adams called a convention that met at the Old South Meeting House. The convention sent a message to Governor Hutchinson, demanding that he force the tea ship to leave the harbor. To do so, of course, would be illegal, as Adams and the convention well knew—once a ship was granted harbor, it could not be turned out again to sea. But Hutchinson did not simply refuse the convention's request, he blocked the harbor so the ship could not leave even if it chose to. When the convention received the governor's expected refusal, Adams proclaimed, "This meeting can do nothing further to save the country."

No sooner had Adams uttered these words than a band of men dressed as Mohawks, screaming war whoops, dashed past the windows of the meeting house and ran to the wharf. There they joined with other bands of white men dressed as Indians and paint-darkened as blacks, numbering together about 150, and rowed out to the tea ship. In three hours time they emptied 342 large chests of tea into Boston Harbor and then withdrew quickly.

"This is the most magnificent moment of all," wrote Sam Adams' cousin, John Adams, of this "Boston Tea Party." "There is a Dignity, a Majesty, a Sublimity in this last Effort of the patriots, that I greatly admire. The People should never rise, without doing something notable and striking. This Destruction of the Tea is so bold, so daring, so firm, so intrepid and inflexible, and it must have so important Consequences, and so lasting, that I can't but consider it as an Epocha in history."

The Boston Tea Party did have important consequences. For Parliament, it was the last straw, the final indignity. No longer would it allow the colonies to insult its authority. New, more stringent measures would have to be adopted to deal with those American upstarts. Boston, and all America, would have to be taught a lesson they would never forget.

Chapter 8 Review

Summary

- In the 18th century the British colonies in America experienced a population explosion. As a result of this population explosion and the expansion of new territory, the social classes began to merge and society began to tear apart at the seams.

- New ideas began to tear society apart. Liberalism and republicanism took root in America. Liberalism made men think that natural, not divine, laws should govern and direct human societies and that individual liberty was the highest ideal of social life. Republicanism made them doubt that anyone had a divine right to political power.

- Beginning in 1734, Jonathan Edwards' preaching inspired the "Great Awakening." This Great

Awakening revived Puritanism and made it into a distinctively American expression of religion. The personal character of the Great Awakening fueled popular sentiment against the establishment of an Anglican bishop for the colonies. The common man saw himself as equal to the educated ministers of the church, which gave rise to another strain of political thought—democracy.

- In 1763 the government of George III tried to strengthen the Acts of Trade and Navigation passed by Parliament to regulate colonial trade.

- Parliament passed the Stamp Act in 1765, and Patrick Henry gave his famous speech against it. The Stamp Act inspired unrest in the colonies.

Chapter 8 Review (continued)

- The passage of the Stamp Act in 1765 caused the Virginia House of Burgesses to pass a set of "Resolves" against the Stamp Act, saying that the colonies possessed all the liberties and privileges possessed by the people of Great Britain. The "Sons of Liberty" formed to protest the Stamp Act and incited mobs against "enemies of liberty."

- Parliament repealed the Stamp Act in 1766 but approved the Declaratory Act, stating that the king and Parliament of Great Britain could "bind the colonies in all cases whatsoever."

- In 1767, Charles Townshend levied external, not internal, taxes, on the colonies, placing new duties on English manufactured items entering America. The colonists did not balk at this, but John Dickinson saw through Townshend's scheme and pointed out that there was a distinction between Parliament regulating trade and Parliament levying taxes to raise revenue for the British government. External taxes for the sake of raising revenue, Dickinson said, compromised the colonies' liberty.

- The colonies entered into the Non-Importation Movement, which boycotted all British and West Indian goods. In 1770, however, the king chose Frederick, Lord North, as his prime minister, and North repealed all the Townshend Acts, but kept a tax on tea.

- The Boston Massacre took place on March 5, 1770. This, along with other events, turned public opinion against the British.

- In 1773 Parliament passed a law that allowed the British East India Company to sell its tea directly to the colonies, creating what the colonists thought was an illegal monopoly on tea. In Boston, a tea ship entered the harbor, and when Governor Hutchinson refused to turn it away, a band of men dressed as Mohawk Indians boarded the ship and emptied the tea overboard.

Key Concepts

hierarchy: a social arrangement in which members of society are designated above and below in the order of rank, honor, power, or authority

paternalism: the practice of treating people in a fatherly manner, especially in regard to their material welfare

interdependence: a relationship in which each member of a society is dependent on another

gentleman: a word derived from the Latin word for "family" or "clan"; a man of a prominent family

Liberalism: a political and social philosophy that emphasizes the freedom of individuals to follow their own desires in their social, religious, and economic life

republicanism: a political ideology that holds that government derives from the authority of the people and is merely the representative and voice of the people, established by the people so they can enjoy security in the free possession of their rights.

Great Awakening: a Protestant revival in colonial America that sparked new interest in religion

Dates to Remember

1734: Jonathan Edwards' preaching inspires the Great Awakening.

1760: the British government tries to strengthen the Acts of Trade and Navigation.

1765: Parliament passes the Stamp Act, and the Virginia House of Burgesses approves a set of Resolves.

1766: Parliament repeals the Stamp Act and passes the Declaratory Act.

1767: Parliament approves the Townshend Acts.

1769: Daniel Boone opens up the Wilderness Road, which became the major route for emigrants heading west.

1770: Frederick Lord North becomes prime minister and repeals the Townshend Acts, but keeps the tax on tea.

1770: The Boston Massacre

1773: Sons of Liberty dump tea into Boston Harbor.

Central Characters

Jonathan Edwards (1703–1758): American theologian and philosopher who stimulated the religious revival known as the "Great Awakening

Patrick Henry (1736–1799): brilliant orator, member of the Virginia House of Burgesses, and a major figure of the American Revolution

Chapter 8 Review (continued)

Samuel Adams (1722–1803): politician of the American Revolution and leader of the Massachusetts "radicals"

John Dickinson (1732–1808): colonial writer who turned the colonists against the Townshend Acts

Questions for Review

1. How did the population expansion of the 18th century contribute to the disintegration of society in colonial America?

2. Describe the three elements of English society (hierarchy, paternalism, and interdependence) and why they did not fully take root in colonial America.

3. How did Daniel Boone's explorations contribute to the disintegration of society in colonial America?

4. What effects did increased trade with England have on society in America?

5. Explain what Liberalism is and how it led to the formation of revolutionary ideas in America.

6. Explain what republicanism is and how it led to formation of revolutionary ideas in America.

7. Compare republicanism with the Catholic medieval view of government.

8. What are the three most important rights that Locke argues for? How do they form the basis of Liberalism?

9. What effects did the Great Awakening have on colonial life and revolutionary ideas?

10. List each of the acts passed by Parliament. Why did these acts incite rebellion in the colonies?

11. How did the colonists think they should be treated by the British government?

Ideas in Action

1. Read St. Thomas Aquinas' treatise, *On Kingship* and compare his views on government with those of the colonial Americans.

2. Read some accounts, fictional and non-fictional, of the Boston Tea Party. Do you think this was a just and proper reaction to Parliament's actions? Why or why not?

3. Read Patrick Henry's most famous speeches. Do these speeches betray the influence of Liberalism and republicanism? Be able to cites specific passages.

Highways and Byways

Tea Time

Tea leaves are grown mostly in the Orient, and tea is classified by region of origin: China, Ceylon, Darjeeling, to name a few. The tea leaves are harvested by hand and then processed so that they can be used as a beverage. The leaves are manufactured in three categories: fermented (black), unfermented (green), and semifermented (oolong). The processing procedure involves four steps. First, the leaves are withered, then rolled, then fermented, and finally dried. The purpose of this procedure is to allow the leaves to dry properly and to allow the chemicals in the leaves to produce the quality peculiar to each type.

We generally associate tea with England and China. Legend says that tea has been known in China since 2700 B.C. At first it was a medicinal drink, but by the 3rd century A.D. it had become a daily drink. In 1610 the Dutch East India Company brought tea to Europe. The beverage was introduced into England by the Portuguese wife of Charles II, who made it a court favorite. In 1706, Thomas Twinings was one of the first to introduce tea drinking to the English. Over the years his business grew until he was selling not only to all of the United Kingdom, but to the American states as well. Twinings tea company still sells tea today.

THE AMERICAN REVOLUTION

"The town of Boston ought to be knocked about their ears and destroyed. *Delenda est Carthago*" So exclaimed one Van, a member of the British parliament, who with other members of Parliament, was debating what to do about the dumping of tea into Boston Harbor, the latest insult to Parliament's authority. Most agreed with Van that the Bostonians needed to be punished, though there were those who believed that punishing the colonies would only make matters worse. One of these latter was Edmund Burke. Burke believed that reconciliation would only come by returning to the way things were between the colonies and the crown before the Stamp Act:

> Revert to your old principles. Leave America, if she has taxable matter, to tax herself. I am not here going into a distinction of rights, nor attempting to mark their boundaries. I do not enter into these metaphysical distinctions. I hate the very sound of them. Leave the Americans as they anciently stood, and these distinctions, born of our unhappy contest, will die along with it.

William Pitt, the Earl of Chatham, who had directed the British to victory during the French and Indian War, urged caution in dealing with America. But being a faithful subject of King George, Chatham opposed American independence. "If I could once persuade myself that they entertain the most distant intention of throwing off the legislative supremacy and great constitutional superintending power and control of the British Legislature," he wrote, "I should myself be the very first person to enforce that power by every exertion this country is capable of making."

Cartoon of Boston Port Act: "Bostonians in Distress"

Parliament Gets Tough

Yet, it was this British legislature that would push matters to the point where independence would seem the only alternative to many American colonists. In March of 1774, Parliament passed the "Coercive Acts," aimed at punishing Boston. The first of these acts, the Boston Port Act, ordered the closing of the port of Boston until the city paid for the dumped tea and

151

for the property of royal officials destroyed by mobs. Even if Boston fulfilled these conditions, said Parliament, the port would remain closed until the king was satisfied that peace and due obedience to the laws were reestablished. To enforce this act, the British fleet would blockade Boston while regulars of the British army occupied the city. Later, after entering Boston, when the British army had to sleep, for lack of accommodations, outside on the commons, Parliament passed the Quartering Act, which required Boston citizens to house and board soldiers and officers.

The Boston Port Act, which was to go into effect on June 1, 1774, proved a great blow to the port city, whose economy depended on trade and fishing. Yet while this first of the Coercive Acts struck at the city alone, the third, the Massachusetts Government and Administration of Justice Act, enraged the countryside; it revoked part of the Massachusetts Bay charter that provided for the popular election (albeit subject to the governor's veto) of members of the colonial council. Instead, the act mandated that all councilors, as well as all inferior court judges, marshals, justices of the peace, and sheriffs were to be appointed by the governor.

Reaction to the Coercive Acts was bitter and violent. If Parliament had passed the Port Act alone, it could possibly have isolated Boston; but with the Massachusetts Government Act, the city's seething discontent seeped into the countryside. Colonists outside the Bay Colony joined in their countrymen's outrage. Meeting at Faneuil Hall, Bostonians drafted a message to the other colonies, calling upon them to join Massachusetts in a "Solemn League and Covenant neither to export to Great Britain, nor to import goods from there." Messages of support began flowing in from other colonial centers, such as Newport, Rhode Island, and Farmington, Connecticut. Farmington citizens erected a pole in honor of "the immortal goddess of Liberty." The town of Brooklyn, Connecticut, told Boston that, though the people of Brooklyn were few and unimportant, they were "ready to march in the van and to sprinkle the American altars with our hearts blood, if the occasion should be."

Outside New England, from New York to South Carolina, colonial leaders called for solidarity with Boston, though many had their doubts about signing on to the Solemn League and Covenant. In Virginia, George Washington wrote that the colonies should stand with Boston so as "not to suffer ourselves to be sacrificed by piece meals." On May 24, 1774, the Virginia House of Burgesses adopted a resolve, drafted by Patrick Henry, Richard Henry Lee, George Mason, and Thomas Jefferson, denouncing the "hostile invasion" of Boston by British regulars and designating June 1 as a day of fasting, humiliation, and prayer.

When Governor Dunmore of Virginia heard of the Burgesses' resolve, he dissolved the assembly. Undaunted, the burgesses reconvened at the Raleigh tavern in Williamsburg and adopted a further resolve; that "an attack made on one of our sister colonies to compel submission to arbitrary taxes, is an attack made on all British America." The burgesses then instructed the Virginia committee of correspondence to contact other colonial committees with a view to summoning a congress of the colonies.

A committee of correspondence in New York had already proposed just such a measure. Unlike New England, however, New York had a large loyalist faction that opposed all drastic measures. Though the New York committee had been dominated by "patriots" (as the more radical called themselves), an equal number of "Tories" (as the patriots named the loyalists) joined the committee and steered it in a more conservative direction. The Tories favored a continental-wide congress, for such a congress would be sufficiently removed from the popular pressures that compelled lawmakers in the colonies to adopt radical measures. With New York and Virginia in favor of such a congress, other colonies soon followed suit. This "Continental Congress," as it was called, was set to convene on September 5, 1774.

Discontent Grows

Despite their dispute with Parliament, the citizens of Boston greeted the British General, Thomas Gage's, entrance into their city with festivity. Flags flew and bells pealed to welcome the new governor and commanding general. If anyone were to head the occupation, the

Bostonians knew, Gage was the best of the lot. Married to a New Jersey woman, Gage was known and liked by the colonists. Even so, after the festivities had ended, Bostonians proffered little help to Gage.

Though governor of all Massachusetts, Gage could really only control Boston. Outside the city, people were sullen and rebellious; they threatened and sometimes assaulted the new judges and officials Gage sent out to them. In Worcester, the citizens assembled on the common and asked the Gage-appointed Judge Timothy Paine to resign, and he complied. When Gage heard this, he considered sending troops to Worcester; but, receiving reports that 20,000 armed Connecticut militia were marching to the town, Gage changed his mind.

So, the citizens of Massachusetts continued to hinder the sitting of courts and the establishment of any royal government outside of Boston. Instead, committees of correspondence met in court houses and assumed governmental powers. In October 1774, an illegal colonial assembly under the presidency of John Hancock met at Concord. Acting as an independent government, the assembly sent out "committees of safety" to collect arms and munitions; and though the convention was not a representative assembly, it levied taxes and trained a state militia composed of farmers and tradesmen. These militiamen came to be called "minutemen" because they could gather quickly on notice of a British attack.

In late June of 1774, Parliament passed another law that inspired dismay and anger in the colonies. This intolerable law was the Quebec Act which, among other shocking provisions, guaranteed to the French in Quebec the freedom to practice the Catholic Faith. It also allowed the French to govern Quebec according to French, not British, laws. A final provision extended the southern border of Quebec to the Ohio River, thus permanently cutting off colonial settlers and land speculators of the 13 seaboard colonies from the rich lands west of the Appalachian and Allegheny Mountains.

British colonists greeted the Quebec Act with a storm of protest. One writer fulminated: "We may live to see our churches converted into mass houses, and land plundred of tythes for the support of Papist clergy." One Bostonian complained that "a superstitious, bigoted Canadian Papist, though ever so profligate, is now esteemed a better subject to our Gracious Sovereign George the Third, than a liberal, enlightened New England Dissenter, though ever so vir-

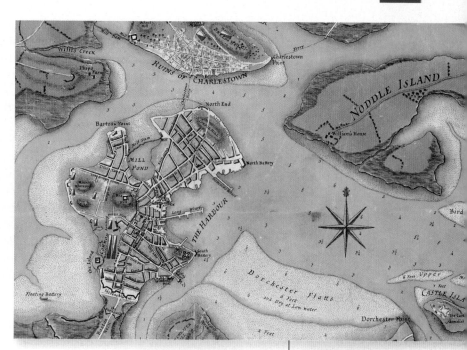

A plan of the town and port of Boston and its environs, with the lines, batteries, and encampments of the British and American armies in 1776

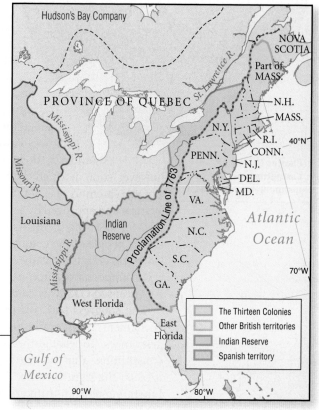

Colonial possessions after the French and Indian War, showing boundaries established by the Proclamation Line of 1763 and the Quebec Act

tuous." Alexander Hamilton of New York worried that the Quebec Act would leave the colonists surrounded by "a Nation of Papists and Slaves." Many were horrified that a good Protestant like George III would permit the Catholic Church to exist in any of his domains. Sam Adams and other Sons of Liberty spread rumors that King George was secretly toying with becoming a detestable papist himself. A Catholic George III, they said, would become as dangerous as the Catholic James II, whom the Glorious Revolution of 1688 had driven from England.

First Continental Congress

As planned, representatives of the various colonies from Massachusetts to South Carolina gathered in Philadelphia on September 5, 1774 to discuss what steps the colonies, acting together, should take in the face of the Coercive and Quebec acts. This "Continental Congress" was a significant meeting, since it was only the second time in their history that the various colonies attempted to act as one. The delegates had to forge a common mind and intent among colonies who had very different histories and customs and were used to looking out for their own interests alone.

The 55 delegates included men who would rise to leadership among the united colonies in the coming contest with Parliament. To Philadelphia came John Jay of New York; Peyton Randolph (elected president of the congress) and Patrick Henry of Virginia; the "two Adamses," John and Sam, from Massachusetts; and Joseph Galloway of Pennsylvania.

Joseph Galloway was one of many loyalists in Philadelphia; yet, he believed that the colonies had genuine grievances against Parliament. He presented a plan to the congress that would give the colonies more autonomy in government while keeping them in the British empire. Galloway suggested the establishment of an American parliament, called the "Grand Council." The British parliament could not pass laws and levy taxes on the colonies without the consent of the Grand Council, whose members would be elected every three years by representatives of the people of the colonies.

Opposing Galloway were those more radical delegates who pushed for a non-importation, non-exportation agreement in solidarity with Boston. These warned that if Congress simply adopted the Galloway plan, Boston would be left to the mercy of the British. The Galloway camp responded that Boston had caused her own problems and should pay the fee for the spilt tea and be done with it. News out of Massachusetts,

Charles Carroll of Carrollton, painting by Joshua Reynolds, 1763

however, soon defeated the hopes of the Galloways and furthered the cause of the radicals.

On September 9, 1774, Congress first heard of the Suffolk Resolves. Drafted by Joseph Warren and approved by several Massachusetts towns, the resolves condemned the Coercive Acts for violating the British constitution, proclaimed Massachusetts a free state, and called on the people of the colony to take up arms if Parliament did not repeal the Coercive Acts. Congress enthusiastically endorsed the Suffolk Resolves and voted to recommend imposing a non-importation, non-exportation agreement, called the "Association," on the colonies. An incensed Galloway called the endorsement "a declaration of war against Great Britain."

The congress had convened to seek redress for colonial grievances against the British parliament; but it could not quite decide upon what reasons it would found the colonies' grievances. To what authority should congress appeal? Should it merely invoke the British constitution, that unwritten body of laws, susceptible to many interpretations? Should it plead the rights granted by colonial charters? Or should it base its arguments on what Liberal republican thinkers called "natural law"?

In the end, the congress appealed to all three authorities. In a *Declaration and Resolves* adopted by the delegates on October 14, 1774, the congress argued that "the inhabitants of the English Colonies in North America" hold their rights "by the immutable laws of nature, the principles of the English constitution, and the several charters or compacts." The first of the rights Congress couched in the language of the social contract: English colonists, says the *Declaration and Resolves*, "are entitled to life, liberty, and property, and they have never ceded to any sovereign power whatever, a right to dispose of either without their consent." The declaration called upon the British constitution and the colonial charters, when it argued that Americans are guaranteed all the constitutional rights of Englishmen, especially since they "by no means forfeited, surrendered, or lost any of those rights" by their emigration to America.

The declaration was directed not only against the Coercive Acts; it excoriated the appointment of judges by governors, the extension of the jurisdiction of the admiralty courts, the abridgment of the right to trial by jury, and the maintenance of a standing army in the colonies during peacetime. The declaration objected to the "establishing of the Roman Catholick Religion in the province of Quebec, abolishing the equitable system of English laws, and erecting a tyranny there, to the great danger, from so great a dissimilarity of Religion, law, and government, of the neighboring British colonies."

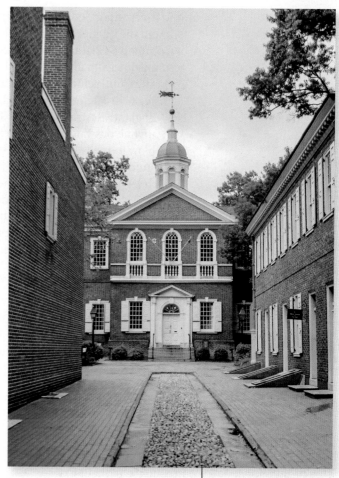

Carpenter's Hall, Philadelphia, where the First Continental Congress gathered

Six days after it adopted the *Declaration and Resolves*, the congress formally approved the Association, calling not only for non-importation and non-exportation, but for a non-consumption of British goods. Unless Parliament repealed the Coercive Acts and met all colonial demands, the united colonies were resolved to block all imports from Great Britain beginning December 1, 1774. If, after another year, by September 10, 1775, Parliament still did not see the light, the colonies would freeze all exports to Great Britain.

On October 26, 1774, delegates to the First Continental Congress, their business completed, returned to their homes.

Parliament Responds

On January 20, 1775, the Earl of Chatham addressed the House of Lords. "What is our right to persist in such cruel and vindictive measures against that loyal and respectable people?" he said, speaking of the Americans. Chatham praised the Americans for their "unexampled patience" and "unparalleled wisdom," though they had been "abused and traduced by Parliament." Another lord, the Duke of Richmond, warned his peers, "You may spread fire, sword and desolation, but that will not be government. No people can ever be made to submit to a form of government they say they will not receive."

America thus had her friends in both the House of Lords and the House of Commons; nevertheless, the majority in both houses favored stern measures against the colonists. King George III, too, was for standing tough. When it was suggested that a royal commission go to America to investigate colonial grievances, the king told Lord North he would have none of it, for it would look as if he feared the American congress. In all their votes, Parliament followed the king. A bill to repeal the Coercive Acts failed by a vote of 82 to 197. In the House of Commons, Chatham introduced a bill that would have made the Continental Congress a permanent legal body and repealed all the troublesome acts. But this bill, which would have given the Continental Congress all it had asked for, went down in defeat.

Instead, in late March 1775, Lord North's Parliament passed another coercive bill, the New England Restraining Act. This act forbade the New England colonies from trading with anyone but England and Ireland; even Scotland was off limits. The act struck a crippling blow to the New England fishing industry by closing off the banks of Nova Scotia and Newfoundland to New England fishermen.

Such legislation further chipped away at whatever loyalty many American colonists still felt for King and Parliament. Indeed, most Americans had not wanted rebellion, much less independence. Even the most radical leaders (with the exception of some like Sam Adams) still hoped for reconciliation between the colonies and the mother country. But reconciliation seemed more and more remote as each side hardened its position.

Enforcement of the Association

Not all colonists were in favor of the measures taken by the Continental Congress. Throughout 1774 and 1775, and even long into the war that followed, only about a third of the colonists strongly supported the more radical partisans of American rights. Among the reluctant, some who initially believed the colonies had genuine grievances, later so strongly opposed the actions of the Continental Congress that they threw in their lot with Britain and King George. Loyalists made up from 20 to 30 percent of the population. Most other colonists, however, were neither loyalist nor strongly patriot, but indifferent. Circumstances might push them one way or the other—say, later, if British forces abused their persons or property, or if overzealous Sons of Liberty threatened them with tar and feathering.

Enforcing the Association for non-importation, therefore, became a matter of some concern to the Continental Congress. Not only was most of the population indifferent or opposed, but the congress itself had a very doubtful legal status. To enforce compliance with the Association, Congress authorized local Committees of Safety to investigate the conduct of citizens suspected of being unsympathetic with its aims. These committees were to administer a "pledge" to honor non-importation; any who refused to take the pledge could be held up to public scorn, threatened with the loss of livelihood or property (or worse consequences) and ostracized from society. The Committees of Safety, of course, were seen to have even less legal authority than the Continental Congress. Neither the committees nor Congress could claim that they derived their powers from the consent of the people as a whole, or even from the majority of the people. In each town the committees were usually composed of self-appointed Sons of Liberty.

Committees used various means to ferret out suspected Tories. They investigated private papers; they spied on their neighbors; they used informers. If one were a loyalist or simply just unsure where he stood, he didn't

The Plight of the Fencesitters

Janet Schaw, a Scotswoman visiting the plantation of the loyalist John Rutherford in Wilmington, North Carolina, in July 1775, described the plight of the uncommitted colonists drawn into a conflict they did not choose. She wrote:

The inclination of this country is however far from being generally for this work [of resistance]. Indolent and inactive, they have no desire to move, even where their own immediate interest calls them. All they are promised is too distant to interest them; they suffer none of those abuses they are told of and feel their liberty invaded only by the oppressive power of the Congress and their Agents, who at this Season are pressing them from their harvest, for they know not what purpose. The Alternative is proposed: Agree to join us, and your persons and properties are safe; you have a shilling sterling a day; your duty is not more than once a month appearing under Arms at Wilmingtown, which will prove only a merry-making, where you will have as much grog a you can drink. But if you refuse, we are directly to cut up your corn, shoot your pigs, burn your houses, seize your Negroes and perhaps tar and feather yourself.

know if and when his neighbors might inform on him to the committee—even for actions as simple as serving British tea to wayfarers in an inn.

The committees punished intransigent Tories in a variety of ways. William Davis of Augusta, Maine, was merely ordered to run about a Liberty Tree three times and publicly denounced as an enemy to the "rights and liberties of America." Others less fortunate were tarred and feathered, or worse.

"The cruelties which are exercised on all those who are in [the rebels'] power is shocking," wrote Ann Hulton, a loyalist from Chester, Massachusetts. "By advice from Kennebec the Committee there had sentenced a Man to be buried alive for wishing success to the King's Troops, and that the sentence had been executed upon him."

Such was the price of loyalty in revolutionary America.

First Blood

British General Gage knew something more was expected of him than simply sitting in Boston and maintaining the blockade. Decisive action was needed to regain control of the Massachusetts country-side. Sentiment amongst the colonists was swinging away from the rebels and toward the old, established ways—and peace. Gage could sense the impatience of the Boston loyalists; a resounding British victory could definitively turn the tide of public sentiment towards the British government, he thought.

Just such an opportunity for action came in the early spring of 1775. Gage's spies informed him that the rebels had cached arms and ammunition at both Worcester and Concord. Worcester was some 50 miles west of Boston, while Concord was only a scant 20. Also, the Massachusetts provincial congress was meeting near Concord. If Gage could get an operation against Concord underway secretly, he not only could seize some valuable munitions but capture some important rebel leaders as well.

In those days, Boston was almost an island, con-nected to the mainland on the west by only a small causeway, or neck, of land. Gage's plan was to divide his force, sending one group on the longer land route across the Boston neck, through Cambridge, and then west, by way of Lexington to Concord. The other would assemble on the Boston common and then by longboat cross the bay to East Charlestown. From Charlestown the British contingent would pursue the same route to Concord. General Gage planned to send 1,800 soldiers, over half of his effective force in Boston.

General Thomas Gage, by John Singleton Copley

Though he tried, Gage could not keep his plans a secret. Boston was full of rebel spies, who noted the preparations. By April 16, 1775, rebels in Concord had been warned to hide their armaments. Dr. Joseph Warren, the rebel chief of staff in Boston, made plans to watch British moves and prepared couriers to warn the countryside once the royal troops began to move. Other rebels arranged signals to warn their friends in Cambridge, across the bay: they would hang two lanterns in Christ Church tower if the "redcoats" were coming by sea; one, if they were moving by land.

Meanwhile, the provincial congress had closed its proceedings in Concord—Gage had lost his chance of seizing that assembly. Two of its most important members, Sam Adams and John Hancock, were, on April 15, making their way to Lexington to visit Hancock's fiancée.

On April 18, when Gage's advance troops were set to embark, the general finally learned that his plan was well known in Boston. Unable to call off the advance, Gage sent couriers to intercept any messengers that might be sent to warn the rebels in Concord. Dr. Warren had already chosen two men to rouse the countryside: William Dawes was to go by way of Boston neck; the silversmith, Paul Revere, was to cross by water to Charlestown.

As two lanterns were being hung in the tower of Christ Church, Paul Revere began paddling his small boat across the Charles River. Though it approached midnight and was dark, Revere was in considerable danger. Around him lay several ships of the British fleet, each with a night lookout. Passing close by the ship *Somerset*, he was, inexplicably, not seen. Landing at Charlestown, Revere took to horse, only to be pursued by two British officers who lay in wait in the shadows of the common. Eluding his pursuers, Revere rode on to Lexington, 12 miles distant, alerting patriots along the way.

In Lexington he found Sam Adams and John Hancock at the house of the Rev. Jonas Clarke. He warned them to flee. There Revere was joined by Dawes and another courier named Prescott. These three took to the road again, only to be waylaid by a small contingent of British troops. Revere was captured, but Dawes and Prescott, eluding the soldiers, continued on to Concord.

The Battle of Lexington, engraving from a contemporary drawing by Ralph Earle, April 19, 1775

Throughout the early morning hours of Wednesday, April 19, "minutemen" militia gathered in Lexington. Commanders warned their men, "Let the troops pass by and don't molest them with out they begin first." Meanwhile, Lieutenant Colonel Francis Smith's contingent of British regulars had crossed the Charles River, marched through Charlestown, and turned west along the road to Lexington. The advance guard under Major John Pitcairn was the first to reach Lexington. Seeing in the unclear light of early morning armed men blocking the road to Concord, Pitcairn ordered his men to halt.

"Ye villains, ye rebels, disperse!" cried Pitcairn to the militia blocking the road. "Lay down your arms!

"Why don't ye lay down your arms?"

At that, the militia began to retreat behind a stone wall that ran alongside the road. Pitcairn ordered a detachment of light infantry forward to intercept the militia before they reached the wall. Suddenly, a few shots rang out from the rebel side, wounding a redcoat and hitting Pitcairn's horse. That was a signal to Pitcairn's men. All the suppressed anger from months of insult and abuse from Boston rebels welled up within them. "The men were so wild they could hear no orders," later wrote an officer, recalling the event. Without orders, Pitcairn's men aimed their muskets and fired a murderous volley into the rebels. When the smoke cleared, of the 60 or so colonial minutemen gathered at Lexington, ten were dead; nine, wounded.

So was the first blood of the Revolution shed. If no rebels had fired, if the British regulars had restrained their rage . . .

The news of the "slaughter" at Lexington spread like wildfire over the Massachusetts countryside. The British had now to march through a countryside seething with anger and the desire for revenge.

Lt. Colonel Smith's troops continued the march to Concord. There, two battalions of militia had already gathered. As the British advanced into town, the militia made a series of strategic retreats across North Bridge and ensconced themselves on a ridge northwest of town. Following the rebels across the North Bridge, the British halted at the foot of the ridge in a face-off with the rebels. Two hours later the rebels began to advance on the redcoats. The British commander, realizing the danger of his position (between a stream and the ridge), ordered his troops to recross the bridge. The militia opened fire, killing four British officers and three soldiers and wounding five others.

British troops entering Concord, Massachusetts, engraving by Amos Doolittle, 1775

Colonel Smith now ordered a retreat to Boston. But as they marched toward Lexington, the redcoats were assailed by an unseen enemy. Fighting Indian-style, the rebels shot at the passing British from behind trees and stone walls, only to retreat further into the woods they knew so well when the redcoats moved to counterattack. Assailed by a continuous fire, the British were soon exhausted and near despair: "[We were] so fatigued," wrote an officer, "that we could not keep flankering parties out, so that we must soon have laid down our arms or been picked off by the rebels at their pleasure."

The road to Boston was marked by the same guerrilla sniping. British regulars, unable to come to grips with the enemy, retaliated with plundering and cruelty, destroying houses from which gunfire came, or was suspected to have come. Men, even women and children, suffered atrocities. When the British finally made it back to the safety of Boston, their losses were 73 killed and 200 wounded. Of the Americans, 49 were killed, 41 wounded.

News of the Battles of Lexington and Concord spread quickly to all the colonies. Soon contingents from other colonies joined the Massachusetts militia in laying siege to Boston. From Connecticut came Benedict Arnold as well as Israel Putnam, with the Connecticut militia. Philadelphia sent five regiments; other militia came from New York and New Hampshire.

Nor was the ominous importance of the fight lost on the colonial leaders. Months, years of waiting were ended; the vital moment had come. In a letter to his brother in law, one Joseph Andrews wrote: "When I reflect and consider that the fight was between those whose

Benedict Arnold, with Québec city in the background, by Thomas Hart, 1776

parents but a few generations ago were brothers, I shudder at the thought, and there's no knowing where our calamities will end."

Ticonderoga and Crown Point

On his way from New Haven to Cambridge, Benedict Arnold met with Colonel Samuel Parsons who was also heading north with his "raiders" to the siege of Boston. Arnold, a wily schemer, an armchair military strategist, and a profoundly ambitious man, had conceived a plan to take the strongest British fort in North America—Fort Ticonderoga. Situated on the western shore of Lake Champlain, Ticonderoga held a rich cache of armaments. It was strategically placed along an invasion route the British might take from Canada, down Lake Champlain, across New York to the Hudson River, and by that river to New York City.

Arnold easily convinced Parsons to embrace the plan to take Ticonderoga, and, arriving in Cambridge, he received a military commission from the Massachusetts Assembly. Unfortunately for Arnold, another adventurer had conceived the same ambition —Ethan Allen, from the Green Mountains in Vermont. A rough frontiersman, tall and gruff, and as self-promoting as Arnold (but in a more flamboyant way), Allen wrangled with Arnold over the command of the expedition. Arnold presented his commission; Allen countered that his "Green Mountain Boys" would follow no one but himself. At last the two headstrong men compromised: they would command the operation together.

On May 9, 1775, the small American force reached the eastern shore of Lake Champlain. Having crossed the lake on a leaking barge, Arnold and Allen, walking side-by-side, led their 83 men to the fortress of Ticonderoga, whose gates, in the early morning hours, were flung wide open. Only a sentry opposed them, and his gun misfired. Striding up to the quarters of the commanding officer, Ethan Allen demanded his surrender. "Come out, you old rat!" he shouted. When the British commander asked by whose authority he should surrender, Allen (at least according to his own account) answered, "In the name of the Great Jehovah and the Continental Congress."

The next day, Arnold and Allen took the British fort at Crown Point unopposed. Taking command of an American sloop, Arnold sailed up Lake Champlain, captured the town of St. John's on the Canadian border, and seized the 70-ton English sloop of war that patrolled the lake. With the capture of St. John's, Lake Champlain came entirely under American control.

Throughout the campaign, Arnold had been scheming to take sole command of the American troops on Lake Champlain. With new recruits, he added to the number of men under his command. While Ethan Allen and his Green Mountain Boys were away on an invasion of Canada, Benedict Arnold took command of the remaining American forces. When Allen returned from his unsuccessful foray, he found Arnold reinforced and in undisputed command.

The Second Continental Congress and Bunker Hill

While Arnold and Allen were busy taking Crown Point, the Second Continental Congress had convened in Philadelphia. This time, all the 13 Atlantic sea-board colonies sent delegates. Among those who came to the City of Brotherly Love were John and Samuel Adams, Patrick Henry, Thomas Jefferson, Richard Henry Lee, George Washington, and Charles

Carroll of Carollton in Maryland (whom John Adams called "a very sensible gentleman, and Roman Catholic, and of the first Fortune in America"). The assembly, under the presidency of John Hancock, met to discuss what should be done in the aftermath of Lexington and Concord.

Though Lexington and Concord put the colonies' relations with Great Britain in a new light, most of the delegates were still not in favor of declaring independence from Great Britain. This was evidenced by their reaction upon hearing the news from Ticonderoga. Lexington and Concord was one thing. It had been essentially a defensive maneuver; but aggressively taking a British fort—that was an offensive act of war against His Majesty, George III! Congress forthwith ordered the Americans to abandon Lake Champlain; and, though it allowed the removal of munitions from Ticonderoga, it ordered them inventoried so that repayment could be made to the king's government upon the re-establishment of peace.

Protests from the New England colonies and New York, however, changed Congress' mind; Ticonderoga was not abandoned. Instead, the Massachusetts Provincial Congress sent reinforcements under Colonel Hinman to Lake Champlain. When Benedict Arnold learned that Hinman was to take command of all the forces, he resigned his command and ordered his 200 to 300 men to disband. Arnold declared he would not serve as second-in-command to any man.

Though Congress protested it was not bucking for independence, it began to act very much as if it were a sovereign government. It designated the motley troops around Boston and at Ticonderoga the provisional army of the United Colonies and made George Washington of Virginia its commander-in-chief. The delegates commissioned the disgruntled Benedict Arnold to go north to Maine and organize patriot resistance in Canada. On the diplomatic side, Congress sent ambassadors to European countries. Three departments of Indian affairs were created, and a treaty was signed with the Shawnee and Delaware Indians.

Congress cherished hopes that Canada would join the struggle against Britain. In hopes of such an alliance, in May 1775, Congress sent an address "to the oppressed Inhabitants of Canada." The address, drafted by John Jay of New York, spoke of "the fate of the protestant and catholic colonies" as being "strongly linked together." It reminded the "Quebeckers" that "the enjoyment of your very religion, in the present system, depends on a legislature [Parliament] in which you have no share, and over which you have no control, and your priests are exposed to expulsion, banishment, and ruin, whenever their wealth and possessions furnish sufficient temptation." The French Canadians, however, had not forgotten that, among other grievances, the First Continental Congress had protested the "establishing of the Roman Catholick Religion in the province of Quebec," or that John Jay's October 1774 "Address to the People of England" expressed "our astonishment that a British Parliament should ever consent to establish in that country [Canada] a religion that has deluged your island in blood, and disbursed impiety, bigotry, persecution, murder and rebellion through every part of the world." The Canadians, bolstered in their opposition by Bishop Briand of Quebec, refused to take Congress' bait. They remained loyal to King George III.

Blood on Breeds Hill

On June 23, 1775 George Washington left Philadelphia to take command of the army of the United Colonies at Boston. En route, he learned that the colonials had closed with the British in the second major battle of the war.

General Sir William Howe, who had taken command of the British troops at Boston in May (General Gage remained as governor), had been planning an assault on Dorchester Heights and Cambridge to scatter the rebel army investing Boston. When the plan became known, General Artemas Ward, who commanded the Massachusetts troops, thought to forestall the attack by placing men and artillery on Bunker Hill on the Charlestown peninsula. From Bunker Hill, Ward thought, he could direct artillery fire on British positions in Boston.

A contemporary depiction of the Battle of Bunker Hill: "A Correct View of the Late Battle at Charlestown, June 17, 1775"

On the night of June 16, 1775, colonial troops under Colonel William Prescott moved in to occupy what they thought was Bunker Hill but was, instead, Breeds Hill. Throughout the early morning hours of June 17, they dug trenches and built a stockade on Breeds Hill. When the sun rose, the British saw the small eminence bristling with colonial militia.

General Howe thought it an easy matter to take the hill—and it should have been, since the colonials had no artillery (it had not arrived), little ammunition, and almost no military discipline. Surprisingly, although the attacking British troops were supported by fire from their own ships in the harbor, they broke against colonial resistance. In the first assault, British grenadiers and light infantry fell before the withering fire of colonials ensconced behind a rail fence. In a second assault, colonials turned back British marines and grenadiers as they tried to storm Breeds Hill. Only in the third assault, when the colonials had run out of ammunition, did the British take the hill. Still, the Redcoats paid a high price for victory: out of the 2,200 engaged, they suffered 1,054 casualties (killed and wounded). The colonials lost 444 killed and wounded out of 3,200 engaged. "A dear bought victory," said British General Clinton of the fight; "another such would have ruined us."

This "Battle of Bunker Hill" inspired the rebels with new confidence. In the wake of the battle, on July 6, Congress issued a "Declaration of the Causes and Necessity of Taking Up Arms." Drafted by John Dickinson and Thomas Jefferson, the declaration listed all the events leading up to the conflict between Great Britain and her colonies. The chief and overriding grievance, however, was the "one statute" (the Declaratory Act of 1766) by which "it is declared, that parliament can 'of right make laws to bind us in all cases whatsoever.'" This statute was most grievous, said the declaration, because such laws would be passed by a body in which the colonists were not represented. It was not that the colonies wanted representation in Parliament (indeed most of Great Britain had no such representation), but they demanded that laws affecting the internal life of the colonies should be made only by their own legislatures. Congress, however, wanted to clarify that it did not seek independence; it meant not "to dissolve that union which has so long and so happily subsisted between us, and which we sincerely wish to see restored."

A lithograph of the Battle of Bunker Hill by Nathaniel Currier, after a painting by J. Trumbull

Two days after approving the Declaration, Congress, urged by John Dickinson, issued the "Olive Branch Petition" as a sort of last-ditch effort to end the conflict. Its message was conciliatory but not abject:

Attached to your Majesty's person, family and government with all the devotion that principle and affection can inspire, connected with Great Britain by the strongest ties that can unite societies, and deploring every event that tends in any degree to weaken them, we solemnly assure your Majesty, that we not only most ardently desire the former harmony between her and these colonies may be restored, but that a concord may be established between them upon so firm a basis as to perpetuate its blessings uninterrupted by any future dissentions to succeeding generations in both countries.

As many expected, the king was not moved by the petition. On August 23, 1775, he issued a declaration calling all subjects to make the "utmost endeavors to withstand and suppress such rebellion and bring the traitors to justice."

The rebellion had gone too far. There was no turning back. It had been sealed by blood.

The Road to Independence

General George Washington had an enormously difficult task before him—to turn the raw militiamen of the several colonies into an effective fighting force. The American soldier had a tremendous sense of independence. It was his custom to fight, as duty demanded, and then return to his farm to provide for his family. Only when he was needed again did he return to fight. Enlistments in New England were mostly for six-month periods, and Washington was hard put to convince the men to stay longer. He was able to get Congress to enlist men for three-year periods, or for the duration of the war—but there were still many in his army who had signed up for shorter stints.

The soldiers had to learn military discipline. Drilling them was essential and one of Washington's chief difficulties. He received help from a foreign volunteer, one Baron Friedrich Wilhelm von Steuben, a Prussian *Junker* (nobleman) who joined Washington's staff in 1777. Baron von Steuben adapted Prussian drill to American needs and later, in 1779, wrote a manual of drill for the American army.

Washington was probably the best choice for commander-in-chief. He inspired confidence with his quiet, reflective, aristocratic Virginian manner. His genuine devotion to the cause for which he fought, combined with his evident concern for the good of his men, inspired their devotion. Many times, when supplies ran short for the army, Washington provided for his men from his own relatively modest Mount Vernon estate. Devoted, sometimes to excess, to the ideal of the republican gentleman, Washington sought to conform himself in all ways to this ideal

George Washington in 1776, by Charles Wilson Peale

Many Diverse Skirmishes

While Washington was busy turning his undisciplined band of militiamen into a disciplined fighting force, battles flared at isolated points throughout the colonies. A British sea captain, driven off from Falmouth (now Portland), Maine, poured red-hot cannon balls on the town, igniting fires that burned it to the ground. A conflagration destroyed Norfolk, Virginia in December 1775—but this time, it was patriots who were the cause. But they so successfully blamed the fire on Governor Dunmore and the loyalists that they enlisted many fence-sitters to the rebel cause.

In North Carolina, Scottish Highlanders who lived on the upper reaches of the Cape Fear River had longstanding grievances against tidewater Carolinians, who were largely patriots. The Highland leaders, Donald MacDonald and Donald McLeod, who were conspiring with British General Clinton, thus, had little trouble whipping up a loyalist uprising. With

Clinton they laid their plans. The general would march from the coast and rendezvous with the Highlanders near Cape Fear.

In early 1776, the beautiful Flora MacDonald, the wife of loyalist Major Allen MacDonald, mounted a snow-white horse and rode through the countryside recruiting her Highlander people to fight for King George III. Flora was already a heroine to the Highlanders, for it was she who had rescued Bonnie Prince Charlie from the British after the Battle of Culloden in Scotland in 1746. The prince, a Stuart, had led a rebellion against King George II, of whose son Flora was now exhorting her people (in Gaelic) to rise in defense. On February 27, 1776, 1,700 Highlanders, clad in kilts and blaring bagpipes, set out to join Clinton. He, however, had been delayed by a storm at sea, and the Highlanders, stumbling on a patriot camp at Moore's Creek near Wilmington, were soundly defeated. Half of the Highland army was killed; 850 were taken prisoner.

In the north, in November 1775, rebel General Richard Montgomery with 1,000 New Englanders marched by way of the Hudson River and Lake Champlain and captured Montreal in Quebec. After a rendezvous with General Benedict Arnold and his 600 Maine militiamen, Montgomery assaulted Québec city, but was repulsed and died in the action.

When in March 1776, General Washington's army occupied Dorchester Heights, investing Boston entirely by land, General Howe decided to abandon the city. On March 17, the British army and hundreds of loyalists were transported by ship to Halifax in Nova Scotia. The army of the United Colonies marched in triumph into the city.

"Of Right . . . Free and Independent States"

It was slow going to convince most Americans that the colonies should break with the mother country and form an independent nation. Even at the close of 1775, George Washington and his officers still drank toasts to King George III—and embraced the illusion that Parliament alone, not the king, was behind all the measures to "suppress their liberties." Their English sense of tradition told them the king could not be aware of Parliament's actions; or, if he were, he had been forced to condone them. By the spring of 1776, however, attitudes had changed. As the progress of war intensified bitter feelings between the colonies and Great Britain, ever more colonists began to entertain thoughts of independence. By the spring of 1776, Washington wrote that he was convinced that independence was the only possible course open for the colonies.

Thomas Paine, painting by Thomas Millière

What changed his mind? A short book—really a pamphlet—called *Common Sense*. The author, a one-time Quaker named Thomas Paine, had only recently, in 1774, come to America from England. A failure in every business endeavor he attempted, Paine in 1776 was making a scanty living as a farmer and mechanic in Philadelphia. Then, in January 1776, *Common Sense* emerged and changed Paine's and the colonists' fortunes forever.

Thomas Paine's book is an eloquent summary of the social contract theory of government. In *Common Sense*, Paine calls human society a "blessing" but even the best government "but a necessary evil." "Like dress," wrote Paine, government "is the badge of lost innocence; the palaces of kings are built upon the ruins of the bowers of paradise." If men were perfectly virtuous, Paine insisted, they would not need government; but because men are vicious, governments are necessary to assure freedom and security. But not any form of government is desirable; according to Paine; only republican governments of elected representatives of the people are just. All other governments—aristocracies, monarchies—are nothing but tyrannies.

Union with Great Britain, wrote Paine, could only be effected by friendship or force; "but it hath so far happened that the first hath failed, and the second hath withdrawn her influence." America, he wrote, does not need Britain to prosper; America's commerce provided the necessities of life, which "will always have a market while eating is the custom of Europe." The king of Britain, argued Paine, had used the colonies solely for his own benefit; and far from being the "Father of his people," as he claimed to be, he was the "hardened, sullen-tempered Pharaoh of England"—as evidenced by the Battles of Lexington and Concord. Further, America, like a child come of age, no longer needed the guidance of Great Britain but deserved emancipation. No more kings, declared Paine, except the king who "reigns above, and doth not make havoc of mankind like the Royal Brute of Great Britain." In America, said Paine, not George III nor any merely human ruler—rather, "THE LAW IS KING." Calling at last upon "ye that love mankind," Paine perorated:

> Ye that dare oppose not only the tyranny but the tyrant, stand forth! Every spot of the old world is overrun with oppression. Freedom hath been hunted round the Globe. Asia and Africa have long expelled her. Europe regards her like a stranger, and England hath given her warning to depart. O! receive the fugitive, and prepare in time an asylum for mankind.

Common Sense and the continuing war were undermining whatever reverence English Americans felt for the king. Though the New England delegates to the Continental Congress were somewhat hesitant, it was not long before they joined Virginia's delegates in calling for independence. The New York and Pennsylvania delegates, however, openly opposed independence; but by clever politicking, Richard Henry Lee and the two Adamses got Congress to pass a resolution over the protests of New York and Pennsylvania—that since the King had excluded "the inhabitants of the United Colonies from the protection of his Crown . . . the exercise of every kind of authority under the said Crown should be totally suppressed, and all the powers of government exerted under the authority of the people of the colonies."

The Declaration of Independence

Between mid-May and early June 1776, the southern colonies, from Georgia to Virginia, all endorsed independence, as did the four New England colonies. Only the Middle Colonies (New York, New Jersey, Maryland, Pennsylvania, and Delaware) held back. On June 2, Richard Henry Lee read to Congress a resolution approved by the Virginia legislature, that "these United Colonies are, and of right ought to be, free and independent states." This resolution notwithstanding, the Middle Colonies would not budge, and the vote for independence was postponed until July 1. In the meantime, a committee of five—Thomas Jefferson, John Adams, Benjamin Franklin, Roger Sherman, and Robert Livingston—were appointed to draw up a formal declaration for independence. The youngest member of this committee, the 33-year-old Thomas Jefferson, was given the task of drafting the document.

John Dickinson was the first to address Congress on July 1, and he spoke out against independence. However, by the next day, July 2, nearly all the delegates were in favor of independence; and when the vote was taken, 12 colonies voted for independence, while the New York delegation abstained. The next step was to adopt Jefferson's draft of a declaration of independence. After emending the document, all the delegates present, except John Dickinson, voted to adopt it, and John Hancock as president of Congress signed it, on July 4, 1776. Over the next month the Declaration was sent to the various colonial legislatures for their approval. Finally, on August 2, the members of Congress signed their names to the document, including John Carroll of Carrollton in Maryland, the only Catholic to do so.

The Declaration of Independence is an eloquent catalog of the causes that, Congress claimed, compelled the colonies to seek independence from Great Britain. It is a "self-evident" truth that all men are created equal, and "that they are endowed by their Creator with certain unalienable Rights, that among these are Life, Liberty and the pursuit of Happiness." This language was drawn from Locke, though Jefferson substituted the phrase, "pursuit of Happiness," for Locke's "property." Jefferson may have derived his wording from another document with which he was doubtless familiar—the first article of the Virginia Bill of Rights, drafted by George Mason and adopted June 12, 1776 by the Old Dominion:

> . . . all men are by nature equally free and independent, and have certain inherent rights, of which, when they enter into a state of society, they cannot by any compact deprive or divest their posterity; namely, the enjoyment of life and liberty, with the means of acquiring and possessing property and pursuing and obtaining happiness and safety.

Once it has established a basis for human liberty and equality, the declaration, in the language of the social contract, goes on to justify political revolution. Governments exist to secure the people's rights and derive their "just powers from the consent of the governed." When a "form of government becomes destructive of these ends, it is the Right of the People to alter or to abolish it, and to institute new Government." No people should do this lightly, however, but only "when a long train of abuses and usurpations, pursuing invariably the same Object evinces a design to reduce them under absolute Despotism." Then, it is the people's "right," "it is their duty, to throw off such Government and to provide new Guards for their future security." The Declaration then lists the alleged "injuries and usurpations" of the king of Great Britain against the colonies.

In its peroration, the declaration lives up to its name—it proclaims the independence of the former colonies from Great Britain:

> We, therefore, the Representatives of the united States of America, appealing to the Supreme Judge of the world for the rectitude of our intentions, do, in the Name, and by Authority of the good People of these Colonies, solemnly publish and declare, That these United Colonies are, and of Right ought to be Free and Independent States. And for the support of this Declaration, with a firm reliance on the Protection of Divine Providence, we mutually pledge to each other our Lives, our Fortunes and our sacred Honor.

On July 9, the Declaration of Independence was read at a public meeting on the common in New York City. Afterwards, the people pulled down a gold-plaited lead statue of George III. Removing the gold, they melted down the 4,000 pounds of lead and made from it musket balls for the Continental—now the United States—army. It would need such munitions. It was one thing to declare for independence, quite another thing to secure it.

A Civil War

Flora MacDonald suffered more than disappointment from the Highlander defeat at Moore's Creek Bridge; her husband, Captain Allen MacDonald, was taken prisoner. And more misfortune followed. Over a year later, the North Carolina Committee of Safety confiscated the MacDonald's property, and members of the committee mistreated Flora's two daughters. They took the girls' rings, and then (Flora wrote), "putting their swords into their bosom, split down their silk dresses and taking them out into the yard, stripped them of all their outer clothing."

Flora MacDonald was but one of the many who maintained their loyalty to King George III. These loyalists included not only former agents of the British government (such as customs men), Anglican clergymen, and some of the very rich, but small farmers, poor craftsmen, fugitive slaves (to whom King George promised freedom if they abandoned their rebel masters), and some scoundrels. In other words, loyalists represented a cross-section of society. Why they were loyal varied, of course, from person to person: some remained loyal out of self-interest (as in New York after the British occupied the city), but others out of conscience, as their sufferings at the hands of rebels proved. Anglican clergymen would not renounce the head of their church; others thought they should not break oaths they had taken to remain the king's faithful subjects. Some loyalists tried to remain neutral, while oth-

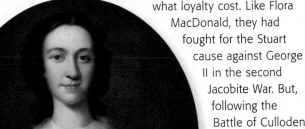

Flora MacDonald, portrait by Richard Wilson

ers joined loyalist regiments that served with the British against the rebels.

July 4, 1776 marked the beginning of a new era of repression against loyalists, who, because of independence, could now be accused of treason. Of course, those who actively supported the king, or were thought to, could expect death; but those who tried to stay neutral in the conflict had cause to fear for their lives. A group of about 175 Scots Catholic Highlanders who had settled around the fortified mansion of Sir John Johnson in the Mohawk Valley in upper New York learned what loyalty cost. Like Flora MacDonald, they had fought for the Stuart cause against George II in the second Jacobite War. But, following the Battle of Culloden, they had taken an oath never to fight against the king—and they were determined to keep it. For their loyalty, they, along with their priest, Father John McKenna, were driven out of New York and forced to take refuge in Montreal.

The American Revolution was truly the first American civil war. Neighbor fought against neighbor, even brother against brother. The Catholic parish of St. Mary's in Philadelphia, for example, divided over the issue of independence and provided both loyalist and patriot regiments. Both loyalists and patriots were guilty of barbaric acts—burning houses, insulting women, murdering the innocent. The bid for American independence stirred bitter animosities that awakened the worst passions in the human breast. Such animosities would linger many years after the war was done.

A Long and Weary War

When General Sir William Howe decided to move his troops from Halifax to New York in June and July of 1776, General Washington had no choice but to abandon Boston and lead his army southward. By August, the United States army, 18,000 strong, held Brooklyn Heights on Long Island while General Howe's British forces occupied New York City and its harbor.

New York was a good base of operations for Howe. It was strongly loyalist, and the harbor was one of the best in the colonies and able to accommodate a large fleet. It was also a good base for operations up the Hudson, and across New Jersey against the American capital, Philadelphia.

Washington and Howe's forces first met in battle on Long Island on August 27, 1776. Having lost 1,000 men, Washington retreated across the East River into Manhatten, finally encamping on Haarlem Heights. When he had established Forts Henry and Lee on either side of the Hudson, Washington moved his forces to North Castle on the Hudson, whence he could easily cross into New Jersey if Howe moved against Philadelphia.

Washington was sure that Howe would march on Philadelphia—the question was, when? If Howe did advance on the capital, Washington knew he had to beat him to the bridge spanning the Raritan River near New Brunswick, New Jersey, or else all hope of defending Philadelphia would be lost. To make sure that he could beat Howe to the Raritan, Washington left about 5,000 men at North Castle and marched the remainder of his army south—maneuvers that provided the British general with a grand opportunity to destroy Washington's army piecemeal. Howe, however, delayed, and Washington was the first to cross the Raritan. On December 7–8, he led his small army over the Delaware River at Trenton. For his part, Howe on December 13 decided to end all campaigning for the winter. He would not venture forth from the comforts of New York City.

Washington now faced a new problem—the enlistment periods for one-half of his army were to expire at the turn of the year. Knowing the American soldier, Washington knew that few would voluntarily re-enlist. To bolster his men's morale and perhaps attract more soldiers to the field, Washington took the offensive. Setting out at 7 p.m. on Christmas Day, 1776, Washington's army marched north along the Delaware to McKinley's Ferry, and thence crossed into New Jersey. Occupying Trenton was a force of auxiliaries, mercenaries from the German state of Hesse. The Hessians were still sleeping off the effects of their Christmas celebration when Washington's forces fell on them in the early hours of December 26, 1776. After a brief resistance, the Hessians surrendered Trenton to Washington. This victory was a morale boost to the American cause; the hated foreigners, whom Britain was paying to fight against her own people, had been soundly whipped. Enlistments rose, and Washington, with a larger, renewed army, planned further offensives.

In early January 1777, Washington's army descended on Princeton, New Jersey. There, British forces almost beat the Americans, but Washington's presence among his men encouraged them to stand firm. Routing the British forces, the Americans took Princeton on January 3.

By the end of January, Washington had taken his army north to Morristown, New Jersey and there camped for the winter. From Morristown, Washington sent out raiding parties to the east, capturing the towns of Hackensack, Elizabethtown, and Newark.

Washington's initial campaigns in 1777 had been encouraging, but the future was still far from certain. Thomas Paine summed up the situation of the war in his paper, *Crisis*, on January 19, 1777:

> These are the times that try men's souls. The summer soldier and the sunshine patriot will, in this crisis, shrink from the service of their country; but he that stands it now deserves the love and thanks of man and woman. Tyranny, like hell, is not easily con-

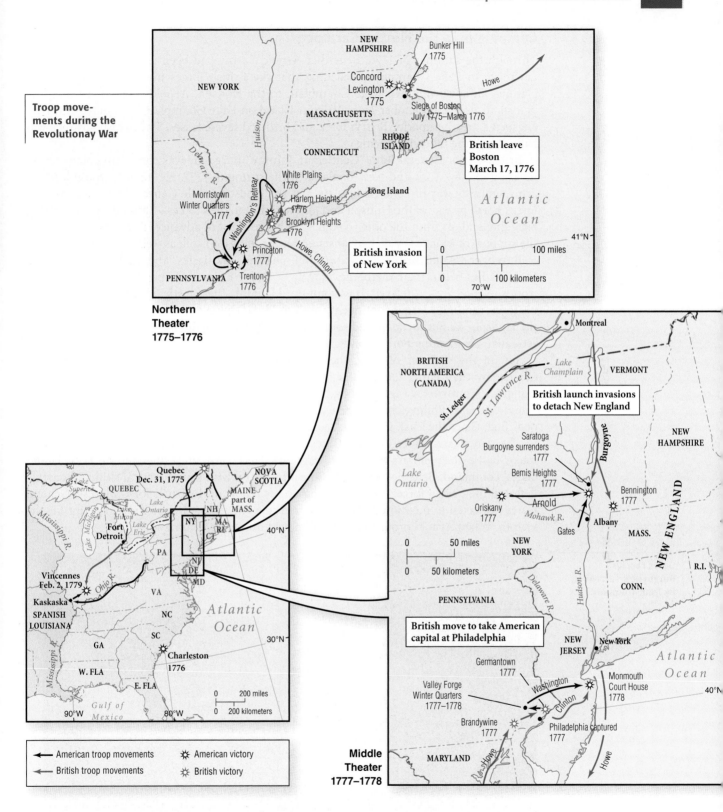

Troop movements during the Revolutionay War

Northern Theater 1775–1776

NEW HAMPSHIRE

NEW YORK

Bunker Hill 1775

Concord Lexington 1775

Howe

MASSACHUSETTS

Siege of Boston July 1775–March 1776

Hudson R.

RHODE ISLAND

CONNECTICUT

British leave Boston March 17, 1776

Delaware R.

White Plains 1776

Long Island

Atlantic Ocean

Morristown Winter Quarters 1777

Washington's Retreat

Harlem Heights 1776

Brooklyn Heights 1776

41°N

Princeton 1777

Howe, Clinton

British invasion of New York

0   100 miles

PENNSYLVANIA

Trenton 1776

0   100 kilometers

70°W

Middle Theater 1777–1778

Montreal

BRITISH NORTH AMERICA (CANADA)

Lake Champlain

VERMONT

St. Ledger

St. Lawrence R.

British launch invasions to detach New England

Burgoyne

NEW HAMPSHIRE

Saratoga Burgoyne surrenders 1777

Bemis Heights 1777

Bennington 1777

Lake Ontario

Oriskany 1777

Arnold

Mohawk R.

Albany

NEW ENGLAND

Gates

MASS.

0   50 miles

NEW YORK

R.I.

0   50 kilometers

Delaware R.

CONN.

Hudson R.

PENNSYLVANIA

British move to take American capital at Philadelphia

NEW JERSEY

New York

Atlantic Ocean

Germantown 1777

Washington

Monmouth Court House 1778

40°N

Valley Forge Winter Quarters 1777–1778

Clinton

Brandywine 1777

Philadelphia captured 1777

MARYLAND

Howe

Howe

Quebec Dec. 31, 1775

NOVA SCOTIA

Lake Superior

QUEBEC

Lake Huron

MAINE part of MASS.

NH

Lake Ontario

NY   MA RI CT

40°N

Mississippi R.

Lake Michigan

Lake Erie

Fort Detroit

PA

Vincennes Feb. 2, 1779

Ohio R.

NJ DE MD

VA

Kaskaska

SPANISH LOUISIANA

NC

Atlantic Ocean

30°N

SC

GA

Charleston 1776

W. FLA

E. FLA

Mississippi R.

Gulf of Mexico

0   200 miles

0   200 kilometers

90°W   80°W

→ American troop movements   ✴ American victory

→ British troop movements   ✴ British victory

quered; yet we have this consolation with us, that the harder the conflict, the more glorious the triumph. What we obtain too cheap, we esteem too lightly; it is dearness only that
gives everything its value. Heaven knows how to put a proper price upon its goods; and it
would be strange indeed if so celestial an article as freedom should not be highly rated.

Campaigns in the North—Saratoga

Through the summer of 1776, Benerdict Arnold's army had been retreating along the St. Lawrence to Lake Champlain. Learning that the British forces under Sir Guy Carleton planned an advance down Lake Champlain to the Hudson, Arnold ordered the building of a small fleet. On October 11, at Valcour Island on Lake Champlain, this makeshift fleet engaged a greatly superior British force and inflicted severe losses. The British advance was halted until the following spring.

British Major General John "Gentleman Johnny" Burgoyne was concocting plans for an invasion of New York and New England in the spring of 1777. He himself would lead his army south by way of Lake Champlain and the Hudson, while General Howe was to send forces north by way of the Hudson and join with Burgoyne's forces—thus effectively cutting New England off from the other colonies. In his southward advance, Burgoyne would have the support of Mohawk Valley loyalists under Sir John Johnson, as well as the Iroquois.

Burgoyne's 4,000 British regulars, 3,000 Hessian auxiliaries, and 1,000 Canadian and Indian allies began their march on June 1, 1777. For his part, General Howe, with 27,000 troops in New York—delayed. It was not until late July that he stirred; and then he divided his force, sending a larger contingent south to Philadelphia and a smaller force north along the Hudson. As Burgoyne moved south along Lake Champlain, the American forces slowly retreated, abandoning Fort Ticonderoga.

Yet, in the summer of 1777, the American army was threatened with a more serious enemy than either Gentleman Johnny and General Howe—the political juggling of Congress. Controversy raged among the delegates over who should command the northern army—General Philip Schuyler, Benedict Arnold, or Horatio Gates? Arnold was the most qualified; Gates the least. Congress decided on Gates.

The Americans under General Gates and the British under Burgoyne finally met in a major battle at Freeman's Farm near Saratoga, New York, on September 19, 1777. Under Gates' command, Benedict Arnold led the attack, and with sound tactical skill and daring, defeated the British forces. But in writing up his report of the battle for Congress, General Gates neglected to mention Arnold's decisive role and, instead, gave himself credit for the victory. When Arnold protested, Gates removed him from command.

Gates receives Burgoyne's surrender, by John Trumbull

After his defeat at Freeman's Farm, General Burgoyne's position worsened day by day. He couldn't retreat and his Indian allies were abandoning him. On October 7, Burgoyne took the only course left open to him—he attacked the American position. In the Second Battle of Freeman's Farm, Arnold took unofficial command of the New England regiments and with them routed the British. Unable to advance or retreat, Burgoyne surrendered to General Gates ten days later.

Advance on Philadelphia

While General Burgoyne was marching south to eventual defeat, ships transporting a British regiment, 18,000-strong, under General Howe had been moving southward along the New Jersey and Maryland coasts and then, having rounded Cape Charles, passed into Chesapeake Bay. Landing 50 miles south of Philadelphia, Howe's force advanced on the city. On September 11, 1777, at Brandywine Creek, the British joined battle with the Washington's army. Washington's 12,000 men were a motley bunch; they had few uniforms and marched into battle wearing sprigs of green as symbols of hope. Their hope, though, had to be deferred. In the ensuing battle, the Americans lost 1,000 men and were forced to retreat. With the British only about 30 miles from Philadelphia, Congress fled the city to Lancaster, Pennsylvania, about 70 miles to the west. On September 26, General Howe marched into Philadelphia. He had captured the American capital!

Bust of Lafayette in the Virginia state capitol, Richmond, Virginia

More ill luck dogged the American cause. Washington, who had withdrawn to the north, attacked Howe's camp at Germantown on October 4 but was defeated with a loss of 1,000. Following this defeat, Washington decided to call it quits for the year and retired to winter quarters at Valley Forge in Pennsylvania. It was a bitter winter for the Americans, who lacked supplies and had to contend with cruel cold. But Howe did not inconvenience himself. Instead of pushing his advantage against Washington, he spent a pleasant winter in Philadelphia, enjoying the polite and refined society of the loyalists in the City of Brotherly Love.

Alliance with France

Of all Europeans, it was the French people who most warmly supported the American Revolution. This at first might seem strange, for France was a highly centralized monarchy—just the kind of government that it seems would most oppose revolution. Yet, it had been only 14 years since the Treaty of Paris gave all of Canada to Great Britain, and many of the French and their king wanted to see their ancient enemy, England, humbled. French intellectuals, and many aristocrats, too, were ardent republicans who looked to America as an experiment in political freedom. Indeed, one French aristocrat, the Marquis de Lafayette, was so committed to the cause of liberty that in 1777 he outfitted a ship and sailed to America. Congress commissioned him a major general in the Continental Army.

Congress, however, had wanted more from France than an occasional soldier; it longed for a military alliance. So it was that Congress sent Benjamin Franklin as its ambassador to the court of Louis XVI. Franklin was popular in Paris. His scientific experiments made him welcome among the intellectuals and earned him a membership in the French Academy of Sciences. His republican manners and the fact that he was a Freemason won him regard in some of the highest circles of French society.

But despite Franklin's charm, and her own itch for revenge, France was reluctant to acknowledge American independence openly—though she sent cargoes of clothing and munitions to Congress and allowed American privateers and naval ships to use French ports. The situation changed, however, with Burgoyne's defeat. The French government worried that the military defeat might move the British government to seek peace with America. Such fears were not baseless; on November 7, 1777, Lord Neville introduced a "conciliatory bill" into Parliament that basically granted the Americans everything the First Continental Congress had asked for in 1774. But, fortunately for the French, members of Parliament did not act on the bill right away. They had to have their Christmas break, and so the vote on Lord Neville's bill was delayed until the new year.

This delay gave Franklin the time he needed. He knew that, once a treaty with France was signed, the American congress could not turn from independence, no matter what Parliament offered. On February 6, 1778, the French government signed two treaties of friendship and commerce with Congress. Under the terms of the treaties, France joined the United States in their bid for independence. France agreed not to claim Canada (which many Americans were eager to annex to the United States), though she would be able to keep her West Indian island possessions; and France and America would grant each other special privileges in trade.

Eleven days later—and 11 days too late—Parliament passed Lord Neville's conciliatory bill. Then, in the spring, Parliament sent a royal commission to New York to negotiate an armistice with Congress. The commissioners were empowered to give in to all American demands, except independence. Congress, however, would not meet with the commissioners unless they first acknowledged American independence. By the end of the year, the commissioners returned empty-handed to England.

The news of the American alliance with France brought other changes: Parliament replaced General Howe with Sir Henry Clinton on May 8, 1778 and ordered the new commander-in-chief to evacuate Philadelphia and concentrate his forces on New York. As Clinton moved across New Jersey, Washington followed, hoping for an opportunity to engage the British in battle. This opportunity came on June 28, 1778, at Monmouth County Courthouse. It was another American defeat. Clinton marched safely into New York, and Washington placed his troops in a half-circle to the north of the city. There he would await the French.

The Dark Years

If the French alliance gave new hope to the American cause, it initially had very little effect on the course of the war. The year 1778 did not witness any victories like the one over Burgoyne the previous year. Instead, the year commenced a period of successive defeats for the patriots in the Deep South.

Savannah, Georgia, occupied by American General Robert Howe and a small force of 700 Continental soldiers and 150 state militia, was the first target of a British offensive. It was a relatively easy catch for the British commander, Colonel Sir Archibald Campbell, and his 3,500 troops. In November 1778, Campbell moved on Savannah and took the city in December. He then pushed farther into the interior and took Augusta, the state capital. By the spring of 1779, the royal governor had been reinstated, and Georgia was again a royal province.

The next target for the British was Charleston, South Carolina. Sir George Prevost and his army composed of East Florida loyalists and Cherokees looted and pillaged across South Carolina. General Benjamin Lincoln, who defended Charleston, would have lost the city had not cavalry under the Polish volunteer Casimir Pulaski arrived and driven off the enemy. Prevost then fell back on Savannah.

The Americans received their first French aid when French Admiral Charles Henri, Comte d'Estaing's fleet of 33 ships with 6,000 troops arrived off the coast of Georgia. Savannah, defended by only 3,200 men, looked an easy catch for the combined American and French assault that occurred on October 9, 1779. The assault, however, was premature, and the allies suffered tremendous losses—among them Casimir Pulaski, cut down by grapeshot while he probed for a weak point in the British lines. He died on board an American ship as it sailed out of the Savannah River. The Americans and French withdrew, and Savannah remained in British hands.

A French map of the siege of Savannah, 1779

Except for the assaults on Savannah and Charleston, the years 1778 and 1779 witnessed little more military action other than raids. The British navy under Sir George Collier ravaged the Chesapeake Bay in May 1779. Collier went on to burn defenseless villages in the Hudson River Valley and then turned south again, following the Hudson into the Atlantic. Sailing eastward through Long Island Sound, Collier landed at New Haven, Connecticut, tried to burn Yale College, but was repulsed by Connecticut citizens. On the American side, John Paul Jones led privateering raids on British ports in his ships *Ranger* and the *Bonhomme Richard*. With the *Bonhomme Richard*, a gift of the French, and four other ships, Jones engaged the British ship *Serapis* in a battle in the North Sea on September 23, 1779. The battle, waged from 6:30 to 10:30 p.m., ended in the sinking of the *Bonhomme Richard*—but not until Jones had forced the surrender of the *Serapis*, which he seized as his flagship.

John Paul Jones' victory, however, was the only bright spot for the Americans in what would prove a year of dismal defeats. In the fall of 1779, Lord Sir Charles Cornwallis, who commanded British forces in the South, conceived a plan to take the Carolinas, which he commenced in the spring of 1780. On April 8, 1780, a British fleet passed the guns of Fort Moultrie and anchored off the city of Charleston while British troops under Generals Clinton and Cornwallis landed south of the city. Caught between the fleet and the army, American General Benjamin Lincoln surrendered Charleston. By July, Cornwallis' troops had taken all of South Carolina and restored the royal governor.

Battle of the
Bonhomme Richard
and the *Serapis*

Meanwhile, Washington sent American troops under General Johann von Kalb south to reinforce the patriots. The troops arrived in North Carolina nearly starved, for the states through which they passed refused to give them food or aid. Then, Congress imposed a new hardship on the southern army when it appointed General Horatio Gates its commander. Ignorant of the countryside, Gates forced his men to march across the pine barrens of North Carolina, where they could find no food. Then, on August 16, Gates led the army into battle with Cornwallis at Camden, South Carolina and was utterly defeated.

More bad news followed the Battle of Camden—the treason of Benedict Arnold. Arnold had not gotten over Gates' snubbing after the first Battle of Freeman's Farm; and though he had received Washington's praise and a general's commission from Congress, Arnold could not forget or forgive. Then, in February 1779, Congress brought charges of misconduct against Arnold. Congress acquitted him of four of the charges but referred the remaining charges to a court-martial that, in January 1780, convicted Arnold of two trivial offenses. Yet, though he was only sentenced to receive a reprimand from Washington, the combined events were too much for his proud and ambitious spirit. His marriage to Peggy Shippen, who belonged to a prominent loyalist family in Philadelphia, perhaps helped sway his affections from the patriot cause. Appointed commander of West Point on the Hudson, Arnold conspired with General Clinton to deliver the post to the British. Arnold's treason became known when patriots captured Clinton's envoy, Major John André, carrying papers from Arnold. André was hanged as a spy while Arnold escaped to the British, who commissioned him a brigadier general.

Meanwhile, with the defeat of Gates, North Carolina lay open to Cornwallis. Supported by Major Patrick Ferguson's 1,400 loyalists, Cornwallis marched north to Charlotte, North Carolina, while Ferguson turned west to harry the patriot settlements of western North Carolina. Ferguson's threats to execute the patriot leaders in that region and lay waste their settlements frightened the settlers of the West into resistance. They hastily formed a militia and called on the men of the new Tennessee settlements over the mountains to join them. On October 7, 1780, at King's Mountain on the border of North and South Carolina, Ferguson's loyalists met the patriot militia, led by the Tennesseans John Shelby and John "Nolichucky Jack" Sevier. In his checkered shirt, Ferguson was an easy target; in the one-hour battle, the Tennesseans cut him down, and his men were routed. Cornwallis, who had counted on Ferguson's joining him in North Carolina, had to withdraw again into South Carolina, where he wintered.

The Tide Turns

Though Congress had appointed Washington overall commander of its army, it had been Congress, not Washington, that had been appointing commanders in the various theaters of the war. Inspired more by politics than military sense, Congress' choices had been mostly dismal. Its appointment of Gates for the southern theater had been disastrous—just as it would have been in the North but for the intervention of Benedict Arnold. With the threat of a new offensive by Cornwallis, Congress at last let Washington choose the southern commander. His choice was Nathaniel Greene, 38-years old, an excellent strategist, and a man who inspired loyalty. Greene chalked up an odd record in the days to come: he lost most of his battles while inflicting greater casualties on the enemy than he himself sustained. At the battle of Guilford Courthouse in North Carolina on March 15, 1781, Greene's forces had to retreat—but with far fewer casualties than Cornwallis, who lost 30 percent of his army! Cornwallis retired to Wilmington. In the summer of 1781, Greene advanced into South Carolina and forced the British and loyalist forces to withdraw into Charleston.

Since December 1780, Benedict Arnold, leading 1,700 loyalist volunteers, had been wreaking havoc in Virginia. In January 1781, he drove (and nearly captured) Governor Thomas Jefferson from Richmond. Cornwallis, with a force of fewer than 1,400 men, moved north from Wilmington into Virginia to take advantage of Arnold's successes. In May he joined Arnold in Petersburg, Virginia.

In June, Cornwallis sent out raiding expeditions and began moving his own force toward Williamsburg, Virginia. Throughout July, General Clinton sent Cornwallis a series of conflicting orders, eventually commanding him to establish a fortified naval station in Virginia. Cornwallis chose Yorktown, situated on a long peninsula formed by the York River, to the north, and the James River, to the south. On August 2, the British entered Yorktown and began building fortifications. Cornwallis had hoped Clinton would join him for a general assault on the South, but from New York Clinton dispatched his refusal. Instead, of leading his forces to Virginia, Clinton sent Cornwallis reinforcements that increased the British army at Yorktown to only 7,000 men.

Yorktown and Victory

The French alliance had been a disappointment to the Americans. Except for Lafayette (who was entirely freelance) and Commodore d'Estaing, France had contributed little to the war effort. General Rochambeau at Newport, Rhode Island, commanded 6,700 French troops; but without a navy to transport and support them, they were of little use to Washington. An added problem was that Congress could not induce the states to send in their quotas of money and men for the army. The United States army was in a dismal state. The men were hungry, ill-clothed, and at times owed two to three years' back pay.

The summer of 1781, however, brought good news from Paris: King Louis XVI promised to commit a major part of his navy to the American cause. Twenty line-of-battle ships under Rear Admiral François Joseph Paul, Comte de Grasse, set sail for the West Indies, where four more ships and 3,000 soldiers awaited him.

Washington, conferring with Rochambeau and, by emissary, with de Grasse, debated whether it would be best to attack Clinton in New York or Cornwallis at Yorktown. The decision was left to de Grasse, who chose Yorktown. With admirable coordination of their forces, Washington, Rochambeau, and de Grasse converged on Yorktown in early September

Cornwallis surrenders his sword to Washington at Yorktown. An 1819 engraving.

1781. There was no aid for Cornwallis, for General Clinton remained in New York, deceived by false reports (instigated by Washington) that the Americans and French would attack the city. On September 5, de Grasse's fleet met a British fleet of 19 ships off Cape Charles at the entrance to the Chesapeake Bay and defeated it. The British fleet, forced to sail to New York for repairs, left Cornwallis without support from the sea.

On September 28, 1781, the siege of Yorktown began. Cornwallis' 8,000 men, blocked seaward by de Grasse's fleet, could not escape by ship; nor could they move by land, surrounded as they were by Rochambeau's 8,000 French troops and Washington's 5,645 regulars and 3,200 Virginia militia. An experienced soldier, Cornwallis knew when he was beaten. On October 17 he sent out the white flag. Two days later, Cornwallis formally surrendered his entire army to the Americans.

First in War

News of the Yorktown victory spread quickly through the states. In the middle of the night, people were dancing in the streets at the reports—the victory, they thought, would bring a speedy end to the war. They were both right and wrong. Yorktown was the decisive battle, but still war would rage for over a year in the West between Indians and rebel militia. Peace did not come until March 12, 1783, when news of the Treaty of Paris reached Washington's forces in Philadelphia.

There were two treaties of Paris. The first, concluded between the United States and Great Britain on November 30, 1782, acknowledged American independence and granted the young republic all lands from the Appalachians to the Mississippi River and (except for Florida) from the Gulf of Mexico to the Great Lakes. The second, the formal treaty signed September 3, 1783, involved not only the United States and Great Britain but Holland, France, and Spain, all whom had waged war on Great Britain. In this treaty, France received little, while Spain received Florida and was assured of the continued possession of Louisiana. Over a year later, on November 25, 1783, the smart, red-clad British regiments evacuated New York City while Washington and his tatterdemalion troops marched in to take possession.

With the war now ended, Washington was eager to return home to Mount Vernon. In December, at Fraunces Tavern in New York, the commander-in-chief dined for the last time with his officers. Following the meal, he filled a wineglass, and holding it aloft, he pledged them: "With a heart full of love and gratitude, I now take my leave of you. I most devoutly wish that your latter days may be as prosperous and happy as your former ones have been glorious and honorable."

Washington shook each of his officers' hands until, coming to his most trusted lieutenant, General Henry Knox, he embraced him, and both wept.

On December 19, Washington entered Annapolis, Maryland, where Congress was then sitting. He came to resign his commission. The grateful Marylanders celebrated him at a great ball four days later. It was there he read his farewell address. "It was a solemn and affecting spectacle," wrote an eyewitness afterwards:

> The spectators all wept and there was hardly a member of Congress who did not drop tears. The General's hand which held the address shook as he read it. When he spoke of the officers who had composed his family, and recommended those who had continued in it to the present moment to the favorable notice of Congress, he was obliged to support the paper with both hands. But when he commended the interests of his dearest country to almighty God, his voice faltered and sunk, and the whole house felt his agitations. After the pause which was necessary for him to recover himself, he proceeded to say in the most penetrating manner, "Having now finished the work assigned me I retire from the great theatre of action, and bidding an affectionate farewell to this august body under whose orders I have so long acted I here offer my commission and take my leave of all the employments of public life."

An engraving of George Washington

Taking leave, he thought, forever of public life, Washington rode away to his home, Mount Vernon, on the Potomac. There he spent Christmas Eve with his wife, Martha, and her grandchildren.

Chapter 9 Review

Summary

- Parliament passed the Coercive acts in March of 1774, incensing the colonists and leading to the creation of the Continental Congress.
- Parliament passed the Quebec Act in June of 1774, further incensing the colonists.

- The Continental Congress met on September 5, 1774 to discuss what steps to take against the Coercive and Quebec Acts. This was the second time the colonies attempted to act as one. Congress soon afterwards endorsed the Suffolk Resolves, which condemned the Coercive Acts. Congress also passed the Declaration and Resolves, which laid out the rights of the colonists.

Chapter 9 Review (continued)

- In March of 1775 Parliament passed the New England Restraining Act, which forbade the colonies to trade with anyone but England and Ireland. This act further chipped away at whatever loyalty was left for the king and Parliament in the colonies.

- British General Gage needed a British victory that would turn public sentiment towards the British government. He heard of rebels caching arms and ammunition at both Worcester and Concord and sent out forces to capture those arms. On April 19, Gage's army met with an army of colonial militia in Lexington. The rebels fired shots at the British, and the British retaliated with a murderous volley, killing ten minutemen and wounding nine others.

- Benedict Arnold, leading a colonial army, took Ticonderoga from the British in May of 1775. Meanwhile, the Second Continental Congress convened in Philadelphia to discuss what was to be done. The Congress designated the colonial army the provisional army of the United Colonies and made George Washington its commander-in-chief.

- The British defeated the colonial army in the costly battle of Bunker Hill in June of 1775.

- On July 6, 1775, Congress issued the "Declaration of the Causes and Necessity of Taking Up Arms," and two days later, the "Olive Branch Petition." The king was not moved by the last petition and issued a declaration calling on all his subjects to withstand and suppress the rebellion and bring the traitors to justice.

- Thomas Jefferson drafted the Declaration of Independence in June of 1776. Congress approved the declaration on July 4, 1776, and John Hancock as president of the Congress signed it on July 4. By August 2, 1776, all of the members of Congress had signed it.

- The Americans and the British met in the Battle of Saratoga on September 19, 1777, and the British were defeated through Benedict Arnold's strategy.

- The French signed two treaties of friendship and commerce with Congress on February 6, 1778.

- In 1780 Benedict Arnold, angry because he was convicted of two trivial offenses, betrayed the Americans to the British.

- The siege of Yorktown began on September 28, 1781. On October 17 British General Cornwallis surrendered to the Americans. Two treaties between Great Britain and the United States were signed on November 30, 1782 and September 3, 1783.

Key Concepts

Tories: Patriot name for the colonists loyal to King George III

Continental Congress: the body of delegates that spoke and acted collectively for the states during the American Revolution

minutemen: militiamen trained to gather quickly on notice of a British attack

Declaration of Independence: document approved by the Continental Congress on July 4, 1776, which announced the separation of the American colonies from Great Britain

Dates to Remember

1774: Parliament passes the Coercive and Quebec Acts. The first Continental Congress gathers (September 5). It approves the Declaration and Resolves.

1775: Parliament passes the New England Restraining Act.

Battles of Lexington and Concord (April 19)

Battle of Breeds Hill (Bunker Hill) (June 17)

Congress issues the "Declaration of the Causes and Necessity of Taking Up Arms," and the "Olive Branch Petition"

1776: the Continental Congress approves the Declaration of Independence (July 4).

1778: France signs a treaty with the United States.

1781: Cornwallis surrenders to the Americans at Yorktown.

Central Characters

Thomas Gage (1721–1787): British general who commanded all British forces in North America at the outbreak of the American Revolution and military governor of Massachusetts (1774–1775)

Joseph Warren (1741–1775): a leader in the American Revolution who drafted the Suffolk Resolves in which the Massachusetts legislature condemned the Coercive Acts and called on the people of the colony to take up arms if Parliament did not repeal the acts

Joseph Galloway (ca. 1731–1803): a loyalist and delegate to the First Continental Congress. He suggested the establishment of an American parliament, called the "Grand Council," under the authority of the British king

Sir William Howe (1729–1814): commander-in-chief of the British army in America during the first years of the revolution

Benedict Arnold (1741–1801): patriot officer who fought for the Americans until 1779, when he shifted allegiance to the British

George Washington (1732–1799): commander-in-chief of the American army during the American Revolution

Thomas Paine (1737–1809): English-American writer whose *Common Sense* was a major influence in moving the Americans toward proclaiming independence from Great Britain

Marquis de Lafayette (1757–1834): French aristocrat who fought for the Americans in the American Revolution

Charles Cornwallis (1738–1805): British general whose defeat at Yorktown brought about the end of the American Revolution

Questions for Review

1. Name and explain the three Coercive Acts and what effects they had on the colonies.

2. What was the Continental Congress and how was it formed?

3. What are the rights listed in the Declaration and Resolves, and what authority did they claim as the basis of their demands?

4. What effects did the New England Restraining Act and the Quebec Act have on the growing rebellion?

5. What events led to the battle of Lexington?

6. Why were the Canadians so opposed to joining forces with the Americans?

7. Why was the battle of Bunker Hill important to the revolution, and what document did it inspire?

8. What was the chief difficulty the American army faced during the Revolution?

9. Briefly summarize Thomas Paine's *Common Sense* and explain why it was so influential.

10. Briefly summarize the Declaration of Independence, what it was calling for, and the principles it cited as the basis for its claims.

11. Explain the two treaties of Paris in 1782 and 1783.

Ideas in Action

1. Read historical fiction or eyewitness accounts of the American Revolution.

2. Read about and discuss the Social Contract Theory on which the Declaration of Independence is based. What positive and negative effects does the Social Contract Theory have on government and the society of America?

3. What would have happened if Cornwallis had not surrendered at Yorktown? Some historians, such as Page Smith, author of *A People's History of the American Revolution*, argue that Great Britain could not have prevented American independence, even if the United States had received no aid from the French. Research and discuss whether the French alliance was decisive to the securing of American independence from Great Britain.

4. Study the claims of patriots, for, and loyalists, against, American independence, and research what Catholic thinkers have said about the right to revolution. In light of Catholic tradition, who had the better cause—patriots or loyalists?

Highways and Byways

Stars and Stripes

The original American flag, adopted in 1777, was supposedly created by a woman named Betsy Ross. According to the received story, a small committee, including George Washington and Betsy's relative,

Chapter 9 Review (continued)

George Ross, went to consult Betsy on the design of a flag, and she was commissioned to make it. Whether this story is true or not, on June 14, 1777, the Second Continental Congress passed the Flag Resolution, stating that "the flag of the thirteen United States be thirteen stripes, alternate red and white; that the union be thirteen stars, white in a blue field, representing a new constellation." This basic design has never changed, except for the addition of stars as new states were admitted into the union. The current version of the flag, adopted in 1960, has fifty stars, but maintains the thirteen alternating red and white stripes, representing the 13 original states.

A NEW NATION

Revolutionary Governments

It was one thing to declare independence. It was another thing to win it. It was another thing yet to secure it. The course of popular revolutions in the next 200 years would follow a general pattern: the establishment of a new regime, followed by confusion, followed by a dictatorship. America's revolution was different and more fortunate. With the end of British occupation, colonial governments, long established, were able to supply the necessary order. Further, the fact that these governments existed testified to the colonials' ability to form effective and lasting governments.

With the Congress' declaration of independence, existing colonial governments began to function as state governments with little or no change to their constitutions. Connecticut would operate according to its original colonial charter until well into the 19th century. Virginia, too, continued to follow its colonial pattern—a legislature that dominated government, a council whose members were appointed by the legislature, and a governor whose veto power had to be supported by the council. This legislature-dominated Virginia government became the model for several other states.

John Adams, by
John Trumbull

Though it had been the radical wellspring of the revolution, Massachusetts, during the revolution, had developed the most conservative organ of government. In 1779, John Adams drafted a new state constitution and submitted it to the townships, which approved it. This constitution set up a house of representatives, elected by the people; a senate, which represented the wealthier citizens; and a popularly elected governor, who could veto acts of the legislature and appoint state officials. The governor appointed the members of an independent judiciary that could decide on the constitutionality of acts passed by the government.

Adams' constitution reflected a strain of republican thought that held that pure forms of government inevitably became corrupt: monarchies became tyrannies; aristocracies hardened into oligarchies; and popular governments collapsed into anarchy. Adams thought the best government is one that has a mixture of monarchical, aristocratic, and popular elements. Such a government would allow each element to check the power of the others. The governor (the monarchical element) could veto laws passed by the legislature (popular in its lower house and aristocratic in its upper house). Since the two houses of the legislature depended on each other for the passage of laws, the aristocrats could not dominate the people, nor the people the aristocrats.

Pennsylvania stood at the opposite end of the political spectrum from Massachusetts, having adopted a unicameral (one-house) legislature with no governor. Many radical thinkers thought this the only proper form of government for a republic. The people ruled through the legislature, they said—so what need was there for another governmental body to check the will of the people? The people's representatives were the best safeguard of popular liberties. Checks and balances reeked too much of aristocracy to suit such populist republicans. So it was that, under its unicameral constitution, Pennsylvania became the most democratic—but also the most dissension-ridden—of the states.

The states differed in their qualifications for the suffrage. All the states limited the vote to white males, except for New Jersey, where women who held property and free blacks could vote. Seven states allowed every white male taxpayer to vote, while the rest established property requirements for voting. Almost every state permitted only property owners to vote for members of the upper house of the legislature. A few states, such as New Hampshire, had test oaths of loyalty for office-holders to keep Catholics and loyalists from holding office.

Bills of Rights

George Mason was one of the most prominent men in Virginia. Not only his vast estates in Fairfax County and the high social standing these gave him, but his extraordinary talents made him very influential in Virginia government. In the heady days of the stamp tax controversy, Mason had drawn up a series of non-importation agreements, which were presented to the Virginia House of Burgesses by his close friend and neighbor, George Washington. In 1774, Mason had drawn up the Fairfax Resolves, calling for a congress of the colonies and a non-importation act against Great Britain.

George Mason was something of a recluse and, at times, disagreeable. Yet, when he thought duty called him to the service of his country, he was ever ready to comply. In 1776, the Virginia burgesses called on him to compose what became, perhaps, his single most important contribution to American government: the Virginia Bill of Rights. On June 12 the burgesses adopted Mason's bill, with but two emendations.

The Virginia Bill of Rights declared "that all men are by nature equally free and independent, and have certain inherent rights, of which, when they enter into a state of society, they cannot by any compact deprive or divest their posterity." These rights, wrote Mason, are "the enjoyment of life and liberty, with the means of acquiring and possessing property, and pursuing and obtaining happiness and safety." The Virginia Bill of Rights further declared "that all power is vested in, and consequently derived from, the people; that magistrates are their trustees and servants, and at all times amenable to them."

Among the protected rights, the Virginia bill listed trial by jury, protection from searches without a warrant, and the freedom of the press. Without disestablishing the Anglican Church, the bill of rights guaranteed "the free exercise of religion, according to the dictates of conscience," since "religion, or the duty which we owe to our Creator, and the manner of discharging it, can be directed only by reason and conviction, not by force or violence."

Other states followed Virginia's example and adopted bills of rights. Pennsylvania's bill of rights mirrored Virginia's but added freedom of speech to freedom of the press, granted foreigners "of good character" the right to own property, and (true to Pennsylvania's Quaker heritage) provided protection for those whom conscience forbade to serve in the military. In 1780, Massachusetts adopted a bill of rights, listing among those enumerated a right to a mixed government.

The First U.S. Constitution

Trying to get the states to agree on a constitution for the new national government proved a difficult task. Having thrown off the British yoke, the states cherished their independence and feared giving too much power to a central government. In July 1776, John Dickinson introduced into Congress the draft of a constitution called the Articles of Confederation and Perpetual Union. This constitution called for a unicameral legislature, called the Congress, to which states would yearly send delegates. It gave the new government power to declare war and make peace, conclude treaties, regulate the coining of money, and decide in disputes between states.

These were the powers the Articles would give the central government. More revealing are the powers the states retained in this their first "social contract." The articles were drawn with special attention to state sovereignty. Article two stated that "each state retains its sovereignty, freedom and independence, and every Power, Jurisdiction and right, which is not by this confederation expressly delegated to the United States, in Congress assembled." To protect the sovereignty of each state, every state, whatever its population, received one vote in Congress. The articles granted Congress no power to collect taxes; instead, Congress had to rely on state contributions for its revenue. Nor did Congress have the power to place duties on foreign trade. Any important decisions—such as declaring war, making treaties, and borrowing money—had to garner the agreement of nine of the 13 states. Further, any change in the articles had to draw the unanimous consent of all the state legislatures.

On November 15, 1777, Congress approved the Articles of Confederation and submitted them to the state legislatures for approval. It wasn't until February 1779 that all the states but one approved the articles. Maryland alone held out.

Why did Maryland prove intransigent? A powerful cadre of land speculators, who had formed the Illinois-Wabash company, had convinced the Maryland legislature to delay ratification of the Articles until the settlement of a land dispute with Virginia. Virginia laid claim to western lands stretching from her southern border northward, and westward indefinitely from the borders of Maryland and Pennsylvania. In the colonial period, the Illinois-Wabash Company had illegally purchased some of this western land from the Indians; now, because Virginia had refused to recognize the company's title to the land, the company wanted Virginia to cede her western lands to Congress.

George Mason

In response to the Illionis-Wabash company's demands, Virginia sent out an expedition (in 1778, while the war still raged) under George Rogers Clark. Clark passed down the Ohio to the mouth of the Cumberland River, and then marched through the wilderness, seizing Kaskaskia, a British fort on the Mississippi in what is now southwestern Illinois. The following year, with the help of a Catholic priest, Clark's company took the settlement of Vincennes on the Wabash River. Virginia used Clark's expedition to validate her claim to the lands west of the Appalachians and south of the Ohio River.

While it was lobbying Congress to federalize the western lands, the Illinois-Wabash Company had entered into negotiations with Spain. The company proposed the separation of the lands west of the Appalachians from the United States, with their formation into a separate republic under the protection of the Spanish king. A few members of Congress who were members of the company supported this plan, as did the French minister in Philadelphia (a share-holder in the company). The conspiracy was discovered, however, and in 1781 Virginia offered to cede her western lands to the United States. Maryland, her chief objection removed, agreed to ratify the Articles of Confederation. The Articles went formally into effect on March 1, 1781, only seven months before Conrwallis surrendered at Yorktown.

Cornwallis

Republican Reforms

Revolutions are typically followed by periods of radical change, especially in laws and government. The American Revolution was, in its effects on society (a theme we shall develop in Chapter 11), as radical as any other. In its effects on law and government, however, it did not appear very revolutionary at all.

At first glance, the abolition of primogeniture and entailment in Virginia might seem quite radical. A law of primogeniture requires that estates be passed down to the first-born son, while entailment forbids an heir to sell an estate to anyone outside one's extended family. Such laws were in force to maintain family lands intact so as not to diminish a family's wealth and status. Virginia republicans, however, thought primogeniture and entailment worked to protect landed aristocracy and so fought to overturn them. Still, the lawmakers succeeded in abolishing primogeniture only when an owner died "intestate" (without a legal will); and, as for entailment, it was never widely favored in America, even among "aristocrats." It was not unusual in the South for planters, particularly of tobacco, to over farm their lands and so destroy their fertility. No one wanted to be tied to such lands, especially when farther westward lay virgin fields of rich fertility to exploit.

More radical, it seems, was the movement to abolish slavery in several northern states. Yet slavery was only abolished in those northern states where it was no longer economically viable—and, even then, many slaves were sold south and not freed at all. But in Massachusetts, in 1781, a court freed Quock Walker, a slave, because the Massachusetts bill of rights "sets out declaring that all men are born free and equal—and that every subject is entitled to liberty, and to have it guarded by the laws, as well as life and property—and in short is totally repugnant to the idea of being born slaves." Other northern states, Connecticut, New Hampshire, and Pennsylvania, declared the children of slaves to be free. New York and New Jersey did not abolish slavery until later; the former in 1799, and the latter in 1804. Father south, no state abolished slavery; still, by 1783, Virginia, Delaware, Maryland, along with all the northern states, had prohibited the foreign slave trade.

Farther

Yet, it was during this very period that slavery was under assault in the South. Every southern state had one or more abolition societies, and several prominent southern leaders were opposed to the institution. They thought it contrary to revolutionary principles. Virginia's governor, Thomas Jefferson, himself a slave owner, worked with other slaver owners to plan a gradual abolition of slavery. North Carolina did not abolish the slave trade but placed a heavy tax on slave imports. In 1787,

A British anti-slavery broadside depicting the conditions on a ship used in the foreign slave trade

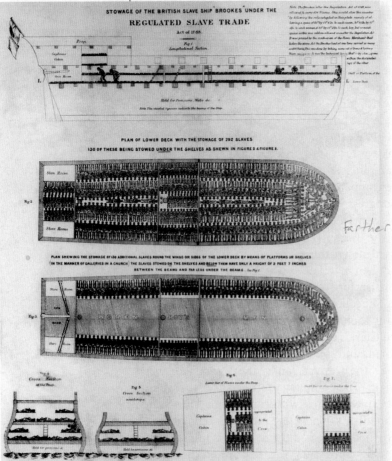

South Carolina passed a law prohibiting the slave trade—though it was repealed it in 1803 because the state found it impossible to enforce.

In 1783, Virginia freed all slaves who had fought for America in the Revolutionary War. The same year, Methodists petitioned the Virginia assembly to abolish slavery entirely because it was "contrary to the fundamental principles of the Christian religion" and violated the Declaration of Independence. Virginia did not go so far as to abolish slavery, for too many influential landowners would not go for it. James Madison, one of the younger generation of revolutionary leaders, perhaps spoke for many slaveholders when he wrote that he would never have possessed the wealth he needed to devote himself to politics had he never owned slaves.

The Revolution and Religion

Possibly more radical even than the moves to abolish slavery was the disestablishment of churches and enactments of freedom of religion in the states. Like most European nations, most of the states had long-established churches—churches recognized by law and supported by taxes. In some cases, governments required attendance at church services. Following the revolution, however, New York, Maryland, and both Carolinas disestablished the Anglican Church. In Virginia, Thomas Jefferson fought for complete religious liberty and disestablishment. Jefferson wanted not only freedom for all religions but what he called in an 1802 letter he wrote to the Baptists of Danbury, Connecticut, a "wall of separation" between church and state.

Jefferson and other republicans called for the disestablishment of state churches because, central to Liberalism, is the conviction that religion is a purely private affair. It has nothing to do with the state, or the state with it. This conviction was rooted in another assumption—that religion is not about truth but is merely private opinion. Indeed, Liberal thinkers in Europe went so far as to call religion "superstition." American Liberals rarely used such language, at least in public; yet, some like Jefferson thought that since religious doctrines could not be proven by reason (that is, by the scientific method), reasonable men could not possibly hold to them. Not all American leaders went as far as Jefferson did in this, but many of the founders held that, at the very least, religious belief and practice should be left entirely to the free choice of individuals—a freedom they never would have accorded to certain political ideas, such as those held by the loyalists.

The Virginia Bill of Rights had called for the "free exercise of religion, according to the dictates of conscience." Yet, in Virginia, tax monies still went to support the established Anglican Church. Jefferson fought vigorously for the disestablishment of the Anglican Church in Virginia. In 1777, the Virginia assembly repealed all laws requiring church attendance and universal support for the established Anglican Church. But Jefferson wanted to go further. He prepared a proposed statute to establish absolute religious liberty and equality for all religions, without state support for any religion. His opponents, among whom were Patrick Henry and George Washington, favored equal state support for all religious groups. Nevertheless, Jefferson prevailed after a ten-year struggle that he later called the severest in his life. In January 1786, the Virginia assembly passed Jefferson's Statute of Religious Liberty:

From Jefferson's Letter to the Danbury Baptists

"Believing with you that religion is a matter which lies solely between Man & his God, that he owes account to none other for his faith or his worship, that the legitimate powers of government reach actions only, & not opinions, I contemplate with sovereign reverence that act of the whole American people which declared that their legislature should 'make no law respecting an establishment of religion, or prohibiting the free exercise thereof,' thus building a wall of separation between Church & State. Adhering to this expression of the supreme will of the nation in behalf of the rights of conscience, I shall see with sincere satisfaction the progress of those sentiments which tend to restore to man all his natural rights, convinced he has no natural right in opposition to his social duties."

> . . . no man shall be compelled to frequent or support any religious worship, place or ministry whatsoever, nor shall be enforced, restrained, molested, or burthened in his body or goods, nor shall otherwise suffer on account of his religious opinions or belief; but . . . all men shall be free to profess, and by argument to maintain, their opinion in matters of religion, and that the same shall in no wise diminish, enlarge or affect their civil capacities.

These rights, said the statute, "are of the natural rights of mankind."

With this statute, wrote James Madison, "was extinguished forever the ambitious hope of making laws for the human mind." Indeed, the statute declared that since God had created the human mind free, any attempt to coerce belief contradicted "the plan of the Holy author of our religion, who being Lord both of body and mind, yet chose not to propagate it by coercions on either, as was in his Almighty power to do." The statute condemned the "impious presumption of legislators and rulers, civil as well as ecclesiastical, who being themselves but fallible and uninspired men, have assumed dominion over the faith of others, setting up their own opinions and modes of thinking as the only true and infallible." Finally, the statute opened up public office to anyone, regardless of religion; for, said the statute, "our civil rights have no dependence on our religious opinions, any more than our opinions in physics or geometry."

Religion in the New Republic

In 1827, Charles Carroll of Carrollton told a Protestant minister: "to obtain religious as well as civil liberty I entered zealously into the Revolution and, observing the Christian religion divided into sects, I founded the hope that no one would be so predominant as to become the religion of the state." Carroll's hope was not disappointed. Though not all states granted complete religious freedom, especially to Catholics, still, a widespread tolerance of Catholics grew up after the revolution. In North Carolina a law had been passed in 1776 that said "no person who shall deny . . . the truths of the Protestant religion . . . shall be capable of holding any Office or Place of Trust or Profit in the civil department within this state." Nevertheless, Dr. Thomas Burke, a Catholic, represented North Carolina in Congress and, in 1781, became governor of the state. In 1800, another Catholic, William Gaston, served in the North Carolina state senate and was elected to the United States House of Representatives. Later, some contested Gaston's proposed appointment to the North Carolina supreme court, because, they said, he denied "the truths of the Protestant religion." Gaston said he denied nothing that was true in the Protestant religion and then asked his critics what those "truths of the Protestant religion" could be? No one ventured an answer, and Gaston was duly appointed a supreme court judge.

In New England the Congregational Church remained quasi-established, since townships appointed ministers to local congregations. But this led to difficulties with the traditional Calvinists, because town selectmen tended to appoint more liberal-minded, this-worldly Unitarian ministers instead of the old hard-line Puritans. In response, Calvinists began setting up their own churches, supported by their members, not the state.

Almost everywhere in the states, churches cut off ties with their mother churches in Europe and formed distinctly American groups. The Anglican Church in America, which had long suffered for a lack of bishops, finally, with independence, obtained one, and from thenceforth was no longer directed from England. In the states it became known as the Protestant Episcopal Church.

The state of the Catholic Church in America was not robust. In all there were about 25,000 Catholics in the United States, centered for the most part in Maryland and Pennsylvania; about 1,500 Catholics lived in New York and 200 in Virginia. Catholics in Pennsylvania, who were mostly English with a few Germans and a growing number of Irish, had benefited from Pennsylvania's traditional religious tolerance. But before the revolution, Catholics in Maryland had lived in fear of the penal laws. The priests in America were Jesuits who, because their flocks could not support them, were forced to make their living as planters. When Pope Clement XIV suppressed the Jesuits in 1773, the Jesuit priests in America could receive no additions to their numbers. By the 1780s they were old, retiring, and spiritless.

The Catholics in English America were under the authority of the bishop of London, called the "vicar-apostolic" because, legally, he could not call himself "bishop" in England (the title was reserved for Anglican prelates). The bishop of London could do little for America, hampered as he was by his essentially illegal status in England. Catholics in the United States needed a bishop, but both priests and people were against it; they were afraid that it would spark a persecution against them. They remembered too well how the colonists had angrily rejected the idea of having an Anglican bishop in America—what would they do if faced with a Catholic one?

Yet, because of the revolution, attitudes towards Catholics had begun to change in the United States. The alliance with France had forced many Protestant Americans to temper their anti-Catholicism. Even Puritan Massachusetts had sent a Catholic priest to work among the Catholic Indians in Maine, which cemented the Indians' bonds with the new country. Still, Catholics who had suffered centuries of persecution, or the threat of persecution, continued to tread warily.

A Bishop for America

One man who understood the new state of things in America better than most was Father John Carroll. Born in Maryland in 1735, John Carroll and his cousin, Charles, had attended the Jesuit school at Bohemia Manor in Maryland before being sent to St. Omer's in France in 1748. Both had entered the seminary, but Charles later decided to study law and returned home to become the lord of Carrollton. John, however, entered the Society of Jesus, taught at St. Omer's and then at Liege in Belgium. He later served as chaplain to Lord Arundel of Wardour in England. After the suppression of the Jesuits, Carroll returned to Maryland and lived at his mother's house at Rock Creek, where he said Mass and from whence he set out to minister to Catholics in Maryland and Virginia.

Dedication "In All Weathers"

The life of a priest in America was not easy. Not only did he have to earn his own bread, but it was his duty to travel long distances to minister to his scattered flock. Maryland priest Father James Moseley described his life in a letter to his brother in London:

> Our journeys are very long, and our rides constant and extensive. I often ride about three hundred miles a week, and never a week but I ride one hundred and fifty to two hundred. In our way of living we ride as much by night as by day; in all weathers, in heats, colds, rain, frost, and snow. You must not imagine that our chapels lie as yours do. . . . They are in great forests, some miles away from any house of hospitality. Swamps, runs, miry holes, lost in the night, etc. this, as yet, and ever will in this country, attend us. Between three and four hundred miles was my last Christmas fare on one horse.

Statue of John Carroll at Georgetown University, Washington, D.C.

JOHN CARROLL
FOVNDER

During the revolution, John Carroll had taken the part of the colonies. In 1776 he had accompanied his cousin, Charles, Benjamin Franklin, and Samuel Chase to Quebec in an unsuccessful attempt to convince the Canadians to join the rebellion. On this trip he earned Franklin's respect and friendship. Throughout the war years, Carroll remained at his mother's house.

The question of an American bishop was raised again after the war. In a declaration to Rome in 1783, Carroll and five other priests resolved that no bishop was needed in the United States. The priests did, however, petition Rome to allow one of their number to serve as a superior, and they nominated Carroll for this position. The pope, Pius VI, approved, and on June 6, 1784, Carroll was named prefect apostolic of the Church in the United States, with the faculties to administer the Sacrament of Confirmation.

One of the greatest problems Father Carroll faced as prefect was a lack of priests. Priests sent from Europe often proved troublesome. Claude Florent Bouchard, **abbé** de la Poterie, a priest from France, for example, settled in Boston in 1788 where he issued a pastoral letter claiming he had special powers from Father Carroll. When it became known that the archbishop of Paris had suspended the abbé before he came to America, Father Carroll too had to suspend him. Bouchard then published an inflammatory tract charging that Father Carroll was working secretly to revive the Jesuits in America.

Father Carroll had to struggle with a peculiarly American form of Church government—trusteeship. Since there had been no established Church government in English America, Catholic laymen, designated *trustees*, had established and funded Catholic congregations and paid priests' salaries. Because of their status, it was not long before trustees began to see themselves as the final authorities in Church matters, hiring priests, and firing them at will if they did not approve of them. This problem became especially troublesome when certain charismatic priests with a gift for eloquence became focal points for factions within the Church, opposing at times Father Carroll's authority. Once, in New York, the trustees refused to allow Father Carroll to say Mass in St. Peter's church, and in Philadelphia, the trustees of a German church led a group of Catholics into schism over a controversy about a priest.

Such troubles finally convinced Carroll and others that someone with more authority than a prefect apostolic was needed to guide the American Church—it needed a bishop. In 1785, Carroll suggested to Rome that the first American bishop be elected by the priests so that it would not appear to Americans that the bishop received his authority from a "foreign power." (The pope, one must remember, was at that time the temporal ruler of central Italy.) Rome agreed. When the American priests gathered to select one of their number to be bishop, they chose John Carroll. On November 6, 1789, Pope Pius VI appointed Carroll bishop of Baltimore with jurisdiction over the entire United States. He was consecrated a year later in England by the Benedictine bishop, Charles Walmesley, at the chapel of Lulworth Castle.

The problems in the American Church did not end because it now had a bishop. Trustees continued to assert their authority, and Carroll still had to rely on foreign priests to staff the churches. Revolution in France was driving a number of priests to American shores. Many of these were worthy men; some were not. Bishop Carroll had to suspend one priest, Abbé Louis Rousselet, who had formed a breakaway parish in Boston after he had engaged in a controversy with his colleague, Father John Thayer. Thayer, a former Puritan minister and a native Bostonian who had become Catholic after a visit to Rome, was Rousselet's temperamental opposite. After his suspension, Abbé Rousselet left America. He ended up in the French West Indian island of Guadeloupe where officials of the French revolutionary government arrested him. He spent his last days ministering to those facing death by guillotine. His regret was that he had to die "without having the efficacious graces of the Sacraments applied to my poor soul."

Before Carroll's appointment as bishop, an Irish priest, Patrick Smyth, had published an attack on Carroll and the American Church in a pamphlet titled, *The Present State of the*

abbé: French, for abbot; also, a title given to a member of the clergy in France

Catholic Missions Conducted by the ex-Jesuits in North America. Smyth, who had served as a priest in Maryland, had felt himself slighted and had returned to Ireland. He accused the former Jesuits in America of living like lords on estates worked by slaves, whom the priests treated cruelly.

The former Jesuits did own slaves. They did not live in luxury. In a letter to Archbishop Troy of Dublin, Carroll refuted the accusation of cruel treatment:

> The few to whom this management is committed, treat their Negroes with great mildness and are attentive to guard them from the evils of hunger and nakedness; that they work less and are much better fed, lodged and clothed, than labouring men in almost any part of Europe; that the instances are rare indeed, and almost unknown, of corporal punishment being inflicted on any of them who are come to the age of manhood; and that a priest's negro is almost proverbial for one, who is allowed to act without control.

At times, it seemed the Catholic Church in the United States was rife with problems. German Catholics wanted a German bishop, and well-established parishes balked at submitting to a bishop's authority. But all was not dark. One bright spot was the establishment of a seminary by four French Sulpician priests and five English speaking students—an endeavor paid for by the Sulpicians themselves. The Sulpician priests also staffed the first Catholic college in America, Georgetown College (now in Washington, D.C.), which opened its doors the same year the seminary did, in 1791.

Perhaps Bishop Carroll's most important contribution to the Church in the U.S. in these early years was the dedication of his new diocese to the Mother of God. One of the bishop's first tasks was to order that the Litany of Loretto, a prayer to Mary, be recited before every High Mass. Her intercession would be needed in the coming years of struggle, triumph, and disappointment for the Church in the United States.

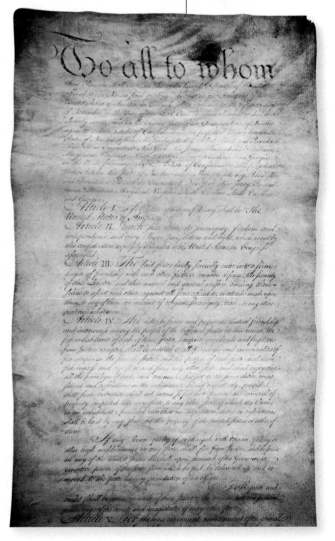

First page of the Articles of Confederation

The Struggle for a New Government

It did not take long for the Articles of Confederation to betray their inadequacies as a model for a national government. States had been unwilling to compromise their newly won independence by giving too much power to the national government, and they would not cooperate with it once it was established. The result was the national government was always in desperate need of money and incapable of resolving conflicts between states.

Since Congress could not tax but only requisition money from the states, it relied on the willingness of state legislatures to supply needed revenues. Only New Jersey refused outright to pay, but other states contented themselves with paying the interest on the debt the national government owed a state's citizens; this meant that Congress received no new revenue, but merely enjoyed a reduced debt burden. Attempts to enhance Congress' taxing power through amendments failed in 1781, 1783, and 1784 because amendments required receiving the consent of all the states—an improbable, if not impossible, hope.

Congress' weaknesses meant it could not fulfill its obligations under the peace bargain with Great Britain. The Treaty of Paris required the United States to respect the property of loyalists; but because Congress was unable to exercise authority over the states, loyalists suffered the loss not only of their property, but, occasionally, their lives as well. While some loyalists had fled to Canada and England, and others had returned to their homes and prospered, many others underwent great suffering in the years following the revolution. This was especially true in North Carolina, where partisan warfare had stoked bitter feeling, since both Tory regiments and patriots under Nathaniel Greene had left devastated farms and plantations in their wake. Loyalists in North Carolina who attempted to recover their property were threatened, sometimes with death. The otherwise moderate George Washington expressed the sentiment of many of his countrymen when he called loyalists "parricides" and "unhappy wretches! Deluded mortals!"

Congress not only failed to protect loyalists, it failed the patriots who had fought for independence. Throughout the latter part of the war, Congress had been inept at supplying the army properly. Now, after the war, the national government still owed large sums of back pay to veteran soldiers. It's not surprising that these former soldiers felt that the government had betrayed them.

Congress could do little to settle state conflicts that threatened to tear the fledgling union apart. New York placed heavy taxes on imports from New Jersey and Connecticut because merchants in those states (whose duties on imports were lower than New York's) had been able to sell foreign goods in New York at prices lower than New York merchants could charge. In retaliation, New Jersey charged New York 30 pounds a month to keep a lighthouse on Sandy Hook at the mouth of the Hudson River. Virginia and Maryland fought over oyster fisheries in the Chesapeake Bay and over who controlled the Potomac River, which Maryland claimed from bank to bank.

Foreign powers humiliated the new government. Despite the Treaty of Paris, Great Britain still retained forts in the northwest—two on Lake Champlain and others at Ogdensburg, Oswego, Niagara, Detroit, and Michilimackinac. When Congress complained of this violation of the Treaty of Paris, the British government retorted that the United States had not honored the treaty, either: debts to Britain had not been paid, and the property of loyalists had not been returned.

Troubles came, too, on account of Spain, which retained the settlements of Natchez and Vicksburg on the east bank of the Mississippi—on U.S. territory, according to the Treaty of Paris. Placing themselves under Spain's protection, the Creek, Choctaw, and Cherokee tribes raided American settlements on the Cumberland and Tennessee Rivers. Western farmers, who had to ship their produce by way of Spanish-held New Orleans and, thence, to the Atlantic coast cities, faced heavy duties on their goods. And, worse, General James Wilkinson of Kentucky and other U.S. citizens were accepting pensions from Spain and scheming to make the West a separate republic under Spanish protection. At the same time, Vermont, which had been denied statehood, was contemplating secession and making overtures to the British in Canada.

The Northwest Ordinance

The states however did cooperate with the national government in the matter of western land claims. Based on their old colonial charters, several of the states had laid claims to lands between the Appalachians and the Mississippi River. Now, they were handing their lands over to the central government. Virginia, which had agreed to the cession of her western lands in 1781, finally ceded them on March 1, 1784. The following year, Massachusetts and Connecticut both ceded their western land claims to the central government. In subsequent years, North Carolina and Georgia followed suit. The formation of western lands into territories of the central government made the United States an imperial power. More importantly (at least for the time), it provided the impoverished Congress with a new source of revenue—land sales to settlers. For instance, the Ohio Company, a group of land speculators, agreed to buy 1,500,000 acres of western land from the government for a dollar an acre.

Acquiring western territories was one discernible achievement in the early years of the American republic. Another was the Northwest Ordinance, a body of laws Congress adopted on July 13, 1787 to govern the territories. The Northwest Ordinance governs United States territories to the present day.

The Northwest Ordinance divided the Northwest (the territories north of the Ohio River and west of the Appalachians) into five regions, each of which eventually became a state. When any of these regions attained a population of 5,000 free males, Congress was to establish a territorial government for it. The government consisted of a representative assembly, elected by the people of the territory; a governor, appointed by Congress; and a council of five chosen by Congress from names submitted by the territorial assembly. All townships in the territories were to be surveyed six miles square and divided into 36 sections, each a mile square, that were to be sold at auction. Section 16 in every township was reserved for the support of public schools. When a region attained a population of 60,000 freemen, it could become a state, equal in rights and privileges to the original states.

A sort of bill of rights formed a part of the Northwest Ordinance. Congress guaranteed territorial inhabitants religious freedom. Settlements had to provide for schools, since, said the ordinance, "religion, morality, and knowledge" are "necessary to good government and the happiness of mankind."

The Northwest Ordinance made provisions for Native Americans living within the western territories:

> The utmost good faith shall always be observed towards the Indians, their lands and property shall never be taken from them without their consent; and in their property, rights, and liberty, they shall never be invaded or disturbed, unless in just and lawful wars authorized by Congress; but laws founded in justice and humanity, shall from time to time be made for preventing wrongs being done to them, and for preserving peace and friendship with them.

The Northwest Ordinance addressed slavery in Article VI:

> There shall be neither slavery nor involuntary servitude, otherwise than in the punishment of crimes whereof the party shall have been duly convicted.

The new ordinance stipulated, however, that slaves who escaped to the territory had to be returned to their masters.

Rebellion in Massachusetts

The years following the end of the war found farmers all over America sinking deeper into debt. In the course of the war, many farmers had made good money selling their crops to the Continental Army. With the coming of peace, farmers lost this lucrative market; and this loss, coupled with the general economic downturn of the time, left them owing money to all sorts of creditors, including the government—debts that they could not repay. In those days, a man could be imprisoned for not paying his debts; and, as today, his land could be seized and sold at auction.

A contemporary drawing of Daniel Shays (left) and Job Shattuck, a fellow rebel. The verse to the left reads "Thro' drifted storms let SHAYS the Court assail/And SHATTUCK rise, illustrious from the Jail/In coward Hands, let legal Powers expire,/And give new Subjects to my sounding Lyre."

Many states, especially in the North, where the debt problem was the most dire, passed laws to relieve the poor farmers. Some states established land banks, which lent a kind of paper money to the farmers that they could use to pay their taxes. Other states passed "stay laws" that postponed the collection of mortgages and other debts. Rhode Island, one of the most radically democratic of the states, passed a law that if a creditor refused to take state paper money in repayment of debts, then his debtors could deposit the money at a local court and the law would consider the debt paid. But creditors did not want paper money; they decided it worthless, as it was not backed by "specie"—gold or silver. Many Rhode Island merchants, therefore, closed shop, or moved to New York or the West Indies.

Things were different in Massachusetts. Unlike the democratic Rhode Island legislature, in the Massachusetts Great and General Court (the state legislature), any relief measure passed by the lower house legislature was defeated by the senate, representing the wealthier coastal counties instead of the poorer western counties. The strongly conservative Massachusetts government refused to issue paper money and insisted that all debts be paid in specie. Specie was hard to come by, and so it took longer for a farmer to earn the money to pay his debts—and his taxes, for that matter, which weighed more heavily on the poor than on the rich. The poor economy compelled merchants to demand payment of debts from shopkeepers, who sought payment from farmers; and since farmers could not pay in specie, they lost their farms, cattle, furniture, and even their freedom to their creditors. In one year alone—1785—92 men were imprisoned for debt in Massachusetts.

The situation became yet more dire when the Massachusetts Great and General Court placed a tax on paper and vellum used for books, deeds, and newspapers. Legal documents also had to be printed on sheets stamped by the commissioner of taxes—a stamp tax! Farmers first responded by requesting relief from the legislature; and when that didn't work, they formed county conventions to state their grievances. They even established committees of correspondence. The irony of the situation was lost on Sam Adams—now a respectable member of the state legislature—who threatened to hang anyone who did the very things he had done against the British government only ten years previous.

In the fall of 1786, groups of farmers in the four western counties and Middlesex County prevented courts from sitting. They hoped they thus could keep the courts from trying any more farmers for debt until the coming of the spring elections that could change the membership of the legislature. In response, Governor James Bowdoin issued a proclamation forbidding unlawful assemblies and ordered out the state militia to disperse the farmers. Meanwhile, Daniel Shays, a poor farmer who had served as a captain of the Massachusetts line regiment during the Revolutionary War, became the leader of the rebellious farmers. Ignoring the governor's proclamation, Shays, along with Luke Day and Eli Parsons, led his farmer regiments in a march on Springfield to prevent the sitting of the state supreme court and seize the federal arsenal there.

When Governor Bowdoin learned of Shays' movements, he ordered General William Shepard (who had fought alongside Shays at Bunker Hill) to garrison Springfield. On January 25, 1787, Shays' men marched on Springfield and attacked Shepard's force,

"The Looking Glass"—a political cartoon from 1787 in support of a new constitution referring to Shays' Rebellion and other events

which had taken its position on a small rise. Shepard had ordered his men to fire over the heads of the farmers, to frighten them; but when the farmers continued their advance, Shepard ordered his men to shoot to kill. After the first volley of militia muskets and artillery, Shays' men broke and fled. Retreating through the snow and bitter cold of a New England winter, they did not form again until they reached Petersham, about 45 miles west of Springfield.

State militia under General Benjamin Lincoln pursued Shays' forces to Petersham where, on February 4, they routed the farmers and took many prisoners. Fourteen of the leaders of the rebellion were sentenced to death (they were eventually pardoned). Shays himself escaped to Vermont, while Eli Parsons fled to New York, where he raised another force. In late February, Parsons led his new force into Massachusetts, where he was joined by more recruits. Seizing supplies at Stockbridge, Parsons' men moved against Springfield, where they confronted a larger force of state militia and fled, leaving two dead and 30 wounded. By March 1787, state militia had crushed the rebellion.

Shays' Rebellion had failed. Yet it may have inspired changes in Massachusetts. An election in the spring brought a new legislature and governor to power. The new legislature passed laws granting relief to the burdened tillers of the soil. The year 1787, too, ushered in a period of prosperity, and farmers became less discontent.

Still, Shays' Rebellion was troubling to many in America: it confirmed their conviction that the current form of the national government was insufficiently powerful to keep the peace. Though the Massachusetts militia had proved quite capable of handling the rebellion, some pointed out that the federal government had been powerless to help. Leaders throughout America were deeply worried about the future of the American union. Only Thomas Jefferson, then ambassador to France, was unruffled. "A little rebellion now and then is a good thing," he wrote from Paris. "The tree of liberty must be refreshed from time to time with the blood of patriots and tyrants."

The Pennsylvania state house, Philadelphia, where the constitutional convention was held

A New Constitution

When, in 1785, delegates from Virginia and Maryland met to settle their disputes over oyster fisheries and the Potomac boundary, they realized they could not reach a resolution on these questions without the cooperation of Delaware and Pennsylvania. Greater issues were at stake than the simple adjustment of trade and boundaries—issues that would require the concurrence of more than just two or three states. The process of addressing such issues was haphazard and difficult under the federal government, for it possessed no way to force states to come to an agreement on controversial points—and having come to an agreement, observe it. The root of the problem was the Articles of Confederation. Something had to be done to reform them.

To this end, Virginia and Maryland called for a convention of all the states to meet in Annapolis, Maryland. But when the convention met in September 1786, only five states had sent delegates. The most the Annapolis delegates could do was call for another convention. Congress concurred and on February 21, 1787 invited the states to send delegates to a convention that was to meet in Philadelphia "for the sole and express purpose of revising the

A General *Faux Pas*

Washington was held in highest esteem by everyone at the constitutional convention. However, Gouverneur Morris declared that he himself was not in awe of Washington. Hearing Morris' boast, James Madison wagered a dinner that Morris would not walk up to Washington, slap him on the back, and say, "How are you today, my dear General?" Morris took up the bet. Afterward, over the dinner Madison had provided for having lost the bet, Morris confessed that after the withering look the general had given him after the slap on the back, he would never again attempt a similar familiarity—not for a thousand dinners.

Articles of Confederation" so that they might "render the federal constitution adequate to the exigencies of government, and the preservation of the Union."

The convention was set to open on May 14, 1787; but, by that date, only a few delegates had appeared in Philadelphia. Eleven days later, delegates from only seven states were present. Delegates from Vermont, New Hampshire, Connecticut, and Maryland trickled in over the next few months. Rhode Island's delegates never showed up.

The delegates that came to Philadelphia represented the aristocracy of the new republic. Many were lawyers, some were college professors, others had served in their state legislatures. They were conspicuous for their youth. Some were in their late twenties, while the leaders, for the most part, were men in their early to late thirties. Among the younger were Alexander Hamilton (just 32), James Madison, Gouverneur Morris, and Edmund Randolph. Others, such as James Wilson, Luther Martin, Oliver Ellsworth, and William Paterson, were in their forties. The "venerable fathers" of the convention included George Washington, then 55, and the octogenarian Benjamin Franklin.

Washington had been unwilling to leave retirement at Mount Vernon—after all, he had taken formal leave of public life after the war ended, and he wondered whether it might not be dishonorable to take up what he had abandoned. Friends, however, convinced the general that he must serve as the convention's president—only he could command the respect necessary to keep order in the convention, they said. Events proved the truth of this. Though, as president, he could not engage in the discussions, Washington served as the unifying force among the disputatious delegates.

The delegates to the constitutional convention held that a "mixed" form of government was the safest form of government, a notion they drew from their study of classical Greek and Roman politics and from the writings of the French Liberal theorist, Montesquieu. This conviction was reflected in the first plan offered to the convention, the Virginia Plan. Introduced by Edmund Randolph just four days after the opening of the convention, the Virginia Plan called for a bicameral (two-house) national legislature. Both the lower and upper houses would represent the states according to population (proportional representation)—that is, the states with larger populations ("large states") would have a greater number of representatives; the "small states"—those with smaller populations —a fewer number. The plan provided that the people would elect members of the lower house, while members of the upper house, the Senate, would be appointed by the lower house from lists provided by the states. The Virginia Plan provided for a national executive and a national judiciary.

According to the Virginia Plan, the legislature would make laws "in all cases to which the separate States are incompetent, or in which the harmony of the United States may be interrupted by the exercise of individual legislation." It would further have the right "to negative all laws passed by the several States, contravening, in the opinion of the National Legislature the articles of Union; and to call forth the force of the Union against any member of the Union failing to fulfill its duty under the articles thereof." These provisions, of course, gave the national government very wide powers over the states; and to assuage the fears of delegates who opposed a strong national government, the plan provided for a Council of Revision that could overturn any acts of the national government that it deemed violated the rights of the states.

The Small States Fight Back

The Virginia Plan was the work of one of two major factions at the convention—the nationalists, those who favored a strong, central government that would dominate the states. The nationalists thought the Articles of Confederation had rendered the national government impotent at home and a mockery abroad. They wanted no mere revising of the articles—as Congress had authorized—but a complete and total overhaul: an entirely new constitution. The nationalists were the more energetic faction; they had organized early and had taken control of the convention. For a time it looked as if they would get everything they wanted.

The other faction, which favored a weak central government and the preservation of state sovereignty, was at first disorganized and unable to stop the forward momentum of the nationalists. The second faction represented the small states, and these were particularly worried by the Virginia Plan's provision for proportional representation. Proportional representation, they thought, would allow the large states to dominate in the national counsels. The small states faction favored equal representation, as the Articles of Confederation provided, where each state, regardless of its size, received only one vote in Congress.

The nationalists, or large state faction, thought it unjust that the small states be treated as the equals of the large states. But they were not worried at first about the small state faction: the nationalists, after all, controlled the convention. Not that there was no opposition to the Virginia Plan—Roger Sherman of Connecticut and Elbridge Gerry of Massachusetts opposed popular elections; they thought that state legislatures should appoint the members of the national legislature. George Mason, James Wilson, and James Madison opposed Sherman and Gerry. Another question was whether the executive should be one man or many, and Edmund Randolph opposed a one-man executive, calling it the "foetus of monarchy." Next came the question whether the people should elect, or the states appoint, the members of the upper house. Madison favored the former; Gerry and Mason, the latter. The upper house, Gerry and Mason said, should represent the commercial and moneyed interests, just as the British House of Lords represented the nobility. And Mason thought that having the state legislatures appoint the members of the upper house would draw the states more into the central government, making them "a constituent part of the national establishment."

Alexander Hamilton, by John Trumbull

For a time it appeared that the nationalists would have their way in the convention. But, then, on June 9, 1787, William Paterson of New Jersey stood up before the delegates and spoke out against proportional representation. If the large states, he said, insisted on proportional representation, then they could forge a union among themselves, without the small states. "Let them unite," he said, "but let them remember that they have no authority to compel the others to unite. New Jersey will never confederate on the plan before the Committee. She would be swallowed up."

Paterson's speech was the first shot in a struggle that would bedevil the rest of the convention. Two days after Paterson spoke, Roger Sherman offered a compromise—each state should have one vote in the Senate and proportional representation in the lower house. A vote of six states to five defeated this compromise. Four days later, on June 15, Paterson submitted a new plan, the New Jersey Plan, which called for a mere revision of the Articles of Confederation and for equal representation of states in the legislature. The introduction of this plan shook up the nationalists—they had not expected such organized resistance from the small states.

William Paterson

On June 18, Alexander Hamilton, a delegate from New York, stood up to champion an eccentric proposal. The national government, he said, should reflect the British constitution. The lower house, like the House of Commons, should be elected, while members of the Senate should serve for life or for good behavior. Hamilton asserted that the executive should also serve for life. As for the states—well, they should be abolished, since, said Hamilton, they were "not necessary for any of the great purposes of commerce, revenue, or agriculture." Instead of keeping the states, Hamilton favored dividing the country into new administrative districts.

Hamilton's proposal was too extreme for the delegates. It was never even brought up for a vote. The New Jersey Plan, however, was; but on June 18 it was rejected, seven states to three, in favor of the Virginia Plan. This did not stop the champions of equal representation, however. The controversy raged on until the entire convention stood at an impasse.

It was on June 28, when all seemed hopeless, that Benjamin Franklin arose and made a surprising request. Addressing Washington, Franklin proposed opening the convention's sessions with prayer.

"I have lived, Sir, a long time," said the 81-year old Franklin, "and the longer I live, the more convincing proofs I see of this truth, that God governs in the affairs of men. And if a sparrow cannot fall to the ground without his notice, is it probable that an empire can rise without his aid?" A delegate, however, explained to Franklin the difficulties of his proposal; the convention had no money to spare for a chaplain—and, besides, if it got out that the delegates had felt it necessary to resort to prayer, the public might think matters must be going badly indeed in the convention! The delegates rejected Franklin's motion.

At Last, Compromise

In the hot, humid weather of a Philadelphia summer, delegates wrangled, tempers flared over the one issue they could not resolve—how states should be represented in the national government. Finally, after delegates from Delaware, New Jersey, and Maryland threatened to return home, Roger Sherman again stood up and again offered his plan—proportional representation in the lower house, equal representation in the senate. The vote on the "Connecticut Compromise," as it was called, was five to five; nevertheless, it was recorded as passing. Many of the nationalists, including Madison and Hamilton, still wanted only proportional representation, but the best they could get, they found, was a compromise.

The convention adjourned on July 26, leaving a committee to draw up the draft of the new constitution. The draft, released on August 6, contained the Connecticut Compromise—the lower house, the House of Representatives, would have proportional representation, while the upper house, the Senate, would admit two representatives from each state. The executive, called the president, would be elected indirectly by the people—that is, the people would vote for electors who, in turn, voted for the president. The number of electors for each state was to be proportional to its population. This measure, the delegates thought, put a buffer between the people and the president, for each elector had the discretion to vote against the will of the people who chose him. Good republicans, the delegates did not trust the wisdom of the common folk, who, they thought, tended to mobocracy. The president would be commander-in-chief of the armed forces and would have veto power over congressional legislation. Only a two-thirds majority in both houses of the legislature could override a president's veto. Finally, the draft established a supreme court whose members, appointed for life by the president with the consent of the Senate, would serve during good behavior. Lifetime terms, the delegates hoped, would free the court from political pressures, such as the need to curry favor with politicians or with the public in elections.

The draft for the constitution, of course, did not end all controversy. Delegates debated over immigration, a standing army, paper money, and property qualifications for public office. The disputes over the perpetuation of the slave trade presaged an important division in the United States in the coming years—the division between North and South. One prominent southerner and slave owner, George Mason of Virginia, called for an end to the slave trade, but delegates from South Carolina and Georgia objected. General Charles Cotesworth Pinckney of South Carolina protested that the economy of his state needed slave labor, and John Rutledge of South Carolina predicted the secession of three states if the slave trade were not continued. The convention therefore adopted a compromise that allowed the foreign slave trade for another 20 years, after which time it would be illegal.

Another controversy surrounded the coercive powers of the national government. Paterson's New Jersey Plan said that if a state ignored an act of Congress, the president should have the power "to call forth the power of the confederate states . . . to enforce and compel obedience." Many delegates, including Madison, objected to this provision, since, they said, it could lead to the forceful domination of the small by the large states. What the delegates decided is embodied in Article 6 of the constitution—the national government could not resort to force but only to the courts of law if states refused to comply with congressional acts.

What resulted from all the debates was a "federal" model of government, that more or less defined the areas where the national and state governments exercised sovereignty. The United States was to have two sovereigns —the states in regards to their internal affairs, and the national government in relation to national matters, such as war and peace, treaties with foreign nations, and international and interstate trade. As one aspect of this sovereignty, the national government would have the authority to lay taxes directly on citizens, bypassing state legislatures, and thus freeing it from monetary dependence on the states.

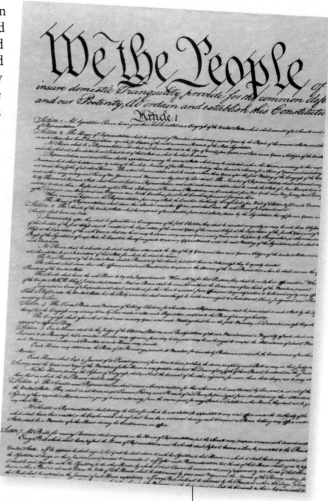

The United States Constitution

Most of the delegates were dissatisfied when they came to sign the constitution on September 17, 1787. All of the New York delegates, except Alexander Hamilton, refused to sign—and Hamilton called the document "a weak and worthless fabric." Luther Martin declared the constitution opposed to liberty, and George Mason refused to sign it, as did Edmund Randolph and Elbridge Gerry. Daniel Carroll, Charles Carroll's brother, called the constitution "the Continental Congress in two volumes instead of one," and Madison declared that "the change which it proposes comes to much less in the addition of New Powers to the Union, than in the invigoration of its Original Powers." Many delegates thought the constitutional convention largely a failure.

Benjamin Franklin, however, held a different view. Wrote an eyewitness:

> Looking towards the President's chair at the back of which a rising sun happened to be painted, [Franklin] observed to a few members near him, that Painters had found it difficult to distinguish in their art a rising from a setting sun. I have, said he, often and often in the course of the Session, and the vicissitudes of my hopes and fears as to its issue, looked at that behind the President without being able to tell whether it was rising or setting: but now at length I have the happiness to know that it is a rising and not a setting Sun.

Fight for Ratification

In the weeks and months following the close of the constitutional convention, many Americans would have demurred at Franklin's optimism. Winning approval from the states for the new constitution would not be automatic or easy. A vigorous opposition awaited the "federalists," as the supporters of the constitution called themselves. Their foes, the "anti-federalists," came from a variety of backgrounds and opposed the new constitution for a variety of reasons. In some cases, they represented the proponents of democracy, optimistic about human nature and hoping for the birth of an ideal age. These feared a strong centralized government with the power to tax; such a government, they thought, would become the tool of the few for the oppression of the many. Others opposed the new government for less worthy reasons, and many opposed it for a variety of reasons that cannot be easily cataloged. A common division was based on age—younger men tended to support the constitution while the older, more established men opposed it. This was true especially in the South, where the strongest opposition to the constitution came from the settled tidewater regions, while the raw western counties supported it.

The constitutional convention called for ratification of the constitution by state conventions, not state legislatures—a savvy move, since a state convention would have a wider representation than a legislature and thus be more likely to include elements more favorable to ratification. Nine states had to ratify, or approve, the constitution before it could go into effect. To reach this threshold was not an easy task, as events proved. For example, Richard Henry Lee, one of the distinguished Virginia Lees, fought to keep Congress from sending the constitution to the various state conventions. He failed, but his and his allies' influence was sufficient to keep Congress from endorsing the proposed constitution.

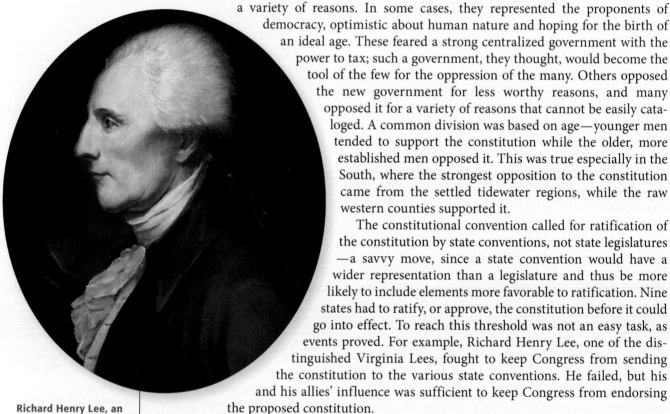

Richard Henry Lee, an anti-federalist

The small states (except for Rhode Island) embraced the new constitution enthusiastically. The first state to ratify it was Delaware, on December 7, 1787. Pennsylvania, though a large state, followed on December 12—the federalists there had organized the state convention before the opposition could mobilize. The New Jersey convention ratified the constitution six days later. In the first two months of 1788, Connecticut and Georgia in turn ratified the constitution.

An important battleground was Massachusetts, one of the most populous states and the major center of the country's shipping and trade. If Massachusetts failed to ratify the constitution, other major states, such as Virginia and New York, would probably also not ratify it. The Massachusetts convention met on January 9, 1788, and at the first vote, 192 delegates opposed ratification while 144 favored it. Sam Adams opposed the ratification until his friends, the Boston shipwrights, convinced him otherwise.

Nathaniel Gorham and Rufus King, the chief proponents of the constitution in Massachusetts, had an uphill battle to fight. Anti-federalists criticized the constitution for its failure to outlaw slavery and because it did not forbid government offices to non-Christians. Those who thought liberty was preserved only if representatives served one-year terms objected to the proposed two-year term for representatives and the six-year term for senators. Still, despite the opposition, on February 6, 1788, Massachusetts ratified the constitution, but only by the narrow margin of 187 to 168. As part of its ratification, the Massachusetts convention requested the addition of a bill of rights to the constitution.

In the spring of 1788, Maryland, South Carolina, and New Hampshire ratified the constitution. Though New Hampshire brought the number of ratifying states to the required nine, that Virginia and New York (the two largest and most powerful states) still held aloof imperiled the future of a federal union under the new constitution. Virginia's anti-federalists included such prominent patriots as George Mason and Patrick Henry. Among the federalists were numbered James Madison, Colonel Henry ("Lighthorse Harry") Lee, the young John Marshall (later to become chief justice of the Supreme Court), Edmund Randolph, and, most important of all, George Washington.

Patrick Henry delivered a long address to the Virginia convention, criticizing the constitution on a number of grounds. He objected to its leading off with "we the people"; "the people gave them [the constitutional convention] no power to use their name," insisted Henry. "That they exceeded their power is perfectly clear." Henry found fault with the office of president ("it squints toward monarchy") and declared that with its new taxing power, Congress will "clutch the purse with one hand and wave the sword with the other." Chiefly, Henry feared that the new government would compromise America's fledgling liberty.

Edmund Randolph refuted Henry. The union of the states, said Randolph, was necessary for the continuance of "our political happiness and existence. Let it not be recorded of Americans," he said, "that, after having overcome the most astonishing difficulties, and after having gained the admiration of the world by their incomparable valor and policy, they lost their acquired reputation, their national consequence and happiness by their own indiscretion.... Catch the present moment ... for it may be lost, never to be regained."

George Mason questioned whether the constitution could govern so wide a territory as the United States while preserving liberty. "There never was government over a very extensive country without destroying the liberties of the people," said Mason. He criti-

Edmund Randolph, a federalist

cized the constitution for failing to outlaw the importation of slaves; at the same time, he criticized it for not sufficiently protecting Southern slave holders from the loss of their "property."

It was probably Washington's support that won the day for the constitution in Virginia. The state convention approved the new government on June 25, 1788 by a margin of only ten votes.

In New York, the opposition —chiefly large landowners led by Governor Clinton—feared the constitution would increase taxes on their properties. Alexander Hamilton and John Jay, joined by the Virginian, James Madison, writing under the pen name "Publius,"

John Jay, by Gilbert Stuart

composed a series of articles for New York journals in defense of the constitution. These articles, later collected into a volume called *The Federalist*, developed the themes of the insufficiency of the Articles of Confederation and the advantages of the constitution. This collection, written by men who had participated in the constitutional convention, has since gained a quasi-official status as an authoritative interpretation of the constitution.

In the first article of what became *The Federalist*, Hamilton invoked a sentiment reminiscent of Winthrop's "city on the hill" and one increasingly prevalent in post-revolutionary America—that the United States has a special mission to all of mankind. If America fails in the cause of free government, who can prevail? "It has been frequently remarked," wrote Hamilton, "that it seems to have been reserved to the people of this country, by their conduct and example, to decide the important question, whether societies of men are really capable or not of establishing good government from reflection and choice, or whether they are forever destined to depend for their political constitutions on accident or force. If there be any truth in the remark, the crisis at which we are arrived may with propriety be regarded as the era in which that decision is to be made; and a wrong election of the part we shall act may, in this view, serve to be considered as the general misfortune of mankind."

In perhaps the most famous of the papers, "Federalist Number 10," Madison addressed the question of factions and interest groups in society and the particular danger they pose to free governments. The remedy to such a danger does not lie in state governments—which, being relatively small, are more prone to factions—argued Madison. A large republic is different. There, unlike in a democracy, the people choose men to represent them in government, and these men, more removed from popular passions, could more equitably than the mass of the people judge matters set before them. Moreover, the vastness of the national republic meant that its factions would be more varied, more spread apart, and less able to join together in a common enterprise. Alluding probably to Shays' rebellion, Madison wrote:

> The influence of factious leaders may kindle a flame within their particular States, but will be unable to spread a general conflagration through the other States. A religious sect may degenerate into a political faction in a part of the Confederacy; but the variety of sects dispersed over the entire face of it must secure the national councils against any dangers from that source. A rage for paper money, for an abolition of debts, for an equal division of property, or for any other improper or wicked project, will be less apt to pervade the whole body of the Union than a particular member of it; in the same proportion as such a malady is more likely to taint a particular county or district, than an entire State.

Yet, despite the eloquence and arguments of *The Federalist*, the anti-federalists remained a very strong force in New York. Perhaps what finally turned the tide in favor of the constitution in that aristocratic state was the realization that if the convention failed to ratify it, New York would be left out in the company of the only other state that had not approved the constitution—Rhode Island, that hated stronghold of radical democracy, which had not even called a state convention! (It would not do so until 1790.) Whatever the reason, New York did finally ratify the constitution by the small margin of 30 yeas to 27 nays.

With the concurrence of all the states but Rhode Island, Congress formally declared the constitution ratified and called for presidential and congressional elections

First in Peace

The first presidential election was a mere formality—all knew that George Washington would be the republic's first president. He ran unopposed and so became the only president in U.S. history to receive the entire electoral vote.

A view Federal Hall, New York City, as it appeared in 1797 (an 1847 lithograph by Henry R. Robinson). It was on the balcony of this hall that Washington was inaugurated president.

In his inauguration address delivered April 30, 1789, President Washington expressed his reluctance to accept the presidency. "Among the vicissitudes incident to life no event could have filled me with greater anxieties," said Washington:

> On the one hand, I was summoned by my country, whose voice I can never hear but with veneration and love, from a retreat which I had chosen with the fondest predilection, and, in my flattering hopes, with an immutable decision, as the asylum of my declining years . . . On the other hand, the magnitude and difficulty of the trust to which the voice of my country called me, being sufficient to awaken in the wisest and most experienced of her citizens a distrustful scrutiny into his qualifications, could not but overwhelm with despondence one who (inheriting inferior endowments from nature and unpracticed in the duties of civil administration) ought to be peculiarly conscious of his own deficiencies.

Washington's task was formidable. He had to turn a written constitution into a working government over a people, many of whom still opposed it. In part to appease the anti-federalists, Washington in his inaugural address hinted that Congress should approve a bill of rights. Accordingly, 12 amendments were presented to Congress, which approved them and sent them on to the states for ratification. By December 15, the required number of states had ratified ten of the 12 amendments, and these became part of the constitution.

The Bill of Rights was seen as a series of checks upon the power of the federal government. Thus, Article I prohibits Congress, but not the states, to make laws that "abridge the freedom of speech, or of the press" or the right to free assembly and petition. It forbids Congress, but not state legislatures, to make a "law respecting an establishment of religion, or prohibiting the free exercise thereof." Article II protects a state's right to a militia and so forbids the federal government from infringing on "the right of the people to keep and bear Arms." Article X enshrines a principle dear to the anti-federalists—the separation of powers in American government, mandating that "powers not delegated to the United States by the Constitution, nor prohibited by it to the States, are reserved to the States respectively, or to the people." Neither this amendment nor any part of the constitution, however, clearly delineates all the respective powers of the federal government or the states—assuring that the question would serve as the grist for many future debates both inside and outside of Congress.

Washington realized his limitations and so attempted to surround himself with a number of talented men upon whom he could rely. Besides John Adams, who was elected vice-president (in those days the candidate who received the second highest number of votes became vice-president), Washington's first administration included Thomas Jefferson as secretary of state, Alexander Hamilton as head of the treasury department, General Knox as secretary of war, and Edmund Randolph as attorney general. Washington made no important decisions without consulting these officials—who formed what became known as his "cabinet."

How to Address a President

Among the issues confronting the first Congress was the question of how one should address a president. Adams, who as vice-president served also as president of the Senate, tended toward the pompous and suggested that everyone address the president as "His Highness the President of the United States of America and the Protector of the Rights of the Same." The more republican and, shall we say, more prosaic Senate rejected this mouthful. They settled on "Mr. President," the form of address used till the present day.

An important task for Washington was composing the Supreme Court. Although the Constitution established the judiciary as the third branch of government, it did not specify how many justices should sit on the court. Thus, on September 24, 1789, Congress passed the Judiciary Act, setting the number of justices at six—one chief justice and five associates. (The number was later increased to nine). The act also established 13 district courts and three circuit courts.

precedent: something done or said that is taken for an instance or example to justify a similar act in the future

President Washington, "with the advice and consent of the Senate," appointed John Jay as the republic's first chief justice. The "Jay Court" is significant for establishing **precedents** for what later became known as "judicial review"—the court's critique of the legal acts of states and the federal government. The first of these precedents was the Supreme Court's decision that a law passed by the Connecticut assembly was unconstitutional; the second was the court's refusal to execute a law passed by Congress. In the latter case, the court said that it was unconstitutional for the federal courts to act as the agents of Congress.

Alexander Hamilton became Washington's most trusted adviser. Hamilton's goal was to see the new federal government well-established and strong. An admirer of the British government, Hamilton worked to set the financial affairs of the federal government upon principles already established in the mother country. For Hamilton, the wealthy (cultured and established families, prosperous merchants, creditors, and successful financiers) were the solid pillars upon which to erect the federal government. He thought that if the federal government established policies favorable to the wealthy, the wealthy would in turn lend their support to the federal government over state governments, which Hamilton wanted to see weakened.

Hamilton advocated a number of policies to put the new government on a sound financial footing. He promoted repayment of both the foreign and domestic debt. He convinced the president and then Congress that, instead of having each state pay its own debts, the federal government should assume and pay off all state debt. Under Hamilton's leadership, the federal government by 1795 had paid off the foreign debt. Hamilton also suggested and lobbied for the creation of a federal bank—the Bank of the United States.

Hamilton wanted to foster domestic manufacturing. In 1791 he issued a "Report on Manufactures" that called for federal protection of the United States' fledgling industries by placing duties on imports of foreign manufactured goods—thus increasing the cost of foreign relative to domestic goods. Hamilton thought import duties would increase the national wealth, encourage the immigration of artisans, spur the invention of new machinery, and create employment for women and children in manufacturing. (Home manufacturing already existed in many states, especially in New England.) But no one favored Hamilton's report—neither southerners, who depended on foreign manufactures, nor northerners, who were enjoying the benefits of free trade, which import duties would effectively end.

Overall, Hamilton's policies were a boon for the coastal cities in Massachusetts, Connecticut, New York, Rhode Island, and South Carolina. In Massachusetts, the prosperity of Boston seeped into the western counties, and so the entire state grew quite complacent toward the Washington administration. In the rest of the country, however, people saw little benefit in Hamilton's policies. Especially in most of the South, they objected to the federal assumption of state debt and opposed the establishment of the Bank of the United States. Patrick Henry well summed up the thoughts of these folk: "to erect, and concentrate, and perpetuate a large monied interest . . . ," he wrote, "must . . . produce one or other of two evils, the prostration of agriculture at the feet of commerce, or a change in the present for the federal government, fatal to the existence of American liberty . . ."

As in the Revolution, Henry was the harbinger of a national movement—one that would affect the complexion of American society.

The Loyal, but Ornery, Opposition

Thomas Jefferson had only just returned to Virginia in November 1789 from serving as United States envoy to Paris when he learned that Washington had chosen him to be secretary of state. It took some convincing, but Washington finally prevailed upon Jefferson to accept the post. The president didn't know it, but by appointing Jefferson he was creating a hornets' nest in his cabinet.

It was not long before Jefferson came into conflict with Hamilton. The two were very different men. Twelve years Hamilton's senior, the 44-year old Jefferson had built for himself quite a reputation and was well known on both sides of the Atlantic. Not only was he famous for having authored the Declaration of Independence, and as a renowned inventor and architect as well, he was a dabbler in all areas of knowledge, including theology (where he displayed a marked agnostic tendency). Hamilton had not achieved such fame, nor was he a polymath. Jefferson and Hamilton differed even in demeanor. Languid, lax in dress and manners, Jefferson was a marked contrast to the well-dressed, tidy, and energetic Hamilton.

Jefferson on Farmers

In his only full-length book, *Notes on the State of Virginia* Thomas Jefferson said this of farmers:

Those who labor in the earth are the chosen people of God, if ever He had a chosen people, whose breasts He made His peculiar deposit for substantial and genuine virtue. It is the focus in which He keeps alive that sacred fire, which otherwise might escape from the face of the earth. Corruption of morals in the mass of cultivators is a phenomenon of which no age nor nation has furnished an example. It is the mark set on those who, not looking up to heaven, to their own soil and industry, as does the husbandman, for their subsistence, depend for it on casualties and caprice of customers. Dependence begets subservience and venality, suffocates the germ of virtue, and prepares fit tools for the designs of ambition . . . [G]enerally speaking, the proportion which the aggregate of the other classes of citizens bears in any State to that of its husbandmen, is the proportion of its unsound to its healthy parts, and is a good enough barometer whereby to measure its degree of corruption.

But Jefferson and Hamilton most differed in their ideas on society and government. Jefferson repudiated Hamilton's favoritism of the wealthy and his admiration for British government—Jefferson was horrified to learn that Hamilton had even been heard to say that he thought corruption an essential part of effective government! Jefferson represented the American democratic idealist. He hoped that the change to republican government and manners would draw mankind to new perfections. He favored the common man, the small farmer, whose independence he thought would form the foundation for free government. While it is true that he did not trust the common man's wisdom and believed that a republican government would foster a "natural aristocracy" that would direct the affairs of the nation, he also believed that defects in the common man could be remedied by free public education. Finally, unlike Hamilton, Jefferson wanted agriculture to be the economic foundation of the United States and mistrusted manufacturers and the artisan and merchant classes.

The New Capital

Section 8, Article I of the Constitution of the United States gives Congress the authority "to exercise exclusive Legislation in all Cases whatsoever, over such District (not exceeding ten Miles square) as may, by Cession of particular States, and the Acceptance of Congress, become the Seat of the Government of the United States . . . " It was George Washington who selected the site for the district on the Potomac River. He favored the site because it lay on the border lands of the northern and southern states, and so would belong to neither section. Ships, too, could ply the waters of the Potomac to the location, and so the capital, to be called Washington City, could have a port and thus be open to Atlantic trade. The president hoped the district would bind the trans-Appalachian West to the Eastern Seaboard and thus keep the West in the Union.

The District of Columbia, ten miles square, was formed from lands donated by the states of Maryland and Virginia and included the existing cities of Georgetown (north of the river) and Alexandria (south of the river). In 1846, Congress re-ceded the portion of the District south of the Potomac, including Alexandria, to Virginia.

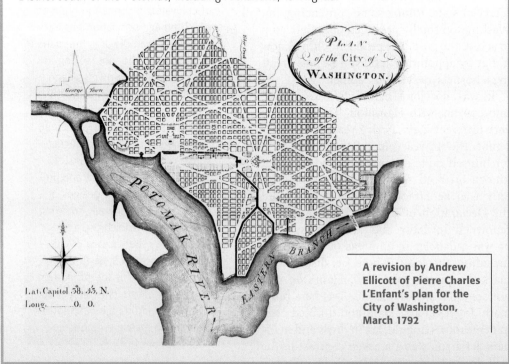

A revision by Andrew Ellicott of Pierre Charles L'Enfant's plan for the City of Washington, March 1792

At first, Jefferson and Hamilton cooperated with each other, as when they both promoted the establishment of a district on the Potomac River for the seat of government—the District of Columbia and the capital city, to be called Washington. But when in December 1790 Hamilton proposed the establishment of the Bank of the United States, Jefferson became his most virulent opponent. When James Madison, who was gradually coming under Jefferson's influence, stood up in the House of Representatives to oppose the chartering of the bank, Washington called together his cabinet to get their opinions. Jefferson argued that while the Constitution allowed Congress "to make all laws necessary and proper" to carry out the federal government's designated powers, it did not allow Congress to do what is merely convenient. The bank, said Jefferson, was not necessary to federal finance and therefore was unconstitutional.

Hamilton countered that if some measure had "an obvious relation" to a power given by the Constitution to the federal government, and was not forbidden by any part of the Constitution, then "it may safely be deemed to come within the compass of the national authority." A bank, according to Hamilton's reasoning, would be constitutional because, even though it was not necessary to federal finance, it had an obvious relation to it, since it facilitated the operation of a constitutional power of the federal government. Hamilton's "loose construction" interpretation of the Constitution triumphed over Jefferson's "strict construction." President Washington signed the bank bill passed by Congress. From that point on, Jefferson mistrusted Hamilton's fidelity to republican liberty. He feared that Hamilton was undermining what Jefferson thought was a great experiment in liberty and would turn the United States into just another corrupt world power.

Jefferson was gracious, a man of what seemed noble and generous ideals. It was these qualities, along with his notable talents and intelligence, that attracted new friends and political allies—among whom was James Madison, who became Jefferson's fast friend and associate. In an obviously politically motivated trip to New York, Madison and Jefferson met with prominent anti-federalists, including Governor Clinton, whose associate, Colonel Aaron Burr, had already been at work turning a club called the "Sons of St. Tammany" into

A Federalist cartoon from 1793 depicting Jefferson's party as a coterie of anarchists in concert with the devil. Jefferson is depicted speaking from a bench.

a political organization aligned with Jefferson's faction. In New York, Jefferson invited the poet Philip Freneau to come to Philadelphia (where the government was then sitting) to start a newspaper in opposition to the Washington government. In return, Jefferson awarded Freneau a government job.

Jefferson and Hamilton differed not only on domestic matters, but foreign policy as well. While both held with the general aims of President Washington—assuring justice for the United States abroad while maintaining peace at home—Hamilton desired U.S. friendship with Great Britain while Jefferson favored France. Jefferson had been in Paris during the first days of the revolution there and sympathized with it. Hamilton (and, incidentally, Washington and Adams) feared the radicalism of the French Revolution and objected to its disdain for law and the tried ways of government. A book, *The Age of Reason*, written by Thomas Payne (who had joined the French revolutionary government) expressed the ideas these men loathed but Jefferson embraced (he had written the introduction for the book). Acccording to Payne, government should rest on the foundation of pure reason alone, not tradition or tried experience.

The breaking out of war between France on the one side and Spain and Great Britain on the other divided Americans; some wanted the U.S. Government lieutenant to back the French, while others wanted support to go to Great Britain. President Washington, however, ignored the bellicose demands of both sides. Instead, he said, America would remain neutral.

The split between Hamilton and Jefferson over the French Revolution mirrored a similar conflict in the nation at large. It gave rise to two political factions. Those who supported Hamilton began calling themselves "Federalists," while Jefferson's party named themselves "Republicans" (not to be confused with the modern Republican Party, which traces its ancestry to the Federalists). Washington deplored such factions but was powerless to stop them. Though not political parties in the modern sense of the word, the Federalists and the Republicans represented the beginnings of what became a characteristic of American politics—the two-party system.

Washington's Second Administration

Washington had wanted to retire at the end of his first term, but at the entreaties of Jefferson and Hamilton, he agreed to stand for a second term. No one opposed Washington in the election of 1792 and, once again, he was elected with a unanimous electoral vote.

In his second administration, Washington faced difficult problems. For one, Great Britain still refused to abandon the forts it held in American territory. More serious, British ships were seizing neutral American ships bound for France and the French West Indies and **impressing** American sailors. Too, the refusal of Spain to allow American farmers passage down the Mississippi jeopardized the union of the western territories with the United States. Then there were the Barbary pirates of the northern coast of Africa who seized unprotected American ships and imprisoned American sailors.

Closer to home, a rebellion of farmers in western Pennsylvania challenged federal power. In 1791, to fund the federal government's assumption of state debt, Congress had laid an **excise tax** on whiskey, which affected the farmers of the Appalachian region, who could only transport their corn by distilling it into spirituous liquors. The tax was especially heavy on small farmers, for they could not afford the flat yearly rate of $54 that larger distilleries paid to get out of the per-gallon tax. When farmers in western Pennsylvania refused to pay the tax and rose in revolt, the Jeffersonian Republican governor of Pennsylvania, Thomas Mifflin, did nothing to hinder them. With Washington's urging, however, Congress called up the militia of four states. Led by Washington, and joined by Hamilton sporting military dress, the militia dispersed the farmers, putting an end to what was jokingly called the "Whiskey Rebellion."

More serious were developments farther west. The British lieutenant governor of Upper Canada (later named Ontario), John Graves Simcoe, built a fort on the Maumee River, 100 miles southwest of Detroit—well within United States territory. Worse, Simcoe was mobiliz-

impress: to force into government service; here, naval service

excise tax: a tax placed on the purchase of a specific good or good, and usually included in the price of the product

A tarred and feathered tax collector is made to ride the rail during Whiskey Rebellion, 1794.

ing and arming the Indians in the Northwest Territory. Fortunately for the United States, the western army of 2,000 men was under the command of Maj. General Anthony Wayne. Called "Mad Anthony" by his men for his reckless courage, Wayne was a consummate strategist and expert in the art of forest warfare, in which he relentlessly drilled his men.

Reinforced by several hundred Kentucky riflemen, Mad Anthony moved north towards the Maumee, fighting Indians in the dense forest lands of Ohio and Indiana. Reaching the Erie Plain, where lay the log cabins and cultivated fields of the Indians, Wayne built Fort Defiance and offered the Indians peace. They refused his offer and retreated to the vicinity of the British fort. There, behind a natural stockade of fallen trees, members of the Miami, Shawnee, Ojibwe, Potawotomi, Sauk and Fox, and Iroquois peoples, along with a contingent of Canadians led by an old loyalist commander, awaited Wayne's advance. On August 20, 1794, Wayne attacked the Indians and Canadians in what became known as the Battle of Fallen Timbers, a short fight that in 40 minutes completely routed the Indian force. Wayne followed up the victory by burning Indian homes and laying waste their fields. At the forks of the Maumee in Indiana he raised Fort Wayne.

A year later, tribes from the region between the Mississippi, the Great Lakes, and the Ohio met with Wayne and signed the Treaty of Greenville. In this treaty, the Indians ceded to the United States the entire southeastern section of the Northwest Territory, as well as the sites of Vincennes, Detroit, and Chicago. In return, they received $20,000 and the promise of a yearly payment of $9,500 in goods.

But the Treaty of Greenville did not end the disputes between the U.S. and Great Britain. To resolve the disputes, President Washington had sent Chief Justice John Jay to negotiate a new treaty with Great Britain; but when Washington saw the treaty, he feared to publish it.

Jay's Treaty, signed November 19, 1794, did contain some provisions favorable to the United States. For one, the British agreed to evacuate all their forts on United States territory by 1796 and granted American ships a limited right to trade with the British West Indies; and while the United States agreed to pay back debts amounting to 600,000 pounds, the British offered 1,317,000 pounds in reparation for the illegal capture of American ships. But other parts of the treaty, Washington knew, would only stoke Republican ire—and they made even Washington wince. For one, the treaty forbade American ships from transporting, as they long had been doing, certain products, including cotton, molasses, and sugar, from the British West Indies to America. It did not press the British to compensate slave owners for slaves taken at the end of the war—Jay was opposed to slavery and did not insist on the provision. Finally, the treaty made no mention of the impressing of American sailors.

Washington asked the Senate to debate the treaty in secret; but Pierce Butler, senator from South Carolina, gave a copy of the treaty to Madison, who leaked it to the press. A storm of Republican protest arose. Jay was called traitor, and when Hamilton tried to defend the treaty in New York, he was met with a hail of stones (which led one Federalist wag to comment that, by trying to knock out Hamilton's brains, the Republicans attempted to "reduce him to an equality with themselves.") Incensed at these insults, Hamilton challenged all Republicans to a duel. Yet, despite the protests, anger, and political theater, the Senate finally approved Jay's Treaty by the required two-thirds majority, and Washington signed it on August 1, 1795.

The Jay Treaty was but one incident that illustrates the growing partisanship in the politics of the new republic. Even before the treaty, Republican attacks against not only the Federalists but even the venerable Washington himself had been increasing in frequency and bitterness. Jefferson, himself, who had resigned as secretary of state in late 1793, wrote to an Italian friend that "men who were Samsons in the field and Solomons in the council" (referring to Washington, Hamilton, and Adams) had been "shorn by the harlot England." After Washington signed the treaty, Nathaniel Ames, a doctor from Massachusetts, wrote in his diary: "Washington now defies the whole Sovereign that made him what he is—and can unmake him again. Better his hands had been cut off when his glory was at its height, before he blasted all his laurels."

The Election of 1796 and Washington's Farewell

Weary with the burdens of office and age, Washington decided not to run for a third term. The election of 1796 saw John Adams and Thomas Pinckney (Federalists) pitted against Thomas Jefferson and Aaron Burr (Republicans). The vote was close; Adams received 71 electoral votes and Jefferson, 68. By the rules of the day, Adams became president, and Jefferson, vice president.

In his farewell address to the nation, delivered September 17, 1796, Washington spoke of his gratitude toward the people he had so long served and expressed the hope that the happiness of the United States would be so preserved as to "acquire to them the glory of recommending it to the applause, the affection and adoption of every nation which is yet a stranger to it." He spoke of the value of the union and the importance of cultivating a national patriotism over local sympathies:

> The name of AMERICAN, which belongs to you, in your national capacity, must always exalt the just pride of patriotism, more than any appellation derived from local discriminations. With slight shades of difference, you have the same religion, manners, habits and political principles. You have in common cause fought and triumphed together; the Independence and Liberty you possess are the work of joint councils, and joint efforts, of common dangers, sufferings and successes . . .

"The continuance of the UNION," Washington said, must be "a primary object of Patriotic desire."

Because of his deep regard for the union of the states, Washington warned against factions, against altering the Constitution except by "an explicit and authentic act of the whole people," and against "the spirit of party in general." Washington praised religion and morality as instruments conducive to political prosperity. "A volume could not trace," he said, "all their connections with private and public felicity . . . reason and experience both forbid us to expect that national morality can prevail in exclusion of religious principle." The president added praises for "institutions for the general diffusion of knowledge," since, he said, they are "essential that public opinion should be enlightened."

One could note a certain sadness in Washington as he bade his country farewell:

> In offering you, my countrymen, these counsels of an old and affectionate friend, I dare not hope they will make the strong and lasting impression I could wish; that they will controul the usual current of the passions, or prevent our nation from running the course which has hitherto marked the destiny of nations. But if I may even flatter myself, that they may be productive of some partial benefit, some occasional good; that they may now and then recur to moderate the fury of party spirit, to warn against the mischiefs of foreign intrigue, to guard against the impostures of pretended patriotism; this hope will be a full recompence for the solicitude for your welfare, by which they have been dictated.

When John Adams had delivered his inaugural address, Washington returned to his home, Mount Vernon. There he engaged in the pursuits of the gentleman farmer for which for so many years he had so longed. In 1798, when war with France threatened, Washington again answered his country's call to command the army, though he said he would not take actual command until war was declared. He never took command. On December 12, 1799, while riding about his plantation in the rain, hail, and snow, Washington caught a severe cold. Two days later he died a peaceful death, in his sixty-seventh year. They buried the "Father of His Country" at Mount Vernon, his home overlooking the broad Potomac River.

Chapter 10 Review

Summary

- With the Declaration of Independence, colonial governments began acting as state governments, each with its own constitution.

- In 1776 George Mason wrote the Virginia Bill of Rights, adopted by the state of Virginia the same year. Other states followed Virginia's example.

- In 1776, John Dickinson, in an attempt to get the states to agree on a constitution for the new national government, introduced into Congress the Articles of Confederation and Perpetual Union. All of the states but Maryland approved the Articles of Confederation by 1779. Maryland ratified them in 1781.

- Following the revolution, religion in the United States underwent changes. In 1786 the Virginia assembly passed Jefferson's Statute of Religious Liberty. The American churches cut off ties with their mother churches in Europe, forming distinctly American groups. In 1784, John Carroll was named prefect apostolic of the Catholic Church in the United States, and bishop in 1789.

- Congress was facing many problems fulfilling its obligations to both Britain and its own people, so many Americans began to see the need for a stronger national government.

- In 1786, Massachusetts farmers, led by Daniel Shays, rose in rebellion against the high debts and taxes that were troubling them. The rebellion was crushed by 1787. This troubled many in America, as they were convinced that the current national government was insufficient to keep the peace.

- In 1787 Congress adopted the Northwest Ordinance, which governs United States territories to this day.

- Virginia and Maryland called for a convention of all the states to meet in September 1786 to discuss revisions to the Articles of Confederation. When only very few delegates came to attend, in February of 1787 Congress called for another convention to discuss revisions to the Articles. During the convention, two factions arose. One faction, the nationalists, called for a strong central government that would dominate the states, with proportional representation of the states in the legislature. The other faction favored a weak central government, the preservation of state sovereignty, with equal representation of the states in the legislature.

- Roger Sherman suggested the "Connecticut Compromise," a plan that called for proportional representation in the lower house and equal representation in the upper house or senate. The compromise was agreed upon and passed, and a committee drafted the new constitution on August 6.

- When 12 out of 13 states had approved the new constitution, Congress formally ratified it and called for presidential and congressional elections

- George Washington was elected the first president of the United States on April 30, 1789, with the entire electoral vote.

- Washington chose Thomas Jefferson and Alexander Hamilton to serve in his cabinet. Around these two men, who had very different visions for the new republic, grew up two parties, the Republicans and the Federalists.

- Congress approved a bill of rights, a series of checks on the federal government. By November 1791, the required number of states approved ten of the 12 provisions in the Bill of Rights, and these became formally part of the Constitution.

- Washington was reelected in 1793, again with a unanimous electoral vote. He retired in 1797, the year Adams became president, with Jefferson as his vice president. Washington died in 1799.

Key Concepts

trusteeship: an American form of church government in which Catholic laymen established and funded Catholic congregations and paid priests' salaries.

Articles of Confederation: the first United States constitution

Northwest Ordinance: a body of laws adopted by Congress in 1787 to govern the territories

nationalists: those who favored a strong, central government that would dominate the states

Connecticut Compromise: the compromise promoted by Roger Sherman that provided for a dual system of representation in the legislature and was used as the basis for the existing Constitution

federalists: supporters of the new Constitution to replace the Articles of Confederation

anti-federalists: opponents of the new Constitution

strict construction: a principal of interpreting the Constitution that says that the federal government only possesses those powers clearly granted it by the Constitution and may do only what is strictly necessary to the carrying out of the powers

loose construction: a principal of interpreting the Constitution that says that the federal government has the authority to act on any measure that bears an obvious relation to a power given by the Constitution to the federal government and is not forbidden by any part of the Constitution

Dates to Remember

1776: George Mason writes, and Virginia approves, the Virginia Bill of Rights.

John Dickinson introduces his Articles of Confederation and Perpetual Union into Congress.

1777: Congress approves the Articles of Confederation.

1779: The Articles of Confederation go into effect.

1786: the Virginia assembly passes Jefferson's Statute of Religious Liberty.

1787: Congress adopts the Northwest Ordinance.

A convention is called to amend the Articles of Confederation (May).

The Constitutional Convention draws up the new Constitution based on the Connecticut Compromise.

1789: Father John Carroll becomes the first Catholic bishop of the United States and dedicates his new diocese to the Mother of God.

George Washington becomes the first president of the United States.

1791: Congress and the states ratify the Bill of Rights.

1797: Washington retires, and John Adams becomes the second president of the United States.

Central Characters

George Mason (1725–1792): American patriot and statesman who wrote the Virginia Bill of Rights

James Madison (1751–1836): a Virginian influential in the planning, writing, and ratification of the Constitution and sponsor of the first ten amendments, the Bill of Rights

John Carroll (1735–1815): first Catholic bishop of the United States

Daniel Shays (1747–1825): leader of Shays' Rebellion in Massachusetts

Alexander Hamilton (1755–1804): New York delegate to the Constitutional Convention and one of three authors of the *Federalist*, written in defense of the Constitution. Hamilton, a leader of the Federalist faction, favored a loose construction of the Constitution.

Roger Sherman (1721–1793): author of the Connecticut Compromise

Thomas Jefferson (1743–1826): George Washington's first secretary of state and the leader of the Republican faction that favored, among other things, a strict construction of the Constitution

Questions for Review

1. What was the significance of the Virginia Bill of Rights?

2. What was Maryland's reason for not ratifying the Articles of Confederation, and how was the problem solved?

3. What were some of the political and social reforms realized in the United States after the revolution?

4. Why did republicans call for the disestablishment of state churches?

5. Briefly explain Jefferson's Statute of Religious Liberty.

6. What were the problems Father John Carroll faced as prefect apostolic of the Church of the United States? Give a brief description of each.

7. What were the inadequacies of the Articles of Confederation?

8. What did the Northwest Ordinance do for the United States?

9. What is the significance of Shay's Rebellion? How did it contribute to the call for a new constitution?

10. Describe the two factions that divided the delegates to the Constitutional Convention.

11. What was the Connecticut Compromise?

12. List the factors that made it difficult for the new constitution to be ratified.

13. What is the Bill of Rights? What did it seek to clarify?

14. What were some of the problems that Washington faced as the first president?

Ideas in Action

1. Read and discuss the Constitution and the Bill of Rights. (Copies of these may be found on the Internet.) How have the ideas presented in these documents played out in the history of the United States?

2. Study the arguments of the anti-federalists. Have their predictions of the kind of government and society the Constitution would create come true? Why or why not?

3. Debate the merits of the ideas of the strict and loose construction of the Constitution.

4. Read Washington's Inaugural and Farewell addresses (also found on the Internet). Does the United States today live up to the ideals that Washington espoused?

Chapter 10 Review (continued)

Highways and Byways

Constitutions throughout the Ages

The United States is not the only country that has a constitution. In fact, all countries have constitutions in some form or another. Sometimes this constitution is a specific document, as in the case of the United States, or sometimes, as in the case of the United Kingdom, the constitution is a collection of documents, statutes, and traditional practices that govern the body politic. Though of different kinds, these constitutions fit the definition of a constitution: a "body of doctrines and practices that form the fundamental organizing principle of a political state."

The idea of a constitution first originated with the Greeks. The Greek philosopher Aristotle writes extensively on constitutions in his works, including *Politics* and *Nicomachean Ethics*. Aristotle's idea of a constitution is an arrangement of offices in a polis, or state. He thought the best constitution is a mixed one that contains elements of monarchy, aristocracy, and democracy. St. Thomas Aquinas took these ideas of Aristotle and adapted them to the medieval world, which was largely monarchical. Aquinas believed that since God is sole ruler of the universe, and men are bound to obey his laws, then the best form of government is that which best reflects this order—a monarchy. During the age of Enlightenment, however, thinkers began to favor governments formed after a republican rather than a monarchical ideal and to prefer written constitutions.

THE FIRST TEST OF THE UNION

The Revolution of 1800

It was May 18, 1797, and President John Adams had concluded his address to Congress. The Senate, it was clear had been won over by Adams' call—to strengthen the national defense. It voted to commend the president for his "vigilance, firmness and promptitude."

"Effectual measures of defense" were needed, the senators said, "to check aggression and prevent war." The House of Representatives, too, voted their support for the president. One representative, however, Matthew Lyon of Vermont, would have none of it. Let the "gentlemen of blood" go, he said; he was too good a democrat. He was not sprung from "the bastards of Oliver Cromwell" or "from the witch-hunting Puritans of New England who persecuted the Quakers and despised all joy."

Patriotic democrat though he was, Representative Lyon would soon find himself at odds with most of the American people. World events involving America would wing public opinion in President Adam's way. Beginning in 1789, the French Revolution was sweeping away the traditional aristocratic and monarchic structure of France. It was not long before revolutionary France was in conflict with the powers of Europe, and in 1796 French ships began attacking American merchant ships. By 1797, the year Adams took office, ships flying the French tricolor flag had captured 700 American vessels. This was why Adams was eager to strengthen the country's defenses and especially to build a navy.

For John Adams' political opponents, the Republicans, revolutionary France stood as a bastion of republican liberty. Ignoring the atrocities committed by the French revolutionary government, Republicans (under the influence of Vice-President Thomas Jefferson) saw the French Revolution, with its cry of "Liberty, Fraternity and Equality," as a continuation of the American Revolution. They rejoiced as they followed the conquests of General Napoleon Bonaparte in Italy—everywhere overthrowing aristocracies and establishing republics. Republicans celebrated France by wearing French liberty caps and setting up liberty poles—the French equivalent of the liberty tree.

Adams' party, the Federalists, despised France and its revolution. The Federalists believed that true liberty was assured only by a sound constitution and by empowering

The Battle between the American Frigate USS *Constellation* and the French frigate *L'Insurgente*, February 9, 1799, during the undeclared naval war with France.

the elite and aristocratic elements of society. Federalists saw in the chaos, atrocities, and upheavals of the French Revolution a confirmation of their mistrust of uneducated and poor people. While tolerating a degree of popular power, Federalists like Alexander Hamilton thought society needed to be built on the landed gentlemen, the bankers, land speculators —what we would call today "business interests."

An event in 1797 only served to confirm Federalist opinion of France. The new French government (the third since 1789) called the Directory had been trying to bribe three American commissioners to Paris—Elbridge Gerry, John Marshall, and Charles Cotesworth Pinckney. In what came to be called the XYZ Affair, three French ministers (hiding their identities under the pseudonyms, X, Y, and Z) said the American ministers could not negotiate with the French foreign minister, Talleyrand, until they paid him about $250,000 and guaranteed the Directory a loan of $10 million. News of this "XYZ Affair" inflamed the American public. The Republicans were embarrassed; Adams and his Federalists, bolstered by public opinion, pushed through their program of national defense.

A 1799 cartoon inspired by the XYZ Affair. A Hydra-headed French Government, at dagger point, demands money from the American commissioners.

By the end of 1798, the United States had built a fleet of 14 ships that began winning victories against French warships and privateers in the Caribbean—a series of incidents that became known as the Quasi-War. At first, President Adams was for war with France; but when it became clear that the French Directory had no desire for war, the president relented and re-established diplomatic relations with France. This decision, along with the events of the previous year, strengthened the Federalists. The congressional election of 1798 gave the Federalists a majority in both the House of Representatives and the Senate.

Opposition from within his own party, however, undermined Adams. Alexander Hamilton had long held a poor opinion of John Adams—he called him "a mere old woman and unfit for a president." Hamilton had influence in the president's cabinet, three of whose members secretly received advice and guidance from him. When Adams was eager for war, Hamilton counseled peace. When Adams favored peace, Hamilton pushed for war. Hamilton, it seems, had grandiose dreams of becoming a sort of American Napoleon. Fearing a French plot to conquer America, Hamilton conceived a plan of leading an army to take New Orleans (then held by France's ally, Spain) while the American navy supported him from the sea.

Two Controversial Acts

Though a little cowed by the XYZ Affair, the Republicans did not let up in their attacks on Adams and the Federalists. Using a network of newspapers, Republicans harshly attacked the president and the Federalist members of Congress. Since many of the editors of these papers were foreign immigrants, the Federalists counterattacked by accusing the Republicans of wanting to give the country over to foreign powers.

The Federalist Congress and President Adams responded to fears of foreign infiltration by passing three acts in 1798. The first, the Naturalization Act, extended from five to 14 years the time a foreigner must reside in the United States before he could become a citizen.

The Alien Act gave the president power for two years to expel any foreigners he wished. The more controversial Sedition Act made it a crime to say or write anything critical of the president or government of the United States "with the intent to defame" or "to bring into contempt or disrepute." The crime was punishable by fine or imprisonment.

President Adams justified the Sedition Act by arguing that when the leaders of government are abused, government itself loses its dignity and force. Twenty-five men were arrested and ten convicted under the act, including several Republican editors. The first man to be indicted, however, was Vermont representative Matthew Lyon. Lyon had almost been expelled from Congress for spitting in Representative Roger Griswold's face while in chambers (Griswold had publicly mocked him). Later, Griswold assaulted Lyon with a stick in the House chamber, and Lyon responded by assailing Griswold with a fire tongs. But the final straw was an article Lyon published in the *Vermont Gazette* denouncing the Sedition Act. Arrested and charged with libel, Lyon was pronounced guilty and sentenced to pay a $1,000 fine and spend four months in jail. Lyon thus was made a Republican martyr.

Dominated by Republicans, the Kentucky and Virginia legislatures approved two important critiques of the Alien and Sedition Acts, and the Constitution itself. The first of these, the Kentucky Resolves (adopted November 16, 1798), was written anonymously by Thomas Jefferson, who as vice president could not honorably oppose the Adams administration's policies in public. The states, said the Kentucky Resolves, did not unite "on the principle of unlimited submission" to the federal government; rather, they formed a "compact" by which they "constituted a general government for special purposes" and "delegated to that government certain definite powers, reserving each State to itself, the residuary mass of right to their own self-government." Since the national government, said Jefferson, was created by a compact among equals—itself and the states—it could not be "the exclusive or final judge of the extent of the powers delegated to itself, since that would have made its discretion, and not the Constitution, the measure of its powers." Since the parties that agreed to the Constitution set up no person or body to stand as a judge between them, "each party," said Jefferson, "has an equal right to judge for itself, as well of infractions as of the mode and measure of redress." Thus, if a state government thought an act of the federal government was unconstitutional it could refuse to recognize—that is, it could *nullify*—the act—until a convention of states could gather to decide on its constitutionality.

The *Virginia Resolves*, composed by James Madison, was a shorter document that followed Jefferson's reasoning.

Other state legislatures roundly condemned the *Resolves* in the winter and spring of 1799. The legislatures argued that since the Constitution provided that "the judicial powers shall extend to all cases arising under the laws of the United States," it was the federal courts and ultimately the Supreme Court, that decided on the constitutionality of any act or law of the Congress of the United States. This reasoning, however, did not convince Jefferson. In a further set of Kentucky Resolves, issued in February 1799, he replied that, since the federal courts are a branch of the federal government, making them the "exclusive judge of the extent of the powers delegated to it [the federal government]" would lead to a despotic federal control over the state governments.

A 1798 drawing of a fight in Congress between Matthew Lyon and Roger Griswold of Connecticut. The verses read: "He in a trice struck Lyon thrice/Upon his head, enrag'd sir,/Who seiz'd the tongs to ease his wrongs,/And Griswold thus engag'd, sir."

The Election of 1800

The Republicans were determined to overthrow Adams and the Federalists in the election of 1800. They again chose Jefferson as their presidential candidate. Jefferson's platform called for a "strict construction" of the Constitution and for a frugal and simple federal government —no multiplication of officers. It opposed a standing army; except in the case of foreign invasion, the state militias, said Jefferson, were sufficient for internal defense, while a navy should only be large enough to protect the coasts and harbors. Standing firmly against the Alien and Sedition Acts, Jefferson emphasized the constitutional rights of freedom of speech and of the press.

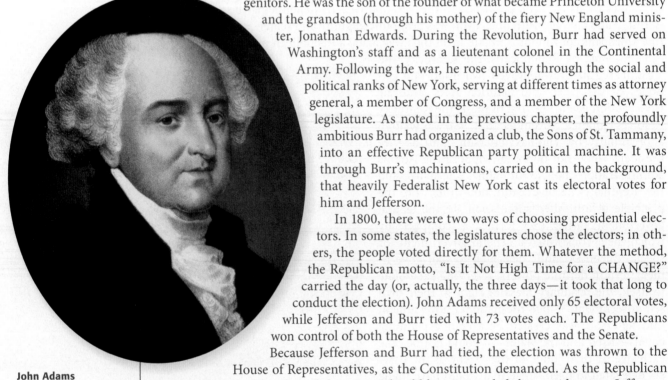

John Adams

The Republican vice-presidential candidate, Aaron Burr, had famous progenitors. He was the son of the founder of what became Princeton University and the grandson (through his mother) of the fiery New England minister, Jonathan Edwards. During the Revolution, Burr had served on Washington's staff and as a lieutenant colonel in the Continental Army. Following the war, he rose quickly through the social and political ranks of New York, serving at different times as attorney general, a member of Congress, and a member of the New York legislature. As noted in the previous chapter, the profoundly ambitious Burr had organized a club, the Sons of St. Tammany, into an effective Republican party political machine. It was through Burr's machinations, carried on in the background, that heavily Federalist New York cast its electoral votes for him and Jefferson.

In 1800, there were two ways of choosing presidential electors. In some states, the legislatures chose the electors; in others, the people voted directly for them. Whatever the method, the Republican motto, "Is It Not High Time for a CHANGE?" carried the day (or, actually, the three days—it took that long to conduct the election). John Adams received only 65 electoral votes, while Jefferson and Burr tied with 73 votes each. The Republicans won control of both the House of Representatives and the Senate.

Because Jefferson and Burr had tied, the election was thrown to the House of Representatives, as the Constitution demanded. As the Republican vice-presidential candidate, Burr should have conceded the presidency to Jefferson, but he would not. Burr's ambition would not allow him to give up the opportunity thus offered him.

The Federalist-dominated House met in the new capital on the Potomac, Washington City, in February 1800 to decide who would be president. Either Burr or Jefferson had to win a majority of the House—the representatives of nine states. This was no easy task. The Federalists, for instance, hoped to block Jefferson's election and then appeal to the Senate to appoint an interim president until new elections could be held. The situation grew serious as the required majority (nine states) failed to materialize for either candidate. It was only reports of threatened insurrections that forced the House to act. After Jefferson gave assurances that he would not tamper with the navy, the House lined up behind him.

Before leaving office in March, John Adams was able to strike out once more at his enemies—and an effective hit it would prove to be. In January, with only two months left in office, the president began to appoint Federalists to the federal courts. When Chief Justice Oliver Ellsworth retired from the Supreme Court, Adams nominated John Marshall of Virginia (Thomas Jefferson's cousin) to succeed him. Though even many Federalists opposed Marshall, the Senate confirmed him in late January. By such appointments, Adams assured the continuance of Federalist principles in what would become an increasingly important branch of the federal government: the Supreme Court.

But despite Adams' coup, Jefferson saw the election of 1800 as marking a fundamental change in American government—he even called it a "revolution." "The Revolution of 1800," he later wrote, "was as real a revolution in the principles of our government as that of 1776 was in its form, not effected by the sword, as that, but by the rational and peaceable instrument of reform, the suffrage of the people."

Society in Turmoil

The Republican victory in 1800 was merely one aspect of greater changes in American society that had begun shortly after the surrender at Yorktown. In the name of the equality of all men, the Founding Fathers had rebelled against a traditional, hereditary aristocracy in favor of a "natural aristocracy" of talent and achievement (which included themselves). Birth, they insisted in good republican fashion, should not confer any privilege; a man should rise in society only if he prove himself worthy of honor and trust. By insisting that all men are created equal, the founders did not mean to imply that men were to remain equal. Others would draw that conclusion, killing, almost at its conception, the social order that the fathers had hoped to establish.

American colonial society had never been as traditional or as hierarchical as European society. As noted in Chapter 9, colonial aristocracy in America had had a hard time living up to the ideal of the leisurely, independent gentleman. Open and cheap land robbed would-be aristocrats of tenants and forced them to engage in ungentlemanly money-making endeavors. Even before the revolution, Americans had been migrating in a slow stream westward, crossing over into the lands west of the Appalachians—despite the fact that the British government had reserved these lands for the Indians.

Colonial society then had always been somewhat tumultuous. The revolutionaries, with their cry of equality and the right of all to the "pursuit of happiness," only stirred up more turmoil. The revolutionaries' appeal to equality, of course, only went so far; for them it was only a condition for the flourishing of a natural aristocracy who, because of their talents and accomplishments, would become the leaders of society. Common, uneducated, and "unenlightened" men, however, began to ask why the "natural aristocracy" should have all the privileges—after all, they asked, were not all men created equal? Were not all men supposed to pursue happiness?

One man who forcefully brought these democratic, rather than classically republican, doubts and musings to the fore was Abraham Bishop. The son of a respected citizen of New Haven, Connecticut, a graduate of Yale University, a lawyer and later school teacher in New Haven, Bishop had taken to penning powerful attacks on the Federalists. The Federalists, he charged, were nothing but aristocrats who for their own advantage cowed the common people into submission. The structure of society, he said, was not natural or ordained by God but was constructed by men; and what men had constructed, men could tear down and then rebuild. These Federalist aristocrats, he admitted, had advantages over the rest of society—they excelled in all the accomplishments of enlightened gentlemen. But that was precisely why they were so dangerous. "Through excessive indulgence we have already a number of men too great for a republic," wrote Bishop. "How happens it, that these great men are so very fit to govern? Internal government is designed to control inordinate passions: great men are most proud, avaricious and tyrannical: will you then select these to curb pride, avarice and tyranny?" The aristocracy, said Bishop, "by circumstances of fortune, birth or superior bestowments of mind, or better education . . . have ceased to be as you; their political condition is immensely variant from yours, they are to govern, you are to be governed. They are well-born, you are base-born!"

Bishop was not alone in his attacks on the aristocracy; throughout the northern states in the 1790s, mechanics, tradesmen, and working men organized Republican societies, which took up the cry against educated men—the natural aristocracy of the founding fathers. "Keep up the cry against Judges, Lawyers, Generals, Colonels and all other designing men, and the day will be ours," they said. Not only learning but the life of leisure was condemned. Leisure became equated with idleness, which George Washington's biographer, Parson Weems, called "the worst of crimes." Rather than leisure, a life of labor became the ideal, at least in the North. To hold his head up in society, one needed to say that he worked for a living.

Love of Commerce

In all this attack on aristocracy, there was no attack on wealth as such. Even though the period following the revolution witnessed greater inequality of wealth than had prevailed before the revolution, both rich manufacturers and poor craftsmen could join forces against the leisured aristocracy. A prosperous manufacturer might be rich, but he became so, and remained so, through his labor. If anything, he was thought to be an example to all working men of what they might become through their own industry. He was a "self-made man," the ideal of all aspiring workmen.

Especially in the northern states, common people had become engrossed in the pursuit of wealth. Why should luxuries and the pleasures of life belong to the aristocracy alone—why should not all men, regardless of their birth or profession, participate in the "good things" of life? After all, everyone was created equal; all were endowed with the right to pursue happiness. So the race to obtain the wealth that purchased luxuries accelerated in the 1780s. After the war it became increasingly evident that internal trade—trade within and between states—could be very profitable. Farming families began to engage in home-based industries along with agriculture to take advantage of this trade. In Worcester, Massachusetts, said Brissot de Warville in 1795, "almost all" the households were "inhabited by men who are both cultivators and artisans; one is a tanner, another a shoemaker, another sells goods; but all are farmers."

Robert Fulton's Clermont commencing its first New York to Albany voyage, 150 miles upstream, August 17–18, 1807. Making an average speed of five miles per hour, the Fulton made its destination in 32 hours.

Despite the opinions of such old revolutionaries as John Adams, who wrote in 1814 that "human nature, in no form of it, ever could bear Prosperity," the new generation glorified it. The new prosperity resulting from the growth of manufacturing—arising, as Adams said, from men's "desire of gain, beyond the supply of the mere necessities of life"—became the theme of national life. Columbia College professor Samuel Mitchill wrote in 1800 that "the voice of the people and their government is loud and unanimous for commerce. Their inclination and habits are adapted to trade and traffic. From one end of the continent to the other, the universal roar is Commerce! Commerce! at all events, Commerce!" Henry Clay, speaking to the House of Representatives in 1812, called commerce "a passion as unconquerable as any with which nature has endowed us."

Since commercial activity required an ability to read and cipher, the passion to engage in commerce led to higher literacy rates. It also led to internal improvements, such as new roads and canals for internal transportation. In 1807, a steam-powered boat called the *Clermont* began plying the waters of the Hudson River between New York and Albany. In 1814–15, the *Clermont's* inventor, Robert Fulton, a native of Lancaster County, Pennsylvania, constructed a 38-ton steam-powered warship, called the *Demologos* (later, the *Fulton*), for the United States government. Thus was the era of steam transportation born.

The desire to engage in adventurous, entrepreneurial business enterprises necessitated a ready access to money. To ease transactions, states began issuing paper notes, which could be redeemed by national gold and silver currency. Banking grew at a phenomenal rate as people demanded more credit. Before 1781, banks were rare in America; by 1790, along with the national bank in Philadelphia, banks had sprung up in New York, Boston, and Baltimore. The decade of the 1790s saw the establishment of 25 banks, while the first decade of the 19th century witnessed the chartering of 62 more by the states. By 1820, the U.S. had more than 300 chartered banks. Fifty years earlier, in colonial times, men had sought loans from the local gentleman; by the 19th century they dealt with financial institutions. While this gave people a sense of independence (since they owed no personal gratitude to a bank), it involved them in an impersonal system that did not treat them as neighbors or dependents but as mere agents in a business transaction. Banks were harder and more unrelenting on borrowers than gentleman lenders had been—who, after all, were making loans to neighbors, not mere customers.

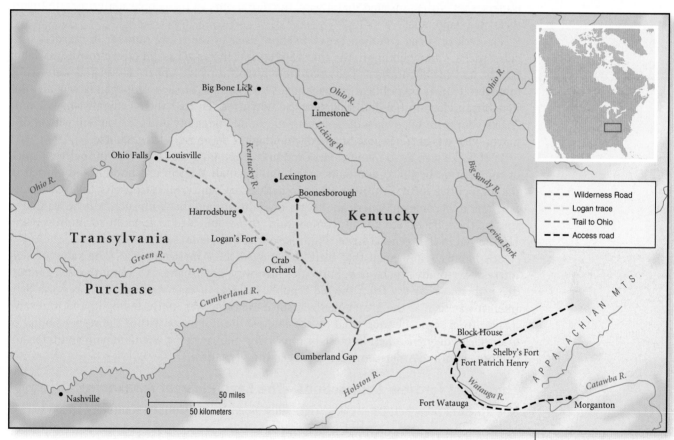

The desire for prosperity fueled emigration. With the opening of the western lands after the revolution, settlers, lured by the hope of richer soil, began pouring across the Appalachians into Ohio, Kentucky, Tennessee, and lands further west. Population growth in the West was swift. By the early 1780s, Kentucky, a territory thinly settled by whites before the revolution, had over 20,000 whites; by 1800, there were 220,000 white settlers, almost all of them emigrants. The population of Ohio grew so rapidly that by 1820 it was the fifth largest state.

Such emigration meant that people were frequently moving. Established settlements in the East saw their old families pack up and leave. Houses and lands ceased to be homes and became merely commodities to buy and sell. It was not unusual for a family to move at least three or four times, each time selling the farm for a profit.

The Wilderness Road, first blazed by Daniel Boone, was the route by which Anglo-American settlers moved west into Kentucky and beyond.

Such movement promoted a greater sense of equality among people while it broke apart the social bonds that held them together. As a Kentuckian wrote to James Madison in 1792, such a mobile population "must make a very different mass from one which is composed of men born and raised on the same spot. . . . They see none about them to whom or to whose families they have been accustomed to think themselves inferior." Neither did they see around them anyone with whom they were connected by blood or marriage. Just as the mobility of American society broke the predominance of the old aristocracy, it dispersed families, undermining the extended family and kinship relationships characteristic of traditional society.

With the breaking apart of the traditional societies of the village and the family, society lost the glue that held people together. Charles Nisbet, an immigrant Scot, wrote in 1787 that the revolution had made "a new world . . . unfortunately composed . . . of discordant atoms, jumbled together by chance, and tossed by unconstancy in an immense vacuum." Society, he said, "greatly wants a principle of attraction and cohesion." All this came about because leaders, said Nisbet, insisted that it was "the moral duty of the people at all times, to insure their own happiness."

The lack of social cohesion began to show itself in the rising number of murders, suicides, thefts, and mobbings in the cities. Street riots increased as did tavern rowdiness, labor strikes, and racial conflicts. The poor grew resentful of the upper classes and were stung to anger at times by political propaganda. One example of such propaganda was an 1801 Republican election handbill that told the downtrodden that their Federalist mayor only "hates you; from his own soul he hates you . . . do your duty and . . . you will get rid of a mayor who acts as if he thought a poor man had no more right than a horse."

With folks seen as so many atoms randomly impinging on each other in society, a spirit of competition began to dominate social life. Elkanah Watson of Rhode Island gloried in the competitive spirit. In 1810 he set up in Berkshire County, Massachusetts, the first county fair, later to become an American institution. Watson said that with such fairs he wanted to spur on the spirit of "envy" and "competition" that would lead to agricultural improvement. He rejoiced in the "general strife" that rose out of individual self-interest.

Self-interest—it seemed that little else moved the American spirit. The value of self-interest was loudly proclaimed; in politics men were not ashamed to admit that self-interest drove them—a far cry from the old republican ideal of disinterested public service. Self-interest was seen as the great equalizer, since everyone was motivated by it; and to receive a favor from someone motivated by self-interest did not carry with it the responsibility of gratitude or deference. Self-interest, or improving one's own lot, would remain an important component of the American ideal of rugged individualism.

The Quest for New Connections—The Second Great Awakening

The itinerant preacher, Peter Cartwright, described Logan County, Kentucky, this way:

> There was not a newspaper printed south of the Green River, no mill short of forty miles, and no schools worth the name. We killed our meat out of the woods, wild; and beat our meal . . . As for coffee, I am not sure that I ever smelled it for ten years.

Logan County was not unlike much of the country west of the Appalachians. Untamed, perilous, uncivilized, the West was being colonized by folks who had cut off all connections with their places of origin and even with their extended families. Cities did not exist—the rough frontier settlements with their wood shanty buildings were mere depots for the isolated homesteads in forest clearings that spread for many miles about. There was little social life for the settlers on these homesteads. Even the parish church structure, typical of the East, could not thrive in this raw land. Many were unchurched, and those who maintained some faith had to wait for a traveling preacher, such as Peter Cartwright, to minister to them.

A frontier Presbyterian church in western Pennsylvania, ca. 1800

The people of the West, it was said, "preferred their whiskey straight, and their politics and religion red hot." Peter Cartwright found that these folk wanted a different style of preaching. Simply being a preacher didn't earn Cartwright any respect—at times he had to "whupp" some sinner in a fistfight before he could tell him of God's love. He also had to cast aside doctrine and appeal to emotion, describing the pains of hell in graphic terms and passionately calling for conversion. This form of revival preaching was not new; Jonathan Edwards had used it to effect several decades before Cartwright. Yet, in the West, it took on a whole new character in what was called the "Second Great Awakening."

It all began in Logan County in the Summer of 1799. The Reverend James McGready, a Presbyterian preacher, was holding a preaching marathon meeting from Friday night to Monday morning at the church at Red River near the Kentucky/Tennessee border. With McGready were three other Presbyterian ministers and one Methodist, John McGee. On Monday, while one of the Presbyterians was preaching, a woman at the other end of the church began crying aloud and shouting. John McGee, feeling an irrepressible urge, also began to preach; but with the woman continuing her shouting, he decided that a greater power than himself was present, and he began exhorting his hearers to submit themselves to God. The room erupted with cries for mercy and shouts of ecstasy. Many fell unconscious to the ground so that, as one observer noted, the meeting ground was "covered by the slain."

The Red River "revival" of 1799 was the first of many such "camp meetings." The most famous of these was the Cane Ridge Revival in Kentucky, which attracted anywhere from 10,000 to 25,000 thousand people—an astonishing number, since the largest Kentucky town, Lexington, numbered only 1,795 souls. The same Logan County enthusiasm, only multiplied many times, was in evidence at Cane Ridge—men and women screamed, shouted, fell unconscious to the earth, shook with violent spasms, rushed from preacher to preacher, singing, laughing, sometimes barking like dogs! The meeting grew more intense as night fell, the lurid glare of campfires and torches illuminating even more frenzied intensity.

Camp meetings of the Cane Ridge sort were repeated all over the West. In the East, such meetings were far tamer; but in both the East and West they represented an attempt by ordinary folk to deal with the revolutionary changes in their society. The deistic, rationalistic philosophies of such Enlightenment figures as Thomas Jefferson could not satisfy the emotional and spiritual needs of the common man; neither could the "orthodox," overly intellectual Protestantism of the Anglicans or the New England Calvinists. Common Americans longed for a direct experience of God, not a philosophical or religious theory. They wanted a God, a "Sweet Jesus," who was personal, close to them, who loved them and

Methodist camp meeting near New York. Created by Provost, published on *L'Illustration Journal Universel*, Paris, 1857

Methodist camp meeting near New York. Created by Provost, published on *L'Illustration Journal Universel*, Paris, 1857

made a rough life comprehensible. Each felt himself (in the words of the hymn first sung during this period) a "poor wayfaring stranger, traveling through this world of woe." They wanted a religion that would stir them to the depths of their being and fill them with an exhilarating ecstasy.

The religion of the camp meetings rejected the old Calvinist predestination and emphasized man's free will. Camp meetings were the logical flowering, in religion, of American democratic optimism, of the belief in equality and rugged self-sufficiency. Man did not have to wait for God but only open himself up to God to feel his presence.

The Second Great Awakening had its moral aspects, as well. Converts were to live upright lives, to reject selfishness and practice disinterested benevolence. Under the influence especially of Charles G. Finney (who held a series of revivals from 1824 to 1837) preachers began to emphasize social justice themes, which led some to found antislavery, temperance, and Bible societies. And as women were often the controlling forces in these societies, their status and importance in society grew.

Charles G. Finney

The Second Great Awakening gave Americans the belief that the United States was a (Protestant) Christian nation; thus politics were not left untouched by this revival. The more deistic, rationalistic leaders began to give way to leaders who gave at least lip-service to more traditional Protestant Christianity. Even some of the rationalists succumbed to religion. Congress, in response to the public's desire for a show of faith, hired a chaplain and passed a law forbidding the delivery of mail on Sunday. Even courts followed suit. In *The People of New York v. Ruggles*, New York chancellor James Kent in 1811 upheld laws against blasphemy.

The Great Awakening, however, ultimately succumbed to rugged American individualism. Though the camp meetings had an ecumenical tone (led as they were by preachers of various Protestant denominations), they ended in creating a large number of new sects, further shattering Protestant Christianity. The revival was also profoundly individualistic. One contemporary wrote that each person was "considered as possessing in himself or herself an original right to believe and speak as their own conscience between themselves and God, may determine." The Baptist Elias Smith wrote in 1809 that men must be "wholly free to examine for ourselves what is truth, without being bound to a catechism, creed, confession of faith, discipline or any rule excepting the scriptures." So it was that people went from church to church, looking for "prophets" and new religious experiences. So it was too that churches began to compete, and fight, for members; Christians argued over doctrine, destroyed each other's meeting houses—and split into more and more sects.

Finally, preachers began appealing to people's self-interest. How else could one maintain a spirit of benevolence in a society that glorified self-interest? Thus was born the idea of "enlightened self-interest," that one should do good because it improves one's prospects in this world, as well as the next. It was not long before the idea of virtue for many degenerated into a useful policy one needs to follow to attain worldly advantage.

The Quest for New Connections—Voluntary Societies

As the traditional bonds of their society disintegrated, Americans began to create new communities by joining together in organizations founded for certain specific purposes. So numerous were these organizations that they became a hallmark of American society. No other country in the world could boast so many volunteer benevolent organizations as the United States.

Many of the founders of the United States had looked upon religion as a means to cultivate in the masses the virtues necessary for a republican order. Churches and other religious groups willingly embraced this vision and began to form societies for various charitable purposes. Though at first wealthy "aristocrats" headed up these societies, in time Americans of more moderate means came to direct them. The purpose of these societies was to serve as watchdogs of virtue so that (as *Columbia* magazine stated it in 1814), "character, that dearest earthly interest of man, will thus be protected, and thousands who are now settling down into incurable habits of licentiousness, will by these means be reclaimed."

Voluntary societies existed both in the rural towns and in the cities. In the latter, they oversaw the construction and maintenance of relief systems for the indigent, hospitals, free schools, prisons, and savings banks for the needy. Though their immediate purpose was to supply for the material wants of men, their goal was ultimately moral—to improve the character of the unfortunate. As time went on, the moral aspect gained even more importance. Societies were founded to reward industriousness and to punish laziness and so strike at the vices that were seen as the necessary causes of poverty. Societies formed to combat the consumption of alcoholic "spirits," gambling, profanity, Sabbath-breaking, and so on. It was thought that by changing the moral character of the poor society could eliminate poverty.

But in the end, despite their high-mindedness, even moral societies had to fall back on the promotion of self-interest. A savings bank established in New York in 1819 was founded "on principles calculated to inspire economy, produce reform, and inculcate a spirit of enterprise and industry, and self-respect, among the laboring classes of the community." All this would happen when members of these classes "saw the progressive increase of the little capital" they had put away.

Voluntary societies ultimately failed to replace the traditional ligaments of society. After a time, membership in them did not involve attending meetings or joining others in common action. Instead, members participated merely by lending monetary support.

The Hope of the World

Liberals like the French thinker Comte Destutt de Tracy did not bemoan the breaking of traditional bonds in America. These bonds only hid what de Tracy thought was the only true bond in society—commerce, buying and selling, economic exchange. Precisely because the United States had given free rein to commerce, de Tracy called the republic "the hope and example of the world."

"Society consists only in a continual succession of EXCHANGES," wrote de Tracy "Commerce and society are one and the same thing." Since in America the bulk of all trade was between states and regions, commerce was one way to keep the union together. Tracy, however, took it further. "Commerce," he said, "that is exchange, being in truth society itself, it is the only bond among men; the source of all their moral sentiments; and the first and most powerful cause of the improvement of their mutual sensibility and reciprocal benevolence."

Yet, if it was unifying the disparate regions of the new federal union, the new commercial society was severing the bond between past and present—the bond of tradition. Men were looking less and less to the past for orientation but always spoke of change, of a more hopeful and better future. In 1809, the political economist Laommi Baldwin summed up the national spirit:

> Everything relative to political economy must be original. Without recurrence to the past, we have to consult futurity; we have every thing to create and little to correct; and instead of remedial institutions formed on retrospective views, we are to establish principles that shall interest posterity.

Noah Webster, painting by James Herring

Another fruit of the commercial society was the growth of the middle class. Americans had neither the elegance of the European aristocracy nor the habits of the European peasant. Americans, it was said, were "mediocre par excellence." Even the definition of gentleman changed—Noah Webster in his 1828 *Dictionary* defined a gentleman as a man "of education and good breeding, of every occupation." Thus in America anyone could be a gentleman—a revolutionary concept, indeed. Everyone, it was thought, had the opportunity to possess enough property to cultivate himself.

The notion of what constituted an education also changed under democratic influences. Unlike their European ancestors, Americans did not think that the point of education is to lead men to the knowledge of the truth and the enjoyment of beauty; rather, a good middle class education in America was supposed to emphasize what is useful. Even that enlightened gentleman, Thomas Jefferson thought that American education should instruct in what pertained "to the common business of life"—such as labor-saving, comfort-increasing inventions, and the political arts. Some revolutionary leaders did not spare even the study of Greek and Latin, long the staples of a classical education. They called them "un-republican," and useless to merchants, mechanics, and farmers.

For many, the wonder of America lay in the fact that this vast mass of people, composed of individuals pursuing only their private interests, could come together in a common will. Many ascribed this to Providence—that God had a peculiar interest in the progress of the United States. The idea behind Winthrop's old "city on the hill" metaphor, now secularized, was applied to the young republic. It became almost a religious belief that America had a special destiny among the nations of the world.

Not all were so optimistic, though. One of the old revolutionary leaders, Benjamin Rush, was highly disillusioned with the course of the republic and regretted the revolution. An ardent believer in the old republican ideal, Rush grieved that the revolution had changed "the principles and morals" of Americans and had brought government under the control "of the young and ignorant and needy part of the community." In 1812 he bemoaned that America was "a bebanked, a bewhiskied, and a bedollared nation." Rush was not alone. Nearly every revolutionary leader ended his life in disappointment—only the wealthy Charles Carroll of Carrollton never lost his optimism.

Even the two architects of the new America, Alexander Hamilton and Thomas Jefferson, came to despair of the future of the country they had helped form. It is understandable that

Hamilton, the foe of democracy, could in 1802 write that, "this American world was not made for me." But what of Jefferson, whose theories and politics did so much to encourage the democratic spirit? He too felt a stranger in the new order. His hopes in the common man were disappointed—he was more self-seeking, more superstitious (that is, religious) than ever. Instead of progressing toward greater enlightenment, people seemed to be growing more barbaric. Towards the end of his life Jefferson felt abandoned, his legacy and contributions all but forgotten. In 1825, at the age of 82, he wrote to a friend that their contemporaries were "all, all dead, and ourselves left alone amidst a new generation whom we know not, and who knows not us."

The Jeffersonian Experiment

The new capitol, Washington, was a swampy, unhealthy place. A morass separated the executive mansion, the "White House," from the unfinished capitol building where Congress met. Counting the boarding house where the members of Congress dwelt in some discomfort, these buildings, plus the new treasury, were all the government structures that existed in the new capital.

In March 1801, President-elect Thomas Jefferson rode a-horseback to the new capitol. No servant or guard attended him. He dismounted his horse and hitched it to the palisades. In keeping with republican standards, his dress was simple but dignified. After taking the oath before the senators and representatives to uphold the Constitution, the new president delivered his address in which he, like Washington, called for unity among citizens:

> Let us, then, fellow citizens unite with one heart and one mind. Let us restore to social intercourse that harmony and affection without which liberty and even life itself are but dreary things. And let us reflect that having banished from our land that religious intolerance under which mankind so long bled and suffered, we have yet gained little if we countenance a political intolerance as despotic and wicked, and capable of as bitter and bloody persecutions . . . every difference of opinion is not a difference of principle. We are all Republicans—we are all Federalists.

Jefferson called on all citizens to support the government of the American union, "the world's best hope," and for all to give way willingly to the decisions of the majority, while respecting the rights of minorities. He called on his fellow citizens to cherish their republican liberty. "Sometimes it is said that man cannot be trusted with the government of himself," said the new president. "Can he, then, be trusted with the government of others? Or have we found angels in the forms of kings to govern him? Let history answer this question." Government, said Jefferson, must be "wise and frugal" while it restrains "men from injuring one another, which shall leave them free to regulate their own pursuits of industry and improvement, and shall not take from the mouth of labor the bread it has earned."

Unlike Washington and Adams, who had sought to impress on people the dignity of the presidential office, Jefferson insisted that he be treated with informality. He considered himself the equal of state governors, refused to be called "Mr. President" (preferring the simple "Mr. Jefferson"), and even greeted foreign dignitaries in his slippers. "If it be possible, to be

Official presidential portrait of Thomas Jefferson, by Rembrandt Peale, 1800

certainly conscious of anything," he said. "I am conscious of feeling no difference between writing to the highest and lowest being on earth."

Marbury v. Madison: A Federalist Coup

Jefferson entered office hoping to reconcile Republicans and Federalists. He did not want to remove Federalists from the government offices; but because his party supporters clamored for rewards, Jefferson replaced some Federalists officeholders with Republicans. Adams' last minute appointments of Federalist justices, however, was another matter to Jefferson. He called the appointments an "outrage to decency" because he thought they violated the will of the people, who clearly had voted for Republican, not Federalist, ideas to prevail in the government. Jefferson thus instructed his secretary of state, James Madison, to withhold several commissions to Adams appointees, including to one William Marbury, whom Adams in the last days of his presidential term had appointed a justice of the peace.

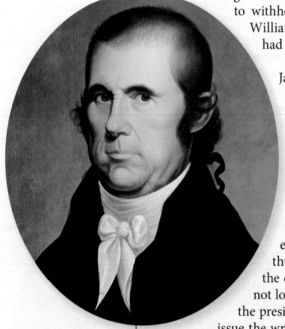

John Marshall, portrait (ca. 1810) by Cephas Thompson (1775–1856), a self taught American painter.

Marbury, however, refused to back down to Jefferson. He sued James Madison, requesting the Supreme Court to command the secretary of state to issue the commission. Marbury appealed to Congress' 1789 Judiciary Act that authorized the Supreme Court to issue a "writ of mandamus"—basically a command (*mandamus* in Latin means "we command") to the executive branch.

Though it seemed a simple matter, much was at stake in this case, *Marbury v. Madison.* Jefferson and the Republicans objected to any assertion of the the Supreme Court's power over the elected branches of government (the presidency and Congress); rather they thought the court should submit to the will of the people, expressed through their elected representatives. *Marbury v. Madison* thus seemed to offer the Republicans a golden opportunity to knock the court down to size. It seemed as if, whatever the result, they could not lose. If the Supreme Court issued writ of mandamus in the case and the president defied it, the court could lose prestige. If the court refused to issue the writ, it would look like it was backing down to the president, and so lose prestige. Whatever happened, it seemed Jefferson would be able to strike a blow against the power of the Supreme Court.

But when, in 1803, Chief Justice Marshall laid down his decision in *Marbury v. Madison,* it was not what anyone expected. First, Marshall declared that the president had no right to withhold Marbury's commission; nevertheless, the chief justice conceded that no body of government could force the president to issue the commission, for, in authorizing the court to issue writs of mandamus, the Judiciary Act of 1789 was unconstitutional and, therefore, void. Jefferson, thus, would not be compelled to issue Marbury his commission nor did he have to submit to a writ of *mandamus* from the court.

The decision in *Marbury v. Madison,* thus, seemed like a triumph for Jefferson; but it really was not—and the president knew it. By declaring a portion of the the Judiciary Act unconstitutional, the Marshall court had implicitly asserted that it had the constitutional authority to nullify laws passed by Congress and signed by the president. In other words, in *Marbury,* Marshall asserted the principle established by Chief Justice John Jay—that the Supreme Court has the authority under the Constitution to review laws passed by Congress and declare on their constitutionality. The Supreme Court, thus, is the supreme interpreter of the Constitution.

Marshal's decision in *Marbury* was directly contrary to Jefferson and the Republicans' view of popular government. For the Republicans, it was unconscionable that a small group of unelected men, serving lifetime tenures, could overturn the will of the people as expressed through their elected representatives. Twenty years later, the decision still rankled with

Jeffersonians; "very irregular and very censurable," he called it. The Federalists, however, rejoiced in Marshall's decision. Indeed, it could be said that, by his last-minute appointment of John Marshall to the court, President Adams had effectively preserved Federalist ideals even in an age when the majority of Americans were showing a preference for Jefferson's rival democratic republicanism.

The Shores of Tripoli

Jefferson did not just fear a powerful Supreme Court; for him, a large military posed a dire threat to republican liberty. Thus, he was not long in office before he ordered the army reduced from 4,000 to 2,500 men. He ordered a reduction in the size of the navy as well and promoted the building of small gunboats over large ships. For Jefferson, the Atlantic was a "moat" large enough to protect the United States from rapacious European powers. Gunboats were all that was needed, he thought, to protect the nation's coasts.

Jefferson's agrarian vision for America, perhaps, led him to overlook the fact that American citizens were engaging in mercantile trade by sea and would want a strong navy to protect their interests when trading far from America's shores. Indeed, American merchants were already experiencing troubles at sea. Since the 1780s, the United States had been paying ransoms to the rulers of Morocco, Algiers, Tunis, and Tripoli in North Africa to guarantee that their "privateers" did not prey on "unprotected" American merchant ships. Jefferson had been only two months in office when the bashaw of Tripoli, who was demanding a hike in the tribute payments, commenced a war on the United States that staggered on for three years. Though Jefferson had reduced the size of the fleet, American naval ships acquitted themselves well against Tripoli's Barbary privateers and even set up an effective blockade of the Barbary ports. In 1804 William Eaton, former American consul at Tripoli, gathered a force of United States navy and marines, 40 Greeks, Arab cavalry, and 100-odd men at Alexandria in Egypt. Crossing the Libyan desert on camels, Eaton's force captured the Tripolitan town of Derna. This victory convinced the bashaw to sign a treaty with the United States.

Sea battle of the Tripolitan War—Lieutenant Stephen Decatur in mortal combat with a captain of Tripoli during the bombardment of Tripoli, August 3, 1804

Beyond the Mississippi

The vigorous Napoleon Bonaparte, First Consul of France, had at last, it seemed, stabilized the government of France following the confusions that had followed the French Revolution. With peace established in France, Napoleon began to harbor the dream of a restoration of French power in North America. In 1800, he entered into secret negotiations with Spain over Louisiana, a vast territory stretching from New Orleans in the south, and westward from the Mississippi to the Rocky Mountains. In return for some European territories, Spain secretly ceded Louisiana back to France in the Treaty of San Ildefonso on October 1, 1800.

This secret cession became public in 1802 when Napoleon sent a French force to take possession of New Orleans and Louisiana (which remained ostensibly under Spanish control). Jefferson and other Americans—Republicans and Federalists alike—were worried. They thought Spanish control of Louisiana troublesome, since the Spanish could easily close off the port of New Orleans to the shipment of American goods. Yet, Spain was weak, and Jefferson hoped that in time Americans could take advantage of this weakness and begin pealing away parts of Louisiana for the United States. French control of Louisiana, however, was another matter altogether, for Napoleon's France was strong and thus a real hindrance to American expansion westward. Hoping to ward off the French threat, Jefferson wrote to the American minister at Paris telling him to warn the French government that "the day that France takes possession of New Orleans . . . we must marry ourselves to the British fleet and nation." This was no idle threat; for Great Britain was Napoleon's greatest enemy in Europe. An American alliance with Great Britain could threaten French possessions in the Americas.

The Louisiana Purchase

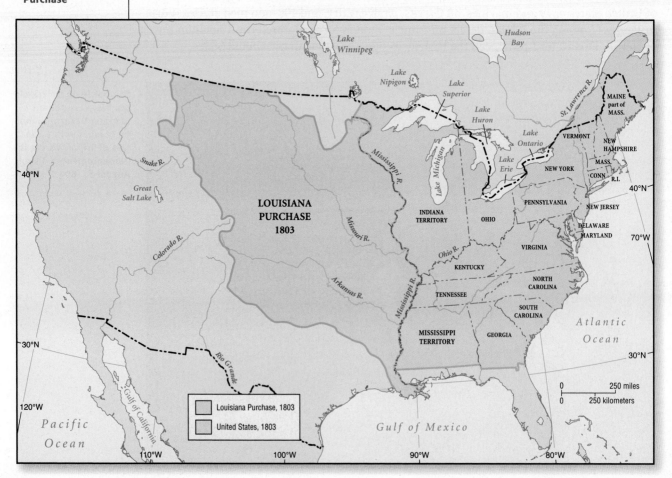

Tensions between France and the United States increased in 1803; the Spanish governor of Louisiana again forbade Americans in the West the right to ship their goods through the port of New Orleans. The president's Federalist rivals clamored for war with France; but Jefferson, eager to maintain peace, instead sent James Monroe to France as envoy extraordinary to help the American consul Robert Livingston negotiate an understanding with France.

Events now took a significant turn. Napoleon was mobilizing for war with Britain, and he feared that, with their superior sea power, the British might seize Louisiana. Moreover, Napoleon needed money. On April 11, 1803, his minister, Talleyrand, approached Livingston and Monroe and offered to sell the whole of Louisiana to the United States. Nineteen days later Livingston and Talleyrand signed an agreement in which France agreed to sell Louisiana to the United States for the bargain price of $15 million.

Jefferson faced a quandary. According to his own political philosophy, the Constitution gave the president no authority to add to national territory by treaty. His lawyers, however, hammered out a justification, worthy of Hamilton, for the purchase; the power to purchase was implied, they said, not actually spelled out, in the Constitution. The reasoning certainly violated Jefferson's strict-constructionism; but his conviction that the U.S. should expand to the west—even, perhaps, to the Pacific—as well as his fear of foreign powers in the West demanded a momentary lapse from constitutional purity. The failure to control New Orleans, he thought, would imperil the continuance of the West in the federal union. "The future destinies of our country hang on the event of this negotiation," said Jefferson. So despite its dubious constitutionality, Jefferson submitted the treaty to the Senate, and it was ratified.

On November 30, 1803, the Spanish government formally transferred Louisiana to France. Three weeks later, France transferred the territory to the United States. By the stroke of a pen, Jefferson had doubled the size of the country.

Lewis and Clark

The vast lands stretching between the Mississippi and the Pacific Ocean held mysteries. Except for the trappers who plied the waters of the muddy Missouri in search of pelts, no white man knew what lay in and beyond the vast plains that sundered settled lands from the great "Stony" Mountains in the West. Few were more curious than Thomas Jefferson about what the lands encompassed by Louisiana territory held—what peoples lived there, what plants and animals.

Jefferson chose two men to lead an expedition of discovery into the newly purchased territories. One, the 29-year old Meriwether Lewis, was the president's personal secretary. His companion, William Clark, 33-years old, was the younger brother of the Revolutionary War hero George Rogers Clark and a veteran of Indian wars in Ohio, including the Battle of Fallen Timbers. These two adventurers gathered a company of over 40 men, the "Corps of Discovery," including soldiers, two French hunters and interpreters, experienced river men, and Clark's black slave, York.

Meriwether Lewis, by Charles Wilson Peale

Jefferson spoke of commerce in his instructions to Lewis and Clark; but more important to the president was scientific knowledge. The Corps of Discovery was to gather information on the animals and plants, the minerals and soil, of the lands through which they passed. The corps was also to describe the culture, religion, mores, traditions, and languages of the Indian tribes it encountered. Though always hungry for knowledge, Jefferson had a practical motive for such research: the president thought the Indians were capable of "progress"; but any attempts at civilizing them must take into account their character and ways.

Lewis and Clark began their voyage up the Missouri from St. Louis on May 14, 1804. Where it enters the Mississippi, the Missouri is a wide river, muddy-brown from the soil churned up by its swift and turbulent waters. Since the expedition traveled in a 55-foot keel boat and two smaller boats called "periaguas," going upstream against the river's current was difficult. The river was swollen from the melting snow, and the icy cold May rains soaked the men to the skin. With adverse winds blowing against them, the expedition sometimes made only three to four miles a day.

About 20 miles from St. Louis, the expedition came across a cluster of about 100 cabins and a Catholic church—the French settlement of St. Charles. While he praised the settlers "careless gaiety" and "amiable hospitality," their "genius and vivacity," and their great endurance, Clark, the enterprising American, could not understand their lack of ambition. The French settlers' efforts were "all desultory," wrote Clark; "their industry . . . without system, and without perseverance." They did not care for trade and progress, he wrote, but were content to live by hunting, fishing, and cultivating their abundant house gardens.

The Corps of Discovery, however, would soon meet peoples more incomprehensible (to them) than the French—the free Indian nations of the West. The Indians Lewis and Clark would encounter along the Missouri River belonged to two families of tribes, each family having similar languages and customs. One, the Algonquin family, had originally inhabited the eastern seaboard but had been pushed west by the Iroquois. The other, the Siouan, comprised a number of tribes that also had been pushed west by the Iroquois. The Algonquian and Siouan tribes were almost always at war with each other and among themselves.

The first tribe the Corps of Discovery encountered was the Kickapoo, an Algonquin nation that had helped George Rogers Clark capture Vincennes during the revolution. Passing the mouth of the Osage River, the expedition moved for the first time into Siouan territory. There they came across a settlement of the Siouan Osage, a tribe that originally inhabited the region of North Carolina and Virginia. The Osage were both hunters and farmers, cultivating pumpkins, corn, and beans. They lived in semi permanent villages, in dome-shaped houses made of saplings and mud. Their warriors, which numbered about 1,500, were tall, handsome men, said Clark, with "fine military capacities."

In June, because of the shifting sandbars in the river, Lewis and Clark's men were forced to pull their heavy barge upstream from the banks. Surrounding them was a land of grass and wooded hills that frequently were visited by sudden and violent rainstorms. The corps passed a Siouan Missouri village wiped out by the

William Clark, by Charles Wilson Peale

Map of Lewis and Clark's route, showing locations of Indian tribes

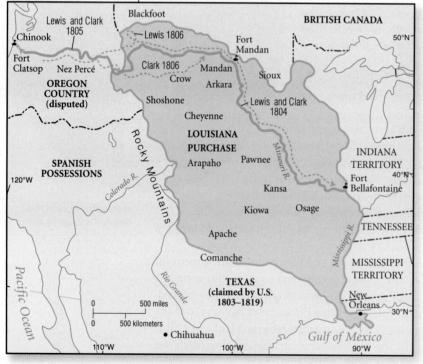

Algonquian Sauk and Fox tribes. The Missouri had been severely reduced by smallpox and now lived with their neighbors, the Oto. Farther on, the expedition encountered signs of the Kansas nation, who were then out hunting buffalo on the plains. Their numbers had been greatly reduced by the Siouan Iowa, allies of the Sauk.

By July 22 the corps had reached the shallow, muddy Platte River, 200 miles from St. Louis. Continuing along the Missouri, they crossed into Pawnee territory. The Pawnee were star-watchers who worshiped the morning and evening stars; and though they believed in many lesser gods, they worshiped a single, omnipotent god, and Mother Earth. Like the other tribes the corps had met, the Pawnee lived by both agriculture and hunting buffalo. They had been pushed across the Mississippi by the Iroquois and forced further west by the Osage.

Beyond the Platte, Lewis and Clark penetrated the vast prairies of the Great Plains. Except for the cottonwood, oak, black walnut, and hickory that grew along the river banks, this land was a treeless, sometimes rolling, sometimes flat expanse of grass. On the prairies the explorers discovered the prairie dog (a large ground squirrel that makes a barking sound) and the prairie dog "towns" of burrows, sometimes stretching for miles. Over the plains ran enormous herds of buffalo, the prey of the Plains Indians, who hunted them by stampeding the herds over the edges of cliffs overlooking the Missouri. After the stampede, the Indians, wrote Lewis and Clark, would "select as much meat as they wish" from the dead or injured buffalo and abandon the rest "to the wolves." The mass of dead buffalo, said Lewis and Clark, created a "most dreadful stench."

On August 3, at Council Bluffs on the Missouri, Lewis and Clark met with representatives of the Oto and Missouri tribes, including six lesser chiefs. Lewis and Clark announced the tidings that the Oto and Missouri were the children of a new "great father" and that the great father wished them to benefit from his protection and from trade with his people. He would provide them more opportunities for trade than the Spanish or French ever did, said the explorers.

Lewis and Clark holding a council with Indians at Council Bluffs; a woodcut illustration from the journal of expedition member Patrick Gass

In late August, Lewis and Clark made their first contacts with the Dakota or Sioux. The explorers were worried, for they had heard much of this tribe and of its cruel and relentless attacks on its neighbors. But the first of these people they met, the Yankton Sioux, were eager for trade and friendship with the United States. Their people were poor, they said; they needed guns and ammunition. The Indians asked for "some of their great father's milk"—whiskey.

Clark described the Yankton Sioux as having "a certain air of dignity and boldness." Fond of decoration, they wore "paint and porcupine quills and feathers . . . with necklaces of white bear claws three inches long." According to Clark, the Sioux "camps are handsome of a Conic form Covered with Buffalo Robes painted different colors and all compact & handsomely arranged." He was describing, of course, the tipi, a kind of housing used only by the

Teton Sioux horse-men, by Karl Bodmer (1830–1834)

Plains Indians. The Sioux lived by hunting buffalo and were excellent horsemen. They frequently raided other tribes to steal their horses.

A little farther up river, the expedition met the Teton Sioux, who lived by hunting buffalo and raiding their enemies, the Mandans, for horses. The Teton had once manufactured pottery but had given it up for the horse-trade. They kept friendly relations with their neighbors, the Arikaras, who were farming folk and supplied the Teton with corn. The farmers among the Arikara were the women, who cultivate the soil with digging sticks made from the shoulder blades of antelope and buffalo and rakes made from reeds fastened to a long handle.

The Teton Sioux mistrusted Lewis and Clark, and at their first meeting, the Teton chiefs were belligerent. When they demanded more whiskey and presents, Clark put on a warlike mien. He told the chiefs that he and his men "were not squaws, but warriors," and "were sent by our great father, who could in a moment exterminate them." According to Clark, "the chief replied that he too had warriors, and was proceeding to offer personal violence to Captain Clark, who immediately drew his sword."

The Indians formed a circle around Clark. His men formed up behind their leader. From the barge, the swivel gun was turned on the Indians. Several tense moments passed before the Teton chief, Black Buffalo, intervened and made his men draw back.

Lewis and Clark spent the next three days with the Teton Sioux. After another incident almost led to violence, the expedition moved farther up river. Fall was upon them, and they decided to find winter quarters with the Mandan. The Mandan proved hospitable and allowed the corps to build a fort, Fort Mandan, outside their village. Mandan villages were made up of permanent "lodges" centered around a sacred cedar post that represented a village hero. Like other tribes, the Mandan believed in "medicine"—a personal spirit or intercessor before the Great Spirit. There was "good medicine" (beneficial spirits) and "bad medicine" (maleficent spirits).

At the Mandan village Lewis and Clark met two whites, George Drouillard and Toussaint Charbonneau, who joined the expedition as interpreters with the Indians. Charbonneau's wife was a Shoshone Indian woman who had been separated from her people in a raid and sold to Charbonneau. This woman, Sacagawea, along with her infant son, joined the expedition; the captains thought she would be valuable in helping them obtain from the Shoshone the horses the expedition needed to cross the Rockies. As events proved, this 17-year old woman would prove very useful to the expedition; for she knew what roots are edible, could describe medicinal plants and serve as an interpreter with the tribes that knew the Shoshonean language.

On April 6, 1805, the corps resumed its journey. Continuing up the Missouri, they passed through hilly lands and then into barren country where were no signs of men. The Missouri now flowed between perpendicular black granite cliffs, 1,200 feet high. Jutting skyward reared "large irregular masses of rocks and stones." Herds of deer and elk thinned, and buffalo were seen no more in this bleak, frowning, though beautifully sublime land. By late May the expedition had reached a place where, for the first time, they could see the Rockies.

Reaching a great fork in the Missouri, the corps divided into two parties, each following a tributary to discover which was the principal stream. Lewis' party, with Sacagawea, followed

A Mandan village, by Karl Bodmer (left), a Mandan chief, by Karl Bodmer (right)

the northern fork, which he named Maria's River (now the Marias), while Clark followed the southern fork, which proved to be the main stream of the Missouri. Proceeding up this fork, by mid June the expedition reached the great falls of the Missouri. The passage around the falls proved most difficult; the explorers suffered from hailstorms; the terrain was broken, the country infested with prickly pear cactus and grizzly bears. It was not until July 4 that the explorers completed the passage. They celebrated their victory, and Independence Day, by drinking off the last barrels of spirits and dancing into the night.

Lewis had hoped that the Rockies would demand only a single passage over high country. What was his disappointment, then, when, on August 12, having become the first Anglo-American to ascend the Continental Divide, he saw before him "immense ranges of high mountains still to the West of us their tops covered with snow." Six days later was Lewis' 30th birthday; marking the occasion in his journal, he mulled over the meaning of his life. He reflected that he had "as yet done but little, indeed, to further the happiness of the human race or to advance the information for the succeeding generation." With "regret" he viewed:

Lewis and Clark on the Columbia River, by Frederic Remington. Sacagawea, her husband, Toussaint Charbonneau, and their baby are pictured behind Lewis and Clark.

> . . . the many hours I have spent in indolence . . . but since they are past and cannot be recalled, I dash from the gloomy thought, and resolved in the future, to redouble my exertions and at least endeavour to promote those two primary objects of human existence by giving them the aid of that portion of talents which nature and fortune have bestowed on me; or in the future, to live for *mankind*, as I have heretofore lived for *myself*.

The day before Lewis' birthday, his party had met a band of Shoshone whose chief, Cameahwait, turned out to be Sacagawea's brother. The Shoshone were a Plains tribe that the Sioux had pushed into the mountains. Short in stature, these Indians wore a costume of animal skins; tufts of their defeated enemies' hair fringed their boots.

Though the Shoshone held absolute sway over their wives and daughters, their government, wrote the explorers, was "perfectly free from restraint. Each individual is his own master, and the only control to which his conduct is subjected, is the advice of a chief supported by his influence over the opinions of the rest of the tribe." Through Sacagawea, Lewis and Clark were able to secure horses from Cameahwait for the difficult descent of the Rockies.

Commencing this descent, the Corps of Discovery passed through the lands of the Nez Percé ("Pierced Nose") nation and of the Flatheads, so named because of their practice of compressing the heads of infants between two boards to give them a flattened appearance. The food for the expedition was the typical Indian fare of the region—roots, salmon (now abundant in the rivers), and plump dogs.

The party discovered that the Indians of the Pacific were different from those of the Plains. They were, according to Clark, short and bowlegged. They lived in long, wooden plank lodges—sometimes over 200 feet long—that often housed several families. They plied the rivers in long canoes, expertly made from redwood. Lewis and Clark discovered that women had a higher station among these tribes than among those east of the Rockies—"they were permitted to speak freely before the men, to whom indeed they sometimes address themselves in a tone of authority." Chinook, Tillamook, Kalamath, and Clatsop were the names of some of these Pacific coast tribes. Following the Columbia, the Corps of Discovery had passed beyond the limits of the Louisiana Purchase territory and entered the Oregon Country—lands claimed by both Great Britain and Spain. When at last the corps had reached the Pacific Ocean, they chose a site amid the misty forests of the Oregon coast for their winter quarters, raising log structures and a palisade they called Fort Clatsop. There they remained until March 23, 1806, when they began their homeward journey.

Passing again over the Rockies, Lewis and Clark parted ways, as they had done on the westward journey; the former, with a part of the company, moved north to the Marias River, while Clark went south by way of the Jefferson and Yellowstone Rivers. Uniting again at the junction of the Little Missouri and Missouri Rivers, the expedition continued down river to the Mandan village, where they parted with Sacagawea. Descending the Missouri, Lewis and Clark reached their point of embarkation, St. Louis, on September 23, 1806. The following February found them reporting to President Jefferson in Washington.

The Sad End of Meriwether Lewis

Jefferson had expected Lewis to compose a detailed scientific account of all that he had observed and experienced on the expedition. Lewis, however, never completed the account. Appointed by Jefferson governor of Louisiana Territory, Lewis could not cope with the challenges he faced. The French, Spanish, and even the American, inhabitants of Louisiana were discontent with American rule. Land speculators and traders fell into conflicts with the Indians. Lewis' drinking problem, already in evidence before he came to Louisiana, was soon exacerbated by a deep depression. Clark, who had accompanied Lewis to Louisiana, wrote to President Jefferson, who recalled Lewis to Washington. Enroute to the capital, Lewis stopped at a road house in Tennessee; and there on October 11, 1809, he shot himself, doing "the deed," wrote President Jefferson later, "which plunged his friends into affliction, and deprived his country of one of her most valued citizens."

Meriwether Lewis, watercolor by Charles Balthazar Julien Fevret de Saint-Memin, 1807

The Virginia Dynasty

The federal government of the early 19th century was not powerful nor did it always evoke loyalty—especially in those who thought their interests were threatened by it. In those days it would have been relatively easy for a state or a group of states to separate from the union, for the federal government took care of only a certain limited number of concerns; the rest fell to the states. Moreover, the patriotism of most Americans still centered on their local region or states. They had not yet developed an American consciousness.

So it was that in 1804 certain New England Federalists, fearing the policies of Jefferson and his Republicans, contemplated separating from the union and forming a "Northern Confederacy of New England and New York." They approached Alexander Hamilton with their plan; but, unable to enlist him in their conspiracy, they turned to Aaron Burr, whom Jefferson had dropped as his running mate for the election of 1804. Deep in the conspiracy, Burr ran against the Republican candidate for the governorship of New York but lost because of Hamilton's opposition. With Burr's defeat, the New England secession movement fell apart.

Aaron Burr

Smarting over his loss and angry with Hamilton for his opposition, Burr wanted revenge. Taking as a pretext a newspaper story that quoted Hamilton saying Burr was "a dangerous man and ought not to be trusted with the reins of government," Burr challenged Hamilton to a duel. Hamilton accepted. The two men met at Weehawken, New York on July 11, 1804. Hamilton fired into the air, but, at ten paces, Burr shot Hamilton dead. He had killed his old rival, but also his own political future. Public opinion turned against Burr, and he went west.

Burr owned land in Louisiana where he hoped to establish a colony of settlers. Together with the Irish adventurer, Harman Blennerhassett, Burr conceived a plan to conquer Mexico—whether for himself or for the United States is unclear. Burr negotiated with Louisiana governor James Wilkinson, who had long been secretly in the pay of Spain, to make Louisiana an independent republic in league with Spain. Establishing headquarters at Lexington, Kentucky, Burr and Blennerhassett began training troops. But betrayed by Wilkinson, Burr was seized and taken to stand trial for treason. Ruling that there was insufficient evidence for treason, Chief Justice Marshall acquitted Burr of all charges. But the American public was not convinced of Burr's innocence; and he, rather than face continued public censure, exiled himself to Europe. There he remained until 1812.

Secession talk did not end with Burr's departure. Dissatisfaction with Jefferson's government intensified when in 1805 the British began seizing American ships engaged in trade with France. Insult was added to violence when British naval captains began boarding American merchant ships to impress sailors. Though the United States was neutral in Britain's war with Napoleon, the British navy justified impressment by claiming that American ships carried British naval deserters. This was often true, though British captains did not shrink from impressing American citizens and black slaves.

In 1806, to strike at French trade, Great Britain issued orders blocking all trade through specified ports in Europe. Napoleon responded in 1806 by issuing the Berlin Decrees, which forbade any country to trade with Great Britain. The British countered Napoleon's move in 1807 by issuing two "Orders in Council": the first prohibited all trade with any port belonging to France or her allies; the second blockaded all European ports that prohibited the entry of British ships. Napoleon retaliated with a further decree on December 17 declaring that any ship searched by the British would be considered enemy property and could be confiscated. Thus caught between British orders and French decrees, American ships soon found themselves barred from most foreign ports.

Tensions increased between Great Britain and the United States when, on June 22, 1807, the British warship, the H.M.S. *Leopard*, fired on the U.S.S. *Chesapeake* ten miles off the coast of Virginia. Americans were outraged; the Federalists clamored for war. Then France began seizing neutral ships—including American vessels. Unwilling to go to war with both Britain and France (or with either of them alone), Jefferson chose instead the more peaceful expedient of an embargo. On December 22, 1807, Congress passed the Embargo Act, which forced all American ships in port to remain in port, lest they be seized by British and French ships. The act struck the port cities of New England and New York hard. Ships sat idle in the shipyards; small ship owners were ruined.

In the congressional election of 1808, every New England state went Federalist. Town councils passed resolutions calling for the repeal of the Embargo Act, some suggesting secession as a recourse if the act were not repealed. Plans were laid for a convention of New England states to consider nullifying the Embargo Act—Federalists were claiming a right championed by Jefferson's Kentucky Resolves! But the convention never met. It did not need to. On March 1, 1809, just three days before the end of Jefferson's second term, Congress repealed the Embargo Act.

Though the Embargo Act had won Jefferson few friends in New England, he was, it seems, still popular elsewhere in the union. In the election of 1808, Jefferson's hand-picked successor and fellow Virginian, James Madison, successfully defeated his Federalist opponent. Virginian Republicans thus remained in control of the federal government.

James Madison

Madison Becomes President

Though he was Jefferson's protégé and a Republican, James Madison's inauguration ceremonies recalled the more pompous displays of the Washington and Adams years. A uniformed militia escorted the president-elect to the capital, where he took his oath of office. Madison promised that he would (continuing Jefferson's policy) keep the United States at peace while he defended the country's honor—a promise he would not fulfill.

Problems with Great Britain and France did not end with the lifting of the Embargo Act. Before Madison took office in March of 1809, Congress had already replaced the embargo with a non-intercourse act forbidding trade with either France or Britain. When he received assurances from the British foreign secretary, David Montague Erskine, that the British government would remove the Orders in Council, Madison, in April, revoked the non-intercourse act against Great Britain. But Britain failed to lift the orders, and Madison reinstated non-intercourse with Great Britain in August. Napoleon aggravated matters by issuing a decree at Rambouillet that said France could seize any American ship that entered a French port. By the time this decree became known in the United States, the French had seized 150 American ships.

By 1810 several Latin American Spanish colonies were in open revolt against the rule of Joseph Bonaparte, whom Napoleon had placed on the throne of Spain. The people of West Florida (the region between the Mississippi and the Pearl River in the modern state of Louisiana)—a congeries of Spaniards, Englishmen, and Anglo-Americans—also rebelled and issued a plan of government on July 17, 1810. After the Spanish governor refused to accept the plan, insurgents seized Baton Rouge on September 23, and three days later a convention declared West Florida independent of Spain.

This newly independent state, flying a flag with a single star, now sought annexation to the United States. The petition evoked a storm of controversy, for adding West Florida would bring another slave-holding region into the United States, something the northern states opposed. Madison was in favor of the annexation. He contended that West Florida had been part of Louisiana all along and so had been purchased in 1803. In the end, West Florida was annexed and added to the District of Orleans, the southernmost part of Louisiana.

Before the controversy between northern and southern states over West Florida could cool, a request for statehood by the District of Orleans reignited it. The District of Orleans covered an area where a particularly degrading slave culture thrived. While the harsher aspects of slavery had mellowed somewhat in the old slave states, the life on the sugar plantations in Orleans was slavery of the worst sort. Here were a breed of greedy pioneers who had little concern for the humanity of the black slave. Driven by often ruthless foremen, the slaves were also oppressed by "black codes," laws that forbade them to congregate, ride horseback, bear arms, or purchase liquor.

Northerners in Congress balked at the idea of adding another slave state to the Union—would this not give the South more representation than the North in national government? In the House of Representatives, Josiah Quincy of Massachusetts was one of the leaders of the opposition to statehood. Professing himself devoted to the union, Quincy said admitting Orleans as a state would dissolve the bonds of union, leaving every state free to go its own way. Others argued that the Constitution only allowed new states to be formed from territories that were part of the United States at the time of the Constitution's ratification. Despite the opposition, the House approved the admission of Orleans as a state and the Senate followed suit. In 1812, the region, under the name "Louisiana," entered the union as the 18th state.

Members of Congress wrangled as well over whether to renew the charter for the Bank of the United States. The long and bitter controversy recalled the debates between Hamilton and Jefferson over the original chartering of the bank. But, unlike the former controversy, the rechartering fight ended in a victory for the anti-bank faction. The charter was allowed to expire. The Bank of the United States was no more.

Portrait of Henry Clay, by Matthew Harris Jouett, 1818

Among the most vehement opponents of the bank was Henry Clay. Ambition had driven Clay, the son of a poor Baptist minister, to study law in Richmond, Virginia under Chancellor George Wythe, who had taught both Jefferson and Chief Justice Marshall. Though tall and awkward, and somewhat long-faced and homely, Clay's eloquence and genial spirit stood him in good stead in his law practice in Lexington, Kentucky. He was elected to the constitutional convention for Kentucky in 1799 and, in 1803, to the Kentucky legislature. Though only 29 years old, Clay was appointed to serve out an unexpired term in the United States Senate in 1806, and again in 1810. In the years ahead, Clay would become the champion of the young and rawboned West against the interests of the slave-holding South.

It was Clay's eloquence that helped seal the fate of the Bank of the United States. He soon joined other voices in the House of Representatives and the Senate in quite another cause—to urge their young country into the second war of her national existence.

The Draw of War

A comet scored the heavens at the moment of his birth, an event that presaged his future greatness. His father, a Shawnee chieftain, named him Tecumseh ("Panther Crossing the Sky"), in token of the omen. From his earliest days, Tecumseh watched as white settlers crossed through the Cumberland Gap, over the mountains, to take his people's country, western Virginia and the rich lands of Kentucky beyond. He saw his people fight these settlers, only to be defeated in battle after battle; his father, Puckeshinwa, fallen in battle; his mentor, the chieftain Cornplanter, shot and killed; his elder brother, Chiksika, slain at his side—all these deaths, and many more, weighed on Tecumseh's spirit. He waxed more bitter and angry against the people that flowed in, in ever increasing numbers, over the mountains. The 26 year-old Tecumseh was among the defeated at Fallen Timbers in 1794; but unlike his fellow chiefs, he had refused to sign the Treaty of Greenville, which handed millions of acres of land over to the United States government for yearly payments of $10,000.

An engraving of the Battle of Tippecanoe

Tecumseh knew that the Shawnee alone, or even an alliance of the northern tribes, were powerless against the whites, whose numbers seemed endless. He conceived of a broader alliance that would join the northern and southern tribes against the whites and prevent them from seizing more Indian land. By 1808 he had formed an alliance with tribes of the western Ohio River Valley. He established the capital for this alliance at Tippecanoe, a settlement on the Wabash River in the Indiana Territory. There warriors gathered and trained for war.

Together with his brother, Tenskwatawa, Tecumseh prepared his people for war. His people held Tenskwatawa in honor; he was called "the Prophet" because of a spiritual awakening that he said had put him in contact with the world of spirits. Tecumseh and the Prophet called on Indians to give up whiskey and no longer to trade with whites. The Indian, they said, must eschew ties with the white men and return to ancestral ways.

The territorial governor of Indiana at the time was William Henry Harrison. In 1809, by intimidation and bribery, Harrison had induced the chiefs of the Miami, Potawatomi, Delaware (Lenape), and Kikapoo to sign a treaty ceding 3 million acres in southern Indiana and Illinois to the United States. Tecumseh had protested this sale; no Indian, he said, could give up the land that belonged to all red men. Wishing to avoid war, the Shawnee chief met with Harrison to induce him to void the treaty and give assurance that the United States would not purchase any more Indian lands. Rebuffed by the governor, Tecumseh prepared for war. In 1811 he went south to draw the Chickasaw, Choctaw, Creek, and Cherokee peoples into his alliance.

Rumors of Indian attacks on white settlements soon reached Governor Harrison. To overawe the Indians or beat them into submission before Tecumseh's return, Harrison gathered 1,000 volunteers and regulars and stealthily moved against the Indian encampment at Tippecanoe. By November 6, 1811, Harrison had established a camp on a wooded hill,

12 miles from Tecumseh's capital. The Prophet, whom Tecumseh had left in command, learned of Harrison's advance. Though Tecumseh had commanded him to instigate no violence, Tenskwatawa made plans to fall on the white man's camp.

Assuring his warriors that his magic protected them from injury and death, Tenskwatawa led an attack on Harrison's camp just before dawn on November 7. Surprised by the onslaught, Harrison's men suffered heavy casualties; but reforming their ranks, they charged on the Indians, forcing them into a swamp that lay between Tippecanoe and the United States camp. With heavy losses on both sides, the battle ended in a draw. The following morning, Harrison marched on the Indian camp—only to find it abandoned. Tenskwatawa had withdrawn by night.

The victory at Tippecanoe made Harrison a national hero. It also ended Tecumseh's hopes for an alliance of Indian nations. With the same spirit by which he forbade the torture of his white enemies during war, Tecumseh spared his brother Tenskwatawa's life. Faced with no other alternative, he led his people into an alliance with the British in Canada. War threatened the uneasy peace between Great Britain and the United States. Perhaps, with British aid, Tecumseh could lead his people to regain what they had lost to the ever encroaching Anglo-Americans.

Triumph of The War Hawks

Relations between the United States and France and Great Britain had been deteriorating. Despite diplomatic moves like the non-intercourse bill, Britain refused to repeal the Orders in Council and continued to board American ships and impress American seamen. Under assurances from Napoleon that French ships would cease seizing American merchantmen, Madison moved Congress to renew the non-intercourse bill (which had lapsed the previous year) against Great Britain but to maintain trade with France. Though Napoleon's promises proved empty (he even ordered the burning of American ships), Madison's policy towards France did not change.

In response to the renewal of non-intercourse, the British navy began blockading the American coast. Madison ordered John Rodgers, commander of the U.S.S. *President*, to protect American shipping. One evening, Rodgers, sailing the 44-gun *President* out of Chesapeake Bay, sighted in the growing darkness what he thought was a British warship. A warship it was, the H.M.S. *Little Belt*. Hailing the ship, Rodgers received a stern reply; then, according to the American account, the smaller *Little Belt* fired on the *President*, hitting the mainmast. The American ship returned fire, and a 15-minute battle ensued, crippling the *Little Belt* and leaving 32 British dead or wounded.

The battle between the *Little Belt* and the *President* whipped up a feverish clamor for war throughout the United States. Anti-English feeling, never really dead since the revolution, was aroused. Members of Congress, called "War Hawks," declared that America had suffered enough insult from Great Britain; it was high time to lesson that haughty nation. *War!* they cried. *War!* they demanded, to humble the proud British lion, to show what free men could do against tyrants—and, as a side benefit, to add British-held Canada to United States territory.

John C. Calhoun

Henry Clay, now a representative and speaker of the House of Representatives, led the fight for war. He was joined by another War Hawk, the 29-year old John Caldwell Calhoun of South Carolina. Calhoun came from a family of middling wealth in Abbeville, South Carolina. His father, Patrick Calhoun, had taught his son a deep distrust of government; that "government was best which," said the elder Calhoun, "allowed the largest amount of individual liberty compatible with social order." After his father's death, the 12-year old John went to live with his brother-in-law, the Rev. Moses Waddell, a Presbyterian minister from whom Calhoun learned the stern Calvinism and almost prophet-like demeanor that came to characterize him. Graduating from Yale University with distinction, Calhoun attended Judge Tapping Reeve's well-respected law school in Litchfield, Connecticut. In 1808–1809 he served in the South Carolina legislature and was elected to the House of Representatives in 1810. Through marriage he obtained a large plantation with many slaves and so came to Washington armed not only with eloquence but social prestige.

In 1811, both Clay and Calhoun fought in Congress to strengthen the navy by building more frigates. The regular army also needed reinforcement, they averred, and were hotly opposed by the anti-war faction in Congress. Finally, the War Hawks prevailed, and Congress voted new internal taxes to finance the military. In April 1812, Congress passed a bill establishing a 60-day embargo against Great Britain. If at the end of that period the British did not remove the Orders in Council and cease the impressment of American sailors, Congress would declare war.

By June it became clear that Britain would not back down, and in the House, Calhoun called for war. On June 1, President Madison, standing before the assembled Congress, asked for a declaration of war. "British cruisers," he said, "have also been in the practice of violating the rights and peace of our coasts. They hove over and harass our entering and departing commerce . . . our commerce has been plundered in every sea." On June 4, the House of Representatives voted 79–49 to declare war on Great Britain, and on June 17 the Senate voted in favor of the declaration. President Madison signed it on June 18.

Only 31 years after Yorktown, the United States was again at war with the mother country, England.

The War of 1812

The United States were ill-prepared for war. In contrast to the British navy, which had more than 100 ships, the Americans had only five frigates. The American army and militia were badly trained or not trained at all, and the generals, mainly veterans of the Revolutionary War, were past their prime.

Commodore Hull on board the *Constitution*

Yet, despite its weaknesses, the small United States navy gained some glory early on in the war. On June 21, Commodore John Rodgers sailed out of New York harbor with the small American fleet and made a sweep of the North Atlantic. In August, Commodore Isaac Hull, in the *Constitution,* captured the British frigate, *Guerriére.* On October 25, Commodore Stephen Decatur, captaining the *United States*, captured the British frigate *Macedonian*, and on December 29, William Bainbridge, on board the *Constitution*, seized the frigate *Java* off the coast of Brazil. These small victories barely annoyed the British power, but they demonstrated the skill and daring of the small American navy and taught a measure of humility to the British, who were exceedingly proud of their sea power.

The land war was not only less successful, it was an embarrassment. Arriving at Detroit on July 5, American General William Hull planned an invasion of Canada with untrained and poorly equipped troops. Crossing the Detroit River into Ontario, Hull avoided attacking Fort Malden, which guarded the entrance into the straits from Lake Erie, but nevertheless issued a call for the surrender of Canada. Meanwhile, British Brig. General Isaac Brock gathered British and Indian reinforcements and, pushing Hull back into Detroit, forced the American general to surrender on August 16. Hull's "invasion" gained the British a foothold in Michigan.

Hull cannot be entirely blamed for this defeat; his commanding general, Henry Dearborn, had sent him no reinforcements. Dearborn, headquartered on Lake

A pro-American cartoon, titled, "A Boxing Match, or Another Bloody Nose for John Bull." King George III (at left) says to Madison, "Stop, stop, stop, Brother Jonathan, or I shall fall with the loss of blood—I thought to have been too heavy for you—but I must acknowledge your superior skill. Two blows to my one! And so well directed too! Mercy mercy mercy on me, how does this happen!!!" To which Madison replies: "Ha ah, Johnny! You thought yourself a Boxer did you? I'll let you know we are an Enterprizeing Nation, and ready to meet you with equal force any day."

Champlain, had been delayed by British agents who were negotiating for peace. The British truly wanted peace, for, occupied as they were with fighting Napoleon in Europe, they had few troops to spare for America. Thus, for at least two years, American troops outnumbered British forces in Canada.

Despite Hull's defeat, the war party in Washington still cherished hopes of annexing Canada. Secretary of War William Eustis ordered General Stephen Van Renssalaer, stationed at Buffalo, New York, to attack British positions across the Niagara River. Van Renssalaer's first attempt on October 10, 1812, a night attack on Queenstown, ended when the first boat to cross the river bore away the oars for the boats yet on the American shore. The second assault three days later, also by night, was more successful. American regulars captured a battery atop some bluffs commanding Queenstown and beat off two British assaults on their position, killing General Brock himself. The American militia, however, refused to cross the river; they had enlisted, they said, not to invade Canada but to defend American territory. Van Renssalaer, they said, would violate their constitutional rights if he forced them to invade. Thus, the militia did nothing while the British overwhelmed and captured the regulars on the Queenstown heights.

The situation did not improve when an Irish general from Virginia, Alexander Smyth, took command. Though he promised the volunteers that he would lead them to a victory that would "palsy the savage hand . . . wielding the scalping knife," and though, by the end of November, he had gathered an army of 4,500 volunteers with 500 Seneca and Cayuga warriors, Smyth's operations were so inept that his men finally refused to obey him. General Dearborn's attempt to advance on Montreal also failed—his troops would just not cooperate.

With the loss of Detroit, the frontier from Ohio to Georgia stood open to attacks from Tecumseh's Indians. Allied with the British, Tecumseh directed a series of raids that terrorized the frontier. Against the Indian threat, Henry Clay in Kentucky led a muster of volunteers, who were placed under William Henry Harrison, commander of the regular army in the Northwest. A more tatterdemalion army could not be found. As later described by a British officer, the American troops wore tattered clothes and "their long hair fell matted and uncombed over their cheeks."

Yet, this unkempt horde were fighters. While Harrison moved with the main body of the army up the Maumee River in northwestern Ohio, General James Winchester, with a division of Harrison's army, captured Frenchtown on the Raisin River in Michigan. But on January 22, 1813, British and Indians under General Proctor assaulted Winchester's position at Frenchtown, forcing the Americans to surrender. After the surrender, Proctor's Indian allies killed and maimed 30 wounded Americans.

Proctor with 1,000 Canadians and 1,200 of Tecumseh's Indians next laid siege to Fort Meigs on the Maumee; but unable to breach the fortifications, they abandoned the fort to hunt-down Harrison, who was encamped on the upper Sandusky River. Enroute lay Fort Stephenson, defended by 160 Americans under George Croghan. Told by Harrison to abandon the fort, Croghan refused: "We are determined to maintain this place, and by heaven we will!" Proctor surrounded the fort with 500 British regulars and 700 Indians, and attacked. Though vastly outnumbered, Croghan's men doggedly fired from behind the palisades at the British, picking off all the officers and one-fifth of the men. Proctor withdrew.

Don't Give Up the Ship

Though unable to spare more troops to fight in America, the British were able in 1813 to free up more of their navy for a naval blockade of the American coast. The blockade bottled up American shipping in ports south of New York. Thinking it only hurt their interests while it benefited the southern states, public opinion in New York and New England went heavily against the war. So opposed were New Englanders and New Yorkers to the war that the governors of the New England states refused to release their state militia to the federal government. Wanting neither to annoy the New Englanders nor jeopardize continued trade with them, the British did not blockade the northern ports.

Throughout the winter and into the spring of 1813, American Commodore Isaac Chauncey with Commodore Oliver Hazard Perry constructed and equipped four small schooners on Lake Erie: three ships with two to four guns and two larger ships, the *Niagara* and the *Lawrence*, with 20 guns each. Their English counterpart, Captain Robert Heriot Barclay, commanded six ships, including the *Detroit*, having 19 guns, and the *Queen Charlotte*, with 17 guns. In April, Commodore Chancey with General Dearborn, commanding 14 vessels with 980 sailors, attacked York (now Toronto) on the northwestern banks of Lake Ontario. The British garrison of 600 surrendered to the Americans, who proceeded to burn the two houses of the provincial assembly, along with a number of civilian houses. The sacking of York opened the way for an American victory on Lake Erie.

In the early spring of 1813 British forces in Detroit invaded Ohio, pushing by summer as far as the Sandusky River, which flows into Lake Erie. Deep as they were in enemy territory, the British relied on support from their fleet on Lake Erie. It was this support that Perry wanted to knock out. On September 10, Perry's small cadre of ships closed with Barclay's fleet. The *Detroit* and the *Queen Charlotte* engaged Perry's flagship, the *Lawrence*, flying a pennant that read, "Don't Give Up the Ship." Though British fire riddled the *Lawrence*, Perry did not give up. Finally, with only one gun operable, Perry abandoned the *Lawrence* and rowed to the *Niagara*. Maneuvering his new flagship between the *Detroit* and the *Queen Charlotte*, Perry fired broadsides from port and starboard. Already heavily damaged from their fight with the *Lawrence*, the two British ships could not sustain the attack of the *Niagara*, and surrendered. "We have met the enemy and they are ours. Two ships, two brigs, one schooner, and one sloop," read a communiqué Perry sent to General Harrison.

Commodore Perry transfers his command from the *Lawrence* to the *Niagra*

With the Americans now in control of Lake Erie, the British were forced to withdraw from Ohio and to abandon Detroit and Fort Malden. Transported across Lake Erie by Commodore Perry, General Harrison pursued Proctor's retreating army in Ontario. On October 5, Proctor made a stand on the north bank of the Thames River, his left flank on the river, and the right flank, made up of Tecumseh and his Indians, skirting a swamp. Richard Johnson, commanding Kentucky cavalry, led the attack on the British position. The British broke and retreated. Johnson himself fell on Tecumseh and his warriors, who guarded the British retreat. The Indian ranks withered in the face of the more disciplined American assault. Tecumseh stood firm and died bravely, with 33 of his warriors around him.

Attempts by Americans to capture and hold points on Lake Ontario and along the St. Lawrence River in the summer and fall of 1813 came to nothing. British and Canadian forces were able to drive the Americans entirely out of Canada, even capturing Fort Niagara in New York, north of Buffalo. Canadians held Fort Niagara until the end of the war.

Throughout 1813 and into 1814, the British tightened their blockade on American ports. Even American naval ships could not sail out of port, and merchantmen-turned-privateers carried on much of the resistance on the sea. American privateer attacks on British shipping were most effective, however; insurance companies in England drove up premium payments because American privateers had sunk so many British merchant ships.

The War in the South

In the South, the War of 1812 was not a struggle against the British but an Indian war. It began when Little Warrior, a Creek follower of Tecumseh, led an uprising that resulted in the slaughter of a white settler and his family. When Creek chiefs ordered the death of Little Warrior and his followers, about 2,000 Creek warriors under the prophet High Head Jim and Josiah Francis, rose up in revolt against the chiefs and went on the warpath in the spring

243

Massacre at Fort Mims

of 1813. With the looming threat of these "Red Sticks" (so named because of their red war clubs), in August 1813, 553 settlers from throughout southern Alabama fled for protection to Fort Mims on the Alabama River, about 40 miles north of Mobile. The Red Sticks attacked the fort in late August; only 15 to 20 of the settlers escaped. Those who did not escape or die, were tortured to death by the Indians.

News of the Fort Mims massacre stirred Tennessee, Louisiana, Mississippi Territory, and Georgia into action. Levies from these regions—2,500 men—were placed under the command of Andrew Jackson of Tennessee. The 46-year old Jackson, known as "Old Hickory" for his tough and unyielding character, was suffering from a wound he had recently received in a brawl with a man he had tried to horsewhip. Now, at the head of his motley troops, he was establishing forts on the Tennessee and Coosa Rivers and began an advance into Red Stick country. His first forays were unsuccessful; his men proved too unruly to command. He gathered a new enlistment and attacked the Red Sticks in their fortress on the Coosa River in Alabama. The Indians fought bravely and stubbornly but were no match for Jackson and his men. Of the 800 Indians in the fort, only 243 escaped into Florida. From the Coosa, Jackson pushed south destroying abandoned Creek villages.

Promoted to major general in command of the military district covering the entire Southwest, Jackson established his headquarters at Mobile. When the federal government ordered him to make a treaty with the remaining Creek, Jackson drove a hard bargain. These Creek were not Red Sticks; in fact, they had aided the government and the white settlers against the Red Sticks. Nevertheless, Jackson threatened to destroy the Creek chiefs with their followers if they did not cede to the United States government all their ancestral lands between the Chattahoochee and Coosa Rivers (eastern Alabama). Faced with such harsh terms, the Creek chiefs signed over their lands to the Americans.

Punish the Parricides!

April 11, 1814, the day Napoleon Bonaparte abdicated the throne of France, marked the end of Great Britain's war in Europe. Britain could now spare troops, some of the best she possessed, for the war in America. The *London Times* on April 15, 1814, expressed British sentiment toward America. "There is no public feeling in this country stronger than that of indignation against the Americans," fulminated the *Times*. America had, by declaring war on Britain in the midst of her struggle against Napoleon, aided the French tyrant. "That a republic boasting of its freedom should have stooped to become the tool of the Monster's ambition; that it should have attempted to plunge the parricidal weapon into the heart of that country from whence its own origin was derived; that it should have chosen the precise moment when it fancied Russia was overwhelmed, to attempt to consummate the ruin of Britain—all this is conduct so black, so loathsome, so hateful, that it naturally stirs up the indignation that we have described."

With Napoleon out of the way, Britain could punish America. In the spring a British fleet bombarded the town of Lewiston, Pennsylvania, on the Delaware River, for 24 hours because the town had refused to give food to the British commander. At Hampton, Virginia, another coastal town, British pillaged houses and molested women. In the far north, the British took northern Maine and annexed it to New Brunswick.

In the Northwest, General Prevost led a British counteroffensive against General Wilkinson, retook Fort George and the Canadian Niagara, and crossing into New York, burned Black Rock and Buffalo. Following this string of defeats, the war department replaced Wilkinson with General George Izard. With American regulars, militia, and Iroquois Indian warriors, Izard assaulted British forts on Lake Ontario and was able to maintain control of Lake Erie.

The Summer of 1814 witnessed a series of British offensives. On July 18, the British vice admiral, Sir Alexander Cochrane, ordered British ships to destroy Atlantic coastal towns and villages. General Prevost, gathering 12,000 British veterans of the Napoleonic wars, marched from Montreal into New York. Like Burgoyne in the revolution, Prevost's plan was to march on New York City by way of Lake Champlain and the Hudson River Valley. Hoping to draw American troops from the Canadian border, Major General Robert Ross planned an attack on the American capital, Washington.

In August, General Prevost's troops were awaiting the arrival of the small British fleet on Lake Champlain to launch an attack on the American fortifications at Plattsburgh, on the New York side of Lake Champlain. The British fleet on Lake Champlain boasted the 37-gun *Confidiance*, three smaller ships, and 12 gunboats. When the British fleet under Captain George Downie reached the harbor at Plattsburgh, they found an American fleet commanded by 30-year old Thomas Macdonough blocking the harbor entrance. In the ensuing battle, Macdonough's ships, outgunned though they were and suffering heavy casualties, forced the surrender of the British fleet. With this defeat, General Prevost lost the heart to advance down the Hudson and retreated into Canada. New York was saved.

The U.S. Capitol after the fire

The city of Washington did not fare so well. In August, 1814, Admiral Cochrane's fleet appeared in Chesapeake Bay. Landing at the mouth of the Patuxent River, British regulars under General Ross followed the riverbank 50 miles northwest until they reached the village of Bladensburg, seven miles from Washington. President Madison, working feverishly to provide a defense for the capital, sent General William Winder to Bladensburg with 5,000 regulars, militia, sailors, and marines to block the route to the city. When Winder decided to fall back on Washington, Madison himself, with his secretary of state James Monroe and other cabinet members and aids, went out to reinforce the small American force left at Bladensburg after Winder's retreat.

On August 24, the British attacked, at Bladensburg; the Americans fought back briefly and then fled. The way to Washington lay wide open to the British. Important government papers, along with the Declaration of Independence, had already been removed from the city, and many citizens had fled (including the president's wife, Dolley Madison, with a portrait of George Washington), when the British marched into Washington. They set fire to the capitol, the White House, the navy yard, and the treasury building. Only the onset of two thunderstorms saved the buildings from utter destruction.

With Washington sufficiently punished, the British fleet carried Ross' regulars north to attack Baltimore. In a coordinated land and sea assault, Ross was to attack the city by land while Cochrane and his fleet reduced Fort McHenry on the seaward side of the city. But because of the delay at Washington, Samuel Smith, commander of the American forces at Baltimore, had had time to plan for defense. He had gathered over 10,000 men to hold defensive positions around the city and strengthened the defenses of Fort McHenry. Above the fort Commander Smith let fly an exceedingly large American flag as if in defiance of the invader.

An American, Francis Scott Key, sailed with the British fleet. He had met with British officers to arrange the release of a doctor whom they had captured and was detained lest he carry back to American forces any news of British movements. Thus it was that, from a British ship, Key witnessed the bombardment of Fort McHenry that began on the morning of September 12 and lasted all day (with little effect on the fortress). When night set in, the bombardment intensified in order to cover a British attack on the city. It was a fearful and

Bombardment of Fort McHenry

furious display, the bombs detonating before they struck the fort—literally bursting in air. Key wondered if, by morning, the fortress would have fallen to the enemy. Throughout the night, though, the light cast by the flashing bombs revealed the great flag still flying over Fort McHenry. Key commemorated this event in a poem, which has come down to us under the title, "The Star Spangled Banner."

While the fleet bombarded Fort McHenry, British forces under Ross attacked the earth fortifications around the city. When Ross was killed by a sharpshooter's bullet, command fell to Colonel Arthur Brooke. The Americans fought bravely but when the British turned the Americans' left flank, they were forced to retreat. Both sides had suffered heavy casualties and the British, weary from marching and dispirited by the death of Ross, did not press into the city. In the end, faced with 15,000 American troops, opposed to his 4,800 British regulars, Colonel Brooke called off the attack. On September 13, the British withdrew from Chesapeake Bay and sailed to the West Indies. There they joined a powerful land and naval force gathered at Jamaica for an assault on New Orleans in Louisiana.

More Secession Talk

Elections in 1814 proved New England's continuing opposition to the war and the Republicans. In 1814, control of the state legislatures went to the Federalists, who insisted that the government's war policy violated New England's interests to benefit Virginia and the South. That Jefferson and Madison were both Virginians demonstrated the southern bias of the federal government, or so New Englanders thought. They decided the government's policy of cutting new states out of the Louisiana territory would only weaken New England's influence in the union. So deep were their fears that many New Englanders welcomed the news of the British assault on New Orleans. They hoped that, with Louisiana falling to Britain, the West would be forced to separate itself from the union, leaving the thirteen original states to operate according to the rules and character of their original constitutional compact.

But some New Englanders went further; they wanted their own states to secede from the union. Caleb Strong, Federalist governor of Massachusetts, even sent an emissary to the British to discuss a separate peace between the Bay State and the mother country. In the fall of 1814, the Massachusetts legislature called on the other New England states to send delegates to a convention that would discuss their position relative to the union. The hope was that, in time, a convention of all the states could be called to revise the Constitution.

Delegates of the New England states were to meet at Hartford, Connecticut. News of the convention worried many throughout the union, for they feared it would call for the secession of New England. The Richmond (Virginia) *Enquirer* voiced the opinion of many that such a course was not possible. "No man, no association of men, no state or set of states *has a right* to withdraw from this Union, of its own accord," said the *Enquirer*. "The same power which knit us

A anti-Hartford Convention cartoon, titled, "The Hartford Convention or Leap No Leap." In this cartoon, King George says to the three figures representing Massachusetts, Rhode Island, and New Hampshire: "O'tis my Yankey boys! Jump in my fine fellows; plenty molasses and Codfishes; plenty of goods to Smuggle; Honours, titles and Nobility into the bargain—"

The Hartford Convention or *LEAP NO LEAP.*

together, can only unknit us. . . . The *majority of states* which form the Union must consent to the withdrawal of *any one* branch of it. Until *that* consent has been obtained, an attempt to dissolve the *union*, or to obstruct the efficacy of its constitutional laws, is Treason—Treason to all intents and purposes."

The Hartford Convention, however, turned out to be a mild affair. Far from calling for secession, the convention only reiterated the grievances of the New England states. When the convention adjourned, New England was no closer to secession than she was before.

The Defense of New Orleans and the End of the War

When General Andrew Jackson in September 1814 learned that a British fleet was about to set sail for New Orleans, he began to gather a defensive force. In December, he arrived in New Orleans with 4,000 men. The British, meanwhile, had set out from Cuba in 50 ships said to be carrying 8,000 soldiers, all veterans of the Napoleonic wars. By early December they had landed at Chandeleur Island in the Mississippi delta, and on December 14 they captured American gunboats on Lake Borgne. Now the British stood only ten miles from New Orleans.

A lithograph of the Battle of New Orleans by Nathaniel Currier, 1842

Faced with an imminent British assault on New Orleans, Jackson declared martial law in the city and ordered all able-bodied men, from French aristocrats to the pirate crews of Pierre and Jean Lafitte, to join in the defense of the city. When Jackson learned that 1,688 British soldiers were approaching New Orleans, he ordered the church bells of the city rung and mobilized 2,200 men to march on the British position while the 14-gun *Carolina* sailed down river. Supported by the guns of the *Carolina*, the Americans forced the British to form up behind a levee.

For the next three days, the British brought up more troops. In late December, their artillery fired hot shot into the *Carolina* and set her afire. On January 8, British commander, Sir Edward Pakenham, ordered a two-pronged attack on the American positions. He sent one detachment to silence an artillery battery under General David Morgan, while another detachment assaulted Jackson's men ensconced behind wood and mud palisades.

Jackson's men—French gentlemen dressed in bright red and blue uniforms, sailors, free blacks, French refugees from Santo Domingo, and volunteers from Tennessee and

Kentucky—were a strange sight to the smartly dressed British regulars advancing in strict military formation. Attacking the American left, these brave veterans were in the open and so were cut down mercilessly by the Americans, firing from behind their fortifications. When Pakenham himself, leading the second charge, was killed, the major general who took command ordered a halt to the attack. The British had lost nearly 2,000 men, killed and wounded, including three generals, 11 colonels, and 75 lower officers, while American casualties stood at only 45.

The British withdrew from New Orleans. Enroute to the West Indies, the expedition was preparing to attack Mobile but desisted when it received the news that the United States and Great Britain were now at peace. The two powers had signed a peace treaty at Ghent, in Belgium, on Christmas Eve, December 24, 1814, two weeks *before* the Battle of New Orleans.

The Fruit of War

British representatives had been meeting since August with an American delegation that included Henry Clay and John Adams' son, John Quincy Adams, to discuss terms for peace. At first British demands were high—they included the establishment of an Indian buffer zone between the United States and Canada and the cession of a large part of Maine to New Brunswick. But as the British public grew more and more weary of the war, the British sought to buy peace at much lower rates. Finally, both sides signed a treaty that accomplished nothing else but peace. Britain did not repudiate the impressment of sailors on American ships, and neither side gained any new territory. Things were just as they were when the war began.

Yet, though the war achieved none of the War Hawks' goals, it did have some beneficial effects. Oddly enough, it led to better relations between the United States and Great Britain. Britain had learned to respect American soldiers and sailors, and both countries realized how much each relied on the other for trade. In the United States, the war created a new spirit of national unity. All sections had helped in the war effort; even New England had contributed her privateers. Though sectional problems would remain and become more intense as the years passed, the war had given Americans a common focus and a mutual endeavor, for the results of which (whatever those were) they were all responsible.

Chapter 11 Review

Summary

- In 1797, the XYZ Affair gave President Adams and the Federalists the impetus to put through their program of national defense.

- The small American fleet engaged in battles against the French, in what became known as the Quasi-War. But when President Adams found out that the French had no desire for war, he reestablished friendly relations with them.

- In response to fears of foreign infiltration, President Adams and the Federalist Congress passed three acts in 1798: the Naturalization Act, the Alien Act, and the Sedition Act. The Republicans responded with the Kentucky and Virginia Resolves, written respectively by Thomas Jefferson and James Madison.

- Running for the Republicans, Thomas Jefferson won the 1800 election. He saw this election, or "Revolution," as he called it, as marking a fundamental change in American government.

- American society after the revolution was undergoing significant social changes. The traditional social order was disintegrating.

Chapter 11 Review (continued)

- The Second Great Awakening began in 1799 with a camp meeting in Kentucky. This Second Great Awakening gave Americans the belief that the United States was a Protestant Christian nation. This religious revival affected politics and laws.

- In an attempt to create new communities in the disintegration of traditional bonds, Americans began to start organizations for certain specific purposes; such organizations have become a hallmark of American society. But these organizations did not solve the problems of social distintegration.

- Under President Jefferson, James Madison withheld from William Marbury the commission for his appointment as justice of the peace, and Marbury sued Madison. The Supreme Court declared that the president had no right to withhold a commission, but no body of government could force the president to issue a commission, thus nullifying the Judiciary Act, passed by Congress and signed by the president. In this decision, the Supreme Court implicitly asserted that it had the constitutional authority to nullify laws passed by Congress and signed by the president.

- In 1803 the Spanish government transferred Louisiana to France, and France in turn sold the territory to the United States.

- In 1804 Lewis and Clark set out on their expedition to explore the lands encompassed by Louisiana. After making their way across the Rocky Mountains to the Oregon Country, the expedition returned in 1806.

- In the election of 1808, Jefferson's hand-picked successor, James Madison, was elected president, keeping the federal government under Republican control.

- The impressment of American sailors by the British, as well as a sea battle between the American ship, the *President*, and the British ship, the *Little Belt*, whipped up a clamor for war in the United States. In June 1812, Congress declared war on Great Britain. The war waged until the signing of a peace treaty at Ghent on December 24, 1814.

Key Concepts

Naturalization Act: the act that extended the time a foreigner must reside in the United States before becoming a citizen

Alien Act: the act giving the president power for two years to expel from the country any foreigners he wished

Sedition Act: the act that made it a crime to say or write anything critical of the president or government of the United States

Kentucky Resolves: an act, authored by Thomas Jefferson, of the Kentucky legislature that said the federal government is not the final judge of the extent of its own powers under the Constitution and asserted a state's right to nullify a federal law it deems unconstitutional

Second Great Awakening: a religious revival that swept the United States in the early 19th century and affected American society and government

embargo: a legal prohibition by a government restricting the departure of ships from some location to another location or country

commerce: a branch of production which deals with the exchange of goods and services from a producer to a consumer

Dates to Remember

1797: the XYZ Affair

1798: the United States builds its first fleet of ships for war.

Congress and President Adams approve the Naturalization, Alien, and Sedition Acts.

1799: the Second Great Awakening begins.

1800: Thomas Jefferson elected the third president of the United States

1803: France sells Louisiana to the United States.

1804: Lewis and Clark begin their expedition.

1808: James Madison elected the fourth president of the United States

1812: Congress declares war on Great Britain, thus starting the War of 1812.

1814: the War of 1812 ends with the signing of the Treaty of Ghent (December 24).

Central Characters

Thomas Jefferson (1743–1826): draftsman of the Declaration of Independence and third president of the United States

Meriwether Lewis (1774–1809): American explorer who co-led the Lewis and Clark Expedition to the Pacific Northwest

William Clark (1770–1838): American explorer who with Meriwether Lewis led the Lewis and Clark Expedition

Sacagawea (1788–1812): Shoshone Indian woman who traveled with Lewis and Clark as an interpreter and guide

Tecumseh (1768–1813): Shawnee Indian chief who directed Indian resistance to white rule in the Ohio River valley and fought against the Americans in the War of 1812

Henry Clay (1777–1852): a United States Senator from Kentucky and one of the leaders of the "War Hawks"

John C. Calhoun (1782–1850): a member of the United States House of Representatives, who, with Henry Clay and other War Hawks, pushed for war with Great Britain

Questions for Review

1. What was the "Revolution of 1800," and what were its effects?

2. What was the significance of the XYZ Affair?

3. What situation prompted President Adams and Congress to pass the Naturalization, Alien, and Sedition Acts?

4. Describe the differences between the Republicans and the Federalists.

5. What was President Jefferson trying to express in his inaugural address when he said, "We are all Republicans—we are all Federalists"?

6. How did commerce in America help bring about the disintegration of traditional society?

7. Why did emigration and the mobility of American society contribute to the disintegration of traditional society?

8. What was the social and political significance of the Second Great Awakening?

9. What did Comte de Tracy mean by calling America "the hope and example of the world?" What did he mean when he said that "commerce and society are one and the same thing"?

10. Explain *Marbury v. Madison* and its significance.

11. What did Jefferson hope to accomplish by sending Lewis and Clark on an expedition through the new uncharted American territory?

12. How was the War of 1812 begun? What events led up to the declaration of war?

13. What did the War of 1812 accomplish?

Ideas in Action

1. Read portions or all of the *Journals* written by Meriwether Lewis and William Clark. While reading the text, map out the path of their expedition.

2. Read Thomas Jefferson's Kentucky Resolves (available on the Internet). Do the ideas expressed in the document make sense given the nature of U.S. government?

3. Read all four verses of Francis Scott Key's "The Star Spangled Banner." What did Key want to express about America in the poem?

Highways and Byways

The National Anthem

Before "The Star Spangled Banner" became the official national anthem of the United States, other songs,

Chapter 11 Review (continued)

including "Hail, Columbia" and "My Country 'Tis of Thee," served as unofficial national anthems. In 1889 "The Star Spangled Banner" was recognized for official use in the United States Navy, and on March 3, 1931 it was made the national anthem by a congressional resolution, signed by President Herbert Hoover.

Francis Scott Key originally called his poem, "Defense of Fort McHenry." He gave the poem to his brother-in-law, Joseph Nicholson, who saw that the words fit the melody of the popular "Anacreonic Song" by the English composer John Stafford Smith.

The "Anacreonic Song" was the official song of the Anacreonic Society, an 18th century club of gentlemen amateur musicians. Key's poem, set to the melody, was published under the title, "The Star Spangled Banner," and soon became very popular. In the early 20th century there were several versions of the song, and President Woodrow Wilson asked the U.S. Bureau of Education to provide an official version. This standardized version, which covers one and a half octaves (and thus is famous for being hard to sing), is the version that is still used today.

12 REVOLUTION IN NEW SPAIN

A California Romance

On an April day in 1806, a ship flying the two-headed eagle, emblem of the Russian Empire, sailed into California's Golden Gate, braving the guns of the Presidio de San Francisco. A message sent from shipboard to the Spanish commander announced the arrival of the Russian ship *Juno,* and her master, Nikolai Petrovich Rezánov, an agent of the Russian-American Fur Company and chamberlain to His Majesty, the Tsar.

Rezánov had sailed from Alaska that spring on a desperate mission. The Russian trading settlement of Sitka was suffering from hunger and was near to collapse. Unable to get supplies from elsewhere, and intent on saving the settlement, Rezánov looked south, to California, known to be a land of plenty. There, he thought, he could get supplies for the struggling colony—and scout out a location for a Russian settlement.

The Spanish authorities were not naïve; they understood the desirability of California and, moreover, they knew how ill-defended it was. From San Diego to San Francisco there were no more than 210 soldiers, stationed at four *presidios* at San Diego, Santa Barbara, Monterey, and San Francisco. What's more, these *presidios* had few working cannon, and their defenses were in poor repair. The Spanish crown knew that any nation with enough resolve could easily conquer this languid country; and it was for this reason, in part, that it forbade trade with foreign countries.

The meeting between the Spanish commander at San Francisco, Captain José Dario Argüello, and Rezánov, was somewhat comic: Argüello was anxious lest the

San Francisco presidio, 1817

Russian discover the weakness of the *presidio,* and Rezánov was trying to hide the conditions at Sitka while he negotiated for a shipload of food. The Spanish commander showed Rezánov generous hospitality, and the lighthearted *Californios* made his stay pleasant; nevertheless, Argüello said there would be no question of trade, even for food.

Meanwhile, the courtly Rezánov charmed the *gente de razón* (members of the upper class) in San Francisco and the local clergy, who all took his part. Still, neither Argüello nor the governor, José Arillaga, would bend. They were not to be corrupted; they would maintain the king's law. But Rezánov found one very powerful advocate—Argüello's 16-year old sister, Doña Maria de la Concepción.

Concepción, or Conchita, as she was called, was courted by sons of the first families of California, for she was very beautiful. Still she fell in love with the charming Russian nobleman, though he was 35 years her senior. Rezánov courted Conchita and finally asked for her hand in marriage. This presented a difficulty; since Rezánov was Russian Orthodox and Conchita was Catholic, their marriage would need permission from the pope and the king of Spain, as well as the Russian church and the tsar. Captain Argüello, however, accepted Rezánov as Conchita's suitor, and the lovers were betrothed.

Matters now were different. Rezánov was not just a Russian agent; he was a member of the Argüello family. The governor could not refuse him the supplies. In May, with the *Juno's* holds filled with food, Rezánov set sail for Sitka. Before his departure, Concepcíon vowed she would never marry another man, and Rezánov promised that he would return for her after he received permission for his marriage from the tsar.

Years passed, and Concepcíon heard nothing from her betrothed, nor any news about him. She remained true to her vow, however, and never married; instead, she entered the third order of the Franciscans and devoted herself to works of charity, finally taking formal vows in 1851, when she was 60 years old. By all accounts she was a joyful, even jolly, sister.

Thirty-six years after Rezánov's departure for Sitka, a famous English traveler named Sir George Simpson visited Monterey. At a banquet given in his honor, Simpson revealed what had happened to Rezánov—he had been killed many years before in Siberia when he was thrown from a horse. He had been riding to Moscow to seek permission for his marriage. As related in the verse version of the story by California author Bret Harte, Sir George, not knowing that Sister Concepcíon was at the banquet, commented, in passing—left a sweetheart, too, they tell me. Married, I suppose, of course!

"Lives she yet?" A deathlike silence fell on banquet, guests, and hall,
And a trembling figure rising fixed the awestruck gaze of all.

Two black eyes in darkened orbits gleamed beneath the nun's white hood;
Black serge hid the wasted figure, bowed and stricken where it stood.

"Lives she yet?" Sir George repeated. All were hushed as Concha drew
Closer yet her nun's attire. "*Señor*, pardon, she died, too!"

The "Golden Age" of California

The story of Conchita and Nikolai Rezánov is the stuff of legend, but it epitomizes a period that has been called California's "golden age," stretching from the late 1780s to the end of the Mexican era in 1848. It is a period yielding a rich harvest for the imagination—an era of holy padres teaching docile Indian converts, proud rancho dons, *caballeros* in colorful costume, and beautiful, dark-eyed *doñas* and *señoritas*. Of course, this picture is somewhat exaggerated and only partially true, like all legend; but like all legend, it reveals something of the truth.

As the story of Conchita and Rezánov illustrates, California was a hierarchical society with clearly demarcated levels of authority. At the pinnacle of the social/political structure was the Spanish governor. Though appointed by the viceroy in Mexico and formally subject to him, the California governor, because of the great distance from Monterey to Mexico City, was practically independent. Hardly any checks were placed on his actions. His power was absolute over all California society, except the missions, which answered to the *padre presidente* alone. Under the governor were the captains of the *presidios* and civil officers, called *comisionados*.

California's social structure was aristocratic. At the top of the social pyramid were the *gente de razón*, the families of more or less pure Spanish blood. The families of government officials, like the Arillagas and the Argüellos, belonged to this group, as did the increasing number of rancho *dons*. Indians who married into this group became members of the *gente de razón* by association, their children thus suffering no stigma. As the story of Conchita illustrates, the *gente de razón* were closely related, and claims of kinship were held sacred—contravening, at times, even the king's law.

The *Californio* aristocrats were noted for their generosity and love of ease. Money meant little to them; they measured their wealth in lands and cattle. The *Californio* don was a proud man who despised all manual labor as beneath his dignity. The only occupations he would countenance were herding cattle and military service. John Bidwell, an American who settled in California, wrote in 1842, "it is a proverb here . . . that a Spaniard will not do anything which he cannot do on horseback."

With such interests, few *Californios* bothered themselves with learning, though there were some educated *dons* and *doñas*. No public system of education existed in California. Some families employed friars to teach their children, while others sent them to school in Hawai'i or the United States.

Below these aristocrats were other "whites," many of whom were illiterate, some of whom were released criminals. The latter made the *pueblos* of Los Angeles, San José, and the short-lived

A view of old Los Angeles, made in 1860

Branciforte wild, unruly places. The number of these "whites," including the *gente de razón*, was never large. Inhabiting only the coastal strip from San Diego to San Francisco, their numbers reached only 970 in 1790, and 3,270 in 1820—and this in an area where millions live today!

The Indians of California were divided between those who lived on the missions and those who did not. Of the former, there were 7,353 neophytes in 1790; over 10,000 by 1800. The number of Indians outside the missions is hard to estimate, since the total number of Indians in California has been in dispute. Earlier estimates reported around 133,000 souls; more recent estimates, about three times that number.

A California Indian, by Louis Choris

Governor Borica, who ruled California for Spain from 1794 to 1800, wrote that the "great country" of California had a good climate, "good bread, excellent meat, tolerable fish . . . plenty to eat." It was "the most peaceful and quiet country in the world." Theoretically, the king of Spain held all land titles to this country; in practice, land was dealt out to its inhabitants. According to Spanish law, the Indians were to receive all land necessary to sustain them. Indeed, the vast mission lands, the best in California, were to be turned over to the Indians when the process of civilizing and Christianizing them was complete. Beginning in 1786, the king's government began giving land grants to non-Indians, having distributed 16 ranchos by 1795. Eventually, the rancho would become the predominant social institution in California.

California inevitably attracted the eyes of foreigners. Beyond founding a Russian settlement in California to supply the pelt-hunting settlements farther north, Nikolai Rezánov wanted a base from which Russia could conquer all of California. Alexander Baranov, the head of the Russian American Fur Company, took up Rezánov's plan and executed the first part of it. In March 1812, a large ship flying the double-headed eagle flag appeared off the coast north of San Francisco. It brought native Alaskan fur hunters and a small number of Russian overseers, who began to construct a fort and settlement on a bluff overlooking a stream that became known as the Russian River. When finished, this settlement, called Fort Ross (probably a shortened form of *Rossiya*—Russia) consisted of a palisade built from large tree trunks surrounded by sixty buildings, orchards, gardens, grain fields, and villages for Alaskans and the local Kashaya Pomo people. Later, the settlers built a Russian Orthodox chapel.

Until 1820, the Russians and Alaskans at Fort Ross were reaping a rich harvest of valuable sea otter pelts. When the number of sea otters drastically decreased because of overhunting, the settlers turned to growing grain and vegetables, which they sent north to the frigid Alaskan settlements. Most of the settlers were not Russian, and among those that were, many intermarried with the Alaskans and the local natives.

Sketch of Fort Ross, 1841, by Ilya Gavrilovich Voznesenskii

It was this Russian settlement, in part, that induced President James Monroe to issue the Monroe Doctrine (see Chapter 13). Americans, at first, were not interested in California, though as the years passed American interest in California would grow quite intense. Most foreign ships, including American ships, that visited the coast of California in the late 18th century were whalers. As the 19th century progressed, however, merchant smugglers increasingly visited California waters, engaging in an illegal trade with the *Californios.*

This contraband trade increased significantly after 1810, when revolutions in Mexico and Central America cut off shipments of goods from Mexico. *Californios* had to fall back on their own resources, which were good, because, due principally to the missions, California was self-sufficient in essentials. Other goods that had been supplied by trade with Mexico were gotten from trade with foreigners.

For *Californios,* the revolutions rocking Latin America in the early 19th century were a distant rumor, and they remained untouched by them for many years. Loyal to the king, the *Californios* assumed the revolutionaries would sooner or later be defeated and effective royal rule restored. One effect of the revolutions was to stop further Spanish settlement into inland California. The great Central Valley and the foothills of the Sierra Nevada had been explored in the period of 1805 to 1811 with an eye to the establishment of more missions; but, without the support of the Spanish crown, nothing further could be done.

California's first brush with revolution came in 1818 when two ships under the French captain, Hippolyte de Bouchard, appeared off the coast. Flying the colors of the rebellious government of Argentina, Bouchard might have come as an "agent of liberation" for the people of California, though he behaved more like a pirate. Having sailed from Hawai'i with a crew mostly Hawai'ian, though sprinkled with other nationalities, all under French officers, Bouchard arrived at Monterey and demanded the surrender of the *presidio* and of all California. The Spaniards responded that they would fight to the death rather than submit. After firing a cannonade, however, the Spanish garrison retreated inland, leaving Monterey to the mercy of the invader, who sacked the *presidio,* plundering and burning the settlement. Sailing south, Bouchard repeated the same performance at Santa Barbara. The inhabitants, as at Monterey, made no counteroffensive, though one José de Guerra marched his handful of men several times around a hill to make his force appear much larger than it was. Continuing southward, Bouchard left California waters, never to return.

Progress and Decline in the Missions

In 1801, a Chumash Indian said Chupu, the god of the Channel Coast, had appeared to him in a dream. The god revealed that the Chumash of the Channel Coast were dying of an epidemic because they worshiped a new god, the god of the Spaniards. All baptized Chumash would die, said Chupu, unless they made offerings to him and washed their faces in sacred water. The message of Chupu's visitation spread secretly among the Chumash of San Buenaventura and Santa Barbara missions—anyone who revealed his coming to the padres would die, said the god. When the padres did find out about Chupu's appearance, the Chumash were alarmed. They feared the god would kill them.

Mission Santa Barbara, in an 1876 photograph by Carleton Watkins

Such was missionary work among the Indians of California: the Franciscans not only had to teach the Gospel to the natives, but to draw them from their stone-age cultures into a highly complex European civilization. Not only native religion but the loosely structured character of native life contrasted sharply with European life. No wonder that, from 1790 to 1800, 700 to 800 neophytes fled from the regimen of mission life to seek refuge among the "gentile" tribesmen; the hardships involved in adapting to new ways were immense. Moreover, bloody feuds among the gentile Indians often involved tribes to which mission Indians were connected, and the friars had to be on the watch to make sure that their converts did not run off and to join their kindred's conflicts.

Though some have charged the mission system with cruelty, there is little evidence of it, at least until 1810. Despite the runaways, the Indians displayed no violent opposition to the missionaries. True, some tribes resisted the friars' invitations to join the missions, but even these showed no deadly hate—and others asked that missionaries be sent among them. The first charges of cruelty, however, came in 1798 when Fray Antonio de la Concepción Horra, a friar who had been dismissed on charges of insanity after having stayed only two months in California, published an attack on the missions. He, along with four Spanish military commanders (including Felipe de Goycoechea, the commander at Santa Barbara *presidio*—whose interest, the friars said, was to circumvent their authority and get cheap Indian labor), charged that the friars forced pregnant women to work in the fields from six to nine hours a day and to engage in other hard labor. The friars, too, said Horra, did not give Indians sufficient time to gather wild fruits, punished them with the stocks and heavy floggings, and deprived them of water.

In 1800, the viceroy in Mexico City ordered Fray Fermín Lasuen, third president of the missions, to respond to these charges. Not only Fray Fermín, but three other California missionary friars wrote refutations of Horra's claims. The friars denied that pregnant women were compelled to perform hard labor; rather, only light labor was required of them, either in the fields or the the mission compound, for only four to six hours a day. Frequently, said the friars, the women were dismissed from work altogether for health reasons. Not only were

A sketch of Mission San Buenaventura from *Life in California*, ca. 1839, by Alfred Robinson

Indians allowed to gather wild fruits, but every Sunday, one-fifth of them were allowed to visit their native *rancherías* for as long as a week or two. As for flogging, deprivation of water, the stocks—these were indeed applied, but only after repeated offenses; and only at Santa Barbara had women been flogged. After an investigation, the viceroy exonerated the missionaries.

By today's standards, any use of the lash seems excessive; at that time, however, corporal punishment was very common and thought unremarkable. California's governor Don José Joaquin Arrillaga wrote that the friars treated their Indian neophytes as they would their own children. Indeed, for the friars, the Indians were children, and like children had to be protected from their own foolish actions and punished for their correction. In his refutation of Horra and Goycoechea, Fray Fermín wrote that the "chastisement which we inflict on the Indians is in keeping with the judgment with which parents punish their own beloved children.

> We have begotten the neophytes for Christianity by means of our labors for them, and by means of Baptism in which they received the life of grace. We rear them by means of the Sacraments and by means of the instruction in the maxims of Christian morals. We therefore use the authority which Almighty God concedes to parents for the education of their children, now exhorting, now rebuking, now also chastising when necessity demands it.

For the most part, the friars corrected Indians with words alone; but more serious infractions (such as sexual sins, theft, or violence) would receive 12 to 25 lashes. Though Governor Felipe de Neve had rarely allowed friars to use soldiers to pursue and capture fugitive neophytes, under later governors, the use of soldiers for this purpose increased, and the captured runaway was flogged. According to Lasuén, a captured, first-offense runaway was "reproached for the transgression of not complying with the obligation of hearing holy Mass on a day of obligation. He is made to see that he has freely subjected himself to this and other Christian duties, and is then warned that he will be chastised if he repeats the transgression." Only if he runs away again does he experience "the chastisement of the lash or the stocks"; and if these punishments are not sufficient, "he is made to feel the shackles, which he wears for three days while he is kept at work." As for women offenders, they "are punished," says Lasuén, "with one, two, or three days in the stocks, according to the gravity of the offense; but if they are obstinate in their evil intercourse, or run away, they are chastised by the hand of another woman in the apartment for the women. Sometimes, though exceedingly seldom, the shackles are put on."

Fray Fermín did not deny that "defects" existed in the California missions and among the missionaries. "We are aware," he wrote, "that we have faults which we hope will be forgiven us." Perhaps among Lasuén's own personal faults was an inability to see the good in native cultures, apart from their faults. While Fray Junípero Serra and other missionaries could praise native peoples, Lasuén, in explaining the difficulties he and colleagues faced, described the California Indians in dark terms, as "a people without education, without government, religion, or respect for authority, and they shamelessly pursue without restraint whatever their brutal appetites suggest to them. Their inclination to lewdness and theft is on a par with their love for the mountains."

Whatever difficulties the missionaries had with their neophytes were compounded by the Spanish settlers, whose encroachments on mission lands the friars had periodically to oppose. Though the friars did not oppose, and even encouraged, the founding of white settlements in California, they came to have a poor opinion of the non-Indian settlements that were established. The settlements did not add to the country's prosperity, they said, and were a detriment to missionary work. How could the friars teach their converts about the importance of attending Mass and other services, when the Spaniards often themselves neglected them—while they would never miss a *fandango*. Though Indians could be flogged for missing some services, the Spaniards received no punishment for the same infraction. It was extremely difficult to convert the heathen in the midst of such Christians, said the friars.

A sketch of Mission San Luis Rey, from *Life in California*, ca. 1839, by Alfred Robinson

The death rate among the California Indians remained extremely high in the first two decades of the 19th century. Diseases such as dysentary, pleurisy, pneumonia, and measles decimated Indian populations in California. A major cause of sickness and death was syphilis, which, the friars said, was spread by the Indians' promiscuous habits. But whatever the causes, "the Indian population is declining," wrote Fray Mariano Payeras, in 1820:

The interior of Mission San Miguel Arcángel, 1939

> . . . They live well free but as soon as we reduce them to a Christian and community life they decline in health, they fatten, sicken and die. Women are particularly affected. It is the sorrowful experience of 51 years that Indians live poorly in the missions. Even when healthy the women lose fertility and their sterility is not apparent in annual reports because in most areas of the province gentiles are still being baptized, one is confused with the other, and the total always increases.
>
> In all missions hospitals have been built, potions have been purchased and medicines

acquired from surgeons of the province and from books. The best *curanderos* and *curanderas* have been procured. In all, it forms a somber calculation of diminution. The population decline is made more notable since in 24 years I have known only two epidemics, that of 1801 and the measles of 1806.

As the number of the coastal Indians that were yet unconverted decreased, missionaries had to go farther afield to find pagan tribes. Soldiers and friars began making expeditions over the Coast Range mountains into the great Central Valley to search out sites for new missions and to roundup fugitive neophytes. In the Tulares, among the lakes and sloughs of the Central Valley, were gentile *rancherías*; some of these were willing to receive the Gospel and welcomed the prospect of missions, but not all.

But with the onset of revolution in Mexico in 1810, government payments and support for the California military garrison ceased. The missions, with their abundant crops, numerous livestock, and general prosperity, began to supply the garrisons. Such conditions seem to have brought added strain on the Mission Indians, and the second decade of the 19th century witnessed an atmosphere of greater tension in the missions. Also many, if not most, of the Indian oral traditions alleging cruelty on the part of the friars date back to this period.

During the second decade of the 19th century, discontent among neophytes and the number of runaways from the missions so increased that the missionaries were alarmed. At Mission San Gabriel, neophytes seemed to be angry over the continued imprisonment in the Santa Barbara *presidio* of certain Indians who in the past had been hostile. The angry *Gabrielleños* (as the neophytes of San Gabriel Mission were called) joined with gentiles in stealing cattle and breaking into mission storehouses. In 1818 there were numerous runaways from the central coast missions, from Santa Barbara to San Miguel. These escaped to the Tulares, in the San Joaquin Valley—a place that the missions' prefect, Fray Mariano Payéras, called "a republic of hell and a diabolical union of apostates."

An 1873 map showing the Tulares and San Joaquin Valley. Tulare Lake is now gone, its waters having been diverted for agriculture.

In a letter written in 1819 to Governor Solá of California, Fray Mariano complained that "a considerable number [of neophytes] have withdrawn from the mild rule of the friars and have become one body with the savages with whom they carry out whatever evil their heart and malevolent soul dictates. . . . The spirit of insolence and idleness is spreading and affecting even the more staid of the neophytes." Payéras wrote that the Indians were losing their fear of the soldiers and all respect for the friars; he predicted the speedy end of the missions if the state of things were to continue. Fearing raids on the missions if nothing were done (the gentiles had learned to use the horse), Payéras called for a grand expedition to collect all the runaways and to punish those Indians guilty of depredations. Indeed, he said, "the whole cause of the desertions lies in the fact that the [presidial] troops have ceased to go after the culprits who are unmindful of their duties." Payéras, however, pleaded with Solá that he "merely restrain the Christians and savages within the bounds of what is just; for in keeping with our sacred calling, which demands kindness and mildness, we solemnly protest that in such expeditions we abhor deaths, mutilations, and whatever is opposed to Christian gentleness." Though delayed that year (for the Santa Barbara runaways had returned), the expedition began in 1819. It was, however, only partially successful.

In a letter written on September 17, 1819, Fray Luis Martínez, a missionary at San Luis Obispo, gives other reasons for the problem of runaway neophytes. "Never before," says Martínez, "has so much watchfulness been necessary with regard to the soldiers. They have come to us without discipline and religion. They have been taught to suffer many hardships, but never for God and the king. They should be relegated to the *presidios*, and an eye should be kept upon them. They should be given some occupation that is not useless and that is calculated to banish idleness, the mother of all vices." Idle soldiers were especially troublesome because they seduced native women or even raped them. Another effect of the soldiers' (as well as of the civilian settlers') idleness was that the burden of the material support of California fell on the missions. "The viceroy ought to be notified with some energy that a territory that cannot support itself, will be still less able to sustain others," Fray Luis complains:

> The missionary is expected to furnish shoes, boots, and even gunsticks. They want him to be tailor, weaver, mason, carpenter, and everything else without having learned it, and this too without support, without aid. Whence shall he obtain the infused science? Then, how can a poor Indian be cheerful, who throughout the year is occupied at work in a mission, when his labor procures for him nothing more than a poor suit of clothes and a blanket since he must labor for others?

But, even if such complaints were not lost on the viceroy in far off Mexico City, there was little he could do to address them. Since 1810, the viceroyalty of New Spain had had to weather waves of violent revolution, and it was all the viceroy could do to preserve his government from complete and utter collapse.

Revolution in Mexico

For many years California remained untouched by events farther south in New Spain. Being a relatively young settlement, California was neither burdened nor blessed with all that had developed since the days of Cortés. As we have seen in a previous chapter, a great and cultured society had grown up in *Nueva España*. Grand cities had arisen, adorned with beautiful churches, universities, and theaters. In New Spain, Europe had been transplanted in American soil and modified by the native influences of the new continent.

But like in any society, the glory of New Spain was tarnished by injustice and structural problems. By 1800, the *peninsulares* or *gauchupines*, those born in Spain, were still relatively few in number, but they controlled the majority of all political offices in New Spain. Next there were the creoles, American born persons of Spanish blood; yet, though these numbered about one million souls—many times the number of the *gauchupines*—they had nowhere near the *gauchupines'* power and influence in government. This, of course, was a source of deep discontent among the creoles, who had come to think they should occupy a position in society that accorded with their dignity and their numbers. The *mestizos*—those of mixed Indian and Spanish blood—had even less political power than the creoles, though the number of *mestizos* greatly exceeded the number of creoles. It is not surprising that they thought themselves oppressed by the Spanish colonial system. The lot of the Indians had

An 1810 French map of New Spain (Mexico)

changed little since the days of Cortés—they remained, for the most part, laborers with little chance of social advancement.

Political corruption was commonplace in New Spain. Offices were bought and sold, and bribery was widespread. Taxation was heavy. Both the government and the Church levied taxes. This hindered private initiative and inspired ill will among some towards both government and Church. The Spanish government maintained economic controls on New World dominions, forcing them to trade almost exclusively with the mother country. Colonial industries that would compete with established industries in Spain were forbidden.

Though from the beginning the Church had sponsored schools and universities, illiteracy remained high in New Spain. Folk traditions—song, legend, and plastic art—however were vibrant, forming a rich cultural substratum from which a refined civilization could arise. Enlightenment and republican philosophies had begun to influence the ruling classes and the creole intellectuals; but because of the Inquisition they had to hold meetings in secret. And because of the *Index of Forbidden Books*, the works of French, Yankee (such as Jefferson and Tom Paine), and other Enlightenment thinkers could not be sold or distributed publicly. But like many a contraband item, these books were smuggled in, abridged into pamphlet form, and widely distributed. The examples of the American and French Revolutions drew many, especially creoles, to embrace Liberal republican political philosophies.

The foregoing paints a somewhat bleak pictures of Spanish colonial society. Care, however, must be taken in evaluating the time. Injustices there were, but also widespread contentment. As in the English colonies, the majority in Spanish America were not seething with revolutionary anger. Most were faithful to the king, even loved the king, while they ignored his laws. People today will chastise the Church for her taxation; but, in the mindset inherited from the Middle Ages, it was thought that, since the Church contributed to the common good (which was both spiritual and material), it was the *duty* of those who benefited from the common good to support the Church. And the people of New Spain did benefit from the Church, not only spiritually but materially as well. It was the Church after all that provided what we today call "social services"—relief for the poor, hospitals, and schools.

Modern people will condemn the Inquisition and the *Index*—but the Spanish saw them as necessary to protect society from false opinions. Error, it was thought, is worse than poverty, worse than death, for error leads men away from what gives life to the soul—truth and moral virtue. Since, according to Catholic tradition, human society exists not simply to ensure material benefits but to help men become good and attain eternal life, error undermines the very purpose of society and government and thus destroys both. In a society that accepted the Catholic faith as absolutely true, it was thought necessary to protect from opinions that would lead men away from the truth and, perhaps, condemn their souls to eternal death.

Prelude to Revolution

It was not conditions *in* New Spain that finally precipitated revolution, but events across the Atlantic. The mother country, Spain, was rocked with civil war.

Carlos IV, who had occupied the Spanish throne since 1788, had become inconvenient to France's Emperor Napoleon, who had brought nearly all of Europe under his sway. An independent Spain did not serve Napoleon's purposes; so, on May 6, 1808, he pressured Carlos IV and his son Fernando VII to relinquish all claim to the Spanish throne, and, in their place, made his brother, Joseph Bonaparte, king. Popular indignation broke out against the new king, and all over Spain, **juntas** were formed to oppose the French. At the end of September 1808, the *juntas* formed themselves into one body, called the *Junta Central Gubernativa del Reino* (Central Governing Body of the Kingdom) and formed a *cortes* (parliament) to represent both Spain and America.

King Fernando VII of Spain, by Luis de la Cruz

junta: (pronounced HOON-tah) a group controlling a government, especially following a revolution

Like the mother country, New Spain rejected Joseph's rule. When Joseph Bonaparte ascended the Spanish throne, the town council of Mexico City asked the viceroy, José de Iturrigaray, to assume the powers of government of New Spain in the name of Fernando VII. The viceroy was willing; a greedy man who had amassed a fortune by illegal means Iturrigaray, hoped to take advantage of the situation and to make himself king of New Spain. The viceroy's essentially illegal action, however, drew the opposition of the *audiencia* of New Spain and a group of 300 *gauchupines* who called themselves the Volunteers of Fernando VII.

The Volunteers wanted to overthrow the viceroy without all the blood and trouble of an armed revolution. So, on the night of September 15, 1808, they broke into the viceregal palace and took Iturrigaray prisoner. The *audiencia* replaced Iturrigaray with a feeble man, nearly 80 years old, Pedro de Garibay.

In the wake of these disturbances, groups called *Caballeros Racionales* (Rational Gentlemen) began meeting throughout Mexico. Since they met to discuss revolutionary doctrines, their meetings were secret for fear of the government's informants and spies. At the same time, agents of Napoleon were active, trying to induce Mexicans to revolt in favor of France.

Knowing Garibay was incompetent to deal with this dangerous situation, the Volunteers petitioned the *Junta Central* in Spain to appoint a new viceroy. The *Junta* complied and chose Archbishop Francisco Xavier de Lizana y Beaumont; but he was little better than Garibay, and, in December 1809, some creoles formed a plot to overthrow the government. The plot failed, and the archbishop was recalled to Spain. In August 1810, the new viceroy, an army officer named Francisco Xavier Venegas, arrived in Mexico. It would not be long before he was embroiled in a contest that would shake Mexico to its foundations.

cura: a priest who has the charge or care of a parish

Priest Revolutionary

A group of creole intellectuals and army officers had been meeting secretly in Querétaro, about 200 miles northwest of Mexico City. Calling themselves the *Academia Literaria* (Literary Academy), the group's aims were ostensibly literary; but their work was really political, for they were working for the overthrow of the *gauchupines* and a Mexico independent of Spain (though ostensibly at least still faithful to Fernando VII.) Among their number were the army officers Ignacio Allende and Juan Aldana, and a priest, the 57-year old *cura* of the nearby village of Dolores, Miguel Gregorio Antonio Ignacio Hidalgo y Costilla.

Padre Hidalgo had long had a reputation for radicalism. Having studied at the Colegio de San Nicolás in Valladolid, not far from Mexico City, he had been ordained a priest in 1778 and later served as rector of San Nicolás. A French scholar, Hidalgo had been drawn to the works of French Enlightenment thinkers, such as Rousseau and Montesquieu—an interest he shared with a close friend, Manuel Abad y Queipo. Because of this interest, in 1800 accusations of heresy were leveled against Hidalgo and Abad, and the Inquisition secretly investigated them both in 1800. Hidalgo, it was charged, among other errors, denied the virgin birth, the perpetual virginity of Mary, and the sinfulness of fornication. (That Hidalgo had children by two different women lends credence to the last charge.) But nothing came of the investigation, and both Hidalgo and Abad were never formally accused of heresy.

When in 1803 Hidalgo became *cura* of the village of Dolores in Guanajuato, he took great interest in the material welfare of the Indians. Leaving the spiritual concerns of the parish to one of his assistants, Hidalgo worked to promote the cultivation of grapevines and olive trees among the Indians and introduced the silk worm. He taught the Indians to make pottery and tan leather—all industries forbidden in America by Spanish law.

By August 1810 Hidalgo and the Querétaro group had a plan in place. In a *coup d'état* they would capture key Spanish government officials and set up a revolutionary government. The date set for the coup was October 1. One of the members of the group, however, turned traitor and revealed the plan to the government. On September 16, an order was issued to seize all the members of the *Academia Literaria*.

corregidor: a chief magistrate

Learning of the betrayal, Doña Josefa Ortiz, the wife of the **corregidor** of Querétaro, but a supporter of the revolutionaries, hurried to Dolores and warned Hidalgo. This was the crucial moment for the *cura*—would he flee, would he surrender and beg clemency, or would he call for resistance? Hidalgo chose the last course. Ringing the bell of the village church, he gathered his Indian parishioners, and from the pulpit, he gave the *grito de Dolores*, the "Cry of Dolores," which, according to one account, reads:

> My friends and countrymen: neither the king nor tributes exist for us any longer. We have borne this shameful tax, which only suits slaves, for three centuries as a sign of tyranny and servitude; [a] terrible stain which we shall know how to wash away with our efforts. The moment of our freedom has arrived, the hour of our liberty has struck; and if you recognize its great value, you will help me defend it from the ambitious grasp of the tyrants. Only a few hours remain before you see me at the head of the men who take pride in being free. I invite you to fulfill this obligation. And so without a fatherland or liberty we shall always be at a great distance from true happiness. The cause is holy and God will protect it. . . .

Long live Our Lady of Guadalupe! Perish the Government! Perish the *gauchupines*!

An image of Miguel Hidalgo, made between 1890 and 1913

Five hundred to 600 men gathered around the priest, and as this band marched from village to village, hundreds and thousands more joined them. By September 21, 50,000 Indians, *mestizos,* and a few creoles were marching with Hidalgo under a banner of Our Lady of Guadalupe that Hidalgo had taken from a church. Armed, some with guns but more with farm tools, the peasant army brutally slaughtered any Europeans, *gauchupines,* or creoles they found in the villages. Hidalgo (now called "Captain General of America"), Ignacio Allende, and Juan Aldama led this ill-disciplined and rag-tag mob toward the city of Guanajuato.

When the army reached Guanajuato on September 28, Hidalgo pledged that he would spare all Europeans if the city surrendered; but the *commandante* had heard of the atrocities committed by the peasant army and refused. Gathering all the royalists and the city treasury into the Alhóndiga de Granaditas (a building to store grain) the *commandante* prepared for a siege. At first the royalists held off their assailants, firing down from the stout stone walls of the granary on the ill-disciplined peasant army. The Alhóndiga was strong enough to hold off the insurgents but for one weak point—its great wooden door. Hidalgo's force set fire to the door and broke into the granary. A bloodbath followed.

"When the insurgents had taken the Alhóndiga," wrote Lucas Alamán, an eyewitness who survived the slaughter, "they gave rein to their vengeance. In vain those who had surrendered begged on their knees for mercy. . . . The building presented a most horrible spectacle. The food that had been stored there was strewn about everywhere; naked bodies lay half-buried in maize, or in money, and everything was spotted with blood."

Mural of Miguel Hidalgo Costilla, by Clemente Orozco, Government Palace, Guadalajara, Mexico

Alhóndiga Granadítas (right) in Guanajuato

It is said that Hidalgo was at first shocked by his "army's" violence but that he came to accept it as a necessary evil. He issued a proclamation, ostensibly to rein in the violence —"Nine Laws to Avoid Disorder and Bloodshed." These "laws" forbade the seizure of "ecclesiastics except in case of high treason" and offered to "respect the security" of the "life and wealth" of the "European [presumably *gauchupine* or creole] who spontaneously surrenders to us." The European, however, who spoke against the revolt or who resisted with arms would be "put to the sword." More bloody was the fifth law, decreeing that "when we are menaced by siege and combat, before engaging in it, and at the same time that we begin hostilities, we shall put the many Europeans who are in our hands to the sword." Americans (creoles, *mestizos*, and Indians) fared no better. Those who defended with arms or "maliciously" hid a European would be "put to the sword." Those "who simply through compassion" hid a European would "suffer the pain of exile and the confiscation of his property." Anyone who informed about "any of the aforementioned crimes" would be rewarded 500 *pesos*.

Following the capture of Guanajuato, Hidalgo's old friend, Manuel Abad y Queipo, now bishop-elect of Michoacán, excommunicated the *cura* of Dolores and all his followers. In his decree of excommunication, Abad lamented that Hidalgo's rebellion threatened to visit on New Spain the same atrocities that had stained the revolution in France, where "two million people . . . a tenth of the French population, young people of both sexes in the prime of life had been killed." Abad raised the spectre of a rebellion in Haiti in 1810, where "anarchy liquidated all the whites, leaving not a single one alive, then liquidated four fifths of the other inhabitants, leaving the final fifth, composed of blacks and mulattos, locked in a mortal struggle." And now, Abad continued, "a minister of the God of Peace, a priest of Jesus Christ, a pastor of souls (I hate to say), the *cura* of Dolores village, Don Miguel Hidalgo (who until now had merited my confidence and friendship) . . . [has] raised the banner of rebellion, lit the torch of discord and anarchy, and persuaded a number of unsophisticated peasants to take up arms." Abad deplored the inscription Hidalgo had attached to the image of Our Lady of Guadalupe: "Long Live our Religion! Long Live our Holy Mother, *Nuestra Señora de Guadalupe*! Long live Fernando VII! Long live *América*! Death to Bad Government!" Abad continued:

> Because our religion condemns rebellion, murder, and the mistreatment of innocents, and because the Mother of God cannot protect criminals, the *cura* of Dolores committed two grave acts of sacrilege when he put that inscription on a banner with the image of *Nuestra Señora*. He likewise insulted and attacked our government and, thereby, insulted our sovereign, Don Fernando VII. He mistreated the king's vassals, disrupted law and order, and violated the oath of fidelity to king and country.

Perhaps ironically, only a few months before Hidalgo's rebellion began, Abad had sent to the king a document in which he called for abolishing Indian tribute payments and class distinctions, as well as for a redistribution of royal lands among the natives. But now that he and other bishops who followed his lead were condemning Hidalgo's rebellion, the Church was made to appear the enemy of the people and the friend of the "oppressive" government. Using the power of religion against Hidalgo (just as Hidalgo had used religion to further revolution), Abad and his brother bishops accomplished little more than to alienate the pro-Hidalgo masses.

During October 1810 Hidalgo gained control of much of central Mexico west of Mexico City. Everywhere, the same mob violence was repeated—which disgusted Hidalgo's commanding general, Ignacio Allende. A professional soldier, Allende valued discipline; Hidalgo, however, could be too lenient with his followers—as when he rebuked Allende for cruelty to the Indians, when Allende was trying to stop the violence of the mob by striking out at them with the flat of his sword. But when it came to the enemy, Hidalgo did not show such complaisance. At Valladolid, a priest canon of the cathedral bravely approached Hidalgo unarmed and made him promise to spare the city. The city was spared, but Hidalgo was so stung to anger that the cathedral (where he wanted to offer thanks) was locked against him that he imprisoned all the *gauchupines* and seized the city treasury. Such arbitrary actions and Hidalgo's tolerance of violence convinced creoles, whom Hidalgo had hoped would rise with the Indians, to instead joined forces with the *gauchupines*.

From Valladolid, Hidalgo moved against Mexico City. On October 3, at Monte de Las Cruces in the foothills overlooking the capital, Hidalgo's 80,000 joined battle with 6,000 Spaniards under General Torcuato Trujillo. Though vastly outnumbered, Trujillo's force inflicted heavy losses on the rebels; still, Hidalgo's overwhelming numbers forced the Spaniards to retreat to Mexico City. That night the lurid glow of the rebels' campfires illumined the hills surrounding the capital.

What to do next? The soldier Allende and others encouraged Hidalgo to strike the city, but Hidalgo hesitated and instead decided to retreat northwest, toward Guadalajara. Demoralized by the loss of a victory that seemed so clearly within their reach, thousands abandoned the rebel army. On November 7, 1810, Spanish troops under General Félix Calleja defeated Hidalgo's remnant of 40,000 men at Aculco.

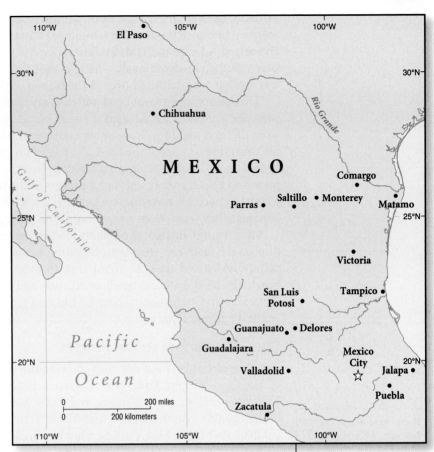

Map of Mexico showing the major cities in 1810

Yet, despite the defeat, the people of Guadalajara greeted Hidalgo and his army with fiestas and proclaimed the priest the liberator of his country. Gradually new recruits began to swell the numbers of Hidalgo's diminished force until it once again boasted over 80,000 men. At Guadalajara, Hidalgo, with the lawyer Ignacio López Rayón, established a government and issued a proclamation granting freedom to slaves and the surrender to the Indians of the lands they cultivated. The Guadalajara government pledged its fidelity to King Fernando VII.

Meanwhile, General Calleja, with 6,000 well-trained and well-armed men, had retaken Guanajuato and was moving against Guadalajara. Against the advice of Allende, Hidalgo chose to meet Calleja's advance by concentrating his entire force at Calderón bridge on the eastern outskirts of Guadalajara. There, on January 14, 1811, Calleja attacked the rebels; his disciplined campaigners held their own against the unruly, concentrated native force. A cannon ball, flying over the heads of the rebels, struck their munitions dump. An explosion rocked the insurgents from behind while angry flames clawed at the heavens. The explosion sparked a grass fire that threw the rebels into confusion. Hidalgo, Allende, and a small remnant of their force retreated through Guadalajara and fled northeast, toward Zacatecas. Calleja entered the city in triumph.

At Zacatecas, a disgusted Allende removed Hidalgo from command of the army. Hoping to connect with rebels in the north and elicit aid from the United States, Allende, with Hidalgo and 1,000 men crossed into the hot and barren deserts of northern Mexico enroute to Texas. On March 21, 1811, near Saltillo, in the wastes of Coahuilla, the small rebel force, betrayed by one of their own, encountered a Spanish force. The Spaniards defeated the rebels and seized Allende and Hidalgo, killing on the spot many of the lesser officers. Allende was later executed ignominiously—he was shot through the back—while Hidalgo, because he was a priest, was delivered over to the bishop of Durango for trial.

"Oh that someone would give water to my head and fountains of tears to my eyes! Or that someone even now would shed the very blood that flows through my pores, not only did I weep day and night for those of my countrymen who have died, but weeping can only bless the unending mercies of the Lord." So began a recantation, dated May 1811, written allegedly by Hidalgo (some have called it a forgery). In it the writer expresses his fear of divine punishment and begs the forgiveness and prayers of those he has wronged. Hidalgo implored those who had joined his revolution to desist and told them to honor the king and obey the priests, "because they watch over you as those who must give account to the Lord for your affairs."

After trying Hidalgo, the bishop of Durango removed his priestly dignity and delivered him to the state for execution. Standing before a firing squad on July 30, 1811, Hidalgo calmly instructed them to shoot him through his right hand, which he placed over his heart. His head, with the heads of Allende and Aldama, were displayed on the walls of the Alhóndiga in Guanajuato, where for the next ten years they remained, a grim warning to all would-be revolutionaries.

Guerrilla Warfare in the Jungles

But severed heads could not stop the revolution. Rebel leaders who had risen in the wake of Hidalgo—Vicente Guerrero, Manuel Félix Fernández (who called himself Guadalupe Victoria, in honor of the Virgin), and Padre Mariano Matamoros—still troubled the peace of the country. Another priest, José María Teclo Morelos y Pavón, had since after the fall of Guanajuato in 1810 been causing trouble. Hidalgo had appointed him to lead the revolution in the south.

Padre José María Teclo Morelos y Pavón

Unlike Hidalgo, who had come from a creole family, Padre Morelos was a poor *mestizo* from Valladolid. He had worked as a mule driver until, in his twenty-fifth year, he began his studies for the priesthood at the Collegio San Nicolás in Valladolid. There he studied natural and moral philosophy under the direction of the rector—Padre Miguel Hidalgo—for whom Morelos conceived a profound respect. After he was ordained a priest, Morelos took a parish in Michoacán.

Morelos had been a priest for over ten years when he was roused by Hidalgo's *grito de Dolores*. Sent by Hidalgo to Zacatula on the Pacific coast, Morelos organized a small force there. A skilled commander, Morelos favored the hit-and-run methods of guerrilla warfare (a strategy well suited to the dense, jungle-like forests where he fought) rather than Hidalgo's pitched battle strategy. The rebels were anonymous. Many of Morelos' soldiers were farmers who worked their fields until they were called—then they became rebel insurgents. When a battle ended, they returned to their fields. To punish and kill off these unknown insurgents, the Spaniards began destroying entire villages. In 1811, Morelos carried out several successful campaigns against Spanish forces and, with fewer than 5,000 men, captured the regions from the valley of Mexico City to the Pacific Coast, failing only to take the highly fortified port of Acapulco. Joined by Padre Matamoros and other rebel leaders, Morelos organized four armies and sent them to various parts of Mexico.

In March 1812, General Calleja marched with an army of 8,000 against Morelos' position at Cuautla, a town about 50 miles southeast of Mexico City. Besieged at Cuautla, an unfortified city built on a low hill, Morelos, Matamoros, and their force of 4,000 resisted Calleja for 73 days. The insurgents were reduced to starvation and forced to eat vermin, soap, and tree bark. Morelos awaited the coming of the spring rains that, he hoped, would spread disease and contagion among the Spanish army, who were not used to jungle conditions. But the rains did not come, and, on May 2, Morelos and the remainder of his army fought their way out of Cuautla. Calleja marched into the city and, finding no rebels, began slaughtering women and children. Meanwhile, Morelos moved south and west, capturing the towns of Huajuapan, Orizaba, and Oaxaca.

Unlike Hidalgo, Morelos had a genius for government. On September 1, 1813, he, with Ignacio Rayón, Carlos María Bustamante, and other revolutionary leaders, assembled a revolutionary congress at Chilpancingo. In September, Morelos delivered to the congress the document, *Sentimientos de La Nación*, in which he laid out his ideas for the government of an independent Mexico. Morelos abandoned any pretense that he was fighting for the rights of King Fernando VII; instead he proclaimed that Mexico's "dependence upon the Spanish Throne has ceased forever and been dissolved."

In line with Liberal republican thought, Morelos declared that the sovereignty of the state proceeds "immediately from the people." Like the revolutionaries leaders who won U.S. independence, he said the government should be divided into legislative, executive, and judicial branches. Laws, said Morelos, "should be such that oblige fidelity, patriotism, moderating opulence and misery." Congress should pass laws to "increase the wages of the poor" and improve "their standard of living, removing ignorance, violence and theft." The congress must abolish torture, said Morelos, and slavery should be "prohibited forever and also distinction between classes, leaving everyone equal, and Americans distinguished from one another only by their vice or virtue."

But unlike Anglo America's revolutionary leaders, Morelos opposed the disestablishment of religion. It is true that he wanted to end tax support for the Church; her ministers, he said, should "be supported by all with only their tithes and offerings, and the people" should not "need to give any more than their devotion and offerings." Yet, Morelos said the new state "neither professes nor recognizes any religion but the Catholic, nor will it permit or tolerate the practice, public or private, of any other." The decree pledged that the government "will protect with all its power, and will watch over, the purity of the Faith and its dogmas and the maintenance of the regular bodies." He further proclaimed December 12, the feast of Our Lady of Guadalupe, "the Queen of our liberty," a national celebration. And while he forbade military expeditions outside the country, an exemption was granted to those who would "extend our faith to our brothers in far away lands."

The congress adopted the *Sentimientos,* proclaimed Mexico independent of Spain, and set about drawing up a constitution. The tide of war, however, began to turn against the rebels. In December, Morelos tried to take the city of his birth, Valladolid; but its able young royalist commander, a creole colonel named Agustín Cosme Damián de Iturbide, drove off the more numerous rebel force. The battle was a disaster for Morelos; Iturbide had even captured Padre Matamoros, Morelos' right-hand, and ordered his execution. Morelos' army disintegrated. In January 1814, government forces under Iturbide forced the rebel army and the new representative congress to flee. When the congress reassembled at Tlacotepec, it removed Morelos as head of the army; after Valladolid, it had lost confidence in him. Morelos, whose chief interest had been to serve the revolution, not himself, complied. Yet, without his leadership, the rebel forces began to break down into factions.

In the fall of 1815, the congress decided to move southeast to Puebla, where the Spanish government forces were weaker. To reach Puebla, however, the congress had to pass through a stretch of royalist-controlled territory, and Morelos took command of the military convoy. On November 5, the convoy met 600 royalist troops. Morelos fought them off long enough to permit the congress to escape but was himself unable to elude capture. Loading him with chains, the royalists marched Morelos in triumph into Mexico City.

Both military and ecclesiastical tribunals tried Morelos. He was charged with treason and with failing in fealty to the king; of ordering the execution of prisoners; of ignoring the excommunication leveled against him by the bishops and the Inquisition; and of having celebrated Mass after commanding troops in battle. (Canon Law forbade clerics to shed blood.) Morelos denied that he had failed in fidelity to the king; rather, he said, Fernando VII had failed in his duty to Mexico and so, in effect, had abdicated. Morelos admitted he had ordered the execution of prisoners but said he had done so by order of the congress and as a reprisal against the vice-regal government. Morelos denied the validity of the excommunications, saying that they were declared against an independent nation, and only the pope or an ecumenical council had the authority to impose such an excommunication. Finally, he denied having celebrated Mass during the revolution.

Condemned by the military tribunal, Morelos was delivered over to the Church court that would degrade him from the dignity of priest. Here the Inquisition intervened and demanded its own trial against Morelos, even though, as an Indian, he did not fall under its jurisdiction. Moreover, since he had already been tried and condemned by another tribunal, the Inquisition should not have tried him again. On November 27, 1815, the court of the Inquisition repeated the old charges and added four new ones: having received communion while under excommunication; failure to recite the divine office while in prison; lax moral conduct (Morelos had had a mistress, who had borne him children); and sending his son to the United States to be educated by Protestants. Morelos answered that he did not recognize the validity of the excommunication, that he had sent his son to a Catholic college in the United States, and that the darkness of the prison would not allow him to read his **breviary**. As to his lax conduct, he admitted it, though he claimed it had caused no scandal.

breviary: a small book containing the divine office: the Psalms, hymns, and prayers said daily by priests and religious

The Inquisition condemned Morelos: he was "a formal heretic, a favorer of heretics, a persecutor and disturber of the ecclesiastical hierarchy, a profaner of the holy sacraments, a traitor to God, the king, and the pope." The sentence deeply affected the priest; fearing not the condemnation of death he expected from the viceroy but the damnation of his soul, he gave information on the state and location of the rebel forces and on the qualities and aptitudes of the rebel commanders.

On November 28, 1815, the viceroy condemned Morelos to die by firing squad. After making his confession, Morelos was blindfolded and led to an enclosure. Commanded to kneel, he fell to his knees, and prayed, "Lord, you know if I have done well; if ill, I implore your infinite mercy." Four shots rang out, and Morelos crumpled to the earth. Seeing his body still moving, the commander ordered another volley.

An Interim of Troubled Peace

For a time it seemed as if revolution had run its course in Mexico. In 1814, Napoleon was defeated by an alliance of European kingdoms, and Fernando VII returned to the Spanish throne. Though he swore to uphold the Liberal constitution adopted by the Spanish *Cortes* in 1812, Fernando suppressed the constitution as soon as he had attained enough power. In New Spain this meant that the local *juntas* that had grown up during the revolution, along with the freedom of speech and of the press guaranteed by the Constitution of 1812, were were swept away. In Mexico, restoration of Bourbon rule annoyed not only the Liberals but also the conservative creoles who had come to enjoy certain of the new liberties. But a simple Liberal/conservative divide did not characterize Mexico in this period; instead, Mexican society was divided between four factions: *gauchupines,* who wanted the old monarchical order; conservative creoles, many of whom opposed the Liberal Constitution of 1812; Liberals who wanted this constitution restored; and radicals who favored independence.

The year 1816 saw the dissolution of Morelos' revolutionary congress by the rebel general Luis Mier y Terán. In April, Juan Ruiz de Apodaca became viceroy and offered amnesty to the remaining revolutionaries, and many accepted it. In January 1817, Luis Mier and José Francisco Osorno surrendered; only small guerrilla bands under Vicente Guerrero and Guadalupe Victoria continued the struggle. Eventually, even Victoria's men abandoned him, and the rebel leader wandered alone in the mountains, evading capture for two-and–a-half years.

However, rebellion in Spain in 1820 forced Fernando VII to restore the Constitution of 1812. Once again Liberal reforms calling for, among other things, the seizure of Church property, an end to the Inquisition, and the abolition of special privileges for clergy and military including the *fueros* (traditional privileges) that preserved the clergy and military from trial except in the ecclesiastical and military courts were imposed on Mexico. The Liberals, of course welcomed the law; but many "clericalists"—conservative creoles and members of the clergy—began to fear that the older order they so loved would be entirely destroyed. Union with Spain, they determined, was dangerous to that order. They began to plot independence.

Agustín Iturbide

One of these conspirators was Don Agustín de Iturbide. In the period after the death of Morelos, Iturbide had gained notoriety for his harsh treatment of captured revolutionaries, having ordered the execution of over 900 insurgents. In 1816 he commanded a regiment that protected wagon trains conveying silver from the mines; but when he was accused of extorting money from the wagon drivers for protection, Viceroy Apodaca removed him from command. For the next four years, Don Agustín remained inactive.

During his forced retirement, Iturbide underwent a kind of religious conversion and attended a retreat at the Jesuit convent at La Profesa, a church in Mexico City. It so happened that La Profesa was a meeting place for influential conservatives, churchmen, and government officials, who, with Don Agustín, began discussing the possibilities for Mexican independence. Iturbide made valuable friendships with many prominent clergymen, who became his advocates with the viceroy. Upon their recommendation, Apodaca gave Iturbide the command of a military expedition against the insurgent, Vicente Guerrero.

The "Bloodless" Revolution

Late one night, shortly before departing for the south to fight Guerrero, Iturbide confided to a friend that he longed to be the liberator of his country—the Napoleon of Mexico. Iturbide's friend was deeply moved—the handsome Don Agustín, his aristocratic bearing, the conviction that seemed to inspire his defense of the Church and the traditional order, drew the admiration and confidence of this friend and many others. He handily became the leader of a party that sought to preserve the old ways, oddly enough, by revolution.

Iturbide marched out to do battle with Guerrero in December 1820. After suffering defeat from rebel forces, Iturbide changed his tactics and began negotiating with the rebel chieftain. Seizing a silver train bound for Acapulco, Iturbide moved on to the town of Iguala. There, in February 1821, he published his *Plan de Iguala,* a blueprint for independence. The plan convinced even the wary Guerrero. The rebel leader met Iturbide at Teloloapán, and the two clinched their alliance with a public embrace.

Agustín Iturbide and Vicente Guerrero embrace

The genius of the *Plan de Iguala* was the way it could unite rebels (like Guerrero) with conservatives, and conservatives with Liberals, in a common cause. It had something for everyone. Its guarantee that the Catholic Church would remain the sole religion of Mexico, that the clergy would maintain their status and properties, and that the head of government would be King Fernando VII (or, if he refused, another member of his family or a member of another Catholic ruling house of Europe) pleased the conservatives. The old insurgents were won over by the plan's abolition of all distinctions between the American born and the *gauchupines*, assuring citizenship to all classes and opening the "door of advancement" to "virtue and merit." The Liberal creoles applauded the plan's design for a representative congress and a constitution. Notably absent was any mention of the rights of Indians and *mestizos;* nor did the plan speak of the redistribution of hacienda lands to the poor. The revolution had changed from an Indian and *mestizo* uprising to a predominately creole war for independence.

Iturbide named his force the Army of the Three Guarantees, after the three guarantees of the *Plan de Iguala*: independence for Mexico, the preservation of the Church, and the equality of *gauchupines* and creoles. Iturbide was not successful at first. Deserted by many of his own troops, Don Agustín faced a stiff royalist opposition. Organized in Masonic lodges, these rich *gauchupines* and pro-Spanish creoles were formidable. But it was not long before it became apparent to them that they would fare better under a conservative Mexican government than a Liberal Spanish regime; and, in April, many royalists and Liberals cast their lot with Iturbide. In May, the rebel army marched into Guanajuato, then into Vallodolid. Guadalajara joined the rebel movement, as did all of the north. By August, only the cities of Mexico City, Veracruz, Perote, and Acapulco remained faithful to Spain.

In late July 1821, a new Spanish viceroy, Juan O'Donojú, arrived in Veracruz but could not leave the besieged city. In the hot, humid summer weather, yellow fever struck O'Donojú's family and attendants. Powerless to move on Mexico City and threatened by plague if he remained in Veracruz, O'Donojú agreed to meet Iturbide at Córdoba. There, in August,

O'Donojú agreed to the *Plan de Iguala*. The revolution was over, and Mexico was independent. O'Donojú went to Mexico City to oversee the withdrawal of Spanish troops from what once had been New Spain.

Independent Mexico

On September 27, 1821, Iturbide led his Army of the Three Guarantees in triumph into Mexico City. With flamboyant chivalry, Don Agustín, mounted on a black horse, marched his army in review past the most beautiful woman in the city. He then proceeded to the

San Juan de Ulúa

viceregal palace, where O'Donojú received the conqueror. In thanksgiving for victory and independence, the archbishop of Mexico offered Masses in the cathedral that had been built by Cortés, almost 300 years before.

At first all seemed to go well for Iturbide. In October the Spanish surrendered Veracruz, Acapulco, and Perote, and their forces retired to the fortress of San Juan de Ulúa, built on an island in the bay of Veracruz. The entire mainland of New Spain, from Guatemala to San Francisco, was independent of Spain.

Yet though Mexico seemed peaceful and unified, factions and dissensions threatened the new country.

Iturbide's revolution established creole dominance in Mexico; yet, the creole class was deeply divided. Many creoles admired the federal system of the United States and wanted to establish a similar government in Mexico. These "Liberals" met opposition from "conservative" creoles, who favored a centralized regime and still hoped that Fernando VII or some other Bourbon prince would take the throne of Mexico. Iturbide, at first, won the support of the more radical Guerrero and of the Liberal creoles and, in accord with the *Plan de Iguala*, called for the election of a congress. It was not long, however, before Don Agustín began to ally himself with the conservative centralists. Thus he alienated old revolutionaries like Guadalupe Victoria and Nicolás Bravo.

The revolution encouraged *mestizo* ambitions, and many *mestizos* were influenced by Liberal republicanism. They favored the abolition of class distinctions and were eager to occupy places in the national bureaucracy. *Mestizos* were powerful in the mountainous south and in the north where *ranchos* rather than haciendas—the large agricultural estates of the wealthy—predominated. Chieftains rose to power in these regions and, despite the central government, held nearly absolute sway. One of these, Juan Álvarez, once a follower of Morelos, was master of the south for 50 years. A check to Liberal republican aspirations, however, was the army. It maintained the *fueros* it held under Spanish rule. Military men were tried in their own courts, which did not respect civilian rights when they were violated by military men. After the revolution, in many parts of Mexico, the military robbed and murdered civilians. Iturbide could maintain the loyalty of the military only as long as he could pay them, but this became a problem for him; for Mexico had very little money.

One target of the Liberals was the Church, which had survived the revolution with all her lands and *fueros* intact. Clergy retained the right to be tried only in their own courts and were free from taxation. The bishops were eager to maintain this state of things and allied themselves with the more conservative and wealthy creoles.

It had long been the contention of Catholic theologians and, indeed, of the Church's magisterium, that the Church is not and cannot be subject to the power of the state. The argument goes like this. Since the Church is a true society, through which the greatest good comes to mankind—eternal salvation, union with God—the Church is supernatural, and thus superior to the state, a society whose purpose is merely to help citizens attain natural goods: peace, access to the means of subsistence, cultural achievement, and, finally, natural moral and intellectual virtue. Though she is ultimately a spiritual society, the Church nevertheless needs material goods to carry out her mission. The Church, for instance, could not decently conduct divine worship without church buildings and liturgical appurtenances. If she is to serve the poor, she needs a certain amount of wealth. In Mexico and throughout the world, the Church operated hospitals and schools, which are and obviously require material goods. Because the Church is superior to the state, the state has no direct authority or power over what belongs to the Church. The state, thus, may not justly confiscate Church property. The difficulty was, however, that at times in New Spain and elsewhere churchmen abused their great wealth and the power great wealth inevitably endows on those who possess it. Liberals claimed that to curtail such abuses, the Church should be divested of her wealth; yet, this claim was often disingenuous, for wealthy Liberals were more interested in seizing Church wealth for themselves than they were in righting the wrongs perpetrated by corrupt and incompetent churchmen.

Liberalism, too, was fundamentally anti-Catholic, for it held that religion is merely a matter of personal opinion and thus should not impinge on the life of society and the state. For Liberals, the state is the highest society to which all things, including religion, should be subject. As we have seen, for Liberals, the greatest human good is individual liberty; all individuals are born in freedom and thus should be free to express, even publicly, whatever religious, philosophical, or ethical ideas they wish. Since, too, all people are fundamentally free, government derives its authority from the people alone, not God.

The Church opposed such ideas. Human beings, said the Church, are created to live in society; they are bound to acknowledge the truth about God and man and, thus, have a moral obligation to confess the true religion, the Catholic faith. Even though they might be established by the people, governments, said the Church, rule by God's authority. And since they derive their authority from God, governments are bound to acknowledge the true God and the religion he has established—the Catholic Church. Unfortunately, in Mexico, the Church's opposition to Liberalism led churchmen to ally themselves with a particular political faction, with which the Church came to be identified. For their part, Liberals had to temper their criticism of the Church, for most Mexicans were faithful Catholics. Even many Liberals (Morelos, for instance) were devoted to the Catholic faith. For this reason, the public stance of Mexican Liberals was to maintain the Catholic faith as the sole religion of Mexico even while they sought to confiscate Church property.

Emperor Agustín

Following his victory, Iturbide began to set up his government—a regency, because ostensibly he only awaited the establishment of a kingdom in Mexico. Taking for himself the titles of *generalissimo* and high admiral, Iturbide nominated a *junta* of five regents, with himself as president. He then began preparations for the election of a congress, as promised in the *Plan de Iguala*.

The congress was elected according to a formula that favored wealthy creoles—most of whom were *Borbonistas* (supporters of the royal Bourbon family and Fernando VII). But by the time the congress first met, in February 1822, it was well known that neither Fernando

VII nor any member of his family intended to ascend the throne of an independent Mexico; the Spanish king, in fact, refused to recognize Mexican independence, and a Spanish garrison remained at the fortress of San Juan de Ulúa as a symbol of his claims. Disappointed in their hopes of a Bourbon king, the *Borbonistas* in congress began calling for a **centralist republic.** They joined forces with the Liberals in congress. Together, they opposed Iturbide.

Political tensions were growing in Mexico City. *Gauchupines* in Mexico City were plotting with the Spanish at San Juan de Ulúa to restore Spanish rule. Life had not been comfortable for *gauchupines* since the revolution. Many among both the creoles and the *mestizos* were turning against all things Spanish—Congressman Carlos María de Bustamante had written a proclamation calling on the Army of the Three Guarantees to avenge the Aztecs whom Cortés had slain at Otumba and Cholula! The conqueror of Mexico had become quite unpopular in the capital—a mob of poor beggars, called *léperos*, stormed the cathedral in Mexico City to desecrate his tomb. They found an empty grave. Cortés' bones had been removed to a secret location.

Not only the *gauchupines* but the congress itself was causing trouble. It delayed writing up a constitution to focus its attacks on Iturbide. The conservatives (*Borbonistas* and others) had long been organized in Masonic lodges of the Scottish rite; now the Liberals (republicans), under the influence of the United States minister, Joel Poinsett, organized themselves in Masonic lodges of the York rite. Both groups of Masons turned their fire on Iturbide. In May, the congress moved to reduce the number of generals in the army and remove members of the regency from military command. It was time for Iturbide to act.

On the evening of May 18, 1822, Pio Mancha, a sergeant in Iturbide's army, raised the cry: *"Viva Agustín I!"* Other soldiers took up the cry, and as they marched through the streets towards Iturbide's dwelling, crowds of *léperos* and others joined them. Gathering around Iturbide's house, the mob demanded that he take up the government of Mexico in place of the Bourbons. This was not the first time there had been calls for Iturbide to assume the crown; ever since September 1821, such calls had been frequent—and Iturbide had issued a manifesto rejecting them. Now, appearing on the balcony of his house, Iturbide again refused the offered kingship. He withdrew into the house to consult the regents; when he

centralist republic: a republic where the preponderance of power lies in the central government rather than in local or state governments

Viva Agustín El Primero!

Emperor Agustín I

returned to the balcony, he announced his decision—he would accept the crown. Bells rang and guns were fired into the air in honor of the new king. The next day, the mobs waited in the streets outside the hall where congress gathered and inside mingled with the congressmen, crying *viva!* to Iturbide and threatening death to any who opposed him. No wonder the congress at last voted to proclaim Iturbide the emperor, Agustín I, of Mexico!

In July, Iturbide and his wife, adorned with jewels, in state entered the cathedral of Mexico City, where the archbishop anointed Agustín I with holy oil. The emperor and empress then mounted their thrones where he, like Napoleon Bonaparte, placed the crown on his own head. For the next month, Don Agustín occupied himself in making Mexico a full-fledged empire, with all the imperial trappings. He established the honorary Order of Guadalupe, endowing 50 grand crosses on favored recipients, along with 100 knighthoods.

Congress, however, remained the emperor's enemy, and now in their midst was the famed Liberal clergyman, Fray Servando de Teresa y Mier. Fray Servando had been deported from Mexico late the previous century for denying the miraculous origin of the image of Our Lady of Guadalupe. He had returned to Mexico in 1821 and taken the seat in congress to which he had been elected. As a congressmen, Fray Servando virulently and effectively attacked Don Agustín, ridiculing the emperor's pomp and the empty titles he had bestowed on his favorites. In retaliation, the emperor imprisoned Fray Servando and 15 other congressmen. This outrage united congress against the emperor. In October 1822, Don Agustín dissolved the congress and replaced it with a smaller, 45-member *Junta Nacional Instituyente,* handpicked by the emperor from the old congress.

But this new reduced congress also bucked and kicked against the emperor; it refused to write up a constitution and vote for taxes. Don Agustín now said he himself would write up a constitution, but he found he had to face more serious problems. His generals were still not happy—without tax revenues, they were not receiving their salaries. The emperor issued paper money to pay them, but this only caused prices to rise, fanning public discontent with the emperor. Agustín's empire tottered; it needed only a slight push to topple it.

Antonio López de Santa Anna

That push came from an army officer, the 27-year old Antonio López de Santa Anna. A native of Jalapa, Santa Anna had served in the royalist army, but hearing opportunity knock, had switched sides and joined Iturbide in 1821. When Iturbide became emperor, Santa Anna went to Mexico City to congratulate him and took to courting Iturbide's unmarried sister, thought he was 27 and she over 60 years old. The emperor and Santa Anna had a falling out, however, and Don Agustín dismissed him in disgrace to Veracruz. In the fall of 1822, Santa Anna sent out a call for the overthrow of the empire and the establishment of a republic. (The formal plan that Santa Anna issued, however, made no mention of ending the empire.) He organized an army of liberation, to which Vicente Guerrero, Nicolás Bravo, and Guadalupe Victoria joined their names and their power. At first, the rebellion was a failure, and Santa Anna planned to flee to Texas. But then everything changed.

Don Agustín's generals began to desert him. In February 1823, one general, José Antonio Echávarri, who had been conducting a desultory siege against Santa Anna at Veracruz, issued the *Plan de Casa Mata,* which laid out two demands: Don Agustín must restore the full congress and the insurgent armies must "attempt no act against [the emperor's[august person, which they respect as inviolable." All of the emperor's generals soon signed on to the plan; even his troops in Mexico City deserted him. On March 4, Emperor Agustín gave in to the inevitable; he summoned the old congress, which met on March 7.

But by the time the congress met, it was clear to Iturbide that he could not continue to exercise his office as he thought he should be able to do. During the rebellion, provincial governments throughout Mexico had begun taking on powers that weakened the control of the central government. Moreover, it was clear that the reformed congress would likely begin debates on whether to maintain the monarchy and the place of the Catholic Church in Mexico. To Emperor Agustín, this placed both the Church and his office at the mercy of the congress; thus, on March 19, 1823, he offered his resignation. The congress accepted it and sentenced him to perpetual banishment. That spring Iturbide and his family took ship for Europe.

Return of the Emperor

Don Agustín's abdication in 1823 was not the end of his dealings with Mexico. A year later, Iturbide, who had gone first to Italy and then to England, informed the Mexican congress that Spain was planning a reconquest of Mexico. Encouraged by reports that the people and the army were behind him, Iturbide offered his services to the Mexican government. He did not await a reply but took ship from England. At sea he likely passed the ship from Mexico that brought the government's reply: if Iturbide should return to Mexico, he must die.

The emperor, his wife, and two youngest children, landed at Soto La Marina on the Tamaulipas coast in the spring of 1824. Proceeding inland to Padilla, Iturbide was arrested by local authorities and immediately sentenced to be shot. With great dignity and courage, Don Agustín took his place before the firing squad. "Fellow Mexicans," he said, "in the moment of my death I recommend to you the love of our country and the observance of our holy religion. . . . I die happy, for I die among you!" Shots rang out, and Don Agustin de Iturbide, the first emperor of Mexico, fell dead to the earth.

The Republic of Mexico

Thirteen years of war had taken its toll on Mexico. About half a million people had been killed, and thousands were maimed and crippled or impoverished or homeless. Fields had been trampled; mines, flooded or abandoned; roads, destroyed. The new government had an enormous task of rebuilding ahead of it; but, as events would prove, it was unequal to the task.

The fall of Iturbide, left conservatives divided and weak. Moderates took control of the government and declared Mexico a republic. In November 1823, Miguel Ramos Arizpe assumed leadership of a new congress and drafted a constitution patterned on the constitution of the United States. The new constitution, proclaimed on October 4, 1824, divided Mexico into 19 states and four territories; each state was to elect its own governor and legislature. Unlike the U.S. constitution, however, the Mexican constitution made no provision for trial by jury—it had never been part of Spanish jurisprudence. Though it forbade the practice of any other religion except the Catholic, the constitution abolished the Church's exclusive control of schools.

According to the new constitution, state legislatures were to elect the president and vice president of the republic. Their choice in 1824 was Guadalupe Victoria for the first office and Nicolás Bravo for the second. Victoria's administration was peaceful, but not on account of his administrative abilities. During his tenure, conservative and Liberal forces were organizing themselves into factions that would over the next 40 years visit confusion on the country. Though his administration was unremarkable, President Victoria did have this distinction, shared by no other 19th century Mexican president: he completed his term and left office as poor as when he entered it.

Chapter 12 Review

Summary

- From the late 1780s to 1848, California enjoyed what is called its "golden age" and attracted the interest of foreigners. In 1812, the Russians came to California and built a settlement at Fort Ross.

- In the early 1800s, the California missions went through a period of progress during which many Indians were converted. The missions experienced difficulties resulting from runaway neophyte Indians and the bad influence of lax Spanish Catholics. In 1810 government payments and support for the California military garrisons ceased, so the missions began to supply the garrisons, bringing strain on the Mission Indians.

- The society of Spanish America was tarnished by injustice, structural problems, and political corruption. The ideas of the Enlightenment and the examples of the American and French Revolutions drew people to embrace Liberal republican political philosophies.

- In the mother country, Spain, civil war was beginning. Napoleon pressured Carlos IV and his son, Fernando VII, to relinquish all claim to the Spanish throne, and made his own brother, Joseph Bonaparte, king of Spain. Indignation broke out against the French, and *juntas* were formed to oppose them.

- New Spain also rejected Joseph Bonaparte's rule, and the town council of Mexico City asked the viceroy, José de Iturrigaray, to assume the powers of government of New Spain in the name of Fernando VII. Iturrigaray was a greedy man, however, and his action drew the opposition of the *audiencia* of New Spain, as well as of the Volunteers of Fernando VII, who broke into the viceregal palace and took Iturrigaray prisoner.

- During this early period of unrest in New Spain, *Caballeros Racionales* began meeting in Mexico to discuss revolutionary doctrines.

- In August of 1810, the priest, Miguel Hidalgo, and the Querétero group of *Caballeros Racionales* planned to capture key government officials and set up a revolutionary government. They were betrayed, but Hidalgo still chose to call for resistance, and by September 21, Hidalgo had amassed an army of 50,000. The army marched on Guanajuato on September 28 and slaughtered many inhabitants of the town. By October, Hidalgo had gained control of much of central Mexico. Hidalgo was captured in March 21, 1811, and later tried and executed.

- After the death of Hidalgo, Padre José María Morelos took command of the revolution. In 1813 Morelos abandoned any pretense that he was fighting for the rights of Fernando VII. He proclaimed that Mexico's dependence on the Spanish throne had ceased forever and been dissolved. He laid out his ideas for the government of an independent Mexico. The congress adopted his plans and set about drawing up a constitution.

- In 1814 Napoleon was defeated, and Fernando VII returned to the Spanish throne. He suppressed the constitution adopted by the Spanish Cortes in 1812.

- In 1816 the rebel general Luis Mier y Terán dissolved Morelos' revolutionary congress. In April of that same year, Juan Ruiz de Apodaca became viceroy and offered amnesty to the remaining revolutionaries.

- Revolution in Spain in 1820 forced Fernando VII to restore the Constitution of 1812. Liberals then demanded reform and determined that union with Spain was dangerous. They began to plot independence.

Chapter 12 Review (continued)

- Agustín de Iturbide published his *Plan de Iguala* with its "Three Guarantees," a blueprint for independence, in 1821. In July of that year a new Spanish viceroy, Juan O'Donojú, arrived in Veracruz, but the city was besieged, so he could not leave. In August he agreed to the *Plan de Iguala*, and the revolution was over, leaving Mexico independent.

- Iturbide began to set up his government, but the Spanish king would not recognize an independent Mexico. In 1822 a mob demanded that Iturbide take up the government of Mexico as emperor. Things did not go well with the new government, and Agustín's empire was falling apart. Congress began calling for a centralist government. Antonio López de Santa Anna organized a rebel army against the new emperor, and on March 19, 1823, Emperor Agustín offered his resignation.

- After the fall of Iturbide, moderates took control of the government and declared Mexico a republic. Miguel Ramos Arizpe assumed leadership of a new congress and drafted a constitution patterned on that of the United States. The constitution was proclaimed on October 4, 1824.

Key Concepts

junta: a group controlling a government, especially following a revolution

Plan de Iguala: the blueprint for independence in Mexico, written by Agustín de Iturbide

Three Guarantees: the assurances of the *Plan de Iguala*: independence for Mexico, the preservation of the Church, and the equality of *gauchupines* and creoles.

centralist government: a republic where the preponderance of power lies in the central government rather than in local or state governments

Constitution of 1824: Mexico's first republican constitution, modeled on the Constitution of the United States of America

Dates to Remember

1808: Carlos IV and his son Fernando VII relinquish all claim to the Spanish throne, and Joseph Bonaparte becomes king of Spain.

In Spain *juntas* are formed to oppose the Bonapartist government.

1810: Padre Hidalgo begins the Mexican Revolution.

1812: Padre Morelos takes over from Hidalgo and publishes his *Sentimientos de La Nación*, his ideas for the government of Mexico. The Mexican congress adopts the *Sentimientos*.

1814: Napoleon is defeated, and Fernando VII returns to the Spanish throne and abolishes the Constitution of 1812.

1820: Fernando VII is forced to restore the Constitution of 1812. The Liberals in Mexico begin to plot independence.

1821: Iturbide publishes his *Plan de Iguala*, and the new Spanish viceroy, Juan O'Donojú, agrees to it, thus establishing Mexican independence.

1822: Iturbide becomes emperor of an independent Mexico.

1823: Iturbide resigns as emperor. Mexico becomes a republic.

1824: The Mexican congress proclaims the Constitution of 1824.

Central Characters

Fernando VII (1784–1833): king of Spain during the Mexican revolution of 1810

Miguel Hidalgo (1753–1811): Catholic priest who first led the rebellion for Mexican independence

José María Morelos (1765–1815): revolutionary priest who assumed leadership of the Mexican independence movement after Hidalgo's death

Vicente Guerrero (1782–1831): a Liberal rebel leader who joined with Iturbide to institute the Plan de Iguala

Guadalupe Victoria (Manuel Félix Fernández) (1786–1843): Liberal rebel leader who became the first president of the republic of Mexico

Agustín de Iturbide (1783–1824): Mexican officer who became the leader of the Mexican independence movement and, as Agustín I, briefly reigned as emperor of Mexico

Chapter 12 Review (continued)

Questions for Review

1. Describe the chief characteristics of the "golden age of California."

2. How was California a hierarchical society?

3. What were some of the difficulties the missionaries were experiencing with the Indians of the missions in California?

4. What conditions led to the Mexican revolution?

5. How did Napoleon's actions in Europe encourage the Mexican revolution?

6. What did Hidalgo achieve during the Mexican revolution?

7. Describe Morelos' idea of government.

8. Describe the *Plan de Iguala* and its Three Guarantees.

9. What were the factions and dissensions that threatened the newly independent Mexico?

10. Explain why the Church cannot be subject to the power of the state.

11. What events led to Agustín I's resignation as emperor.

12. Describe the 1824 constitution of Mexico.

Ideas in Action

1. Read the 1824 Constitution of Mexico (this can be found in the Internet) and compare it to the American Constitution. How do they differ and how are they alike?

2. Choose one of the California missions and research its founding, the region wherein it was built, the Indians who inhabited it, and the work the missionaries and the Indians did.

Highways and Byways

The Green, White, and Red

During Mexico's war for independence, a number of flags were used to represent the struggle. When the country finally achieved its independence under the *Plan de Iguala*, the tricolor of green, white, and red became the official flag of Mexico. The design may have been influenced by the French flag, also a tricolor (of red, white, and blue); but the colors of the Mexican flag were thoroughly Mexican. The green symbolizes independence; white, the Catholic religion; and red, union. These three elements represent the "Three Guarantees" of the *Plan de Iguala*: independence from Spain, preservation of the Catholic Church, and the equality of all Mexicans. In the center of the flag, on the white field, is an emblem that depicts the foundation myth of the ancient Aztec empire: an eagle with a snake in its talons and beak, standing on a cactus that grows out of rocks in the middle of water. Over the years, various renditions of this scene have been used by the many different regimes. In one version, when Mexico was an empire, the eagle is depicted wearing a crown.

GOOD FEELINGS AND HARD TIMES

The Catholic Church in the Early 19th Century

For months she had watched him grow weaker and weaker. With determination and cheerfulness she had striven—despite her own sorrow and fears—to prop up his flagging spirit; but their financial worries, the long voyage, the detention in quarantine in Pisa, had exacted a heavy tribute of the sick man's heart. And now he was dead, and she and her daughter were alone in a foreign land.

She had married William Magee Seton nine years earlier, in 1794, at the Episcopal St. Paul's Church in New York City. By him she had given birth to five children. Before her marriage she was Elizabeth Ann Bayley, daughter of Dr. Richard Bayley, a professor and health officer for the Port of New York, and of Catherine Charlton, daughter of an Episcopalian minister of Staten Island. While providing her all comfort, Elizabeth Ann's father had not neglected her education, nor was she an indifferent student. She read avidly, especially in religion and history. Probably through her mother's influence, Elizabeth conceived a great love for Sacred Scripture, taking a special delight in the Psalms.

Elizabeth Ann Seton

Besides the love of her husband, marriage brought Elizabeth a new and deep friendship. Rebecca Seton, William's sister, became the "friend of her soul." Together they went about doing charitable work among the poor of the city until people began to call them the "Protestant Sisters of Charity." In 1797, at the age of 23, Elizabeth and Rebecca founded the Society for the Relief of Poor Widows with Small Children.

Tragedy soon dogged the steps of the Setons. Business troubles followed the death in 1798 of William's father, a rich merchant, and Elizabeth and William were left to raise William's orphaned siblings. Then, in 1801, Elizabeth's beloved father died. In great anxiety she prayed for him, offering to God even the life of her infant daughter for his salvation. Then, in 1803, William had fallen ill, and Elizabeth and their eldest daughter set sail with him for Italy where they hoped his health would improve.

After her husband's death, the Filicchi family, William's business associates in Pisa, befriended Elizabeth Seton, and she stayed on in Pisa for two more years. There she encountered the beauty of Catholic culture in the church buildings of Italy. Through the example and influence of Antonio Filicchi, Elizabeth grew slowly convinced of the truth of the Catholic Faith. Returning to America, she began to correspond with Jean-Louis Lefébvre de Cheverus, who later became bishop of Boston. Cheverus was a kindred spirit and helpful correspondent for Elizabeth Ann. Living in a two-room shack, Bishop Cheverus chopped his own firewood and dispensed charity to the poor of Boston. His zeal for souls would later move him to travel on foot to minister to the Indians of Maine, and even to learn their language. Now he labored for the soul of a young, aristocratic widow, and his labors, joined with her prayers and fasting, were not in vain. On Ash Wednesday, March 14, 1805, Father Matthew O'Brien of St. Peter's church in New York City received Elizabeth Ann Seton into the Catholic Church.

With five children to support, and with little of her husband's fortune left, Elizabeth's conversion was not worldly wise. Her Protestant friends and relatives abandoned her. She found employment teaching for a school opened by an English Catholic; but when that was forced to close because of rumors that it was seeking to make converts, Elizabeth, with the help of some friends, opened a boarding house for the boys of a Protestant school. But when, through her influence, Elizabelth's youngest sister-in-law converted to the Faith, the New York legislature threatened to expel her from the state. After much suffering, Elizabeth Seton accepted an invitation from Father Dubourg of St. Mary's Seminary in Baltimore to open a school for girls in that city.

She arrived in Baltimore in 1808 and opened her school next to St. Mary's Seminary. Soon several other women joined her, and together they formed a quasi-religious community. The same year a convert from Virginia offered Elizabeth Ann and her community $10,000 to found a school for poor children. Buying a farm just outside Emmitsburg, Maryland, the community moved in June 1808. In 1812, the community adopted the rule of the Sisters of Charity of St. Vincent de Paul; and, against her wishes, the sisters elected Elizabeth as their superior.

Many were the hardships of the life at Emmitsburg. Mother Elizabeth lost two of her daughters, Anna and Rebecca, but her fervor and zeal carried her through all difficulties and sorrows. Soon members of her community took charge of an orphan asylum in Philadelphia (1814).

When her sisters elected her superior for the third time in 1819, Mother Elizabeth protested that they had elected the dead. She lived for the next two years, suffering from heart problems. When she died in 1821, she was only 46 years old, but her religious community, then numbering 50 sisters, lived on after her. She is buried in the basilica bearing her name in Emmitsburg.

Ambrose Maréchal

Crisis in the American Church

The bickering of national factions, and American individualism, compromised the unity of the Catholic Church in the United States in the early 19th century. When John Carroll, archbishop of Baltimore, died in 1815, the largely Irish Catholic population east of the Appalachians fell under the rule of bishops who were mostly French. Though the Irishman Leonard Neale succeeded Carroll in Baltimore, Neale's coadjutor and successor was Ambrose Maréchal, a Frenchman. French Sulpicians controlled the seminary at Baltimore; the bishops of Bardstown, New Orleans, and Boston were all French. The Irish, who boasted the best and most accomplished preachers of the day, wondered why Rome passed them over for Frenchmen—for "foreigners."

Both Archbishop Neale and his successor, Ambrose Maréchal, had trouble dealing with the trustees of the Catholic church in Norfolk, Virginia, and Charleston, South Carolina. The trustees were making extraordinary demands. Having control over parishes and their finances, trustees throughout the United States had for years wanted the authority to choose their own priests. Now, in Norfolk and Charleston, the trustees demanded the right to choose their own bishops as well! The situation tended dangerously toward schism.

Dr. Simon Felix Gallagher, the pastor at Charleston, was a brilliant orator, as were so many Irish priests. He was also a drunkard. Archbishop Carroll, and now Neale, had written letters urging him to abstain, but to no avail. Yet, despite his alcoholism, Gallagher was beloved in Charleston; and so the news that Neale wanted to remove him in favor of his assistant, Joseph Pirot Cloriviére—a Frenchman—met with much protest. In 1816, Neale suspended Gallagher; but when the trustees later drove Cloriviére out of the parish, Gallagher, claiming that the French priest had abandoned the flock, again took over the parish.

Catholics in Norfolk were also irate on account of a controversy with their bishop. In 1817, the year Ambrose Maréchal became archbishop of Baltimore, the trustees, calling themselves the "vestrymen of the Roman Catholic Apostolic Christian Congregation" of Norfolk, sent a petition to Rome asking that the Irishman, Rev. Thomas Carbry, be made bishop of Norfolk. In their letter, the trustees claimed an "inalienable right of patronage" by which they could elect their own bishops. Two years later, on January 4, 1819, Carbry forwarded to a Father Hayes in Dublin a letter from the trustees of Charleston, South Carolina. The letter instructed Hayes to go to the Jansenist bishop of Utrecht and be consecrated the bishop of Charleston. The bishop of Utrecht was not in union with the Catholic Church, though he had valid orders and so could ordain priests—and consecrate bishops. Asking Hayes to seek ordination from the bishop of Utrecht was thus a schismatic act.

Hayes, it seems, was no schismatic. He forwarded the letter to Rome, where authorities grew so alarmed upon reading it that they agreed to appoint Irish bishops for Norfolk and Charleston. Norfolk fell to Patrick Kelly, who resigned after two years because of controversies with the cantankerous trustees. Charleston received John England whose thick skin and talent for appeasement assured him a longer career.

England in the South

Though Bishop John England's diocese covered an enormous territory—the states of South Carolina, North Carolina, and Georgia—his flock was small—no more than 15,000 souls. Yet, though the number of Catholics in his diocese were few, the challenges they presented him were great. His task, as England saw it, was to acquiesce as much as possible in what he deemed his people's just demands while maintaining his episcopal authority. This was no easy task, and it led to other difficulties. Because of the measures he undertook to defuse his people's opposition, he earned the stern disapproval of his brother bishops in America.

But then Bishop England objected to these bishops as well. The French clergy, he thought, made the Catholic faith seem foreign, almost exotic, to most Americans. The French "cannot understand," he wrote in a letter to Rome in 1825, "why it [the Faith] should be made to appear assimilated to American principles." To remedy this "French problem," England sought to bring priests from Ireland to serve his parishes; but when these turned out to be the men their bishops wanted to be rid of, England opened "The Philosophical and Classical Seminary of Charleston" to train his own priests.

In an attempt to assimilate the Faith to "American principles," Bishop England in 1823 drew up a constitution for his diocese. To Rome, he wrote, "I do not know of any system more favorable to the security of religious rights and of church property than that of the American law. . . . I prefer it to the law of almost every Catholic country with which I am acquainted." He set up a "congress," with purely advisory powers, made up of a Convocation of Clergy and a lay House of Representatives. Yet while praising republicanism, he did not entirely adopt it for the running of his Church. In particular, he attacked trusteeship; he cut off the trustees' financial power by abolishing the fees they charged people for occupying pews in church. (This practice was called "pew rent.") To strike this problem at its roots, England ordered the abolition of pews in churches, where this was practicable (after all, pews are a Protestant invention) and commanded that they be excluded from all new churches.

To foster the unity of the Catholic Church in the United States, John England asked his metropolitan, Archbishop Maréchal, to call a synod of bishops in Baltimore to discuss establishing uniform regulations for governing the dioceses of the Church in America. Maréchal, who looked askance at England's innovations and held to the traditional autonomy of bishops, refused. His successor, Archbishop James Whitfield, however, did call a synod, in 1829; but at this First Council of Baltimore, the American bishops ignored England's calls for uniform regulations for the Church in America.

The front page of the *United States Catholic Miscellany* from 1829

Bishop England worked diligently to advance not only the spiritual, but the cultural good of his people. He compiled a catechism and a missal in English, and he established a book society in each parish. He also founded the first Catholic magazine in the United States, called the *United States Catholic Miscellany,* and contributed articles to it.

The bishop of Charleston cared for both the white and black members of his flock. In 1830, he established the Sisters of Our Lady of Mercy who, he said, were "to educate females of the middling class of society; also to have a school for free colored girls, and to give religious instruction to female slaves; they will also devote themselves to the service of the sick." England celebrated an early Mass for blacks every Sunday and preached to them at Vespers. When he had a choice whether to preach to the wealthy whites or the blacks, he chose to preach to the blacks.

Bishop England was a great orator and even addressed Congress in Washington to rebut President John Quincy Adams's claim that Catholicism is incompatible with republican institutions. "We do not believe," said England, "that God gave to the Church any power to interfere with our civil rights, or our civil concerns . . . I would not allow to the pope, or to any bishop of our Church, the smallest interference with the humblest vote at our most insignificant ballot box."

Bishop England worked hard for his people, riding long miles over his vast diocese to offer Mass and to preach. His personal life was marked by a spirit of poverty; he wore shoes until the soles were worn away. His episcopate was significant in the history of the United States, for his spirit of accommodation came to dominate a large section of the American Catholic Church—a spirit that sought assimilation into the surrounding culture instead of a peaceful (but not necessarily quiet) opposition to it.

The Church on the Frontier

When the French Sulpician priest, Benedict Joseph Flaget, learned that he was to be bishop of Bardstown in distant Kentucky, his heart sank. Falling to his knees before his superior, he begged not to be sent. Flaget's superior, however, was unmovable. "My lord bishop," he replied, addressing Flaget by his new title, "you should be in your diocese!"

In the late 18th century, only two secular priests served French Catholics in their western settlements of Vincennes (on the Wabash River) and Kaskaskia (on the Mississippi). Six other priests rode the rounds ministering to Catholics in Kentucky and Tennessee, who met in ten small log cabin churches. Because the scattered Catholic population could expect only rare ministrations from a priest, laymen took over many clerical functions—reading prayers on Sundays, administering baptism, and registering marriages. Sometimes these laymen exceeded their powers, for instance by giving homilies or spicing up the worship celebrations (for instance, with a brass band)—issues the new bishop of Bardstown would often have to deal with.

An Attractive Offer

A recruiting advertisement for the American missions, circulated in France, described the conditions for missionaries on the American frontier: "We offer you: No salary; No Recompense; No Holidays; No Pension. But: Much Hard Work; a Poor Dwelling; Few Consolations; Many Disappointments; Frequent Sickness; a Violent or Lonely Death; an Unknown Grave."

Bishop Flaget arrived in Bardstown in 1808. When this bishop (whom Henry Clay called "the best representative of royalty off a throne") was not on horseback visiting Catholics in his large diocese, he lived like the poorest peasant. His dwelling was a 16 square-foot log cabin, with only a bed and a writing desk. With his priests, he lived the strenuous life.

Other bishops eventually joined Flaget in the West. They were mostly French, since the majority of Catholics west of the Appalachians were French. Among the more interesting was Bishop Simon Bruté de Remur. Bruté was 14 years old when the Reign of Terror gripped France, and he used to accompany disguised priests as they ministered to Catholics in the prisons. After studying medicine, Bruté decided to become a priest. Ordained a Sulpician, he went to America and for many years taught at Mount St. Mary's College in Maryland. There he was called the "Angel of the Mount" on account of his reputation for holiness; but he was also known for his vast library, and his eccentricity.

In 1834, when he was in his fifties, Bruté became bishop of Vincennes. There he brought his large library of books; but he found he had little time for reading. He became a horseback priest and generously dispensed material goods to those in need, living himself on the barest necessities. In his short reign of five years, Bruté established two seminaries.

Benedict Joseph Flaget

An intriguing figure of the Catholic frontier was a "Mr. Smith" (in those days priests in America went by the title of "Mister" instead of "Father"). Smith, whose given name was Prince Demetrius Augustin Gallitzin, was born at the Hague in Belgium in 1770. His father, a Russian ambassador, was the friend of such Enlightenment figures as Diderot, d'Alembert, and Voltaire. Gallitzin's mother was a Prussian who later in life became a fervent Catholic. Once she cornered the German poet, Johann Wolfgang von Goethe and tried to convert him. Goethe fled the house to escape her, but she followed him, jumped into his carriage, and continued pleading for his soul—much to the poet's embarrassment.

With such a mother, it is not surprising that Prince Gallitzin himself became Catholic at the age of 17. His father showed little concern over his son's conversion—"Mitri always wants to go against wind and tide," he said. The prince served in the Austrian army and was on his way to further advancements when he visited the United States in 1792. There he entered Bishop Carroll's seminary and three years later was ordained a priest. Though his father wanted him to return to Europe, where there was more opportunity for ecclesiastical advancement, Gallitzin decided to remain in America. Taking the common and more pronounceable name, "Mr. Smith," in 1799 he headed west over the Alleghenies to work with Catholics in western Pennsylvania.

The Basilica of the Sacred Heart of Jesus, Conewago, Pennsylvania, built between 1785 and 1787. Gallitzin spent the first five years of his priesthood here, from 1795 to 1799.

There he founded a settlement, really a Catholic colony, called Loretto. Using his own wealth he bought land, selling it at one-fourth its price to lay Catholic settlers. He built a flour mill and a saw mill for the settlers. Though receiving installments of money from his mother, Gallitzin fell into debt; but someone always intervened to save him from ruin. Once the Russian ambassador to Washington, Baron von Tuyl, invited "Mr. Smith" to dinner on the very day that he was due to repay a loan of $5,000. During the dinner (at which Henry Clay was also a guest) the baron took out the note for the loan—and used it to light his cigar. Gallitzin's royal connections were helpful. A gift of $10,000 from the king of Holland erased all of Gallitzin's debt.

Though he always retained his military spirit and insisted on rigid discipline from his people, Gallitzin was well loved. Later in life, though partially paralyzed from a fall, he continued to minister to his flock, in winter riding about in a sled. It was thus that the priest, Peter Henry Lemcke, met him. Lemcke had been warned about Gallitzin—"he's a singular old saint; many others have tried to live with him, but it seems as if no one could get along with him." When Lemcke first saw the prince, Mr. Smith was sitting in his sled, dressed in an old overcoat and with a broken and beaten peasant's hat on his head. He was reading a book.

"Are you really the pastor of Loretto?" asked Lemcke, walking up to him.

"Yes, I am," replied this singular priest.

"Prince Gallitzin?"

At that, Gallitzin laughed loudly. "Yes, I am that very exalted person."

Lemcke remained with Gallitzin and in 1836 founded another settlement like Loretto. Lemcke wanted to call it Gallitzin, but the old prince vehemently objected. So Lemcke named the village Carrolltown instead.

The "Era of Good Feelings"

It had been over two years since the Battle of New Orleans. "Old Hickory" still held the city under martial law—and defied the secretary of war in Washington to do anything about it. Though this was a clear instance of insubordination, the administration of President James Monroe more or less tolerated it. Washington had reasons to treat the stubborn, insubordinate Andrew Jackson gently; trouble was again flaring in "East Florida" (the modern state), and the government needed Jackson. He was a very effective general, perhaps the best the country had.

On April 23, 1816, Jackson wrote to Mauricio de Zuñiga, Spanish commandant at Pensacola in Florida: "A Negro Fort erected during our late war with Britain has been strengthened since that period, and is now occupied by upwards of two hundred and fifty Negroes, many of whom have been enticed away from the service of their masters—citizens of the United States . . . "

East Florida had been a troublesome place since 1812 when, with the secret encouragement of Washington, a group of Anglo settlers (mostly from Georgia) had settled there. Calling themselves the "Patriots," these settlers had seized Amelia Island with the aid of U.S. gunboats and then marched on San Agustín, which was protected by a garrison of only 400 Spanish soldiers. The situation grew more complicated when Seminole Indians, suffering from Anglo-American inroads on their lands, and a group of blacks who had escaped from plantations in Georgia began attacking plantations on the St. John's River. A bloody struggle ensued that pitted the Patriots, U.S. federal troops, and Georgia state militia against blacks and Seminoles under the chieftain Bowlegs. The war ended in 1816 when the Patriot

The site of Fort Gadsden, near the Apalachiola River in Florida

leader, Buckner Harris, was killed and the remainder of his followers made peace with the Spaniards.

The "Patriot War" was over, but trouble with blacks and Seminoles continued. In November 1814, Colonel Edward Nicholls, claiming he was an agent of the British government, built a fort on a bluff overlooking the Apalachicola River in East Florida. This fort became known as the "Negro Fort" when it was taken over by escaped black slaves who used it as a base from which they raided cattle and sheep ranches in Georgia, terrorizing white settlers. Forests surrounded the Negro Fort, and in its rear lay a swamp. Along the banks of the Apalachicola for many miles stood fields tilled by blacks and Indians, and in the forests a multitude of sheep and cattle wandered.

General Jackson told the Spanish commandant at Pensacola that failure on Spain's part to control the Negro Fort would "compel" the United States "in self-defense to destroy [it]." Never one to level an idle threat, Jackson sent U.S. troops under General Edward Gaines and boats under Lieutenant D. L. Clinch into Spanish territory to destroy the troublesome fort. In 1816, a small flotilla of boats appeared on the Apalachicola beneath the fort and opened fire. Unable to breach the stout fortifications, Lieutenant Clinch ordered a discharge of hot shot to set the fort ablaze. A large explosion followed when a ball struck the fort's powder barrels. Within the fort, 270 men, women, and children perished.

The Negro Fort had been destroyed, but peace was not achieved. Gregor MacGregor, a Scotsman who dreamed of an independent Florida republic, gathered a band of followers and forced the surrender of Spanish troops on Amelia Island. Encouraged by MacGregor, the Seminole took to the warpath in the Spring of 1817. With the cry, "Negro Fort!" the Indians raided white settlements, killed settlers, and drove off their cattle. General Gaines retaliated by attacking and destroying Seminole villages. General Jackson, with President James Monroe's permission to invade Spanish Florida, marched with Tennessee volunteers against St. Mark's on Apalachiola Bay. There naval forces under Lieutenant Isaac McKeever joined him, and together they captured St. Mark's and took possession of Apalachicola Bay. From St. Mark's, Jackson marched over 100 miles east to the settlement of Chief Bowlegs on the Suwannee River. But he failed to capture the chief.

It was when he returned to Fort Gadsden (built on the site of the Negro Fort) that Jackson heard very vexing news. The Spanish governor, who had gathered many Indians at Pensacola, was protesting Jackson's invasion of Spanish territory! The irascible general's response was direct. He marched on Pensacola and captured the town, along with the governor and his troops.

Of course, Jackson's bold act brought protests from the Spanish ambassador in Washington, Don Luis de Onís. President Monroe and his cabinet met to consider Don Luis' demands—that the U.S. troops leave Florida and that the insubordinate Jackson be punished. It was a ticklish matter, for Jackson was popular; but failure to discipline him might lead to war with Spain. After deliberation, both the president and his cabinet finally decided to punish the headstrong Jackson. Only Monroe's secretary of state, John Quincy Adams, had defended Jackson. After all, he said, Spain could not control her own Indians.

Matters might have ended there had not Congress met to decide whether it too should censure Jackson. Henry Clay warmly called for censure. He eloquently warned the House of Representatives that to acquit Jackson would be "a triumph of the spirit of insubordination, a triumph of the military over the civil authority, a triumph over the powers of the House, a triumph over the Constitution." Yet, in the end, the representatives declined to censure the general. Jackson was too popular. His campaign in Florida had made him a hero, especially in the South and the West. Clay's advocacy of censure made Jackson his implacable enemy.

The "war" against the Seminoles formally ended in 1818, and a year later Spain ceded all of East Florida to the United States in return for $5 million and a settlement of the disputed border between the Louisiana Territory and Spanish Texas. In 1821, when Florida formally became a U.S. territory, Jackson was made its military governor.

"We Are All Republicans . . . "

It was a strange political mutation.

James Monroe, by Samuel F. B. Morse

With the close of the war with Britain, the Republicans, once champions of state over national government, became, instead, ardent nationalists. They even began adopting policies championed by their defeated enemy, the Federalists, including Hamilton's policy on manufacturing. In 1816, the Republican-controlled congress rechartered the National Bank (which Republican opposition had killed) and voted for a tariff on foreign manufactured products—both strongly nationalist measures.

Changes during and after the War of 1812 in part explain the transformation in Republican policies. Since Americans had not been able to obtain such British products as iron, spun cotton, and grain during the war, in the North, native American industries had arisen to provide them. Now, with peace, British products again flooded the American market, jeopardizing the infant American industries. Already, thousands of factory workers had been laid off, and soup kitchens and charitable organizations in the cities were overwhelmed with the numbers of the needy. Others lay in debtor's prisons. Many citizens began demanding tariffs—duties added to the cost of the product—on imported goods that competed with goods American industries could produce in sufficient quantities.

In Congress, Senators Clay and John C. Calhoun supported a bill to place a 20 percent duty on such imports. New England merchants, who profited from importing European goods, however, opposed the bill. The merchants' champion was the 34-year old representative from New Hampshire, the eloquent Daniel Webster. But despite his oratorical skills, Webster could not carry the day. The tariff bill passed both houses of Congress, and President James Madison signed it into law.

Though they had opposed rechartering the Bank of the United States in 1811, Calhoun and Clay became its champions in 1816. The small banks that had sprouted up all over the country were highly unstable. Americans had an insatiable desire for money to fund their multitudinous business ventures, and banks had been issuing notes to keep up with demand. These notes were supposedly backed up by gold and silver, but this was all too often not the case. One bank had issued $395,000 in notes but had only $27,000 in gold and silver specie to redeem them. The National Bank was seen as a way of stabilizing this situation.

Clay and Calhoun favored rechartering the bank because they saw it was a way to fund internal improvements—roads and canals. When lands formerly held by Tecumseh and the Creeks had been opened to settlement, a new wave of emigrants swept over the Appalachians. Such emigration eventually gave rise to the states of Indiana (admitted in 1816), Mississippi (1817), Illinois (1818), and Alabama (1819). In order better to unite these regions with the East, and to ease emigration west (and trade heading east), roads and canals were necessary, or so it was argued. When some countered that the Constitution did not give the federal government the power to fund internal improvements, Calhoun delivered a very Hamiltonian refutation; the guide, he said, to interpreting the Constitution should be "good common sense" directed toward to the general welfare. Clay and Calhoun convinced Congress to fund the National Road, which eventually ran from Fort Cumberland to Vandalia, Illinois.

The Supreme Court under Chief Justice Marshall furthered the trend toward nationalization in a case involving the state of Maryland and the Bank of the United States. Maryland had taxed the Baltimore branch of the National Bank, thus treating it as it would a state bank. In the 1819 court case, *McCulloch v. Maryland*, the state argued that Congress had no power to charter a bank, because such a power is not included in the "necessary and proper" clause of the Constitution. Chief Justice Marshall disagreed. In his decision, supported by the majority of the court, Marshall argued that the union is the government of the people, that it "emanates from them. Its powers are granted by them and are to be exercised directly on them, and for their benefit." The chief justice echoed Hamilton's theory of implied powers, writing that while federal powers are limited, "let the end be legitimate, let it be within the scope of the Constitution, and all means which are appropriate, which are plainly adapted to that end, which are not prohibited, but consist with the letter and spirit of the Constitution, are constitutional."

The elections of 1816 and 1820 displayed a remarkable political unity that, together with a generally good economy, seemed to justify calling the time, "The Era of Good Feelings." In 1816, James Monroe, Madison's secretary of state, took the presidency with 183 electoral votes, while Rufus King, the candidate of the almost defunct Federalist Party, won only 34 electoral votes. Monroe was Madison's hand-picked successor, as Madison had been Jefferson's, and was the fourth Virginian to win the presidency. Four years later, the election of 1820 seemed to underscore further America's political unity; Monroe won relection with 231 electoral votes, one shy of the 236 vote total. That vote was cast for John Quincy Adams, but only so that Washington alone would have the honor of receiving a unanimous electoral vote. No Federalist had opposed Monroe.

The Death Knell of the Union

Eighteen-nineteen was not a good year. A business panic ending in a depression paralyzed the nation. The Bank of the United States had demanded payment from state banks on all the notes they had issued and refused to renew any mortgages. State banks collapsed one by one, and the national bank seized thousands of properties in the West because their owners failed to pay the mortgages. It was a bitter period for the entire country, but mostly for the West; for while the East recovered within a year or two, the West's sufferings continued well into the mid-'20s. Many were apprehensive, for the situation could spark a secession movement in the West.

Slaves using the first cotton gin

A bill introduced into Congress the same year awakened another rivalry—between North and South. Formerly part of the Louisiana territory, Missouri had been settled by folks from the South who had been drawn by the good bottom land along the Missouri and Mississippi rivers. Since Missouri had been open to slavery, settlers brought their slaves with them; and so it was that in their proposed state constitution the people of Missouri forbade emancipation and prohibited free blacks from entering the state. The underlying North-South sectional rivalry revealed itself when Representative James Tallmadge of New York introduced an amendment to the Missouri bill to prohibit the further introduction of slaves into Missouri and provide that all children born to slave parents at the time the state constitution was established should be free when they turned 25.

The Tallmadge amendment stirred up a storm of protest in both the House and Senate. Southerners denounced what they called unconstitutional restrictions and restraints introduced as criteria for admitting new states. The Tallmadge amendment, they said, violated the property rights of slave holders in Missouri and, in effect, prohibited slave owners from carrying their "property" into the territories. Yet, beneath this constitutional palaver lurked both political ambition and a deep-seated fear. Southerners feared that if slaves could not be transported into the territories, or new slave states were not admitted to the union, then blacks would come to outnumber whites in the existing slave states (as they already did in some regions of the South). Once the slaves realized their power, a bloody slave revolt, so dreaded by southern whites, might come to pass.

The slavery question, like a coiled snake, had always been with the union. It had arisen in the Constitutional Convention of 1787 and had been lulled to sleep by compromise; now, in 1819, it once again warned of danger and destruction. Controversy would be more difficult to quiet than in 1787, for then one could argue that slavery was growing obsolete and would die a natural death. But the invention of the cotton gin in 1791 by Eli Whitney of New Haven, Connecticut had changed all that. Suddenly the laborious and time-consuming task of separating seeds from cotton fiber was made simple, and slaves once again became profitable—at least in South Carolina, Georgia, and the Gulf States, where cotton was grown. Formerly, it took almost 1,000 slaves to process 1,000 pounds of cotton a day for a relatively small profit for the cotton grower; now, one cotton gin could do the work of 1,000 slaves—and the extra labor could be sent to do field work and so increase the number of acres devoted to cultivation. In this way, the cotton gin, worked by slaves and fed by slaves harvesting cotton in greatly expanded fields, phenomenally increased production. In ten years (1791–1801) cotton exports from the South increased from only 189,500 pounds (before the gin) to 41,000,000 pounds (after the gin). Cotton thus became the source and the foundation of the wealth of the southern states.

Political rivalry exacerbated North/South relations. Because the North in 1820 had a population of 5,152,000 people, as opposed to the South's 4,485,000, in the House representatives of the North outnumbered those from the South, 105 to 81. That's why the Missouri bill with the Tallmadge amendment handily passed the House of Representatives. But in the Senate, the number of southern and northern representatives was equal—11 states each—which explains why the bill failed in the Senate. The South feared that unless Missouri came in as a slave state, the North would end up dominating both the House of Representatives and the Senate; for Maine, a northern and "free" state, was seeking admission at the same time Missouri was.

Antislavery sentiment was not particularly strong in the North at this time. In fact, the only antislavery journal in the country, the *Philanthropist*, was published by a southerner and was distributed mostly in the South. So, though some in the North denounced slavery as unchristian and unconstitutional, it was the political rivalry that prevailed in the current contest. Some northerners saw the Missouri issue as a way of creating a "solid north" that would "snatch the scepter from Virginia." Desire for political dominance was thus the predominant factor inspiring northern opposition to the admission of another slave state to the union.

The controversy over Missouri was not settled in 1819 but awaited the seating of the 16th Congress, in 1820. The Senate passed a compromise bill that established the latitude 36 degrees, 30 minutes (the southern boundary of Missouri westward) as the division between slave and free territory, and allowed masters to retrieve any slaves who escaped into free territory. The House defeated a similar bill but approved an amended bill on account of House Speaker Henry Clay's cajoling and arm-twisting tactics. This "Missouri Compromise" allowed Missouri to submit its constitution, slavery and all, to Congress; at the same time, it admitted Maine as a free state, thus maintaining an equal representation of North and South in the Senate. The Missouri Compromise quieted sectional wrangling for another 30 years. The compromise, however, cost several congressmen their seats in the next election; for many, both in the North and South, were not pleased with it.

Some thought the fight over Missouri a bad omen for the future. "I take it for granted," wrote John Quincy Adams, "that the present question is a mere preamble—a title-page to a great, tragic volume." The 80-year old Thomas Jefferson wrote, "this momentous question, like a fire bell in the night, awakened and filled me with terror. I considered it at once the death knell of the Union." The compromise, he said, was "a reprieve only, not a final sentence," for the slavery question would not go away. "We have the wolf by the ears, and we can neither hold him, nor safely let him go. Justice is in one scale and self-preservation in the other."

Jefferson held that the states, not the federal government, should decide the slave question for themselves. He himself would be pleased if slavery could be ended through emancipation and expatriation to Africa; but popular passions, once awakened, would not be quieted. Disunion, he said, would come. "I regret," said Jefferson, "that I am now to die in the belief, that the useless sacrifice of themselves by the generation of 1776, to acquire self-government and happiness to their country, is to be thrown away by the unwise and unworthy passions of their sons, and that my only consolation is that I live not to weep over it."

A Warning to Europe

In 1815, the Americas had only two independent governments—the United States and Haiti. But, beginning in 1816, a series of revolutions so rocked Spanish America that by 1822 nearly all of America, from the border of Canada south to Tierra del Fuego, was divided into independent nations. José de San Martín had "liberated" La Plata (the Argentine), Chile had declared independence under Bernardo O'Higgins, Simón Bolívar had established the Republic of Great Columbia (modern Columbia, Ecuador, Venezuela, and Panama), and Mexico was free under the rule of Agustín Iturbide. At first President Monroe was unwilling to recognize these new nations. But he changed his mind in 1823 when France invaded Spain.

King Fernando VII of Spain chafed under the constitution Spanish Liberals had forced on him. He wanted to rule as an absolute monarch, and his Bourbon cousin of France, the restored King Louis XVIII, decided to help restore him to power. France invaded Spain and with Fernando overthrew the power of the Spanish parliament, the Cortes. With his power restored, it was rumored that Fernando, with the French, would invade the New World to crush the incipient republics that were formerly his domains.

Worried about Bourbon intentions, Great Britain in 1823 approached the United States and suggested an alliance. Was it not in the interests of both to keep France out of America? On the advice of both Madison and Jefferson, Monroe was willing to sign on to an alliance with Britain; but the secretary of state, John Quincy Adams, voiced his opposition to the plan. The United States, Adams said, should spell out its own policy, not "come in as a cockboat in the wake of the British man-of-war." The United States, he said, should issue terms to both France, and Spain—and Great Britain as well.

Monroe spelled out Adams' policy, since called the Monroe Doctrine, in a message to Congress delivered December 2, 1823. While the United States, Monroe said, would not interfere "with the existing colonies or dependencies of any European power," nevertheless, the American continents, "by the free and independent condition which they have assumed and maintain, are henceforth not to be considered as subjects for future colonization by any European powers." The United States, said Monroe, "should consider any attempt" of European nations "to extend their system [of government] to any portion of this hemisphere as dangerous to our peace and safety."

The Monroe Doctrine told Europe that its days of colonizing the Americas were over. None of the European powers, only the United States, was henceforth to be hegemon in the Western Hemisphere.

The Democratic Revolution

John Quincy Adams

Unlike the election of 1820, where Monroe ran basically unopposed, in 1824 four candidates, all Republicans, vied for the presidency. The Era of Good Feelings was over; each candidate represented a particular interest or faction competing to dominate the republic. John Quincy Adams represented New England interests and the remnants of the old Federalist Party. William H. Crawford was the candidate favored by Congress. Then there was Henry Clay, who might have stood for the West and South had not Tennessee nominated General Andrew Jackson, war hero and the model of the self-made man.

Jackson appealed to the western pioneer. Born in a log cabin on the Carolina frontier, General Andy had climbed and fought his way out of poverty to become a war hero, a rough-hewn (from hickory, it was said) Tennessee gentleman, and the owner of a plantation complete with slaves. He was the symbol of success to the hard-scrabble western farmer and frontiersman. If Andy Jackson could rise in the world, why, so could any hard-working man with gumption! As a member of Congress from Tennessee in 1796–97, he had been an opponent of President Washington. Elected to the Senate in 1797, he resigned a year later and served as a state supreme court judge in Tennessee until 1804. A violent, quarrelsome man, Jackson carried two bullets in his body gotten in duels, the second in a tavern in Nashville where, after being shot, he fell down a flight of steps.

In the election of 1824, Jackson carried New Jersey, Pennsylvania, and most of the South and West, winning 99 electoral votes. John Quincy Adams—a round, balding, reserved man—came in second, with 84 electoral votes, while Crawford and Clay finished third and fourth. Because no candidate received a clear majority (51 percent) of the 261 electoral votes, the election was thrown to the House of Representatives, where Clay gave his support to Adams and so assured his election to the presidency.

Foul! Corrupt Bargain! cried Jackson and his supporters. Adams, they said, took the election by bribery, a claim seemingly justified by the new president's appointment of Clay as his secretary of state. No sooner was the election of 1824 over than Jackson and his supporters began campaigning for 1828. Two Jackson men, James Buchanan of Pennsylvania and Martin Van Buren of New York, led a relentless political war against the new president, accusing him of corruption and claiming that the people had been robbed of their rightful president—Andrew Jackson.

Van Buren later admitted privately that the charge of corruption was spurious. Adams was one of the last representatives of classical republican probity. On taking office, he not only refused to indulge in the "spoils system," removing political opponents from appointed offices, but even gave appointments to Jackson men. Adams was a thoroughgoing nationalist, a proponent of federally funded internal improvements and even scientific expeditions. He wanted to make Washington the national center of research and learning; but his efforts in this, and in trying to establish a naval academy, were thwarted by Congress at every turn.

Adams was a republican dinosaur in a new, democratic age. Changes were altering the complexion of America. In 1825, the Erie Canal was completed, joining Lake Erie with New York City and making New York the most populous city in the union. However, this canal would soon be obsolete; for outside Quincy, Massachusetts (the president's birthplace), a horse-drawn carriage on rails had been built—the first instance of the railroads that would shortly span the country. Democracy, the rule of the common man, was everywhere in the air; the voice of republicanism with its "natural aristocracy" was drowned out by a discordant clamor about the rights of the people.

Andrew Jackson

Jackson led a party of men who had themselves risen from the bottom of society. They wanted to give the common man his chance to rise, unhindered by the pretensions of aristocracy, natural or otherwise. They were not the party of the downtrodden but of the poor who wanted to rise in society. They called for the removal of property qualifications in voting, and a universal suffrage for all free white males. They favored free public education. Jackson and his boys spoke the language of the common man, painting all issues in thick strokes of black and white. Often unscrupulous politicians among Jackson's followers and allies used such tactics to appeal to the baser instincts of the masses, encouraging narrowness and bigotry against those who were not of the white and Protestant majority. Other Jacksonians, though, were honestly moved by an ardent zeal for equality.

The demise of republicanism in the United States was symbolized by the deaths of two of its champions—John Adams and Thomas Jefferson. Though once bitter political enemies, Jefferson and Adams had reconciled later in life and for years had been carrying on a correspondence. Now, on July 4, 1826—the fiftieth anniversary of the signing of the Declaration of Independence—both stood at the verge of death. Jefferson lay in a coma at his home at Monticello, attended by a young kinsman. At midnight of July 3–4, the old statesman awoke, and turning to his kinsman asked: "Is this the fourth?" When the young man nodded, yes,

Jefferson breathed a sigh of contentment and fell again into unconsciousness. At noon he passed from this life. At the same hour, hundreds of miles north, in Quincy, Massachusetts, the dying Adams was awakened by a cannon blast and a shout from the public square. When a speaker delivering an oration in honor of the Fourth proclaimed the words, "Independence forever!" Adams turned to his attendant, a granddaughter, who bent her ear to hear his whispered words. The old patriot gasped, and breathed, "Thomas—Jefferson—still—surv—" and said no more. That evening, the second President of the United States quietly passed away.

The People's President

The presidential campaign of 1828 was the nastiest to date. Jacksonian newspapers spread false stories about corruption in the Adams' administration; and pro-Adams papers returned fire, spreading stories of Jackson's shady past. The result was predictable—Jackson carried the entire West and South, Pennsylvania, and most of New York, winning 178 electoral votes; Adams received only 83 electoral votes. This was the first election where the vote split along class lines, the wealthier supporting Adams and the poorer sort backing Jackson.

Jackson purged the government of Adams appointees with a ruthlessness never before known in the United States. Adams' supporters were swept from office—a precedent that would be followed in all future administrations. Jackson's cabinet was made up of mediocre men, except for his secretary of state, Martin Van Buren. Called "Little Van" because he was short, and the "Little Magician" for his cunning, Van Buren proved a consummate political operator who was not opposed to using devious means to amass more power for himself.

Little Van's first target was Vice President John C. Calhoun.

Cartoon depicting Andrew Jackson hanging opposition candidate, President J.Q. Adams

Andrew Jackson being sworn in as president by Chief Justice John Marshall

It all started—Jackson's opponents would say, fittingly—in a Georgetown tavern owned by one O'Neale. O'Neale's daughter, Peggy, was a fine looking lass, whose good looks and flirtatious ways attracted a host of Washingtonian men, including one of her father's boarders, Tennessee senator John H. Eaton. Though married to a navy purser, Peggy was rumored to have had a long-standing affair with Eaton, who used his influence to keep her husband at sea for longer and longer periods of time. When Peggy's husband died in 1829, she lost no time in marrying Eaton. All of Washington buzzed with the unseemly scandal.

Jackson, who made John Eaton his secretary of war, was an ardent, if perhaps naïve, defender of Mrs. Eaton's honor. He grew enraged when cabinet members' wives snubbed her at gatherings. Since the chief snubber was Mrs. Calhoun, Little Van confided to the president that Vice President Calhoun was behind all the "dishonorable" treatment of Peggy Eaton. Calhoun was already in bad blood with the president over some revelations that he had urged court-martialing Jackson when the general had invaded Spanish Florida in 1817. Now the rogue was insulting a member of the "fair sex"! This was too much for the president to bear.

But despite Jackson's chivalrous concern for Mrs. Eaton's honor, the affair surrounding her was a vexation for him. Little Van, however, had the remedy for the distemper. One day when Jackson was venting his spleen against the Calhoun men in the cabinet, Van Buren offered to resign and to convince Eaton to resign as well. When the president refused to hear of this, Van Buren confided that his own resignation would allow the president to ask for the resignations of the rest of the cabinet, and Jackson could reconstitute his cabinet with new men and so be rid of the Peggy problem That's just what happened. Eaton and Van Buren's resignation was followed by the resignations of the rest of the cabinet. Little Van had lost his cabinet position, but had won the heart of Old Hickory. In the election of 1832, he would run in place of Calhoun as Jackson's vice-presidential candidate.

An 1831 Cartoon depicting Andrew Jackson collapsed in his chair as his cabinet scurries away

The "Tariff of Abominations" and Nullification

By the 1820s, South Carolina was having hard times. The opening up of the Gulf Coast states to cotton growing had brought an increase in cotton production, leading to lower prices for cotton on the market and a decrease in profits for South Carolina growers. Because South Carolina planters had for years and years been planting only cotton on the same land, the soil had become depleted. Lower yields and decreasing prices spelled economic disaster for the South Carolina growers.

Added to this were the tariffs that, since 1816, Congress had been imposing on foreign imports to protect manufacturers in the North. Because the South had little manufacturing, southern growers were dependent on foreign imports, for which they had to pay increasingly higher prices because of ever-increasing tariffs that benefited primarily New England. The South Carolina growers began to blame the tariffs for their impoverishment. The Tariff of 1828 proved the final straw. Calling it the "Tariff of Abominations," South Carolinians denounced what they thought was an attempt to rob the South to benefit the North. A South Carolina senator claimed that because the tariff adversely affected the profits Britain made from exporting goods to America, the British were forced to buy less cotton from the South. Great Britain was the South's biggest cotton customer.

With little to do as vice president, John Calhoun found a new outlet for his considerable energy in fighting the tariff. Though he had supported the first protective tariff in 1816, he now thought that tariffs were bringing poverty to the South and sectional strife to the union. He worked out a new political doctrine, called "Nullification," to help his home state, South Carolina, defend herself against federal encroachments on her interests. Calhoun's Nullification was something of a development of Jefferson and Madison's nullification doctrine found in the Kentucky and Virginia Resolves.

According to Calhoun, states were equal partners with the federal government in a social contract, whose terms were spelled out in the Constitution. As an equal partner in this contract, each state had as much right as the federal government did to interpret the terms of the contract. If a state deemed a federal law contrary to the Constitution, said Calhoun, the state could nullify the federal law within its borders. Calhoun's nullification doctrine was more radical than anything the Kentucky and Virginia Resolves had proposed. Jefferson and Madison had held that a convention of states could nullify a federal law, not an individual state by itself.

Calhoun set forth his nullification theory anonymously in the "South Carolina Exposition and Protest," which was subsequently approved and adopted by the South Carolina legislature. But the state legislature did not take the next step and call a convention to discuss nullifying the Tariff of 1828 since Calhoun urged them to wait to see whether or not Congress would vote to reduce the tariff.

South Carolina's endorsement of nullification did not go unnoticed. In December 1829, a congressional debate on a Connecticut senator's proposal to put a brake on the sale of western lands turned into a forum on constitutional theory. For weeks senators expended eloquence on constitutional themes; crowds gathered in the Senate chambers to hear the debates, which began to turn on whether liberty or union was the fundamental value of the American republic. On January 26, 1830, Senator Daniel Webster of Massachusetts delivered a reply to a South Carolina senator, in the presence of Vice President Calhoun. In this speech, Webster criticized the "South Carolina doctrine" and delivered a peroration that would inspire future unionists:

> I have not allowed myself, Sir, to look beyond the Union, to see what might lie hidden in the dark recess behind. I have not coolly weighed the chances of preserving liberty when the bonds that unite us together shall be broken asunder. I have not accustomed myself to hang over the precipice of disunion, to see whether, with my short sight, I can fathom the depth of the abyss below; nor could I regard him as a safe counselor in the affairs of this government, whose thoughts should be mainly bent on considering, not how the Union may be best preserved, but how tolerable might be the condition of the people when it should be broken up and destroyed.

Webster said the preservation of the union offered "high, exciting, gratifying prospects . . . for us and our children . . . God grant," he prayed, that when his eyes "turned to behold for the last time the sun in heaven," he would not see "him shining on the broken and dishonored fragments of a once glorious Union; on States dissevered, discordant, belligerent; on a land rent with civil feuds, or drenched, it may be, in fraternal blood!" No, he hoped to behold . . .

> . . . the gorgeous ensign of the republic, now known and honored throughout the earth, still full high advanced, its arms and trophies streaming in their original lustre, not a stripe erased or polluted, nor a single Star obscured, bearing for its motto, no such mis-

erable interrogatory as "What is all this worth?" nor those other words of delusion and folly, "Liberty first and Union afterwards"; but everywhere, spread all over in characters of living light, blazing on all its ample folds, as they float over the sea and over the land, and in every wind under the whole heavens, that other sentiment, dear to every true American heart—Liberty and Union, now and for ever, one and inseparable!

But eloquence alone could not dispel the threat (or promise, depending on how one saw it) of nullification. Congress gave South Carolina grounds for testing Calhoun's theory in 1832 when a new tariff, pushed by Henry Clay, removed sections of the Tariff of Abominations, though maintaining its high duties on iron and textiles. Such a compromise was not good enough for South Carolina. The state election of 1832 brought states' rights men into the South Carolina legislature, which now called a state convention to consider nullifying the new tariff. On November 24, 1832, the South Carolina convention issued an order of nullification that said the new tariff act was "unauthorized by the Constitution of the United States, null, void, and no law, nor binding upon the State, its officers or citizens." This ordinance forbade federal officers to collect customs duties in South Carolina after February 1, 1833 and threatened secession if the federal government tried to enforce the tariff.

Jackson, though a defender of states' rights and an enemy of tariffs, was not about to tolerate this defiance of federal law. He reinforced Forts Sumter and Moultrie in Charleston harbor, ordered revenue cutters to collect duties on imports if customs officials refused to do so, and on December 10 issued to the people of South Carolina a proclamation that condemned the right of secession. "Whether it be formed by compact between the States, or in any other manner," wrote Jackson, "it [the federal government] is a government in which all the people are represented, which operates directly on the people individually, not upon the States." Jackson flatly denied a right to secession, since, his proclamation said, each state in entering the union had "parted with so many powers as to constitute, jointly with the other States, a single nation." According to Jackson, a state "cannot possess any right to secede, because such secession does not break a league but destroys the unity of a nation."

But South Carolinians were not about to be cowed by the man they now derided as "King Jackson." Though other Southern states opposed the doctrine of nullification, South Carolina was determined to resist even to the shedding of blood, it seemed. In response to the president's proclamation, the state legislature approved the nullification ordinance and raised a volunteer force. Jackson responded by saying he would send troops into the state at the first sign of resistance. At this tense moment, Congress intervened. On March 2, 1833, Congress adopted a proposal made by Henry Clay to scale down customs duties; at the same time, it debated a force bill that would

Cartoon deriding Jackson as "King Jackson"

grant Jackson the authority to use the army and the navy to collect customs duties if South Carolina refused to acknowledge the judgment of the courts.

The debate on the force bill was, as could be expected, rancorous. In the Senate, Vice President Calhoun delivered an address defending nullification and the right of secession. To force the majority (the North) to "consult the good will" of the minority (the South), a state required the right, said Calhoun, to interpose itself between its citizens and unjust and unconstitutional congressional laws. The contest between North and South was a contest between "power and liberty." If the South did not defend its interests, said Calhoun, its fate would be "more wretched than that of the aborigines whom they have expelled, or of their slaves." To his fellow Southerners, Calhoun said that if they persevered in their fight for freedom, their section "will become distinguished for its patriots and statesmen." But if they don't persevere, "if we prove unworthy of this high destiny, if we yield to the steady encroachment of power, the severest and most debasing calamity and corruption will overspread the land."

Daniel Webster fired his stentorian eloquence in reply to Calhoun. Nullification, he said, struck "a deadly blow at the vital principle of the whole Union" and would lead to "the dismemberment of the Union and general revolution." Evoking the America-as-Messiah theme that would become the staple of unionist rhetoric, Webster declared that, to the world, "it must seem incredible and inconceivable" for "a single state" to "rush into conflict with all the rest . . . and thus break up and destroy the world's last hope."

Congress passed the Force Bill, and Jackson signed it, along with Clay's tariff bill. On March 11, the South Carolina convention again met and repealed the ordinance of nullification. "Thus dies nullification and the doctrine of secession, never more to be heard of," crowed Jackson in a letter to James Buchanan, now ambassador to Russia.

In just 30 years, during the final days of this same Buchanan's term as president, first South Carolina and then six other southern states would vote to secede from the Union.

The Slayer of Monopoly

"This worthy President thinks that because he has scalped Indians and imprisoned judges, he is to have his own way with the Bank. He is mistaken."

So boasted Nicholas Biddle, president of the Bank of the United States. Jackson was a dyed-in-the-wool opponent of the National Bank, which he thought a dire and certain threat to the security and liberty of the people. He was determined to slay this fearful monster, whose clever and powerful champion was this same Nicholas Biddle.

Biddle certainly had many resources to hand. Allied with Jackson's political enemies, he had several congressmen in the bag, including Daniel Webster, who was a director of the bank and several thousands of dollars in debt to it. Other congressmen received no-interest loans from the bank that they could pay back when they received their salaries from the government. The bank gave loans on very favorable terms to influential journalists, who, by no odd coincidence, championed the institution in their papers.

The election campaign of 1832 provided a forum on the popularity of the National Bank. The Republicans had split into rival parties, with Jackson's wing organizing itself as the Democratic Party,

U.S. capitol in the 1830s

which at its first convention nominated Jackson and Van Buren as its presidential and vice presidential candidates. This party, because it championed states' rights and opposed the bank, became especially popular among westerners and southerners. These folk wanted easier credit and more paper money to fund the land speculation to which they were addicted, and the Bank of the United States made both of these items harder to get. The other Republican wing organized itself as the National Republican Party and nominated for president Henry Clay, long a proponent of the bank. The election, like the one in 1828, witnessed processions, dramatic oratory, and fireworks displays. One French traveler likened a pro-Jackson parade to religious processions he had seen in Mexico.

Ironically, Jackson was a firm opponent of both easy credit and paper money. Still, the South and West carried him into a second term, along with a House of Representatives favorable to his views. But even before Jackson's second inauguration on March 3, 1833, battle had been joined between the president and pro-bank forces. Four years before the bank's expiration date in 1836, Congress voted to recharter it. Jackson vetoed the bank recharter bill. In a message to Congress, he explained his reasons. The National Bank, said Jackson, represented an invasion of states' rights and was a monopoly that would favor the rich and foreign investors over hardworking farmers, mechanics, and shopkeepers. The bank, he declared, led to the "prostitution of our government to the advancement of the few at the expense of the many."

Congress could not override the president's veto, but the bank fight was far from over. The bank's rechartering deadline of 1836 lay ahead. Who would prevail then, none could say. Jackson, however, did not want to wait another four years to find out. He knew there was more than one way to skin a rat—and he came up with a way of killing the bank with or without congressional approval. In 1833, Jackson ordered his treasury secretary to remove all government funds from the Bank of the United States and deposit them in local banks. Without government deposits, the Bank of the United States could not operate, and it closed its doors.

Yet, though he had killed the national bank, Jackson unwittingly helped establish the very monopolistic forces he had hoped to subdue. Clever financiers soon reestablished themselves—this time on Wall Street in New York City—and laid the foundations of a financial power more far-reaching and unshakeable than that of that "monster," the Bank of the United States.

Trails of Tears

Democracy exacerbated a problem that had bedeviled European Americans since the days of Columbus—what to do about the Native Americans? France had more or less left the Indians to their ancestral ways. The French had traded with them, sent missionaries to them, but otherwise left them alone. Spain's policy, on the other hand, was to draw the Indians into Spanish society—to make them equal subjects (in theory, at least) of the Spanish crown. The monarchical, authoritarian Spanish regime could control, to some extent, the greed and cruelty of its white subjects in America. Too, the Spanish government encouraged, and Spanish settlers did not oppose, intermarriage with Indians, with the result that the majority of Latin Americans came to be neither pure European nor pure Indian, but a mix—*mestizo*.

In democratic Anglo America, the same solutions France and Spain had used were not so ready to hand. For one, the American frontiersman had a seemingly limitless hunger for land. Indian lands, though guaranteed by federal treaties, proved too tempting to the hordes of settlers who were continually crossing the Appalachians. Whites encroached on Indian lands, settled on them, and treated the "savages" cruelly, even murdering them when it suited their purposes. The federal government was generally powerless to hinder violations of its treaties; its authority came from the very people who perpetrated the outrages.

Intermarriage with Indians, as well as blacks, was repugnant to most Anglo-Americans, though some might use Indian and black women for pleasure. Two very different races, very different cultures, vied for the same land; and, lacking a spirit of accommodation, one or the other had to be the loser.

Those in the U.S. government who were friendly to the Indians formulated the only policy they thought could save them from extermination. The government, they said, should give eastern tribes lands west of the Mississippi in return for the lands they vacated in the East. A removal policy was first formulated under President Monroe that granted the option of citizenship to half-breeds and full-blooded tribesmen with well-developed farms; all other Indians would receive compensation for their lands and be moved west—voluntarily, it was said. The humane John Quincy Adams showed little sympathy for this policy, and little was done about it during his administration. But with Jackson, the sinewy champion of the democratic frontiersman, the removal policy took on new life.

In 1830, Congress passed the Indian Removal Act, authorizing the president to give eastern Indians lands for settlement in the unorganized Louisiana Territory. The act stipulated that the president would compensate Indians for their old lands, including any improvements they had made on them, and that he would pay all the expenses of their removal, plus the amount needed for one year's subsistence in their new home. For his part, Jackson, who approved the act, promised that he would force no tribe to leave its lands involuntarily.

Black Hawk

Black Hawk

Because the culture of the tribes in the "Old Northwest" was semi-nomadic, their clash with white settlers and their settled farming culture was severe. Between 1829 and 1843, the nations of the Shawnee, Delaware, Wyandot, and others accepted offers of removal to the new West. But unscrupulous federal agents often cheated these Indians of the just compensation for their lands. Some agents got chiefs drunk and convinced them to sign away their lands; other agents simply did not pay them what their lands were worth.

Moreover, the journey west was fraught with hardship; for being used to living off the land, the Indians were not in the habit of making sufficient provision for the future. Some could not make the journey in one season and so were exposed to bitter winter weather that killed many Indians. Cholera and measles took their toll, and tribes arrived in their new homes with their numbers significantly reduced. Buying the equipment needed to farm the land the government had given them exhausted their resources, and the tribes were reduced to the most abject poverty.

In 1829, a portion of the Sauk and Fox nation in Illinois Territory had agreed to move west of the Mississippi. Black Hawk, a chief of the Sauk and Fox, however, refused to leave his ancestral tribal seat at the mouth of the Rock River in Illinois. In his youth, the 63-year old chief had distinguished himself as a mighty warrior and had fought on the side of the British during the War of 1812. In 1816, he, though not a chief, had signed a treaty that in part affirmed an 1804 treaty in which his people had surrendered their lands to the United States. Black Hawk, however, later said he had not known that the 1816 treaty ceded any land at all.

Black Hawk made alliances with other tribes to resist the whites. When white settlers arrived at the Sauk village in 1831, Black Hawk prepared to drive them out; but threatened by state militia, he and his followers escaped across the Mississippi. The militia burned the Indian village to the ground. Later that year, at a peace conference with Illinois Governor John Reynolds, Black Hawk and his followers agreed to leave Illinois forever.

In their new home, Iowa, a hard winter and the threat of the Sioux reduced the Sauk and Fox to starvation. The following spring, looking for a place to plant corn to feed his people, Black Hawk recrossed the Mississippi. The reappearance of the Sauk and Fox in Illinois alarmed Governor Reynolds; Indians friendly to the whites had told him that Black Hawk and his starving band of warriors, old men, women, and children threatened an uprising. Governor Reynolds called out the state militia; he told Black Hawk to return to Iowa. When Black Hawk refused, General Henry Atkinson, with the Sixth United States Cavalry, and General Winfield Scott with 1,000 infantry, set off in pursuit of the Indians. State militia (in which a young man named Abraham Lincoln led a company) and Indian enemies of the Sauk and Fox reinforced the regular army.

On May 14, 1832, Black Hawk and 40 warriors routed some disorganized state militia, and then began attacking isolated white settlements, killing whomever they found. In a battle on June 25, Black Hawk again defeated militia forces, but suffering heavy losses himself, fled north into Wisconsin. Black Hawk now sought peace with the whites; but when his overtures were ignored, he tried crossing the Wisconsin River, where he lost 68 warriors in a battle with whites.

Retreating with his remaining warriors and the band of starving women and children, Black Hawk arrived at the confluence of the Mississippi and Bad Axe Rivers. The Indians tried crossing the Mississippi, but a steamboat sporting a six-pounder fired a deadly hail of shot into the Indian encampment. Now the Sauk and Fox were cornered by a force of U.S. army regulars, state militia, and Indian allies led by Colonel Zachary Taylor. Though Black Hawk sent out a flag of truce, the whites attacked on August 3, 1832, slaughtering warriors, women, and children. Black Hawk himself survived the battle, but his branch of the Sauk and Fox was annihilated.

Following Black Hawk's defeat, the United States government seized all Sauk and Fox land in Illinois and eastern Iowa. Terrified by what happened to Black Hawk and his people, other tribes fled Illinois and Wisconsin for the West.

The Five Civilized Tribes

Unlike other Indian tribes in Anglo America, the Choctaw, Creek, Chickasaw, Cherokee, and Seminole of the old South had adopted much of white culture; they had established farmsteads and, in many cases, embraced the Christian faith. Still, these five "civilized tribes," as they were called, were in the way of white settlement. Despite federal treaties, the states of Georgia, Alabama, and Mississippi claimed they had jurisdiction over tribal lands, and they doled them out to white settlers.

Sequoyah, by C.B. King, 1836

As with the native peoples in the North, the removal of the southern tribes to the West brought suffering and death. The Choctaw in Mississippi were the first to accept the federal offer of resettlement in the Indian Territory and by 1833 had removed to their new lands in what is now Oklahoma. In 1832, the Creek in Alabama signed a treaty and followed the Choctaw west. Their case had been desperate: white settlers had encroached on their land, sold them whiskey, and destroyed their property. When false reports of a Creek uprising spread, federal troops rounded up the Creek and forced them to move west. The Chickasaw of Mississippi fared better, though many of their people died on the long trek to their new home.

The Cherokee, whose lands lay in northern Georgia, eastern Tennessee, western North Carolina, and northern Alabama were the most civilized of the civilized tribes. George Gist, a half-breed whose Indian name was Sequoya, had invented a Cherokee alphabet, allowing his people to print a Bible, various books, and a weekly newspaper, the *Cherokee Phoenix*, all in the Cherokee language. Many Cherokee had become Christian and had built roads, houses, and churches. They even drew up their own constitution and had an elected legislature to govern their affairs.

John Ross in 1838

White settlers, however, had long been encroaching on Cherokee lands. In 1828, gold was discovered in Cherokee country, and white encroachments on tribal lands increased until, by 1830, about 3,000 white settlers were occupying Cherokee lands. The legislature of Georgia for its part ignored a 1791 federal treaty that had acknowledged the Cherokee as an independent nation; instead, the state encouraged the dispossession of the Cherokee. In 1832, the Supreme Court under Chief Justice Marshall ruled that Georgia had no authority over the Cherokee because they constituted a sovereign nation; but the state legislature denounced the court and ignored the ruling. In this case, President Jackson did not back federal authority with threats of force, or anything else; he took Georgia's side. "John Marshall has made his decision," Old Hickory said. "Now let him enforce it."

When Georgia held a lottery to dispose of Cherokee lands to whites, a delegation under Chief John Ross went to Washington in 1835 to plead the Indians' case. Ross, whose Indian name was Coowes Coowe, was the son of a Scottish loyalist and a mother who was one-fourth Cherokee. The Cherokee returned with a treaty of removal that they submitted to a tribal council that met at Red Clay, Tennessee. Ross and others opposed the treaty, and the entire council rejected it. To prevent Ross' return to Washington, Georgia officials had him imprisoned, and to hide this breach of justice, suppressed the publication of the *Cherokee Phoenix*.

For the Cherokee, a period of terror followed. Whites, including justices of the peace, crossed into Cherokee territory; they destroyed property, assaulted and flogged Cherokee men and women with cowhide, hickory sticks, and clubs. But though the Cherokee suffered abuse and murder, the majority under John Ross held fast—they would not leave their lands. Finally, in order to avoid intervening in state affairs and so risk another secession movement—and to save the Cherokee from extermination—the federal government decided to break its treaty with the Cherokee and force them to move west.

In May 1838, General Winfield Scott, commanding U.S. forces, began the forced expatriation of the Cherokee to Indian Territory. According to an eyewitness, soldiers "were sent to search out with rifle and bayonet every small cabin hidden away in the coves or by the sides of mountain streams." Indian men "were seized in their fields or going along the road, women were taken from their [spinning] wheels and children from their play." Roughly 15,000 Cherokee were forced to follow their "trail of tears"; and a sorrowful trail it proved to be. By the time they reached Indian Territory, about 4,000 Cherokee had died. But the loss of their ancestral lands was as bitter as death to them. "My poor and unhappy countrymen," lamented one Cherokee, were "driven by brutal power from all they loved and cherished in the land of their fathers to gratify the cravings of avarice."

Farther south, in Florida, the Seminole had also signed a treaty of removal with the U.S. government. The treaty however presented a major stumbling block to the Seminole—it stipulated that all blacks living among them would be sold into slavery. Many escaped slaves had found refuge among the Seminole and had married Indian women; and their chief, Osceola, refused to abide by the treaty. Jackson, not one to back down, especially to "savages," told the Seminole that they must go willingly, or in chains.

The Seminole would not go willingly or in chains. The war that followed was bloody. Poorly armed, the Indians fought guerrilla-style in the swamps and thick forests against a vastly superior American force. Still, Osceola was able to destroy Fort King, killing its commander, Wiley Thompson, who had taken Osceola's half-black wife prisoner. Then began raids on plantations, so effective that the civilian population fled to the cities and area forts. In the spring of 1837, U.S. general Thomas Jessup met the Seminole at a peace conference at Fort Dade. Assured that they and their black members could leave Florida peacefully, the tribe signed a treaty of removal. But when white slave owners appeared at the fort, the Seminole, smelling treachery, repudiated the peace and again took to the warpath.

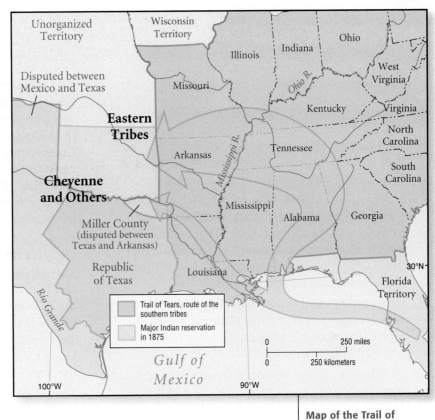

Map of the Trail of Tears

Finally, the army adopted a more devious measure. In the fall of 1837, General Jessup met with Osceola under a flag of truce. While Jessup spoke with the chief, his men quietly surrounded the Seminole camp. Osceola and his men were taken prisoner and sent to Fort Moultrie in South Carolina.

The capture of Osceola, however did not end the Seminole resistance. The war would last another five years until the United States, in desperation, simply gave up the struggle. The war had cost the United States government $20 million and the lives of 1,500 soldiers, not to mention the untold numbers of civilian dead. Some of the Seminole finally did remove to Indian Territory, though a large number remained in Florida, living in the depths of the Everglades swamps. No peace treaty had been signed, so these Seminole remained officially at war with the United States well into the 20th century.

Osceola

Osceola himself died only a few months after arriving at Fort Moultrie. He had been treated with every respect, been allowed to use the officers quarters, and had free rein of the fort. He had become something of a celebrity, sitting to have his portrait painted by the famous artist George Catlin and mixing with the finest of Charleston society. Yet, despite all the dinners, the plays, and the attention received from prominent whites, Osceola remained a stranger, a tragic figure. One woman named Mary Boykin, who had seen him at the theater in early January 1838, painted with her pen this portrait of the chieftain:

> His was the saddest face I ever saw. Under that red skin it seems there was a heart to be broken . . . For the poor savage—there is no friend. It seemed to me that my country had not dealt magnanimously with these aborigines of the soil. And I found the dignified Osceola a sad spectacle.

Chapter 13 Review

Summary

- After the death of her husband, Elizabeth Ann Seton became Catholic and opened a school for girls in Baltimore. She was joined by other women, and they adopted the rule of the Sisters of Charity of St. Vincent de Paul.

- John England, Catholic bishop of Charleston, South Carolina, favored reforms that would render the expression of the Catholic faith better assimilated to American principles. His spirit of accommodation came to dominate a large section of the American Catholic Church.

- Other bishops and priests, including Benedict Joseph Flaget and Demetrius Gallitzin, worked hard among the pioneer Catholics, founding seminaries and Catholic settlements.

- Florida was a troublesome place, and the government had problems with the Seminole and the blacks, particularly from the Negro Fort. U.S. troops destroyed the Negro Fort in 1816, but trouble again arose from the Seminoles. The first war against the Seminole finally ended in 1818, and Spain ceded all of East Florida to the United States. Florida formally became a territory in 1821.

- After the War of 1812, British products again flooded the American market, jeopardizing infant American industries. Many citizens demanded tariffs on imported goods and Congress approved a tariff bill.

- In 1816 Calhoun and Clay began supporting the rechartering of the Bank of the United States. In 1819, in *McCulloch v. Maryland*, Maryland argued that Congress had no power to charter a bank. Chief Justice Marshall and the Supreme Court disagreed. In his decision, Marshall argued that the union is the government of the people, that it "emanates from them. Its powers are granted by them and are to be exercised directly on them, and for their benefit."

- James Monroe won the elections of 1816 and 1820. The Monroe years have been called "The Era of Good Feelings" because there was remarkable political unity and a generally good economy in the United States.

- The year 1819 awakened the rivalry between the North and the South. In the dispute over whether Missouri should be a slave or free state, Congress in 1820 passed a compromise bill (the Missouri Compromise) and allowed Missouri to submit its constitution, slavery and all, to Congress, while admitting Maine as a free state, thus maintaining an equal representation of North and South in the Senate.

- Fernando VII of Spain, with the help of King Louis XVIII of France, overthrew the power of the Spanish parliament, the Cortes. It was rumored that Fernando, with the French, would invade the New World, so Great Britain approached the United States in 1823 and suggested an alliance. This resulted in the Monroe Doctrine, in which the United States told Europe that its days of colonizing the Americas were over.

- The election of 1824 saw several different factions dividing the Republican Party. John Quincy Adams won the election after it was thrown to the House of Representatives.

- Andrew Jackson defeated Adams in the election of 1828, and he purged the government of Adams' appointees. Such a thorough purge was something new, but it would become the standard practice in future administrations.

- South Carolina was struggling economically, which it blamed on tariffs on foreign imports. After Congress passed the Tariff of 1828, the "Tariff of Abominations," John Calhoun published his thoughts on a new political doctrine called "Nullification." Congress removed sections of the Tariff of Abominations, but this did not satisfy South Carolina, and a state convention passed an order of nullification. When South Carolina threatened secession, Congress passed a new tariff bill as well as a force bill in 1833. South Carolina repealed the ordinance of nullification.

- The election campaign of 1832 found the Republicans split into rival parties, with Jackson's wing calling itself the Democratic Party. The other wing called itself the National Republican Party.

- To destroy the Bank of the United States, which Congress rechartered in 1832, President Jackson ordered his treasury secretary to remove all government funds from the bank and deposit them in local banks. Without government deposits, the Bank of the United States could not operate, and it closed its doors.

- In 1830 Congress passed the Indian Removal Act to allow whites to settle in the West without the resistance of the native Indians. Many of the tribes went peacefully, but some of them fought back, including the Sauk and Fox under Black Hawk, the Cherokee, and the Seminole. All but the Seminole were finally forced to remove to the new Indian Territory in the West.

Key Concepts

Missouri Compromise: a bill voted into law by Congress in 1820 that allowed Missouri to submit its constitution, slavery and all, to Congress; at the same time, it admitted Maine as a free state. It drew a line across the country. To the north of the line, no slave states could be formed while slavery was permitted in the territories to the south of this line. The compromise help quiet North-South sectional strife for another 30 years.

Monroe Doctrine: President James Monroe's declaration that any attempt by European nations to exercise hegemony in the Americas would be considered dangerous to the peace and safety of the United States. The doctrine declared that American territories that had won their independence would thenceforth be presumed free from European interference.

tariff: a duty placed on the price of imported or exported goods

Nullification: a legal theory developed by John C. Calhoun that states that a state has the right to nullify, or invalidate, within its borders any federal law that the state has deemed unconstitutional.

Dates to Remember

1808: Elizabeth Ann Seton arrives in Baltimore and opens her school for girls.

1819: Spain cedes all of East Florida to the United States.

1820: Congress passes the Missouri Compromise.

1823: James Monroe delivers the Monroe Doctrine.

1828: Congress passes the "Tariff of Abominations," and Calhoun publishes his nullification doctrine.

1830: Congress passes the Indian Removal Act.

1833: Congress passes the Force Bill, and South Carolina repeals its ordinance of nullification.

Central Characters

Elizabeth Ann Seton (1774–1821): first native-born American to be canonized by the Catholic Church and the founder of the Sisters of Charity

John England (1786–1842): an American bishop who favored reforms that would render the expression of the Catholic faith in the United States better assimilated to American principles

James Monroe (1758–1831): fifth president of the United States. Monroe issued the Monroe Doctrine and presided over the period called the "Era of Good Feelings"

Andrew Jackson (1767–1845): military hero and the seventh president of the United States. Jackson was the first president to come from the West and the first to gain office by a direct appeal to the mass of voters. He founded the Democratic Party.

John C. Calhoun (1782–1850): vice president in Jackson's first administration and creator of the Nullification doctrine

Questions for Review

1. What are Elizabeth Ann Seton's greatest contributions to the American Catholic Church?

2. What compromised the unity of the American Catholic Church in the early 19th century?

3. Why did Bishop England want to assimilate the Catholic faith to American principles?

4. Why did Congress agree to lay tariffs on trade with Britain?

5. What was the "Era of Good Feeling," and why is it so called?

Chapter 13 Review (continued)

6. What was the predominant factor in the North's opposition to the admission of another slave state into the union in the early 19th century? Why did the South want Congress to continue to allow the admission of slaves states to the union?

7. What was the Missouri Compromise and what did it accomplish?

8. What aspects of social and political life in the 1820s and '30s showed that Americans were moving away from the ideals of republicanism?

9. Explain Calhoun's doctrine of Nullification and how it differs from the similar doctrine espoused by Thomas Jefferson and James Madison.

10. Explain the views of both the proponents and opponents of the National Bank.

11. What was the Indian Removal Act, and why was it passed? How was it abused?

Ideas in Action

1. Read a life of Elizabeth Ann Seton, Bishop John England, or of any other Catholic figure mentioned in this chapter.

2. The question of whether or not to assimilate to American culture was to become very controversial to Catholics living in America. What dangers could arise for the Catholic faith from such assimilation? What benefits? Could one detect any of those dangers or benefits already in the early 19th century?

3. Based on your understanding of the United States Constitution as a "social compact," does Calhoun's theory of Nullification make sense? Was he right that states were equal partners in the compact and thus had as much right as the federal government to interpret its terms? Why or why not?

4. Was the "democratic revolution" of Andrew Jackson a logical development of principles of the American Revolution, or did it depart from those principles? Why or why not?

5. On a map, follow the routes of the various "Trails of Tears," marking the route each nation or tribe took to the Indian Territory.

6. What alternatives to Indian removal did the federal government have, given the character of American government at the time? Were there any alternatives?

Highways and Byways

The Trail of Tears

The Trail of Tears is one of the most tragic events of American history. It evokes the collective suffering of the affected Indian peoples—the Southwest Indians and, especially, the Cherokee nation. The French philosopher Alexis de Tocqueville, who came to America in the early 19th century, said he witnessed the Choctaw removals in 1831. He writes in his book, *Democracy in America*:

> In the whole scene there was an air of ruin and destruction . . . one couldn't watch without feeling one's heart wrung. The Indians were tranquil, but somber and taciturn. We . . . watch the expulsion . . . of one of the most celebrated and ancient American peoples.

Today the Trail of Tears is a National Historic Trail, designated as such by Congress in 1987 in memory of the Indians who suffered and died during the removal. The trail includes 2,200 miles of routes that span portions of nine states and traverse both land and water.

WAR AND UNCERTAIN PEACE IN MEXICO

Part I: An Unstable Republic

Guadalupe Victoria was a hero. His years spent in the mountains, deserted even by his followers, endowed him with the aura of romance. But his glory faded during his years as president of the Republic of Mexico. Of course, his task was immense—to unite a country divided by deep class distinctions, dependent on a powerful military, simmering with opposed ideas of government and society. Moreover, the only authority recognized by New Spain in 300 years—the king of Spain—had been cast aside; why, then, would anyone respect a new, untried authority when there seemed no good reason to do so?

George Canning, by Richard Evans

The congress elected in 1823 was composed of mostly creole intellectuals enamored of Anglo-American notions of government. The problem was that Mexico had always been a country whose government was centralized in the king; it thus had no traditions of local, self-government, as had the English colonies to the north. The 1824 federalist constitution drawn up by the new congress not only provided for a decentralized, federal system but extended the suffrage to every male, including millions who could not read and, in many cases, not even speak, Spanish. Thus, fraud and coercion of voters were rampant in the first elections.

Mexico had strong factions that could resist, and did resist, government interference. The military jealously guarded its *fueros*, or traditional rights. Many of the large creole landowners had joined the revolution to be free of the power of the *gauchupines* and would brook no domination by the republican government. Then there was the Church, which held vast lands; and, while the Church devoted much of her possessions to charitable purposes—education, missions, hospitals—some, among both the secular and religious clergy, used the Church's prestige for personal enrichment.

The problem for President Victoria was that he had to keep the military happy by paying their salaries; but he had insufficient tax revenues to do that and to provide for the other needs of the country. Altogether, the government's expenses ran to about 18 million *pesos* a year, but taxes were bringing in only 9 million *pesos* annually. Victoria could not propose taxing the wealthy landowners—they would never stand for that; nor could he tax the Church, since her traditional privileges left her free of government interference in such matters. Victoria thus had to take out foreign loans, and the British government was all too willing to oblige him.

George Canning, who had become Great Britain's foreign secretary in 1822, saw Mexico as a lucrative market for British business. When Spain, in a confederacy of European nations called the Holy Alliance, had threatened to reconquer Mexico, Canning recognized Mexico's independence. Canning's diplomat in Mexico, H. G. Ward, seeing Victoria's money problems, convinced the president to accept two loans of three million pounds each from British banking houses. Though much of the money never reached Mexico, and much of it was ill spent after it did, the loans did help shore up Victoria's unstable government. But, more ominously for the future, the loans helped make Mexico a British economic satellite. Deeply in debt to Great Britain, Mexico had no choice but to allow British business interests to acquire large portions of Mexico's trade and to permit British capital to develop mines for extracting the country's rich mineral wealth. Soon, France and Germany were investing in Mexico. Though politically independent of Spain, Mexico was losing her economic freedom to northern Europe.

Federalists and Centralists

The United States' opportunity to seize some of the investment spoils from Mexico was hampered by the first U.S. ambassador to independent Mexico, Joel Roberts Poinsett. Poinsett's zeal for Anglo-American style democracy and his interference in Mexican politics had made him suspect to the Mexicans. Some wondered if the ambassador were trying to destabilize Mexico so that the United States could seize some of Mexico's northern states. Such fears were not assuaged when, in 1827, Poinsett suggested the sale of Texas to the United States. Many Mexicans thought their neighbor to the north was not to be trusted.

Poinsett's introduction of York Rite Masonry helped organize the Liberal faction in Mexican politics. Though the creole *moderados* (moderates) dominated the congress, the influence of the Liberals, called *puros* or *Yorkistas* (because they followed the York rite of Masonry), was growing. Among them were some of the most prominent intellectuals of Mexico—José Luis Mora, an economist and theoretician; Lorenzo de Zavala, the *mestizo* governor of the state of México; and Valentín Gómez Farías, a physician from Zacatecas and the leader of the *puros*.

A bust of Lucas Alamán

The most prestigious of the conservatives (called *Esconcistas,* because they followed the Scottish rite of Masonry), was Lucas Alamán. Alamán believed Mexico should continue its tradition of centralized government; he opposed the division of Mexico into states on the model of the United States. He favored bringing in a foreign monarch to rule Mexico; and if that weren't possible, he wanted to see the establishment of a home-bred authoritarian regime.

Though he had joined those who had favored overthrowing Iturbide, Nicolás Bravo shared Alamán's opinions on government. Though during the revolution Bravo had been an ardent supporter of independence and had served under Morelos, he did not favor radical social change. Now, in 1827, fearful of Poinsett's influence and the too Liberal policies of Victoria's government, Bravo mounted a rebellion, calling for a return to centralized government, the abolition of Masonic lodges, and the deportation of Poinsett. But another old revolutionary, Vicente Guerrero, leading government troops, put down the rebellion, and Bravo went into exile.

The conservative and Liberal divisions mobilized for the election of 1828. The *Esconcistas* supported the *moderado* Gómez Pedraza for president, while the *Yorkistas* backed Vicente Guerrero. Though Guerrero was the more popular candidate, Pedraza won the election with ten states to nine (each state had one vote in electing the president). It was suspected, however, that Pedraza (who had been secretary of war) had strong armed the state legislatures, and Guerrero refused to concede the election to him.

But in Veracruz, Antonio López de Santa Anna would not tolerate a Pedraza victory. Santa Anna was a political chameleon who had wavered between the conservatives and the Liberals. Sensing now that power lay with Liberalism, Santa Anna unfurled the banner of rebellion. Guerrero, he proclaimed, was the rightful president. "How could I see in cold blood," declared Santa Anna, with his wonted bombast, "the republic converted into a vast Inquisition? Santa Anna will die before being indifferent to such disasters." Santa Anna's proclamation was a bit premature, and government troops drove him into Oaxaca. There he barricaded himself in a monastery.

Though Victoria's term of office had not expired, it was Pedraza who responded to Santa Anna's declaration by arresting *puros*, including the governor of the Mexico City district, Lorenzo de Zavala. The arrests angered the Liberals, who, across the country rose in rebellion against Pedraza. Led by Zavala, soldiers at the prison of La Acordada in Mexico City rebelled in November, and for four days fighting raged in the city streets. The *léperos*, ever ready to further the rule of chaos, attacked and burned El Parián Market, the chief marketplace of the capital, destroying the many shops of foreign merchants there. From early morning until late afternoon of December 4, 1828, the *léperos* controlled the city. Finally Pedraza, finding his cause hopeless, fled the city and went into exile. The triumphant Liberals, led by Zavala, marched into the presidential palace, abandoned by all save President Victoria, the impotent figurehead of the republic.

By the end of January 1829, the rebellion was over. Congress met and proclaimed Guerrero president and a conservative, Anastasio Bustamante, vice-president. Peace was restored, but not for long.

Vicente Guerrero, a posthumous portrait from 1850, by Anacleto Escutia

The Hero of Tampico

The same year Guerrero became president, a fleet of Spanish ships carrying Spanish troops set sail from Cuba, bound for Mexico. Their quest, by order of King Fernando VII, was to land on the coast of Mexico and reconquer the country for Spain. Land they did, on the Tamaulipas coast, and they seized the fortress of Tampico. There the fleet abandoned the army (the admiral had quarreled with its commander) and returned to Cuba. At Tampico, the Spanish troops, unused to the sultry, swampy coast, soon succumbed to yellow fever, and many died.

The news of the invasion caused alarm in Mexico City. President Guerrero, given near dictatorial powers because of the danger, told General Santa Anna at Veracruz, just down the coast from Tampico, to advance against the invader. Fortunately for Santa Anna, by the time he reached Tampico, the Spanish force had been so reduced by disease that it surrendered to him after only a brief engagement.

The victory, such as it was, made Santa Anna suddenly very popular—the people haled him the "Hero of Tampico!" He had saved the fatherland from the hated *gauchupines*! Santa Anna now awaited an opportune moment to use his newly won fame to advance his political fortunes.

El Parián Market in Mexico City, early 19th century

He did not need to wait long. President Guerrero, a *mestizo* of Spanish, Indian, and African heritage who did not speak Spanish well, faced stiff opposition from the creole conservative centralists. It was no secret that the president hated creole society, yet he conducted no purges of his opponents; rather, he had pardoned those who had opposed him and allowed Nicolás Bravo back into the country. Still, the conservatives denounced Guerrero, saying he was an atheist, a Mason, and an enemy of religion. On a misty night in late 1829, troops commanded by Vice President Bustamante crept along the Guadalupe causeway that led into Mexico City and seized the capital. Guerrero fled the city and took refuge in the mountains of the south where, years before, he had waged guerrilla war against Spanish troops.

Learning of the *coup d'état*, Santa Anna, who fancied himself the "Napoleon of the West," issued a dramatic pronouncement against Bustamante and the conservatives: "I shall stubbornly oppose those who, on any pretext whatever, would temerariously hurl from the presidential chair the Illustrious General, Citizen Vicente Guerrero, and they will succeed in doing so only over my dead body, when I shall have perished defending the Chief Magistrate of the Nation!"

Santa Anna's bluster, though, was mistimed. Soon the entire country, with the exception of only a few Liberals under General Juan Alvarez, accepted Bustamante as president. Giving way to necessity, Santa Anna retired to Manga de Clavo, his estate near Veracruz, and bided his time.

Bustamante's administration was able to bring an end to banditry and smuggling and stabilize government finances. But, though reluctant to use violence against political opponents, Bustamante found that the conservatives who surrounded him, including Lucas Alamán, wanted drastic measures taken against Liberals. In the name of public order, troops armed with bayonets and cannon surrounded congress. The army removed Liberal governors and legislatures in 11 states, suppressed newspapers, and jailed, shot, or exiled leaders of the *puros*.

But the government could do little about Guerrero, who, with General Juan Alvarez, was ensconced in the southern mountains. Guerrero, with his old comrades, resisted the government until, after about a year, General Bravo defeated him in battle at Chilpancingo. Guerrero retired to Acapulco, where he took refuge on an Italian ship, the *Colombo*, commanded by a friend. But the captain, loving money more than friendship, took Guerrero prisoner and sold him to the government for 50,000 gold *pesos*. Proclaimed mentally incapable of governing, Guerrero was imprisoned. On February 14, 1831, he repeated the story of Hidalgo and Morelos, dying by firing squad in Cuilapa, in the state of Michoacán.

The execution of Guerrero and the repression of Liberals sparked a rebellion of the northern states in 1832. Santa Anna, again seeing an opportunity, seized Veracruz and proclaimed the *moderado* Gómez Pedraza (whose term would have ended that year) the rightful president. Seeing resistance hopeless, Bustamante relinquished power and went into exile. After installing Gómez Pedraza as provisional president on January 3, 1833, Congress proclaimed Santa Anna "Liberator of the Republic" and "Conqueror of the Spaniards." On March 30 they elected him president and the radical Liberal, Valentín Gómez Farías, vice president.

Santa Anna loved pageantry. As he triumphantly entered the capital, four carriages filled with ladies holding pictures and tokens of his victories greeted him. However, though loving the dash and grandeur involved in seizing power, the Hero of Tampico did not relish the tedious duties associated with actual governing. On inauguration day, Santa Anna informed Congress that he was too sick to attend the ceremonies and returned to his hacienda, Manga de Clavo, to revel in the joys of cock-fighting and gambling. Santa Anna was still president, but the actual job of governing fell to Gómez Farías.

Thus, Gómez Farías had free reign to put through his radical agenda. First, in the summer and autumn of 1833, Congress issued indictments against members of Bustamante's government, chasing Lucas Alamán into hiding. Then the vice president pushed through Congress a series of laws designed to weaken the Church's power. These laws abolished the compulsory payment of tithes to the Church; allowed monks and nuns to renounce their vows; transferred the oversight of education from the Church to the state; and ordered the secularization of the missions in California. The government enforced these measures even though the Constitution of 1824 had pledged Mexico to protect the Catholic religion "by wise and just laws, and prohibit the exercise of any other whatever."

Gómez Farías next went after the military. Congress reduced the size of the army and the number of officers and deprived the military of its *fueros*. Such acts roused the ire of one Colonel Ignacio Escalada; he called on "the Illustrious Conqueror of the Spaniards, General Don Antonio López de Santa Anna" to rise and defend the "privileges of the clergy and the army, which are threatened by the usurping authorities." Thus the conservatives, crying *Religión y Fueros!* called on the Liberal Santa Anna to defend traditional rights. Santa Anna, however, who from time to time assumed presidential powers in the capital, took no action against Gómez Farías' policies. Unsure which way the political wind blew, Santa Anna retired once again to Manga de Clavo. He only awaited a sign to indicate the course he should follow.

He soon received his sign. In April 1834, the military garrison at Cuernevaca issued a plan, calling for the expulsion of the Liberals and the protection of religion. Moreover, the Church pronounced its support for the Napoleon of the West. Throughout Mexico, provincial leaders lined up behind Santa Anna, who had discovered that he was a conservative. Soon Gómez Farías was in flight to New Orleans, and the Liberal government was scattered. Santa Anna marched into Mexico City, dismissed Congress, and for the next eight months ruled as military dictator, abolishing state legislatures and governors and replacing them with generals.

Valentín Gómez Farías

By December 1834, Santa Anna had completely purged the government of Liberals. He called a new congress, whose members he hand-picked himself. The new congress replaced the republican Constitution of 1824 with a new instrument that set up a *Poder Conservador*—a committee of citizens, who were to see to it that the executive, legislative, and judicial branches did not encroach on each other. The *Poder* had supreme power and was accountable to no one—not even Congress. The *Poder Conservador* would, in the next few years, be the arbiter of who should be president.

But again growing tired of government (and, perhaps, fearing to lose the good graces of his supporters if he remained too long at the reins of government), Santa Anna again retired to Manga de Clavo, leaving the government in the hands of his vice-president, General Miguel Francisco Barragán.

Remember the Alamo!

The large number of Anglo-Americans who had settled in a northern territory of Mexico called Tejas were unhappy. The great upheavals in Mexico, along with the inefficiency of Mexican officials, annoyed and frustrated them. Then there was the sheer foreignness of Mexican law. For one thing, it did not provide for trial by jury, a right every Anglo-American held dear—it had never been a part of Spanish legal tradition. And there was no **common law**. Furthermore, Tejas (or, as the Anglo settlers called it, Texas) was not even its own state but formed the northern portion of Coahuilla. Anglo-Texans chafed—they could not even be decently self-governing!

common law: a body of law that arises from custom or precedent—prior judicial interpretations of written law

Yet, these "Texians," as they were called, had chosen to emigrate from their native country and into the rich Mexican lands watered by the Trinity, Brazos, and Colorado Rivers, so they really couldn't complain—not too much. But by 1833, the Anglo-Americans greatly outnumbered Mexicans (called *Tejanos*) in Texas. Before 1823, there had been about 3,000 non-Indian *Tejanos* in Texas; ten years later, largely on account of Anglo immigration, the number of non-Indians had grown to between 20,000 and 30,000.

In the last years of her rule, Spain had encouraged immigration of U.S. born Americans of English, Irish, and Scots Irish extraction to Texas, hoping by this means (oddly enough) to keep the United States from seizing the largely unpopulated territory. In 1821, a Connecticut Yankee named Moses Austin had received a large land grant in Texas from the Spanish king. Austin had been something of a rolling stone: he had been a dry-goods merchant in Philadelphia and Richmond, and after buying lead mines in Virginia, he went to Missouri to pioneer lead mining there. In St. Louis, he had become a banker before setting his sights on Texas.

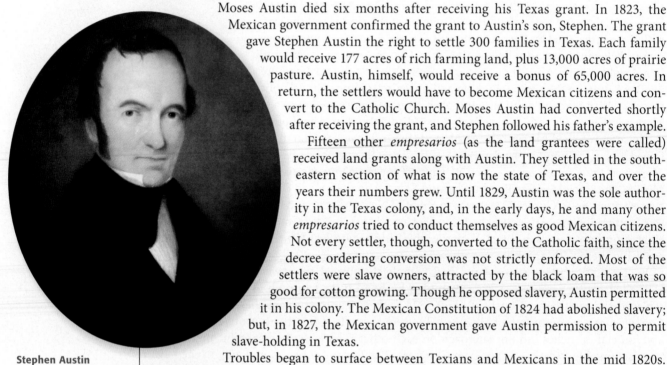

Stephen Austin

Moses Austin died six months after receiving his Texas grant. In 1823, the Mexican government confirmed the grant to Austin's son, Stephen. The grant gave Stephen Austin the right to settle 300 families in Texas. Each family would receive 177 acres of rich farming land, plus 13,000 acres of prairie pasture. Austin, himself, would receive a bonus of 65,000 acres. In return, the settlers would have to become Mexican citizens and convert to the Catholic Church. Moses Austin had converted shortly after receiving the grant, and Stephen followed his father's example.

Fifteen other *empresarios* (as the land grantees were called) received land grants along with Austin. They settled in the southeastern section of what is now the state of Texas, and over the years their numbers grew. Until 1829, Austin was the sole authority in the Texas colony, and, in the early days, he and many other *empresarios* tried to conduct themselves as good Mexican citizens. Not every settler, though, converted to the Catholic faith, since the decree ordering conversion was not strictly enforced. Most of the settlers were slave owners, attracted by the black loam that was so good for cotton growing. Though he opposed slavery, Austin permitted it in his colony. The Mexican Constitution of 1824 had abolished slavery; but, in 1827, the Mexican government gave Austin permission to permit slave-holding in Texas.

Troubles began to surface between Texians and Mexicans in the mid 1820s. Mexico revoked a land grant to an *empresario* in Nacogdoches, Haden Edwards, who had attempted to seize *Tejano* lands for Anglo settlers. His followers protested and proclaimed the independent Republic of Fredonia, complete with its own red and white flag. The would-be revolutionaries, however, fled when the Mexican army arrived on the scene to put down the rebellion.

The Fredonia episode, however, brought about a change in Mexican policy toward Anglo settlement. Lucas Alamán, for one, thought it foolish to allow so many Anglos into Texas; it would end, he said, in the annexation of Texas to the United States. Then, in 1829, President Guerrero issued a decree abolishing slavery in Mexico, a move aimed, at least in part, at Texas, since slavery existed nowhere else in Mexico. A year later, under President Bustamante, Alamán issued another decree forbidding further Anglo settlement in Texas. The Decree of 1830 also ordered the collection of customs duties along the Texas/Louisiana border, thus burdening the trade of the Texians with the United States. The sending of troops to enforce the decree, along with a further crackdown on smuggling, drove the Texians to the verge of revolt.

Ardent federalists, the Texians, along with many *Tejanos*, bitterly disliked Bustamante's centralist regime. Texian leaders, including Stephen Austin, were Masons and had, in 1828, petitioned for the establishment of the York rite in Texas—thus showing their support for the apparently-Liberal Santa Anna's rebellion. In this way they hoped to gain some concessions from the radical Gómez Farías. Stephen Austin undertook the long, arduous journey to Mexico City to ask Farías to seek a repeal of the Law of 1830 and to make Texas a separate state from Coahuila. Farías refused Austin's request. Austin then wrote a letter to the

Texians, telling them to establish a state legislature, in spite of the government in Mexico City—for which that government threw him into prison, where he remained for a year and a half.

Among the chief motivations for Texian discontent with Mexican rule was the fear that the Mexican government might enforce the slavery decree of 1829 even in Texas. Immigrants from the United States had come to Texas to escape the poverty they had known in their home states. Texas' rich soil, so suited to cotton growing, held out to them the promise of riches. These hardscrabble farmers hoped that they, too, could become wealthy planters. This dream of riches necessitated slavery—or so the people thought. "Texas must be a slave country," wrote Stephen Austin not long after Guerrero issued his 1829 decree. "Circumstances and unavoidable necessity compels it." And, besides, said Austin, "it is the will of the people there."

The Texians, too, feared that talk of emancipation would inspire slave revolts—as had happened on the island of Santo Domingo in the Caribbean in 1813 and ended in a bloodbath for the island's white, French population. So it was that Mexico's emancipation measures inspired thoughts of revolt among the Texians. Writing from Matamoros on the Rio Grande in January 1830, Captain Henry Austin described the effects of Mexican emancipation measures on the Texians. "We have rumors here," he said, "of a revolutionary disposition in the people of Texas on account of the decree freeing all slaves in the Republic."

Meanwhile, no one was enforcing the immigration measures of the Law of 1830, and Anglos continued to pour into Texas from the U.S. Unlike earlier settlers such as Stephen Austin, who counseled peace with Mexico, many of the newcomers were unwilling to put up with Mexican rule and formed a "war party" in the territory. One of these latter was Sam Houston.

Six feet, two inches tall and broad of chest, Houston was an old friend of Andrew Jackson, had served in the Creek War, and had worked as an agent to help move a band of Cherokee from East Tennessee to Indian Territory. In 1818, after Secretary of War John C. Calhoun rebuked him for appearing before him dressed as an Indian (and for charges of official misconduct), Houston resigned as agent and went to practice law in Nashville. After serving one term in Congress, Houston was elected governor of Tennessee in 1827; but two years later, after his wife of three months left him, Houston resigned his governorship and went to live among the Cherokee. The Indians adopted him as a member of their tribe and gave him the unflattering epithet, "Big Drunk." In 1832, at the age of 39, he went to Texas, where he became a Mexican citizen and a Catholic. Houston was an important member of the convention that had petitioned the Mexican government for the separation of Texas from Coahuila.

Sam Houston, ca. 1850, by Thomas Flintoff

Revolution

In his latest transformation—into a conservative dictator—Santa Anna had decided that he had to do something about Texas. Liberalism was triumphant there. The laws were not being observed. Anglo-Americans, like a barbarian horde (that's how the Mexicans saw them), were crossing the border illegally. To remedy the situation, Santa Anna sent an army under General Martín Perfecto de Cos north to enforce obedience to the law. Learning of Santa Anna's plans from Lorenzo de Zavala, who had gone north to warn the Texians of the general's approach, Stephen Austin, now released from imprisonment, called on Texians to take up arms. Sam Houston was made general of a Texian army. In early October 1835, Cos arrived with 1,200 troops at San Antonio de Bexár; he fortified the city,

Map of Mexican Texas

including the old Franciscan mission church, San Antonio de Valero, known as the Alamo. Throughout October and November, armed Texians and some *Tejanos* arrived at San Antonio de Béxar and lay siege to the city.

On December 4, Texian colonel Benjamin R. Milam gathered the Texian army and, the next day, assaulted Cos' position in the city. For five days battle raged as the Texians pushed their way into San Antonio. Finally, on December 10, Cos surrendered. The Texians occupied the city and fortified the Alamo.

Santa Anna had had second thoughts after he sent Cos to Texas; he decided that he wanted the glory of crushing the Texian revolution for himself. Establishing his headquarters at San Luis Potosí, about 260 miles northwest of Mexico City, Santa Anna impressed Indians and other "recruits"—men who had known nothing of army service before—until he had built up a sizable force. The government had no money to finance an army, so Santa Anna took out loans at ruinous interest rates. He manufactured munitions and requisitioned horses and carts. Whipping the men into some semblance of discipline, Santa Anna drove them north across the deserts of Coahuila, toward Texas.

Those who know nothing of deserts may not understand how bitterly cold they can be in winter. Both men and animals in Santa Anna's army suffered terribly from cold, hunger, and disease. Still, the ever implacable Hero of Tampico forced them on until, having left behind many dead, the Mexican army stood, half starved, outside the walls of the Alamo.

Meanwhile, the Texians at the Alamo were quarreling over how to conduct the war and changed their commander almost daily. The garrison, numbering only about 150 men, eventually fell to the command of 27-year-old William Barrett Travis. Born in South Carolina, Travis had spent many years in Alabama, where he had become a lawyer and a Mason. Abandoning his wife, son, and unborn daughter, Travis went to Texas in 1831, where he set up a law practice and joined those who were conspiring for independence from Mexico. Houston had ordered Travis to evacuate the Alamo, but he was determined to remain. He ordered the fortification of the mission to prepare for the assault he knew would come.

Defending the Alamo with Travis were both Texians and *Tejanos*—among them the frontiersman David Crockett and James Bowie, famous for his long hunting knife. Bowie had come to Texas in 1830. Before that, both he and his brother, Rezin (pronounced like *reason*), had engaged in illegal slave smuggling in Louisiana (the pirate, Jean Lafitte, was their supplier) and in land speculation. Shortly after coming to Texas, James Bowie was baptized a Catholic and married into a prominent San Antonio family. Over the next few years he gambled, engaged in land speculation, and earned the ill will of Stephen Austin, who thought him a charlatan. Bowie, though, had distinguished himself as a brave leader in the battle of Béxar against General Cos.

David Crockett

David Crockett was a late-comer to Texas, having arrived at the lag end of 1835. Already a legendary frontiersman, Crockett had fought in the Creek Wars and had served in Congress as a representative from Tennessee, where he distinguished himself as an opponent of Jackson's Indian removal policy. When in 1835 he lost his congressional seat to a Jackson man with a peg-leg, Crockett told friends, "Since you have chosen to elect a man with a timber toe to succeed me, you may all go to hell and I will go to Texas." And to Texas he went, arriving just in time to join Colonel Travis at the Alamo.

On February 23, 1836, Santa Anna with 3,000 ragged troops laid siege to the 150 defenders of the Alamo. For two weeks, Travis refused to surrender. Finally, in the early hours of March 6, Santa Anna ordered the trumpeter to sound the *deguello*—the ancient signal used in the Spanish wars against the Moors, signifying "take no prisoners." The assault began. Travis died early on in the battle, with a single bullet through the head. Bowie, whom sickness had confined to bed, had his skull shattered by six bullets. Almost all the defenders died within a few hours, and Santa Anna commanded that those who had been captured must be shot. It is uncertain what happened to David Crockett. One account by an eyewitness, the Mexican officer José Enrique de la Peña, says that Crockett was among the captured. De la Peña continues that, after his plea for his life was refused, Crockett was bayoneted and then shot. He died bravely, without complaint.

A few days before the Alamo massacre, a convention of Texians had met at Washington-on-the-Brazos, 200 miles east of San Antonio de Béxar, and proclaimed Texas an independent republic. They appointed David Burnet provisional president, and as vice president they chose Lorenzo de Zavala, the former governor of the state of México. Sam Houston, hearing that Santa Anna's army had turned east and was terrorizing the population as it advanced, ordered a general retreat. The entire population of Texas was in flight before the victorious Santa Anna.

The grand conqueror, hearing that the provisional Texas government had removed to Harrisburg at the mouth of the San Jacinto River, thither led his force to bag Houston's army and the rebellious government at once. Santa Anna met Houston and his small army at Lynchburg Ferry on the San Jacinto, and a face-off ensued between the two armies. A day passed, and no action. Santa Anna, whose tent sat on a small rise not far from the enemy's lines, lay down to take a conqueror's well-earned *siesta*. He had posted no sentries or pickets, so the first notice he received of Houston's attack was the impassioned shout, "Remember the Alamo!" He had barely time to escape. Houston's small force, with a loss of only three dead and 18 wounded, destroyed the Mexican army—400 died, 200 were wounded, and 730 were taken prisoner. Next day, the Texians captured Santa Anna; they found him hiding in high grass, clad in a blue shirt, white trousers, and red slippers.

The Battle of San Jacinto ended the war. To assure his release, the conquered Napoleon promised to recognize the independence of Texas. Santa Anna did not return home directly but went on to Washington where he met with President Jackson. After a cordial meeting, Jackson sent Santa Anna home by ship. Arriving in Mexico, Santa Anna retired to Manga de Clavo, his loss of Texas having assured his loss of the presidency. Anastasio Bustamante succeeded Santa Anna and Barragán as president.

Though the Mexican government refused to acknowledge Texas' independence, it did nothing to win back the rebellious territory. Texas remained an independent republic.

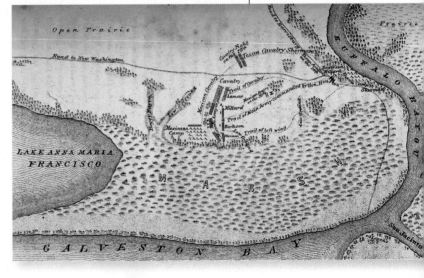

Map of the San Jacinto battle ground

Military Anarchy

Monsieur Remontel, a French citizen, owned a pastry shop in the Tacubaya section of Mexico City. One night, a group of Mexican officers entered his shop, locked him in his back room, and devoured all his pastries. The enraged pastry cook, unable to get satisfaction for his loss from the Mexican government, appealed to his own government for justice. Remontel was not the only one to complain of property loss; other French citizens in Mexico had had property destroyed when the *léperos* sacked Mexico City's El Parián market in 1828. It was ostensibly in response to its citizens' plight that France demanded compensation from Mexico—600,000 *pesos*—an amount Mexico said it could not pay. So, in 1838, a French fleet appeared off Veracruz and blockaded the port from April to November. On November 26, the fleet bombarded the fortress of San Juan de Ulúa. The fortress soon surrendered, and a new war, called the Pastry War by the Mexicans (in honor of Monsieur Remontel) commenced.

The bombardment of San Juan de Ulúa could be heard at Manga de Clavo. It had been a year since Santa Anna had returned from Texas in disgrace; now, the conqueror saw a way of redeeming his fortunes. Mounting his white horse, he rode to Veracruz and then, by skiff, paddled out to the fortress of San Juan de Ulúa to convince the French commander to surrender it. When this failed, Santa Anna returned to Manga de Clavo. Receiving a military command from President Bustamante, Santa Anna prepared his forces and then marched proudly and defiantly into Veracruz.

Bombardment of San Juan de Ulúa

Early one morning, as Santa Anna slept, the French sent a landing party into the city. Awakened by shouting and firing in the streets, Santa Anna, clad only in his underwear, barely escaped to the outskirts of the city. There he organized his forces and marched again into the city where the Mexican troops engaged French marines, who were fighting from behind a barricade. After several hours, the French began withdrawing to the fortress. Santa Anna, proclaiming victory, led a charge against the retreating foe. But then, a cannon ball, fired from a French ship, struck him below his left knee, shattering his leg.

After this brief military exchange, the French withdrew from Veracruz. (There was no need for them to remain, for the Mexican government payed the 600,000 *pesos* compensation). The now one-legged Santa Anna sent a dispatch to Mexico City announcing that he had repulsed the French advance; he had saved the Fatherland! The timing was perfect. Mexico was suffering, not only from the Pastry War, but from a severe financial crisis. Moreover, Indians were attacking creole villages in Sonora and Chihuahua; and Yucatan in the south and Mexican states in the north were threatening secession. Two generals, José Urrea and José Antonio Mejía, had risen up in revolt, threatening Bustamante's government. Only the "Hero [now] of Veracruz" could save the country. The *Poder Conservador* begged him, once again, to take up the reins of government.

Carried by carriage to the capital, Santa Anna played the part of the a hero injured in his country's services. Pallid and unsmiling, languidly waving his hand, Santa Anna witnessed the affection of his country: rockets were fired, speeches were given; triumphal arches adorned his route. Upon Santa Anna's arrival in the capital, the *Poder Conservador* proclaimed him *Benemerito de la Patria* ("Well Deserving of the Fatherland") and made him president. Hearing that General Mejía had taken Veracruz, Santa Anna sent troops against him and defeated the rebel. Condemned to execution, Mejía said, "Santa Anna is doing to me what I should have done to him; only he is shooting me three hours after my capture, while I should have shot him in three minutes!"

It did not take long, however, before Santa Anna grew bored with government; once again he returned to Manga de Clavo. No sooner had he gone than Nicolás Bravo, whom he had left in charge, faced a new insurrection. Gómez Farías had returned from exile in New Orleans and called for a restoration of the federal Constitution of 1824. For 11 days fighting raged in the streets of Mexico City until it became clear that neither side could prevail—and that neither side had received the blessing of Santa Anna. Both sides proclaimed a truce, and Gómez Farías went again into exile while Anastasio Bustamante re-assumed the presidency.

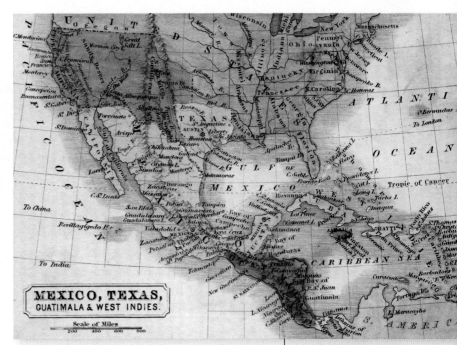

Mexico after the Texas Revolution

But Bustamante was unable to raise enough money to pay the military, and in 1841, he faced another revolt. Generals Mariano Paredes and Gabriel Valencia issued a proclamation against the government. They were soon joined by Santa Anna himself. Marching from Veracruz, *El Benemerito de la Patria* entered the capital; for 28 days street fighting rocked the city. In desperation, the conservative Bustamante sought Liberal support by proclaiming a restoration of the Constitution of 1824, but it was too late. Bustamante fled into exile. Santa Anna, riding triumphantly into the city, assumed the office of dictator.

With absolute power at his disposal, Santa Anna's extravagance fully blossomed. His revenues far exceeded the exactions of his predecessors. He coerced loans from the Church, raised import duties by 20 percent, sold mining concessions to English investors. With the increased revenue he built a new theater in the capital, *El Gran Teatro de Santa Anna*; raised a statue of himself, with one hand pointed towards Texas (and, it was noted, the national mint); paved the capital's streets; built a new market; and recruited a personal bodyguard of 1,200 men, decking them out in sumptuous uniforms. The year 1842 was a continual fiesta, with "His Serene Highness" (as Santa Anna was addressed) at the helm. His left leg was disinterred from its burial place at Manga de Clavo and carried in state to the capital, where it was re-interred in the cathedral cemetery. The capital reveled in holidays, celebrating Santa Anna's birthday, independence day, and other occasions. Solemn Masses were sung in thanksgiving.

The taxation to provide for all this pageantry, however, drained the country's wealth, and discontent swelled. With the election of a *moderado* congress in June 1842, and tired of the complaints issuing from all quarters, Santa Anna again returned to Manga de Clavo, leaving Nicolás Bravo at the head of government. Bravo dissolved Congress and established a *Junta* of Notables that, in 1843, drew up a new constitution that established the president as a virtual dictator. In January 1844, the *junta* asked Santa Anna to resume the presidency. But his return to Mexico City was short-lived; once again, he retired, leaving General Valentín Canalizo in charge.

When, in June 1844, the news that Texas was again requesting admission to the United States reached Mexico City, Santa Anna once more took power. With a loan of 3 million *pesos* coerced from unknown sources, Santa Anna ordered a levy of 30,000 soldiers, mostly Indians pressed into service, to lead in war against the United States. This time, however, his extravagance had reached its limit, and General Mariano Paredes proclaimed a revolution against him in Jalisco.

Gathering his army, Santa Anna marched against Paredes, but bad news from the capital forced his return. Mexico City had risen against him; the *léperos* had even disinterred his leg and was dragging it ignominiously through the streets! Little by little, and then in large numbers, Santa Anna's own troops deserted him. Fleeing with only his cook and two adjutants in tow, Santa Anna sought refuge in the mountains of Veracruz. There he was discovered and captured. Instead of shooting him, however, the government allowed *El Benemerito de la Patria* to go into exile in Havana, Cuba, where he was supposed to remain for the next ten years.

A California Interlude

Back in January 1822, Governor Sola of Alta California had written the governor of Baja California about certain documents he had received reporting the progress of the revolution in Mexico. "Such documents," in Sola's opinion, "are printed in a country of dreamers, since independence is a dream. Day by day their presses will turn out absurdities by the thousand; but you and I, aware that the immortal, incomparable Spanish nation has many and great resources with which to make herself respected, must look with contempt on such absurd views."

Map of Mexican "Upper or New California" in 1838, showing locations of missions, settlements, and presidios

Sola was no prophet. Not three months had passed since he wrote the letter when he received dispatches from Mexico announcing the establishment of Iturbide's regency. By April 9, 1822, members of the ruling *junta* of California decided that they should swallow their royalist scruples and take the oath of allegiance to Mexico. It had only been two years since they had sworn allegiance to the Spanish Constitution of 1812; but they knew that, despite its "many and great resources," Spain could not hold California if she did not hold Mexico. Necessity was, after all, necessity.

Convincing the friars might be more difficult, for, if royalist sentiment was strong among *Californios* as a whole, it was strongest among the Franciscans. Acknowledging Mexican independence was a struggle for them; but some, like Fray Vicente Sarriá, after much reflection, took the oath. "May God grant that all may be for the best," said Fray Vicente. On April 11, the *junta* and the soldiers gathered at Governor Sola's house in Monterey and formally took the oath. Fray Mariano Payeras, prefect of the missions, then preached a sermon, and the day ended with *vivas*, the firing of guns, and music.

More festive still were the celebrations when Don Agustín's representative, the cleric Agustín Fernandez de San Vicente, arrived in Monterey in late September. Fernandez officiated at the ceremony at which the Spanish flag was lowered and the Mexican flag raised. "*Viva la Indepencia Mejicana!*" they cried, to the firing of artillery and the music of drum and fife. "*Viva el Emperador Agustín I!*" Church services, then races and feasting followed, and the day concluded with a grand ball.

A little over a year later, Luis Argüello, who had replaced Sola as governor, learned that eight months earlier *El Emperador* Agustín I had resigned and a new government was in place. What this all meant was, perhaps, unclear to Don Luis. Under Agustín I, the *Californios* had obtained representation in the Mexican congress and had established their own assembly, the *diputación*. What changes would the new government bring? Whatever the future, Don Luis did what he had to do—he formally acknowledged the new federalist government of Guadalupe Victoria.

Argüello was only a provisional governor. In 1825, Colonel José María Echeandía arrived from Mexico to replace him. Echeandía had not been long in California before he began to strike at the integrity of the missions by commencing a process of secularization. His first move, on July 25, 1826, was to proclaim the emancipation of any neophytes who could prove capable of functioning as full citizens of Mexico. The immediate effects of the decree were not promising. The decree, along with Echeandía's harangues on liberty that he delivered to the wondering neophytes, created discontent, and the Indians at the southern missions of San Juan Capistrano and San Luis Rey refused to work as they had formerly. Some of the Indians who qualified for and took advantage of emancipation fell into drunkenness or squandered what wealth they had in gambling.

The threat of secularization was nothing new; in fact, it had always been an expectation of the mission system. The friars' function was not only to Christianize the Indians but to educate them to take their full place in Spanish society. When this was completed, the government would turn over mission lands to the Indians and replace the friars with secular clergy. In 1813, the Spanish Cortes had ruled that all missions ten years old or older should be turned over to the bishop "without excuse or pretext whatever, in accordance with the laws"—that is, they were to be secularized. The law was never enforced in California, for the vice-regal government judged that California's mission Indians were not yet ready for secularization.

The California friars, however, opposed secularization. The California Indians had a very simple culture when Serra arrived, and ten years could never have been a sufficient period of time in which to prepare them to function in a European society. Still, with the arrival of Echeandía, the friars prepared themselves for the inevitable—though they tried to stave it off. These were different times; their old missionary college at San Fernando could not supply them with new missionaries, as it had before; in California, the soldiers had ceased to respect the friars. The missions, it seemed, had entered their twilight. What the future held, none could say.

Indian neophytes at the missions could sense the changes brought about by the Mexican Revolution. Since the supply ship from San Blas had stopped coming in 1811, Indian laborers had borne the burden of feeding the soldiers and their families, and they were weary. Moreover, the soldiers, who had less fear of the friars, had grown more careless toward the Indians and at times mistreated them cruelly. The fact that the unconverted Indians, or gentiles, having learned the use of the horse, had grown emboldened in their attitude towards the Spanish population, made the neophytes even more restless and discontent.

A corridor of La Purísima Concepcíon Mission, as it appeared in 1937

This smoldering discontent flamed into violence on February 21, 1824. What exactly happened is unclear, but it seems to have started when one Corporal Cota ordered the flogging of a neophyte at Mission Santa Inés. The Indians rose, the few soldiers at the mission defended themselves and the friar, and several mission buildings were burned. The next morning,

Mission Santa Inés, as it appeared in 1904

alférez: a junior officer; an ensign or second lieutenant

when Sergeant Anastasio Carrillo arrived at Santa Inés with a small force, he found that the hostile Indians had fled to the nearby mission, La Purísima Concepción.

Purísima had been the scene of another uprising on February 21. Throughout the afternoon and the night, Corporal Tiburcio Tapia, with four or five men, defended the soldiers' families and the friars against an Indian attack, until their powder ran out. During the affray, the Indians killed four travelers, Dolores Sepulveda and his companions, en route to Los Angeles, while losing seven of their own number. The next morning, the Indian insurgents sent Tapia and Fray Blas Ordáz (who had the reputation of living an irregular religious life) to Santa Inés to warn Carrillo not to approach Purísima; if he did, the Indians would slaughter the soldiers' families. Carrillo's answer is unknown, but the Indians finally released the families. The other friar at Purísima, Fray Antonio Catarino Rodriguez, remained to minister to the rebels.

Reinforced by Indians from Santa Inés and from other missions, the Purísima Indians prepared to defend themselves. They sent messengers to other missions and to the gentile tribes, fortified the mission, mounted a decrepit cannon, and waited for the inevitable assault. At Santa Barbara, on Sunday, February 22, Fray Antonio Ripoll and Fray Antonio Jaime succeeded in quieting the neophytes and ordered the soldiers at the mission to withdraw to the *presidio*. But, at the *presidio*, when Captain José de la Guerra heard that two of the soldiers had been wounded in a tussle with the Indians, he marched on the mission, and a three-hour fight ensued in which two Indians were killed, three wounded. When Guerra retired to the presidio, the Indians took whatever they could from the mission (respecting, however, the church itself), and fled to the mountains. They had begged Fray Antonio Jaime, who was sick in bed, to go with them, but he had refused. On the same afternoon, **Alférez** Maitorena arrived with Guerra's troops and, in the next two days (against the friars' protests) sacked the Indians' houses and killed several Indians in cold blood. By the end of February, the rebels had fled to the Tulares.

The news of the Indian revolt frightened the governor at Monterey. He sent 100 men south under Lieutenant Mariano Estrada and Alférez Francisco de Haro to join with Captain de la Guerra in an assault on Purísima. In the early morning hours of March 16, the Mexican cavalry fanned out to left and right, while the rest of the force opened fire on the mission walls. Within, the neophytes, numbering about 400, returned fire with the old cannon, a few swivel guns, muskets, and arrows, but they were no match for the Mexican regulars. The Indians tried to flee, but the cavalry prevented them. Finally, Fray Antonio Rodriguez interceded for the Indians, and, at 10:30 a.m., the battle was over. Guerra and Estrada condemned seven of the neophytes to death for the murder of the Sepulveda party and sentenced the four ringleaders of the revolt—Mariano, Pacomio, Benito, and Bernabé—to ten years labor in the *presidio*, followed by perpetual banishment. The seven condemned to death received the sacrament of Penance and the Eucharist before they were shot.

With the defeat at Purísima, the Indian revolt lost steam. A few smaller operations were conducted against the remaining rebels in the Tulares, but the danger was over. By the intercession of Fray Antonio Ripoll and Fray Vicente Sarría, the governor extended a general pardon to the rebellious Indians, and by June 16, 1824, California was again at peace.

The Fall of the California Missions

When Governor Echeandía ignored Monterey and set up his government at San Diego, he created a good deal of ill will in the north of California and awakened latent rivalries between the south and the north. But the governor proved he could unite the interests of the leaders of both parts of Alta California when, in July 1830, he lay before the *diputación* a plan to secularize the missions.

Echeandía proposed that, beginning with the missions nearest the presidios, the government should take control of the *temporalities* (lands and anything having to do with economic production) from the missionaries and deliver them to salaried officials. The friars would function essentially as parish priests, or they could depart to establish new missions in the interior. The neophytes would be granted a share in the mission lands. The plan, which would basically hand control of the the neophytes and their lands over to a small group of *Californios* who had long wanted to seize the missions to exploit them, was approved by the *diputación* and then sent to Mexico City for approval.

One flaw in Echeandía's plan was that, earlier the same year, March 8, 1830, President Anastasio Bustamante had appointed Colonel Manuel Victoria the new governor of Alta California. Victoria, however, did not arrive in San Diego until late November or early December—and when he did, he discovered, to his chagrin, that Echeandía was not there to hand over the office to him. Traveling north, Victoria entered Santa Barbara—but still no Echeandía. What Victoria did discover—and provoked his wrath—was a decree Echeandía issued from Monterey on January 6, 1831 (a month after he knew Victoria had arrived), ordering the secularization of the missions.

José Castro

Victoria proceeded north again and came to Monterey, where on January 31 he took the oath of office as governor. The next day, he suspended Echeandía's secularization decree as opposed to the will of President Bustamante and the supreme government. Victoria then worked to establish California's government on a sound basis—at least in the opinion of Bustamante's conservative government. He suspended the *diputación*, saying its members had not been elected legally, and ordered several executions of persons convicted of serious crimes. For these measures—but primarily for countermanding the decree of secularization—Victoria earned the ill-will of such prominent and Liberal *Californios* as the northerners Mariano Vallejo, José Sanchez, Juan Bautista Alvarado, and José Castro; and the southerners, Pío Pico of Los Angeles, his brother-in-law, Juan Antonio Carrillo, and Juan Bandini of San Diego. Victoria hadn't been in office a year when the southerners, including Echeandía, rose in rebellion against him. Though the governor's forces routed the rebels, Victoria himself was wounded. Before returning to Mexico, Victoria made over the governorship to Echeandía.

Mariano Vallejo

With Victoria's departure, Pío Pico of Los Angeles, as senior member of the *diputación*, claimed the governorship. But northerners did not not want a southerner to rule them; they named as governor Agustín Vicente Zamorano, who established himself at Monterey. Further south, Echeandía also refused to recognize Pico and continued to rule in San Diego. So, until 1833, with the arrival from Mexico of Brevet Brig. General José Figueroa, California had three governors—one at San Diego, another at Los Angeles, and the third at Monterey.

Figueroa came to California with several Franciscan friars belonging to the missionary College of Zacatecas; it would be their task to take over the government of the northern missions, while the southern mission remained under direction of the aging Fernandinos. The new governor was also given the task, by order of Gómez Farías' government, to secularize the missions; but when he presented the law to the California *diputación*, that body ruled that the governor had no authority to execute the law.

The problem with this law for the *diputación*, it seems, was that it would not allow prominent *Californios* to benefit from the breaking up of the missions, for it would merely turn them into pueblos and divide the lands among the neophytes. A plan proffered by Figueroa on August 2, 1833 was more to *diputación's* liking. This plan, which would divide

Pío Pico in later life

mission lands among the neophytes, did not entrust control of the lands to them but handed it over to *mayordomo* administrators. That these administrators were either members of the *diputación* or their close associates and kindred was not surprising. The control of the temporalities of ten out of the 19 missions thus passed from the hands of the friars to the likes of Pío Pico, Carlos Carrillo, Juan Bandini, and Mariano Vallejo.

Under Figueroa's secularization plan, half of the mission lands were to go to the Indians and half to the *Californios*, but this was not how things turned out. Not fully assimilated into European culture, most of the Mission Indians did not attempt to farm their lands nor did they know how to manage them. In a few years, the mission lands, became the possession of prominent *Californios*, who plundered them of their wealth, while the mission Indians were scattered; or if they remained on the missions, they were forced to labor for their new masters, often for no pay. Many Indians fell into the vices the friars had tried to guard them from—idleness, drunkenness, and prostitution. The administrators, who cared little or nothing for the neophytes' souls, permitted them to neglect their religious duties; indeed, some administrators seemed bent to make the life of the remaining friars as difficult as possible. Thus, the missions themselves began their swift descent into decay.

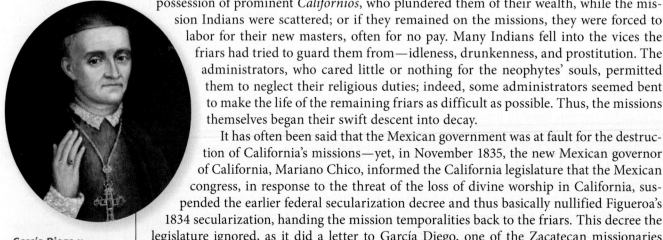

García Diego y Moreno, first bishop of the Diocese of Two Californias

It has often been said that the Mexican government was at fault for the destruction of California's missions—yet, in November 1835, the new Mexican governor of California, Mariano Chico, informed the California legislature that the Mexican congress, in response to the threat of the loss of divine worship in California, suspended the earlier federal secularization decree and thus basically nullified Figueroa's 1834 secularization, handing the mission temporalities back to the friars. This decree the legislature ignored, as it did a letter to García Diego, one of the Zacatecan missionaries whom the Mexican government named the first bishop of Baja and Alta California in September 1836. In this letter, the Mexican secretary of the interior reiterated that the government had suspended secularization and returned the missions to the friars.

In a letter dated September 25, 1837, Fray Narciso Durán of Mission Santa Barbara, expressed his opinion that Figueroa had acted "contrary to his own judgment" in putting forward his secularization plan; but, said Fray Narciso, the *diputación* threatened to rebel if the "pusillanimous" governor went against their wishes. Then the friar, who had worked in the missions for 31 years, made a dire prediction for Mexican California. He wrote:

> How must not such enormous wrongs cry to Heaven for vengeance? And how can this land escape being, in time, the battlefield on which the chastisements of God may camp, who cannot remain deaf to the cries of the poor? Of God, in fine, who tells us through the royal prophet that *faciet judicium inopis et vindictam pauperum*? ["He shall make judgment for the needy and vindicate the poor"—Psalm 139:13 (Vulgate).]

Comic Opera Wars

The secularization of mission lands, along with the Mexican government's approval of more land grants to white settlers, increased the number of private ranchos in California. These great cattle ranches centered on the hacienda—a long one-story adobe building, sometimes with porticoed wings enclosing a courtyard, but always with a shaded verandah. Rancho dons were noted for their extravagant hospitality to strangers, their rodeos, bull fights, balls, and feasting. Besides cattle raising, which was practically his sole occupation, the *Californio* filled his hours with singing and dancing.

For some in California, politics added a needed spice to an otherwise quiet, pastoral life. Before his death in 1836, Figueroa had appointed José Castro as civil governor; nevertheless, Lt. Colonel Nicolás Gutiérrez, a companion of the former governor, decided to unite civil and military affairs under himself. It was 1836, and centralism was triumphant in Mexico. When Governor Mariano Chico left only three months after arriving from Mexico, handing

A View of Mission San Diego

In 1835, Richard Henry Dana, an American, visiting San Diego mission, described it as "a number of irregular buildings, connected with one another, and disposed in the form of a hollow square, with a church at one end . . ." The mission, however, was but a shadow of its former glory. "Just outside of the buildings, and under the walls," wrote Dana, "stood twenty or thirty small huts, built of straw and of the branches of trees grouped together, in which a few Indians lived. Entering a gateway, we drove into the open square, in which the stillness of death reigned. We rode twice round the square, in the hope of waking up someone." Only one friar remained at the mission, and he, said Dana, provided the party with "the most scrumptious meal we had eaten since we left Boston."

Bell tower of Mission San Diego in 1936

the government back to Gutiérrez, certain Liberal *Californios*, tired of rule by non-*Californios*, rose in revolt. Led by Juan Alvarado of Monterey and José Castro, *Californios*, Indians, and Anglo-American foreigners under Isaac Graham, attacked the governor's residence in Monterey. When his house was struck by a cannon ball, Gutiérrez decided he had had enough and retired to Mexico.

The rebels were triumphant. Juan Alvarado's uncle, Mariano Vallejo, became *comandante general*, and Alvarado convinced the *diputación* to proclaim California an independent state, at least until centralism was overthrown in Mexico. But the south objected, opposed independence, and denounced the foreign influence of Isaac Graham and his cohorts. Leading an armed force south, Alvarado brought the southerners over to his views; but, only a short time later, in a bid for power, Los Angeles joined San Diego in adopting the centralist constitution. Not to be outmaneuvered, Alvarado also adopted the centralist constitution, and, not long after, the Mexican government recognized him and Vallejo respectively as governor and *comandante general* of both Californias, *alta y baja*.

With the forces in the south cowed—at least for the time being—Alvarado and Vallejo turned their eyes east. They were uneasy about the future of California. Anglo-Americans were arriving overland, an Anglo-American expedition had surveyed the Sacramento and San Jacinto Rivers, and the Swissman, Johann August Sutter, who had bought Russian properties at Fort Ross, had established his own, nearly independent domain, which he called New Helvetia, on the Sacramento River. More soldiers, more Mexican colonists were needed in California, Vallejo told Mexico City. Mexico's answer was Brig. General Manuel Micheltorena, who arrived as governor at Los Angeles in August 1842 with 300 troops. Marching thence to Monterey in October, the new governor heard the shocking news that seemed to confirm Vallejo's fears—

The American navy had captured the capital!

Juan Bautista Alvarado

Commodore Thomas ap Catesby Jones, commander of the United States Pacific squadron, had received intelligence that Mexico and the United States were at war. Sailing for the California coast, Jones, in his flagship, the *United States*, with another ship of the squadron, the *Cyane*, entered Monterey bay on October 19 and demanded the surrender of the garrison. Juan Alvarado, who was still acting governor, agreed to the surrender, saying his small force and decrepit artillery could not stand up to Jones' 800 men and 80 cannon. However, the following day, realizing his mistake—the U.S. and Mexico were *not* at war—Commodore Jones returned California to the Mexican officials. The Mexican flag, which had been lowered, was again raised, and both sides fired salutes in each other's honor.

Though the whole affair ended amicably, with fiestas, dances, and courteous visits, the Jones episode was ominous. It showed how easily a foreign power could seize the rich land of California.

Part II: The Draw of the West

He was a holy man and a miracle worker. He was said to be a prophet. Though infirm with severe rheumatism, Fray Magín Catalá tirelessly served Mission Santa Clara de Assís, near San José—preaching, visiting the sick, living an austere life—just he had done since the 1790s. He predicted, it is said, the growth of San Francisco (then a few adobe dwellings called Buena Vista) into a great metropolis; it was said he foretold the Gold Rush and the San Francisco earthquake of 1906. Seeing "foreigners"—Anglo-Americans—coming into California, Fray Magín predicted they would bring disaster upon Indians and *Californios* alike by undermining the Catholic foundations of the *Californio* society. A noted historian of the California missions, Zephyrin Engelhardt, recorded the gist of Fray Magín's words, culled from those who heard him:

> Another flag will come from the East and the people that follow it will speak an altogether different language, and they will have a different religion . . . On account of their sins the Californians will lose their lands and become poor, and many of their children's children will give up their own religion. The Indians will be dispersed and will not know what to do, and they will be like sheep running wild . . .

Fray Magín died in 1830 and so did not live to see the secularization of the missions and the scattering of his beloved Indian flock. Perhaps he knew nothing of the steady push westward that characterized the restless young republic far to the east. Since the purchase of Louisiana and the expedition of Lewis and Clark, Anglo-Americans, impatient of the civilized East, had been flowing into the Mississippi Valley and across that great river into the wide lands beyond. Many found their way into Texas, but others thrust into the plains and the Rocky Mountains. These latter were not settlers but hunters and trappers who searched for the haunts of the beaver, whose pelts the East coveted for hats, gloves, and other clothing.

Mountainy Men

These "mountainy" men, as they were called, were a rough lot, for they had to be; the Far West in those days was a dangerous place. Indian tribes, wild and free, still wandered the plains, and fearsome beasts, like the irascible grizzly bear, lurked in the woods. Clad in skins, the mountainy men lived like Indians, even taking Indian women to wife. The mountainy men sold furs to either General William Ashley's Rocky Mountain Fur Company or the company owned by the German immigrant, John Jacob Astor. In Canada and in the "Oregon Country" (covering the modern states of Oregon, Washington, and Idaho and the province of British Columbia), the British Hudson's Bay Company employed trappers, who deposited their furs at the company's post of Vancouver on the Columbia River.

The mountainy men boasted not a few colorful characters in their number. One of these was Hugh Glass. A famous hunter and Indian fighter, Glass nearly met his Maker near the forks of the Grand River in what is now South Dakota when a grizzly tore and lacerated his body "in a fearful rate." Left for dead in a cabin with a few provisions by his companions, John Fitzgerald and Jim Bridger, Glass nevertheless managed to lift himself from his cot and drag himself outdoors to find berries and water. After recuperating for ten days, Glass went in pursuit of his faithless companions, walking and crawling over 100 miles to Fort Kiowa on the Missouri River, where he arrived looking the very image of death. From Fort Kiowa, Glass went to Fort Benton. There he found Bridger, whom he forgave on account of his youth. Glass, however, was not about to pardon Fitzgerald (who had taken the famous rifle with which Glass had killed many Indians). Hearing Fitzgerald had entered the military, Glass pursued him to Fort Atkinson on the Red River. En route, Arikara Indians attacked the Glass party, killing everyone but Glass. At Fort Atkinson, Glass found Fitzgerald, and would have killed his old companion had not others begged for his pardon. Glass spared Fitzgerald's life and, in return, received back his old rifle.

John Jacob Astor

A grizzly nearly killed another mountain man, Jedediah Strong Smith, who was trapping in the Rockies in the winter of 1823. Badly injured, Smith was being nursed back to health by his two companions when Indians attacked the party, killing all but Smith, who had hid in the underbrush. With only his rifle, knife, flint, and a Bible, Smith survived by eating the beaver he found in traps and drinking water from a stream. Once he killed a buck and survived off the meat until it turned rotten. Finally, when Smith was starved and near death, others of his trapper companions found him.

Earlier that year, Jedediah Smith had joined General Ashley's trapping expedition to the Yellowstone. Pushing up the Missouri in a keel boat, Ashley's expedition was forced to turn back when fierce Arikara warriors attacked them. Deciding the Missouri was too dangerous a route, Ashley hit upon on a new system of collecting furs. He equipped pack trains with pots, tobacco, whiskey, coffee, gunpowder, and other necessaries, which he sold to trappers. So provisioned, the trappers, who before had worked in larger companies, went off into the mountains in bands of two or three to trap during the fall, winter, and spring. In the summer the small parties gathered and met the pack trains at a specified spot, called the rendezvous, where they recklessly spent all the money they made from furs and, generally, whooped it up.

Map of the West by Jedediah Smith

After he recovered from his injuries, Jedediah Smith, along with Thomas Fitzpatrick, received permission from Ashley's partner, Andrew Henry, to operate as free trappers. Gathering a party of 18 men, Smith and Fitzpatrick trapped in the Wind River and Sweetwater regions, in what is now Wyoming. Hearing from Indians of the many beaver in the Green River Valley, in what is now eastern Utah, Fitzpatrick set off south and discovered a wide pass that made a graded ascent through the Rockies. This was the famous "South Pass" through which immigrant wagon trains would in a few years make their passage over the mountains to the fertile lands of Oregon beyond.

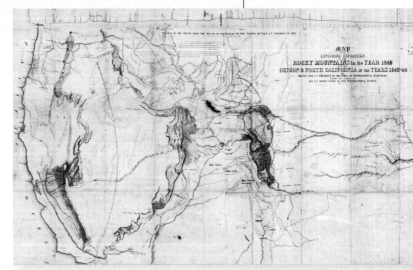

The Green River Valley proved a rich hunting ground, so rich that, by 1826, Ashley had made his fortune and sold his fur trading company to Smith and his partner, William Sublette. While Sublette concerned himself with fur trading, Smith was more interested in exploration. In the summer of 1826, with 18 men and 50 horses, Smith set out to see if he could find a route through the Rockies to California. Smith wrote in his journal:

> In taking the charge of our western Expedition, I followed the bent of my strong resources of wealth and bring to light those wonders which I readily imagined a country so extensive might contain. I must confess that I had at that time a full share of that ambition (and perhaps foolish ambition) which is common in a greater or less degree to all the active world. I wanted to be the first to view a country on which the eyes of a white man had never gazed and to follow the course of rivers that run through a new land.

Departing from the Great Salt Lake southwestward, Smith's company followed the Sevier River in the Wasatch Range and then crossed the Escalante Desert. They passed through the country of the Ute Indians and into the wastelands where the primitive Piute dwelt. Reaching the cliffs overhanging the Colorado, the party followed the river until they reached the settlements of the Mojave tribe. An agricultural folk, the Mojave raised wheat, squash, corn, beans, and melons.

The Mojave told Smith that the Spanish settlements of California (which they frequently raided) lay to the west but ten days distant. However, crossing into the desolate Mojave Desert, Smith soon found that the Indians had deceived him. He returned to the Colorado and so intimidated the Mojaves that they allowed him two Indian guides—runaways from San Gabriel Mission—who willingly accompanied him. Smith and his party followed the dry Mojave River bed westward and southward and then crossed the San Bernardino Mountains at El Cajon Pass. "I was approaching," wrote Smith, "a country inhabited by the Spaniards, a people of different religion from mine and possessing a full share of bigotry and disregard of the right of a Protestant that has at times stained the Catholic Religion. . . . They might perhaps consider me a spy imprison me persecute me for the sake of religion or detain me in prison to the ruin of my business."

Arriving at San Gabriel Mission, however, Smith learned that his fears were unfounded. Cordially greeted by Fray José Bernardo Sanchez, the party was shown every kindness, though their Indian guides were locked up and flogged as runaways. Smith, a teetotalling Protestant, was somewhat shocked at the "wine in abundance" at the mission, which "made our fathers quite merry." But Smith soon learned that, according to Mexican law, his party had to be detained. In early December, Governor Echeandía summoned him to San Diego and told Smith to leave the country by the same way he came.

But Smith was determined to find a route through the Sierra Nevada. When

Choir loft at Mission San Gabriel

he had gotten far enough away from the Spanish settlements, he turned west instead of east, and crossed the Sierra Nevada at Tehachapi Pass, making the steep descent into the San Joaquin Valley, whence he continued northward, trapping. In May 1827, Smith turned west, and leaving behind certain members of his party, crossed the Sierra Nevada and passed into the "desolate waste" that is now Nevada. If it had not been for the kindness of the tribes he met on the way, Smith and his party would not have survived the scorching desert. In July he arrived at the rendezvous at Bear Lake.

Smith had promised to retrieve the men he had left behind in California; so only a few weeks after the arrival at Bear Lake, he set out on another expedition. At the Colorado, the Mojave, who had been told by Echeandía to guard the approach to California, fell on Smith's party, killing ten of his

Cañon de Las Uvas (Tejon Pass), about 1868

men. Traversing the Mojave Desert and the San Bernardino Mountains to San Gabriel, Smith continued westward through the region that is today covered by sprawling Los Angeles and its suburbs and then turned north, crossing the mountains by the Cañon de Las Uvas, and descended into the San Joaquin Valley. He pushed ever northward through California's great Central Valley. Needing supplies, he crossed the Coast Ranges to Monterey, where government officials did not detain him because American ships in port posted bond for him. After finding the men he had left behind on the first expedition, Smith continued north into Oregon, where he wintered at British Fort Vancouver. In the spring, he and his men followed the Columbia eastward, then continued up the Snake River. At last they met some of Sublette's men at what is now Jackson Hole, Wyoming.

Yankees West

Jedediah Smith may have been the first Anglo-American to cross into California westward, over land. Other Anglo-Americans, however, had come to California before Smith's explorations in 1826 and 1827—but by sea. Some of these Yankees settled in California, and though few in number, became influential by conducting the business end of things in the territory. A few married into prominent *Californio* families. Abel Stearns, a hide and liquor smuggler, married the beautiful daughter of a southern California rancho owner and ended up becoming the richest man in the region around Los Angeles. As in Texas, a foreigner could remain in California if he swore allegiance to the Mexican government and became Catholic. Abel Stearns did both.

But the number of Anglo-Americans in California was bound to increase following Smith's explorations. On the trail Jedediah Smith had blazed through the Sierra Nevada, fur trappers now began to come overland to California to hunt the abundant beaver in her rivers and streams. Dirty and unruly, the trappers were unwelcome to the Mexican authorities, who jailed them—if and when they could catch them.

Far less dirty and unruly was the Swissman, Johann August Sutter, who in 1834 had left his homeland—and his wife and five children—to escape his debts. When Sutter arrived in California in 1839, he became an ally of Governor Alvarado, who gave him a large tract of land on the Sacramento River. There Sutter built a "fort" where, as a Mexican official, he was to guard the inland settlements against the inroads of unruly Americans, Indians, and other undesirables. But instead, Sutter became

Johann August Sutter

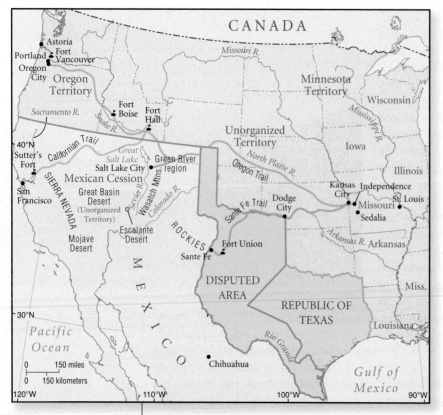

Map of emigrant trails into California and Oregon

a friend to the emigrant parties of Anglo-Americans that, in the 1840s, were flowing across the continent in ever increasing numbers, into California.

Anglo-American interest also focused on the Oregon Country farther north. The Oregon Country had, since 1818, been held jointly by the United States and Great Britain; before 1832, trappers of both the Rocky Mountain Fur and the Hudson's Bay Companies had been hunting beaver in the rivers and streams of this region. In 1834, American Protestant missionaries, Jason Lee and his companions, settled in the rich Willamette Valley near modern Salem. There they joined with former employees of the Hudson's Bay Company and began raising wheat and cattle. On July 5, 1843, at Champoeg, they drew up a compact for governing their small colony.

"Oregon Fever" struck white settlers in Iowa, Missouri, Illinois, and Kentucky when they learned of the rich lands to be had in the Willamette Valley. Gathering at Independence, Missouri, wagon trains of pioneers began the long, overland trek westward across what became known as the Oregon Trail. They generally gathered in May, pushed on to Fort Leavenworth in Kansas, and then followed the course of the River Platte to the Rockies. Thanks to the trapper Thomas Fitzpatrick, the pioneers crossed the Rockies through the easy gradient of South Pass; then traversing the Wyoming basin, they skirted the Gros Ventre and Teton ranges, following the westward flowing rivers. When at last they reached the Snake River, many built rafts to float their wagons to the Columbia.

The journey to Oregon was long, full of dangers from Indians, the elements, starvation, and disease. Many a wagon, separated from the main train, took the wrong path and was lost. If all went well, settlers who left Independence in May could reach the Willamette Valley by November. Despite the dangers, however, 5,000 emigrants arrived in Oregon between the years 1842 and 1845.

A strange religious group also contributed to the Anglo-American settlement of the West. In 1830, a book appeared, purporting to be a revelation of Jesus Christ to the natives of North America. It was called the *Book of Mormon*, and its promoter, Joseph Smith, claimed to have received it in the form of golden tablets from an angel on a hilltop in New York state. Smith said he could translate the ancient characters on the tablets by the aide of special glasses the angel had given him. The tablets, Smith said, conveyed a revelation of the restored gospel, lost for centuries; and, he averred, he was the prophet of a restored church, called the Church of Jesus Christ of Latter Day Saints.

The Latter Day Saints, or the "Mormons," were not welcome in New York, and so they moved on to Kirtland, Ohio, then to Missouri, and then, in 1839, to Nauvoo, Illinois. In Nauvoo, Smith received a "revelation" that God wanted to reestablish polygamy. Whether for this or for the promise that good Mormon men would one day become gods, the Latter Day Saints won converts in both the northern states and in England. Their swift growth, however, and their peculiar religious practices earned them the keen dislike of their neighbors, and in 1844 a group of "gentiles" (as non-Mormons were called) attacked Nauvoo and killed Joseph Smith. Brigham Young, who took on the office of prophet (and five of Smith's 25 widows), organized groups called "Avenging Angels" and for two years waged bitter war on the "gentiles."

Waging war on one's neighbors, however, does not make for easy cohabitation, and so in 1846 Brigham Young led his followers on a journey west to the "promised land." In July 1847, the pioneer band of saints reached the basin of the Great Salt Lake—a forbidding desert region, sandy, with alkali deposits dotting the landscape. Young chose this region, which he named Deseret, because it was then part of Mexico—and he figured no other whites would want to settle it. Under Young's autocratic command, the Mormons built irrigation canals to bring water from the surrounding mountains and established a system of small farms. Young, who accumulated a large fortune from all this, forbade speculation in land and made laws repressing all "heresy" and "schism." He also provided for foreign and domestic missions and helped finance transatlantic and transcontinental immigration to Deseret. By the end of 1848, about 5,000 Mormons had settled in Deseret.

Manifest Destiny and the Road to War

In May 1836, John C. Calhoun said: "there [are] powerful reasons why Texas should be part of this Union." The southern states, he said, "owning a slave population, were deeply interested in preventing that country from having the power to annoy them." With other southerners, Calhoun feared an independent Texas could not maintain the institution of slavery by itself; and if Great Britain should annex Texas, slavery would end there. No fugitive slave agreement, as the South had with the North, would exist with an independent Texas; and if slavery were abolished in Texas, slaves in the states could easily escape there. Some southerners, too, thought admitting Texas would provide, as one Senator McDuffie said before his colleagues on May 23, 1844, "a safety valve to let off the superabundant slave population from among us." Texas annexation, McDuffie continued, would "at the same time improve their [the slaves'] condition; they will be more happy, and we shall be more secure. But if you pen them up within our present limits, what becomes of the free negroes, and what will be their condition?"

Southerners had another reason to favor Texas' annexation. As in 1820, Calhoun and other southerners feared the political dominance of the North. To date, there were 13 slave and 13 free states; but with Florida remaining the only potential slave state, and with

Westerward the Course of Empire Takes Its Way, by Emanuel Leutze. This painting, which hangs in the U.S. Capitol in Washington, D.C., expresses the spirit of Manifest Destiny.

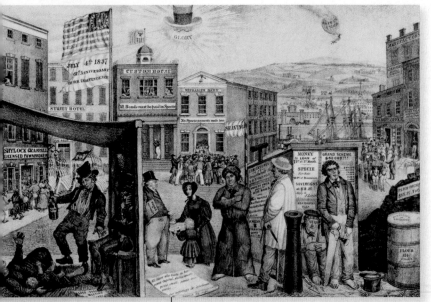

A cartoon that depicts the impact of the financial Panic of 1837. The illustration shows a bank run, homeless woman and child, unemployed men, a closed factory, and a sheriff's auction.

Wisconsin, Iowa, and Minnesota, all free territories, waiting in the wings for statehood, Southerners feared to lose their power in the Senate as they already had in the House. Texas, they thought, could be divided into several slave states and so provide their section the representation it needed to maintain its power in the national councils.

The growing number of antislavery "abolitionists" in the North, of course, disagreed. They wanted to keep Texas out of the union. Indeed, many thought the whole Texas revolution had been a plot by slaveholders for the extension of slave territory. In November 1837, the Vermont legislature protested the admission of any states that allowed domestic slavery. President Martin Van Buren, however, had a different reason for opposing the annexation of Texas; he was engaged in delicate negotiations with Mexico at the time, and Mexico was very sensitive about the issue. The annexation issue was brought before Congress in 1838 and was defeated after a three-week anti-annexation speech by Senator John Quincy Adams.

Sam Houston, president of the Republic of Texas, was eager for annexation into the United States; but if he could not get it, he would settle for protection and aid from either France or Great Britain. Texas' finances were worse off than Mexico's. Moreover, the financial panic of 1837 that hit the states had brought more debt-ridden small planters into Texas, increasing its Anglo-American population to 50,000.

The financial panic, which began in 1837 and lasted to 1841, had important political effects. Because he was president when the panic hit, Martin Van Buren was blamed for it. His opponent in the election of 1840, nominated by the Whig party (a coalition of conservative Republicans and remnants of the Federalist Party), was William Henry Harrison, the Hero of Tippecanoe. Harrison and his vice-presidential candidate, John Tyler, an old-fashioned Virginia Republican, ran on no platform; instead, the Whigs paraded "Old Tippecanoe's" military record. "Tippecanoe and Tyler, too!" they cried. When a Democratic journalist sneered that "Old Tip" would prefer to retire to his log cabin if he had $2,000 and a barrel of hard cider, the Whigs took up the sneer and ran a campaign centered on log cabins and hard cider. They attacked Van Buren for his "aristocratic" New York ways:

> Let Van from his coolers of silver drink wine,
>   And lounge on his cushioned settee;
> Our man on his buckeye bench can recline,
>   Content with hard cider is he.
>
> Then a shout from each freeman—a shout from each State,
>   To the plain honest husbandman true,
> And this be our motto—the motto of Fate—
>   "Hurrah for Old Tippecanoe!"

But, despite the democratic appeal of the campaign, Harrison won the popular vote by only a small margin (though he captured 174 more electoral votes than Van Buren). But President Tip had not long for this world. Refusing to wear coat

lame duck: an elected official or group of officials whose term of office will soon end or who continue in office after the election, but before the inauguration, of a successor

joint resolution: a legislative measure that, like a bill, requires a majority vote of both the House and the Senate before it can have the force of law. A joint resolution requires also the approval of the president, except when it proposes a constitutional amendment; in that case, the resolution requires a two-thirds majority in both houses of Congress and ratification by three-fourths of the states. Joint resolutions differ from bills in that they are usually drafted to address a temporary problem—such as a presidential request for a limited use of military force.

or hat at his inauguration (it was a bitterly cold day), the 70-year-old Harrison caught pneumonia and died a month after taking office. John Tyler then became president and proved himself more of a Democrat than a Whig. It was not long before he was repudiated by his old party and allied himself with the states' rights Democrats.

Tyler joined John C. Calhoun and other Democrats and pressed for the annexation of Texas. A **lame-duck** president (he was nominated by neither the Whigs nor the Democrats in 1844), Tyler wanted Texas admitted to the Union before the end of his term. He resorted to a constitutionally questionable move—Congress approved the annexation, not by passing a bill of annexation but through a **joint resolution**. On February 28, 1845, just a few days before he left office, Tyler informed Sam Houston that Congress had approved Texas' admission into the union.

The Goading of Mexico

The presidential election of 1844 pitted James K. Polk, a Democrat and the governor of Tennessee, against the Kentucky Whig senator, Henry Clay. The Democrat Polk had not only favored annexing Texas (which Clay had opposed), but was convinced that it was the United States' "manifest destiny" to stretch from the Atlantic to the Pacific. The conviction that the country's boundaries should reach ever westward—that it had almost a divine mandate to do so—had seeped into the American popular mind. Rich lands lay in Oregon and in fabled California. Many thought the latter was not ruled well by the Mexicans, who couldn't realize its potential. California was ripe for the taking, and rather than let France or England take it (rumor said they wanted it), the United States must seize it.

HARRISON AND PROSPERITY

VAN BUREN AND RUIN

A detail of an anti-Van Buren pamphlet, with the title: "The Contrast: or Plain Reasons Why William Henry Harrison Should Be Elected President of the United States and Why Martin Van Buren Should Not Be Re-elected. By An Old Democrat."

An anti-Democratic Party cartoon depicting Jackson leading the party into ruin in the election of 1844. Of course, the Democratic Party secured the presidency and both houses of Congress in this election.

President Polk wanted California but did not, if at all possible, want to go to war to get it. The Mexican government, however, had broken off diplomatic relations with the United States over Texas and so would pay no attention to Polk's proposals to buy California. When Texas formally accepted annexation in July 1845, Polk again proposed buying California. Since it had defaulted on the payment of debts it owed American citizens for destroyed property, Mexico, Polk suggested, should give California to the United States in lieu of the debt payment. It seemed a good business deal to Polk, but the proud Mexicans thought it an insult to their honor.

Polk did not understand the Mexican temperament. In late November 1845, he told John Slidell, the U.S. minister to Mexico, to offer the California debt forgiveness swap, as well as an unspecified amount of money, to President José Joaquin Herrera. Slidell was also to suggest that Mexico recognize the Río Grande as the southern boundary of Texas. To round off the deal, the minister was to offer $5 million for New Mexico.

President Herrera refused to meet with Slidell, but he did suggest that an understanding could be reached on these questions as long as some means were found to assuage Mexican national pride. Herrera's reply did not please General Mariano Paredes, who led a coup d'etat against Herrera in early 1846 and drove him from office. Neither did it please Polk. Further and more stringent measures had be taken, he thought. If money could not buy California, he would have to resort to war to get it.

Polk knew that to galvanize American support for the war, he had to make it look that Mexico had provoked it. In July 1845, he had sent General Zachary Taylor and a detachment of the regular army to the Nueces River in Texas to guard the border with Mexico. Now, on January 13, 1846, having learned of Herrera's refusal to meet with Slidell (but not of Paredes' revolt), Polk ordered Taylor to cross the Nueces and proceed to the Río Grande. This was a provocative act, for Mexico had never recognized Texas' claim to the Río Grande boundary but insisted that everything between the Río Grande and the Nueces belonged to Mexico. (Indeed, Texas had never exercised any authority south of the Nueces, which had formed its border with the Mexican state of Tamaulipas.) By late March, Taylor was on the Río Grande. Moreover, he had **blockaded** Matamoros, a city at on the south bank of the Río Grande and clearly within Mexico's borders.

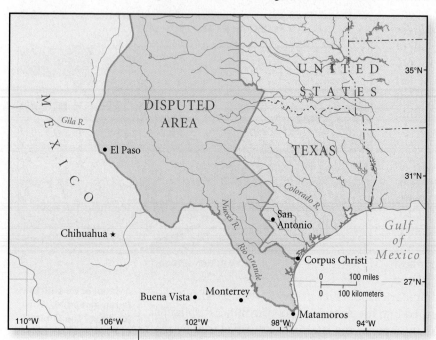

The Texas/Mexico border showing the disputed boundary lines: Mexico said Texas' southern boundary was the Nueces River, while Texas said it was the Rio Grande

blockade: the isolation of a particular area by troops or warships to prevent the passage of persons and supplies to and from that area

The Pathfinder's Plot

In the December of 1845, a party of about 16 armed men led by Captain John Charles Frémont of the United States Army Corps of Topographical Engineers arrived at Johann Sutter's fort on the Sacramento River. Frémont's party included the explorer and trapper, Kit Carson.

It was Frémont's second journey into California. He had first come to California in 1843 through Nevada, westward over the Sierra Nevada, and through central and southern California. From California, he made his way home via Santa Fé in New Mexico. Frémont

"54 40 or Fight!"

The possession of the "Oregon Country"—the vast western territory that included modern British Columbia, as well as the states of Washington, Oregon, and Idaho—had long been a matter of dispute between the United States and Great Britain. In 1818, both powers had agreed to a joint occupation of the territory, but this only deferred the question of who possessed it. It did not settle it. The "Oregon Question" came up again during the Texas annexation fight when John C. Calhoun suggested linking the annexation of Oregon with that of Texas in order to appease the Northerners. In 1844, President Taylor had approached British prime minister, Lord Aberdeen, with a plan to divide Oregon along the latitude of 49 degrees. Aberdeen, however, refused to give up Fort Vancouver, which lay north of that line, and so the talks came to nothing.

In his annual message to Congress in December 1845, President Polk said

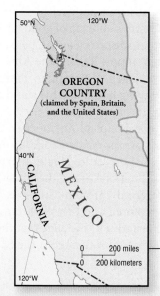

Map of the Oregon Country

the latitude 54 degrees 40 minutes was the "clear and unquestionable" boundary of American Oregon. (This boundary would have given all of the Oregon Country to the U.S.) Polk also asked Congress to end the 1818 joint occupation agreement with Great Britain. Both measures, if approved, would threaten war with Great Britain at the very time Polk was contemplating war with Mexico.

Polk, however, was shrewder than to fight a war with two powers at once. When Lord Aberdeen suggested that Oregon be divided along latitude 49 degrees north to Puget Sound, Polk accepted the compromise. The Senate however was not so agreeable. Expansionists pushed for all of Oregon: "54 40 or Fight!" was their cry. But, at last, on June 15, 1846, the Senate accepted the compromise. Like Polk, they had discovered that they did not want a war with Great Britain—especially now that they were at war with Mexico.

wrote a detailed report of his expedition that not only gave details of topography, flora, and fauna, but revealed the feeble hold Mexico had on California. The report won fame for Frémont as the "Pathfinder."

Frémont's father-in-law was the pro-expansionist senator from Missouri, Thomas Hart Benton; the former ambassador to Mexico, Joel Poinsett, was Frémont's patron. After Frémont returned from his first expedition in 1844, Poinsett introduced him to both General Winfield Scott, who promoted Frémont to captain, and to President Polk. It was with the backing of such powerful men that Frémont undertook his second expedition into California. Ostensibly it was just another topographical expedition, like the first.

From Sutter's fort, Frémont journeyed through the San Joaquin Valley, looking for a party of his men that had crossed the Sierra Nevada by a different route than his. When he could not find them, he returned to Sutter's fort. From Sutter's, he went by launch to Yerba Buena (later named San Francisco), and then down to Monterey, where he visited Thomas Larkin. Yankee merchant and United States consul to California, Larkin held the trust of Mexican officials, though all the while he was privy to secret information from the United States unfavorable to Mexican interests. In one such message, Larkin would receive in October 1845, President Polk told the consul that if the people of California "should desire to unite their destiny with ours, they would be received as brethren."

John Charles Frémont

When he learned that Frémont had entered California with a corps of armed men, the Mexican *commandante general*, Don José Castro, was suspicious. In answer to Castro's inquiries, Frémont said he was a captain in the United States Army Corps of Engineers surveying "the nearest route from the United States to the Pacific Ocean." He had entered California to take on supplies. Castro accepted this explanation. But Frémont lingered in California. Setting up camp at the abandoned Laguna Seca rancho, about 13 miles from San Jose, he was rejoined by the rest of party (some 44 men) and began receiving visits from Anglo-American settlers. From the rancho, he set out to explore the countryside. Castro again grew suspicious and this time sent a pointed message to Frémont. While traipsing through the Salinas Valley, Frémont received Don José's missive. It was clear and unequivocal—leave California at once!

Frémont decried Castro's "breach of good faith." He and his men did not leave California; instead they built a stockade near Gavilan peak, in sight of Mission San Juan Bautista, where Castro was drilling his troops. Raising the American flag over the stockade, Frémont defied Castro for three days. Then, decamping, Frémont headed north towards Mount Shasta, enroute to Oregon. Having had made his stand against the Mexican despot, Frémont could leave California with his honor intact.

But Frémont did not complete his journey. At Klamath Lake, on May 8, he heard the sound of hoof beats. Two horsemen rode up to Frémont to inform him that Lieutenant Archibald H. Gillespie of the United States marines was following him with important missives. Turning south, Frémont met Gillespie at nightfall. What did the missives contain? "The information received through Gillespie," wrote Frémont years later, "absolved me from my duty as an explorer, and I was left to my duty as an officer of the American Army, with the further authoritative knowledge that the Government intended to take California." Retracing his steps, Frémont returned to the Sacramento River, where he awaited the next act in the drama.

The Bear Flag Revolt

Californio factions could not bury their differences even to face a common foe. Even the California government was divided. In the north, at Monterey, Castro held the office of military *commandante general*, while in the south, at Los Angeles, Pío Pico occupied the office of civil governor. Castro controlled the army, the custom's house, and the revenue it brought in; Pico had the support of the *diputación*, which met in Los Angeles. Pico and Castro mistrusted each other. They were on the verge of leading troops against each other when news reached them that Anglo-American settlers in Sonoma, north of San Francisco Bay, had risen in revolt.

The revolt had begun in this way. On May 30, 1846, Frémont had sent two messengers out to rouse Anglo-American settlers to his camp on the Sacramento. "Notice is hereby given," said the notice, "that a large body of armed Spaniards on horseback, amounting to 250 men, has been seen on this way to the Sacramento Valley, destroying crops, burning the houses, and driving off the cattle. Captain Frémont invites every free man in the valley to come to his camp at the Buttes immediately." Of course, it was all a lie; but it was the first assault in the "neutral conquest" Frémont had planned for California.

About a week later, news reached Frémont that some men sent by General Castro had requisitioned 200 horses at the rancho of Mariano Guadalupe Vallejo in Sonoma. Without delay, a band of Frémont's men, under Ezekial Merritt, rode out and, the next day, captured the horses at Murphy's Rancho, south of Sutter's fort. After driving the horses to Frémont's camp, Merritt gathered about 20 men and rode to Sonoma.

Sonoma, showing the town plaza and the flag pole on which the Bear Flag was raised. Historic American Buildings Survey, by George Gibbs, 1851.

At dawn of Sunday, June 14, General Vallejo awoke to find his house surrounded by the most disagreeable-looking men—all armed, many dressed in buckskin, some without shirts, some shod, others not. They were Merritt's men, and Vallejo, knowing he could not resist the rabble, quietly surrendered. Taking Don Mariano and others prisoner, Merritt's men escorted them to Sutter's fort, where Frémont, who claimed no involvement in the action, ordered them confined.

The Anglo-American settlers, now in full revolt in the north, were a motley band. Some were respectable farmers, but others were mere adventurers; others were bloodthirsty, unruly denizens of the unruly West. The revolt, which lacked all cohesion, might soon have fallen apart had it not been for William Brown Ide, a Massachusetts Yankee, who organized the disparate band. On the very day of Vallejo's capture, Ide raised a flag—white, with a red flannel horizontal stripe at the bottom, a star in the upper left-hand corner, and rather pig-like Grizzly Bear image right of the star—and proclaimed the independent "California Republic." Unable to receive help from Commodore John B. Montgomery on the *U.S.S. Portsmouth*, anchored off San Francisco (his government, said Montgomery, was not yet at war with Mexico), Ide nevertheless issued a proclamation declaring that the settlers had been driven to revolt by the "principles of self-preservation . . . the love of truth, and the hatred of tyranny."

Sutter's Fort in 1849

Three days later, at Santa Clara, General Castro learned of the revolt at Sonoma. Issuing a proclamation that called on *Californios* to "arise in mass, divine providence will guide us to glory," he gathered three divisions, totaling 160 men. Some younger *Californios*, led by a 22-year-old barber, Juan Padilla, and the school keeper, José Ramón Carrillo, commenced unofficial hostilities against the "Bears," as the insurgents were called.

Early in July, Frémont decided to drop his neutral façade. On July 4 he arrived in Sonoma, where an Independence Day celebration was in full swing, complete with the booming of cannon, a reading of the Declaration of Independence, and a fandango. The next day, Frémont took command of the Bears saying he would lead them in the struggle to "free" California from the "usurper" Castro. The Pathfinder knew he was acting illegally—he, a United States army regular, had received no news of a declaration of war against Mexico. Six days later, though, when he was at Sutter's fort, he received news that legitimized his act. Commodore John Drake Sloat, commander of the United States Pacific squadron, had taken Monterey and raised the stars and stripes on July 7. This meant only one thing—Mexico and the United States were at war.

Blood on the Río Grande

President Polk's patience had about worn out. On March 12, 1846, Slidell had again tried to meet with the Mexican foreign minister and again was refused. Though the Mexican minister hinted that he would be willing to meet with an *ad hoc* minister other than Slidell to discuss the annexation question, Polk thought his response insincere. Was not the U.S. offering Mexico a good business deal? Didn't the Mexican government need the money? Polk simply could not understand the Latin spirit that preferred honor to profit. To sell California would be to admit weakness—and the Mexicans would not admit weakness. Disgusted, Polk prepared a message to Congress asking for a declaration of war based on Mexico's unpaid claims to American citizens and the Mexican government's slighting of Slidell.

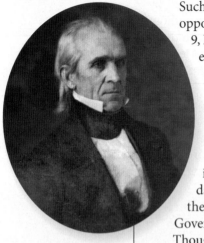

President James K. Polk

"Old Rough and Ready"

"Old Fuss and Feathers"

Such "provocations" would, perhaps, have been too meager to convince Polk's Whig opponents in Congress to support war; but better motives were forthcoming. On May 9, Polk learned that his strategy had paid off—he had goaded the Mexicans into what even the Whigs would admit was an act of war. On April 25, Mexican cavalry had crossed the Río Grande and skirmished with United States dragoons, leaving several Americans dead. American soldiers had been slain on "American soil"! Polk spent the next day preparing his war message to Congress.

"The cup of forbearance had been exhausted, even before the recent information from the frontier," Polk said to Congress on Monday, May 11, 1846. "After reiterated menaces, Mexico has passed the boundary of the United States, has invaded our territory, and shed American blood upon American soil." And two days later, Congress, after some debate, approved a declaration of war. "By act of the Republic of Mexico," read the declaration, "a state of war exists between that Government and the United States."

Though the states bordering the Mississippi welcomed the conflict—they would contribute 49,000 volunteers in the course of the war—the original 13 states were not so enthusiastic. Even in the South, elder statesmen thought the annexation of Texas was enough. Calhoun, for one, rightly foresaw that opening up new territories west of Texas would revive the controversy over slavery in the territories, an issue that he hoped had been put to rest. Antislavery folks opposed the war, which, they said, was nothing more than a grab for more slave territory. And though they voted credits for the war, the Whigs generally opposed it. One of their number questioned the president's rationale for the war—that the Mexicans had invaded American territory. Polk, said a congressman from Illinois, named Abraham Lincoln, could provide no justification for the claim that the Río Grande was the border of Texas. And the president, said Lincoln, "is [so] deeply conscious of being in the wrong; that he feels the blood of this war, like the blood of Abel, is crying to Heaven against him." Delivered when the war was 20 months old, Lincoln's speech cost him his re-election, for Illinois favored the war.

Following the attack on his forces, General Zachary Taylor had crossed over the Río Grande and engaged General Mariano Arista in battle. The accuracy of the Americans' guns proved too much for the Mexican army, equipped as it was with more primitive weapons, and General Arista withdrew from Matamoros. Taylor occupied Matamoros and sent dispatches to newspapers in the U.S. announcing his victory. Then, for two months, "Old Rough and Ready," as Taylor was called, refused to move. He waited in Matamoros for supplies and reinforcements while thousands of his men died from measles and dysentery. In September, having received a few reinforcements, Taylor moved against Monterey in Sierra León, capturing the city after a three-day battle. Then advancing into Coahuila, he encamped at an exposed position near Saltillo—and remained there for the next four months.

Polk was not happy with Taylor's progress and what Polk thought his incompetence; but what displeased the president even more was the general's penchant for sending dispatches announcing his victories to newspapers. Generals who did that sort of thing were spoiling for the presidency, Polk knew; and since Taylor was a Whig, the president did not want to give him a platform for the election of 1848. So it was that Polk gave over the command of the war to Maj. General Winfield Scott, generously supplied him with arms and provisions, and turned over to him half of Taylor's troops. Though a Whig, "Old Fuss and Feathers" (as Scott's men called him) had none of the charism of "Old Rough and Ready." A vain martinet, Scott could not even earn the affection of his soldiers—how could he ever appeal to voters?

Battle of Buena Vista, "From a sketch taken on the spot by Major Eaton, Aid De Camp to Genl Taylor . . ."

Napoleon Returns

By August 1846, the Mexican president, General Mariano Paredes, was in despair. United States troops had invaded his country, defeating Mexican forces in battle after battle. Without victories, Paredes knew he could not hope to hold on to power. The general found comfort only in inebriation and partook more frequently of the bottle. The last thing Mexico needed at this juncture was a drunk president. In August, an insurrection pushed Paredes from power and placed Gómez Farías and the *puros* again at the helm of government. Immediately, Farías reestablished the Constitution of 1824 and called for the assembling of the congress.

Farías planned to raise the needed funds to outfit an army by confiscating Church lands. But where was he to find a general capable of leading this army to victory? Farías could think of no one better than the Napoleon of the West, General Santa Anna. It was a somewhat desperate move to bring the old general back, but like Paredes had been, Farías was desperate. Besides, Santa Anna's political principles were flexible enough to accommodate him to Liberalism—if it were to his advantage. In exile in Havana, Santa Anna gladly received the news of his rehabilitation. The old rascal was even able to fool Polk into granting him a pass through the American blockade of the Mexican coast. Santa Anna promised to make terms favorable to the United States, once he again assumed the presidency of Mexico.

So it was that Santa Anna, dressed in sober habiliments befitting a republican, reentered the capital, assumed the presidency, and set off for San Luis Potosí to raise an army, leaving Gómez Farías in charge of the government. By January 1847, Santa Anna had raised an army of 25,000 (mostly Indian conscripts), which he financed from his own fortune and by confiscations. These men he marched north (himself in a carriage drawn by eight mules and carrying a cage with gamecocks—the general was quite addicted to gambling) to meet General Taylor at Saltillo.

Despite orders from Winfield Scott, Taylor had not moved from his exposed position on the plain at Saltillo. It was in this indefensible position that Taylor on February 21 received unwelcome news—Santa Anna was bearing down on him. Obeying orders at last, Taylor burnt his stores and retreated to a mountain pass near a hacienda named Buena Vista. There Santa Anna and Taylor's armies clashed in a bloody battle in which the Mexicans gained an initial advantage but were soon mowed down by the superior firing power of the American guns. When night fell, Santa Anna withdrew, leaving his fires burning. The Americans, fearing a renewal of the attack the following day, were relieved next morning to find their enemy had withdrawn. Taylor did not order a pursuit.

Sending messengers ahead to announce his "victory," Santa Anna led his army south to Mexico City. He found the capital torn by a civil war that had erupted when creole militia (called *Polkos* for their love of dancing) rose up to defend the Church from confiscations. Santa Anna quelled the rebellion and removed Gómez Farías from office, replacing him with a *moderado*, General Pedro María de Anaya. Promising to exact no further confiscations, Santa Anna convinced the Church to give him 2 million pesos. With this money he outfitted an army that he planned to lead, not against Taylor but a new threat in the east. For General Winfield Scott had landed at Veracruz.

Scott's Invasion

While Taylor rested at Saltillo, and General Scott was planning his strategy for the war, the U.S Navy under Commodores Sloat and Stockton seized, one by one, the coastal pueblos of California. Both Castro and Pico were making plans to resist the invader; but, finding little support among the *Californios,* both men fled California without firing a shot. For a time it seemed the *Californios* would acquiesce to the conqueror; but then Archibald Gillespie, whom Stockton had left in command at Los Angeles, proclaimed martial law and imprisoned 20 *Angeleños* who had spoken out against American rule. Incensed by Gillespie's high handedness, *Californios* under Andrés Pico and José Maria Flores rose up against the Americans. Having few arms besides long lances tipped with metal points, the *Californios* used their superb horsemanship to bloody the noses of the invaders in a few small engagements. Further resistance, though, was futile, and in mid-January 1847, *Californio* leaders signed the Cahuenga Capitulations, surrendering to the United States forces.

The conquest of California, however, was merely a sideshow to what became the main act of the war—General Winfield Scott's invasion of Mexcio. Scott's plan of war was a daring one (though some might have called it foolish); he would take Veracruz, and following Cortés' old invasion route, march across the sultry plains, climb the lofty sierra, and assault Mexico City. Relying as it did on a 350-mile supply line, Scott's strategy tempted disaster, for the enemy could easily cut off the American supply line. Fortunately for Old Fuss and Feathers, the Mexicans were so disunited that they could not muster sufficient numbers at any one time to crush Scott's small force of 12,000 men.

Battle of Churubusco, by J. Cameron, 1847

On March 9, 1847, Scott's forces, transported by naval ships, landed at Veracruz, which surrendered after a siege and bombardment lasting two weeks. From Veracruz, Scott marched to the fortified mountain pass of Cerro Gordo, where the Mexican National Road began its climb into the *sierra*. There Santa Anna and his men awaited him. Since the pass was guarded on both sides by high hills, it, looked as if the Americans would have to make a dangerous frontal assault on the Mexican lines. But then, one Captain Robert E. Lee discovered how to flank the Mexicans by placing men on the left-hand slope that was thought inaccessible. Attacked from front and left, the Mexican forces broke and retreated. The pass belonged to Scott.

As "Old Fuss and Feathers" moved on Puebla, confusion reigned in Mexico City. All parties mistrusted Santa Anna, but, it seemed, there was no one else to whom they could turn. Oddly, there was someone who did trust the old charlatan—President Polk. The president still believed that Santa Anna would keep his word and surrender. Polk even forwarded $10,000 to the general as an expression of his confidence in him.

On August 9, the bells of the cathedral in Mexico sounded the alarm—the Americans were approaching the capital! The following day, the American troops crossed the Continental Divide and beheld through the mountain mists the beautiful Mexican capital. But the approach to the city proved difficult and bloody. United under Santa Anna, the Mexicans fought doggedly for every inch of ground. But always in the forefront of battle, Santa Anna would brook no competition for glory, even if it spelled defeat. For instance, he ordered General Gabriel Valencia, who held a strong position, to retreat. When Valencia refused, Santa Anna removed his own troops from Valencia's command, leaving him to his fate—a humiliating defeat.

On August 20, 1847, 3,000 Mexicans died in the battle of Churubusco, less than ten miles from Mexico City. The United States suffered severe losses—179 killed, 879 wounded—mostly from the fire of the San Patricio Battalion. The San Patricios were mostly Irish immigrants, but in their number they included Germans, Italians, French, Scots, Poles, and even escaped American slaves. Most of them were Catholic. They had signed up with the United States army to fight in Mexico, but their Protestant officers had treated

A contemporary lithograph depicting the Storming of Chapultepec

these immigrants with undue harshness. The United States army provided no Catholic chaplains, and some officers forced the Catholics to attend Protestant services. Though some of the San Patricios may have been attracted by Mexican offers of land if they deserted, others had decided that they could not fight for a Protestant against a Catholic country. Such was the motivation of their leader, John Riley of County Galway, Ireland. At Churbusco, as in the other battles in which they fought, the San Patricios proved courageous and skilled soldiers; but they could not beat back the American advance. At the battle's end, the Americans captured 83 San Patricios, 72 of whom were court-martialed for desertion. Of that number, 50 were sentenced to be hanged, while 16 were to be flogged and branded on the cheek with the letter "D"—for deserter. Though condemned by court-martial, Riley and several others were spared execution by General Scott because they had deserted before Congress had declared war on Mexico. Instead, they were flogged and branded.

The Americans prepared a more exquisite torture for 30 of the 50 San Patricios condemned to death. The officer in charge of their execution, Colonel Harney, had the condemned arranged in a line along a common gibbet, facing the Mexican fortress of Chapultepec, which American forces were then assaulting. Harney told the San Patricios that they would live until they saw the American flag flying above Chapultepec's battlements. In defiance, the condemned cheered the still flying Mexican flag.

It was September 13. Scott had granted Santa Anna a fortnight's truce to consider terms of surrender. When Santa Anna refused the terms, Scott renewed his assault. Chapultepec was the last obstacle standing between the U.S. forces and the Mexican capital. Abandoned by Santa Anna, the few defenders of Chapultepec could not withstand the American assault. In their number were the boys of the Mexican military academy, since called *Los Niños Heroes* (the boy heroes), who fought doggedly, but futilely, against the invader. All were killed as the Americans scaled the fortress walls. Soon the Mexican flag was lowered over Chapultepec. In its place hung the Stars and Stripes.

That evening, the American forces broke through the walls of Mexico City. Santa Anna retired to Guadalupe while American forces and the Mexicans engaged in desperate street fights. Two United States lieutenants, Raphael Semmes and Ulysses S. Grant, mounted howitzers on roofs and belfries, riddling the enemy below with deadly fire. Finally, on the morning of September 14, 1847, the city government let fly the white flag. The ragged and bloody American forces, led by two generals (one wearing only one boot) marched into the plaza in front of the cathedral that Cortés had built. A few minutes later, General Scott, splendidly clad, his sword gleaming, rode in triumph into the plaza leading a company of dragoons. The cheers of the soldiers greeted their victorious commander.

Guadalupe Hidalgo

The conquest of the Mexican capital did not lead immediately to peace. On the night of September 14, snipers picked off American soldiers as they retired to their sleeping quarters. Santa Anna and the *puros* planned to gather new forces to cut Scott off from Veracruz. In the weeks and months following the conquest of the capital, guerrilla warfare, carried on by patriots and bandits both, assailed the American forces, while Santa Anna led an unsuccessful attack on U.S. forces at Puebla.

The *moderado* congress, however, wanted peace. Some of the northern Mexican states were threatening secession during the long months following the capture of Mexico City,

Map showing all the new territories added to the United States, including the ones ceded from Mexico

and in the south Mayan Indians in the Yucatán were carrying on a rebellion with arms supplied by British merchants in Belize. From Querétaro, about 100 miles from the capital, Manuel de la Peña y Peña, chief justice of the Mexican supreme court and the acting president, opened up negotiations. At first, the U.S. demands were so severe that the Mexican government refused to consider them. But, with the U.S. government threatening to renew the war, Peña y Peña and the congress at last agreed to sign a treaty U.S. and Mexican representatives had ratified on February 2, 1848 at the town of Guadalupe Hidalgo, about 150 miles north of the capital.

The Treaty of Guadalupe Hidalgo is the only treaty in U.S. history to open with an invocation of God: "In the name of Almighty God." In this treaty, Mexico agreed to cede Alta California and New Mexico (including Arizona, western Colorado, Utah and Nevada) to the United States for $15 million and affirmed the Río Grande as the southern boundary of Texas. In return, the United States would assume all unpaid debts owed by Mexico to American citizens. The treaty guaranteed the rights of Mexicans residing in the ceded territories. Their property, said the treaty, "shall be inviolably respected," and they "shall be maintained and protected in the free enjoyment of their liberty and property, and secured in the free exercise of their religion without restriction." Grants of land made by Mexico to individuals, said the treaty, shall "preserve the legal value which they may possess; and the grantees may cause their legitimate titles to be acknowledged before the American tribunals."

Thus Mexico lost more than half of her territory and the United States were able to fulfill what they deemed their "manifest destiny" to extend from "sea to shining sea." There were some, particularly slaveholders in the Gulf States, who wanted Congress to demand the whole of Mexico; and Polk himself confided to his diary, "if the treaty was now to be made, I should demand more territory." But in the end Polk thought it best to leave well enough alone. The Senate ratified the treaty on March 10, 1848.

As for Santa Anna, pursued by Texas Rangers, who sought revenge for the Alamo, the old general was forced to flee into the mountains. But, as usual, good luck was his. Given safe conduct by the Americans, Santa Anna sailed for Jamaica, his new home in exile. Only five years would pass, however, before the Napoleon of the West would return and play his last performance on the stage of poor Mexico.

Chapter 14 Review

Summary

- In 1828, Gómez Pedraza, running against Vincente Guerrero, won the election for president in Mexico. Antonio López de Santa Anna would not tolerate a conservative in power and mounted a rebellion against Pedraza. The rebellion ended in 1829. and Congress proclaimed Guerrero president.

- King Fernando VII sent troops to Mexico to reconquer the country for Spain. The Spanish troops were not used to the sultry, swampy Tamualipas coast, and they succumbed to yellow fever, and many died.

- In late 1829, the conservative party denounced Guerrero, and troops seized Mexico City, forcing Guerrero to flee, and making Vice President Bustamante president. Bustamante began to sup-

press the Liberals, and this, combined with the execution of Guerrero in 1831, sparked a rebellion in the northern states in 1832. Santa Anna seized Veracruz and proclaimed Pedraza the rightful president. Bustamante relinquished power and went into exile. Santa Anna was elected president, though he claimed to be ill and returned to his hacienda, Manga de Clavo. While he was gone, his vice president, Gómez Farías put through a radical Liberal agenda.

- In 1834, in response to Farías' actions, conservatives called for the expulsion of the Liberals and the protection of religion. Under the leadership of Santa Anna they completely purged the government of Liberals. Santa Anna called a new congress, which replaced the Constitution of 1824 with a new

Chapter 14 Review (continued)

instrument that set up a *Poder Conservador*—a committee of citizens, who were to see to it that the executive, legislative, and judicial branches did not encroach on each other.

- Americans began to receive land grants in Texas from the Mexican government, and a large number of Anglo-American began to settle there. These settlers did not like the laws of Mexico, and trouble began to surface between them and the Mexicans in the mid 1820s. Santa Anna decided he had to do something about the Anglo settlers in Texas, so he sent in an army to enforce obedience to the law. Stephen Austin called on Texians to take up arms. In 1836 Santa Anna and his troops laid siege to the Alamo. All of the Texians defending the fort were slaughtered. Later at the battle of San Jacinto, Santa Anna was captured, and the war ended. To assure his release, Santa Anna promised to recognize the independence of Texas.

- In response to the property loss of French citizens at the hands of Mexicans, France demanded compensation from Mexico. When Mexico failed to comply, the Pastry War commenced. The war ended when Mexico paid the demanded amount to the French.

- In 1841 Santa Anna became dictator of Mexico when a revolt was raised against Bustamante. When discontent against Santa Anna swelled, he retired to Manga de Clavo.

- Santa Anna again took power in 1844 when Texas again requested admission to the United States. This time his extravagance reached its limit, and a rebellion forced him into exile for ten years.

- In 1836 Liberal *Californios* rose in revolt and declared California an independent state. *Californios* in the south of California objected, however.

- "Mountainy" men, including Hugh Glass, Jedediah Smith, Thomas Fitzpatrick, and Jim Bridger, began to explore the Far West. Fitzpatrick discovered the South Pass through the Rockies, and Smith discovered a route through the Sierra Nevada.

- "Oregon Fever" struck white settlers in Iowa, Missouri, Illinois, and Kentucky, and thousands of people went west to settle the rich lands in Oregon's Willamette Valley.

- Mormonism arose in 1830, and members of the new religion settled in Nauvoo, Illinois. When their peculiar religious practices earned them the dislike of their neighbors, the Mormons went west with Brigham Young in 1846 to the "promised land," the basin of the Great Salt Lake of Utah.

- Convinced that it had a "manifest destiny" to stretch from the Atlantic to the Pacific, the United States decided it must seize California before any other country did so. President Polk offered to buy the region from Mexico but was refused. He decided he would have to go to war to get it, and he managed to manipulate events so that it seemed as if Mexico had started a war against the United States. In 1846 the United States declared war on Mexico. The war ended after the Americans took Mexico City and both sides signed the Treaty of Guadalupe Hidalgo.

Key Concepts

puros: a name given to the Mexican Liberals

fueros: traditional rights and privileges accorded to certain groups in society, such as (in Mexico) the Church and the military

Poder Conservador: in Mexico, a committee of citizens whose job it was to see that the executive, legislative, and judicial branches of the government did not encroach on each other

common law: a body of law that arises from custom or precedent—prior judicial interpretations of written law

Manifest Destiny: the conviction that the United States had almost a divine mandate to stretch from the Atlantic to the Pacific

Dates to Remember

1822: *Californios* take an oath of allegiance to newly independent Mexico.

1829: President Guerrero issues a decree abolishing slavery in Mexico.

1833: Gómez Farías pushes through the Mexican congress measures that compromise the independence of the Church in Mexico.

1834: Santa Anna purges the government of Liberals and sets up a new congress that replaces the Constitution of 1824 with a *Poder Conservador*.

1836: Battle of the Alamo

Santa Anna surrenders to the Texians at San Jacinto and grants independence to Texas.

1846: Brigham Young leads the Mormons to the Great Salt Lake.

The United States declares war on Mexico.

1848: The Treaty of Guadalupe Hidalgo ends the Mexican-American War.

Central Characters

Vincente Guerrero (1782–1831): Liberal president of Mexico and hero in Mexico's efforts for independence

Valentín Gómez Farías (1781–1858): leader of the Mexican Liberals, notable for the social reforms that made him the enemy of the clergy, army, and the conservatives

Antonio López de Santa Anna (1794–1876): army officer and statesman, at various times president and dictator of Mexico, who presided during the Texas revolt and the Mexican-American War

Jim Bridger (1804–1881): American fur trader, frontiersman, and scout

Jedediah Smith (1798–1831): trader and explorer, the first American to enter California from the east and to return using an overland route

John Charles Frémont (1813–1890): American military officer and explorer who supported the Bear Flag revolt in California

Zachary Taylor (1784–1850): American general during the Mexican-American War

Winfield S. Scott (1786–1866): American general who conquered Mexico City during the Mexican-American War

James K. Polk (1795–1849): 11th president of the United States, under whose leadership the United States entered the Mexican-American War

Questions for Review

1. What events or situations sparked the rebellion of 1828 in Mexico? What was the outcome of the rebellion?

2. What did Gómez Farías do to cause the rebellion of 1834 in Mexico?

3. Why were the Anglo-Americans in Texas so opposed to Mexican government? How did this opposition lead to rebellion in Texas?

4. What is the significance of the Pastry War?

5. Briefly describe the condition of California under Mexican rule.

6. Who instigated the secularization of the California missions? What were their motives? What were the results of the secularization?

7. Who were the "mountainy men" and what did they achieve in the American West?

8. What is Manifest Destiny? What did it entail for California and Oregon?

9. What was the Bear Flag Revolt, and what was John Charles Frémont's role in it?

10. What events or situations led to the United States declaring war on Mexico?

11. Summarize the provisions of the Treaty of Guadalupe Hidalgo.

Ideas in Action

1. Explore why Mexico's government was so unstable in the first half of the 19th century? What form of government, do you think, would have brought stability to Mexico? Why?

2. Using a map of the western United States, chart the routes taken by the mountainy men.

3. Research the histories of some of the regions mentioned in the history of the mountainy men.

4. Read stories or life accounts of such men as David Crockett and Jim Bowie.

5. Stage a debate on the morality of the United States' declaration of war on Mexico in 1846. Consult the *Catechism of the Catholic Church*, paragraphs 2258–2330.

Highways and Byways

Jim Bowie's Knife

Jim Bowie's knife, known as the Bowie knife, is a very popular knife even today. It is a fixed-blade fighting knife and has several recognizable and characteristic features. The common use of the name refers to any large sheath knife with a cross guard and "clip point,"—the appearance of having the end third of the blade "clipped" off, creating a convex shape.

The historical Bowie knife did not have a single design but was a series of knives improved over time by Jim Bowie. The earliest version was made by Jesse Clifft at Rezin Bowie's request. It looked like a common butcher knife and was based on a Spanish knife. The Bowie knife first became famous in the Sandbar fight in which James Bowie fought several men and was stabbed, shot, and beaten half to death, but managed to triumph using his large knife. After the Sandbar Fight, the Bowie brothers became famous and received requests for their large knives. An 1847 article says that the Bowie knife was originally made in order to have a close combat weapon that one could wear. The cleaver-like blade had enough weight to give the blade sufficient force in a slashing attack. The Bowie knife was then and now made in a variety of sizes.

15 ON THE EVE OF DISUNION

Part I: **Ambitious Country Boys**

In some ways, not much had changed by 1850.

In the upper Midwest and Northeast—whether in New England, New York, Pennsylvania, or in the broad lands stretching between the Allegheny Mountains and the Mississippi River—Americans were living as they had at the turn of the century. Most engaged in subsistence farming—their produce went primarily to support the family; only the excess was sold on the market. Most others—merchants, storekeepers, craftsmen, and small bankers—dwelt in the small towns and villages that dotted the countryside.

Yet, despite their quiet rural life, northern Americans had not lost any of their industriousness and bustle. The same ferment that had peopled the old Northwest, hewed farmsteads out of the dense forests, raised towns where, a few years before, only the Indian and the savage beast had roamed—this same ferment drove farmer and townsman to strive after what seemed to be the limitless promise of progress and advancement. And, as before, if one could not improve his condition where he lived, he could always move farther west.

Life in the North was a buzz of activity. Foreign visitors to America commented on how Americans had little regard for leisure or entertainments. It seemed that they considered time not spent working a mere waste. Men and women labored six days a week, and even Sunday was not really a day of rest. The Puritan ethic, prevalent almost everywhere, forbade playing and entertainments on the Sabbath. Families attended services and then spent the day engaged solely in sober, pious activities, such as Bible reading.

That a Puritan ethic should predominate in the North is not surprising, since much of the immigration into the old Northwest had come from New England. Fleeing the rocky soils of his native state, many a New England farmer had sought richer loams westward. Yankees had settled the interior of New York and Ohio, they had pushed their way into Illinois, Indiana, Michigan, Minnesota, and Iowa. Wherever they settled, their spirit of thrift

A view of the Erie Canal, from 1829

and industry prevailed. Of course, others peopled the Northwest too—Pennsylvanians, Kentuckians and, increasingly, German and Scandinavian immigrants. But New England's culture held sway.

With the Indian threat pushed westward, across the Mississippi, the states of the Old Northwest had grown more settled and civilized. The Erie Canal had not only opened Ohio, Illinois, Indiana, and Michigan to the East, it had given rise to new urban centers. Cleveland grew up as a port on Lake Erie. Chicago, though numbering only 400 souls, became a hub of transport; goods would go from there by way of the Great Lakes to Buffalo, and thence eastward by the Erie Canal. Farther south, transports took flour and pickled pork from Cincinnati down the Ohio to the Mississippi. The Old Northwest, by 1850 called the "Near West," prospered in trade and agriculture and grew in population. It was not long before its importance was felt in the controversies that wracked the nation.

The Gears of Progress

The building of the Erie Canal gave rise to similar projects in other states. Since the federal government had given up funding internal improvements in the 1830s, state governments took up the task of building canals. Sometimes the state itself would construct the canal; often, it would grant monopolies to private corporations to do so. In any event, canals were dredged all throughout the North. Pennsylvania built a rather impressive canal that wound from the eastern part of the state, over the Alleghenies, to Pittsburgh. To pull barges and boats over higher elevations, the canal engineers designed stationary steam engines. By the first half of the 19th century, northern energy had dug thousands of miles of canals.

How pleasant it must have been to travel by canal, moving slowly along over placid water, surrounded by peaceful rural scenery! No sound of motors or horns, only the plash of water, the warbling of birds, the occasional song of the bargemen. In some ways, the canals did not match the restless spirit that produced them.

Railroad transportation, however, did.

Though, in 1850 most freight still traveled by way of canals, increasing railroad traffic spelled the eventual demise of that kindly system. Trains were faster and could carry freight in winter; canal barges were ice-bound for several months until the spring thaw. The Hudson River Railroad soon stretched the 160 miles from New York City to Albany; and the New York Central ran from Albany to Buffalo. By 1856, rails connected New York City with Chicago, bringing swift growth to the latter city. To the south, the Pennsylvania Railroad connected Philadelphia to Pittsburgh; in 20 years it would render the state's canal system obsolete.

Improved transportation allowed for increased industrial output. In the first half of the 19th century, textile factories rose along rivers whose currents powered the large looms that wove cotton into cloth. By 1840, there were about 1,200 cotton factories in the United States. Lawrence, Massachusetts and Woonsocket and Pawtucket, Rhode Island, produced woolen products—blankets, flannel, and coarse worsteds. By 1850, 1,500 wool factories had been built in the United States. Iron production in the United States grew more slowly, though by 1850 American factories were producing over 540,000 tons of pig iron. Other factories in the North produced machine tools, firearms, furniture, wooden clocks, and other products. Connecticut tinware and wooden ware were distributed throughout the United States by Yankee peddlers.

The Yankee enterprising spirit gave rise to a number of inventions. In 1846 Elias Howe invented the sewing machine—which would take the manufacture of clothing from tailors and the home and put it in factories for mass production. In 1834, Cyrus McCormick of Virginia invented the mechanical reaper. In 1832, Samuel F.B. Morse invented the electric telegraph, and eleven years later, Ezra Cornell built a telegraph line between Baltimore and

Washington. Morse's first message sent over the telegraph to a friend in Baltimore on May 24, 1844, was, "What hath God wrought!" A humbler invention was John Rand's creation in 1841 of the collapsible metal tube for paints (and now for many other things, including toothpaste).

Manufacture was not confined to large factories. Throughout New England, farmers were engaged in home-based manufacture when not occupied in the fields. Among the most important products of home manufacturing were shoes and boots, for no process to produce them in large quantities yet existed. In winter months, crews of local farmers gathered in workshops to work on materials supplied by a local merchant. A boy was often hired to read to the working men, to help while away the hours.

With increased manufacture and transportation came the growth of eastern cities. Between 1820 and 1850, the combined populations of New York, Philadelphia, Baltimore, and Boston grew from 293,500 to around 943,000. Population increase in the cities during the 1840s out-stripped westward migration in numbers and importance to the life of the nation. Though many native-born Americans moved to the cities, a goodly percentage of urban growth can be attributed to immigration of foreigners from England, Germany, and, especially, famine-ravaged Ireland.

A steam engine and passenger train from the the Mohawk & Hudson Rail Road, the first passenger steam train in the United States, 1830

A view of Philadelphia in the 1840s

Immigration

The United States had attracted immigrants from foreign countries since independence from England. By 1850, however, immigrants were flooding into the country when, only 30 years before, their numbers were a mere trickle. In the 1820s, 129,000 immigrants landed on the shores of the United States; in the 1830s this number had climbed to about 540,000—mostly Irish, followed by Germans, with a smattering of English. In the 1840s, however, the number of immigrants nearly tripled. What caused this sudden surge in immigration?

The Irish potato famine, for one. In 1845 a massive failure in the potato crop in Ireland (potatoes were the staple of the Irish diet) forced many Irish to choose between starvation and immigration. Wars and revolutions in Europe also convinced many central Europeans to seek their fortunes across the Atlantic. Many of these immigrants came to America to escape dire poverty. Some, such as the skilled craftsmen, came because they had fallen on hard times in their countries; others, because they thought that in America they would find greater opportunities for social advancement. Some, particularly Germans, sought a greater freedom to practice their religion than they enjoyed in their homeland. A few came as missionaries. Such were the German Lutherans who settled Frankenmuth and Frankentrost in Michigan—who came to America in 1846 to convert the Chippewa Indians. When the United States government moved the Chippewa west, these Germans remained in their settlements and farmed.

Immigrants faced many hardships in their passage to America. Packed on ships like so much merchandise, they endured the ocean crossing, assailed by hunger and disease. In New York harbor, where most immigrants arrived, both native born Americans and sometimes even their own countrymen who had come over earlier, cheated and swindled them. Despised by both natives and earlier immigrants, the new immigrants often faced physical assault, beatings, and even murder. Forced to take the lowest-paying, most laborious, and often most dangerous work, immigrants dwelt in the worst parts of the city—in vermin and disease-ridden ghettoes. Great numbers of immigrants died of disease, from bad liquor, or from being ground-down by labor beyond the endurance of man.

The older Americans' disdain for immigrants had a long history. Thomas Jefferson, for instance, believed American democracy needed protection against what he called "the unbounded licentiousness" of immigrants who would "infuse in [the United States] their spirit, warp and bias its direction, and render it a heterogeneous, incoherent, distracted mass." Many an American shared the view of the prominent New Yorker, George Templeton Strong, who in his diary described his impression of the immigrants he saw seeking naturalization. They were, wrote Strong, "enough to turn a man's stomach. . . . Wretched, filthy, bestial-looking Italians and Irish, and creations that looked as if they had risen from the lazarettos of Naples for this special object; in short, the very scum and dregs of human nature filled the clerk of CP [Common Pleas] office so completely that I was almost afraid of being poisoned by going in. A dirty Irishman is bad enough, but he is nothing comparable to a nasty French or Italian loafer."

Immigrants were blamed for disease, crime, the poverty of their ghettos, and prostitution. These charges had some foundation, though they were often grossly exaggerated. In large part, immigrants succumbed to disease, lived in impoverished areas, and were reduced to crime because of exploitation by the "natives." The cruelty of poverty can inspire a cruel response.

Natives complained that a very large percentage of immigrants were unskilled laborers who only swelled the ranks of those requiring public aid. This was true, but these unskilled laborers also provided a pool of cheap labor for the capitalist class. The Irish, in particular, competed with free blacks (whose condition was the most wretched) for the lowest paying jobs.

Immigrant violence often spurred a native reaction. Irish thugs attacked Whig voters and free blacks. But the American-born were often the instigators of violence; the immigrants were dangerous in their eyes not only for their poverty, their ignorance or their foreign ways, but for their religion. Since a large number of both German and Irish immigrants were Catholic, they threatened (thought the natives) one of the safeguards of American liberty: the Protestant religion.

Nativist fear gave rise to a new political party, called the American Republican Party, later the Native American Party, or American Party (Know-Nothings). The American Republicans wanted tighter restrictions on immigration and a requirement that a foreigner live 21 years in the United States before he could apply for citizenship. (The law at the time required only five years' residence.) It was not long before such political agitation led to rioting.

Some particularly nasty riots arose over the Bible. In 1843, the Philadelphia school board agreed to the request of the Catholic bishop there to allow Catholic students in city schools

AMERICAN CITIZENS!

We appeal to you in all calmness. Is it not time to pause? Already the enemies of our dearest institutions, like the foreign spies in the Trojan horse of old, are within our gates. They are disgorging themselves upon us, at the rate of HUNDREDS OF THOUSANDS EVERY YEAR! They aim at nothing short of conquest and supremacy over us.

A PAPER ENTITLED THE

AMERICAN PATRIOT.

IN FAVOR OF
The protection of American Mechanics against Foreign Pauper Labor.
Foreigners having a residence in the country of 21 years before voting.
Our present Free School System.
Carrying out the laws of the State, as regards sending back Foreign Paupers and Criminals.

OPPOSED TO
Papal Aggression & Roman Catholicism.
Foreigners holding office.
Raising Foreign Military Companies in the United States.
Nunneries and the Jesuits.
To being taxed for the support of Foreign paupers millions of dollars yearly.
To secret Foreign Orders in the U. S.

We are burdened with enormous taxes by foreigners. We are corrupted in the morals of our youth. We are interfered with in our government. We are forced into collisions with other nations. We are tampered with in our religion. We are injured in our labor. We are assailed in our freedom of speech.

☞ **The PATRIOT is Published by J. E. Farwell & Co., 32 Congress St., Boston, And for Sale at the Periodical Depots in this place. Single copies 4 Cents.**

A short-lived nativist paper, called the *American Patriot*, from 1852. The text says the paper is "opposed to: Papal Aggression & Roman Catholicism; Foreigners holding office . . . Nunneries and the Jesuits." It declares "We are burdened with enormous taxes by foreigners. We are corrupted in the morals of our youth. We are interfered with in our government. We are forced into collisions with other nations. We are tampered with in our religion. We are injured in our labor. We are assailed in our freedom of speech." In the picture, Catholics are depicted as holding signs that say, "Americans shan't rule us" and "We are bound to carry out the pious intentions of his holiness the Pope."

to use the Catholic Douay-Rheims translation of the Bible in place of the Protestant King James Version. Before this, Catholic students were required not only to read the King James in school but had to endure textbooks that attacked their religion. The school board's ruling stirred up a campaign against Catholics. A Protestant clergy association spread pamphlets warning Philadelphia citizens that the Catholics were subverting free American government and trying to remove the Bible from public schools. The pamphlets proclaimed, "the Pope reigns in Philadelphia."

The Irish reacted violently to this bigotry. During the Philadelphia city election of 1844, Irish Catholic mobs assaulted American Republican voters at polls in Irish Catholic districts. On May 6, American Republicans staged a mass meeting in Kensington, a district inhabited by Scots-Irish Protestants and Catholic Irish. Rioting ensued, and some Catholics attacked rioters with stones and guns, killing a young boy who was holding an American flag. The American Republicans staged another rally, and on May 8 marched into Kensington, burning 30 houses, a convent, and the churches of St. Michael and St. Augustine. Two hundred Irish families were left homeless, 60 people were injured, and 40 killed. Another riot on July 4 had to be put down by "blue jackets" from the *U.S.S. Princeton.*

If the prevailing Anglo-American culture had a hard time digesting the Irish, it had an equally hard time with the Germans. Unlike the Irish, though, the German immigrants were not uniformly poor: they were farmers

An anti-Immigrant cartoon, ca. 1850, showing two men with barrels as bodies—one, representing the Irish (labeled "Irish Whiskey"); the other, a German (*Lager Bier*). They are carrying a ballot box—signifying that immigrants "steal the vote." In the background, a crowd riots at a polling place.

and artisans; some were Liberal political refugees and intellectuals. German-speaking colonies arose in New York, Baltimore, and Cincinnati. By 1850, Milwaukee was predominately German. Germans settled St. Louis in large numbers, and the city became noted for its many fine breweries.

Germans, and Scandinavian immigrants as well, generally did not remain in the cities; they settled the land and farmed. Chicago became the terminus for immigrants who were heading west, and settlements sprang up in which immigrants were assailed by poverty and epidemics; in 1849, cholera carried off one-half the population of Swedish immigrants in a settlement outside Chicago. Throughout the Near West Germans and Scandinavians settled in farming communities, some of which would remain for over 100 years.

Anglo-Americans had no more respect for Germans than they had for the Irish. But then the Germans could be very pigheaded. Though often materially successful, Germans held on to their traditions and language—often refusing to learn English. Though much anti-German sentiment was mere bigotry, the Germans themselves, as one of their own, Moritz Busch, explained, were partly responsible. Anglo-Americans, said Busch, despised Germans for their "thickheaded peasant's conceit" and their "factionalism." This factionalism was evident when German "Greys" (older, established immigrants) ostracized and took advantage of more recent immigrants (the "Greens"), many of whom were political refugees and intellectuals. Germans were also divided by religion, and even language, since Germany was home to many different dialects of the same tongue.

The German unwillingness to assimilate often stemmed from a distrust and fear of the corrosive moral and individualistic tendencies of American culture. German religious colonies, both Protestant and Catholic, sought to shield themselves from a culture which they thought threatened the integrity of their own religious cultures. When the Lutheran missionary

German immigrants board a steamer in Hamburg for the voyage to America.

society that sponsored the Frankenmuth, Michigan settlement heard a rumor that the missionaries there were adopting American dress, they were appalled. Were the Frankenmuthers abandoning their religion? One missionary, Frau Loesel, wrote to her mother, to assure her: "We know nothing other than to be German, German in doctrine and faith, German in our calling and dress, German in our work and household as far as possible. . . . We are a German Lutheran mission congregation which is concerned with the honor of God and the salvation of souls." Such a vigilance over keeping traditional ways led to the preservation of dialects of German in some places even to our own day.

German Catholic immigrants continued a tradition begun by Prince Gallitzin—the founding of distinctly Catholic communities. In 1836, Father Johann Bredeick sent his brother, Friedrich, to America to buy land for a Catholic settlement. Friedrich bought 92 acres in Ohio that became the basis of the Delphos Colony, settled in three successive phases, in 1842, 1843, and 1844. Many similar colonies were founded, usually under the direction of a priest who often exercised a tight control over community life.

Perhaps the most interesting was St. Nazianz in Wisconsin, founded by Father Ambros Oschwald in 1854. In Germany, Father Oschwald became known for his studies in herbal medicine, his reputed power of supernatural healing, and his eccentric visionary utterances based on the Apocalypse in the Bible. In 1849, the archbishop of Baden condemned Oschwald's book, *Mystischen Schriften* ("Mystical Writings"), which predicted the advent of the New Jerusalem before the year 1900, and removed Oschwald from his parish. The same year, Oschwald organized his followers in the Spiritual Magnetic Association, which he placed under the patronage of St. Gregory Nazianzen. It was an economic downturn in the Black Forest region of Germany, however, that induced Oschwald and his followers to emigrate to America.

In Manitowoc County, Wisconsin, Oschwald organized a settlement whose core members were celibate men and women who lived a common, monastic life. Families were included in this arrangement, sharing all material goods in common with the celibate members. Other families who joined the settlement and could own private property also participated in the religious life of the community (including daily Mass, the recitation of some of the hours of the Divine Office in German, and Catholic religious customs peculiar to southwestern Germany).

Father Ambros Oschwald

At the center of community life was the parish church, which included a dispensary for Oschwald's herbal remedies. Oschwald wrote for the settlement a constitution called the Statutes that regulated the public morality of St. Nazianz and laid down provisions for the needy, "so that the poor shall receive the same care as the rich." The celibates in the community took in orphans and opened a school. Later, in 1871, Oschwald established a seminary. Unlike in Germany, Oschwald had good relations with his local ordinary, the bishop of Milwaukee; and, it seems, he de-emphasized or abandoned his apocalyptic utterances.

St. Nazianz demonstrated that, while many immigrated to America for mere material gain, others came so they could freely follow the path of faith. "We did not come to America to become rich," Father Oschwald insisted, "but to save our souls."

Centers of Culture, Hives of Discord

The growth of industry and the influx of foreign immigrants dramatically changed the character of the great northern cities. From relatively small provincial towns they grew into teeming metropolises and reverberated with a confusion of tongues. In the great cities of New York, Boston, and Philadelphia, opulence and middle-class respectability contrasted with abject poverty and destitution. If the American cities symbolized the concentrated energy of the nation, they also represented the despair of many of the country's rootless masses.

Walt Whitman

"The whole of New York," someone remarked, "is rebuilt about once in ten years." It was an exaggeration, but not much of one. New Yorkers were continually pulling down older buildings to make way for newer ones in that restless city. New York was a business center; New Yorkers valued speculation, trade, and manufacturing, and had little truck with literature or the arts. Still, the arts were there. Edgar Allen Poe spent some time in New York as a literary editor. The poet William Cullen Bryant edited the *New York Evening Post*, while the *Literary World* and the *Democratic Review* sought to create a native American poetry. Walt Whitman wandered the streets of the city, drinking at Pfaff's tavern and writing democratic verse without meter. Samuel F.B. Morse founded the National Academy of Design in the city, where painters Thomas Cole and Asher B. Durand turned from conventional depictions of Bible scenes then popular and began to paint the American landscape, such as the dramatic scenery of the nearby Catskill Mountains.

One of New York's sons was the first American to receive widespread literary recognition. Washington Irving, intensely interested in the old Dutch culture of New York, immortalized it in 1809 in *A History of New York from the Beginning of the World to the End of the Dutch Dynasty by Diedrich Knickerbocker*, and in stories such as *The Legend of Sleepy Hollow* and *Rip Van Winkle*. Irving had served as secretary of the American legation in London under President Andrew Jackson and as minister to Spain under President John Tyler. This experience taught him an admiration for the traditions of European civilization and made him a critic of American culture, which he thought was bent only on a pursuit of the "Almighty Dollar." Another critic of the American democratic scene was New Yorker James Fenimore Cooper, author of *The Deerslayer* and *The Last of the Mohicans*.

Another New York son, Herman Melville, received little recognition in his day for his literary work. His first book, *Typee*, was published in England but had little success in his own country. His masterpiece, *Moby Dick*, which tells the story of Captain Ahab's relentless and maniacal quest after a great white whale, received little notice for over 60 years after it was published. Today it is considered an American classic. *Billy Budd*, another Melville novel, went unpublished during his lifetime, though it is widely admired today.

While New York was known for its hustling energy, Boston had about it a conservative and elegant staidness. The winding avenues and antique Georgian buildings of Boston contrasted markedly with New York's ruler-straight streets and dirty brownstone structures. The presence of Harvard University and Boston's aristocratic upper class lent the town the dignity of tradition. Among Boston's literary figures were Henry Wadsworth Longfellow, who became America's favorite poet; the physician Oliver Wendell Holmes, who wrote witty verses and the popular *Autocrat of the Breakfast Table*; and the poet James Russell Lowell.

But as noted, there was a dark side to American city life. The vast underclass lived in sordid conditions. Riots, caused by racial, religious, or class strife, were common, especially in Philadelphia, which, despite its old colonial dignity, was notorious for its sometimes near-lawless conditions. Northern American cities were torn by an acquisitiveness that extended even to religion. Churches, especially Episcopal churches, were often funded by selling pew space; thus, those too poor for such donations were unwelcome in many churches. Only the Catholic churches were everywhere open to all, the lowly and destitute as well as the wealthy.

Poor neighborhoods were filled with drunkenness, filth, and prostitution; epidemics were rampant. One Philip Hone noted that the cholera epidemic that swept New York City in 1849 started "in Orange Street, in the abodes of filth, destitution, and intemperance, in houses where water was never used internally or externally, and the pigs were contaminated by the contact of the children."

"In New York," wrote Reverend David Macrae, "all that is best and all that is worst in America is represented. Fling together Tyre and Sidon, the New Jerusalem, Sodom and Gomorrah, a little of heaven, and more of hell, and you have a faint picture of this mighty Babylon of the New World. City of

Washington Irving

A view of New York, from above Union Square, 1847

colossal wealth and haggard poverty; city of virtue, with an abortionist occupying the most palatial residence in Fifth Avenue; city of churches and Bible houses, where one of the foremost citizens is a man who keeps his wife on one side of the street and his mistress on the other." David Macrae could have penned a similar description of the other great metropolises of the northern United States.

Politics

New York had been the most aristocratic state in the 18th century; by 1850, it had become the most democratic. This was because it was the most populous. The old Hudson River *patroons* had found it increasingly difficult to control the great numbers of New Englanders, Germans, and Irish who had swelled the population of the "Empire State." Many of these had found a home in the Democratic Party, which trumpeted the cause of the common man against the interests and power of the rich.

The New York Democratic Party had fallen under the sway of what became known as the Albany Regency. Formed by Martin Van Buren, the Albany Regency was made up mostly of transplanted New Englanders who had been won over to Jackson's cause in 1824. Little Van's consummate political skills made the Regency the power center of New York politics. It controlled the state senate and extended the unique organizational structure that had come to characterize the Democratic Party to the towns and cities. The structure was in some ways not very democratic; for though the Regency protested that it fought for "the people" against organized wealth, it insisted that the people, for their own good, had to be controlled by powerful party "bosses."

Martin Van Buren

The New York Democratic Party system became the model for all party systems across the union. Each locality had its own caucus, and caucuses sent representatives to county conventions that, in turn, sent representatives to state conventions. There were also district conventions for congressional elections, and every four years, national conventions where the party would vote on its platform and choose its candidate for president. The strength of the caucus system was that it was able to bring to prominence rural leaders who might otherwise have had no opportunity to enter politics. But in the cities the caucuses were dominated by powerful bosses and were riddled with corruption.

Political bosses and corruption became the notorious marks of Tammany Hall, Aaron Burr's old Republican political "club" and the power base of the "Democracy" in New York City. No sooner had the New York state legislature passed a law permitting **universal manhood suffrage** in 1827, than Tammany Hall began recruiting immigrants right off the boat. Party representatives would help immigrants find work and lodging and, in a matter of days, rush them through the naturalization process that, by federal law, was supposed to take five years. Not surprisingly, Tammany Hall and the New York City Democratic Party became dominated by Irish. Prominent members of "The Wigwam" (Tammany's nickname) were "Honest John" Kelly, "Slippery Dick" Connolly, "Mike" Walsh, and John Morrissey, a prize fighter.

universal manhood suffrage: the right of all male citizens to vote

Differing opinions on various issues divided members within both the Democratic and Whig parties. Most folks' interests were still local, and so the art of party leadership required making a platform of general principles upon which the membership could agree, while convincing them, for a time, at least, to ignore the issues that divided them. While this worked for the most part, there was one issue that would split the national Democratic Party, it seemed, beyond repair. That issue was slavery.

The Sectarian Spirit

They called the region of central New York state along the Erie Canal, "The Burned-over District." This region, peopled by New England immigrants, had experienced so many fiery religious revivals that men likened it to a war-torn land. Central New York witnessed the birth of odd religious movements that would give American Protestantism a rather exotic look.

Joseph Smith, founder of the Mormon sect, came from central New York. Then there was Mother Ann Lee of New Lebanon, New York, who said God had revealed to her that the original sin was Adam's "knowing" of Eve. So, she founded colonies of men and women, who lived together in celibacy. These "Universal Friend," or "Shaker" communities became famous for their efficient organization and their unique furniture. The sect grew only by conversion and adoption of orphans—for, of course, Shakers had no babies. New communities were formed from Mother Ann's original community, though the Shakers never experienced any great growth.

Then there was William Miller of Hampton, New York, who had worked it out that Christ would return sometime in 1843 or 1844. When, under pressure from his followers, he settled on October 22, 1843, he convinced thousands to sell their goods, don white robes, and so await the advent of Christ—the Second Coming—on hilltops and rooftops. He lost a large number of followers when Christ did not appear as expected, but many remained with him, and were known as Millerites or Adventists.

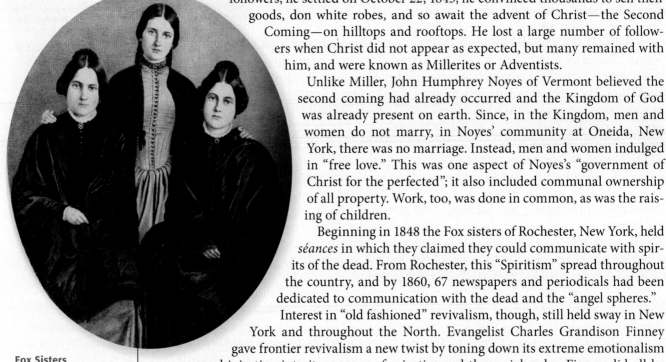

Unlike Miller, John Humphrey Noyes of Vermont believed the second coming had already occurred and the Kingdom of God was already present on earth. Since, in the Kingdom, men and women do not marry, in Noyes' community at Oneida, New York, there was no marriage. Instead, men and women indulged in "free love." This was one aspect of Noyes's "government of Christ for the perfected"; it also included communal ownership of all property. Work, too, was done in common, as was the raising of children.

Beginning in 1848 the Fox sisters of Rochester, New York, held *séances* in which they claimed they could communicate with spirits of the dead. From Rochester, this "Spiritism" spread throughout the country, and by 1860, 67 newspapers and periodicals had been dedicated to communication with the dead and the "angel spheres."

Interest in "old fashioned" revivalism, though, still held sway in New York and throughout the North. Evangelist Charles Grandison Finney gave frontier revivalism a new twist by toning down its extreme emotionalism and injecting into it a concern for justice and the social order. Finney did all he could to shake people out of what he thought was their religious torpor; he held services at late and early morning hours and encouraged impromptu prayer. Henry Ward Beecher, first in Indianapolis and later in New York, carried the social message further. "How hateful," he said, "is that religion which says, 'Business is business and politics is politics and religion is religion is religion!' Religion is using everything for God; but many men dedicate themselves to the Devil and shove religion in to the crooks and crevices of time and make it the hypocritical outdrawing of their leisure and their laziness." Beecher attacked corrupt judges from the pulpit and ardently denounced slavery.

In New England, reaction to Puritanism's stress on man's total depravity threw many into Unitarianism. Like the Greeks of St. Paul's day, Unitarians tripped at the stumbling block of the central Christian doctrines of the Incarnation and the Trinity. Such doctrines were not "rational" to the Unitarian. Against the Trinity, Unitarianism insisted on the unity of God;

Fox Sisters

An illustration of Johnny Appleseed, from *Harper's Monthly*, 1845

Henry Ward Beecher and his daughter, Harriet Beecher Stowe

Ralph Waldo Emerson

and against grace and sin, Unitarians taught the radical goodness of man and his ability to improve himself by his natural powers alone.

Closely related to Unitarianism were the doctrines of the 18th-century Swede, Emanuel Swedenborg. Swedenborgianism, which found adherents in America, taught that God and Satan are engaged in an eternal struggle and that God is present in all things. Swedenborgians rejected Original Sin. One of Swedenborg's disciples was Johnathan Chapman. With "long dark beard and black sparkling eyes, quick and restless in speech and gesture," clothed in a coffee sack with holes for his head and arms, and wearing a cooking pot for a hat, Chapman wandered about through Pennsylvania, Ohio, Indiana, and Illinois, handing out Swedenborgian pamphlets and planting apple trees. Johnny Appleseed, as he was called, refused to kill living creatures. Once when a Methodist preacher asked, "where is the barefoot wandering Christian who is on his march to the Kingdom of Heaven?" Johnny raised one naked foot and said, "Here, my man, here he is!"

Despite Johnny Appleseed and his trees, Swedenborg's doctrines won few adherents in America, though they influenced a rather prominent American literary figure—Ralph Waldo Emerson. Discontent with traditional New England Protestantism, Emerson became a Unitarian minister. Later abandoning the ministry altogether, Emerson became a sort of lay preacher for a movement called Transcendentalism. In his popular speeches and essays, Emerson emphasized that every individual could become enlightened and improved by his own efforts alone. "The highest revelation is that God is in every man," he told rapt audiences. "Life is an ecstasy," was the central tenet of his doctrine.

Emerson's Transcendentalist optimism, his exhortations to find God and truth in nature, had a profound effect on the antebellum North and led to what is called the "New England Renaissance." Prominent among the Transcendentalists was Henry David Thoreau, the author of *Walden* (1854), a description of, and meditation

Henry David Thoreau

on, his time spent in a small cabin on Walden Pond outside Concord, Massachusetts. Thoreau was a naturalist. He believed men had to simplify their lives to be aware of the world around them; only thus could they discover what is essential to human happiness and contentment. His essay, "On Civil Disobedience," written after a night spent in jail for refusing to pay his taxes (in protest of the Mexican-American War), would in years to come inspire revolutionaries against oppressive regimes worldwide.

Though never a true Transcendentalist, Nathaniel Hawthorne, a native of Salem, Massachusetts, was associated with the movement. His short stories and novels explore the darker aspects of New England Puritanism. His greatest novel, *The Scarlet Letter*, wrestles with what is good and bad in Puritanism, and shows how suffering can bring redemption. (Hawthorne's daughter, Rose, became a Catholic. Later in life, moved by the suffering of the sick, she founded congregation dedicated to care of dying cancer patients—the Dominican Hawthorne Sisters.)

American Protestant religion in the North thus presented a wide divergence in faith and practice—from relatively orthodox faith to the almost atheistic and pantheistic tenets of Transcendentalism. "In America," wrote an observer of the time, "everyone worships the Deity after his own fashion; not only the mode of worship, but even the Deity itself, varies. Some worship God, some Mammon; some admit, some deny Christ; some deny both God and Christ; some are saved by living prophets only; some go to heaven by water, while some dance their way upwards. Numerous are the sects, still are the sects much divided." Religion mirrored the disintegration seen in other aspects of American society.

Nathaniel Hawthorne

Reform and More Reform

Partly because of the influence of men like Charles Finney and Henry Ward Beecher, some American Christians turned their attention from mere soul saving and interior religion to engagement in crusades to right the wrongs of society. For instance, seeing that many poor folk in the cities and in the countryside went without churches and religious instruction, missionary societies formed to spread religion among the lower classes. Personal piety, though, did not form the entire agenda of these societies; they aimed to inculcate the values of the middle class in the down-and-out. Sunday school classes instilled not only Christianity, but cleanliness. Children were expected to come tidy and well-dressed to their lessons, and those children whose parents could not afford such finery were given the proper, "respectable" clothes to wear.

An allegory of the "demon alcohol," temperance propaganda from the 1830s, by George Cruikshank

Reform-minded Christians formed various societies to improve the spiritual and material conditions of the poor. There were societies to feed the hungry. There were societies to reform prostitutes. There was even a "Society for the Encouragement of Faithful Domestic Servants." After a time, some reform-minded folks began to question whether it was good to give handouts to the poor. Only struggling workmen, they argued, should receive aid in the form of public works jobs—at which they would, of course, be paid, but at substandard wages.

Other reform movements were not purely religious in character. One of the most influential was the movement to abolish slavery (a topic we shall treat in another place); another was Temperance. Americans had become notorious for their love of liquor—whiskey, rum, beer, and wine—and for drunkenness, a vice that many believed had become a serious social problem. A vocal minority began to push for legislation forbidding the production, importation, possession, and use of alcoholic beverages. Unless the "demon rum" were abolished, they said, America would never achieve her promised greatness. Between 1846 and 1856, Maine, Vermont, New Hampshire, Massachusetts, Rhode Island, Michigan, Delaware, Iowa, and Pennsylvania passed laws either restricting or prohibiting entirely the sale and use of alcohol. Though some of these laws were later repealed, or declared unconstitutional by state courts, they showed that the Temperance movement was a powerful political force.

Lucy Stone

Many of the women involved in Temperance were advocates for women's suffrage, a movement that began in Seneca Falls, New York, in 1848. Lucy Stone of Massachusetts, a leader of this movement, had since childhood been indignant over the way American men treated women. A woman, for instance, was not allowed into college and was unable to hold property in her own name. Stone studied Greek and Hebrew to discover what the Scriptures really said about wifely subjection. She attended college at Oberlin, Ohio—then the only college to admit women—and by 1848 was lecturing in an antislavery society. In 1850 she led the call for the first women's rights convention, held that year in Worcester, Massachusetts. When she married Henry B. Blackwell five years later, he agreed that she would keep her own surname. Susan Brownell Anthony was another Massachusetts daughter who fought for women's suffrage. Originally an antislavery crusader, after 1854 Anthony began agitating for women's rights. Later she founded a weekly paper, *The Revolution*.

Amelia Jenks Bloomer, a New Yorker, saw a reform of women's dress as a way of improving women's lot in society. She came up with an idea for a short skirt over loose trousers, gathered at the ankles, to ease women's work. These "bloomers," as they came to be called, became an object of derision, and only the bravest suffragettes wore them in public.

Susan B. Anthony, about 1855

Two closely allied movements were anti-death penalty and prison reform. The former was partially successful—Maine abolished the death penalty in 1837, as did Rhode Island in the 1850s. The prison reform movement sought to make prisons more humane and to direct their efforts towards reform rather than punishment. Measures favored by reformers included the enforcement of silence on prisoners (so they could think on their ill deeds), the distribution of Bible tracts among them, and the introduction of useful labor into prisons.

Dorothea Lynde Dix of Maine wrote story books for children and taught school; but in 1841 she began to investigate the condition of the insane poor in New England asylums and was appalled with what she discovered. At the age of 39, this quiet, reserved woman began a campaign to reform asylums. Her efforts between 1845 and 1852 led to the establishment of hospitals for the insane both in the North and in nine southern states. She even went to Europe and persuaded both Queen Victoria and Pope Pius IX to reform asylums in Great Britain and the Papal States.

A cartoon from an 1851 issue of the English magazine *Punch*, showing smoking women in bloomers. The caption for the picture reads, "Bloomerism—an American custom"—"Some American women appeared in the streets of London in a tunic and trousers, confirming a certain brassy stereotype." Smoking at the time was considered unbecoming to women.

Other reform movements were not quite so successful. A peace movement, for one, did not attract much attention; neither did vegetarianism, despite the enduring fame of Sylvester Graham. Graham led a campaign in New York against white bread and invented, as a substitute, a whole wheat cracker, since called the Graham Cracker.

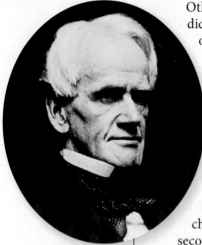

Horace Mann

Horace Mann Meets Dagger Jack

Among the reform movements of the first half of the 19th century, one movement, for educational reform, has had the most lasting effects. Churches—both Catholic and Protestant—had provided most schools in America, whether elementary, secondary, or collegiate. In the early 19th century, there were more secondary academies and colleges in the South than in the North and almost all of them charged fees. In New England, some elementary and even secondary schools were free, though many parents were ashamed to send their children to them, for it marked them as poor. In the 1820s Boston had two free secondary schools.

A growing number of people became convinced that the state should provide free schools for all citizens—after all, they said, isn't education necessary for citizens in a republic? Among those calling for free schools was Horace Mann, chairman of the Massachusetts board of education. Mann believed that no one, regardless of wealth, should go without education. He also believed that religious instruction—particularly Bible reading—should be part of the school day. The problem was that, since the state would provide the schools, they could not espouse the tenets of any one religious group. Thus, instruction, thought Mann, should be in the "common truths" of Christianity alone.

The problem of course was that when one removes from the Christian religion doctrines that are peculiar to any one religious group—such as infant baptism, belief in sacraments or the Trinity—what one ends up with is something like Unitarianism. It was for this reason that the "mainline" Protestant denominations—such as the Episcopalians, the Presbyterians, and the Lutherans—opposed nonsectarian schools. Such Protestant groups already had their own schools and opposed any watering-down of their doctrines. They supported, not free "common" schools, but public support of denominational schools. They were not about to acquiesce to state-sponsored Unitarianism.

But other Protestant groups, like the Methodists, Baptists and Congregationalists, supported state-funded nonsectarian "common" schools. In part, this was because of nativist reaction to the Catholic Church. Bitterly anti-Catholic books had appeared in the 1830s, including *Awful Disclosures of the Hotel Dieu Nunnery of Montreal*. This work, purportedly written by an escaped nun, "Maria Monk," alleged that Catholic nuns lived immoral lives. The book, concocted by Protestant ministers and a renegade Catholic priest, represented the sentiment of many Protestants and helped fuel movements to keep the state from funding denominational schools—for it would then have to fund not only Protestant but Catholic schools as well.

Gradually, Protestants began to view free public schools as a defense against "papistry." Many proponents of the common school were prominent Protestant ministers. When in 1841, John Hughes, the Catholic bishop of New York, led the fight for public funding of Catholic parochial schools, the Methodist journal, *Christian Advocate*, published a series of articles called, "The Common Schools, the Antidote of Jesuitism." A Baptist journal, the *Watchman*, argued that "if the children of Papists are really in danger of being corrupted in the Protestant schools of enlightened, free and happy America, it may be well for their conscientious priests, to return them to the privileges of their ancestral homes, among the half-tamed boors of Germany . . ."

Bishop Hughes (called "Dagger Jack" for his vigorous manner) was something of a reformer in his own right; he instituted schools, programs, and social reforms intended to reclaim the poor Catholics of New York. With the help of religious sisters, impoverished girls were trained in domestic and marketable skills; those who were caught in prostitution were given protection and schooling. When in 1841 the public school officials of New York refused Hughes' request for public funding of parochial schools, he formed a separate political ticket against both the Whigs and Democrats for the election of 1842. Though garnering only 2,200 votes, the bishop's ticket cost some Whigs and Democrats the election. These defeats changed the composition of the state legislature, which passed a school law providing for a completely secular public school system, without religious instruction.

Despite opposition, the principles of the common school movement spread. Gradually many states provided free public elementary schools for all children, and after a time, free public secondary schools as well. But the Catholic and Missouri-synod Lutheran parochial school systems continued—and drew criticism from nativists: the Catholic system for its "un-American papistry," the Lutheran system for its insistence on maintaining German language and customs.

The second half of the 19th century would witness another struggle between those who insisted on common schools and those who wanted to maintain their parochial institutions.

Archbishop Hughes, by Mathew Brady

The Quest for Utopia

Some reformers were not content just to tinker with existing society; like John Humphrey Noyes, they wanted to erect perfect communities that could be an example to all the world of how mankind should live. Such reformers were working to establish a Utopia. Unlike the communities founded by Noyes or the Shakers, however, many of the new Utopian communities were not religious in inspiration; they were founded on the conviction that men could recreate their world by their own natural powers, without God.

Robert Owen had tried to revolutionize the running of his cotton mill in New Lanark, Scotland, by giving his workers a large share in both the management of the company and the company itself. He dreamed of a system of "unrestrained cooperation on the part of all members for every purpose of social life." Lack of want, he said, led to happiness, and happiness to virtue, whose end was enlightenment.

In 1825, Owen bought 30,000 acres from the Rappites, a religious community in Indiana. Renaming the property New Harmony, Owen established his experimental community there. At New Harmony, all land and the means of production were held in common. In order to learn more "enlightened" ways of behaving and thinking, children were raised and educated apart from their parents. Religion was to have no part at New Harmony and, after a time, Owen declared even marriage to be an anachronism. About 1,000 men and women came to New Harmony. But it was not long before disharmony shattered the settlement; despite Owen's well-ordered rule, disputes over religion and government led to the community's demise in 1828. Owen himself lost four-fifths of his fortune on the venture.

Robert Owen, by William Henry Brook

More successful were the "phalanxes" inspired by the thought of the Frenchman, Charles François Marie Fourier. Fourier believed that virtue came from the unrestrained indulgence of human desires. In order to remove the "false" restraints on human action, Fourier thought society should be reconstructed on the basis of cooperation rather than competition. He thought society should be divided into departments, or phalanxes, of 1,600 persons each. Each phalanx would hold land for cultivation of crops, the chief occupation of its members, though they could pursue other avocations according to their pleasure. Fourier wanted no fixed jobs for anyone. Like Owen, Fourier abolished marriage; but unlike Owen (whose system he despised), Fourier allowed for some private property. Albert Brisbane, a journalist, introduced Fourier's ideas to America. In the 1840s the U.S. had 41 phalanxes. Most of them failed.

George Ripley founded the Institute of Agriculture and Education at Brook Farm, Massachusetts in 1841. He wished, he said, "to prepare a society of liberal, intelligent, and cultured persons, whose relations with each other would permit a more wholesome and simple life than can be led amidst the pressure of our competitive institutions." Brook Farm became a haven for young Transcendentalists; and Nathaniel Hawthorne lived there for a time. Young farmers, seamstresses, and mechanics, along with intellectuals and artists, formed the community.

Brook Farm concentrated much energy on education. Instead of stuffing "our children with dry facts, overloading their memory, while leaving their higher faculties dormant," as a member, Georgiana Bruce put it, Brook Farm tried to stimulate children's imaginations and expand their reasoning and intuitive faculties. Work on the farm was mixed with study; leisure time was enlivened by plays, concerts, poetry, and dramatic readings. Adults cultivated a spirit of concern for one another.

"Often in these years that are darkening around me," wrote Hawthorne in his *Blithedale Romance*, a satire on Brook Farm, "I remember our beautiful scheme of a noble and unselfish life, and how fair in that first summer appeared the prospect that it might endure for generations, and be perfected as the ages rolled by, into a system of a people and a world. . . . More and more I feel we struck upon what ought to be a truth. Posterity may dig it up and profit by it." Eventually, Brook Farm became a Fourier phalanx. The colony dispersed after a great fire in 1847.

A great irony of the Brook Farm experiment is that a number of its members became Catholic. One was George Ripley's wife, Sophia. Another was Orestes Brownson, a journalist who had wielded his pen in defense of the poor and working class laborers in New York City. "The unpolished, vehement, and positive" Brownson, as Georgiana Bruce called him, would become a prominent figure in the American Catholic Church in the years to come. Another Transcendentalist, Isaac Hecker, who had been part of the short-lived, vegetarian community of Fruitlands, also entered the Church. Hecker became a priest and the founder of the Paulist congregation.

Orestes Brownson

"How could they take such a step," asked Georgiana Bruce of the converts. "What induced them to do it? . . . Perhaps it was the disappointment of the breaking up of our hopes. Perhaps the speculative intellect needed rest . . ." Or, perhaps, it was the realization that a society of love and cooperation requires a firmer foundation than refined culture, individual freedom, and sublime hope.

Part II: Cavaliers of the Left Bank

The churning turmoil of the American North ended abruptly at the Ohio River. Across the Ohio, on its southern bank, dwelt a very different society. Alexis de Tocqueville, a French traveler through the United States in the 1830s, recorded his impressions of the two banks of the Ohio:

Undulating lands extend upon both shores of the Ohio, whose soil affords inexhaustible treasures to the laborer; on either bank the air is equally wholesome and the climate mild. . . . Upon the left [southern] bank of the stream the population is sparse; from time to time one descries a troop of slaves loitering in the half-desert fields; the primeval forest reappears at every turn; society seems to be asleep, man to be idle, and nature alone offers a scene of activity and life.

"From the right bank," continued Tocqueville, "a confused hum is heard, which proclaims afar the presence of industry; the fields are covered with abundant harvests; the elegance of the dwellings announces the taste and activity of the laborers; and man appears to be in the enjoyment of that wealth and contentment which is the reward of labor."

To what did Tocqueville attribute the difference between the north and south banks? The south bank had slavery; the north bank did not. "These different effects of slavery and freedom" to Tocqueville not only explained the differences of North and South but also "many of the differences which we notice between the civilization of antiquity and that of our own time."

The North and South however differed not only because of slavery, but for other reasons as well, some cultural, others economic. The Puritan spirit of New England dominated the North, for, as we have noted, much of the Near West had been settled by pioneers from New England. These settlers brought to their new homes New England social and political organization, but, more importantly, the New England mindset. Puritanism began as a revolt against the (to them) all-too-Catholic state Church of England. Puritanism had always implied a questioning and rejection of tradition and custom. This questioning of tradition had led many New Englanders away from Puritanism's more rigid doctrines into Unitarianism and other systems, but the native distrust of received tradition remained and had been intensified by democracy. New Englanders, and with them, the North, had moved from a trembling faith in the Sovereign Will of God to an enthusiastic embrace of the radical freedom that allowed the individual to decide for himself what is true and good.

This spirit of individualism, as we have seen, produced new inventions and opened up a wilderness. Individualism, along with New England's rocky soil, had induced men to become merchants and manufacturers. Though the North still remained largely agrarian, industrial concerns and interest in making money were becoming dominant there. This was evident even in agriculture, where farmers were becoming speculators, buying farms only to improve them and sell them at a higher price. In the North, the social revolution that was changing the society of America showed no signs of slowing down; on the contrary, it was accelerating.

The South was different. It had undergone its pioneer phase, its rapid and disordered scramble towards the West; and southerners were still pushing west, along the Santa Fe Trail, into New Mexico and California. Yet, in the southern lands, the pioneering spirit left in its wake nothing like the restlessness and ferment of the North. Instead, southern society seemed to grow drowsy and sleep. Vast tracts of dense woods remained, broken only occasionally by large and small plantations. Roads remained in poor condition. The enterprise to build factories, to dig canals, and lay railroads seemed utterly lacking.

The rich agricultural lands of the South, its temperate climate and abundant water, were made for farming. The northernmost southern states—Maryland, Virginia, North Carolina, Kentucky, much of Tennessee—produced for the most part cereal crops and tobacco. Along the coasts of South Carolina and Georgia, and in the swampy lands of Louisiana, sugar cane and rice predominated. But a great deal of the South, from

Alexis de Tocqueville

An idealized picture of a plantation in the Deep South

South Carolina into Georgia, throughout the black soil lands of the Gulf states into Texas, up the Mississippi, along the Red River—in these lands King Cotton held sway. Eli Whitney's invention of the cotton gin had allowed cotton growing to spread across the continent and made cotton the largest export, not only of the South, but of all the United States. In 1820, the cotton kingdom produced 334,000 bales of cotton; by 1860 this figure had risen to 3.8 million bales—two-thirds of all U.S. exports.

This wealth of cotton had several effects. For one, it helped keep the South an agricultural land. Growers did not invest money in trade or manufactures, or even in improving the buildings on their sometimes vast plantations. Because cotton growing quickly depleted the soil, plantation owners were continually investing in new lands to replace the exhausted ones. As long as new lands were there for the taking, few cotton growers concerned themselves with wise management of the soil, and this contributed to the move westward, into the Gulf states and Texas. Too, the cotton gin had made slavery profitable, so much of a plantation owner's profits went into buying new slaves to work his expanding domain. The non-cotton southern states became supply depots for the cotton states, providing them with food, mules, and more black slave labor.

These facts explain the material reasons for what some would call southern backwardness, but others, southern agrarianism. Yet, though material conditions contribute to human society and culture, they do not absolutely determine it. What a people think the highest and most important goods—what, most importantly, they think about God and their relationship to him—has a greater effect in forming a culture than merely the character of their land and climate. Southerners, by and large, had certain ideas about how society should be constituted, about how life should be lived. These ideas influenced how they saw themselves, how they ordered their life, how they tried to direct their government—it even influenced their belief in God and how they worshiped Him.

Tradition, Honor, Custom

Unlike Americans of the North, who reveled in newfangledness, the people of the South regarded themselves as conservative and preservers of tradition. In particular, they saw themselves as carrying on the traditions of European, specifically English aristocratic society. Indeed, many a southern gentleman believed himself not merely to be a descendant in spirit, but also in blood to European "cavaliers." "The southern Gentleman comes of a good stock," wrote Daniel R. Hundley in 1860:

> Indeed, to state the matter fairly, he comes usually of aristocratic parentage; for family pride prevails to a greater extent in the South than in the North. In Virginia, the ancestors of the Southern Gentleman were chiefly English cavaliers, after whom succeeded the French Huguenots and Scotch Jacobites. In Maryland, his ancestors were in the main Irish Catholics—the retainers and associates of Lord Baltimore—who sought in the wilds of the New World religious tolerance and political freedom. . . . Throughout the entire extent of the South, (for the new Southern States have been settled almost wholly by emigrants from those named above,) wherever you meet with the Southern Gentleman, you find him *hijo dalgo*, as the Spaniards phrase it.

There were, however, "many notable exceptions," said Hundley. "There are scattered throughout all the southern States many gentlemen of the genuine southern character, whose ancestry was only in part of the cavalier stock."

Two books were, in part, responsible for the belief that southern gentlemen came from cavalier stock. One was *The Cavaliers of Virginia*, written in 1832 by William A. Caruthers; the other, *Lettres sur l'Amérique du Nord*, written by Michel Chevalier four years later.

Chevalier argued that while northern Americans descended from Oliver Cromwell's Puritan Roundheads, the settlers of Virginia came from the cavaliers who followed the Stuart king, Charles I. On the strength of these works, many a southerner—whether a rich plantation owner or poorer planter—believed he sprang from aristocratic stock. This was, of course, not true; most southerners descended from English, Scots, and Irish of the middle and lower classes. Some, especially in the Carolinas, came from England into America as indentured servants, scarcely above the status of slaves.

The South actually had few "old families." The Washingtons, Lees, and Randolphs of Virginia; the South Carolina descendants of the 17th century Huguenot refugees; the old Creole families of Louisiana—these were the closest thing the South had to old family, landed aristocracy. Most rich landowners, especially in the Gulf states, had been up-and-coming men who had made it rich on cotton. Some were transplanted Yankees. The example of Jefferson Davis was not unusual. Born in a log cabin in Kentucky, Davis served in the army, distinguishing himself at the Battle of Buena Vista during the Mexican War. Afterwards he married General Zachary Taylor's daughter, Sarah. (She died three months after their marriage.) Leaving the military, Davis devoted himself to growing cotton and soon became one of the richest planters in Mississippi. Yet, despite their backgrounds, Davis and others who were not old aristocracy devoted themselves with varying degrees of success to the aristocratic ideal.

Yet, even though they were not blood descendants of European gentry, southern gentlemen were their spiritual descendants. Like the Spaniards, who longed to become *hidalgos* (landed gentlemen) in the New World, many a southerner strove to become an aristocrat. Southern society was a conscious attempt to continue Old World European social and cultural traditions in the New World. Since aristocracy was part of these traditions, it too had to be transplanted to American soil.

In southern eyes, the aristocrat differed markedly from the rich northern merchant, speculator, or industrialist. The southern aristocrat, it was thought, was wealthy, but he did not "chase the Almighty Dollar" like his northern counterparts. In fact, according to the southern aristocratic ideal, while wealth was necessary for one to live the leisurely life of a

A horse race at Jacksonville, Alabama

gentleman, wealth did not make him a gentleman. Unlike in the North, where the patterns of life and the social order were continually being altered to accommodate wealth-making, in the South wealth existed to support a particular model of life.

"Chivalry" summed up those traits that made a man a gentleman in southern eyes. Like the legendary knights of old, the southern gentleman was to cultivate refined manners. He was to foster the spirit of *noblesse oblige* by which he showed kindness and deference to inferiors. In fact, "the natural dignity of manner peculiar to the southern Gentleman," said Hundley, was "doubtless owing to his habitual use of authority from his earliest years; for while coarser natures are ever rendered more savage and brutal by being allowed the control of others, refined natures on the contrary are invariably perfected by the same means, their sense of the responsibility and its incident obligations teaching them first to control themselves before attempting to exact obedience from the inferior natures placed under them."

Hospitality towards guests and strangers also marked the southern gentleman. In their written accounts, travelers through the South noted the graciousness with which both rich and humble southerners received them. One plantation owner would post on a nearby road a slave whose duty was to invite passers-by to enjoy the hospitality of his master's house. Southern chivalry demanded, as well, a lofty respect for women, at least white women. In true chivalric fashion, southern men venerated the fairer sex, competed for their favor in "tournaments" where gentlemen displayed feats of horsemanship, showed deference to them, and defended their honor. A toast made at a celebration of Georgia's 100th anniversary was typical—"Woman!!! The center and circumference, diameter, and periphery, sine, tangent and secant of all our affections!"

The southern gentleman's sense of honor could brook no insult to his name or family. A duel to the death was the proper way to erase an insult, though many resorted to less noble avenues of revenge, such as horse-whipping or stabbing. Though he could tolerate a good deal of laziness or shiftlessness from his "domestics," the southern gentleman could not countenance a slave who crossed him or resisted his will. Honor demanded that a gentleman aid both his rich and poor kinsmen, even those distantly related to him.

A southern gentleman's fidelity to family was to find its fulfillment in love for his country. He was to have a lofty public spirit that would compel him to military service or to a run for the legislature. Public-mindedness might decide his avocation, such as lawyering or medicine. But though such avocations might draw him to the towns or to the federal capital, the southern gentlemen always longed to return to his rural plantation home. "No matter what may be a southern Gentleman's avocation," said Hundley, "his dearest affections usually center in the country. He longs to live as his fathers lived before him, in both the Old World and the New."

That the ideal of the southern gentleman did not always match reality is, in some ways, unimportant; for the ideal shows what kind of man the southerner expected himself to be. Still, the reality rarely lived up to the ideal. Except for a very few, southern gentlemen had little time for leisure. Often occupied with the affairs of his plantation, with the responsibilities arising from owning many slaves, the typical planter found his day consumed by a thousand cares. His wife, too, shouldered many burdens and responsibilities. She was hostess, she directed the life of the household, she bandaged the minor injuries of her household "servants." The realities of the still largely unhewn character of American life kept most planters from achieving their ideal of being a leisured, landed aristocracy.

Human weakness, too, and the inability fully to come to terms with the fact that southern society depended on the misery of men condemned to unending, involuntary servitude compromised the southern aristocratic ideal. The southern gentleman did not love slavery; but he saw it as a necessary foundation for the sort of life he cherished. This was not the only reason he defended slavery, but it was an important one. That the southern gentleman could rise to his ideal only on the backs of his degraded brothers was the fatal assumption that undermined the noble aspirations of this real and would-be "aristocracy."

Southern Social Classes

Only about 15,000 southern families could be called "gentry"; yet, their ideals set the tone for southern society. To greater or lesser degrees, most southern whites followed the code of chivalry espoused by the gentry. One did not need to be a planter to show deference to women. Kinship relations—the extended family, as we would call it today—remained important at all levels of southern white society. One lived not only nearby his mother, father, brothers, and sisters, but his uncles, aunts, great uncles and great aunts; first, second, third, and so on, cousins; and kinsmen for whose kinship relationship the English language has no name.

Unlike in the North, where people seemed constantly on the move, in the South, families settled down and became identified with the regions in which they lived. This rootedness in a place begat pride of family, which the southerner George Fitzhugh praised as the origin of patriotism:

> Families are the most conservative of all institutions. The "son of nobody" belongs to no place or country. Men whose kin and ancestry for hundreds of years have resided in the same section, love their country and may be relied on in times of difficulty. Family pride begets patriotism, and is the only reliable source from whence it arises. . . . Those who have most ties, like the ancient oak, that has been putting forth roots for centuries, are the men to cling to and defend their country . . .

Most southern white families belonged to the class of yeomen farmers. Such farmers owned their own land and the buildings on them. They raised cash crops—tobacco, sugarcane, or cotton—and grazed cattle, kept hogs, and grew much of their daily food. The farmer worked in the fields, alongside the half dozen or so slaves he might own; these shared their master's dinner, often at the same table with their master's family. But while many yeomen farmers were slave owners, thousands more were not. Most southern whites owned no slaves.

Unlike the great planters, who relied on New York banks for loans to buy land and slaves, the yeoman farmer in the South lived fairly independently. The yeoman farmer and his family lived in a log cabin or a simple frame house. Hominy (a type of corn) was their staple food, to which they would occasionally add hog meat and "critters" (raccoons, squirrels, and other small game that could be hunted), collard and mustard greens, and fruit in season. The women made the family's clothing at their own looms. Like the gentry, the yeoman farmer did not read much beyond the Bible and the newspaper, if he read at all; schools of any sort were scarce in the South. The yeoman's entertainment was outdoor sports, hunting, and fishing.

Town dwellers were relatively few in the South, for the simple reason that, unlike the North, towns were few and far between. The only cities of any size were Richmond, Virginia; Charleston, South Carolina; Atlanta, Georgia; and New Orleans, Louisiana. The rest were small towns or mere meeting places (such as churches or courthouses) for the surrounding farm families.

Below the yeomen farmers was a class of people derisively called "poor white trash," "crackers," and other unfortunate names. Despised by more respectable whites, these illiterate, unskilled, and uncultured folks despised and envied their "betters" in turn. They also hated blacks, many of whom lived in more dignity and orderliness than the "rednecks." The only thing that connected "poor white trash" to culture and civilization was their white skin. They lived in tiny cabins with dirt floors, had a bad diet—sometimes eating the clay soil itself—and suffered from hookworm which they caught by going barefoot. Less than ten percent of the population, these unfortunate folk were the frontiersmen left behind in the wake of the great wave of western migration.

Few foreign immigrants came to the South. Unwilling to compete with slave labor, or to be placed on the same social level as black labor, most foreign immigrants chose to settle in the North. The absence of manufacturing centers in the South needing cheap labor was another factor that kept many immigrants from settling there.

Though sometimes confused with "poor white trash," the mountaineers, or "hillbillies" of the South were an entirely different sort of people. Fiercely independent, they lived in the mountain valleys or on the hillsides of the Appalachians and, westward, in the Ozarks. There they subsisted by farming small plots of corn and by hunting and fishing. The mountaineers had little contact with society outside the mountains. They were thus able to keep alive, even well into the 20th century, their unique and rich English and Scots heritage: ancient folk songs, Elizabethan ways of speaking, and old English and Scots customs. They even preserved a stringed instrument forgotten everywhere else—the mountain dulcimer.

Literature and Learning

Much has been made of the fact that the South had more illiterates than the North. The illiteracy rate was higher in the South—almost all southern blacks and at least 20 percent of whites could not read or write. No common school movement agitated for public schools in the South. The South (especially the Atlantic seaboard states) had more academies and colleges than the North; but these charged fees and so were the domains of the southern gentlemen and out of the reach of the yeoman farmers. Lack of literacy, however, does not spell lack of culture. The southerner had a rich culture of folk customs, songs, oral traditions, and stories.

Southern tastes tended toward the Romantic and medieval. Many a southerner enjoyed a night reading the Scottish Romantic novelist and poet Sir Walter Scott's tales of medieval knights-errant and of Jacobite chieftains who fought in the cause of the Stuart kings in England and Scotland. But Sir Walter Scott and other favored writers were not southern, not even American. The antebellum South experienced no renaissance of literature like that of New England and New York. Virginia could boast of the often gloomy imagination of Edgar Allen Poe, who was raised in Richmond. Charleston could claim William Gilmore Simms, who wrote ten romances, including the historical novel, *The Yemassee*, between 1834 and 1842. But beyond these writers, the South had no outstanding literary figures until the 20th century.

Edgar Allan Poe

If the literature of the South was sparse, this may be because the southern genius had long been turned toward politics. One thinks of Thomas Jefferson, James Madison, and other leading lights of the revolutionary period. But after 1820, even this penchant for political writing was squandered in defending the institution of slavery against real and perceived northern threats.

The antebellum South did however produce a number of gentleman amateur scientists. John James Audubon, author of *The Birds of America* and *The Quadrupeds of North America*, was born in Santo Domingo (now Haiti) in the Caribbean and, afterward, lived in Louisiana and Kentucky. Doctor Edmund Ravenel of Charleston became a leading authority on shells, while his cousin, Henry Ravenel, published a book on fungi in 1853. The Georgia planter, Louis Le Conte, kept a botanical garden at his plantation. He was the father of the famous geologist, Joseph Le Conte. Edmund Ruffin, whom legend would say fired the first shot on Fort Sumter, studied soil chemistry and published a book on the subject in 1832.

Ruffin agitated for better methods of cultivation to restore the fruitfulness of Virginia's tidewater soils. Finally, United States naval commander, Matthew Fontaine Maury of Virginia, published a highly respected and definitive book, *The Physical Geography of the Seas*, in 1855.

Religion

If southern society had aristocratic ideals, its religion had a decidedly democratic flavor. The Protestant Episcopal Church (the U.S. branch of the Anglican Communion) attracted mostly members of the old families and had since the Second Great Awakening remained stagnant in numbers. Except for Maryland and Louisiana, and outside of the larger cities, few Catholics lived in the South. Anti-Catholic prejudice, combined with a live-and-let-live attitude amongst Catholics, kept most southerners outside the Church. Instead, most middle class southerners flocked to evangelical sects, particularly the various Methodist and Baptist groups.

As in the North, Protestant groups in the South had splintered into hundreds of sects; unlike northerners, however, southerners did not form strange, fringe religious movements like Noyes' Oneida group and Miller's Adventists. They also were not drawn to Unitarianism or movements that only stressed natural morality apart from God's grace. Though at times intensely emotional, southern religion was classically Bible-based Protestant and conservative.

A kind of Puritan narrowness of morals had descended on southern evangelicalism since the Second Great Awakening. In this region, which would later be called the Bible-belt, evangelical preachers inveighed against liquor, card playing, and dancing. Though spared the agitation of prohibitionist suffragettes, religious southerners, particularly the women, demanded that believers abstain from the "sins" of drinking, gambling, and idleness.

Illustration of a Great Spotted Woodpecker, by John James Audubon

Southern Politics

As we have seen, the ideal of aristocracy colored the society of the Old South. But one place it did not hold sway was the ballot box. General Andrew Jackson of Tennessee had been quite popular in the South. His "Democracy" had inspired the yeoman farmer with the hope of achieving a higher social status and the belief that he could rise to higher social position; moreover, Jacksonian Democracy had spread the conviction that since common men were in the majority, they should have more than just a voice in government. They should control the government. So, even if one was an aristocrat, if he wanted public office, he had to show himself a friend of radical democracy. In most parts of the South, this meant one had to be a candidate of the Democratic Party. The South had its Whigs, but on the whole, Jacksonian Democracy held sway.

But despite this democratic fervor, the ideal of aristocracy still held its own in the South. Though in Alabama and Mississippi the yeoman class controlled the government, in other states one had to be connected to one of the great families to obtain political office. Yet, even aristocrats had to show they were the willing servants of the public that elected them. This was true not only in state government, but in the House of Representatives in Washington. A politician, if he wanted public office, had at least to appear attentive to the interests of those he represented.

Thus, the ideals of aristocracy and gentility dominated the cultural imagination of the South, but the interests of the people held sway in politics. This contradiction expressed and exacerbated a longstanding rivalry between large planters and yeoman farmers, especially in regions like western Virginia, where backwoods mountaineers and poor farmers bitterly resented the power and position of the tidewater aristocracy. A similar opposition reigned in the upland districts of eastern Tennessee and in the hills of northern Alabama.

The "Peculiar Institution"

"Colonel Chaney had lots and lots of slaves," reminisced Harriet McFarlin Payne of Arkansas, herself a former slave . . .

> . . . and all their houses were in a row, all one-room cabins. Everything happened in that one room—birth, sickness, death, and everything, but in them days niggers kept their houses clean and their door yards too. These houses where they lived was called "the quarters." I used to love to walk down by that row of houses. It looked like a town, and late of an evening as you'd go by the doors, you could smell meat a-frying, coffee making, and good things cooking. We were fed good and had plenty clothes to keep us dry and warm. . . . If all slaves had belonged to white folks like ours, there wouldn't been any freedom wanted.

"No, sir, he wa'n't good to none of us niggers," said William Colbert, describing his former Georgia master, years after the Civil War. Colbert remembered how his master had beaten his brother, January, because he had been an hour late for his work. "Massa" was angry; he stript January's shirt off, and said, "'Now, nigger, I'm going to teach you some sense.'"
Colbert continued:

> With that he started laying on the lashes . . . January, he never said nothing, and the massa keep a-beating till little streams of blood started flowing down January's chest, but he never holler . . . I sat on my mammy's and pappy's steps a-crying. The niggers was all gathered about, and some of 'em couldn't stand it; they had to go inside their cabins. After while, January, he couldn't stand it no longer hisself, and he say in a hoarse loud whisper: "Massa! Massa! Have mercy on this poor nigger."

A young slave in rags, ca. 1863

So run two very different accounts of slave life in the South. Slavery was not everywhere the same. Many slave owners were considerate and kind masters; others, if only a relative few, were cruel and sadistic. As William Colbert said, "The peoples was the same as they is now. There was good ones and bad ones. I just happened to belong to a bad one." Jefferson Davis, one of the "good ones," allowed his slaves a large measure of self-government, even permitting them to form their own juries to try petty offenses. Davis' experience of slavery induced him to believe that it was a benign institution—and that it should be spread, through conquest, to Latin America. Another "good one," John Hampden Randolph of Louisiana, hired a physician to care for his slaves, while Mrs. Ann R. Page of Virginia devoted her life to her slaves' welfare. However, there were few checks on those masters who drove their slaves like beasts. And even the best of masters resorted to cruel floggings or mutilation to force his slaves to obedience.

Unlike his counterpart in Spanish America, the Anglo slave owner exercised absolute power over his black slave. He could treat him well, or he could beat him till he was nearly dead. Some states had laws against excessive cruelty, but they were rarely enforced. Two forces kept slavery more or less humane, when it was humane: fear of retaliation from the slaves and ostracism by neighbors who treated their slaves well. The owner could sanction the marriage of slaves, as Harriet Payne said Colonel Chaney did, or he could tear a husband from his wife, a child from his mother, and sell each of them to different masters far from their homes. Slaves dreaded being sold "down south" to the factory-like cotton plan-

Verse from "My Old Kentucky Home"

The cruel separation suffered in slave families was immortalized in Stephen Foster's song, "My Old Kentucky Home." The song speaks of how such separations affected both slaves and the families to whom they "belonged."

> O the young folks roll on the little cabin flo'
> So merry and happy and bright.
> Just a few mo' days, I'll be goin' out de do'
> Then my old Kentucky Home: goodnight!
>
> Weep no more, my lady, o weep no more today
> We will sing one song for my old Kentucky home
> For my old Kentucky home far away.

"Negro Life at the South," 1859

tations of the Gulf States where slaves labored long hours in work gangs and suffered the worst cruelties.

Slavery had gradually disappeared from Catholic Europe in the Middle Ages; it reappeared in the expansion of the 16th century and the greed that accompanied colonization of the Americas. Slavery and the slave trade have been common in Africa for centuries, perpetuated by inter-tribal warfare. The Europeans were merely new customers in the tribal slave market. If he survived the filthy, inhumane, and brutal voyage across the Atlantic, the black man discovered that his life as a slave in America was not without its advantages; sometimes, in America, he was better housed, clothed, and fed than many peasants in Europe. Yet, he was still a slave, and Christians, whose ancestors had once freed slaves, now profited by their misfortune.

Like their white masters, slaves recognized different classes among themselves. Slaves distinguished themselves by how long they had been in America. Some slave families had been in America for 200 years; then there were blacks—"Gullahs" they were called—who had recently been smuggled illegally into the country from Africa. Slaves distinguished themselves by the work they did. Domestic slaves, such as butlers, maids, and "mammies" held a privileged place on the plantation, and they knew it. They were often intimate with their "white folk"; mammy suckled and raised her master's children; the old butler gave his opinions on his master's guests, and was heeded! Below the domestic slaves were the skilled craftsmen and artisans—carpenters, blacksmiths, and barbers—who earned wages and could purchase their freedom with the percentage of the money they earned for their masters. Below these were field hands to whose lot fell all the hard, monotonous work on the plantation. Field hands made up the majority of the slave population.

A small number of free blacks lived in the South. The dwellings of these folk were interspersed with those of whites in the cities and towns, and lower class whites often intermingled socially with their free black neighbors. Upper class whites, though they frowned on any interracial mixing, themselves had dealings with the few prosperous free blacks. A few free blacks, such as Andrew Durnford of Louisiana, owned slaves. Durnford worked his plantation with 75 slaves, whom he bought and sold as readily as any white slave holder. He and other slave-holding blacks looked down on their enslaved brothers as much as any white man did.

A pre-Civil War illustration of a slave auction

Before 1822, southerners looked upon slavery as a necessary evil. Some, like George Mason and Thomas Jefferson, wanted to see a gradual emancipation of the slaves and their repatriation to Africa. Things began to change, however, in 1822. An attempted slave insurrection in Charleston led by a freed black man, Denmark Vesey, awakened fears of slave revolt. The specter of Haiti, where black leader Jean Jacques Dessalines had massacred whites 15 years earlier, frightened southern whites. States began to tone up their "black codes" (laws governing the conduct of slaves). Blacks were forbidden to assemble or to leave their quarters after curfew; and bands of armed men patrolled roads by night. Every state, except Maryland, Kentucky, and Tennessee, passed laws forbidding masters to teach their slaves to read and write, since literate slaves learned to long for a better life. Despite the ease with which they mixed socially with their slaves, white southerners lived in fear of them. There were enough isolated cases of stealthy murder of white masters or mistresses to keep the fear alive. "It is like a smothered volcano," wrote Mrs. Lawrence Lewis of Woodlawn, Virginia. "We know not when, or where, the flame will burst forth, but we know that death in the most repulsive forms awaits us."

A growing antislavery sentiment in the North spurred some southerners to a positive defense of slavery. Thomas R. Dew of Virginia, a professor at William and Mary College, wrote a pamphlet in 1832 arguing that slavery had produced the civilizations of ancient Greece and Rome. The Hebrew prophets, Dew argued, and St. Paul as well, had sanctioned the institution. In two works, *Cannibals All!* and *Sociology for the South,* George Fitzhugh argued that the black man was less human than the white European. John C. Calhoun held that civilization required a subject race.

Still, as late as 1831, the Virginia legislature was contemplating a gradual abolition of slavery. The agitation for abolition came from some of the old Liberal families and from western regions where slavery was less important economically. W. B. Preston of western Virginia introduced a resolution that "it is expedient to adopt some legislative amendment for the abolition of slavery." The time, however, was yet unripe for such measures. It was voted down, 73 to 58.

After 1831 all legislative attempts to abolish slavery in the South ceased. That year, a slave in Virginia led a short-lived but bloody insurrection against the whites.

Nat Turner, a field slave, believed God had called him to rise against the whites. "I heard a loud noise in the heavens," he later recounted (in prison) to the white lawyer Thomas R. Gray (who edited Turner's comments), "and the Spirit instantly appeared to me and said the Serpent was loosened, and Christ had laid down the yoke he had borne for the sins of men, and that I should take it on and fight the Serpent." With four men he could trust—Henry, Hark, Nelson, and Sam—Turner laid his plans. At 2 a.m. on August 21, 1831 (about three years after his vision) Turner and his men broke into the house of Joseph Turner—"who," Nat recounted, "was to me a kind master, and placed the greatest confidence in me; in fact, I had no cause to complain of his treatment to me. . . ."

Turner continues:

> Hark got a ladder and set it against the chimney, on which I ascended, and hoisting a window, entered and came down stairs, unbarred the door, and removed the guns from their places. It was then observed that I must spill the first blood. On which armed with a hatchet, and accompanied by Will, I entered my master's chamber; it being dark, I could not give a death blow, the hatchet glanced from his head, he sprang from the bed and called his wife, it was his last word. Will laid him dead, with a blow of his axe, and Mrs. Travis shared the same fate, as she lay in bed. The murder of this family five in

number, was the work of a moment, not one of them awoke; there was a little infant sleeping in a cradle, that was forgotten, until we had left the house and gone some distance, when Henry and Will returned and killed it.

From the Turner house Nat and his companions took "four guns that would shoot, and several old muskets, with a pound or two of powder."

So began an insurrection that in the end claimed 55 lives. More slaves joined Turner's band until it numbered 40 men. With guns, clubs, axes, and swords, they attacked several houses, shoot-

A contemporary wood-cut of the Nat Turner Rebellion

ing, stabbing, beating, and hacking to death the inhabitants. They spared neither women, nor the old, nor children. The next day, state militia scattered Turner's band when they tried to attack the nearby town of Jerusalem. The following morning, state and federal soldiers repulsed Turner and his small band when they attacked a farm house. Turner escaped, went into hiding on the Travis plantation, until, betrayed by two black women, he was found and captured. The Southampton County Court tried Turner and, on November 4, condemned him to death. On November 11 he was hanged, and then skinned. In all, the state of Virginia executed 55 blacks, exiled many others, and acquitted a few. White mobs, in retaliation for the rebellion, "without trial and under circumstance of great barbarity," as a contemporary account said, murdered over 200 blacks who had taken no part in the rebellion.

With slavery, in Jefferson's words, southerners had caught "the wolf by the ears"; they could "neither hold him, nor safely let him go." Despite the defenses of slavery, many southerners realized its profound injustice. Slave auctioneers were despised in the South, and, wrote Mary Boykin Chestnut, "most people detest overseers." One overseer, who Mrs. Chestnut said was "an exception," expressed what many in the South would, at least, have thought. "I never knew a Negro to be murdered or burnt," he said in 1861, in the midst of the Civil War. "But if the Marsters are bad or drunken, look out. Slavery is a thing too unjust, too unfair to last. Let us take the bull by the horns, set 'em free, let 'em help us fight to pay for their freedom."

A fine sentiment. But without the determination to bring it to fruition, emancipation would remain only a wistful dream.

Part III: The Far West

Gold!

It was January 1848. The Treaty of Guadalupe Hidalgo had not yet been signed, but the war with Mexico was effectively over. California remained what it long had been—a sparsely settled Mexican frontier province. Except for the American flag that waved over the plazas and the presence of American troops, there was little evidence that California now belonged to the United States of America.

That was soon to change.

Johann Sutter had hired a carpenter named James Wilson Marshall to build him a saw mill on the American River, which flows from the Sierra Nevada southwestward into the Sacramento. One day, January 24, Marshall saw in the millrace "something shining . . . I reached my hand down and picked it up. It made my heart thump, for I was certain it was gold. The piece was about half the size and shape of a pea. Then I saw another piece in the water. After taking it out I sat down and began to think right hard." Marshall told Sutter of

A reproduction of a ca. 1850 daguerreotype showing James Marshall standing before the mill, where he discovered gold

his find, and Sutter thought to keep the matter a secret. However, he told his servants, who spread word of the discovery. Soon, the *California Star*, a small paper in San Francisco, got wind of it. But E.C. Kemble, the *Star's* editor, thought the rumors of gold a "sham, as superb a take in as ever was got up to guzzle the gullible."

A few days after the *Star* dismissed the news of gold, a man came to San Francisco from Sutter's fort and paid for goods with gold. This convinced Sam Brannan, the *Star's* owner, that there might be more to the rumors. He went to Sutter's fort and, discovering that the reports were true, returned to San Francisco to plan his strategy. Though he thought there probably was not much gold at the mill, he decided that publicizing the strike would sell newspapers. One day, in May, he strolled down Montgomery Street in San Francisco, holding a bottle of gold nuggets over his head. "Gold! Gold! Gold on the American River!" he cried.

A few days later, the *Star* reported, "the stores are closed and places of business vacated, a large number of houses tenantless." The citizens of San Francisco had abandoned the town for the gold mines. News spread to Monterey. "My messenger sent to the mines has returned with specimens of the gold," wrote Walter Colton, whom Commodore Stockton had named *alcalde* (mayor) of the town.

He dismounted in a sea of upturned faces. As he drew forth the yellow lumps from his pockets and passed them around among the eager crowd, the doubts, which had lingered until now, fled. All admitted they were gold, except one old man, who still persisted they were some Yankee invention got up to reconcile the people to the change of flag. The excitement produced was intense; and many were soon busy in their hasty preparations for a departure to the mines . . . the blacksmith dropped his hammer, the carpenter his plane, the mason his trowel, the farmer his sickle, the baker his loaf, and the tapster his bottle. All were off for the mines, some on horses, some on carts, and some on crutches, and one went in a litter.

A sailing card, advertising transport to California by clipper ship

The Donner Party

It was only two years earlier, before the great rush to the West, when the most famous tragedy of western migration occurred. The Donner Party originally set out from Independence, Missouri in May of 1846. In November, an early snowfall prevented the party's crossing the final mountain pass (since called Donner Pass) through the Sierra Nevada. Of the 79 members of the party, only 45 survived the winter of 1847. And they survived because they ate the bodies of their dead comrades.

An 1846 picture of "Starvation Camp," with stumps of trees cut down by the Donner Party

Word now spread by ship to Hawai'i, and then south into Mexico and Chile. In September, U.S. Navy lieutenant Edward Beale arrived in Washington with 230 ounces of gold. In November, California's territorial governor sent to Washington $3,000 in gold nuggets along with his official report of the gold strike. The federal government put the gold on display, and the East Coast awakened to the hope of promised riches.

"The frenzy continues to increase every day," wrote George Templeton Strong from New York. "It seems as if the Atlantic Coast was to be depopulated, such swarms of people are leaving it for the new El Dorado." Strong of course exaggerated; but, between December 1848 and January 1849, 61 ships set sail from the East Coast carrying 3,000 eager gold seekers. Gold fever spread so swiftly that by the end of 1849, 700 ships had carried 45,000 passengers to California. Some of these took the long (six to eight month), tedious route around Cape Horn. Others sailed to Panama, and crossing the isthmus, awaited ships to carry them along the Pacific Coast to San Francisco. Cholera and malaria assailed those who crossed by way of Panama; many never reached the gold fields.

Other gold seekers came by land to California—some in Conestoga wagons drawn by two to six mules or oxen, others pulling their belongings in push-carts or wheelbarrows. Emigrants braved the Indian threat of the Plains, the lofty terror of the mountains, and the parched and burning desolation of the deserts. Guided by experienced trappers, such as Jim Beckworth, Thomas Fitzpatrick, and Etienne Provost, the "Forty-niners" (so-called because they came in 1849) faced innumerable dangers—starvation, thirst, disease, wild animals, hostile Indians, and their own gullibility and foolishness. We hear of those who, following some deceptive Indian guide, took a "short cut" to the gold fields—and never were seen again. One group who took a "short cut" nearly died of thirst and starvation in a California desert valley, which they christened "Death Valley." Others arrived in the Sierra Nevada after the autumn snows had fallen, and many froze or starved to death. Those who survived did so by the generosity of the California mining towns, which sent them money and supplies.

Emigrants took many routes to California. From Independence, Missouri, they followed the Platte River to Fort Laramie, and from Fort Laramie they crossed the Rockies over South Pass to the Humboldt River. From the headwaters of the Humboldt, the trail passed though

Gold mining in California, an 1849 Currier & Ives lithograph

miles of desolate desert to the Truckee River, following that river into the Sierra Nevada. From the Sierra, the trail descended into the Sacramento Valley. Other emigrants followed the southern Santa Fe Trail, which crossed New Mexico into Arizona, and then followed the Gila River to Yuma on the Colorado. From the Colorado, it traversed the desert to San Bernardino, a Mormon outpost, and from thence to a new American settlement called El Monte. From El Monte and Los Angeles, emigrants continued north to the gold fields.

Gold-hungry adventurers followed the American River into the Sierra Nevada. They panned and sluiced gold out of the river and its tributary streams and knocked it out of rocks. Soon new gold strikes had been made north on the Sacramento River, and farther north on the Trinity and Humboldt Rivers, all the way to the Oregon border. The mining camps that sprang up overnight in the gold fields were colorful places where all ranks of society were reduced to a common level. The camps had professors, doctors, lawyers, even European nobility mixing with the common farmer and mechanic. Blacks were accepted as equals in the camaraderie of the camps.

The miners who made their fortune were generally the clever or unscrupulous, who organized and used the labor of others. Most miners however did not even break even. Some left the gold fields to become carters, run boarding houses, or operate stores. Though most came to California for only as long as it took them to strike it rich, many were so utterly ruined that they could not afford to return to their homes.

The height of the California gold rush was from 1849 to 1853. During that period, miners dug or panned or sluiced $220 million in gold out of California's waters and soil.

Democratic Chaos

It seemed all the world had come to California. Hawai'ians, Mexicans, and Chileans had been the first to arrive at the gold fields from outside the territory. Then came the thousands of Americans from the East Coast and the Middle West. Even Europeans caught gold fever,

A view of San Francisco and its bay, ca. 1860

and hundreds of emigrants arrived from Asia. The population of California multiplied at a phenomenal rate, in five years increasing over tenfold, to 223,856 people.

The port of San Francisco bristled with masts. The village had swollen from a meager population of 500 in 1848 to over 25,000 to 35,000 people by 1850. Hastily constructed frame structures, some with canvas sides, covered the peninsula. Settlers erected schools, churches, theaters, and a public library. Enterprising individuals published magazines and newspapers. But the city had more than its share of saloons, brothels, and gambling parlors—and criminals and charlatans. "Robberies and murders were of daily occurrence," wrote Amos Delano. Crime was so frequent that citizens finally organized a vigilance committee in 1851. When vigilantes caught someone committing a crime, they hastily gathered a jury and tried, condemned, and executed the perpetrator on the spot. Such swift frontier justice was effective. Despite its rough citizenry, San Francisco in a matter of a few months achieved a lower crime rate than long-established cities in the East.

If San Francisco attained some measure of law and order, chaos reigned everywhere else. Throughout California, said a contemporary observer, "human character crumbled and vanished like dead leaves." In Sacramento, hoodlums deliberately started fires that killed over 300 people and left thousands homeless. When attempts were made to put out the fires, the arsonists ignited wood shavings to keep them ablaze. To stem such violence, Sacramento, with the growing cities of Oakland and San Jose, followed San Francisco's example and adopted vigilance committees. But in the camps and in the mining settlements (bearing such names as Murderer's Gulch, Delirium Tremens, Whiskey Diggings, Hangtown, and You Bet) crime was epidemic. "Organized bands of thieves," said Amos Delano, "existed in the towns and in the mountains."

Another kind of thievery, speculation, set prices on all sorts of goods soaring. Leases on hotels and gambling houses ran $100,000 a year in San Francisco. Store space rented for $1,000 a month. Lots in Sacramento, that in 1848 sold for $200 were going for $30,000 a year later. Even such small goods as pickaxes sold for $200 each, and a barrel of whiskey cost $18,000.

California's population had grown so swiftly that in June 1849 the territorial governor called for a constitutional convention. The 48 delegates who gathered in Monterey in

September included mostly older residents; among these were Mariano Vallejo and seven other *Californios*. Despite the large number of southerners in the territory, the constitution the delegates crafted declared California a free state and adopted a clause from Mexican law that allowed married women to own property apart from their husbands. Only about 13,000 voters approved the new constitution in November, and it was sent to Congress for ratification; but even before ratification, elections were held for governor, state legislature, United States representatives and senators. In September 1850 word reached California that Congress had admitted the territory as a state of the federal union.

Yankee California

Though they themselves had only recently come to California, Anglo-American miners did not take kindly to "foreign" miners. Mexicans, for one, were able miners, and the Yankees were envious. In 1850, the state legislature placed a miner's tax—$20 a month—on all foreigners, and bands of Yankee miners made sure the foreigners paid it. It was not long before most Mexicans left the state to escape the burdensome tax. The state legislature passed laws limiting the immigration of Chinese and Japanese into California.

In northern California, the influx of Yankee miners overwhelmed the old *Californio* population. The provision of the Treaty of Guadalupe Hidalgo that recognized old Mexican and Spanish land grants became a problem. For one, the ranchos covered immense tracts of land, and the old records describing the boundaries were ambiguous. Yankee emigrants, moreover, simply squatted on rancho lands. In 1851, Congress passed a law that required a federal board or commission to approve all land grant titles. To prove their claims to their lands, *Californios* had to carry on litigation in courts. To pay their lawyers' fees, they were forced to sell off large tracts of their land.

An Agua Calienta (Cahuilla) woman and her children, 1903. She is shown with a *metate*, a stone used for grinding grain

In 1856, Pablo de la Guerra, addressing the California legislature, pleaded the case of the *Californios*: "they are the ones who had been sold like sheep," he declared, "those who were abandoned and sold by Mexico . . .

. . . They do not understand the language which is now spoken in their own country. They have no voice in this Senate, except such as I am now weakly speaking on their behalf . . . I have seen old men of sixty and seventy years of age weeping like children because they have been cast out of their ancestral home. They have been humiliated and insulted. They have been refused the privilege of taking water from their own wells. They have been refused the privilege of cutting their own firewood. And yet those individuals who have committed these abuses have come here looking for protection, and, surprisingly, the Senate sympathizes with them. You Senators do not listen to the complaints of the Spanish citizens. You do not sufficiently appreciate their land titles and the just right to their possessions.

If Mexicans and *Californios* fared badly under American rule, the lot of the Indians was worse still. Under Mexican rule, even after the secularization of the missions, Indians, though often grossly mistreated, played a role in Californian society as *vaqueros* (cattle herders or cowboys) on the ranches. The Yankees, however, thought the Indians were poor laborers and decided they were useless. Yankees in the Sacramento Valley murdered Indians without provocation; and since California (unlike the Mexican) law wouldn't allow Indians to testify against whites in court, such murders went unpunished. Violent tribes incited Yankee fears and vengeance; the Mojave, Yumas, and Apaches in the south, the Modocs, Klamaths, and Pit River Indians in the north, raided white settlements and killed miners. White retaliations were often brutal; they slaughtered not only the men, but the women, the old, and young children.

Californians could not agree on what to do about the Indians. Some suggested setting up reservations for them, but land developers did not want to abandon prime real estate to "savages." Some suggested killing the Indians off. "It is a mercy to the red devils to exterminate them, and a saving of many white lives," said an editorial in the *Chico Courant* in 1866. The Indian population of California would decrease throughout the remainder of the 19th century, shrinking from 150,000 in 1845 to a mere 16,000 in 1900.

The Gold Rush and the great influx of population mostly affected the northern part of California. In the south, from San Luis Obispo to San Diego, life continued to center on cattle ranching. There were Yankee settlers in the south, and Los Angeles had as much violence and murder as any northern town; yet, outside the towns, the old rancho culture continued and even prospered for a short period. Cattle prices had risen, and *vaqueros* drove herds to the north where they sold them for a profit. But many a rancho don wasted his money in extravagant spending and in gambling, and some lost their lands to high interest rates on loans they had taken out to pay for their extravagance.

California represented a new era in the history of the United States. Settled by both northerners and southerners, it belonged really to no section but was a meeting place for both. The dream of Fray Junípero Serra and the Franciscan friars of a Christian Indian commonwealth had given way, and in its place new men conceived another dream—the dream of an order founded on the equality of (at least) white men and the desire of individuals to better their condition in this world. This dream of course characterized all of the United States, but it would find in the years to come perhaps its fullest flowering in California—the land where the spirit of the Gold Rush has never died.

Chapter 15

Summary

- By the 1850s, in the northern United States, increased productivity, industrialism, and the growth of eastern cities came with the dawn of the canals and the railroads. Manufacturing was accelerated with the invention of such technology as the sewing machine, the mechanical reaper, and the telegraph.

- By 1850, immigrants were flooding into the country, increasing the number of people in the cities. The immigrants often succumbed to poverty, disease, and violence. Some Irish immigrants became involved in politics, while many Germans founded their own communities.

- By 1850 New York had become the most democratic state when, before, it was the most aristocratic. The New York Democratic Party had fallen under the sway of what became known as the Albany Regency. The New York Democratic Party system became the model for all party systems across the union.

- The sectarian spirit took hold of the North and gave American Protestantism an exotic feel. Sects splintered, leading to the formation of new sects.

Chapter 15 Review (continued)

- Reform-minded Christians began to form various societies to improve the spiritual and material condition of the poor and society in general. These included societies promoting temperance, women's suffrage, and asylums for the mentally insane.

- A movement arose in the first half of the 19th century that called for free public schools, partly to provide an education for all Americans, and partly to defend Protestant society against "papistry."

- Some reformers sought to create Utopias in order to reform society. These Utopias included Robert Owen's New Harmony, Charles François Marie Fourier's phalanxes, and George Ripley's Brook Farm. All of these experiments eventually failed.

- In his popular speeches and essays, Ralph Waldo Emerson emphasized that every individual could become enlightened and improved by his own efforts alone. He said, "the highest revelation is that God is in every man," and "Life is an ecstasy." Emerson's Transcendentalist optimism, his exhortations to find God and truth in nature, had a profound effect on the antebellum North and led to what is called the "New England Renaissance."

- Life in the South was very different from that of the North. The South not only had slavery but lacked the restlessness and spirit of growth that characterized the North. Southerners viewed themselves as conservatives and sought to preserve tradition to form an aristocratic society. The ideal of the southern gentleman was one whose wealth existed to support a particular mode of life, who was chivalric, hospitable, and faithful to his kindred.

- There were several classes of whites in the South: the gentleman, the yeoman farmer, the "poor white trash," and the "hillbillies" of the mountains. Literacy was low in the South, and religion was not as affected by a wild sectarianism. In politics, the interests of the people held sway.

- Slavery was a common institution in the South. Some slave owners treated their slaves well, while others were cruel and sadistic. By 1831 the Virginia legislature was considering a gradual abolition of slavery, which was voted down. In the same year, Nat Turner, a field slave, led a short but bloody insurrection against the whites in Virginia.

- In 1848 in California, a carpenter named James Marshall found a lump of gold while building a mill on the American River. His find inspired thousands of people to come to California to find gold. California grew very quickly in size, and a cultural chaos reigned.

- In 1850 California became a state. Californians did not take kindly to the "foreign" Hispanics, Chinese, Japanese, and Mexicans, and the state legislature placed a miner's tax on all foreigners, forcing Mexicans to leave the state.

- Many *Californios* held land grants; but since the boundaries of these grants were ambiguous, Congress passed a law that required a federal board or commission to approve all land grant titles. *Californios* had to sell off large tracts of their lands to carry on the litigation.

- The Indians of California fared far worse than the *Californios*. The Yankees regarded them as useless and often murdered them. Through the remainder of the 19th century, the Indian population in California dwindled significantly.

Key Concepts

Shaker: a member of a religious sect founded by Ann Lee in the 19th century. Shaker teaching emphasized simplicity, celibacy, and work.

Adventist: member of a group of Protestant Christian churches that are distinguished by their emphasis on the belief that the personal, visible return of Christ is close at hand

Unitarianism: the ideology of a religious sect that calls for rationalism and denies the Trinity

Transcendentalism: a movement of writers and philosophers who asserted the essential unity of all creation, the innate goodness of man, and the supremacy of insight over logic and experience in the discovery of truth

New England Renaissance: the period beginning in the 1830s when American literature came of age as an expression of the national spirit

suffrage: the right to vote

universal manhood suffrage: the right of all male citizens to vote

Utopia: an ideal community whose inhabitants exist under seemingly perfect conditions

Dates to Remember

1831: Nat Turner instigates his slave insurrection.

1832: Samuel F.B. Morse invents the electric telegraph.

1843: the potato famine hits Ireland, sending many Irish immigrants to America.

1848: Lucy Stone begins the women's suffrage movement.

James Marshall finds gold at Sutter's Mill in California.

1850: California becomes a state.

Central Characters

Samuel F.B. Morse (1791–1872): inventor of Morse code and the electric telegraph

Ann Lee (1736–1784): religious leader who formed the Shakers

Ralph Waldo Emerson (1803–1882): American poet and leading exponent of Transcendentalism

Henry David Thoreau (1817–1862): American essayist, poet, and philosopher, renowned for his works *Walden* and "On Civil Disobedience" as well as for being a vigorous advocate of civil liberties

Nathaniel Hawthorne (1804–1864): American novelist and short-story writer, known for *The Scarlet Letter* and *The House of Seven Gables*

Lucy Stone (1818–1893): American pioneer in the women's suffrage movement

Dorothea Dix (1802–1887): American educator, social reformer, and humanitarian

Nat Turner (1800–1831): black American slave who led the only major slave rebellion in U.S. history

Questions for Review

1. How did the Puritan ethic contribute to the spirit of industrialism?

2. Name some of the hardships the immigrants faced in America, and why they faced them.

3. Why did Thomas Jefferson think that democracy in America needed to be protected against immigrants?

4. Why did nativist Americans fear immigrants?

5. How did the influx of immigrants change the character of the northern cities?

6. What is the sectarian spirit, and how was it displayed in the United States?

7. Briefly describe each of the religious sects mentioned in this chapter.

8. What were the traits that were thought to characterize the southern gentleman?

9. Describe the different conditions under which slaves lived in the American South.

10. How did the Gold Rush change the character of California?

Ideas in Action

1. Read some of the literature of the New England Renaissance; for instance, essays by Emerson, some of Nathaniel Hawthorne's short stories, and Thoreau's *Walden* or "On Civil Disobedience." Discuss how these works reflect Transcendentalism.

2. Read about Samuel Morse, and learn how to do Morse code.

3. Listen to the songs of Stephen Foster and other songwriters of the time—and, if you can, perform them yourself.

4. This chapter describes the cultural characteristics of the major sections of the United States by 1850. Do these characteristics still apply to these regions today? How and how not? What section do you think has been most influential? Why?

5. Did American society in 1850 reflect the kind of social order the founding fathers of the United States had envisioned for the new country? Why or why not?

Chapter 15 Review (continued)

Highways and Byways

Morse Code

Morse code refers to two systems for representing letters, numbers, and punctuation by an arrangement of dots, dashes, and spaces. Each character is represented by a series of dots and dashes, and these codes are transmitted as electrical pulses or visual signals. The first system was invented by Samuel F.B. Morse for electrical telegraphy. It was improved by his assistant and partner, Alfred Vail, some time later.

It soon became evident that Morse code was useful only for the English language, since Morse did not provide codes for letters with diacritic marks (marks that change the sound value of a letter, like the umlaut in German). Some languages, for example, use more than the 26 letters that the English alphabet uses. To remedy this, International Morse Code was invented by a conference of Europeans in 1851. It is called Continental Morse Code. Similar to the original Morse code, International Morse Code is simpler and more precise. For example, International Morse Code made the dashes a constant length instead of the variable lengths used by the original. International Morse Code has not changed much since it was invented, and it has been used extensively since. It was used in World War II, as well as the Korean and Vietnam wars. It was in constant use by the shipping industry and for the safety on the seas up until the early 1990s.

16 A HOUSE DIVIDED

"I will be as harsh as truth and as uncompromising as justice. On this subject, I do not wish to think, or speak, or write with moderation. No! No! Tell a man whose house is on fire, to give a moderate alarm, tell him to moderately rescue his wife from the hands of the ravisher; tell the mother to gradually extricate her babe from the fire into which it has fallen, O but tell me not to use moderation in a cause like the present. I am in earnest—I will not excuse—I will not retreat a single inch—

"AND I WILL BE HEARD!"

And William Lloyd Garrison was heard. His journal, the *Liberator*, carried his voice throughout the North and into the farthest reaches of the South. His message was not merely "anti-slavery"; he demanded the immediate freeing of all black slaves. "Woe to this guilty land . . . !" cried Garrison. "IMMEDIATE EMANCIPATION can alone save her from the vengeance of Heaven, and cancel the debt of ages." This was radical talk that ruffled the North and galvanized the South in an opposition inspired by fear.

The Goad of Abolition

Garrison, a printer and writer, had been promoting total abstinence from alcohol in Boston when he met Benjamin Lundy. Lundy, who had founded an anti-slavery society in 1815, inspired the young Garrison, then in his mid-twenties, to join the anti-slavery cause. A year later, in 1829, Garrison joined Lundy in Baltimore and with him edited *The Genius of Universal Emancipation*, a journal Lundy had been publishing since 1821.

Masthead of *The Liberator*, 1844

Lundy was a gradualist; that is, he believed slavery should be abolished, but slowly, over time. He also believed that Americans should colonize emancipated slaves somewhere outside the United States. Garrison, at first, accepted these ideas; but, as the years wore on, his mind began to change. He took to promoting immediate emancipation and argued that blacks should remain in America as full and equal citizens of the United States. By 1830, Garrison and Lundy had parted company, and, in 1831, Garrison, with Isaac Knapp, founded in Boston another journal—*The Liberator*.

When, in 1831, Nat Turner's rebellion erupted in Virginia, Garrison wrote that the uprising was "what we have long predicted . . ." "The first drops of blood," he wrote, "which are but a prelude to a deluge from the gathering clouds, have fallen . . ." Not only the South, said Garrison, was responsible for the violence, but "the people of New England and of all the free states. The crime of oppression is national. The South is only the agent in this guilty traffic."

But Garrison aimed his most fiery rhetoric at southerners. "Ye patriotic hypocrites!" he fulminated. "Ye accuse the pacific friends of emancipation of instigating the slaves to revolt. Take back the charge as a foul slander. The slaves need no incentive at our hands."

Garrison aimed at the very center of southern fears—the terror of slave insurrection. Southerners laid the blame for slave insurrection at the feet of Garrison and other abolitionists. Garrison's rhetoric, southerners believed, posed a real threat to their safety. Moreover, Garrison's call for immediate emancipation of slaves, without compensation to their masters, struck at the very foundations of the southern economy. Such a course would have ruined the South, which depended on slave-harvested and processed cotton as its chief export.

Other slavery opponents understood the practical problems of emancipation—and it was thus that they promoted gradual emancipation with compensation to the owners. The gradualists called themselves "anti-slavery" and distinguished themselves from the more radical men like Garrison, who became known as "abolitionists."

William Lloyd Garrison

The Challenge of Anti-slavery

The anti-slavery movement, both in its moderate and abolitionist manifestations, arose from evangelical Protestant revivalism. Slavery was seen as the crowning evil in a nation riddled with moral corruption, and fighting slavery was an act of repentance. anti-slavery adherents were usually allied with other reform movements in society—with the temperance movement, for instance, and the women's rights movement.

One of the most active anti-slavery reformers was Theodore Dwight Weld of Connecticut. Weld had been converted to evangelical Christianity by Charles Grandison Finney and had worked with the Rev. Sylvester Graham in his campaign against white bread. Weld had traveled to the Gulf of Mexico in 1831–32 to observe slavery conditions first hand.

In 1833 Weld, along with Garrison, Arthur Tappan, and others, formed the American Anti-slavery Society, whose publication, *The Emancipator*, became the most widely read of the anti-slavery journals. The society attracted the rich New York businessman, Arthur Tappan, and the poet John Greenleaf Whittier, who headed the society's New York branch. Standing upon the "Declaration of Independence and the truths of divine revelation," the society's "Declaration of Sentiments" admitted that the federal constitution did not grant the federal government the authority to interfere with slavery; so, instead of agitating for political change, the society dedicated itself to moral persuasion to change the hearts of both northerners and southerners. But such positions were no comfort to the South, since the society held that all laws that protected slavery were null and void.

John Greenleaf Whittier in the 1830s

Angelina Grimké and her older sister, Sarah, the daughters of a Charleston, South Carolina, judge, had grown up in the South and so had witnessed slavery first-hand. Their experience made them prominent anti-slavery advocates; but Angelina, in particular, lent her energies to the "emancipation" of women as well. Theodore Weld, Angelina's fiancée, wrote to her trying to dissuade her from dividing her energy between anti-slavery and women's rights. "In a debating society when a boy," he wrote, "I took the ground that sex neither qualified nor disqualified for the discharge of any functions mental, moral, or spiritual; that there is no reason why woman should not make laws, administer justice, sit in the chair of state, plea at the bar or in the pulpit, if she had the qualifications . . ." But, wrote Weld, so many "unspeakable responsibilities rest on you—on YOU!" that "you" must leave the "lesser work" to others.

Angelina explained in her reply why she thought the causes of women and slaves were connected. "Reformations," she said, are "bound together in a circle like the sciences; they blend with each other like the colors of the rainbow; they are parts only of our glorious whole and that whole is Christianity, pure practical Christianity."

The currents of anti-slavery and other reform movements met and coalesced at Oberlin College in Ohio (founded in 1833). In 1834, Theodore Weld, who had taught at Lane Theological Seminary in Cincinnati, withdrew to Oberlin with 20 of his students when the seminary's trustees forbade any discussion of slavery. In 1835, the year Charles Grandison Finney came to teach theology there, Oberlin became the first U.S. college to admit black students. The college had also been the first in America to educate women together with men; in 1841, three women graduated from Oberlin with bachelor of arts degrees that were comparable to degrees men received in other universities.

Angelina Grimké

The anti-slavery movement was, not surprisingly, mostly made up of whites; but former slaves worked for emancipation as well, traveling to anti-slavery conventions, telling of their experiences in slavery. Their eloquence was arresting—inspiring tears and sometimes laughter—annealing the resolution to fight. One of these black speakers was Frederick Douglass, the son of a white man and a black mother.

In Maryland, his master's wife had taught Douglass as a young man how to read and write, and these skills had opened for him a whole new world and kindled in his heart a longing for freedom. Douglass put his learning to practice and began forging passes for slaves who wanted to escape north. Though his master, William Freeland, was kind to him, Douglass himself attempted an escape in 1836, but was suspected and jailed. He was later released on lack of evidence.

Freeland later sent Douglass to serve Hugh Auld in Baltimore as a ship's caulker. In 1838, disguised as a sailor, Douglass escaped by train to New York City. He ended up in New Bedford, Massachusetts and in 1841 gave an extempore speech before an anti-slavery meeting in Nantucket. This proved to be the beginning of his career as a lecturer on the anti-slavery circuit. Douglass' eloquence and learning led some to call him an imposter, and to refute the charge, in 1845 Douglass published the *Narrative of the Life of Frederick Douglass, An American Slave*. From 1845 to 1847 he went to England and Ireland to lecture—and avoid capture.

Douglass was not the only black man to fight in the struggle against slavery. James Holly was a free black and Episcopalian minister who advocated that blacks move outside the boundaries of the United States and set up a republic of their own. He wanted to show whites that blacks were capable of self-government. After his visit to Haiti, Holly encouraged free blacks to move there, advice he himself finally took in 1861. William Nell, another free black, worked to desegregate Boston schools, a goal he saw accomplished in 1855.

Frederick Douglass, age 29

Black women too joined the struggle against slavery. One was Isabella Baumfree, a tall, spare woman of great dignity, who called herself "Sojourner Truth." Sojourner had belonged to a New York slaveholder, who had raped her. When New York passed its manumission law,

Sojourner Truth

she became free. Sojourner said that she talked with God, and he had told her to preach against slavery. Leaving everything behind, she became a sojourner, a wanderer, preaching against slavery with spell-binding eloquence. "I sets up my banner," she said, "an' then I sings, an' then folks always comes up round me, an' then I preaches to 'em. I tells them about Jesus, an' I tells them about the sins of his people. A great many always comes to hear me; an' they're right good to me, too, an' say they want to hear me again."

For Sojourner Truth, the fight for justice did not rely solely on human powers, but on God. Once, at an abolition meeting at Faneuil Hall in Boston, she shared the platform with Frederick Douglass. After eloquently detailing the wrongs of slavery, Douglass concluded that the slaves had no hope of justice except what "their own right arms" could win them. When he finished, Sojourner broke the silence in the hall. "Frederick," she called out, "is God dead?"

Cannibals All!

In 1831, southern state legislatures began passing more stringent laws governing the activities of slaves. This was a direct result of the Nat Turner rebellion, but it was in part a response to growing anti-slavery and abolitionist agitation in the North. Garrison's tirades against slave holders—accusing them all of barbaric cruelty—struck southerners hard. Instead of changing their hearts, Garrison's assaults put their backs up and set them on the defensive.

Southerners responded to abolitionist attacks and even used the Bible to justify slavery. After all, they argued, the Old Testament patriarchs owned slaves, and St. Paul told slaves to obey their masters; how, then, could slavery be a moral evil? When abolitionists, unable to find a clear Biblical condemnation of slavery, began arguing that slavery violated the natural equality of man, some pro-slavery apologists took another tack. John C. Calhoun, for instance, argued that a subject race was needed to serve civilization. "Many in the South," wrote Calhoun, "once believed that slavery was a moral and political evil. That folly and delusion are gone. We see it now in its true light and regard it as the most safe and stable basis for free institutions in the world."

George Fitzhugh, a lawyer and small planter from Virginia, responded to abolitionists like Garrison by pointing to northern hypocrisy. "We are all, North and South, engaged in the White Slave Trade, and he who succeeds best, is esteemed most respectable," Fitzhugh wrote in his book, *Cannibals All!* By the "white slave trade," Fitzhugh was referring to the inhuman treatment of immigrant workers in northern factories. The "White Slave Trade," said Fitzhugh, "is far more cruel than the Black Slave Trade, because it exacts more of its slaves and neither protects nor governs them . . . The profits, made from free labor, are the amount of the products of such labor, which the employer . . . takes away, exacts, or 'exploitates' from the free laborer." The slave owner, however, receives smaller profits from slave labor, said Fitzhugh, "because the master allows the slave to retain a larger share of the results of his own labor." White slavery, said Fitzhugh, is more cruel, for it leaves "the laborer to take care of himself and family out of the pittance which skill or capital have allowed to retain."

"'Property in man' is what all are struggling to obtain," concluded Fitzhugh. Yet he argued slaves were better cared for than white laborers. Why, he asked, should not capitalists "be obliged to take care of man, their property, as they do of their horses and their hounds, their cattle and their sheep? Now, under the delusive name of liberty, you work him, 'from morn to dewy eve'—from infancy to old age—then turn him out to starve. You treat your horses and hounds better. Capital is a cruel master. The free slave trade, the commonest, yet the cruelest, of trades."

Cannibals All! was a powerful indictment. Though it could not and did not justify southern slavery, it pointed out an inconsistency in many anti-slavery minds; in their concern for the black slaves of the South, they paid scant attention to the plight of free laborers—black and white—in the North.

In general, northerners themselves were scarcely more welcoming of their anti-slavery and abolitionist brethren than were

CANNIBALS ALL!

OR,

SLAVES WITHOUT MASTERS.

BY

GEORGE FITZHUGH,

OF PORT ROYAL, CAROLINE, VA.

" His hand will be against every man, and every man's hand against him."—GEN. XVI. 12.
"Physician, heal thyself."—LUKE IV. 23.

RICHMOND, VA.
A. MORRIS, PUBLISHER.
1857.

Title page from Fitzhugh's work, *Cannibals All!* The quotations from Scripture read: "His hand shall be against every man, and every man's hand against him" (Genesis 16:12) and "Physician, heal thyself" (Luke 4:23).

southerners. Moreover, most northerners, and a good number of anti-slavery people, were opposed to full social and legal equality for blacks, slave or free. The very thought of intermarriage with blacks appalled them. Then there was the economic aspect of the question. Northern textile manufacturers benefited from the fruits of slavery—the abundant cotton crop of the South. Northern merchants, too, had, for a long time, been involved in the African slave trade, and continued, illegally, to smuggle in slaves from Africa.

In the North, free blacks occupied the lowest rung on the social ladder. They lived in squalid ghettos, segregated from the predominately white community. They competed with poor whites, particularly Irish immigrants, for jobs and suffered periodically from riots and violence from the Irish and other groups. The poor living condition of blacks in the North led Fitzhugh to opine:

> The aversion to negroes, the antipathy of race, is much greater at the North than at the South; and it is very probably that this antipathy to the person of the negro, is confounded with or generates hatred of the institution with which he is usually connected. Hatred to slavery is very generally little more than hatred of negroes.

It might seem to us today that anti-slavery was a cause that at least a large percentage of American Christians would have embraced. But the reality was that the reaction of most religious groups to slavery was tepid, if they did not oppose anti-slavery and abolition both. Mainline Protestant churches in the North remained neutral on the slave question. In 1836, the Congregationalists rejected immediate emancipation, as did the Methodists. The Presbyterians said slavery was a political, not a moral, issue; later they would divide into northern and southern branches over the question. Episcopalians and Lutherans also took a neutral stance.

The Catholic position was complicated by the fact that the Church in America had been founded in Maryland, south of the Mason-Dixon. "The public opinion of the Catholic body," wrote the convert Orestes Brownson, "is formed mainly by the Catholics in the Border Slave States, and the Catholics in these states, including the District of Columbia, are intensely southern in their character and sympathies, and bitterly hostile to New-England, or to the 'Yankees.' Their southern sympathies, and hatred of Yankees or New Englanders are diffused through the entire Catholic body even in the New-England states themselves." Maryland Jesuits had owned slaves, as did some bishops and the Ursuline sisters of New Orleans. The "black code" of Louisiana, hearkening back to both French and Spanish law, held that masters were to respect the marriages of blacks and to provide them the freedom to observe holy days, which, in those days included freedom from manual labor. This code, though, was often ignored. Some Catholics engaged in slave smuggling—though popes had condemned it.

The Catholic position on slavery can in part be explained by the fact that Catholics were engaged in their own struggles against nativist bigotry. Catholics, too, were for the most part Democrats, a party that had an enormous power base in the South. Further, though Catholic theologians taught that it is immoral to enslave an innocent free man, one is not, they said, necessarily bound to abolish a condition of slavery or to free people already reduced to a condition of slavery. If freeing slaves would lead to greater evils that would seriously harm the common good—if, say, their freedom meant economic ruin for all, both slave and free—then one was not bound to emancipate them. A master had to treat his slaves as

The Pope on Slavery

In 1839, Pope Gregory XVI issued a letter, *In Supremo,* against the slave trade. It reads in part:

We . . . do vehemently admonish and adjure in the Lord all believers in Christ, of whatsoever condition, that no one hereafter may dare unjustly to molest Indians, Negroes, or other men of this sort; or to spoil them of their goods; or to reduce them to slavery; or to extend help or favor to others who perpetrate such things against them; or to exercise that inhuman trade by which Negroes, as if they were not men, but mere animals, however reduced into slavery, are, without any distinction, contrary to the laws of justice and humanity, bought, sold, and doomed sometimes to the most severe and exhausting labors; and, moreover, the hope of gain being by

Gregory XVI

that trade proposed to the first captors of the Negroes, dissensions, also, and as it were, perpetual wars are fomented in their countries . . .

Gregory's was not the first papal condemnation of slavery and the slave trade. In 1435, Pope Eugene IV in *Sicut Dudum* condemned the enslaving of black people in the Canary Islands. Responding to abuses in the New World, Pope Paul III condemned the enslavement of Indians and the confiscation of their property in the 1537 pontifical decree, *Sublimis Deus.* Likewise, between 1591 and 1741, Popes Gregory XIV, Urban VIII, and Benedict XIV joined their voices to the condemnations of slavery. In 1815, Pope Pius VII tried to convince the European powers at the Congress of Vienna to outlaw slavery.

human beings, not mistreat them, not buy and sell them, not forbid them to marry, divide families, or deprive them of the benefits of religion; but, he need not free them. Most Catholics agreed with their neighbors that, at least, immediate emancipation would lead to grave social ills. In an attempt to explain Pope Gregory XVI's 1839 letter on slavery, Bishop John England of Charleston said that the pope was condemning the slave trade, not domestic slavery. While Bishop England himself did not favor the continuance of "domestic slavery," he thought abolition merely a political question, not a moral necessity. This was the general view of most American Catholics.

Two Catholics in Ireland—the patriot hero Daniel O'Connell and Father Theobald Mathew—urged Irish Catholics in America to enlist in the abolition cause. American Catholic voices, however, were stronger. Orestes Brownson opposed any movement that would contravene the Constitution. An unsigned editorial in the *Metropolitan*, the diocesan paper of the archdiocese of Baltimore, said in 1855 that the abolition movement had produced only one result: to render laws against slaves "more severe than ever," neutralizing "all attempts to ameliorate the condition of the Negro . . . [T]he emancipation of the slave has been retarded, perhaps for a century." The editorial said Catholics "must ever stand aloof from the abolition movement, and in their own way labor to effect the great end; and few we think . . . will entertain any other opinion than our own, that if slavery ever is abolished, it will be by the Catholic Church in her own calm, steady, lawful way."

Illustration of the Alton, Illinois riot

Opposition to the anti-slavery and abolition movement in the North at times broke out in violence. In 1835, a mob tied a rope around William Lloyd Garrison's neck and led him through the streets of Boston. The police saved him, and he spent a night in jail. Farmers whipped the English abolitionist, Charles Stewart, out of Plainfield, Connecticut. Mobs attacked an anti-slavery meeting in the Pennsylvania Hall for Free Discussion in Philadelphia. After burning down the hall, they then went on to assault free blacks.

Elijah Lovejoy became the most celebrated of abolitionist martyrs. He had left St. Louis, Missouri, to settle in Alton, Illinois, just across the Mississippi, to escape opposition to his church paper, *The Observer*, which carried his anti-slavery editorials. But Illinois proved no refuge for the reformer. A mob in Alton destroyed his printing press in 1837. Later, they destroyed a second press. When Lovejoy bought a third press, securing it in a warehouse under armed guard, a mob attacked the warehouse. Shooting broke out, one of the assailants was killed, and the mob withdrew. When Lovejoy opened the door of the warehouse, five shots rang out, and he fell, dead.

The death of Lovejoy, and the sufferings of others abolitionists, did not retard an increase in the ranks of anti-slavery societies. Their membership, by 1840, had swelled to 150,000.

Politics or No Politics

For years, the Quaker Thomas Garrett's home in Wilmington, Delaware, had been a way-station for slaves who wanted to escape to the North and freedom. Thousands had been given refuge and aid by Garrett, on account of which slave owners offered a $10,000 reward for his capture. In 1848, authorities in Delaware, a slave state, arrested and tried Garrett. The jury's verdict—Garrett was guilty of stealing slaves from their masters. When Garrett heard his sentence (he was ordered to sell his home and business) he addressed the court with all Quaker solemnity:

"Judge, now that thou hast relieved me of what little I possessed, I will go home and put another story on my house. I want room to accommodate more of God's poor."

Turning to the court, Garrett then deliverd an hour-long oration against slavery. When he had finished, one of the jurors approached him and said, "Give me your forgiveness, and let me be your friend."

"Freely given," replied Garrett, "if thee ceases to be an advocate of the iniquitous system of slavery."

Garret's friends bought his property at auction and restored it to him. He took to welcoming fleeing slaves as before and sent them on their way again, north.

Garrett's was just one station in what became known as the Underground Railroad. He was one "conductor" in the organized system that, in defiance of the Fugitive Slave Law, helped slaves escape north and thence into Canada. The Underground Railroad ran from Virginia and Kentucky along certain routes, house to house, into the North. An escaping slave followed the north star by night and hid by day until he met a conductor, who would, by various disguises and stratagems, help him to the next station. It was a dangerous business. Slave-hunters and many other perils pursued escaped slaves. Since the Fugitive Slave Law allowed slave-hunters to pass the Mason-Dixon and the Ohio in pursuit of their quarry, the fugitive slaves were not safe until they reached Canada.

When Harriet Tubman of Maryland learned in 1849 that she was to be sold following her master's death, she set off after the north star and freedom. She reached Philadelphia but then returned a year later to bring out her family—brothers and cousins, mother and father. In the ensuing years, she returned to the South 19 times. In all she led 300 slaves to freedom.

Harriet Tubman said she did not fear capture. "I had reasoned dis out in my mind," she said, "that there was one of two things I had a right to, liberty or death; if I could not have the one, I would have de oder; for no man would take me alive; I should fit for liberty as long as my strength lasted, and when de time come for me to go, de Lord would let dem take me." She carried, concealed beneath her dress, a revolver that she was determined to use against anyone who stood in her way. Once, when one of the escaping slaves in her party panicked, threatening to turn back and betray them all, she placed the gun to his head. "Dead niggers tell no tales; you go on or die," she told him.

Harriet Tubman (far left) with family members and others she helped to escape

The Underground Railroad represented the ultimate nonpolitical response to slavery and was espoused by the likes of William Lloyd Garrison. But some began to think that more was needed than heroic escapes and efforts to change slaveholders' hearts; they began to look towards politics. In 1835 abolitionists began sending petitions to Congress, asking it to abolish slavery in the District of Columbia. Because of southern opposition, however, Congress rejected the anti-slavery petitions without reading them.

In 1836, Congress passed the first of its "gag resolutions"—that all petitions relating to slavery or abolition should be "laid on the table"; that is, ignored. John Quincy Adams, then a representative from Massachusetts, vigorously opposed the gag resolution, calling it "a violation of the Constitution of the United States, of the rules of this House, and the rights of my constituents." Galvanized into resistance against the gag, abolitionists sent tens of thousands of petitions into Congress, all of which were tabled. In the end, the sheer amount of unrelenting abolitionist opposition to the gag resolutions had its effect—Congress repealed the resolutions in 1844.

By 1844 one could detect a definite split in the anti-slavery ranks. Some, like Garrison, eschewed politics; others, however, began to form organized political resistance to slavery. James Birney, a southerner converted by Weld to the abolitionist cause, organized the first anti-slavery party in the United States, the Liberty Party, in 1839. Birney ran for president the following year but garnered only 7,000 votes. Four years later, though, he ran again and received 62,000 votes.

Though an important founder of the abolitionist movement, Garrison's rejection of politics weakened his influence among anti-slavery people. Indeed, not only would Garrison not sully himself with politics, he did not wish to dirty himself any longer with the federal union. "The issue is this," he said in 1855: "God Almighty has made it impossible from the beginning, for liberty and slavery to mingle together, or a union to be founded between abolitionists and slaveholders—between those who oppress and those who are oppressed. This Union is alien; the American Union is a sham, an imposture, a covenant with death, an agreement with hell, and it is our business to call for a dissolution . . . . I say, let us cease striking hands with thieves and adulterers, and give up to the winds the rallying cry, 'No union with slaveholders, socially or religiously, and up with the flag of Disunion.'" Such rhetoric only served to distance Garrison further from the mainstream of the movement he had founded.

They Awakened a Slumbering Evil

Calhoun had been right. The old senator from South Carolina had predicted that the vast new territories won from Mexico in the last war would re-awaken the sectional controversy over slavery in the territories. As early as 1846, talk of what to do with conquered California, New Mexico, and Utah stirred up the old rivalry—would these territories be open to slavery or not? One congressman answered with a definite no. On August 8, 1846, Representative David Wilmot of Pennsylvania submitted his "Wilmot Proviso" to Congress—a proposal to forbid any introduction of slavery into territories where it did not already exist. The proposal immediately became a focal point of controversy.

Of course, southern representatives strenuously protested the Wilmot Proviso. President Polk, trying to restore peace, proposed extending the Missouri Compromise line to the Pacific—territories north of that line being free, those south of it, open to slavery. This seemed a sensible solution, but the slavery controversy had gone too far to allow hardliners on either side of the issue to acquiesce to it—"to retreat a single inch." Moreover, new theories about the legality of slavery in the territories forbade any consideration of extending the Missouri Compromise to the west.

On the anti-slavery side, many argued that Congress had a moral duty to forbid slavery in the new territories. Slavery, they said, should be confined to the southern states, where it would, eventually, die out. On the pro-slavery side, Senator John C. Calhoun declared the Missouri Compromise itself unconstitutional. Since the union, said Calhoun, was a partnership of northern and southern states, the territories belonged equally to all the states; Congress therefore could not forbid settlers from bringing their "common law property" into any territory. Congress, Calhoun concluded, had the constitutional duty to protect slave property, like any other property.

The question of slavery in the territories remained unresolved when Polk left office on March 4, 1849. Leaving California, New Mexico, and Utah unorganized territories, Congress contented itself with admitting Oregon as a free territory in 1848.

An exhausted President Polk had decided not to run for a second term in 1848, and so the Democrats settled on Lewis Cass of Michigan as their candidate. Cass was a proponent of what became known as popular, or "squatter," sovereignty—that the people living in a territory should themselves decide whether it would be be slave or free. The Whig candidate, General Zachary Taylor, though a southerner and a slave owner, was nevertheless not strongly pro-slavery. Having never before even voted in a presidential election, Taylor's political views were unknown, an asset in those controversial times. He was simply an able general—"Old Rough and Ready," the hero of the Battle of Buena Vista in the Mexican War! General William Henry Harrison had won the Whigs the presidency in 1840; another general might win it for them in 1848.

Anti-slavery thus found no home in either major party. Under the slogan, "Free Soil, free speech, free labor, and free men," disaffected Democrats from New York, members of James Birney's Liberty Party, and anti-slavery Whigs formed the Free-Soil Party. Hearkening back to the Ordinance of 1787, which forbade the introduction of slaves into the Northwest Territory, the Free-Soilers argued that Congress could forbid slavery in any territory. They wanted to "limit, localize and discourage" slavery. Martin Van Buren was the Free Soil candidate for president.

It was an ugly, bitter campaign. James Fenimore Cooper wrote campaign articles for the Democrats, while John Greenleaf Whittier penned salvos for the Free-Soilers. The former

John C. Calhoun

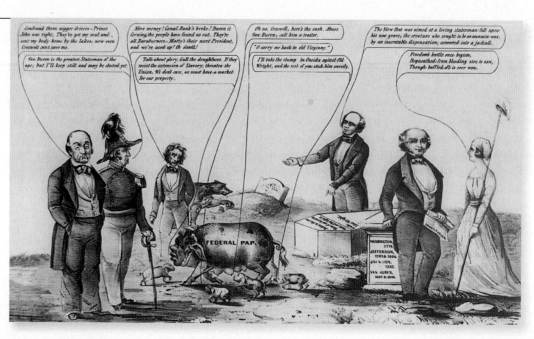

A pro-Free Soil, pro-Van Buren political cartoon, election of 1848

Illinois representative, Abraham Lincoln, campaigned for Taylor and the Whigs, arguing that supporting Free Soil would only throw the election to the Democrats. Banners, buttons, campaign biographies, and satirical ballads promoted the candidates and mocked their rivals. One piece of doggerel ran:

> Come, ye hardy sons of toil,
> And cast your ballots for Free Soil;
> He who'd vote for Zacky Taylor,
> Needs a keeper or a jailor.
> And he who for Cass can be
> He is a Cass without the C;
> The man on whom we love to look
> Is Martin Van of Kinderhook.

Despite the dire predictions, Free Soil did not split the Whig vote. Instead, "Little Van" pulled votes from Cass in New York, and the state went for Taylor. Though the electoral margin was small, the people chose Old Rough and Ready for their president.

Lewis Cass

President Taylor turned out to be an able, if uninspired, executive. Convinced that the whole slavery issue was so much political hash, Old Rough and Ready was eager to get on with organizing the new western territories and admitting California into the union as a state. The new, 31st Congress (with 112 Democrats, 105 Whigs, and 12 Free Soilers in the House), was however bitterly divided over the question of slavery in the territories. Southern senators, in particular, resolutely opposed the admission of California as a free state. "I trust we shall prevail in our resistance until the restoration of all our rights," wrote Calhoun to his daughter, "or disunion, one or the other, is the consequence. We have borne the wrongs and insults of the North far too long. It is time they should cease." While Calhoun was concerned for southern rights, some of the younger, more radical southerners opposed a free California because they dreamed of establishing a slave-holding empire stretching from the Atlantic to the Pacific. Other southerners had no such grandiose dreams; they merely feared that they would lose power in the Senate (where North and South still had equal representation) if California and the other territories were admitted to the union as free states.

The old senator from Kentucky, the 73-year-old Henry Clay, sought to break the impasse over the admission of California. On January 29, 1850, he stood before the Senate and proposed a compromise, known to history as the Compromise of 1850. Congress, said Clay, should admit California into the union as a free state but organize territorial governments in New Mexico and Deseret (Utah) without any reference to slavery, thus allowing slaveholders to bring slaves into those territories. As a sop to the southerners, Clay offered a new, stricter fugitive slave law; and as a concession to the abolitionists, he proposed abolishing the slave trade in the District of Columbia.

The aged and ailing Calhoun opposed Henry Clay's compromise. Too weak to address the Senate himself, the old, indomitable South Carolinian had his speech read for him by Senator James Murray Mason of Virginia. "I have, senators, believed . . . that the agitation of the subject of slavery," said Calhoun, "would, if not prevented by some timely and effective measure, end in disunion." The union, he declared, was "permanently and hopelessly [being] converted into the means of oppressing, instead of protecting" the South. His solution? The North must allow for a change in the Constitution, establishing two presidents, one for the South and one for the North. Only then, said Calhoun, would southern interests be secure.

Henry Clay

The Other Clay

The author of the great Compromise of 1850 had a lesser-known cousin, Cassius Marcellus Clay, also of central Kentucky, who was a strict abolitionist and had no use for the word "compromise." Once when pro-slavery hecklers disrupted an event where he was to deliver a passionate defense of abolition, Cassius Clay stepped up to the podium and said, "For those who accept the laws of Almighty God, I give you this—[and he pulled out a Bible and placed it on the table beside him]—and for those who accept the laws of man, I give you this—[and he pulled out a copy of the Constitution and placed it on the table]—and for those who accept neither the laws of God nor the laws of man, I give you these." Whereupon he drew out two loaded revolvers and placed them before him on the podium. Then he proceeded to speak without further interruption.

Cassius Clay, by Mathew Brady

Three days later, on March 7, crowds filled the galleries of the Senate chambers to hear Daniel Webster reply to Calhoun. Webster, his huge frame shrunken with age, his once golden voice now weakened and faltering, eloquently argued for Henry Clay's compromise. "I wish to speak today," began Webster, "not as a Massachusetts man, nor as a northern man, but as an American, and a member of the Senate of the United States. . . . I speak today for the preservation of the Union. 'Hear me for my cause.'" Webster challenged John Mason; reminding him that his grandfather, George Mason, had condemned slavery as an evil, while his grandson and other southerners like him called it a great blessing. As for disunion—"Peaceful secession!" Webster cried. "What would be the result?

Where is the line to be drawn? What states are to secede? What is to remain an American? What am I to be? An American no longer. Am I to become a sectional man, a local man, separatist, with no country in common with the gentlemen who sit around me here? . . . Heaven forbid!. . . . I would rather hear of natural blasts and mildews, war, pestilence, and famine, than to hear gentlemen talk of secession. To break up this great government! To dismember this glorious country! . . . No, Sir! There will be no secession!

Senator William H. Seward of New York argued for anti-slavery men who opposed the compromise. While Congress had the power, he admitted, to establish slavery in the territories, "there is a higher law than the Constitution which regulates our authority over the domain"—the law of God. He continued: "All measures which fortify slavery or extend it, tend to the consummation of violence; all that check its extension and abate its strength, tend to its peaceful extirpation."

The fight over Clay's compromise went on for weeks. Southern opponents of the compromise suffered a set-back with the death of Calhoun in March. No senator had the stature to fill the place left vacant by the old South Carolinian. Then, on July 4, 1850, President Taylor, after sitting two hours in the sun listening to some long-winded oratory, and consuming great quantities of iced water and cucumbers, came down with a bad case of gastroenteritis. Treated by incompetent doctors, Old Rough and Ready succumbed five days later. His vice-president, the inept Millard Fillmore, succeeded him as president.

By September, Clay's compromise had been cut into five separate bills. Assisted by Stephen A. Douglas, the short, intensely ambitious Democratic senator from Illinois, and by other Democrats, Clay was able to get enough support for the five bills to see them pass in the Senate and the House of Representatives in early September. President Fillmore signed the bills, and the Compromise of 1850—the last great compromise between North and South—became law.

Ichabod

In the North, outrage greeted the news of Clay's compromise. Though Democrats, on the whole, embraced it, Free-Soilers and abolitionists denounced it, and many Whigs, whether anti-slavery or not, decried it. For anti-slavery folk and escaped slaves, the most vexing part of the compromise was the new, strengthened Fugitive Slave Law.

The Fugitive Slave Law effectively removed any legal protection runaway slaves had in the North. According to the law, an owner need not be present or sign any affidavit to prove that a black man seized in the North was indeed his slave—the claim of the slave hunter himself was sufficient evidence. The accused could not testify in court on his own behalf nor even call witnesses to testify for him. Even harder to take was the fact that slave hunters and the law could call on passersby to help capture a runaway; any who refused—even from conscience—could suffer heavy penalties. Helping a fugitive to escape, hiding him, or attempting to free him from custody, brought on heavy fines or imprisonment.

A Lament for Webster

Shortly after Webster's famous March 7 speech, John Greenleaf Whittier wrote a poem that epitomized abolitionists' disillusionment with Webster. Whittier called the poem, "Ichabod," Hebrew for "inglorious":

So fallen! so lost! the light withdrawn
    Which once he wore!
The glory from his gray hairs gone
    Forevermore! . . .

Of all we loved and honored, naught
    Save power remains;
A fallen angel's pride of thought,
    Still strong in chains.

All else is gone; from those great eyes
    The soul has fled:
When faith is lost, when honor dies,
    The man is dead!

Then, pay the reverence of old days
    To his dead fame;
Walk backward, with averted gaze,
    And hide the shame!

Daniel Webster

The Fugitive Slave Law eclipsed even the fame of Daniel Webster, for he had supported it as part of the compromise. Abolitionists had thought Webster one of them, and now he had betrayed them! Yet, though the "divine Daniel" was no friend of slavery, he would accept it as a price for the union—for him, the mystical embodiment of liberty.

The Fugitive Slave Law spread terror among escaped slaves. Many fled north to Canada, where the slave hunters could not reach them. Others formed secret vigilance committees for mutual protection. In Christiana, Pennsylvania, William Parker, a black man, formed such a committee. He soon found a use for it.

Edward Gorsuch was known in Maryland for his kindness to his slaves—he had even freed some of his older servants. However, when four of his slaves escaped, Gorsuch, his son, and others pursued them into Pennsylvania. The four fugitives had found refuge with William Parker, whose house Gorsuch and his men surrounded. The escaped slaves inside Parker's house taunted their master and sang a heroic spiritual—

I will die on the field of battle
    Die on the field of battle,
With glory in my soul.

Soon, a party of blacks, members of Parker's vigilance committee from Christiana, surrounded Gorsuch's party. They attacked the white men, beat Gorsuch senseless, and severely wounded his son. The slaves escaped. Southerners decried the assault, saying that if Pennsylvania did nothing about it, the southern states should secede.

In the deep, cotton South, the Compromise of 1850 had brought little peace. There, the two major parties, the Democrats and the Whigs, for a short time disappeared, to be replaced by a Southern Rights Party (which favored secession) and a Union Party (which did not). The electoral contests in every cotton state found candidates from these parties vying for office. The Unionists, however, carried the day in every cotton state, except one: South Carolina went to the Southern Rights Party.

The Passing of the Guard

By 1852, the Whig Party was approaching the last stages of its demise. It was a presidential election year, and the prospects looked grim for the party. Broken into northern and southern, anti-slavery, pro-slavery, and union-only factions, the Whigs limped toward the election.

Daniel Webster, though 72-years old and sick, thought he would try, one last time, to win his party's presidential nomination. It was a sad spectacle. The old senator's ambition would not allow him to rest in his past glories; his friends could not dissuade him. His rivals for the party nomination were the incumbent president, Millard Fillmore, and General Winfield Scott. Henry Clay, ailing at Ashland, his home in Kentucky, threw his support to Fillmore. The Whigs, though, hoping that another general would win them the election, settled finally on Scott. "Old Fuss and Feathers" was an unfortunate candidate. He had been a kindly and lucky general, but his vanity and pomposity could attract little popular support.

Disillusioned with Scott, many southern Whigs bolted the party and joined the Democrats. At their convention in Baltimore, the Democrats rejected some of their more energetic candidates (such as Stephen A. Douglas of Illinois) and settled on a "dark-horse," Franklin Pierce of New Hampshire. Pierce had had a distinguished military career, having won the rank of brevet general in the Mexican-American War; but little else besides was known about him. The campaign of 1852 was as nasty as any that preceded it, though the result was probably more easily foretold. Pierce won the presidency with 254 electoral votes. Old Fuss and Feathers had garnered only 42.

The election of 1852 marked the end of the Whig Party. Henry Clay did not live to see this outcome, nor did Daniel Webster survive to say, "I told you so" to those who nominated Scott instead of him. Clay, the author of two compromises that cemented the union in times of crisis, died at Ashland on June 29, 1852. Webster passed away four months later, on October 24. Their passing, as well as Calhoun's two years previous, marked the end of an era. No statesmen of their stature, it seemed, were left to succeed them. "From the old heroic race to which Webster, Clay and Calhoun belonged," bemoaned George Templeton Strong, "down to the rising race of Sewards and Douglases and Fishes is a dismal descent."

The year 1852 saw the publication of a controversial book. In *Uncle Tom's Cabin*, Harriet Beecher Stowe of Connecticut told a story of black slaves, their white masters, and the misery that slavery thrust on all of them. Some of the southern slaveholders in Stowe's portrayal are kindly and good men—a fact, she wrote, she drew from real life. But the protagonist, Uncle Tom's, last owner, Simon Legree, would become in the popular imagination the epitome of the cruelty of the slave system. Stowe wrote in the epilogue to *Uncle Tom's Cabin* that God's wrath would not be long withheld from America for the sin of slavery, a sin, she said, for which both the North and the South were responsible. She urged, however, that there was still time to right the wrong:

Franklin Pierce

> A day of grace is yet held out to us. Both North and South have been guilty before God; and the Christian church has a heavy account to answer. Not by combining together, to protect injustice and cruelty, and making a common capital of sin, is this Union to be saved,—but by repentance, justice and mercy; for, not surer is the eternal law by which the millstone sinks in the ocean, than that stronger law, by which injustice and cruelty shall bring on nations the wrath of Almighty God!

The impact of *Uncle Tom's Cabin* was great. Southerners denounced the book, saying that Stowe had never visited the South (which was true, she had known only a few slaveholders) and could not know the true character of their "peculiar institution." Mary Chestnut (whose husband was a slave holder and a senator from South Carolina) spoke of Uncle Tom's story as "invented or imagined by Mrs. Stowe." Moreover she wrote that an overseer of her acquaintance had said of Simon Legree that "he had not seen many of that sort. If there were any, 'money couldn't buy 'em.'" In the opinion of those living south of the Mason-Dixon Line, Stowe's book was a libelous attack on their section— and but another example of the ill will the North held for the South.

Prosperity and Growth, Despite Saber-rattling

Harriet Beecher Stowe

The seething animosity between North and South notwithstanding, the early years of the 1850s were prosperous for both sections. In the North, industrial development continued, railroads were built, wages rose. The future seemed so rosy that in 1853 the *United States Review* crowed that, in the next half-century, "machinery will perform all work—automata will drive them. The only task of the human race will be to make love, study, and be happy." In the South, tobacco production increased, and cotton was demanding ever-higher prices on the market. The Tredegar Iron Works (run by slave labor) in Richmond, Virginia and cotton mills in other states represented the first halting attempts at industrialization in the South. Though nowhere as numerous as in the North, railroads began to join major cities in Georgia and Tennessee, and connections linked New York with New Orleans.

Despite the rumblings of secession, American idealism was not dead. The "Young Americans," a movement of men, old and young, sought to find new ideals to inspire civic leadership to support democratic revolutions the world over. They even talked of the U.S. annexing Ireland and Sicily. By their inspiration, in 1849 the legislatures of New York, Ohio, and Indiana called for national action against Austria because the Habsburg emperor had crushed a nationalist revolution in his kingdom of Hungary. Daniel Webster, at that time secretary of state under President Fillmore, reflected the spirit of the Young Americans by writing a condescending letter to Emperor Franz Josef: "The power of this republic [the United States] at the present moment is spread over a region, one of the richest and most fertile on the globe, and in an extent in comparison with which the possessions of the House of Hapsburg are but a patch on the earth's surface."

The Young Americans' ideals found their way into President Franklin Pierce's cabinet. Under the influence of his secretary of state, William L. Marcy, and the secretary of war, Jefferson Davis, Pierce came to favor **filibustering** expeditions against Spanish Cuba—adventures that President Taylor, before him, had frowned on. Davis, like many southerners, wanted the United States to annex slave-holding Cuba as compensation to the South for the loss of California as a slave state. In 1848, Narciso López, a former Spanish general and ex-governor of Madrid, led an independence movement in Cuba against Spanish rule. Defeated, he fled to the United States. Two years later, López led a force of mostly American volunteers from New Orleans into Cuba, but was defeated and captured. Spanish authorities executed the entire force.

In response to American filibustering, Spanish authorities in Cuba began seizing suspicious American merchant ships. In 1854, they seized the American ship, *Black Hawk*, and detained it in Havana, confiscating its cargo of cotton. This was a pretext for war, according to Jefferson Davis. Pierce, who wanted Cuba, tried to incite the Spaniards to declare war on the United States, but the Spanish government did not take the bait; instead, it apologized for the seizure of the *Black Hawk*. Undaunted, Pierce called on his ambassadors to England, France, and Spain—James Buchanan, John Mason, and Pierre Soulé—to draw up a policy to govern the United States' relations with Cuba. The result was the Ostend Manifesto of 1854.

The Ostend Manifesto declared Cubans were "now suffering under the worst of all possible governments, that of an absolute despotism." Moreover, and incidentally, this government made it impossible for the United States to suppress the African slave trade. The United States should buy Cuba from Spain, said the resolution; but (it continued), if Spain refused to sell Cuba, the U.S. would be justified "by every

filibuster: to carry out revolutionary activities in a foreign country

An 1850 satiric illustration of Narciso López, titled, "Gen'l Lopez the Cuban Patriot Getting His Cash." The caption at the bottom has López saying, "Well! We have not Revolutionized Cuba, but then we have Got what we came for, my Comrades came for Glory, I came for Cash, I've Got the Cash, they've Got the Glory, & I suppose we're all satisfied. I'm O_P_H for the United States again. Can't live under a Military Despotism."

GEN. LOPEZ THE CUBAN PATRIOT GETTING HIS CASH

law, human and divine," and by the principle of self-preservation, in taking it from Spain. Yet, the manifesto's belligerent and self-righteous tone fell short of its desired effect. It did not lead to war with Spain.

From Words to Blows

American westward settlement had mostly neglected the open prairies. Settlers preferred the forested lands where they could find more water, and trees provided lumber for building and for fuel. When they did settle the prairies, most emigrants chose the river bottoms where grew stands of cottonwood, hickory, and other trees.

This settlement pattern, however, began to change in the mid 1850s with the increased construction of railroads. Instead of relying on cumbersome, slow-moving wagon trains for supplies, settlers could receive what they needed, quickly, by rail. One such railroad, the Illinois Central, when completed, ran from Chicago to Cairo, Illinois, and thus opened up the Illinois prairie for settlement.

The 1850s witnessed the definitive triumph of the noisy railroad over the peaceful, idyllic canal. With California and Oregon filling up with settlers, Americans began to dream of a trans-continental railroad. Different routes were proposed. The most promising seemed to be the southern route, since it would pass through already organized territories. Starting in New Orleans, the route would follow the Red River, and then run through Texas and New Mexico to the Gila River. Following the Gila, the railroad would pass through Yuma on the Colorado River, and from Yuma, traverse the Southern California desert to its destination in San Diego.

Secretary of State Jefferson Davis advocated the southern route because it would connect the South to the West. Because the route would pass through the Gila River valley, which was Mexican territory, Davis persuaded President Pierce to buy it from Mexico. Mexico agreed to the sale, and in 1854 the Gadsden Purchase (named for James Gadsden, the U.S. ambassador to Mexico) added the territory south of the Gila River and west of the Río Grande (in what is now Arizona and New Mexico) to the United States.

But Davis' southern route faced powerful opposition in the Senate. Stephen A. Douglas, senator from Illinois, had been speculating in western lands and in Chicago real estate. Partly to realize greater profits on his investments and partly to add to his own political prestige, Douglas began to champion a central route for the transcontinental railroad. This route would run from St. Louis, up the Kansas and Arkansas Rivers, climb over the Rockies to the Great Salt Lake, and then follow the California trail over the Sierra Nevada to San Francisco. There was one catch to Douglas' plan, however; the railroad needed to pass through organized territories, and the Nebraska territory between Missouri and Utah had no territorial government.

The "Little Giant"

Such an obstacle could not daunt Stephen Douglas, known to his senatorial colleagues as the "Little Giant" for his short stature and mighty political organizing abilities. In 1854, Douglas introduced a bill to split and organize the Nebraska territory into two separate territories—Kansas and Nebraska. The Little Giant knew he needed southern support for this Kansas-Nebraska bill, so he proposed that the territories should be organized without any reference to slavery. Instead, the people who settled the territories would decide whether they would accept slavery among them or forbid its introduction.

Popular or "squatter" sovereignty was what Douglas was proposing for Kansas and Nebraska. But, whatever one called it, Douglas' proposal slashed at the weakening bonds of the union, for it would implicitly overturn the Missouri Compromise; the new territories lay north of longitude 36 degrees, 30 minutes, from where slavery was supposedly forever banned. This was bad enough, but, to add insult to injury, Douglas took the further step of supporting a bill, presented to the Senate by Senator Dixon of Kentucky and Senator Atchison of Missouri, that would explicitly repeal the Missouri Compromise.

Opposition to the Kansas-Nebraska bill was hot in Congress. One southern senator, Sam Houston of Texas, attacked the bill because it would violate treaties with Indian tribes to whom the U.S. had guaranteed Kansas and Nebraska for "as long as grass shall grow and water run." Few congressmen, however, cared a whit about Indian treaties; other concerns—slavery or freedom, a southern or central railroad line—took precedence.

In the end, Douglas' political engine broke through all opposition in Congress, and both houses passed the Kansas-Nebraska Act on May 25, 1854. President Pierce gladly signed the bill, and it became law. Kansas and Nebraska were organized as territories under popular sovereignty.

A "Political Map of the United States," 1854. The map states it was "designed to exhibit the comparative area of the Free and Slave States and the territory open to slavery or freedom by the repeal of the Missouri Compromise." Free states are in red; slave states, in grey. The territories are green, except for Kansas, which appears as white. The Missouri Compromise line runs in white from the southern border of Kansas westward to California.

A Year of Troubles

It was a year of troubles, was 1854. It was a year of economic depression. It was a year of unrest. Besides the upheaval over slavery, in the cities a smoldering resentment of the poor against the rich was growing more evident. And now the Kansas-Nebraska Act had shredded a 30-year compromise that had held the union together. What future was in store for the nation?

Anti-slavery Democrats in Congress—Joshua Giddings, Salmon Chase, Charles Sumner, and Gerrit Smith—denounced the Kansas-Nebraska Act in an "Appeal of the Independent Democrats in Congress to the People of the United States." They called the act a "gross violation of a sacred pledge." Citizens, they declared, might resist the act, "for the cause of freedom is the cause of God." Other Democrats showed their disgust for the Democrats' support for the Kansas-Nebraska Act by leaving the party.

Lafayette Hall, Pittsburgh, Pennsylvania, where the newly established Republican Party held its first convention in February 1856

Throughout the North—in New England, the Midwest, and the states along the northern Mississippi—voices began to call for state conventions to stem the spread of slavery. Conventions of anti-slavery men met in Maine, Vermont, Michigan, and Massachusetts. A convention in Massachusetts, featuring Charles Francis Adams (John Quincy's son), drew up a platform for what they called the Republican Party. The platform proclaimed "that no man can own another man . . . That slavery must be prohibited in the territories . . . That all new States must be Free States . . . That the rights of our colored citizens going to other States must be protected."

Fearing that popular sovereignty might claim Kansas and Nebraska for slavery, northerners organized emigrant aid societies to settle anti-slavery men in those territories. The societies raised $100,000 to finance settlements of thousands of ardent, and not-so-ardent, anti-slavery families in Kansas and Nebraska.

The upheavals of the time revived old anti-immigrant and anti-Catholic nativism. Since the 1840s, harassment of immigrants, and Catholics in particular, had abated. Now, once again, many Americans saw both groups as threats—the Catholics to the Protestant ideas of freedom (as "papists," it was said, they served a foreign prince), and the immigrants to the availability of jobs to poorer, Protestant whites. Some German immigrants had introduced revolutionary communism into America and were publishing journals (in German) calling for an uprising of the working class.

Charles B. Allen of New York had in 1849 founded a secret patriotic society called the Order of the Star Spangled Banner, that developed into the American "Know-Nothing" Party. Its goal was to support the election of anti-immigrant and anti-Catholic politicians to public office. Members of the order took oaths of secrecy; and, when asked anything about the order, were to reply "I know nothing" (for which they earned the dubious nickname, the "Know-Nothings.") In 1852, the order showed some influence at the polls. By 1854, it had become a serious force in politics.

That year the "Know-Nothing" Order organized itself into a political party, called the American Party. The Whigs had disappeared, and the only major party, the Democratic, was the party of the immigrants and Catholics. (To nativist disgust, Democratic President Pierce had even appointed a Catholic to be his postmaster general.) The only recourse for nativists, then, was to form their own party. In the off-year elections of 1854, the American "Know-Nothing" Party almost took control of the state of New York. In Massachusetts,

Know-Nothings secured the governorship, the entire Senate, and all but two seats in the House of Representatives. In 1855, they won victories in Rhode Island, New Hampshire, and Connecticut. The same year, Know-Nothing officials were elected in Maryland and Kentucky, as well as Tennessee, New York, California, Georgia, Alabama, Mississippi, Louisiana, and Texas. It seemed that the American Party could become a real rival to the Democratic Party. With the elections of 1856 just around the corner, Know-Nothings were sure they could capture even the presidency.

Bloody Kansas

Even before the Kansas-Nebraska Act had been signed into law, Missourians had been crossing the border onto the plains of Kansas. The territory was still Indian land, but such a technical legal detail had rarely influenced the settlement patterns of American emigrants. The government would eventually open any Indian territory to white settlement, if enough white Americans wanted it that way.

The Missourians in Kansas were pro-slavery. But with the passage of the Kansas-Nebraska Act, settlers from the Northeast, funded by emigrant aid societies, poured into Kansas to make sure the territory would be free-soil, not slave. Soon, the majority of settlers were free-soilers, and desperate pro-slavery southerners saw Kansas slipping from their grasp.

President Pierce appointed Andrew Reeder of Pennsylvania as the first territorial governor of Kansas and Samuel Dexter Lecompte as the territory's first chief justice. As chief justice, Lecompte organized the first election for a territorial representative to Congress. Over 1,500 armed Missourians crossed the border to vote for pro-slavery candidates, overwhelming the votes of the free-soilers. During the election for the territorial legislature in March 1855, the same thing happened—Missourians assured a pro-slavery majority in the legislature. The new legislature, which then met at Leavenworth, adopted the laws of Missouri for Kansas, made it a crime to speak or write against slavery, and decreed that anyone helping a slave to escape from his master would be executed.

Hoping, however, to maintain peace in the territory, Governor Reeder dissolved the territorial legislature. But President Pierce, who favored the pro-slavery forces, removed Reeder and replaced him with a pro-slavery governor, William Shannon. The free-soilers, meanwhile, had set up their own legislature in Topeka that, in December 1855, drew up a free-state constitution that excluded all blacks, free or slave, from Kansas. The Topeka legislature chose state officials and sent a delegation to Congress.

In the midst of all this political wrangling, armed bands of pro-slavery men had been stopping wagons of emigrants from the Northeast, arresting free-soilers, and threatening anybody opposed to a pro-slavery future for Kansas. Hearing rumors of a large pro-slavery military force assembling in Missouri, free-soilers appealed to President Pierce for help, but he ignored them. Pierce blamed the emigrant aid societies for all the trouble in Kansas and gave his full support to the pro-slavery Leavenworth assembly. To counter pro-slavery violence, emigrant aid societies began sending supplies of Sharps repeating-rifles to Kansas free-soilers.

The stage was now set for a full-scale conflict. Major Jefferson Buford of Alabama, with 300 volunteers, marched into the territory to aid the pro-slavery forces. Governor Shannon welcomed Buford and designated his force the Kansas Militia. Strengthened by 500 more men, in May 1856, Buford's militia descended on Lawrence, a free-soil town, confiscated the arms of the citizens, and destroyed printing presses, the public library, and the Free State Hotel. Emigrant aid societies responded to such violence by sending more money and settlers into Kansas. In Kansas itself, the reaction was far more bloody. An ardent abolitionist, John Brown, who lived at Osawatomie with his four sons and 60 other settlers, had come to Kansas to stop any westward tide of slavery. Now, in retaliation for the sacking of

John Brown, about 1856

Lawrence and the murder of free-soilers, Brown led a party to the pro-slavery settlement at Dutch Henry's Crossing on Pottawatomie Creek, seized five men, and gunned them down in a mass execution.

For the next several months, bloody warfare, like a prairie fire, ignited the Kansas-Missouri border. Free-soil violence now equaled pro-slavery violence. Northern "Jayhawkers" pitted themselves against Missouri "border ruffians" with such names as Kickapoo Rangers, Doniphan Tigers, and Lecompton Guards. Terrible were the stories that reached the East of murders, highway robberies, pillage,

Cartoon of Preston Brooks' attack on Sumner

and arson. "Bloody Kansas" demonstrated how deep the chasm between the North and South was growing.

Nor was violence confined to the frontier. In Washington, D.C., on May 19, 1856, Charles Sumner, the talented, handsome anti-slavery senator from Massachusetts, eloquently condemned the "crime against Kansas" before the assembled Senate. Sumner scurrilously attacked Senator Andrew James Butler of South Carolina, saying he courted "the harlot slavery," and called Stephen Douglas "the squire of slavery, ready to do its humiliating offices." Two days later, Butler's cousin, Preston Brooks, a congressman from South Carolina, stood up and denounced Sumner on the Senate floor for insulting not only Butler but South Carolina as well. Then with a stout stick, Brooks proceeded to beat the Massachusetts senator senseless.

Butler's choice of weapon was pregnant with meaning. According to the southern code of honor, a "gentleman" would have been challenged to a duel, not beaten like a dog—or a slave! Charles Sumner did not recover for another next three years, so badly was he wounded. The North, of course, denounced the violence and made Sumner a hero, while many southerners praised the "chivalry" of Preston Brooks for defending the honor of his state and his kinsman.

A House Divided

The mid-term elections of 1854 were an ominous warning to the Democrats and President Pierce. The newly formed Republican Party took 105 seats in the House of Representatives, and the Know-Nothings claimed 40 seats, leaving only 74 seats to the Democrats. Such a victory encouraged the Republicans to think that in 1856 they might capture not only Congress but the presidency as well.

President Pierce's first worry, however, was not about a Republican rival, whoever he might be; within his own Democratic Party, ambitious Democrats were challenging Pierce for the party's nomination. Stephen Douglas, for one, was eager for the honor. So was Pierce's ambassador to England, James Buchanan, who had come out in front as the party favorite. Douglas and Pierce teamed up to try to wrest the nomination from Buchanan, but to no avail. Though the vote was close, the Democratic convention nominated James Buchanan for president and John C. Breckinridge of Kentucky for vice-president.

The Republican convention, meeting in June 1856 in Philadelphia displayed all the spirit and enthusiasm of youth. Nominating John C. Frémont, the "Pathfinder," as their candidate

The Great Republican Reform Party cartoon. An anti-Fremont satire. Representatives of various perceived radical groups approach Frémont, who makes them this promise: "You shall have what you desire, and be sure that the glorious Principles of Popery, Fourierism, Free Love, Woman's Rights, the Maine Law [i.e. temperance], and above all the Equality of our Colored brethren, shall be maintained; If I get the Presidential Chair."

for president, the delegates approved a platform that struck out at both slavery and the Mormons, declaring that it is "both the right and the duty of Congress to prohibit in the Territories these twin relics of barbarism, polygamy and slavery." The delegates came up with a catchy party slogan for the campaign: "Free soil, free speech, and Frémont."

Throughout the North, zealous Republicans campaigned for "The Pathfinder"; among them was the 47-year old Abraham Lincoln. Lincoln, who had stepped out of politics after he lost the re-election to Congress for opposing the Mexican-American War, now returned to the fray refreshed and with new ideas. Not only did he stump for Frémont, but he expatiated on the Declaration of Independence, how it declared that all men were created equal. Congress, he argued, had the authority to prohibit slavery in the territories. Lincoln was ambitious. Senator Douglas was up for re-election in two years, and Lincoln was hoping to challenge him. The response to his speeches was encouraging, for everywhere he went, great crowds gathered to hear him.

For their part, the Democrats and Buchanan bitterly lashed out at the "Black Republicans," as they called them, accusing them of fomenting disunion. In the South, newspapers ran snippets of Republican speeches to prove how dangerous Republicans were. One snippet, from a speech by Joshua Giddings of Ohio, ran: "I look forward to the day when there shall be a servile insurrection in the South; when the black man . . . shall assert his freedom and wage a war of extermination against his master." Another Republican, James Watson Webb, said his party would have to "drive back the slaveocracy with fire and swords." Wielding such quotations, southern leaders declared that if Frémont were elected, the southern states would have to seek their own safety outside the Union.

In the election, Buchanan carried every slave state, except Maryland, which fell to the Know-Nothing Party. In the North, he carried every state except Pennsylvania, Illinois, and Indiana. The final vote tally was 174 electoral votes for Buchanan to 114 for Frémont. The popular vote was close: 1,838,000 for Buchanan to 1,340,000 for Frémont. Only 1,200 of Frémont's votes came from slave-holding states. If Frémont had triumphed in every northern state, he could have beaten Buchanan. The seriousness of the possibility was not lost on southerners. The North formed a block that could control, not only the House of

Representatives, but the presidency as well. If the South lost its footing in the Senate, it would be completely at the mercy of North and its interests.

Dred Scott and Lecompton

It had been over ten years since Dred Scott, a slave, had laid suit for his freedom. In the early 1840s, his master, Dr. John Emerson, had followed his army commission to a post in Illinois, taking Dred Scott with him. From Illinois, Emerson went next to Fort Snelling on the west bank of the Mississippi, a free territory, according to the Missouri Compromise. There Scott and his wife remained, hired out by their master, while the sickly Emerson went from post to post. In 1843, Emerson died, and his wife, who lived in Missouri, received his property, along with Dred Scott and Scott's wife, Harriet.

Dred Scott was convinced that because he and his wife had lived in free territory, they were free. A judge in Missouri agreed—Dred Scott and his wife, he said, were indeed free by the provisions of the Missouri Compromise. Mrs. Emerson appealed the ruling to the Missouri Supreme Court, which, after ten long years, ruled in her favor. Undaunted, Dred Scott's lawyer appealed the case to the United States Supreme Court. The justices agreed to hear the case in 1856.

Dred Scott, about 1857

The chief justice at the time was Roger Taney. Appointed by Andrew Jackson to the court in 1834, Taney had had a long and distinguished career as a justice. He was something of a rarity: he was Catholic and a slave owner who had freed all his slaves. As a young lawyer in Maryland, he had defended a Methodist minister who had been hauled into court for preaching against slavery and in the defense appealed to the Declaration of Independence. Slavery, Taney said at the time, is "a blot upon our national character." A Jacksonian Democrat to the bone, Taney despised the money interests who, he said, sought "to destroy the spirit of freedom and manly independence in the working classes of society."

But Chief Justice Taney and four of his associate justices (all southerners) were worried over the growing rift in the union. First, the Missouri Compromise, then the Compromise of 1850, then the Kansas-Nebraska Act—all had failed to bridge the divide. Where the various acts and legislation had failed, the Supreme Court might succeed, thought the nearly 80-year old Taney. Like many Americans, his first concern was for the union; compared to preserving the union, slavery was but a side issue for Taney.

On March 6, 1857, the Supreme Court published its decision in the Dred Scott case. Writing for the majority, Chief Justice Taney maintained that neither the Declaration of Independence nor the Constitution had the slave population in mind when it spoke of citizens and their rights. "A negro, whose ancestors were imported into this country, and sold as slaves could not be a citizen, nor was he included in the words 'all men' in the Declaration of Independence." Blacks, Taney argued, "had been for more than a century before regarded as beings of an inferior order, and altogether unfit to associate with the white race, either in social or political relations; and so far inferior that they had no rights which the white man was bound to respect; and that the Negro might justly and lawfully be reduced to slavery for his benefit." As a black man, and therefore excluded from the purview of the Constitution, Dred Scott had no legal right to sue in the courts of Missouri, according to Taney. Whether or not Dred Scott had lived in free territory, he was still a slave, wrote Taney, for the Constitution guaranteed a man his property, and slaves were property.

Roger Taney

There was more. Chief Justice Taney declared that when the Constitution gave Congress the right to make laws for the territories, it referred only to those territories lying east of the

Mississippi River, since Louisiana had not yet been purchased. The Missouri Compromise was, thus, an unconstitutional exercise of congressional power.

The Dred Scott decision thus nullified the Missouri Compromise and so opened up all the territories to slavery—even those, like Oregon, which had been declared free. Furthermore, besides nullifying the Missouri Compromise, the decision toppled popular sovereignty in the territories, since it said the Constitution protected the "property" of any slaveholder anywhere, even in free territory. Many southerners were, of course, pleased with the decision, since it gave them what they sought—equal rights with the North in the territories. Northerners, whether anti-slavery or not, were outraged at what appeared an exercise of raw judicial power in favor of the "slaveocracy."

Another event served to widen the chasm between North and South. In June 1857, delegates to a constitutional convention in Lecompton, Kansas drew up a pro-slavery constitution to send to the United States Senate for approval for statehood. Most of the convention delegates were pro-slavery, chosen according to a census from which free-soil citizens abstained. The delegates made no provision for a popular vote on the Lecompton constitution, and they approved it, despite the territorial governor's veto and in spite of free-soil protest. Though President Buchanan at first supported a popular vote on the constitution, he later reneged. On February 2, 1858, he urged Congress to admit Kansas into the Union under the pro-slavery constitution.

Senator Stephen Douglas led the Democratic opposition to President Buchanan. To admit a state under a constitution that had not been ratified by popular vote violated Douglas' doctrine of popular sovereignty. The "Little Giant" was playing a dangerous game, however; in opposing the president, he could alienate southerners, whose votes he needed if he hoped to win the presidency in 1860. On the other hand, to support the president, he would need to repudiate his doctrine of popular sovereignty and, perhaps, alienate the northern Democrats, whom he represented. He gambled and chose to oppose the president, with fatal consequences for him, as we shall see, in the election of 1860.

"Honest Abe" versus the "Little Giant"

Abraham Lincoln, about 1860

The man Illinois Republicans chose for their senatorial candidate in the midterm elections of 1858 was tall, ungainly, and just plain homely. But he could speak and rivet the attention of his listeners. In the speech that initiated his campaign, this man, Abraham Lincoln, told Republicans gathered in Springfield that "a house divided against itself cannot stand."

> I believe this government cannot endure, permanently half slave and half free.
>
> I do not expect the Union to be dissolved—I do not expect the house to fall—but I do expect it will cease to be divided. It will become all one thing, or all the other.
>
> Either the opponents of slavery, will arrest the further spread of it, and place it where the public mind shall rest in the belief that it is in the course of ultimate extinction; or its advocates will push it forward, till it shall become alike lawful in all the States, old as well as new—North as well as South.

"A house divided" was a powerful image, taken from Scripture—Christ's answer to the Pharisees when they accused him of casting out demons by the power of Beelzebub. The image resonated with Lincoln's listeners. But the speech, published in the South, inspired a different reaction. Southerners saw it as a declaration of the North's hostility towards the South.

Lincoln's Democratic rival for the Senate, "Judge" Stephen Douglas, tore into his opponent with all the power and irony for which he was famous. Douglas accused Lincoln of being a "nigger worshiper" who wanted equality with blacks because he wanted (God forbid!) to marry with blacks! Lincoln protested against that "counterfeit logic," saying: "[just because] I do not want a black woman for a slave, I must necessarily want her for a wife. I need not have her for either. I can just leave her alone."

Lincoln did not find trading salvos with Douglas over a distance satisfying; he wanted to take on the "Little Giant" face to face in the public arena. So it was that Lincoln initiated a challenge, which Douglas accepted—the candidates would meet in seven public debates in different parts of the state. These debates would prove to be a remarkable display of oratorical and logical skill where the audience sometimes would have to follow complicated, reasoned arguments. It's a wonder that anyone came to hear them.

But they did come, and in large numbers. Twenty thousand came from round about, and from distant towns by rail, to hear the first debate at Ottawa on August 21. Senator Douglas spoke first, attacking Lincoln's character with back-handed compliments on Lincoln's drinking and gambling ability. He reminded his listeners that, while in Congress, Lincoln had opposed the Mexican-American War, for which he had justly lost his seat. Douglas attacked the "House-divided" speech, claiming it fomented disunion, and accused Lincoln of wanting equality between "Negroes" and whites. "I am opposed to negro citizenship in any form," said Douglas to the cheering crowd. "I believe this government was made on the white basis. I believe it was made by white men, for the benefit of white men and their posterity instead of conferring it upon negroes, Indians and other inferior races . . . I do not question Mr. Lincoln's conscientious belief that the negro was made his equal, and hence his brother [laughter], but for my own part, I do not regard the negro as my equal, and positively deny he is my brother . . ."

Lincoln did not deny that, in certain respects, blacks might be inferior to the white man, "but in the right to eat the bread without leave of anybody else, which his own hand earns, he is my equal and the equal of Judge Douglas, and the equal of every living man." Great applause greeted this thrust. Lincoln continued saying that the "Judge" had criticized the statement that a house divided against itself cannot stand; but "does the Judge say it can stand? . . . If he does, then there is a question of veracity, not between him and me, but between the Judge and an authority of a somewhat higher character." The audience erupted in laughter and applause.

The question over slavery in the territories occupied a central place in the debates. Douglas had a certain, practical wisdom in his proposal of popular sovereignty; practically and strategically speaking, it was unlikely that any of the western territories, even Kansas, would become slave states. They did not possess the soil and climactic conditions for the crops that made slave labor so valuble. (Southerners themselves admitted this.) Even the most likely candidates—New Mexico and Arizona—would probably not attract many slave owners who, it seemed, did not want to risk their "property" by moving them to the frontier, and so close to the Mexico, where slavery had been abolished.

For Lincoln, though, the question of slavery in the territories was not fundamentally a practical or strategic one; it was a moral one. "The Republican Party," said Lincoln at Quincy on October 13, "think it wrong

> . . . we think it is a moral, a social and political wrong. We think it is a wrong not confining itself merely to the persons or the states where it exists, but that it is a wrong in its tendency, to say the least, that extends itself to the existence of the whole nation. Because we think it wrong, we propose a course of policy that shall deal with it as a wrong. We deal with it as with any other wrong, in so far as we can prevent its growing any larger, and so deal with it that in time there may be some promise of an end to it.

Though he refrained from demanding immediate emancipation, Lincoln appealed to principles that were higher than any written law, higher even than the Constitution. Lincoln appealed to the "inalienable rights" of man as expressed in what was, for him, the creed that defined the United States—the Declaration of Independence. If all men were created equal and endowed with inalienable rights, then these rights belonged to all men, black as well as white. This high moral stance endeared Lincoln to anti-slavery folk throughout the North and contributed to his swift rise in the ranks of the Republican Party.

Southerners, however, found little comfort in Lincoln's statements. His policy on slavery meant that, sooner or later, the South would be condemned to permanent minority status and become politically powerless against a triumphant North, to which the South saw itself as economically and culturally opposed—and not only on account of slavery. The debates also turned the South against Douglas, for the "Judge" had failed to come out unequivocally in support of the Dred Scott decision. Henceforth, the Little Giant could rally only the northern Democrats. Southern Democrats abandoned him in disgust.

Illinois was pleased with Douglas' snub of the Supreme Court and returned him to the Senate. Lincoln, though defeated, was not crushed. The campaign had assured him a prominent place in the western Republican Party and sparked interest in him in the East. He had lost the Senate, the lesser prize, but in less than two years he would again pit himself against Douglas in a contest for the greatest political prize of all—the office of president.

John Brown's Body

John Brown, 1859

Old Osawatomie John Brown, now sporting a long, gray beard and bearing the alias Shubel Morgan, had returned to Kansas. He had been in Chatham, Ontario in May 1859 meeting with 12 white and 24 black abolitionists, including Harriet Tubman; they had been discussing a plot of Brown's for a violent revolution to free the slaves. Back in Kansas, John Brown was again causing trouble. Answering a plea for help from a slave who was to be sold at auction, Brown, his sons, and others crossed over into Missouri, freed the slave (along with five of his fellow slaves), and stole some horses and a wagon. Proceeding to another farm, Brown's party freed five more slaves, killing a white man who opposed them. When the government placed a $500 bounty on Brown's head, the old abolitionist again fled to Canada.

In Canada, Brown met with New England abolitionists who had become convinced that only violence could free the slaves. Brown laid out his plan. He would capture the federal arsenal and gun factory at Harper's Ferry, Virginia, and establish it as the center of a fugitive slave republic, from whence he would lead a general slave insurrection. Compelling, charismatic, with blue-gray eyes flaming with zeal, the gaunt John Brown stirred the hearts of his hearers. Gerrit Smith, Joshua Giddings, and Samuel Gridley Howe supported his desperate plan. But Frederick Douglass said he would have no part in it.

It was night, on October 16, 1859, when John Brown with 13 whites (including three of his sons) and five blacks assaulted the federal arsenal at Harper's Ferry. Killing an army major, they seized the arsenal and then proceeded to round up the prominent citizens of the town. Fifty slaves, freed by Brown, joined him in the railroad roundhouse where they were besieged by the Jefferson Guards of the Virginia state militia. A bitter fight ensued in which, one by one, Brown's men fell dead around him. "Brown was the coldest and firmest man I ever saw in defying danger and death," wrote Lewis Washington, one of the besieged who survived. "With one son dead by his side, and another shot through, he felt the pulse of his dying son with one hand and held his rifle with the other, and commanded his men with the utmost composure, encouraging them to be firm and to sell their lives as dearly as they could."

It was a hopeless defense. The next day, October 18, Colonel Robert E. Lee and a contingent of United States marines battered down the doors of the roundhouse and took a wounded Brown and three others prisoner. Lee delivered them to Richmond, where they were to stand trial for treason.

Brown refused the insanity defense his lawyer had prepared for him, and the court condemned him to death. Unruffled and unrepentant, Brown addressed the court:

> Now, if it is deemed necessary that I should forfeit my life for the furtherance of the ends of justice, and mingle my blood further with the blood of my children and with the blood of millions in this slave country whose rights are disregarded by wicked, cruel, and unjust enactments—I submit; so let it be done!

No general slave revolt followed Brown's action or his execution by hanging on December 2, 1859. The South, however, reeled with fear of slave insurrection and blamed the radical agitation of abolitionists for Brown. Though northern leaders like Lincoln, Douglas, and Seward condemned Brown's raid, the South could not, or would not, put any confidence in their sincerity. What southerners heard were the voices of abolitionists, who, for years had condemned all slave holders as immoral monsters, proclaiming Brown a martyr—a man they believed would, if he could, have bathed the South in blood. They heard the voice of a man as respectable as Ralph Waldo Emerson, proclaiming Brown "that new saint."

John Brown's Harper's Ferry insurrection on October 17 1859 Captain Albert's militia fire on Brown's insurgents from the railroad bridge.

It cant stop me for I built it

You find me in dis yer Fence Massa Daglis.

...can I get over this Rail Fence

Election 1860 cartoon, showing Lincoln competing with Douglas in a race to the White House. Douglas says, "How can I get over this Rail Fence?" while Lincoln boasts, "It can't stop me for I built it"—referring to his reputation as a rail splitter. A black man, his head poking up through the fence, says, "You find me in dis yer fence, Massa Daglis."

Brown's death, said Emerson, "will make the gallows glorious like the cross."

The Election of 1860

Even though Lincoln had lost his bid for the Senate, his debates with Douglas had made him nationally famous. A new prospect opened up for his ambition—the Republican nomination for the presidency. In 1859 and into 1860, Lincoln traveled the Midwest, giving speeches at Columbus, Milwaukee, Indianapolis, and other towns. Everywhere he attacked Douglas' popular sovereignty doctrine, appealed to the Declaration of Independence, and reiterated his insistence that the territories be closed to slavery. He composed a campaign autobiography where he described himself as "on the average a hundred and eighty pounds; dark complexion with coarse black hair, and grey eyes—no other marks or brands recollected."

In February 1860, Lincoln delivered one of the most important speeches of his career at Cooper Union Hall in New York City. The rough, homespun lawyer from Springfield, Illinois, had captured the West; but how would he play before New York Republicans? These easterners were refined; they were intellectual, cultured anti-slavery folk, temperance advocates, Free-Soilers, and Know-Nothings. If Lincoln could impress them (and they were hard to impress) he could probably take the Republican nomination.

About 1,500 people, including such notables as William Cullen Bryant and Horace Greeley, gathered to hear his speech. Lincoln was conservative. He condemned John Brown's raid. He invoked the Constitution, the Northwest Ordinance, and appealed to the fathers, arguing that Congress indeed had the power to prohibit slavery in the territories. "As those fathers marked it [slavery]," he declared, "so let it again be marked, as an evil not to be extended, but to be tolerated and protected only because of and so far as its actual presence among us makes that toleration and protection a necessity."

The Cooper Union Hall Speech was, for the most part, a cold didactic speech; but when he called on his audience to hold to their principles, Lincoln hit a note of grandeur. "Neither let us be slandered from our duty," he declared, "by false accusations against us, nor frightened from it by menaces of destruction to the government, nor of dungeons to ourselves. Let us have faith that right makes might, and in that faith let us to the end dare to do our duty as we understand it." Though his hearers were not at first impressed by Lincoln's gangly and cadaverous appearance, by the conclusion of Lincoln's speech, they had a very favorable impression of him. Cooper Union had made him a leading contender for the Republican party's presidential nomination.

Meanwhile, the Democratic Party was badly split between supporters of Senator Douglas and popular sovereignty and the southern members who insisted on an extreme pro-slavery platform. Among these southern Democrats were cotton state delegates, like Jefferson Davis, who hoped for a split convention. If there were two Democratic candidates, the election could be thrown to the House of Representatives. But others, "fire eaters" they were called, hoped the election would usher in a Republican president and so push the South to secede from the Union.

When in April 1860 the Democratic convention gathered in Charleston, South Carolina, cotton state delegates, led by Jefferson Davis, demanded a platform calling for the establishment of black codes in all territories. William L. Yancey of Alabama wanted another platform declaring for the morality of slavery. When the convention rejected an extreme pro-slavery platform, delegates from the eight cotton states withdrew. The remaining delegates could not agree on a candidate, and they adjourned to Baltimore, where, in June, they nominated Stephen Douglas for their presidential candidate. Those who had seceded at Charleston formed a rival convention, adopted an extreme pro-slavery platform, and nominated John C. Breckenridge of Kentucky for president and Senator Joseph Lane for vice-president.

The Republican convention met in Chicago in May and adopted a platform that enshrined the doctrine of the Declaration of Independence that all men are created equal, and condemned disunion. It proclaimed freedom to be "the normal condition of all the territory of the United States," and declared that Congress should ban slavery in the territories. Beyond the slavery issue, the platform also called for "appropriations by Congress for River and Harbor improvements of a National character"; a free land grant homestead act for the West; and for "adjustment" of "imposts as to encourage the development of the industrial interest of the whole country"—that is, increasing the tariff on foreign manufactured goods, which the South still vehemently opposed. These planks betrayed a purely northern sectional bent and a growing orientation toward the interests of commerce and manufacturing—the interests of the North.

Old line conservative Whigs and others, worried about the decay of the union, formed a third party called the National Constitutional Union and nominated John Bell of Tennessee for president and Edward Everett of Massachusetts for vice-president. The National Constitutional Union styled itself as the only party "a gentleman could vote for."

The union was like a ship, breaking up at sea; still, the parties campaigned as if it were just another election year. Republicans marched through the streets carrying fence rails for Abraham Lincoln, the "rail-splitter" candidate. They appealed to the prejudices of the northern working classes by asking, "Can a free laboring man expect to get two dollars a day when a slave cost his master but 10 cents?" Douglas Democrats hired fat little boys to march through the streets as "Little Giants"; and Douglas, violating all custom, went out on the road campaigning for himself and for popular sovereignty as the salvation of the union.

As the election progressed, it became clearer that the nation might get Lincoln, a "Black Republican" (as southerners called him) for president. In the South, there was more talk of secession. Only a month before the election, the Charleston *Mercury* warned that, if Lincoln were elected, the North would once again plunder the South with a new and higher protective tariff. Abolitionism, it said, would rule the country and undermine slave property, "the foundation of all property in the South." "When security in this is shaken," said the *Mercury*, "all other property partakes of its instability."

Some abolitionists objected to Lincoln because he did not go far enough in combating slavery and assuring equal rights for blacks in the North. At an anti-slavery meeting at Framingham, Massachusetts, on July 4, 1860, an ex-slave, Ford Douglass, declared, "I am a colored man; I am an American citizen, and I think I am entitled to exercise the elective franchise. I am about 28-years old, and I would like to vote very much. . . . No party, it seems to me, is entitled to the sympathy of anti-slavery men, unless that party is willing to extend to the black man all the rights of a citizen."

Abraham Lincoln won the election of 1860, with a majority of the electoral votes: 180. Stephen Douglas, though he came second in the popular vote (1,376,957 votes to Lincoln's 1,866,452), finished last in the electoral college, capturing only Missouri's 12 electors. John C. Breckenridge finished second, taking all the cotton states, with 72 electoral votes, while John Bell won Virginia, Kentucky, and Tennessee, giving him 39 electoral votes.

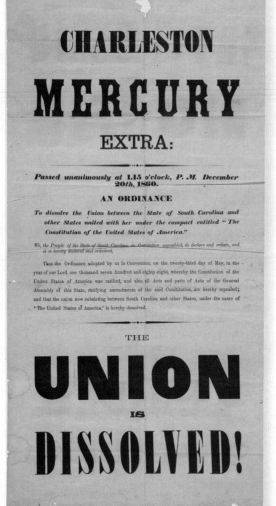

The election of 1860 presents an interesting snapshot of the U.S. at the time. Though he won the election, most Americans did not favor Lincoln; the vote totals of the three other candidates combined exceeded Lincoln's by about one million. Lincoln also won by taking the North—hardly a vote was cast for him south of the Mason-Dixon line. This was ominous because, even if only one candidate had secured the electoral vote not given to Lincoln, it would come to only 123 electoral votes, 57 fewer than Lincoln's total. The election of 1860 demonstrated that a solid North could capture and control the presidency.

The election results did give one encouraging sign—John Bell and Douglas had done very well, even in the cotton South. In Alabama, for instance, the combined vote for Bell and Douglas was 41,526 compared to Breckinridge's 48,831. Thus, support for the union was still quite strong even in the very deep South.

The Union Is Dissolved

Mere smoke without a fire—this is what Lincoln and others thought southern threats to secede upon the election of a "Black Republican" amounted to. They were wrong. Though union sentiment was strong in the South, the fear of northern domination and the desire to escape from a situation where they felt the accusing finger of guilt for an institution many southerners truly believed wrong, was stronger. Enthusiasm for secession was strongest in the cotton South, and at its most intense in South Carolina.

"The Tea has been thrown overboard," cheered the Charleston *Mercury*, the day after the election; "the revolution of 1860 has been initiated." Men took off from work to follow the election results and cheered every notice of Lincoln's success. That night fireworks celebrated disunion, and within a few days, South Carolina's two federal senators, James Chestnut, Jr., and James Hammond, sent in their resignations. The state legislature summoned a state convention to meet December 17 to discuss whether South Carolina should remain in the union. It was a foregone conclusion. On December 20, the South Carolina convention voted unanimously that "the Union now subsisting between South Carolina and other States, under the name of 'The United States of America' is hereby dissolved."

Before South Carolina's state convention met, letters had been coming in to President-elect Lincoln asking for his leadership at this crisis of the union. What were his intentions towards the South? What would he do in the event of secession? It was well known that Lincoln thought secession was illegal. For Lincoln, the union formed a consolidated nation, not a federation of states where the national government held some authority over individuals, but where the states retained final sovereignty. This was well known, as were his assurances that he did not favor interference with slavery in the South; but men begged for some reassurance now, not references to the dead letter of past speeches. Some in the cotton South, such as Jefferson Davis and Alexander Stephens of Georgia, did not favor secession. They would remain in the union if they received the assurances they wanted from Lincoln.

Lincoln, however, remained stonily silent. He did write a letter to Alexander Stephens on December 22, but prefaced it with the words, "For your eyes only":

> Do the people of the South really entertain fears that a Republican administration would directly, or indirectly, interfere with the slaves, or with them about their slaves? If they do I wish to assure you . . . that there is no cause for such fear—The South would be in no more danger in this respect than it was in the days of Washington. I suppose, however, this does not meet the case—You think slavery is right and ought to be extended while we think it is wrong and ought to be restricted—That I suppose is the rule—It certainly is the only substantial difference between us.

The letter probably would not have met "the case," but it was never given the chance to do so, for it was never published. Soon state conventions in Mississippi, Florida, and Alabama voted for secession, and on January 19, Alexander Stephen's state, Georgia, left the union. On January 26, Louisiana seceded, and on February 1, despite the pleas of Sam Houston, Texas severed its ties with the United States. The cotton South had left the union.

South Carolina's "Ultimatum," an editorial cartoon showing South Carolina governor Francis Pickens' threatening secession against President Buchanan. Currier & Ives engraving

A New Nation

President James Buchanan did nothing while state after state seceded from the union. Though urged to action by General Winfield Scott, Buchanan did not threaten South Carolina with military intervention as Andrew Jackson had done during the nullification crisis; but then Buchanan wasn't Jackson. He had hoped for a peaceful, uneventful administration; and here he was faced with the supreme crisis of his country's history.

Though Buchanan did nothing, and Lincoln was silent, others attempted reconciliation. Senator John Crittenden suggested a compromise that would revive the Missouri Compromise line and compensate slaveholders for escaped slaves who could not be recovered. Virginia, which held a state convention in readiness to discuss secession, called a peace convention. Delegates from 21 states (not including the seceded states) met in Washington for two weeks in February. With former president John Tyler presiding, the convention discussed how to draw the seceded states back while keeping the southern "border" states in the union. They drew up seven constitutional amendments, including one that stipulated that Congress would never by law or amendment interfere with slavery in any state. Congress passed this amendment on February 27 and submitted it to the states. Ohio immediately ratified it.

Yet none of these compromise measures had any effect. Delegates from the eight seceded states met in Montgomery, Alabama, on February 8 to discuss how they would unite under their own federal government. They formed a provisional Congress of the "Confederate States of America" and drew up a provisional constitution that would prove little different from the permanent constitution adopted a year later. The Constitution of the Confederate States of America opened with the preamble, "We, the people of the Confederate States, each State acting in its sovereign and independent character . . ." to make it clear that states, not the people as a whole, established this government.

The new constitution differed little from the United States Constitution, except in lengthening the term of the president to six years and forbidding his reelection. Also, unlike the United States Constitution, it forbade tariffs and the appropriations of "money for any internal improvement intended to facilitate commerce." The Confederate constitution prohibited the passage of federal laws "denying or impairing the right of property in Negro slaves" and opened all territories to slave holders. However, despite the fire-eating dreams of some southerners for the revival of the foreign slave trade, the new constitution forbade the "importation of Negroes of the African race, from any foreign country, other than the slaveholding States or Territories of the United States of America."

On February 9, the delegation of six states elected Jefferson Davis and Alexander Stephens as respectively provisional president and vice president of the new government. Davis arrived in Montgomery for his inauguration on February 16. That night, addressing a crowd that had gathered under the balcony of his hotel, Davis admitted that the nation might "be ushered in the midst of a storm," but ultimately the southern confederacy would enter "the harbor of constitutional liberty and political equality." Davis continued:

> We fear nothing . . . because, if war should come, if we must again baptize in blood the principles for which our fathers bled in the Revolution, we shall show that we are not degenerate sons, but will redeem the pledges they gave, preserve the rights they transmitted to us, and prove that southern valor still shines as bright as in 1776.

The crowd grew ecstatic at the words of their president, who declared that he would resign the presidency and take to the field of battle, if his country needed him. In the midst of the cheers, William L. Yancey, a leading fire-eater and the man who had introduced Davis to the crowd, declared that, in Davis, the South had been blessed with "the statesman, the soldier, and the patriot" it needed. In the exhilaration of the moment, with the future dimmed by mists of uncertainty, Yancey declared, speaking of Davis: "The man and the hour have met."

The New President

Abraham Lincoln left Springfield, Illinois, on February 11, 1861, on a meandering train journey through the northern states that would end in Washington, D.C. and his inauguration. Along the way, he made several stops, addressing crowds eager to catch a glimpse of

Jefferson Davis' inauguration in Montgomery, Alabama

their new president and, perhaps, gain some reassurance from him about the future. Lincoln however gave no clear indication of how he would handle the crisis, and many left without being reassured.

March 4, 1861 was a somber inauguration day in Washington, D.C. Crowds gathered outside the capitol building with its unfinished rotunda, oppressed by uncertainty; many doubted the ability of the man who now took the oath of the office from Chief Justice Taney. Moving to the lectern to deliver his inaugural address, Lincoln removed his hat. Senator Douglas, who stood close by, seeing the president could find no place for his hat, stepped forward and held it for him.

In his address, Lincoln said that southern apprehensions that "by the accession of the Republican Administration, their property and their peace, and personal security are to be endangered," were groundless. "Indeed," he said, "the most ample evidence to the contrary has all the while existed, and been open to their inspection," and he quoted from his speeches and from the Republican platform. The union of the states, Lincoln insisted, "is perpetual. Perpetuity is implied, if not expressed, in the fundamental law of all national governments"; thus any attempt by one or a few states to secede was illegal, "insurrectionary and revolutionary, according to the circumstances." Further, if the federal government is a compact, said Lincoln, then, if it is to be dissolved, both sides in the compact must agree to its dissolution. In regards to the southern states that had seceded, Lincoln declared he would not surrender to them any property held by the federal government and would collect all federal duties and imposts; "but beyond what may be necessary for these objects, there will be no invasion—no using of force against, or among the people anywhere."

Lincoln concluded, addressing the South:

> In *your* hands, my dissatisfied fellow countrymen, and not in *mine*, is the momentous issue of civil war. The government will not assail *you*. You can have no conflict, without being yourselves the aggressors. *You* have no oath registered in Heaven to destroy the government, while I shall have the most solemn one to "preserve, protect and defend" it.
>
> I am loath to close. We are not enemies, but friends. We must not be enemies. Though passion may have strained, it must not break our bonds of affection. The mystic chords of memory, stretching from every battle-field, and patriot grave, to every living heart and hearth-stone, all over this broad land, will yet swell the chorus of the Union, when again touched, as surely they will be, by the better angels of our nature.

Fort Sumter

Lincoln's secretary of state, William H. Seward, had little confidence in the abilities of his boss. After all, Seward had been a prominent senator, an anti-slavery leader, and might have won the Republican nomination had he not had powerful enemies in the party. And what was Lincoln? Though eloquent, he was nothing but a small-town lawyer from the raw West. What did he know about statecraft?

The problem that confronted the new administration in its first few weeks was a volatile one. Since proclaiming independence, southern states had seized federal forts and arsenals lying in their territory. Only two forts remained in the control of federal forces: Fort Pickens in Pensacola, Florida, and the yet unfinished Fort Sumter in Charleston harbor. The Confederate government had demanded the surrender of these forts, since they constituted in the mind of the government the presence of foreign troops in Confederate territory. For the federal government to maintain them would be a tacit act of aggression.

President Buchanan had sent a ship with provisions and reinforcements to Sumter, but the guns of the South Carolina militia that held the forts surrounding Charleston harbor had turned it back. The problem of Sumter and Pickens now fell to Lincoln, and Seward thought that he himself—not that bumbling lawyer from the West—was the man to handle it.

Commissioners from President Davis arrived in Washington in March to discuss the surrender of Castle Pinckney and Fort Sumter. Though he refused to meet with them in person, Seward told a go-between that in a few short days the troops at Fort Sumter would be withdrawn. So certain was Seward that he could control Lincoln's cabinet and Lincoln himself, that he had no doubt that this would be the case.

Seward held sway in Lincoln's cabinet; thus, when the president met with cabinet members to discuss what to do with Sumter and Pinckney, five of the seven members recommended abandoning the forts. Such a gesture, argued Seward, would send a message of reconciliation to the South. Lincoln, however, had other ideas. He would hold the forts, he said; and though he would not send reinforcements to Sumter, he would attempt to supply the fort with provisions.

With all due formality, Lincoln sent a telegraph message to Governor Pickens of South Carolina, informing him that he was sending provisions, but no reinforcements or armaments, to the garrison at Fort Sumter. Commanding Confederate forces around Charleston was General Pierre Gustav Toutant Beauregard of Louisiana. With news of the approach of a provision ship, the question over what to do with Sumter reached a crisis point, and President Davis telegraphed Beauregard to send a message to Major Robert Anderson, commander at Fort Sumter, demanding the surrender of the fort. If Anderson refused to surrender, he was to be informed that Confederate shore batteries would open fire on him at once.

On April 11, a group of Beauregard's staff officers crossed by boat to Sumter. They presented their general's terms to Anderson, who replied he could not surrender Sumter without due instructions from his government. As the Confederate officers departed, Anderson admitted that his garrison, without new provisions, could hold out only a few days. Beauregard communicated this news to Davis, who replied that if they could get assurances from Anderson that he would surrender when his food supply ran out, then they would refrain from bombarding the fort.

But Anderson would give no assurance of surrender; he told the Confederates that he would surrender only if he were not reprovisioned in the next few days. The staff officers, thinking it pointless to confer with Beauregard on this reply, passed a written note to Anderson: "By authority of Brigadier General Beauregard, commanding the Provisional Forces of the Confederate States, we have the honor to notify you that he will open the fire of his batteries on Fort Sumter in one hour from this time." It was then 3:20 on the morning of April 12.

One hour and ten minutes later, a mortar from Fort Johnson fired from across the harbor. The missile arched into the dark morning sky, looking "like the wings of a firefly," as one Confederate gunner put it. Reaching the apogee of its path through the sky, the missile descended and exploded right over Fort Sumter. Then all the Confederate batteries opened fire, shaking the night with hellish explosions, lighting the heavens with wrathful fire. Spectators watched from the rooftops of Charleston, some weeping, some rejoicing, others praying. The war had begun, and there was no turning back.

The firing continued throughout the day, with no casualties on either side. The relief ship arrived outside Charleston harbor; but being unable to reach the fort, it turned back. Finally, the next day, April 13, Anderson, his ammunition exhausted, surrendered. Under the terms of surrender, Beauregard allowed Major Anderson and his soldiers to fire a last salute to the Stars and Stripes before they lowered it.

What horrors lay ahead, stemming from this first assault, none then could tell. To many a short-sighted southerner, only glory and honor, and a vindication of southern rights, awaited the first trial of arms that was Fort Sumter. "The bloody trial of strength must be essayed," said the Charleston *Mercury* after the event. "The sword must cut asunder the last tie that bound us to a people, whom, in spite of wrongs and injustice wantonly inflicted through a long series of years, we had not yet utterly hated and despised. The last expiring spark of affection must be quenched in blood. Some of the most splendid pages in our glorious history must be blurred. A blow must be struck that would make the ears of every Republican fanatic tingle, and whose dreadful effects will be felt by generations yet to come. We must transmit a heritage of rankling and undying hate to our children."

Chapter 16 Review

Summary

- The anti-slavery movement in the United States became a major political force. It included such anti-slavery proponents as Benjamin Lundy, William Lloyd Garrison, and Angelina Grimké, as well as former slaves, such as Sojourner Truth and Frederick Douglass. The antislavery movement split into two factions, the "anti-slavery" and the "abolitionist." The movement made enemies in the southern states.

- In 1835 abolitionists began sending petitions to Congress asking it to abolish slavery in the District of Columbia. This caused Congress to pass the first of its "gag resolutions" in 1836, which, because of

Chapter 16 Review (continued)

unrelenting abolitionist opposition, was repealed in 1844.

- James Birney organized the first anti-slavery party in the United States, the Liberty Party, in 1839.

- When David Wilmot submitted his "Wilmot Proviso" to Congress, he awakened the sectional controversy over slavery in territories. The territories in question were the territories newly acquired from the war with Mexico.

- In January of 1850 , Henry Clay proposed the Compromise of 1850. By September his bill had been cut into five separate bills. President Fillmore signed the bills that same month. The North greeted the Compromise with anger, especially the strengthened Fugitive Slave Law. The Fugitive Slave Law especially frightened escaped slaves, some of whom formed secret vigilance committees for mutual protection.

- In 1852, Harriet Beecher Stowe published a controversial book, *Uncle Tom's Cabin*, with its portrayal of what would become the standard of the cruel slave owner, Simon Legree. Stowe's book elicited a storm of protest in the South.

- The early years of the 1850s were prosperous for both the North and the South. American idealism was renewed with the "Young Americans." The president, Franklin Pierce, favored filibustering and tried to instigate a war with Spain.

- In 1854, Jefferson Davis, who promoted a southern transcontinental railroad route, persuaded President Pierce to purchase from Mexico the territory south of the Gila River and west of the Río Grande. Mexico agreed to this purchase, known as the Gadsden Purchase.

- In 1854, Stephen Douglas introduced a bill to divide and organize the Nebraska Territory into two separate territories—Kansas and Nebraska. Congress passed the Kansas-Nebraska Act on May 25, 1854. The territories were organized under the concept of Popular Sovereignty.

- In 1854, the anti-immigrant, anti-Catholic American or "Know-Nothing" Party became a powerful force in politics.

- Northerners feared that Popular Sovereignty might claim Kansas and Nebraska for slavery, so they organized emigrant aid societies to settle anti-slavery men in these territories. Soon the majority of settlers were free-soilers. Free-soiler and pro-slavery rivalry resulted in bloody warfare in Kansas.

- In 1857 the Supreme Court published its decision in the Dred Scott case. In his decision, Chief Justice Roger Taney said black men were excluded from the purview of the Constitution and were the property of their owners. In his decision, Taney nullified the Missouri Compromise, thus opening up all the territories to slavery.

- In 1858 Congress attempted to admit Kansas into the union under a proslavery constitution, thus creating a wider chasm between the North and South.

- In 1859, John Brown sought to instigate a violent revolution to free the slaves by assaulting the federal arsenal at Harper's Ferry, Virginia. Brown was arrested and hanged.

- Abraham Lincoln won the presidential election of 1860. Following the election, South Carolina seceded from the union, followed by seven other southern states. The congress of the new Confederate States of America drew up a provisional constitution and on February 9, 1861 elected Jefferson Davis and Alexander Stephens respectively as provisional president and vice president.

- In 1860, the Confederate government demanded that the United States remove all its troops from forts in Confederate territory. When Fort Sumter in Charleston harbor refused to surrender to the Confederate government, Confederate troops fired on it on April 12, 1861, thus beginning the Civil War.

Key Concepts

anti-slavery: the name referring to proponents of a gradual emancipation of the slaves

abolitionists: proponents of immediate emancipation of the slaves

Know-Nothings: the nickname for members of the American Party that opposed immigration, especially Catholic immigration, to the United States

Underground Railroad: a network of secret routes and safe houses that helped black slaves to escape to freedom

Free-Soilers: member of the Free-Soil Party that opposed the introduction of slavery in the new territories

Popular Sovereignty: the political doctrine that said that a territory's settlers alone should decide whether it should or should not permit slavery

filibuster: to carry out revolutionary activities in a foreign country

Dates to Remember

1846: David Wilmot submits his "Wilmot Proviso" to forbid the introduction of slavery into new territories.

1850: Congress approves the Compromise of 1850.

1852: Harriet Beecher Stowe publishes *Uncle Tom's Cabin.*

1854: The Pierce administration issues the Ostend Manifesto.

In the Gadsden Purchase, Mexico sells to the United States territory south of the Gila River and west of the Río Grande.

Stephan Douglas introduces the Kansas-Nebraska bill.

1857: the Supreme Court publishes its decision on the Dred Scott case.

1859: John Brown attempts a violent revolution to free the slaves, but is captured and killed.

1860: Abraham Lincoln elected president

South Carolina secedes from the Union.

1861: Confederate troops fire on Fort Sumter.

Central Characters

William Lloyd Garrison (1805–1879): an American journalist who helped lead the abolitionist campaign against slavery

Frederick Douglass (1818–1895): a former black slave who was one of the most eminent antislavery leaders of the 19th century

Sojourner Truth (1797–1883): an African-American evangelist and reformer who used her religious fervor to further the abolitionist movement

Stephen A. Douglas (1813–1861): politician, leader of the Democratic Party and senator from Illinois, who favored the cause of Popular Sovereignty in the territories; Democratic candidate for president in the 1860 election

John Brown (1800–1859): an American abolitionist whose raid on the federal arsenal at Harper's Ferry, Virginia, in 1859 and subsequent execution made him a martyr to the anti-slavery cause

Abraham Lincoln (1809–1865): 16th president of the United States whose election led to the secession of southern states from the union

Questions for Review

1. How did the anti-slavery movement differ from the abolitionist movement, and what where the main ideas of each?

2. How did George Fitzhugh's *Cannibals All!* answer northern criticisms of southern slavery?

3. What was the position of American Catholics on slavery in the first half of the 19th century? What actions did the Church take or not take on slavery, and why?

4. Explain the controversy between North and South over the new western territories. What constitutional and moral arguments did each side make?

5. Did Henry Clay's Compromise of 1850 solve the controversy between North and South over slavery? Why or why not?

6. Explain the importance of *Uncle Tom's Cabin* in the controversy over slavery.

7. Explain the controversy over the Kansas-Nebraska bill and how it contributed to the slavery controversy.

8. How did the Dred Scott decision fuel the slavery debate? What effect did it have on the relationship between the North and the South?

9. Briefly explain both Lincoln and Douglas' views on slavery as expressed in their debates during the Illinois senatorial campaign of 1858.

Chapter 16 Review (continued)

10. Why did South Carolina decide to secede from the union?

Ideas in Action

1. Research the history of the Know-Nothings and their effect on the Catholic Church in the United States.

2. Study the history of the Underground Railroad and chart the paths slaves took to freedom.

3. Study the arguments for gradualism and immediate abolition, and stage a debate between students who hold, one or some to gradualism, and one or some to immediate abolition.

4. Read a fictional or eyewitness account of the opening of the war. Compose your own imaginary eyewitness account of the war's opening from whatever perspective you wish.

5. In his first inaugural address, Abraham Lincoln said secession is illegal because the union "is perpetual. Perpetuity is implied, if not expressed, in the fundamental law of all national governments." Research what the secessionists thought about the right to secession; how would they have answered Lincoln? What constitutional arguments would they have used? Given what you know about the Constitution and the powers it grants to the federal government and reserves to the states, who do you think had the better argument—Lincoln or the secessionists?

Highways and Byways

Singing the Slaves Free

The anti-slavery movement was not just speeches. Many songwriters and poets became involved in the movement, lending a musical touch to the movement. Meetings often opened with song. A fugitive slave, William W. Brown, compiled a collection of songs in 1848, *The Anti-Slavery Harp: A Collection of Songs for Anti-Slavery*. This collection included songs such as, "Am I Not a Man and Brother" and "Slave's Lamentation." These songs were often set to popular tunes. In the preface to the book, Brown writes, "The demand of the public for a cheap Anti-Slavery Song-Book, containing Songs of a more recent composition, has induced me to collect together, and present to the public, the songs contained in this book." The book is dedicated to "all true friends of the Slave."

The famous poets of America also lent their talents to the anti-slavery movement. John Greenleaf Whittier wrote a dedication poem for the May 1838 opening of the Pennsylvania Hall in Philadelphia, an abolitionist meeting place, as well as a volume of poems entitled *Anti-slavery Poems: Songs of Labor and Reform*. And of course there is a plethora of songs and poems about the antislavery hero, John Brown. No movement would be complete without its songs.

17 A BROTHERS' WAR

A Leap into the Unknown

"My permanent object is this struggle to save the Union, and is not either to save or to destroy slavery." So wrote Abraham Lincoln to newspaper editor Horace Greeley on August 22, 1862, well over a year into the struggle now known as the Civil War. When Lincoln wrote Greeley, it appeared the president would fail to achieve his object. The union, it seemed, was doomed; the separated southern states would maintain their independence.

The war had dragged on longer than many initially thought it would. In the beginning, many believed a northern victory would be swift, a mere 90-day affair. Lincoln himself seemed to believe this. On April 15, 1861, he called for 75,000 volunteers to serve a mere three-month stint to put down combinations "too powerful to be suppressed by the ordinary course of judicial proceedings" and "to cause the laws to be duly executed." Winfield Scott, general and chief of the United States army, thought more men were needed, and for a longer time; he urged the president to raise an army of at least 300,000 for a two to three-year stint of service. Lincoln would not follow Scott's suggestion, for the president still seemed to think the uprising of the southern states a mere insurrection.

Abraham Lincoln, shortly after his election

Confederate President Jefferson Davis' objective—to maintain the independence of the Confederate States of America—gave him, at least initially, a more realistic view of the war. After all, he could gauge Lincoln's determination to maintain the union, while Lincoln could not understand the southern will to resist. A little over a month before Fort Sumter, President Davis had called for 100,000 volunteers to defend the southern states.

With the secession of Virginia on April 17, 1861, the Confederate government moved its capital from Montgomery, Alabama, to Richmond. Now the two presidents, Davis and Lincoln, were separated by a scant 100 miles of Virginia soil—soil that would drink the blood of countless thousands before their struggle would end. So different were these men. Davis was the refined southern aristocrat, with all the virtues and vices of his class. He had honesty, a devotion to duty, a deep sense of honor; but he was often aloof, overly sensitive on small points that touched on his dignity, impatient with those who opposed him, and tactless. Lincoln remained the rough westerner, peppering his conversation with homey stories and coarse jokes; willing to humble himself to subordinates to obtain a greater goal; somewhat unconcerned about using unworthy means to obtain a desired end, but acting with a keen, hard-headed astuteness. While Davis fought merely for his country's

Horace Greeley

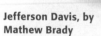

Jefferson Davis, by Mathew Brady

independence, Lincoln battled to maintain a union that he saw as "the city on the hill"—the messianic hope of the world.

The two presidents possessed very different resources for waging war. The white population of the North, for one, was 18.9 million in contrast with the South's 5.5 million. Northern industry could produce the arms and provisions needed by the Federal army. The South had little industry—only Richmond's Tredegar Iron Works could produce armaments at the beginning of the war. Southern wealth was in cotton and other agricultural products, which the South could use to purchase arms and provisions in Europe. But Europe was an ocean away.

Given the Confederacy's inferiority in numbers and industrial output, it looked as if to win the war it would, sooner or later, need the support of the great foreign powers, Great Britain and France. The South knew it had an important bargaining chip—cotton. It was generally thought that if the South could not sell its cotton to Europe, European textile mills would fall idle and lay off workers. The resulting unrest would induce Great Britain and France to put pressure on Lincoln to end the war.

Perhaps the South's greatest asset was the spirit of many of its men, who saw themselves as fighting to protect their homes and native states. Sam Watkins of Columbia, Tennessee, spoke for many a southern man when he said he fought because he believed in states' rights and because "the South is our country, the North is the country of those who live there." And Davis could place these men under the command of the cream of the United States army's officer corps, who had left the U.S. army to fight for the South.

Lincoln's call for volunteers finally induced the wavering Virginia State Convention to vote for secession; Virginia would not consent to the subjugation of her southern sister states. With Virginia went a number of America's most able military men, including Lt. Colonel Robert Edward Lee. The son of Revolutionary War hero "Lighthorse Harry" Lee, Robert E. Lee was deeply attached to the union. But although Lincoln offered him the command of the entire northern army, Lee refused it; he would not fight against his friends, family, and native state. At Arlington, his home overlooking the Potomac and Washington City, Lee resigned his commission in the United States army.

One advantage the Union had over the Confederacy was its navy. It was the commander of the U.S. army, General Winfield Scott, who early in the war hit upon what would prove an effective use of this advantage. Use it, he advised Lincoln, to establish a blockade of the coast and seize control of the Mississippi; that way, the Federals could cut off the South's trade with Europe and eventually starve the Confederates into submission. Many mocked this squeezing of the Confederacy, calling it Scott's "anaconda strategy." Himself feeling popular pressure to secure a quick victory over the South, Lincoln saw he could not rely on Scott's strategy alone. Still, the "anaconda" formed a part of Lincoln's plan of conquest. This was to establish a blockade of the southern coast and capture key positions on the western rivers; at the same time, three forces would invade the South: one, east of the Appalachians; another, west of the Appalachians and east of the Mississippi; and a third, west of the Mississippi.

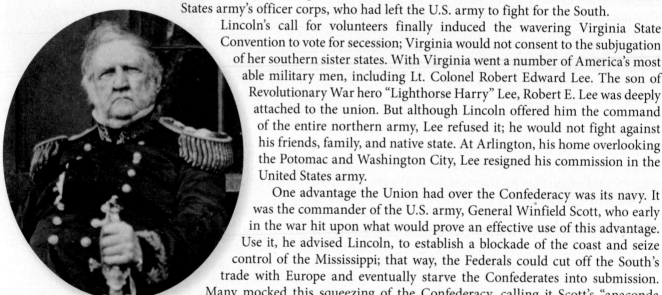

General Winfield Scott

The task before Lincoln was immense. For one thing, the Federal navy had only 40 ships to blockade the long southern coastline, stretching from the Potomac to the mouth of the Río Grande in Texas. The regular army had only 16,257 officers and men, and the three-month volunteers were rough and untrained. On May 3 Lincoln called on state governors to provide 40,000 three-year recruits, but these men would need training. How to fund all this

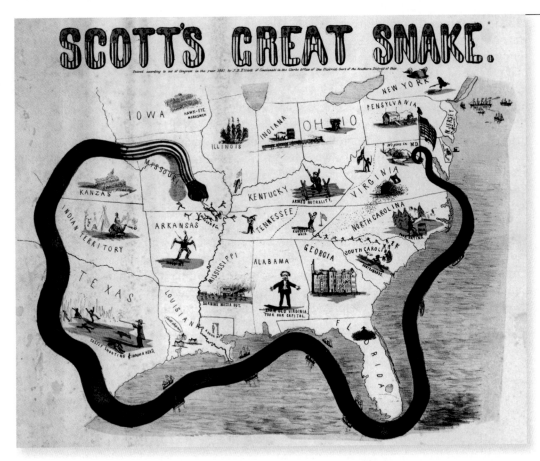

was a problem that Congress would solve by what some would say was an unconstitutional means—an income tax—as well as a national banking system. By the end of 1862, the federal government was spending $2.5 million a day on the war.

Battle for the Border

Lincoln's first task was to secure for the union the neutral border states—Maryland, Kentucky, Delaware, and Missouri. Delaware, with few slaves, had shown no signs of seceding. Kentucky, however, had a strong secessionist faction and could as easily go Confederate as remain in the union. Lincoln thought an insistence that Kentucky contribute to the war effort against the South would goad that state into secession. He thus assured Kentucky that he would respect her neutrality. No Federal troops would cross over onto Kentucky soil.

Missouri was divided between southern and union sympathizers, among the latter the numerous German population around St. Louis. Though in February 1861, a state convention voted to stay in the union, Governor Clairborne Jackson refused to send troops to Lincoln and plotted to seize the Federal arsenal in St. Louis. The commander of the arsenal, Nathaniel Lyon, got wind of the plan and with Federal troops broke up a state militia encampment at St. Louis. Promoted to brigadier general and to the command of Federal troops around St. Louis, Lyon then marched on Governor Jackson, driving him from the state capital, Jefferson City, into the southern regions of Missouri.

Maryland was a special worry for Lincoln, for if that state seceded, Washington would be cut off from the North. Lincoln thought he had to secure Maryland at any cost. Maryland's governor, Thomas B. Hicks, stood stoutly for the union, but the state had many secessionists. To forestall an irregular meeting of the state assembly, which secessionists would dominate, Hicks called a regular session of the assembly to meet on April 26. During the session, Hicks called for Maryland's neutrality, and the legislature decided that it had no legal right to call a state convention to consider secession. This was a victory for Lincoln. He had contemplated sending in troops to arrest members of the Maryland legislature if need be to halt a movement toward a state convention.

Still, Lincoln did not rest content with Maryland's acquiescence to the union. He adopted harsher measures to silence secessionist voices in the state. On April 27, he ordered Scott to suspend the writ of *habeas corpus* "for the public safety" along the military line that ran through Maryland to Washington. A legal protection guaranteed by the Constitution, *habeas corpus* assures the right of anyone imprisoned to be brought before a court so it might examine the reasons for imprisonment. *Habeas corpus* is a "privilege," says Article 1 of the Constitution, which "shall not be suspended, unless when in Cases of Rebellion or Invasion the public Safety may require it." Lincoln said such conditions prevailed in Maryland.

But Chief Justice Taney disagreed with the president. The military had arrested John Merryman, who was recruiting men for the Confederate army, and had locked him up in Fort McHenry in Baltimore. When Taney sent a United States marshal with a writ of *habeas corpus* for Merryman, Maj. General George Cadwalader, commanding the Federal forces in Baltimore, refused to allow him to serve it. The president, said Cadwalader, had suspended the writ. Taney replied that "the president under the Constitution of the United States can-

A map of the United States and the Confederate States of America, with neutral states, at the beginning of the Civil War

not suspend the privilege of the writ of *habeas corpus*, nor authorize a military officer to do it." Only Congress could order a suspension of the writ, said the chief justice. Lincoln disagreed and ignored Taney. Lincoln said that the Constitution allows the writ to be suspended in periods of rebellion; and, in his opinion, he as president had the duty to suspend it. "Are all the laws, but one, to go unexecuted," said Lincoln, "and the government itself to go to pieces lest that one [*habeas corpus*] be violated?" It has been claimed that Lincoln at one point issued a warrant to arrest Taney, but it was never served.

It was Cadwalader's predecessor, Brig. General Benjamin F. Butler, who, without direction from General Scott, had placed Baltimore under martial law. A former Massachusetts Democratic politician, Butler had abandoned politics to take command of the 8th Massachusetts Infantry. In early May 1861, after taking and fortifying Federal Hill, overlooking Baltimore, Butler had, again, on his own authority, established martial law over the city. Butler closed newspapers with a secessionist bent, confiscated arms, arrested men suspected of Confederate leanings, and imprisoned ministers who in church services omitted prescribed prayers for the president of the United States. The outcry against Butler's acts was great, and on May 15 Winfield Scott sent him to Fort Monroe on the Chesapeake Bay. But the government did not undo what Butler had wrought, and martial law continued under his successor, Maj. General Cadwalader.

So, by fair means or foul, Lincoln made fast Maryland's ties to the Union. But he could not keep Tennessee and Arkansas in the union. Both seceded in early May 1861. North Carolina followed them into the Confederacy later the same month.

From Words to Blows

The war seemed a thrilling and glorious adventure to young men, North and South. Tens of thousands answered the calls for enlistment. In the North, Yankee boys left farms and shops for the army; Irish, Germans, Italians, and Scots enlisted. The Federal army grew with additions of state militia and private militia groups, some of whom sported colorful uniforms. "Zouave" units wore uniforms of red and blue, with the Turkish tasseled fez for head wear. A Scottish highlander militia from northern New York decked themselves out in kilts. Mexican units from Texas, wearing ponchos and sombreros, gave an Hispanic flavor to some southern units.

The soldiers had not yet tasted the bitterness of war. Thousands upon thousands continued to enter the service as the Confederate and union governments called for more and more

Robert E. Lee's house at Arlington, with Federal occupying soldiers

soldiers. On May 3, Lincoln called on the states to provide 42,000 three-year volunteers. Almost two weeks later, on May 16, 1861, the Confederate Congress authorized the recruitment of 400,000 volunteers, and still recruiters turned away southern men eager for the fight; there was just no room for them.

On May 24, "the sacred soil of Virginia" was "polluted" by the "abolition hosts" of a "reckless and unprincipled tyrant." So said General Pierre Gustav Toutant Beauregard, who commanded Confederate forces in Virginia. He was speaking of the first Federal assault on Confederate territory—the seizure of Arlington Heights and Alexandria, across the Potomac from Washington. In June, more Virginia soil was "polluted" when General

George Britten McClellan led a Federal force into the state's western mountain counties, which stood strongly for the union. McClellan encountered a smaller force under Confederate General Robert E. Lee and forced the southern commander to evacuate the region. Mocked as "Granny" and "Evacuating" Lee by southern newspapers, Robert E. Lee returned to Richmond, where he took up a desk job. For his part, McClellan won widespread fame for robbing the South of a region rich in coal. On June 11, western Virginia organized a pro-union government and sent representatives to Washington. The region would later secede from Virginia to form the state of West Virginia.

About this time, one leader of the "abolition hosts" began pushing the war in a direction Lincoln said he did not want it to go. Though he had supported the nomination of Jefferson Davis for president in 1860, General Benjamin Butler had more recently remade himself into a liberator of slaves. Slaves were crossing the Federal lines at Fortress Monroe on the Chesapeake Bay, thinking the Federals would grant them liberty, and Butler was not turning them away. "Contraband of war," he called them. By late spring, Butler was harboring about 1,000 slaves, using them for all sorts of menial tasks around Fortress Monroe.

Throughout the North, men were spoiling for a fight, for some decisive action that would bring this foolish secessionist experiment to a quick end. In Washington, Lincoln felt the pressure of public opinion and urged General Irvin McDowell, who commanded Federal troops in Washington and northeastern Virginia, to find and do battle with the Confederate army. About 60,000 Confederate soldiers defended Virginia, with 22,000 of them under General Beauregard at Centreville, a scarce 25 miles from Washington. McDowell told the president he would move on Beauregard when his troops were sufficiently trained, but to do so now—why, his men were still too green! "You are green," replied the president, "but they [the Confederates] are green, also you are all green alike." Lincoln wanted action, especially since the Federal army's 90-day stint of service was almost up.

July 18, 1861, when the Federal army, 37,000 strong, marched out of Washington, was like a holiday Not only soldiers, but carriages full of congressmen, senators, ladies, and eminent citizens, all with picnic lunches, advanced on the Confederate position at Manassas Junction. The picnickers were going to watch their union boys "whup the rebels." The soldiers themselves partook of the holiday spirit. Many of them broke rank, running off into the woods and fields to gather wild berries or drink water. It was a sultry, hot day. War was a frolic for them, a long walk in the woods.

Three days later, the Federals reached Bull Run, the creek across which lay the Confederate army. It was nine o'clock Sunday morning when McDowell ordered his men to cross the creek. He led 18,000 men against the Confederate left flank in a plan to destroy it; he then would crush the entire army between the two flanks of his own. The whir of bullets passing over their heads astonished the green Federal recruits, but they felt little fear. Though they began to see wounded men carried back across the lines, still they little felt the horror of their task and situation.

Confederate General Joseph Eggleston Johnston had arrived at the scene of battle, and, since he outranked Beauregard, took command of the army. Seeing from the rising dust and smoke to the west that McDowell was concentrating his attack on the left flank, Johnston began to reposition his force westward. But it seemed all too late; the badly outnumbered Confederates on the left flank had broken and were in retreat before the triumphant Federals. "We've whipped them," cried the Yankees, "We'll hang Jeff Davis to a sour apple tree! They are running. The war is over." The onlookers from Washington rejoiced to witness the downfall of the Confederacy.

The Confederates retreated to a new position on a hill, called Henry's Hill after the family whose house stood on its crest. There reinforcements awaited them: South Carolina troops led by Wade Hampton and Georgia regiments under Colonel Francis Stebbins Bartow. Five Virginia regiments soon arrived, commanded by Brig. General Thomas Jonathan Jackson. He posted his men on the brow of the hill.

About noon, the Federal onslaught began. The Confederate regiments, badly disorganized, were ready to break. Colonel Bartow died from a bullet wound while trying to rally his men. The South Carolinian, General Barnard Bee, in desperation rode up to Jackson: "General, they're beating us back," he said. Jackson was cool. "Sir," he replied, "we will give them the bayonet." Bee rode to a party of stragglers, and standing in his stirrups, cried, "Look! There is Jackson standing like a stone wall! Rally behind the Virginians!" A bullet struck Bee in the stomach, and he fell to the ground, dead.

With Jackson as its anchor, the Confederate line held. Reinforcements under Colonel Jubal Early arrived, and at about 4 p.m., the Confederates counterattacked. "Yell like furies!" cried Jackson to his men, and for the first time men heard the chilling, half-savage Confederate battle cry, the "Rebel Yell." The Federal retreat became a rout; soldiers fled in confusion, casting away their weapons. The Warrenton Turnpike, running from Manassas to Washington, was clogged with soldiers and with carriages filled with terrified ladies and gentlemen fleeing for the safety of the capital.

"We have whipped them!" General "Stonewall" Jackson exulted. "They ran like sheep! Give me 5,000 fresh men and I will be in Washington City tomorrow!"

Federal cavalry at Sudley Ford of Bull Run, from a glass negative, by George N. Barnard, July, 1861

Young Napoleon

A Confederate assault on Washington was just what Lincoln and others feared. Yet, despite the fact that the road to Washington was open, General Johnston would not move on the federal capital. His troops were still too undisciplined to storm Washington's fortifications. Instead, Johnston fortified his own position at Centreville and trained his men.

First Manassas (or Bull Run, as the North would name it), claimed 4,500 Federals and Confederates killed, wounded, and captured. It awakened in Lincoln and the North the realization that the war would not be a quick affair but a long, drawn out struggle. Lincoln thus called on the states to supply him with 100,000 three-year volunteers. He replaced General McDowell with a commander he thought could win battles, Maj. General George McClellan.

McClellan arrived in Washington resplendent with the glory of his victories in western Virginia. He took the disorganized Federal army and disciplined it, instilling in the men a new spirit of confidence and pride. He worked around the clock, displaying devotion and a spirit of sacrifice. He led his men in reviews before the president, and the gaunt Lincoln seemed to pale in glory by comparison to McClellan. McClellan's men, who loved him, took pride in their commander, calling him affectionately, "Little Mac." Northern newspapers praised the new general of the "Army of the Potomac," dubbing him the "Young Napoleon," an identification McClellan warmly embraced and promoted.

George McClellan, by Mathew Brady

Struggle for the Border States

While McClellan was training his troops in and around Washington, secessionist and union forces fought in Missouri. In late June, Lincoln had appointed John C. Frémont overall commander in the West, and the Pathfinder had established his headquarters in St. Louis. Frémont's task was to prepare an invasion along the Mississippi to New Orleans and so divide the western from the eastern Confederate states. Meanwhile, Nathaniel Lyon and his union force had driven Missouri's governor, Clairborne Jackson, into Arkansas and now waited in Springfield for reinforcements from Frémont. A motley band of secessionists, some of them armed only with ancient flintlocks, were organized under former Missouri governor and one-time congressman, Sterling Price. Price had had no use for secession; but when forced to choose between his home state and the union, he chose Missouri—for whose sake he fought, not the Confederacy. A gentleman, Price wanted hostilities confined to the contending armies. (He later arranged an agreement with Frémont to end guerrilla warfare, stop arrests for political opinion, and spare civilians and their property. The Federals later repudiated this agreement.)

Told that Frémont could spare no soldiers, Lyon decided to move on the secessionist forces under the command of Price and Confederate General Ben McCulloch. The two armies met at Wilson's Creek on August 10, 1861, in a pitched battle in which Lyon was killed and the Federal forces routed. Price led his men to Lexington, in the central-western part of the state, and took the city.

But more troublesome for Lincoln than Lyon's defeat was the Federal commander's headstrong behavior. Without consulting Washington, Frémont had issued a proclamation freeing all slaves owned by Missouri secessionists. Such a decree in a neutral state threatened Lincoln's war strategy, for it could tip the scales of public opinion in neutral Kentucky toward the Confederacy. If Kentucky seceded, important points on the Ohio and Mississippi would fall to the Confederacy and threaten the success of Lincoln's western strategy. This must not happen, and Lincoln immediately repudiated Frémont's decree.

If Lincoln was treating Kentucky gently, so was Jefferson Davis. Kentucky, neutral or Confederate, stood as a buffer zone between the northern armies and Tennessee. If Kentucky went fully to the union, all of central Tennessee, along with Mississippi and Alabama, lay open to a Federal advance. Davis wanted to do nothing to tip Kentucky to the union.

Meanwhile, Confederate General Leonidas Polk (an Episcopalian bishop before the war) was worried about the buildup of Federal forces in Illinois. Federals under Brig. General Ulysses S. Grant were massed at Cairo, Illinois, and Federal gunboats threatened from St. Louis. Fearing a Federal advance into Kentucky, Polk marched his forces into the state in early September and took and fortified Columbus, a city on a bluff overlooking the Mississippi.

General Leonidas Polk

U.S. Grant quickly reacted to Polk's move and captured Paducah on the Kentucky side of the Ohio. The move was decisive, for now the union controlled the mouth of the Tennessee River, which provided a road to the heart of the central Confederate states. And Grant had this advantage—it was Polk, not he, who first violated Kentucky's neutrality.

Polk's invasion of Kentucky ended the state's neutrality. In September 1861, the strongly pro-union Kentucky legislature met and asked for federal military aid against the Confederates. Kentucky would receive that aid, and more. Kentuckians soon discovered that the end of neutrality meant an end to their political freedoms. All over the state, U.S. marshals arrested men on the mere suspicion of disloyalty. In Confederate-occupied regions of the state, suspected pro-union sympathizers were likewise arrested and imprisoned.

Maryland, too, felt the heavy hand of Washington. Emboldened by the Confederate victory at Manassas, southern sympathizers in Maryland again agitated for secession. In September the state assembly was set to meet in special legislative session, and Lincoln feared it would vote for Maryland's withdrawal from the union. To forestall this, Lincoln sent troops into Baltimore and arrested and jailed the mayor and 31 legislators. Lincoln held them in jail for two months, long enough to assure the election of a pro-union majority to the legislature in November.

With Kentucky and Maryland firmly in his grasp, Lincoln faced a new annoyance. The summer had passed, it was now well into the autumn, and McClellan showed no sign of advancing on Johnston at Centreville. Republicans in Congress were growing impatient—when would the general move? McClellan said his preparations were not complete. Besides, his intelligence agent, Allan Pinkerton, had informed him that Johnston had at least 150,000 men at Centreville. (In reality Johnston had not even half that number.) McClellan said he himself needed at least 270,000 men, and until he got that number, it would be foolish to engage Johnston in battle.

Congress was not impressed by this argument, and the Senate and House set up the Joint Committee on the Conduct of the War to investigate McClellan and his strategy. Though publicly opposed by Congress, and privately scorned by the Young Napoleon, Lincoln decided to back his general. In early November he allowed Winfield Scott to retire as general and chief of the Federal army and replaced him with McClellan.

General Joseph Johnston

Advance and Retreat

The autumn passed and the cold of winter blanketed the earth. New Years' Day 1862 came and went, and still McClellan wouldn't move on Johnston at Centreville. Not just McClellan, but General Don Carlos Buell, ensconced in Lexington, Kentucky, and General Henry Wager Halleck, who had replaced Frémont in Missouri, would not heed Lincoln's exhortations to engage Confederate armies. In desperation, the president contemplated taking command of the armies himself!

Finally, on January 27, 1862, Lincoln issued General War Order Number 1, which commanded a general movement of all land and sea forces on February 22, George Washington's birthday. Lincoln told McClellan that he must move on Manassas, but the general balked at attacking so "strong" a position. Instead, he asked permission to transport his army southward to the Rappahannock River, toward Richmond—leaving, of course, a sufficient force to guard Washington. Lincoln approved the plan, and McClellan began preparations for what would be a massive coordination of both land and sea forces, for the great northern army would have to move by sea transport down the Potomac, along the coast of Virginia, to the mouth of the Rappahannock.

McClellan with his army of over 120,000 men could have moved on Manassas and overwhelmed Joe Johnston's host of less than half that number. Johnston, himself, thought his position at Centreville a weak one, and abandoned it, leaving his dread fortifications behind —tree trunks painted to look like cannon and mounted on caissons. When it became known that Johnston's artillery were wood "Quaker guns," McClellan became

Civil War battles in Virginia and Maryland

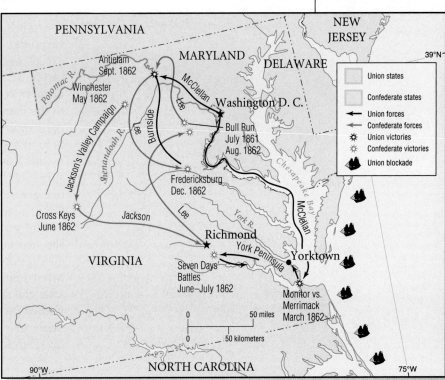

a laughing stock. Senator Ben Wade, chairman of the Joint Committee on the Conduct of the War, told Lincoln that anybody would be a better general than McClellan. "Wade," Lincoln replied, "anybody will do for you, but I must have somebody."

With Johnston taking his position on the Rappahannock, that "somebody," McClellan, had to change his plans. He decided on a movement farther south, to the York Peninsula, with a direct line of march along the James River to Richmond. This move would threaten the Confederate capital and so force Johnston from his position on the Rappahannock, only 50 miles from Washington. Lincoln agreed to McClellan's plan and removed him from general command of all the federal forces so he could concentrate on his new task—deploying the "Army of the Potomac" southward to the doorstep of the Confederate capital.

What U.S. Stands For

General Ulysses S. Grant, at least, had not been idle. While McClellan was making and changing his plans for an advance on the South, Grant, with the support of gunboats commanded by Commodore Andrew Foote, was pushing up the Tennessee River. On February 6, Confederate Fort Henry on the Tennessee, its walls hammered by Foote's gunboats, fell to Grant's 15,000 Yankees.

Grant's next target was Fort Donelson on the Cumberland River. While Foote's gunboats pushed down the Tennessee to the Ohio River, whence they could steam up the Cumberland, Grant's army marched the 15-odd miles to Fort Donelson. The Confederate force of 15,000 men at Fort Donelson was commanded by Generals John Floyd and Simon Bolivar Buckner, both of whose soldierly qualities Grant despised. Also at the fort were the second-in-command, Gideon Pillow, and a slave-trader-turned-cavalry officer, Nathan Bedford Forrest.

Commodore Foote's gunboat bombardment failed to reduce Donelson, and Grant lay siege to the fortress. On February 15, Pillow tried to cut an escape route to Nashville through Federal lines but failed, despite the hard work of Forrest's cavalry. With the escape route closed, the Confederate generals discussed whether to surrender. Both Floyd and Pillow refused to surrender the fortress and, that night, fled Fort Donelson, leaving Buckner to seek terms of surrender from Grant. Forrest and his 700 men, however, refused to be included in the surrender, and escaped through the backwaters of the Cumberland to Nashville.

Period map of Fort Donelson and its environs

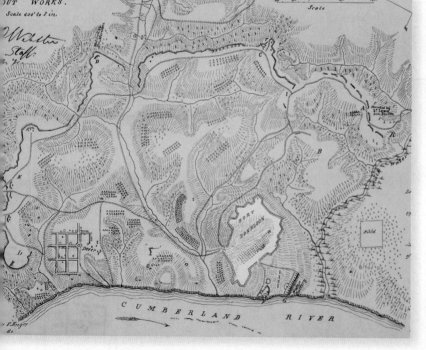

Grant's reply to Buckner's request for terms of surrender was simple and direct: "No terms except unconditional and immediate surrender can be accepted. I propose to move immediately on your works." Buckner surrendered the fortress to the mercy of Grant. When news spread about the capture of Fort Donelson, Grant became a hero in the North. The "U.S." in U.S. Grant, folk in the North exulted, stood for "unconditional surrender"! Lincoln, pleased that at least he had one general who accomplished something, made Grant a major general of volunteers.

The surrender of Forts Henry and Donelson shocked everyone, both North and South. Now all the interior of Tennessee and Alabama and Mississippi lay open to Federal armies. Four days after the fall of Fort Donelson, Foote's gunboats pushed up the Cumberland and took Clarksville, Tennessee. They were now only a day's journey by river from Nashville, the state capital, and

Bedford Forrest, who commanded the Confederate army there, knew he couldn't withstand both Grant's army and that of General Buell, which could easily reach Nashville by rail from Bowling Greene, Kentucky. Forrest withdrew his troops from Nashville on February 23. Just 24 hours later, Don Carlos Buell's federals marched into the state capital.

U.S. Grant continued his drive south along the Tennessee River.

Battle of the Iron Monsters

Stephen R. Mallory, Jefferson Davis' navy secretary, knew that the Confederacy was at a disadvantage as far as ships were concerned. The union had not only started out with more ships than the Confederates, but northern industry and shipyards could build more of them faster than the Confederates could. President Buchanan, to placate the South, had abandoned the naval shipyard at Norfolk, Virginia; but, before leaving, the Federal navy had scuttled the ships they were leaving behind. The Confederacy thus had a naval secretary and no navy.

Mallory knew he could never match federal sea power by building ships. What he needed was ships that, though fewer in number, could take on the federal navy, regardless of its numbers. If he had a fleet of iron-armored ships, thought Mallory, he need not fear the wooden union ships. So, in the fall of 1861, the Confederates raised the hull of the naval frigate *Merrimack* from the waters of Norfolk harbor, riveted iron plates upon it, and cut ten gun holes along the port and starboard sides of the vessel. The *Merrimack* (renamed the *Virginia*), was transformed into what looked like a great iron-shelled turtle.

News of the ironclad *Virginia* terrified the North. "Who is to prevent her dropping her anchor in the Potomac . . . and throwing her hundred-pound shells into [the White House] or battering down the halls of the Capitol?" asked Gustavus Fox, assistant secretary of the Federal navy. Something had to be done before the his ships were shot to splinters! Federal navy secretary Gideon Welles appealed to the Swedish-born inventor, John Ericsson, who came up with a design for a flat, iron-clad vessel, with one revolving turret sporting two guns. On January 30, 1862, the union ironclad, dubbed the *Monitor*, set sail from the shipyards on the East River in New York southward toward Norfolk to face its rival, the *Virginia*.

Nothing was seen of the CSA *Virginia* until March 8, 1862, when it steamed up the Elizabeth River from Norfolk into Hampton Roads. Several Federal ships lay at anchor in the Roads. It was laundry day for the Federal sailors, and the USS *Cumberland* was festooned with drying clothes when the *Virginia* attacked, ramming the ship with its metal beak and then firing a broadside against it at point-blank range. While its balls bounced harmlessly off the sides of the *Virginia*, the *Cumberland* suffered such damage that she sank in shallow water. The *Virginia* next attacked the *Congress*, setting her afire, and then assailed the *Minnesota*, driving her aground. It now grew towards night, and the *Virginia* withdrew to Norfolk.

The next morning at 7 a.m., when the *Virginia* steamed out from Norfolk to finish the job she had begun on the *Minnesota*, she met an unexpected rival—the *Monitor*. A battle ensued, the two iron-clads pounding each other, but neither able to sink the other. After four-and-half hours, the *Virginia* withdrew. It would be her last battle; for, two months later, the Confederates blew her up when they had to abandon Norfolk. The *Monitor*, on the other hand, was the first of many Federal iron-clads. The battle in Hampton Roads on March 8 opened a new era in naval warfare, an era of steel and steam.

Battle of the *Monitor* and *Merrimac*

Maneuvers in the East, Bloodshed in the West

It took over 400 vessels to ferry the immense Army of the Potomac, 121,500 strong, from its base near Washington to Fort Monroe. McClellan's army reached Fort Monroe in mid-March and began its slow advance up the York Peninsula. On April 5, McClellan's advanced guard reached Yorktown where, some 80 years earlier, Cornwallis had surrendered to Washington.

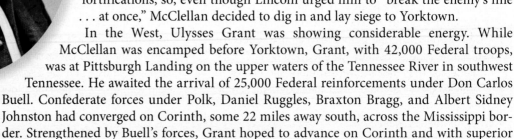

Joe Johnston's Confederates lay between the Army of the Potomac and Richmond. At Yorktown itself, John Bankhead Magruder generalled 11,000 men. Magruder, knowing he was vastly outnumbered by union forces, fell back on his flair for the theater. By scattering artillery fire and marching his men across the same clearing several times, Magruder made it seem that he possessed far more than 11,000 men. He fooled McClellan, who believed no fewer than 100,000 men lay across the Confederate lines. It would be foolish, McClellan thought, to challenge such a host, ensconced as it was behind fortifications; so, even though Lincoln urged him to "break the enemy's line . . . at once," McClellan decided to dig in and lay siege to Yorktown.

In the West, Ulysses Grant was showing considerable energy. While McClellan was encamped before Yorktown, Grant, with 42,000 Federal troops, was at Pittsburgh Landing on the upper waters of the Tennessee River in southwest Tennessee. He awaited the arrival of 25,000 Federal reinforcements under Don Carlos Buell. Confederate forces under Polk, Daniel Ruggles, Braxton Bragg, and Albert Sidney Johnston had converged on Corinth, some 22 miles away south, across the Mississippi border. Strengthened by Buell's forces, Grant hoped to advance on Corinth and with superior numbers (67,000 to the Confederate's 40,000) destroy the Confederate western army. Buell, however, had not arrived by April 6, and Grant alone had to contend with the energetic and brave Confederate general, Albert Sidney Johnston, overall commander of the Confederate forces at Corinth.

Ulysses S. Grant

A.S. Johnston knew his untrained troops could probably not withstand Grant and Buell's combined force. His only hope was to destroy the Federal army piecemeal; to strike at Grant before Buell arrived. Filled with Napoleonic dreams, Pierre Toutant Beauregard, second in command, drew up the battle plans—which were too complex for raw troops. The movement from Corinth to Pittsburgh Landing was so badly carried out that Beauregard worried the Confederates had lost the element of surprise he had counted on. As it turned out, despite Confederate bumbling on the morning of April 6, the Federals didn't know that their enemy was encamped only a mile away.

It was a bright, pleasant spring morning—one of those mornings when rest seems to pervade the air. The Federals soldiers were polishing their muskets, cleaning their shoes and uniforms, enjoying a quiet contentment. Then suddenly—gunfire and artillery shattered morning peace. Confederates descended on the unsuspecting Federals, throwing them back into into their ranks, forcing them to retreat. The rebel soldiers only paused long enough to grab some food from the enemy camp—they had not eaten in 24 hours.

Albert Sydney Johnston

William Tecumseh Sherman, who had returned to the Federal army after a winter of melancholy that had sent him home, commanded a brigade of Ohioans on the extreme right of the Federal line. Sherman and his men held a hill near which stood a small Methodist log church called Shiloh (meaning "peace"). The Sixth Mississippi under William Hardee assaulted the hill; 425 men marched, rank upon rank, against Sherman and were cut down by musket and artillery fire. The bullets and canister slaughtered 325 of the rebels, but they pushed on, forcing the green Yankee troops to flee before them. Hardee took the hill of Shiloh and again advanced.

Battle of Shiloh, by Thure de Thulstrup, 1888. Restoration by Adam Cuerden

In the middle of the line ran a sunken road where Federal troops from Iowa and Illinois held out against Confederates, advancing under Braxton Bragg. The numerous rebel assaults that broke against the sunken road gave the lie to General Johnston's boast to Beauregard, "We are sweeping the field and I think we shall press them to the river." Thousands of Confederates died along this center line, which became known as the "Hornet's Nest."

Another bloody battle raged around a peach orchard on the right of the Confederate line. Albert Sidney Johnston himself led the charge that finally broke the Federal line there. But the victorious Johnston was struck by a minie ball behind the knee. Absorbed in fighting, however, he didn't notice the wound; but the bullet had cut an artery, and his boot filled with blood. Suddenly he fell from his horse—he had lost too much blood. He died that afternoon.

The Confederate command now fell to Beauregard, who continued to press on the Federal center at the Hornet's Nest. The Yankees held out on the sunken road until half-past five in the evening and then retreated. The evening, however, had advanced too far for Beaureagard to follow up on the victory. As the shadows of night descended on the field, the din of musket and cannon died away. Punctuated only by the fire of gunboats, lobbing missiles on the Confederates lines, the cries of the wounded and dying in the fields filled the air with a dreadful dissonance.

The Confederates had pushed Grant all the way back to Pittsburgh Landing and might have finished him off the next day had not Buell arrived that night with reinforcements. The Confederates now numbered only 30,000; the Federals, 50,000. Beauregard, seeing the odds against him, ordered a retreat to Corinth. The Battle of Pittsburgh Landing, or Shiloh, had been the single, bloodiest day of the war, though bloodier days would follow. Of the roughly

100,000 men who fought at Shiloh, nearly 25,000 were wounded and killed. Thousands of men filled the ranks of the dead.

The Capture of New Orleans

The Confederate army in the West could not retrieve its losses in Tennessee and Kentucky. With Beauregard in retreat in Mississippi, General Halleck, in command of the Federal army in the West, could carry on the conquest of the Mississippi Valley.

The next objective for the Federals was Fort Pillow on the Mississippi, north of Memphis, Tennessee, over 80 miles south of the Confederate fortress, Island 10, which Union forces had recently conquered. Halleck thought that if he could take Corinth, he could control the railroad to Memphis, and then the Confederates would be forced to abandon Fort Pillow. Halleck, however, did not trust the operation to Grant. Instead, he removed Grant from command of the army at Pittsburgh Landing because, Halleck said, Grant had taken to heavy drinking. With the addition of troops under General John Pope, Halleck's army numbered 100,000 men.

It took one month for Halleck to move his army the 22 miles into Corinth—where, when he arrived, he discovered that Beauregard had withdrawn farther south. Though he had not fired a shot, Halleck proclaimed a great victory. So pleased was Lincoln at this news, and with the capture of Memphis six days later, that he promoted Halleck to General-in-Chief of the Federal Armies.

The capture of Corinth, though, had not been the only good news for Lincoln. In April, a Federal naval fleet of 24 ships commanded by Admiral David Glasgow Farragut, a pro-union southerner, had entered the Mississippi River where it pours into the Gulf of Mexico. Between the mouth of the Mississippi and New Orleans, over 100 miles to the north, stood Fort Jackson and Fort St. Philip, facing each other across the river. The forts seemed formidable obstacles—and Farragut was unable to reduce them after a six-day's bombardment by gunboats. Farragut then decided he would run his fleet through. "The passing of the forts," he wrote, "was one of the most awful sights and events I ever saw or expect to experience . . . [it] seemed as if all the

Admiral David Farragut

"The Splendid Naval Triumph on the Mississippi, April 24, 1862," a Currier & Ives print

artillery of heaven were playing upon the earth." Though he lost four ships, Farragut successfully ran the forts. The only other opposition he faced was offered by a squadron of eight ships, six of which were sunk. New Orleans, itself, offered no resistance, and Farragut captured and occupied the city on April 25, 1862.

With New Orleans in the bag, Farragut pushed farther up river, taking Baton Rouge, Port Hudson, and Natchez. The only Confederate stronghold remaining in the Mississippi Valley was Vicksburg, Mississippi, 400 miles north of New Orleans. Set on a bluff 300 feet high, and surrounded by swampy ground, Vicksburg was a formidable fortress. Vessels sailing down river could not get past its guns nor could an army trudge through the swamps that surrounded it to besiege its fortifications. Vicksburg was important, for if the Federals did

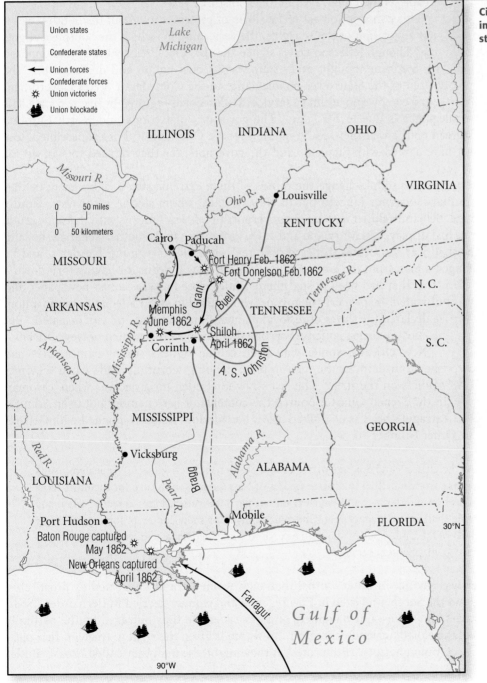

Civil War battles in the western states

not take it, they couldn't control the Mississippi, and if the Confederacy lost it, the southern nation would be split in half. "Vicksburg is the nailhead [that] holds the South's two halves together," said Jefferson Davis.

The Reign of the Beast

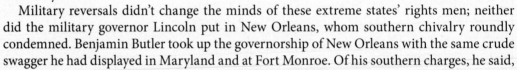

By mid-April 1862, the military prospects of the Confederacy looked grim. Not only was the Army of the Potomac encamped less than 70 miles from the Confederate capital, Richmond, the Confederacy hadn't enough soldiers to carry on the war. Faced with the unraveling of the war effort (and the end of their nation's existence), the Confederate congress passed two laws on April 16. The first extended the enlistment of men already in arms for the length of the war; the second conscripted all able-bodied men, ages 18 to 35, for three years' service.

This conscription act met a storm of protest throughout the South—was it not a violation of states' rights, the very cause for which the South was fighting? Though Jefferson Davis signed the law, Vice-President Stephens opposed it. Stephens thought every state was its own nation and declared that "the citizen of the State owes no allegiance to the Confederate States Government . . . and can owe no 'military service' to it except as required by his own state. His allegiance is due to his State." The governors of Georgia and North Carolina agreed and vowed they would ignore the law. One-half of those conscripted, too, must have agreed with Stephens and the governors, for they refused to sign up for military service.

Benjamin Franklin "The Beast" Butler, by Mathew Brady

Military reversals didn't change the minds of these extreme states' rights men; neither did the military governor Lincoln put in New Orleans, whom southern chivalry roundly condemned. Benjamin Butler took up the governorship of New Orleans with the same crude swagger he had displayed in Maryland and at Fort Monroe. Of his southern charges, he said, "they shall fear the stripes if they do not reverence the stars in our banner"—and he hanged a man from the United States Mint in New Orleans for having torn down a U.S. flag that had been posted there. Butler closed a secessionist newspaper and confiscated the property of anyone who refused to swear allegiance to the union. He declared the slaves of disloyal planters "manumitted and emancipated." But his most notorious offense was one that involved the women of New Orleans.

New Orleans women had been calling Butler's troops names; they had shown disdain for the men in blue, stepping scornfully aside when they met soldiers on the street. The last straw for Butler, however, was when a woman in the French Quarter poured the contents of her chamber pot over Admiral Farragut's head as he walked below her window. Butler responded with General Order Number 28:

Confederate vice-president, Alexander Stephens

As the Officers and Soldiers of the United States have been subject to repeated insults from the women calling themselves ladies of New Orleans, in return for the most scrupulous non-interference and courtesy on our part, it is ordered that hereafter when any female shall, by word, gesture, or movement, insult or show contempt for any officer or soldier of the United States, she shall be regarded and held liable to be treated as a woman of the town, plying her trade.

Butler was saying, in other words, that such women could be treated as prostitutes. Throughout the South, and even in Europe, men and women decried Butler's order. "Shall our mothers, our wives, our daughters and our sisters be thus outraged by the ruffianly soldiers of the North," cried Beauregard, "to whom is given the right to treat, at their pleasure . . . as common harlots?" But protest as they might, the man they called "Beast" Butler

Bird's eye view of New Orleans, as it appeared in 1880

was secure; the South could not retake New Orleans, nor would Lincoln chastise Butler for his order. Not for his insults to womanhood, nor his confiscating private property, but only for supposed embezzlement, would the president later dismiss Butler from his New Orleans post.

On to Richmond!

McClellan had been besieging Yorktown for almost a month before he decided to attempt an assault on the Confederate position. But on the night of May 3, 1862—the day McClellan had put his guns in position for an assault—the Confederates struck the Federals with a barrage of artillery fire. The next morning, however, the Confederates did not follow up their attack. McClellan soon discovered the reason: Johnston had withdrawn his troops in the night under cover of the artillery. Yorktown was deserted.

McClellan followed Johnston cautiously. On May 5, the two armies met in a brief engagement before Williamsburg, the old Virginia capital, and again the Confederates retreated. Johnston's army dug in before Richmond. By May 24, McClellan drew up lines five miles from the Confederate capital—and halted. Still convinced Johnston's army outnumbered his, McClellan waited for reinforcements under Irvin McDowell to arrive from the Rappahannock.

McDowell, however, was not coming. The very day McClellan reached his position before Richmond, McDowell marched his army westward to the Shenandoah Valley. General Thomas "Stonewall" Jackson with 17,000 men had been leading Federal generals Frémont and Nathaniel Banks in a wild dance in the Shenandoah Valley and the Blue Ridge. Jackson, who believed it was a man's "entire duty to pray and fight," was a strict, old-line Presbyterian who worshiped the Old Testament God of battles. This eccentric general, who dressed shabbily and went into battle sucking on lemons (for his health), was a relentless taskmaster with his men; he led them in divine service almost every day and forced them to make long, swift marches. But his men were proud to be "Old Jack's boys"; and, because of the intense (some would have said, crazed) gaze of his blue eyes, gave him the nickname, "Old Blue Light."

In the Shenandoah Valley Jackson struck Yankee forces hard and then quickly withdrew—seeming to disappear. At Winchester, Jackson defeated Banks and drove his army to the Potomac. In little over a month, Stonewall Jackson's men had marched 400 miles, seized Federal supplies, and left in their wake 7,000 Federal casualties. When Washington sent McDowell to deal with Jackson, "Old Blue Light" achieved one of his goals—to keep McDowell's 40,000 Federals from reinforcing McClellan. "He who does not see the hand of God in this," declared Jackson, "is blind, sir, blind!"

Rainfall had swollen the waters of the Chickahominy River, running northeast of Richmond. McClellan's army was so situated that the Chickahominy divided it, with the smaller number of the Federal troops on the south side of the river. Johnston saw this as an opportunity—he would attack the smaller force and hopefully be able to destroy McClellan's army piecemeal. On Saturday, May 31, Johnston struck McClellan's left in the battle of Fair Oaks or Seven Pines. It was a bloody, inconclusive engagement in which the South lost 6,000 men and the North, 5,000. Johnston himself, seriously wounded, was forced to relinquish command of the Confederate army.

Robert E. Lee

Jefferson Davis, perhaps, did not regret the loss of Johnston. He and the general had never gotten along; both were proud, headstrong, and easily offended. They had rarely addressed each other directly but only through the mediation of a man they both implicitly trusted—General Robert E. Lee. Now Davis chose Lee to take Johnston's place. Many in Richmond groaned over the president's choice—"Old Granny Lee," the general with a desk job; "Evacuating Lee," the general who had high-tailed it out of western Virginia! But Lee was made of sterner stuff than his critics thought. Taking command, he renamed the army, the Army of Northern Virginia—to indicate his goal of retaking all of Virginia. And he declared his resolve to Davis: "Richmond," said Lee, "must not be given up. It shall not be given up."

Lee's first task was to learn the disposition of McClellan's army. He sent out James Ewell Brown ("Jeb") Stuart with 1,700 cavalry to reconnoiter the Federal position. The dash and flair of Jeb Stuart recalled the English cavaliers of Charles II. Bearded and with a large white feather stuck in his hat, Stuart chivalrously courted the favor of fair ladies and basked in their applause. For three days Stuart and his horsemen rode a 150-mile circuit around McClellan's army, taking 170 prisoners and appropriating 300 horses and mules. Philip St. George Cooke, who was Stuart's father-in-law and fought for the North, pursued the cavalier and his men but could not catch them.

J.E.B. Stuart

With information provided by Stuart, Lee laid his plans. Generals D. H. Hill, A.P. Hill, and James Longstreet, with the greater part of the army, would strike McClellan's right wing, drawn up in front of Mechanicsville, across the Chickahominy. Jackson, who was advancing from the Shenandoah Valley, would move around the right flank of the Federal line, striking it from behind. These combined forces, Lee hoped, would crumple and utterly destroy the enemy's right wing. Meanwhile, Magruder, with only a mere fraction of the Confederate troops, would protect Richmond. The fear was that McClellan would realize that so few men stood between him and Richmond and would crash through their lines and take the capital. To prevent this, Magruder was to put on one of his theatrical displays to fool McClellan into believing that a large host defended the capital.

On June 26, Lee struck McClellan's right wing at Mechanicsville. The battle did not go as planned, for, inexplicably, Jackson arrived late. Still, the two Hills, Longstreet, and Jackson (when he arrived) pushed Federals under Fitz Hugh Porter from their position in front of Mechanicsville, while Magruder (with his theatrics) immobilized McClellan. Though he lost 1,500, Lee would not let up. The next day he struck Porter at Gaines' Mill, forcing the Federals to take up a position in Boatswain's Swamp. The following day, June 28, Porter withdrew across the Chickahominy, and the rest of McClellan's forces retreated to Savage Station.

Savage Station—it was aptly named, for the fighting there on June 29 was savage and bloody. So was the fighting, the next day, near Frayser's Farm. McClellan, fearing what he thought Lee's overwhelming numbers, kept retreating towards the James River and the safety of his gunboats. On July 1, the Confederates tried to take the Federal position on Malvern Hill, but riddled by shot from Yankee artillery, they were driven off. The next day, McClellan removed to Harrison's landing on the James River, where the artillery of his gunboats protected him.

So ended the series of battles called the Seven Days—a week of fearful loss for both sides, but especially for Lee. He had lost 20,000 men. Lincoln visited McClellan at Harrison's Landing. The general told the president he needed 50,000 more men—or maybe 100,000—otherwise he could not beat Lee. Lincoln told McClellan those numbers were not available and that he should return to Washington. So it was that the Army of the Potomac took ship down the James River and by September was steaming up the Potomac to Georgetown. Richmond was saved.

Field Hospital at Savage Station

Suppress the Miscreant!

"Let us look before us and not behind. Success and glory are in the advance, disaster and shame lurk in the rear!" So General John Pope told his new command—the troops of Frémont, Banks, and McDowell. The government in Washington had brought Pope from the West, where, Pope claimed, soldiers were used to seeing the *backs* of their enemies.

Lincoln had brought this boastful but energetic general east because of his frustration with slow-moving generals like McClellan and McDowell. Perhaps Pope would do something. And Pope did do something—he put in place Lincoln's more stringent war policy; not just the Confederate army, but civilians were to suffer for secession. In July General Pope issued general orders:

First, citizens of union-occupied territory in Virginia were to be held responsible for any guerrilla activity in their region—whether they were responsible for it or not.

Second, any male citizen who refused to take an oath of allegiance to the United States would have to leave his home and cross over to enemy lines; and if he returned, he would be "subjected to the extreme rigor of military law."

Third, those who took the oath of allegiance, and then violated it, would be executed.

General John Pope

Pope also issued orders commanding his soldiers to "subsist off the countryside"—that is, to take what food they needed from Virginia citizens. When the inevitable abuses arising from such an order occurred, Pope issued a corrective order, declaring: "it is to be distinctly understood that neither officer nor soldier has any right whatever, under the provisions of that order, to enter the house, molest the persons, or disturb the property of any citizen whatsoever." Those who did so would be "severely punished."

The threat of these corrective orders was worse than their execution—noncompliers were not shot; but the original order—that the Federal troops were to live off the land—was enacted with a vengeance. Federal troops seized Virginians' livestock and grain, entered houses, looted and pillaged. Army stragglers took Pope's order as permission to do as they wished with civilian property. So bad was the depredation that one Federal officer lamented, "the lawless acts of many of our soldiers are worthy of worse than death." Southerners roundly condemned Pope's orders; they had hoped the war could be fought according to civilized codes, and now Lincoln's government was removing the barriers civilization had erected to stave off the brutality of war. Lee, at Richmond, said simply that his army needed to suppress the "miscreant," General Pope. Dividing his army, Lee marched north to drive the "miscreant" from Virginia.

Jackson with 25,000 men met Pope's army at Cedar Mountain in Virginia on August 9, 1862, and fought him to a standoff. Then Old Blue Light led his army on a two-day, 56-mile march around Pope's right flank, cut the rail line to Washington, and looted and burned the Federal supply depot at Manassas Junction. Pope, who thought Jackson was in retreat, went after him with only half of his force, about 30,000 men. He found Jackson's roughly 20,000 men holding a stony ridge overlooking the old Manassas battlefield.

Pope attacked Jackson on August 29 in an attempt to drive him from the ridge. Stonewall's men fought doggedly, and though the Federals momentarily broke their line, the rebels drove them back. That night, reinforcements reached both Pope and Jackson; Lee had arrived with Longstreet and 30,000 troops, while Pope's force grew by another 20,000. The next morning, Pope again attacked Jackson's position and was again repulsed. Then Lee sent Longstreet's five divisions in.

Stonewall Jackson, by Nathaniel Routzhan

Pope's army broke, retreated, and took a position on the Henry House hill, where, just a little over a year before, Jackson had stood firm like a stone wall. Night fell, and, the next day, Pope retreated to Centreville. The Confederates had once again defeated the Yankees on the fields of Bull Run.

Pope had failed, and Lincoln soon sent him west to fight the Sioux in Minnesota. With no other general in the offing, Lincoln placed Pope's army again under McClellan. General

Lee, meanwhile, thought it hopeless to attack Pope's defeated army, which had fled into the Washington fortifications, and instead moved his tatterdemalion army north into Maryland. He hoped, thereby, to draw Federal armies out of Virginia and to recruit Marylanders who, he believed, were sympathetic to the southern cause.

Lincoln Contemplates Emancipation

Through the actions of Federal commanders like Butler, who confiscated slaves in southern territory, and by the simple fact that slaves flocked to invading Federal armies, the war was slowly changing from a simple war to preserve the union into a war to free the slaves. Congress, dominated by extreme anti-slavery Republicans called the Radicals, had passed a law in March 1862 that forbade army officers to return fugitive slaves to their owners. Later, in April, under Radical Republican influence, Congress abolished slavery in the District of Columbia and, in June, prohibited slavery in the western territories. Said one member of Congress, "only the damndest of 'damned abolitionists' dreamed of such a year ago. John Brown's soul is marching on, with the people after it."

Though he had insisted that the sole goal of the war was to preserve the union, not to free slaves, Lincoln had for a while been secretly contemplating a declaration to emancipate slaves in the rebellious states. He was certainly opposed to slavery and had tried to abolish it in the border states by offering slaveholders there $400 for each slave along with shipment of the freedmen to Africa or Central America. This offer, refused by slaveholders, was condemned by free blacks, who said that the United States, not Africa or Central America, was their home. Yet, Lincoln was not moved solely by humanitarian concern— emancipation, he thought, could further the war effort. By freeing the slaves in the Confederate states, Lincoln could strike a blow at the southern economy and, perhaps, prevent European nations from recognizing the Confederacy—for what king, prince, or president in enlightened Europe would wish to align himself publicly against an anti-slavery struggle?

Emancipation, too, could turn the war into a crusade for liberty and perhaps rekindle enthusiasm for the struggle in the North. The extent of the war and its bloodiness had dampened enthusiasm in the North. There was even a growing sentiment that peace should be concluded and the South be allowed to follow her own destiny. Emancipation might be just the thing to galvanize the North and weaken the South—but to what else could it lead? Would it enkindle a bloody slave revolt? And what was to be done with the millions of released slaves? Where would they live? How would they be fed and clothed? Would they be able to support themselves?

All these questions, though, were still academic. Before he could issue a proclamation of emancipation, Lincoln needed a military victory; without a victory, emancipation would appear a gesture of weakness, not of strength. Lee seemed unstoppable, and in the West, General Braxton Bragg had invaded Kentucky, taken Lexington, and sworn in a secessionist government there. Lincoln needed a victory—but who could give it to him?

Sharpsburg

Lee's men, said a Maryland woman, were "a most ragged, lean and hungry set of wolves." Yet, she conceded, "there is a dash about them the northern men lacked."

"This body of men," said another woman, moved "along with no order, their guns carried in every fashion, no two dressed alike, their officers hardly distinguishable from the privates . . . Were these the men that had driven back again and again our splendid legions?"

Lee was marching north, but it was not clear where exactly he planned to go. Behind him, following, came the ever-cautious McClellan. He needn't have been so careful; Lee had divided his army, sending Jackson to Harper's Ferry to capture the Federal garrison there. McClellan's army numbered 95,000, while Lee had only 18,000 with him. But McClellan was cautious, even after one of his soldiers found, wrapped around some cigars lying in a meadow where the Confederates had camped, a copy of Lee's general orders. "Here is a paper

Map of the Battle of Sharpsburg (Antietam), from *Atlas to Accompany the Official Records of the Union & Confederate Armies, 1861–1865*

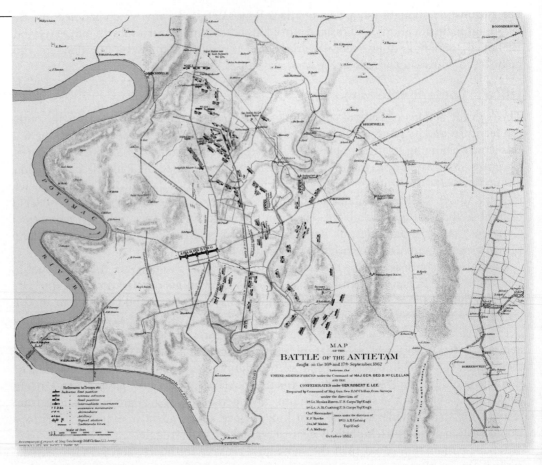

with which, if I cannot whip Bobbie Lee," said McClellan, "I will be willing to go home." Still, he delayed 18 hours before he ordered an attack.

Lee had taken up his position on a ridge east of Sharpsburg, Maryland, near to where Antietam Creek flowed on its meandering course to the nearby Potomac. Late in the morning of September 15, 1862, McClellan's force arrived on the heights of the eastern bank of Antietam. The number, wrote Longstreet, "increased, and larger and larger grew the field of blue until it seemed to stretch as far as the eye could see."

McClellan might have destroyed the southern army that day, or the next—but he hesitated, and while he hesitated, Jackson returned, taking up the Confederate right wing, opposite Federal general Joseph Hooker. The Federals still outnumbered Lee by about 50,000 men, but it would be harder to defeat him now.

At 6 a.m. on the morning of September 17, 1862, Hooker's division emerged from the woods and began marching across a wide cornfield. Jackson's men held a rise on which stood a white-washed Dunker Church. (The Dunkers were a pacifist German sect, so named because they baptized adults by immersion.) Exposed to Confederate fire, Hooker's men nonetheless began to push Jackson's men back towards the church. Then came the counter-attack—Texans led by John Bell Hood descended on the Yankees, forcing them back across the cornfield. For hours both sides contended for that cornfield, and by 10 a.m., 8,000 lay dead and wounded.

In the center of the line, two Confederate brigades under Colonel John B. Gordon held a position on a sunken road that soon became known as Bloody Lane. For hours Federals hurled themselves against the Confederates, only to be brutally cut down, charge after charge. Finally, some New Yorkers found a rise from which they could fire down on the Confederates in the Sunken Road and began "shootin them like sheep in a pen." Under such blistering fire, the Confederate center broke and retreated. The day could have been

McClellan's, but he, again, hesitated to press his advantage.

On the extreme Confederate right, General Ambrose Burnside with 12,500 Federal troops contended with General Robert A. Toombs for a stone bridge over the Antietam. Though vastly outnumbered, Toombs' 400 men commanded a butte overlooking the stone bridge and kept Burnside at bay for three hours. But finally, the Confederate line broke and fled towards Sharpsburg.

This was the most dangerous moment for Lee, for Burnside's men could cut off his line of retreat and destroy his army. But then, to the south, Lee espied a cloud of dust. "Whose troops are those?" he asked his attendant, for he feared they might be Federals. Peering through the spyglass, his attendant answered:

Lincoln with McClellan at Sharpsburg

"they are flying the Virginia and Confederate flags, sir." A.P. Hill, wearing the bright red shirt he always wore into battle, was leading 3,000 men from Harper's Ferry. Many of Hill's men wore captured blue jackets, so Burnside's men held-off firing on them. Hill's men crashed into Burnside's flank. The beleaguered Burnside asked McClellan for reinforcements but received the reply, "It would not be prudent."

Burnside withdrew to the stone bridge, and night fell. With his line of retreat open, Lee withdrew his army across the Potomac. He had lost 10,318 men, one-fourth of his army. The Federal dead and wounded numbered about 13,000.

Thenceforth and Forever Free

"God bless you and all with you," wrote Lincoln to McClellan after the Battle of Sharpsburg (or Antietam). "Destroy the rebel army if possible." But September passed, and McClellan still did not pursue Lee. On October 1, Lincoln ordered McClellan to pursue Lee. McClellan obeyed—but only after another 18-day delay.

Allan Pinkerton, Lincoln, and Maj. General John A. McClernand at Sharpsburg. Photograph from glass negative, by Alexander Gardner, October 3, 1862

Though not a decisive victory, the Battle of Sharpsburg (or Antietam) was still a victory for the North; McClellan had held the field while Lee retreated. It was for just such a victory that Lincoln had been waiting—"God," he said, "had decided in favor of the slaves." On September 22 he issued the Preliminary Emancipation Proclamation:

> On the first day of January, in the year of our Lord one thousand eight hundred and sixty three, all persons held as slaves within any State, or designated part of a State, the people whereof shall then be in rebellion against the United States, shall be then, thenceforth, and forever free.

This proclamation, of course, did not free all the slaves—only those living in the states "in rebellion." It also did not immediately free any slaves—the Confederacy had three months to decide whether it would lay down arms. Southerners saw this proclama-

First reading of the Emancipation Proclamation before Lincoln's cabinet, July 22, 1862. Left to right: Edwin Stanton, Salmon Chase, Lincoln, Gideon Wells, Caleb Smith, William Seward, Montgomery Blair, Edward Bates.

tion as inviting a slave revolt. In an article, "Civilized Warfare," published in 1863, the Reverend Joseph Cross spoke for many southerners when he wrote, "O that Mr. Lincoln could see himself as others see him!" Cross approvingly quoted an Irish paper, the *Belfast News Letter*, which said:

> If Mr. Lincoln were a Brahmin we could understand him . . . The law promulgated by Mr. Lincoln is like that of Menu, which declares that the Brahmin is entitled to all that exists in the universe by his primogeniture and eminence of birth. This eminent Yankee claims sovereign sway from Staten Island to the Rocky Mountains. . . . His Emancipation proclamation is nothing more nor less than a premium for murdering men and outraging women. It is the most odious and atrocious outburst of brutal and cowardly vindictiveness that ever emanated from a pagan or "christian" tyrant.

Southerners were horrified. The Emancipation Proclamation, they thought, not only struck at their economy, but the safety of their women and children. Jefferson Davis echoed this sense of horror. He called Lincoln's proclamation the "most execrable measure recorded in the history of guilty man."

Many abolitionists were not satisfied with the proclamation, since it exempted the Border States. But others saw its true import—it put slavery on the road to quick extinction; for how could the Border States maintain slavery when it was everywhere else abolished? It also changed the very character of the war. No longer was it a struggle for something called the "Union." It now became a fight for human freedom.

Kill 'Em All

A partial compensation for Lincoln for the inaction of General McClellan was the news from the West that on October 8 Don Carlos Buell had stopped Braxton Bragg's invasion of the North by defeating him at Perryville, Kentucky. Yet, McClellan was still a thorn in

Stone Wall, Marye's Heights

the president's side. On October 25, he finally began following Lee but was keeping a good distance from him. By early November, Lincoln's patience had been exhausted. He removed McClellan as commander of the Army of the Potomac and replaced him with Ambrose Burnside.

The progress of the war, however, was but one of Lincoln's troubles. The mid-term congressional election of 1862 had gone to the Democrats. Northerners were dissatisfied not only with the conduct of the war but with Lincoln's suspension of civil rights in Maryland and his seizure of telegraph lines in the North. Not only did Republicans lose to Democrats in congressional elections but also in legislative elections in New York, Pennsylvania, Ohio, Indiana, and in Lincoln's home state, Illinois. A Democrat took the governorship of New York.

Meanwhile, Ambrose Burnside was leading the great Army of the Potomac (120,000 strong) towards Richmond. By early December, he had reached the Rappahannock River, opposite Fredericksburg. Burnside's plan was to cross the river and occupy the hills overlooking the town. Unfortunately, the war department had been tardy in sending him pontoon bridges, so he could not move his army across the river. The delay cost him dear, for Lee placed his own army of 75,000 men on Marye's Heights, the hills above Fredericksburg—a commanding position from which it would be hard to dislodge them.

In the calm before the battle, Confederate and Federal pickets traded tobacco, newspapers, and coffee, floating them across the river on little rafts. Once a Federal band struck up the tune, "Dixie," bringing cheers from the rebels. All that changed on December 11, when Federal artillery opened fire on Fredericksburg (whence most of the citizens had fled, by Lee's advice.) With pontoon bridges in place, the Federals began crossing the river in long lines, looting and vandalizing the city as they passed.

Fredericksburg follow-ing the battle

On December 13 the assault began. Burnside wanted to break the Confederate left, which commanded Marye's Heights; but the Confederates held an impregnable position—they stood, six lines deep, infantry and artillery, along a sunken road running behind a stone wall. The wall skirted the crest of the hill, and between the hill and Fredericksburg lay a sloping plane the Federals had to cross in their attack. Burnside's order to take Marye's Heights was "murder, not warfare," as one soldier put it. First Edwin Vose Sumner's divisions, then "Fighting Joe" Hooker's, bravely stormed the Confederate line, only to be cut down by crisscrossing artillery and musket fire. In 14 assaults, line upon line fell, no soldier in blue coming within 100 yards of the wall. Nine thousand men died in trying to take Marye's Heights, a dismal display. Lee, observing the carnage, said, "It is well that war is so terrible, we should grow too fond of it."

The assault on Jackson's position on the Confederate right was also a failure; and as night settled and the winter mists crept up from the river, the moans and cries of the thousands of wounded, like the lamentations of lost souls, drifted across the field. By morning, many of the wounded had frozen to death; their naked bodies, stripped of clothing by needy Confederates, lay, stretched stiff, on the frozen earth.

When Burnside withdrew from Fredericksburg, the Confederates were aghast at the destruction the Yankees had wrought on the town. "Fredericksburg is in ruins," wrote Jeb Stuart. "It is the saddest sight I ever saw." One of Jackson's men asked him what should be done with men who did such things. Jackson's reply was laconic. "Kill 'em. Kill 'em all," he said.

Chapter 17 Review

Summary

- At the beginning of the war, many Americans believed it would be over swiftly. With that assumption, Lincoln called for 75,000 volunteers. General Winfield Scott wanted up to 100,000, but Lincoln would not follow his suggestion, thinking the uprising in the South a mere insurrection that he could easily crush.

- Virginia seceded on April 17, 1861, and the Confederate government moved its capital from Montgomery, Alabama to Richmond, Virginia.

- The South was inferior to the North in numbers and industrial output and needed the support of foreign powers, Great Britain and France, to supply its arms. The South had an important bargain-ing chip, cotton. The South's greatest assets were the spirit of its men and its commanding officers, including Lt. Colonel Robert E. Lee.

- The North's greatest advantage was its navy. Lincoln planned to blockade the southern coast and seize control of the Mississippi River, therefore cutting off the South's trade with Europe and eventually starving the Confederates into submission.

- Lincoln's first task of the war was to secure for the union the neutral border states of Maryland, Kentucky, Delaware, and Missouri. In order to silence secessionist voices in the divided state of Maryland, on April 27, 1861, Lincoln ordered the suspension of the writ of *habeas corpus* "for the public safety" along the military line that ran through Maryland to Washington. This caused

Chapter 17 Review (continued)

indignation in the state, and Chief Justice Taney said that only Congress could order suspension of the writ. But Lincoln would not heed him.

- In May the Confederate congress authorized the recruitment of 400,000 volunteers. Still, recruiters turned away southern men eager for the fight because there was just no room for them.

- In June, General George McClellan forced Lee to evacuate Virginia's western mountain counties, which stood strongly for the union. On June 11, western Virginia organized a pro-union government and sent representatives to Washington.

- General Benjamin Butler, though he had supported nomination of Jefferson Davis in 1860, had more recently remade himself into a liberator of slaves. Slaves were crossing Union lines at Fortress Monroe on Chesapeake Bay, and Butler was not turning them away. By late spring he was using about 1,000 slaves for menial tasks around the fortress.

- At the first Battle of Bull Run, or Manassas, Confederate forces defeated the Federal army, which retreated toward Washington. This battle awakened people to the fact that the war would not be a quick affair, but a long, drawn-out struggle.

- In September 1861, Confederate general Leonidas Polk marched his forces into Kentucky, thus ending the state's neutrality. The state went to the union. When southern sympathizers in Maryland again agitated for secession, Lincoln arrested and jailed the mayor and 31 legislators, replacing them with a pro-union majority.

- In January of 1862, Lincoln issued General War Order Number 1, commanding a general movement of all land and sea forces on February 22, 1862.

- The unconditional surrender of Forts Henry and Donelson made General Ulysses S. Grant a northern hero and opened the interior of Tennessee and Alabama to Federal armies.

- On April 16, 1862, the Confederate congress passed two laws. The first extended the enlistment of men already in arms for the length of the war, and the second conscripted all able-bodied men between the ages of 18 and 35 for three years' service. This conscription law met a storm of protest, and many states declared it was a violation of states' rights.

- General Johnston was wounded in the battle of Fair Oaks or Seven Pines and was forced to relinquish command of the Confederate army. President Davis chose Robert E. Lee to take his place. Lee renamed the army the Army of Northern Virginia to indicate his goal of retaking all of Virginia. He marched out to defend Richmond against the Federal army under the command of General George B. McClellan.

- Following the series of battles called the Seven Days, with fearful losses on both sides, McClellan asked Lincoln for more men. Lincoln told him the numbers were not available, and he should return to Washington. The Army of the Potomac left Richmond.

- General Pope issued three general orders, and commanded his soldiers to "subsist off the countryside"—that is, to take what food they needed from Virginia citizens. This measure was enacted with vengeance, and Lee marched out to drive the "miscreant" from Virginia. The two armies met in the Second Battle of Bull Run or Manassas, in which the Confederates were victorious.

- Lincoln began to turn his thoughts towards freeing the slaves. After a marginal victory in the Battle of Antietam or Sharpsburg, Lincoln issued the Preliminary Emancipation Proclamation on September 22, 1862.

Key Concepts

habeas corpus: a writ, or legal action that requires a person under arrest to be brought before a judge or into a court so it might examine the reasons for imprisonment

Dates to Remember

1861: Lincoln calls for volunteers.

Virginia secedes from the union (April 17).

The first Federal assault of the war: the seizure of Arlington Heights (May 24)

First Battle of Bull Run or Manassas (July 21)

1862: the Battle of Shiloh (April 6)

The Confederate congress passes a conscription law (April 16).

Chapter 17 Review (continued)

1862: The Battle of Seven Days (June 26–July 1)

1862: Lincoln issues the Preliminary Emancipation Proclamation (September 22).

Central Characters

Jefferson Davis (1808–1889): president of the Confederate States of America

Robert E. Lee (1807–1870): commander of the Army of Northern Virginia

George McClellen (1826–1885): the general who reorganized Federal forces in the first year of the American Civil War and served as both commander-in-chief of the Federal army and as commander of the Army of the Potomac

Thomas J. Jackson (1824–1863): "Stonewall" Jackson, the general who was one of the most skillful tacticians in the Confederate army

Ulysses S. Grant (1822–1885): the general who successfully commanded the Federal armies in West

Questions for Review

1. What was Abraham Lincoln's main objective in the war?

2. Describe the personalities of Abraham Lincoln and Jefferson Davis and how they differed.

3. What were the South's greatest assets in the war?

4. What were the North's greatest assets in the war?

5. Why did Lincoln find it necessary to secure the neutral states for the union?

6. What significance did the First Battle of Bull Run (Manassas) hold for the war?

7. What was the significance of Vicksburg? How could its capture by the Federal army change the course of the war?

8. Why did General Lee change the name of his army. What events led him to do so?

9. Why did Lincoln decide to make slavery an issue in the war?

10. How did the Preliminary Emancipation Proclamation change the character of the war?

Ideas in Action

1. Read some fictional or eyewitness accounts of civilian life in the American Civil War and discuss the effects the war had on civilians both in the North and South.

2. Stage a debate between students, with some taking the side of the South and others taking the side of the North over the right of the southern states to resist the military might of the Federal government. Might there have been another position than than these?

3. Did Lincoln violate the Constitution when he ordered the suspension of the right of *habeas corpus* in Maryland? Why or why not? Was his action morally justified?

4. Imagine you are a northerner or southerner, either a soldier or civilian, during the Civil War, and write an account of your experiences.

Highways and Byways

The Heroes of West Point

Ulysses S. Grant, Robert E. Lee, Stonewall Jackson, Jefferson Davis—all of these American Civil War leaders were graduates of the prestigious West Point. One of the oldest armed service academies in the world, the United States Military Academy, or West Point Academy, is an institution of higher education for training commissioned officers for the U.S. Army. West Point was founded in 1802 as a school for the U.S. Corps of Engineers. It was proposed by General Henry Knox in 1776, but it was not until 1802 that Congress passed the act to establish the academy. The academy is situated in Orange County, New York, overlooking the Hudson River. During its early years, the academy suffered from lack of organization and discipline. It was not until the Mexican-American War that the academy gained prominence as it its graduates proved themselves in battle for the first time. West Point continues to be a prestigious school for military officers.

18

TO THE BITTER END

Catching Copperheads

On December 31—New Years Eve, 1862—abolitionists, both white and black, gathered in Music Hall in Boston to await the turning of the year and the dawn of what they hoped would be a new age of freedom. None of the "states in rebellion" had laid down their arms; and so, as Lincoln warned in his Emancipation Proclamation, they must pay the price. Their slaves, come January 1, 1863, should be "forever free." The tolling of midnight was for Frederick Douglass, William Lloyd Garrison, Harriet Beecher Stowe, and for all those in Music Hall, the long-awaited moment, the culmination of all their labors. Douglass greeted the new year with tears of joy.

Throughout the South, however, little changed, though Federal officers read Lincoln's proclamation to joy-befuddled fugitive slaves in the "contraband camps." They were free! As before the proclamation, many slaves sought the union lines, while others remained on their masters' plantations and farms. No slave insurrections troubled the South; and though the economy suffered, it was on account of the ever-tightening Federal blockade rather than escaping slaves.

Though abolitionists could bask in the joy of emancipation, others in the North were growing weary of a war that seemed no nearer its stated objective—preserving the union. The Midwestern states in particular were rife with opposition to the war. Fathers advised their sons to desert the army and come home; newspapers publicly called for military desertion. Let the South go their own way, many midwesterners thought; they did not want to fight a war for "niggers" or for New England merchants and industrialists whose interests, they thought, the war chiefly benefited. Some of these "Southern sympathizers," called "Copperheads" by their Yankee compatriots, spoke openly in favor of the Midwest joining the South in a struggle against the Northeast.

Lincoln thought such opposition required stern measures. On September 24, 1862, Lincoln ordered the suspension of *habeas corpus* throughout the North. All who openly encouraged resistance to enlistment or were "guilty of any disloyal practice affording aid and comfort to the rebels" were to be subject to martial law. Lincoln was

A southern cartoon by Adalbert J. Volck, 1864, depicting Abraham Lincoln as a devil, with demons around him, writing the Emancipation Proclamation and trampling on the Constitution

Freed slaves escape to Union lines shortly after the issuance of the Emancipation Proclamation

extending what he had done in Maryland to the entire North, and his military authorities throughout the North acted with zeal. Throughout the course of the war, 13,000 northerners would be imprisoned and have their right of *habeas corpus* denied them.

Lincoln now exercised a power that even many kings had failed to achieve. "Copperheads" and Democrats denounced the president as a despot and tyrant. Clement Vallandigham, an Ohio Democrat, led the opposition to Lincoln in his state. As a member of Congress in 1861, Vallandigham had delivered a speech against Lincoln's suspension of *habeas corpus* in Maryland (Congress had been debating, and finally voted to support, the suspension); now Vallandigham was running for governor of Ohio on a peace platform that called for an immediate armistice with the South.

The military governor of Ohio ordered Vallandigham arrested—an act Governor Horatio Seymour of New York called "cowardly, brutal, infamous. It is not merely a step," Seymour said, "toward Revolution, it is revolution . . . our liberties are overthrown." A military court tried and convicted Vallandigham of treason; but instead of having him killed (and made a martyr), Lincoln ordered Vallandigham banished to the South. Eventually Vallandigham took ship to Canada, where he continued his run for governor of Ohio, publishing manifestos from Windsor, Ontario.

Homespun and Chicory

Southerners, too, had their own quarrels with *their* president, Jefferson Davis. The conscription act was but one example of his "tyranny," as was his failure to delegate authority and his attempt to manage the war and his generals down to the smallest details. Eventually Davis, too, would think it necessary to ask Congress to suspend the writ of *habeas corpus* in Richmond and other areas of the South. Congress suspended the writ in 1864; and though arbitrary imprisonments occurred, as in the North, Davis was not as vigorous in exercising martial law as Lincoln.

On the whole, the southern government was less vigorous than its northern counterpart, but not for lack of zeal. The Confederate Congress held all their sessions behind closed doors—and this was a good thing. They were a cantankerous lot, riddled with factions, and frequently opposed to President Davis. Being "southern gentlemen," congressmen were quick to take offense, and fighting with umbrellas, knives, and revolvers marred many a legislative session.

The Confederate Congress voted taxes that weighed heavily on the people of the South. All landowners were required to pay one-tenth of their produce to the government in return for valueless Confederate paper money. Military agents who requisitioned cattle and crops left impoverished farmers in their wake; for this reason, many farmers hid their grain or drove their cattle into the woods. Rich landowners objected not only to giving a tenth of their cotton or other crops, but to government impressment of their slaves.

With the scarcity of food and other necessities in the cities, merchants hiked prices to exorbitant levels. In Richmond, a barrel of flour that sold for $70 in the fall was going for $250 in January. Not only merchants, but some rich planters continued to trade with Northern merchants, thus "aiding and abetting the enemy."

To supply its army with arms and its people with food, the South used a small fleet of blockade runners that sneaked through the Federal blockade to carry cotton to the British islands of Bermuda and Nassau and returned laden with manufactured goods, luxury items, and, most importantly, rifles. (Blockade runners brought 600,000 rifles into the South during the course of the war.) The arrival of a blockade runner into port was an occasion of joy to citizens weighed down as they were by want and fear.

Southern women bravely embraced deprivation for a cause they thought not only just, but holy. Women spun and weaved their own cloth to make "homespun" dresses for themselves and "homespun" uniforms for the army. Women collected the family's urine to make nitre for gunpowder. They gathered raspberry leaves for tea and ground chicory for coffee. Southern women ardently embraced the southern cause, at times inspiring their men with their own courage. At times, a southern girl would steal away from home, clothe herself as a man, and join the army.

"Let us Cross Over the River"

The turn of the year 1863 found the Army of the Potomac mired in Virginia clay at Falmouth, on the left bank of the Rappahannock, opposite Fredericksburg. The morale of the men was low—they had not been paid in months, the camps were rife with sickness, the food was bad, and Burnside was still in command. At least a quarter of the men were absent without leave, and the rest, who stayed, waited sullenly for an end to the rain, snow—and mud.

The Army of Northern Virginia still stared defiance from the hills above Fredericksburg. Their case however was more desperate than the Federals'. In ragged clothes and without shoes, with even less food and pay than their Northern brothers, rebel soldiers were in a miserable state. Many (about 40 percent) were absent without leave, some answering desperate appeals from hungry family at home, others just sick of the blood, cold, and mud.

Prospects brightened for the Army of the Potomac in the spring when Lincoln replaced Burnside with General Joseph Hooker. Called "Fighting Joe," Hooker boasted that his "plans" were "perfect." "May God have mercy on General Lee, for I will have none," he boasted. Hooker boosted his men's morale, not only with fighting words but by cleaning up the camps and, more importantly, by supplying them with food and pay.

Hooker had a good plan to destroy the Army of Northern Virginia, once and for all. He would divide his enormous force—185,000 men—and while a large

The road to Gettysburg, December 1862– July 1863

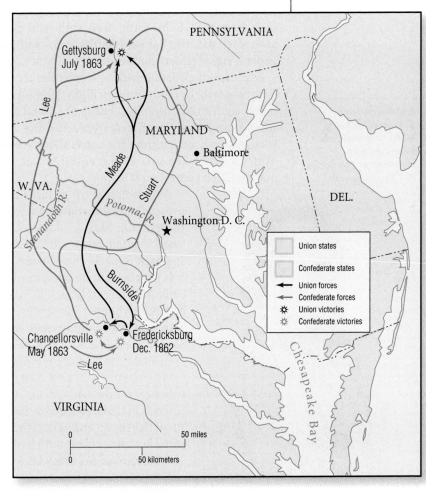

General Joseph Hooker

A photograph of
Stonewall Jackson,
taken seven days
before he was
wounded at the Battle
of Chancellorsville

contingent under General Sedgwick pretended to make a frontal attack on Lee at Fredericksburg, Hooker would secretly lead another, larger force northwest, cross the Rappahannock farther upstream, and attack Lee from the rear. In this way, Hooker thought he and Sedgwick, like a hammer and anvil, could between them crush the Confederate Army of Northern Virginia.

General Robert E. Lee, however, was not fooled. He had an uncanny ability to read the character of his opponent and guess what he might do. After Hooker began his march up the river on April 27, Lee did a daring act—he divided his small force of 60,000, leaving 10,000 to face Sedgwick at Fredericksburg, while he led the remainder west to face Hooker. Military strategists thought dividing a smaller force in the face of a larger one the height of foolishness, but Lee was not governed by textbook strategy. He was in a desperate situation that called for desperate measures.

By May 1, Hooker had crossed the Rappahannock and had led his force through what locals called the "Wilderness"—a thick, dark, and tangled forest. Hooker made his headquarters at Chancellorsville—not a town, but a large house that stood amid a clearing in the Wilderness—and began to move on Confederate lines. Then, inexplicably, he ordered his men back to Chancellorsville. Why? Years later he explained: "I just lost confidence in Joe Hooker."

Meanwhile, Lee was moving against Hooker. Stonewall Jackson, scrapping for a fight, convinced Lee to divide his army yet again—Jackson leading 26,000 to attack Hooker's right flank. Lee agreed, and on May 2 Jackson moved his army 14 miles until it stood poised to attack Hooker's flank. Hooker ignored reports of rebel movements. That evening, about 5.30 p.m., while the Federals were relaxing around their fires, deer leaped from the woods into the camps. Behind the deer, with wild cries banishing peace, came Jackson's rebels. Overwhelmed, the Yankees fell back in confusion. By nightfall, Jackson had pushed the Federal right flank two miles back to Chancellorsville.

Success only whetted Jackson's appetite. He would not rest. He was determined to make a night attack. In the waning twilight, Jackson and several of his officers rode out to reconnoiter the Yankee lines. But within the Confederate lines, Jackson's men were skittish, and when Jackson and the officers were returning, they mistook them for a Yankee patrol. Shots rang out. Jackson fell from his horse, shot once through the right hand and twice in the left arm. He was taken to a field hospital, where the surgeon decided that he would have to amputate the general's left arm.

When Lee heard of Jackson's misfortune, he said, "he has lost his left arm, but I have lost my right." Yet, with or without Jackson, Lee had a battle to fight. On May 3, Sedgwick crossed the Rappahannock and pushed the small Confederate force from Marye's Heights. The Confederates kept falling back but held the Federals at Salem Church. At the same time, Hooker was making blunder after blunder. He still had 70,000 troops; he could have rallied them and beaten the outnumbered rebels. But Hooker was scared; Lee had whipped his spirit. The Rebels pushed the Yankees back; they retreated, abandoning the Chancellorsville clearing. Confederate artillery shelled the house, setting it ablaze. Other shells ignited the woods. The fires consumed the helpless wounded.

The next day, May 4, Lee again divided his army, sending the greater number to the aid of the Confederates at Salem Church. The reinforced Confederates drove Sedgwick back over Marye's Heights, through Fredericksburg, and across the Rappahannock. Lee now reunited his entire force for a final blow, but Hooker wouldn't give him the chance. On May 6, Hooker moved his army back across the river and took up quarters again at Falmouth.

"My God! My God! What will the country say?" exclaimed Lincoln when he heard the news of Hooker's defeat. Hooker's casualties were high—17,000 men lost. Lee's were less, though they were a greater blow to him—13,000 men, one-quarter of his army.

Another blow to Lee was the news that Stonewall Jackson had come down with pneumonia. He lay at a nearby farmhouse; his wife, Anna, by his bedside. When he was conscious, Old Blue Light was confident he would survive—"the Almighty has yet a work for me to perform," he said to Anna. Yet, on Sunday, May 10, when Anna told him that the surgeon said he would not last the day, Jackson merely said, "Very good, very good. It is all right. It is the Lord's day; my wish is fulfilled. I have always desired to die on Sunday."

Throughout the day, Jackson dozed on and off. A little after three, he awoke in a delirium: "Order A.P. Hill to prepare for action!" he said. "Pass the infantry to the front . . . Tell Major Hawks—" He fell silent, smiled, and closed his eyes. "Let us cross over the river," he murmured, "and rest under the shade of the trees." And Stonewall Jackson died.

Vicksburg

Set atop its high bluff overlooking the Mississippi, the town of Vicksburg seemed to rear its head in derision at the many failed Federal attempts to take it. But failure did not discourage General Ulysses Grant. In the autumn of 1862, he set off south with 45,000 men to take this last Confederate stronghold on the Mississippi. With him marched William Tecumseh Sherman, his inseparable companion and ally.

Joe Johnston now commanded Confederate forces in the West, and a hard time he had of it. He simply did not have enough men to protect this vast territory (stretching between the Appalachians and the Mississippi), much less to drive the invader Federals out of it. Johnston had put General John C. Pemberton with 31,000 men at Vicksburg. Pemberton was a Pennsylvanian who had embraced the southern cause; yet, southerners did not trust him—he was still a Yankee, for all his southern sentiments. So, even though he was an able general, Pemberton couldn't inspire his skeptical men with confidence.

View and map of Vicksburg, 1863

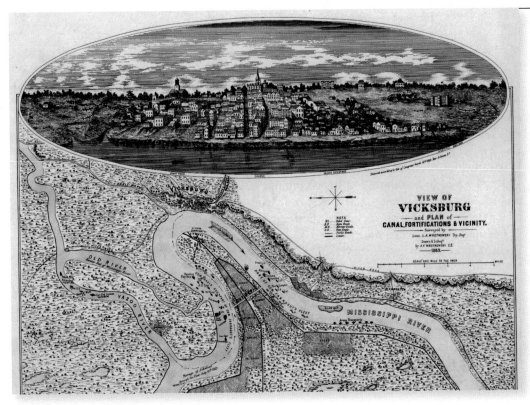

By the end of January 1863, Grant and Sherman had reached Young's Point, 20 miles upriver from Vicksburg. The land between the Federal army and Vicksburg was cut by the Yazoo River and was swampy. Grant attempted to dig canals so that Admiral David Porter's boats could ferry the army over to the bluffs that could command Vicksburg, but the attempt failed. Finally, after several months of failure, Grant hit upon a desperate plan. He would march his army down the west bank of the Mississippi while David Porter's gunboats shot their way past Vicksburg. South of the town, Grant would meet Porter, who would ferry the army across the river. Grant would then move his army around Vicksburg and attack it from the east. The plan, however, posed a big problem; for in moving his army to the east of Vicksburg, Grant would cut himself off from all communication with Sherman and the North, and his line of retreat would be severed.

Everything worked as planned, and on April 30, while Sherman pretended to assault Vicksburg from the north, Porter's boats blasted past Vicksburg and then ferried Grant's army onto the east bank of the river. Over the next three weeks, Grant fought five battles, each time defeating his enemy. Marching eastward, Grant captured Jackson, the capital of Mississippi (that Johnston had abandoned), and then moved westward against Vicksburg. In late May, Grant invested Vicksburg; but when he tried to take the city by force, its defenders beat him back. Two more times Grant assaulted Vicksburg, but failed to take it. Finally, he lay siege to the city. Now Pemberton and his men were trapped. Federal artillery daily lobbed bombs into the besieged town.

Jefferson Davis was worried—losing Vicksburg, the Confederacy would be split in two. He urged Lee to send General Longstreet west to relieve Vicksburg, but Lee had what he thought was a better idea. He would lead the Army of Northern Virginia once again in an invasion of the North. Crossing the Potomac, he would carry the war from the blood-soaked soil of Virginia into Pennsylvania. Harrisburg would be Lee's target and then Philadelphia, and then, maybe, Washington itself. With the capital threatened, Lee was certain Lincoln would call Grant east, thus breaking off the siege of Vicksburg. Davis approved Lee's plan, and in late May, the Army of Northern Virginia, now 70,000 strong, commenced its invasion of the North.

"Help Me Fight These People"

Lincoln did not want Hooker to think of attacking Richmond. "Your proper target," said the president, "is not the Confederate capital, but the Confederate army—Robert E. Lee's army." So, while Lee moved northward from the Rappahannock, the Army of the Potomac under Hooker moved north too, keeping always between Lee and Washington. In June, Lee's army crossed the Potomac, capturing York, Pennsylvania on June 28.

Meanwhile, Hooker had quarreled with General Halleck, the Federal general-in-chief, and had asked to be relieved of his command. Lincoln accepted Hooker's resignation, and on June 28 replaced him with Maj. General George Meade, who took command of the Army of the Potomac, now encamped around Frederick, Maryland.

Lee had left war-torn and ravaged Virginia in part because his army was in desperate need of food. Southern Pennsylvania was ripe with produce and wore the aspect of contented prosperity. The weary and hungry Confederates saw it as a garden of delights. Lee allowed his men to commandeer animals, food, and wagons, but strictly forbade them to pillage and loot. They had to pay for everything they took, said Lee—albeit with worthless Confederate scrip. Some Confederates ignored Lee' orders, for they wanted to take vengeance on the North for what the Yankees had done in Virginia. Soldiers seized free blacks—men, women, and children—to drive them back again into slavery. For the most part, however, Lee's men obeyed his orders.

Lee was marching into Pennsylvania blind—for he had not heard from his cavalry general, Jeb Stuart, for several days, and Stuart was (as Lee called him) the "eyes" of the army. Without Stuart, Lee did not know that Meade had moved his army to Emmitsburg, Maryland, just across the Pennsylvania border. Lee would soon learn the disposition of Meade, but by accident.

An infantry commander in A.P. Hill's division had moved into the town of Gettysburg, Pennsylvania, because Hill heard he could find a supply of boots there. It was July 1, 1863. There, too, came General John Buford with Federal cavalry sent north by Meade to feel out Lee's position. Finding the Confederates at Gettysburg, Buford decided he would contest their advance into the town while awaiting a reinforcement of infantry under General John Reynolds, who was not far away. A.P. Hill had no reason to fight at Gettysburg except that the enemy was there; and being pugnacious, Hill too was determined to do battle. When Reynolds arrived in Gettysburg he found a small but brisk battle going on. Reynolds also had no reason to engage the enemy at Gettysburg—in fact, his orders from Meade indicated that he should perhaps fall back if he met the enemy. Reynolds, though, was also a fighter, and he was determined he would hold the town. But he was killed by a stray bullet early in the battle, and Hill pushed Buford's men back through Gettysburg.

Matters might have gone ill for the Federals had not General Winfield Scott Hancock arrived and rallied the retreating soldiers on the high ground south of Gettysburg—Culp's Hill and Cemetery Ridge. When Lee, who had heard the distant sounds of battle, arrived, he ordered his entire army to converge on Gettysburg. Having surveyed the lay of the country, Lee saw that he had to take the high ground and ordered General Richard S. Ewell to seize Culp's Hill on the Federal right, "if practicable." Ewell commanded Jackson's old division, and if "Stonewall Jackson" had been there, he might have made the attack at once. But Ewell delayed, not certain it was "practicable" to take the hill. Culps Hill thus remained in Federal hands.

General James "Old Pete" Longstreet, whom Lee called "my old warhorse," wanted to march his division around the union left and get between the Federals and Washington. He thought it advisable to take a strong defensive position away from Gettysburg and await a Federal attack. But without Stuart to tell him the lay of Meade's army, Lee was unwilling to do this. "No," said Lee, "I am going to whip them [here], or they are going to whip me."

Throughout the evening and into the night of July 1 the combined Federal and Confederate armies converged at Gettysburg. By the next day, 65,000 Confederates faced a Federal host, numbering 85,000. When Longstreet arrived, Lee ordered him to advance on the Federal left and to take two hills that commanded Cemetery Ridge—Little Roundtop and Big Roundtop. Lee's plan was for Longstreet to attack the Federal left, while A.P. Hill

Map of the Gettysburg battlefield, 1863

assaulted its center on Cemetery Ridge, and Ewell moved on Culp's Hill. Longstreet's advance, which was to be secret, was however somewhat roundabout, and it wasn't until 2:30 in the afternoon that he was in position. Still, he delayed.

Meanwhile, Stuart had returned to greet an angry Lee. "I have not heard from you for days," said Lee, "and you are the eyes and ears of my army."

Chastened by the general's anger, Stuart defended himself. "I have brought you 125 wagons and their teams, general."

"Yes," replied Lee, "and they are an impediment to me now." Noticing Stuart's surprise and shame, Lee softened. "Let me ask your help," he said to Stuart. "We will not discuss this matter further. Help me fight these people."

At 4 o'clock, Longstreet at last advanced. His division commander, John Hood, sent two Alabama regiments against Little Round Top, which was held by only 350 men, the 20th Maine, under Colonel Joshua Lawrence Chamberlain—in civilian life a college professor. Chamberlain took his orders to hold Little Round Top "at all hazards" with the utmost seriousness. Some 3,500 Confederates assailed the 20th Maine; the fighting surged back and forth, and to save his left flank, Chamberlain formed his men at right angles in a "V" formation. Finally, when his men were nearly out of ammunition, Chamberlain ordered them to fix bayonets, and charge the Confederates. Taken by surprise, the Confederates broke and fled. Chamberlain had held Little Round Top, but with a loss of nearly one-third of his men.

Elsewhere—in the "Wheat Field," "Devil's Den," and the "Valley of Death"—the fighting was bitter. Minie balls flew thick like a shower of hail. Yet, by the close of day, the Federal flanks held. Ewell had been driven back from Culp's Hill; Jeb Stuart had been checked from reconnoitering the Federal right by a young Federal cavalry commander named George Armstrong Custer. Little Round Top had been reinforced.

After this day of failures, Longstreet urged Lee to retreat, but Lee would not. You will attack the Federal center on Cemetery Ridge tomorrow, he told "Old Pete." Though only a low rise, Cemetery Hill was nevertheless a strong position; to attack it, the Confederates would have to march without cover across a large open field in the face of the powerful Federal artillery. Federal troops lay behind a stone wall that ran the length of the ridge. It was almost as strong a position as Marye's Heights was in the Battle of Fredericksburg.

Longstreet tried to dissuade Lee. "General Lee," he said, "there never was a body of 15,000 men who could make that attack successfully." But Lee's fighting spirit was up. "The enemy is there, General Longstreet," he said, "and I am going to strike him."

Longstreet and Lee chose General George E. Pickett of Virginia to lead the assault. The 38-year-old general, though something of a dandy (he wore his hair in ringlets, richly perfumed) rejoiced that the glory of the assault would be his and eagerly awaited the commencement of the attack. He would lead his own division, and two others—13,000 men in all.

First, though, the union center had to be "softened," and at one in the afternoon Confederate artillery began a savage barrage on Federal lines. Though the guns fired high, Confederate fire wreaked havoc and death within the Federal lines. General Hancock, who commanded the Federal center, rode on horseback in the front of his lines to calm his

Pickett's Charge, by Thure de Thulstrup

men. One of his lieutenants told him not to expose himself so, but Hancock replied, "There are times when a corps commander's life does not count."

Federal artillery answered the Confederate barrage. After about two hours, though, the union commander silenced his guns to conserve ammunition for the assault he knew would come. Longstreet could delay no longer, though he was loath to order the attack. When Pickett eagerly inquired whether now was the time, Longstreet merely nodded. Pickett penned a hasty note to his fiancée—"If Old Peter's nod means death, then good-bye and God bless you, little one."

Many a southern schoolboy would come to relive this moment in his mind—the high-water mark of southern chivalry. Pickett's words would echo down the years: "Up men and to your posts! Don't forget today that you are from old Virginia!"

And in silence they marched from the cover of the woods along Seminary Ridge where Lee's headquarters lay. In well ordered ranks they advanced, a mile in length, red battle-flags waving, arms glistening in the sun, across the wide-open field, toward the stone wall. "It was the most beautiful thing I ever saw," wrote one union officer. They marched "with the step of men who believed themselves invincible," a union private recalled. Their lines contracted from a mile to a half-mile in length. After crossing the Emmitsburg Pike, they regrouped and continued marching on and on.

Union artillery opened fire, punching large holes in the Confederate line. But still they came on. Seeing the destruction the cannons caused, union soldiers taunted their enemy with cries of "Fredericksburg! Fredericksburg!" But still, in ordered ranks, they came on. The invincible Army of Northern Virginia! Bobby Lee's men! Two-hundred yards from the wall, all hell-fire was loosed on them—11 cannon, 1,700 muskets—cutting down men like grain at harvest. Most never reached the wall, but Brigadier General Lewis A. Armistead did. The North Carolinian and his men engaged the enemy in hand-to-hand combat, broke the union lines. But Armistead was shot as he tried to turn the union artillery, and his men were captured or killed.

Battle dead at Gettysburg

The Confederates broke and fled. Over half of them, 6,500 men, had fallen or been taken prisoner. As Lee watched in horror the shattered remnant of his army return, he cried out, "All this has been my fault—it is I who have lost this fight." He feared a union counterattack, and finding Pickett, ordered him to rally his division for defense. Pickett, his exaltation turned to despair, looked in dazed wonder on Lee: "General Lee," he said, "I have no division now."

The next day, July 4, came in a shower of rain, as if to wash away the memory of the Battle of Gettysburg. Combined Federal and Confederate casualties numbered 51,000. That afternoon, Lee retreated, and Meade, fearful of Lee's remaining strength, let him go. Late that night an exhausted, defeated Lee recalled Pickett's Charge. Never had men fought so bravely, he said. If only they had had better support, they might have, they just might have . . . He paused, then loudly cried out his sorrow, "Too bad! Too bad! Oh—too bad!"

The Confederacy Cut in Half

Gettysburg was not the only bad news Jefferson Davis had received. On July 4, the very day the Army of Northern Virginia began its retreat across the Potomac, Vicksburg fell to Grant.

It had been a long siege. Daily, for over a month, Federal artillery, 200 guns, had battered the city by land, while gunboats fired at it from the river. To escape that rain of fiery death,

Confederate prisoners
at Gettysburg

civilians dug into the yellow chalk hillsides—lived in caves—while their houses above them were blasted to timber. Though wild reports spread throughout the South of women and children maimed and killed by falling shells, only 12 civilians were killed during the course of bombardment; 30 were wounded. As food supplies ran low, civilians and soldiers ate mules, horses, dogs, and even rats. Sickness spread among the troops defending Vicksburg. By late June, one-half of the Confederates were listed as sick.

Yet, Grant could not take the city, and the defenders vaunted their defiance from its battlements. On July 2, the *Vicksburg Citizen* boasted that the "Great Ulysses—the Yankee Generalissimo surnamed Grant—has expressed his intention of dining in Vicksburg on the Fourth of July. . . . Ulysses must get into the city before he dines in it. The way to cook a rabbit is 'first catch the rabbit.'"

But the *Citizen's* confidence was misplaced. By early July, Confederate General John Pemberton had received a note signed, "Many Soldiers." "The army is now ripe for mutiny, unless it can be fed," said the note. "If you can't feed us, you'd better surrender us, horrible as the idea is, than suffer this noble army to disgrace themselves by desertion." Pemberton decided that it was indeed time to surrender. He would hand over Vicksburg on July 4, Independence Day, for he thought that then he could hope for the best terms from the Yankees

Though the North rejoiced at the fall of Vicksburg, the union soldiers who had invested it did not—at least not much. As one Southern minister said, "they knew that we surrendered to famine, not to them." Over the courthouse now flew the Stars and Stripes instead of the Stars and Bars. Vicksburg had been taken, the Mississippi now belonged to Lincoln, and the Confederacy was cut in half.

In the Wake of Gettysburg

Before the fall of Vicksburg and Lee's retreat from Gettysburg, the southern armies had seemed to be advancing in the East and holding their own in the West. With continued successes, perhaps Great Britain or France would recognize the Confederacy; and Lincoln then would have to agree to peace or face war with European powers. Gettysburg and Vicksburg changed all that. Lee was back in Virginia, and the Mississippi River was a Federal highway. The blockade grew more and more efficient, and the hope of European intervention grew dim. Lincoln needed another supreme effort, it seemed, to topple the Confederacy. The problem was, he needed more troops.

In March, Congress had passed a conscription act that allowed the president to draft into service men between the ages of 20 and 45. With enlistments way down, Lincoln enacted the conscription act, and in July called for 300,000 men to serve for three-year stints. One provision of Lincoln's draft, however, drew the opposition of Radical Republicans in Congress: if a man could come up with a $300 "commutation fee" or could find someone to serve in his place, he could avoid the draft. This law, declared Pennsylvania congressman Thaddeus Stevens, "is a rich man's bill made for him who can raise his $300 and against him who cannot raise that sum."

The draft gave an occasion for all sorts of corruption. Brokers for substitutes set up shop, taking a fee to find substitutes for men with means. Some doctors, for a hefty fee, diagnosed non-existent diseases. It seemed the poor working class man alone would fill the ranks of the army and become cannon fodder for the union. The Irish in the cities, who resented the

Nuns and the Civil War

Taking no sides in the conflict between the North and South, thousands of Catholic nuns tended the sick and wounded during the war. There were no official records kept of such volunteers, and so it is impossible to know just how many women made up the "Sisters of Mercy," as all nuns—whatever their order—were commonly called. The record of their service is to be found in convent archives, soldiers' personal letters, private diaries, and letters to newspapers of the time. It is known, however, that thousands of sisters volunteered, freely and without pay, for nursing duty in many locations on both sides of the Mason-Dixon line: New York, Boston, Pittsburgh, Baltimore, Washington, Philadelphia, Charleston, Richmond, Nashville, Vicksburg, Memphis, Atlanta, New Orleans, and Gettysburg.

Tending Confederates and Yankees, Catholics and non-Catholics, black and white, the sisters worked in field hospitals, on hospital boats, in prisons, and in larger military hospitals. They tended the wounded, even on the battlefields. Universally, it was noted that the sister-staffed hospitals were clean and orderly.

The training the sisters had received to work in Catholic schools, orphanages, and hospitals put them in an elite—the small group of nurses prepared for rigorous duty. And their unwavering self-discipline and religious devotion gave them the mental and emotional strength to cope with the horrors they saw. The sisters normally arrived at their posts with complete corps of expert executives, medical and surgical nurses, trained dieticians, and insanity experts.

Indeed, death rates at military hospitals typically dropped dramatically after sisters arrived to assume nursing duties. More than once, through tender and persistent care, the sisters were credited with saving the lives of men whom doctors had given up for dead. In some instances, overworked surgeons refused to treat men they felt had no hope of surviving. Some soldiers believed, as a letter in a Baltimore newspaper stated, "that had the Sisters been here from the beginning, not a man would have died."

Detail from the Nuns of the Battlefield Monument, Washington, D.C.

Daughters of Charity from Emmitsburg, Maryland, were on the Gettysburg battlefield on July 4, the day after the fighting ended, and remained in the area for months at various hospitals. Sixteen sisters and a priest left Emmitsburg for Gettysburg, taking refreshments, bandages, sponges, and clothing. Their journey by wagon brought them up the Emmitsburg Road, which Pickett's Charge had crossed on July 3. The dead of both armies lay so thick that the wagon driver could hardly avoid driving over bodies.

In Gettysburg, the sisters paired off and scattered throughout the battlefield and among the many hospitals set up in public buildings. "The White Cornette of the Sisters of Charity fluttered like Angels' wings," wrote a witness. One Sister Petronilla Breen was seen seated on a shattered tree stump, "hurriedly preparing the compresses necessary to staunch the flow of bullet-spilt blood." So many men needed attention that the sisters contacted their convents in Emmitsburg and Baltimore to ask that more nuns be sent north to Gettysburg. One of the Sisters of Charity from Emmitsburg, Sister Camilla O'Keefe, was assisting a surgeon in the Methodist church. The surgeon sent Sister Camilla to a Sanitary Commission facility for more bandages. "But the Methodist church doesn't have nuns," the Sanitary Commission representative protested. "It does today," Sister Camilla replied.

There is a Civil War monument in Washington, D.C., that depicts 12 women in various religious habits. These twelve represent the 12 religious orders that were known to have sent sisters to nurse and tend the soldiers of both the Union and the Confederacy. Above the plaque is inscribed: "They comforted the dying, nursed the wounded, carried hope to the imprisoned, gave in His Name a drink of water to the thirsty."

(Credits: Michael F. Fitzpatrick, a photo collector in Annapolis, Maryland, became interested in researching the contributions of the sister nurses when he acquired some pictures of nuns from the Civil War period. His extensive and fascinating article on the topic appeared in the *Civil War Times*, Volume XXXVI, #5, October, 1997. Part of Michael Fitzpatrick's article and photographs was reprinted in *Canticle* Magazine, Volume 7; reprinted with permission of *Canticle* Magazine, *Civil War Times* and the author)

Draft riots in New York City, 1863

blacks because they competed for their jobs and who felt generally kicked around, especially resented the draft.

On July 11, the first names of draftees were drawn in New York City. It was the same day that names of casualties at Gettysburg were posted. Festering resentment now found an occasion for expression. Irish mobs attacked the draft office, destroyed files, and finished the job by razing the building. For the next three days, the mobs wandered the streets, rioting, breaking into stores and businesses, and looting. Black neighborhoods were their special target; mobs set fire to black boarding houses, a black orphanage, and a black church. Archbishop John Hughes of New York, who had supported the draft, intervened on July 17, appealing to his flock to stop the rioting. Finally troops, veterans of Gettysburg, restored order. The killed numbered 105.

Jayhawkers and Bushwackers

Bloody guerrilla struggles raged along the border of Missouri and Kansas. Brigadier General James H. Lane, formerly a United States Senator from Kansas, thought Missourians were "wolves, snakes, devils." "Damn their souls," he said, "I want to see them cast into a burning hell." Lane and his band of pro-union *banditti* called "Jayhawkers" did their best to see that this happened. Crossing the border into Missouri, the Jayhawkers raided and set fire to settlers' houses, burnt and plundered towns.

Missourians thirsted for vengeance. Forming themselves into bands called "Bushwackers," they did unto Kansans what Lane had done unto them. The most formidable and bloody Bushwacker band was led by Confederate Captain William Clarke Quantrill, whose Bushwack Raiders took and sacked Lawrence, Kansas on August 21, 1863. While Quantrill ate a hearty breakfast at a local hotel, his men pillaged the town and murdered 150 men and boys. The Raiders escaped back into Missouri, leaving Lawrence in flames.

General Thomas Ewing, Jr., who commanded Federal forces in Missouri, wanted to put an end to Quantrill. To keep Missouri settlers from supplying the Bushwackers (as some did), Ewing issued General Order 11, commanding the inhabitants of three Missouri counties driven from their homes. Federal troops forced 10,000 men, women, and children from their homes, which Jayhawkers then plundered and burnt. As groups of refugees crossed the open prairies, Jayhawkers attacked them and looted their wagons. The three Missouri counties were soon called the "Burnt District."

General Sterling Price, leading 12,000 Confederate regulars, thought the Missourians' desire to revenge such outrages gave him an opportunity to win the state back for the Confederacy. Though unable to gain significant support from General Edmund Kirby Smith in Arkansas, Price invaded Missouri in September, pushing as far as the northwestern part of the state. At Westport on October 23, 1864 he met a powerful Federal army under General Samuel Curtis and was routed. Fleeing through eastern Kansas, Price and his men made a 1,400 mile march into Texas.

The battle of Westport was the last major Confederate action west of the Mississippi, for Quantrill had fled with Price to Texas. Some of Quantrill's men returned and made sporadic guerrilla raids into Kansas, but these were more the actions of bandits than of armies. After the war was over, Quantrill's legacy haunted Kansans in the persons of two former Raiders—the outlaw brothers, Frank and Jesse James.

Jesse James

The Black Soldier

Frederick Douglass thought that if a black man could serve in the Federal army there would be "no power on earth which can deny he has earned the right to citizenship in the United States." Like other abolitionists, both white and black, Douglass hoped that the United States government would enlist black soldiers into the Federal army. In September 1861, he asked:

> Why does the government reject the Negro? Is he not a man? Can he not wield a sword, fire a gun, march and countermarch and obey orders like any other?

In the same article, Douglas made the surprising claim that "there are at the present moment many Colored men in the Confederate Army doing duty not only as cooks, servants and laborers, but real soldiers, having muskets on their shoulders, and bullets in their pockets, ready to shoot down any loyal troops and do all that soldiers may do to destroy the Federal government and build up that of the traitors and rebels." Douglass based this claim on reports he had received after First Manasses or Bull Run—and he used it as propaganda to pressure the federal government to induct blacks into its service

The Confederate Congress did not officially allow blacks to serve as soldiers, though thousands of blacks, free and slave, served in the Confederate ranks throughout the war. Most of these, however, were servants and laborers, used to relieve the white soldiers from drudgery and free them to fight; and most blacks, it appears, were pressed into service. But some of them may have served as soldiers bearing arms.

After Gettysburg and Vicksburg, some prominent Confederate leaders proposed an official recruitment of blacks into the Confederate army. General Patrick Ronayne

Cleburne wrote that the Confederacy "immediately commence training a large reserve of the most courageous of our slaves and further that we guarantee freedom within a reasonable time to every slave in the South who shall remain true to the Confederacy in this war." Other southerners, though, agreed with Howell Cobb of Georgia, who insisted that "you cannot make soldiers of slaves, or slaves of soldiers! The day you make a soldier of them is the beginning of the end of the revolution. And if slaves seem good soldiers, then our whole theory of slavery is wrong." So great was the opposition to recruiting slaves into the army that Jefferson Davis shelved the idea—at least for a time.

Lincoln supported recruiting blacks into the Federal army, but many Federal generals opposed it. The battle of Milliken's Bend, Louisiana, on June 7, 1863, however changed their minds. In this fight, Federal soldiers, both black and white, fought bravely against a superior force of Confederates. By the end of the war, free blacks from the North, along with escaped slaves from the border states and the Confederacy, had joined the Federal army to the number of 185,000. But though they had proven their worth in battle, these black soldiers still did not receive equal pay to the whites and were not given the same clothing allowances. White doctors, too, were loath to operate on black patients, and many black soldiers died for lack of attention. The Confederate government, too, did not recognize blacks who served in the union army as soldiers and so refused to include them in prisoner exchanges. Instead, the Confederate government ordered that black Federals captured in battle were to be shot.

Twelve illustrated cards narrating the journey of a slave from plantation life to the struggle for liberty, for which he gives his life, as a Union soldier, and for which he is crowned with laurels by Columbia, ca. 1863

The Battle for Central Tennessee

In the six months following a battle fought at Murfreesboro, Tennessee, on December 30, 1862, the Federal and Confederate armies had reached a stand-off in central Tennessee. Murfreesboro had been indecisive. Neither Federal general William Rosecrans, nor Confederate general Braxton Bragg had won an advantage. Afterwards, except for occasional skirmishes, the two armies did nothing but stare each other down.

Lincoln wanted Rosecrans to do something, but "Old Rosy" (as his men called him) said he needed more men and supplies. Finally, in June, threatened with removal from command if he stayed inactive any longer, Rosecrans began a series of bloodless flanking maneuvers in which he drove Bragg south, 80 miles, to Tullahoma, and then to Chattanooga, near the Georgia border.

Rosecrans' movements threatened to drive a wedge between the eastern tier of Confederate states and those west of the Appalachians, and President Davis was worried. After conferring with General Lee, Davis withdrew Longstreet and 12,000 men from the Army of Northern Virginia and sent them west. Since Ambrose Burnside had taken Knoxville, Tennessee, Longstreet could not take the more direct rail route through East Tennessee, and so his men had to be transported through the Carolinas and Georgia, and north toward Chattanooga. Bragg, however, had been reinforced by other Confederate regiments so that his force now equaled that of Rosecrans.

In September, to draw Rosecrans out of Chattanooga, Bragg began to move his army south into Georgia along the Chickamauga Creek. The plan worked. Rosecrans, thinking Bragg was retreating, began to pursue the Confederate army. On September 20, 1863, Bragg struck Rosecrans hard, though he was unable to destroy the Federal army as he had hoped. The next day, reinforced by Longstreet and 6,000 men from the Army of Northern Virginia, Bragg again attacked Rosecrans. Taking advantage of a break in Federal lines, Longstreet routed two Federal corps, and the entire northern army began a confused retreat towards Chattanooga. Had it not been for General George Henry "Pap" Thomas' stubborn withdrawal, the Confederates might have wrought worse damage on the Federal ranks. For his steadfastness, Thomas earned the title, the "Rock of Chickamauga."

But Bragg did not follow up his victory with another attack, and a disgusted Longstreet called for his removal. "I am convinced," declared Old Pete, "that nothing but the hand of God can help as long as we have our present commander." Jefferson Davis traveled to Chattanooga to settle the dispute that now developed between his generals. But though all the generals voiced their disapproval of Bragg, Davis decided to keep him. Better Bragg then, say, Beauregard or Joe Johnston, thought the president. And, besides, Davis liked Bragg.

Lincoln, too, was not pleased with his general, Rosecrans. In October, he appointed Ulysses Grant as the commander of all Federal armies between the Mississippi and the Appalachians, and Grant decided to replace Rosecrans with Pap Thomas. Grant infused a new spirit into the defeated Federals at Chattanooga—by filling their bellies. Since the battle, they had lived in filth and without sufficient food. Grant opened up supply lines and fed his army.

Though the Confederates were as hungry as the Federals had been, they still provided Grant a formidable challenge. Bragg occupied a strong position east of Chattanooga—the

Battle of Chickamauga

six-mile-long Missionary Ridge, anchored to the south at the 2,000-foot high Lookout Mountain. Bragg had placed artillery on Lookout Mountain, dug in rifle pits along the slopes and trenches along the base of Missionary Ridge. Altogether, it looked as though the Confederates held an impregnable position.

Despite the appearances, Grant and Pap Thomas decided to attack. After Sherman arrived in mid November with four divisions, Grant began his assault on Missionary Ridge. On November 24, Sherman attacked the left flank of the rebel line while General Hooker struck at the right. While Sherman was turned back, Hooker led his men stealthily up the slopes of Lookout Mountain, swathed in dense fog that rose from the Tennessee River. In this "Battle Above the Clouds," Hooker's men forced the Confederates from the mountain. By day's end, the Stars and Stripes flew from the peak of Lookout Mountain.

The next day, Grant ordered Thomas' men to capture the first line of Confederate trenches skirting the base of Missionary Ridge. Thomas overran the trenches and then stopped, waiting for further orders. During the lull, one of Thomas' generals, Philip Sheridan, the son of an Irish immigrant, pulled a flask from his pocket and toasted the Confederate gunners on the ridge with, "Here's at you." The rebels didn't appreciate the compliment and returned Sheridan's toast with artillery fire, spattering Sheridan and his officers with dirt. Sheridan was furious. "That was ungenerous!" he cried out. "I'll take your guns for that!"

Summit of Lookout Mountain, ca. 1864

Without orders, Sheridan led his men up the steep slope of Missionary Ridge. Shouting "Chickamauga!" Sheridan's men climbed like furies, sometimes on hands and knees, sometimes pulling themselves upward with sticks and bayonets, always in the face of heavy fire. They seemed unstoppable. Grant watched with wonder—"who ordered those men up the hill?" he asked. "No one," answered an aide. "They started without orders. When those fellows get started, all hell can't stop them."

Some of the Confederates broke and fled; then it turned into a major route. Sheridan's men took Missionary Ridge, and 4,000 prisoners. The Confederates thus lost Chattanooga, and the way stood open for a Federal advance into Georgia.

Address at Gettysburg

Five days before the battle of Missionary Ridge, Abraham Lincoln came to Gettysburg to dedicate a cemetery to the union dead there. Yet, president though he was, he was not to be the principle speaker. Edward Everett, the 70-year old former governor of Massachusetts, was to deliver the principle address while Lincoln was to add only some "appropriate remarks."

Everett, a florid orator, spoke for nearly two hours. When at last Lincoln rose to speak, he offered only a short speech he had penned on the back of an envelope, probably while Everett spoke.

"Fourscore and seven years ago, our fathers brought forth on this continent a new nation, conceived in liberty, and dedicated to the proposition that all men are created equal." These famous words encapsulated Lincoln's—and, indeed, many Americans'—vision of the federal union. Other nations had been founded on a common culture or race; they were in many ways like an extended family; but the United States had been founded on a proposition—an idea demanding a response: human equality. Not culture, not race;

Lincoln at Gettysburg. Lincoln can be seen center left, just to the left of a tall man in a top hat.

U.S. Grant, by Mathew B. Brady

not soil or blood, but a belief defined America. For Lincoln, as for many Americans, this idea had been set forth in a kind of creed, the Declaration of Independence.

"Now we are engaged in a great civil, testing whether that nation, or any nation so conceived and so dedicated, can long endure." For Lincoln, the war then being waged was significant not just for America, but for the world. It had universal significance. Could a nation, dedicated to the creed of equality, survive? The fate of the United States, the Union, (which Lincoln elsewhere called the "last best hope of earth") would be the test.

The men who died at Gettysburg, said Lincoln, "gave their lives that that nation"—the hope of mankind, a sort of secular version of Winthrop's "city upon a hill"—"might live." Their deaths, not any consecration or dedication, said Lincoln, hallowed the ground. Their sacrifice would be remembered:

The world will little note, nor long remember what we say here, but it can never forget what they did here. It is for us the living, rather, to be dedicated here to the unfinished work which they who fought here have thus far so nobly advanced. It is rather for us to be here dedicated to the great task remaining before us—that from these honored dead we take increased devotion to that cause for which they gave the last full measure of devotion—that we here highly resolve that these dead shall not have died in vain—that this nation, under God, shall have a new birth of freedom—and that government of the people by the people, for the people, shall not perish from the earth.

The Twilight of the War

When he was young, U.S. Grant had been thought a failure. His father, Jesse Grant, a tanner by trade, thought his boy, who withdrew from others and was a might too sensitive, so impractical that he sent him to West Point to train for a military career. "A military life had no charms for me," Grant later wrote, and he was an indifferent student, graduating at the middle of his class. Though he thought it wicked, Grant fought in the Mexican War; for he held it his supreme duty to serve his flag.

In 1848, Grant married Julia Dent, to whom he was deeply devoted. When the army transferred him to a Pacific post without his wife and children, he was lonely, began drinking too much, and contemplated leaving the army. In 1854, he did just that—resigned his commission and returned to Missouri and his Julia. He tried his hand at several occupations—farming, bill collecting, real estate—and failed at them all. Finally he ended up clerking in his brother's leather store in Galena, Illinois. There the war found him, and Grant went from failure to the victories of Donelson, Vicksburg, and Chattanooga.

It was (on the outside, at least) a very different Grant that entered Washington in March 1864 to take up a commission that no one had held since George Washington. Grant was to be Liet. General, having command over the entire U.S. army. Grant was the toast of the capital; everyone wanted to see and shake hands with the small, shy general who had so soundly whipped the rebels in the West. But Grant was uneasy in Washington. He longed to be out on the field of battle, not in drawing rooms.

Grant's nemesis was a man whom his classmates at West Point called "The Marble Model" because he had never earned a single demerit there. While Grant had arisen from very humble beginnings, Robert E. Lee was a scion of one of the first families of Virginia. His father was "Light Horse" Harry Lee, one of George Washington's most trusted officers, who had married Mary Custis, Martha Washington's granddaughter. "Light Horse" Harry had squandered much of the family fortune and then skipped off to the West Indies, but Robert's mother brought him up to be a gentleman, teaching him "to practice self-denial and self-control" and to love honor.

Robert E. Lee

Lee did not love secession or slavery (he had freed his father's-in-law slaves and never owned any of his own), but his sense of honor induced him to follow Virginia out of the union. His obligation, he believed, was first to his people and his state. He later said, "I did only what my duty demanded. I could have taken no other course without dishonor. And if it were all to be done over again, I should act in precisely the same manner." Lee, however, was more than a marble man; he enjoyed music, dancing, and fine food. Though always faithful to his wife, Lee took pleasure in the attentions of ladies, who thought him handsome and dignified. His chief defect was a terrible temper, which he took great pains to control; even so, once roused, Lee withered offenders with the cold, white intensity of his furious, silent stare.

Lee knew he was up against something new in Grant—that at last he faced a relentless, vigorous campaigner. Outnumbered, Lee would try to hold fortified positions against which Grant must hurl and break his army. Lee hoped by this strategy to make the price of war so high in northern blood that the North would tire of the war and call for peace. Lincoln was up for election in November 1864; perhaps enough war tragedy would bring a new, more peace-minded president into office.

Grant had his own strategy. He thought the Federal armies had operated independently of one another for too long. He intended to coordinate all the armies, east and west, in a combined assault on the Confederacy. Grant would send General Franz Sigel to capture the Shenandoah Valley, the breadbasket for Lee's army, while Benjamin Butler moved up the James River toward Richmond. Grant himself, with General Meade and 110,000 men of the Grand Army of the Republic (as Grant's army was now called), would pursue the Army of Northern Virginia, 60,000 strong, while, in the west, Sherman advanced from Chattanooga to Atlanta, Georgia.

Grant's plan was a good one, and the new general could boast of triumphs in the West. Still, some veterans of the Army of the Potomac were not convinced Grant could carry it off. Grant may have been victorious against other Confederates, they said, but he had "never met Bobbie Lee and his boys."

Into the Wilderness

In early May 1864, the Grand Army of the Republic broke camp at Brandy Station, near Culpeper, Virginia, and began its march south. Lee and his army were encamped in the Wilderness outside of Chancellorsville where, almost a year and half earlier, they had beaten Hooker and lost Stonewall Jackson. Grisly reminders of that battle greeted the advance guard of the Federal army as it marched onto Chancellorsville battleground; a heavy rain had fallen, washing away the soil from the shallow, hastily dug graves, uncovering the skeletons of the fallen. In the firelight, "the dead were all around us," remembered a Federal private; "their eyeless skulls seemed to stare steadily at us."

The fighting that erupted at noon the next day, May 5, swelled the hosts of the dead. The dense forest, the thickets, snared the smoke of rifles and artillery and threw both

Confederates and Federals into confusion. Friends fired on friends in the smoky darkness, and the lines were very close. "It was a blind and bloody hunt to the death, in bewildering thickets, rather than a battle," wrote one soldier.

The second day of the battle, Federals under General James Wadsworth broke through the Confederate center. Lee, seeing the danger, was worried; but General John Gregg's Texans, part of Longstreet's command, rushed in to plug up the hole. "Attention, Texas Brigade," shouted Gregg to his men, "the eyes of General Lee are upon you, forward march." Lee, hearing Gregg's command, raised himself up in his stirrups, took off his hat, and earnestly exclaimed, "Texans always move them." "When Lee pronounced these words," remembered one of the Texans, "a yell rent the air that must have been heard for miles around. . . . A courier riding by my side, with tears coursing down his cheeks, exclaimed, 'I would charge hell itself for that old man.'" Gregg's men stoutly contended with Wadsworth's men. Of the 673 Texans that went into the fight, only 223 survived.

Grant showed no emotion during the battle. Even when Confederate John B. Gordon smashed the Federal right, he said nothing, but quietly whittled a stick with a small knife. That night, though, as brush fires raged through the Wilderness and the death screams of the wounded filled the air; as the realization that, with 17,000 dead and wounded, he had lost the battle to Lee—that night, in his tent, Grant, all alone, wept. But the next morning, he was the same, impassive general. "Whatever happens," he had told Lincoln, "we will not retreat." He would continue to push south, toward Richmond.

A Dance of Death

Lee predicted that Grant would continue to push south, and where he would go next. So it was, when Grant's army arrived at Spotsylvania Courthouse, the Army of Northern Virginia was there to meet it. In the early dawn of May 12, Winfield Scott Hancock attacked the Confederate center at a "U" shaped redoubt that would soon be called the "Bloody Angle." Hancock's assault pushed the Confederates back. Lee, seeing the danger, rode forward to lead the counterattack himself. When General Gordon saw Lee imperiling himself, he called to his men, who rushed forward, forcibly turned Lee's horse, Traveller, and brought him back within the lines. Then they rushed against the redoubt, forcing the Yankees back. For hours, until midnight, the Confederates and Yankees fought over the Bloody Angle until a multitude lay dead, some piled on top of each other, four deep. Days afterwards, as the fighting at Spotsylvania continued, these bodies, decaying, filled the air with a horrid stench.

Grant again withdrew. His strategy was to push toward Richmond, always moving south and east to get around Lee's flank. Lee, guessing Grant's strategy, always kept ahead of him; but he knew more had to be done. "We must destroy this army of Grant's before he gets to the James [River]," said Lee. "If he gets there, it will become a siege, and then it will be a mere question of time."

On June 3, Grant attacked Lee's position at Cold Harbor on the Chickahominy River. "It was not war; it was murder," remembered a rebel general afterwards. Sixty-thousand Federals smashed into the Confederates, who, well entrenched, beat off their assailants. Five to seven thousand Federals were butchered, most within the first eight minutes of battle. Many of the dead were unrecognizable; only little slips of paper they had affixed to their uniforms could identify them. Grant admitted that the attack at Cold Harbor was a mistake. Some in the North agreed and began to think his whole campaign was a mistake. In just 30 days of fighting, Grant had lost 50,000 men. Of course, these were easily replaced, for the North seemed able to supply almost an unlimited number of soldiers. Still, Grant was not as popular as he had been. But Lincoln, despite the criticisms, stood by his general. For Grant fought.

Because Grant was only a few miles from Richmond, Lee assumed that city would he his next target. Lee, for once, was wrong. Grant feinted towards Richmond, but his real target

Collecting the Dead, Cold Harbor

was Petersburg, a major rail and communications center. If he took Petersburg, Grant could isolate Richmond and starve it into submission.

Lee's misjudgment almost proved fatal. On June 15, the advance guard of Grant's army, 16,000 men under General W.F. Smith, reached Petersburg, which was guarded by a mere 3,000 men under General Beauregard. But Smith moved too slowly; by the time he began his assault, Lee had reinforced Beauregard. The Confederates beat back the Federal attack.

Both armies converged on Petersburg, which was soon ringed with trenches. For the next ten months the Confederates and Petersburg were besieged, and Grant's campaign stalled. Once again, Northerners thought the war was a failure. Newspapers called Grant a butcher.

The presence of Jubal Early in the lower Shenandoah Valley didn't help matters, either. Lee had sent Early north to push Federal troops out of the Shenandoah Valley, to invade Pennsylvania, extracting tribute from towns there, and to harass Washington. Jubal Early routed General Sigel in the Shenandoah. On July 11, he attacked Fort Stevens in the Washington suburbs but was beaten back by the Second Rhode Island. On July 30, he took Chambersburg, Pennsylvania and demanded a $500,000 ransom. When the city refused to pay it, Early burned the city's business district to the ground.

On to Atlanta

General William Tecumseh Sherman, commanding the 98,000-strong Grand Army of the West, had set out on May 6, 1864 from Chattanooga, Tennessee into Georgia. His goal was to capture Atlanta, the second most important manufacturing center of the Confederacy. In pursuit of this goal, Sherman was relentless: "War is the remedy our enemies have chosen," he said, "and I say let us give them all they want; not a word of argument, not a sign of let-up, no cave in till we are whipped—or they are."

Opposing Sherman, with only half the number of Sherman's men, was Joe Johnston. Johnston hoped to coax Sherman to attack where he hoped he could score a significant defeat, or, at least, slow Sherman's advance. To hamper the Federal supply line, Johnston sent Bedford Forrest and his cavalry into Sherman's rear to wreak havoc on railroads, bridges, and tunnels. Yet, despite the thoroughness of Forrest's

William Tecumseh Sherman

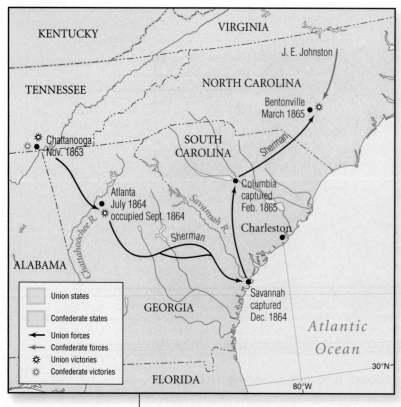

Sherman's march

work, Sherman's efficiency and his army's manpower triumphed—railroads, bridges, even tunnels, were quickly repaired.

Sherman's progress was slow. Instead of risking frontal attacks on Johnston's army, Sherman sent the Army of the Tennessee, under General James McPherson, to flank the rebel army, thus forcing it to retreat deeper into Georgia. Sherman's progress was slow—too slow for him. He was eager to strike the enemy. When, in mid June, the Confederates dug in on Kennesaw Mountain (only 20 miles from Atlanta.) Sherman ordered 13,000 men to attack the Confederate position. On June 27, the Federals stormed the fortified mountain, only to be beaten back with heavy casualties. Sherman saw, and admitted, his mistake, and swore he'd never repeat it—and he didn't. Returning to his flanking strategy, Sherman pushed Johnston closer and closer to Atlanta.

Jefferson Davis, who had never liked Johnston, thought his general was not fighting hard enough to save Atlanta. On July 17, Davis replaced Johnston with John Bell Hood of Kentucky, a soldier who had lost a leg and the use of his arm in battle. Johnston's men loved him, and so it was only with reluctance that they received Hood. Not everyone shared Davis' confidence in Hood. "Hood is a bold fighter," said Lee. "I am doubtful as to other qualities necessary."

Hood was, indeed, "a bold fighter." On July 20, he led a daring attack on Sherman at Peachtree Creek outside of Atlanta. But the Confederates were driven back. Two days later, when Hood heard that Sherman had sent McPherson to Decatur (a town east of Atlanta) and that McPherson was moving on Atlanta from that position, he moved south to counter him. Hood met McPherson in what became known as the Battle of Atlanta, on July 22. For hours the fierce fighting was inconclusive. Then McPherson rode by mistake into a knot of Confederates. They ordered him to surrender, but tipping his hat to them, he turned his horse and galloped toward Federal lines. Shots rang out, and McPherson fell, dead.

With McPherson gone, General John "Black Jack" Logan took command. Riding up and down the Federal lines, he shouted, "McPherson and revenge, boys, McPherson and revenge!" instilling a renewed spirit, as of their fallen leader, in the men. They charged, and within a half hour, drove Hood's men from the field.

After failing again to defeat Sherman at Ezra Church, Hood withdrew within the fortifications of Atlanta. He had lost 20,000 men in one week. So stout were Atlanta's defenses, that Sherman did not dare a frontal attack. Instead, he lay siege to the city, shelling the Confederate trenches and the houses and buildings beyond. Atlanta was entirely cut off from supplies and, if they were to be had, reinforcements.

The siege lasted one month. On August 31, Sherman attacked Atlanta from the south along the Macon and Western Railroad. The next day, Hood, deeming he could not save Atlanta and his army both, evacuated the city. Sherman had taken Atlanta.

To Remain A Barren Waste

The taking of Atlanta was not the only good news to reach Lincoln and Grant. General Phil Sheridan, whom Grant had sent into the Shenandoah Valley with 45,000 men to hunt down

Jubal Early, finally met the rebel commander in battle at Winchester on September 19. Early had not only been threatening Pennsylvania towns, railroad supply lines, and Washington; but, his presence in the lower Shenandoah Valley, near the Potomac, had dampened the spirits of the North. At Winchester, though Early, with about 15,000 men, fought doggedly, he was finally forced to withdraw.

But Winchester was not the end of Early. Almost a month later, he attacked Sheridan's forces encamped at Cedar Creek, while Sheridan himself was 20 miles away. The battle became a rout as Early drove the Yankees from their camps. When Sheridan, who had heard of the attack, finally arrived, he rode amongst his disorganized men, urging them to reform their ranks and counterattack. The presence of their commander emboldened the Yankees. They began to cheer, but Sheridan cried out, "God damn you! Don't cheer me! If you love your country, come up to the front! There's lots of fight in you men yet! Come up, God damn you! Come up! We will lick them out of their boots!"

And lick them they did, driving Early and his outnumbered men from the field. Early's force was utterly routed and broken. This was his last fight in the Shenandoah Valley. That Virginia garden now belonged to the Yankees.

But it would not remain a garden for long. In late August, Grant had told Sheridan, "if the war is to last another year, we want the Shenandoah Valley to remain a barren waste." The lieutenant general did not want the valley supplying the Confederate capital or its armies. Sheridan obeyed Grant with earnest thoroughness; he destroyed over 2,000 barns filled with wheat, hay and farming implements, drove off 4,000 head of cattle, and killed about 3,000 head of sheep. In retaliation for the "murder" of a Federal lieutenant, John R. Meigs, Sheridan declared that all houses in a five-mile radius were to be destroyed. "Tomorrow I will continue the destruction," he declared. "When this is completed, the Valley . . . will have but little in it for man or beast."

Maj. General Philip Sheridan, by Mathew Brady

A McClellan campaign poster

A Lincoln-Johnson campaign poster

These victories—the capture of Atlanta, the routing of Early—sealed the presidential election of 1864. Only two months before, Lincoln had thought his chances for reelection dim. The Democratic candidate was General George McClellan, who criticized Lincoln's policies. A McClellan victory would have heartened the South; for, War Democrat though he was, McClellan was running on a platform that called for peace. By November, however, it had become clear that the Confederacy was in the final stages of dissolution—that Lincoln's war policies were succeeding. In the election, Lincoln, thus, took every state, except Delaware, Kentucky and New Jersey, and won 54 percent of the popular vote. Receiving the election results by telegraph, Lincoln exulted. "I give thanks to the Almighty for this evidence of the people's resolution to stand by free government and the rights of humanity," he said.

March to the Sea

On November 7, 1864, the day before the northern elections, Jefferson Davis addressed the Confederate Congress:

> There are no vital points on the preservation of which the continued existence of the Confederacy depends. There is no military success of the enemy which can accomplish its destruction. Not the fall of Richmond, nor Wilmington, nor Savannah, nor Mobile, nor of all combined, can save the enemy from the constant and exhaustive drain of blood and treasure which must continue until he shall discover that no peace is attainable unless based on the recognition of our indefeasible rights.

These were brave words, but they betrayed desperation. They hinted at irregular, guerrilla warfare continuing until the North grew so tired of blood that it would concede southern independence. The regular channels of government in the South were fast falling apart. Even in the face of Sherman and Grant, some Southern governors obstructed the Confederate draft; the governor of Georgia said it violated states rights. The armies were in desperate need of soldiers, and records showed that from 100,000 to 200,000 men were absent. Davis had gone to Macon, Georgia in September to appeal to men to return to duty, but to no avail. As one Confederate senator from Texas noted, the people's "confidence was gone, and hope was almost extinguished."

In this the twilight of the war, Federal generals were proving more relentless. In September, Sherman ordered all civilians to evacuate Atlanta and arranged a ten-day truce with Hood to allow them to pass through Confederate lines. Both the mayor of Atlanta and Hood protested; such an evacuation, they said, would bring heavy suffering to civilians, especially to the infirm and the old. "The unprecedented measure you propose transcends, in studied and ingenious cruelty, all acts ever before brought to my attention in the dark history of war," wrote Hood to Sherman. The Yankee general, however, was unmoved by appeals to antique chivalry. "Gentlemen," he replied, "You cannot qualify war in harsher terms than I will. War is cruelty and you cannot refine it . . . You might as well appeal against the thunderstorm as against these terrible hardships of war."

When the civilians had evacuated the city, Sherman ordered one-third of Atlanta burned. Then, on November 16, Sherman left Atlanta behind, and with 60,000 of his men, began a march, eastward, to the sea. This was a daring act, for Sherman was cutting himself off from his supply base and from all communication with the North. He had conferred with both Grant and Lincoln before commencing this march, and both, though doubtful, had approved it. Sherman explained that his great army would live off Georgia's rich farmlands. His goal was the seacoast town of Savannah, where he could reestablish contact with the North.

Jefferson Davis

Ruins of railroad round-
house at Atlanta, after
its capture by Sherman

Hood did not follow Sherman. Hood assumed that if he threatened Tennessee, Sherman would follow him. Hood planned to march through Tennessee, into Kentucky, and go all the way to the Ohio. On November 30, at Franklin, Tennessee, Hood led 13 charges against Federals under Pap Thomas and suffered a bloody repulse, losing one-fourth of his army. On December 15, Thomas attacked Hood at Nashville and routed the Confederates. Hood's army was splintered and destroyed, and a central railway hub fell to the Federals. The Confederate army of the West was no more. Only scattered cavalry units and militias were left to contend with the victorious Federal army.

Meanwhile, Sherman's advancing columns were laying waste the countryside, plowing a furrow, 40 miles wide, of destruction. Sherman had ordered that his troops respect private property, but nobody (not even he himself) took his order seriously. Sherman had said he wanted to "make Georgia howl." "We cannot change the hearts of these people of the South," he wrote, "but we can make war so terrible . . . and make them so sick of war that generations [will] pass away before they again appeal to it."

Sherman's was a war of vengeance, rapine, and cruelty. What was not stolen was wantonly destroyed. "As far as the eye could reach," remembered one woman, "the lurid flames of burning [houses] lit up the heavens. . . . I could stand out on the verandah and for two or three miles watch as they came on. I could mark when they reached the residence of each and every friend on the road." Yankee soldiers stole from white and black alike. They killed so many cattle that "the whole region stunk with putrefying death carcasses." Soldiers frightened white women, sometimes molesting them; black women were treated less kindly. "The cruelties practiced on this campaign toward the citizens have been enough to blast a more sacred cause than ours," wrote a Federal corporal. "We hardly deserve success."

Thousands of escaping slaves followed in the wake of Sherman's army. They hardly dared venture too far from the Federal army for fear of roving Confederate militia and cavalry units who might return them to slavery or simply kill them. Within Federal lines things were not easy for slaves, either. Many Federal officers and men had no sympathy with freeing slaves. Disease, starvation, and exposure took their toll on hundreds of blacks.

For the duration of the march, neither Lincoln nor Grant had heard anything from Sherman. Finally, on December 22, Lincoln received a telegram. It was from Sherman: "I beg to present you as a Christmas present the city of Savannah, with 150 heavy guns and plenty of ammunition; also, about 25,000 bales of cotton."

With Hood's army destroyed and Georgia devastated from Atlanta to the sea, only Lee's army now stood between Lincoln and complete victory.

"With Malice Toward None"

"Fellow-Countrymen: At this second appearing to take the oath of the presidential office there is less occasion for an extended address than there was at the first."

It was inauguration day, March 4, 1865. Abraham Lincoln, standing before the now-finished capitol, spoke of the encouraging progress of the war. He recalled that on this day, four years earlier, "all thoughts were anxiously directed to an impending civil war. All dreaded it, all sought to avert it." Both unionists and secessionists, he said, "deprecated war, but one of them would make war rather than let the nation survive, and the other would accept war rather than let it perish, and the war came."

What caused the war? "All knew," said Lincoln, "that this interest" —the slave interest—"was somehow the cause of the war." Though his government had sought nothing more than to limit the "territorial enlargement" of slavery, "the insurgents [for the strengthening and enlargement of that institution] would rend the Union even by war." No one, said Lincoln, thought the war would be so great or so long, nor did they think the end of slavery would be its fruit. Each side prayed to "the same God" for success:

It may seem strange that any men should dare to ask a just God's assistance in wringing their bread from the sweat of other men's faces, but let us judge not, that we be not judged.

The prayers of both could not be answered. That of neither has been answered fully. The Almighty has His own purposes. "Woe unto the world because of offenses; for it must needs be that offenses come, but woe to that man by whom the offense cometh." If we shall suppose that American slavery is one of those offenses which, in the providence of God, must needs come, but which, having continued through His appointed time, He now wills to remove, and that He gives to both North and South this terrible war as the woe due to those by whom the offense came, shall we discern therein any departure from those divine attributes which the believers in a living God always ascribe to Him?

Abraham Lincoln, by Alexander Gardner

Lincoln thus suggested that the fault of slavery rested not on the South alone; but North and South had to atone for it. The president closed his address with a promise of reconciliation:

With malice toward none, with charity for all, with firmness in the right as God gives us to see the right, let us strive on to finish the work we are in, to bind up the nation's wounds, to care for him who shall have borne the battle and for his widow and his orphan, to do all which may achieve and cherish a just and lasting peace among ourselves and with all nations.

Among those listening to Lincoln's address was a young actor, John Wilkes Booth. A renowned Shakespearian actor as well as an ardent southern partisan, Booth thought Lincoln a tyrant and had warned that re-election would make him a king. Booth, it seems, had worked as a spy in the southern interest but had never entered the southern army, for which, as he confessed to his diary, he deemed himself a coward. Booth wanted to strike a blow for his country—a blow directed against the president himself.

Booth gathered a band of conspirators at a boarding house in Washington. He had concocted a plan; he and his companions would kidnap Lincoln and exchange him for southern prisoners of war. It was known that the president and his wife sometimes slept at the Soldiers Home on the outskirts of Washington. One March night, Booth and his accomplices, all with masks, rode out to the Soldiers Home, thinking to seize Lincoln. To their chagrin, the president was not there. A discouraged Booth returned to his plotting.

"So goes the world," he lamented. "Might makes right."

John Wilkes Booth

Stamping Out the Sparks of Rebellion

The Confederates had been certain that Sherman would have to stay put in Savannah. In Georgia, winter rains turned the dirt roads to mud; he could not possibly bring an army over them. But the relentless general disappointed them. Sherman ordered his men to hew down forests of timber with which they built cordon roads that crossed muddy and swampy land. Nothing, it seemed, could stop Sherman as he turned his army north to invade the heart of "Secessia"—South Carolina.

"When I go through South Carolina," said Sherman, "it will be one of the most horrible things in the history of the world. The devil himself couldn't restrain my men in that state." The same determination that had devastated Georgia now laid waste to South Carolina; the Federal soldiers had punished secession in its branch, now they would kill it at the root. On February 17, Sherman presented another prize of war to Abraham Lincoln; he had captured

George A. Atzerodt, a Lincoln assassination conspirator

Ruins of Charleston, South Carolina

Columbia, the capital of South Carolina. Like Atlanta, Columbia was set ablaze, though it is unknown by whom. Sherman blamed retreating Confederates, while Columbia citizens said it was Sherman's drunken soldiers that started the fires.

On the very day Sherman took Columbia, Fort Sumter fell to the Federal navy.

In the Carolinas, only 20,000 Confederates now opposed Sherman's army. Joe Johnston commanded this small body of rebels, keeping just ahead of Sherman as the Federal army advanced into North Carolina. At Bentonville, North Carolina, on March 19, Johnston decided he would attack Sherman's army before the forces of General John Schofield, who was advancing from the sea, reinforced it. Johnston smashed into Sherman's right wing, but, after three days, was forced to withdraw. Now, with only 18,000 men, Johnston withdrew to Raleigh, the capital of North Carolina, to await further developments.

Fall of Richmond

The Confederacy was fast dissolving. Still proclaiming his devotion to states' rights, the governor of Georgia was threatening to secede from the Confederacy and to seek a separate peace with the United States. The governor of North Carolina, too, was unyielding; he had tens of thousands of uniforms which he refused to give up to the Confederate government. Davis was near despair. "If the Confederacy falls," he said, "there should be written on its tombstone: Died of a Theory"—the right to secession.

The military situation was grim. In front of Petersburg, Grant kept extending his trenches to the left, and Lee, to keep from being flanked, was forced to extend to the right. But while Grant had 125,000 men, Lee's force had dwindled to a mere 35,000. Daily, men were deserting the Confederate lines. Some left because hunger and want threatened their families back home; others, because hunger and want had reduced them to desperation or despair. Those that remained had to man trench works spanning 53 miles. By late March 1865, these men formed a skeleton force.

Lee asked the Confederate government for more men and supplies, but there was none it could give. Lee next asked Congress to reconsider a plan it had rejected the year before—to recruit black slaves into the Confederate army. Grant them their freedom, if they will serve, said Lee, and see if they will fight for us instead of our enemies. Moved by Lee's appeal, on March 13 the congress approved a call for the enlistment of 300,000 black soldiers. Soon, black recruits were training with white soldiers in the streets of Richmond.

It was, however, too little, too late. Lee knew he couldn't hold out at Petersburg much longer. His one hope to save his army would be to join Joe Johnston in the hills of North Carolina. To do that, Lee had to punch a hole through Grant's lines, and on March 25, he ordered General John Gordon to do just that. Gordon was at first successful, but then he was driven back. On April 1, Federal cavalry and infantry under Phil Sheridan, rounding Lee's flank, met and routed a Confederate division led by George Pickett. Grant now understood the weakness of Lee's army and ordered a general assault on the Confederate trenches for the next day at 4:30 a.m.

Though they doggedly defended their lines, the Confederates could not withstand the Federal assault that Sunday morning, April 2. Grant's men overran the Confederate trenches, killing the defenders, some of whom were old men and boys as young as 14. A.P. Hill, one of Lee's trusted generals, died in this assault, shot through the heart.

That morning, while he attended service at St. Paul's Episcopal church in Richmond, Jefferson Davis received a note from the parish sexton. As he read, the president's face grew pale. It was from General Lee: "My lines are broken in three places. Richmond must be evacuated this evening."

Davis ordered the records of the Confederate government collected and placed in rail cars; the government would remove to Danville, 140 miles south, from where it would continue the struggle. That evening, as the last train pulled out of Richmond with the president and his cabinet on board, retreating Confederates set fire to the city while mobs plundered

A stereo photograph of two women in black in ruined Richmond, April 1865

and ransacked buildings. Confederate Admiral Raphael Semmes destroyed the Confederate fleet on the James River, while, in the city, fire consumed the Confederate States' arsenal, setting off rounds of explosions.

The next day, April 3, Federal troops marched into a ruined, smoking Richmond. Blacks swarmed into the streets, jubilantly greeting their deliverers. That day, President Lincoln with his son, Tad, arrived by steamer. As Lincoln walked through the streets of the former Confederate capital, black people surrounded him, weeping, dancing, crying out in joyful shouts, straining to touch him. "I know I am free for I have seen Father Abraham and felt him," cried one man. The president seeing some of the men kneeling before him, said, "Don't kneel to me. You must kneel to God only, and thank Him for your freedom."

Retreat to Appomattox

Having abandoned Petersburg, Lee's army was moving southwestward, along the Appomattox River. On April 3, they reached Amelia Courthouse, where Lee had expected to find supplies and the Richmond troops waiting for him; but nothing and no one were there. He spent a day there, combing the neighborhood for food. The next day, assailed by Federals (for Grant's infantry and cavalry under Meade and Sheridan followed him), Lee continued on, now moving further westward to round Grant's flank. Everyday, discouraged soldiers, tired of hunger and the threat of death, threw down their arms and deserted. Some, unarmed, continued to follow Lee; others the Yankees captured, too tired and dispirited to resist.

At Sayler's Creek, on April 6, Sheridan and Meade attacked Lee's ranks, overwhelming the rear guard. Lee lost 8,000 men, nearly a third of his army. The next day, Grant sent a message to Lee, telling him that the fall of Petersburg "must convince you of the hopelessness of further resistance." To save himself from the "responsibility of any further effusion of blood," Grant asked Lee to surrender his army. Lee wondered what "the country" would think if he surrendered, to which his aide replied, "Country be damned! There is no country. There has been no country, for a year or more. You're the country to these men." Though his numbers were dwindling, Lee replied to Grant that it was not yet time to surrender.

Marching west as he was, toward Lynchburg, Lee had little hope of ever joining Johnston. His path merely led to the mountains where, if he desired, he and his men could continue the struggle as guerrilla warriors. There, for long years, they could harry Federal cavalry, who would ravage the land in search of them. Such a prospect did not appeal to Lee. Still, as long as there was hope, he would continue. At Appomattox Courthouse, he knew, supplies from Lynchburg awaited his starving troops. If only he could get there before Grant.

It was Sheridan who spoiled this last hope. The hard-fighting general, astride his horse Rienzi, arrived at Appomattox Courthouse before Lee and captured the supplies. With Sheridan now before him, and Meade advancing behind him, Lee was trapped. But, still, he would not give up without one last fight. He sent General Gordon to break through Sheridan's lines. On April 9, Gordon struck, pushing union cavalry from their position; but then, mounting a hilltop, Gordon saw despair. Before him, line upon line, stretched a sea of unconquerable blue. There was no escape that way but death.

Lee would not needlessly sacrifice his men. "There is nothing left for me to do but go and see General Grant," said Lee to his aide, "and I would rather die a thousand deaths." His aide replied, "What would history say?" To which, Lee: "But that is not the question, Colonel; the question is, is it right to surrender this army? If it is right, then I will take all the responsibility."

A white towel on a stick preceded the Confederate messenger across the Yankee lines. A horseman, waving his hat, delivered a note to General Grant. He opened it and asked an aide to read it. He read the note: Lee would surrender, it said. "No one looked his comrade in the face," noted an eyewitness of the scene. "Finally, Colonel Duff, chief of Artillery, sprang upon a log [proposing three cheers]. A feeble hurrah came from a few throats, when all broke down in tears."

Lee and Grant met at the house of Wilmer McClean at Appomattox Courthouse. McLean had moved from his house in Northern Virginia when it had become the center of a great battle, the First Battle of Manasses. Now, in McClean's parlor, the war would end. At two separate tables sat Grant and Lee, two very different men. Lee, dressed in his pressed dress uniform, gloves and with ceremonial sword, looked as if he would attend a ball; Grant, in mud-spattered pants and boots, and wearing a private's dirty shirt, looked as if he had just ridden through the night, as indeed he had. Lee showed no emotion, noted Grant, but sat, "a man of much dignity" and "impassible face."

Even though he could demand harsh terms, Grant was kind and generous. He reminded Lee that they had met once before during the Mexican war. (Legend has it that Lee had

Surrender and capitulation of Lee at Appomattox

upbraided Grant for his slovenly appearance.) Lee noted that he could not remember Grant's face. "Our conversation grew so pleasant," said Grant, "that I almost forgot the object of our meeting . . . General Lee called my attention to the object."

Grant's terms were generous. No unconditional surrender. Lee's men, he said, could keep their side arms, their personal possessions, and their horses, for it was the time for spring planting. "Each officer and man will be allowed to return to his home, not to be disturbed by the United States authorities," as long as they were peaceful and kept the laws. Grant said he would provide rations for Lee's men, and the two commanders signed the terms of capitulation. Then standing, they shook hands. Lee mounted Traveller and returned to his men. When Federal soldiers began to cheer, Grant angrily checked them: these men are again "our countrymen," he said. "We do not want to exult over their downfall."

Lee rode back to his camp, his head sunk upon his breast. But hearing his men cheer, "he raised his head," said one observer, "and hat in hand he passed by, his face flushed, his eye ablaze." As he rode by, some gently stroked the sides of Traveller, and all cheers turned to weeping in his wake. One old man, a veteran of battles, cried out, "I love you just as well as ever, General."

Lee passed into his tent; the Army of Northern Virginia, into legend.

Assassination

In Washington, fireworks displays punctuated the news of Lee's surrender. Lights shone in the windows of the White House and of government buildings, and the dome of the illumined capitol flamed in triumph over the city. Crowds gathered around the White House, hoping to hear a speech from the president; but when Lincoln came out on the balcony, he asked only that the band play "Dixie." "We fairly captured [the song] yesterday," said Lincoln. "It is our lawful prize."

Lincoln promised the crowd that he would deliver a speech the following evening.

But, if the crowds that gathered the next evening in the White House grounds came to hear the president give a rousing victory speech, they were disappointed. Lincoln spoke, instead, on the reconstruction of the southern states after the war, their reintegration in the union. In 1863, he had enacted a reconstruction program for the conquered areas of Louisiana—a program, he thought, that might prove a model for the other states once the "rebellion" was over. This plan specified that if 10 percent of the people of Louisiana swore allegiance to the union, they could establish a state government and constitution. In Louisiana, Lincoln said, 12,000 people had done this. They had adopted a new state government and a new constitution; they had approved emancipation; they had established public schools for both whites and blacks; and they had empowered their legislature to grant the franchise to blacks. What's more, the Louisiana legislature had approved the 13th Amendment to the Constitution. In January 1865, Congress had approved the amendment, which would abolish slavery throughout the United States.

Lincoln admitted he had hoped for more. He had hoped that reconstructed Louisianans would simply give the franchise to the blacks, not merely authorize the legislature to do so. Yet, he was satisfied enough with the results. "These twelve thousand persons," he said, "are . . . fully committed to the Union, and to perpetual freedom in the state—committed to the very things, and nearly all the things, the nation wants—and they ask the nation's recognition and its assistance to make good their committal."

If only Congress would recognize them—if only Congress would agree to sit representatives from Louisiana, the country might be well on the way to reconciliation. Yet, Lincoln lamented, there were those in Congress, of his own party, who favored extreme measures and desired to punish the southern states more. Lincoln said he could not approve of their

The last photograph of Abraham Lincoln, by Abraham Gardner, April 9, 1865

spirit of vengeance, though he did agree with their goal—the union of the country and the full inclusion of blacks as citizens.

Lincoln had wanted a full reconciliation, without malice. He had even proposed that Congress appropriate $400 million to compensate slave holders for their loss in "property." His cabinet had rejected this proposal, and in their meeting, held Good Friday, April 14, 1865, Secretary Stanton was proposing his own plan for reconstruction: military governments in all the states, with self-government to follow, and the delay of black suffrage. Lincoln gave his tentative approval to Stanton's plan, saying that he hoped self-government might be reestablished in the southern states by December. Until the next cabinet meeting, which would be the following Tuesday, Lincoln said cabinet members should study the matter.

Meanwhile, John Wilkes Booth, deeply depressed over the news of Lee's surrender, heard that that Good Friday evening, Mr. and Mrs. Lincoln, with General and Mrs. Ulysses S. Grant, were to attend a performance of the English comedy, *Our American Cousin*, at Ford's Theater. Booth reflected that, as an actor, he had access to the backstage of the theater. Kidnapping had failed; but, there was assassination. Lincoln and Grant taken down together, and Booth the hero-avenger of his country's honor!

That evening, Mr. and Mrs. Lincoln arrived late to the play. The Grants had not come but instead had taken a train to Philadelphia. When the president and the first lady entered the presidential box, the play stopped long enough for the orchestra to play, "Hail to the Chief." Then the play resumed. Mrs. Lincoln, her hand in her husband's, noticed that he seemed to enjoy the comedy well.

Booth was in a local bar, drinking brandy. He had gathered his conspirators; while he struck at the president, they would take care of the vice-president, Andrew Johnson, and Secretary Stanton. As he contemplated the fearful act he planned, Booth poured himself some more brandy.

When he arrived at the theater, Booth asked a scene-shifter to hold his horse. He climbed the steps to the presidential box, a derringer in his right hand, and a dagger in his left. On the stage, a woman had accused the "American Cousin," Asa Trenchard, of being ignorant of the manners of good society. "Don't know the manners of good society, eh?" said the coarse Trenchard, "Well, I guess I know enough to turn you inside out, you sockdoligizing old man-trap . . ."

A roar of laughter rose. It was Booth's signal. Leaping into the box, he fired his derringer, point-blank, into the back of Lincoln's head, slashed at one of the president's party with his dagger, and jumped to the stage below, breaking his left leg in his fall. Waving his dagger, Booth shouted to the astonished audience the motto of Old Virginia, *Sic semper tyrannis!* ("Thus always to tyrants!") Then, stumbling off, he mounted his horse and rode away.

Soldiers carried Lincoln to a nearby boarding house. There he lay, unconscious, the bullet lodged behind his right eye. At the head of the bed stood his son, Robert, bearing himself well but occasionally breaking down into sobs. The end was not long delayed. The next morning, April 15, 1865, at 7:22 a.m., Abraham Lincoln passed from this life.

Final Surrender

The war was not yet over. Scattered bands of Confederates still held on in Tennessee and along the Gulf and in the West, across the Mississippi. Near Raleigh, North Carolina, Joe Johnston was contemplating how he might surrender his 18,000 infantry. When he met President Davis at Greensboro, Johnston said that "it would be the greatest of human crimes for us to continue the war." He told Davis he should "exercise at once the only function of government still in his possession and open negotiations for peace." Davis told Johnston that

John Wilkes Booth leaps from the presidential box with knife in hand. The print inaccurately depicts Lincoln standing.

the Federals would not recognize his authority. He told Johnston to treat with Sherman for an honorable peace.

Davis would not surrender. He was fleeing south by rail, hoping to be able to reach Texas where he and his cabinet could form an effective center of resistance. But he was not naïve. As his train steamed southward toward Georgia, a fellow traveler remarked that the Confederate cause was lost. "It appears so," replied the weary but resolute Davis. "But the principle for which we contended is bound to reassert itself, though it may be at another time and in another form."

That time was not then. On April 17, two days after Lincoln's death, Johnston and Sherman met at a little log cabin outside Durham, North Carolina. Implacable in war, Sherman proved magnanimous in peace. Both he and Johnston worried that the war might degenerate into a guerrilla struggle. The next day, Confederate secretary of war, John C. Breckenridge joined the two generals, and they signed a treaty that called for a generous reconciliation between the warring sections.

Sherman's treaty allowed Confederate soldiers, from the Atlantic to beyond the Mississippi, to return home with their weapons, which they would deposit at their state capitals. There the weapons might remain so the states could defend themselves against rebel guerrilla insurgents. State governments should be reorganized, said the treaty, once state officers then holding office should swear allegiance to the Constitution of the United States. The treaty also guaranteed southerners "their political rights and franchises, as well as the rights of person and property as defined by the Constitution of the United States and of the states respectively." Andrew Johnson, who had succeeded Lincoln as president, rejected this treaty, which was more conciliatory even than Lincoln's proposals for reconstruction. The new president told Grant that Johnston must surrender under the same terms given to Lee. On April 26, Sherman met with Johnston again, and the Confederate general signed the new terms of surrender.

West of the Appalachians, Pap Thomas' army was stamping out the last sparks of Confederate resistance. His cavalry corps under James H. Wilson had defeated Bedford Forrest and then had swung into Georgia. At Irwindale, Georgia, on May 10, Wilson captured Jefferson Davis. The Confederate president was sent, a prisoner, to Fortress Monroe in Virginia.

West of the Mississippi, in Shreveport, Louisiana, Confederate General Edmund Kirby Smith had determined on continued resistance. For some weeks, citizens meetings in Texas called for the enlistment of all males, black and white, and the arming of women. On May 13, about 100 Federals, blacks and whites, clashed with a small force of Confederates at Palmito Ranch, near Brownsville, Texas. It was the last Confederate victory—and the last battle of the war. Thirteen days later, Edmund Kirby Smith surrendered the Confederate Trans-Mississippi army to General Canby at Baton Rouge.

A desolate silence now reigned from Texas to Virginia. The bloody fratricidal war was done.

Chapter 18 Review

Summary

- Northerners were growing weary of the war and wanted to let the South go its own way. Fathers and newspapers encouraged soldiers to desert. Lincoln thought such opposition required stern measures, and on January 1, 1862, he ordered suspension of *habeas corpus* throughout the North. All who openly encouraged resistance to enlistment or disloyalty were subject to martial law.

- Southerners had quarrels with their own president, Jefferson Davis, who, apart from the conscription act, attempted to manage the war down to the last detail. In 1864, Davis asked Congress to suspend the writ of *habeas corpus*. The Confederate congress voted heavy taxes on the people of the South. The military requisitioned crops and impressed slaves; and prices went up in the cities.

- In May 1863, Lee defeated Hooker at Chancellorsville and lost Stonewall Jackson.

- Grant attempted to capture Vicksburg but was beaten back. Davis was worried and urged Lee to send General Longstreet to relieve Vicksburg. Lee had what he thought was a better idea: he would invade the North.

- In late May 1863, the Army of Northern Virginia commenced its invasion of the North. At Gettysburg, Lee was defeated by the Federal army under General Meade.

- On July 4, 1863, Vicksburg fell to Grant after a long siege. The Federals now controlled the Mississippi River, and the South was divided in half.

- In March 1864, General Grant took on the rank of Lieut. General of all the Federal forces. In May, he commenced his campaign against Lee and the Army of Northern Virginia. The campaign ended in Grant laying siege to Petersburg, Virginia, a siege that lasted ten months.

- William Tecumseh Sherman took Atlanta on September 1–2, 1864. General Sheridan drove the Confederates out of the Shenandoah Valley in Virginia and laid waste to it. Because of these victories, Lincoln was reelected in 1864.

- After burning one-third of Atlanta, Sherman marched towards the sea and the seacoast town of Savannah, where he could reestablish contact with the North. Along the way he laid waste to the countryside. He captured Savannah on December 22, 1864.

- From Savannah, Sherman marched into South Carolina, devastating it as he had Georgia. He captured Columbia, the capital of South Carolina, on February 17, 1865. The same day Fort Sumter fell to the Federal navy.

- With only a skeleton of his army left, Lee asked the Confederate government to induct black slaves. On March 13 the congress approved a call for the enlistment of 300,000 black soldiers.

- On April 2, 1865, Grant's forces overran Lee's trenches before Petersburg. As the Confederate government removed to Danville, Grant's army captured Richmond.

- On April 6, 1865, after a battle at Sayler's Creek in which Lee lost nearly a third of his army, Grant sent him a message asking him to surrender his army. Lee refused. Enroute to Appomattox Court House, Lee, cut off by Sheridan in front and Meade behind,

Chapter 18 Review (continued)

decided to meet with Grant. On April 9, Lee and Grant met at Appomattox Courthouse, and Lee surrendered his army.

- John Wilkes Booth, a southern partisan, was determined to assassinate both Lincoln and Grant. While the president was enjoying a play at Ford's Theater in Washington, Booth shot him in the back of the head. Lincoln died the next morning, April 15, 1865.

- On April 17, 1865, Johnston and Sherman, joined by Confederate secretary of war, John C. Breckenridge, signed a peace treaty that called for a generous reconciliation between the North and the South.

Key Concepts

Copperheads: the name given to northerners who favored letting the southern states go their own way and who were said to sympathize with the cause of the South

Jayhawkers: irregular troops who terrorized southern sympathizers in Missouri

Bushwackers: irregular troops who terrorized northern sympathizers in Kansas

Dates to Remember

1863: the Emancipation Proclamation goes into effect (January 1).

The battle of Gettysburg (July)

Lincoln delivers the Gettysburg Address (November 19).

1864: Grant begins his campaign against Lee in Virginia.

Sherman captures Atlanta (September 1).

Lincoln is reelected.

Sherman captures Savannah (December).

1865: Sherman captures Columbia, the capital of South Carolina (February).

Grant captures Richmond (April).

Lee surrenders his army to Grant (April 9).

John Wilkes Booth assassinates Lincoln (April 14).

Johnston and Sherman sign a peace treaty (April 17).

1865: Last battle of the Civil War at Palmito Ranch, Texas (May 13)

Central Characters

George Meade (1815–1872): American army officer who defeated Lee's army at Gettysburg, Pennsylvania

George Edward Pickett (1825–1875): Confederate army officer who led "Pickett's Charge" at the Battle of Gettysburg

William Tecumseh Sherman (1820–1891): the Federal general who captured Atlanta and Savannah in Georgia and Columbia, in South Carolina

Ulysses S. Grant (1822–1885): Lieut. General in command over the entire U.S. army

John Wilkes Booth (1838–1865): American actor who assassinated President Abraham Lincoln

Questions for Review

1. Why were people in the North growing weary of the war and encouraging soldiers to desert?

2. What hardships did the Confederate government and army place on the people of the South during the course of the war? How did these hardships affect the course of the war?

3. What was Lee's objective in his invasion of the North?

4. Explain the significance of the battle of Gettysburg to the war.

5. Explain the significance of the capture of Vicksburg to the Confederate war effort.

6. Briefly summarize the ideas Lincoln presented in his Gettysburg Address. Have they been influential?

7. Considering that Lee was against slavery and secession, why did he fight for the Confederacy?

8. Why was Sherman so ruthless in his campaigns in Georgia and South Carolina?

9. Describe the main ideas of Lincoln's proposed reconstruction of the South.

10. What was Booth's motivation for assassinating Lincoln?

Chapter 18 Review (continued)

Ideas in Action

1. Listen to the songs and music of both the North and the South created during the war. Discuss how these songs embody the spirit and the ideas of each side.

2. Read and discuss the Gettysburg Address. How do Lincoln's ideas of America and the union reflect those expressed by Daniel Webster in his speeches? Do Lincoln's ideas of America influence Americans in our own day?

Highways and Byways

The Bank Note of the South

The dollar currency of the Confederate States of American was issued just before the start of the American Civil War by the newly formed Confederate government. Unlike the United States dollar, the Confederate denomination was not backed by hard assets but by a promise to pay the bearer after the war. This promise of course banked on the prospect of southern victory and independence. This worked for a while, until the war began to go against the Confederates. When that happened, confidence in Confederate currency waned, producing inflation. By the end of the war, the currency was practically worthless.

The Confederate dollar, or "Greyback," is now a prized collector's item. There are many versions of the Greyback, due to the lack of skilled engravers, printers, and secure printing facilities. Some bills portray engravings of leading Confederates, historical figures, or images of slaves, while others depict images of gods and goddesses. Since there were many different types of Confederate notes, and since banks could issue their own notes, counterfeiting became a problem in the Confederate states. These counterfeits, however, are just as valuable to a collector today as a genuine Confederate bank note.

LIBERALISM TRIUMPHS IN MEXICO

Divisions that Run too Deep

The war with the United States had exhausted Mexico. The sure sign of this was that from 1848 to 1853 there were no revolutions. In 1848, the *moderado* Congress restored José Joaquin Herrera as president. He held office until 1850, when General Mariano Arista (who had lost Matamoros to Taylor in the Mexican-American War) was elected. The transition from Herrera to Arista was peaceful—the first peaceful transition since Guadalupe Victoria took office in 1823. It would be the last for many years.

It seemed Mexico's constitution, the Constitution of 1824, was insufficient to combat the chaos into which the country had fallen. Mexico did not need a weak, republican instrument of government at a time when states, and regions within states, were hurling away from the center. Despite the fact that both Presidents Herrera and Arista made considerable strides in improving Mexico's finances and foreign debt situation, their country was breaking into small and yet smaller states. Districts seceded from states to form new states; local caciques (political leaders) interpreted laws and made laws as they saw fit; and politicians sold themselves out for bribes. At the same time, commerce was dead, and in the capital police had the duty of clearing away the dead bodies of those who had died of starvation, while troops quartered in the city pillaged and plundered at will.

Throughout the country, peace and security were wistful dreams. Far to the south, in Yucatán, one-half of the population had died because of a brutal war between Mayan Indians and local *hacendados*. In the far north, Indian tribes from Texas and Arizona raided Mexican settlements, brutally murdering the populace. As bad were the Anglo-American filibusters, who hoped to stir up revolt along the borders. From north to south, bandits infested the countryside.

Santa Ana

What Mexico needed, thought the aged conservative, Lucas Alamán, was order—and order imposed by a powerful, central authority. Preferably, this should be a foreign prince, some scion of the houses of Habsburg or Bourbon; and such a prince Alamán and other conservatives sought to get. They negotiated with the Spanish court in Madrid but were told that they needed, first, to take control of Mexico's government. For that the conservatives needed a stopgap, some dictator who would impose order and maintain it until the hoped-for prince should come.

But whom should they choose for their dictator? Alamán was no fool, nor was he corrupt; but he could discover no one who could summon up the authority necessary to act as dictator, except one man—and this man was a gamble, and Alamán despised him. Still, in the end, it was the old war-horse, Antonio López de Santa Anna, that the desperate conservatives chose for their leader. In January 1853, in a *coup d'etat,* they overthrew Arista, and in April Santa Anna returned from exile in Venezuela for his last fling on the national stage.

With Lucas Alamán as head of his cabinet, Santa Anna got off to a fairly good start. Plans were laid for the building of roads and telegraphs and for colonizing new lands. The army grew to 90,000, and Spanish and Prussian officers came over from Europe to drill and train the men. A purge against Liberals was most thorough—soldiers removed Liberal governors, Liberal newspapers were suppressed, while Liberal leaders sought refuge in New Orleans.

"In your hands," Alamán told Santa Anna, "lies the happiness of the fatherland." Alamán was ailing. Having finished his great work, *Historia de Mexico* (for which he is chiefly remembered), the old conservative died on June 2, 1853.

With Alamán gone, Santa Anna laid his hands on the happiness of the fatherland. Taking the title, "His Most Supreme Highness," he resumed his old, dissolute ways, giving concessions of money to friends and thus depleting the treasury; outfitting himself with uniformed escorts, "Lancers of the Guard of the Supreme Powers"; wallowing in pleasures, and raping the resources of the fatherland.

The conservatives' gamble had failed. They had misread the man and the times, for their Liberal foes were of a new generation: sterner, harder, more relentless. The conservatives had proved too conservative and were unprepared to meet the struggle that was to come.

Clericals and Anti-Clericals

It had been over 40 years since Hidalgo's *grito* had shattered the peace of New Spain. And with the change of years came a change in Mexican Liberalism. The old Liberals believed in constitutional government; they believed in decentralized government; they favored *laissez-faire* in economics—the insistence on private and of unrestrained economic activity. While some, like Valentín Gómez Farías, had called for the secularization of Church lands as well as the secularization of schools, many Liberals wanted to maintain the Catholic faith as the sole religion of Mexico and, like Morelos, professed themselves devout Catholics.

The new generation of Mexican Liberals had studied in secular schools and, instead of belonging to one of the creole families, were of the rising *mestizo* class. Just as the creoles had coveted the political power of the *gauchupines,* so now the *mestizos* desired to possess the political power that accorded with their place in the population—after all, weren't they the majority? So it was that many *mestizos* turned their eyes on the wide Church lands as a source of new wealth for themselves. With land they could achieve the age-old Spanish dream of *hidalguería*—the life of the landed gentry. Many local caciques joined the Liberal ranks, for a weak, decentralized national government would not interfere with the power they wielded in their region.

But there were those who had an idealistic devotion to Liberal doctrines and did not espouse them merely for reasons of self-interest. They saw Mexico as a land locked in the past, a medieval anachronism in a dynamic, progressive world. The chief obstacles to progress, they believed, were the Church and the military that with their *fueros* (traditional privileges) retarded individual enterprise and true political reform. Some of the more radical faulted the Church for the "superstitions" by which, they said, the priesthood controlled the people through fear. These "anti-clericals" thought that if Mexico were to take her place in the family of nations, she must free individuals from the structures that restricted their enterprise and freedom. Thus, both the military and the Church must be brought under the control of the state. The state alone would direct all society toward the proper secular good.

Among these more principled Liberals was the governor of Michoacán, Melchor Ocampo, a scholar and scientist and a disciple of French radical thinkers, including Rousseau and Voltaire. Another was Ocampo's friend, Santos Degollado, who served in Ocampo's government and was professor of law in Morelia. A third was the governor of Oaxaca, Benito Juárez. A Zapotec Indian, Juárez did not speak Spanish until the age of 12. After going to Oaxaca as a servant, Juárez attracted the attention of a wealthy creole patron, who sent the boy to school to study for the priesthood. Deciding he had no vocation, Juárez turned to law. As governor of Oaxaca, he was known for his honesty, efficiency, and for his simple, democratic manners. His short stature, his reserved and quiet demeanor, hid the power that would raise him to leadership among the Liberals.

In Mexico City, intellectuals and artists founded an academy to encourage the development of a peculiarly Mexican literature, for which they chose an old revolutionary, Andrés Quintana Roo, honorary president. Politics was among the interests of these men, who spoke of literature and in the cafés of the city laughed at creoles. Guillermo Prieto, who would become Mexico's national poet, held forth as much on Liberal politics as on poetry. Ignacio Ramírez, who glorified Mexico's Aztec past, spewed venom on her Catholic present.

The conservatives, or "clericals," as they came to be called for their support of the Church, are usually characterized as representing the generals, the wealthy creoles, and the clergy; but as the character of Liberal policies became clearer through their effect on the lower classes, many Indians flocked to the conservative standard. The conservatives stood for centralized authority, the maintenance of the hacienda system, and the preservation of military and ecclesiastical *fueros.* It is not unusual for historians to portray the conservatives or clericals as selfish oppressors or as men whose only interest was to maintain their status in society and to keep the poor man down. One cannot be so naïve as to deny the entire truth of such charges, but neither can he accept so simple a portrayal of a cause that stirred men to their depths and for which they gave their lives. Men's motives are often mixed, and every good cause attracts unworthy adherents.

Melchor Ocampo

As we explained in Chapter 12, Mexican society enshrined characteristics of the Spanish society from which it sprang. *Fueros,* or traditional rights, were accorded not only to the Church and to the military, but also to cities and, even, in a sense, to the Indians. Under Spain, Indians were immune from prosecution under the Inquisition, and tribes held *ejidos,* or corporately held lands, as a perpetual right. Towns, too, held corporate lands, as did the Church. The hacienda was a kind of personal domain where the *hacendado,* as a quasi-independent lord, governed the Indians under his care. *As conceived,* the hacienda was an attempt to establish a working relationship between two very different cultures. *As practiced,* however, it was subject to many abuses.

To a modern American, it may seem strange that the Church would fight doggedly to maintain control of land, mere real estate. Is not the Church a spiritual institution? Indeed, it can be documented all too well that, in holding lands and political power (for the Church had haciendas), some churchmen fell into sins of greed, covetousness, exploitation of the poor, and sordid worldliness. It was not unusual for priests to charge, sometimes exorbitantly, for administering the sacraments, especially marriage. Yet, the Church fought for a principle when it contended that the state had no right to seize Church property. That principle was that the state does not have authority over the Church, that the Church is not the subject or the servant of the state. The Church could divest herself, if she wished, of lands and money—*temporalities,* as they were called; but no human institution had the authority to force the Church to make such a concession. The Church in Mexico was fighting for her independence and sovereignty.

Guillermo Prieto

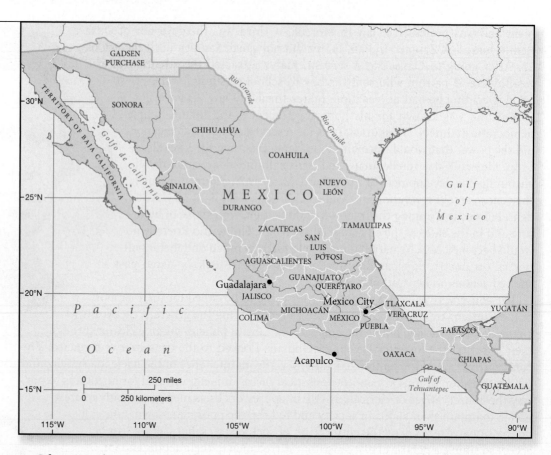

The Republic of Mexico, after 1848

Of course, the situation in Mexico was complicated by the fact that, under the Spanish *patronato real,* the king held a good deal of control over the Church and its lands; so, it did not seem out of the ordinary for the state not only to determine *how* Church lands were to be used but *whether* the Church should own land. There was, however, no transference to the Mexican government by Rome or Madrid of the *patronato;* and, furthermore, as we shall see, unlike the Spanish king, the Liberals claimed jurisdiction over more than just the Church's temporalities.

The Liberals wanted to eradicate from society any intermediate bodies between the state and the individual. They wanted the state to be not only the highest but the only real authority in society. In this way, they thought, individuals would be free to pursue each his own good without hindrance. At its best, Mexican conservatism was a defense of an older order of society where groups in society had rights with which the state could not interfere.

Revolution of Ayutla

Santa Anna's suppression of Liberals forced many of them into exile in New Orleans. Melchor Ocampo was there, working as a potter, as was Benito Juárez, who found employment as a cigarette roller. But from the south came news that would draw them back to Mexico. *Guerrilleros* in the state of Guerrero had risen against His Most Supreme Highness. Juan Álvarez, who had fought with Morelos, led the rebels, along with the creole Ignacio Comonfort, whom Santa Anna had dismissed as collector of customs at Acapulco. In March 1854, the rebel leaders issued the *Plan de Ayutla,* which called for a temporary dictatorship of the leader of the revolutionary forces, to be followed by a free election.

Santa Anna's attempt to crush the rebellion was not impressive. Álvarez's *guerrilleros* slowly withdrew before the dictator's advancing army. At Acapulco, Comonfort refused to surrender, so Santa Anna contented himself with burning Indian villages and shooting Liberals. He then returned to the capital, proclaiming victory. Meanwhile, the money in the treasury was nearly depleted, and the Church would give Santa Anna no money; so, the dictator turned to the United States for help. Though the United States government supported the Liberals (Comonfort received supplies from the north), it could not pass up the opportunity to gain more territory. On December 30, 1853, Santa Anna had agreed to sell the Mesilla Valley (now southern Arizona) to the United States for a sum of $10 million. The Gadsden Purchase (named for James Gadsden, ambassador to Mexico), which went into effect on June 30, 1854, allowed Santa Anna to pay his army for at least another year.

But Santa Anna's days were numbered. Santos Degollado was organizing guerrilla bands in Jalisco. Caciques, such as Manuel Doblado in Guanajuato and Santiago Vidaurri in Nuevo León, expelled Santa Anna's officials from their territories. Northern Mexico declared for the *Plan de Ayutla,* and soon the entire east coast joined the revolution. Santa Anna could see that all was up with him. In August 1855, he climbed into his carriage, as if going for a ride, and drove out of Mexico City. At Veracruz he boarded (ironically enough) the ship *Iturbide* and on August 17 set sail for Venezuela.

The conservatives in the capital appointed a president to take Santa Anna's place, but their power base was broken. Juan Álvarez, who as chief of the revolution had organized a Liberal government at Cuernevaca, marched in triumph into Mexico City on November 14, 1855.

The Reform

Forty years as a guerrilla leader did not make Juan Álvarez a statesman. That he was half Indian and half black did not endear him to the populace of Mexico City. A month hadn't passed before Manuel Doblado threatened rebellion against him. In December Álvarez resigned, and Ignacio Comonfort became president.

Though allied with the extreme Liberals, Comonfort was a moderate at heart. Hating war and desiring peace above all, he hoped to win over conservatives to his government. This was impossible, however, for Comonfort's government had inherited Álvarez's minister of justice, Benito Juárez. Before Álvarez had left office, Juárez had issued a set of laws, the *Ley Juárez,* which restricted cases tried by ecclesiastical courts to members of the clergy. Before, certain wealthy creoles had obtained the privilege to be tried in Church courts. The *Ley Juárez,* which also attacked military *fueros,* had contributed to Álvarez's downfall.

The *Ley Juárez* was mild, and somewhat reasonable. What followed proved far worse. Under the conciliating Comonfort, Juárez was working for a complete overthrow of traditional Mexican society. This "Reform," as it came to be called, showed its radicalism with the issuance of the *Ley Lerdo* in June 1856. Inspired by Juárez and drafted by Miguel Lerdo de Tejada, the *Ley Lerdo* was an attempt to spur economic progress and increase government revenues by the secularization and sale of Church lands. According to the law, the Church was, henceforth, forbidden to own land, and all lands held by the Church were to be sold. Though the proceeds of the sales would go to the Church, the *Ley Lerdo* placed a heavy sales tax on all transactions, the proceeds of which were to go to the government.

Ley Lerdo, however, did not just target Church lands; it forbade any corporate body to hold land. Henceforth, only individuals were permitted to own property. Cities, thus, had to sell their lands. Even *ejidos,* held by tribes since the time of Cortés, were to be broken up and sold to individuals. The results of all this were disastrous. Though a few secular clergy

Miguel Lerdo de Tejada

bought Church-owned haciendas, most creoles refused to participate in the break-up of Church property. Mostly, it was foreign capitalists from Great Britain, France, Germany, and the United States who could afford Church lands and the taxes attached to their sale; these bought up the lands and so formed a new wealthy ruling class. Many a disappointed *mestizo*, unable to afford Church lands, "denounced" Indian *ejidos* to the government and bought the land for a pittance. In the autumn the government tried to remedy this by ruling that Indian community lands were to be divided amongst members of the tribe, but it did no good. The Indians had no tradition of private ownership—theirs was a system of tribal, communal property ownership; so it proved easy for the unscrupulous to cheat the natives of their land, often after plying them with alcohol.

The secularization of Church lands was to have a dire effect on the economy and society of Mexico. Church haciendas were generally better managed than those owned by lay *hacendado* families, who often squandered their patrimony in two or three generations. Moreover, the revenue from ecclesiastical haciendas did not go merely to enrich churchmen but funded public charities, hospitals, schools, and colleges. The Church also functioned as a sort of bank, loaning money at low rates of interest. Secularization swept away all these benefits.

Ley Lerdo met conservative resistance. In Mexico City, a priest, Francisco Xavier Miranda, formed the *Directorio Conservador Central* and, in disguise, began traveling about the country to coordinate generals and guerrilla leaders in common opposition to Comonfort's government. Throughout the country religious orders such as the Franciscans and the Dominicans refused to accept the new laws, and their monasteries became centers for intrigue and the cache of munitions. In September, Comonfort ordered the destruction of the Convent of San Francisco (built by Cortés) because the friars there opposed the laws. Four hundred workmen assembled around the old convent but were fearful of touching it. Finally, a city councilman took a crowbar and attacked the walls, and goaded by Liberal harangues and stirred by Liberal songs, the workmen began to tear down the ancient structure. The Convent of San Francisco made way for one of the more prosaic works of man—city streets.

Not only creoles, churchmen, and generals protested *Ley Lerdo*; many Indians, seeing the loss of their *ejidos* and the assault on their religion, rose in rebellion. Tomás Mejía, a chieftain from the Sierra Gorda, about 175 miles north of Mexico City, joined Padre Miranda and one Miguel Miramón in seizing control of the city of Santiago, in the state of Querétaro in October 1856. The rebellion spread through San Luis Potosí, Michoacán, Tlaxcala, and the country about Veracruz. Comonfort responded to the rebellion with vigor and by March 1857 peace reigned again in Mexico—though an uncertain peace it was.

Tomás Mejía

A New Constitution

While the clericals raged against the new laws, a convention of mostly moderate creoles and *mestizos* was meeting in Mexico City to draw up a new constitution. Though the U.S.-inspired Constitution of 1824 had proved unworkable in Mexico, most of the convention delegates remained enamored of Anglo-Saxon democracy and wanted another try at imposing it on Mexico. Some, the more radical, however, agreed with delegate Arriaga that it was pointless to impose political reforms without economic reforms. "This people cannot be free or republican, much less prosperous," fulminated Arriaga, "though more than a hundred constitutions and thousands of laws proclaim abstract rights, beautiful but impractical theories, in consequence of the absurd economic system." Arriaga, perhaps, did not consider that imposing a foreign economic system on a country can be as disastrous as imposing an alien political order.

Miguel Miramón

The new constitution, though, did not reflect Arriaga's radicalism. It was merely a revision of the Constitution of 1824; only it further centralized the government. The new constitution abolished the senate (seen as too aristocratic), reducing the congress to one house, which had the power to remove state governors for cause. The constitution gave the supreme court the power to decide state elections and made all federal elections for president indirect—the people would vote for electors (government employees appointed by the president) who would, in turn, vote for the president.

The new constitution enshrined *Ley Lerdo* and *Ley Juárez* and added further anti-clerical laws. According to a provision forbidding **peonage**, the government permitted monks and friars to break their vows. Another provision removed education from the hands of the Church. Delegates hotly debated the question of religious liberty and the place of the Catholic Church in the new order. During these debates spectators filled the galleries, some waving green banners that read, "Long Live Religion, Death to Tolerance!" Others held yellow banners, inscribed with the words, "Down with the Rich Who Fight Liberty of Conscience!" In the end, the constitution contained neither a provision allowing religious liberty nor one establishing the Catholic Church as the religion of Mexico. The constitution was completed in February 1857. Unable to walk by himself, the aged Valentín Gómez Farías, the father of the Liberals, was carried into the chambers to be the first to swear allegiance to the new government. Kneeling, he swore on the Holy Gospels to obey the constitution. This act inspired the fervor of the delegates; they cried out in ovation to the old man, "We swear! We swear!"

But in Querétaro, conservative insurgents issued a *pronunciamento*:

> A handful of men without faith, without religion, without principles, possessed by cruelty and vengeance, breathing death and destruction, have put their heavy foot on the neck of the Mexican nation! They have reversed the order by which societies should be guided, and for more than a year their heavy chains have bound the fatherland. These impious men would take away our Religion, and their foul lips have blasphemed the name of the Almighty. They have insulted our priests and thrown them into jail; they have destroyed our temples and turned them to profane uses. These sacrilegious men, full of avarice, have seized the goods of the Church and have reduced her ministers to beggary. What is worse, they have impiously mocked at the excommunications and anathemas of the Church. They are preparing mourning, bloodshed, devastation, and rapine for the Mexican Nation, and, finally, they will complete our ruin if Divine Providence does not watch over good Mexicans!

And across the ocean, Pope Pius IX added his voice to the condemnation of the Liberal government:

> The Chamber of Deputies, among the many insults it has heaped upon our Most Holy Religion and upon its ministers, as well as upon the Vicar of Christ on Earth, has proposed a new constitution containing many articles, not a few of which conflict with Divine Religion itself, its salutary doctrines, its most holy precepts, and with its rights . . . For the purpose of more easily corrupting manners and propagating the detestable pest of **indifferentism** and tearing souls away from our Most Holy Religion, it allows the free exercise of all thought and opinion. . . . And so that the Faithful who reside there may know, and the Catholic world may understand, that We energetically reprove everything the Mexican government has done against the Catholic Religion, against its Church, its sacred ministers and pastors, and against its laws, rights and properties, We raise our Pontifical voice in apostolic liberty . . . to condemn, reprove, and declare null and void everything the said decrees and everything else that the civil authority has done in scorn of ecclesiastical authority and of this Holy See.

peonage: the condition where a person, called a *peon*, is held to perform labor for another

indifferentism: the belief that people do not have the duty to believe in God by worshiping in and practicing the one true religion

Engraving of Pope Pius IX

In declaring the new anti-clerical laws null and void, the pope implicitly blessed resistance to the government. The Church in Mexico followed Pius and excommunicated all who swore allegiance to the constitution. Bishop Clemente de Jesús Munguia of Michoacán openly condemned provisions of the constitution allowing freedom of the press and federal authority over the clergy, as well as the notion that all governmental authority proceeds from the people, not from God. Canon Antonio Reyere y Lugo called on the people of Puebla to resist "the enemies of Religion who are attacking the independence and sovereignty of the Church."

Canon Reyere ruled Puebla in place of its exiled bishop, Antonio Pelagio Labastida y Dávalos. From Cuba, Bishop Labastida encouraged the resistance and expressed well his and other clericalists' undying opposition to the Liberal order. "I have resolved, not only from today, but since the day of my consecration," wrote the bishop, "to suffer any sacrifice and to undertake, with the grace of God, every trial, rather than violate in the slightest degree my conscience and the solemn vow I have made to God."

The War of the Reform

President Ignacio Comonfort did not like the new constitution. He thought it placed too many strictures on the power of the president. It also placed too many restrictions on the Church, and Comonfort wanted to placate and conciliate the conservatives, not further alienate them. Seeing the president waver, the conservatives tried to win him over to their cause; but Comonfort, now alienated from his own party, would not link his fortunes with his former enemies. He became a man without a party.

In the Autumn of 1857 Comonfort asked the new congress to suspend civil liberties and work on a revision of the constitution. Congress refused. But, in Tacubaya, Félix Zuloaga, a gambling house cashier turned general, thought he would take Comonfort up on his offer. Proclaiming the *Plan de Tacubaya* (a Comonfort dictatorship), Zuloaga captured Mexico City in December. Comonfort adopted the *Plan de Tacubaya*, declared an end to the Constitution of 1857, and allowed Zuloaga to imprison Vice President Benito Juárez. The archbishop and clergy embraced Zuloaga's cause and approved his *Plan*.

Félix Zuloaga

The Liberals in the provinces refused to acquiesce in this *coup d'etat*. Santos Degollado organized an army of resistance in Michoacán and Jalisco. Seventy members of congress, who had fled Mexico City, gathered in Querétaro and declared that, since Comonfort had turned traitor, the imprisoned Juárez, as vice president, was now president. Confronted with this resistance, Comonfort changed his mind, released Juárez, and gathered an army to resist Zuloaga. But when desertions left him with an army of only 550 men, on January 21, 1858, Comonfort fled into exile in the United States.

Declared president by the conservatives, Zuloaga repealed the reform laws and marshaled clericalist generals to resist the Liberals. Meanwhile, in Querétaro, Juárez claimed the presidency and fled to Guadalajara, where, in March, Zuloaga's troops captured him. Juárez would then and there have died by firing squad had not the poet Gabriel Prieto intervened. Crying, "brave men do not assassinate," Prieto thrust himself between the firing squad and their target. The soldiers, lowering their rifles, relented, and Juárez escaped to the Pacific coastal town of Manzanillo.

Juárez appointed Santos Degollado general of the armies in the west and then took ship to Panama. From Panama he sailed by way of Havana to New Orleans, and from thence, to Veracruz. In Veracruz, Juarez organized his cabinet, which included the leading Liberals Melchor Ocampo, Guillermo Prieto, Ignacio Ramírez, and the brothers Lerdo de Tejada—Miguel and Sebastián.

Meanwhile, the conservative forces were coalescing their resistance under the Indian chieftain Tomás Mejía, the chivalrous general Miguel Miramón, and the brutal Leonardo Márquez. The year 1858 witnessed mostly conservative victories. Miramón and Márquez drove the Liberal general Santiago Vidaurri, from Nuevo León and occupied San Luis Potosí. Thence they marched against Degollado, and Márquez captured Guadalajara, while Miramón subjugated the Pacific coast. Liberal caciques, forced into the mountains, carried on guerrilla warfare against their conservative foes.

But divisions now appeared among the conservatives. In December 1858, troops in Mexico City overthrew Zuloaga, who had lost the confidence of the clergy, and Miguel Miramón became president. Two months later, President Miramón marched on Veracruz to drive out the Liberals and so gain the customs duties that flowed in through that port. But he was unable to capture that well-defended city and withdrew to save his men from yellow fever. While Miramón was withdrawing from Veracruz, the Liberal General Degollado moved on Mexico City, but he delayed at Tacubaya and Chapultepec. There General Márquez joined battle with him on April 11, 1859 and in four hours decimated the Liberal army. After the battle, Márquez not only ordered, by Miramón's command, the execution of all captured officers but went beyond the president's command and killed all of the prisoners, including a group of medical students who had come to care for the wounded on the battlefield. For his brutality, Márquez became known as the "Tiger of Tacubaya."

Initially, the conservatives had most of the advantages in funding and personnel. They had the better, more experienced generals. The Church, stripping sanctuaries of all rich ornament save for the sacred vessels, provided them money. The Liberals, however, controlled the customs duties coming through the port of Veracruz—and these monies would continue to flow when the Church's riches were exhausted. The Liberals also had tenacious leaders who were not discouraged by defeat.

In July, Juárez, wanting a share of the Church's wealth and wishing to strike a powerful blow against the enemy, issued the Laws of the Reform. Drafted by Miguel Lerdo de Tejada, the Laws of Reform ordered the complete confiscation of all Church lands, the immediate suppression of all men's monasteries, and planned the gradual demise of women's monasteries and convents by forbidding the entrance of new sisters. Juárez struck at marriage by defining it as merely a civil contract instead of acknowledging it as a sacrament. Unlike *Ley Lerdo*, the Laws of the Reform ordered Church lands to be divided among small landowners, though this did these landowners little good. In the heat of war, local caciques sold Church lands to the highest bidder. Once again, confiscated Church lands swelled the wealth and power of a new Mexican oligarchy.

Benito Juárez

With the issuance of the Reform Laws, the civil war grew even bloodier. Liberal caciques shot priests who would not administer the sacraments to their troops and executed monks and friars caught fighting for the conservatives. Churches captured by Liberal forces had their altars stripped, their interiors gutted, and their relics and images burned in bonfires. Property owned by citizens of the United States, France, Great Britain, and Spain suffered as well from the depredations of *guerrilleros*, both conservative and Liberal.

The destruction of foreign-owned property provided the opportunity for foreign intervention. France, Great Britain, and Spain recognized Miramón's government, while the United States favored the Liberal cause and recognized Juárez's. In December 1859, Melchor Ocampo signed a treaty with the United States that would have given the Yankees a right to intervene in Mexican affairs. The McLane-Ocampo Treaty would have spelled a significant loss of Mexican sovereignty, but the U.S. Senate refused to ratify it.

Yet, the United States aided Juárez in other ways. In the Winter of 1860, while Miramón invested Veracruz by land, a Cuban ship flying a Mexican flag was proceeding to blockade the port of Veracruz when a commander of a U.S. warship seized it because, he claimed, he thought it was a pirate. That same winter, Juárez received an important shipment of munitions from the U.S. Such shipments would continue, despite the Civil War, for Abraham Lincoln had long admired Juárez. When Juárez had fled the capital at the beginning of the War of the Reform, Lincoln had sent him a message expressing hopes "for the happiness, prosperity, and liberty of yourself, your government and its people." In his journal, General Phil Sheridan wrote that, during the war, the United States army "continued supplying arms and munitions to the Liberals, sending as many as 30,000 muskets from Baton Rouge alone."

The tide of war began to turn against the conservatives in the spring and summer of 1860. They had nearly exhausted the resources of the Church, and without the customs duties from Veracruz, they could not fund their struggle much longer. Soldiers began to desert the conservative armies. In August, three Liberal generals converged on Miramón's small force at Siloa and, with a three-to-one advantage in men, destroyed the conservative army. While Miramón withdrew into the Valley of Mexico, Liberal *guerrilleros* in the south under the command of Marcos Pérez captured Oaxaca.

In the autumn Liberal *guerrilleros* converged on Mexico City, hemming Miramón in on all sides. In late December, Miramón cut his way through the investment to engage General González Ortega at San Miguel Calpulalpan, about 75 miles northeast of the capital. There, just three days before Christmas, was fought the decisive battle of the war. After only two hours, Ortega destroyed Miramón's forces, and the conservative president barely escaped back into Mexico City. There, he debated whether he would hunker down for a siege or flee the city. When Ortega appeared before the city and demanded unconditional surrender, Miramón decided his course. He fled by night to Jalapa on the Gulf of Mexico, where he remained in hiding until he went into exile in France.

On January 1, 1861, Ortega entered Mexico City in triumph. Eleven days later, a black carriage carried Benito Juárez, an expressionless, taciturn figure, into the capital.

A Short-Lived Peace

Benito Juárez believed in the rule of law. Despite the disastrous state of Mexico—the empty treasury, non-existent commerce, ruined agriculture, and continued resistance from conservative guerrilla forces—Juárez would not do what others in his place would have done: he would not become dictator. The Mexican president saw himself as the defender and upholder of the Constitution of 1857; how then could he himself violate it, even for what seemed a just cause?

Though he banished five bishops and the Spanish ambassador, Juárez offered amnesty to all conservatives who had resisted him in the late war, if they agreed to lay down their arms. He even allowed complete freedom for the press, permitting the publication of the conservative *El Pajaro Verde,* a periodical that routinely attacked his government. Such acts of clemency disgusted Melchor Ocampo, who resigned his place in the cabinet over the issue and returned home to his farm in Michoacán.

Liberal though he was, Juárez faced opposition from the Liberal congress that assembled in May 1861. This body—peppered with eloquent orators such as Sebastián Lerdo de Tejada and Ignacio Altamirano—obstructed the president at every turn. They used any excuse to criticize him. In the autumn, 51 congressmen signed a petition demanding that Juárez resign in favor of his vice-president, Gabriel Ortega; but they were opposed by 52 congressmen, who signed a counter-petition. Juárez, thus, narrowly escaped being overthrown by members of his own party.

Porfirio Díaz

Meanwhile, conservative generals—Márquez in the central provinces and Tomás Mejía in Querétaro—would not accept the defeat of their cause. In June 1861, Márquez and his *guerrilleros* raided Michoacán and captured Melchor Ocampo. True to form, the "Tiger of Tacubaya" had Ocampo shot. Santos Degollado asked, and obtained, Juárez's permission to avenge the death of Ocampo—and Márquez captured Degollado as well and had him executed. Márquez continued his depredations, unchecked by the government, until, at San Cosme, near the capital, Liberal commanders Ignacio Mejía and Porfirio Díaz drove him into the mountains.

Added to the problem of conservative insurgency was the 80-million *peso* debt Mexico owed France, Spain, and Great Britain. Though he did not shirk responsibility for the debt, Juárez knew that is was impossible for Mexico in its depressed state to meet such a financial obligation; so in July 1861 he decreed a suspension of all debt payments. The three European powers would not accept this expedient and agreed they would together occupy the port of Veracruz. In December 1861, Spanish troops under General Prim landed at Veracruz; in January, British and French forces joined them.

The three European powers, however, could not agree on a common course of action. Though Great Britain and Spain had pledged not to make war on Mexico, the French ambassador, Dubois de Saligny, it seemed, wanted to goad the Mexicans into attacking the allied powers. Despite the common proclamation of the three powers that they had come to lend Mexico "a friendly hand" and to "preside at the grand spectacle of your regeneration," Saligny's continued insistence on the immediate payment of 12 million *pesos* appeared to cloak more bellicose intentions. Finally, in April 1862, the British and the Spanish decided that the French wanted war and withdrew, leaving Veracruz in the possession of the French.

What were the French up to, anyhow?

Empress Eugeníe

Exiles in Paris

Empress Eugeníe, like so many women in Paris, found the young Mexican diplomat charming. José Manuel Hidalgo was a tragic figure to the French aristocrats, for he had lost his estates in Mexico to the Liberals. Through Hidalgo, Eugeníe met other Mexican exiles who had likewise suffered. There was José María Gutiérrez de Estrada, whom the Liberals had hunted out 20 years earlier for proposing a monarchy. There were Padre Francisco Xavier Miranda, Don Antonio Pelagio Labastida y Dávalos (bishop of Puebla), and Juan Almonte, one of Santa Anna's old generals. The tale of their woes moved the devoutly Catholic, but somewhat capricious and high strung, Eugeníe to embrace their cause.

Eugeníe's husband was Napoleon III, nephew to the first of that name. In 1852 this latest Napoleon had been proclaimed emperor of France and, to live up to the expectations of his name, was eager for foreign adventures of glory. To him Eugeníe introduced the Mexican exiles. The emperor listened to their stories and resolved to vindicate the honor of monarchy by sending an expedition to Mexico to deliver it from Liberal bonds. Of course, Napoleon would need a king to replace the hated Juárez, but whom should he choose? Among the many unemployed princes of Europe, Napoleon finally decided to offer the kingdom—nay, the empire!—of Mexico to Archduke Maximilian von Habsburg, brother to the emperor of Austria.

But first Napoleon had to secure Mexico. Thus it was that he had sent 6,000 French troops under General Charles Ferdinand de Lorencez to Veracruz, ostensibly to secure repayment of debts but really to instigate a war. Reports from the French ambassador

Napoleon III

to Mexico, Dubois de Saligny, encouraged Napoleon. Juárez was a monster, wrote Saligny; the Mexicans, chafing under Juárez's tyranny, would welcome the French and rise against the oppressive Mexican government. How Saligny knew all this, isolated as he was at his post in Veracruz, the emperor, perhaps, did not bother to ask. But believe it he did.

But if the Mexicans were to rise with the French, they were a long time in flocking to their standard. General Lorencez did receive some reinforcements—one day General Márquez marched into the French camp with a band of very ragged *guerrilleros;* but that was all. Still, Lorencez had to do something or leave Mexico; so gathering his army and Márquez's men, the French general began his campaign of conquest by marching on Puebla.

Ignacio Zaragoza commanded the Mexican army in Puebla. A bunch of former *guerrilleros* commanded by amateur generals, armed with antique weapons that Guadalupe Victoria had bought 40 years before from the British (who had used them against Napoleon I), the Mexican force was not formidable. Still, Lorencez's attack did not come off as he had wished. Storming the center of Puebla's fortifications, pushing his troops across an open ditch and over a brick wall, climbing up the steep slopes of the Cerro de Guadalupe, Lorencez led his men to the slaughter. He lost, that day, May 5, 1862, 1,000 men and was forced to withdraw to Veracruz. It was a day the Mexicans would remember, a day they would celebrate thenceforth every year as the festival, *Cinco de Mayo.*

Such a defeat was, needless to say, not encouraging to Emperor Napoleon. But he would not give up. He sent more troops to Mexico. Soon the French army numbered some 34,000 men, to which was added a force of about 20,000 Mexican conservatives. While, for seven months, the new French general, Élie Frédéric Forey, gathered and prepared his force, Juárez worked feverishly to build up a defense. Deprived of the customs duties out of Veracruz, the Mexican president levied taxes and forced loans from the Mexican people. González Ortega, with 30,000 men at Puebla, strengthened the fortifications of the city, making it impregnable. Ignacio Comonfort, returned from exile, commanded the army in the field.

General Bazaine attacks the fort of San Xavier during the siege of Puebla.

Still, all the preparations were insufficient to counter the power of the French. In the late winter of 1863, Forey moved on Puebla and invested the city on March 16. Though impregnable, Puebla was not sufficiently supplied with foodstuffs to withstand a long siege. For two months its defenders resisted until they ate every animal in the city and exhausted their ammunition. On May 16, Ortega surrendered. Forey sent the Mexican army and its officers to Veracruz, to ship them off to France. Two Mexican generals did manage to escape. They were González Ortega and the Indian guerrilla leader, Porfirio Díaz.

Juárez had sworn to defend the capital; but finding he had only 14,000 men and no reliable general to lead them, he withdrew from Mexico City to San Luis Potosí on May 31. On June 10, General Forey and his French and Mexican army entered the capital.

The French Occupation

The clergy of Mexico City joyously greeted the entrance of General Forey; conservatives hoped it was the dawn of a better day. But Forey, it turned out, was not the savior they wanted. Two days hadn't passed since he entered the capital before he issued a proclamation declaring that confiscated Church lands would remain in the hands of those who currently possessed them. (Many of the owners of church property were French nationals.) An outcry of protest went up from the clergy. They threatened to suspend the public administration of the sacraments—a powerful threat in that Catholic country. But Forey was not one to cringe at threats. If the clergy, he said, closed church doors, he would blow them open with artillery!

With the French in control of the capital and advancing to take the surrounding cities, a delegation of Mexican exiles, in October 1863, visited Miramare, the castle of the Archduke Maximilian in Trieste. There they found the tall, fair-haired scion of the House of Habsburg

Maximilian von Habsburg, by Franz Xaver Winterhalter

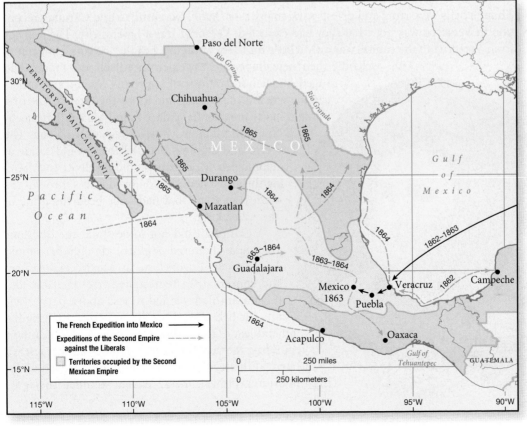

The Second Mexican Empire, with invasion routes of French forces, 1861–1867

and his short, dark-haired, and beautiful wife, Princess Marie Charlotte Amélie, or Carlota. José María Gutiérrez de Estrada, who led the delegation, told Maximilian of Mexico: "It is a budding plant," he said, "entitled to a place in the sun." Maximilian, he said, could be the country's redeemer! This must have appealed to the romantic archduke; but he was not to be taken in so easily. There was honor to be considered, and right. "A Habsburg," he told Gutiérrez, "never usurps a throne." Maximilian said he wanted a document proving that a majority of the Mexican people wanted him to assume the throne of their country.

Maximilian would get his document. Learning of the archduke's ultimatum, General Forey called a "Supreme Council" of conservatives—hardly a representative majority of the people—who issued a call for Maximilian to take up the rule of Mexico. The naïve archduke was fooled and in April 1864 accepted the imperial crown of Mexico. He and Carlota set sail for Mexico and landed at Veracruz on May 28.

Meanwhile, Juárez had moved north from San Luis Potosí to Saltillo, and from Saltillo to Monterey. There he was in the country controlled by General Santiago Vidaurri, his old ally in the War of the Reform. But that wily Liberal, instead of giving Juárez the revenues from the customs house at Piedras Negras, declared his support for Maximilian. When other Liberal leaders, Doblado and Ortega, called on the president to resign, Juárez fled into Texas.

By March 1864, the Liberal cause was tottering. Comonfort had been killed in battle; other Liberal generals had fled to the United States. Juárez controlled only the very far north, while the 74-year-old Juan Álvarez controlled his old stomping grounds, Guerrero, and Porfirio Díaz dominated Oaxaca. But though they controlled the cities, the French could not master the countryside. There, from the dense forests of the south, northward to the mountain fastnesses, Liberal *guerrillero* bands held sway.

The Tragedy of Maximilian and Carlota

Though bells were rung and priests sang many a *Te Deum,* Maximilian and Carlota's reception in Veracruz was not what they had expected. Veracruz was a Liberal city. The journey from Veracruz to the capital was only a little more encouraging, but the Indians came out to welcome their new emperor. In Mexico City itself, the French had arranged for demonstrations of support—*léperos* and others casting wreaths of flowers, paid for by the French. The first night in the presidential palace found Maximilian sleeping on a billiard table, the bed bugs were so bad. The emperor and empress decided they would reside at Chapultepec, Montezuma's old residence overlooking the city. There they enjoyed walks through the cypress gardens that had once been the pride of the Aztec king.

Maximilian did not understand the divisions that had shattered Mexico, though he should have. As in Europe, so in Mexico: Liberalism and conservatism represented irreconcilable ideals. Maximilian wanted to rise above party divisions. He had sent a message to Juárez, inviting the Liberal leader to lay down his arms and join him in rebuilding Mexico. Juárez understood the character of the struggle better than the emperor and pledged undying opposition. Other Liberal leaders sounded the same

Charlotte (Carlota) of Belgium

defiance. From the fastnesses of Guerrero, old Juan Álvarez declared, "I still live, men of the coast, I who have ever led you to fight against tyrants."

The problem was that Maximilian, if not a Liberal, had Liberal leanings. He tried to conciliate men who would never accept conciliation and so ended up alienating his friends. Instead of building his government on the conservatives who had brought him to Mexico, Maximilian wanted to base his rule on the *moderados*. He even placed in his cabinet men who had been followers of Gómez Farías. When the papal nuncio presented the emperor with six points calling for the repeal of the Laws of the Reform and the restoration of Church lands, Maximilian and Carlota both refused to consider them and sent the nuncio packing. Later Maximilian sent a delegation to Rome to discuss his policy of appeasing the Liberals, but discussions went nowhere. He even contemplated granting Mexico complete freedom of religion—a concession other Liberals, such as Morelos, had opposed.

Conservative opposition soon mounted against Maximilian. Labastida y Dávalos, now archbishop of Mexico City, led the clerical opposition to the emperor, and Padre Miranda denounced him. They should not have been surprised at Maximilian; Napoleon III was no conservative—so why would he have chosen a conservative as his puppet emperor? What Napoleon wanted was clear—Mexican silver and a repayment of the debts owed France. What did it matter to him whether the Mexican emperor were a conservative or not?

It soon became clear to Maximilian that he had little real power in his empire. General François Achille Bazaine, who now commanded the French forces, listened only to Napoleon, who ordered the general to send French officials to take over the collection of customs at Veracruz and placed a French financier over the treasury department. With Liberals despising him and the conservatives turned against him, Maximilian was entirely dependent on the French emperor.

Emperor Maximilian I

But, despite these disappointments, Maximilian and Carlota zealously threw themselves into their new roles as emperor and empress. They threw lavish banquets, planned to build a theater and an academy of sciences in Mexico City, and laid plans for the capital's beautification. They tried to become Mexicans in every way; they ate Mexican food and wore Mexican dress (Maximilian often decked himself out in sombrero and the button down trousers of a *charro*—a cattle rancher). The emperor sometimes walked the streets unattended—an odd spectacle to Mexicans who were used to the extravagance of an Iturbide or a Santa Anna. On September 16, 1864, Maximilian journeyed to Dolores to honor Independence Day and the memory of Hidalgo.

And, despite the continuing poverty of the people and the government and *Juarista* guerrilla raids on the Valley of Mexico, Maximilian's first year of rule showed encouraging signs. The Mexican people, while not enthusiastically embracing the new government, were at least content to have some peace and order after so much war. As long as he had enough French money, Maximilian could win over even *Juaristas* by giving them government jobs. The military situation was also encouraging. In September, Bazaine conquered Nuevo León and Coahuila. Juárez, now almost a lone fugitive in the mountains of Durango, fled to Chihuahua and then to Paso del Norte (now Ciudad Juárez) on the Río Grande. In February 1865, Bazaine, who had turned south, captured Oaxaca, forcing Porfirio Díaz to surrender himself and his army. By spring of 1865, only Guerrero and Michoacán had significant guerrilla opposition, while Juárez barely held on in the far north.

The problem for Juárez was that, without the aid of the United States, he was nothing —and the United States was engaged in a civil war and so could send him little help. This changed in April 1865, for that month Robert E. Lee surrendered at Appomattox Court House, and the union was triumphant. With the defeat of the South, the U. S. government could turn its attention to its neighbor to the south.

God Save the Emperor!

Not only France was interested in the wealth of Mexico. With the end of the Civil War, the United States began to covet the rich wealth of the mineral mines south of the Río Grande. As Secretary of State Seward saw it, the United States had to secure the good will of the Mexican people, lost during the Mexican-American war. Only then could Anglo-American businessmen invest in and develop the rich resources of Mexico. By 1865, said Seward, the United States "wanted dollars more and dominion less."

United States' policy was twofold—to free Mexico from foreign domination and to aid Juárez. Seward, who began to press Napoleon to withdraw his troops from Mexico, found the emperor not unwilling. Napoleon had found that his Mexican adventure had brought him no profit. It was highly unpopular among the French people; and with the threat of Prussia in Europe weighing on his mind, Napoleon was eager to bring his army home. Though he had promised Maximilian that French troops would remain to the end of 1867, and though he had indicated that he would support the Mexican emperor until his power was established, Napoleon reneged and assured Seward that he would begin to withdraw the French army.

Direct U.S. aid to Juárez was also forthcoming. General Sheridan began amassing American troops on the Río Grande; ammunition dumps were placed at strategic locations for the use of Juárez's men. With American support and with arms, Juárez's army began to grow. But the United States also aided Juárez politically. In the autumn of 1865, Juárez's term of office came to an end, and without the possibility of a general election, he could not be re-elected. General González Ortega, who had been living in New York City, claimed that he, as vice president and head of the Mexican supreme court, was by constitutional right the president of Mexico. But Ortega was seized and imprisoned by U.S. authorities before he could reach Mexico, thus assuring Juárez's continued leadership.

Maximilian had not been informed of, much less consulted about, the withdrawal of the French army. When he learned of the projected withdrawal, Maximilian sent emissaries to Napoleon, but to no avail. Perhaps to appease his conscience, Napoleon ordered Bazaine to make one last attempt to crush Juárez. Severity against the Liberals, Bazaine told Maximilian, was necessary to defeat them. In October 1865 he urged Maximilian to publish a decree ordering the execution of anyone caught resisting the imperial forces. Believing false reports that Juárez was in retreat, Maximilian issued the edict, ordering the execution of all "bandits."

"From this day forward," read the edict, "the struggle will be between the honest men of the nation and the gangs of criminals and bandits. There will be no more indulgence for those who burn towns, for those who rob, and for those who murder peaceful citizens, poor old folk, and defenseless women." This decree, however, harmed Maximilian's cause, for when the imperialists executed the *Juarista* general José María Arteagra Magallanes. The act inspired universal indignation against the emperor.

In March 1866, Bazaine began his withdrawal from the north—from Monterey, Saltillo, and Tampico. In his wake came the *Juarista* armies, who occupied the territories Bazaine abandoned. In the capital, Maximilian was forming a Mexican army, strengthened by volunteers from Belgium and France. In July, Bazaine informed Maximilian that the

French army would withdraw in 18 months—would the emperor not abdicate and fly this wretched country? Without the French, all seemed hopeless, and Maximilian contemplated abdication. But Carlota reminded her husband of his honor. Was not abdication mere cowardice? And was he not a Habsburg? Remembering his and his family's honor, and his sworn word to rule Mexico, Maximilian relented. He would not abandon his post.

Carlota was determined to play her part to save her husband's throne. In July she left the capital, by way of the road from Mexico City to Veracruz, braving the perils of the bandit-infested route. Arriving in Veracruz, she took ship for France—she would plead with Napoleon to relent in his decision to remove the French army from Mexico. In Paris, the Empress Eugeníe told Carlota that she would not be allowed to see the emperor; he was sick, she said. When Carlota threatened to force her way into the palace, Eugeníe

Empress Carlota, by Franz Xaver Winterhalter

relented. Twice Carlota visited Napoleon and pleaded her husband's cause; twice, though he wept, Napoleon made no promises.

Carlota then went to Rome to seek the pope's aid. Pius IX's secretary told her that Maximilian had only himself to blame; he had alienated himself from the Mexican conservatives by refusing to repeal the Reform Laws. Poor Carlota had now reached the limits of her strength. The emotional drain, the fear of what was to come, proved too great for her. When met with the pope himself, she threw herself on her knees before him and cried that Napoleon was trying to poison her. Refusing to return to her hotel, she spent the night in the papal palace. The next morning she was escorted to her hotel where, fearing poisoning, she refused to eat or drink anything her servants brought her. In October, her brother, the Count of Flanders, fetched her and gave her over to the care of doctors. They pronounced her insane.

When Maximilian heard of Carlota's insanity, he again thought of abdication. He wished to rush to her side. In October 1866, he drafted an abdication proclamation and went to Orizaba, between Puebla and Veracruz. There he remained for six weeks, contemplating what course he should take while studying botany and entomology. There the conservative generals, Leonardo Márquez and Miguel Miramón, who had returned to Mexico, pleaded with him not to abdicate. More influential, though, was a German priest, Padre Fischer. Though a disreputable man (since his ordination he had fathered a family of illegitimate children) Fischer could move the heart of the emperor. Was the emperor to forget Carlota's sacrifices for Mexico's imperial throne? Would not abdication stain the Habsburg family honor? Such appeals moved Maximilian; at the end of November 1866, he said he would remain and fight for his throne.

In February 1867, General Bazaine sailed from Veracruz. Maximilian had now to rely on an army of 15,000 to 20,000 Mexicans with some European volunteers. This force was

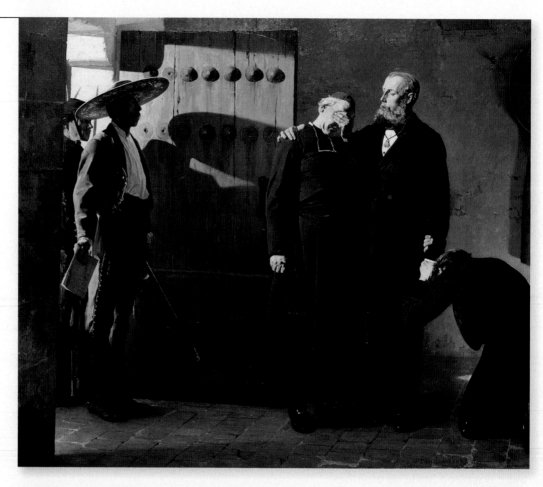

The Last Moments of Maximilian, Emperor of Mexico, by Jean-Paul Laurens

divided between Puebla and Querétaro, where Miramón and the Indian Tomás Mejía commanded. Meanwhile, the Liberal armies under the command of generals Escobedo, Riva Palacio, and Corona were advancing on Santiago, in Querétaro, while another force under Porfirio Díaz moved on Puebla. Now Maximilian began to show himself a true Habsburg. Taking supreme command, the emperor went to Querétaro to face the advancing enemy. With him went Leonardo Márquez and Santiago Vidaurri.

Resting in a valley surrounded by hills, Santiago de Querétaro was unsuitable for defense. The imperial army was small, numbering only eight to nine thousand men. When General Escobedo appeared before the city, Miramón counseled the emperor to strike before the remainder of the Liberal force under Riva Palacio and Corona arrived. Márquez, though, counseled against this; attack them when they are all together, he said, and destroy them all at one blow! Maximilian listened to Márquez but came to rue it. Soon about 40,000 *Juaristas* surrounded Santiago de Querétaro, cutting off all supplies of food. In March, Maximilian sent Márquez and Vidaurri with 1,200 men to cut through the *Juarista* lines and go to Mexico City for reinforcements.

But Márquez did not follow orders. Turning from Mexico City, he went to relieve the siege of Puebla. Learning of Márquez's approach, Díaz assaulted Puebla and took it on April 4. He then gave chase to Márquez and routed him. Abandoning his men, Márquez fled to Mexico City. Díaz followed and lay siege to the capital.

At Santiago de Querétaro, Maximilian earned his men's applause by sleeping wrapped in a blanket like a common soldier and by continually exposing himself to danger. When Escobedo offered to give Maximilian safe conduct through the lines, the emperor refused. He would share the fate of his men. The situation was now most desperate. Maximilian and

Execution of Emperor Maximilian, by Edouard Manet

his generals decided that the only hope for the army lay in fighting their way out of Querétaro and joining Tomás Mejía's Indians in the Sierra Gorda. Midnight, May 14, would be the time of their escape. But the emperor had a traitor in his midst—Miguel López. López, one of Maximilian's constant companions, now convinced him to delay the escape. López had been carrying on secret negotiations with Escobedo and had agreed to betray the imperial army. All he asked was that Escobedo pay him a fee and spare Maximilian's life.

At 3 a.m. on the morning of May 14, López allowed *Juaristas* to pass through the entrenchments he guarded. When the enemy had taken possession of the town, López urged Maximilian to escape. The emperor refused. He would not abandon his generals. Instead, he joined Tomás Mejía and his small force on the Hill of Bells. But seeing the hopelessness of resistance, Mejía and the emperor surrendered with the dawn.

Juárez wanted to make an example of Maximilian—his fate would be a warning to other foreign powers who might think to invade Mexico. Juárez ordered seven officers to try Maximilian in a rigged court. Maximilian was guilty of killing Mexican citizens by his decree of October 1865, declared the court martial. He was sentenced to be shot.

Pleas for leniency from the crowned heads of Europe came to Juárez—would he not spare the life of Maximilian? But Juárez had made up his mind. On the morning of June 19, 1867, soldiers awakened Maximilian in his room in the convent of the Capuchins in Santiago. He showed no fear of death—such cowardice was unbecoming to a Habsburg. They led him to the Hill of Bells, where Miguel Miramón and Tomás Mejía awaited him. Clad in black civilian clothes, Maximilian placed a scarlet piece of cloth over his heart; there, he said, the gunmen should take their aim. Facing the firing squad, he said, "I forgive everyone. I pray that everyone may also forgive me, and my blood which is about to be shed will bring peace to

Mexico. *Viva México! Viva la Indepencía!*" Shots rang out. Maximilian staggered backward and fell to the ground, dead. Miramón and Mejía followed him in death. Their last words: "God save the Emperor!"

A few days later, Porfirio Díaz took Mexico City. The war was over. Santiago Vidaurri was shot as a traitor. Leonardo Márquez escaped. He would live for 40 more years as a pawnbroker in Havana. Carlota, the Empress of Mexico, lived until 1927 but never recovered her sanity. She spoke often of her husband, of his imperial glory. The "Sovereign of the Universe," she called him.

From Republic to Dictatorship Again

Clad in black and riding in a black carriage, Benito Juárez reentered Mexico City. He returned to power in a Mexico torn and impoverished by war. Most of the men who had fought with him in the War of the Reform and against Maximilian, were dead—or, like Prieto (who had supported Ortega), in disgrace. Juárez's old companion, Sebastián Lerdo de Tejada, still lived and became his closest associate.

On returning to power, Don Benito put aside some of his Liberal scruples. Though reelected president in 1867 by wide margins, Juárez faced constant opposition from the new Liberal congress. With an empty treasury and decreased foreign investment, Juárez could brook no opposition, constitutional or otherwise. He began to interfere in congressional elections to get representatives favorable to him elected. He used his popularity and prestige to force through congress an amendment to the federal constitution, adding a senate to congress. Juárez increased presidential power by another amendment that required a two-thirds vote to override a presidential veto. Juárez also further centralized the Mexican government by taking power from local caciques.

Under Juárez, Mexico experienced the beginnings of industrial development and a growth of commerce that brought more money into the national treasury. Unfortunately, foreigners controlled much of this growth. The circulation of the money gotten from the seizure of Church lands along with the 3 million francs left in Mexico City by the French helped spur this development. In 1873, with Juárez's support, British engineers completed the railroad line running from Veracruz to the capital.

The Laws of the Reform had removed education from the jurisdiction of the Church and placed it into the hands of the state. Juárez now planned a system of free secular public schools. He established a committee led by the scientist Gabino Barreda. Barreda traveled to Paris to study under the French thinker Auguste Comte, whose stilted and materialistic Positivist system became the basis of Mexican education. Juárez took the old Jesuit college of San Ildefonso in Mexico City and turned it into the National Preparatory School. He required *hacendados* to build schools on their estates.

Don Benito's soul knew no sentimentalism—some would have said, it knew no gratitude. One of his first acts after the war was to reduce the size of the army. At war's end, there were 90,000 soldiers in the army that had restored Juárez to power; with stoic indifference, Juárez dismissed two-thirds of them without a pension and with barely a word of thanks. Because of this, Juárez faced several revolts of former soldiers throughout the years of his rule. He crushed these uprisings ruthlessly, executing all captured soldiers as traitors.

Though, to some degree, the lot of the Indians did not worsen under Juárez (he gave up any attempt to turn them into farmer proprietors and protected their remaining *ejidos*), other *campesinos* (field workers) fared badly. Juárez's government needed money. He continued the old policy of refusing to turn Church lands over to the poor men who worked

President Juárez

them, selling them instead to rich *hacendados* who had supported the Liberal cause. There were a good number of these rich Liberals, for Liberalism wasn't so much a movement for the poor man as it was an assault on the Church and traditional society. Liberalism believed that the old Catholic society put too great a check on individual initiative; Liberalism stood for individual "freedom." That such individuals were rich landowners didn't matter for many Liberals; the important thing was that, between the state and the individual there be no organized societies (the Church, the military, cities with *fueros*, trade guilds) to hamper individual freedom and curtail state power.

Dispossessed peasant farmers did not see matters in the same light. If there were the Liberal rich, there were many conservative poor. Many of these, along with anti-*Juarista* soldiers, were driven into banditry. Juárez faced revolts led, some by Liberal military leaders, some by peasants, some by Indians. Soon Juárez faced opposition, not only from the "right" but from the "far left." In 1868 Plotino Rhodakanti, a peasant leader of peasants, who called Jesus Christ "the divine socialist of humanity," rose in revolt against Juárez. Another, Julio López, led an insurrection "to destroy the present vicious state of exploitation" and replace it with a socialist state. Juárez used federal troops to crush both uprisings.

Other troubles assailed Juárez. In southern Yucatan, the Mayan Indians had established an independent state following their 1847–1855 war against local landowners. In the north, the Apache, pressed as they were by Anglo settlers in Arizona and New Mexico, attacked northern Mexican settlements. Raids by bands led by the Apache Cochise and his successors, Victorio and Ju, brought about the death of many Mexicans.

The Election of 1871

Porfirio Díaz, the Indian Liberal revolutionary, had no public grievance against Juárez; his was personal, for Juárez had snubbed him. At the close of the war against Maximilian, Díaz had spent large sums of money on flowers and banners to welcome Juárez into the capital. He had gone out to meet Juárez at Tlalnepantla—and what did he, Don Porfirio, the general who had won the greatest victories in the war; what did he get for his pains and expense? A mere nod from the president, who then drove on without even offering Díaz a seat in his carriage! Later, when Juárez offered him a generalship to help put down insurrections of dismissed soldiers, Díaz refused it. He would not fight against his former comrades-in-arms. Instead, he returned to Oaxaca to his hacienda of La Noria, which the state government had given him. In 1867, Díaz ran against Juárez for the presidency, but lost For the next four years, he remained at La Noria, growing sugarcane, while friends organized a *Porfirista* party.

Then came the election year of 1871. When Juárez announced that he would run again—for a fourth term—Don Porfirio saw his chance. Declaring that Juárez was trying to establish a dictatorship, Díaz announced his own candidacy. Others also raised this cry against Juárez, including Sebastián Lerdo de Tejada, his old friend, who also decided to run for president as well. When the election results came in, neither of the three candidates had a clear majority. The election was thrown to congress, which chose Juárez as president and Lerdo as vice president and president of the supreme court.

The *Porfiristas* would not accept this result. The governor of Oaxaca, Felix Díaz, Don Porfirio's brother, organized resistance with caciques in the mountain districts stretching from Sonora to Tehuantepec on the Pacific coast in the state of Oaxaca, and rose against the government. *Juarista* forces, led by Sostenes Rocha, put down the rebellion in the capital, shooting down 200 rebels. Rocha then crushed the rebellion in Oaxaca (where Felix Díaz was killed) and forced the caciques into the mountains. Don Porfirio, disguised as a priest, fled to the north, where he found refuge amongst Indians in the mountains of Nayarit.

Though Rocha had crushed the rebellion by the spring of 1872, Benito Juárez did not long enjoy the victory. On the evening of July 18, 1872, the quiet and relentless Liberal chieftain succumbed to a heart attack and died while working at his desk in the National Palace. He was 66 years old. Lerdo de Tejada succeeded to the presidency in his place.

El Porfiriato

In an election held in the autumn of 1872, Lerdo was elected to a full four-year term as president. He had had the support of the *Juaristas;* even the conservatives were more or less behind him. To establish peace, Lerdo extended pardon to the *Porfiristas.*

It was not long however before Lerdo lost the heart of the people. He was arrogant and overused government power. Many believed he gave too many concessions to U.S. railroad barons who wanted to penetrate into Mexico—though, in reality, he had forbidden them to extend their lines into Mexico, a move which cost him the support of the U.S. government.

In 1876, Lerdo announced he would run for reelection as president. Porfirio Díaz, banking on popular discontent with the president, gathered money and recruits in the United States and proclaimed the *Plan de Tuxtepec,* calling for more local democracy and no presidential reelection. Under this banner, Díaz captured Matamoros on the Río Grande, but was driven back into the United States by the *Lerdista* general Mariano Escobeda. Disguised as a Cuban doctor, Díaz took ship for Veracruz and from there returned secretly to Oaxaca. There he began confiscating property to raise an army against Lerdo.

Though half of Mexico was now in rebellion against, him Lerdo held elections. With only half the states voting, Lerdo proclaimed himself president. Meanwhile, Díaz and Manuel González defeated the *Lerdistas* at Tecoac and moved on the capital. It was October 1876. Lerdo, seeing the game was up, fled by way of Acapulco to the United States. Díaz entered Mexico City and assumed the provisional presidency.

So began *el Porfiriato,* the long dictatorship of Don Porfirio Díaz. This Liberal champion of democracy and no re-election would rule Mexico for all but four of the next 35 years—and for those four years the acting president, his general, Manuel González, would be the puppet of his power. There would be peace and prosperity (at least for some) in Mexico, but at the price of oppression and foreign domination by the United States and other powers. By his policy of *pan ó palo*—"bread or the club"—Don Porfirio would reward his "friends" and mercilessly destroy his enemies. Such tyranny, though, would have its day of reckoning; neither foreign money nor paternalistic cruelty would save Don Porfirio from the groundswell of discontent that would topple him from his throne—and plunge Mexico once again into a bloodbath of ideological hatreds.

Chapter 19 Review

Summary

- The war with the United States had exhausted Mexico, and a sign of this was that there were no revolutions from 1848–1853. However, Mexico had fallen into chaos, and the Constitution of 1824 was insufficient to combat the chaos. States were breaking up into smaller and smaller states. Commerce was dead, and local *caciques* made laws as they saw fit.

- Lucas Alamán thought that Mexico needed order imposed by a powerful, central authority, such

as a foreign prince. He and other conservatives negotiated with the Spanish court but were told they needed to take control of the Mexican government first. The conservatives needed some dictator who would impose order and maintain it until the hoped-for prince would come. In desperation, the conservatives chose Santa Anna for their leader, and in January 1853 they overthrew President Arista. Santa Anna took control of and reformed the government and removed Liberals everywhere. But when Alamán died, Santa Anna resumed his old,

Chapter 19 Review (continued)

dissolute ways, and the country fell into ruin again and Liberals were emboldened.

- A change came in Mexican Liberalism. The new Liberals believed that the Church and military were the chief obstacles to progress and must be brought under the thumb of the state. The Church fought to maintain its lands and property, while the Liberals sought to make the state not only the highest but the only real authority in society.

- In 1854, *guerrilleros* in the state of Guerrero, led by Juan Álvarez and Ignacio Comonfort, rose against His Most Serene Highness (Santa Anna). In March the rebel leaders issued the *Plan de Ayutla*. Santa Anna attempted to crush the rebellion. Comonfort refused to surrender, and Santa Anna contented himself with burning Indian villages and killing Liberals.

- In 1855, Northern Mexico declared for the *Plan de Ayutla*, and when the entire east coast joined the revolution, Santa Anna drove out of Mexico City and took a ship to Venezuela. Juan Álvarez marched in triumph into Mexico City on November 24, 1855.

- Ignacio Comonfort became president after Álvarez resigned in December 1855. Comonfort was a moderate at heart, and he wanted to win over conservatives to his government. This became impossible because Álvarez's minister of justice, Benito Juárez, issued two sets of laws, called the *Ley Juárez* and the *Ley Lerdo*. Creoles, churchmen, and many Indians rose in rebellion against the new laws, but were crushed in 1856.

- At the same time, a convention met in Mexico City to draw up a new constitution. The new constitution was merely a revision of the Constitution of 1824, and it further centralized the government.

- The constitution was completed on February 5, 1857. The conservatives greeted the constitution with a *pronunciamento*, and Pope Pius IX condemned the Liberal government and declared the new anti-clerical laws null and void, implicitly blessing resistance to the government. The Church in Mexico excommunicated all who swore allegiance to the constitution.

- In 1857, Félix Zuloaga captured Mexico City, proclaiming the *Plan de Tacubaya*, a Comonfort dicta-torship, and declared an end to the Constitution of 1857. By that time, Comonfort was alienated from the Liberal party but would not link fortunes with his former enemy. When the Liberals rose in resistance, Comonfort changed his mind and gathered an army to resist Zuloaga. Desertions rendered his army too small, and Comonfort fled into exile to the United States in 1858.

- Declared president by the conservatives, Zuloaga repealed the laws of reform and marshaled clericalist generals Tomás Mejía, Miguel Miramón, and Leonardo Márquez to resist the Liberals.

- In July 1859, Juárez issued the Laws of Reform.

- With the issuance of the Reform Laws, the civil war grew bloodier, and foreign-owned property was destroyed. This provided the opportunity for foreign intervention. France, Great Britain, and Spain recognized the conservative government, while the United States favored the Liberal cause. The United States sent arms and munitions to the Liberal Mexicans, even throughout the American Civil War.

- In spring and summer of 1860, the tide of war began to turn against the conservatives. In the autumn Liberal *guerrilleros* converged on Mexico City. On January 1, 1861, Ortega entered Mexico City in triumph.

- As president, Juárez would not become dictator. He offered clemency to all those who had opposed him, if they laid down their arms. He faced opposition from the Liberal congress. Fifty-one congressmen signed a petition demanding that he resign, but they were opposed by 52 congressmen, and Juárez escaped being overthrown by his own party.

- The conservatives rose again, but they were driven back by Liberals into the mountains. Added to that, Mexico owed an 80-million *peso* debt to France, Spain, and Great Britain, whose troops occupied the port of Veracruz. France seemed to want war and tried to goad Mexico into an attack. Finally the British and Spanish withdrew, leaving Veracruz in the possession of the French.

- Empress Eugeníe of France, enamored of the Mexican exiles, introduced their cause to her husband, Napoleon III. Napoleon resolved to take

Chapter 19 Review (continued)

up their cause and deliver Mexico from Liberal bonds. He had first to secure Mexico, so he sent in 6,000 troops under General Charles Ferdinand de Lorencez, ostensibly to secure repayment of debts but really to instigate a war.

- On May 5, 1862, Lorencez led his army against Ignacio Zaragoza in Puebla. Lorencez lost and was forced to withdraw to Veracruz. That day has been commemorated as the festival, *Cinco de Mayo*.

- In March of 1863, González Ortega surrendered Puebla to the new French commander, Élie Forey, after a long siege. Finding that he did not have enough men, Juárez withdrew from Mexico City on May 31, and on June 10, the French and Mexican army entered the capital.

- In October 1863, a delegation of Mexican exiles went to the Archduke Maximilian von Habsburg and offered him the throne of Mexico. Maximilian, in April 1864, accepted the imperial crown of Mexico.

- Maximilian did not understand the divisions that had shattered Mexico, and since he had Liberal leanings, he built his government on the *moderados* instead of the conservatives who had brought him to Mexico. He refused to repeal the Laws of Reform. Conservative opposition soon mounted against him. Despite setbacks, Maximilian's first year of rule showed encouraging signs, and as long as he had enough money from the French government, he could maintain the peace.

- After Robert E. Lee's surrender in 1865, the United States again turned its attention towards Mexico. Its policy was twofold—to free Mexico from foreign domination and to aid Juárez. General Sheridan began amassing American troops on the Río Grande, and with American support and arms, Juárez's army began to grow.

- When Maximilian found out that Napoleon was planning to withdraw French troops, he sent emissaries to Napoleon, but to no avail. Napoleon ordered Bazaine to make one last attempt to crush Juárez. Bazaine urged Maximilian to be severe against the Liberals, and in October 1865, Maximilian published a decree ordering the execu-

tion of anyone caught resisting imperial forces. This decree harmed Maximilian's cause, however, and inspired universal indignation against the emperor.

- When French troops began to withdraw, Maximilian began to lose hope and contemplated abdication. His wife, Carlota, convinced him not to give up, and she went to France to plead with Napoleon, who gave her no assurances. She went next to Rome and pleaded for the pope's aid, which was refused to her. Reaching the end of her strength, she was pronounced insane. Again Maximilian contemplated abdication but was again convinced not to abandon the throne.

- In 1867, without French aid, Maximilian and his small army fought against the larger Liberal army. Due to a traitor, Maximilian was forced to surrender. Juárez wanted to make an example of him, and he tried Maximilian in a rigged court and sentenced him to be shot on June 19, 1867. A few days later, Porfirio Díaz took Mexico City and the war was over.

- In 1871, when Juárez ran again for a fourth term as president, Porfirio Díaz, who had been snubbed by Juárez, declared that Juárez was trying to establish a dictatorship and announced his own candidacy. When Juárez was again elected, rebellion broke out from the *Porfirista* party and was quickly suppressed. Juárez died soon after on July 18, 1872, and Sebastián Lerdo de Tejada, president of the supreme court, became president in his place.

- Lerdo soon lost the heart of the people and when in 1876 he announced he was going to run for reelection, Díaz gathered money and recruits in the United States and proclaimed the *Plan de Tuxtepec*, calling for more local democracy and no reelection. In October Lerdo fled, and Díaz entered Mexico City and assumed the provisional presidency.

Key Concepts

cacique: a political leader

guerrillero: member of a guerrilla group

peonage: the condition where a person, called a *peon*, is held to perform labor for another

indifferentism: the belief that people do not have the duty to believe in God by worshiping according to and practicing the one true religion

Dates to Remember

1853: Santa Anna overthrows the government and becomes dictator.

1855: a rebellion overthrows Santa Anna, and Juan Álvarez becomes president.

1857: the Mexican congress approves the Constitution of 1857.

1861: Benito Juárez becomes president of Mexico.

1862: Napoleon III of France resolves to deliver Mexico from Liberal bonds and sends forces to Mexico.

1863: the Liberal army surrenders to the French, and a delegation goes to Archduke Maximilian von Habsburg to offer him the throne of Mexico.

1864: Archduke Maximilian accepts the imperial crown of Mexico.

1867: Maximilian is forced to surrender to the Liberal army and is executed.

Benito Juárez resumes the presidency.

1876: Porfirio Díaz becomes president of Mexico.

Central Characters

Lucas Alamán (1792–1853): Mexican politician, historian, and leader of the Mexican conservatives

Juan Álvarez (1790–1867): revolutionary leader and provisional president of Mexico

Ignacio Comonfort (1812–1863): Mexican politician, soldier, and president of Mexico

Benito Juárez (1806–1872): president of Mexico and the protagonist of the Reform. He fought against foreign occupation under Emperor Maximilian.

Napoleon III (1808–1873): nephew of Napoleon I; the emperor of the French who took up the cause of the Mexican conservatives

Maximilian I (1832–1867): emperor of Mexico who attempted to liberate Mexico from the Liberals but failed and was executed

Princess Marie Charlotte Amélie (Carlota) (1840–1927): Maximilian's wife and empress of Mexico

Porfirio Díaz (1830–1915): revolutionary soldier and president of Mexico

Questions for Review

1. How did Mexican Liberalism change after Santa Anna became dictator of Mexico?

2. How have the Mexican conservatives been characterized, and what did they really stand for?

3. Why did the Church fight to maintain control of lands and privileges? What was the main principle behind the Church's defense of her rights?

4. What goals did the Mexican Liberals want to achieve?

5. What were some of the effects of the secularization of Church lands had on the economy and society of Mexico?

6. Briefly describe *Ley Juárez* and *Ley Lerdo* and what effects they had.

7. What was France's motivation in helping Mexico?

8. What was the United States' motivation in helping Mexico?

9. Why was Emperor Maximilian unable to secure the throne of Mexico?

10. Were Juárez and the Mexican Liberals successful in achieving their goals for Mexico? Please explain.

11. How did Porfirio Díaz come to power in Mexico? Did he fulfill his promises to the Mexican people? Please explain.

Ideas in Action

Compare the ideas of the Mexican Liberals with those political and social doctrines of the founders of the United States. How are they the same and how do they differ, if at all?

Chapter 19 Review (continued)

Highways and Byways

The House of Habsburg

The House of Habsburg was one of the principal sovereign dynasties of Europe from the 15th to the 20th century. Habsburgs occupied the throne of the Holy Roman Empire for centuries and provided kings for at least eight countries in Europe. The family derived its name from Habsburg Castle, a fortress built in the 1020s in what is now Switzerland by Werner, bishop of Strasbourg, and his brother-in-law, Count Radbot. Radbot's son, Werner I, was the first to bear the title of Count of Habsburg.

The Habsburgs first became a major power in Germany and then, in the 1400s, began to expand their connections through marriage to the royalty of other countries. In the 16th century, the house separated into the senior Habsburg Spain and the junior Habsburg Monarchy branches. The senior branch ended when Carlos II of Spain died in 1700 and was succeeded by Felipe V of the House of Bourbon. In 1740 the junior branch began to go extinct when the last of the male line, Holy Roman Emperor Karl VI, died. The branch went completely extinct in 1780 when Karl VI's eldest daughter, Maria Theresia, died. She was succeeded by the Vaudemont branch of the House of Lorraine when her husband, Franz of Lorraine, was recognized as emperor. The new house was called the House of Habsburg-Lorraine, though it was still referred to as the House of Habsburg. It continues to this day as the dynastic successor to the original House of Habsburg.

20 RECONSTRUCTION AND THE GILDED AGE

Part I: **Traitors or Fellow Citizens?**

Though the federal government, at first, promised to parole Confederate President Jefferson Davis, Radical Republicans in Congress and public opinion in the North branded him a traitor; so Jefferson Davis paid the debt of a traitor at Fortress Monroe, in a prison cell kept lit day and night and under constant vigilance. Other Confederate leaders might likewise have suffered (and, indeed, Alexander Stephens was imprisoned for a short time); but Lee, Johnston, and other Confederate generals had the sworn word of Generals Grant and Sherman to protect them. Jefferson Davis had no one to take his part.

Imprisonment tested the proud spirit of a man who had been a general, then a senator, and finally a president. One day the commander of Fortress Monroe ordered Davis shackled after he threw a plate of food in the face of the guard who brought it to him. After the chains were placed on his arms and legs, the tall, genteel Davis sat down on his cot and wept.

Davis did receive some unexpected comfort while in prison. Pope Pius IX, who had in Italy been battling a Liberalism similar to that of Juárez in Mexico, sent Davis a portrait of himself, with the papal signature and the inscription, "If any man will come after me, let him deny himself, and take up his cross, and follow me."

The cross symbolized the suffering of Davis

Illustration of Jefferson Davis in his cell at Fortress Monroe

and of thousands in the South, both white and black. "When the war closed in 1865," wrote the Scottish minister Rev. David Macrae, "the South presented a spectacle of wreck and prostration probably without parallel in modern times. . . . The people had shared in the general wreck, and looked poverty-stricken, careworn and dejected." The economy was devastated. Solitary chimneys and burnt-out houses and buildings gave witness to the ravages of war. Once proud gentlemen and their ladies took up menial jobs, while others rooted through trash for subsistence. Confederate veterans, some wounded, returned home to find their wives and children starving. Destitution was everywhere, in cities, in the villages, in the fields, and in the hearts of the people. Davis, in his humiliation, had become a symbol of the fallen southern nation.

To escape federal rule, a small number of southerners left their homes. Some of these expatriated to Brazil, taking with them whatever slaves who were willing to go with them; others joined Bedford Forrest, Jubal Early, and John Magruder in Mexico to fight for the Emperor Maximilian. Some moved north. Some fled even farther. Old Edmund Ruffin, who, legend has it, had fired the first shot on Fort Sumter, declared he could never live under Yankee rule and shot himself in the head. Others—the majority—remained in their native states, trying to rebuild their fortunes.

According to David Macrae (a northerner), most southerners were not sorry to see slavery end. "The South," he said, "feels like a man who has been subjected against his will to a severe operation—an operation which he thought would kill him, which has terribly prostrated him, from which he is doubtful if he will completely recover, but which being fairly over, has given him prodigious relief." Many southerners, though, probably agreed with a unionist southern man that though "the death of slavery is recognized" by southerners, "we don't believe that because the nigger is free he ought to be saucy; and we don't mean to have any such nonsense as letting him vote. He's helpless and ignorant, and dependent, and the old master will still control him."

The "Negro Question"

Indeed, the "Negro Question" would occupy the South—and the North—for the next 12 or so years. It would be the centerpiece of "Reconstruction"—the process of reintegrating the southern states into the union. Many southern whites were determined that, if the black man was free, he would not be equal. Southern whites feared (as they had feared under slavery) that if blacks were not "kept down," they would perpetrate bloody war on whites. The presence of black federal troops in the South did not assuage such fears. A bloody insurrection of former slaves, 30 years after their emancipation, in British Jamaica aroused southern fears, and the examples of black government in Haiti and Liberia were not encouraging. Though whites outnumbered blacks almost three to one in the South, in some areas blacks were in the majority. What, fearful whites asked, would happen if those blacks gained political power?

miscegenation: the mixing of races

Southern whites feared **miscegenation**. They thought (as did most Northerners) the black race inferior to the white; thus it was imperative that inter-racial marriages be avoided. One cannot escape the irony that, already, the number of mixed race persons (called mulattos, quadroons, and octaroons) was quite large in the South; yet, to the southern mind, since such persons came from illicit unions, they could not claim social equality with whites. To give equality to blacks, whether of pure or mixed ancestry, might, many feared, open up the door to legal, marital unions between whites and blacks and to a thorough mixing of the races. The result, some southerners said, would be to cut the South off from the family of white nations and to turn it into "another Mexico."

The desolation wrought by Federal armies in the South, the dislocation of many free blacks who had followed those armies and who now congregated around military outposts in the larger cities, produced great problems. The federal government established the Freedmen's Bureau (a branch of the war department) to pass out emergency rations of food (to both whites and blacks) and to integrate blacks into white society. The bureau founded schools for blacks throughout the South and helped support the founding of four black colleges. The bureau encouraged the many wandering freedmen to return to their former masters and work for wages.

The condition of blacks in the South varied. Some blacks had never left their old plantations, even when able to; others, following in the wake of the Federal army, had fled from their old homes. Many blacks were eager to work for wages, while others equated freedom with idleness. Many black families suffered from starvation, as some whites were unwilling to hire black men who had children.

Blacks had their own social classes. Those who had been house slaves or who had been freemen before the war had adopted more of white culture than those who had been field slaves. Often, the habits of those they deemed less cultivated embarrassed educated blacks. In particular, black forms of worship, which were very emotionally-charged and accompanied often by wild cries and shouts, appalled those blacks who had adopted more of white culture. A black sub-culture was developing among the poorer, less-educated people from which the more "cultured" blacks were excluded. Excluded, also, by whites, these blacks inhabited a lonely no-man's land in society.

Blacks more assimilated to white culture tried to raise the poorer blacks to what they thought a higher level of culture. Benjamin Montgomery, one of Jefferson Davis' former slaves, rented out two of Davis' confiscated plantations, Hurricane and Briarfield, to free blacks. By 1870 the project was so successful that the farmers could buy their plots of land and be independent. Still, not men like Montgomery, but black preachers became the leaders of black society. Belonging themselves to the black sub-culture, the preachers understood the hearts of their people.

Freedmen greeted wage earning at first with joy; but they soon learned that being a free wage earner carried certain disabilities. For one, former masters, now employers, paid freedmen as small a wage as possible, which was often not enough for their needs. Too, under slavery, a master would feed, clothe and house sick, injured, or elderly slaves; now, under freedom, employers turned out the infirm to fend for themselves. Other, healthier men were always available for hire. Many freedmen, too, had little notion of the value of money and wasted it on luxuries bought at the plantation store, leaving them little for necessities. Despite its evils, slavery was a world built on personal relationships that somewhat softened its rigors. The new, wage-earning world could be cold and pitiless.

As a branch of the war department, the Freedmen's Bureau operated within areas where occupying Federal armies held sway. Outside those areas, the lot of freedmen was not much changed; in fact, it was arguably worse. Fear of blacks led to violence against

A pro-Freedman's Bureau cartoon from *Harper's Magazine*, showing the bureau, represented by a Federal soldier, standing between angry whites and freedmen.

Anti-Freedman's Bureau cartoon. It reads: "THE FREEDMAN'S BUREAU! An agency to keep the Negro in idleness at the Expense of the White Man. Twice vetoed by the President, and made a law by Congress. Support Congress & you support the Negro. Sustain the President and you protect the White Man." The president referred to was Andrew Johnson.

blacks. Freedmen who were too "uppity," who dared to assert their equality, or who even looked a white man in the eye, were beaten, sometimes killed. Cases there were of black men violating white women—for which offense they would be lynched by bands of whites. But more often innocent blacks shared the fate of the guilty just on suspicion of wrongdoing, or for simply acting "uppity."

The worst violence against blacks was found in parts of the South, such as eastern Tennessee, where there had been few plantations and where unionist sentiment had been strongest during the war. Blacks, by and large, fared better among the "old master" class and in the plantation South. Poor whites tended not only to fear but to hate blacks; they saw blacks as competitors for their place in society and blamed blacks for the war and the subsequent destruction of their homes. The old masters wanted to keep blacks down but tended to maintain a paternalistic care for them. Men who had been kind masters maintained the loyalty and affection of many of their former slaves.

White violence was not only directed against blacks but against other whites, as well. Unionists suffered in some parts of the South at the hands of Confederate veterans, and Confederates suffered in areas that had been predominately unionist. Confederate hate was also directed against "scalawags"—southerners who cooperated with Federal occupying forces, Republicans, or the Freedmen's Bureau. Some southerners, such as General James Longstreet, who had joined the Republican party, cooperated with the North in order to ease the lot of their fellow southerners. But others did it for mere gain and sometimes suffered bitterly for their greed.

More despised than the scalawags, if possible, were the "carpetbaggers"—Northerners who had moved South either to help freedmen or, more typically, to profit off southern misfortune. Named carpetbaggers because they were said to have come south with all their belongings in a satchel made from two squares of carpet, these Northerners bought up old plantations at depressed prices or established businesses and built factories. Eventually they would play leading roles in southern politics while native southerners were excluded from voting and holding office.

A cartoon depicting President Lincoln and Vice President Johnson working together to stitch up the union. The caption reads: "The 'Rail Splitter' at Work Repairing the Union." Johnson, sitting astride a globe, says, "Take it quietly UNCLE ABE and I will draw it closer than ever!!" And Lincoln says, "A few more stitches ANDY and the good old UNION will be mended."

President Johnson's Reconstruction

Andrew Johnson had been a teacher in east Tennessee before he entered politics. Like so many in that region of his state, Johnson had resented the power and influence of the great planter aristocracy that occupied the fertile lands to the west. Elected to the Senate, Johnson was an ardent unionist; so, when Tennessee seceded from the union, Johnson insisted on keeping his seat in the Senate. President Lincoln had made Johnson wartime governor of Tennessee for his loyalty, and (though Johnson was a Democrat) had chosen him as his running mate in 1864.

As vice-president, Johnson had said that treason must be made odious and traitors punished and impoverished; but as president he continued Lincoln's policy of binding up the wounds of the union with "charity towards all" and "malice towards none." Two members of his cabinet shared Johnson's desire to reinstate the southern states as full members of the union. Both Secretary of State William H. Seward and Secretary of the Navy Gideon Welles thought it was high time to restore the constitutional order of the United States to what it had been before the war. Though anti-secessionists, Seward and Welles were for clearly defined states' rights. They believed that, while the federal government might punish individuals for traitorous conduct, it could not punish states—for, they said, hadn't the federal government gotten its authority from the states in the first place?

Edward M. Stanton, the secretary of war, disagreed. With his allies, Thaddeus Stevens in the House of Representatives and Charles Sumner in the Senate (the same Sumner whom Preston Brooks had beaten senseless back in 1856), Stanton thought the South should be more severely punished for the war. But these men, along with the Radical Republican faction in Congress (who had given Lincoln sorrow during the war), did not long simply for revenge; they wanted to reconstruct the social order in the South, giving blacks full equality and voting rights with whites. To this end, they wanted to extend the power of the federal government beyond what many believed its constitutional limits. But such legal scruples were of little moment to the Radicals, who interpreted the Constitution in light of their ideals. "Anything for human rights," as Sumner said, "is constitutional."

Andrew Johnson, by Mathew Brady

Thaddeus Stevens had been in Congress since 1848. As an anti-slavery Whig from Pennsylvania, he had opposed the Compromise of 1850 and the Fugitive Slave Law. Reelected in 1856 as a Republican, Stevens, with his strong, uncompromising manner and stinging wit and sarcasm, became the most powerful man in the House of Representatives. Stevens pronounced the southern states conquered provinces and said they should be treated as such. He wanted to humble the proud, planter aristocracy by turning their estates over to their former slaves. "Strip a proud nobility of their bloated estates, " he said, "reduce them to a level with plain republicans; send them forth to labor, and teach children to enter the workshops or handle the plow, and you will thus humble the proud traitors. Teach his posterity to respect labor and eschew treason. Conspiracies are bred among the rich and vain, the ambitious aristocrats."

Stevens identified the good of the nation with the good of the Republican party. This, in part, induced him to push for black suffrage while denying the suffrage to southern white "rebels." Blacks, he was sure, would vote Republican; southern whites, Democratic. If southern Democrats united with northern Democrats, the Republican party might lose control of Congress. To avoid this, Stevens had pushed Congress to deny seats to representatives from Lincoln's "ten percent" states and vehemently fought Johnson's plan of reconstruction.

Thaddeus Stevens, by Mathew Brady and Levin Corbin Handy

In June 1865, President Johnson appointed provisional governors for the southern states. These states, he said, were to call conventions to draw up new state constitutions that, said Johnson, had to declare secession illegal and abolish slavery. Southern whites, said Johnson, would be allowed to vote under the new constitutions, but not those who had served as civil officers in the Confederacy, had been governors of seceded states, had been general officers in the Confederate army and navy, or whose wealth had exceeded $20,000. Even among these groups, army and naval officers, and the rich, could obtain a pardon if they swore oaths of allegiance to the union. Among the first to avail himself of this provision was Robert E. Lee. Many others followed his example.

Johnson enacted his reconstruction package without summoning Congress to a special session. He even ignored a letter sent him by Thaddeus Stevens in July asking Johnson to do nothing until Congress convened in December. Stevens could not like the new southern state constitutions; for, though granting blacks freedom, they did nothing more for them—neither granted them civil rights nor the right to vote. Meanwhile, Republicans and members of the Freedmen's Bureau in the South were reporting hundreds of instances of

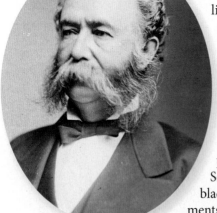

violence and cruelty against freedmen, unionists, schoolteachers, and those who went south to help the blacks.

When Congress assembled in December 1865, the Republican majority established the Joint Committee on Reconstruction to investigate reports of abuse coming out of the South. Meanwhile, every southern state, except Texas, had held elections and by January had functioning state governments. That the new southern legislatures had a large number of former Confederate officers troubled the Radical Republicans. Stevens' men bristled at southern acts of defiance—the governor of Mississippi, for instance, refused to fly the national flag over the state capitol and, in several instances, legislators publicly equated Yankees with vandals. Worse than all this, though, were the black codes—laws passed by southern legislatures to keep blacks "in their place." Though such prominent men as Robert E. Lee in Virginia and General Wade Hampton in South Carolina counseled the new state governments to grant civil rights to blacks and even the suffrage to literate and intelligent blacks, the new governments, dominated by middle and lower class whites, passed laws that prohibited blacks from voting and from serving as jurors. Some of the black codes prohibited black men to assemble, made it illegal for them to own firearms, and established the pillory and flogging to punish them.

Wade Hampton, by Mathew Brady and Levin Corbin Handy

The black codes contained elements of old laws against vagrancy and embodied in law the customs of slavery times. The codes utilized regulations for ex-slaves enacted in the British West Indies, as well as Federal regulations for freedmen. The black code of Mississippi, for instance, mandated that black minors under the age of 18 "who are orphans, or whose parent or parents have not the means or who refuse to provide for and support said minors" be apprenticed to a "competent and suitable person." This "person," said the code, must "protect the interest of the minor," furnish him "sufficient food and clothing," treat him "humanely," provide him "medical attention in case of sickness," and "teach, or cause to be taught, him or her to read and write." In Louisiana, blacks were to contract themselves out every year to whatever employer they wished; but they were forbidden to leave their employers for the time specified by their contracts.

Some black codes, however, contained measures to protect freedmen's rights. The Louisiana black code required employers to honor contracts with freedmen under threat of being "fined an amount double that due the laborer . . . to be paid to the laborer." Any "cruelty or neglect of duty on the part of the employer," said the code, "shall be summarily punished by fines . . . to be paid to the injured party." Both employers and employees could seek justice from the courts—but since no black could serve as juror or judge, he had to rely on the justice and good will of the very men who wanted to keep him down.

The severity of black codes varied from state to state—Mississippi's, Louisiana's, and Florida's were the harshest;

A cartoon deriding Johnson as "King Andy I." Beside the crowned Johnson, Secretary of State William H. Seward directs the execution of Thaddeus Stevens.

those of Virginia, North Carolina, and Georgia were more benign. Because of strong unionist influence, Tennessee had no black code.

Whether mild or harsh, the black codes were not calculated to please the likes of Stevens and Sumner, who wanted immediate and complete equality for blacks in the South. To undermine the governments that established these codes, Radical Republicans in Congress assailed President Johnson's reconstruction policy. In February 1866, Congress passed the Freedmen's Bureau Bill, extending the life of the bureau and expanding its powers. With characteristic courage and stubbornness, President Johnson vetoed the bill. He objected that the bill contained "provisions which . . . are not warranted by the Constitution and are not well suited to accomplish the end in view"—to secure to freedmen "the full enjoyment of their freedom and property and their entire independence and equality in making contracts for their labor." Johnson, in particular, criticized the bill because he said it unconstitutionally maintained martial law in peacetime. He cited Article 6 of the Constitution: "in all criminal prosecutions the accused shall enjoy the right to a speedy and public trial by an impartial jury of the State and district wherein the crime shall have been committed." Further, said the president, by passing a law governing 11 states, while refusing to seat their representatives, Congress was violating the principle of no taxation without representation.

Undaunted by the president's veto, Congress in March passed the Civil Rights Act. "All persons born in the United States and not subject to any foreign power," said the act, ". . . are hereby declared to be citizens of the United States." As citizens, such persons, regardless of their color or "previous condition of slavery," are guaranteed the "full and equal protection of the law." Johnson vetoed the act. The power to confer state citizenship, said the veto message, "is just as exclusively with the several states as the power to confer the right of Federal citizenship is with Congress." Johnson said the bill gave the federal government powers that had been "considered as exclusively belonging to the States. They all relate to the internal police and economy of the respective States. They are matters which in each State concern the domestic condition of its people, varying in each according to its own peculiar circumstances and the safety and well-being of its own citizens." Johnson objected to transferring state court cases to federal tribunals. "The question here naturally arises, from what source Congress derives the power to transfer to Federal tribunals certain classes of cases embraced in this section," wrote Johnson. The bill "undoubtedly comprehends cases and authorizes the exercise of powers that are not, by the Constitution, within the jurisdiction of the courts of the United States."

In sum, Johnson called the Civil Rights Act revolutionary. The act, he wrote . . .

> . . . is another step, or rather stride, toward centralization and the concentration of all legislative powers in the National Government. The tendency of the bill must be to resuscitate the spirit of rebellion and to arrest the progress of those influences which are more closely drawing around the States the bonds of union and peace.

Despite so stern a warning, Congress overrode the president's veto on April 9, 1866.

Radical Republican themselves doubted the constitutionality of their Civil Rights Act. Their doubts were confirmed in April by the Supreme Court decision, *Ex Parte Milligan*. Though a Lincoln appointee, Chief Justice Salmon P. Chase, with the entire court, ruled that Lincoln's wartime suspension of *habeas corpus* throughout the union had been unconstitutional. Since the Constitution applies to rulers and people both in peace and wartime, said the court, "martial rule can never exist when the Courts are open and in the proper and unobstructed exercise of their jurisdiction." This decision vindicated Johnson, who immediately suspended military court trials of civilians throughout the South.

Charles Sumner

Stevens, Sumner, and the Radicals were checked but not defeated. In July they were able to override the president's veto of the Freedmen's Bureau bill; but the key to their victory ultimately lay in the insertion of the 14th Amendment into the Constitution. This amendment, approved by Congress in June 1866, embodied the essence of the Civil Rights Act and gave the federal government unprecedented powers over the states.

The 14th Amendment for the first time linked state with national citizenship. "All persons," it read, "born or naturalized in the United States, and subject to the jurisdiction thereof, are citizens of the United States and of the State wherein they reside." Further, the amendment assured equal treatment for all citizens. It says:

> No State shall make or enforce any law which shall abridge the privileges or immunities of citizens of the United States; nor shall any State deprive any person of life, liberty, or property, without due process of law; nor deny to any person within its jurisdiction the equal protection of the laws.

The amendment contained language (inserted by Thaddeus Stevens) directed at breaking the political power of former rebels in the southern states: no one, it said, who "shall have engaged in insurrection or rebellion against" the United States, "or given aid or comfort to the enemies thereof" shall be eligible to hold political or judicial authority either in federal or state governments. And striking out at President Johnson's pardon of Confederate generals and soldiers, the amendment said only *Congress* "may by a vote of two-thirds of each House, remove such disability."

"The Congress shall have the power to enforce, by appropriate legislation, the provisions of this article." This clause of the 14th Amendment would in the future, give the federal government almost unlimited sway over the states. In future years some would argue that the federal government, not state governments, should be the final defender of citizens' rights.

Though not an immediate victory (for three-fourths of the states had still to ratify it), the 14th Amendment assured that the Radical Republicans' dream of equality would live on long after their political power ended. It also seemed to confirm the fear of Welles, Johnson, Seward, and many others—that the prewar republic, with its balance of state and national sovereignty, was giving way to a new, centralized political order: an imperial republic.

Radical Reconstruction

On August 20, 1866, President Johnson declared the end of the "insurrection"—the Civil War. "Peace," he said, "order, tranquility and civil authority now exist in and throughout the whole of the United States."

The Radical Republicans had some grounds to disagree. In May, a brawl between white state police and black soldiers in Memphis had mushroomed into a bloody race riot. After the black soldiers retired to their encampment, the white police assaulted blacks throughout the city, killing 48 and wounding eight—including inmates of the Freedmen's Bureau hospital.

In New Orleans, the Republican reconstruction governor, J. Madison Wells, had called a state constitutional convention, to be composed of white Republicans and blacks, to amend the state constitution to grant blacks the suffrage. On May 1, the day the convention was scheduled to meet, a mob, led by the sheriff (an ex-Confederate general), attacked a large group of blacks. When the blacks fled, the mob hunted them down, crying, "God damn you, not one of you will escape from here alive." The casualty count that day was 48 killed, 68 badly wounded, and 98 slightly injured.

Such riots not only assured the passage in Congress of the 14th Amendment but weakened northern support for Johnson. Clergymen, the press, and business leaders turned

Race riot in Memphis, May 1866

against the president. But Johnson remained undaunted. During the Congressional election of 1866, he stumped through the Midwest for Democratic candidates. Before crowds of westerners, many of whom cared not a lick for the "nigger problem" and who had axes to grind against the industrial northeast (the Republican stronghold), Johnson attacked Congressional Republicans, whom he called the enemies of states' rights. By refusing to seat southern state delegates, Congress, said Johnson, had lost its constitutional authority to act.

The Republicans gave as good as they got. "Jefferson Davis is in the casemate at Fortress Monroe," declared Charles Sumner, "but Andrew Johnson is doing his work. Witness Memphis, witness New Orleans." In the end, the Republicans proved the more persuasive; in December, Congress convened with a larger, veto-proof Republican majority.

Thomas Nast cartoon of the New Orleans riots. In the door way is President Johnson, crowned

Segregation in the North: cartoon from 1856 depicting a black man in Philadelphia being expelled from a railway car

The Radicals did not wait long to use their enhanced power. From December to March 1867, the Joint Committee on Reconstruction presented testimony after testimony of abuse of freedmen and unionists, as well as southern lack of cooperation with the Freedmen's Bureau and the military. The South was still in dire need of "serenity and peace," said the committee, which must come by means of changes in "organic law as shall determine the civil rights and privileges of all citizens in all parts of the republic" and "shall place representation upon an equitable basis."

By "representation upon an equitable basis," the committee report meant black manhood suffrage. Not surprisingly, this was a very controversial issue. Since the war, several northern states had voted, by wide margins, to withhold the suffrage from the few blacks within their borders; only in New England could blacks vote. Even many abolitionists did not favor of giving the vote to freedmen. William Lloyd Garrison in his *Liberator* wrote that he thought it was too soon to grant freedmen the suffrage. Richard Henry Dana thought slavery had debased the freedmen; they needed first learn to read and write, he insisted; but, even then, "the greatest good of the greatest number of people" in the South should decide the issue of black suffrage—and the greatest number were white.

Frederick Douglass, however, argued that blacks are not "naturally, or practically, or in any important sense inferior to anybody on this globe." They, thus, should be granted the suffrage. "What I ask for the Negro," said Douglass, "is not benevolence, not pity, not sympathy, but simply *justice*." He begged Garrison and other abolitionists not to abandon the struggle for black people. In the North, in Illinois, Indiana, and Ohio, blacks could not testify in a court of law, said Douglass; and in the South, "the very fact that the Negro has been used to defeat this rebellion and strike down the standard of the Confederacy will be a stimulus to all the whites' hatreds, to all their malice, and lead them to legislate with greater stringency toward this class than ever before."

The Radical Republicans were of the same mind as Douglass, and in 1867 they took reconstruction out of the hands of the president. In a Reconstruction Act, passed in March, Congress disbanded all southern state governments then functioning and divided the South into five military districts under five generals, all of whom answered to U.S. Grant. The Reconstruction Act gave the military the authority to purge state governments of "disloyal" members, for Congress had ruled that ex-Confederates could not serve in public office. Under Congressional Reconstruction, southern states had to call conventions to draw up new state constitutions to guarantee black civil rights and the right to vote. Blacks would have a voice in choosing delegates to the constitutional conventions. Congress further decreed that before any reconstructed southern state could be readmitted to the union, its legislature had to ratify the 14th Amendment.

Reconstruction Governments

"Satraps," "despots" were the names southern whites gave U.S. Grant's governor-generals. Indeed, some of the generals were out to punish "rebels" and "traitors," in some cases suppressing Confederate veterans organizations and parades and even historical societies. But worse than all this to the humbled whites was that only blacks and "loyal" whites could vote. Under Congress' Reconstruction, South Carolina, Alabama, Florida, and Mississippi had more black than white voters. In South Carolina, blacks dominated the state constitutional convention.

Some of the black leaders that met to draw up South Carolina's constitution were accomplished, well-educated men. Among them were Robert Brown Elliott, who claimed he had studied at English schools and at Eton College, Oxford. Though no record exists of him attending those schools, Elliott clearly had had a classical education and could speak several languages. Another black leader, Francis Cardozo, was the son of Isaac Cardozo, a free black of Charleston before the war who had become an economist, a newspaper editor, and a prominent writer. Isaac's son, Francis, helped establish Freedmen's Bureau schools and was the principal of Avery Institute, a private college for blacks. Other prominent blacks included William Whipper, a lawyer from Pennsylvania, and Martin Delany. Delany had been accepted to Harvard Medical School, though he never attended; white students there refused to study with a black man. Before the war, Delany had recommended resettling former slaves in Santo Domingo in the Caribbean; since the war, he had been helping freedmen establish farms around Hilton Head, South Carolina.

The speeches of Delany, Whipper, Elliott, and other blacks during the constitutional convention were calm, reasoned, and articulate. They were well seasoned with New England radical thought. These men called not only for free public schools (which South Carolina had never had) but for mixed-race schools. Francis Cardozo's suggestion that education be compulsory brought on an objection from another black delegate, Robert De Large, who thought such a measure impossible to put into operation. Elliott, however, backed up Cardozo. It is "republicanism to educate people without discrimination," said Elliott. "The question is not white or black united or divided, but whether children shall be sent to school or kept at home." The state, not the parents, according to Elliott, should decide how children must be employed during the day.

Martin Delany as a major in the Civil War

Delegates considered the important question of how freedmen could obtain land. William Whipper opposed confiscation, and the convention voted that the state would pay for any lands distributed to freedmen. Whipper also suggested that the new constitution give women the right to vote—a measure that was defeated. The convention, though, drew up the first divorce law South Carolina had ever had and provided for direct election of the governor, who, under the old constitution, had been appointed by the legislature.

Though blacks did not dominate other southern state constitutional conventions, a few black legislators gained prominence outside of South Carolina. Among them was James Rapier of Alabama, who had attended the University of Glasgow in Scotland. Another was James Lynch, who became Mississippi's secretary of state.

The state elections of 1867 were the first in which blacks were to vote—and many wondered how the experiment would work out. In registering freedmen to vote, one not only had to reckon with the violence of whites but with the inexperience of the freedmen themselves. Having been slaves, most blacks did not really understand what it was to be a citizen.

Black men and white who worked to register black voters labored to convince them to vote Republican. One Mary Jones tells of "a Yankee Negro" speaker who assured his black audience that, next year, the government would take land from the whites and distribute it among the blacks in 40 acre parcels. Others

Freedmen voting

appealed to the simple fact that the Republicans would look after black interests, unlike representatives of the "old master class," who only wanted to keep blacks down.

In 1867, 700,000 blacks registered to vote in the South while white registered voters numbered only 40,000. Many whites, in protest against the Reconstruction governments, simply refused to register or to vote. The result was that southern governments became predominately Republican, with a large number of blacks serving in the state legislatures and on governors' staffs. Some of these blacks were competent to serve; others were not, and thus, white "carpetbaggers" used them as pawns in the greater political struggle.

Southern Whites Fight Back

On a cold December evening in 1865, a group of young, former Confederate soldiers in Pulaski, Tennessee, decided they would form a club, a secret society. It was not to be anything serious, it seems; after all, the titles they took for the various officers were downright ridiculous. The leader of the group would be called the "Grand Cyclops," while other officers would bear such titles as "Grand Dragon" and "Grand Magi." Members would go by the absurd name of "Ghouls." When it came to naming the club itself, one member suggested the Greek word *kuklos* (meaning "circle")—just to make the whole business sound mysterious. Another suggested adding "clam" to the name, from which combination they arrived, at last, at the name, "Ku Klux Klan."

The members adopted an elaborate, but silly, ritual for their club. They also began riding through the streets of the town by night, dressed in white sheets. When these night rides created a stir among townsmen—and, especially, frightened superstitious freedmen—the Klan added a white pointed mask to their costume. It is not clear when the group went from being a social diversion for bored young men to a kind of vigilante group, but it was not long before hooded men in white sheets began visiting black cabins at night to warn their frightened inhabitants to be good—that is, keep their place. Soon simple warnings turned to violence directed against "uppity" blacks.

"Visit of the Ku Klux," by Frank Bellew, 1872

The Ku Klux Klan grew and spread to other states. Men, prominent in the Confederacy as politicians and generals, joined the white-sheeted ranks. General Nathan Bedford Forrest, who became the first "Grand Wizard" of the order, described the Klan as "an institution of Chivalry, Humanity, Mercy and Patriotism" whose purpose was to resist the inroads of the northern conqueror into southern society. Since blacks were seen as the tools by which Yankee carpetbaggers were crushing white southerners, blacks would have to be warned to mind their behavior. Such warning went beyond mere terrorizing—Klan members and their imitators (for anyone could don a white sheet and hood) beat and murdered blacks who would not submit to their demands. They also attacked white unionists, carpetbaggers, and scalawags. Soon, bands of blacks and unionist whites were clashing in bloody struggles with Klansmen.

In April 1867, Klan leaders gathered in Nashville to decide how they would respond to Congress' Reconstruction Act. They created an elaborate chain of command, at the head of which was the "Grand Wizard." Throughout the spring and summer, sheeted nightriders appeared throughout the South, terrorizing blacks to keep them from voting. These sheeted vigilantes began to use not only whips but guns on particularly stubborn individuals. Murders and instances of cruel violence increased. Black and white radical politicians were threatened; some were shot; others had their houses burnt down. Other groups arose, imitating the Klan—the Knights of the White Camelia and numerous others. Groups of blacks began to form to protect the persons and property of those who received threatening warnings from the Ku Klux.

The Klan formed an "Invisible Empire" that successfully resisted the attempts of Reconstruction governments to suppress it. In some counties, the Klan was the de-facto government. Though many southern whites deplored the Klan's violence, they welcomed its intervention. They saw blacks as tools of the northern radicals to undermine white southern culture and independence.

Elizabeth Merriweather and her husband Minor had freed their slaves before the war (at great financial loss to themselves) and paid for their passage to Liberia. Now, after the war, she noted that, before the Klan, white southerners "felt powerless, in the face of over-whelming military forces, to prevent the carpetbaggers from using the Negroes as tools with which to exploit the South to the point of utter ruin and desolation." Under the carpetbaggers, she said, "the ignorant Negroes became intolerably insolent and overbearing." For instance, they began "sitting by white women in street cars," they went to the polls to vote, they were "elbowing white men off the sidewalks, etc." Such effronteries, to the white southern mind, presaged worse things to come; but then the Klan came and ended, said Merriweather, the "orgy of misrule and oppression." It saved the South "from such a devastation as no country has seen since the Duke of Alva laid waste the lowlands of Holland!"

Through 1868, and into 1869, Congress and Reconstruction governments adopted harsher measures to deal with the Invisible Empire, hunting down Klansmen and establishing martial law in Klan-dominated counties. In 1869, Bedford Forrest ordered the Klan disbanded, and it ceased to exist as a centralized organization, though local chapters continued to threaten, torture, mutilate, and kill their opponents. In 1871, Congress passed legislation that removed state jurisdiction in the South over murder, assault, and robbery, and expressly forbade night riding and the wearing of masks and white sheets. Yet, by 1871, the Klan was already growing obsolete. It died of its own accord in the mid 1870s.

An 1868 cartoon by Thomas Nast depicting the South as a skeleton, holding a gun to prevent blacks from voting

Gunning for the President

Thaddeus Stevens and other Radical congressman, like Benjamin "the Beast" Butler, had for some time been openly talking about impeaching President Johnson. The problem was they could not convincingly charge the president with treason, bribery, or other "high crimes and misdemeanors"—offenses that, according to the Constitution, justified the removal of a president from office following impeachment. But though they couldn't rid themselves of Johnson, the Radicals could chip away at his power.

The Radicals had an ally and confidant in the president's cabinet—Secretary of War Edwin M. Stanton. To prevent Johnson from dismissing Stanton, the Radicals pushed through Congress the Tenure of Office Act in March 1867. The act required the president to seek the "advice and consent" of the Senate, not only when appointing cabinet members (which the Constitution requires), but even when dismissing them. This act was certainly unconstitutional, as it encroached on executive powers; but the Radicals were riding high and feared no one.

Such a Congressional grab for power only stiffened Johnson's will to resist. In August 1867, he ordered Stanton to resign. Stanton refused and stubbornly awaited the convening of Congress in December. Johnson, however, appointed Ulysses S. Grant as temporary secretary and then proceeded to remove Generals Sheridan and Daniel Sickles from the military districts they commanded in the South, replacing them, with Generals Winfield Scott Hancock and E.R.S. Canby, both known to be more sympathetic to the South.

The Senate gathered for the impeachment trial of Andrew Johnson, *Harper's Weekly*, 1868

The Radicals were fighting mad when Congress convened in December. They refused to recognize the dismissal of Stanton (at which point, Grant resigned), and the House called for the impeachment of the president. The vote for impeachment failed. But, though he was courting danger (for Thaddeus Stevens was out for blood), Johnson would not back down. He replaced Stanton with another secretary of war, and when Stanton refused to vacate his office in the War Department, rumor had it that Johnson would call out the marines to evict him.

Stevens would tolerate no more opposition from the president. In February, he renewed his call for impeachment. "There is a moral necessity [for impeachment] for which I care something, and there is a party necessity for it, for which I care more," Stevens told *Blackwood's Magazine.* "In fact," Stevens continued, "the party necessity is the moral necessity; for I consider that when the Republican party dies this country will be given over to the so-called Democracy, which is worse than the devil." Stevens and Butler drew up the charges against Johnson. The president, they said, had removed Stanton without the Senate's advice and consent and had in his speeches attacked the Republican Congress. Benjamin Butler "waved the bloody shirt" of an Ohio carpetbagger flogged by the Ku Klux Klan in Mississippi and said Johnson was responsible for such injustices. In the end, Stevens and Butler got their way. On February 24, 1868, the House of Representatives voted, 126 to 47, to impeach President Johnson "of high crimes and misdemeanors in office."

Chief Justice Salmon Chase presided over the first presidential impeachment trial ever held in the Senate. Johnson was represented by some of the ablest council in the country, who proceeded to destroy the prosecution's case. Still, Johnson was not out of danger, for Radical Republicans dominated the Senate as well as the House. In the end, on May 16, 1868, seven Republicans voted to acquit Johnson, bringing the vote to 35 Senators for conviction, 19 against—just one vote shy of the required two-thirds majority needed to convict a president.

Yet, though he had failed to oust the president, Stevens did succeed in neutralizing his power. With only ten months left in office, and with little chance that the Democrats would nominate such an unpopular man for president in the election of 1868, Johnson could do nothing to stem the triumphant tide of Radicalism. By the summer of 1868, eight southern states (North Carolina, South Carolina, Georgia, Florida, Alabama, Louisiana, Arkansas, and Tennessee) voted to ratify the 14th Amendment and were admitted into the union. On July 9, 1868, that amendment had been ratified by enough states to become part of the Constitution.

The same month the 14th Amendment became law, Thaddeus Stevens gave his last address to Congress. He was 76 years old and so sick that he had to be carried into the House chambers. Americans live "in a political Eden," he told his fellow Congressmen; "all we have to do is avoid the forbidden fruit, for we have not yet reached the perfection of justice." This "forbidden fruit" was racial and class prejudice, which Congress could avoid, said Stevens, if they but "fling away ambition and realize that every human being, however lowly born or degraded, by fortune is your equal and that every inalienable right which belongs to you belongs also to him." If his colleagues only realized this, said Stevens, "truth and righteousness will spread over the land."

Stevens died the following month, convinced that his life and work had been a failure. A few days before his death, he told a journalist that "with all this struggle of years in Washington, and the fearful sacrifice of life and treasure, I see little hope for the Republic." Ironically, some of his enemies in the South and in the president's cabinet might have said something similar, but for very different reasons.

Part II: **President Grant and the Gilded Age**

It was not at all clear that the Republicans could take the presidency in the election of 1868.

The late war encouraged the idea that the only rift in the country was along the Mason-Dixon and the Ohio River. This was not the case. The Appalachians marked another division between the increasingly industrialized Northeast and the predominately agricultural Middle West. One could also note gaping chasms in the large cities between the wealthy and the swarms of poor workmen, many of whom were Irish immigrants.

The Republican party's insistence on Negro suffrage and civil rights did not appeal to many westerners and poor, working class Irish. The yeoman farmer of the West had never had any love for blacks. The Irishman, subsisting at the bottom of the social pyramid, saw free black labor as competition for his paltry wages. Yet, the "Negro Question" alone did not determine the political views of these men. The Republicans favored the interests of the industrialists and the Wall Street men—bankers and speculators—of the East by insisting that the value of money be based on gold **specie** and by calling for high tariffs on imported manufactured goods. Specie-backed currency increased the buying power of the dollar (for it made each dollar worth more), but it also made the dollar harder to come by. Western farmers and small businessmen favored the paper currency that had been issued during the war. Since each paper dollar was worth less than a dollar in specie, its purchasing power was less. Such "cheap" money thus forced prices up by increasing the number of dollars in circulation, and this benefited small shopkeepers and farmers, or so they thought.

specie: money in coin, either in gold or silver

A Tilden-Hendricks campaign poster

Ulysses S. Grant

The Democratic platform seemed tailor-fit for those who were dissatisfied with Republican rule. It demanded "immediate restoration of all the States to their rights in the Union under the Constitution, and of civil government to the American people"—thus, attacking Reconstruction and the Republican disregard for states' rights. The Democrats called for amnesty "for all past political offenses, and the regulation of the elective franchise in the States by their citizens." It demanded the "abolition of the Freedmen's Bureau" and an end to the "usurpation of Congress" and the "despotism of the sword." The Democrats favored a tariff only for the purpose of tax revenue, not for protection of industry.

The Republicans, though, had one advantage over the Democrats—their presidential candidate was the war hero, Ulysses S. Grant. The Democrats, abandoning Johnson for Horatio Seymour, could not compete against the popularity of Grant. Grant captured 214 electoral votes, while Seymour garnered only 80. Even had the still unreconstructed states (Virginia, Mississippi, and Texas) added their 23 votes to Seymour, he could not have won. The disparity of the popular vote, though, was not so great: 3,015,071 for Grant, 2,709,613 for Seymour—a difference of less than 310,000 votes.

"I shall on all subjects have a policy to recommend, but none to enforce against the will of the people," said Grant in his inaugural address in March 1869. The general-president stated that the object of government policy should be "the greatest good to the greatest number," and such a policy "required security of person, property, and free religious and political opinion in every part of our common country, without regard to local prejudice." To Grant, though, it belonged, not to the states, but to the federal government, to protect and foster the "greatest good of the greatest number." The states, in his opinion, were to function as instruments of the national government. In his commitment to centralization, Grant aligned himself with the Radical Republicans in Congress.

Grant's commitment to centralization transcended national boundaries. In a speech he gave at Birmingham, on a visit to England, Grant expressed his fond hopes for an international tribunal that would peacefully resolve disputes between nations. "Nothing should afford me greater happiness," said the president, "than to know that, as I believe will be the case, at some future day, the nations of the earth will agree upon some sort of congress which will take cognizance of international questions of difficulty and whose decisions will be as binding as the decisions of our Supreme Court are upon us. It is a dream of mine that some such solution may be." The old general had, perhaps, seen too much of the horror of war to think it a fit arbiter of international disputes. (His former enemy, Robert E. Lee, then president of tiny Washington College in Lexington, Virginia, had, it seems, also grown sick of war. "The greatest mistake of my life," said Lee, "was taking a military education.")

Grant's espousal of a dominant national power reflected a new epoch in United States history, one inaugurated by the Civil War. Increasingly people would say the United States "is" instead of, as previously, the United States "are." This grammatical shift indicated that the United States "were" becoming a consolidated nation, not a union or confederation of sovereign states. This consolidation had been the goal of Alexander Hamilton and, to some extent, of George Washington. Commitment to the decentralization favored by Thomas

Jefferson and his party was withering. It had made its first formal assault in the Virginia and Kentucky Resolves of the 1798/99; it had been nurtured by the men who supported the Hartford Convention, by John C. Calhoun and nullification, and by the sentiment of much, perhaps most, of the country, North and South. The Civil War had dealt it a fatal wound; and though there were yet many who championed the doctrine of "states' rights," their numbers would dwindle and their cause languish.

Nowhere was Grant's conception of national power more in evidence than in his advocacy for equal rights for blacks. His commitment to black equality appeared in his appointment of black men to posts in his administration. In his inaugural address, Grant called for ratification of the 15th Amendment, which would extend the suffrage to blacks nationwide. Like 14th Amendment, the proposed amendment extended the power of Congress over questions that had formerly been the domain of the states. It forbade the United States or any state to deny or abridge the right to vote purely "on account of race, color, or previous condition of servitude;" and decreed that "the Congress shall have the power to enforce this article by appropriate legislation."

An 1870 poster celebrating the passage of the 15th Amendment

Congress had passed the 15th Amendment on February 26, 1869, shortly before Grant took office. Charles Sumner and other Radicals, however, had opposed the amendment because, they said, it did not go far enough to protect the rights of blacks. While the amendment did not allow states to withhold suffrage from blacks merely because of their race and color, it said nothing about discrimination based on other grounds—such as the ability to read or to pay a **poll tax**. Sumner argued that unless the amendment specified that a state could not discriminate in voting on account of education or wealth, it would become a dead letter. States would raise obstacles to voting that few blacks could overcome.

Yet, despite the objections, abolitionists saw the amendment as the fulfillment of all their labors. The American Anti-Slavery Society in May 1869 called it "the capstone and completion of our movement." Blacks could now, they thought, achieve equal rights with the vote. When the amendment was ratified in February 1870, William Lloyd Garrison, who had awakened the anti-slavery movement over 40 years earlier, dissolved the American Anti-Slavery Society. "We have lived to see as great a miracle as ever we had read of," exulted Garrison. "Who ever dreamed of seeing a nation, as it were, born in a day? Ten years ago the slave power seemed to be able to defy God." Garrison prophesied: "I believe it is the will of God, that those States shall pass under the control of the colored people, and that they will lead off in a career of prosperity and honor and glory for our country."

The mid-term elections of 1870 saw several blacks elected to Congress, including Joseph Rainey, Robert Elliott, Ranier and Richard Cain—all of South Carolina; John Lynch of Mississippi; and James Rapier of Alabama. These black congressmen aligned themselves with the Radical Republicans. In his maiden speech to Congress, Elliott opposed a bill granting amnesty and the franchise to unreconstructed southern whites.

This, the 41st Congress, and its predecessor, passed three "force acts" in 1870, 1871, and 1872, to compel southern whites to respect the right of blacks to vote. The years of Reconstruction had embittered many more southerners against "Yankee carpetbag"

poll tax: a fixed amount of money a person has to pay in order to vote

government and against the blacks who, they thought, served as the tools of that government. Ku Klux Klan-style groups continued to intimidate, threaten, and murder blacks to keep them from the polls. Some black legislators were injured and murdered. But despite the force acts, the federal government could not control these "white knights" of the "Invisible Empire." Southern white resistance was too elusive, too widespread.

The force acts had the further effect of alienating some Republicans from the Radical cause. The German congressman from Missouri, Carl Schurz, for one, began to believe that federal interference was subverting republican government. He decried the interference of "National Government into local affairs on every possible occasion," and "even to disregard and throw aside the most fundamental safeguards of popular rights for the correction of passing abuses." Schurz believed the doctrine of states' rights to be "the embodiment of true and general self-government" and was "convinced that this is the prevailing sentiment among the American people."

Carl Schurz

Corruption

The Civil War had shown that, despite the heroes and courageous deeds, war is bloody and horrible. And war takes its toll not only in dead and mangled bodies, in devastated lands and desolated cities, but in the moral life of a people. Political and business corruption, as well

Our Neighbor to the North

Since the American Revolution, many Americans, from common folk to statesmen, had wanted to annex Canada. Annexation had been one of the goals of the War Hawks in 1812; and though, at that time, the attempt had failed, the dream never died. After the Civil War, the goal of annexation could unite even the likes of President Johnson, Secretary Seward, Senator Sumner, and U.S. Grant.

Canada had been troublesome to the union during the Civil War. Confederate spies and commissioners had operated north of the border and from Canada had even raided a Vermont town. Clement Vallandigham had published his manifestos against the Lincoln government from Windsor, Ontario. After the war, however, the tables had turned. Irish nationalists in New York City, members of the Irish Revolutionary Brotherhood, the "Fenians," had conceived a plan: they would invade Canada, seize possession

of it, and hold it hostage for Ireland's independence from Great Britain. Seven Fenian "invasions" of Canada occurred between 1866 and 1871, the most important being an invasion of the Niagara Peninsula in June 1866.

Fort Erie, across the Niagara River from Buffalo, New York, had been abandoned by British troops for over 40 years. In the early morning hours of June 1, 1866,

Battle of Ridgeway

(continued)

"General" John O'Neil and 1,500 Irish soldiers crossed the Niagara River and raised the green Fenian flag over the fort. The same day, warned of the invasion by the British consul in Buffalo, about 2,000 British regulars and Canadian militia converged on Chippewa, about 13 miles northwest of Fort Erie. Learning that a lone Canadian militia unit was approaching his position, O'Neil marched inland to destroy it before it could join the main body of the British and Canadians. On the morning of June 2, the Fenians took a defensive position on raised ground called Limeridge and awaited the militia.

When the the Canadian militia reached Limeridge, it attacked the Fenian position. At first, the Canadians drove the Irish back; but when a few Irish soldiers on horseback appeared, the militia, who were all infantry, thought the Irish had cavalry and began to withdraw. The Fenians, seeing their confusion, charged, and the militia retreated, suffering ten dead and many wounded.

Knowing that a larger militia force awaited them, the Fenians retreated to Fort Erie, from whence they drove out a contingent of soldiers that had been posted there since their withdrawal. But failing to receive reinforcements, the Fenians withdrew to the U.S. side of the Niagara River, where they were all promptly arrested. United States authorities, however, soon released the insurgents and paid their train fare to their homes.

Though unsuccessful from the Irish point of view, the Fenian raids led to important changes in Canada. For some time, Canadian "Federationists" had been calling for a certain degree of self-rule and independence from Great Britain. As an independent nation, Canada would have less to fear from United States expansionists. Canadian elections in 1866 brought Federationist victories in New Brunswick and Nova Scotia. These provinces, along with Ontario and Quebec, sent delegates to London to discuss the idea of a federation with British government authorities.

Queen Victoria, by John Jabez Edwin Mayall

These meetings culminated in the British North American Act of 1867. Under this act, the "Dominion of Canada," as it was to be called, would conduct its domestic affairs separately from Great Britain while remaining subject to Her Majesty, Queen Victoria. The British government, though, would still control Canada's foreign affairs. Parliament would appoint a governor general to represent the queen in Canada.

The Dominion of Canada was inaugurated on July 1, 1867, with Sir John Macdonald as its first premier. Like Great Britain, Canada had a two-house parliament. Unlike the United States, each province was not conceived of as sovereign; the Canadian federal government appointed all provincial governors. Gradually other provinces joined the original provinces: British Columbia in 1871 and Prince Edward Island in 1873. In 1869, Canada obtained the Northwest Territories from the Hudson's Bay Company.

The United States Congress viewed the creation of the Dominion of Canada "with extreme solicitude"; for, after all, it was not a purely republican but a "monarchical confederation." Expansionists in the United States saw the formation of the dominion, especially when it eventually spread from the Atlantic to the Pacific, as a definite check to their dreams of annexation. On their northern border stretched a new, and different, constitutional order—a model of what the United States might have become had they remained under the rule of Great Britain.

Several disputes regarding fishing rights and border questions still remained between Canada and the United States. Under President Grant, these questions were settled amicably in 1872 in the Treaty of Washington. Though a lion in war, Grant proved to be capable administrator in peace. The two great English-speaking countries of North America would be able to occupy the continent, without war, for generations to come.

A large squatters' settlement with wood homes and an office "selling lots" near Central Park, New York City, 1869

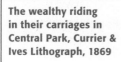

The wealthy riding in their carriages in Central Park, Currier & Ives Lithograph, 1869

as widespread immorality, often characterize post-war periods. The post-Civil War epoch in American life was no exception to this rule—especially in the cities.

It was Mark Twain who christened the period after the war; he called it the "Gilded Age." It was time of material prosperity, which, like a thin layer of gold covering a baser metal, hid a multitude of ills. Wealth there was but also dire poverty; the working poor, beggars, rag pickers, jostled the well-heeled and affluent in the larger cities. While an aura of respectability wreathed the houses of the rich, the sordid stench of vice invaded the dwellings of the poor. The Scottish minister David Macrae was troubled over the growing immorality in the North. He noted that "free-love" relationships between men and women were not uncommon and that in one year Chicago had 250 divorces (out of a population of 300,000). Abortions, he said, were easily obtainable. "It is impossible," he wrote, "for any one to travel in the States without becoming aware of the frightful prevalence of this practice. The papers swarm with advertisements for the requisite medicines . . ." Macrae said he knew of 30 doctors in one northern city who practiced abortion.

The Bowery district of New York City was notorious for its gambling dens, saloons, and brothels—some brightly lit, showy, with festively-clad "hostesses"; others, dark holes with cheap liquor, low crime, and disease. Into these dark streets wandered the poor and the rich; the common workingman mingled with the captain of business and the politician. On the streets, a multitude of rag-pickers, dealers in old clothes, and hucksters of every sort plied their trade

All of this, in some measure, is unremarkable—cities have always had bad districts and more than their share of vice. The problem in New York, and in other American cities, was that the city government was in cahoots with the criminals. Police, judges, the board of supervisors, the mayor—many profited from the black trades in the city. Embezzlement of public funds was rampant among office holders, some of whom turned tidy sums from digging into public coffers. Meanwhile, the poor lived in rank tenements and in shantytowns. It is estimated that over 55 percent of the population of New York City lived in the city's slums.

New York City had no cultural unity; it was a babel of foreign tongues, a city of immigrants. Of the 942,293 dwellers of New York in 1870, 419,094 were foreign born. Irish, Germans, blacks, and others, all with competing interests, pulled at the unity of the city. How could anyone hold such a disparate population together? One man gave his solution: "This population," he said, "is too hopelessly split up into races and factions to govern it under universal suffrage, except by the bribery of patronage and corruption."

The man who said this stood at the center of a ring of corruption that encompassed first New York City, then the state of New York itself. William Magear Tweed, called "Boss" Tweed, was 28 years old in 1851 when he was elected a New York City alderman. After serving one term as a United States Representative, Tweed established himself as a pillar of respectability by bringing about the downfall of the city's corrupt mayor, Fernando Wood. From 1858 to

A tenement house in New York, 1869

Broadway in New York City, 1876

William Magear "Boss" Tweed

graft: gaining money or other gain in an illegal or dishonest manner

Jay Gould

1871, Tweed established his power through the Democratic party political machine, Tammany Hall, and enriched himself through **graft**. With these funds he "patronized" public officials, civil servants, and others, so they would do his bidding. The Tweed Ring (which included Mayor A. Oakey Hall, Peter B. Sweeney, and Richard "Slippery Dick" Connolly), besides skimming tax money, reduced taxes for some to buy favors and issued bonds at high interest rates. Some have estimated that the amount of money stolen from the city at this period amounted to $45 million, while others place the sum at closer to $200 million.

By 1868, Tweed had gained control of the state Democratic Party. Now his influence spread to Albany, and some feared it would eventually reach all the way to Washington. One of his accomplices, Jim Fisk, had worked as a peddler, a tavern waiter, a circus barker, and a dry-goods salesman until he struck it rich by dealing in army contracts during the war. Fisk joined with banker and financier Jay Gould and started the Erie Railroad, from which the two men stole investment money. Fisk and Gould connived with men high in the Grant administration to help them in a scheme to corner the gold market. They wanted the Grant administration to hold back from issuing government gold on the market so that Gould and Fisk, who had invested extensively in gold, could drive up the price of gold. Grant, however, released government gold on the market, which led to an economic panic. The resulting scandal sullied President Grant's reputation.

Indeed, corruption tainted nearly everyone in Grant's administration, even the members of his cabinet. Business interests (railroads, oil, textiles, iron, steel) "patronized" United States Senators—such leading Republicans as James G. Blaine of Maine (called by admirers, "the Plumed Knight"), Chauncey Depew of New York, Matthew S. Quay of Pennsylvania, and Joseph B. Foraker of Ohio. These party leaders became quite wealthy on such "patronage," which they justified as forging the bonds that Alexander Hamilton thought were so important between government and business. Others, however, held a different opinion. Senator James W. Grimes of Iowa for his part thought the Republican party in 1870 was "going to the dogs" and had become "the most corrupt and debauched political party that has ever existed."

The year 1871 saw the downfall of Boss Tweed. Though he controlled most of the city's newspapers (through "contributions" to their publishers), the *New York Times* published evidence obtained from a city bookkeeper revealing the extent of Tweed's embezzle-

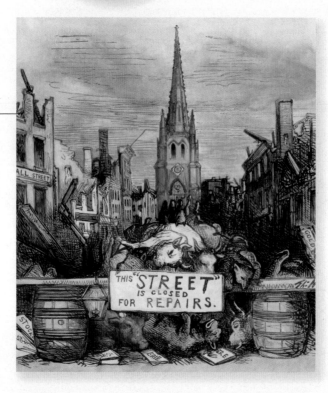

A cartoon by Thomas Nast depicts Wall Street devastated by the 1869 panic caused by Fisk and Gould's conniving. The cartoon's caption reads, "What a fall was there, my countrymen!"

ments. Boss Tweed fell, but it would not be long before others took his place. As George Templeton Strong noted, "When we the people learn (among other things) to consider wealth basely acquired and ignobly enjoyed a reproach and not a glory, we shall have a right to hope for honest rulers."

Grant's Second Term

Disillusioned with Radical rule and corruption in the civil service and government, Carl Schurz and others split from the Republican Party and held their own convention in May 1872. Calling themselves Liberal Republicans, they ended up endorsing the Democratic candidate for president, the old newspaper editor, Horace Greeley. Both Liberal Republicans and Democrats opposed "any re-opening of the questions settled by the 13th, 14th, and 15th amendments." They called for "the immediate and absolute removal of all disabilities imposed on account of the Rebellion" and affirmed that "local self-government, with impartial suffrage, will guard the rights of citizens more securely than any centralized power."

The Liberal Republican/Democratic platform reflected the sentiment of many in the country who were tired of Reconstruction. Still, Grant won reelection in 1872, taking all but six states. The popular vote was 3.6 million to 2.8 million.

Democrats however had a field day with the revelations of political corruption that surfaced during Grant's second administration. In September 1872, private letters revealed a huge scandal involving senators, representatives, and the Crédit Mobilier Company. Promoters of the Union Pacific Railroad had organized Crédit Mobilier to divert government funds from railroad construction to themselves. During Grant's first administration, Crédit Mobilier promoters distributed shares among members of Congress and to Vice President Schuyler Colfax, to keep them from investigating the company. Democrats exposed the Crédit Mobilier scandal, along with cases of corrupt administration practices in the executive department.

Another scandal surrounded the "Whiskey Ring" in St. Louis. Members of the ring, together with Grant's private secretary and friend, General Orville Babcock, and treasury officers defrauded the government of millions of dollars in tax revenues. The Navy Department, too, had taken its share of the swag: for instance, a million feet of lumber slated for the Boston shipyard turned up

In this Thomas Nast cartoon from *Harper's Weekly* supporting Democratic presidential candidate Horace Greeley, President Grant dances while Tweed applauds.

A Thomas Nast cartoon depicting New York City chamberlain Peter Sweeny, Tammany Hall boss William Tweed, controller Richard 'Slippery Dick' Connolly, and Mayor Oakey Hall as vultures

missing. Washington had become the pinnacle of a great pyramid of corruption that encompassed state, city, and local governments, as well as big business.

Though surrounded by corruption on all sides, President Grant was personally untouched by it. Still, he did little to stop it, despite his promise "to let no guilty man escape." Babcock escaped, as did others. Grant could not think ill of a friend.

State capitals, North and South, had their share of graft, embezzlement, and bribery. Reconstruction governments spent extravagantly and so racked up large state debts. Members of the old aristocracy, carpetbaggers, and black politicians profited from the corruption. Even prominent black leaders like Robert Brown Elliott sold themselves for bribes. One black politician said, "I've been sold in my life 11 times. This is the first time I ever got the money."

The frenzy for money resulted in too rapid an expansion of the economy, stock manipulation, and a proliferation of get-rich-quick schemes, all of which helped bring on the Panic of 1873. For the next six years the country was in the grip of an economic depression that left thousands out of work and looking for jobs or living on public assistance. The panic brought about the failure of the Freedman's Savings Bank, which had held the hard-earned wealth of many an industrious freedman. All that they had worked to save was gone.

Yet, few probably shed tears for the plight of the poor freedman. White folk were themselves in trouble and thoroughly sick of Reconstruction. Politicians, sensing the wind-change, cared little now whether blacks received equal rights or the suffrage. Only a few—the aging Charles Sumner in the Senate and President Grant among them—cared a straw for the 13th, 14th, and 15th amendments.

An 1874 book, *The Prostrate State: South Carolina Under Negro Government,* helped seal the fate of Reconstruction. The author, James Shepherd Pike, had been a politician from Maine and had served as Lincoln's minister to the Netherlands. Though an old anti-slavery stalwart, Pike thought blacks an "ignorant and servile race," unfit for governing. Still, in *The Prostrate State,* Pike reported that black politicians compared favorably with their white colleagues; some black politicians even excelled in the political art, which made him reflect that one could anticipate a "future for the race quite different from that bred from the old pro-slavery idea of universal inferiority." Yet, Pike argued that the typical black "is a child of vice and ignorance and superstition in South Carolina as well as in Africa." The old aristocratic order had been replaced by "the rude form of the most ignorant democracy that mankind ever saw, invested with the functions of government. . . . It is barbarism overwhelming civilization by physical force. It is the slave rioting in the halls of his master, and putting his master under his feet. And, though it is done without malice and without vengeance, it is nevertheless none the less completely and absolutely done."

Southern white resistance to Reconstruction was bearing fruit. In the state elections of 1874, Democrats took control of the reconstructed governments in Texas, Arkansas, Mississippi, and Alabama. Because of disillusionment with Republicans, some blacks had opted to vote what was familiar into power—the old master class. Other black voters succumbed to intimidation to vote Democratic or to keep away from the polls altogether. White militiamen, members of "rifle clubs," "redshirts," and others scoured the countryside terrorizing, beating, and murdering known and suspected black Republicans. In Grant Parish, Louisiana, whites attacked and murdered 200 blacks. When this happened in Coahoma County, Mississippi in 1875, the governor asked for federal troops. But though Grant favored enforcement of Reconstruction civil rights laws, his attorney general told the governor that "the whole public are tired out with these annual autumnal outbreaks in the South." Mississippi received no Federal troops and had to rely on its own militia.

But Radical hopes were not entirely dead. Since 1870, old Charles Sumner had been pushing a civil rights bill that would entitle to everyone, regardless of race, the use of public facilities, such as theaters, inns, trains, and stages. In 1874, Sumner again introduced the bill, this time appending a section calling for amnesty for all Confederate officers and generals.

The debate over the bill was lively, pitting Alexander Stephens, formerly vice-president of the Confederacy and now a senator from Georgia, against Robert Elliott, the black representative from South Carolina. Stephens had opposed the Klan in his state and supported suffrage for property-owning blacks; but he opposed this Civil Rights Act as another attempt to change southern society and undermine states' rights. Elliott said that he considered Stephens an "adversary" because he opposed the "full enfranchisement" of the black race. Stephens, he said, "now offers his Government, which he has done his best to destroy, a very poor return for its magnanimous treatment, to come here and seek to continue, by the assertion of doctrines obnoxious to the true principles of our Government, the burdens and oppressions which rest upon five millions of his countrymen . . ."

Poor Sumner did not live to see the fruit of all his labor, for he died in early March of 1874. Almost a year later, on March 1, 1875, Congress passed his Civil Rights Act, and President Grant signed it into law. But the passage of this act was only a short-lived victory, for now the country was more than determined to move beyond the era of Reconstruction and to leave the black man, with all his paper civil rights, to fend for himself.

Robert Elliott delivering a speech in favor of the Civil Rights Act in the House of Representatives.

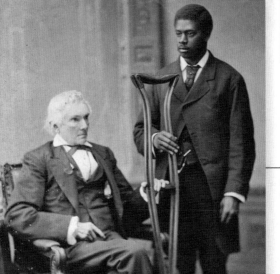

Alexander Stephens and a black servant

End of Reconstruction

By the election year 1876, two factions divided the Republicans: the "Liberals," who wanted an end to Reconstruction and a reform of the civil service, and the "Stalwarts," who were pleased with the status quo and supported the continued enforcement of Reconstruction laws. The two factions, however, were able to agree on a compromise candidate for president—Rutherford B. Hayes. In the war, Hayes had served as a brigadier general under Sheridan, and after the war, had been governor of Ohio, where he had so distinguished himself for his honesty that he earned the epithet, "Old Granny." The Republican platform called for the "permanent pacification of the southern section" and affirmed as a duty the "complete protection of all its citizens in the free enjoyment of all their rights." It hinted at women's suffrage by calling for "respectful consideration" of the "honest demands of women for additional rights, privileges and immunities."

For their part, the Democrats nominated New York governor Samuel J. Tilden, who had helped break up the Tweed Ring. The Democratic platform called for "reform"; and while it affirmed the equality of all citizens (presumably black and white), it tied reform to states'

An 1874 Thomas Nast cartoon that alludes to an old Copperhead slogan, "The Union as it was, the Constitution as it is," and attacks white alliances that wanted to overturn Reconstruction

Rutherford B. Hayes

rights. "Reform," said the platform, "is necessary to . . . establish, in the hearts of the whole people, the Union . . . now to be saved from a corrupt centralism."

Associated as they were with government corruption, the Republicans had an uphill battle to win the election of 1876. Though they "waved the bloody shirt" (aligning Democrats with treason during the war), Republicans couldn't pull the votes they had in the past. When the results first came in, it seemed that Tilden had won. But returns from Oregon were disputed, and in three southern states (South Carolina, Florida, and Louisiana) Reconstruction governors threw out thousands of Democratic votes, saying they were fraudulent. With these states under his belt, Hayes would have 185 electoral votes to Tilden's 184; but even with them, he trailed Tilden in the popular vote by about 250,000.

A Congressional electoral commission of eight Republicans and seven Democrats met to decide what to do about the disputed results from the South. They sent "visiting statesmen" to the South—and these statesmen, it seems, made a deal with southern Democrats. The Democrats agreed to recognize the election of Hayes if the Hayes administration agreed not to force the South to honor the 15th Amendment guaranteeing black voting rights. On March 2, 1877, the commission voted on party lines to reject Democratic returns from the three southern states; and, two days later, Rutherford Hayes became president of the United States.

Whether or not a deal had been made with southern Democrats to get him elected, President Hayes acted in their interest. A case in point occurred in South Carolina, where voters elected two rival governors—former Confederate general Wade Hampton, who represented the "Redeemers" (advocates of white rule in the South), and Federal general Daniel H. Chamberlain. Chamberlain took the oath of office, but the state supreme court ruled in favor of Hampton. Federal troops then barred Hampton from entering the state house in Columbia. On April 10, 1877, Hayes helped to decide the South Carolina impasse by ordering the withdrawal of Federal troops from the state capitol. Without the support of Federal bayonets, Chamberlain could not maintain his claim, and Hampton became governor. Two weeks later, Hayes ordered the evacuation of federal troops from New Orleans, ushering in white southern rule in that city.

Such acts effectively ended Reconstruction. Except in Texas, state governments in the South fell under control of members of the Confederate officer class. "Redeemer" governors such as Wade Hampton, however, promised to respect the civil rights of blacks, and for almost two decades blacks continued to vote in large numbers, and a few even sat in state legislatures. On the surface, at least, race relations were amicable, as visitors to the South noted. They would not remain so. It would not be long before demagogues reawakened the spirit of white supremacy, and using it for their own purposes, ushered in a new era of suffering for the Negro.

Summary

- The Federal government promised parole to Confederate President Jefferson Davis, but he was viewed as a traitor, so he was kept in a prison cell at Fortress Monroe. While he was in prison he received a picture of Pope Pius IX with the inscription, "If any man will come after me, let him deny himself, and take up his cross, and follow me." This gift symbolized the sufferings of Davis and thousands in the South, where destitution reigned.

- In the South, the "Negro Question" was predominant during Reconstruction. The Southerners feared that their freed slaves would obtain too much political power; they especially feared miscegenation. The Federal government established the Freedmen's Bureau to pass out emergency rations of food and to integrate blacks into white society.

- Freedmen greeted wage earning at first with joy, but they soon learned the disabilities it carried. Before, slave owners cared for their slaves even when sick, but employers did not care for their workers. Freedmen earned very low wages.

- In the Federal government, opinions differed on how the South should be treated. Some, such as President Andrew Johnson, thought the South should be treated with kindness and gentleness and southern states admitted back into the union. Others, including Edwin M. Stanton, Charles Sumner, and Thaddeus Stevens, thought the South should be more severely punished for the war.

- In June 1865, President Johnson appointed provisional governors for each of the southern states, and told them to call conventions to draw up new state constitutions that had to declare secession illegal and abolish slavery. By January each southern state except for Texas had functioning state governments. The Radical Republicans objected because the new governments had a large number of former Confederate officers, who enforced blacks codes, laws to keep blacks "in their place."

- These black codes did not please Stevens and Sumner, who wanted immediate and complete equality for the blacks. Radical Republicans assailed President Johnson's reconstruction policy by passing the Freedmen's Bureau Bill in 1866, which President Johnson vetoed. Congress passed the Civil Rights Act in March, which President Johnson also vetoed. Congress overrode the president's veto on April 9, 1866.

- In April 1866, the Supreme Court decision, *Ex Parte Milligan*, ruled that Lincoln's wartime suspension of *habeas corpus* had been unconstitutional.

- In July the Radicals were able to override the president's veto of the Freedmen's Bureau, and in June of 1866 Congress voted to approve the 14th Amendment, linking state with national citizenship.

- Although President Johnson declared the end of the war on August 20, 1866, race riots still troubled the South. These riots not only assured the passage of the 14th Amendment but weakened northern support for Johnson. In 1867 the Radical Republicans took Reconstruction out of the hands of the president. In a Reconstruction Act, Congress disbanded all southern state governments and divided the South into five military districts under five generals.

- Under Congress' Reconstruction, there were more black than white voters, since only "loyal" whites could vote. In South Carolina, blacks (many of them educated men) dominated the state constitutional convention.

- The state elections of 1867 were the first in which blacks could vote. The number of blacks who voted far outnumbered the number of whites. Republicans came to dominate southern state legislatures.

- In 1865 a group of young, former Confederate soldiers decided to form a secret society (which they called the "Ku Klux Klan") merely for their entertainment. Eventually the group became a sort of vigilante group, and the hooded men in white sheets began visiting black cabins to frighten the inhabitants to keep their place. They even killed blacks who presented any problems. The group died out on its own by 1870.

- Radical Republican congressmen wanted to impeach President Johnson, but they needed some offense on which to try him. In March 1867

Chapter 20 Review (continued)

Congress passed the Tenure of Office Act, which required the president to seek the advice and consent of the Senate when appointing and dismissing members. When Johnson violated this act, the Radicals called for his impeachment. The House of Representatives voted to impeach the president, but the Senate acquitted him. Although the Radicals had failed to oust the president, they had neutralized his power.

- By 1868, eight southern states voted to ratify the 14th Amendment and were admitted into the union. On July 9, 1868, the amendment became part of the Constitution.

- Ulysses S. Grant won the presidential election of 1868 for the Republicans. He was committed to centralization and expressed hopes for an international tribunal that would peacefully resolve disputes between nations. His espousal of a dominant national power reflected a new epoch in United States history. The United States was becoming a consolidated nation.

- Grant called for the ratification of the 15th Amendment, extending the suffrage to blacks nationwide. Congress approved the amendment on February 26, 1869 and it was ratified the following year.

- The period after the war was characterized by political corruption, and Mark Twain called it the "Gilded Age." New York City was a major center of this corruption.

- After Grant's reelection in 1872, several scandals in his administration were brought to light. President Grant did little to stop the corruption, however.

- A frenzy for money resulted in a too rapid expansion of the economy which brought on the Panic of 1873.

- In the state elections of 1874, Democrats took control of several reconstructed state governments. Radical hopes were not dead, however, and Sumner again introduced his Civil Rights Act. On March 1, 1875, Congress approved it, and President Grant signed it into law.

- In 1876 Rutherford B. Hayes became president. President Hayes removed federal troops from the state capital of South Carolina and evacuated federal troops from New Orleans. These acts ended Reconstruction in the South.

Key Concepts

Reconstruction: the process by which the southern states were to be readmitted to the union after the Civil War; the period in which this reconstruction took place

miscegenation: the mixing of races, especially through marriage

scalawags: southerners who cooperated with federal occupying forces

carpetbaggers: northerners who moved south either to help freedmen or to profit off southern misfortune

poll tax: a fixed amount of money a person has to pay in order to vote

specie: money in coin, either in gold or silver

graft: obtaining money or other gain in an illegal or dishonest manner

Dates to Remember

1865: President Johnson appoints provisional governors for the southern states and calls on them to draw up new state constitutions.

1866: Congress passes the Freedmen's Bureau Bill, the Civil Rights Act, and the 14th Amendment. President Johnson declares the end of the war.

1867: blacks are allowed to vote for the first time.

1868: Radicals attempt to impeach President Johnson.

Ratification of the 14th Amendment

Ulysses S. Grant becomes president.

1870: Ratification of the 15th Amendment

1873: an expansion of the economy brings about an economic panic.

1875: Congress passes the Civil Rights Act and President Grant signs it into law.

Central Characters

Andrew Johnson (1808–1875): 17th president of the United States, who took office after the assassination of President Abraham Lincoln. The Reconstruction policies he favored angered the Radical Republicans and led to his impeachment.

Charles Sumner (1811–1874) and Thaddeus Stevens (1792–1868): Radical Republican leaders in Congress who wanted to reconstruct the social order in the South, give blacks full equality and voting rights with whites, and extend the power of the federal government beyond what many believed its constitutional limits.

William Magear Tweed (1823–1878): New York politician, known as "Boss" Tweed, who with his "Tweed Ring" cronies plundered New York City of large amounts of money

Jay Gould (1836–1892): American financier who started the Erie Railroad and embezzled investment money from it

Rutherford B. Hayes (1822–1893): 19th president of the United States who brought Southern Reconstruction to an end

Questions for Review

1. Describe the condition of the South after the Civil War.

2. Describe the condition of blacks in the United States after the war.

3. What was President Johnson's policy towards the South, and how did it embitter the Radicals towards him?

4. What did the Radical Republicans think should be done with the South?

5. Why was the 14th Amendment so important for the Radical Republicans?

6. What is the 15th Amendment? Did it affect both the North and the South? Please explain.

7. What were the various attitudes toward black equality both in the North and South?

8. Briefly explain the Civil Rights Act.

9. How did the government of the Dominion of Canada differ from the government formed by the United States Constitution?

10. What did President Grant's espousal of a dominant national power reflect? How did this affect the United States?

11. What did Mark Twain mean by calling the postwar period the "Gilded Age"?

12. What events brought about the end of southern Reconstruction?

Ideas in Action

1. If you were the president of the United States, what would you have wanted to do with the South after the war? Come up with what you think would be a fair treatment and defend it.

2. Examine the U.S. Constitution in regards to what it says about the powers granted to the federal government and state governments. In light of this, defend whether you think that Radical Republican policies after the Civil War were in accord with the Constitution or not.

3. In light of what Catholic theology and papal teaching said about slavery at the time, were Radical Republican policies concerning the status of freedmen more in accord with Catholic teaching or not? Address the same question in light of subsequent Church teaching on human freedom (for instance, the *Catechism of the Catholic Church*, 1730–1742 and 2401–2449).

Highways and Byways

Writing in Color

Literature has always had a major impact on society. It was no different during and after the Civil War, especially where blacks were concerned. During these periods, the blacks in cities organized literary and musical societies, which impacted both their culture and that of the whites. When the Civil War broke out, many blacks used their pens and voices to convince

Chapter 20 Review (continued)

President Lincoln that, since the war was a war to end slavery, the black man should be able to enlist and fight. Their agitation brought 180,000 black soldiers into the Federal army. Reconstruction saw black writers promoting the ideal of racial equality. William Wells Brown in *My Southern Home* and Frederick Douglass' *Life and Times of Frederick Douglass* foretold progress for the freedman, while Frances Harper's collection of poems based on her travels amongst the freedmen, *Sketches of Southern Life,* countered a popular white stereotype that the freedmen were all lazy and incompetent. The literature of black culture may not have alone raised the black man from his despised state, but perhaps it encouraged the black man to better his position through its promotion of equality and opportunity.

21 A NEW AMERICA IS BORN

Part I: The Passing of the Red Man

"Nothing lives long except the earth and the mountains."

White Antelope, old gray-head, arms folded, sang his death song: "Nothing lives . . ."

The ancient chief, leader of the people, refusing refuge within the banks of the murmuring creek bed, boldly faced the onslaught of the white-faces, unresisting. The whizzing bullet, whether aimed deliberately or fired recklessly, struck the old man, and he fell, like an ancient, towering pine cut down in the distant forest.

"Nothing lives long . . ."

Some would have said that White Antelope's people, the Arapaho, had lived far too long, scouring the plains in pursuit of the herds of buffalo that fed them and clothed them. It was a new age; the white man was advancing, had been advancing, for over 20 years across the hunting grounds of the Arapaho, the Cheyenne, and the Sioux. Not many years had passed since gold had been found in the mountains of Colorado, and the white man's city, Denver, had swelled with thousands of fortune seekers. The shiftless Indian (as the whites thought him), intent only on hunting and war, just wasted this land, just wasted it. He must submit to the white man (whose destiny it was to take the land) or die.

The white men of the West despised, and often hated, the "inhuman savages," as they called the Plains Indians. The Indian, they

An illustration of the Sand Creek Massacre by a Cheyenne eyewitness, Howling Wolf

said, was treacherous, bloodthirsty, cruel, and he stank. Though the white man himself could be cruel and bloodthirsty, his religion and culture condemned both cruelty and blood thirst. The Indian, particularly the warlike plainsman, thought it no indignity to treat an enemy with the utmost cruelty—brutally torturing the living, mutilating and scalping the bodies of the dead. As the white men were driving the Sioux, the Cheyenne, and the Arapaho from their hunting grounds, so had those tribes driven off other, weaker tribes who had dwelt on the plains before them. Yet, when white folk justified broken treaties, cruelty, and massacres by pointing to Indian savagery, it was not so often offended virtue, but greed, that spoke.

When the United States government concluded treaties with Indian nations, offering them reservations and government subsidies of food in return for land across which whites could travel or on which they could settle, the intent was to get the Indian out of the way. Such was the intent of the treaty of Fort Laramie, signed September 1, 1851, with the Sioux, Shoshone, Assiniboine, Crow, Arikara, and Pawnee tribes; such may, too, have been the point of the treaty signed at Fort Atkinson on the Arkansas River with the Comanche and the Kiowa, and of the treaty of Fort Benton in Washington Territory. As the government saw it, moving Indians to reservations was the first step in civilizing them, but it proved to be the beginning of their decline. As the mountain man and Indian friend, Thomas Fitzpatrick, noted in 1854:

> They [the Indians] are in abject want of food half the year. The travel upon the [Oregon Trail] drives the buffalo off or else confines them to a narrow path during the period of migration, and the different tribes are forced to contend with hostile nations in seeking support for their villages. The women are pinched with want and their children are constantly crying with hunger.

Arapaho camp. In the background, buffalo meat drying

The Arapaho and the Cheyenne under Black Kettle had signed a treaty with the United States in 1861; the tribes exchanged hunting lands for subsidies and a small reservation in the area of Sand Creek, Colorado. The reservation, however, proved so poor that the Indians could not feed themselves, and they were dying from epidemics. Cheyenne warriors then began raiding white ranches, stealing cattle. Following one such raid in the spring of 1864, angry white settlers called out the militia, which fired on a band of innocent Cheyenne. This incident led to a general uprising of the Cheyenne and Arapaho, who, in two weeks time, killed and mutilated 200 white settlers and emigrants.

Black Kettle knew that his people could not long withstand the power of the United States military, and he approached Major Scott Anthony at Fort Lynn with an offer of peace. Anthony, replying that he had no authority to make peace, told Black Kettle and his people to return to the reservation. The Indian chief, thinking he had received a promise of protection from Anthony, returned to Sand Creek, 40 miles from Fort Lynn.

Meanwhile, a former Methodist minister and anti-slavery man, John Chivington, set out at the head of the Third Colorado Volunteers to obey orders "to pursue everywhere and destroy the Cheyenne and Arapahos." In the early dawn of November 29, Chivington and his men reached Black Kettle's encampment, where 700 Cheyenne and Arapaho men, women, and children lay sleeping. The soldiers fell on the unsuspecting Indians and began their work of slaughter. The Indians, recovering from their initial shock, fought back doggedly and pushed back the assault. The fighting continued until about four in the afternoon when the soldiers completely overcame the Indians' defense. Then, according to reports, the soldiers mutilated the corpses of Indian men, women, and children.

Two hundred Indians, most of them women and children, died in this "Sand Creek Massacre." Though Black Kettle escaped, many a brave warrior, including White Antelope, lay among the dead. The massacre did not end the war, and sporadic fighting continued even after Black Kettle and other chiefs agreed in a truce in 1865 to move to a reservation in Kansas. Two years later, they signed another treaty, trading their Kansas reservation for two smaller reservations in Indian Territory.

Dissatisfied Cheyenne under the chieftain Roman Nose, however, continued resistance. When the government failed to deliver provisions to the Cheyenne reservation, many of the Indians joined Roman Nose, crossing into Kansas, killing settlers. In the fall of 1868, Colonel George Armstrong Custer led a winter campaign against the Cheyenne. Crossing over into the Cheyenne reservation in Indian Territory, Custer attacked Black Kettle's village, even though the chief had kept peace with the white man and was flying a white flag over his tipi. "Both the chief and his wife fell at the river bank riddled with bullets," one witness wrote. "The soldiers rode right over Black Kettle and his wife and their horse as they lay dead on the ground, and their bodies were all splashed with mud by the charging soldiers."

Blackrobe

His father feared that he would become a shiftless wanderer—perhaps a soldier of fortune, or worse. His father proved partly right. At seminary school in Belgium, Pierre-Jean De Smet fell under the spell of a wanderer in distant, marvelous lands. Charles Nerinckx told stories of dense, virgin forests in a far away country called Kentucky, of the strange red men who wandered these forests, of their great nobility and unaccountable savagery. For Nerinckx, as for other missionary priests, these strange, outlandish men and women were not so many savages to be gotten out of the way but a ripe field of souls, white unto harvest. This wanderer priest inspired the young Pierre-Jean. He, too, would become, as his father feared, a wanderer in the wilds, but not a shiftless one. Nor would he seek a fortune that moth or rust consumes, but the incomparable treasure of human souls.

Pierre De Smet came to America in 1821. He entered the Jesuit novitiate at Whitemarch, Maryland, but two years later joined some Jesuits who set up a new establishment on the frontier, at Florissant near St. Louis, Missouri. In 1831, four years after De Smet's ordination to the priesthood, Indians from the distant Rocky Mountains arrived in St. Louis seeking a "blackrobe" to return with them to teach their people. Some Iroquois, who had come to live among the Flathead tribe in what is now Montana, had told these western Indians of the Christian faith and the black robed priests who had brought that faith to the Iroquois in the distant years when France ruled in the New World. The Jesuits in St. Louis said they had no priests to spare for such a far-off mission. Still, over the next seven years, three more delegations arrived from the West. Finally, in 1839, the Jesuits agreed to send a missionary and chose Father De Smet for the task.

During the previous year, De Smet had been busy at the mission he had founded for the Pottawatomie at Council Bluffs. He seemed to have a powerful influence over the Indians. Besides caring for the Pottawatomies' souls, he had arranged a truce between them and the Sioux, who raided their settlements. He also worked to impress upon the Indians the importance of abandoning their nomadic, hunter life for the settled existence of farmer folk. Besides the benefits an agricultural life

Pierre-Jean De Smet, by Mathew Brady

would bring in terms of civilization, De Smet thought that it was the only way the Indians could survive in a world increasingly dominated by white men. He favored the model of the Reductions of Paraguay—settled, self-ruled communities of Indians, separated from the influence of white men.

With great joy, the Flatheads and the Pend d'Oreilles received Father De Smet in their Rocky Mountain fastnesses. Having promised them a mission, De Smet returned to St.

A sketch of a village of the Kansas people, by Father De Smet

Louis, visiting the Crow, Gros Ventre, and other tribes on his way. The following year, 1841, De Smet and another Jesuit, Nicholas Point, returned to Flathead country and established a mission there, St. Mary's on the Bitter Root River. Over the next five years, De Smet visited Europe, seeking missionaries and soliciting funds. Returning to America, he established another mission to the Kalispel people on Puget Sound in the Oregon Country and made peace between the Blackfeet and the Crow and other tribes among whom there had been continual war. So great was their respect for this "blackrobe" that the Blackfeet agreed to a mission, which Nicholas Point founded among them.

De Smet wanted to remain among the Indians, but his Jesuit superiors decided, instead, to send him back to St. Louis. But De Smet's work for the Indians was not over. Because of the large influx of white settlers traveling across the plains to California and Oregon, the Indians were growing more restless and hostile. The government called a gathering of the tribes to the Creek Valley, near Fort Laramie, for 1851, and requested De Smet's presence. The blackrobe helped to make peace between the United States government and the Sioux, Shoshone, Assiniboine, Crow, Arikara, and Pawnee tribes, thousands of whom had gathered at Fort Laramie.

Yet, as we have noted, the treaties signed with the various tribes in the early 1850s did not last. In another treaty signed in 1851, the government had convinced the Sioux in Minnesota to sell their lands for the paltry sum of $3 million (12 cents an acre). The government promised that part of this sum, given in payments of about $125,000 a year, would pay for subsidies of food and clothing. But the government gave over half of an original lump payment of $555,000 to Indian traders who had helped conclude the treaty with the Sioux. The Sioux, who were ignorant of the value of money and whose culture knew nothing of thrift, wasted their subsidies; and when game became scarce because of increasing white settlement, the Indians became more and more destitute.

Though many of the Sioux had adopted white man's dress, lived in framed houses, and had taken to farming, their sense of injury increased, and the realization that they had been cheated of their lands gradually dawned on them. Nevertheless, government reports spoke in glowing terms of civilizing the Sioux, and the Indians generally had friendly relations with the surrounding whites. But in August 1862, while the country was in the grip of the Civil War, the government delayed the Sioux's yearly subsidy payment. This had happened before, causing great suffering among the Indians; but this time the Minnesota Sioux rose in revolt under their chief, Little Crow, and attacked white settlements, torturing, killing, and mutilating everyone within them. In the course of the war, the Sioux killed and captured about 1,000 whites.

In desperation, the government appealed to De Smet to pacify the Indians. The Sioux trusted the priest, and he understood the ill treatment they had received from the whites. He arrived at Fort Berthold on the Missouri River in the Dakota Territory in July where many Indians had gone to take refuge from the Sioux. When the Sioux in great numbers appeared on the riverbank opposite the fort, De Smet decided to go out and parley with them, though those in the fort warned him to fear for his life. The Sioux would have killed any other white man, but not De Smet. After a three-hour parley with the Indians, he returned to the fort unharmed.

When however he learned that General Sully planned only to punish the Sioux and that the government had no intention of honoring its promises, De Smet refused to negotiate for them further with the Indians. The military drove the Sioux out of Minnesota into the Dakota Territory, and the war ended on Christmas day, 1862, with the execution of 38 Sioux men in Mankato, Minnesota.

What's To Be Done with the Indians?

The Indian question became increasingly more important after the Civil War. The long cherished plan for a transcontinental railroad—delayed by the war—could now be realized. An act of Congress in 1862 gave the Union Pacific Company 20 square miles of land for every mile of track it laid. The railroad, which was to stretch from Omaha on the Missouri River westward across the central plains and over the Rocky Mountains, would pass through the hunting grounds of the Plains Indians. It was imperative, therefore, to make peace with and obtain land from the tribes through whose lands the rails would run.

Meanwhile, the army was building a series of forts along the Bozeman Trail, which ran from the South Platte in Colorado into Sioux lands in Wyoming, to protect miners and settlers en route to gold fields in Montana. But Red Cloud, chief of the Oglala Sioux, would not tolerate such a military intrusion. The stream of settlers would have to be stemmed, Red Cloud knew, lest the western Sioux share the fate of their brothers in Minnesota and lose their hunting grounds. In 1866, Red Cloud led a series of attacks on the trail forts, climaxing in the massacre of 80 United States soldiers with their commander, Captain William Judd Fetterman, outside Fort Phil Kearney in Wyoming.

William Fetterman was a cocky soldier with a distinguished Civil War record. In December 1866, Colonel Henry Carrington had sent Fetterman to guard a detail of men bringing in wood for the construction of the Bozeman Trail forts. When the Sioux attacked the "wood train," Fetterman drove them off. Then, ignoring Carrington's order not to pursue the Indians, Fetterman and his column went after them. Crossing a ridge, he fell into an Indian ambush. Hearing distant gunshots, Carrington sent a cavalry detail to reinforce Fetterman. It arrived too late. Not one of Fetterman's men was left alive. Pools of frozen blood stood among the dead and mutilated bodies of soldiers.

Red Cloud (right) and American Horse, by John C. H. Grabill, 1891

The news of the Fetterman Massacre deeply troubled the country. It caused General William Tecumseh Sherman, who, since the Civil War, had been commanding the military Division of the Missouri (stretching from that river to the Rocky Mountains) to change his opinion of the Indians. Before, he had been their defender against the greedy, grasping white settlers. Now, he wrote: "I do not understand how the massacre of Colonel Fetterman's party could have been so complete . . . We must act with vindictive earnestness against the Sioux, even to their extermination, men, women and children. Nothing else will do."

The hero of the Atlanta campaign lived to regret those words.

Red Cloud's assaults on the Bozeman Trail forts kept the regiments posted in them in a constant state of fear. The government was at a loss what to do. Father De Smet, again working among the Indians, drew up a long list of Indian grievances that he sent to Washington. Peace with the Indians, he said, could be achieved if the government employed honest agents. The old abolitionist guard agreed with De Smet; but, since they had never lived amongst the western Indians, their prescriptions were more idealistic than the priest's. They favored a different tactic than that of the military, which believed that Indians had first to be pacified

General Sherman with commissioners meeting with Indian chiefs at Fort Laramie, 1868

(conquered), then treated with fairness. The Eastern reformers wanted the government to take a conciliating approach towards the Indian—a position which earned them the ire of many a western settler who believed the only good Indian was a dead Indian.

On the heels of the news of the Fetterman Massacre, Congress created a non-governmental organization called the Indian Peace Commission. The members of the commission included prominent reformers and General Sherman. In 1868, the commission came out with a report that recommended a "hitherto untried policy of endeavoring to conquer [the Indian] by kindness," while it warned of the serious threat that a "handful of savages" posed to the march of civilization and progress. That same year, members of the commission traveled to Fort Laramie. The government asked Father De Smet to convince the Sioux leaders to attend the conference, and he, old and ailing though he was, agreed.

Father De Smet, who had set out for Fort Laramie with the peace commissioners, broke from them en route and began a lonely walk across the treeless wilderness of the plains. Traversing even the torrid Badlands of South Dakota, De Smet finally arrived at last at an encampment of about 5,000 Sioux, led by Sitting Bull. Meeting with Sitting Bull and three other chiefs—Four Horns, Black Moon and No Neck—De Smet convinced them to send representatives to the peace conference.

The commissioners and the representatives of the Sioux concluded the Treaty of Fort Laramie in May 1868. The treaty gave the Sioux an enormous tract of land, centering on the Black Hills (a sacred spot to the Sioux) in South Dakota, as well as a yearly subsidy of food and clothing. The treaty forbade all white settlement on Indian land. Any Indian who wanted to farm would be provided with 360 acres of land, plus seed and farming implements. The United States government, too, would provide schools to which the Indians agreed to send their children. In return, the Indians had to abandon any claim to lands that lay outside their reservation and agree to "withdraw all opposition to the construction of the railroads now being built on the plains."

The commissioners concluded similar treaties with the Comanche, Kiowa, Arapaho, and Southern Cheyenne; with the Crow, the Ute, the Bannock, and the Shoshone; with the Navajo and the Snake. It all seemed a grand achievement—peace with the Indians had been achieved! Or so it was thought.

How feeble the peace proved to be.

Reservations or Assimilation?

Within a year of the peace treaties with the Plains Indians, a cherished hope of many Americans came to pass—the transcontinental railroad had been completed. It had been a kind of race. While the builders of the Union Pacific, setting out from Omaha, were grading the soil of the plains and laying the sleepers upon which the steel ribbons of track would run, workers on the Central Pacific had set out from Sacramento, California, laying track across the Central Valley, over the Sierra Nevada, and into the Great Basin deserts. On May 10, 1869, the two railroads met at Promontory Point, near the Great Salt Lake in Utah. There they drove in a gold spike to mark the completion of the railroad that linked East and West.

Over the next 15 years, Congress chartered other railroads across the vast expanse of the West. The Northern Pacific ran from Lake Superior to Portland, Oregon. The Southern

Pacific traversed the far South, from New Orleans, across Texas, New Mexico, Arizona, and into Southern California. From Los Angeles, it turned north and ran, by way of the San Joaquin Valley, to San Francisco. Taking a route between the Southern and Union Pacific railroads, the Santa Fe Railroad ran from Atchison, Kansas, to Santa Fe, New Mexico, and thence, passing by way of Albuquerque, crossed Arizona and the Mojave Desert, to San Bernardino, California. From San Bernardino it turned south to San Diego.

The railroads brought increased white settlement to the West. Railroad companies advertised for settlers to whom they sold land on credit, and whom they then transported to their property. Many a new town sprang up along the rail routes, and many an older town mushroomed into a city. The railroads turned such settlements as Omaha, Kansas City, Duluth, Oakland, Portland, Seattle, and Tacoma into important population centers.

With increased white settlement, the question of what to do with the Indians became more pressing than ever before. Indian hostilities had not ceased on the plains. The railroads frightened away game and, most importantly, buffalo—and, what was worse, professional hunters, often from the windows of the trains themselves, shot down buffalo by the hundreds. The Kansas Pacific Railroad, for example, chartered excursions out to Forth Leavenworth for the very purpose of hunting buffalo. For the Plains Indians, buffalo were

The meeting of the Union Pacific and Central Pacific railroads at Promontory Point, Utah, May 10, 1869. Painting by Thomas Hill

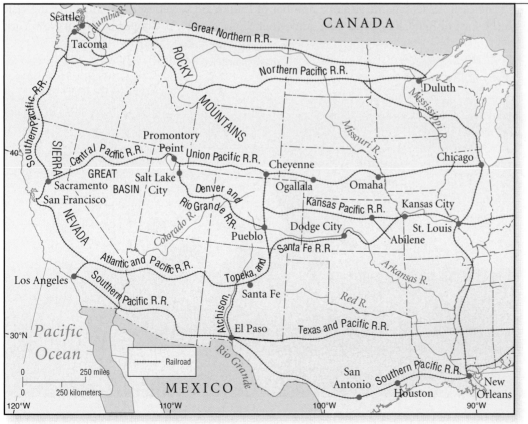

Railroad routes across the western United States

Buffalo skulls waiting to be ground down into fertilizer, 1870s

a source of food, clothing, and shelter; white hunters, on the other hand, killed buffalo, sometimes for their valuable hides, sometimes for their tongues, and sometimes just for sport, leaving the carcasses to rot.

The loss of buffalo led to new revolts among the Southern Cheyenne, the Comanche, and the Kiowa, halting westward traffic on the trails. General Philip Sheridan directed the campaign against the Cheyenne and the Arapaho in which Colonel Custer killed Black Kettle and his warriors. While Custer engaged in no wanton killing of women and children, others did. In Wyoming, on January 23, 1870, Colonel E.M. Baker and his men attacked a village of the Piegan people, killing 173 Indians, mostly women and children.

With the outbreak of hostilities, the debate over the Indian question grew more intense. Some easterners echoed the western voices that called for extermination. The Literary and Debating Society of Mastersville, Ohio—long a center of reform and abolitionism—offered as a topic of debate, "Should the Uncivilized Indians be Exterminated?" Others wanted to see an end to the reservation system and a break up of the Indian tribes so they could be absorbed by white society. The Congregationalist minister, Lyman Abbott, spoke for such assimilationists when he wrote, "let us understand once for all that an inferior race must either adapt and conform itself to the higher civilization, wherever the two come in conflict, or else die. This is the law of God, from which there is no appeal."

The early 1870s saw the rise of a number of Indian aid societies, especially after the visit to the East of Red Cloud, Red Dog, and other Sioux chiefs. At Cooper Union in New York

Sioux warriors on the Plains, by Edward Curtis, 1905

City, Red Cloud told the gathered crowd about the corruption of Indian agents sent out to the reservations. "I don't want any more men sent out there who are so poor that they think only of filling their pockets. We want those who will help to protect us on our reservations, and save us from those who are viciously disposed toward us."

President Grant had said he would have peaceful passage for emigrants across the plains "even if the extermination of every Indian tribe was necessary to serve such a result." Such a statement was probably born of frustration, for Grant intended to treat the Indians with justice and kindness. He appointed General Francis A. Walker as commissioner of Indian Affairs. Walker's report to Grant in 1872 was melancholy:

> Every year's advance of our frontier takes in a territory as large as some of the kingdoms of Europe. We are richer by hundreds of millions, the Indian is poorer by a large part of the little that he has. This growth is bringing imperial greatness to the nation; to the Indian it brings wretchedness, destitution, beggary.

Walker and Grant saw the reservation system as a means to civilize the Indians. While the natives lived off rations and what they could produce for themselves, the government would provide them schools in which they could be trained in the rudiments of American culture. Grant removed the corrupt Indian agents, replacing them with Christian ministers. Father De Smet learned of this new policy at a government conference on Indian affairs he attended in 1870. But to his disappointment, of the 43 ministers appointed, most were Quakers and only four were Catholic. "In the whole of the affair," wrote De Smet, "the Indians have not been consulted as to the religion they desired to belong to." De Smet's dream of Indian missions based on the Reductions of Paraguay was not to be. With this sadness he died, three years later, on May 23, 1873.

War Among the Lava Beds

Dry lava beds and sagebrush thickets cover the plateaus of northeastern California and southeastern Oregon. Surrounding this desert land rise mountains covered with pine forests. This region was the home of the Modoc Indians. Along the shores of Tule Lake and on the banks of the Lost River, they dwelt in dome-like dwellings made of reeds and grass.

Whites who settled in the Lost River area did not want the Modoc around; they demanded that the U.S. government remove them to a reservation on the Klamath River. This reservation, where the government put the Modoc, was already shared by the Snake and Klamath tribes. The Modoc and the Klamath spoke a similar language, but they were enemies. Suffering abuse from the Klamath, some Modoc, under the leadership of Kientpoos, left the reservation and returned to the Lost River region. Kientpoos, called "Captain Jack" by the whites, demanded a reservation on the Lost River. The white settlers would never agree to this, so the Indian superintendent, Alfred Meacham, persuaded Captain Jack and the Modocs to return to the Klamath River reservation. But, as before, the Klamath harassed the Modoc. In April 1869, Captain Jack and about 370 Modocs returned to the Lost River. This time they refused to leave.

Kientpoos ("Captain Jack")

Over the next three years, settlers in the Lost River region did not let up on their demands. The Modoc had to leave! Finally, in November 1872, Major Green at Fort Klamath ordered troops to round up Captain Jack and his people and bring them back to the reservation. Unwilling to fight white troops, Captain Jack agreed to return to the reservation and, even, lay down his arms. But then an altercation between a Modoc man and a soldier turned into

A photograph of Modoc women. The women standing is Tobey Riddle, who, according to the picture's caption, was "the Squaw who cautioned General Canby of his impending fate." She stands between an Indian agent and her husband, Frank Riddle (left).

a general fight. The Modoc fled, and soldiers burned their village.

In retaliation, a small band of Modoc led by "Hooker Jim" killed 14 white settlers. The main body of the Modoc, under Captain Jack, fled to the dry lava beds on the shores of Tule Lake. Scored with deep trenches, the lava beds formed a natural fortress where the 50 or so Modoc men, women, and children could defend themselves. They soon needed to. On January 16, 1873, the Modocs beat back about 300 soldiers advancing against their stronghold and inflicted many casualties.

Captain Jack now hardened his position. Unless he was promised a reservation on the Lost River, he would not surrender. The U.S. government would not agree to this demand. Nevertheless, President Grant appointed a peace commission to meet with the Modoc chief. The commissioners, who included General E.R.S. Canby and Indian superintendent Meacham, were to meet with Captain Jack and four other Modocs. All Indians and whites were to come to the meeting unarmed. But on the morning of April 11, when Canby, Meacham, and the peace commissioners entered the peace tent, they found eight Modocs instead of the five they had expected. What's more, three of the Modocs, including Captain Jack, were clearly armed. Captain Jack again demanded a reservation on Lost River, and when the commissioners refused, he pulled out a revolver and killed General Canby. The other two armed Modocs killed two commissioners and severely wounded Meacham. Only one commissioner escaped unharmed.

The Modoc now fled south to another lava flow where they could find water—soldiers had cut them off from their water supply. In the early morning of May 10, the Indians staged a surprise attack on the troops who had encamped at a dry lake bed, but were driven off. Following this repulse, the Modoc broke up into small bands and fled in different directions. The army soon caught up with Hooker Jim, who promised, in return for his own safety, to help them find Captain Jack. On June 1, the whites at last tracked down Captain Jack, and the Modoc chieftain surrendered himself to them.

Though he had murdered 14 settlers, Hooker Jim was granted amnesty; it had been the price of his betrayal. President Grant pardoned the two Modocs who had helped Captain Jack kill the peace commissioners, and they were imprisoned at Alcatraz Island in San Francisco Bay. But there would be no mercy for Captain Jack. Though Meacham pleaded for the chieftain's life ("white men in California and Oregon," he said, were "more responsible for the blood of General Canby than Captain Jack himself"), popular opinion forbade clemency. Captain Jack was hanged on the morning of October 3, 1873. The government removed his Modoc followers far from their home, settling them at the Quapaw Agency in Indian Territory. The remainder of the Modoc remained on the Klamath Reservation.

Slaughter on the Little Bighorn

Though he had graduated at the bottom of his class at West Point, Colonel George Armstrong Custer had so distinguished himself during the Civil War that he had won the admiration and gratitude of General Philip Sheridan. Since July 1866, when he was appointed to command the Seventh Cavalry in the West, Custer had earned the reputation of a skilled Indian fighter. This reputation was bolstered by a good dose of dash and histrionics—a small band of musicians accompanied his expeditions, and he always had a journalist tagging along to report on his heroic deeds.

Reports had reached military authorities that the Sioux were raiding the Pawnee in the lands south of those guaranteed to the Sioux by the Treaty of Fort Laramie. General Sheridan recommended to Sherman that the army establish a military post on the reservation to watch and control the activities of the Sioux and Cheyenne. Custer was chosen to lead a reconnaissance of the reservation to ascertain where such a fort might be located. Dressed in buckskin, Custer led a force of 1,200 men, including a 16-man band of musicians, along with miners and geologists. The latter were going to ascertain whether there was anything to reports of gold coming out of the Black Hills.

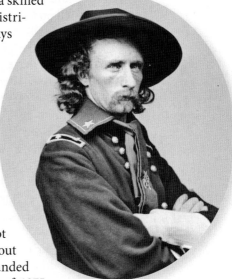

As it turned out, Custer's party did find gold in the Black Hills, though not much. Western newspapers, however, exaggerated the reports, and soon about 800 miners had entered the Black Hills illegally, while many more demanded that the government open up the land for prospecting. In the summer of 1875, agents of the government met with leaders of the Sioux to offer them money in return for the Black Hills. Though the Black Hills were sacred to the Sioux, several chiefs, including Red Dog and Red Cloud, were in favor of selling the land. But when they were told the sale price—$400,000 a year for mining rights and $6 million to buy the land—they refused to negotiate further. It was not enough money.

George Armstrong Custer

The government now decided to play tough—if the Sioux would not sell the Black Hills for the amount offered, they would receive no further subsidies of food. Sioux warriors now began to rally around Crazy Horse, Sitting Bull, and other chiefs who refused to compromise. Sitting Bull was a **shaman** and had a reputation for unwavering courage. Crazy Horse had been a great warrior since his youth and had fought at the side of Red Cloud in his wars against the forts on the Bozeman Trail. Crazy Horse was determined not to trade his people's traditions for wealth; he refused to accept any sale of the sacred Black Hills. The 1,200 Sioux and Cheyenne warriors who gathered around him agreed.

shaman: an Indian medicine man

The Indian Bureau now ordered all the Cheyenne and Sioux to gather at Fort Laramie. It was winter. The snow lay so deep and the cold was so bitter that only one tribe was able to make the journey to the fort. General Sheridan, though, would not take snow or excessive cold as an excuse. Those tribes, he said, who had not come to Fort Laramie were to be considered, henceforth, enemies of the United States of America.

Sioux Indians, Joe Merrivale, Young Spotted Tail, Antoine Janis, Touch-the-Clouds, Little Big Man

Sheridan planned his campaign against the Sioux. It would include a three-pronged attack that would converge at the junction of the Bighorn and Yellowstone rivers. Meanwhile, Sitting Bull had summoned Sioux and Cheyenne warriors to his camp on Rosebud Creek near the Little Bighorn. There, he led them in the Sun Dance, imploring the Great Spirit to send them victory. Sitting Bull himself tore one hundred strips of flesh from his arms and chest and then fell into a trance in which he said he saw soldiers falling into the Sioux camp, like a myriad locusts, from the sky.

Crazy Horse took Sitting Bull's vision as an omen of victory. At the head of his warriors, he fell on General George Crook's division as it advanced up Rosebud Creek in Montana on June 16, 1876 to attack Sitting Bull's camp. The fight between the Sioux and Crook's soldiers lasted until nightfall, when Crazy Horse abandoned the field. Crook claimed victory, though he turned back, making no further advance against Sitting Bull.

General Alfred Terry, who commanded another of Sheridan's divisions, had concluded that Sitting Bull was encamped on the Little Bighorn River. Sending Colonel John Gibbon up the Bighorn, he ordered George Custer and the Seventh Cavalry to ride up the Little Bighorn to flank the enemy if Gibbon attacked. On June 25, 1876, Custer spotted the Sioux and Cheyenne village on the Rosebud River, but instead of waiting (as he was ordered) for Gibbon's larger force, he decided to take the village himself. He did not realize that the village contained 4,000 Indians, over a third of whom were warriors.

Custer divided his own force into three divisions. He sent one division under Captain Frederick Benteen to the northern end of the valley to prevent the Indians from escaping by that route. Custer ordered Marcus Reno and his division of 175 men to cross the river and attack the north end of the village, while he himself, with the remaining 210 men, attacked the southern end.

Reno, crossing the Little Bighorn, soon found himself assailed by 1,000 Sioux warriors. Vastly outnumbered, he ordered his men to fight dismounted while retreating across the river. By the time he had retreated to the bluffs on the east side of the river, Reno had lost half of his men. On the bluffs, Reno held his position against the swarming hosts of warriors until Benteen reinforced him and took command.

While Reno was retreating, Custer moved down the east side of the river. As he prepared to attack the village, an overwhelming force of Indians swarmed over a nearby ridge. Custer tried to dispose his small force for defense, but before he could do so, another wave of warriors under Crazy Horse assailed him. The fight lasted less than an hour.

The next day, scouts from General Terry and Colonel Gibbon discovered the remains of Custer and his men. Their naked and mutilated bodies lay strewn across the field. There lay the dead horses whose bodies Custer and his men had used as shields against the relentless fire of the Indians. In the midst of all this carnage lay the body of Custer himself, stripped

Custer's last stand at the Battle of the Little Bighorn

naked, but not mutilated. Some say the Indians had refrained from harming the body in respect to so a great a warrior.

The slaughter of Custer's force at the Little Bighorn seemed to fulfill the promise of Sitting Bull's vision. But while the Sioux exulted, voices throughout the United States clamored for revenge. In August, Sheridan reinforced General Terry, who set out after the Sioux and Cheyenne. During this campaign, Colonel Nelson A. Miles drove Chief Gall and Sitting Bull into Canada, while throughout the winter of 1876–77, General Crook pursued Crazy Horse. Worn down, his people starving, Crazy Horse surrendered to Crook in May 1877.

As for Sitting Bull—though he was offered a pardon if he agreed to settle on a reservation, he defiantly refused to leave Canada. But four years later, with the buffalo almost gone and his people starving, Sitting Bull returned to the United States, surrendering his gun at Fort Buford. Proud to the end, he said he wanted it to be remembered "that I was the last man of my tribe to surrender his rifle."

"I Will Fight No More, Forever"

As he lay dying, Old Joseph, a chieftain of the Nez Percé tribe, admonished his son. "This country holds your father's body," he said. "Never sell the bones of your father and mother."

Old Joseph had been engaged in a long struggle to keep his people on their land, the Wallowa Valley in northeastern Oregon. Since the days of Lewis and Clark, the Nez Percé had maintained peace and friendship with the whites who came to Oregon, first in small, but then in ever-increasing numbers. As the settlers encroached on Nez Percé lands, Old Joseph, a Christian convert, continued to counsel peace. Still, he was sorely tried.

In 1855, Old Joseph and other chiefs had signed a treaty with the United States in which they surrendered certain of their lands in return for subsidies and the guarantee that they

Chief Joseph and his family, about 1880

could keep the Wallowa Valley as their home. But since settlers continued to encroach on the Wallowa Valley, government agents approached the Nez Percé in 1863 to negotiate another treaty. Some of the chiefs signed the treaty; but Old Joseph refused. He would not surrender the sacred Wallowa Valley. The Senate ratified the treaty in 1867, but Old Joseph still refused to leave the Wallowa Valley. On his deathbed he told his son not to abandon his people's homeland.

Hinmaton-Yalatkit ("Rolling-Thunder-in-the-Mountains"), called "Young Joseph," succeeded his father as chief in 1871. Following his father's example, the new Chief Joseph maintained his people on their land while counseling peace with white settlers. Keeping the peace became increasingly more difficult. For one, Joseph refused to adopt farming. ("The earth is our mother," he said. "She should not be disturbed by hoe or plough. We want only to subsist on what she freely gives us.") However, the white settlers, who continued to encroach on Nez Percé lands were more than willing to "disturb" Mother Earth and to graze their cattle on her grasses. Tensions between two such different cultures were bound to increase.

In 1876, an army commission, including General Oliver Otis Howard, met with Chief Joseph to persuade him to sell the Wallowa Valley and move his band to the Lapwai Reservation in Idaho, where Nez Percé had already gone. When Chief Joseph refused, the commission gave him a month to withdraw voluntarily to the reservation; if he continued to refuse, he would suffer force. Since he had few warriors, Joseph knew resistance was futile. In sorrow he abandoned the graves of his father and mother, and with his people, crossed the Snake River into Idaho.

Tragedy awaited Joseph in Idaho. Some of the young warriors, angry over the loss of their ancestral lands, rode out from the band and killed 20 white settlers, burned their farms, and raped their women. Fearing harsh retaliation from the whites if he remained in Idaho, Joseph decided to cross the Rockies with his band and, if possible, flee into Canada. When word of the massacre reached him, General Howard with 110 soldiers and volunteers marched out from Lapwai. Finding the Nez Percé at White Bird Canyon, Howard rejected Joseph's offer of peace and ordered an attack on the Indians. Though outnumbered, the Nez Percé killed 34 of their assailants and wounded four.

Continuing their flight, Joseph and the Nez Percé followed the Clearwater River to its source in the Bitter Root Mountains. Howard, in pursuit with 400 soldiers and 180 Indian scouts, attacked Joseph again in July but was unable to hinder him from crossing the Bitter Roots into Montana. From there, the Nez Percé crossed the Continental Divide and encamped in Big Hole Valley in southwestern Montana. There, Colonel John Gibbon attacked them one early morning, killing men, women, and children; but the warriors rallied, forcing Gibbon's men into defensive positions. Joseph and the Indians continued their flight.

The Nez Percé's odyssey took them through Yellowstone and then, north, towards Canada. In October, only 40 miles from the border, they were attacked by 600 soldiers from Fort Keogh led by General Nelson Miles, whom the Indians repulsed with heavy casualties. Miles, though, laid siege to the Nez Percé encampment, and, a few days later, Howard arrived, ending all hopes of escape. Joseph, with only 120 cold and hungry warriors, decided to surrender. To General Howard, Chief Joseph sent a message: "I am tired of fighting . . .

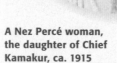

A Nez Percé woman, the daughter of Chief Kamakur, ca. 1915

> Our chiefs are killed . . . The old men are all dead . . . He who led the young men is dead. It is cold and we have no blankets. The little children are freezing to death. My people, some of them, have run away to the hills and have no blankets, no food. No one knows where they are—perhaps they are freezing to death. I want to have time to look for my children and see how many of them I can find. Maybe I shall find them among the dead.
>
> Hear me, my chiefs, I am tired. My heart is sad and sick. From where the sun now stands, I will fight no more forever.

Joseph's people were distributed between reservations in Indian Territory, Idaho, and Washington. Joseph himself would never again see the Wallowa Valley. He died at the Colville Reservation in Washingon 27 years later, in 1904.

War in the Southwest

After ten years of terrorizing white settlements in Arizona, Cochise, the leader of the Chiricahua Apache, at last surrendered:

> The war had begun in 1861 on account of a cocky U.S. army lieutenant named George Bascom. Some Apaches had kidnapped a white child, and Bascom ordered Cochise and five other Apaches to appear for questioning. When Cochise and his companions denied know-

ing anything about the kidnapping, Bascom ordered them imprisoned. A fight ensued, and Cochise escaped by cutting his way through the canvas side of Bascom's tent. Bascom held Cochise's wife, son, and two nephews prisoner.

Up until the Bascom incident, Cochise had kept peace with the United States. He and his people had abandoned the roving life and begun raising cattle to supply the white forts and settlements with beef. At first, the Apache obtained their beef from raiding Mexican settlements south of the border (an age-long Apache practice), but after a time they were raising their own cattle. Relations between whites and Apaches had been cordial—until the kidnapping.

After he fled from Bascom, Cochise attacked the Butterfield Stage, wounding one white man and killing another. That same evening, Apaches killed eight Mexicans, taking two white prisoners. Cochise kept the prisoners—one of them a willing one, the manager of the stage station, who knew Cochise—and offered Bascom the captives in exchange for his wife and family. What happened next is uncertain—either Bascom killed the Indians, and Cochise retaliated by killing the captives, or Cochise first killed the captives; but soon the Chiricahua again went on the warpath. Settlers, both adults and children, were brutally murdered in the Indian onslaught. Abandoned, burned out ranches were all that remained of white settlement in the region north and south of the Gila River.

Apache warriors, about 1906, by Edward S. Curtis

During the Civil War, when troops were removed to fight in the East, the Apache held sway in Arizona. Even after the war, Cochise and his warriors eluded capture, hiding in their strongholds in the Dragoon Mountains, from whence they set out on forays to raid and pillage and kill. In 1871, General George Crook took command of the Department of Arizona. He assured Cochise that he and his people could remain in their ancestral mountains and not be sent to the Tularosa Reservation in New Mexico, where other Apache had gone. The United States government, however, refused to honor Crook's promise and ordered the Chiricahua to Tularosa. Cochise again went on the warpath.

Cochise finally surrendered in the spring of 1872 when the government established a reservation for his people in the Chiricahua homeland. The Apache, however, were unwilling to take to farming and again began making raids into Mexico. On one such raid, Cochise was wounded. When he returned to the reservation, the wound grew infected and he died, June 8, 1874.

With Cochise dead, the Apache warriors no longer felt his restraining hand. Settlers began to complain that Indians were stealing their horses and cattle. In 1876, when the government ordered the removal of the Chiricahua to the San Carlos Reservation in a barren desert region of Arizona, the Apache again rose in revolt under the shaman, Goyathlay ("One Who Yawns"), called Geronimo. For the next six years, Geronimo and his warriors raided white settlements, spreading terror throughout the region. In 1882, General Crook again took command of the Department of Arizona and set out with 5,000 troops and 500 Indian scouts in pursuit of Geronimo. In January 1884, Geronimo surrendered, and Crook settled the Apache on the San Carlos Reservation.

At San Carlos, Geronimo chafed under the restraints and privations of reservation life. In May 1885, he fled with 35 men, eight boys and 101 women. Crook again set out in pursuit.

He chased Geronimo into Mexico, where at Cañon de los Embudos, the shaman again surrendered to Crook. But as they approached the United States border, Geronimo and a small band eluded Crook's watch and again escaped.

General Nelson A. Miles, who now replaced Crook, pursued Geronimo into his mountain stronghold in Sonora, Mexico. In September 1886, at a peace conference at Skeleton Canyon in Arizona, Miles told Geronimo that, if he surrendered, he would be sent to Florida, where his family had already been taken. But Miles assured Geronimo he would be able to return eventually to Arizona. With this assurance, Geronimo surrendered for the last time.

The government did not honor Miles' promise. Taken to Florida, Geronimo did not see his family for over seven months. He remained in Florida until 1894, when he was sent, not to Arizona, but to Fort Sill in the Indian Territory. There he remained until his death in 1909.

A Change in Indian Policy

Geronimo, about 1907

Throughout the 1870s, the voices of those who called for reform of the country's Indian policy grew more insistent. That their government had broken treaty after treaty with the Indians and had settled them on the poorest lands; that the Indians were not improving, not growing more civilized, but were becoming more degraded, weighed on the consciences of these reformers. A book published in 1881 by Coloradan Helen Hunt Jackson, *A Century of Dishonor,* helped fan the flames of reform. Clergymen, statesmen like Carl Schurz, journalists, and others joined in the cause to better the condition of the Indians.

The reformers' goal was simple—to civilize the Indians. Civilization meant Christianization. It meant teaching the Indians to read and write and cipher. It meant getting them to settle down as farmers. Many reformers thought this goal could best be achieved if the tribes were broken up and individuals were given their own plots of land to cultivate. Property ownership was the means, they said, to make the Indians into American citizens and, ultimately, assimilate them into white American culture.

The problem was that the Indians, with their tribal culture, could not easily adjust to western civilization. Indians had no tradition of private property ownership—all property belonged communally to the tribe. The Spanish found they could adjust to this reality by granting *ejidos* that preserved communal ownership; but the Anglo-American, it seems, could not imagine any such concession to tribal culture. Another problem was that Indian men thought it an indignity to farm; such lowly business they left to the women.

The Dawes Act (named after its sponsor, Senator Henry L. Dawes of Massachusetts), passed by Congress in 1887 (with the support of reformers and land speculators), embodied many of the reformers' ideals. The act allowed the president to authorize the break-up of reservations into individual homesteads when he received sufficient evidence that the Indians in question wanted it. Each family, said the act, would receive a homestead of 160 acres. Any reservation lands remaining after every family had received its allotment was to be sold to white settlers, the money from the sale to be held in trust for the tribe. The Dawes Act exempted the Five Civilized Tribes in Indian Territory from this break-up and allotment.

The breaking-up of the reservations began in 1891. Within one year, Indian lands had been decreased by 12 percent. (By 1932, Indians had lost two thirds of the 138 million acres they possessed in 1887.) Though Indians received homesteads, they did not benefit from them. They knew nothing of the monetary value of land, and land speculators easily took advantage of them. The Omaha and Winnebago in Nebraska, for instance, leased their lands for eight to ten cents an acre to a real estate syndicate, which turned around and re-leased the lands to white farmers for one to two dollars an acre. Tribal timberlands suffered the

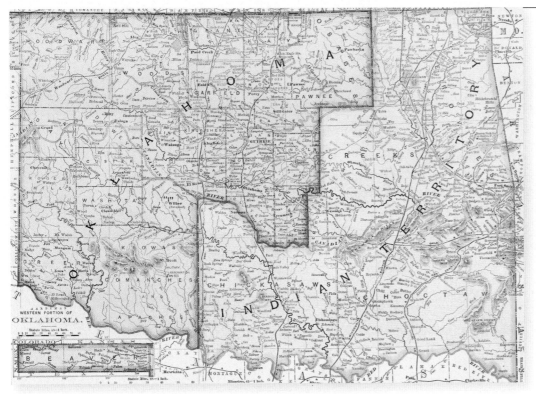

A 1900 Map of Indian Territory and Oklahoma Territory. Both territories, excluding the "panhandle," had formed Indian Territory. But, in the 1870s, organized bodies of white settlers moved into the Indian Territory, in violation of Federal law. Though the government forced most of these settlers to leave, eventually Congress, in response to public pressure, opened up 3,100 square miles of the western Indian Territory to white settlement. Eventually, this new Oklahoma Territory ballooned to include half of the original Indian Territory. By 1893, most even of Indian Territory was opened to white settlers and then dissolved, with lands assigned to the various tribes. The entire territory became the state of Oklahoma in 1907.

same fate. Though passed ostensibly to "improve" the Indians, the Dawes Act set in motion forces that would reduce tribes to even greater destitution.

Finale at Wounded Knee

One day Sitting Bull had a vision. He saw a meadowlark. The bird alighted on a small hill near where he was sitting. The meadowlark spoke. "Your own people will kill you," it said.

Times were hard on the Sioux reservations. The government had reduced food subsidies it had guaranteed by treaty. A feeling of desperation spread among the Sioux; humiliated, they were not even receiving the price of their humiliation.

In their desperation, the Sioux, Cheyenne, Arapaho, and other plains tribes had taken to a new ritual called the Ghost Dance. In 1889, a Nevada Paiute named Wovoka had said he had been taken up into heaven where the Great Spirit told him of a soon-to-come renewal of the world—a great flood would destroy the white men and restore everything to what it was it was before they came. Dead Indians, said Wovoka, would return to life; game would abound. Those who performed a ritual called the Ghost Dance would become immortal—the bullets of the white man could not penetrate their bodies.

Sitting Bull in 1881

The Ghost Dance frightened white settlers and Indian agents. But, though charged with emotion, it is unclear that the dance forebode any violence. Indeed, Wovoka had told his followers to remain at peace with white and red men alike. But the Ghost Dance had the effect of uniting in a bond of hope tribes who were otherwise enemies. And the strangeness of the ritual, coupled with the growing Indian unrest, made white men uneasy.

Big Foot's camp, three weeks after Wounded Knee Massacre, with bodies of four Lakota Sioux wrapped in blankets in the foreground

Authorities at Standing Rock Sioux reservation feared that Sitting Bull would join the Ghost Dancers and further agitate the Indians. On December 19, 1890, before dawn, Sioux reservation police (all of them Indians) broke into Sitting Bull's cabin to arrest him. A fight broke out that left six police and eight of the Sioux who defended Sitting Bull, dead. Sitting Bull too was among the dead; one of his own people had shot him through the head.

The news of Sitting Bull's death whipped the Sioux up into even greater agitation. Fearing a military attack, many Sioux fled the reservation. They were pursued by several thousand soldiers, who finally surrounded them and moved them to a camp near Wounded Knee Creek in Montana. The next day, the soldiers ordered the Indians to surrender their rifles—and they did, stacking them in the center of the camp. The soldiers, however, were not satisfied. They began to search Indian tents for more arms. This angered the Indians, and the shaman, Yellow Bird, goaded them to resistance. The bullets of the white men, he told the warriors, could not hurt them, for they had joined in the Ghost Dance.

Return of Casey's scouts from the fight at Wounded Knee

Then a Sioux warrior resisted surrendering his rifle. A struggle ensued. A rifle's report was heard; it was unsure from where it came. The Indians grabbed what arms they could, while the surrounding soldiers fired deadly barrages into the Indian camp. The Indians returned fire but, despite the promises of Wovoka, many were shot down. When the battle was done, about 150 Sioux, mostly women and children, lay dead.

Though some sporadic fighting continued after Wounded Knee, within two weeks the Sioux had returned to their reservations.

So ended the last armed engagement between United States soldiers and the America's indigenous peoples. The great Indian wars, which, for over 200 years had formed Anglo-America's heroic, though brutal, epic of adventure, in which the exotic names of Pontiac, Tecumseh, Black Hawk, Sequoia, and Crazy Horse are recorded—those struggles, at Wounded Knee, came to a dismal and inglorious close.

Part II: **The New Age of Steel**

John Brown's body lies a-mouldering in the grave. . . .
Out of his body grows revolving steel,
Out of his body grows the spinning wheel
Made up of wheels, the new, mechanic birth,
No longer bound by toil
To the unsparing soil
Or the old furrow-line,
The great, metallic beast
Expanding West and East,
His heart a spinning coil,
His juices burning oil,
His body serpentine . . .

So, over a half century later, wrote the American poet, Stephen Vincent Benét. The Old South was dead, its aristocratic and agrarian ideals buried in the debris of war. The war, the crusade for which John Brown had been the prophet, had created a new era that steam and steel would dominate. The agrarian America, of which Jefferson had dreamed; the land of sturdy, thrifty, and independent yeomen farmers; an order of rough equality birthing a "natural aristocracy"—all this was giving way. If the "Revolution of 1800" had validated the Jeffersonian ideal, the revolution of 1861–65 had inaugurated a Hamiltonian reality.

Railroad Revolution

Of course, this change didn't occur immediately. For the remainder of the 19th century, and well into the 20th, the mass of Americans still lived and worked on small farms. Small country towns, not large metropolises, still dominated the American landscape and imagination. The Homestead Act, passed in 1862, gave a stimulus to the creation of farms by opening up the Great Plains to settlers. Under this act, the federal government granted 160 acres of public land to any settler who could afford to pay a small fee and resided on the land for five years.

Not only the Homestead Act but the transcontinental railways stimulated a new wave of agricultural growth. The railroad companies sold the vast lands the government had given them to settlers. All along the shining rails, from the Mississippi to California and Oregon, rose new towns, surrounded by farmlands burgeoning with wheat and corn. Despite drought, heat, blight, and locusts, settlers, speaking a myriad of languages, broke and tamed the rich soil of the Great Plains.

The railroads helped create one of the romantic legacies of the West—the cowboy and the cattle drive. Longhorn cattle, which the Spaniards had abandoned over 100 years previous, had bred until thousands wandered the plains of Texas. Soldiers returning home from the war began herding the wild cattle, and soon northern and western Texas was parceled out to large ranches. Texas ranchers also discovered that the rich grasses of the vast plains between the Rockies and the Mississippi could feed thousands of head of cattle on long drives. Cattle could be driven from Texas to railheads and transported to market by rail car and locomotive.

Thus were born the great cattle drives, immortalized by literature and, later, motion pictures. Along such trails as the Chisolm and the Abilene, cattle drivers, called cowboys or (if Mexican) buckaroos (from the Spanish *vaqueros*), moved cattle to the railheads of the Kansas Pacific, at Abilene, Kansas; the Santa Fe, at Dodge City, Kansas; and the Union Pacific at Ogallala, Nebraska. From these centers, rail cars transported cattle to slaughterhouses in Kansas City or Chicago. By means of the newly invented refrigerator car, Texas beef was then transported to markets in the East, and, thence, by ship, even to Europe.

But the very force that helped make the cattle drives brought about their demise. By 1885, the plains were so crossed by railroads and criss-crossed by the barbed-wire fences of settlers that the free range was gone. During the harsh winter of 1886–87, thousands of cattle froze to death, and good pasture neces-

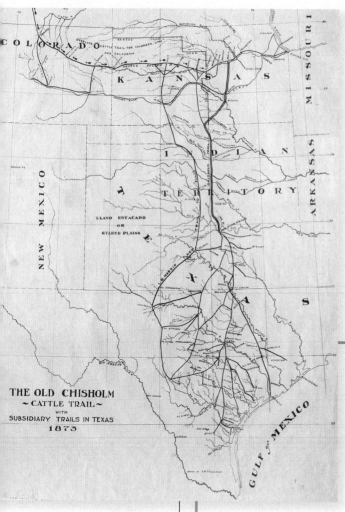

THE OLD CHISHOLM
~CATTLE TRAIL~
WITH
SUBSIDIARY TRAILS IN TEXAS
1875

Map of the Chisholm Trail, "with subsidiary trails in Texas," 1875

The Cattle Drives

Throughout fall and winter, great herds of cattle ran free on the Texas plains. In spring, cowboys rounded them up and distributed them between ranches according to brand marks, and then branded the young cattle, dividing among the ranches any motherless calves (called "mavericks" or "dogies"). Leaving the breeding cattle to graze at home for another year, the cowboys then rounded up the three- and four-year old cattle for the drive north.

A group of 12 cowboys and a "horse wrangler" (who managed their horses) drove a herd of about 2,500 longhorns on the 1,200 to 1,500 mile trek to the rail heads. The life of the cowboy was arduous. Shaded from the hot sun by wide-brimmed sombreros, cowboys moved cattle (about 10–20 miles a day). Day and night, cowboys had to ride around the perimeters of the herd, guarding it against stampedes and prairie fires and from such human predators as cattle rustlers and Indians. When they reached the towns at the end of the trails, the cowboys were paid, and then they whooped-it up, squandering their money in the "cow-town" saloons and gambling houses.

A cowboy in Sturgis, Dakota Territory, by John C. Grabill, 1888

sary for the long cattle drives became increasingly more scarce. Ranches themselves became contained, and the wandering cowboy became a domestic "hand." Yet, that brief epoch of the cattle drives became an image of freedom and strenuous action that has inspired the imagination. Theodore Roosevelt, who bought a ranch in the Dakotas in 1883, wrote in his *Autobiography* of his three years on the range:

> In that land we led a free and hardy life, with horse and with rifle. We knew toil and hardship and hunger and thirst; and we saw men die violent deaths as they worked among the horses and cattle, or fought in evil feuds with one another; but we felt the beat of hardy life in our veins, and ours was the glory of work and the joy of living.

Western cattle and the railroads changed the agricultural economy of the East. Traditionally, both in Europe and America, cattle had been raised in the areas where the people who consumed them lived. Now, with cattle shipped from the West, cattle raising declined in the East. Not just railroads, but industrial development in the East, would have its effect on agriculture as a whole. Except for the great plantations, most farms had been subsistence farms—growing a number of different crops, first, for the consumption of the farmer's family, then for sale on the market. To use the new farming machinery, farms had to become larger (for the machinery was expensive) and produce almost solely for the market. Instead of growing a number of crops, farmers increasingly specialized in one or a few crops—wheat and corn, for example. Hundreds, thousands of acres of corn and of the swaying, golden heads of wheat now covered the prairie where the Indian and buffalo once had roamed.

A publicity photo from the 1915-1925, demonstrating Bell's first ◄elephone

What made this all possible—the railroads, the new farm machinery—was cheap steal. The Bessemer converter, invented in the 1850s by the English engineer, Sir Henry Bessemer, converted iron ore into steal at a relatively low cost. In the ore fields of the northern and southern Appalachians, of Michigan and Minnesota, men mined the iron ore that went by rail to Chicago, Cleveland, Toledo, Ashtabula, Milwaukee, Pittsburgh, and Birmingham. In 1867, the United States produced 20,000 tons of steel. In the ensuing years, this number grew exponentially, so that by 1895, the country produced 6 million tons of steel, and 10 million tons only five years later

dynamo: a generator of electricity

Other breakthroughs came with the harnessing of electricity. In 1876, Alexander Graham Bell introduced his invention, called the "telephone," at the Centennial Exhibition in Philadelphia. Bell, and his partner, Theodore Vail, organized the Bell Telephone Company and provided telephone service in the cities. Since little electricity was necessary for the transmission of messages, telephone systems could be set up relatively easily in cities. Electric lighting systems were another matter. After the war, another inventor, Charles F. Brush, developed a **dynamo** capable of providing power to arc lamps, and in the late 1870s, early 1880s, Wabash, Indiana became the first American city to replace gas lamps with electric light.

An Ohioan, Thomas Alva Edison, had moved from his home state, where he had owned an electrical engineering business, to New Jersey. There, in Menlo Park, he set up a laboratory in which he, with other scientists and engineers, studied electricity and experimented with its uses. In the mid 1870s, Edison developed a "phonograph" or "speaking machine"—a cylinder covered with tin foil and turned by a crank. On October 21, 1879, Edison developed a light bulb that had a loop of carbonized cotton glowing in a vacuum. This was the incandescent light bulb.

Thomas Edison in his laboratory in West Orange, New Jersey, about 1901

The growth in manufacturing transformed many northern cities into "mill towns." This growth, of course, had been noted before the war; but in the second half of the 19th century, it accelerated. Large brick factories, powered by burning bituminous coal, their cylindrical towers belching steam and smoke, reared defiant of all that would impede the material progress of the nation. The Northeast was filled with these factory towns, but the Midwest was not laggard. Pittsburgh, Pennsylvania; Youngstown and Akron, Ohio; Milwaukee, Wisconsin; St. Louis, Missouri; and not to forget the country's largest city after New York, Chicago, Illinois—all these cities testified that a new America had arisen like a phoenix from the ashes of the antebellum union; an America born and nurtured in the recesses of the Yankee Northeast; a nation whose blood was a melting, transforming fire and whose sinews were a gray, cold, and tempered steel.

Cutthroat Competition

No rules governed the business world in the North after the war. It was a free-for-all where the acquisitive passions were let loose and where the primal law of survival held sway. Like atoms flying in a void from every direction, businessmen, inventors, speculators, and investors, following their own interests, struck each other in their career, deflecting the weaker from the trajectory of prosperity.

The post-war era was a time of wild speculation, of rapid production, of ruthless competition. Nowhere was the spirit of the age more clearly displayed than in the railroad companies. Railroads fought each other relentlessly, lowering rates and fares to drive each other out of business. Sometimes this competition would take on a comic character. When Cornelius Vanderbilt of the New York Central and Hudson River Railroad lowered rates on cattle to one dollar a head to undercut his rival, Jim Fisk, Fisk took advantage of the situation—he bought up a large number of cattle and shipped them by Vanderbilt's line. While these rate wars could be advantageous to those who shipped goods or traveled by rail, they often had dire effects on the companies themselves. Because of rate wars and stock manipulation, many railroads went bankrupt.

A daguerreotype of Cornelius Vanderbilt, about 1844–1860

Railroad and other companies did not shrink from manipulating government in order to make a profit or control a market. With vast funds at their disposal, railroad companies coerced and bribed state lawmakers; in California and New Hampshire, they practically controlled state government. Mining companies followed suit, bribing judges who heard suits over rival claims. Since railroads had practically unlimited control over the regions through which they ran, and which depended on them for the shipment of goods and crops to market, farmers and merchants had to rely on their mercy—which was often not forthcoming. Railroads could raise and lower their rates at will, and the farmer or merchant had no other recourse than to pay them.

"At this period," wrote Thomas W. Larson in his book *Frenzied Finance* (published 1905), Americans found they could "by the exercise of a daring and cunning of a peculiar, reckless and low order, so take advantage of the laws of the land and its economic customs as to create for themselves wealth, or the equivalent, money, to practically an unlimited extent, without the aid of time or labor or the possession of any unusual ability coming through birth or education." This climate brought instability to the market—companies rose and fell, the value of bonds plummeted, the rivalry of manufacturers led to overproduction—and this brought a glut of products to the market resulting in dramatic falls in prices. These factors combined to create a financial "panic" (as depressions were then called) in 1873 and, another one 20 years later.

To stabilize the marketplace somewhat, rival manufacturers and producers entered into agreements whereby they maintained prices at a certain level and divided business and profits among themselves. But because members of such "pools" did not keep their word

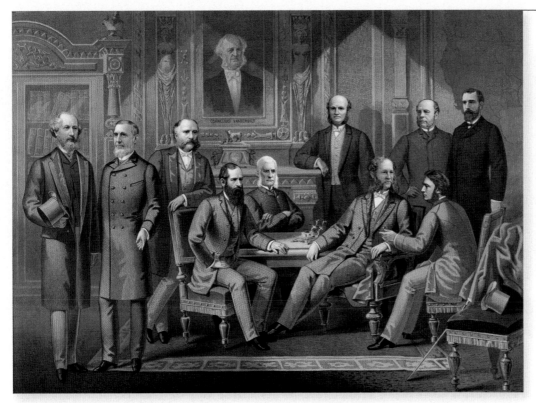

Kings of Wall Street, 1882. Left to right: Cyrus Field, Russell Sage, Rufus Hatch, Jay Gould, Sidney Dillon, Darius Ogden Mills, William H. Vanderbilt, August Belmont, George Ballou, James R. Keene

but, under cover of it, undercut their partners, these agreements often did not last long. What's more, some state governments had declared such business combinations illegal. A better form of business combination was soon found—one that would not only stabilize the market, but corner it as well: the "trust."

A trust is a combination in which companies or firms hand over, or "entrust," their securities and power to a central board of "trustees." Such trustees did not form a company incorporated under the laws of any state; thus, they were not subject to the same restraints as normal companies. Thus, trusts, if they grew large enough, could dominate and control markets.

Such a combination was the Standard Oil Trust, formed by John D. Rockefeller in 1882. Rockefeller had been in the oil refining business since 1863. In 1870, with his brother William and other partners, Rockefeller formed the Standard Oil Company. The oil refining business in those days was subject to fierce competition. Dangerous fires, too, often broke out in refineries. Rockefeller set out to group smaller companies together, to economize their business practices and improve their technology. To do this, Rockefeller and his allied refiners organized the South Improvement Company and convinced the Pennsylvania, Erie, and New York Central railways to lower shipping prices for them while upping rates for competitors. South Improvement then offered to buy its competitors' companies (when they could no longer compete) by offering them money or stock in Standard Oil. By such methods, and by others (such as assailing competitors with lawsuits until they went bankrupt), Rockefeller had by 1878 gained control of over 90 percent of the oil refineries in the United States. In 1882, Rockefeller's Standard Oil Trust governed 39 corporations in various states.

John D. Rockefeller, about 1872

Another man who amassed great wealth during this period was a Scotsman named Andrew Carnegie. Andrew was only 13 when in 1848 his father brought him to America. Employed by the railroad, the young Carnegie rose in the business world and was the first to introduce sleeping cars for the railroads. After observing the Bessemer process in Europe and foreseeing the coming demand for iron and steel, Carnegie invested in iron and in 1875 built the Edgar Thomson Steel Works near Pittsburgh. There he produced steel rails. By 1888, Carnegie had bought out the steel works in Homestead, Pennsylvania, and had gained control of coal and iron fields, a 425-mile long railway, and a line of Great Lakes steamships.

Andrew Carnegie, about 1861

Laissez-faire and Regulation

The evolutionary theory of the English naturalist Charles Darwin, which was sweeping the scientific world during the late 19th century, seemed a justification for the unregulated competition of the business world. According to Darwin, more complex life forms develop from less complex ones through a process of natural selection in which only the fittest, most adaptable, species survive. Many in the late 19th century thought that economics operated in the same manner; in business, they thought, only the fittest should survive. Far from implying any injustice, such survival led, it was thought, to the progress of human society. The men on top were on top because they deserved to be on top. What's more, it was ultimately better for everyone that they were on top.

Such a philosophy dovetailed nicely with a concept of *laissez-faire,* a French phrase meaning, "let do." Proponents of *laissez-faire* believed that businessmen should be able to pursue their economic interest as they wished with little or no government interference. An influential proponent of the Darwinian and *laissez-faire* school of economics was William Graham Sumner, a professor of sociology at Yale University. Sumner thought that populations inevitably grow too large for their food supply and thus suffer want and starvation. In order to overcome this natural state of affairs, he said, men invent things and engage in activities that lead to the further progress of the human race. To interfere with this natural cycle—say, by coming to the aid of the less fortunate—said Sumner, is to diminish man's potential. "If we should try by any measures of arbitrary interference and assistance," he wrote, "to relieve the victims of social pressure from the calamity of their position we shall only offer premiums to folly and vice and extend them further."

Sumner was deeply conservative in the sense that he thought men should maintain the social institutions they have inherited. "We are inheritors of civil institutions," he wrote, "which it has cost generations of toil and pain to build up, and we are invited to throw them away because they do not fit the social dogmas of some of our prophets." Sumner eschewed ideals, declaring that they (and religion, for that matter) were in conflict with science. Hard-nosed scientific facts, thought Sumner, pointed to the soundness of the developing economic order. "The concentration of wealth," he wrote, "is indispensable to the successful execution of the tasks which devolve upon society in our time."

Among those who rejected the *laissez-faire,* Darwinian view of society and its economic order was Lester Ward—called the father of American sociology. Ward thought that men by scientific investigation could come to understand how society works and learn how to order and direct it to control the disorderly effects of economic competition and ameliorate suffering. Religion, he thought, could not accomplish this, since it had hindered true morality by trying to make men good through fear. Ward thought society (that is, government), armed with scientific knowledge, could create an "organization of happiness." "It is the duty of society, in its collective capacity," he wrote, "so to regulate the phenomena of the social aggregate as to prevent, as far as possible, the advancement of a small class at the expense of a large one."

Since individual free enterprise had driven much of American life, Americans tended to favor a *laissez-faire* view of business. This, coupled with their fear of government power, made Americans hesitant to use law as a means to rein in even the worst abuses of business. Nevertheless, faced with the power that trusts possessed to corner and control a market, states began to try and break these combinations. They were largely unsuccessful. New York, for instance, sued a branch of the Sugar Trust, only to have it regroup later under a new organization and a new name—the American Sugar Refining Company—and eventually control 85 percent of sugar production in the United States. New York's attorney general, David Watson, tried to break up Standard Oil, arguing that "a society in which a few men are the employers and a great body of men are merely employed or servants is not the most desirable in a republic; and it should be as much the policy of the laws to multiply the numbers engaged in independent pursuits, or in profits or production, as to cheapen the price to the consumers." Watson, however, failed to force Standard Oil to sell off many of its holdings. Rockefeller simply gave the controlling board a new name—"liquidating trustees" (board members entrusted with selling property)—and business went on as before. The state couldn't interfere with Standard Oil as long as the trustees were (if only on paper) doing what the state ordered them to do: sell off property.

"The Bosses of the Senate," depicting the trusts as the masters of the U.S. Senate. A cartoon by Joseph Keppler from the journal, *Puck*.

When states failed to regulate business, the federal government got into the act. In 1887, Congress passed the first Interstate Commerce Act to regulate "unreasonable" railroad rates and the pooling of companies across state borders. The act established the Interstate Commerce Commission. When, however, the federal courts said the commission could review railroad rates, but not fix them, it lost its teeth. In 1890, Congress passed the Sherman Antitrust Act, which declared monopolies and business combinations that hindered interstate trade illegal. This act also was largely ineffectual; the five years following the passage of the act saw the formation of at least 25 new trusts throughout the country.

Theodore Roosevelt, in his *Autobiography,* summed up this period of rapid business expansion and centralization. The post-war United States saw, he said, witnessed . . .

> . . . a riot of individualistic materialism, under which complete freedom for the individual . . . turned out in practice to mean perfect freedom for the strong to wrong the weak. . . . The power of the mighty industrial overlords . . . had increased with giant strides, while the methods of controlling them, . . . through the Government, remained archaic and therefore practically impotent.

The Laborer's Plight

Andrew Carnegie saw clearly that the growth of big industry and corporations in Europe and the United States had worked revolutionary changes. "The contrast between the palace of the millionaire and the cottage of the laborer . . . today measures the change that has come with civilization," he wrote in the *North American Review*. This change has come at a high cost, said Carnegie; the intimate relationship between master and apprentice had been broken and, in its place, had risen the factory, the mine, and the counting house, where "thousands of operatives [labor] of whom the employers can know little or nothing, and to whom the employer is little better than a myth." Such a situation, said Carnegie "breeds mutual distrust" and "friction between the employer and the employed, between capital and labor, between rich and poor."

Carnegie thought these ills were the unfortunate but inevitable result of the "law of competition." "It is to this law that we owe our wonderful material development, which brings improved conditions in its train," he wrote. And in true Darwinian strain, he added that, "while the law may be sometimes hard for the individual, it is best for the race, because it insures the survival of the fittest in every department." The compelling problem facing the modern age, said Carnegie, is not the way men gain wealth, but "the proper administration of wealth, so that the ties of brotherhood may still bind together the rich and the poor in harmonious relationship."

Carnegie thought he had found the answer to this dilemma. The rich, he said, should use their excess wealth for the good of society. They should endow schools, museums, and other cultural establishments to help the poor to better themselves. In his lifetime, Carnegie set-up the Carnegie trusts which, to this day, fund cultural and intellectual endeavors. But Carnegie dismissed private charity. It violates, he said, the law of competition and the survival of the fittest. And, while he could be a kindly employer, Carnegie was not opposed to holding down his workers' wages, or laying them off, to increase profits.

Offering possibilities for betterment, however, did not afford any relief for the immediate needs of the typical working man and his family. Workers labored long hours (12 to 14 hours a day) for little pay, in dirty and dangerous conditions. Not only a father, but his wife and even his young children (eight years old and up) labored in the "dark Satanic mills" of the industrialists. Periods of unemployment, caused either by slumps in the business cycle or by the introduction of labor-replacing machinery, threatened workers with homelessness and starvation.

Bad industrial working conditions were nothing new in America. The spirit of *laissez-faire*, of free, untrammeled enterprise, had held sway in the rough young country since its earliest days. This spirit tended to reduce workers to the status of machines, mere means to an end—a large profit margin for the employer and the investors in his company. Just as an industrialist would try to pay the lowest price possible for his machines, so he would pay the lowest wage possible to his employees. Since there were so many men who wanted work, the employer could always find someone who would work for what he wanted to pay. The abundance of cheap labor, too, made many an employer careless of the safety of his shop—if a worker became injured on the job, his boss simply dismissed him and found another to take his place.

As we have noted, the industrial workers in antebellum America were chiefly the native born, free blacks, and immigrant Irish. After the war, new laborers, such as farmers' sons escaping to the city and discharged soldiers, entered the industrial workforce. In the 1860s, the number of immigrants from the British Isles began to decrease while the number of immigrants from the European continent grew. Russians, other Slavs, Italians, and southern and eastern Europeans, as well as laborers from China, made up an increasing share of the swelling num-

A boy, Raoul Julien, had been working in the Chace Cotton Mill in Burlington, Vermont, when Lewis Wickes Hine took this photograph in 1909

ber of immigrants entering the United States—from 300,000 in 1866 to 789,000 in 1882. In terms of yearly numbers, immigrants from the British Isles declined in percentage from 45 percent of all immigrants in 1861–70 to 18 percent in 1891–1900, while the number of continental Europeans in the same period increased from 0.1 percent to over 50 percent.

Because of this immigration, large cities, such as New York, Philadelphia, Pittsburgh, and Chicago, babbled in a multitude of tongues. These cities, of course, had already German and Irish neighborhoods, but to these were added Russian, Italian, Slavic, and Chinese enclaves. When a native Anglo-American entered such sectors of his native city, he must have felt as if he were walking into a foreign country!

Tenements of the poor on the Lower East Side of New York City, early 1900s

But whether they were foreigners or native born, laboring families lived in squalid conditions. Packed in tenements with bad ventilation, dark, dingy, and dirty, families often lived, six to eight people, in a single, small room. The New York labor commissioners reported that tenants "cook, eat, and sleep in the same room, men, women, and children together. Refuse of every description makes the floors damp and slimy, and the puny, half-naked children crawl and slide about it." In Fall River, Massachusetts, 500 persons in a tenement had access to only a single bathroom—and those who couldn't use this privy would dispose of their excrement where they could. No wonder "consumption" (tuberculosis) and infectious diseases took a heavy toll of urban laboring families, especially children.

Hell's Half Acre—a row of houses at the edge of a mill settlement in Alabama, by Lewis Wickes Hine, 1910

A Lewis Wickes Hine photograph, 1912, of Mrs. Tony Racioppo, who in her tenement apartment at 260 Elizabeth St., 1st floor rear, New York City, is finishing pants

This wretched existence put new pressures on family life, and many families did not survive the strain. Though the farm had its own hardships, the rural homestead was the center of a family industry. Labor united, rather than dispersed, family members. Father, mother, and each child had his function on the farm, and all worked together toward a common goal. In the cities, however, each family member went about his own individual task, and long hours of labor separated parents from their children, who then grew up without guidance. Gangs of youth roamed the streets, and the young fell to dissolute living and, too often, crime. Women who were single or who had lost their husbands and had no extended family, sometimes cohabitated with men not their husbands or in their desperation turned to prostitution.

The industrial worker left the squalor of his or her home six days a week for the misery of the workplace. Unlike craftsmen of old, who worked in small shops in which often friendship and even a family spirit prevailed between the master, his journeymen and apprentices, the typical 19th century worker labored in large factories built for machines, not men, where he was merely one "unit of labor" to his employer. The older craftsman could engage in interesting work and had the satisfaction of being involved in the whole process of production. If he were, say, a silversmith, he might design a teapot, make the mold into which he would pour the molten silver, and give his work the finishing touches. Such a worker was an artist in the truest sense. But with the

"Breaker Boys" during a noon hour break at a South Pittston, Pennsylvania coal mine, by Lewis Wickes Hine, 1911

invention and increasing use of machinery in the 19th century, workers only engaged in one small aspect of production, and the teapot or the hat or the dress was the work of many hands, not one. In this system, the worker became merely a cog in a great wheel—and an expendable cog, at that.

And to all this drudgery and squalor, industrialization added another misery—indignity. Men often suffered the trial of seeing themselves replaced by women and children, whom employers could work longer and pay less. Children between eight and 14 years old performed the labor of men, ten to 11 hours a day. Women worked long hours sewing in hot, badly ventilated rooms, sometimes behind locked doors. Industrialism showed no mercy to the delicacy of women or the tenderness of youth.

And all this was undertaken for pay that was hardly adequate to supply the necessities of life. Employers deducted money from their workers' meager pay for company housing and medical care. In some factories and coal mines, workers were paid in scrip that they could use only to buy goods in stores owned by the company. Company stores charged such exorbitant prices for goods that workers would end their year in debt to their employers.

On Strike

Deep in the bowels of the earth, men and boys labored in darkness to extract the precious substance that powered the machines and engines of industrial America. The flickering flames of torches illumined their faces, blackened with coal soot. Their lungs drew in the dust of ancient creatures and vegetation long dead. Danger threatened the miners always. If the pumps that pushed water from the mines failed, the shafts could flood and drown the miners. Methane gas, often found in the mines, could ignite and explode. Furnaces in shafts below the miners created drafts that expelled the methane; but if these furnaces should ignite their timber-lined vents, the whole mine could be engulfed in fire.

Such a disaster occurred in 1869 at Avondale in the anthracite coal region of Pennsylvania. On the morning of September 6, a worker sounded the alarm when he discovered that one of the ventilating furnaces had ignited its wooden shaft. The column of flame with terrible swiftness rushed to the surface; above the ground, the earth spewed fire. Fire crews from Scranton, Wilkes-Barre, and surrounding areas rushed to the scene, but little could be done. When, finally, the fire had died down and rescue crews could descend into the mine, a lurid sight met their eyes.

The miners who had not escaped had tried, to no avail, to shut themselves off from the lethal methane gasses freed by the failure of the ventilation system. "Fathers and sons were found clasped in each other's arms," wrote Andrew Roy, state inspector of Ohio's mines, in 1876. "Some of the dead were kneeling, as if in the attitude of prayer; some lay on the ground with their faces downward, as if trying to extract a mouthful of fresh air from the floor of the mine; some were sitting with clasped hands, as if they had vowed to die with each other; and some appeared to have fallen while walking."

Such were the dangers coal miners faced, for the pittance of a wage.

Irish Catholic mine workers had been organized since 1836 in chapters of the Ancient Order of Hibernians, an Irish fraternal organization. Among these workers, a smaller group, called the Molly Maguires, took to agitating for better working conditions and better wages. Against them were ranged a coalition of coal and railroad companies called the Anthracite Board of Trade, under the leadership of Frank Gowen of the Philadelphia and Reading Railroad Company. Gowen employed "coal and iron" police to keep rebellious miners in line. Called the "Pennsylvania Cossacks" by the miners, these police committed murders and other crimes to intimidate their opposition.

The Molly Maguires responded in kind. During the "Long Strike" of 1875, when miners agitated for higher wages and better working conditions, the Mollies used threats, beatings, and murder against their opposition—mine superintendents, bosses, and the Cossacks. They obstructed train traffic, pushed engines off the rails, and destroyed property. Some

Burning of the Lebanon Valley Railroad bridge during the Great Strikes of 1877

"Sixth Regiment Fighting its way through Baltimore," an engraving from the front cover of *Harper's Weekly*, August 11, 1877.

say that it was the Cossacks that were responsible for a good deal of the violence ascribed to the Mollies; more miners than company operatives, it was said, died from violence. But the violence finally served to discredit the miners' cause. Both during and after the strike, Catholic priests and bishops condemned the Molly Maguires, both for their violent ways and because they required their members to take secret oaths. Archbishop John Wood of Philadelphia excommunicated Molly Maguire members.

The Long Strike ended in failure for the miners, but the violence continued. Cossacks and Mollies settled down into a two-year period of quasi-guerrilla war. Frank Gowen hired agents of the Pinkerton Detective Agency to infiltrate the Mollies to obtain evidence against them—and the "Pinks," some say, were responsible for much of the violence ascribed to the miners. Evidence brought by one Pinkerton agent, James McParlan (who was working for Gowen), led to the conviction and execution of 19 men said to be Mollies in June 1877. Other Mollies ended up serving prison time. These convictions broke the power of the Molly Maguires.

Only a month after the execution of the Mollies, the Baltimore and Ohio Railroad announced that it was cutting wages that were already at a level barely able to support a family. Workers pleaded with the owners of the Baltimore and Ohio, who merely ignored them. On July 16, railroad workers near Baltimore, Maryland went on strike. Other workers connected with the railroad joined them, as did railroad workers in other cities. Strikes and demonstrations broke out in Martinsburg, West Virginia; Philadelphia and Pittsburgh; Columbus and Cincinnati; Chicago; and St. Louis, Missouri.

So began the Great Strikes of 1877, long remembered in the history of labor agitation. Strikers not only paralyzed the railroads of the North—the lifelines of industry—but created considerable unrest in the cities. Not only men ("respectable" tradesmen among them), but women and young girls composed the throngs of workers in the cities. In Pittsburgh, armed strikers pushed engines from their tracks and defied state militia called out to pacify them. One state militia general found himself confronted by an angry mob when he tried to carry out his orders to arrest one of the ringleaders of the strike. Then someone in the mob cried out, "At them, boys! At them! Give them hell!" The militia general ordered his men to open fire, killing 16 and wounding several others. "The sight presented after the soldiers ceased firing was sickening," wrote a reporter for the *New York Herald*. "Old men and boys attracted to the [scene of the standoff] . . . lay writhing in the agonies of death, while numbers of children were killed outright. Yellowstone, the neighborhood of the scene of the conflict, was actually dotted with the dead and dying; while weeping women, cursing loudly and deeply the instruments which had made them widows, were clinging to the bleeding corpses."

When militiamen from Pittsburgh heard of the slaughter, they threw down their arms and joined the strikers. Soon the remainder of the Pennsylvania militia found itself besieged in a railroad roundhouse, while strikers and others who had just joined the fray pillaged city shops for weapons. Four-thousand strikers and others, unable to dislodge the militia, set fire to the roundhouse. The militia finally withdrew, while mobs burned railroad property and commenced a general looting of the city.

The country had never seen such an "insurrection." By July 30, the strikes had spread to the coal fields, crippling industries and foundries that relied on coal. Railroad workers in Trenton and Newark, New Jersey, also quit work. Many Americans were appalled not only by the violence but by what they thought was the workers' temerity. After all, some thought, how could they complain? Their wages, though small, were but a sign of their inferior abilities, and so they were only receiving their due. Even so stalwart an anti-slavery man as the Rev. Henry Ward Beecher, after praising the "heroism of railroad employees" and admitting the right of every man to withhold his labor, still condemned any concerted effort that interfered with the labor of others. The strikers, the *New York Times* reported Beecher saying to congregants at Plymouth Church in Brooklyn, "had put themselves in an attitude of tyrannical opposition to all law and order and they could not be defended."

Henry Ward Beecher

Beecher continued: "The necessities of the great railroad companies demanded that there should be a reduction of wages. There must be a continual shrinkage until things come back to the gold standard, and wages, as well as greenbacks, provisions and property, must share in it." This erstwhile defender of the poor slave could find, it seems, no sympathy for the plight of wage workers. Their problem, he said, was that they needed to be trained in "self-denial." Beecher (said the *Times*) continued that "it was true that $1 a day was not enough to support a man and five children if a man would insist on smoking and drinking beer." Such a family, if it were prudent, "may live on good bread and water in the morning, water and bread at midday, and good water and bread at night (continued laughter)." Though he admitted that real hardship existed, Beecher insisted that "the great laws of political economy could not be set at defiance."

The Great Strikes ended when President Rutherford Hayes decided to treat the strikes as an insurrection and sent the United States army under General Winfield Scott Hancock into Pittsburgh. Hundreds of millions of dollars of property had been destroyed because of the Great Strikes, and many Americans now grew fearful of communist and socialist infiltration.

Still, the strikes brought some benefit to workers. The Baltimore and Ohio Railroad set up a relief association for workers that provided them and their families insurance (50 percent of the average monthly salary) in the event of illness, death, or on-the-job injury.

The Pullman Palace Car Company purchased 4,000 acres near Chicago to build a workers' community called Hyde Park and hired landscape architects to design a town that included shopping centers, a playhouse, and gymnasium. The company, however, established rules for the town that strictly governed the inhabitants' conduct and gave them no voice in local governance—policies that served only further to alienate the workers living there.

Organized Labor and the Beginnings of Labor Reform

Those who suspected communist influence in labor agitation were not entirely wrong. Some unions were indeed affiliated with the Communist International, which was working for a general, worldwide proletarian revolution. Other unions were affiliated with the Black International, an anarchist organization. Such leftist organizations generally flourished wherever German immigrants had settled—in Wisconsin, for instance, or Chicago. But they hardly represented the majority of the American labor force.

Print depicting Terence Powderly, with other leaders of the Knights of Labor

A German paper in New York City, *Die Freiheit* ("Freedom"), espoused the cause of revolutionary anarchism. It belonged to Johann Most, a German revolutionary who had arrived in New York City from London in 1882. Most, who had been imprisoned several times in Germany for revolutionary activity, worked to organize an anarchist workingman's party. In Pittsburgh he organized the International Working People's Association (IWPA) and issued a manifesto that told workers, "it is . . . your right, it is your duty, says Jefferson—'to arm!'" Later he moved the headquarters of the IWPA to Chicago, where in *Die Freiheit* he published instructions on how to make dynamite.

The Knights of Labor, founded in 1869, was the first labor organization that tried to unite all workers in one big union. The Knights were not communist or anarchist; but they proposed an end to the wage system in favor of an "industrial cooperative system" where workers would share in the ownership and profits of companies. Terence Powderly, an Irish Catholic who became grand knight of the union in 1881, was something of a visionary. He wanted the Knights to ally themselves with causes that promoted "personal liberty and social equality." Powderly also wanted his union to unite with the temperance movement and encouraged local union councils to form cooperative business enterprises.

Under Powderly, the Knights of Labor gained some victories. An 1884 railroad strike the Knights organized in the Southwest forced Jay Gould to concede to some union demands. In 1885, Congress passed a law favored by the Knights, forbidding the importation of foreign contract labor—like the Chinese laborers in the West. But Powderly in some ways was too visionary, and he tended to treat the Knights of Labor as if it were his own personal union. His opposition to clemency for the Haymarket anarchists and his impracticality severely weakened the Knights of Labor at the height of their influence and membership. In the 1880s the Knights gave way to another powerful union.

This union was the American Federation of Labor (AFL). One of the founders of this union, Samuel Gompers, a British subject of Jewish and Flemish background, worked at a cigar shop in New York's Lower East Side and was a member of a cigar makers union. Unlike Powderly, the eminently practical Gompers eschewed ideas on how to change the economic and social order and concentrated only on goals that could be immediately achieved. Gompers led his union out of the Knights of Labor, and in 1886 he and other labor leaders formed the AFL as a national federation of craft unions to represent skilled workers in factories. Gompers became chairman of the new organization whose more humble goals were shorter work hours and higher wages.

Gompers' call for a general strike to campaign for an eight-hour work day brought him into opposition with Powderly (who thought the issue too political since it might require laws to enforce it) and the IWPA, which favored revolutionary, not piecemeal, change. In the end, the Knights of Labor and the anarchists fell into line and pushed for the eight-hour day in opposition to almost every sector of society. Both liberal and conservative newspapers and journals opposed the eight-hour workday. Henry Ward Beecher thought it a scandal that workers should be paid for working ten hours when they had only worked eight. Gompers answered such objections by arguing that the eight-hour day would actually increase worker productivity, since it would allow a worker longer periods of rest. Such an argument could not move Beecher, who seemed to take the dimmest view of the moral character of workers. The eight-hour day, he said, is "a charitable scheme for the benefit of saloon keepers."

Samuel Gompers

The eight-hour day, though, received the support of President Grover Cleveland and of some senators and representatives. The campaign was, on the whole, successful; companies began to scale back the number of hours workers labored—some to the desired eight hours, others to nine hours, a day. This was a major victory for Gompers' AFL and for the labor movement in general.

Throughout the 1870s and '80s, various state legislatures began passing laws to regulate the treatment of workers. In 1874, Massachusetts passed the Ten-Hour Act for women and children in factories. Nine years later, New York, at the urging of Gompers, of then-governor Grover Cleveland, and of Theodore Roosevelt, began investigating cigar manufacturing in tenement houses. Roosevelt reported that cigar manufacturers housed a family and lodgers in a single room where they lived and rolled cigars. Subsequent legislation by the state of New York was designed to break down these and other sweat shop operations.

The New York state supreme court, however, struck down this legislation. "It cannot be perceived, how the cigar-maker is to be improved in his health or his morals by forcing him from his home and its hallowed associations and beneficial influences to ply his trade elsewhere," said the court. Besides, the court continued, such legislation interfered with the profitable use of property without any demonstrable public benefit. Other courts echoed the New York state supreme court's decision. Beginning about 1886, courts began overturning state business regulation laws on the basis that they violated the freedom of contract.

Religion and the Labor Question

Though the number of religious sects in the United States was myriad, Americans in the late 19th century evinced a rather uniform Protestant set of mind. Religion dominated America, and so it is not surprising that it should influence, and be influenced by, the problems of capitalism and labor.

Most Protestant Christians in the United States maintained a conservative attitude towards the labor question and tended to side with the men who controlled capital. As we have seen, Henry Ward Beecher tended to take a dim view of the workingman's character.

Haymarket

The Winter of 1885–86 was bitterly cold. Thousands were out of work, and soup kitchens did not have provision enough to feed all the hungry. Workers at Cyrus McCormick's factory in Chicago had gone on strike, and McCormick had locked them out. With the protection of police and Pinkerton detectives, McCormick had hired other workers to replace the strikers. The strikers derisively referred to these workers as "scabs."

Several strikes had gone off badly in Chicago in recent months; police chief John Bonfield had not shied from using violence to suppress them. But in the weeks before May 1, 1886, labor leaders had pulled off a series of successful public meetings. Prominent among these leaders were two anarchists, August Spies, a German immigrant, and Albert Parsons. Born into a prominent Southern family, Parsons had joined the Confederate army at the age of 13. After the war he had found his way to Chicago, where he became involved in union agitation and socialism. Employers had blackballed Parsons because of his role in the Great Strikes of 1877.

On Sunday, May 1, 1886, 30,000 gathered in Chicago for a peaceful labor rally. The next day, another rally was held in front of the McCormick factory to protest the lockout. In the midst of the rally, McCormick's scabs began coming out the building, for they had been given a half-holiday to celebrate McCormick's acceptance of the eight-hour day (which had been among the strikers' demands). The angry strikers turned on the scabs and forced them back into the building. Soon over 200 police arrived at the scene and attacked the strikers with their billy clubs, killing one striker and wounding six others.

It was not long before the rumor spread that the six wounded strikers had been killed. In response to the rumor, August Spies printed a broadside that read, "REVENGE! Workingmen! to Arms!" Spies printed another flier, calling for a mass meeting, to be held May 4 at Haymarket Square, to protest police violence. The first proof of this flier carried the injunction, "Workingmen arm yourselves and appear in full force!" but Spies ordered that line expunged. Of the 20,000 fliers printed, maybe only 200–300 contained this line.

At 8 p.m. on May 4, Spies addressed a few hundred workers gathered at Haymarket Square. As he warmed to his subject, he began denouncing McCormick and challenged the workers. "The families of twenty-five or thirty thousand men are starving because their husbands and fathers are not men enough to withstand and resist the dictation of the thieves on a grand scale," he cried.

Albert Spies' "Revenge" broadside, printed in English and German

Albert Parsons next addressed the slowly growing crowd. "I am not here for the purpose of inciting anybody," he declared. "It behooves you, as you love your wife and children, if you don't want to see them perish with hunger, killed or cut down like dogs in the street, Americans, in the interest of your liberty and your independence, to arm, to arm yourselves." The people applauded and cried, "We will do it, we are ready now!"

A rainstorm drove away many of those gathered, and at 10 p.m., when about 180 police arrived, only 300 to 400 remained. The rally had been peaceful, but the police captain ordered it to disperse. No sooner had he spoken than someone threw a bomb into the ranks of police, killing one officer and injuring sixty others. The police fired into the crowd. In the aftermath, one striker lay dead, 12 others were wounded.

(continued)

Explosion in the Haymarket

Newspaper accounts of the Haymarket episode made it appear that the bomb-throwing had been part of a well-orchestrated anarchist plot. In the weeks that followed, police arrested socialists and anarchists in Chicago and suppressed their newspapers. Among those arrested were August Spies and another anarchist leader, Samuel Fielden. Albert Parsons, who had gone into hiding, decided to give himself up. "I could not bear to be at liberty knowing my comrades were here and were to suffer for something of which they were as innocent as I," he said.

Thirty-one radical leaders were indicted as accessories to the bombing. Eight of these—Spies, Parsons, Fielden, Louis Lingg (who manufactured bombs similar to the one thrown in the Haymarket), Oscar Neebe, Michael Schwab, Adolph Fisher, and George Engel—were put on trial. Throughout the trial, the judge displayed a bias against the defendants and made rulings favorable to the prosecution; and though no evidence linked the eight to the bombing, the jury found them guilty. All but Oscar Neebe (sentenced to 15 years in prison) were condemned to die by hanging.

In his address to the court, Spies declared that he had been convicted simply because he was an anarchist, because he believed the "state of castes and classes—the state where one class dominates over and lives upon the labor of another class . . . is doomed to die, and make room for a free society, voluntary association, or universal brotherhood, if you like . . . If death is the penalty for proclaiming the truth, then I will proudly and defiantly pay the costly price! Call in your hangman! Truth crucified in Socrates, in Christ, in Giordano Bruno, in Huss, Galileo,

still lives—they and others whose number is legion have preceded us on this path. We are ready to follow!"

Lawyers for the eight anarchists appealed their case to the Illinois state supreme court, but the justices upheld the verdict of the lower court. A group of lawyers, among whom was old Benjamin ("the Beast") Butler, next appealed the case to the United States Supreme Court. Given the irregularities of the case, they thought it certain that the court would hear the case and grant a writ of error. They were wrong. The justices refused to consider the case.

The only hope left for the condemned men was a governor's pardon. Illinois governor Richard Oglesby long vacillated between letting the court's sentence stand and commuting the death sentences to life imprisonment. The plight of the seven men had become of national interest to labor, with Samuel Gompers weighing in for pardon and Terence Powderly calling for justice to take its course. (Powderly himself it seems was trying to deflect criticism that the Knights of Labor were socialist radicals.) Oglesby said if enough businessmen came out for pardon, he would feel assured that he could grant it. Indeed, enough businessmen would have supported a pardon had not the rich and powerful Chicagoan, Marshall Field,

Four Chicago anarchists on their way to their execution by hanging, at Cook County jail, November 1887

(continued)

voiced his opposition to clemency. Against the powerful Field, no businessmen spoke in favor of pardoning the convicted anarchists.

Governor Oglesby finally opted for compromise; he commuted Schwab and Fielden's sentence to life imprisonment. Spies, Fischer, Parsons, and Engel were led to the scaffold on November 11, 1887. (Lingg had committed suicide in jail by blowing off a dynamite cap in his mouth.) "There will come a time when our silence will be more powerful than the voices you strangle today!" Spies cried from the gibbet. His comrade, Fisher, shouted, "Hurrah for anarchy," while Engel chimed, "This is the happiest day of my life!" The trap doors then gave way beneath the condemned, but Parsons had just time enough to raise his voice: "Let me speak . . . Let the voice of the people be heard!"

Other Protestants saw wealth as the reward of virtue, especially industriousness. William Lawrence, Episcopalian bishop of Massachusetts (whose Trinity Church in Boston the wealthy richly endowed), taught that not only does wealth *not* lead men into immorality, but, "in the long run, it is only to the man of morality that wealth comes . . . . Godliness is in league with riches," he said. "To seek for and earn wealth is a sign of a natural, vigorous, and strong character." A Congregational minister, William Makepeace Thayer, echoed the Rev. Lawrence when he declared, "We might say that religion demands success." Such men looked askance at or positively condemned unionism as introducing an un-American, and therefore, un-Christian and even socialist system into the country.

But the late 19th century saw a growing number of Christian justifications for unionism and even socialism. Lyman Abbott, who had succeeded Henry Ward Beecher at Plymouth Congregational Church in Boston, believed that, while industrial competition had been necessary and had produced many good results, it was time for the competitive spirit to give way to "new principles of cooperation and more equitable income distribution." With Henry Codman Potter, the Episcopalian bishop of New York, Abbott formed the Church Association for the Advancement of the Interests of Labor, which mediated strikes and encouraged church members to patronize businesses that had fair labor practices.

Other Christian thinkers began to think that sin was not merely individual but that societies had sinful structures that fostered and perpetuated sin in the lives of individuals. George Herron, pastor of a church in Burlington, Iowa, held such a view and saw socialism as the means of curing the ills of society. Herron condemned "the condition of competition" as "inconsistent with both Christianity and democracy." He insisted that "the people must finally own and distribute the products of their own labor." Herron, with other Christian socialists, saw the democratic state as the means to bring about social reform. "The state," Herron said, "is the only organ through which the people can act as one man in the pursuit of righteousness." The state, Herron said, must be "born again" and "delivered" from "pagan doctrines of law and government, from commercial and police conceptions of its functions, from merely individualistic theories of freedom."

Some North American Catholic bishops, priests, and laity objected to labor unions because they thought unions espoused ideas and encouraged practices that could harm the faith of their Catholic members. The bishops of Quebec, for instance, sought from Rome a condemnation of the Knights of Labor because members were required to take secret oaths modeled on the rituals of Freemasonry, which the Church had condemned. Unions, too, brought Catholics together with non-Catholics (Protestants and, it was feared, radicals) who could lure them away from the Church.

James Cardinal Gibbons, the archbishop of Baltimore, however, came to the defense of the Knights of Labor. In a document called the "Memorial," Gibbons assured the Holy See that the oaths Knights took, though secret, were not binding like Masonic oaths. Terence Powderly, Gibbons said, had pledged his devotion to the Church, and it was clear to the cardinal that the Knights plotted nothing against the government. The "Memorial" had two effects. First, it saved the Knights from Rome's condemnation. Secondly, when it was leaked to the newspapers, Gibbons and the other bishops who signed it were celebrated as friends of labor.

But the chief contribution of the Catholic Church to the labor question came not from America, but from Rome. On May 15, 1891, Pope Leo XIII issued an encyclical letter, *Rerum Novarum* ("Of Revolution"). In *Rerum Novarum,* Pope Leo applied traditional Catholic teachings on the nature of property, wealth making, justice, and charity to the contemporary situation of labor and capital. The result was a masterpiece of balance, avoiding the extremes of *laissez-faire* Liberalism and of socialism, both of which Leo condemned.

In *Rerum Novarum,* Leo taught that, since God gave mankind the earth "to serve the common interests of all," every person has a natural right to the fruits of the earth. Yet, said Leo, "God is said to have given the earth to mankind in common, not because he intended indiscriminate ownership of it by all, but because he assigned no part to anyone in ownership, leaving the limits of private possessions to be fixed by the industry of men and the institutions of peoples." With private property, all can share in the goods of the earth, since the owners are sustained by their property, while "those who lack resources supply labor, so that it can be truly affirmed that the entire scheme of securing a livelihood consists in the labor which a person expends either on his own land or in some working occupation."

Pope Leo XIII

Thus, argued Leo, human beings have a right to private property, and workers, in particular, have a right to a wage that "shall not be less than enough to support a worker who is thrifty and upright." Such a wage, said the pope, must "be sufficient to enable [the worker] comfortably to support himself, his wife, and his children," and, "if he be a sensible man, to practice thrift" by which he can "put by some little savings and thus secure a modest source of income." In affirming the right to private property, the pope condemned socialism; but in promoting a just wage, he condemned any treatment of workers as mere cattle or machines. To secure a just wage, Leo noted, workers had the right to organize themselves into unions. Peaceful strikes were permissible, but on no occasion should workers embrace violence as a just means to secure their rights. Employers, too, had to respect their workers' right to organize and give way to their just demands. Workers, said the pope, should be treated as human beings; they must not be overworked, nor should children be forced to labor like adults or work placed upon females as if they were adult men.

Leo, however, envisioned a state of society that would transcend the divisions of capitalist and worker. "Law," he wrote, "ought to favor [the right to private property] and, so far as it can, see that the largest possible number among the masses of the population prefer to own property." Leo, thus, hoped for a society where not only a few owned productive property (such as farms, shops, machinery, etc.), but one in which as many workers as possible were property owners. In response to the theory of *laissez-faire,* he assigned a role to the state as the architect of the social order—the authority to set down the parameters of law by which the various groups in society operate in justice according to their own proper principles. Thus, since the state is composed, first, of families, then of other smaller societies, the role of the government should be to help each of these bodies operate in the best manner possible, without in any way taking over, or interfering in, their proper functions.

In a certain sense, Pope Leo agreed with Thomas Jefferson that the state exists so men might secure their rights to life, liberty and happiness. But unlike Jefferson, Leo defined what he meant by liberty and happiness. Following Catholic tradition, he said the use of material goods has one end—the practice of virtue; thus, happiness is living a virtuous life. "Assuredly," Leo wrote, "since social good must be of such a character that men through its acquisition are made better, it must necessarily be founded chiefly on virtue."

Leo insisted that the Church has to be involved in solving social problems; for it is the Church alone that infallibly teaches men and nations how they ought to live. "Without hesitation We affirm," wrote the pope, "that if the Church is disregarded, human striving will be in vain.

> Manifestly, it is the Church which draws from the Gospel the teachings through which the struggle can be composed entirely, or after its bitterness is removed, can certainly become more tempered. It is the Church, again, that strives not only to instruct the mind but to regulate by her precepts the life and morals of individuals, that ameliorates the condition of the workers though her numerous and beneficent institutions, and that wishes and aims to have the thought and energy of all classes of society united to this end, that the interests of the workers be protected as fully as possible.

Chapter 21 Review

Summary

- As white settlers moved into the West, the question of what to do about the Indians came more to the fore. To solve the problem, the United States government made treaties with Indian nations to get them out of the way of white settlement. The Indians were moved to reservations and were given government subsidies and a sum of money for their land.

- The Arapaho and Cheyenne under Black Kettle signed a treaty in 1861 and were moved to a reservation. The reservation was so poor that the Indians were dying, and Cheyenne braves began raiding white ranches, causing the settlers to call out the militia. This led to a general uprising of the Cheyenne and Arapaho. Black Kettle signed a treaty in 1865 and went to a reservation. Dissatisfied Cheyenne continued the resistance.

- The Jesuit priest, Pierre De Smet, came to American in 1821 and began to work among the Indians. He had a powerful influence over the Indians, and they trusted him. He established missions among the Indians and made peace between warring nations.

- In 1862 the government delayed a yearly subsidy payment to the Sioux, and the nation rose in revolt under their chief, Little Crow. The government appealed to Father De Smet to pacify the Indians. When De Smet learned that the government had no intention of honoring its promise to the Indians, De Smet refused to negotiate any further.

- After the Civil War, the long cherished plan for a transcontinental railroad could be realized. The railroad would, however, have to pass through Indian lands, so it was imperative to make peace with the Indians.

- The army began building forts along the Bozeman Trail, which ran through Sioux lands, to protect miners and settlers en route to gold fields in Montana. In 1866, Captain William Fetterman fell into an Indian ambush, and he and his men were slaughtered.

- Congress created a non-government organization called the Indian Peace Commission. In 1868 the commission recommended conquering the Indian by kindness. They called for a peace conference in 1868. The commissioners and the Sioux concluded the Treaty of Fort Laramie in May and concluded similar treaties with other nations.

- On May 10, 1869, the Union Pacific and the Central Pacific railroads met at Promontory Point in Utah and drove in a gold spike to mark the completion of the first transcontinental railroad.

- With the transcontinental railroad came an increasing number of settlers into the West, and the Indian problem became even more pressing. The early 1870s saw the rise of a number of Indian aid societies.

- When white settlers came to the lava beds of northeastern California and southeastern Oregon, they demanded the removal of the Modoc, the inhabitants of that region. The government complied and removed the Modoc to a reservation on the Klamath River. This reservation was already shared by the Snake and Klamath tribes, who were enemies of the Modoc. The Klamath harassed the Modoc, and the Modoc chief, Captian Jack, demanded lands elsewhere, but he was refused. The Modoc fled to the dry lava beds on the shores of Tule Lake and were pursued by the U.S. army. Finally Captain Jack was betrayed by one of his own. He surrendered and was hanged.

- When Colonel Custer and his men found gold in the Black Hills, the government offered the Sioux money in return for the Black Hills. The price was not high enough, so the Sioux refused. The government decided there would be no further subsidies for food for those who refused to compromise. When Sioux warriors began to rally around Crazy Horse, Sitting Bull, and others, the Indian Bureau ordered all Cheyenne and Sioux to gather at Fort Laramie. Because of extreme cold, most of the tribes did not come to Fort Laramie. A war followed with the Sioux and Cheyenne. When Colonel Custer and his men were slaughtered by Sioux led by Crazy Horse, people throughout the United States clamored for revenge. Crazy Horse surrendered in May 1877, and Sitting Bull surrendered four years later.

- Before he died, Old Joseph, chief of the Nez Percé tribe, told his son never to sell the tribal lands in the Wallowa Valley. His son, Young Joseph, refused at first to sell the Wallowa Valley; but when a U.S. commission gave him a month to withdraw peacefully, Chief Joseph complied. When some of his young warriors, angry at their loss, killed white settlers, Joseph fled over the Rockies with his people toward Canada. Along the way they were attacked several times by U.S. cavalry, and finally Joseph surrendered.

- After a long war with the United States, Cochise, chief of the Chiricahua Apache, surrendered and went to the reservation the government had set aside for his tribe. There he died. The Apache were unwilling to take to farming and made raids in Mexico. When the government ordered their removal to a desert region of Arizona, the Apache

rose in revolt under Geronimo. Geronimo surrendered in 1884, and the Apache settled on the San Carlos reservation. Geronimo escaped several times until he was finally captured and removed to Florida.

- In the 1870s reformers called for civilizing the Indians. The reformers thought the best way to do that was to break up the tribes and give individuals their own plots of land. Congress passed the Dawes Act in 1887 that authorized the break-up of reservations into individual homesteads. The Indians, however, could not easily adjust to western civilization because they had no tradition of private ownership. This Dawes Act reduced tribes to greater destitution.

- When the Sioux began to practice the Ghost Dance to make themselves immortal, white authorities were frightened. This, coupled with growing Indian unrest, caused the authorities to fear that Sitting Bull would join the Ghost Dancers and further agitate them. On December 19, 1890, Sioux reservation police broke into Sitting Bull's cabin to arrest him. A fight ensued in which Sitting Bull was killed by one of his own people. The Sioux fled the reservation, pursued by soldiers. At Wounded Knee, the soldiers ordered the Indians to surrender their rifles, and a struggle ensued that ended in a massacre. This was the last armed engagement between the United States and an Indian nation.

- In the West the railroads helped create one of America's romantic legacies—that of the cowboy and the cattle drive. The brief epoch of the cattle drives became an image of freedom and strenuous activity.

- Western cattle and the railroads changed the agricultural economy of the United States. Farms were increasingly no longer subsistence farms and became larger due to the use of new machinery.

- With the harnessing of electricity came other new breakthroughs. In 1876 Alexander Graham Bell invented the telephone. Charles Brush developed a dynamo capable of providing power to arc lamps, replacing gas lamps with electric light. Thomas Edison developed the phonograph and the incandescent light bulb.

Chapter 21 Review (continued)

- In the business world of the North after the war there was wild speculation and rapid production. Overproduction brought on financial panics.

- To stabilize the marketplace somewhat, manufacturers came up with the "trust." With his own trust, John D. Rockefeller controlled 90 percent of the oil refinery business in the United States.

- In order to combat abuses associated with trusts, Congress passed the first Interstate Commerce Act in 1887 and the Sherman Antitrust Act in 1890. Both were largely ineffective.

- The plight of the urban laborer was deplorable. Men, women, and children worked long hours for a mere pittance, and families lived in squalid conditions. In 1877 the "Great Strikes" disrupted business throughout the eastern United States and ended when President Rutherford Hayes sent in the United States army. The strikes brought some benefits to workers, but still their situation was far from ideal.

- Labor groups called unions began to form in America, starting with the Knights of Labor. This group gave way to the American Federation of Labor (AFL) in 1886. The AFL helped realize the passage of eight-hour work day laws in many states.

- Religion began to take an interest in the labor issue, and the late 19th century saw a growing number of Christian justifications for unionism and even socialism. On May 15, 1891, Pope Leo XIII issued an encyclical letter, *Rerum Novarum*, presenting the Catholic teaching on property and labor.

Key Concepts

trust: a combination in which companies or firms hand over, or entrust, their securities and power to a central board of trustees

evolution: a theory in biology that postulates that various types of plants, animals, and other living things have originated from other preexisting types and that the differences that distinguish them come from modifications in successive generations

laissez-faire: French phrase meaning, "let do"; the idea that economic actors should be able to pursue their economic interests as they wish with little or no government interference

labor union: a combination of workers in various industries who unite to bargain over wages, benefits, and working conditions

Dates to Remember

1869: the Union Pacific and the Central Pacific meet at Promontory Point, completing the transcontinental railroad.

1876: the Battle of the Little Bighorn

Alexander Graham Bell invents the telephone.

1877: the Great Strikes

1879: Thomas Edison invents the incandescent light bulb.

1886: Samuel Gompers forms the American Federation of Labor.

1887: Congress passes the first Interstate Commerce Act.

1890: Congress pass the Sherman Antitrust Act

The massacre at Wounded Knee

1891: Pope Leo XIII issues *Rerum Novarum*.

Central Characters

Pierre-Jean De Smet (1801–1873): Jesuit missionary whose efforts to Christianize and pacify Indian tribes made him their beloved "Blackrobe"

Crazy Horse (1842–1877): Sioux chief who was an able tactician and warrior in the Sioux resistance to the white man's invasion of the Great Plains

Chief Joseph (1840–1904): a Nez Percé chief who led his followers in an attempt to escape to Canada

Cochise (d. 1874): a Chiricahua Apache chief who led his people's resistance to American settlement in the U.S. Southwest

Geronimo (1829–1909): a Chiricahua Apache leader who led the Apaches' defense of their homeland against the United States

Wovoka (1858–1932): American Indian religious leader who initiated the Ghost Dance cult

Alexander Graham Bell (1847–1922): Scottish-born American inventor who invented the telephone

Thomas Alva Edison (1847–1931): American inventor who invented the incandescent light bulb

John D. Rockefeller (1839–1937): American industrialist and founder of the Standard Oil Company

Andrew Carnegie (1835–1919): Scottish-born American industrialist and philanthropist who led the enormous expansion of the American steel industry

Terence Powderly (1849–1924): American labor activist who led the Knights of Labor from 1879 to 1893

Samuel Gompers (1850–1924): American labor activist who served as the first president of the American Federation of Labor

Pope Leo XIII (1810–1903): the pope who addressed the issues of economic justice in the encyclical *Rerum Novarum*

Questions for Review

1. What did Americans in the West think of the Indians?

2. Explain the general character of the treaties made with the Indian nations.

3. What made Pierre De Smet's mission to the Indians so successful?

4. How did the transcontinental railroad affect the fate of the Indians of the West?

5. Why didn't the reformers' goal of assimilating the Indians into western civilization succeed?

6. Why didn't the Indians benefit from the homesteads they received under the Dawes Act?

7. How did the cowboy and the cattle drive embody the American ideal?

8. How did technology change the agricultural economy of the United States?

9. Explain what a "trust" is and how it affected the economy of late 19th-century America.

10. Explain Darwin's natural selection theory and how proponents of *laissez-faire* used it to justify their economic theory.

11. How did *laissez-faire* and Darwinian natural selection affect the lot of workers in the late 19th century?

12. What is a labor union? How do craft unions (like the AFL) differ from unions like the Knights of Labor?

13. Outline the major ideas of Pope Leo XIII's encyclical, *Rerum Novarum*.

Ideas in Action

1. Read and discuss Pope Leo XIII's encyclical, *Rerum Novarum*. Examine labor issues of the late 19th century and our time in light of the encyclical.

2. Read Owen Wister's *The Virginian*, a story of the cowboy legend. How has the legend of the cowboy influenced how Americans think of themselves and their nation?

3. Research one of the Indian nations in this chapter, looking at such things as its traditions, religion, and how the nation changed over the course of history.

4. The Franciscan historian of the California missions, Zephyrin Engelhardt, thought that in certain respects the reservation system worked out by the United States government was similar to the Spanish mission system as exemplified by the California missions—but, he thought, there were very fundamental differences as well. What were those similarities? What were the differences? Which system was better in terms of treatment of the native Americans?

Highways and Byways

The Hat that Makes the Man

Everyone knows that the cowboy's most important accoutrement after his horse and his gun is his hat. The hat is what sets the cowboy apart. It defines who he is. The cowboy uses his hat to shield his face from sun and wind. He uses it as a receptacle from which to drink water. And, of course, the hat gives the cowboy that dashing look that made Molly fall in love with her Virginian.

Chapter 21 Review (continued)

The cowboy hat is made of fur-based felt, straw, and sometimes leather. The general structure of the hat is a tall, rounded crown and a wide, flat brim, often customized by creasing the crown and rolling the brim. The first cowboy hat was created in 1865 by J.B. Stetson. Stetson called his hat the "Boss of the Plains." He was the first to market his "Boss of the Plains" to cowboys, and the hat has remained a universal image of the American West.

At a time when a hat was indispensable to every man's wardrobe, Stetson focused on high-quality hats that last a long time. There is a story that in 1912 the battleship *U.S.S. Maine* was raised from Havana harbor, where it had sunk in 1898, and a Stetson hat was found in the wreckage. It had been in seawater for 14 years, exposed to mud and plant growth; but when the hat was cleaned off, it appeared to be undamaged.

Indestructible or not, the cowboy hat has remained the symbol of the cowboy and the West even to this day, immortalized as a symbol by the likes of Buffalo Bill Cody, John Wayne, and Ronald Reagan. It is still well-loved by cowboys and city slickers alike.

22 THE END OF THE CENTURY

Part I: Confusion and Crisis in American Religion

"I want you just to ask yourselves this question, Do you believe in Christ?" The preacher was warming to a sermon that would bring, before the end of the evening, hundreds to the "altar." "Do you believe he was the Son of God? Do you believe he was the God-man? Do you believe he was with God before the morning stars sang together and voluntarily left heaven and came down into this world? Whose Son was he? Was he the Son of Man and the Son of God? Who was he, the God Man? That is the question."

Indeed, that was the question Dwight L. Moody asked continually of those who came to his revival meetings. Who is Christ? What is He to you? "Why don't you love Him? . . . O, sinner, do you think well of Christ today? Love Him today! Give your souls to Him this blessed afternoon, the last Sabbath of this blessed month! This day and this hour let us press into the Kingdom of God!"

Dwight Moody had turned to preaching after a successful career in business. From city to city he traveled, preaching to thousands in the style of the old revivalists. His meetings were lively, with mass hymn singing and the escorting of the converted to the altar where

Dwight L. Moody preaching at the Clermont Rink, New York City

they would give themselves to Christ. Moody always had an inquiry room where those troubled by sin could meet with counselors. Unattached to any denomination, Moody encouraged his converts to seek out the church of their preference where the good work, begun by the revival, might be completed.

The Crisis of Protestantism

Moody represented a strain of Protestantism to which, to one degree or another, most Americans still adhered. This more "conservative" religiosity was centered around Bible reading, personal devotions such as private and family prayer, and "Sabbath" observance. It was a religion still heavily tinged with the Puritan ethic that glorified hard work and sobriety and frowned on "vain" pleasures (card playing, for instance, drinking intoxicating liquors, dancing, and other "carnal" pastimes). Despite the emotional excesses of the revival meetings still popular in the countryside, in small towns, and even on college campuses, the mainstream Protestantism of America was a pretty stiff and rigid affair that identified piety with a narrow and work-a-day middle class propriety.

Relying on an overly simplistic interpretation of Biblical texts, this traditional American Protestantism faced new struggles in the latter half of the 19th century. Darwinists mocked these religious folk for their insistence that God created the earth in seven, 24-hour solar days, because Genesis seemed to say so. Since, according to Darwin's theory, the evolution of species to their current complexity required millions upon millions of years, Darwinists told believers it was absurd to hold that the earth was only around 6,000 years old, as the Bible seemed to indicate. Unable to defend their beliefs on scientific grounds, believers attacked science itself as diabolic. Without an adequate philosophical or theological tradition, many Protestants shrank from the task of reconciling science with the faith that it seemed to contradict.

Of course, many devotees of science were no more willing to reconcile their ideas with religion. To them, religion was nothing but superstition. Religion, they believed, had to give way to reason and science. Many had begun to think empirical science—knowledge derived from measurement, observation and experimentation—was the highest form of knowledge. If mankind would only cast aside religion and other prejudices, they thought, science could lead mankind to untold heights of power, prosperity, and happiness. Men and societies, they believed, had to cast aside ignorance and the bondage of the past, and set out on the road of progress. After all, it was not the middle ages anymore—it was the 19th century!

Protestant Christianity was certainly on the defensive against the triumphant optimism of the proponents of reason and science. These optimists were the heirs to Enlightenment thinkers such as the two Thomases (Jefferson and Paine) who believed in man's basic decency and in the maxim that there is no sin, only error. In the face of this optimistic worldview, the cold Calvinistic religiosity of America, with its emphasis on man's depravity seemed not only irrational and stiff, but even cruel.

Henry Adams

The cities experienced the biggest defection from religion. John Quincy Adams' urbane grandson, Henry Adams, wrote of "his aching consciousness of a religious void." Adams wondered if "any large fraction of society cared for a future life, or even for the present one." Of course, many did still care about a future life, but concern over the present life was ever the stronger. A Japanese convert to Christianity expressed his disappointment upon visiting, in 1884, what he thought would be a "lofty, religious, Puritanic" America. This convert had heard so often "about the superiority of the Christian civilization over that of the Pagan," that he expected America to be a "Holy Land." But what did he find? "A land of mammon-worship and race-distinction!" he said.

A sign of the continued vibrancy of American Protestantism was American involvement in the foreign missions. By 1888, Japan had 450 missionaries, most of whom were American. One-third of China's 1,500 missionaries was American. India, though, had the largest number of American missionaries. In all these countries, American missionaries (the majority of whom were women) spread not only their faith but their notions of equality and democracy. Sun Yat-sen, the leader of the Chinese revolution in the early part of the 20th century, attributed the success of the revolution above all to Christianity. "Along with its ideals of religious freedom," said Sun Yat-sen, Christianity "brings a knowledge of western political freedoms, and along with these it inculcates everywhere a doctrine of love and peace. These ideals appealed to the Chinese; they largely caused the Revolution and they largely determined its peaceful character."

Back home, in America, Protestantism continued to splinter into more and more groups. There were still folks who were preoccupied with the second coming of Christ, though the Millerites or Adventists had given up predicting a date for the event after their disappointment in 1843. A former Congregationalist turned Adventist, Charles Taze Russell, taught that Christ had already come, invisibly, in 1874, and would return again in 1914. Russell said the Bible taught that the number of the saved was 144,000 but that others who bore witness to "Jehovah" could escape annihilation (Russell rejected the doctrine of hell) and dwell on a new earth. Russell founded the Watchtower Bible and Tract Society to disseminate his teachings. His followers, known at first as "Russellites," later became known as Jehovah's Witnesses.

Many Americans of this period were attracted to the New Thought movement. New Thought held that all unhappiness was merely a mental state that right thinking could overcome. New Thought practitioners spoke of a "mind cure" in which, by meditation in tranquil and harmonious surroundings, one was brought into contact with "that Divine Energy we call God." New Thought tapped into the late 19th century's craze for science. Though essentially non-Christian, it eventually took on some Christian overtones.

Portrait of Charles Taze Russell, from his tombstone

Among those who tried to explain notions of mind cure using Christian terminology was Mary Baker Eddy. Born in 1821 in New Hampshire, Mary Baker was a pious girl who studied Greek, Latin, and Hebrew and taught Sunday school. In 1843 she married George Washington Glover, a Charleston merchant, and moved south. Glover died only six months after their marriage. After freeing Glover's slaves, Mary returned to New Hampshire to her parents' house, where, despite continual ill health, she occupied herself in teaching and studying.

Mary Baker Glover married again, in 1853, this time to a New Hampshire dentist named Daniel Patterson. It was a bad marriage and ended ten years later when Patterson abandoned her. During this period Mary met Phineas Quimby, a "healer," who purportedly cured her of her ailments. Quimby, she said, helped her to see that "there is a cause and effect in the spiritual world as in the natural . . . I know there is a science of health, a science of life, a divine science of God." In 1866, she fell on an icy street and was severely injured. Two days later, Mary Glover said that she read an account of healing in the Gospel of Matthew and experienced an immediate recovery.

From this experience, Mary Baker Glover developed her ideas that sickness and death are only deceptions and that the mind could control matter and bring about healing of the body. Glover began to operate as a healer and taught others how to become healers—at $300 for a 12 half-day course. In 1870 she published a pamphlet, "The Science of Man," in which she declared, "In the nineteenth century I affix for all time the word Science

Mary Baker Eddy, in 1882

to Christianity; and error to personal sense; and call the world to battle on this issue." In 1877 she married Asa Gilbert Eddy, one of her students. Three years before Eddy's death in 1882, Mary Baker Eddy founded the Church of Christ, Scientist, whose followers became known as Christian Scientists.

Mary Baker Eddy's new religion experienced a surprising growth; and her principal book, *Science and Health with Key to the Scriptures*, was widely read. Even such a cynical soul as Mark Twain was attracted to this rather odd faith, though he had enough wit to see the ludicrous side of it. Mrs. Eddy, he insisted, had stolen her doctrines from Phineas Quimby and with these ill-gotten gains had marketed "a religion which has no hell; a religion whose heaven is not put off to another time . . . but begins here and now, and melts into eternity." Christian Science, said Twain, was "the Standard Oil of religion."

Further Left and Farther Out

A rather singular event occurred at the World's Columbian Exposition and World's Fair, held in Chicago in 1893 to celebrate the 400th anniversary of Columbus' discovery of America. Besides featuring displays of the great 19th century industrial and scientific achievements, the exposition showcased religions. The "Parliament of Religions" featured presentations, not only by leaders of the various Christian and semi-Christian religions in the United States, but by leaders of world religions as well. Judaism, Islam, Buddhism, and Hinduism had each its spokesmen at the Parliament. Among the more exotic speakers was Swami Vivekananda, an East Indian monk who had spent many years near Calcutta contemplating not only the sacred traditions of Hinduism, but the teachings of Christ, Muhammad, and the writings of such Western philosophers as Kant, Hegel, and Schöpenhauer. Swami Vivekananda had come to the conclusion that science and religion must forge a new union with each other and that material progress was not contrary to spiritual enlightenment. Vivekananda's message at the Parliament of Religions struck a sympathetic chord in the hearts of those Americans who stood in the tradition of transcendentalists like Ralph Waldo Emerson. "Allow me to call you, brethren, by that sweet name—heirs of immortal bliss—yea, the Hindu refuses to call you sinners," said Vivekananda. "Ye are the children of God, the sharers of immortal bliss, holy and perfect beings. Ye divinities on earth—sinners! It is a sin to call a man so; it is [a] standing libel on human nature . . ."

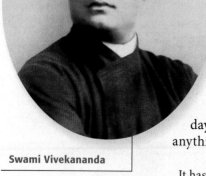

Swami Vivekananda

For Vivekananda, no religion had an exclusive hold on the truth. On the last day of the parliament, he told his listeners: "If the Parliament of Religions has shown anything to the world it is this:

> It has proved to the world that holiness, purity, and charity are not the exclusive possessions of any church in the world, and that every system has produced men and women of the most exalted character. In the face of this evidence, if any dreams of the exclusive survival of his own religion and the destruction of others, I pity him from the bottom of my heart, and point out to him that upon the banner of every religion will soon be written, in spite of resistance: "Help and not Fight," "Assimilation and not Destruction," "Harmony and Peace and not Dissension."

syncretism: a combining of religious or other beliefs and practices

The Swami's **syncretism** had already found many adherents in the United States—in fact, it was one of the driving forces behind the Parliament of Religions. Many Americans had become interested in eastern religions, particularly Hinduism, and had taken up the practice of yoga. In 1873, the Polish Madame Blavatsky had come to New York City, bringing with her Theosophy. The Theosophical Society, which she and others founded with Henry Steel Olcott and William Judge, sought to create a new religion that brought together Hindu, Buddhist, and Christian beliefs. To the Theosophist, God's workings in man are primarily internal; anything external, religions and churches included, are but shadows of this interior work of God.

Spiritism—communication with spirits of the departed—remained popular in the United States and, along with temperance, served as the undercurrent of several fringe movements. One of these was the Free Love movement, which had a number of divisions but generally held that traditional marriage bonds were oppressive and that men and women should be joined only by the "affinity" they feel for one another. Free lovers did not necessarily espouse promiscuity, but they held that men and women should speak openly about sexuality and not establish any artificial rules governing their relations with one another. Free lovers wanted to place male-female relationships on a more "scientific" footing, and so they favored widespread use of contraception. Though it attracted a large number of former abolitionists, the Free Love movement promoted eugenics—the theory that only the fittest men and women (and often the fittest races) should be allowed to breed in order to produce a master race.

Henry Steel Olcott

Free lovers and Free Love communities could be found not only in New York City (where one might expect to find them), but in Massachusetts, Kansas, Iowa, Illinois, Minnesota, and California. There even was a rural Free Love movement, with one of its centers in Valley Falls, Kansas. There the National Liberal League, led by Moses Harman, published the journal, *Lucifer*, which carried articles promoting Free Love and other eccentric causes. But *Lucifer* was but one of many Free Love journals; indeed, there were so many Free Love journals that in 1873 Congress passed the Comstock Act, prohibiting the sending of obscene material through the mail system.

Lucifer and Moses Harman helped form the vanguard of the Free Thought movement, which championed science against what it deemed religion's oppression of the human mind. "The God of the Bible," wrote Harman in *Lucifer*, "had doomed mankind to perpetual ignorance—they would never have known Good and Evil if Lucifer had not told them how to become wise as the gods themselves. Hence, according to theology, Lucifer was the first teacher of science."

Allied with both Free Love and Free Thought was anarchism. An anarchist convention held in Pittsburgh in 1883 summed up the goal of American anarchism—"the destruction of the existing class government by all means, i.e. by energetic, implacable, revolutionary, and international action." Anarchists hoped for a society wherein the individual conscience would be the final judge of the justice of all laws. Some anarchists, like Moses Harman, stressed the independence of the individual; others, like the Russian Jewess Emma Goldman, hoped for a condition in which all property was held in common. Both kinds of anarchists, however, looked forward to an age of anarchy, which would be ushered in by violence. "The law of force against force," wrote Harman, "or the gospel of dynamite will not usher in the millennium of anarchy, but it will help prepare the way for that blessed era." Dynamite, said Harman, is the great equalizer.

Helena "Madame" Blavatsky, in 1889

Related to anarchism were various communitarian attempts to create an alternative to capitalism. Burnette Haskell, who, to fight religion, had formed a secret society called the Illuminati Foundation, turned his energies in 1886 to founding a community that would be, he said, the "purest and most radical democracy." Haskell located his community, Kaweah Colony, in the Tulare County portion of the Sierra Nevada in California. Kaweah Colony did not survive, in large part because of the establishment, in 1891, of Sequoia National Park and its extension to include the colonists' lands, to which they had no legal title.

Similar colonies met similar fates. Liberal, Missouri, broke up when the settlement's free thinkers drove out the free lovers. Fountain Grove, California, was the site of a utopian experiment led by the Swedenborgian minister, Thomas Lake Harris. Harris wanted a community based both on socialism and mysticism. Crowning himself primate and king of the colony, Harris issued daily instructions to his people in the form of poems. Though he finally claimed to be immortal, Harris was forced to leave Fountain Grove because of accusations that he was using his exalted powers to lure women into adultery. He returned to New York City and died in 1906. Harris must have been a persuasive fellow; for, after his death, his wife and their friend, Edwin Markham, waited three days for Harris to rise from the dead.

In his book, *The Human Drift*, King Camp Gillette argued that competition is the source of the evils in America. He proposed a plan "whereby the people gradually absorb and eventually come into complete possession of the world and its wealth." Gillette envisioned a world in which large corporations would be owned by the workers, who would have to work only five years to obtain the "credits" necessary for them to spend their days in the pursuit of learning and culture. He foresaw that the population of the country would be gathered into a single city. They would dwell in high rise buildings, to open up land for parks and recreational and educational centers. Gillette promoted his ideas, not only in his book but in his weekly magazine, *Twentieth Century*, and through Twentieth Century Clubs that he organized across the country.

Ironically, while attacking capitalism and all its works, King Camp Gillette discovered he could improve on the straight-edge razor that men used to shave—and nick—themselves in his day. Gillette's invention of the "safety razor" revolutionized shaving and made King Camp one of the prominent capitalists of the country. Though he never abandoned his socialist ideals, Gillette's name became, in time, more associated with grooming than with movements to found utopia.

Thomas Lake Harris

Can One Be Both Catholic and American?

Except for the period of the Revolution, when Americans felt some benevolence toward Catholics, it had not been easy being Catholic and American. American Catholics, whose settlement on the Atlantic seaboard stretched back to the days of Lord Baltimore, had long experienced intolerance and outright hostility; but when the Irish and other non-English Catholics came to the United States, racial bigotry intensified religious intolerance.

Though Catholics have never proposed the overthrow of the United States Constitution nor have acted (as some Protestants have alleged) under secret orders from the pope to subvert American institutions, real sources of tension have existed between Catholic doctrine and American ideals. The bishops in the United States have recognized the tension and, at times, have tried to downplay certain aspects of Catholic teaching that could irritate Protestant neighbors. For instance, a few bishops protested when the convert Orestes Brownson wrote in his *Review* that the pope holds indirect authority over the state; yet, Brownson was merely repeating ancient Catholic dogma that the pope has the authority to dictate both natural and supernatural truth to the state—as when the Church tells governments that no state can justly pass laws permitting abortion. Still, American bishops, especially Bishop Michael O'Connor of Pittsburgh, thought Brownson's statements on papal authority "inopportune."

Certain actions of the reigning pontiff in Rome made life in America more difficult for Catholics. When Pius IX became pope in 1846, both Europeans and Americans haled him as a Liberal hero. Following his election, Pius had instituted an elective advisory senate for the Papal States, had granted amnesty to political prisoners and exiles, and had broken down

King Camp Gillette

the barriers to the Jewish ghetto. Many thought he favored the cause of Italian union that would bring the various states, duchies, and principalities that made up Italy under one government; but, when Pius refused to support the king of Piedmont's war against the Catholic emperor of Austria, the tide of public opinion turned against him. Driven from Rome in 1848 by the revolutionaries for refusing to fight Austria, Pius returned in triumph with the aid of the French in 1850. His subsequent rejection of political Liberalism together with his refusal to relinquish the Papal States to a united Italian state, earned Pius stern denunciation in both Europe and America.

Pope Pius was not one to back down to the world. In 1864, he issued the encyclical *Quanta Cura,* to which he appended a "Syllabus of Modern Errors." This syllabus was a list of propositions the pope had condemned. For instance, the pope condemned the proposition that "every man is free to embrace and profess that religion which, guided by the light of reason, he shall consider true . . ." He condemned propositions supporting socialism, communism, Protestant biblical societies, and secret societies. Certain errors the pope condemned seemed to strike at the heart of American civic life. For instance, the pope condemned the notion that "the Church ought to be separated from the State, and the State from the Church." In condemning the proposition, "the Roman Pontiff can, and ought to, reconcile himself, and come to terms with progress, liberalism and modern civilization," the pope seemed to make himself an enemy of all "progress."

Though a majority of American bishops publicly supported the "Syllabus," most of them did not publish the document. The one who did was Martin John Spalding, archbishop of Baltimore. Spalding said he had read the papal documents from which Pius had culled the condemned propositions and so knew their context. He attacked the English and American press that had taken pains, he said, "to mutilate and disfigure [the *Syllabus*] through a faulty translation. Spalding said the pope had not condemned democracy and religious freedom as practiced in America but was addressing attacks on the Church by extreme Liberals in Europe.

Orestes Brownson

An anti-Catholic cartoon by Thomas Nast, depicting bishops as crocodiles threatening America's school children by opposing common or public schools. *Harper's Weekly*, May 8, 1875

Concern over the often delicate relations between Catholics and Protestants in the United States led some American bishops (along with certain bishops in Europe) to oppose as "inopportune" the definition of papal infallibility at the Vatican Ecumenical Council, convened in Rome in December 1869. Archbishop Spalding did not, it seems, doubt the truth of the doctrine of infallibility but worried that defining the doctrine would widen the rift between Catholics and Protestants. Most of the American bishops seemed to agree with Spalding, though a handful did indeed doubt the truth of the doctrine. But when in 1870 the Vatican Ecumenical Council defined the doctrine of papal infallibility, every American bishop submitted to the decision.

Though the cultural center of Catholicism in the United States for a long time remained in the South and, thus, was dominated by the old English Catholic society, the Catholics Protestant Americans knew best were the poor Irish immigrants. The Irish generally worked in factories in the cities, in mines, or on the railroads. Bigotry against them, especially in New England, was intense. In metropolises like New York City, the Irish by sheer force of numbers gained control of city politics and were able to attain some social advancement. Their Boss Tweed-style politics, though, did not endear the Irish to the hearts of "native" Americans. The cartoonist, Thomas Nash, depicted the Irish takeover of Tammany Hall as an attempted papal conquest of the United States.

Irish immigration began to dwindle following the Civil War, and the number of German and continental European Catholic immigrants to the United States increased. As in the years before the war, German immigrants who came to America generally were wealthy enough to buy land, and they crossed the Alleghenies to settle in German communities in

An anti-immigrant cartoon from the 1860s. "The Great Fear of the Period: That Uncle Sam May Be Swallowed by Foreigners." The cartoon shows an Irish and a Chinese immigrant devouring Uncle Sam. In the last frame, the Chinese immigrant devours the Irish immigrant.

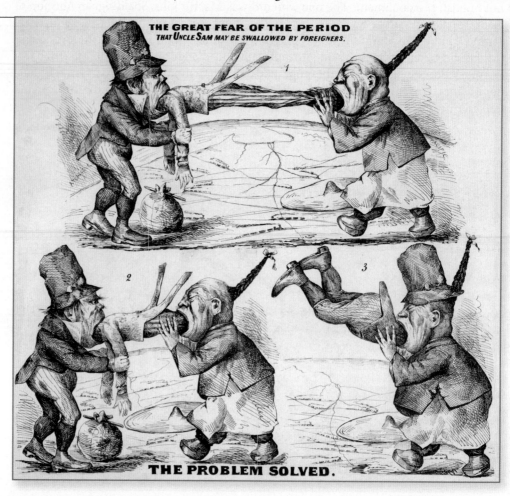

the Midwest. These German communities were either mixed, with Protestants and Catholics, or of a single religion. German Catholics brought over their own priests and proved quite successful in building churches and parish schools. They maintained German as their primary spoken language and formed cultural enclaves separated from the Anglo American population.

The unquestioning confidence American Catholics seemed to repose in their clergy rankled with Protestant Americans. An uncritical acceptance of whatever the priest might say or do is perhaps not surprising for the time—for most American Catholics were not educated, and their priests were. Protestant Americans, too, found it difficult to understand the religious obedience of priests to their superiors. The Catholic Church, of course, like any society, has to have levels of authority, which demand conscientious obedience; but the American Protestant, reared in a religion that stresses almost solely the individual and his response to God, could not comprehend an obedience that appeared to him to be nothing else than abject slavery.

The mere increase in the American Catholic population was probably enough to frighten the Protestant nation—even without the *Syllabus of Errors*. In 1852, Catholics in the United States numbered about 1,600,000; according to the census of 1880, that number had increased to 6,832,954. If one compares this to the recorded numbers of the two largest Protestant denominations (Methodists, 3,286,158; Baptists, 2,430,095), one can appreciate the fear of non-Catholics reared in anti-Catholic traditions. Though Protestants as a whole were still the majority in the U.S., the Catholic Church had become the single largest Christian denomination in the country.

It was said at the time that the Catholic population may have been considerably larger had not so many immigrants fallen away from the Church upon coming to America. Estimates of apostate Catholics in 19th-century America range as high as 10 million or 20 million. The priest Andrew Arnold Lambing of Pittsburg wrote in 1872 that the chief causes of defection were public opposition to the Faith (including barriers to social advancement) and mixed marriages between Catholics and non-Catholics. Lambing wrote:

> There are in nearly if not every state of the Union persons who never saw a Church nor heard Mass on Sunday. How, it may be asked could they have the practical knowledge of religion to bear them safely through the stormy sea of life in America? No: it is a tear and a prayer that I have for the poor immigrants, rather than a word of censure or blame. Their great numbers, the unexampled growth and spread of Catholicity in this country, and the inability of the Church to furnish a sufficient body of laborers for the 'Fields already white for the harvest,' precluded the possibility of meeting the wants of the numerous and widespread flock . . .

Despite Catholic numbers, only a few Catholics were eminent in politics and in the financial world. Though one could cite the example of Orestes Brownson's *Review* and a number of other English language Catholic journals and newspapers, Catholics held slight prominence in the literary world of 19th-century America.

Understanding the importance of Catholic literature, the Second Plenary Council of bishops at Baltimore had in 1866 encouraged the development and growth of a distinctly Catholic press. The seven archbishops, 38 bishops, three mitred abbots, and over 120 theologians who met in Baltimore discussed, of course, much more than Catholic literature. The clergy and the Catholic people, divided by several racial and language groups, needed to forge a more perfect unity. Yet, despite their proclamation of fidelity to the pope, the bishops were unable to attain the unity of mind and purpose that Archbishop Spalding, for one, desired. The quest for unity would be even more severely challenged in the years following the Baltimore synod.

Years of Bitter Controversy

Tensions between German Catholics and their predominately Irish hierarchy shook the unity of the Catholic Church in the United States throughout the latter part of the 19th century. German Catholics had, on the whole, remained resolutely separate from the mainstream of America by segregating themselves in German-speaking communities in rural areas and, in cities, by maintaining German national parishes. Though most members of the American hierarchy were Irish, German bishops ruled in such centers as Milwaukee, Cincinnati, and other midwestern dioceses. German priests, too, had the reputation for being better trained than their English-speaking counterparts, partly because the German priests often belonged to religious orders or had studied in Europe. Yet, because the Church in America had taken on such an Irish character, Germans complained that Irish and other English-speaking bishops were marginalizing them.

For instance, German priests complained that their national churches were not accorded regular parish status and thus did not have the security that English-speaking parishes had. John Ireland, archbishop of St. Paul, Minnesota, Bishop John Keane, and James Gibbons, archbishop of Baltimore, opposed the German claims. In 1887, Rome ruled that German parishes should be made permanent but ignored other demands made by the German clergy.

Rome's decision was a victory for Archbishop Ireland, Bishop Keane, and Cardinal Gibbons, who represented what might be called the "progressive" wing of the Catholic Church in the United States. These bishops wanted Catholics to embrace American culture. They praised American political institutions, American liberty, and American progress and material civilization. Gibbons, and especially Keane and Ireland, thought that though America could learn much from the Catholic Church, the Church, too, could benefit by her association with democratic American society. It is not surprising, then, that these prelates favored cultural assimilation and opposed foreign enclaves amongst the faithful.

Archbishop John Ireland

German Catholics opposed the agenda of Ireland, Keane, and Gibbons, not merely on national grounds, but because they thought that by maintaining their national languages and customs, they were preserving the integrity of their Catholic faith. Two bitter opponents of the progressives were Nicholas Gonner of Dubuque, Iowa, the editor of the newspaper, *Katolischer Western*, and the priest Anton H. Walburg of St. Augustine's Church in Cincinnati. In his 1889 pamphlet, *The Question of Nationality*, Walburg criticized American culture—characterized, he said, by sectarianism, extreme individualism, divorce, and free love—and praised the Irish and the Germans. Though he admitted that, eventually, all immigrants would be Americanized, he did not want to push the process. "Transition from one nationality to another is always a dangerous process," argued Walburg, "and it will not do to hasten it, and to force foreigners to Americanize." If American culture is ever to be converted, he said, "it must be done by the clergy and population already Catholics. The most efficient portion of our Catholic body are of foreign birth and training, and will be for some time to come."

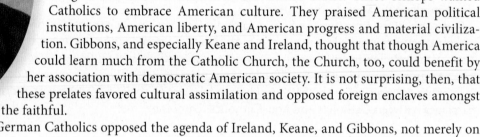

Not just Germans opposed the progressives, however. Bernard McQuaid, bishop of Rochester, New York, and Michael Corrigan, archbishop of New York City, feared the effects of a democratic, pluralist society on Catholics. They became vehement opponents of, especially, the eloquent and charismatic Archbishop John Ireland, who had become the spokesman for the progressive Catholics in the United States.

Bishop Bernard McQuaid

One battleground on which progressives and "preservationists" waged war was the question of education. Priests and laymen in the Midwest (especially the Germans) attacked common (i.e. publicly supported) schools as godless. They opposed the growing state gov-

Not Entirely Optimistic

Though generally positive and optimistic about American civilization, James Cardinal Gibbons was not blind to its less desirable aspects. In his book, *Our Christian Civilization*, first published in 1889, Gibbons gave statistical evidence that supported at least one of Father Walburg's claims—that American society was characterized by a culture of divorce. Gibbons deplored what he termed the "reckless facility with which divorce is procured" in the United States. "Each State," he wrote, "has on its statute books a list of causes, or rather pretexts, which are recognized as sufficient ground for divorce *a vinculo*. There are in all twenty-two or more causes, most of them of a very trifling character, and in some States, as in Illinois and Maine, the power of granting a divorce is left to the discretion of the judge."

From a "special Report on the statistics of marriage and divorce made to Congress by Carroll D. Wright in February, 1889," Gibbons condensed what he called "startling facts." Among these facts was that the number of divorces in the United States went from 9,937 in 1867 to 14,800 in 1876, and from 15,687 in 1877 to 25,535 in 1886. In the first nine-year period, 1867-1876, the coun-

James Cardinal Gibbons

try saw 122,121 divorces nationwide; during the second nine-year period, 1877-1886, 206,595 divorces. "That is to say," Gibbons observed, "the divorces in the latter half were 69 percent more than those in the first half. The population between 1870 and 1880 increased only by 30 percent. The divorces in 1867 were 10,962, and in 1880, they were 19,663, and . . . they are in 1886 more than two and one-half times what they were in 1867."

Gibbons contrasted the U.S. divorce rate with that of other countries. "Our neighbor Canada," he wrote, "presents a far more creditable attitude on this subject than we do. From 1867 to 1886 inclusive, only 116 divorces were granted in the Dominion of Canada, or an average of less than six every year in a population of four millions. During the same period of twenty years, there had been only eleven divorces in all Ireland." The population of the United States in 1890 was nearly 63 million.

Gibbons concluded that, based on the divorce statistics, "it is painfully manifest that the cancer of divorce is rapidly spreading over the community, and poisoning the fountains of the nation. Unless the evil is checked by some speedy and heroic remedy, the very existence of family life is imperiled."

ernment policy of compulsory education, saying that, since God has given parents the right to educate their children, the state could not enforce school attendance—at least in schools to which the parents objected. These critics called for a Catholic school system free from all state control and aid.

Many of the preservationists already enjoyed well-established parochial schools. In the East, however, where Catholics were poorer, the financial burden of maintaining parochial schools was great. Some bishops favored a solution where state monies would go to support the teaching of secular subjects in Catholic schools and for maintaining school buildings. This happened in Poughkeepsie, New York, where the state supported a Catholic school—but only because religious activities and instruction were relegated to periods outside school hours. The problem with such an arrangement was that religion could not permeate and direct the life of the school; but many saw such an arrangement as the only way to maintain Catholic schools.

Archbishop Ireland laid out his position on common and parochial schools in a talk given at the National Education Association's annual meeting, held in St. Paul in July 1890. Ireland told the assembled delegates that not only did he support common schools (and wished there was no need for parochial schools) but he thought that, even though the primary right to educate children belonged to parents, society needed compulsory education laws. Without state laws, he said, many children would receive no education. The archbishop said he favored state aid for secular instruction in parish schools; and, when it was necessary, he approved of the arrangement where Catholic schools acted as public schools between 9 a.m. and 3 p.m., and offered religious instruction only outside official school hours. Ireland, however, criticized the state school because it "tends to eliminate religion from the minds and hearts of the youth of the country." He said he hoped to add to the public system the "splendor and majesty of religious instruction."

The Catholic press roundly criticized Ireland for his National Education Association talk. The archbishop, they said, granted the state, not parents, the superior right to educate children.

Further controversy arose when Archbishop Ireland permitted one of his priests, Father James J. Conry, to arrange for a public school board to take over Immaculate Conception parochial school in Faribault, Minnesota. Another of Ireland's priests, Father Charles Corcoran of St. Michael's in Stillwater, made a similar arrangement with a local school board. About the same time, a pamphlet by Thomas Bouquillon, a moral theologian at Catholic University in Washington, D.C., defended the thesis that the state, as well as the parent, had the right to insist on the education of children. The Jesuit priest, René Holaind, wrote a pamphlet criticizing Bouquillon. It is the parents, not the state, that have the prior right to educate their children, said Holaind. While visiting New York, Archbishop Ireland defended the Faribault-Stillwater arrangements in an interview with the New York *Herald* and praised Bouquillon's pamphlet, while criticizing Holaind's.

The Faribault-Stillwater arrangements, however, began to cause Archbishop Ireland some trouble. In Rome, the influential Jesuit journal, *Civilta Cattolica*, attacked the Bouquillon pamphlet and Archbishop Ireland. Pope Leo XIII then set up a commission to study the Faribault-Stillwater matter and Ireland's speech before the National Education Association. Ireland, at the urging of friends in Rome, sent to Rome a long defense of his position. On April 21, 1892, Rome announced that agreements like Faribault-Stillwater were to be tolerated—a victory for Ireland, or, at least, so his friends interpreted it. In a subsequent letter, however, the pope told the American bishops to establish parochial schools and did not promote solutions such as those tried at Faribault and Stillwater.

Still, in 1892, Rome seemed to favor the American progressives. When the pope appointed a permanent Apostolic Delegate for the United States to help reconcile the dissenting parties, he chose the man Ireland suggested, Archbishop Francesco Satolli. When Satolli arrived in the United States in 1893, he supported recommendations for Catholic schools, very similar to ones Ireland had made. The Apostolic Delegate chose a priest working in St. Paul as his secretary. On the whole, it seemed as if the cause of the progressives was in the ascendancy in the American Church.

A Phantom Heresy?

Archbishop Satolli had come to the United States, in part, to accompany maps and charts from the Vatican Library that would be on display at the 1893 World's Fair and Columbian Exposition in Chicago. The United States bishops had planned a Catholic Columbian Congress in conjunction with the World's Fair, where Catholic laymen and clergy would address a variety of topics. Archbishop Ireland was appointed the bishops' representative to work with the laymen at the congress.

Ireland had been involved in a similar lay congress four years earlier in Baltimore. There he had pointed to the work he hoped American Catholics would undertake—"to make America Catholic, and to solve for the Church universal the all-absorbing problems with which religion is confronted in the present age." He said the Church had the answers for

Participants of the Parliament of World Religions

what chiefly concerned the modern world—"reason, education, liberty, the amelioration of the masses." American Catholics, he said, were to show the world how to reconcile the Faith with democracy and social progress. Laymen, he insisted, had a special part to play in this task. "Priests," he said, "are officers, laymen are soldiers."

> The hardest fighting is often done by the soldier in the warfare against sin and error, the soldier is not always near the officer, and he must be ready to act without waiting for the word of command. Laymen are not anointed in confirmation to the end that they may merely save their own souls, and pay their pew rent. They must think, work, organize, read, speak, act, as circumstances demand, ever anxious to do good to their fellow-men.

During the Chicago Columbian Congress, Archbishop Satolli seemed to share Ireland's optimism about America. Satolli told laymen that they needed to go forth into the world "in one hand bearing the Book of Christian Truth and in the other the Constitution of the United States."

Besides the maps and charts from the Vatican, Catholics had other displays at the Chicago World's Fair—such as the Catholic Educational Exhibition, featuring pictures, pamphlets, and books from Catholic institutions throughout the United States. A Catholic school for blacks in Pine Bluff, Arkansas, displayed various crafts made by the children. Such participation in an essentially secular event was unobjectionable. The same could not be said for Catholic participation in the Parliament of World's Religions, which began September 11. Bishop McQuaid echoed the sentiments of many Catholics when he protested that the parliament put "the Catholic Church, the religion of Christ, with its unerring teaching" on the same footing "with every pretense of religion."

Cardinal Gibbons, who opened the parliament by reciting the Lord's Prayer, had himself pressed for Catholic participation in the assembly. And he had received the hearty endorsement of Archbishop Ireland and Bishop Keane.

In defense of the parliament, Keane wrote:

Palace of Mechanic Arts and lagoon at the 1893 World's Columbian Exposition, Chicago, Illinois, by Frances Benjamin Johnston

It is only by a friendly and brotherly comparison of convictions that reasonable men can ever come to an agreement about the all-important truths which are the foundation of religion, and that an end can be put to the religious divisions and antagonisms which are a grief to our Father in Heaven. Such an assemblage of intelligent and conscientious men, presenting their religious convictions without minimizing, without acrimony, without controversy, with love and truth and humanity, will be an honorable event in the history of religion and cannot fail to accomplish much good.

But Bishop McQuaid remained unconvinced. Two years after the parliament, he wrote, "of late years, a spirit of liberalism is springing up in our body . . . that if not checked in time, will bring disaster on the Church. Many a time Catholic laymen have remarked that the Catholic Church they once knew seems to be passing away, so greatly shocked are they at what they see passing around them." It seems Pope Leo at least belatedly shared McQuaid's sentiments, for he forbade future participation in such ecumenical gatherings.

Only a month after the Parliament of the World's Religions, Ireland was in Baltimore preaching for the Vespers service held in honor of Cardinal Gibbons' silver jubilee as a bishop. Referring to the great inventions of the time, Ireland declared, "Let all things be new, is the watchword of humanity today, and to make all things new is humanity's strong resolve . . . To conquer the new world to Christ, the Church must herself be new, adapting herself in manner of life and in method of action to the conditions of the new order, thus proving herself, while ever ancient, to be ever new, as truth from heaven is and ever must be . . ." The age, said Ireland, "became hardened in its secularism, and taught itself to despise and hate religion" because it had been "irritated by the isolation and unfriendliness of the Church." Ireland said he preached "the new, the most glorious crusade. Church and age. Unite them in the name of humanity, in the name of God."

Throughout 1893 and 1894, the progressives and Archbishop Ireland continued to receive Rome's favor. Ireland's belief that the Church should adapt herself to the times seemed to mirror Pope Leo XIII's policy towards France. The pope had urged the French clergy, who had long opposed the French republican government for its official atheism, to reconcile themselves with it. Those among the French clergy who favored this approach were encouraged by Ireland, and one of their number, Abbé Felix Klein, translated Ireland's speeches into French.

In 1895, however, the tide seemed to turn against the progressives. Pope Leo issued an apostolic letter to the Church in the United States. In *Longinqua Oceani*, Pope Leo praised American liberty and the freedom the United States accorded the Catholic Church; but with this praise, came a warning: "It would be very erroneous to draw the conclusion that in America is to be sought the type of the most desirable status of the Church or that it would be universally lawful or expedient for State and Church to be, as in America, dissevered and divorced."

Archbishop Ireland, it seemed, held somewhat different views from the pope on the relation between Church and state. In a homily he gave in April 1896, Ireland spoke glowingly of the relations between Church and state in America. "The Church recognizes as her own sphere faith and morals," he said. "She possesses and claims no mission in civil and political matters. The State appropriates to itself civil and political matters and assumes no authority in the domain of faith and morals. There is no room for conflict between Church and State; both move in separate and distinct spheres." Throughout his speech, Ireland repeated the phrase, "Separation of Church and State! Most assuredly . . ."

Bishop Keane, too, favored separation of Church and state. Writing in the March 1898 issue of the Paulist journal, *The Catholic World*, Keane said European Catholics found "a condition in which the church neither seeks patronage nor fears persecution" to be "almost inconceivable"; nor could they "imagine a separation of church and state" where "each leaves and is bound to leave the other free and independent in the management of its own affairs;

each, however, respecting the other, and giving the other moral encouragement and even substantial aid when circumstances require or permit."

Such a "physical separation of church and state, would be in reality their moral union," said Keane—and he continued: European Catholics would, he said, "acknowledge that a moral union of the kind would probably be more advantageous to both church and state than a union which would tend to blend and entangle their functions, with probable confusion of wholly distinct ends and methods, likely to prove pernicious to both sides." The American, said Keane, could assure the European "that, considering the circumstances of the times," a "moral union" of church and state (as Keane said existed in the United States) "is the only practicable or even desirable one." Keane then evoked *Longinqua Oceani,* as if the pope's warning in *Longinqua Oceani* indicated approval of the Church/state relations in America:

> From this we can understand with how great wisdom our Holy Father, Leo XIII, has warned us that we must beware of proposing as a norm for the nations at large the conditions which we find so satisfactory and so advantageous to the church in our country. Their situation, traditions, tendencies, dispositions, are totally different, and what fits us admirably would not fit them at all.

More Than a Moral Union

In *Immortale Dei,* Pope Leo clarified what it means for Church and state to be "happily united in concord." The state, he said, "is clearly bound to act up to the manifold and weighty duties linking it to God, by the public profession of religion." But not just any religion suffices, said the pope, but only that religion "which God enjoins, and which certain and most clear marks show to be the only one true religion" —in other words, the Catholic faith. Just as "it is a public crime to act as though there were no God," so it is, said the pope, "a sin for the State not to have care for religion as something beyond its scope, or as of no practical benefit; or out of many forms of religion to adopt that one which chimes in with the fancy; for we are bound absolutely to worship God in that way which He has shown to be His will." Far, therefore, from being separate, Church and state between them have "a certain orderly connection, which may be compared to the union of the soul and body in man . . .

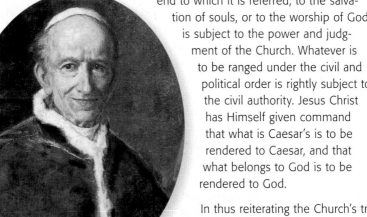

Pope Leo XIII in 1885

the two has for its proximate and chief object the well-being of this mortal life; the other, the everlasting joys of heaven. Whatever, therefore in things human is of a sacred character, whatever belongs either of its own nature or by reason of the end to which it is referred, to the salvation of souls, or to the worship of God, is subject to the power and judgment of the Church. Whatever is to be ranged under the civil and political order is rightly subject to the civil authority. Jesus Christ has Himself given command that what is Caesar's is to be rendered to Caesar, and that what belongs to God is to be rendered to God.

In thus reiterating the Church's traditional teaching on Church and state, Pope Leo was not ignoring the peculiar circumstances confronting Catholics in a secular, pluralistic society like the United States. He was, however, in a more general fashion, teaching what he would later write in *Longingua Oceani*—namely, that "it would be very erroneous to draw the conclusion that in America is to be sought the type of the most desirable status of the Church or that it would be universally lawful or expedient for State and Church to be, as in America, dissevered and divorced."

> The nature and scope of that connection can be determined only . . . by having regard to the nature of each power, and by taking account of the relative excellence and nobleness of their purpose. One of

Keane and Ireland's views could only infuriate their critics. The Church had traditionally taught that, though Church and state operate in separate spheres, these sometimes overlap; in such cases, the Church, as the guardian of man's highest good, should take preeminence and the state follow the lead of the Church. We have seen how Pius IX condemned the proposition that the Catholic religion should not be the only religion of the state. Pope Leo XIII, too, in his 1885 encyclical, *Immortale Dei*, proposed something more than the kind of "moral union" of Church and state suggested by Keane.

In *Immortale Dei*, Leo praised the "time" when "States were governed by the philosophy of the Gospel. Then it was," said the pope, "that the power and divine virtue of Christian wisdom had diffused itself throughout the laws, institutions, and morals of the people, permeating all ranks and relations of civil society. Then . . . Church and State were happily united in concord and friendly interchange of good offices."

A sign that the tide had turned in favor of Ireland and Keane's opponents in the American Church came in September 1896 when Rome removed Keane as rector of the Catholic University in Washington, D.C. Since the university's founding in 1889, Keane had filled its posts with progressives like himself. Keane's removal stunned the progressives. It was rumored that the now-Cardinal Satolli, who had once been so friendly to Ireland, was responsible for Keane's removal. Indeed, over the past year, Satolli had seemed to cool towards Ireland and the progressives. A sign of the legate's new attitude was his support for the right of German Catholics in America to retain their language and customs.

But what brought the controversy between progressives and their opponents to a head was Abbé Felix Klein's publication of a French translation of *The Life of Father Hecker*. A Paulist priest and close associate of Father Isaac Hecker, Walter Elliott, wrote the original English version of this work that first ran in installments in the Paulist periodical, *The Catholic World*, beginning in April 1890. The subject of the book, Isaac Hecker, had lived at Brook Farm and Fruitlands; but, having become disillusioned with Transcendentalism, he had converted to the Catholic Church. Ordained a Redemptorist priest, Hecker eventually founded his own religious congregation, the Paulists, dedicated to converting America to the Catholic faith. Paulists took no vows and engaged in the active apostolate, especially printing. Isaac Hecker died in 1888.

Bishop John Keane

An inspiration to such men as Ireland and Keane, Hecker loved America's institutions and believed that his country had a quasi-messianic destiny to spread free government to the world. He thought that by permitting its citizens a large degree of freedom, the United States was ushering in a new era where the Holy Spirit would inspire and strengthen individuals as never before. The original English version of Elliott's biography quoted the Paulist founder as saying that "the increased action of the Holy Spirit, with a more vigorous co-operation on the part of the faithful, which is in process of realization, will elevate the human personality to an intensity of force and grandeur productive of a new era to the Church and to society—an era difficult for the imagination to grasp, and still more difficult to describe in words, unless we have recourse to the prophetic language of the inspired Scriptures." According to the *Life*, Hecker had said:

> The form of government of the United States is preferable to Catholics above all other forms. It is more favorable than others to the practice of those virtues which are the necessary conditions of the development of the religious life of man. This government leaves men a larger margin for liberty of action, and hence for co-operation with the guidance of the Holy Spirit than any other government under the sun. With these popular institutions men enjoy liberty in working out their true destiny. The Catholic Church will, therefore, flourish all the more in this republican country in proportion as her representatives keep, in their civil life, to the lines of their republicanism.

Abbé Klein edited Elliott's text and shortened it significantly for the French version, thus bringing to the fore certain of Hecker's ideas. According to the French biography, Hecker asserted that the Church must adjust herself to modern civilization and should de-emphasize such "passive" supernatural virtues as humility and obedience and emphasize the "active" natural virtues, such as courage, prudence, and justice. Individuals, too, according to the French biography, had less need of external guidance from the Church than in former times, since the Holy Spirit had been poured out abundantly in the modern world. The Church, according to the biography, must grant greater freedom to individuals to follow the lead of their own minds and consciences—though it asserted that the external guidance of the Church remained necessary. In a preface to the French Hecker book, Abbé Klein compared the Paulist founder to Benjamin Franklin, Abraham Lincoln, and St. Theresa, and said he manifested the superiority of the Anglo-Saxon race.

Father Isaac Hecker

In an introduction that appeared in both the English and French versions of Hecker's *Life*, Archbishop Ireland held Hecker up as an example of the reconciliation of the Church and the modern age. Hecker, wrote Ireland, "laid stress on the natural and social virtues." The archbishop continued:

> The American people hold these in the highest esteem . . . Truthfulness, honesty in business dealings, loyalty to law and social order, temperance, respect for the rights of others, and the like virtues are prescribed by reason before the voice of revelation is heard, and the absence of specifically supernatural virtues has led the non-Catholic to place paramount importance upon them . . .
>
> The Church is nowadays called upon to emphasize her power in the natural order. God forbid that I entertain, as some may be tempted to suspect me of doing, the slightest notion that vigilance may be turned off one single moment from the guard of the supernatural. For the sake of the supernatural I speak. And natural virtues, practised in the proper frame of mind and heart, become supernatural. Each century calls for its type of Christian perfection. At one time it was martyrdom; at another it was the humility of the cloister. To-day we need the Christian gentleman and the Christian citizen. An honest ballot and social decorum among Catholics will do more for God's glory and the salvation of souls than midnight flagellations or Compostellan pilgrimages.

Abbé Charles Maignen

Conservatives, both in the United States and France, roundly condemned the French Hecker biography. Critics called Klein, Ireland, and Keane (who had become associated with the ideas set forth in the biography), "Americanists," and their ideas, "Americanism." *La Pere Hecker est-il un Saint?* ("Is Father Hecker a Saint?"), a pamphlet by the French Vincentian priest, Abbé Charles Maignen, attacked Ireland and the Americanists and received the *imprimatur* in Rome. The controversy over the Hecker book and Americanism grew so rhetorically violent that at last, the pope himself decided to look into it.

Pope Leo's response to the crisis was to issue, on January 22, 1899, the encyclical, *Testem Benevolentiae Nostrae (Concerning New Opinions, Virtue, Nature and Grace, With Regard to Americanism)*. Addressed to "Our Beloved Son, James Cardinal Gibbons," the encyclical expressed the "good will" the pope felt toward the American episcopacy and "the whole American people . . ." Moreover, said Leo "we have often considered and admired the noble gifts of your nation which enable the American people to be alive to every good work which promotes the good of humanity and the splendor of civilization." Still, Leo said, the purpose of his letter was not "to repeat the words of praise so often spoken," but "to suppress certain contentions which have arisen lately among you to the detriment of the peace of many souls."

The pope noted how the French Hecker book had "excited not a little controversy, on account of certain opinions brought forward concerning the way of leading a Christian life." Leo then assailed Americanism. He said he disapproved of any attempt to de-emphasize any Catholic doctrine in order more easily to reconcile the Church with the modern age. "Let it be far from anyone's mind," wrote Leo, "to suppress for any reason any doctrine that has been handed down. Such a policy would tend rather to separate Catholics from the Church than to bring in those who differ." Leo said it was false to say that the Church's "supervision and watchfulness" should be "in some sense lessened," allowing the faithful "each one to follow out more freely the leading of his own mind and the trend of his own proper activity." On the contrary—the "confounding of license with liberty" in the modern world, said Leo, "the passion for discussing and pouring contempt upon any possible subject, the assumed right to hold whatever opinions one pleases upon any subject and to set them forth in print to the world, have so wrapped minds in darkness that there is now a greater need of the Church's teaching office than ever before, lest people become unmindful both of conscience and of duty."

The pope dismissed the distinction between "active" and "passive" virtues; all virtues are active, he said. The "disregard" of supernatural virtues in favor of natural ones was, the pope said, a short step "to a contempt of the religious life which has in some degree taken hold of minds." One may not hold that religious "vows are alien to the spirit of our times, in that they limit the bounds of human liberty; that they are more suitable to weak than to strong minds; that so far from making for human perfection and the good of human organization, that they are hurtful to both."

Towards the end of the encyclical, Pope Leo wrote that he did not object to the name *Americanism* "if by this name are to be understood certain endowments of mind which belong to the American people, just as other characteristics belong to various other nations, and if, moreover, by it is designated your political condition and the laws and customs by which you are governed." But if the name "be so understood that the doctrines which have been adverted to above are not only indicated, but exalted," said the pope, "there can be no manner of doubt that our venerable brethren, the bishops of America, would be the first to repudiate and condemn it as being most injurious to themselves and to their country. For it would give rise to the suspicion that there are among you some who conceive and would have the Church in America to be different from what it is in the rest of the world."

Testem Benevolentiae effectively killed Americanism, at least for a time. American bishops were quick to repudiate the doctrine. In March 1899, Cardinal Gibbons, writing to the pope, said he knew of no one—at least, among educated American Catholics in the United States—who held to Americanism. Archbishop Ireland, too, published his acceptance of *Testem Benevolentiae* but later denied that anyone held to the condemned doctrines; the pope's letter, he said, was a blessing in that it freed Americanists from a heresy to which they had never adhered. Abbé Klein also accepted the pope's letter and removed the French Hecker biography (against Ireland's objections) from publication.

Other American Catholics followed Ireland's and Gibbons' lead. They denied the very existence of Americanism—at least in the United States—and using Abbé Klein's phrase, called it a "phantom heresy." This was not the opinion, however, of two archbishops —Michael Corrigan of New York and Frederick Xavier Katzer of Milwaukee. Both prelates thanked the pope for killing the Americanist heresy in the shell. In Rome, *Civilta Cattolica* not only insisted on the existence of the Americanist heresy but accused American bishops of hiding their approval of the condemned doctrines.

Part II: **The Triumph of the Dynamo**

Henry Adams, great-grandson of President John Adams, stood in awe of all he saw at the Chicago World's Fair. He wrote in his autobiography, *The Education of Henry Adams* (speaking of himself in the third person), that at the World's Fair "he found matter of study to fill a hundred years, and his education spread over chaos . . . The Exposition itself defied philosophy. One might find fault till the last gate closed, one could still explain nothing that needed explanation." The exposition buildings, built around a lagoon, were all of simulated white granite or marble, and at night almost glowed in the electric light that illumined them. Some buildings had gold domes; and one, a crystal dome. Atop the dome that graced the Palace of Arts reared an enormous statue of a lady with spread wings. Adams called the fair "a scenic display, Paris had never approached it." That the fair occurred in Chicago—the brash, new slaughter town of the Midwest—was "more surprising . . . than anything else on the continent, Niagara Falls, the Yellowstone Geysers, and the whole railway."

But what truly amazed and befuddled Adams, heir as he was to an antique and (he thought) antiquated American family, was the display of America's industrial might. The enormous dynamos (generators converting mechanical energy to electricity), displayed at the fair, inspired awe:

> To Adams the dynamo became a symbol of infinity. As he grew accustomed to the great gallery of machines, he began to feel the forty-foot dynamos as a moral force, much as the early Christians felt the Cross. The planet itself seemed less impressive, in its old-fashioned, deliberate, annual or daily revolution, than this huge wheel, revolving within arm's length at some vertiginous speed, and barely murmuring—scarcely humming an audible warning to stand a hair's-breadth further for respect of power—while it would

Exposition grounds at the 1893 Columbian Exposition

not wake the baby lying close against its frame. Before the end, one began to pray to it; inherited instinct taught the natural expression of man before silent and infinite force. Among the thousand symbols of ultimate energy the dynamo was not so human as some, but it was the most expressive.

Exultation and Depression

The Chicago World's Fair was a triumphant declaration that a new age had come—an age that the New World would dominate. The mechanical expositions were displayed not only to awe the likes of Henry Adams but to show old and tottering Europe the energy and power of America. What was truly amazing was that almost all the inventions displayed—the

dynamos, the telephones, the great steam engines—had been born in the 30 or so years since the Civil War. Could any previous century—nay, millennia—boast such mechanical achievements?

The World's Fair was not the only witness to the wealth generated by Americans since the Civil War. The bustling American cities of both the East and the Midwest showcased American prosperity. On account of fires and population growth, Eastern cities and Chicago had been largely rebuilt since 1870. New brownstone and brick buildings, monotonous but solid, lined the streets of America's metropolises. The rich built their roomy, if gaudy, mansions in the whimsical American Victorian style. With the development of steel frames for buildings, the peculiarly American skyscraper began defining the skylines of

"Newspaper Row" in New York City, 1903. The World Building rises on the extreme left.

American cities. In Chicago the Auditorium Building rose ten stories, beaten only by the 375-foot, 26-story World Building in New York, built in 1890. For the first time, rivers were spanned by steel bridges, including the famous Brooklyn Bridge over the East River in New York City.

And who claimed the responsibility for all the new industrial power, all the luxury and convenience items it produced? The politicians. The Republicans, the "Grand Old Party," had been in power almost continually since the retirement of James Buchanan in 1860. For many, being Republican was practically identical with being American. Democrats were, in the memorable words of the Rev. Burchard, the party of "Rum, Romanism, and Rebellion." Republican government, Republican policies, had fostered business (many businessmen had certainly fostered Republican politicians); and, if in a neo-Hamiltonian world, the Republicans had been the party of business, they had to be the party of America, as well.

After serving one term as president, Rutherford Hayes decided not to run again in 1880. The Republicans instead nominated James A. Garfield, a reforming congressman, for their presidential candidate, and for their vice-president, a Stalwart named Chester A. Arthur. In the election, Garfield handily beat the Democratic candidate, General Winfield Scott Hancock, but he had hardly time to enjoy the spoils of victory. Only four months after his inauguration, a disappointed office seeker, crying, "I am a Stalwart! Arthur is President!" shot Garfield. The president died on September 19, 1881, more from the attentions of his doctors than from the assassin's bullet.

A Currier & Ives lithograph of New York harbor as seen from the Brooklyn Bridge

An 1880 Presidential election cartoon, showing candidates James A. Garfield, Chester Arthur, Samuel J. Tilden, and David Davis standing on their "records," published in *Puck*, June 16, 1880

The Stalwart, Chester Arthur, now became president; but, much to Stalwart chagrin, he instituted a reform of the civil service. Patronage had run amok since the days of Grant, and every civil service office was subject to the spoils system. Arthur inaugurated the classified civil service, which removed a certain number of civil service offices from the influence of political patronage and required appointees to pass a competency examination. Still, only a small number of offices were so "classified"; and though in years to come that number would grow, so would the number of offices open to patronage.

Arthur did not run in 1884, and the Republican nomination went to James Gillespie Blaine, called the "Plumed Knight" by his friends and admirers. The nomination of Blaine, plumed or not, was unacceptable to Carl Schurz and other reform-minded Republicans. Called "Mugwumps" by their enemies, they bolted from the party and vowed they would support any candidate the Democrats nominated. The Mugwumps cheered the Democrats' choice of Grover Cleveland, who had been known for his integrity as governor of New York. What's more, Tammany Hall hated him. What could be better? "We love him for the enemies he has made!" said one Mugwump. Reports surfaced during the campaign of the shady profits the Plumed Knight had made through his political office in Congress; and though Republicans dredged up a

An account of President Garfield's assassination attempt, from *Frank Leslie's Illustrated Newspaper*, October 8, 1881.

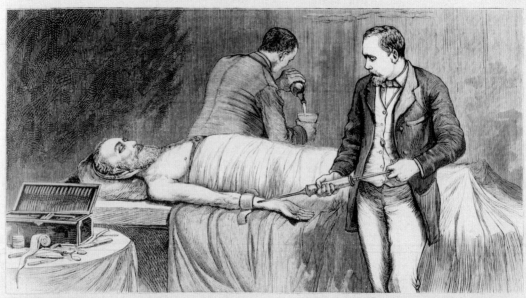

EMBALMING THE BODY OF THE DECEASED, ON THE MORNING OF SEPTEMBER 20TH.

DEATH OF PRESIDENT GARFIELD.
THE NATION'S GREAT AFFLICTION.

THE suddenness of the death of President Garfield seems to have been more surprising to his physicians and attendants than to the public. So few were the minutes that elapsed between the actual loosening of life's bands and the dissolution that his most constant watchers were, for a time, unable to realize the fact that this most remarkable struggle was at an end.

On the fatal night it was the turn of his old companion-in-arms, Judge Advocate-General Swaim, to watch the President. He had been with the sufferer a good deal of the time from three o'clock in the afternoon. A few minutes before ten o'clock he left Colonel Rockwell, with whom he had been talking for some minutes in the lower hall, and proceeded up-stairs to the President's room. On entering, General Swaim found Mrs. Garfield sitting by the bedside. There were no other persons in the room. He said to her, "How is everything going?" She replied, "He is sleeping nicely." He then said, "I think you had better go to bed and rest," and asked her what had been prescribed for him to take during the night. She replied that she did not know; that she had given him milk-punch at eight o'clock. The general then said: "If you will wait a moment I will go into the doctor's room and see what is to be given during the night?" She replied: "There is beef-tea down-stairs. Daniel knows where to get it."

General Swaim continued his narrative: "I then went into the doctor's room. I found Dr. Bliss there, and asked him what was to be given during the night. He answered: 'I think I had better fix up a list and will bring it in to you pretty soon.' I then went back into the sick-room and had some little conversation with Mrs. Garfield. She felt the President's hand and laid her hand on his forehead and said: 'He seems to be in a good condition,' and passed out of the room. I immediately felt his hands, feet and knees. I thought that his

TRANSFER OF THE REMAINS TO THE FUNERAL CAR, AT ELBERON.

knees seemed somewhat cold, and got a flannel cloth and heated it at the fire and laid it over his limbs. I also heated another cloth and laid it over his right hand, and then sat down in a chair beside his bed. I was scarcely seated when Dr. Boynton came in and felt the President's pulse. I asked him how it seemed to him. He replied: 'It is not as strong as it was this afternoon, but very good.' I said, 'He seems to be doing well.' 'Yes,' he answered, and passed out. He was not in the room more than two minutes. Shortly after this the President awoke. As he turned his head on awakening I rose and took hold of his hand. I was on the left-hand side of the bed as he lay. I said, 'You have had a very comfortable sleep.' He said, 'Oh, Swaim, this terrible pain,' placing his right hand on his breast, over the region of the heart.

"I asked him if I could do anything for him. He said, 'some water.' I went to the other side of the room and poured about an ounce and a half of Poland water into a glass and gave him to drink. He took the glass in his hand, raising his head as usual, and he drank the water very naturally. I then handed the glass to the colored man, Daniel, who came in during the time I was getting the water. Afterward I took a napkin and wiped his forehead, as he usually perspired in awaking. He then said, 'Oh, Swaim, this terrible pain! Press your hand on it.'

"I laid my hand on his chest. He then threw both hands up to his side and about on a line with his head, and exclaimed, 'Oh, Swaim, can't you stop this?' and again, 'Oh, Swaim!'

THE DEATH-BED SCENE.

"I then saw him looking at me with a staring expression. I asked him if he was suffering much pain. Receiving no answer, I repeated the question, with like result. I then concluded that he was either dying or was having a severe spasm, and called to Daniel, who was at the door, to tell Dr. Bliss and Mrs. Garfield to come in immediately, and glanced at the small clock hanging on the chandelier nearly over the foot of his bed and saw that

THE TRIBUTE OF THE STUDENTS OF PRINCETON COLLEGE — THE RAILWAY TRACK STREWN WITH FLOWERS.

story that Cleveland had fathered an illegitimate child—and Cleveland himself admitted it—nothing could salvage Blaine's candidacy for the presidency. Cleveland became the first Democratic president elected in 28 years.

The rotund Cleveland did not live up to the stereotype that fat folks are jolly. Conservative and unbending, Cleveland was not given to compromise. During his term, he vetoed or "pocketed" 413 bills passed by Congress—even those supported by members of his own party. Thinking gold the only sound basis for money, he opposed the free coinage of silver allowed under an 1878 congressional law called the Bland-Allison Act. The president also favored reducing the tariff, which supplied two-thirds of public revenue.

In the 1888 presidential election, Cleveland ran against the Republican, Benjamin Harrison. Though a grandson of "Old Tippecanoe" and a Civil War brigadier general in his own right, Harrison was too dour to succeed at a "log cabin and hard cider" campaign. He only won the election by carrying the electoral votes of the state of New York. Cleveland beat him in the popular vote by a margin of 100,000.

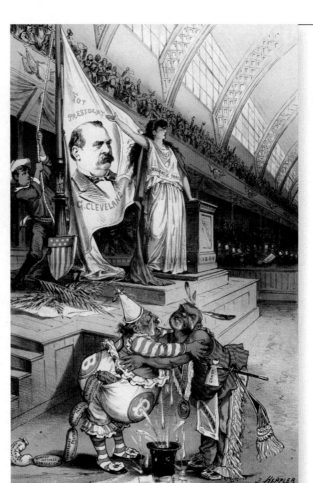

Grover Cleveland and a female figure labeled "Democratic Party," at the 1884 Democratic National Convention in Chicago, Illinois

President Harrison came into office with a Republican majority in both houses of Congress. Under the speakership of the powerful Republican representative, Thomas B. Reed, Congress passed the Sherman Silver Purchase Act (1890), which increased the coinage of silver—a measure Cleveland would have stoutly opposed. Manufacturing interests showed their clout with the Republicans with the passage of the McKinley Tariff of 1890. Sponsored by the Ohio Republican congressman, William McKinley, the tariff increased duties on foreign imports, thus raising the protective barrier for American business. But when the price of domestic goods rose, people blamed the tariff, and during the congressional elections of 1890, the Republicans, who had supported it, took a big hit. The Democrats won a majority in the House, while the Republicans barely maintained their majority in the Senate. The turning of the tide in 1890 washed Grover Cleveland back into office in 1892.

Benjamin Harrison

On May 1, 1893, Cleveland was in Chicago to open the World's Fair. Present with him were dignitaries from around the world, including the Queen of Spain, and a throng numbering around 250,000 people. About noon, the president pulled a golden lever that set the dynamo engines humming. Thousands of flags unfurled around the lagoon, bands began playing, and golden drapery fell from the golden figure representing the "Republic." It was a moment of triumph for the Gilded Age and the American capitalist order.

Administration build-
ing at the World's
Columbian Exposition,
Chicago, on opening
day, May 1, 1893

So it was somewhat ironic that, in a matter of weeks following the opening of the World's Fair, a series of bank failures collapsed the county into a deep depression—the Panic of 1893. Over the next several months, millions lost their jobs, and thousands wandered homeless. Many who, only months before, proudly strutted their prosperity, found themselves bankrupt and ruined. The business cycle had run its course from boom to bust, and discontent was rife. As the president and the politicians argued over the causes of the bust and proposed solutions, an increasing number of citizens began to think only one solution was possible or desirable: a complete overhauling of the country and its institutions.

Fire from the Plains

Hard times had already been the lot of farmers before the Panic of 1893. Kansas was a case in point. In 1881, the price of wheat and corn had been at an all-time high. Then, in Kansas, local prosperity had financed the large-scale building of railroad lines and a rash of spending on civic improvements in small towns. More farmers began to settle the arid regions of western Kansas, buying land on credit, hoping for the large returns that would compensate, and more than compensate, for their investments. But then came the drought of 1887. Crops withered, banks foreclosed, and about half the population of Kansas pulled up stakes and headed east.

Not only Kansans, but farmers across the country were suffering by the late '80s. With the introduction of machinery, such as McCormick's mechanical reaper, farmers became more productive. (In 1880, with only 15 percent of arable land in the U.S under cultivation, they were providing 30 percent of the world's grain.) But increased production meant more crops on the market—and demand from consumers was not keeping up with the rate of production. This meant lower prices for farm goods, and lower prices led to a growing number of farm failures. Increasing railroad transportation costs, unpredictable markets, the money supply, and high interest rates on loans played their part in this, but so did the farmer's desire to "get ahead." The allure of turning grain into gold induced the farmer to mortgage his possessions, to gamble on the future. And, too often, it was the farmer who lost.

Gradually, as more and more farms went bust, the holdings of those that survived grew larger. Those who could afford machinery, and thus, replace labor, fared better than those who had to pay "hands" to work their fields. In the Deep South, where land was given to a single cash crop—cotton—the farmer's plight was extreme. The merchants, from whom farmers had to borrow money, often demanded that the land be put to cotton instead of other crops—thus perpetuating cultivation practices that destroyed the fertility of the soil. As things stood, the farmers sold their cotton cheaply to mill owners (who, themselves, sold it again for high prices); thus, a drastic fall in prices meant the farmer had to sell his cotton for even less and so did not make enough money to pay his mortgages. The merchants who had made the loans would then foreclose on the land. Often, they kept the farmer on as a tenant—working land that had formerly been his own.

Like laborers in the cities, farmers had been forming alliances to protect their interests. One such alliance was the National Grange of the Patrons of Husbandry, founded by Oliver Hudson Kelley in 1867. The Grange proved an effective way of organizing farmers to resist both the middlemen who bought their crops and the railroads, who shipped them. Granges supported political candidates who took control of state legislatures, which then passed laws regulating freight rates. Much of this legislation, though, was not well conceived and so it was easy for courts to rule against it in favor of the railroads.

A detail from a Grange poster from the early 1870s

The Grange and others farmers' alliances undertook direct action by organizing cooperative enterprises to cut out middlemen. Farmers organized cooperative stores, marketing arrangements, and, in a few cases, cooperative manufacturing plants for farm equipment—but the opposition of the railroads forced most of these to close. In some cases, railroads refused service to communities that they thought particularly uppity.

For the elections of 1890, farmers' alliances organized candidates for state and national elections. Kansas seethed with political unrest. Mary Lease, a lawyer and a member of the farmers' Alliance Lecture Bureau, moved audiences with her beautiful voice, described as "a deep rich contralto, a singing voice that had hypnotic qualities." "What you farmers need to do is to raise less corn and more HELL!" Lease purportedly told her audiences, "We wiped out slavery, and by our tariff laws and National Banks began a system of white wage-slavery worse than the first. Wall Street owns the country. It is no longer a government of the people, by the people and for the people, but a government of Wall Street, by Wall Street and for Wall Street. The great common people of this country are slaves, and monopoly is the master. The West and South are bound and prostrate before the manufacturing East . . ." Another alliance speaker, Jeremiah ("Jerry") Simpson, ran for Congress against the incumbent Republican, nicknamed Prince Hal. Simpson gloried in how the Republican lampooned him as the "Sockless Socrates" and used it to appeal to the people. He beat Prince Hal and went to Congress in his stead.

Some members of southern farmers' alliances thought the best way to wrest power was to unite blacks and whites in a common front against the mercantile, manufacturing, and railroad interests. Tom Watson, a Georgia "populist" politician, accused both Democrats and Republicans of using racial fear to keep the poor whites under their thumbs. "You might beseech a Southern white tenant to listen to you upon questions of finance, taxation, and transportation," he said:

You might demonstrate with mathematical precision that therein lay his way out of poverty into comfort; you might have him "almost persuaded" to the truth, but if the merchant who furnished his farm supplies (at tremendous usury) or the town politician (who never spoke to him except at election times) came along and cried "Negro rule!" the entire fabric of reason and common sense which you had patiently constructed would fall.

Other alliance members thought it necessary for farmers to unite with industrial labor against the common enemy. On July 4, 1892, about 1,500 delegates from farmers' alliances, the Knights of Labor, and other groups gathered in Omaha, Nebraska to form a new political party—the People's or Populist Party. The preamble of the party's platform read:

> Assembled on the anniversary of the birthday of the nation . . . we seek to restore the government of the Republic to the hands of the "plain people," with which class it originated. We assert our purposes to be identical with the purposes of the National Constitution; to form a more perfect union and establish justice, insure domestic tranquility, provide for the common defense, promote the general welfare, and secure the blessings of liberty for ourselves and our posterity.

graduated income tax: a tax that increases as the income of the tax-payer increases; those who make a higher income pay a higher tax, while those who make a lower income, pay less.

initiative and referendum: legal provisions where voters can initiate legislation directly (without the legislature) and directly repeal existing legislation

To accomplish these goals, the Populists called for the popular election of United States senators; the government ownership of railroads, telegraphs, and telephone systems; and a **graduated income tax.** Populists also supported **initiative and referendum,** and the free and unlimited coinage of silver. The Populists thought that by maintaining the gold standard, government was enriching moneylenders and bond holders and, in turn, impoverishing farmers, who were forced to sell their crops for less because the dollar was worth more. The Populists thought the introduction of silver into the currency would decrease the value of the dollar and thus inflate the prices of goods sold on the market, thus benefiting the farmers.

Another measure espoused by the Populists was the prohibition of both speculation in land and its monopolization. "All land now held by railroads and other corporations in excess of their natural needs," said the Populists, "and all lands now owned by aliens should be reclaimed by the government and held for actual settlers only."

The Populists ran General James Baird Weaver as their presidential candidate in the election of 1892. He lost, of course, but carried four states. Many farmers and laborers voted for Grover Cleveland because they mistrusted the inexperience of the Populists. Like every third party in the history of the United States, the Populists were unable to take the prize of the presidency, though they sent some representatives to Congress. Still, like many third parties, the Populists championed issues that, later, one or both of the major parties would adopt and have enacted into law. To that degree, the Populists were hardly insignificant.

The Populists represented a last ditch effort to turn the country again in the direction of a Jeffersonian republic. Though the farmers that filled the ranks of the Populists were not quite the independent yeomen farmers that Jefferson had envisioned—they were too dependent on outside markets and modes of transportation—yet, they represented the agrarian ideal of the rugged individual and of small, people-controlled government that has always had its place in Americans' vision of themselves. This would not be the last time this ideal would be invoked. As an ideal, it is still alive today.

Jim Crow

The attempt to unite poor whites and blacks in a common political movement in the South was doomed to failure from the start. The poor southern white man, who occupied the lowest wrung of the white social ladder, intensely feared blacks. As long as they were slaves, blacks had posed no threat to the poor white's social status, however lowly that was; but, now black freedmen jostled with the poor white for his place, and to keep the black man out, the poor white had to keep him down.

Between 1875 and 1890, southern governments had by and large maintained the black franchise. There was even little social segregation. Blacks could ride on the same trolleys, eat in the same restaurants, and generally mingle freely with whites. What segregation there was—in churches and schools—was largely of the blacks' own choosing. The roughly 15 years following the end of Reconstruction had their share of bigotry and racial tension, but under the rule of the old planter class (men like Wade Hampton in South Carolina), state governments recognized and maintained black rights.

One hopeful sign following Reconstruction was the founding of a black school at Tuskegee, Alabama, in 1881, by Booker Taliaferro Washington, a native of Franklin County, Virginia. Born a slave, Washington had attended night school after the Civil War while working in a salt furnace and then a coal mine in West Virginia. He attended the Hampton (Virginia) Normal and Agricultural

Booker T. Washington

institute from 1872 to 1875, where he later taught. In 1881, Washington became the director of a new school for blacks at Tuskegee. Under Washington, the "Tuskegee Normal and Industrial Institute" went from a small school meeting in a small building and a church to become the nation's foremost industrial school for blacks.

Booker T. Washington believed that only by educating themselves could blacks attain any true equality in white society. He believed blacks shouldn't demand that equality but prove themselves worthy of it. If the old planter aristocracy had remained in power, perhaps Washington's ideas would have become reality. The old planters—the "Bourbons," as they were called—though, had abdicated much of their social responsibility in the years following the war. Those Bourbons that maintained power eventually found that power threatened by a political rising of the lower classes, stirred by fear and by the doctrines of the Populists.

It was not long before Populist demagogues realized that they could attain power by appealing to the basest instincts of the lower classes—in this case, their hatred of blacks. Throughout the 1890s, Populist politicians unfriendly to blacks drowned out the voices of Populists who wanted to unite blacks and whites in their movement. In the name of the people, and with their support, the racist Populists took control of state governments in the lower South. Between 1890 and 1908, Populist-controlled state governments altered their constitutions without submitting them to popular vote and enacted poll taxes, literacy tests, and other measures that hindered black people from voting. Louisiana had 130,334 blacks voting in 1896; by 1904, that number had shrunk to 1,342.

In the 1890s, first the governments in the Deep South, and gradually other southern state governments, began passing segregation laws. These came to be known as "Jim Crow" laws after a black character in musical shows, who danced to a song with the refrain, "Jump, Jim Crow." Restaurants, churches, schools, and public conveyances were, thenceforth, segregated by law. To prevent racial mixture, some laws forbade whites and blacks to enter each other's houses—unless of course the blacks worked for the whites as servants.

In 1896, Jim Crow Laws received the sanction of the highest cout in the land. In *Plessy v. Ferguson*, the majority of the U.S. Supreme Court ruled in what became known as the "separate but equal" doctrine that a Louisiana law forbidding blacks to ride with whites in the same parts of a public conveyance was constitutional, as long as the accommodations provided blacks were equal to those provided whites. The question of constitutionality, said the court, came down to whether "the statute of Louisiana is a reasonable regulation, and with respect to this there must necessarily be a large discretion on the part of the legislature. In determining the question of reasonableness it [the legislature] is at liberty to act with

A cartoon criticizing literary tests for blacks. The caption at bottom reads, "The Color Line Still Exists—in this case."

reference to the established usages, customs and traditions of the people, and with a view to the promotion of their comfort, and the preservation of the public peace and good order." The lone dissenter on the court, Justice John Marshall Harlan, wrote, "the statute of Louisiana is inconsistent with the personal liberty of citizens, white and black, in that state, and hostile to both the spirit and letter of the Constitution of the United States."

The Jim Crow era witnessed the grim spectacle of public lynchings. As part of vigilante justice, lynching was common in the West where there were few established courts and police. Not only blacks, but whites, Mexicans, Indians, and Chinese were lynched—mostly on charges of horse stealing, rape, robbery, and murder. Still, out of the number of those lynched between 1889 and 1918, blacks held the majority. The lynching of blacks occurred not only in the South, but in Ohio, Indiana, and Illinois. Not only grown men but women and even young children gathered to watch the executions.

Rape was the typical offense for which lynching was the punishment; however, for the most part, the charge was unproven. Lynching parties did not rely on due process—otherwise, they might have brought their grievances before the courts. Yet, as the darkness of Jim Crow deepened, courts and sheriffs became no refuge for black folks. As evidence of this sad fact, over 21 years would pass before any white man was even arrested for lynching a black man.

Homestead

"Have you read it?"

The two young men turned to see "the Girl," as they called her, as she entered the flat. She was agitated; her eyes had a "peculiar gleam," as one of the men, named Alexander, later recalled. "What is it?" he asked.

"Homestead," she answered. "Strikers shot. Pinkertons have killed women and children . . ."

"Her words," Alexander later recalled, "ring like the cry of a wounded animal, the melodious voice tinged with the harshness of bitterness—the bitterness of helpless agony." Alexander Berkman was an anarchist who longed to strike a blow for workers against their capitalist oppressors. He and "the Girl"—Emma Goldman—ran a small restaurant in Worcester, Massachusetts, that was a meeting-place for radicals like themselves. Both he and Goldman were Jewish emigrants from Russia, where they had imbibed their revolutionary doctrines. Berkman thought the Homestead strike could be used to spark the revolution of the proletariat, the cause for which he lived. He was resolved to carry out the supreme revolu-

Alexander Berkman

tionary sacrifice—*attentât*. Political assassination. By *attentât* an anarchist could show his love for the workers, for he would not only do away with their enemy but deliver himself up for their sakes. The assassin commits his bloody deed; he is captured, tried and, ultimately, executed. The news of his sacrifice spreads and inspires the masses to conceive new ideas of liberation.

With Emma's help (she prostituted herself to earn the money to buy a gun for him) Berkman set out for Pennsylvania.

The Homestead iron works were owned by Andrew Carnegie, who prided himself on his kindly treatment of his workers. He had built the town of Homestead, near Pittsburgh, to provide decent housing for them. In his book, *Triumphant Democracy*, he had written that workers had the right to unionize and even to strike. Furthermore, wrote Carnegie, employers should not bring in strikebreakers or hire scabs to replace striking workers. Such actions he thought violated a truly democratic system.

Carnegie followed his words with actions. In 1887, when workers at his Edgar Thompson plant walked out over Carnegie's plans to link their wages to the price of steel on the market, Carnegie assured them he would hire no workers to replace them. His admission of the workers' genuine grievances won the workers over to him. Carnegie worked out a contract with their union, the Amalgamated Association of Iron, Steel and Tin Workers, still tying their wages to steel prices but specifying that when the price of steel fell, wages would fall at a much slower rate.

However, by 1892, Carnegie was semi-retired, enjoying life at a castle he had bought for himself in his native Scotland. He had left the operation of his Homestead steel company to Henry Frick, owner of the Frick **Coke** Company. Frick had none of Carnegie's charm and none of his, though partial, regard for the workers. On June 30, 1892, the contract with the Amalgamated Association of Iron, Steel and Tin Workers union expired, and Frick proposed a new contract that would cut the workers' wages to $22 a month. The union demanded $24 a month, but Frick would not budge a penny over $23. When workers hanged Frick in effigy, the tycoon shut down the factory and brought in deputies to guard it. When the workers demanded the removal of the deputies, Frick sent two boatloads of armed Pinkertons up the Monongahela River to guard the factory.

When, on July 6, the Homestead workers heard the Pinkertons were coming, they threw up barricades, and some of the workers armed themselves. Men, women, boys, and girls were in the number of those who contested the landing of the 284 "Pinks," armed with Winchester rifles. "Don't land, or we'll brain you!" cried the crowd of workers. When the Pinks attempted to land, the workers rushed forward to seize their guns. A Winchester fired, and then the Pinkertons fired a volley into the crowd. The workers answered with gunfire, forcing the Pinkertons back into their boats.

For 12 hours more the fighting continued until the Pinkertons, worn out by heat and exhaustion, surrendered. The workers led them triumphantly through the streets of Homestead to the town jail. Though the workers had promised the Pinkertons protection, crowds of women attacked the captured gunmen with stones and other missiles. The workmen hurried the Pinkertons into the safety of the jail.

The governor of Pennsylvania responded to the events of July 6–8 by sending state militia to Homestead. With the coming of troops to guard the works on July 12, Henry Frick began hiring scabs to keep production moving. The striking workers remained sullen and defiant.

Alexander Berkman arrived in Homestead shortly before the arrival of the militia. It was a bleak, factory town he saw, where "thick clouds of smoke" shrouded "the morning with somber grey," where the air was "heavy with soot and cinders" and carried a "nauseating" smell. "In the distance," Berkman continued, "giant furnaces vomit pillars of fire, the lurid flashes accentuating a line of frame structures, dilapidated and miserable . . . the homes of

Henry Frick

coke: the residue left after coal is destroyed by distillation; used as fuel

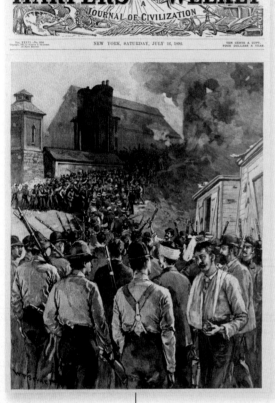

Homestead Strike, from the cover of *Harper's Weekly*

the workers who have created the industrial glory of Pittsburgh, reared its millionaires, its Carnegies and Fricks."

On July 23, a well-dressed Berkman walked into Frick's office.

Two men are seated at the end of a long table. Berkman calls out Frick's name. He notes his victim from the look of terror on his face. The assassin carefully aims his revolver and shoots. Frick falls, and cries, "Murder! Help!" Berkman again fires at Frick, but misses; a third time, and his gun misfires. Though struck on the head, Berkman pulls a dagger and slashes at Frick's legs. Finally overcome, the assassin is forced to look into the eyes of his victim. "His face," wrote Berkman, "is ashen gray; the black beard is streaked with red, and blood is oozing from his neck. For an instant a strange feeling, as of shame comes over me; but the next moment I am filled with anger at the sentiment, so unworthy of a revolutionist."

Frick survived the attempted assassination. The 143-day-long strike at Homestead ended in a victory for the company. Carnegie, his reputation somewhat tarnished by the episode and chastened by Frick's actions, offered pensions to the leaders of the strike, who had lost their jobs; and, after his retirement, Carnegie established a relief fund for Homestead workers. Since Frick did not die, Alexander Berkman was deferred the martyrdom he had hoped for. Instead of execution, he was sentenced to 22 years in prison, only 14 of which he would actually serve. He also learned that the workers did not appreciate his sacrifice. While in jail, before his trial, Berkman explained to a striker, who was also in custody, that "it was for you, for you people that I . . ."

The striker interrupted Berkman. "You better not talk that way in court, they'll hang you," he said—not knowing that that was just what Berkman wanted. The steel workers, he continued, "don't believe in killing; they respect the law." They would "have nothing to do with Anarchists," said the striker.

Depression

President Cleveland attacked the Panic of 1893 in a manner true to form. In his campaign he had committed himself to a "sound and stable currency"—that is, the gold standard. It was the adulteration of the currency with silver, he thought, that had depleted the country's gold reserves and had brought on the depression. One month after he had opened the World's Fair, President Cleveland summoned a special session of Congress to repeal the Sherman Silver Purchase Act. Though opposed by the silver mining lobby, which stood to benefit from the coinage of silver, Cleveland was triumphant, and the silver purchase act was repealed.

The repeal of the silver purchase act angered Populists and the farmers who had voted for Cleveland, though it pleased business mightily. The farmers were convinced that Cleveland had sold out to Wall Street; the president's subsequent receipt of a loan of gold from the tycoon J.P. Morgan and the Rothschilds only confirmed the farmers' suspicions. But while Cleveland was able to push through such "pro-capitalist" measures as the repeal of the Sherman Silver Purchase Act, he was unsuccessful in his attempt to induce Congress to reduce tariffs.

According to Samuel Gompers, the Panic of 1893 put three million men and women out of work. Many families were left homeless, and some workers turned vagabond, wandering the county through the long, cold winter months. Despite the obvious hard times, many of those who had been little affected by the depression despised the out-of-work as lazy and

Mother Jones

One of the more colorful of the labor leaders of this period was a woman, Mary "Mother" Jones. In Ireland, Mary Jones' grandfather had fought against British rule and was hanged for it. Forced to flee to America to escape punishment for his own revolutionary activities, Mary's father brought her to Toronto, where, as a young woman, she taught in a convent school. Upon moving to Chicago, Mary Jones worked as a sempstress. She moved again to Memphis Tennessee in 1861, where she married an iron worker who was a stalwart member of the Iron Molders' Union.

In 1867, tragedy struck. Mary Jones lost her husband and their four young children to Yellow Fever. And tragedy continued to dog her. Having returned to Chicago, she lost all her possessions to the Great Fire of 1871 that destroyed over three square miles of the city. She again took work as a sempstress and became involved with the Knights of Labor. Thenceforth, union activism remained the chief occupation of her life.

Dressed in black serge and white lace, her gray hair pulled up in a bun, Mother Jones looked like anybody's

Mother Jones

grandmother. She was, however, a powerful agitator for labor rights. She realized the importance of women in the struggle; she would tell workers' wives, "the wife must care for what the husband cares for if he is to remain resolute." She was present as an organizer for the United Mine Workers at their strike at Arnot, Pennsylvania in 1899-1900. There, she gathered the miners' wives, 3,000 strong, who, armed with mops and buckets, marched on the scabs who had taken their husbands jobs. The women attacked the scabs with their mops and beat on their buckets, finally driving them, frightened, away. "From that day on," wrote Mother Jones, "the women kept continued watch of the mines to see that the company did not bring in scabs. Every day women with brooms or mops in one hand and babies in the other arm wrapped in little blankets, went to the mines and watched that no one went in. All night long they kept watch. They were heroic women."

Mother Jones finally helped bring the strike to a successful conclusion by convincing the farmers around Arnot, who had been cool towards the strikers, to join forces with them. Met with such determined, united resistance, the mining company finally agreed to the strikers' demands.

shiftless. Recalling the Homestead strike, many feared more violence, and even revolution. Yet, there were others who sympathized with the plight of the unemployed.

Among the sympathetic was Jacob Coxey of Massillon, Ohio. A farmer, horsebreeder, and owner of a quarry that produced silica sand (used in the production of steel), Jacob Coxey was not one of the unfortunate poor. Still, he identified himself with their plight. He dreamed of the United States as a Christian commonwealth and believed that the federal government should take measures to relieve the poor. Coxey said Washington should issue government bonds to fund national work

Coxey's Army

programs to employ the unemployed—programs such as building roads and other public works. The federal government catered to the rich and powerful, Coxey argued; why shouldn't it have at least an equal concern for the working classes?

In 1894, Coxey announced plans for an Industrial Army that would march from Ohio to Washington, where it would stage a peaceful demonstration to call on the federal government to do something for workers. One of those who joined "General" Coxey was Carl Browne of Calistoga, California. Browne, who arrived in Ohio costumed in buckskins with silver-dollar buttons and sporting a flowing beard, parted in the middle, had met Coxey the previous year at the Chicago World's Fair. A Theosophist, Browne claimed to be the reincarnation of both Christ and the Greek historian Callisthenes. As if to prove the point, Browne carried with him a picture he had painted himself; it was a portrait of Christ (who looked very much like Browne), with the words: "PEACE ON EARTH Good Will toward men! He hath risen!! BUT DEATH TO INTEREST ON BONDS!!!"

Most of the reporters who had gathered to report on General Coxey's march, laughed at it. Their laughter changed to wonder, however, when hundreds of workers gathered in Massillon, and to even greater wonder when the "army" actually commenced the march, with the General and Browne in the vanguard. It was Easter Sunday, 1894. With Coxey went three of his female relatives, styling themselves Faith, Hope, and Charity, and one of his sons, Jesse Coxey, dressed in a blue and gray uniform in token of the reconciliation of North and South. (Shortly before the march, Coxey's wife had given birth to another son, whom Coxey named "Legal Tender." Both mother and newborn joined the march.)

As Coxey's army moved onward, others joined and swelled their ranks. News of the march filled many with apprehension—was it the harbinger of revolution? Yet, the march remained peaceful, trudging through Pennyslvania and then Maryland, where the roads were muddy from spring rains. When the army finally reached Washington in May, it found a police guard blocking its way to the capitol. Coxey and Browne tried to reach the steps of the capitol, but police clubbed Browne to the ground and arrested Coxey before he could deliver his prepared address. He was charged with walking on the grass.

A few days later a sympathetic Populist representative read Coxey's address to Congress. "The Constitution of the United States guarantees to all citizens the right to peaceably assemble and petition for redress of grievances, and furthermore declares that the right of free speech shall not be abridged," declared the address. "Up these steps," it continued, "the lobbyists of trusts and corporations have passed unchallenged on their way to committee rooms, access to which we, the representatives of the toiling wealth-producers, have been denied.

> We stand here to-day in behalf of millions of toilers whose petitions have been buried in committee rooms, whose prayers have been unresponded to, and whose opportunities for honest, remunerative, productive labor have been taken from them by unjust legislation, which protects idlers, speculators, and gamblers: we come to remind the Congress here assembled of the declaration of a United States Senator, "that for a quarter of a century the rich have been growing richer, the poor poorer and that by the close of the present century the middle class will have disappeared as the struggle for existence becomes fierce and relentless.

As if in confirmation of Coxey's charge that the federal government catered to the rich, in July 1894, President Cleveland sent federal troops to quell a strike at the Pullman rail car works outside of Chicago. Cleveland's act was of doubtful constitutionality; for, while the Constitution gives the federal government the authority to protect states "against domestic Violence," it specifies that intervention shall by done "on Application of the Legislature, or of the Executive" of the state. The problem was, not only did Illinois governor John Altgeld not request the intervention of federal troops, he had publicly opposed it.

George Pullman, the owner of the luxury rail car company, had cut the number of workers in his factory from 5,500 to 3,300 and then lowered the wages of those that remained by 25 percent. What was worse, while lowering their wages, Pullman refused to reduce the rents workers paid in the company town he had built and which he touted as a model community. When workers asked for a corresponding reduction in rents, Pullman replied, "none of the reasons urged as justifying wage reduction by it as an employer can be considered by the company as a landlord." A day later, three of the workers who led the protest were fired.

The firing of the three members of the committee of protest was the last straw. On May 10, the Pullman workers voted to strike. A day later, Pullman closed the factory—he had, he said, been running the company at a loss just to keep his workers employed; their decision to strike absolved him of any further responsibility towards them. Following the closing of the factory, the American Railway Union (ARU—which represented 465 local unions), at the urging of its president, Eugene Victor Debs, called on its members to refuse to handle Pullman cars on railways across the country. Meanwhile, Pullman met with the General Managers Association, a "union" of the owners of 24 railroads, and convinced them to resist the ARU's boycott of Pullman cars. When railroad workers refused to handle Pullman cars, members of the General Managers Association promptly fired them.

On July 2, at the urging of Richard Olney, Cleveland's attorney general, the federal circuit court in Chicago issued a "blanket injunction" against obstructing the operation of the railroads and holding up the mail. President Cleveland himself authorized the swearing-in of 3,600 special deputies, to be armed and paid by the General Managers' Association. When news of this action reached the strikers, rioting broke out. With the pretext of the riots, Cleveland ordered federal troops into Chicago. The first troops arrived on Independence Day, July 4, 1894.

Eugene V. Debs

The next day, Governor Altgeld protested Cleveland's action. "So far as I have been advised," the governor wrote the president, "the local officials have been able to handle the situation. But if any assistance were needed, the State stood ready to furnish a hundred men for every one man required, and stood ready to do so at a moment's notice." The federal government, said Altgeld, "has been applied to by men who had political and selfish motives for wanting to ignore the State Government." Altgeld protested that Cleveland's action violated "a fundamental principle of our Constitution"—local self-government, where "each community shall govern itself so long as it can and is ready and able to enforce the law, and it is in harmony with this fundamental principle that the statute authorizing the President to send troops into States must be construed."

Despite Altgeld's protest, federal troops remained in Chicago. On July 7, Debs, who ignored the federal court injunction, and other leaders of the ARU were arrested and later convicted of contempt of court for violating an injunction. When the AFL and Samuel Gompers refused to support the Pullman strikers, the ARU, on July 12, offered to end the strike if Pullman rehired all his workers regardless of whether they had participated in the strike or not. Pullman refused, and by early August the strike was broken.

After his conviction, Debs appealed to the Supreme Court, which ruled against him. The justices said the federal government has the implied power to remove any obstacles to interstate commerce. During his six-month prison stint, Debs read Karl Marx and other socialists. He would become, in the next few years, one of America's leading socialists.

The Pullman strike convinced many Americans that the struggle of labor and capital could have revolutionary repercussions if nothing were done about it. Class conflict, they feared, could lead to revolution and, perhaps, to the overthrow of American institutions. While the Pullman strike turned many against the claims of labor, others began to study how to harmonize the conflicts between capital and labor within the prevailing capitalist system. The question for most concerned Americans was not whether to overthrow the capitalist system but how to save society from the upheavals resulting from the struggle of labor and capital.

The Triumph of Capitalism

Since the Pullman strike served to sour many Americans against all things radical and seemingly radical, the congressional elections of 1894 saw Republicans and even Democrats striking out at Populists. Election results were disappointing to the Democrats and the Populists: Republicans were back in control of the House of Representatives, and the Populists had suffered a number of serious defeats.

The Democratic convention for the presidential election of 1896, however, was dominated by men who wanted to turn the party in a Populist direction. They championed a graduated income tax and were opposed to a national bank currency; but most of all, they called for the free coinage of silver. Addressing delegates who favored a gold standard, the 36-year old delegate from Nebraska, Congressman William Jennings Bryan, speaking for the silver **bimetallists**, declared, "When you come before us and tell us that we are about to disturb your business interests. . . . We say to you that you have made the definition of a business man too limited in its application." The employed laborer, the "attorney in a country town," the "merchant at the cross-roads store," the farmer—all these are businessmen, said Bryan, and *he* came to speak for them.

bimetallist: someone who favors a two-metal standard (silver and gold) for money

Bryan came to tell the Democratic delegates that they had better listen to the men of the farms, the men of the vast plains that were his home. "You come to us and tell us," continued Bryan, "that the great cities are in favor of the gold standard; we reply that the great cities rest upon our broad and fertile prairies. Burn down your cities and leave our farms, and your cities will spring up again as if by magic; but destroy our farms and the grass will grow in the streets of every city in the country."

To those who argued (as did the Republicans), that the United States could not adopt a gold and silver standard while the rest of the world used a gold standard, Bryan gave the triumphant response that, instead of the United States following the world, the world would have to follow the United States. "If they dare to come out in the open field and defend the gold standard as a good thing," declared Bryan, "we will fight them to the uttermost. Having behind us the producing masses of this nation and the world, supported by the commercial interests, the laboring interests and the toilers everywhere, we will answer their demand for a gold standard by saying to them: You shall not press down upon the brow of labor this crown of thorns, you shall not crucify mankind upon a cross of gold."

This "cross of gold" speech won William Jennings Bryan the Democratic nomination for president and turned the party in the direction of Populism. For their part, the Republicans nominated William McKinley, the congressman from Ohio who had sponsored the McKinley Tariff Act in Congress in 1890. McKinley's fellow Ohioan, Mark Hanna, a big businessman who wanted the Republican party to promote business interests, had personally groomed McKinley for presidential candidacy. The platform on which McKinley ran was solidly for protective tariffs and "unreservedly for sound money." "We are unalterably opposed to every measure calculated to debase our currency or impair the credit of our country," said the Republican platform. "We are therefore opposed to the free coinage of silver, except by international agreement with the leading commercial nations of the earth, which agreement we pledge ourselves to promote, and until such agreement can be obtained the existing gold standard must be maintained."

McKinley (called the "advance agent of prosperity" during the campaign) argued that the Panic of 1893 had been caused by the repeal under Cleveland of the McKinley tariff measure. Through Mark Hanna, the Republicans received large contributions from metropolitan banks, insurance companies, and railroads. In some cases, employers ordered their workers to vote for McKinley or lose their jobs. Bryan, for his part, went on a speaking tour around the country, traveling 13,000 miles, making 600 speeches—an extraordinary number. Still, for all his labors, Bryan, whom Republicans accused of "proposing to transfer the rewards of industry to the lap of indolence," could not beat McKinley. Though he took the South and West, Bryan won only 176 electoral votes to McKinley's 271. Nor was the popular vote close: Bryan received 6,502,925 votes; McKinley, 7,106,779.

Three years before the election, Henry Adams had written that the adoption of the gold standard under Cleveland had marked the triumph of capitalism—the victory of all Adams had contemplated in awe at the Chicago World's Fair. It was the triumph of the dynamo. Speaking of his own feeble opposition to the new forces, Adams wrote this epitaph:

> He had stood up for his eighteenth century, his Constitution of 1789, his George Washington, his Harvard College, his Quincy, and his Plymouth Pilgrims, as long as any one would stand up with him. He had said it was hopeless twenty years before, but he had kept on, in the same old attitude, by habit and taste, until he found himself altogether alone. He had hugged his antiquated dislike of bankers and capitalistic society until he had become little better than a crank. He had known for years that he must accept the regime, but he had known a great many other disagreeable certainties—like

Two dynamos, ca. 1920

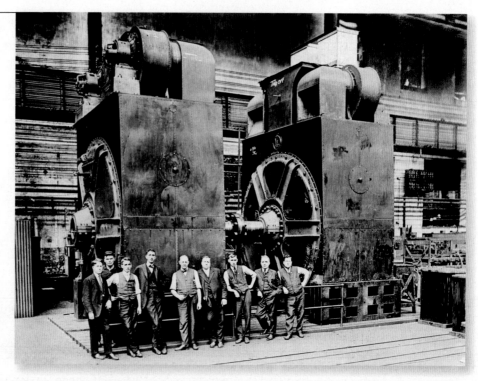

age, senility, and death—against which one made what little resistance one could. The matter was settled at last by the people. For a hundred years, between 1793 and 1893, the American people had hesitated, vacillated, swayed forward and back, between two forces, one simply industrial, the other capitalistic, centralizing, and mechanical. In 1893, the issue came on the single gold standard and the majority at last declared itself, once for all, in favor of the capitalistic system with all its necessary machinery. All one's friends, all one's best citizens, reformers, churches, colleges, educated classes, had joined the banks to force submission to capitalism; a submission long foreseen by the mere law of mass. Of all forms of society or government, this was the one he liked least, but his likes or dislikes were as antiquated as the rebel doctrine of State rights. A capitalistic system had been adopted, and if it were to be run at all, it must be run by capital and by capitalistic methods; for nothing could surpass the nonsensity of trying to run so complex and so concentrated a machine by Southern and Western farmers in grotesque alliance with city day-laborers, as had been tried in 1800 and 1828, and had failed even under simple conditions.

Chapter 22 Review

Summary

- American Protestantism faced new struggles in the latter half of the 19th century: Darwinism and the materialist worldview.

- American religion and philosophical movements continued to split into different groups, including New Thought, Christian Science, and Theosophy.

- New movements were entering American society. Among these were Free Love, Free Thought, and anarchism.

- In the Catholic Church a controversy arose as to whether Catholic and American ideals are reconcilable when Pope Pius IX condemned certain errors that seemed to strike at the heart of American civic life. Despite this, the Catholic population grew,

Chapter 22 Review (continued)

and the Catholic Church became the single largest Christian group in the country.

- Tensions between German and Irish Catholics began to shake the unity of the Catholic Church in the U.S. in the latter part of the 19th century. Among the controversies of the time was the question of to what degree Catholics should assimilate into American culture.

- The "progressives" and the "preservationists" in the Catholic Church in America waged war on the question of education. Some wanted a Catholic school system free from state control and aid, while others would accept state aid and even partial state control of Catholic schools.

- At the World's Fair, an ecumenical Parliament of World Religions was held. Cardinal Gibbons encouraged Catholic participation. But others, such as Bishop McQuaid, disagreed. After the conclusion of the Parliament, Pope Leo XIII forbade future participation in such ecumenical gatherings.

- Archbishop Ireland preached that in order to conquer the new world to Christ, the Church must be new, adapting herself to the new order. At first, Ireland and the progressives received favor from Rome, but in 1895 the tide turned against them when Pope Leo XIII issued the apostolic letter to the Church in the United States, *Longinqua Oceani*.

- The controversy between the progressives and their opponents came to a head when Abbé Felix Klein published a French translation of *The Life of Father Hecker*. Conservatives both in the United States and France condemned the Hecker biography, and critics began to call Klein, Ireland, and Keane "Americanists," and their alleged ideas, "Americanism." The controversy grew so heated that Pope Leo decided to look into it. Leo issued the encyclical, *Testem Benevolentiae Nostrae*, condemning Americanism.

- The Republicans nominated James A. Garfield as their presidential candidate, and he won the election of 1880. Four months after his inauguration, a disappointed office seeker shot Garfield, and his vice president, Chester A. Arthur, became president.

- Grover Cleveland won the election of 1884, the first Democratic candidate to win the presidency in 28 years. The Republican Benjamin Harrison, however, won the presidential election of 1888. Under President Harrison Congress passed the Sherman Silver Purchase Act and the McKinley Tariff. When the price of domestic goods rose, people blamed the tariff, and the Republicans took a big hit in congressional elections. Grover Cleveland triumphed in the presidential election of 1892.

- President Cleveland opened the World's Fair on May 1, 1893. Weeks later, a series of bank failures collapsed the country into the Panic of 1893.

- Farmers suffered during the panic, especially in Kansas. The introduction of machinery had increased farm productivity, and demand from consumers was not keeping up with the rate of production. As farms went bust, the holdings of those who survived grew larger.

- Farmers began forming alliances, such as the National Grange of the Patrons of Husbandry, to protect their interests.

- In 1892 delegates from the farmers' alliances, the Knights of Labor, and other groups formed a new political party, the People's or Populist Party.

- In the South there was an attempt to unite poor whites and blacks in a common political movement. This attempt failed, and the Populists soon realized that they could attain power by appealing to the white lower class hatred of the blacks. In the 1890s, southern state governments began to pass segregation laws, known as "Jim Crow" laws.

- Andrew Carnegie retired to his castle in Scotland, leaving the operation of his Homestead, Pennsylvania steal company to Henry Frick. In 1892, Frick proposed a new contract that would cut the workers' wages. When the union demanded more, Frick shut down the factory and sent for Pinkertons. When the Homestead workers heard the Pinkertons were coming, they threw up barricades and armed themselves. A fight ensued, and the governor of Pennsylvania sent in state militia.

- Meanwhile, Alexander Berkman, an anarchist and immigrant from Russia, was determined to carry out the supreme revolutionary sacrifice—political assassination. On July 23, 1892, he walked into Frick's office and attempted to kill him. Frick

Chapter 22 Review (continued)

survived, and Berkman was sentenced to 22 years in prison.

- President Cleveland committed himself to a sound and stable currency, the gold standard. A month after opening the World's Fair, he summoned Congress to repeal the Sherman Silver Purchase Act.

- During the Panic of 1893, three million men and women were out of work. Jacob Coxey dreamed of the United States as a Christian commonwealth and believed the federal government should undertake measures to relieve the poor. In 1894 Coxey formed plans for an Industrial Army that would march from Ohio to Washington, D.C., and stage a peaceful demonstration to call on the federal government to do something for workers. The army left on Easter Sunday 1894. When it reached the steps of the capitol, Coxey was arrested before he could deliver his address.

- In 1894, a strike broke out at the Pullman rail car works outside of Chicago. When Pullman fired three members of a committee of protest, the Pullman workers voted to strike, and Pullman closed the factory. This caused the American Railway Union to call on its members to refuse to handle Pullman cars.

- On July 2, 1894, the federal circuit court in Chicago issued a blanket injunction against obstructing the operation of railroads and holding up the mail. President Cleveland authorized the swearing-in of special deputies. This caused the strikers to riot, and Cleveland sent in federal troops. When the AFL refused to support the strikers, the strike was broken.

Key Concepts

New Thought: a mind-healing movement that held that all unhappiness and suffering are merely a mental state that right thinking can overcome

syncretism: a combining of religious or other beliefs and practices

theosophy: a syncretist religious philosophy that sought to bring together the insights of the various world religions

Free Thought: a movement that championed science against religion's alleged oppression of the human mind

Free Love: a movement that held that traditional marriage bonds were oppressive and that men and women should be joined only by the affinity they feel for one another

anarchism: a cluster of doctrines and attitudes centered on the belief that government is both harmful and unnecessary

graduated income tax: a tax the rate of which increases as the income of the taxpayer increases; those who make a higher income pay the tax at a higher rate, while those who make a lower income, pay at a lesser rate.

initiative and referendum: legal provisions where voters can initiate legislation directly (without the legislature) and directly repeal existing legislation

Jim Crow law: any of the laws that enforced racial segregation in the South between 1877 and the 1950s

Dates to Remember

1881: assassination of President Garfield

1884: Grover Cleveland elected president.

1890: Congress passes the Sherman Silver Purchase Act and the McKinley Tariff.

1892: the Homestead strike

1893: President Cleveland opens the World's Fair in Chicago.

A financial panic strikes the nation.

1894: Jacob Coxey and his Industrial Army march out to Washington to stage a peaceful demonstration

The Pullman strike

1895: Pope Leo XIII issues the apostolic letter, *Longinqua Oceani.*

1899: Pope Leo issues *Testem Benevolentiae Nostrae.*

Central Characters

Dwight L. Moody (1837–1899): prominent American evangelist of the late 19th century

Mary Baker Eddy (1821–1910): Christian religious reformer and founder of the denomination known as the Church of Christ, Scientist (Christian Science)

Blessed Pius IX (1792–1878): the pope who issued the Syllabus of Errors and during whose reign the doctrine of papal infallibility was authoritatively defined

John Ireland (1838–1918): the archbishop of St. Paul, Minnesota, who promoted the integration of Catholics into American culture

James Cardinal Gibbons (1834–1921): archbishop of Baltimore and the leading Catholic churchman in the United States in the late 19th century and early 20th century

Leo XIII (1810–1903): the pope who issued the encyclical *Testem Benevolentiae Nostrae* against Americanism

Isaac Hecker (1819–1888): Catholic priest who founded the Paulist Fathers and promoted an integration of Catholicism and American ideals

Grover Cleveland (1837–1908): 22nd and 24th president of the United States

William Jennings Bryan (1860–1925): congressman from Nebraska and presidential candidate who led the Democratic Party to embrace Populism

Alexander Berkman (1870–1936): Russian-American anarchist who attempted the assassination of Henry Frick

Jacob Coxey (1854–1951): American political figure who led the "Industrial Army" to Washington, D.C., to convince the government to give aid to the unemployed in the Panic of 1893

Questions for Review

1. Describe the two strains of Protestantism prevalent in America in the latter half of the 19th century.

2. How did Dwight L. Moody contribute to either of these strains?

3. What did the science-religion controversy center on? Explain the views of each side.

4. Briefly describe each of the new religious movements in the late 19th century.

5. What tensions existed between Catholic doctrine and American ideals in the late 19th century?

6. What were the main issues in the German-Irish controversy in the American Catholic Church of the late 19th century?

7. Explain the views of the progressives and the preservationists in the American Catholic Church in the late 19th century.

8. What is Americanism? Was it merely a "phantom heresy"? Please explain.

9. Explain Father Isaac Hecker's views about the Catholic Church in the modern world and how he influenced such men as Archbishop Ireland.

10. What were the effects of the Panic of 1893? What movements came out of it?

11. How and why were Jim Crow laws instituted in the South?

12. What did the Pullman strike reveal about the status of laborers in late 19th-century America?

Ideas in Action

1. Why do you think American culture gave rise to or fostered so many religious, philosophical, and social movements?

2. Read and discuss *Testem Benevolentiae Nostrae*. Is its message still relevant today?

3. Read accounts of the World's Columbian Exhibition and how it influenced American society.

4. Think about and discuss the constitutionality of President Grover Cleveland's sending of troops into Illinois to quell the Pullman strike. Do you think that Governor John Altgeld was right—that Cleveland violated the Constitution by sending in troops even though Altgeld did not request them? Or was what Cleveland did in accord with the Constitution, because, as the Supreme Court argued, he was intervening to protect interstate commerce? Is it clear which side was right?

Chapter 22 Review (continued)

Highways and Byways

The Golden Age of World's Fairs

The first world's fair was Great Britain's Great Exhibition, held in London in 1851. Queen Victoria's husband, Prince Albert, understood the potential value of an exhibition to showcase Britain to the rest of the world and hoped it would lead to more sales of British goods abroad. The building for the fair was designed by a greenhouse builder, Joseph Paxton. His iron-and-glass structure was called the Crystal Palace, and it greatly delighted attendees. The Crystal Palace displayed scientific and technological marvels from different countries as well as other works of art and craftsmanship. The fair was a success, and six million people attended. Indeed, Britain's world fair was such a success that it was imitated, and the period between 1880 and World War I is remembered as the golden age of fairs.

The United States fairs were inspired by those held in Europe. The first American fair was modeled after Britain's Great Exhibition. A Crystal Palace was built in New York to showcase the Industry of All Nations. The fair did not draw as many people as Britain's, however, and it ended with substantial monetary loss. Twenty years passed before another exposition was held in the United States. The World's Columbian Exposition, held in Chicago in 1893, was the most significant fair in United States history. Eager to outdo France's fair, the organizers of the Columbian Exposition tried to make everything bigger and more imposing. The architecture of the structures built for the fair shaped American architectural styles for the next 25 years. The Columbian Exposition marked the peak of the golden age of fairs; no later exposition could ever match it.

23 AT THE CROSSROADS

Republican Empire

The thought of intervening in a war between Spain and Cuba did not sit well with President McKinley for probably a rather simple reason—Mark Hanna (the man who had made McKinley president) and the big business interests opposed it. Neither finance nor manufacture would gain anything from a free Cuba. Perhaps humanitarian issues were at stake—but such concerns were not the "bottom line" for business nor for the very pro-business McKinley administration.

Conditions had been particularly bad in Cuba since 1825, when the Spanish government granted the captains general (the military governors of the island) special powers to prevent Cuba from falling into the hands of newly-independent Mexico or Colombia. Throughout the 1850s, Cuba had suffered from a corrupt government that had inspired revolutionary opposition. Three rival factions divided the Cuban people: the *separatists*, who favored independence from Spain; the *reformists*, who simply wanted a reform of colonial government; and the defenders of the status quo. These last were mostly *peninuslares*.

In 1868, separatists seized the occasion of the deposition of Queen Isabel II of Spain to spark a revolt against Spanish colonial rule. The separatists proclaimed a republic, whose government passed laws guaranteeing freedom of religion and the abolition of slavery. For ten years the rebels and government forces under General Emilio Calleja waged relentless and bloody war against each other, with atrocities on both sides. In February 1878, the rebels accepted the Convention of Zanjón that, while maintaining Cuba as a Spanish colony, granted amnesty to the insurgents, called for reforms in government (including autonomy for Cuba—or dominion status, as Canada had with Great Britain), and proclaimed the gradual abolition of slavery. Abolition of slavery began in 1880 and concluded in 1893, when General Calleja issued a proclamation that, henceforth, blacks were to have the same civil status as whites.

An 1898 cartoon of the Cuban rebellion, depicting King Alfonso XIII of Spain cowering on his throne as the Cuban Moloch prepares to devour the Spanish Fleet

Still, discontent was rife in Cuba. For one, the Spanish government in Madrid raised taxes in Cuba to pay for the recent war. Autonomy too was only apparent, since the governor-general ultimately controlled all political offices in the colony, elective or not. Liberals demanded the separation of military and civil power, true colonial autonomy, and assurance of personal and property rights. About 40,000 Cubans, dissatisfied with the government and the depressed state of the Cuban economy, emigrated to the United States. These émigrés formed *juntas* throughout the United States to foster a revolution in their home country. The *juntas* were allied with a *Gran Junta* in New York City.

In 1895 separatists under José Julián Martí and other leaders instigated a rebellion against Spain. Madrid sent General Valeriano Weyler y Nicolau to Cuba to crush the rebellion. Weyler earned the title, "Butcher," for the brutal way he suppressed the rebellion. He removed non-combatants from their homes and gathered them into villages and towns under military surveillance. Though they were told to cultivate the land, the peasants suffered from hunger and disease. Thousands died. The rebels were hardly better than Weyler; they laid waste to the countryside until it was desolate.

Opinion in the United States was solidly on the side of the rebels. In American eyes, the Cubans were fighting for independence, just as the English colonists had done in 1776. Newspapers owned by William Randolph Hearst and his rival, Joseph Pulitzer, were hot for American entrance into the Cuban war. A true humanitarian feeling inspired the war fervor, though much of it was headstrong and foolish. Many Americans saw war as a way of spreading America's "enlightened" institutions and commerce to the "benighted" Cuban people. Though McKinley's ambassador to Madrid, General Stewart Lyndon Woodford, was opposed to war, other members of the president's administration wanted it. Among these was the American consul to Havana, General Fitzhugh Lee, a former Confederate officer and nephew to Robert E. Lee. Another was the assistant secretary of the navy, the New Yorker Theodore Roosevelt. "No national life is worth having," declared Roosevelt in a public oration, "if the nation is not willing, when the need shall arise, to stake everything on the supreme arbitrament of war, and to pour out its blood, its treasures, its tears like water rather than to submit to the loss of honor and renown."

"Remember the Maine!"

Queen Liliuokalani, about 1887

It was not because he opposed foreign intervention on principle that McKinley opposed intervention in Cuba. For instance, McKinley wanted to annex the Hawai'ian Islands, where wealthy owners of pineapple plantations (themselves the descendants of New England missionaries) had overthrown the last queen, Liliuokalani. In 1893, when the revolution that ousted Liliuokalani took place and Hawai'i became a republic under President Sanford Dole, President Harrison had introduced an annexation treaty into the Senate. President Cleveland withdrew the treaty after he discovered that the Hawai'ian revolution was not a popular uprising but the work of a few Americans with the aid of United States troops. Cleveland called the overthrow of Queen Liliuokalani an unlawful subversion and declared the United States could never countenance it. Such scruples did not bother McKinley. In 1897, the Republican president submitted to the Senate a second treaty for the annexation of Hawai'i.

For Mark Hanna, for American business and, therefore, for President McKinley, the big difference between Hawai'i and Cuba was that the Hawai'ian islands, almost 2,500 miles off the western coast of the United States, were a profitable center of trade. Cuba, on the other hand, held no business interest. American businessmen, and their politicians were for the most part uninterested in heeding the cry of the "oppressed."

But in McKinley's favor, it must be remembered that never had the United States, by a formal declaration of Congress, intervened in a war between foreign powers, for ideals or anything else. Except for the Mexican War, the United States had maintained the role for which Jefferson had hoped—to be an isolationist power. What's more, by late 1897, even idealistic reasons for entering the Cuban struggle were seemingly gone. The Spanish government, having decided to become more conciliatory, recalled Weyler and released Cuban citizens detained in Weyler's concentration camps. What's more, Spain offered Cuba a measure of home rule. The worst abuses had been abolished, and Americans should have rested easier.

But they didn't. War fervor remained strong with Pulitzer, Hearst, with the Cuban exiles in America, and with the American consul to Havana, Fitzhugh Lee. Fearing the collapse of Spanish power would expose American citizens in Havana to danger, Lee asked that Captain Charles Sigsbee and the battleship *Maine* be dispatched to Havana harbor. The steaming of an American battleship into Havana harbor, foreign territory, was technically an act of war, though Spain carefully ignored the provocation. Spain did not want war with the United States.

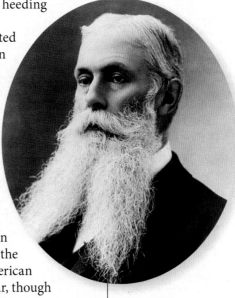

Sanford Dole

Then, on February 15, 1898, the *Maine* exploded, with a great loss of life. The event stirred up war fervor in the United States to a fever pitch. Though there was no proof the Spanish were responsible, pro-war Americans used the explosion to whip up public animus against Spain. Hearst's sensational headline on February 18—"Whole Country Thrills with the War Fever yet the President Says, 'It Was an Accident'"—lambasted the still vacillating McKinley. The people's cry, "Remember the Maine!" began to move Republicans in the direction of war—not so much for patriotic reasons but because they feared that if they ignored the popular clamor, Democrats might take control of Congress in the election of

The *U.S.S. Maine* enters Havana harbor, three weeks before the explosion that would destroy her.

"The Spanish Brute," a political cartoon published in *Judge* in reaction to the sinking of the warship, Maine, 1898

1898. Finally, the decision of a naval court of inquiry that an external submerged mine destroyed the *Maine* convinced most Americans that the Spanish were responsible. McKinley now had no choice but to cry, however feebly and reluctantly, "Remember the Maine!"

A "Splendid Little War"

The day after the naval court of inquiry gave its findings on the *Maine* explosion, President McKinley wired demands to Madrid. Spain, he said, must make an immediate armistice with Cuba, release all Cuban prisoners, and accept the United States as mediator between herself and Cuba, if peace talks between the two sides should break down. Spain found these conditions excessive and gave what McKinley thought an unsatisfactory reply to American Ambassador Woodward. On April 1, Archbishop Ireland, at the request of the pope, met with President McKinley to try to make peace. Ireland's efforts failed, for Spain did not fall into line with McKinley's demands. Though Spain promised an armistice on April 9, Congress still pressed for war.

On April 11, 1898, President McKinley asked Congress for a declaration of war against Spain. Though, mentioning Spain's proffered armistice, the president (who still wanted peace) noted: "If this measure attain a successful result, then our aspirations as a Christian, peace-loving people will be realized. If it fails, it will be only another justification for our contemplated action." Six days later, the House of Representatives passed a resolution demanding that Spain grant Cuba its independence. The Senate soon concurred, and on April 22, McKinley ordered the blockade of all Cuban ports—an act of war. On April 24, Spain declared war on the United States, and, the next day, the United States issued a declaration of war saying Spain must "relinquish its authority and government in the Island of Cuba and withdraw its land and naval forces from Cuba and Cuban waters."

The people of the United States entered this "splendid little war" (as Secretary of State John Hay called it) as if they were going on a country picnic. Young men enthusiastically answered the government's call for 125,000 volunteers; by May, 124,776 men had entered the ranks of the armed forces. William Jennings Bryan raised a volunteer regiment, and Assistant Secretary of the Navy Theodore Roosevelt resolved that he would not sit out the war behind a desk. He told naval secretary John D. Long and President McKinley as much. Roosevelt was to serve as lieutenant colonel in the First United States Volunteer Cavalry, under the command of Colonel Leonard Wood. This cavalry unit, nicknamed the "Rough Riders," was made up of western cowboys and frontiersmen, eastern athletes, and the sons of prominent citizens.

In the weeks following the destruction of the *Maine*, Roosevelt had worked hard to strengthen the navy. He maneuvered to have George Dewey appointed commander of

Joseph Pulitzer's newspaper, *The World*, lauds Dewey's defeat of the Spanish fleet in Manila harbor.

the United States Asiatic naval squadron; Roosevelt knew Dewey would prove energetic in the event of war. When, on February 25, a weary Secretary Long decided to take a day off, he left Roosevelt in charge of the naval office. Though Long specifically told his assistant secretary to attend only to routine business and to do nothing to affect "the policy of the Administration," Roosevelt set to work, ordering the repair of ships, the moving of ammunition and coal, and the preparation of men for combat. What's more, he cabled instructions to Commodore Dewey in the event of war breaking out. When Long returned to work, he was surprised, and not a little disgruntled, at what Roosevelt had done. The secretary, however, rescinded none of Roosevelt's orders.

Roosevelt's preparations paid off. Dewey's fleet had been anchored in Hong Kong, but when war broke out, the British government (which held Hong Kong) ordered the fleet to leave. Dewey's fleet steamed to Manila in the Philippines (a Spanish possession) where it met a decrepit Spanish fleet and destroyed it on May 1, 1898. On May 7, Dewey wired Washington: "I control bay completely, and can take city at any time, but I have not sufficient men to hold." The capture of Manila Bay made Dewey a national hero. So popular was he that a candy company named a chewing gum after him. They called it "Dewey's Chewies."

The Spanish fleet under Admiral Pascual Cervera had set sail on April 30 for Cuba from the Cape Verde Islands. Though American ships had been on the lookout for the coming of the Spanish fleet, on May 17 Admiral Cervera was able to sail secretly into Santiago Harbor, on the southern coast of Cuba. On May 29, the American fleet formed a blockade of Santiago, bottling Cervera up in the harbor. United States marines then landed and established a beachhead at Guantanamo Bay, 40 miles from Santiago.

It seemed as if the war might end abruptly with these naval victories—which was sad news to Theodore Roosevelt. "It will be awful if we miss all the fun," he lamented. Roosevelt took up his command in San Antonio, Texas, on May 15. Unused to military command, he was eager for his men to like him. One hot day, in the midst of drills, he treated his men to

Santiago de Cuba during the Spanish-American war, 1898

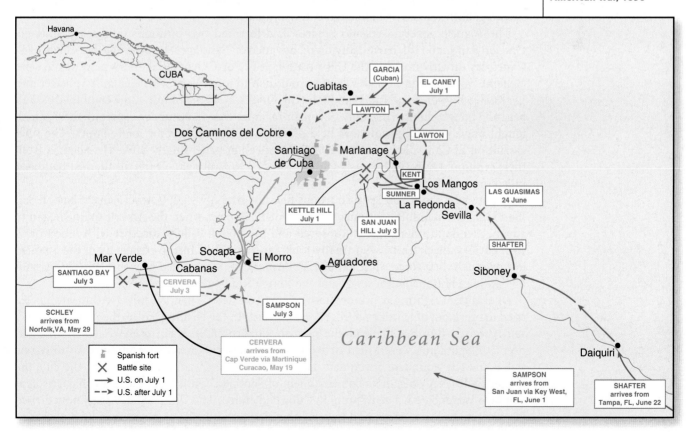

Theodore Roosevelt and his Rough Riders on San Juan Hill

drinks at a local resort. Colonel Wood found out about this and was irate. Roosevelt took Wood's rebukes in good spirit, calling himself "the damndest ass within ten miles of this camp." On May 29, the Rough Riders set off for Tampa Bay, Florida, the embarkation point for Cuba.

Unlike the Navy, the American army was poorly prepared for war. Confusion reigned in the camp at Tampa on the day of departure for Cuba. Troops were ill equipped and untrained. Unprepared for the swampy, hot, and humid climate of Cuba, thousands of United States soldiers would die, more from disease than from enemy bullets. The Rough Riders were something of an exception to this. Roosevelt had equipped them with khaki uniforms instead of the standard issue wool. His men carried Krag-Jorgensen rifles, which used smokeless gunpowder.

The Rough Riders formed a part of the 18,000-strong force that from June 22–27, 1898 landed at Daiquiri, 18 miles east of Santiago. No Spanish troops contested the American landing. Though the Captain General of Cuba had about 200,000 available troops on the island, he had only 13,000 in Santiago itself. The first battle between American and Spanish troops was at the stronghold of Las Guásimas outside Santiago, on June 24. Though Spanish troops defended themselves with Mauser rifles, they soon abandoned their entrenchments. Pursuing the Spanish, American general "Fighting Joe" Wheeler (a Confederate general in the Civil War) cried, "We've got the damn Yankees on the run!" Roosevelt and his Rough Riders were the first to gain the enemy's abandoned entrenchments.

The Spanish general, Arsenio Linares, had fortified two positions outside of Santiago. One, on San Juan Hill, barred any direct advance on Santiago; the other, at the village of El Caney, lay directly north of the U.S. position at El Pozo. General Shafter's plan was to send General H.W. Lawton to take El Caney and then to join forces with Generals Wheeler and J.F. Kent, who were assaulting San Juan Hill. On the morning of July 1, the combined assault began. Though numbering only 520 men (against the 4,500 under Lawton) the Spanish fought bravely and doggedly and held off the American forces for many hours. The final assault on El Caney, led by General A.R. Chaffee's brigade, finally drove the Spanish from their position. Only 100 Spanish soldiers escaped to Santiago. Nearly all the rest had been killed or wounded.

Meanwhile, about 700 Spanish troops held the roughly 15,000 Americans at bay on San Juan Hill. The standoff continued until about 12:30 p.m., when the American line began to advance without orders. It was Roosevelt and the Rough Riders, together with the 9th and 10th cavalry, black units, who finally took San Juan Hill. In the engagement, the Spanish lost over half their force while about 1,500 Americans were killed or wounded. This assault on San Juan Hill made Roosevelt and the Rough Riders national heroes.

Intermittent fighting continued for the next two days. Then, on July 3, Admiral Cervera tried to break out of Santiago harbor with his fleet. In the ensuing battle, the American navy sank the four ships that made up the Spanish squadron. Cervera himself was taken prisoner; over 500 Spaniards were killed or wounded. American casualties amounted to only one killed and ten wounded. Seven days later, with the American army besieging the city, the United States Navy began its bombardment of Santiago. On July 17, the Spanish garrison at Santiago surrendered. The fighting in Cuba had ended. The United States army now turned its attention to Puerto Rico and invaded the island on July 25.

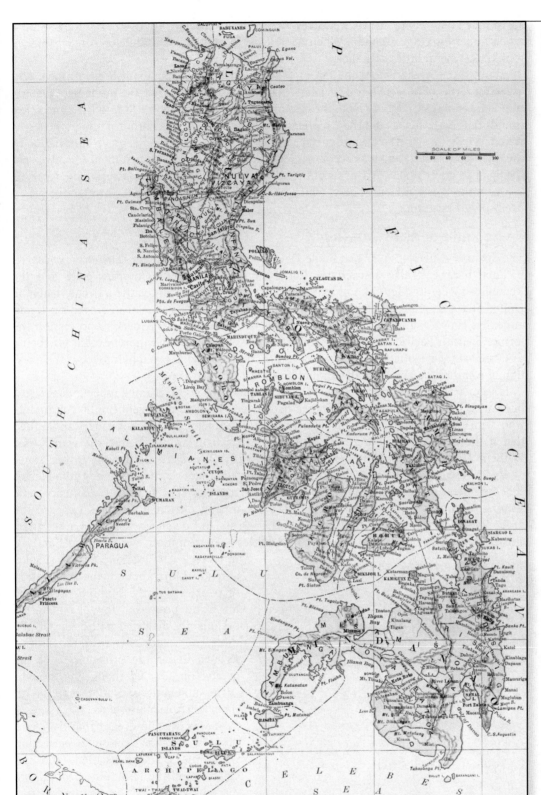

A late 19th-century map of the Philippines

In the Philippines, Commodore Dewey had been building up an invasion force until, by July 31, he had 11,000 men under Major General Wesley Merritt in readiness, with 5,000 more on the way. On August 7, Dewey and Merritt sent a note to Spanish Captain General Fermín Jaudenes in Manila that bombardment of the city might begin any time after 48 hours. Jaudenes was in a tight place. Though he had 13,000 troops in Manila, he was surrounded not only by American forces, backed by a superior fleet of ships, but by Filipino rebels under Emilio Aguinaldo. When American forces attacked Manila on August 13, they took the city with little resistance.

About three weeks before the fall of Manila, on July 26, the Spanish government had asked for terms of peace. Four days later, McKinley issued his terms: the immediate evacuation and relinquishment of Cuba; the cession to the United States of Puerto Rico and other islands in the Marianas; and the American occupation of Manila harbor. Though the terms were hard, Spain signed a preliminary peace on August 12, 1898. This grave humiliation to the once-powerful nation was accompanied by a protest: the relinquishment of Cuba, said the Spanish government, "strips us of the very last memory of a glorious past and expels us . . . from the Western Hemisphere, which became peopled and civilized through the proud deeds of our ancestors."

Peace and the War's Aftermath

The Spanish-American War had made Dewey, the Rough Riders, and Theodore Roosevelt national heroes. It also assured for Roosevelt the governorship of New York and the Republican vice-presidential nomination in 1900. More importantly, the war had made the United States an imperial power. In July 1898, the United States Senate approved the treaty annexing Hawai'i, and the course of the war had brought into America's possession the former Spanish Pacific island of Guam. The annexation of the Philippines that was being discussed at the negotiations in Paris was more controversial. It brought into focus the question of whether the United States should become a colonial power.

It seemed to many Americans that the Philippines would be granted independence, just like Cuba. Indeed, Dewey had welcomed back exiled Filipino insurgent Emilio Aguinaldo, who, with other rebel leaders, had begun organizing a republic. But other Americans argued that if the U.S. did not annex the Philippines, Germany would; before the war, Kaiser Wilhelm II had offered to buy the islands from Spain. Others argued that the United States needed a base of operations in the Far East, while still others claimed that the United States economy required colonial expansion and new markets for American manufacturers. Among these was Henry Demarest Lloyd, a prominent journalist who had exposed the monopolistic tactics of Standard Oil and other trusts and defended the Haymarket anarchists. "American production has outrun American consumption," wrote Lloyd, "and we must seek new markets for the surplus abroad." Lloyd thought the subjugation of peoples like the Filipinos necessary for world progress. "It will be a great prelude to the fraternalization of the races," he wrote, "to have *all* the inferior nations under the protectorate of the greater ones." And though he thought such subjugations would bring with them "terrible abuses and faithlessness . . . it was an idle dream that we could progress from perfection to perfection while the Chinese ossified, and the Cubans and the Philippine people were disemboweled, and the Africans continued to eat each other . . ."

Other Americans, however, opposed an imperial America. Among these was the famous author, Mark Twain, who on June 15, 1898 formed the Anti-

Filipino insurgent leaders. Emilio Aguinaldo is seated, third from right.

Uncle Sam stands between departing American soldiers and American women arriving to western- ize the natives of the Philippines, 1900.

Imperialist League. Other prominent anti-imperialists included William Jennings Bryan and Andrew Carnegie. These would have agreed with the words of the reform lawyer, Moorfield Storey, who asked, "Why should Cuba with its 1,600,000 people have a right to freedom and self-government and the 8,000,000 people who dwell in the Philippine Islands be denied the same right? . . . It is said that there is a war necessity or that we need indemnity. Can we extract our expenses from the enslaved people whom we intervened to help? . . . Is the commandment, 'Thou shalt not steal, qualified by the proviso, 'Unless it is necessary'?"

In the end, it was economic and strategic arguments that moved McKinley to deny Filipino independence. Arguing (as Dewey had reported) that, since the Filipino republican government represented only a fraction of the population, it could not keep order, McKinley pushed for the annexation of the Philippines. The president explained to a delegation of Methodists that he had decided to take the Philippines in order "to educate the Filipinos and uplift and civilize and Christianize them"—forgetting, perhaps, that the vast majority of Filipinos had imbibed Spanish culture and were Catholic. Despite the protests, the United States agreed to pay $20 million for the Philippine islands in the peace treaty with Spain, signed in Paris on December 10, 1898.

The annexation of the Philippines created new problems for the United States. The Filipino insurgents wanted independence, not a new master. To crush the Filipino revolt that now had turned against them, Americans before long resorted to measures that they had condemned when done by Spain. The United States military imitated Weyler by establishing concentration camps throughout the islands. American troops burnt Filipino towns and vil- lages and destroyed crops. The military used torture techniques, introduced by the Spanish, to extract information from captured prisoners, including priests. Anglo soldiers tended to despise the shorter, dark-skinned, Catholic Filipinos. Only black American soldiers treated them with respect.

The October 27, 1900, *Literary Digest* reported that Catholic sentiment—at least as evi- denced by the Catholic press—was "almost unanimously in favor of . . . anti-imperialism." Many Catholics, it seems, feared that the United States occupation of the Philippines threat- ened the Catholic Church there. Yet, despite such Catholic opposition, the *Digest* said it appeared "a large number of influential members of the hierarchy" supported McKinley's policies in the Philippines. Among these were Placide Chapelle, archbishop of New Orleans

Filipino prisoners of war in a courtyard, about 1899

and papal envoy to the Philippines, who argued that not only would Spain have sold the Philippines to another power if the United States had not annexed the islands, but that "the islands are very valuable commercially, and, above all things, they furnish the key to the trade with China." Archbishop Chapelle insisted that the Philippines "should be ours on moral, legal, commercial, sociological, and religious grounds."

Cardinal Gibbons too supported the annexation, even though it meant that in the Philippines the Catholic faith would be placed on an equal footing with other religions. Writing in the March 8, 1900 *New York Sun*, Gibbons said he thought "the government which we enjoy in the United States is the best government for us in the Philippines. The Catholics do not ask any special protection or privileges. All they would ask is a fair field and no favor . . . I know of no objection [to U.S. policy in the Philippines] among people of my religion on religious grounds." In an interview published in the October 20, 1900 *Sun*, Archbishop Ireland claimed that Pope Leo XIII had told him that he was "pleased with the relations of the American government to the church in Cuba and the Philippine islands." If Leo XIII did indeed express these sentiments, it may have been because the constitution established by Aguinaldo's government in 1899 called for separation of Church and state. During the insurrection, Aguinaldo's government imprisoned Catholic priests and religious.

With the occupation of the Philippines, the United States began to exert its influence in the Far East. In 1899, Secretary of State John Hay announced a "open door policy" in regards to China to assure that the United States would not be edged out of the Chinese market by Russia, Great Britain, France, and Japan. When the Boxer Rebellion—an uprising on the part of traditional elements in Chinese society—broke out in June 1900, the United States participated in a joint expeditionary force to relieve Peking. In July of that year, Secretary Hay issued a circular letter setting forth U.S. policy toward China. China, declared Hay, was not to be divided up between the European powers, nor was the principle of equality between trading countries to be violated.

In the Caribbean, the United States made Puerto Rico a territory with the right to become a state or to declare for independence, according to the wishes of the majority of Puerto Ricans. Six thousand United States troops under General Leonard Wood occupied Cuba for three years following the war. The occupation helped the Cubans to recover from the wars of the previous years, and American reform of sanitary conditions wiped out an ancient pest—malaria. In 1900, a constitutional convention drew up a constitution for Cuba patterned on that of the United States. The convention agreed to grant the United States

Guantanamo Bay for a naval base and adopted the Platt Amendment, which gave the United States the right to "intervene" in Cuban affairs "for the preservation of Cuban independence" or to keep order. United States military occupation of Cuba ended in 1902.

The Reign of Teddy

Imperialism was an important issue in the election of 1900. Should the United States take on colonies? Many prominent Americans—including Grover Cleveland, William James, Mark Twain, and William Vaughn Moody—said no. The Democratic candidate for president, William Jennings Bryan, said no. But McKinley and his vice-presidential candidate, Theodore Roosevelt, voiced a resounding yes. Dressed as a Rough Rider, Teddy was going about the country stumping for himself and McKinley. The war victory, the economic prosperity that had begun in 1897, and the vibrant power of Roosevelt's personality were more than Bryan could overcome. His issues of anti-imperialism and free silver could not win the day. McKinley and Roosevelt garnered 292 electoral votes with a 900,000 plurality in the popular vote, while Bryan took only Colorado, Idaho, Montana, Nevada and the "Solid South"—155 electoral votes.

In April 1901, soon after his inauguration, McKinley began a rail journey around the country, speaking to cheering crowds about the prosperity and glory of America. Later that year, Roosevelt and his family took a trip to the Adirondack Mountains in New York. The energetic Teddy must have found the vice presidency somewhat boring after his stint as governor of New York. Then, he had worked to root out corruption in government and thereby won an enemy in Senator Thomas Platt, head of the Republican machine in the state. Platt had for years handed out the political "contributions" of big business to the various Republican office holders in the state and didn't want the "bull in the china closet," as he called Roosevelt, to interfere with what had been a rather comfortable system. It was Platt who pushed to have Roosevelt run for vice president at the Republican party convention—to get him out of New York. Mark Hanna opposed this move; when he saw that the convention wanted Roosevelt for vice president, he said, "Everybody's gone crazy! What's the matter with all of you? . . . Don't any of you realize there's only one life between that madman and the Presidency?"

Roosevelt was certain that the vice presidency destined him for political oblivion. He wanted to be president himself, but the governorship of New York was a more obvious stepping stone to that office than the vice presidency. He contemplated studying law again. Circumstances, however, worked out differently than he or anyone (except for maybe Mark Hanna) expected. On September 6, 1901, an anarchist's bullet struck President McKinley at a public reception for the opening of the Pan-American Exposition in Buffalo, New York.

When Roosevelt received the news, he came to Buffalo; but, as the president seemed to be recovering, he returned to the Adirondacks. But McKinley's wound became infected, and gangrene began to set in. On September 14, while sitting in a meadow in the Adirondacks, Roosevelt saw a runner coming up the trail. "I instinctively knew he had bad news, the

William McKinley, center foreground

Theodore Roosevelt, dressed in his Rough Rider uniform

worst news in the world," Roosevelt later wrote. McKinley was dead, and Roosevelt was to be sworn in as president.

Mark Hanna's fears had come to pass—that "mad-man" was president! While riding on McKinley's funeral train, Hanna fumed: "I told William McKinley it was a mistake to nominate that wild man at Philadelphia. I asked him if he realized what would happen if he should die. Now look, that damned cowboy is President of the United States!"

Progressivism

The new president represented an ideology that had its roots in Populism but had abandoned Populism's rejection of the industrial order. The great strikes at the end of the 19th century had demonstrated that something was awry in the relationship between workers and owners, but the violence of the strikes served to discredit any radical solution to the problem. To many it appeared that big industry was here to stay; that the best anyone could hope for was a bettering of the conditions of labor, not an overthrow of, or any radical change in, the existing order. Those who thought this way came to be known as *progressives.*

The progressives represented the optimistic strain of American thought—one that held that man is basically good in his inclinations and becomes bad on account of bad institutions and laws. In America, they argued, such institutions and laws had created conditions of grave injustice. The progressives pointed out that, despite the return of prosperity beginning in 1897, *real wages*—that is, a workman's earnings minus his rent and other expenses—actually had declined throughout the 1890s and into the 1900s. The average real wage between 1900 and 1914 was $10.73 a week, which, given the rise in the costs of living, was actually less than what a worker earned in 1890. Brooks Adams, Henry's brother, argued in his book, *A Theory of Social Revolution* (1913), that revolutions arose when governments were so rigid they were unable to reform such abuses. Progressives argued that revolution could come to the United States unless something were done to better the lot of the working class.

Still, Roosevelt could lament that not all progressives were really progressive. "Half of them," Roosevelt wrote, "are really representative of a kind of toryism, which wishes to attempt the impossible task of returning to the economic conditions that obtained 60 years ago"; they wanted, in other words, "to bust trusts" and break up large businesses. "The other half," continued Roosevelt, wishes "to recognize the inevitableness of combination in business, and meet it by a corresponding increase in governmental power over big business."

In Roosevelt's mind, if business is big, government must be as big, or bigger, in order to regulate business. Such talk disturbed "tories" such as William Jennings Bryan, who liked neither big business nor big government.

Progressive policies first influenced state governments. The progressive Robert La Follette was elected governor of Wisconsin in 1901, and by his policies Wisconsin became one of the most progressive states in the union. In 1903, he pushed through the state legislature a law that called for taxing railways according to their value. The following year, the legislature passed another La Follette-sponsored law that subjected all nominations for public office to a direct vote of the people. In 1905, Wisconsin began to regulate railroads in the state. That same year, La Follette resigned as governor upon being elected to the United States Senate.

A number of journalists furthered the progressive agenda. Dubbed **"muckrakers"** by Roosevelt, these journalist uncovered the muck of corruption in industry and politics. Their number included Lincoln Steffens, Ida Tarbell (who took on Standard Oil), and Upton Sinclair. As "muckrakers" suggests, Roosevelt thought ill of these writers. Muckrakers were concerned, he declared, with "that which is vile and debasing." Roosevelt said, "I want to let in light and air, but I do not want to let in sewer gas." The muckrakers, Roosevelt thought, "make gross and reckless assaults on character" and see the world as "nothing but muck."

muckrakers: this name is derived from a passage in John Bunyan's *Pilgrim's Progress:* "The Interpreter takes them apart again, and has them first into a Room where was a Man that could look no way but downwards, with a Muck-rake in his hand."

Robert La Follette, by J. C. Strauss

If William Jennings Bryan represented the "far right" of progressivism, and Roosevelt the center, the socialists occupied the left. Less extreme than the communists and the anarchists, the socialists worked at the local level to promote municipal ownership of public utilities, such as waterworks and gas and electric plants. Throughout the first decade of the 20th century, Socialists increased their political clout. By 1911 they had won mayorships in about 18 cities; and they nearly took the mayoral seats of Cleveland and Los Angeles. The Socialist Party weekly journal, *Appeal to Reason,* featured the writing of the man who had led the Pullman strike and who ran as the Socialist candidate for president in 1900—Eugene V. Debs.

Debs had long advocated industrial unionism as opposed to the craft union model championed by Samuel Gompers and the AFL. Debs, and others, argued that, since industry was growing increasingly more centralized, so must unions. Under the Gompers' model, unions, divided up among the various crafts or trades, did not always work in concert together if one or a few went on strike. Such a policy, said Debs, allowed industry to take a divide-and-conquer approach to labor activity and provided no representation for unskilled laborers. If all workers were united under one union, Debs argued, then a strike could cripple a particular industry, thus forcing owners to meet the union's demands. Gompers countered that such an approach never had worked (he referenced the Pullman strike) and always brought more repressive measures against workers in its wake. Only craft union strikes had succeeded, he said.

The Western Federation of Miners and other western unions provided the strength for the formation of the Industrial Workers of the World in 1905. That year, at their founding convention, the "Wobblies," as the Industrial Workers were nicknamed, adopted an industrial union organization that united workers of all trades and industries, both skilled and unskilled. The leaders of this movement were William D. "Big Bill" Haywood, Daniel De Leon, W.E. Trautman, Eugene V. Debs, and a Catholic priest (noted for packing a Colt .45 pistol), Father Thomas J. Hagerty. Both Mother Jones and Emma Goldman became supporters of the IWW.

The Industrial Workers of the World grew rapidly. By their second convention in 1906, the Wobblies numbered 100,000 workers. Political differences among the members (there were socialist, anarchist,

Emma Goldman with Alexander Berkman

and trade unionist Wobblies) led eventually to major splits in the IWW's ranks. The Western Federation of Miners, the largest single union with over 25,000 members, left the union in 1907, and in 1909 the IWW split into two rival groups, each calling itself the IWW: one based in Chicago; the other, in Detroit. The Chicago-based IWW, the only branch finally to survive, adopted a platform for action that favored class conflict between workers and owners. "Between these two classes," declared the union in 1909, "a struggle must go on until the workers of the world organize as a class, take possession of the earth and the machinery of production and abolish the wage system."

Father Hagerty, who wrote the organizational plan for the IWW in 1906, declared at the convention of that year that, "in spite of petty national lines, in spite of international division lines, the workers of the world over are coming together on the ground of their common working class interest, without regard to race, color, creed or flag, and they are coming together because the earth and all the earth holds, and all its possibilities are theirs." Here Father Hagerty echoed a passage in Pope Leo XIII's *Rerum Novarum:* "God gave the whole human race the earth to use and enjoy . . ." The IWW, however, adopted methods opposed to

IWW poster

the letter of the pope's encyclical. The Wobblies said they would embrace "any and all tactics" that would "get the results sought with the least expenditure of time and energy," and encouraged sabotage of employers' property, if it were necessary to achieve their ends. The Wobblies' embrace of class conflict was in marked opposition to Pope Leo, who wanted to see employers and workers joined together in a spirit of justice and friendship.

It is not perhaps surprising, then, that Father Hagerty, who said, "the working class and the employing class have nothing in common," eventually left the priesthood and the Catholic Church.

Perhaps if the Catholic Church in the United States had been more assiduous in seeking to apply the principles of *Rerum Novarum* to problems in their country, Hagerty and other Catholics would not have embraced socialism as the means of helping workers. Catholics, for the most part, had kept aloof from the main currents of American life; and though many Catholics were workers and union members, Catholic leaders had not been conspicuous in efforts to solve the labor crisis. Some bishops were friendly to labor unions; others, fearing what they saw as the unions' socialist and anarchist tendencies, opposed them.

But a few American Catholics involved themselves in the labor question. One of these was Father John Augustine Ryan of the archdiocese of Saint Paul, Minnesota. In his younger years, Father Ryan had been influenced by Populist leader Ignatius Donnelly. Ryan later wrote a book, *A Living Wage,* on the Church's teaching about just wages. A professor at the Catholic University of America, Ryan, at the request of Archbishop Ireland, returned to St. Paul to teach at the diocesan seminary and continued his work in behalf of the working classes.

Father Peter E. Dietz of Cleveland was another priest who sought to apply the ideals of *Rerum Novarum* to the American scene. Dietz was convinced that Catholic priests could help Catholic laymen form Catholic worker organizations to aid in a just resolution of the labor question. Of German parentage, Dietz joined a German Catholic social justice organization, the St. Louis-based *Deutscher Römisch-Katholischer Central-Verein von Nord-Amerika* (the German Roman Catholic Central Union of North America) and edited the English language section of their publication, *Central Blatt and Social Justice.* Dietz, however, came into conflict with the businessman Frederick P. Kenkel, the dominant figure in the *Central Verein,* and later left the organization for a Catholic laborers society called the Militia of Christ for Social Service. This organization met in conjunction with conventions of the American Federation of Labor, and its membership was made up of Catholic AFL members.

Dietz and Kenkel disagreed over how *Rerum Novarum* should be applied to the American scene. Dietz has been called a "reformist"—that is, he did not favor any fundamental changes in the organization of the American economy but simply a bettering of the worker's status in the existing system. Dietz was more of a progressive than Kenkel (for one thing, Dietz wanted *Central Blatt and Social Justice* to go to an entirely English format). Kenkel envisioned a more radical transformation of the American economy, along the lines championed by the late bishop of Mainz, Germany, Wilhelm Freiherr (Baron) von Ketteler (1811–77) and promoted by the German shoemaker-turned-priest, Adolph Kolping. In part to combat the influence of socialism among German-speaking immigrants in the United States, Kenkel proposed what is called a "corporatist" model of industrial organization. According to this model, cooperative unions would be formed that included both owners and workers in a given industry, somewhat along the lines of medieval guilds. The cooperative unions would be controlled and directed by workers and owners both and would oversee any conflicts that arose between them, without strikes. Government would step in only when the internal structure of the union was unable to bring a conflict to resolution.

The beginning of the 20th century, thus, saw the first attempts by Catholic Americans to apply the wisdom of the Church to the special problems of their country. While the reformist approach of Dietz, Ryan, and others would gradually come to dominate Catholic efforts at social justice in the United States, the views of Ketteler, Kolping, and Kenkel would find their expression in authoritative Catholic teaching—in the encyclical, *Quadragesimo Anno* of Pope Pius XI, written to commemorate the 40th anniversary of *Rerum Novarum,* in 1931.

Trust-Buster

It was to the British ambassador that Roosevelt confided his "feeling of contempt and anger for our socially leading people." The president said felt disdain for their "lives which vary from rotten frivolity to rotten vice." This might be said to be an odd feeling for one who had, himself, grown up surrounded by wealth and privilege. The 43-year old president (the youngest to that date to be inaugurated) came from an old Dutch New York family that had been prominent in mercantile, banking, and importing interests for generations. As a child, Theodore had had governesses and private tutors, had benefited from family trips to Europe, and had attended Harvard University. With inherited family wealth he had built a mansion at Sagamore Hill at Oyster Bay on Long Island.

Yet, despite his privileged background, Roosevelt had, throughout his political career, promoted reform in favor of the common man and against corruption. In 1881, only six weeks into his first term as a New York state legislator, Roosevelt had made a motion to impeach a highly respected judge who had gone too easy on certain financiers, whom Roosevelt deemed members of what he called "the wealthy criminal class."

Roosevelt's political career was temporarily halted by his vigorous opposition to the nomination of James G. Blaine as the Republican candidate for president in 1884. After the death of his first wife, Roosevelt retired to work a ranch he had bought in western Dakota. After three years on the range, he returned to New York, where he ran, unsuccessfully, for mayor of New York City. President Harrison appointed Roosevelt to the United States Civil Service commission, where for six years he battled defenders of the spoils system. In 1895, Roosevelt and his second wife, Edith, returned to New York City, where he served as president of the Police Board. He returned to Washington, D.C., to serve as Assistant Secretary of the Navy under McKinley.

Roosevelt's high spirits upon taking office were scandalous to some. After all, people said, because of the circumstances (McKinley's assassination and all), Roosevelt should at least try to hide his pleasure at becoming president. With characteristic energy, Roosevelt began immediately to reform how the nation conducted business. He started first with what was closest to home—the lot of federal workers in Washington, D.C. Roosevelt decreased the number of hours federal employees worked to eight hours a day, 48 hours a week, and established for them a minimum wage and workman's compensation. Though no federal employees were children, Roosevelt abolished child labor in Washington. The federal government, he thought, should set an example for the rest of the nation.

In 1904 Roosevelt would say that though the "Giver of Good" had richly blessed the American people, "the conditions which have told for our marvelous material well being . . .

Theodore Roosevelt

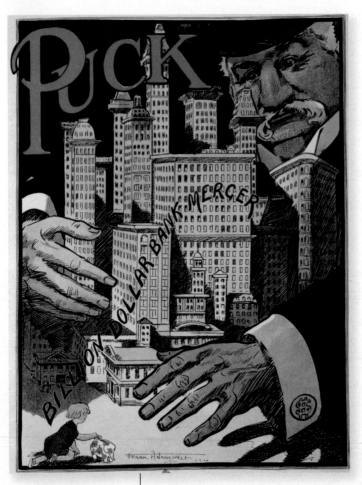

A 1910 cartoon in the magazine, *Puck*, portraying J. P. Morgan as a man holding more financial power than the U.S. government

have also brought the care and anxiety inseparable from the accumulation of great wealth in industrial centers." If the nation, he said, failed to solve the problems associated with capitalism, "the cause of free self-government will rock to its foundations." Where the states were powerless to deal effectively with the inequalities spawned by capitalism—where they were incapable of assuring to the common man what he deserved, that is, a "square deal"—there the federal government, said Roosevelt, should step in to secure the general welfare of the nation.

In his first message to Congress on December 3, 1901, the new president announced that he would not only enforce existing laws to break up trusts but would push for legislation that would give the federal government more power to inspect and regulate business involved in interstate trade. This was not mere talk. When J.P. Morgan moved to consolidate three railroads in a trust called the Northern Securities Corporation, Roosevelt directed his attorney general to prosecute the tycoon for violating the Sherman Anti-trust Act.

But Morgan took the whole matter in stride. "Send your man to my man, and they can fix it up," said Morgan to Roosevelt, as if he were striking a deal with just another businessman. Roosevelt wouldn't negotiate with Morgan on those terms. Instead, the prosecution went forward. On April 9, 1903, the United States circuit court in St. Louis ordered that the Northern Securities Company be dissolved. Almost a year later, the United States Supreme Court, in a five to four decision, upheld the ruling. Roosevelt had busted Morgan's trust.

With this victory under his belt, Roosevelt next brought suit against the American Tobacco Company and Standard Oil. With the president's urging, Congress in February 1903 set up a department of commerce and labor that included a bureau of corporations to gather facts for enforcing anti-trust laws. Outraged business leaders cried that the president was a revolutionary, that he would destroy the social structure and the institution of private property! J.P. Morgan groused that "Roosevelt had not acted as a gentleman."

The Democrat newspaper publisher, Joseph Pulitzer, disagreed. In his paper, *The World*, Pulitzer exulted that Roosevelt "has subjugated Wall Street." And he continued: "If Roosevelt had never done anything else, and if he had committed a hundred times more mistakes, and if he were one hundred times more impulsive, changeable, unpresidential in dignity, loud and vociferating in manner and speech . . . if he had done nothing else except to start the great machinery of the government and the most powerful force and majesty of the law in the direction of prosecuting these great offenders, he would be entitled to the greatest credit for the greatest service to the nation."

Roosevelt and Labor

Though Roosevelt fought for a "square deal" for the common man, he could be critical of the efforts of labor unions to achieve the same goal. Roosevelt objected to what he thought were the "arrogant and domineering attitudes" of unions and opposed the idea of a closed shop (where every worker was required to the join the shop's union). Still, unions were necessary, he thought; workers, he said, "have the right and the duty to combine to protect themselves and their families from want and degradation." Roosevelt reasoned that moral betterment went hand-in-hand with material betterment. "A fall in wages, an increase in hours, a deterioration of labor conditions," he said, "means wholesale moral as well as economic degeneration, and the needless sacrifice of human lives and human happiness, while a rise of wages, a lessening of hours, a bettering of conditions, mean an intellectual, moral and social uplift of millions of American men and women."

In 1902, a strike among workers in the anthracite coal region of Pennsylvania once again brought the labor question to the forefront of the public mind. Miners, led by John Mitchell, were demanding higher pay and better working conditions; but owners, led by J.P. Morgan and George F. Baer of the Philadelphia and Reading Railroad, refused to negotiate with them. As summer turned to autumn and the threat of a winter without coal for heating loomed, the standoff between the workers and the mine owners presaged disaster. Progressive senator Henry Cabot Lodge urged Roosevelt to do something to end the crisis. The president saw he had no constitutional authority to interfere, since the coal miners were not a trust. But he thought something had to be done. "I could not," Roosevelt later told his

Cartoon from the May 23, 1906 issue of *Puck*, "The Infant Roosevelt and the Standard Oil Serpents.

sister, "more see misery and death come to the great masses of the people in our large cities, and sit by idly, because under ordinary conditions a strike is not a subject for interference by the President, than I could sit by idly and see one man kill another without interference because there is no statutory duty imposed upon the President to interfere in such cases."

In October, Roosevelt called on owners and the leaders of the United Mine Workers to meet with him. John Mitchell asked Roosevelt to set up a tribunal where representatives of both labor and management could arbitrate the strike. The owners derided the proposal. They didn't want arbitration but insisted that Roosevelt, like Grover Cleveland before him, send in federal troops to end the strike.

The owners' intransigence was hard to crack. But Roosevelt had another plan. If the owners would not agree to arbitration, Roosevelt would send in federal troops to operate the mines. One congressman, when he heard the plan, objected, "What about the Constitution . . . What about seizing private property for public purposes without due process of law?" Roosevelt (saying he drew his inspiration from Lincoln, who had faced a similar crisis) turned to the congressman, took hold of his shoulder, looked him squarely in the eyes, and in his high-pitched voice nearly shouted, "The Constitution was made for the people and not the people for the Constitution."

Roosevelt, as it turned out, did not need to use troops. After much wrangling with the owners, who refused to allow a representative of labor on the arbitration board, Roosevelt appointed to the board one E.E. Clark, whom he described as an "eminent sociologist." This seemed to placate the owners, who didn't realize that Clark was the very labor man Roosevelt had originally hoped to appoint. Roosevelt added a sixth member to the board—John Lancaster Spalding, Catholic bishop of Peoria, Illinois.

While the arbitration board investigated the situation, the coal workers returned to their jobs. The arbitration board decided that the workers would receive a ten percent increase in their pay and a decrease in their work hours.

Industry had suffered another humiliating defeat at the hands of Roosevelt.

Roosevelt and the Family

"I do not want to see us Americans forced to import our babies from abroad. I don't want to see the stock of people like yourself and my family die out." Thus, Roosevelt's answer to a woman, a mother of six, who criticized his stance on artificial contraception. Roosevelt was a severe critic of those who in his day were encouraging the use of contraception—a practice that not only Catholics but most Christians in the early 20th century condemned as immoral. For Roosevelt, contraception struck at the root of the most fundamental institution of society—the family.

Roosevelt saw the family as the cornerstone of the nation, the basic unit of society. "The nation is nothing but the aggregate of the families within its borders," he wrote. It is "the most fundamental, the most important of all relations" in society. He thought that the family, springing from the union of man and woman in marriage, demands the assiduous care of both husband and wife. Though he praised the woman's role as mother as the more important in the family—so important that he thought a wife should be treated as "the full equal of her husband"—Roosevelt insisted that fathers should be deeply involved in the rearing of their children. The "highest ideal of the family," he said, is found "only where the father and mother stand to each other as lovers and friends," who each assume the full responsibility for good of offspring. This, said Roosevelt, is their highest calling:

> [N]o other success in life, not being President, or being wealthy, or going to college, or anything else, comes up to the success of the man and woman who can feel that they have done their duty and that their children and grandchildren rise up to call them blessed.

Home of the Palia family, Buffalo, New York. The boy, Amorica, center, worked with his mother in a canning factory in summer. Photograph by Lewis Wickes Hine, February 1910

As Roosevelt saw it, the American family in his day was threatened by two evils: a decrease in the birthrate among the "native," Anglo population, and divorce. According to statistics drawn from the U.S. Census, between 1880 and 1920, the U.S. birthrate fell by over 30 percent, with an especially sharp decline in the Northeast. The U.S. population was growing, but relative to the influx of immigrants, the percentage of what Roosevelt called the "native stock" fell from 67 percent in 1880 to 56 percent in 1910. As for divorce, the number of failed marriages had increased threefold between 1890 and 1910. Such statistics in Roosevelt's mind presaged disaster for the nation.

Though Roosevelt worried about the dwindling of what he called his own "race," he was not what we today would call a "racist." A healthy people, he said, procreates; and if a people is so flaccid in spirit that it abandons this duty, then, perhaps, it needs "the infusion into it of the blood of other races that have not lost the virile virtue." Roosevelt in particular praised the people of South America for their fecund family life and predicted that, by the end of the 20th century Spanish speaking people would come to outnumber Anglos in California and the Southwest. To a gathering of progressive Christian theologians in 1911, Roosevelt spoke these hard words:

> If you do not believe in your own stock enough to wish to see the stock kept up, then you are not good Americans, you are not patriots, and . . . I for one shall not mourn your extinction; and in such event I shall welcome the advent of a new race that will take your place, because you will have shown that you are not fit to cumber the ground.

Roosevelt blamed social conditions in part for the decline of family life. "Uncontrolled industrialization and urbanization," he said, had far more dire effects on family life than war. He deplored the "ruin of motherhood and childhood by the merciless exploitation of the labor of women and children." And though he asserted that women had a right to education and to careers that hitherto had been closed to them, he wanted to protect their role in the home. He thus opposed those feminists who despised the role of the stay-at-home mother and promoted contraception. The issue of contraception, said Roosevelt, was "the most serious of all problems, for it lies at the root of, and indeed itself is, national life."

Roosevelt promoted policies that he thought would strengthen the material basis of family life. Because he thought farm life important to the moral fiber of society, he favored a progressive tax to break up large agricultural estates so more tenant farmers could themselves become landowners. He favored changing tax rates to favor families: income and inheritance tax rates, he wrote, "should be immensely heavier on the childless and on families with one or two children, while there should be an equally heavy discrimination in reverse, in favor of families with over three children." He thought the United States should adopt something like Germany's social welfare system that allowed all families to access health care. He approved of a "family wage" so that heads of families (whether male or female) could support them in sufficiency. He wanted to find a way to support widowed mothers or those whose husbands had deserted them, so that they could stay at home to raise their children.

Roosevelt's knowledge of the life of the very poor—the "submerged tenth" of American society—led him to sympathy; he did not include them in his condemnation of the willfully infecund. As for the rest of Americans—if they embraced contraception, they did so "from viciousness, coldness, shallow-heartedness, self-indulgence, or mere failure to appreciate aright the difference between the all-important and the unimportant." Roosevelt told the progressive Christians ministers that he did "not wish to see this country a country of selfish prosperity where those who enjoy the material prosperity think only of the selfish gratification of their own desires, and are content to import from abroad not only their art, not only their literature, but even their babies." Those men and women who bring children into the world—it is these, said Roosevelt, who "dare to live nobly and bravely" in the service of their country.

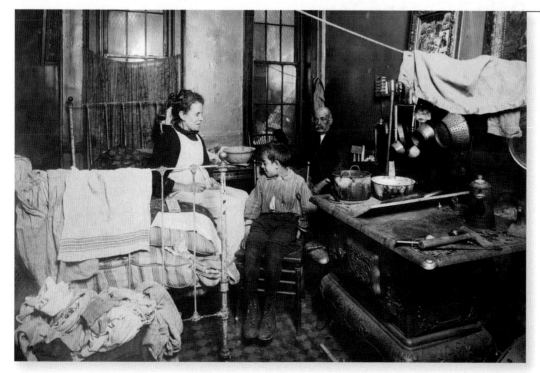

A family in a New York City tenement apartment, 1913, by Lewis Wickes Hine, 1913

Conservation

Gifford Pinchot remembered the wild domestic scene that greeted him at the governor's mansion in Albany when he came to spend an evening with then Governor Theodore Roosevelt and his family. Roosevelt was lowering his children out of a window on the second floor of the mansion, which was under attack by imaginary Indians. When the sanguinary struggle had done, Roosevelt engaged Pinchot in a boxing match, which the governor lost. Defeated, but still buoyant, Roosevelt only then sat down with Pinchot to discuss the object of the visit—conservation.

Gifford Pinchot remained Roosevelt's counselor on conservation of the nation's natural reserves into the latter's presidency. Pinchot drafted the section of Roosevelt's first address to Congress that dealt with conservation. Roosevelt, though, did not need Pinchot or anyone else to convince him of the need of conserving the country's forests and regions of great natural beauty. The passion

Gifford Pinchot, by Pirie MacDonald

for conservation had been instilled in the president during his travels in the West. He believed forests had to be preserved from ranchers and timber companies that were looting federal public lands of their rich harvest of wood. Certain areas of natural beauty—the Grand Canyon, Yosemite, Niagara Falls—Roosevelt believed were national treasures that had to be kept pristine for the edification of future generations.

At Roosevelt's urging, Congress set aside 150 million acres of unsold federal lands as national forest reserve. Roosevelt fostered federal irrigation projects that by 1915 would add a million and a quarter new acres to the nation's arable land. Under the Roosevelt presidency, five national parks and two national game reserves were established, preserving such monuments as Niagara Falls, the Grand Canyon, Crater Lake, the New Mexico petrified forest, and the Blue Ridge Mountains. In 1906, the National Monuments Act set up 16 national monuments, including Muir Woods in California and Mount Olympus in Washington state.

Only A Second Term

Since the man holding the White House was progressive, the Democrats decided to nominate a conservative presidential candidate for the election of 1904. Their choice of conservative New York judge Alton B. Parker, instead of progressive William Jennings Bryan, drew the votes of conservative Republicans who feared a second Roosevelt term; but the Democrats' move failed to pull in the common people, who believed Teddy Roosevelt was a good, honest man who fought for them. Parker took the Solid South, which always went Democratic, but garnered only 140 electoral votes. Roosevelt won 336 electoral votes and so could boast the widest margin of victory of any president in the history of the United States, except Washington.

During the campaign, Roosevelt made a promise that he would later regret. "I believe in a strong executive," he said. "I believe in power; but I believe that responsibility should go with power and that it is not well that the strong executive should be a perpetual executive." Thus, he would not violate "the wise custom which limits the President to two terms . . . Under no circumstances," Roosevelt declared, "will I be a candidate for or accept another nomination." Having given his word, Roosevelt would not turn back; for, as he wrote in 1900, "honesty is . . . an absolute prerequisite to efficient service to the public. Unless a man is honest we have no right to keep him in public life, it matters not how brilliant his capacity."

In his second term Roosevelt somewhat tempered his trust-busting ways. He was coming to think that trusts were here to stay. There were "good trusts," he thought, like the International Harvester Corporation, which he thought helped rather than hindered the business life of the country. It was bad trusts, held by what he called "malefactors of great wealth," that were the enemy. Their problem was not their size, he thought, but their underhandedness and dishonesty. The challenge, he believed, was to regulate bad trusts, not destroy them. Roosevelt's view would be echoed by the Supreme Court in the coming years. In future decisions, the court would rule that a monopoly violated the Sherman Anti-Trust Act, not simply because of its size, but because it "unreasonably" affected interstate trade, and so was in "restraint of trade."

But Roosevelt found it increasingly difficult to get Congress to pass bills to increase federal power over interstate trade. Such bills, introduced in the House, invariably died in the Senate, dominated as it was by conservative Republicans called the "Stand-Patters" (so named from a 1902 speech by Mark Hanna when he encouraged Ohio Republicans to "stand pat and continue Republican prosperity.") Roosevelt's promise not to run for a second term weakened his influence in the Congress during the last half of his administration. Congressmen realized that, soon enough, someone other than Roosevelt would be doling out political patronage.

Still, Roosevelt was able to push through Congress some important progressive legislation. The Hepburn Act, passed in 1906, extended federal regulation from interstate railroads to steamship, express, and sleeping car companies. The bill allowed the Interstate Commerce Commission to determine maximum rates such companies could charge. The companies could appeal the commission's decision to the courts, but the burden of proof was put on the companies.

It was a novel that inspired another Roosevelt victory in his second term. Upton Sinclair, one of Roosevelt's detested "muckrakers," had not meant his book, *The Jungle,* to be an exposé of conditions in the meatpacking industry. The book was about unjust treatment of workers. The reader, however, did not go away from the book horrified at the inhuman treatment of men but with a sick sensation for what went into meatpacking. Readers learned that the great meat packers processed decaying beef and pork, poisoned rats, and human excrement into their food products. Floor level, open vats, near where men worked, sometimes received human victims who were boiled down into lard that was sold to the public. At least, so said Sinclair.

Upton Sinclair

Roosevelt decided to have the meat industry investigated. The result was a report of what Roosevelt called the "hideous" conditions in the meatpacking plants. The president wanted a meat inspection act, which Congress was reluctant to pass. But Roosevelt was relentless. He said he did not want to release the report to the public but would if Congress proved stubborn. Finally, Roosevelt made public a part of the report, and Congress agreed to approve the bill he wanted, on June 30, 1906. This "Pure Food and Drug Act" provided for federal inspections of the food and drug industry and forbade the manufacture, sale, or transportation of adulterated food or drugs.

In such ways, Theodore Roosevelt continued, and accelerated, a tendency toward the centralization of power in the federal government that began with Abraham Lincoln. In this, Roosevelt seemed to follow Alexander Hamilton; yet, Roosevelt pushed centralization, not to enrich a few elite, but to secure the political and economic freedom of the many. In this, he reflected Jefferson (for whom, incidentally, Roosevelt had little respect.) Whether a more vigorous central government was an effective response to the problems brought on by rapid industrialization and consolidation into monopolies and trusts, only time would tell.

The Panama Canal

In his inaugural address, Roosevelt developed his ideas about the place of the United States in the world. "Much has been given us," he said, "and much will rightfully be expected from us . . . We have become a great nation, forced by the fact of its greatness into relations with

Cartoon, "The Big Stick in the Caribbean Sea"

the other nations of the earth, and we must behave as beseems a people with such responsibilities. Towards all other nations, large and small, our attitude must be one of cordial and sincere friendship. We must show not only in our words, but in our deeds, that we are earnestly desirous of securing their good will by acting toward them in a spirit of just and generous recognition of all their rights."

However, the president continued, justice and generosity required strength. "While ever careful to refrain from wrongdoing others," he said, "we must be no less insistent that we are not wronged ourselves. We wish peace, but we wish the peace of justice, the peace of righteousness. We wish it because we think it is right and not because we are afraid. No weak nation that acts manfully and justly should ever have cause to fear us, and no strong power should ever be able to single us out as a subject for insolent aggression."

Roosevelt had said about the same thing many times before but in fewer words: "There is a homely adage which runs: 'Speak softly, and carry a big stick; you will go far.'" Roosevelt almost always spoke softly when dealing with the leaders of other nations. The fear expressed when he took over from McKinley, that he would draw the nation into war, proved unfounded. Once he became president, Roosevelt did all he could to avoid war. He had granted Cuba her independence, as McKinley had promised, and had only intervened once to restore order on the island, as the Platt Amendment allowed the United States president to do. Roosevelt also allowed the Philippines to establish a degree of self-rule, though a United States governor still presided over the island nation.

Yet, Teddy was not averse to using the "big stick" whenever he thought he needed to. He proved this in the case of Colombia.

Talk of a canal connecting the Atlantic and the Pacific, so that ships would not have to travel the long route around Cape Horn, was nearly as old as the presence of Europeans in the New World. A French company had attempted to dig such a canal across the narrow Isthmus of Panama, which was then part of Colombia; but after $260 million spent and hundreds of lives lost, it had abandoned the attempt. The French company was eager to sell its interests in the canal and, it turned out, the Roosevelt administration was eager to buy. There were those in the United States, though, who wanted to build a canal through Nicaragua. Though the Isthmian Canal Commission under McKinley had specifically rejected this option, its proponents had not been silenced. Roosevelt wanted to make sure that Panama, not Nicaragua, would be the sight of the canal.

On June 28, 1902, the Senate passed the Spooner Act, which authorized the president to pay the French company $40 million for the concession to build the canal across the Isthmus of Panama. Since the Spooner Act specified that, unless Colombia ceded land across the Isthmus to the United States "within a reasonable time," the president should pursue the option of a canal across Nicaragua, Roosevelt knew he had little time to act. But all seemed to go well. The Colombian *chargé d'affairs* in Washington signed a treaty that gave the United States a 100-year lease of a ten-mile wide canal zone, stretching from the Gulf of Mexico to the Pacific, for a payment of $10 million and $250,000 a year rent. All that was needed was the approval of the Colombian government.

chargé d'affairs: a diplomatic representative

Roosevelt wielded the big stick over Colombia through his secretary of state, John Hay, who, in a veiled way, told the Colombian government that they had better approve the canal treaty, or else. The Colombian government, however, ignored these threats and rejected the treaty on August 12, 1903. Colombia had just recently come out of a civil war and was sensitive to any slight to her sovereignty. The treaty specified that Colombia would have to cede her sovereignty over the canal zone to the United States; this was unthinkable to the Colombian government. What's more, the United States had bought the canal concession from the French company without consulting the Colombian government. This too, said Colombia, was a violation of her sovereignty.

But Roosevelt had a card up his sleeve. He met with Philippe Bunau-Varilla, the leader of revolutionaries in Panama who wanted their state to secede from Colombia. Bunau-Varilla asked Roosevelt if the United States military would prevent Colombian troops from landing in Panama in the event of a revolution. "I can't say," replied the president, "but I have no use for the Colombian government after what it has done." Of Bunau-Varilla, Roosevelt wrote, "he's a very able fellow, and it was his business to find out what he thought our

Government would do. I have no doubt that he was able to make a very accurate guess and to advise his people accordingly. In fact, he would have been a very dull man had he been unable to make such a guess."

If Roosevelt was purposely vague, the French company agent in Washington was all too clear: he told the Panamanian revolutionaries to proceed, assured of U.S. assistance. On October 19, 1903, three U.S. vessels of war were ordered to anchor off the coast of Panama. On November 2, U.S. military commanders were instructed to occupy

A cartoon satirizing Roosevelt's machinations to attain canal rights in Panama

the Panama Railroad if a revolution broke out. The justification given for this command was a treaty the U.S. had signed with Colombia, allowing American troops to protect the Panama railroad if any danger threatened it. Yet, rather conveniently, by seizing the railroad, U.S. troops could stop the advance of Colombian troops into Panama.

On November 3, the secretary of state in Washington cabled the United States consul in Panama: "Uprising on Isthmus reported. Keep Department promptly and fully informed."

The consul cabled back: "No uprising yet. Reported will be in the night."

That evening, again the consul cabled the secretary of state: "Uprising occurred tonight 6; no bloodshed. Government will be organized tonight."

Except for the death of a Chinese man from a shell lobbed into Panama City by a departing Colombian gunboat, the Panamanian revolution was bloodless. This was, perhaps, partly because a landing party from the *U.S.S. Nashville* prevented Colombian troops from advancing against the revolutionaries. On November 3, the new Republic of Panama declared its independence. Three days later, Secretary Hay recognized that independence.

On November 18, the new Republic of Panama leased the canal zone "in perpetuity" to the United States "to the entire exclusion of the exercise by Panama of any . . . sovereign rights, power or authority." The price paid by the United States for this cession was what Colombia would have received if she had approved the treaty.

With the canal zone in his hands, Roosevelt was eager to get to digging. He first employed private engineers; but when these proved inadequate to the task, he appointed Colonel George W. Goethals to direct the excavation of the canal. Goethals was autocratic, but effective. The canal project began in 1907; by 1914, the Panama Canal was open to commercial traffic. Six years later it was completed. With exuberant and almost boyish high spirits, Roosevelt himself went to Panama to inspect the work—and so set a new precedent. He was the first U.S. president while in office to travel outside the boundaries of his country.

Boats move through Panama Canal at the Culebra Cut (Gaillard Cut), which crosses the continental divide, about 1915.

Into the World

Roosevelt didn't wield the big stick only over Colombia. In 1902, when Great Britain, Germany, and Italy blockaded the coast of Venezuela because that country's dictator refused to pay a debt he owed them, Roosevelt intervened. Using the Monroe Doctrine as his basis, Roosevelt gently, but firmly, negotiated with Kaiser Wilhelm II of Germany to submit his claims to the Hague Tribunal. Kaiser Wilhelm, impressed by the American president, agreed, and the case was submitted to the Hague.

The Hague Tribunal was the fruit of a peace conference that had met at The Hague in Holland from May to July 1899. This conference had adopted a number of conventions to govern the settling of international disputes and warfare. The tribunal was a kind of court to settle any international quarrels before they erupted into war. Theodore Roosevelt warmly supported the Hague Tribunal and became the first world leader to submit a case to it for arbitration.

In his annual message to Congress in 1904, Roosevelt developed the theme of the Monroe Doctrine as it applied to nations in the Caribbean. "Chronic wrongdoing" in these nations, he told Congress, "or an impotence which results in a general loosening of the ties of civilized society . . . may force the United States, however reluctantly, in flagrant cases of such wrongdoing or impotence, to the exercise of an international police power." This "Roosevelt Corollary" to the Monroe Doctrine was an initiative to take the country where it did not, as yet, want to go. Since 1789, the country had mostly followed Washington's advice of staying out of international conflicts, of "isolation," as it would be called. Roosevelt, however, believed it was time the United States assumed what, he thought, was its rightful place as a world power.

Roosevelt applied his corollary to the Dominican Republic in 1904 when that small island nation, through the corruption of its public officials, had to renege on its debts to European creditors. Fearing European intervention in the Caribbean, Roosevelt declared the United

States had to assume the responsibility of making sure "backward" states like the Dominican Republic paid their debts. He established a fiscal protectorate over the Dominican Republic, dedicating 55 percent of that nation's customs revenue to the retirement of the debt. The remainder of the revenue went to the domestic concerns of the small nation.

But the United States would soon learn that the Roosevelt Corollary would involve the country in more than just fiscal supervision. The small nations of Latin America were highly unstable; frequent revolutions rocked these countries, and soon the United States was by Roosevelt's policy forced to establish not only fiscal but military protectorates over them. The burden became so great that in 1930 the government formally revoked the Roosevelt Corollary.

The Russian and Japanese delegations gathered for peace talks at Portsmouth, New Hampshire

Roosevelt loved foreign affairs and involved himself in disputes with foreign countries with a keen relish. In 1905, he intervened in the war between Russia and Japan, bringing both countries to the bargaining table. With careful, tactful diplomacy and much patience, Roosevelt maneuvered representatives of the Russian and Japanese governments, meeting in Portsmouth, New Hampshire, into signing a peace treaty on September 5, 1905. For helping to end this bloody war, Roosevelt received the Nobel Peace Prize and, it was reported, won the admiration and praise of Pope Pius X. "This is the happiest news of my life," said the pope. "Thank God for President Roosevelt's courage." Posterity, though, would not remember this peace treaty so fondly, for it established Japanese power in Manchuria and the Pacific and fanned anti-American feeling among the Japanese, who blamed the United States of robbing their country of territorial acquisitions in Asia. The final results of Roosevelt's good intentions would play themselves out in the Pacific theater in 1939–45.

This peace treaty was not Roosevelt's last dealings with Japan. Reports that, in San Francisco, Japanese children were being segregated from white children in schools roused keen anti-American feeling in Japan. Roosevelt was able to defuse the tense situation by reaching a "gentleman's agreement" with the Japanese foreign minister in 1907: from then on, the Japanese would discourage further immigration to the United States. The Root-Takahira agreement also specified that the United States, Japan, and the European powers would maintain equal trading status with China (called the "Open Door" policy) and that the military status of the United States and Japan would remain unchanged in the Pacific.

Roosevelt's diplomacy reached even into Europe. France was extending her sway over the North African nation of Morocco, and Germany was challenging it. At a conference at Algeciras in 1906, Roosevelt mediated the dispute, which might have erupted into a European-wide conflict. He was finally able to bring both countries to an agreement that called for an independent Morocco that would, nevertheless, be policed by France and Spain. Many in the United States did not approve of Roosevelt's intervention in purely European affairs. In ratifying the peace convention, the Senate added an amendment specifying that the peace convention involved no departure from traditional American foreign policy which forbade participation by the United States in political questions that are entirely European in their scope.

The strength of Roosevelt's Big Stick policy depended on the United States maintaining a strong army and navy. As assistant secretary of the Navy under McKinley, Roosevelt had built up the strength of the American fleet; now as president, he worked to increase the efficiency and effectiveness of the other branches of the military. For one, he appointed men of merit to command positions rather than those who had more seniority. This angered many in the military, but it improved the timbre of the armed forces.

In 1908, Roosevelt sent a naval squadron of 16 battleships under "Fighting Bob" Evans on a grand voyage south along the Atlantic coast, around Cape Horn, and across the Pacific to Auckland, New Zealand; Sydney, Australia; and Yokohama, Japan. The point of this voyage was to test the ships on a long voyage across the Pacific but more to demonstrate to the American people the need for a strong navy. He also wanted to send a "soft" warning to Japan not to violate the Root-Takahira agreement. This time, the big stick behind the soft voice was the young fleet of powerful American warships. And as other countries would realize, this was a mighty stout stick, indeed.

The Waning of Teddy's Reign

In 1906, a young army lieutenant named Douglas McArthur asked Roosevelt what made him so popular with the American public. Roosevelt replied that his popularity was due to his ability "to put into words what is in their hearts and minds but not their mouths." Roosevelt had never been a formal, stiff president; his boisterousness, his broad, toothy smile, his sheer virility had endeared him to the common folk. He was always speaking his mind on a variety of subjects, even on those that didn't fall under his duties as president. Newspapers carried stories about him continually, usually on the front page—even embarrassing ones, as when he wrote to the wife of the ambassador to Italy asking her to lobby the pope to make Archbishop Ireland a cardinal. Such foibles made Roosevelt approachable. His honesty and sincere desire to help better the lot of the common man made Roosevelt admired.

Clifford Berryman's Roosevelt cartoon, with the caption, "Drawing the Line in Mississippi"

Roosevelt's popularity extended into popular culture. In 1902, while hunting in Mississippi, Roosevelt spared the life of an orphaned bear cub. Clifford Berryman, a cartoonist with the *Washington Post*, drew a cartoon depicting Roosevelt in hunting suit, gun in hand, holding his hand aloft in a gesture of refusal while a man in the background holds a bear cub on a leash. A toy store owner and his wife saw the cartoon and sewed a toy stuffed bear, displaying it in their shop window. The toy bear became immensely popular, and Roosevelt permitted the bear's designer to name it after him. Thus, the "Teddy Bear."

In 1907, another financial panic swept the country, and the business interests blamed it on Roosevelt's progressive policies. Roosevelt, in characteristic style, fought back, laying blame for the panic on "the speculative folly and flagrant dishonesty of a few men of great wealth." The answer, he said, was not less progressive legislation but more. "Our laws," said Roosevelt, "have failed in enforcing the performance of duty by the man of property toward the man who works for him, by the corporation toward the investor, the wage-earner, and the general public."

Roosevelt probably could have secured another term as president; at the Republican convention in 1908, a 49-minute demonstration of delegates—marching around the convention hall carrying Teddy Bears and crying "four, four, four years more!"—showed that

A 1909 Puck cartoon depicting Roosevelt handing his "policies" over to Taft

devotion to him was strong. But Roosevelt would not break the promise he made in 1904 not to seek another term. The plain folk of the nation believed in him, said Roosevelt, and he did not want to "destroy their ideal" of him. Instead, he championed the candidacy of his secretary of war, William Howard Taft. Taft had been a judge and had served as governor of the Philippines from 1900 to February 1904, when he became Roosevelt's secretary of war. Though Taft's chief ambition was to sit on the Supreme Court, the ambition of his wife and the support of Roosevelt compelled him to seek the office of president. With Roosevelt's support, Taft could not fail to win the nomination, which he secured after only one ballot.

Since the nomination of a conservative candidate like Judge Parker had failed in 1904, the Democrats chose William Jennings Bryan—again—for their presidential candidate. Disgruntled conservatives who, four years earlier had abandoned Roosevelt for Parker, now returned to the Republican fold and Taft. But, though Bryan pulled one million more votes in the election than Parker had four years earlier, he succeeded in taking the electoral votes of only the Solid South, Nebraska, Colorado, Nevada, and Oklahoma. It was Roosevelt's appointed successor, William Howard Taft, who became president.

The 50-year-old Roosevelt, his term of office ended, returned to his beloved home, Sagamore Hill. "Am I ashamed to say," he said, "I do not miss the White House or being President, one bit." His wife Edith and he, he said, "are enjoying every hour; the walks through the woods in the snow, the red sunsets across the Sound, the brilliant moon, the great log fires indoors." But the strenuous life still called and the lure of a great adventure. In a month he would leave behind the pleasures of a quiet home and be off to hunt big game in Africa.

California Goes Progressive

California had been one of those states where a cadre of very rich men had taken control of state government. From 1879 onward, the "Big Four"—Collis P. Huntington, Leland Stanford, Mark Hopkins, and Charles Crocker (organizers of the Central and Southern Pacific railroads)—kept a tight control of government policies in the Golden State. When Collis Huntington, the last of the Big Four, died in 1900, control of the government passed to Edward H. Herrin, who controlled the state for the next decade.

The unstable character of California society meant no opposition to the political *status quo* had much chance of succeeding. Since the 1870s, California had experienced a number of economic booms. Silk worms were introduced into the state because some speculated that California could become a center for silk production. When that boom busted, cotton growing became the rage. When that failed, the growing of citrus became the next way to strike it rich. This boom, however, had some longevity after farmers joined together in cooperatives to solve problems such as overproduction and high freight rates that had driven many other farmers out of business.

When, in 1885, passenger rates on trains running between Kansas City and Los Angeles dropped dramatically (even to one dollar one way), California experienced a tourism boom. This led, in Southern California, to a real estate boom. Price of land skyrocketed, new towns were laid out, fraud abounded. It is said that real estate agents fixed oranges to the spines of the Joshua Tree (a desert yucca plant), took pictures of a grove of these ersatz citrus trees, and sent them back east to unsuspecting buyers who didn't know they were being sold barren desert ground, not an orange grove. Like most of the other booms, the real estate boom went bust in the late 1880s.

The turn of the century saw an oil boom, an agricultural boom, and a progressive boom. In 1906, the state Republican Party convention was entirely controlled by William Herrin and the corrupt political boss of San Francisco, Abraham Ruef. The following year,

"The Curse of California," a lithograph depicting the railroad as an octopus holding state economic interests (wine, fruit growing, agriculture, mining, etc.) in its tentacles. Looking out from the eyes are (left) Leland Stanford and Mark Hopkins (right), both of the Southern Pacific Railroad.

Republican newspaper editors, lawyers, and others who wanted reform in government met in Oakland and formed the Lincoln-Roosevelt League. The league pledged itself to support progressive candidates for public office, to a reform of the state legislature, to a direct primary (where the people voted for party candidates), and to popular election of senators.

The Lincoln-Roosevelt League did not have to look far to find corruption that cried out for reform. The San Francisco government, which had been under the control of a political organization headed by Eugene Schmitz and Abraham Ruef, was notoriously corrupt,

Abraham Ruef (left), following his conviction and sentence to San Quentin prison

(continued)

wallowing in graft money received from underworld establishments and large businesses. When the great earthquake and fire of April 18, 1906 devastated San Francisco, Schmitz and Ruef did everything they could to profit from the tragedy.

With the aid of William J. Burns, head of the United States secret service (personally recommended by Theodore Roosevelt), the Lincoln-Roosevelt League convinced the grand jury to bring indictments against Ruef, Schmitz, the San Francisco board of supervisors, as well as other prominent San Francisco citizens. The grand jury investigation lasted two years; but, despite the evidence against them, nearly every one of those indicted escaped conviction on some technicality. Ruef, however, was sentenced to 14 years in prison (only four of which he would actually serve). Schmitz too was convicted, but an appeals court nullified the conviction.

Though the grand jury investigation failed to bring about what they wanted, the Lincoln-Roosevelt League

Hiram Johnson

had enough evidence of corruption to run a successful political campaign against the Old Guard. The league nominated Hiram Johnson as their candidate for governor in 1910. Johnson stumped across the state from the Oregon border to San Diego in a motorcar, calling on voters to "kick the Southern Pacific out of politics." The Progressives won the election with large majorities, and Hiram Johnson became governor.

In the coming years, the California legislature passed a number of progressive measures. Under Governor Johnson, the legislature established initiative and referendum, the recall of public officials, as well as the popular election of United States Senators. The government adopted a Public Service Commission that gave the state government power over railroads, gas, and electricity. From being one of the most politically corrupt, California had become one of the most progressive states in the union.

Bull Moose

Standing only five-feet, ten and a half inches tall, but weighing over 300 pounds, William Howard Taft was the largest president ever to occupy the White House. So large was he that a special bathtub had to be constructed in the White House to hold him. But though imposing in girth, Taft was not imposing in character. He was honest, he was methodical; but he had not the electric personality of his predecessor and friend, Teddy Roosevelt. Taft was no politician; he was a judge who had never held an elective office before becoming president. Still, in his own plodding way, he was intent on carrying out Roosevelt's program of reform.

Almost from the beginning, Taft alienated the progressives—a bunch that, Roosevelt himself admitted, had to be kept in line by a strong personality. In choosing his cabinet, Taft selected no progressives; he even replaced a Roosevelt man, James R. Garfield, with Richard A. Ballinger as head of the Department of the Interior—a move that would cost him dear, later on.

Taft's campaign pledge to reduce tariffs was progressive enough. The issue, though, became mixed up with attempts by progressive Republicans to oust conservative "Uncle Joe" Cannon from the speakership of the House. When Cannon, Representative Sereno E. Payne, and Senator Nelson W. Aldrich visited Taft after the inauguration and pledged their support for tariff reduction, Taft promised, in turn, not to back those who wanted to remove Cannon.

William Howard Taft

Aldrich, Cannon, and Payne kept their promise, in a manner of speaking—a tariff bill *was* introduced into the House by Payne and into the Senate by Aldrich. The problem was, this Payne-Aldrich Tariff placed higher rates on imports than had even the tariff of 1897, which progressives so loathed. Taft suggested some changes in the tariff bill that lowered rates, maintained free trade with the Philippines, and established a board to study if and how much protection was really necessary—and all these provisions, and others suggested by the president, were added to the bill. Still, the bill did not reduce tariffs in any way acceptable to progressives.

Leading progressives, such as Senator La Follette and others, expected the president to veto the Payne-Aldrich Tariff bill; they had, they said, enough votes in Congress to sustain the veto. What was their dismay, then, when Taft not only signed the bill but even called it "the best tariff bill that the Republican party passed"! The progressives were stunned, and the first wedge was driven between them and the president.

Then came the accusations leveled against Secretary of the Interior Richard Ballinger by Gifford Pinchot, the head of the Forestry Service. Pinchot alleged that Ballinger had given over valuable coal lands in Alaska to the Morgan-Guggenheim syndicate for its exploitation and private profit. Taft fired Pinchot (Roosevelt's old friend) in 1911 for insubordination toward Ballinger and then referred the question of Ballinger's guilt to Congress. The muckrakers supported Pinchot and stirred up public opinion against Ballinger. Finally, though Congress exonerated him of any charges of wrongdoing, Ballinger resigned as secretary of the Interior. For supporting Ballinger, Taft was abandoned by the progressives.

Richard Ballinger

Ironically, however, Taft's record for progressive legislation was as good, if not better, than Roosevelt's. He supported the Mann-Elkins Act of 1910 that strengthened the Interstate Commerce Commission by granting it the power to suspend transportation rate increases until the railroads could prove the increases were reasonable. The number of prosecutions for violations of the Sherman Anti-Trust Act under Taft's attorney general were double those under Roosevelt's. Taft supported two progressive-inspired amendments to the Constitution, both of which won approval by Congress during his administration. The first, the 16th Amendment, would give power to Congress "to lay and collect taxes on incomes from whatever source derived, without apportionment among the several States and without regard to any census or enumeration." The second, the 17th Amendment, provided for the popular election of United States Senators.

In the area of conservation, Taft accomplished much. He set up reserves on federal oil lands to prevent their private exploitation. Taft, further, asked Congress for the authority to place coal lands in reserve. He established a bureau of mines to protect the nation's reserves of precious metals. Taft's head of the Forestry Service purchased extensive timber lands for preservation in the Appalachians. In his four years as president, Taft accomplished more for conservation than Roosevelt had in his seven years.

Taft's chief problem was that he was an inept politician—and that he was not Roosevelt. Since 1900, real wages had been declining; while the retail cost of food had risen 30 percent, industrial wages had risen only one percent. In 1910 came a sharp increase in the cost of living that was blamed on the Payne-Aldrich Tariff. In the elections that year, Democrats took control of the House of Representatives and made significant gains in the Senate. In the eyes of progressives, it was Taft who was responsible for this, and he could not dispel the suspicions against him.

The Big Game Hunter Returns

Roosevelt had had what he would have called a "bully" time traipsing about Africa, hunting big game. From Africa he had gone to Europe, where he and Edith were wined and dined by the crowned heads of Europe. Everywhere he went, enthusiastic, cheering crowds met him. At the Sorbonne in Paris on April 23, 1910 he gave a speech that, he said, "produced an effect that is really a little difficult for me to understand." Roosevelt was altogether flummoxed by how Europeans received him. "I have been treated as if I combined the functions of visiting sovereign, of distinguished stranger with a wide range of intellectual interests, and of popular orator," he wrote Henry Cabot Lodge:

> The combination has been almost too much. The various sovereigns have vied with one another in entertaining us . . . The popular reception, however, has been even more remarkable. I drive through dense throngs of people cheering and calling, exactly as if I were President and visiting cities at home where there was great enthusiasm for me . . . I have been much puzzled by it.

Roosevelt in Africa

President Taft had an explanation for the enthusiastic reception of the man he still called his friend. "It illustrates," said Taft, "how his personality has swept over the world . . . It is the force of his personality that has passed beyond his own country and the capitals of the world and seeped into the small crevices of the universe."

When Roosevelt returned to New York in June 1910, his boat was escorted by destroyers, a battleship, and pleasure craft. Five hundred Rough Riders escorted their former commander in a parade through the streets of the city. Though he intended to return to Sagamore Hill to take up duties as an editor of the *Outlook*—a magazine that espoused his views—the numerous invitations he received to travel around the country and speak lured him from the comforts of the domestic hearth into the public eye. In 19 days he made a 5,500 mile tour of 14 states and speechified until he was hoarse.

The Roosevelt that had returned was more radical than the Roosevelt that had left America two years earlier. During his time in Africa he had refined and developed his political ideas into what he now called the "New Nationalism." The centerpiece of his political thinking was what he called "social justice," which entailed the reforming of society by political action. "I stand for the square deal," he told an audience at Osawatomie, Kansas on August 31, 1910. What did Roosevelt mean by a "square deal"? I mean not merely that I stand for fair play under the present rules of the game, but . . . for having those rules changed so as to work for a more substantial equality of opportunity and of reward for equally good service. . . . We must drive special interests out of politics."

According to Roosevelt's more radical views, the rich man "holds his wealth subject to the general right of the community to regulate its business use as the public welfare requires." For Roosevelt, the requirements of the public order required the policing action of the state. To compel politicians to take on business interests and the rich, Roosevelt now supported the radical measures of initiative and referendum—and even the public recall of judicial decisions (though this last one, he admitted, was merely the lesser of two evils). But the guiding principle for Roosevelt was popular control of government. "The only safe course to follow in this great American democracy," he said in Columbus, Ohio, "is to provide for making the popular judgment really effective. When this is done, then it is our duty to see that the people, having the full power, realize their heavy responsibility for exercising that power aright."

"We Stand at Armageddon"

"I have had a hard time," Taft had written Roosevelt in May 1910. "I have been conscientiously trying to carry out your policies." Roosevelt, with his ideas of social justice, was growing increasingly critical of his old friend. Taft's appointees to the Supreme Court had nullified much progressive social legislation in the states. Pinchot, Garfield, and their friends now had Teddy's ear, and their criticisms of Taft widened the breach between the friends.

In 1911, Robert La Follette and other progressives formed the National Progressive Republican League. La Follette, who was the spokesman, became the League's candidate for the Republican nomination in 1912; but La Follette was unable to build up much support outside the Mississippi Valley, and in early 1912 he appeared to suffer a nervous breakdown when giving a speech before a national newspaper convention. The disastrous speech sealed La Follette's political fate; and many of his supporters abandoned him.

Though Roosevelt had said he "emphatically did not want" the Republican nomination for president in 1912, the entreaties of La Follette's former followers, newspaper editors, and others that he run, coupled with his disgust at what he thought was Taft's poor performance as president, began to win him over to the idea. When seven progressive state governors wrote him and asked him to run, Roosevelt thought he had no choice. "I will accept the nomination for President if it is tendered to me," he said, "and I will adhere to this decision until the convention has expressed its preference." When a reporter in Columbus, Ohio asked him if he would run, Roosevelt answered, "My hat is in the ring."

Roosevelt knew that the Republican Party bosses would never support his candidacy, so he made sure his name was placed in the running in the 13 states that had popular primaries. (In most states primaries were still controlled by party delegates.) Though he knew that he could never secure the nomination by this means alone, he thought a show of popular support might convince the national convention that he was the man they had better run if they wanted to win. Whether he felt confident of his chances or not, he went to the Republican convention in Chicago saying he felt "like a bull moose."

The Republican convention was divided between supporters of Taft, Roosevelt, and La Follette. Taft and Roosevelt did not spare each other—Taft accusing the ex-president of wanting to stir up class conflict, and he accusing Taft of ungratefulness and of biting the hand that fed him. As he had expected, Roosevelt made an impressive showing in the 13 states with popular primaries, receiving 278 delegates to Taft's 46 and La Follette's 36. Still, the Republican leadership stood with Taft, as did delegates from boroughs in the South. Since the leadership controlled the seating of delegates, nearly every contested seat was given to a Taft man. The result was that Taft was re-nominated with 547 votes, while Roosevelt received only 107, and La Follette, 41.

A 1912 cartoon depicting Roosevelt charging Taft, who is seated on the White House. The caption reads: "Stop! Look!! Listen!!" and quotes "Professor Sam of the Department of Physics," saying: "Gentlemen, we are about to witness what really happens when an Irresistible Force meets an Immovable Body."

Before the final vote had been tallied, Roosevelt, knowing his Republican candidacy was a lost cause, instructed his followers to walk out of the convention. They formed the Progressive Party (nicknamed the "Bull Moose Party," after their leader), which held its convention in Chicago on August 5. The convention delegates displayed all the fervor of a religious revival. Roosevelt's followers paraded around the convention hall, singing "Onward Christian Soldiers" and other stirring songs, and when their leader appeared, they cheered him for nearly an hour. And Teddy addressed them with the unction of a prophet. Whether they win or lose the election, Roosevelt declared, they "shall not falter," and "the movement itself will not stop." He continued:

> Our cause is based on the eternal principle of righteousness . . . you men who . . . have come together to spend and be spent in the endless crusade against wrong, to you who face the future resolute and confident, to you who strive in a spirit of brotherhood for the betterment of our nation, to you who gird yourselves for this great new fight in the never-ending warfare for the good of mankind, I say in closing . . . We stand at Armageddon and we battle for the Lord.

Indeed, Roosevelt expected a kind of Armageddon if Progressive policies were not triumphant. "If the Romanoffs of our social and industrial world are kept at the head of our Government the result will be Bolshevism," he said, "and Bolshevism means disaster to liberty, writ large across the face of this continent." To forestall the triumph of Bolshevism, Teddy and the Progressives called for the popular election of United States Senators; the adoption by states of initiative, referendum, and recall; equal suffrage for men and

A 1912 cartoon depicting Roosevelt and his "Bull Moose Party" as "The Latest Arrival at the Political Zoo." The elephant looking over the wall says, "Suffering Snakes, How Theodore has changed." Scrawled on the barrel are the words, "For stock purposes, compliments of the Harvester Trust."

women; popular recall of judicial decisions; and automatic Supreme Court review of any rulings made by lower federal courts declaring a business policing act of a state legislature was unconstitutional.

In social legislation, the Progressives favored laws "looking to the prevention of industrial accidents, occupational diseases, overwork, involuntary unemployment, and other injurious effects incident to modern industry." They wanted to give to the state and federal governments authority over the "fixing of minimum safety and health standards for the various occupations." They called for the "prohibition of child labor"; "minimum wage standards for working women"; the "general prohibition of night work for women"; an eight-hour work day for women and young workers; the establishment of the eight-hour day "in continuous twenty four-hour industries"; and the "protection of home life against the hazards of sickness, irregular employment and old age through the adoption of a system of **social insurance** adapted to American use." As for conservation, the Progressive platform called for public control of the "remaining forests, coal and oil lands, water powers and other natural resources still in state or National control (except agricultural lands)."

"The doctrines we preach," declared Roosevelt, "reach back to the Golden Rule and the Sermon on the Mount. They reach back to the commandments delivered at Sinai. All that we are doing is to apply those doctrines in the shape necessary to make them available for meeting the living issues of our own day."

The Campaign of 1912

The Democratic Party that met in Baltimore in June 1912 was, as ever, a motley bunch. That a single party could hold together a coalition of such disparate and even conflicting elements was, in a way, amazing. Progressives, under the leadership of William Jennings Bryan; Irish Americans of the large cities of the East and their immigrant cousins; ex-Confederates and agrarians of the South; old conservative Grover Cleveland types; and the newspaper tycoon William Randolph Hearst—all these formed a party that had only once since the Civil War dropped below 43 percent of the popular vote but had only twice won a presidential election. The problem had been, and still was, a lack of leadership.

The problem of no leadership plagued the 1912 convention. Since it was controlled by conservative forces, few thought there was any chance that a progressive candidate could secure the presidential nomination. But since the conservatives were divided between three candidates, Bryan saw an opportunity; he put all his influence behind the progressive governor of New Jersey, Woodrow Wilson, and won him the nomination on the 46th ballot.

Wilson, a native of Staunton, Virginia, had for most of his life been an academic. In 1902 he became president of Princeton University in New Jersey and sought to break the culture of social privilege that characterized the school and make it more democratic. He was largely unsuccessful. Still, Wilson's speeches, addresses, and the articles he wrote won him a national reputation, and in 1910 the conservative political bosses of New Jersey offered him the nomination for governor. Having won the gubernatorial election by a large margin, Wilson set out to fulfill his campaign promise to bring progressive reform to the state.

Little distinguished the platforms of the Progressive and Democratic parties in 1912. What did distinguish them were their respective candidates. Roosevelt was an Old Testament prophet proclaiming the "New Nationalism" amid an industrial wilderness. Wilson, with his "New Freedom," said about the same things as Roosevelt did but sounded less like a revival preacher and more like a Unitarian minister. The "rule of justice and right," he said, must govern the questions of tariffs, trusts, and the demands of labor. With the high moral tone that characterized him, Wilson said things like: "we must effect a great readjustment and get the forces of the whole people once more into play," and "we need no revolution, we need no excited change; we need only a new point of view and a

Woodrow Wilson

---

social insurance: a public program that insures, or provides protection, against risks arising from the economy, such as income loss due to sickness, old age, or unemployment. Sometimes social insurance is called social security.

new method and spirit of counsel." Against two progressive candidates, the third wheel, Taft, appeared hopelessly conservative. For one, he was a poor politician, and he did not take well to attacking Roosevelt. Once, after delivering an anti-Roosevelt speech, he wept. "He was my best friend," Taft said. What's more, with his talk of limited government, of the separation of powers, Taft had little chance of capturing the imagination of the electorate in 1912.

Like Roosevelt, Americans were fearful of "Armageddon." Eugene Debs, the Socialist party's presidential candidate, was gaining steam; in the final vote tally Debs would win six percent of the popular vote, the highest ever for a Socialist candidate in U.S. history. IWW strikes in Lawrence, Massachusetts, dramatized the plight of textile workers who made only $10 for working a 54-hour week. The reality of such misery was cast in the lurid light of labor demonstrations where Wobblies waved red flags and sang the communist *International*—

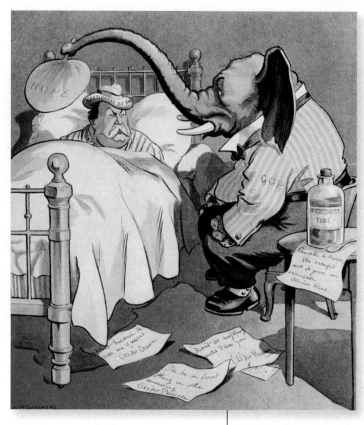

A cartoon from the August 1912 *Puck*, titled, "Sitting Up with A Sick Friend." The Republican elephant with the fan "Hope" comforts a sick Taft, lying in bed with a "Reactionary Ice Bag" on his head. On the table, under a bottle of "Progressivism Tonic," is a note from "Old Dr. Root" (probably Elihu Root, Theodore Roosevelt's secretary of state) that reads, "Caution to Nurse: Be careful not to give an overdose."

> Arise, you prisoners of starvation!
> Arise, you wretched of the earth!
> For justice thunders condemnation.
> A new world is in birth.
> No more tradition's chains shall bind us.
> Arise, you slaves, no more in thrall!
> The earth shall rise on new foundations.
> We have been naught, we shall be all.
> 'Tis the final conflict;
> Let each stand in his place.
> The international working class
> Shall be the human race.

Such talk convinced many common folk that the nation either reform itself or be engulfed in revolution.

So, in the election of 1912, a progressive victory was almost certain. But by splitting the Republican party, Roosevelt had alienated many of his former supporters, some of whom accused him of suffering from messianic delusions. In November, then, Wilson won the election with a landslide of 435 electoral votes, while Roosevelt (carrying California, Michigan, South Dakota, Washington, Minnesota, and Pennsylvania) garnered only 88 electoral votes. Taft came in third, carrying only Utah and Vermont. The popular vote was much closer: Wilson, 6,285,214 votes; Roosevelt, 4,126,020; Taft, 3,483,922. Perhaps if Roosevelt had not split the Republican party, Taft might have won the election.

More significantly, the defection of progressives from the Republican party in 1912 proved permanent. In the coming years, the Republicans would become the party of conservatism, while the Democrats drew all the progressive elements in American politics. Though they won 12 seats in Congress, the Progressive Party, with only Roosevelt to hold it together, could not survive. The election of 1912 proved to be Roosevelt's last foray into national politics. He would decrease, while Wilson and the Democrats increased. Still, the principles of government championed by Roosevelt would live on; progressivism was here to stay. For that reason, Theodore Roosevelt has been, for good or ill, one of the most pivotal figures in American history.

Roosevelt Shot

In Milwaukee, the crowds that came to hear the Bull Moose candidate speak were aghast. He stood before them at the rostrum, his shirt soaked with blood. "Colonel Roosevelt has been shot. He is wounded," had said the presiding officer standing at the candidate's side.

Shortly before Roosevelt had entered the auditorium, a saloon-keeper, who had nursed a grudge against him since the days he had been police commissioner in New York, pulled out a gun and shot him in the chest. Fortunately for Roosevelt, the bullet hit his steel glasses case and had to pass through a thickly folded copy of the speech he would give that night and so was deflected from striking his heart.

Struck by the bullet, Roosevelt fell; but he quickly got up. He told the crowds not to hurt the assailant and then he spat on his hand to see if he were bleeding from his lungs. Seeing no blood, Roosevelt

"We are against his politics, but we like his grit," New York Herald, 1912

insisted on proceeding to the auditorium to give his speech.

Standing at the rostrum and hearing the expressions of horror from the crowd, Roosevelt said, "I don't know whether you fully understand that I have just been shot; but it takes more than that to kill a Bull Moose!" He then held up his speech, showing the crowd where the bullet passed. "The bullet is in me now, so that I cannot make a very long speech, but I will try my best."

Despite continuous appeals that he seek the aid of a doctor, Roosevelt spoke for an hour and a half. The *New York Herald* later ran a cartoon showing Roosevelt with a bullet-torn sheet of paper in his hand. The caption read, "We are against his politics, but we like his grit."

Roosevelt afterwards took the shooting in stride. "I did not care a rap for being shot," he wrote in a letter. "It is a trade risk, which every prominent public man ought to accept as a matter of course. For eleven years I have been prepared any day to be shot."

Big Government

"MY FELLOW CITIZENS: There has been a change of government. It began two years ago, when the House of Representatives became Democratic by a decisive majority. It has now been completed. The Senate about to assemble will also be Democratic. The offices of President and Vice-President have been put into the hands of Democrats. What does the change mean?" The new president, Woodrow Wilson, posed this question to the people gathered to hear his inaugural address. The change meant, he said, "much more than the mere success of a party"; it meant that the nation sought to use the Democratic party "to interpret a change in its own plans and point of view."

Wilson praised the industrial and material development of the nation. He drew attention to the "great system of government, which has stood through a long age as in many respects a model for those who see to set liberty upon foundations that will endure against fortuitous change, against storm and accident." Yet, he asserted that "evil has come with the good." Americans have been wasteful with nature. They have not "stopped thoughtfully enough to count the human cost" of the nation's "industrial achievements." Furthermore, "the great Government we loved has too often been made use of for private and selfish purposes, and those who used it had forgotten the people."

The duty that lay before the American people, said Wilson, "is to cleanse, to reconsider, to restore, to correct the evil without impairing the good, to purify and humanize every process of our common life without weakening or sentimentalizing it.

There has been something crude and heartless and unfeeling in our haste to succeed and be great. Our thought has been, "Let every man look out for himself, let every generation look out for itself," while we reared giant machinery which made it impossible that any but those who stood at the levers of control should have a chance to look out for themselves. We had not forgotten our morals. We remembered well enough that we had set up a policy which was meant to serve the humblest as well as the most powerful, with an eye single to the standards of justice and fair play, and remembered it with pride. But we were very heedless and in a hurry to be great.

Wilson then laid out his agenda: a reformed tariff, aid to agriculture, conservation of forests and water-courses, the study and perfection of the means of putting government "at the service of humanity." The "first duty of law" said Wilson, "is to keep sound the society it serves. Sanitary laws, pure food laws, and laws deterring conditions of labor which individuals are powerless to determine for themselves are intimate parts of the very business of justice and legal efficiency."

Wilson, however, made it clear that he proposed no revolutionary changes, as least as far as business was concerned. "We shall deal with our economic system as it is and as it may be modified," he said, "not as it might be if we had a clean sheet of paper to write upon; and step by step we shall make it what it should be . . . Justice, and only justice, shall always be our motto."

Wilson's peroration was characteristic of him:

This is not a day of triumph; it is a day of dedication. Here muster, not the forces of party, but the forces of humanity. Men's hearts wait upon us; men's lives hang in the balance; men's hopes call upon us to say what we will do. Who shall live up to the great trust? Who dares fail to try? I summon all honest men, all patriotic, all forward-looking men, to my side. God helping me, I will not fail them, if they will but counsel and sustain me!

Wilson came to the presidency amidst a general feeling of optimism about the future. Though problems still plagued the nation, Americans felt they could deal with and master them. What was needed, it was believed, was good, progressive legislation. Laws and a vigorous federal government could address the inequalities and make smooth the way for material progress to better conditions for everyone. Perhaps a lasting peace between nations was attainable through moral progress and by means of such a tribunal as The Hague that could deal with disputes between nations.

Wilson was an eloquent speaker and aptly expressed the moral aspirations of his time. Unlike Roosevelt, though, the new president was more effective at the rostrum than in person. He loved humanity but had difficulty dealing with common people, to whom he appeared aloof. Roosevelt, who had been a rancher, could speak to the common man on a personal basis, for he had worked and lived with him. Wilson displayed his warmth and keen sense of humor among his family and close friends; but to others he was, in the words of Franklin Lane, his Secretary of the Interior, "clean, strong, high-minded, and cold-blooded."

Progressive Legislation

Wilson revived a practice that had died with Jefferson: in person he addressed both houses of Congress together instead of appointing another to read his address to them. This was necessary for Wilson, for he was ineffective when dealing with lawmakers one-on-one. He lacked the "bull moose" quality of speaking softly but carrying a big stick. It was his eloquence that would carry through Congress the legislation he wanted.

One of Wilson's first acts was to call Congress into special session to consider two items of legislation. The first was reducing the tariff on foreign imports. Though Republicans would balk, Wilson knew he could count on the support of many Democrats in both House and

Senate, and on Progressives. On October 3, 1913, Congress passed the Underwood Tariff, which enacted the lowest rates on foreign imports since the Civil War. But the most significant part of Underwood was not its tariff provisions (though these were significant), but the fact that a graduated federal income tax was appended to the bill and became law.

This federal income tax was not the first of its kind. During the Civil War, both the federal and Confederate governments levied income taxes; the former, a tax of three percent on "annual gains, profits or incomes from any source whatsoever" between $600 and $10,000 a year; the latter, on incomes of $500 or more a year. The federal tax was later changed to a flat rate of ten percent and then abolished in 1872. In 1894, during the panic, the federal government levied a tax of two percent per year on businesses and individual incomes over $4,000, but the tax never went into effect because the Supreme Court declared an income tax unconstitutional in *Pollock v. Farmers' Loan and Trust Company*.

In a five-to-four decision, the justices in *Pollock* declared the federal income tax to be a direct tax on individuals and this, they said, was forbidden by Article 1, Section 9 of the Constitution: "No **Capitation**, or other direct, Tax shall be laid unless in Proportion to the Census or Enumeration herein before directed to be taken." Taxing income on personal property, said the court, is the same as taxing property, and the Constitution only allows a direct federal tax on property to be levied in proportion to the population of each state. The income tax of 1894 laid a direct tax on citizens, regardless of state boundaries.

The 16th Amendment, ratified in February 1913, amended Article 1, Section 9 of the Constitution and so nullified the Supreme Court's 1895 decision. The new Underwood income tax levied a tax of one percent on individuals (with incomes exceeding $3,000 per year) and married couples (with incomes over $4,000 a year), with an added tax (surtax) of one to six percent on incomes exceeding $20,000 a year. Corporations were taxed at one percent a year. These were rather low rates, and most Americans were unaffected by the income tax; but that would change over time.

The Underwood Tariff has been called one of Wilson's most important achievements. The second piece of legislation passed under the special session of Congress in 1913 has been called another of his triumphs. Since the days of Andrew Jackson, the United States, unlike other industrial countries, had no central bank that governed the activities of local banks. Many claimed the lack of a central bank made the supply of money "inelastic"—that is, unable to adjust to the needs of production and consumption. Lack of elasticity, it was said, led to periodic panics and depressions. Local and state banks maintained no uniformity with one another. Thus, many argued, a central bank was needed to maintain uniformity in the issuing of money and credit across the nation.

One difficulty was that Jackson's spirit was still alive among the American people, and, in particular, in the Democratic party. Thus, the challenge was to create a central bank that wasn't centralized—or, at least, didn't appear to be centralized. The result was the Federal Reserve Act, adopted by Congress on December 23, 1913. The Federal Reserve Act divided the country into 12 districts, each with its own Federal Reserve bank. These banks were private but were governed by a Federal Reserve Board, whose members were to be appointed by the president. The Federal Reserve could issue bank notes, or paper currency. It could also govern the amount of credit local member banks could issue and the amount of interest they could charge on loans. The Federal Reserve was created to regulate the supply of money and credit so they could expand when production slowed and remain stable when production increased

Wilson sponsored other progressive legislation that further extended federal power over business. Wilson pushed for, and Congress passed, the Federal Trade Commission. In 1914, Congress passed the Clayton Anti-Trust Act of 1914, which Samuel Gompers called "labor's charter of rights," since it declared that labor unions had never been, in themselves, unlawful combinations; that strikes, boycotts were not, as such, violations of federal law; and that federal courts could not use injunctions (as during the Pullman strike) in labor disputes. Other legislation included a law granting workman's compensation for the federal civil ser-

capitation: a direct, uniform tax the government imposes on each person; a poll tax

vices and a law forbidding the interstate commerce in products derived from child labor. This last law the Supreme Court declared unconstitutional.

The centralization of the nation under the federal government that began under Abraham Lincoln had continued apace throughout the 19th century. At first a growth in federal power was justified as a means of securing the rights of freemen in the South, and the passage of the 14th Amendment was a watershed moment in this connection. In the latter part of the 19th century, government did little to intervene in the affairs of big business that had begun to dominate the nation, except, at times, to break the power of labor's opposition. With Teddy Roosevelt things changed. Government grew and centralized to meet the challenges of a centralized business class. Woodrow Wilson continued this progressive trend and solidified it; but he was not its culmination. The coming years would see a further growth and centralization of government in the United States and prove that big government, like big business, was seemingly here to stay.

An anti-income tax cartoon from 1913, showing a turkey labeled, "Income Tax Litigation." The caption reads, "Lawyers at least have plenty to be thankful for."

Chapter 23 Review

Summary

- Discontent and factions divided the people of Cuba, and separatists sparked a revolt against Spanish rule. Because of this and a depressed economy, Cubans emigrated to the United States where they formed *juntas* to foster revolution in Cuba. Americans in the United States were in favor of the revolutionaries, but President McKinley was hesitant to go to war because business interests opposed it.

- The explosion of the *Maine*, an American battleship, in Havana harbor stirred up war fever in the United States. McKinley tried to avoid war, but Congress pushed for it. Finally, on April 11, 1898, McKinley asked Congress for a declaration of war against Spain. The House of Representatives passed a resolution demanding that Spain grant Cuba its independence. When McKinley ordered the blockading of all Cuban ports, Spain declared war on the United States.

- Roosevelt and his Rough Riders captured San Juan Hill, which made them national heroes. In July the American army besieged the city of Santiago. The Spanish surrendered, thus ending the fighting in Cuba.

- The American army invaded the island of Puerto Rico on July 25. Meanwhile, Commodore Dewey, with the help of Filipino rebel forces, took the city of Manila in the Philippines on August 13.

- On July 26, the Spanish government asked for terms of peace. McKinley issued his terms, and though they were hard, Spain signed a preliminary peace on August 12, 1898.

- In July of 1898, the United States Senate approved the treaty annexing Hawai'i. A discussion about whether the Philippines should be annexed or not was taken up. Some thought it necessary to subjugate peoples like the Filipinos in order to achieve world progress, while some opposed an imperial America. Mark Twain formed the Anti-Imperialist

Chapter 23 Review (continued)

League. Despite protests, however, the United States agreed to pay $20 million to Spain for the Philippine islands in December 1898. The Filipino insurgents did not want annexation, however; they wanted independence. This situation resulted in a struggle between United States forces and Filipino insurgents in the Philippines.

- After occupying the Philippines, the United States began exerting its influence in the Far East. U.S. Secretary of State John Hay announced an "open door policy" in regards to China in 1899 to assure Americans that they would not be edged out of the Chinese market by other nations. During the Boxer Rebellion in 1900, the United States participated in an expeditionary force to relieve Peking.

- In the elections of 1900, McKinley was reelected, with Theodore Roosevelt as his vice president. In 1901 an anarchist's bullet killed President McKinley, and Roosevelt was sworn in as president.

- President Roosevelt represented an ideology that called for protections for workers and a regulation of business for the sake of justice but conceded that big industry was here to stay. Roosevelt thought the best anyone could hope for was a bettering of the conditions of labor instead of an overthrow of or any radical change to the social order.

- In 1905 industrial workers formed the Industrial Workers of the World, an industrial union organization that united workers of all trades and industries, both skilled and unskilled. Socialism, too, began to attract adherents in America.

- Throughout his political career, Roosevelt promoted reform in favor of the common man against corruption. When he became president, he announced that he would enforce the laws to break up trusts. When J.P. Morgan moved to consolidate three railroads in a trust called the Northern Securities Corporation, Roosevelt prosecuted him, and on April 9, 1903, a United States circuit court dissolved the Northern Securities Corporation. Roosevelt next brought suit against the American Tobacco Company and Standard Oil and set up departments of commerce and of labor, with a bureau to gather facts for enforcing anti-trust laws.

- A strike amongst coal workers in Pennsylvania in 1902 brought the labor question to the forefront of the public mind once again. John Mitchell, the leader of the strike, asked Roosevelt to set up a tribunal where representatives of both labor and management could arbitrate the strike. The owners derided the request and wanted Roosevelt to send in federal troops. Roosevelt did not send in troops but set up an arbitration board that investigated the situation, returned the workers to their jobs, and decided that the workers would receive a ten percent increase in their pay and a decrease in work hours.

- Roosevelt was a strong proponent of the family and critical of those who encouraged small families. He promoted policies that he thought would strengthen the material basis of family life.

- Roosevelt was reelected to a second term in 1904. During his second term he tempered his trust-busting ways somewhat. He continued and accelerated a tendency toward the centralization of power in the federal government.

- The Roosevelt administration was eager to build a canal connecting the Atlantic and the Pacific. On June 29, 1907, the Senate passed the Spooner Act that authorized the president to pay a French company for the concession to build the canal across the Isthmus of Panama. The only thing needed was the approval of the Colombian government, but the Colombian government refused to cooperate. Fortunately for Roosevelt, revolutionaries in Panama wanted their state to secede from Colombia, and the United States offered its support to the revolutionaries. On November 3, 1903, the new Republic of Panama declared its independence, and on November 18, Panama leased the canal zone to the United States.

- Roosevelt did not wield his "big stick" policy only over Colombia. When Great Britain, Germany, and Italy blockaded the coast of Venezuela, Roosevelt intervened, negotiating with Kaiser Wilhelm II of Germany to submit his claims to the Hague Tribunal.

- In 1904, Roosevelt developed his corollary to the Monroe Doctrine that would allow the United States to intervene in the affairs of other North and South American nations.

- In 1908, Roosevelt did not run again, and the presidency went to his friend, William Howard Taft.

President Taft alienated Roosevelt's allies, the progressives, though his administration is responsible for a number of progressives policies.

- In 1910 Roosevelt returned from hunting in Africa, where he had refined and developed his political ideas into what he called the "New Nationalism." Though he said he did not want the Republican nomination for president in 1912, various entreaties and circumstances won him over to the idea. Losing the nomination to Taft, Roosevelt ran on the Progressive Party ticket. The presidency went to the Democrats with the election of Woodrow Wilson.

- The 16th Amendment, ratified in February 1913, amended Article 1, Section 9 of the Constitution and so nullified an 1894 Supreme Court decision that declared an income tax unconstitutional.

- President Wilson passed two pieces of legislation that have been called his most important achievements. Under Wilson, Congress passed the Underwood Tariff on October 3, 1913, which enacted not only the lowest rates on foreign imports to date, but a graduated federal income tax as well. On December 23, Congress passed the Federal Reserve Act.

Key Concepts

imperialism: the policy of extending a nation's power and dominion by acquiring foreign territory or establishing indirect control of the political life of another country

Progressivism: an American political movement that, like Populism, sought the regulation of business through government action to remedy abuses and to benefit workers and the citizenry as a whole. Unlike Populists, however, Progressives did not seek any radical change for the social order.

social insurance: a public program that insures, or provides protection, against risks arising from the economy, such as income loss due to sickness, old age, or unemployment. Sometimes social insurance is called social security.

Dates to Remember

1898: the American battleship *Maine* explodes in Havana harbor (February 15).

1898: President McKinley orders a blockade of all Cuban ports (April 22).

Spain declares war on the United States (April 24).

Commodore Dewey captures Manila Bay in the Philippines (May 1).

The Spanish garrison at Santiago surrenders, ending the fighting in Cuba (July 17).

The United States signs a peace treaty with Spain (December 10).

1901: Death of President McKinley. Theodore Roosevelt becomes president.

1903: Panama leases the canal zone to the United States.

1909: William Howard Taft becomes president.

1912: Woodrow Wilson defeats Taft and Roosevelt in the presidential election.

1913: Congress passes the Underwood Tariff and the Federal Reserve Act.

Central Characters

William McKinley (1843–1901): 25th president of the United States. He led the United States in the war against Spain that acquired Puerto Rico, Guam, and the Philippines for the United States.

Theodore Roosevelt (1858–1919): 26th president of the United States. He championed progressive policies in the domestic sphere and steered the nation toward an active role in world politics.

William Howard Taft (1857–1930): 27th president of the United States. He alienated the progressives and later his friend, Theodore Roosevelt, but continued the progressive legacy he had inherited from Roosevelt.

Woodrow Wilson (1856–1924): 28th president of the United States. He championed progressive policies and signed laws establishing an income tax and the Federal Reserve system.

Questions for Review

1. Why did the United States go to war with Spain?
2. What did the war with Spain achieve for the United States?

Chapter 23 Review (continued)

3. Why was the United States interested in the annexation of Hawai'i and the Philippines, but not Cuba?

4. Explain how the International Workers of the World differed from unions like the American Federation of Labor.

5. Describe the contributions American Catholics made to the labor question.

6. How did Progressivism as a movement differ from Populism?

7. What were Roosevelt's policies on industry and trusts?

8. What two evils did Roosevelt see as threatening the American family? How did he think the country might address those threats?

9. Why were Roosevelt and others eager to build a canal in Panama?

10. What are some of Roosevelt's achievements in international affairs?

11. Why did progressives disapprove of President Taft? Were their criticisms entirely just? Please explain.

12. Describe Roosevelt's "New Nationalism."

13. What, according to Woodrow Wilson's first inaugural address, was the duty that lay before the American people? How does this duty tie into Wilson's agenda of reform?

Ideas in Action

1. Research the ideas of the American imperialists and anti-imperialists (such as Mark Twain) of the late 19th and early 20th centuries. Stage a debate between proponents of American imperial expansion and those opposed to it.

2. Roosevelt justified the use of the United States military as a "police power" to intervene when grave imbalances occurred in neighboring North and South American nations. He thought that it was time for the United States to take its rightful place in the world. If, as the Declaration of Independence says, all government must arise from the consent of the governed, how can Americans justify intervening in the political and economic affairs of foreign nations?

3. Discuss Roosevelt's opinion that, at times, the president must go beyond the powers granted him by the Constitution to address a crisis in national life. Recall, that Roosevelt cited the example of Abraham Lincoln in support of his position. Are such actions by a president every justified? Why or why not?

4. Roosevelt thought the powers of the federal government needed to be as extensive, or more extensive, than the power of business, in order to regulate business. Given that governments exist to promote and protect the common good, was Roosevelt correct?

5. Research the culture of either Puerto Rico, Cuba, Hawai'i, or the Philippines and what effect the United States has had on those cultures.

Highways and Byways

The Jumping Flea

People often associate the ukulele, a small member of the guitar family, with Hawai'i. The ukelele is, in fact, a 19th century Hawai'ian version of the "machete," a small guitar-like instrument introduced into Hawai'i by Portuguese immigrants. The name "ukulele" translates roughly as "jumping flea," perhaps so named because of the movement of the player's fingers over the strings. The last queen of Hawai'i, Liliuokalani, is said to have translated the name as "the gift that came here," from the words *uku* (gift or reward) and *lele* (to come). Hawai'i's King Kalakaua (1836–1891) was an important figure in the establishment of the ukulele in Hawai'ian music and culture. As a patron of the arts, the king incorporated the instrument into performances at royal gatherings.

The ukulele is generally made out of wood, and it usually has four strings, originally made from catgut. Sometimes the strings are doubled, giving the instrument six to eight strings—a version of the instrument called a taropatch ukulele. Ukuleles come in four different sizes: soprano, concert, tenor, and baritone. The soprano is the most common size and is the standard in Hawai'i. Since its introduction in Hawai'i, the ukulele has spread throughout the world, including countries such as the United States, Canada, Japan, and Great Britain.

THE SECOND MEXICAN REVOLUTION

To Throw Down the Mighty

The centennial celebration on September 16, 1910 of Hidalgo's *grito de Dolores* was a lavish affair. Mexico's president, Don Porfirio Díaz, spared no expense (he spent 22 million *pesos*) to commemorate Mexico's independence from Spain. Banquets, military parades, historical pageants, and Don Porfirio himself decked out in his handsome military uniform, solemnized this great day. Still, the celebrations of the day seemed to have less to do with Hidalgo and his ragged Indian army than with the achievements of Don Porfirio himself who, dictator that he was, had brought Mexico into the 20th century.

Foreign leaders had nothing but praise for Díaz. Among them was Theodore Roosevelt's secretary of state, Elihu Root. In 1907, he offered this toast to the president of Mexico:

> If I were a poet I should write eulogies; if I were a musician I should compose triumphal marches; if I were a Mexican I should feel that the steadfast loyalty of a lifetime would not be too much to give in return for the blessings he has brought to my country. But as I am neither poet, musician, nor Mexican, but only an American who loves justice and liberty, and hopes to see their reign among mankind progress and strengthen and become perpetual, I look to Don Porfirio Díaz, the President of Mexico, as one of the great men to be held up for the hero worship of mankind!

This was high praise, indeed! What had Díaz done to deserve it? For one thing, he had brought peace to Mexico. Since 1876, Mexico had suffered from no civil war. Peace in Mexico had been good for foreign investors, who no longer worried that their property might be confiscated by the next rebel army that "pronounced" against the government. Mexico had become a treasure trove for foreign railroad companies, industrialists, and mining interests.

Porfirio Díaz

Don Porfirio believed that investments of foreign capital in Mexico were necessary if Mexico ever were to be modernized and "civilized." His government paid six to nine thousand *pesos* to foreign railroad companies (chiefly from the United States) for every kilometer of railroad track they laid down. Since the Mexican government made no demands as to where the tracks should be laid, just that they were laid, railroads were built to benefit American commerce, not the people of Mexico. Díaz commissioned real estate corporations to survey government-owned lands and allowed them to take one-third of those lands as their payment. Díaz's government sold the remainder of the land to generals, politicians,

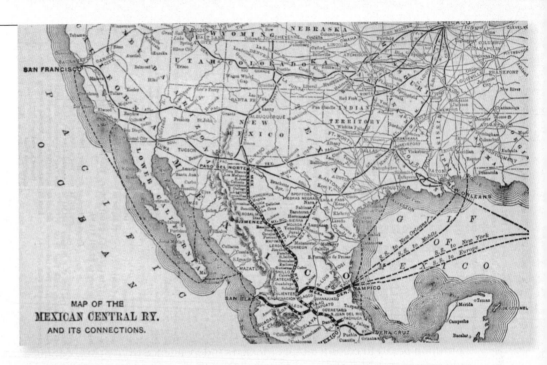

A late 19th century map showing the route of the Mexican Central Railroad and its connections. The map demonstrates how railroads in Mexico were built to facilitate trade with the United States.

MAP OF THE
MEXICAN CENTRAL RY.
AND ITS CONNECTIONS.

and U.S. capitalists. In this way, most government lands fell into the hands of foreigners, and rich and powerful Mexicans.

Though much of the government lands were not arable, they had rich mineral deposits. When the Mining Code of 1884 gave landowners the rights to the minerals below the surface, more American capitalists invested in Mexico. They mined the rich lodes of silver, gold, copper, lead, and zinc and exploited the oil fields; but this wealth mostly did not enrich the Mexican people; it passed into the coffers of American companies north of the border. By the turn of the century, foreign investors owned most of the wealth of Mexico. American investors, more than any others, profited hugely off Mexico. United States Steel, Standard Oil, McCormick, Doheny, and other American capitalists owned three-fourths of all mines and one-half of all the oil fields in Mexico.

Under Díaz, many *mestizos* rose to wealth and prominence, in part through the confiscation of Indian lands. In 1888 and 1902, the Díaz government enforced the *Ley Lerdo*, which forbade any but individuals to own land, and many Indian tribes had to surrender *ejidos* (communally-held lands) that had been theirs since the days of Cortés. When some Indian tribes resisted, they were brutally crushed by the military and by *rurales*, former bandits who served as Díaz's police. In the state of Hidalgo, *rurales* galloped over the heads of recalcitrant Indians, buried up to the neck in their native soil. The Yaqui in the north and the Mayas in the south were reduced to virtual slavery after the government crushed their rebellions. The Mayas were forced to work in slave gangs on plantations to produce henequen for American rope companies and chicle for American manufacturers of chewing gum.

The sale of government lands and the confiscation of Indian lands led to a great disparity in wealth in Mexico. By 1910, fewer than 3,000 families controlled about one-half of Mexico. Though some—albeit few—native Mexicans profited, foreigners controlled the lion's share of the plantations (producing sugar, coffee, henequen, cotton, rubber, and tropical fruits) and the textile, iron, and steel mills. Though this prevented most Mexicans from owning property, Díaz was able to placate members of the middle class by giving them well-paying government jobs. Between 1876 and 1910, the government bureaucracy grew by about 900 percent. As for the governing classes, Díaz either controlled the generals and states' governors or played rivals against each other to keep them weak or bribed them with offices, monopolies, and government contracts. No one could be elected to office unless he had

received the president's blessing; thus, the congress was filled with Don Porfirio's yes men. Díaz controlled the lower classes by brute force. *Pan ó palo*—"bread or the club"—is how Don Porfirio described his peculiar form of crowd control.

Under the influence of Carmen, his young and beautiful wife, and her father, interior secretary Romero Rubio, Díaz had even made peace with the Church. Like many Liberals, Rubio's attitudes toward freedom and the hated Catholic Church changed when he became wealthy. With Rubio's support, Carmen's confessor arranged a meeting between Díaz and Mexico's archbishop, Antonio Pelagio Labastida y Dávalos. Don Porfirio and Archbishop Labastida reached a secret agreement. In return for non-enforcement of the anti-clerical Laws of the Reform, Labastida agreed to allow Díaz to approve all Church appointments. The archbishop would also see to it that priests preached submission to the Díaz government.

The secret agreement allowed the Church in Mexico once again to acquire property. The Church built schools; men's and women's monasteries and convents spread across the land. Clergy received better training in seminaries, and from the 500 or so native clergy in the days of Juárez, the number of priests swelled to 5,000, though a large number of these were not Mexican but Spanish, French, and Italian. These clergy began mobilizing the laity, oversaw the the expansion of the Catholic press as well as Catholic education. Yet, despite these benefits, the Church became subservient to the dictator, who could enforce the Laws of the Reform against her any time the bishops or priests fell out of line. Allying herself with Díaz, too, eventually alienated the Church from many of the people who groaned under the weight of the dictatorship.

But if the Catholic Church in Mexico did not directly challenge the Díaz regime, sectors of it began taking a serious and critical look at the society Don Porfirio had created. Inspired by German Catholic social thought and, more importantly, Pope Leo XIII's 1891 social encyclical, *Rerum Novarum,* the younger generation of priests and laity both began to turn their attention to questions of social justice. Indeed, it was Catholic priests and a few bishops who, in the waning years of Díaz's regime, were the leaders of the movement for social justice in Mexico. Their consciences awakened, Catholics formed Catholic Workers Circles and held social justice congresses in Puebla (1903), Morelia (1904), Guadalajara (1906), and Oaxaca (1909). Based on a study of working class conditions, the Oaxaca congress sternly condemned "the unseemly, harsh, despotic, and arrogant manner in which the workers

A street market in
Mexico City, 1885 (left),
Peons in Mexico City
(right)

in the factories are treated with grievous damage to their dignity." But more pointed was
Querétaro's Bishop Banegas y Galván's assessment of the times. Speaking of the working
conditions that many Mexicans endured, Bishop Banegas said:

> The worker, in return for this terribly exhausting labor, receives between 18 and 25
> *centavos* a day, which is paid partly in seeds and partly in cash, and even with these low
> wages, there are some landowners who find ingenious ways of reducing them further
> . . . We understand Socialism . . . You rich men, there is no way open; either you must
> open your hearts to charity and reduce the hours of work and increase wages, or you are
> accumulating hatred and resentment . . . and your riches and yourselves will be buried.

But, though he had himself risen from a humble condition, President Díaz was deaf to
such warnings; for Carmen Díaz had worked another transformation in her husband. Don
Porfirio, half Indian, had been a rough *guerrillero;* his wife made him a refined "creole"
gentleman. She taught him manners, how to eat at table, how to behave in polite society.

This external transformation of Don Porfirio mirrored a transformation in his government. A group of young men who had grown up since Juárez's revolution were changing the
complexion of the administration from a *mestizo* to a creole dominated one. Called *científicos,* these young men believed that the good of Mexico lay in the material progress that came
through the application of science to social and economic life. Believing the Mexican people
incapable of Liberal democracy, the *científicos* enthusiastically embraced the Díaz dictatorship. Since they believed the Mexican people barbarous, these young men thought civilization could only come to Mexico through the rule of the "white" creole aristocracy and the
importation of foreign capital.

After 1895, the leader of the *científicos* was José Ives Limantour, the son of a French
immigrant. After Limantour became director of the treasury in 1893, the Mexican economy
prospered. For the first time in history, the Mexican government was bringing in more revenue than it was paying out. Railroads were nationalized; harbors, government buildings,
theaters were built; telegraph and telephone lines spanned the land. Illiteracy decreased.
Poetry and the arts flourished. Even the capital, Mexico City, was cleaned up and modernized: the streets, cleared of beggars and *léperos,* were lit with electric lights, and streetcars

carried people hither and yon. With all the improvements, all the new, white marble buildings, Mexico City was becoming (some said) the Paris of the New World.

Thus, Don Porfirio became the toast of the world. (Some American businessmen even said that, instead of the progressive Teddy Roosevelt, Washington needed a man like Díaz.) The great centennial celebration went off without a hitch, and Don Porfirio, it seemed, had reached the acme of his glory.

Though Díaz celebrated the memory of Hidalgo on September 16, 1910, his administration had crushed the very people whose cause Hidalgo had championed. The rural poor, reduced to practical slavery, suffered

President Díaz (at left) during the Mexican centennial celebration

from ignorance, want, and hunger. Shorn of their lands, Indian peons had only the pittance paid them by rich *hacendados* to rely on for their subsistence. Under Limantour prices had doubled; and with their buying power drastically decreased, the peons sank into wretched poverty.

The poor working in the factories, though better paid than the rural workers, were still in grievous want. Yet their spirits were not crushed; they were growing revolutionary. Immigrants from Spain were telling their Mexican comrades of anarchism. Those Mexicans who had gone to the United States in search of work had joined the anarchist International Workers of the World ("Wobblies") and were returning to Mexico with subversive ideas. Socialism, too, began to spread among the ranks of the factory workers. Between 1900 and 1910, these movements inspired the formation of unions and strikes. Though the Díaz government harshly suppressed these strikes, it could not hide the fact that beneath the glittering pageantry of the Great Centennial all was not as well with Mexico as Díaz and the "civilized" world had supposed.

The Fall of Don Porfirio

Resistance to *El Porfiriato*—Díaz's regime—had already begun south of Mexico City, in the tiny state of Morelos.

Since the 1880s, Morelos had become a major producer of sugar cane, and haciendas had been seizing the lands of small farmers and Indian *ejidos*, forcing their owners to work as peons on the ever-growing sugar-cane plantations. One such hacienda was *El Hospital,* which threatened lands held by the peasants of the village of Anencuilco. *El Hospital* would have successfully absorbed the small property around Anencuilco as it, and other haciendas, had successfully done with Indian lands before but for one unexpected factor: a man named Emiliano Zapata.

Emiliano Zapata, the son of a *mestizo* share-cropper and small landowner, did not share the poverty of the Indians among whom he lived. Emiliano was known far and wide as a successful horse trainer—a profession that could have earned him more money and brought a higher social status in nearby Mexico City, had he chosen to go there. Money and social status, though, did not move Zapata; the cause of justice and freedom for his people did. Born into a family that had fought under Juárez against the imperialists, Emiliano had from infancy imbibed ideals of liberty for the small man and small landowner—though Juárez himself had, in the end, betrayed these ideals. For Zapata, however, *Juárismo* did not include a disdain for

Emiliano Zapata

the Catholic faith. Emiliano and his men would go into battle with images of Our Lady of Guadalupe pinned to their sombreros.

Elected to lead the defense committee of Anencuilco in September 1909, Zapata decided to meet head on the threat of *El Hospital*. Under Zapata's lead, the villagers peacefully reoccupied land the hacienda had seized and then divided it among themselves. Such a bold deed spread Zapata's fame throughout the state of Morelos.

A sense of imminent change was abroad in Mexico in 1909 and 1910. In the United States, *Pearson's Magazine* published an interview with Don Porfirio—the "Thrilling Story of President Díaz, the Greatest Man on the Continent."—wherein Don Porfirio told journalist James Creelman that he thought that Mexico, at long last, was ready for democracy. What's more, Díaz, who had been president of Mexico for most of 34 years, said he would not run for president in 1910! Perhaps Díaz thought the interview would be read only north of the border, but Mexicans south of the border read it and were astonished. The interview encouraged Díaz's opposition to express their views publicly.

Francisco Madero

Díaz's opposition included a rather unlikely figure for the political part he was to play. A small man (five-feet, two inches tall), Francisco Madero came from a rich Mexican family that controlled vast lands in the northern state of Coahuila. Educated in both France and the United States, Francisco was the family odd-ball: he was a teatotaller, a spiritualist, and a vegetarian. While managing the family's cotton plantation, he spent the profits on building houses and schools and providing medical services for his peasant workers. In 1908, Madero wrote a book in which he suggested that the country return to the Constitution of 1857 and that Díaz not seek re-election. The book, mildly stated though it was, made Madero a popular figure.

President Díaz, perhaps, thought the puny Madero could cause him no real trouble. In 1909, Díaz did nothing while Madero toured the country making speeches. When Madero founded a newspaper and began forming anti-re-election clubs, Díaz still did nothing. In April 1910, a convention of anti-re-electionists nominated Madero as their presidential candidate. If Diaz, then, did not take Madero seriously, he did a month later when 30,000 *Maderistas* converged on the National Palace in Mexico City to protest the Díaz regime. In June, Díaz had Madero arrested and imprisoned.

Thus it was, on September 16, 1910, the centennial of the *grito de Dolores,* that the 80-year old Don Porfirio could celebrate his achievements and rejoice in his seeming security. He did not recall, perhaps, that Hidalgo's *grito* ended in the bloodbath of the Alhóndiga or the overthrow of Spanish power.

Two weeks later, Díaz and his vice-president, the *científico* Ramón Corral, were re-elected.

Events now began to move swiftly. On October 7, Madero, released on bail, fled to Texas. There he declared the elections null and void, published the *Plan de San Luis Potosí*, and proclaimed November 20 as the day the people of Mexico should rise against Díaz.

Madero's insurrection, however, did not come off as hoped. In Morelos, Zapata had been unmolested in organizing revolutionary forces, but Díaz suppressed the *Maderista* uprisings throughout the rest of Mexico. A discouraged Madero went to New Orleans to set sail for Europe. It seemed he would become just another Mexican exile, sipping tea in a Parisian café. But *this* sad fate would not be his. In New Orleans, he heard news that would change his and Mexico's destiny.

In Chihuahua, a northern desert state owned almost solely by one family, a storekeeper named Pascual Orozco had heeded Madero's *grito* and had organized *vaqueros* into a guerrilla force. A bandit leader, christened Doroteo Arango but known to his men as Pancho Villa, joined Orozco. On November 27, 1910, Orozco and Villa defeated Mexican federal troops at Pedernales and seized control of southern Chihuahua. They then cut the railroad

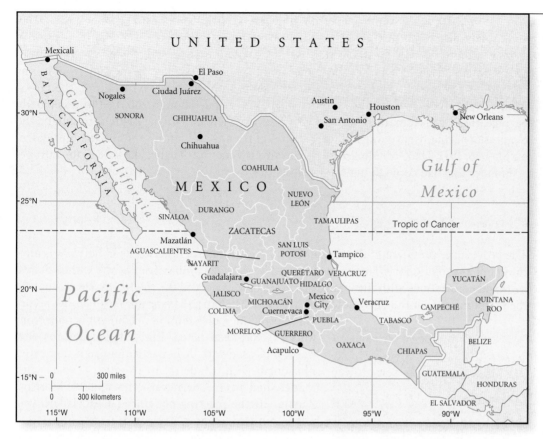

Map of Mexico in the years of the Mexican Revolution

between Chihuahua City and Ciudad Juárez on the Mexican-American border. With a full-fledged rebellion in place, Madero crossed the border into Mexico on February 14, 1911 and joined the rebels in Chihuahua.

In the south, on March 11, Zapata struck a blow for the revolution by taking the village of Ayala in Morelos. This relatively unbloody victory (the *Zapatistas* merely disarmed local police; the villagers were already on their side) was followed by others more bloody. By April 1911, guerrilla forces in Sonora, Sinaloa, Durango, Puebla, Guerrero, Veracruz, Tabasco, Oaxaca, and Yucatán had risen against Díaz.

The *cientifico* leader José Limantour had been in Europe when the revolution broke out. He now returned to Mexico, on the way meeting with Madero's representatives in New York City and with the Mexican ambassador to the United States, Francisco de la Barra. Back in Mexico, Limantour took control of the government and promised reforms. He sought an armistice with Madero, Orozco, and Villa, who were then besieging Ciudad Juárez. Under the influence of his family, Madero was willing to sign an armistice and even allow Limantour to remain in the government; but Francisco Vásquez Gómez, formerly physician to Díaz's family and Madero's vice-presidential candidate, laid down more demands. Among these was a call for Díaz to resign and another to expel all *científicos* from the congress. Limantour refused Vásquez Gómez's demands. Fighting once again broke out between rebel and federal troops outside Ciudad Juárez. The revolution now ran swiftly toward victory. Madero ordered his men to desist, but Orozco and Villa ignored him. Rebel forces forced their way into the city and after much bitter fighting, forced the federals to surrender on May 10. Two days later, in the south, Zapata took the city of Cuautla after a week of fighting. Elsewhere, state capitals fell to rebel *guerrilleros*.

Pancho Villa

On May 21, 1911, Vásquez Gómez laid down the rebel demands: the resignation of Díaz and Limantour and the appointment of Francisco de la Barra as provisional president until elections could be held. When these terms were read in Mexico City, crowds gathered around the National Palace demanding Díaz's resignation. The old president, suffering from tooth-ache, refused to step down. His only answer came from his troops, firing into the crowd from the National Palace and the towers of the cathedral. Though 200 died in this bloody barrage, the crowds remained until rain at last drove them away. That night, at midnight, the old president finally gave way to the entreaties of friends and family and resigned. At dawn, on May 26, 1911, Díaz left Mexico City by train to Veracruz. Thence, he set sail for Europe.

El Porfiriato had come to inglorious close.

Chaos Returns

The provisional president of the revolutionary government, Francisco de la Barra, was any-thing but a revolutionary. This man, who had been Díaz's ambassador to the United States, had tight connections with the wealthy families of Mexico and the *científicos*. He was hardly the man to carry out the only radical provision of Madero's *Plan de San Luis Potosí*—agrar-

Francisco Madero (front row, center) with other rebel leaders

ian reform, the redistribution of land to the poor from whom it had been taken. Emiliano Zapata, for one, was not pleased with de la Barra and had become dis-illusioned with Madero. In August, Zapata and Madero had met in Cuernevaca, the capital of Morelos. Zapata left the meeting convinced that Madero was not committed to agrarian reform.

Zapata was not alone in distrusting Madero; some of the Mexican bishops were wary of him as well, though not for the same reasons as the Morelos revo-lutionary. In a May 28, 1911 letter to the archbishop of Mexico City, José de Jesús Ortiz y Rodriguez, the archbishop of Guadalajara, lamented that "we will no longer be able to depend on the tolerance and the spirit of conciliatory supervision of the illustrious General Díaz, who has been until now our only defense under God." But Archbishop Ortiz did not express the sentiments of the many clergy who sup-ported Madero, nor of the Catholic people, who rejoiced over Díaz's overthrow.

The Catholic Response

Even before Díaz's overthrew, some Catholics who were dissatisfied with the state of things in Mexico were seeking greater involvement in social change. In Mexico City, a group of socially prominent and politically well-connected Catholics formed the *Circulo Católico Nacional* (CCN, National Catholic Circle) to discuss how and when to establish a specifically Catholic political party.

Many socially concerned Catholics, however, were wary of the CCN; they feared the well-placed, economic elite of Mexico would come to dominate it. Many of these social Catholics joined a group formed by a medical doctor, José Refugio Galindo—the *Operarios Guadalupanos* (OG—Guadalupan Workers). Between 1909 and the end of 1911, over 100 OG organizations, with hundreds of members, were founded in 20 states and federal ter-ritories, mostly in central and western Mexico. These groups, formed of small member cells, were not under centralized control; but, rooted as they were in local parish structures, they were able to form a network that allowed them to take concerted action. Parish OG groups provided study groups on social problems, artisan and worker circles, and health care services. Some cells promoted public morality through theater, while others published newspapers. In 1909, the OG opened two rural credit and savings establishments to provide affordable credit to the poor.

Guadalajara became the intellectual center of the OG movement. Among the intellectual lights of the Guadalajara OG were Canon Miguel de la Mora (soon to become bishop of Zacatecas) and Miguel Palomar y Vizcarra, considered the leading Catholic intellectual in Mexico. In 1909, with the blessing of Mexico City's archbishop, José Mora y del Rio, Palomar founded a journal, *Restauración Social* (Social Restoration), which discussed such social justice issues as what constitutes a just family wage. Indeed, such social questions dominated the OG. Members studied the social encyclicals of Pope Leo XIII and published newsletters analyzing Mexico's social problems in light of Catholic social justice teaching. Some solutions were radical; for instance, in June 1914, an OG leader, José Encarnación Preciado, suggested that social Catholics espouse an agrarian reform that would divide large haciendas among workers, who would contribute to bonds that would reimburse former owners. As for how it would organize the state, the OG did not call for the overthrow of the republic or for direct clergy involvement in government. Rather, the OG hoped for a more democratic state structure, resting on universal manhood suffrage. It hoped for a government, controlled by Catholic laity that would respect the institutional Catholic Church in Mexico as a freely operating body in the greater society. In a word, the OG favored what has been called "Christian democracy"—a form of society where the Church and state have clearly defined spheres but are united in mutual cooperation and recognition.

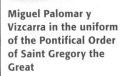

Miguel Palomar y Vizcarra in the uniform of the Pontifical Order of Saint Gregory the Great

Shortly after Díaz's fall from power, members of the OG and CCN formed what has been called Mexico's first modern political party—the *Partido Católico Nacional* (PCN—the National Catholic Party). During the brief period of its existence (1910–1913), the PCN was able to take advantage of the OG's parish-based network to form an effective political movement. At its first convention, the PCN decided not to run its own presidential candidate in the October 1911 election but to throw its support to Madero. But, despite Madero's urging, the party did not support his vice-presidential candidate, José Maria Pino Suárez, because they thought him opposed to Catholic principles. Instead, for vice president, the PCN nominated Francisco de la Barra. Madero and Suárez triumphed in the election, held in October 1911. But while PCN candidates won important elections in some states, the party lost in most of the national races. Only in Jalisco did the PCN's de la Barra win more votes than Suárez.

"A Wicked Despotism has Fallen!"

Though he had sparked a revolution, Madero was no radical. He was committed to a restoration of the freedoms guaranteed under the Constitution of 1857 (freedom of the press, of conscience, of assembly, etc.) and he wanted all Mexicans to exercise full voting rights. That he wanted to prune back severely the privileges of foreign capitalists was not radical; his family, like the rich Mexican capitalist class to which they belonged, wanted a larger share of the wealth of Mexico than they had under Díaz, and measures against foreign capitalists would provide it for them.

Francisco de la Barra

Madero was heavily influenced by his family, for many of his kindred had come to live with him in the National Palace. Especially influential was the president's brother, Gustavo. Though President Madero's gentle, vegetarian soul shrank from executing enemies, Gustavo used heavy-handed tactics worthy of Don Porfirio himself against the regime's foes. Gustavo Madero gathered his own gang of thugs and interfered in elections. Other Madero relatives ensconced themselves in the government, where they carried on the *científico* policies from the days of Díaz.

Mexican insurgents
with a homemade
cannon, 1911

Yet, the freedom of speech and of the press guaranteed by Madero encouraged more radical elements to organize. Trade unions again appeared. In the capital, the *Casa del Obrero Mundial* (House of the World Worker) became a center for intellectuals who promoted socialist and Marxist ideas. Tolerance of such radicalism alarmed wealthy Mexicans and foreign investors. When the radical lawyer Luis Cabrera openly promoted a plan to break up large estates, one began to hear talk among the wealthy and powerful of overthrowing Madero. To the wealthy and well-heeled, Mexican and foreign, it seemed that the mild Madero could not keep order in the country.

Emiliano Zapata, who, since the resignation of Díaz, had been living in retirement in the village of Ayala in Morelos, decided it was time to re-ignite the revolution. On November 25, 1911, Zapata proclaimed the *Plan de Ayala* as the standard of the renewed struggle. After listing Madero's various "tyrannical" acts, the *Plan* demanded the president's resignation. The *Plan* recognized the Chihuahuan Pascual Orozco as chief of the revolution; and if he should not "accept this delicate post . . . recognition as Chief of the Revolution will go to General Don Emiliano Zapata."

It was the *Plan de Ayala's* radical provisions for land redistribution that were of chief interest to the revolutionaries. Since, it said, "the immense majority of Mexican pueblos and citizens are owners of no more than the land they walk on, suffering the horrors of poverty without being able to improve their social condition in any way," the plan called for the redistribution of one-third of lands, timber, and water to the landless, with compensation to the owners. But those "landlords, *cientificos,* or bosses" who opposed the plan in any way would lose all their lands, which would go to pensions for widows and orphans of those who died in the revolution. "We are not personalists," declared the *Plan*, "we are partisans of principles and not of men! Mexican People, support this plan with arms in hand and you will make the prosperity and well-being of the fatherland."

Madero could not understand the significance of Zapata and his plan. To newspapers that wondered if they should publish the plan, Madero quipped: "Yes, print it, so everybody will know how crazy Zapata is."

Zapata was not alone in raising the standard of revolution. In Chihuahua, Pascual Orozco pronounced against Madero; but the president sent General Victoriano Huerta to deal with the rebel, and Orozco fled to the United States. Other rebels, though decidedly more conservative, also rose against Madero—Bernardo Reyes and Felix Díaz (a kinsman of Don Porfirio). Like Orozco's, their uprising ended in defeat. Madero, however, did not execute Reyes and Díaz but, instead, gave them comfortable jail quarters in Mexico City.

Pascual Orozco

Not only the revolutionaries were turning against Madero. Government manipulation of the election of 1912 finally turned the National Catholic Party against the president. PCN candidates had taken a large share of the vote in central and western Mexico, especially Jalisco and Zacatecas. They won control of large cities, including Puebla and Toluca. Such success worried powerful Liberals, who persuaded the Mexican government to annul the results of many of the elections where the PCN had prevailed. Of the hundreds of seats they had won, the PCN were able to maintain control of only 23. Such chicanery, of course angered party members; one of the PCN's most prominent journalists, Trinidad Sánchez Santos, called for Madero's assassination. The bishops of Mexico, however, demanded obedience to the government, and the PCN acquiesced.

Despite the discontent of revolutionaries and political Catholics, Madero might have weathered the swelling storm had he not earned the distrust and opposition of American capitalists and the U.S. government. The American ambassador to Mexico, Henry Lane Wilson, and his boss, President Taft, were highly displeased with Madero's opposition to American capital. Ambassador Wilson (associated with American business interests opposed to the Madero family) told his government that Mexico was "seething with discontent" under Madero; and he advised American nationals that they were no longer safe in Mexico—even though most of the country was at peace. Wilson advised Washington to place American troops along the Mexico-U.S. border.

On February 9, 1913, troops from Tacubaya rebelled against Madero. Led by Bernardo Reyes (who had been released from prison), they marched on the National Palace. Expecting no resistance, the rebels were surprised by machine gun fire spraying them from the palace. It was Sunday and hundreds of churchgoers were on their way to Mass. Gunfire cut down 200–300 civilians, caught between the rebels and the palace. Reyes, too, was killed.

Henry Lane Wilson

Since he had sent his most trusted general, Felipe Angeles, south to fight Zapata, President Madero was forced to rely again on the services of General Huerta, a man whom he had publicly humiliated. (Madero had dismissed Huerta, a notorious drunkard, after he refused to account for the one million pesos he was given to fight Orozco.) For nine days, February 9–18, Huerta, from the palace, and General Félix Díaz, from the citadel, lobbed shells at each other across Mexico City's main business district. Few of the shells hit their intended targets but killed or maimed many civilians. When General Felipe Angeles, arriving from Morelos, proceeded to attack Félix Díaz from the west, Ambassador Wilson intervened; Angeles' guns, he said, were too close to the U.S. embassy. Angeles moved his forces north of Díaz's position, only to discover that someone had removed the focus lenses of his guns.

On February 18, 1913, while Huerta was away from the palace, at lunch with Gustavo Madero, the palace guard arrested the president and his cabinet. When news reached Huerta that the *coup d'etat* had succeeded, he arrested Gustavo Madero, turning him over to Díaz, who had him tortured to death. The same day, Huerta, Felix Díaz, and Ambassador Wilson signed the "Compact of the Citadel" at the U.S. embassy. Huerta was provisional president, while Díaz was to succeed him in the next election. "A wicked despotism has fallen!" Wilson exulted to the U.S. state department.

But what to do with Francisco Madero? Huerta had promised to send Madero into exile but instead kept him confined in the palace. Though Wilson had protested that, as ambassador, he could not interfere in Mexico's internal affairs, he counseled Huerta to do whatever he thought necessary for the good of the country. On February 22, Madero and Vice President Pino Suárez, enroute from the presidential palace to the prison, were forced out of the carriages that conveyed them. The official story was that they were shot while attempting to escape.

Fire from The North

Mexico's new president, Victoriano Huerta, was the anti-Madero. He was no teetotaller; in fact, he spent a good part of his day drunk. He was not tenderhearted but treacherous and cruel. To assure his absolute sway over Mexico, Huerta replaced several state governors with generals faithful to him. He conducted a purge of the congress, jailing over 100 representatives who opposed his regime. One congressman, Belisario Dominguez, a senator from Chiapas, spoke out publicly against Huerta; he was later found dead. He had been shot.

Soldiers fighting in
the February uprising
against Madero

Ambassador Wilson had hoped that a good cabinet, whose members he would help select, could go far to rein in the beastly Huerta, but it was no use. The conservative, responsible men whom Wilson had chosen (some were in favor of social and agrarian reform) soon resigned in disgust. And Huerta's cronies in the congress successfully thwarted any measures they proposed.

When he had come into power, Huerta secured the PCN's acquiesence to his regime by promising the party 100 seats in the congress. He pledged that if a PCN candidate won the planned presidential election in October 1913, he would uphold the results. Both the Church and the party had expressed their disapproval of Huerta; but, then again, for good or ill, he was the government. It seemed that little good would come from opposing him. One could attempt a revolution, but it was doubtful whether a revolution would succeed. This, it seems, was the reasoning that led the PCN leadership to strike a bargain with Huerta. It was a disastrous bargain. As we shall see, Huerta was not about to concede an election to any opponent. Moreover, as the only party left after the purge of the congress, the PCN lost its independence and became tainted with the reputation of being *Huertista*. In the end, Huerta turned on the PCN. In early 1914, Huerta arrested the PCN president, Gabriel Fernández, and exiled him. Its alliance with Huerta killed the PCN. It would not survive the end of the Huerta regime.

It was not long before Huerta's dissipation and cruelty inspired a new uprising. While the president was terrorizing the capital, Venustiano Carranza, the governor of Coahuila, was stirring up rebellion in the north. Carranza was a conservative constitutionalist—a *Maderista*,—and his *Plan de Guadalupe* demanded nothing more radical than the overthrow of Huerta and the restoration of the Constitution of 1857. His rebellion, however, was drawing him into an alliance with elements that would give it a more revolutionary character.

For other chiefs, besides Carranza, were in open rebellion against Huerta. In the north, in Sonora, General Alvaro Obregón had organized his own revolutionary army. Besides being a master of military strategy, Obregón (a former mechanic and farmer) had a democratic, down-to-earth manner that endeared him to his men. His soldiers, like those of Carranza, were drawn from the untamed elements found in the vast deserts of the north. But unlike Carranza's general, Pablo González, Obregón discouraged looting, pillage, and rapine in his army.

To assert his leadership of the revolution, Carranza called himself "First Chief of the Constitutionalist Army." Though Obregón was his rival, Carranza sought an alliance with the Sonoran general; for, at the very least, Obregón was more trustworthy than the less respectable, but otherwise effective, rebel leader who had joined the push against Huerta: Pancho Villa. Obregón accepted Carranza's leadership, and the "First Chief" crossed over into Sonora, establishing his government at Nogales, on the U.S. border. Villa had served under Huerta in the campaign against Pascual Orozco; and Huerta, who hated Villa, had accused him of desertion and ordered his execution. Pardoned by Madero, Villa was at last able to escape into the United States. It was from north of the border that on March 13, 1913, Villa and eight companions re-crossed the Río Grande into Chihuahua. Gathering a force of vaqueros, bandits, and assorted no-accounts (whom he called his *dorados*), Villa seized control of all Chihuahua, except the cities. Villa and his *dorados* were like a blind force of nature, killing and pillaging, terrorizing the countryside. When at last he conquered the cities of Chihuahua, Villa and his men looted churches, killed priests, and turned wealthy and middle class families from their homes to wander the barren wastes of the north. The bandit chieftain established his own government at Chihuahua City, in the center of the state.

Though he could be brutal, Villa was brave and something of an idealist. Like Zapata, he redistributed the lands of the rich among his peon followers. He built schools. When his *dorados* were not fighting, Villa set them to work, cleaning streets and operating electric plants. Villa even printed large quantities of paper money. Though officially allied with Carranza, Villa remained a free operator, so the "First Chief" had little confidence in him.

Venustiano Carranza

In the south, Emiliano Zapata operated alone. With his cry of *Tierra y Libertad!* (Land and Liberty!) Zapata was gradually extending his sway towards the Pacific coast, into Puebla and the state of México, and into the federal district itself. Though his followers continued to burn haciendas and kill their managers, *Zapatista* violence was not random; rather, it was directed by the political goals of the *Plan de Ayala*. Zapata's army did not destroy for the mere pleasure of looting.

Throughout Mexico, small-time generals were rising, overthrowing their local *hacendados* and political bosses. Many of these revolutionary generals were ambitious peons who gathered small armies around themselves. Unlike Zapata, they cared little for justice. If they managed to escape the firing squad, they themselves became petty tyrants over the regions they dominated.

In Mexico City, Huerta's closing of the House of the World Worker in May had either forced radical intellectuals into hiding or into revolutionary ranks. A number of radicals went north to Carranza in Nogales to serve him in what became known as the "Red Battalion." Others, like the anarchist orator Antonio Díaz Soto y Gama, went over to Zapata. These intellectuals forced Carranza, against his inclination, to adopt radical goals for his revolution. When in the summer of 1913, Villa acknowledged Carranza as his revolutionary chief, the two leaders declared that the revolution would be directed against both the dominance of the wealthy landholders and the power of the Church.

The Men of the North

That the revolution was turning anti-clerical could hardly have been a surprise to any Mexican. For, while Madero did not strike out at the Church's liberty, there were those among his supporters who favored the anti-clericalism of Benito Juárez and the *Ley Lerdo*. Conflict between the Church and the secular powers was nothing new in Mexico. It was the renewal of this conflict that Archbishop Ortiz feared when he said Porfirio Díaz had been the Mexican Church's "only defense under God."

It was not surprising that the revolution was turning anti-clerical—especially given the men who now directed it. Both Carranza and Obregón were from the north, from among a population that in many areas had historically little contact with the Catholic Church. We think of Mexico as a deeply Catholic country, but that characterization better fits what is called "Old Mexico," the regions of central Mexico, southward. The influence of both Spanish culture and the Church had been intense in Old Mexico. Not so in the regions of the far northern frontier—Sonora, Chihuahua, Coahuila, and Nuevo León. In many areas of these regions, the Catholic Church's influence had been vestigial. As a federal general, J. B. Vargas, later told a *Cristero* leader, "I'm from the frontier, and in my village the Catholic Church is hardly known."

Alvaro Obregón

Because of their isolation from Spanish culture and the Church, the men of the north were inclined to admire the United States. Anglo-America was alluring. It had a stable government. It was prosperous. The American people seemed to have a dynamism and drive that the people of Old Mexico lacked. Anglo-American culture was not so ancient or, in many ways, as civilized or beautiful as Mexican culture. But it was an effervescent new wine that the men of the north hoped would burst the old wine skins of what they deemed a tired and spent Mexican society.

An attack on Old Mexico necessitated an assault on the Catholic Church. The men of the north were convinced that it was the Church that in large part hampered Mexico's full entrance into an American-style prosperity. The United States was still a predominately Protestant country, and the men of the north thought it was Protestantism that was responsible for the political and economic prosperity of the U.S. It was necessary, therefore, if Mexico was to adopt a more U.S.-style culture, that the Catholic Church be gotten out of the way.

So it was that men like Carranza and Obregón encouraged Protestant proselytizing and the establishment of Protestant congregations in Mexico. It is not surprising that many U.S. Protestants, who saw the revolution as a crusade against the Catholic Church, zealously supported the new revolutionary movement. Such support was not merely monetary; many American Protestants—indeed sometimes whole congregations and their pastors—left hearth and home to go fight in the Constitutionalist army.

The Fall of Huerta

The new president of the United States, Woodrow Wilson, strongly disapproved of Victoriano Huerta. Though he was determined not to intervene directly in Mexico's internal affairs, President Wilson wanted to apply pressure to convince Huerta to step down. Thus in the summer of 1913, Wilson forbade the sale of arms to Mexico. He recalled Henry Lane Wilson (whose part in Huerta's climb to power the president found appalling) and sent John Lind to Mexico as his personal envoy.

Lind urged Huerta to hold free elections and to step down as president. Huerta seemed to acquiesce and, in the October 1913 elections, he was not listed as a candidate. But when Huerta declared the October election null and void and did not step down, President Wilson decided he had had enough. He removed the arms embargo against Mexico and began arming Carranza and the Constitutionalist forces.

President Wilson adopted a policy of "watchful waiting," as he called it, toward Huerta. "By a little every day," said Wilson, "his power and prestige are crumbling, and the collapse is not far away."

But Wilson soon found an opportunity to take more direct action. In April 1914, Mexican authorities arrested American sailors who had landed in a forbidden zone at the Gulf port city of Tampico. They were loading gasoline. Though the sailors were released with apologies after only half an hour, Admiral Henry T. Mayo declared that the Mexican government had gravely insulted the United States. To atone for the insult, said Mayo, the Mexican commandant must honor the American flag with a 21-gun salute—a humiliating condition. The Mexican commandant refused. Huerta, swelling with pride for the fatherland, also refused. An angry President Wilson,

Victoriano Huerta

learning that a German ship was bringing arms to Veracruz, ordered Mayo to seize the port. Mayo bombarded Veracruz and took the port, with a loss of only 21 marines. The Mexicans did not fare so well; 200 Mexican soldiers died in the fray, as well as many civilians, including women and children.

The Tampico incident and the capture of Veracruz made Huerta a hero—he had stood up to the United States for the fatherland! The general uttered wild threats of invading the

United States, and even of conquering Washington. Carranza, too, condemned the seizure of Veracruz as a violation of the Treaty of Guadalupe Hidalgo. Though he might offend a potential ally in Woodrow Wilson, Carranza could not ignore the insult offered to his country.

But Wilson proved more than a potential ally to Carranza. With American arms, the Constitutionalists were able, time after time, to defeat Huerta's federal forces. Obregón from Sonora and Villa and his *dorados* from Chihuahua were engaged in a sort of race to reach Mexico City. But Villa's rough-hewn bandit generalry was no match for Obregón's brilliant strategy. Villa, too, broke with Carranza, who refused to send him any coal to power the trains that were carrying his *dorados*. Stranded at Zacatecas, Villa could only look on as the combined armies of Alvaro Obregón and Carranza's general, Pablo Gonzalez, advanced from Querétaro against the capital.

On August 10, 1914, the federal garrison in Mexico City offered its surrender to General Obregón. Five days later—the feast of the Assumption of Mary—Obregón led his army in triumph into the city. As for Huerta, he fled northward, eventually crossing the border into the United States.

The Revolution Turns Radical

The overthrow of Victoriano Huerta could not bring peace to Mexico. After victory, the divisions that had all the while plagued the revolutionary forces now became clearly pronounced, with *Villistas* and *Carranzistas* each accusing the other of betraying the struggle. General Obregón, after installing Carranza in the presidential palace, went north to negotiate with Pancho Villa. The two revolutionary chieftains agreed that Carranza should serve only as provisional president until elections could be held. Carranza apparently agreed to this (for him) unwelcome plan, though he secretly was looking for some way to hold onto power. He suggested holding a convention of rebel leaders in Mexico City—safely within his own sphere of influence—to discuss the all-important question of the presidential succession.

When General Obregón delivered Carranza's plan to Pancho Villa, the bandit rebel had him arrested and threatened to shoot him. Luckily for Obregón, Villa changed his mind and, instead of killing the general, invited him to dinner. During the meal, the two agreed (against Carranza) that the convention be held, not in Mexico City, but in Aguascalientes—within *Villa's* sphere of power. Afterwards, Villa apparently thought he could not trust Obregón and again ordered him killed. By this time, Obregón was on a train to Mexico City. When the train began, unaccountably, to slow, Obregón guessed treachery. With the members of his staff, he took control of the engine, cut the telegraph wires, and so made his escape to Carranza in Mexico City.

The Aguascalientes convention was, thus, from beginning to end a Villa affair. *Zapatistas, Villistas,* and an odd assortment of radical intellectuals gathered there in November 1914 to discuss the future shape of the republic and to nominate a provisional president. Villa rejected the suggestion that both he and Carranza step down; the delegates rejected Villa's suggestion that they shoot both him and Carranza. They ultimately agreed on Eulalio Gutiérrez, whom the intellectuals favored because he stood for civilian rule and democracy. Villa liked Gutiérrez, too—because he could control him.

Meanwhile, Obregón had thrown in his lot with Carranza, who had withdrawn to Veracruz. (U.S. forces had evacuated the city only a week before.) Pancho Villa and Emiliano Zapata, with their armies, now converged on Mexico City, which waited in terror of their approach. Villa and his men marched into the city with all the bravado and brutality for which they had become famous. But Zapata and his men provided a striking contrast to the rapacious *dorados*; instead of pillaging and looting the capital, the *Zapatista* peasants begged their bread at the doors of the rich.

Zapata, whose chief care was for his home state of Morelos, soon withdrew from the capital. Villa remained in Mexico City, ostensibly President Gutiérrez's general, but really his keeper. When Gutiérrez escaped early in 1915, Villa appointed another provisional president to take his place. But Villa himself was not long for the capital. By the end of January, Obregón's forces had defeated *Villista* forces in Puebla. Villa withdrew to the north while Obregón entered the capital.

The civil war now took a strange turn. Carranza had been seen as the more conservative rebel, while Villa drew the radicals to his camp. Carranza, however, needed the support of the people; thus, at the suggestion of Luis Cabrera, he proclaimed a series of agrarian reforms. Carranza decreed that all lands illegally seized from Indian villages be returned to the villages. If the villages needed more land, they could apply to the newly formed National Agrarian Commission, which had authority to seize hacienda lands. Carranza formed an alliance with the House of the World Worker, promising to aid its efforts to unionize workers and to support it in disputes with employers. Branches of the House of the World Worker began to spring up throughout Carranza-controlled areas of Mexico, and House radicals provided six "red battalions" to fight for Carranza. With Carranza tilting towards the left, conservative elements apparently felt they had no choice but to rally around Pancho Villa. American businessmen arrived at Villa's headquarters, and President Woodrow Wilson and his secretary of state, William Jennings Bryan, threw their support to Villa against Carranza.

Villa (left) and Zapata (right) in the presidential palace, Mexico City

Yet, despite the flow of U.S. arms to Villa, the bandit-chieftain's dash and élan were no match for the studied strategy of Alvaro Obregón. In the spring, Obregón dug in behind trenches and barbed wire near the city of Celaya in Guanajuato state and waited for Villa. In April 1915, the headstrong Villa attacked Obregón's entrenched position in one of the bloodiest battles ever fought on Mexican soil. For three days, Villa's forces assaulted enemy lines, only to be driven back and brutally cut down. It was a brave but futile attempt, and Villa finally withdrew and fled northward toward Chihuahua. Throughout the summer and autumn of 1915, as Obregón pursued him northward along the railroad, Villa's once strong army dwindled away. Villa's defeat at Celaya made any hope of continued U.S. support for him doubtful. And it marked the beginning of his decline.

Throughout the spring of 1915, control of Mexico City passed back and forth between Zapata and the *Carranzista* commander, General Pablo González. In August, with reinforcements from Obregón, González was finally able to drive Zapata and his forces from the Federal District. González now resolved to starve Zapata and all Morelos into submission. His men burnt haciendas, destroyed sugar plantations, and looted far and wide. Yet, though he laid waste that rich land, González was unable to capture Zapata, who had withdrawn to the safety of the *sierra*.

In the United States, American business interests with property in Mexico were putting pressure on President Wilson to intervene in the Mexican civil war. Cardinal Gibbons, speaking for American Catholics, urged the president to step in; Gibbons had heard reports that Carranza's forces were shooting priests and desecrating churches. Wilson, however, did not send troops into Mexico; instead, he issued moral lectures to the Mexicans on the blessings of constitutions and the rights of foreigners. But in October, Wilson shifted his support from Villa to Carranza, diverting all arms shipments to the victorious Constitutionalist forces.

To Villa, Wilson's decision to support the Constitutionalists was simply betrayal. Then, in November 1915, *Carranzista* forces used a rail line, passing through U.S. territory, to launch a surprise attack on Villa's army at Agua Prieta on the border with Arizona. Villa wrote to Zapata that, thenceforward, he would no longer kill his Mexican brethren; he would turn his fury instead on "traitor Americans."

Villa soon fulfilled his pledge. In January 1916, some of Villa's men stopped a train at Santa Ysabel in Chihuahua and killed several Americans on board. In March, Villa himself led a raid across the border. At Columbus, New Mexico, a border town, Villa killed 16 American citizens. Other Mexican bandits followed Villa's example, and in retaliation both American citizens and American lawmen began killing innocent Mexicans north of the border. Facing an upcoming election, Wilson knew he had to do something. In the spring, he sent an American force under General John "Black Jack" Pershing into Chihuahua to capture Villa, dead or alive. But Pershing, ignorant of the desert wilderness that Villa knew so well, found he could not capture, much less find, the bandit chief.

President Carranza and the Constitution of 1917

Though by the spring of 1916, most regions of Mexico had recognized Carranza as provisional president, the country was far from peaceful. The states, practically independent, were divided among a number of chieftains who ruled as dictators over their small territories. Many a chieftain used Carranza's agrarian decree as an excuse to appropriate land. Revolutionary chieftains, once peons themselves, thus became rich and waxed as tyrannical as any strutting *hacendado* of the Díaz regime. Mexico had not been freed; she had just put on new masters.

Carranza was unable to keep order in Mexico. His hot-headedness alienated whatever able men he had gathered into his cabinet, including General Obregón, who retired to private life. Throughout Mexico, and even in the Federal District, generals, greedy for gain, looted houses and killed civilians. Pershing's invasion of northern Mexico cast shame on the president.

In the autumn of 1916, President Carranza called for a constitutional convention to revise the Constitution of 1857. Carranza merely wanted to strengthen the power of the president, but he was unable to dominate the convention, which met at Santiago de Querétaro

Insurrectionists in Mexico

in December. The party backed by Alvaro Obregón controlled the convention and, in six short weeks, produced a constitution notable for its rejection of Liberal *laissez-faire* business doctrines, its espousal of agrarian reform, and its relentless anti-clericalism.

The constitution promulgated in 1917 decreed that no individuals or corporate entities could directly own land, and, especially, water and subsoil minerals in Mexico. All land belonged to the whole people of Mexico, even if it was divided up among many users. This meant that the state (the representative of the Mexican people) could take land (albeit with compensation) from its current owners if the good of "the people" demanded it. Article 27 of the constitution, which embodied this doctrine, also declared that seizures of *ejidos* under *Ley Lerdo* were null and void, and, if they needed to, *ejideros* could take land from neighboring haciendas.

Article 123 of the new constitution established some of the most progressive labor legislation in the world. Among other measures, the article limited the workday to eight hours, abolished child labor, declared the right of workers to organize unions, and called on employers to give workers a share in profits. Both articles 27 and 123 assured that workers and peasants would support the new government.

But among the most controversial provisions of the Constitution of 1917 were those that dealt with the Church.

As we have seen, under Díaz, the Church in Mexico had made some progress in restoring her fortunes. She had regained the property she had lost under Juárez and was once again able to establish religious congregations of men and women. But just as important was the fact that many of her children were turning their attention to the needs and concerns of modern men. As we have seen, Leo XIII's *Rerum Novarum* had awakened Mexican Catholics to the plight of workers and peasants and to the need for social reform. The formation of the Catholic Party had been part of this awakening, as was the founding of its auxiliary association, the League of Catholic Students. The League established youth centers in cities throughout Mexico, as well as the Catholic Student Center in Mexico City. In January 1913, the Catholic Great Workers' Diet that met at Zamora suggested labor reforms similar to those found in Article 123 of the 1917 constitution; and in Mexico City the Jesuit priest, Alfredo Méndez Medina, founded Mexico's first real trade union. The bishops moreover were strongly supportive of such labor organizing. Also in 1913, Catholics had formed the *Asociacion Católica de la Juventud Mexicana* (ACJM—the Catholic Association of Mexican Youth) whose brightest lights were to be two young laymen: Anacleto Gonzáles Flores and Rene Capistrán Garza.

Yet, despite such Catholic attempts to address the social question, Mexican revolutionaries still thought the Church the enemy of progress. The clergy, the revolutionaries charged, had aided Huerta in the overthrow of Madero; and, as we have seen, the only congressmen who served during Huerta's reign were members of the Catholic Party. Too, had not the Church been Don Porfirio's ally? This proud institution of oppression, the revolutionaries thought, must be humbled and broken. The notable exception to this revolutionary anti-clericalism was Emiliano Zapata. Zapata supplied priest chaplains for his men and ordered them to respect churches. Later, the Morelos chieftain gave refuge to the exiled Bishop Fulcheri of Zamora, who was said to be Zapata's confessor.

To undermine the Church's power, the Constitution of 1917 allowed the state to seize Church property; it decreed church buildings the property of the state. Priests had to register with the government; state governments could limit the number of priests within their jurisdictions, and foreigners could not serve as priests in Mexico. The constitution prohibited monastic vows and outlawed monastic orders. It forbade the holding of public religious ceremonies outside of church buildings, and it sought to eradicate the influence of religion in education, even in the now-compulsory primary grades. Children would, henceforth, be taught the secular doctrines of the revolution, not the teachings of Christ.

No Re-election

Carranza was not the author of the more radical provisions of the Constitution of 1917, and he did nothing to enforce them. Indeed, it would have been difficult to deprive foreign companies of their land and mineral rights, for they would appeal to their governments for redress. Both the Church and the landowners resisted the government's reforms. Too, even if Carranza had possessed the power to enforce the Constitution, he had not the desire.

But when Carranza did exercise power, he used it against radicals. He did nothing to redistribute lands to the peasants; he actively suppressed workers' attempts to organize unions. He closed the House of the World Worker in Mexico City and arrested one of its most powerful leaders, Luis Morones.

Given Carranza's violations of the new constitution, one might have expected some general to "pronounce" against him; but Mexico was exhausted by revolution; and, besides, Carranza had pledged that he would not seek re-election.

But more radical elements were not quiet. In May 1918, Luis Morones, released from prison, travelled to Coahuila as a delegate to a convention that had gathered to form a labor union. This union was meant to be anything but radical; indeed, it was to function as an arm of of Carranza's power. Morones, however, was able to wrest control of the convention and the organization it founded—the *Confederación Regional Obrera Mexicana* (Regional Confederation of Mexican Workers—CROM). Morones and a secret cadre of leaders, called *Grupo Acción,* came to control CROM. In 1919, *Grupo Acción* organized the Mexican Labor Party to support Alvaro Obregón for president.

Emiliano Zapata still lived to trouble Carranza. Though he lay waste to Morelos, General Pablo González could not capture Zapata. Unable to break Don Emiliano's power by waging war, González resorted to treachery. Zapata received a message from one Jesús Guajuardo, a colonel in González's army. Guajuardo claimed he was willing to desert the federal army and join his regiment to Zapata's rebel force. Zapata was justly suspicious; but when Guajuardo captured a detachment of González's troops and had them shot, Zapata changed his mind. Would Guajuardo have done so were he not sincere? Zapata arranged a meeting with the colonel at the hacienda of San Juan Chinameca.

A flourish of trumpets greeted Zapata as he, with ten of his followers, rode into San Juan Chinameca on April 10, 1919. Hardly had the trumpets fallen silent, however, when a barrage of gunfire cut-down Zapata and his men. Zapata died instantly. Guajuardo's men loaded his body onto a mule and took it to Cuautla, where they dumped it in the street.

"Men of the South, it is better to die on your feet than live on your knees"—this had been Zapata's call to resistance. Zapata was dead, but his struggle lived on. Indeed, his followers, who said that Zapata had not died at San Juan Chinameca, told that they could see him at times, mounted on his white horse, riding the *sierra* of Morelos. Zapata was dead, but not *Zapatismo.*

Librado Rivera and Enrique Flores Magón, two anarchists associated with Emiliano Zapata

With Zapata gone and Villa a mere bandit annoyance in far-off Chihuahua, Carranza could now attend to consolidating his political power. He knew he could not simply repudiate his pledge not to run a second time for president; but he could back a candidate whom he could easily manipulate once he was in power. Since Carranza, as president, controlled the Mexican political machine (free and honests elections were still only a wistful dream), his candidate would handily win the presidency in 1920—that is, as long as no one intervened.

But someone did intervene. When Carranza tried to break a railroad strike in Sonora, the governor, Adolfo de la Huerta, declared his state's independence. In April 1920, de la Huerta and Plutarco Elías Calles, once an elementary school teacher and the former governor of Sonora, issued a plan calling for the removal of Carranza and the appointment of a provisional president until elections could be held. Marching south, the army of the north, led by Alvaro Obregón, met no opposition, for even Carranza's closest allies had deserted him. Confronted by an overwhelming resistance, Carranza fled the capitol for Veracruz, taking with him five million *pesos* in gold and silver from the national treasury. When at Veracruz his train was attacked by one of his own commanders, Carranza fled north to Tampico. Carranza at last met his fate in a remote Indian village. His guide (who had promised to protect him) murdered him as he lay sleeping in a hut.

With Carranza gone, Obregón and his army entered Mexico City. De la Huerta was sworn in as provisional president and served until November, when Alvaro Obregón became president.

Revolution and Counter-Revolution

The government that replaced Carranza in 1920 was able to bring some peace to Mexico. Pancho Villa was bought off by the gift of a hacienda in Durango. The *Zapatistas* laid down their arms when the government assured them they could keep whatever lands they had taken in Morelos. President Obregón, unlike Carranza, seemed a friend to labor and radical agrarian aspirations—so much so that one could hear disgruntled businessmen in the United States complaining that the president of Mexico was a "Bolshevist."

President Obregón

Obregón, however, was not *too* radical, and he was no Bolshevist. For instance, though he did not suppress organized labor, he recognized only one union, the CROM of Luis Morones. Government boards that arbitrated strikes recognized only CROM strikes as legal; actions by independent unions (such as Marxist or anarchist unions, or the various Catholic workers organizations) failed to pass muster. This was all to the liking of Morones, who wanted to bring all unions under the CROM umbrella. With his gang of thugs, called his *palanca,* or "lever," Morones murdered rivals and terrorized business owners. Morones and other CROM leaders became so corrupt that employers could pay them off to avoid strikes—or worse consequences. Morones in time became so rich that he decked his fingers with costly diamond rings—which he claimed he kept as a monetary trust for the workers. CROM's core power structure, *Grupo Acción,* built for its members a sumptuous country estate, complete with swimming pools, and bought hotels and factories through third parties. At the same time, though workers' wages did rise, they barely reached subsistence level.

Obregón's land reform measures were, to some extent, even less satisfactory. Though he established the *Confederación Nacional Campesina* (National Farm Workers' Confederation) under the former *Zapatista,* Antonio Díaz Soto y Gama, he did little more to further agrarian reform. Free villages could apply to the government for lands; but since the initiative was entirely theirs, few did. The Indians often feared what the *hacendados* would do to them if they applied for land, and some priests told them that the government's land reform was thievery. Even when Indians obtained land, they could not purchase the seed and farming implements needed to work it. To take out loans was out of the question, since interest rates were too high. In all, Obregón's government distributed three million acres of land to 624 villages, only a small portion of the lands that remained in private hands.

Obregón did encourage education. José Vasconcelos, to whom Obregón entrusted his education program, was committed to *Hispanidad,* the ideal of Spanish culture. He built over 1,000 schools in rural villages throughout Mexico. He also had translated great European classics into Spanish, and had them printed in inexpensive editions.

Though Obregón and the men who surrounded him used socialist terminology, their policies were anything but Marxist or Bolshevist. Under Obregón, a new class of Mexican capitalists sprang up; and though many *hacendados* held on to their wealth, a new ruling class merely replaced the old. Obregón formed a dictatorship that was native-born Mexican. He ruled in a manner reminiscent of Don Porfirio, playing off rival groups against each other. In the states his governors were, more often than not, corrupt. The military maintained its time-honored privileges.

Though, as a revolutionary general, he had been among the principal supporters of the anti-clerical provisions of the Constitution of 1917, as president, Obregón adopted a more or less tolerant attitude toward the Church. In 1923, he wrote to the bishops that his government's social program "is essentially Christian, and it is complementary to the fundamental program of the Catholic Church." Here, the president was apparently trying to reconcile the social program of the Church—the chief rival of the revolutionary program—to his own. Yet, despite this overture, Obregón continued to back Protestant missionary endeavors in Mexico, and his government gave direct support to Protestant missions. In 1922, Protestant missionaries from the United States assisted over 700 Protestant congregations in Mexico that served about 22,000 people. By 1926, American Methodists were running 200 schools in Mexico, while Protestants had taken control of the ministry of education. And American Protestants reciprocated Obregón's friendship. "Millions of Americans feel for you and pray for you while you struggle to unloose the grip of the Roman Catholic Church upon your great country." So said a letter to Obregón from the Episcopal churches of Toledo, Ohio, and Taylor, Pennsylvania.

But if Obregón got on well with U.S. Protestants, his relationship with their government was troubled. Washington refused to recognize him as Mexico's president, primarily because Article 27 of the 1917 constitution threatened the possessions of American investors in Mexico. The Harding and Coolidge administrations considered Obregón's government the advanced guard of Soviet Communism in America. Obregón had declared that Article 27 did not apply to mineral rights foreigners possessed from before 1917, but Washington wanted the guarantee written in a treaty. Obregón refused.

But Obregón needed U.S. friendship if his hand-picked candidate for president were to succeed him without trouble in 1923. Plutarco Elías Calles, now a leftist member of the president's cabinet, faced opposition from members of the congress, military leaders, and *hacendados.* Without U.S. support, civil war could again erupt, with Washington siding with Calles' enemies.

Plutarco Elías Calles (center) with President Coolidge (right) and former President (then Supreme Court justice) Taft (left)

Obregón finally gave in to Washington's demands, and President Calvin Coolidge recognized his government on August 23, 1923.

U.S. aid was critical in the rebellion that arose over the election of 1923. Calles' rival candidate, Adolfo de la Huerta, claimed the election had been rigged in favor of Calles (which it had been) and raised the standard of revolt. It was a violent uprising, and the rebels nearly captured Mexico City; but Obregón, with aid from the United States, crushed the rebellion. De la Huerta fled to Los Angeles, California, where he took up his old profession of music teacher. Plutarco Elías Calles succeeded Obregón as president.

Calles Takes Control

While Obregón, fearing to jeopardize his power, had been wary of pushing revolutionary social reforms, Calles was more resolute. In the four years he held the presidency, Calles distributed eight million acres to 1,500 villages and established agricultural banks to provide loans for the new farmers. Calles more firmly allied himself with labor than had Obregón. The new president promoted public hygiene and improved sanitation. He instituted irrigation projects to put more land into cultivation. He continued Vasconcelos' education policies, building more schools in rural areas. Calles—at least at first—seemed genuinely committed to social reform along the lines envisioned by the Constitution of 1917; but it was not long before the basic corruption of his regime undid his would-be radicalism.

Calles ruled as an absolute dictator. He worked to concentrate power in his own hands and was ruthless to those who opposed him. Those who dared oppose him were usually executed, or they "committed suicide" in prison. Calles' dictatorship was more bitter and relentless than Don Porfirio's had been.

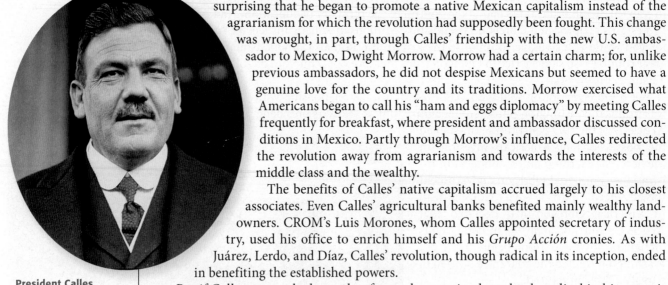

Though he called himself a socialist, Calles little by little warmed to Liberal capitalist ideas and policies. His closest associates were wealthy capitalists, and so it was not surprising that he began to promote a native Mexican capitalism instead of the agrarianism for which the revolution had supposedly been fought. This change was wrought, in part, through Calles' friendship with the new U.S. ambassador to Mexico, Dwight Morrow. Morrow had a certain charm; for, unlike previous ambassadors, he did not despise Mexicans but seemed to have a genuine love for the country and its traditions. Morrow exercised what Americans began to call his "ham and eggs diplomacy" by meeting Calles frequently for breakfast, where president and ambassador discussed conditions in Mexico. Partly through Morrow's influence, Calles redirected the revolution away from agrarianism and towards the interests of the middle class and the wealthy.

The benefits of Calles' native capitalism accrued largely to his closest associates. Even Calles' agricultural banks benefited mainly wealthy landowners. CROM's Luis Morones, whom Calles appointed secretary of industry, used his office to enrich himself and his *Grupo Acción* cronies. As with Juárez, Lerdo, and Díaz, Calles' revolution, though radical in its inception, ended in benefiting the established powers.

President Calles

But if Calles succumbed on other fronts, he remained resolutely radical in his opposition to the Church. Though Catholics had proven they could adjust to new circumstances and propose remedies to modern problems, it was in the interest of the revolutionaries to portray them as reactionaries—and it must be admitted, many Catholics, lay and clergy, played into the stereotype. Still, the Church was proposing reforms that were, in some cases, similar to those of the revolutionaries, but in other cases, different and even more radical. Following the lead of Leo XIII's *Rerum Novarum,* Catholics were proposing solutions that would preserve traditional Mexican society rooted in the Catholic faith while allowing it to adjust it to meet the demands of a new age. Revolutionaries like Calles hated traditional society. It was thus they sought the destruction of that body that sought to preserve it—the Catholic Church.

The Church Bells Fall Silent

The Church in Mexico had suffered waves of persecution since 1914. Revolutionaries had used Huerta's tolerance of the Church and the fact that the Catholic Party had acquiesced to Huerta's government as evidence that the Catholic Church was counter-revolutionary. Despite the engagement of many Catholics in seeking solutions to social ills, the Catholic mutualist societies and labor unions, the revolutionaries dusted off the old *Juarista* anti-clericalist slogans and used them with a vengeance.

Though an anti-clerical, Obregón had been selective in applying the anti-clerical articles of the Constitution of 1917. He had forbidden all religious ceremonies held outside the confines of church buildings. When the papal representative to Mexico attempted to dedicate a monument to Christ the King, Obregón had him expelled. Obregón broke up a Eucharistic congress. Moreover, Obregón's reign witnessed anonymous acts of terror against religion. In February and June 1921, bombs exploded at the archiepiscopal palaces in Mexico City and Guadalajara. On November 14, 1921, a bomb hidden in a bouquet of flowers placed before the image of Our Lady of Guadalupe in the basilica in Mexico City, went off. The explosion wrought significant damage to the church; but the image of Mary, protected only by glass, was unharmed.

Calles had nothing of Obregón's restraint but vigorously applied the anti-clerical articles of the constitution. On June 14, 1926, he decreed that priests who wore their clerical garb in public were to be fined 500 *pesos*; they could be imprisoned for five years if they criticized the government. Calles closed two seminaries and seized Church-run orphanages and homes for the aged. By March 1927, Calles had closed 83 monasteries of male and female religious. He even attempted to establish a national, non-papal Church. In the states, governors followed their president's lead. For example, in January 1925, the governor of tropical Tabasco, Garrido Canábal (who had named his children Lucifer and Lenin) decreed that he would allow only six priests in his territory. In October Canábal granted only "married" priests over the age of 40 permission to remain in Tabasco.

Faithful Catholics, however, refused to submit to this violence. Since 1918, Anacleto Gonzáles Flores, a lawyer in Jalisco, had been writing books and articles detailing his vision of a Catholic social and political order for Mexico. The *Maestro*, as Flores' admirers called him, opposed democracy (he thought Mexico was not ready for it) but called for the popular methods of individual sacrifice and non-violent civil disobedience to oppose the government. To unite Catholics, he formed the *Union Popular*, whose journal, *Gladium* (Latin for "sword"), was reaching 80,000 readers by 1924.

In the autumn of 1925, Pope Pius XI denounced Mexico's revolutionary government, but he did not call on Mexican Catholics to undertake direct political resistance; rather he said they should concentrate on actions of a more religious, social, and cultural character. Some Mexican Catholics, however, concluded that nothing but political action would stop Calles from achieving his goal—the complete destruction of the Catholic Church in Mexico. This was the stance of the *Liga Nacional Defensora de Libertad Religiosa* (National League for the Defense of Religious Liberty) and its zealous leader, René Capistrán Garza. Founded in 1924, the *Liga* took a combative stance against the government's anti-Catholic measures.

The tension between Church and state came to a head in early 1926. On February 4, the newspaper *El Universal* published on

Anacleto González Flores (front center) with other members of the *Union Popular*

its front page an interview with Archbishop Mora y El Río of Mexico City in which he condemned the anti-clerical legislation of the Constitution of 1917. That the interview was nine years old mattered little to the anti-clericals—here was an assault on the foundations of the government! Calles was outraged. On July 2, he issued a penal code which laid down penalties for those who violated the constitution's anti-clerical articles. Calles insisted that all priests in Mexico register with the government—a measure preparatory to exile, or worse. He deported 200 foreign-born priests and religious. Thus, the president had thrown down his greatest challenge yet; how would the Church respond?

With defiance.

On July 14, the bishops gave their support to a measure Capistrán Garza and the *Liga* had called for—an economic boycott. Catholics boycotted movies or plays and gave up the use of government transportation. Catholic teachers refused to teach in public schools. But though many Catholics participated in the boycott, it was unsuccessful; for wealthy Catholics would have no part in it.

interdict: a sanction or punishment placed by the Church on a city or region. When a land is under interdict, no public rites of the Church, including public Masses, may lawfully be said. Priests, however, may privately administer necessary sacraments.

With the approval of Pope Pius XI, the bishops turned to another, more trenchant measure. They would place an **interdict** on Mexico. All public worship would cease, they threatened, if the government did not rescind its order for the registration of priests. Instead, priests would go into hiding and celebrate Masses and other rites in secret. Calles refused to budge from his demands, and the bishops carried out their threat. At Vespers on July 31, 1926, all public religious ceremonies ceased; the next day, no public Masses were said in all Mexico. Though Calles seized church buildings to keep them open (so the "superstitious," at least, could light their votive candles), for the next three years no Church bells, anywhere in Mexico, sounded their call to worship.

The Peasants Rise

The bishops had calculated that an interdict would rouse faithful Catholics against the government. They did not realize how terrible the response would be. From August to September 1926, spontaneous armed uprisings occurred, north of the capital, in west-central Mexico. In Guadalajara, 400 armed Catholics barricaded themselves in the church of Our Lady of Guadalupe. The insurgents stoutly defended themselves and only surrendered when they ran out of ammunition, leaving 18 dead and 40 wounded. Though other uprisings also ended in failure, they gave evidence that devotion to the Faith in Mexico was far from dead. Indeed, it was growing revolutionary.

The *Liga Defensora* caught the wind of revolt and decided to try organizing a full-scale rebellion On January 1, 1927, Capistrán Garza issued a call to arms: *A la Nación*—"To the Nation." The response was immediate. Anacleto González Flores, though he had been urging peaceful means, gave his approval to the rebellion, and thus the *Union Popular* entered the fight. On January 2, at San Miguel El Alto in Jalisco, Miguel Hernandez and Victoriano Ramirez organized a force of ranchers and farmers, armed with old guns, clubs, machetes, and axes. Similar uprisings occurred in Nayarit, Guanajuato, Zacatecas, and in Colima, chiefly among small farmers and ranchers, share croppers and laborers. Like the *Zapatista* peasants (some of whom joined the rebellion), the peasants of central Mexico had risen—this time in defense of the Church.

In the early battles, the insurgents were victorious against local forces but were defeated when they confronted the federal army—which led the federal commander in Jalisco, General Jesús Ferreira, to boast that he would conduct, not a campaign, but a hunt in the state. But in the Pacific coastal state of Colima he met his match in the person of an ex-seminarian and leader of the ACJM, Enrique de

Cristero leaders of the Castañon regiment

Jesús Ochoa. When Ochoa removed his insurgent force from Colima city to Caucentla on the border of Jalisco, Ferreira met him there—and was repulsed.

Because of the insurgents' war cry—*Viva Cristo Rey!* ("Long live Christ the King!")—the Federals, perhaps in mockery, named them *Cristo-reyes* or *Cristeros*. But though they might despise them for being peasants, Federal commanders learned to their dismay that the *Cristeros* had a number of gifted leaders. These were not militarily trained but were men of the common trades who discovered in the crucible of conflict a gift for strategy and command. Along with Ochoa were Jesús Degollado, a druggist; José Reyes Vega and Aristeo Pedroza, priests; and Victoriano Ramirez and Miguel Hernandez, ranch hands. Under such leaders, in the early months of 1927, *Cristero* forces won significant victories against crack federal cavalry at San Francisco del Rincón in Guanajuato, and at San Julián in Jalisco.

Martyrs for Christ the King

From his mother, Miguel Pro had learned to love the poor. On account of his father, a mining engineer, Miguel felt a sense of solidarity with the working class. So it was that when he entered the Jesuit novitiate at the age of 20, he was destined to disprove the old Liberal canard—that priests are moneygrubbers who ally themselves with the rich.

Mexican law forced Miguel Pro to leave Mexico, because he was a Jesuit. He studied in the United States, Spain, Nicaragua, and Belgium; but, because of stomach disorders, he returned to Mexico in 1925—a year after his priestly ordination. Living with his family, he carried on an underground ministry in Mexico City during the interdict, saying Mass, hearing confessions, and administering the other sacraments.

Padre Pro's brothers were active members of the *Liga Defensora*. On November 13, 1926, a car belonging to them was used in an assassination attempt on Calles; and though the Pro brothers had not been involved, they, along with Padre Pro, were arrested and imprisoned. Though no evidence convicted them of complicity in the assassination attempt, all were sentenced to death. Standing before the firing squad, Padre Pro prayed that God might forgive his executioners; then, with arms outstretched in token of the cross, he cried, *Viva Cristo Rey!*

Miguel Pro was not the first, or the last, priest to die under the revolution. Falsely accused of promoting the *Cristero* revolt, Padre Cristóbal Magallanes Jara was condemned to Miguel Pro's fate. Before he was shot, Magallanes distributed his scanty possessions among his executioners. After giving them absolution, he said, "I am innocent and I die innocent. I forgive with all my heart those responsible for my death, and I ask God that the shedding of my blood serves toward the peace of our divided Mexico." In April 1927, a parish priest of Totolan in Jalisco, Padre Sabas Reyes, suffered patiently while his

Picture of a martyr priest. An inscription on the picture reads: "Señor Don Francisco Vera, an elderly priest, shot in Jalisco for celebrating Mass."

hands and feet were burned, his bones broken, and his skull fractured. Finally, he was taken to the town cemetery to be shot. Four times the rifles fired, and at each report Reyes cried out, *Viva Cristo Rey!*

Not only priests but laymen suffered for their religion. David Roldan, Salvador Lara, and Manuel Morales, all laymen, were arrested with Padre Luis Batiz on August 15, 1926 at a town in Zacatecas. Even when offered their freedom, all refused to recognize the legitimacy of Calles' anti-clerical laws. Because Morales had children, Padre Batiz asked the soldiers to free him. Morales, however, preferred death. "I am dying for God," he said, "and God will care for my children."

These are but a few examples of the many who in Mexico died for the Faith in the late '20s and early '30s. Some were soldiers who at the last minute refused to carry out the execution of Catholics and were themselves executed. All displayed the spirit of the priest of Union de Tula in Jalisco who, when asked "Who lives?" answered not with the words that would save his life, "Long live the supreme government," but with the cry, "Christ the King and Our Lady of Guadalupe!" Three times he was asked the same question, and thrice he gave the same reply. For his courage, the priest died by hanging.

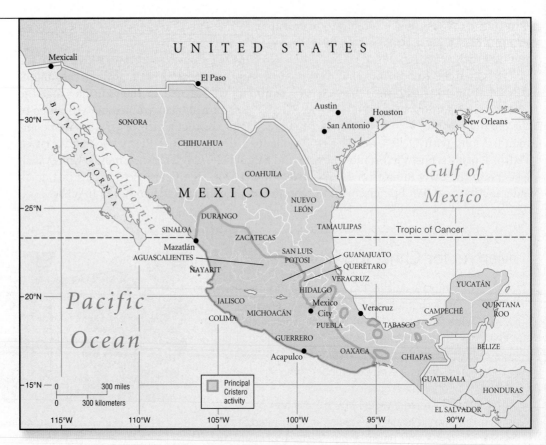

Areas of principal Cristero activity

To address a constant problem the *Cristeros* faced—a shortage in armaments—an underground arms network grew up in Mexico City to supply the insurgents. Women, members of the "Brigades of St. Joan of Arc," strapped gun belts under their dresses, passed through federal check points, and bravely crossed the lines to deliver ammunition to the rebels. Such an arms supply was not sufficient, however, and Capistrán Garza went to the United States to solicit funds to purchase more arms.

While Garza was in the United States, *Cristero* leaders adopted various methods to fill their empty war coffers. In the regions they controlled, they levied taxes on the people. They requisitioned the goods of large landowners. They attacked trains. Some *Cristero* commanders abducted wealthy men and demanded ransom for them; in the three years of the rebellion, six of these hostages were executed when the demanded ransoms did not materialize. Not all *Cristero* commanders, however, resorted to such measures. As Ezequiel Mendoza told his soldiers:

> We must be as brave as lions, but not tyrannical, as they [the federals] are towards us. We must be honest at all times. We will take from their goods what we need to live and fight, but we must not steal other men's goods. All the world's goods come from God, and we must not make bad use of this. If we take what is his in order to live and defend what is truly the cause of God, it is not stealing; we have only disposed of our own goods as those of our Father . . .

But, beginning in March 1927, the *Cristero* rebellion began suffering setbacks. The government, convinced that González Flores was the linchpin of the rebellion, had orders out for his apprehension. Having obtained evidence of his whereabouts, on March 3, 1927 federal secret police, along with city police agents, raided four homes in Guadalajara, the capital of Jalisco. They found the *Maestro* in one of the homes, along with his close associate, Luis Padilla, and two young men, Jorge and Ramon Vargas, the sons of the householder.

Throughout the night and early morning hours, the police tortured Flores and the three men, suspending them by their thumbs, whipping them, tearing at their bodies with bayonet points. Despite their pain, the four refused to reveal any of their plans or the whereabouts of their fellow *Cristeros*. Seeing they could get nothing out of them, the police lined them up for execution. It was noon, April 1, 1927. The four comrades faced their death with courage. Before the shots rang out, their leader, Anacleto González Flores, uttered these words: "I die, but God does not die. *Viva Cristo Rey!*" At Flores' funeral, thousands lined the streets of Guadalajara to pay their respects to the fallen hero.

The body of Anacleto González Flores, with his wife and children

The death of Flores did not stop the momentum of the rebellion—but a deed done by the priest-commander, José Reyes Vega, nearly did. Padre Vega was not a sterling character. He was none too strict with his vow of celibacy nor in his obedience to Canon Law, which forbade priests to take up arms. On April 19, 1927, Vega lost his brother in a raid the priest had led against a train. In revenge, Padre Vega ordered several train cars doused with gasoline and set afire. Fifty-one civilians died in the burning.

Vega's brutal act turned public opinion against the *Cristeros*. The federal General Ferreira marched into the Los Altos region of Jalisco and laid waste to 6,000 square miles, confiscating food and livestock. The peasants of the region, whether *Cristero* or not, he rounded up and placed in concentration camps. Then Capistrán Garza resigned from the *Liga Defensora* in July after failing to raise support for the rebellion in the United States. Both bishops and lay Catholics in the United States had been cold to Garza; one bishop even told him to get a job. The wealthy American Catholic, William F. Buckley, was at first willing to support the *Cristeros;* but when a bishop urged him against it, Buckley changed his mind. Without arms, the rebellion could not continue, and by summer it appeared that it was over.

The Uprising Rekindled

The *Cristero* rebellion would have died in the summer of 1927 but for one man—the guerrilla leader, Victoriano Ramirez. *El Catorce* ("the Fourteen") men called him for a legendary feat—that after breaking out of jail, he single-handedly killed 14 members of a posse sent out to arrest him. With the fame of this legend and a keen grasp of guerrilla tactics, Ramirez rekindled the rebellion in the Los Altos region of Jalisco There he found ready followers; for, not only had Los Altos all along been been the center of the rebellion, but its people had suffered harsh repression by the government. Federal troops had forced the native population to leave their homes and go into concentration camps. In this way the government thought it could keep the peasants from supplying the *Cristeros* and, moreover, confiscate their food and livestock.

Enrique Gorostieta y Velarde

With the rebellion again in full swing, the *Liga Defensora* decided that the scattered *Cristero* forces needed coordination and military discipline. They turned thus to a retired general, Enrique Gorostieta y Velarde, to take on overall command of the rebellion. Gorostieta, however, did not embrace the aims of the *Cristeros*. The mercenary general (he demanded twice the salary a federal general would receive) was a Liberal and a Freemason and mocked the religion for which the *Cristeros* died. But Gorostieta opposed Calles. His dream, it seems was to establish a truly Liberal republic that enforced separation of Church and state but did not interfere with religious belief or practice.

Believer or not, Gorostieta was an able commander. He turned the ragged bands of *Cristeros* into a disciplined army. The rebellion that had seemed dead now took on new life. *Cristero* forces grew to between 40,000 and 50,000 men and throughout 1928 defeated federal forces time and again on the field of battle—and this, despite the fact that the United States was supplying the federals with arms. President Calles thus had no choice but to see the *Cristeros* for what they were: a serious challenge to his government.

Who Were the Cristeros?

Gorostieta was not the only unbeliever to enter the ranks of the *Cristeros*; other leaders joined the insurgents to further their own aims. Even some of the rebellion's true adherents had mixed motives; for, other considerations (such as frustration over the slow pace of agrarian reform or, even, a hankering for adventure) influenced a would-be insurgent. Still, considering the movement as a whole, it was the religious motive that was paramount. Too, as we have seen, middle class, professional men (such as Capistrán Garza and Anacleto González Flores) were central to the rebellion; nevertheless the rank and file of the *Cristero* insurgent army (which included women and children as well as adult men) were drawn mostly from the peasant classes—the same sort of men who had followed Emiliano Zapata.

Calling the *Cristeros* peasants should not invoke disdain. For, though roughly 60 percent of them had never attended any school, like other peasant societies, they had a rich and evocative oral culture. The dialect of Spanish spoken in Jalisco (the center of the rebellion) would have been hard for a city-dwelling Mexican of the period to understand; but it was not, on that account, an inferior instrument of expression. The Spanish spoken by many of the *Cristeros* was essentially the Castilian dialect of the 15th–16th centuries, the period of some of Spain's greatest literary achievements. It had a large vocabulary drawn in part from the Gospels and the literary works of the Middle Ages. Yet, though their culture was oral, these *Cristero* peasants were not uninterested in literary works. Indeed, many of them taught themselves to read and indulged, not only in devotional books, but textbooks on law and even such subjects as astronomy. Moreover, it was not unusual for those who were literate

Cristeros **from Nayarit**

to read to their companions in camp or while they were engaged in work. Even the illiterate insurgent had an intellectual curiosity.

Some among the peasant *Cristero* leaders—when circumstances called them to it—discovered an aptitude for political organization. To maintain order in the liberated regions of Jalisco, Colima, Zacatecas, and Michoacán, *Cristero* leaders had to establish governments that, though led by military men, were nevertheless democratic in character. Religion inspired these civil governments to crack down on immoral behavior, including speculation in trade. For instance, General Manuel Michel, who was both military and civil leader in southern Jalisco, did not allow drunkenness, gambling, and prostitution among his troops, and insisted that they say a daily rosary. If wealthy *hacendados* refused to supply his army,

Gathering in the "Catholic Pueblo of Tlalpujahua" calling for the repeal of an anti-clerical law

he seized from them whatever he needed. He punished severely dealers in maize and other foodstuffs who tried to make money over and above a just return for their product and services. "Those who are making money," said one *Cristero* leader, "are our enemies, the maize dealers, and that is not what we want, it is not the time to be making money and sucking the blood of the people who are sacrificing themselves for the Cause of God."

"Sacrificing themselves for the Cause of God"—this phrase aptly sums up how the *Cristeros* saw themselves. Still, it would be mistaken to think of all *Cristeros* as holy or as strict followers of Catholic moral precepts. The fact that General Michel had to forbid gambling, drunkenness, and prostitution among his men demonstrates that they were not strangers to these vices. And though in many regions, such as Jalisco, the peasants had benefited from sound catechesis and a vibrant sacramental life, in others (where priests had been few or even nonexistent) the Catholic faith was confused with Indian pagan beliefs and practices.

Still, the *Cristeros* were men committed to their Catholic religion, which they encapsulated in the phrase, the "Kingship of Christ." They did not rise up against the government because of any natural proclivity for revolution, for these peasants had a deep regard for constituted authority and were profoundly patriotic (they continued to carry the Mexican tricolor flag in battle, but emblazoned with the image of Our Lady of Guadalupe). They rose because the civil authority had dared to assert itself against *Cristo Rey*. It had threatened to starve their souls by removing their priests, who alone could effect the Sacramental Bread that feeds men with God. Calles, they thought, was the servant of Freemasonry, Protestantism, and the United States—the great northern nation that had stolen vast amounts of territory from Mexico, that (as some *Cristeros* themselves had experienced) mistreated Mexican workers within its borders, and was now allied with those who would kill Mexico's very soul. And though most of their bishops opposed their uprising, the *Cristeros* saw themselves as the defenders of the Church, joined in the epic battle that had first pitted the Archangel Michael against the enemy of mankind. ". . . All history is the history of this war," said the *Cristero*, Ezequiel Mendoza:

> Woe to the tyrants who persecute Christ the King! They are the beasts in human shape of whom the Apocalypse speaks! . . . Now the Calleses are pressing us, they say it is because we are bad, because we are stubborn in wanting to defend the honor and glory of Him who died naked on the highest Cross between two thieves, because He was the worst of all humans because He did not wish to submit to the supreme lord of the earth.

Like *Cristo Rey*, the *Cristeros* refused to submit to the "lord of the earth" or his minion, Plutarco Calles.

"I Have Opened the Churches of Mexico"

The year 1928 was an election year, and, as every election year, it witnessed military insurrections against the government. When Calles had crushed these, he proposed that Alvaro Obregón succeed him in the presidency; their plan, it seems, was to take turns holding the office. Obregón easily won the election in the summer of 1928 but never took office. While in a restaurant on July 17, 1928, Obregón agreed to have his portrait drawn. While sketching the president-elect's portrait, the artist, José de León Toral, took out a gun and shot him in the face.

Toral was a Catholic, but many blamed Calles for Obregón's assassination. (Toral was unconnected to any Catholic group; he was a freelance assassin. Besides his own execution, only one other Catholic was arrested and imprisoned for "complicity" in the murder: an abbess called La Madre Conchita.) Calles faced the crisis by summoning state governors and military leaders to the capital, where he pledged that, from thenceforth, Mexico would not be ruled by personalities but by laws. Calles pledged to steer Mexico toward true democracy.

Calles, of course, could not constitutionally succeed himself as president, so the congress appointed Emilio Portes Gil, the former governor of Tamaulipas, as provisional president of the republic. Calles, though, remained at the center of power—self-dubbed the *jefe maximo* (supreme leader) of the revolution. Thus, after Portes Gil took office in December, it was Calles who wielded power.

As we have said, over the years, Calles had fallen more and more under the spell of the U.S. ambassador, Dwight Morrow. Morrow, who envisioned an American-style capitalist future for Mexico, had been urging Calles to abandon the revolution's agrarian policies and institute instead the direct sale of land for cash—a policy that would benefit the wealthy. Morrow also saw that the *Cristero* uprising was not good for business and urged Calles and President Portes Gil to come to an understanding with the Church. Father John J. Burke, the legal adviser to the United States bishops, supported Morrow's reconciliation effort. In 1929, Morrow and Burke arranged a secret meeting between themselves, along with the pope's delegate, exiled Msgr. Leopoldo Ruiz y Flores, bishop of Michoacán, as well as Portes Gil.

Most of the Mexican bishops had never backed the *Cristero* rebellion. In part this was because of a reticence to ally themselves with any political movement that they feared could compromise their position. Too, it was far from clear that the *Cristero* uprising could succeed—if for no other reason than that the U.S. government was backing Calles with money and arms. If the *Cristeros* were victorious, would the U.S. tolerate a Catholic government in Mexico, if such a regime came to be? And if they did not succeed, the prospect of a guerrilla war without any foreseeable end could jeopardize the interests of the Church, not help them.

Thus, with Morrow as facilitator and the warm support of Pope Pius XI, the government and the Mexican Church at last came to an agreement—*Los Arreglos*, "the arrangements." If the rebellion ended, the government said it would grant amnesty to all *Cristeros* who laid down arms; it pledged to restore their residences to priests and bishops, require civil registry of only some of the clergy, and allow religious instruction in churches (though not in schools). The *Arreglos* were announced on June 27, 1929. The next day, church bells were ringing once again throughout Mexico, and Dwight Morrow crowed (to his wife): "Betty, do you hear that? I have opened the churches of Mexico."

The *Cristeros*, in the meanwhile, had suffered further setbacks. *El Catorce*, accused of writing treasonable letters to a federal commander (his accuser, some think, was a federal spy), was court-martialed and executed. In March 1929, *Cristero* forces failed to take Guadalajara; and though on April 19 they beat the federals at Tepatitlán in Los Altos, Padre Vega took a bullet in the head, and died. On June 2, Gorostieta, who

Cristeros

had been vying for complete control of the rebellion, was shot down in an ambush. Still, the *Cristeros* were far from beaten, and only in obedience to their bishops and the pope did they lay down their arms in the summer of 1929.

Thus ended Mexico's last major peasant rebellion. The cause of religion had been vindicated, or so it seemed. Events proved, however, that the Church's woes in Mexico were far from over. No sooner had the *Arreglos* been issued than the government violated them by ordering the execution, on July 3, 1929, of the *Cristero* leader, Padre Aristeo Pedroza. And the betrayal continued. By the end of 1929, the government had executed all but two of the *Cristero* leaders in Guanajuato and Zacatecas. Between 1929 and 1935, 5,000 *Cristeros* (officers and men) were executed. Many of those who survived fled into the desert, tried to lose themselves in large cities, found refuge in states with governors sympathetic to their plight, or crossed the border into the United States.

The Revolution Becomes Institutional

Interim President Portes Gil at least appeared more revolutionary than his boss, Plutarco Elías Calles. During his short term in office, Gil accelerated the pace of agrarian reform and cut off government funding from the corrupt, but powerful, CROM. But if Gil lent his support to independent unions—even those with a Communist bent—this was merely a political maneuver to crush CROM and Luis Morones. After rendering CROM toothless, the government (that is, Calles) proceeded to smash the independent unions. Communist unions suffered the most in this assault.

In the election of 1929, *Obregonistas* and *Callistas* joined forces in a new party, *Partido Nacional Revolucionario* (PNR). The PNR was not to be a political party in the usual sense —it was not to be one party among many; it was to be the sole party of Mexico. Government employees had to pay a fixed proportion of their salaries to support the party. It would run presidential candidates who would be mere fronts for the real ruling power of the republic—Plutarco Elías Calles. Given the corruption in Mexican politics, a "National Revolutionary Party" would be certain to win every election.

This was the case in 1929. An "anti-re-electionist" candidate, the education reformer José Vasconcelos, opposed the PNR candidate, a non-entity named Pascual Órtiz Rubio. Like

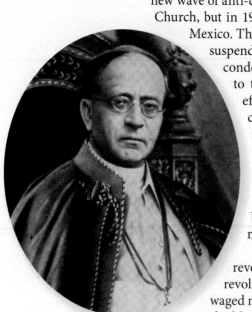

José Vasconcelos

Madero, Vasconcelos toured the country, giving public addresses to thousands. He seemed a relatively popular candidate. But election results, announced in November, gave Vasconcelos a mere 20,000 votes to over one million for Órtiz Rubio. Like Madero, Vasconcelos fled into the United States and called for revolution. No one answered his call, however, and he remained an exiled writer living north of the border.

The *jefe maximo*, Plutarco Calles remained the sole power in Mexico. In Cuernevaca, surrounded by wealthy *Obregonistas* and *Callistas*, in league with foreign capitalists, Calles dictated government policy by daily telephone calls to the presidential palace in Mexico City. Calles had now fully succumbed to Ambassador Morrow's influence. After returning from a trip to Paris in June 1930, the *jefe maximo* declared that the revolution's agrarian policy had been a failure—giving land to peasants, he said, was bad economics. This meant, of course, that President Órtiz Rubio halted all further land distribution to Indian villages and peasant proprietors. The president, however, soon overstepped his bounds by attempting to remove officials who were Calles' friends. In September 1932, after receiving word from Cuernevaca, Órtiz Rubio resigned from the presidency to be succeeded by a man more agreeable to the *jefe maximo*—Abelardo Rodríguez, a banker and gambling house owner.

While Órtiz Rubio was still president, the government (that is, Calles) again enacted a new wave of anti-clerical legislation. States had already been violating the *Arreglos* with the Church, but in 1931, the federal government undertook to limit the number of priests in Mexico. The Holy See opposed the archbishop of Mexico City's intended response, to suspend public worship; but Pope Pius XI did issue the encyclical, *Acerba Animi*, condeming the violation of the *arreglos* while calling on the faithful to submit to the government. But the government's anti-clerical campaign had dire effects. Riots and priest shootings increased. State governors closed churches. By 1935, only 305 authorized priests remained to minister to the millions of Catholics throughout the entire Republic of Mexico.

The assault on the priesthood was not Calles' last strike against the Church. In 1934, he issued his *Grito de Guadalajara*, declaring, "we must now proceed to . . . the psychological revolution; we must penetrate into, and take possession of, the consciences of children and the young people, because they belong and should belong to the revolution . . ." The government must enforce, said Calles, "socialist education."

This latest assault on the traditions of Catholic Mexico inspired a new revolt among about 7,500 former *Cristeros* in six regions of Mexico. This revolt—the "Second" they called it (but not the "Second *Cristiada*")—was waged not just against the state, but the Church, for many *Cristeros* felt their bishops had betrayed them in 1929 by signing on to the *Arreglos*. Fought in the savage sierras of Nayarit, Oaxaca, the Sierra Gorda, and the Sierra de Puebla, the Second, unlike the *Cristiada* of 1926–29, was both a terrorist and guerrilla struggle. Among its victims were school teachers, the agents of Calles' "socialist education" policy. By 1937, insurgents had killed 100 teachers and wounded or mutilated 200 others.

Forces, though, were at work which would shake and finally topple Calles' power. Younger men who had grown up during the revolution were not content to see the struggle end in a triumph for capitalism, native or foreign. Beginning in 1933, these men, who were heavily influenced by Communist theories, grew more influential in the PNR. This new power structure in the party saw to it that agrarian reform was reactivated and transferred from the the states to the authority of the federal government.

Pope Pius XI in 1930

Calles saw he had to appease the young leftists in the PNR, so he lent his support to the candidacy of Lázaro Cárdenas in the election of 1934. Calles, perhaps, did not realize what the election of Cárdenas presaged for the continuance of his power as the unofficial dictator of Mexico.

The Cárdenas Years

Lázaro Cárdenas' presidency began as an all-out war against the *Callistas*. The new president pushed agrarian reform, sympathized with strikes, and closed illegal gambling houses owned by Calles' friends. Cárdenas dismissed Calles' hand-picked cabinet members, and by forming coalitions with various anti-Calles groups, gradually isolated the *jefe maximo* in the PNR. Cárdenas final victory came in April 1936 when he deported both Calles and Luis Morones to Texas.

Lázaro Cárdenas

Once firmly established as head of the PNR, President Cárdenas sought to consolidate his power. He organized peasant militias. He admitted into the PNR delegates of unions and the peasants and then reorganized the party entirely, changing its name to *Partido Revolucionario Institucional* (PRI—the Institutional Revolutionary Party). The new party was to represent peasants, the workers, and the army.

No other Mexican president advanced agrarian reform like Cárdenas. By 1933, only 19 million acres had been distributed to peasants; between 1935 and 1940, Cárdenas' government distributed 45 million acres of land to 750,000 peasant families and to 12,000 villages. Mexican agriculture was still dominated by haciendas, but, because of Cárdenas' policies, 17.5 million acres went to *ejidos* and 19.5 million to private owners. In 1910, 95 percent of the land had been held by *hacendados*; by 1940, that percentage had shrunk to 60 percent.

The increase of peasant and *ejido* ownership of the land created its own problems. Since the agricultural methods applied by many *ejideros* were inefficient and only a small proportion of Mexico is arable (and of that much had been lost to erosion), food production could not keep up with the dramatic increase in population—five million in 20 years. Thus, Mexico had to import food. Cárdenas countered this problem by encouraging better agricultural methods and by the establishment of cooperatives to boost efficiency; but progress was slow.

In 1936, representatives of Mexico, the United States, and other Latin American countries met at a conference in Buenos Aires, Argentina. At this conference, the United States agreed that no American state should intervene in the internal affairs of another American state. This, albeit temporary, agreement served Cárdenas' purposes, for foreign capitalists with property in Mexico opposed his economic policies. To these men, the president was nothing but a Communist. Cárdenas, indeed, allowed the Russian Communist revolutionary Lev Trotsky refuge in Mexico after he had fallen out with Josif Stalin, and the Mexican government openly supported (as did many in the U.S.) the Communist-dominated Republican side in the Spanish Civil War. Still, Cárdenas did not call for state ownership of all industries; he seemed to favor employee ownership of businesses—not a Communist notion but nevertheless one all too radical for capitalist sensibilities.

Cárdenas found occasion to test the Buenos Aires non-intervention agreement in 1937. Workers in foreign-owned petroleum companies had gone on strike, and Cárdenas supported their demands. The government ordered the companies both to raise the workers' wages and begin appointing Mexicans to managerial positions in their companies. This seemed fair enough, for these companies had profited off Mexican oil for many years, with little benefit to the ordinary Mexican. But while the companies agreed to the wage increase, they resisted the other demands.

Ávila Camacho (seated right) with U.S. President Roosevelt

Cárdenas answered their defiance in May 1938 by confiscating all foreign-owned oil properties in Mexico. The companies called on the United States to intervene, but President Franklin Delano Roosevelt, true to the Buenos Aires agreement, refused. Cárdenas nationalized the oil properties into the Mexican Petroleum company. The state-owned oil-company suffered at first from inefficiency but also from a boycott when tankers refused to ship Mexican oil overseas. Cárdenas, however, found Nazi Germany, Fascist Italy, and imperialist Japan ready customers for his oil, and these powers set up a bartering arrangement in which oil was traded for the machinery Mexico needed to modernize her industries.

Though himself a virulent anti-Catholic, Cárdenas understood the utter failure of Calles' anti-clerical policies. In February 1936, he denounced those who placed "the religious problem above all the problems of the national program . . . [A]nti-religious campaigns," he said, "will only provoke a prolonged resistance and will definitely retard economic growth." Several days after Cárdenas gave this speech, seven governors commanded the reopening of churches in their states. Over the next several months, churches reopened in Mexico City, Veracruz, Nayarit, and Jalisco.

Though anti-clerical laws remained on the books under Cárdenas, most were not enforced. Indeed, relations between the government and the Church improved in the late '30s, with the Church coming out in favor of many government policies. Luis Maria Martinez y Rodriguez, who became archbishop of Mexico City in 1937, publicly urged support for the government in its fight with the oil companies. The government of Mexico, however, remained officially anti-Catholic, and it remained a crime for priests and religious to appear in public in clerical attire.

Government anti-clericalism inspired a new movement among former *Cristeros* and other Catholics—*Sinarquismo*. The *Sinarquistas* insisted that Mexico should acknowledge the Catholic religion and the country's Spanish heritage. They favored hierarchical government rather than democracy (which admittedly did not exist in Mexico) and called for the establishment of industrial organizations that included both workers and owners. In the matter of industrial organization, they followed Pope Pius XI, who, in his encyclical *Quadragesimo Anno*, proposed that in such organizations workers and employers could peacefully arbitrate their differences without the rancor that leads to and results from strikes. (Such organizations will be discussed in more detail in Chapter 26.) The *Sinarquistas* and other groups formed a political party, the *Partido Acción Nacional* (PAN—National Action Party; *pan* in Spanish means "bread"). But since the PRI controlled national and state elections, the PAN served as little more than an avenue for dissent—dissent that was often put down by violence.

End of the Revolution

Except for riots on election day, the year 1940 saw the first peaceful transition of power in Mexico in many years. The new president, Ávila Camacho, had been a PRI candidate but was a centrist in comparison to Cárdenas. Camacho, for one thing, favored industrial growth according to capitalist principles; and, what was more extraordinary, the new president publicly proclaimed himself a Catholic. Still, Camacho's regime did not change the essentially anti-clerical character of Mexican government. If the anti-Catholic laws were not stringently enforced under Camacho, they, nevertheless, remained on the books.

A mural by the Mexican artist Diego Rivera depicting the major figures of the Mexican Revolution

With the advent of Ávila Camacho and his more conservative policies, the Mexican revolution effectively ended. The party of the revolution, the PRI, became revolutionary in name only. In reality, it was a despotism that imposed its candidates and policies on the Mexican people. Mexico, as the PAN declared, was a sham democracy, a one-party government whose legitimacy rested on the pretense of popular suffrage. The struggle for the poor and downtrodden masses had ended only in setting up new oppressors. Thus the political fruits of the revolution.

The cultural and economic effects of the revolution however were significant. The revolution did allow more of the poor to own land. By the 1940s, over one-half of Mexico's arable land was held by *ejidos* and by small farmers. The revolution however did little to change the traditional condition of the Mexican people. About two-thirds of the people remained agricultural workers. Despite the government's education program, most Mexicans over the age of ten were still illiterate. Indeed, many Indian tribes still spoke their tribal tongues; some knew no Spanish and lived in the conditions that had prevailed among their peoples for centuries. Because of the revolution, however, Mexicans, most of whom were at least part Indian, began to identify themselves with their Indian heritage. Both Liberals and conservatives of the 19th century had embraced European models as their guide; the Liberals looked to Anglo-Saxon traditions, while the conservatives looked to Spain. The revolution made many Mexicans take pride in their Indian heritage.

And, despite itself, the revolution had made many Mexicans more Catholic. As in ancient Rome, so in Mexico: the blood of martyrs was the seed of the Church. It has been said that Mexicans were more Catholic in 1925 than they had been in 1910. The revolution had forced many to embrace the religion in which they had been born. Still, the revolution had shackled the Church. With dramatically fewer priests, many Mexicans, though devout, remained poorly catechized.

Yet, the Faith remained strong in Mexico and, in the years to come, inspired new calls for social justice against a repressive regime.

Chapter 24 Review

Summary

- Under President Porfírio Díaz, Mexico enjoyed a period of peace. Díaz invited foreign capital into Mexico and gave American landowners rights to land. He made peace with the Catholic Church, making a secret agreement with the Church in Mexico that would allow him to approve all Church appointments. Due to this, the Church became subservient to the government and alienated herself from the people by allying herself with Díaz. Sectors of the Church in Mexico, however, began to take a serious and critical look at Díaz's society, and Catholics formed Catholic workers circles and held social justice congresses.

- A new transformation came about in Díaz's government due to a group of young men called *científicos*. As a consequence, workers were in grievous want and working conditions were poor. Workers were growing revolutionary, however, as new ideas, including anarchism and socialism, spread to Mexico, inspiring the formation of unions and the calling of strikes.

- In the south of Mexico, resistance to Díaz's regime was beginning, led by Emiliano Zapata. Zapata organized a defense committee in 1909, after which the villagers of Anencuilco peacefully seized hacienda lands and divided them amongst themselves.

- More resistance arose in the form of words from Francisco Madero, who wrote that the country should return to the Constitution of 1857 and Díaz not seek re-election. In 1910, anti-re-electionists nominated Madero as their presidential candidate. *Maderistas* converged on the National Palace in Mexico City to protest the Díaz regime, and Madero was arrested. Two weeks later, Díaz was re-elected.

- On his release from prison, Madero fled to Texas, where he declared the elections null and void and published the *Plan de San Luis Potosí*, calling on the people of Mexico to rise against Díaz. Forces began to gather under Pascual Orozco and Pancho Villa, and on November 27, 1910, they defeated federal troops, thus beginning a full-fledged rebellion.

- The *científico* leader, José Limantour, took control of the government in Mexico City, and sought an armistice with the rebel leaders. Madero was willing to sign an armistice but was persuaded not to, and laid down more demands. The revolution ran swiftly towards victory. Díaz's friends and family finally convinced him to resign.

- The provisional president, Francisco de la Barra, was not able to carry out the radical provisions of Madero's plan, and many people came to distrust Madero himself. Catholics in Mexico, dissatisfied with the state of things in Mexico, formed the National Catholic Circle and the Guadalupan Workers.

- Zapata decided it was time to reignite the revolution. On November 25, 1911, he published the *Plan de Ayala* as the standard for the renewed struggle. On February 9, 1913, the rebellion began.

- After the capture and execution of Madero, Victoriano Huerta became president. Huerta was dissipated and cruel and inspired a new uprising, led by Venustiano Carranza, Alvaro Obregón, and Pancho Villa.

- The revolution began to take an anti-clerical turn. Carranza and Obregón were from the northern regions of Mexico, where in many areas there had been historically little contact with the Catholic Church. Revolutionaries' opposition to traditional Mexican culture drew them into an attack on the Church, which they believed hampered Mexico's entrance into American-style prosperity.

- Woodrow Wilson, the president of the United States, disapproved of President Huerta, and began arming Carranza and the Constitutionalist forces. With the aid of the United States, the revolutionaries forced the federal garrison in Mexico City to surrender, and five days later, Obregón marched his army in triumph into the city.

- The overthrow of Huerta, however, did not bring peace to Mexico, and divisions that had plagued the revolutionary forces became clearly pronounced. The *Villistas* and the *Carranzistas* accused each other of betraying the struggle. Carranza suggested holding a convention of rebel leaders in Mexico City, where he could control it. Villa wanted to hold the convention in Aguascalientes, where Villa could control it. Villa and Zapata then marched on Mexico City, beginning a civil war.

- In the United States, business interests with property in Mexico, as well as Catholics, urged President Wilson to intervene in the Mexican civil war. President Wilson gave his support to Carranza, causing Villa to turn on the Americans, who, he thought, had betrayed him.

- By the spring of 1916, most regions of Mexico recognized Carranza as provisional president, but the country was far from peaceful. Carranza could not keep order and alienated many of his cabinet. In the autumn Carranza called for a constitutional convention to revise the Constitution of 1857. The new Constitution of 1917 was very controversial, especially in regards to the Church.

- Carranza used his power against the radicals, which caused radical elements to flare up in opposition to him. When Carranza tried to break a railroad strike in Sonora, the Sonoran governor, Adolfo de la Huerta, declared his state's independence, and he and Plutarco Calles issued a plan calling for the removal of Carranza. Carranza fled, and Obregón and his army marched into Mexico City, where Obregón was sworn in as president.

- Obregón appeared to be a friend to labor and radical agrarian aspirations, and businessmen in the United States complained he was a "Bolshevist." Obregón needed U.S. support if his hand-picked candidate for president, Plutarco Calles, were to succeed him without trouble in 1923, so he gave in to Washington's demands, and President Calvin Coolidge recognized his government in August 1923. A rebellion broke out over the election of 1923. The rebellion was quickly crushed with the aid of the United States, and Calles became president.

- Calles ruled as an absolute dictator and remained resolutely in opposition to the Church. He vigorously applied the anti-clerical articles of the 1917 constitution. On June 14, 1926, he decreed that priests who wore their clerical garb in public were to be fined, and he closed seminaries, monasteries, and Church-run institutions.

- Faithful Catholics refused to submit to this violence. The lawyer Anacleto Gonzáles Flores formed the *Union Popular* to unite Catholics. In the autumn of 1925, Pope Pius XI denounced Mexico's government but did not call on Mexican Catholics to undertake violent resistance. Some Catholics, however, thought no peaceful resistance was possible, and Rene Capistrán Garza founded the *Liga Defensora de Libertad Religiosa* (National League for the Defense of Religious Liberty) in 1924 against the government's anti-Catholic measures.

- When a newspaper published an interview with the archbishop of Mexico City wherein he condemned the anticlerical legislation of the Constitution of 1917, Calles was outraged and issued a penal code that laid down penalties for those who violated the anti-clerical articles. The Church responded with defiance, and on July 14, the bishops gave their support to an economic boycott. When that did not work, the bishops received the approval of the pope to place an interdict on Mexico, causing all public worship to cease.

- Beginning in August 1926, spontaneous armed uprisings occurred throughout Mexico. On January 1, 1927, the *Liga Defensora* issued a call to arms. Under leaders such as Miguel Hernandez and Victoriano Ramirez, insurgent forces fought the federal army. The federals named the insurgents *Cristeros*.

- The rebellion suffered from setbacks and would have died in the summer of 1927 had not Victoriano Ramirez, nicknamed *El Catorce*, rekindled the rebellion. The *Liga* decided the scattered Cristero forces needed coordination and military discipline, and Enrique Gorostieta y Velarde took on the command of the rebellion, training the *Cristeros* into a disciplined army.

- In 1929, the American ambassador, Dwight Morrow, encouraged Calles to come to an agreement with the *Cristeros*. With the support of the pope, the government and the Mexican Church came to an agreement, the *Arreglos*, announced on June 17, 1929. The Mexican Church's woes were far from over, however, as the government violated the *Arreglos* by executing *Cristero* leaders.

- Though new presidents came into office, Calles remained the sole power in Mexico. In 1931 the federal government enacted a new wave of anticlerical legislation, closing churches and enforcing "socialist education." This inspired a new revolt among for-

Chapter 24 Review (continued)

mer *Cristeros*, waged also against the Church, which they thought had betrayed them.

- A new party formed with the elections 1929, the *Partido Nacional Revolucionario* (PNR). A new power structure in the PNR began to diminish Calles' power in 1933. When Lázaro Cárdenas became president, he waged political war against Calles. In 1936 Cárdenas deported Calles and Luis Morones to Texas.

- In 1936, representatives of Mexico, the United States, and other Latin American countries met in conference, agreeing that no American states should intervene in the internal affairs of another American state.

- Though anti-Catholic himself, Cárdenas in 1936 denounced those who placed the religious problem above all the problems of the national program. He allowed churches to reopen throughout Mexico. It still remained a crime for priests to appear in public in clerical attire, however. This inspired a new movement among Catholics, *Sinarquismo*. The *Sinarquistas* and other groups formed a political party, the *Partido Acción Nacional (*National Action Party), or PAN.

- The election of Ávila Camacho in 1940 was the first peaceful transition of power in Mexico in many years. With the election of Camacho, the Mexican revolution effectively ended.

Key Concepts

interdict: a sanction or punishment placed by the Church on a city or region. When a land is under interdict, no public rites of the Church, including public Masses, may lawfully be said. Priests, however, may privately administer necessary sacraments.

Bolshevism: the doctrine of the Bolshevists, those who espoused Marxist Communism and sought the violent overthrow of capitalism

científico: a member of a group of officials in Mexico who advocated the practical application of scientific methods to problems in society and industry

Plan de Ayala: Emiliano Zapata's plan that called for land redistribution in favor of the peons

Cristero: a member of the insurgent army that fought against Calles' enforcement of the anti-clerical articles of the Constitution of 1917

Dates to Remember

1909: Emiliano Zapata and the villagers of Anencuilco peacefully reoccupy hacienda lands.

1910: Francisco Madero publishes the *Plan de San Luis Potosí* and calls on the people of Mexico to rise against President Díaz.

1911: revolutionary forces rise against Díaz. Díaz resigns, and Madero becomes president.

1912: Zapata renews the struggle by publishing the *Plan de Ayala* (November 25).

1913: palace guard arrests Madero and his cabinet, and Victoriano Huerta becomes president (February 18).

1914: after the United States offers its support to revolutionary forces, the federal garrison in Mexico City surrenders to Alvaro Obregón. President Huerta flees Mexico City (August 10).

The Aguascalientes Convention

1917: Promulgation of the Constitution of 1917

1920: Adolfo de la Huerta and Plutarco Calles call for the removal of Carranza. Obregón becomes president.

1924: Calles becomes president.

1926: Calles enforces the anti-clerical articles of the Constitution of 1917.

The bishops of Mexico call for an economic boycott (July 14).

The interdict on Mexico goes into effect, and all public religious ceremonies cease (July 31).

1927: Capistrán Garza issues a call to arms. The *Cristeros* rise against Calles.

1929: the Church and the Mexican government come to an agreement (June 27).

The *Cristeros* lay down their arms.

1934: Lázaro Cárdenas becomes president, ending Calles' unofficial dictatorship.

1936: representatives of Mexico, the United States, and other Latin American countries meet and draw up the Buenos Aires non-intervention agreement.

1938: President Cárdenas nationalizes Mexican oil properties into Mexican Petroleum.

Central Characters

Emiliano Zapata (1879–1919): the leader of the Mexican Revolution in the south, 1910–1919

Francisco Madero (1873–1913): politician and revolutionary, who became president of Mexico after the ouster of the dictator, Porfirio Díaz

Pancho Villa (1878–1923): the leader of the Mexican Revolution in Chihuahua and a major rival to Carranza and Obregón

Victoriano Huerta (1854–1916): the general who overthrew Madero and became president of Mexico. He was driven from power by by Venustiano Carranza and Alvaro Obregón.

Venustiano Carranza (1859–1920): revolutionary leader who called the constitutional convention that drew up the Constitution of 1917

Alvaro Obregón (1880–1928): general and president, who restored order to Mexico after the overthrow of Venustiano Carranza

Plutarco Elías Calles (1877–1945): anti-clerical president of Mexico who moved from agrarian radicalism to become a champion of Mexican capitalism. His enforcement of the anticlerical provisions of the Constitution of 1917 inspired the *Cristero* uprising.

Dwight Morrow (1873–1931): United States ambassador to Mexico who greatly influenced President Calles and helped bring the *Cristero* uprising to an end.

Blessed Anacleto Gonzáles Flores (1888–1927): Catholic lawyer and a leader of the resistance to the government's anti-clericalism. Executed during the *Cristero* war, he was beatified as a martyr by Pope Benedict XVI in 2005.

Rene Capistrán Garza (1898–1974): founder of the National League for the Defense of Religious Liberty during the *Cristero* war

Victoriano Ramirez ("El Catorce") (late 1880s–1929): a guerrilla leader who rekindled the *Cristero* war in Jalisco. He was called *El Catorce* ("the Fourteen") for his legendary feat of single-handedly killing 14 men who were sent to arrest him.

Enrique Gorostieta y Velarde (1889–1929): Mexican general who was given overall command of the *Cristero* forces and formed them into a disciplined army

Lázaro Cárdenas (1895–1970): president of Mexico who ended Calles' unofficial dictatorship

Questions for Review

1. What problems troubled Mexico during Porfirio Díaz's regime?

2. How did the policies of the *científicos* affect the Mexican government and society during the years of Porfirio Díaz's regime?

3. What situation stirred Emiliano Zapata to lead a revolt in Morelos?

4. How did Catholics respond to societal problems in Mexico both during the years of Díaz's regime and afterward?

5. Why did those who had supported President Madero at last stir up a revolution against him?

6. Why and how did the revolution against Huerta turn anti-clerical?

7. How did the United States affect the course of the revolution?

8. What were the principles of the Constitution of 1917?

9. Describe the events that caused the *Cristero* uprising.

10. What chiefly motivated the *Cristeros* in their uprising?

11. Why were the bishops of Mexico hesitant to back the *Cristeros*?

12. How did the PNR weaken Calles' power?

13. What was the significance of the Buenos Aires non-intervention agreement?

14. What were the cultural, religious, and economic effects of the Mexican Revolution?

Chapter 24 Review (continued)

Ideas in Action

1. Study a map of Mexico and identify the regions and places mentioned in this chapter.

2. Listen to *corridos* (Mexican ballads) that tell of events and persons of the Second Mexican Revolution and the *Cristero* uprising. What do these ballads tell us about how the Mexican people view these struggles?

3. Read literature about the *Cristero* war, such as Elizabeth Borton de Treviño's *The Fourth Gift*.

4. Read the lives of the martyrs of the *Cristero* war.

5. How did the policies pursued by Plutarco Elías Calles epitomize the ideals of Liberalism, especially Mexican Liberalism?

6. Was the *Cristero* uprising a just war, according to the principles of Catholic just war doctrine? (See the *Catechism of the Catholic Church*, 2258–2317)

Highways and Byways

A Child-Martyr of the Cristero War

As does every war, the *Cristero* war involved many children. One of these was José Sánchez del Río. José was 14 years old when the *Cristero* war broke out. His brothers went to fight, but neither José's mother nor the *Cristero* general, Prudencio Mendoza, allowed him to enlist. When José insisted that he wanted to give his life for Jesus and and thus attain Heaven, the general relented and allowed him to be the flag bearer to the *Cristero* army.

The *Cristeros* gave José the nickname Tarcisius after an early Christian saint who was martyred while trying to protect the Eucharist. He soon was given an opportunity of living up to this name. In a battle with federal forces, José gave his own horse to a general whose own horse had been killed. Seeking cover, José fired at the federals until he ran out of ammunition and was captured.

Two of José's childhood friends watched as his captors ordered José to renounce his faith in Christ under threat of death, but he refused. His tormentors tried to break José's resolve by cutting off the bottoms of his feet and making him walk around the town, but he would not abandon his faith. When they said to him, "If you shout, 'Death to Christ the King,' we will spare your life," José cried out repeatedly, "*Viva Cristo Rey!*" A soldier then led José to his grave, and there the commander shot him. Just before he died, José drew a cross in the dirt and kissed it. He was canonized by Pope Francis on October 16, 2016.

THE WAR TO END ALL WARS

War in Europe—Should America Fight?

An ocean and nearly a continent away from America, the Habsburg heir to the dual monarchy of Austria-Hungary, Archduke Franz Ferdinand, and his wife Sophie were visiting the provincial capitol of Sarajevo in Bosnia. Franz Ferdinand was not popular with Austrians, Magyars, or Serbians—the peoples who made up the empire over which the Emperor Franz Josef, his uncle, ruled. Franz Ferdinand had, since his marriage to Countess Sophie Chotek, a woman of lower rank, grown reclusive and distant to all but his most immediate family. Furthermore, his ideas of reforming the empire, of turning it into a triple monarchy where the Slavs would have equal voice with the Austrians and the Hungarians, stoked opposition among certain interests who liked things the way they were. The people of the little country of Serbia were also not pleased with Franz's proposed reforms. They wanted the two Serbian provinces, Bosnia and Herzegovina (which Austria-Hungary had annexed in 1908), to join Serbia. They feared that if Franz Ferdinand's reforms came off, the Serbians of Bosnia and Herzegovina would be content to remain in the empire.

So it was that members of the Serbian terrorist group, the "Black Hand," were in Sarajevo on the day (June 28, 1914) the archduke and his wife rode through the streets of the city in a motorcade. As the motorcade passed along the main street of the city, a member of the Black Hand threw a bomb towards the car that was conveying the archduke and his wife. The bomb missed the royal couple. Somewhat ruffled by the event, Franz Ferdinand and Sophie continued on to the mayor's palace, where they were given a formal welcome. Following this reception, the motorcade continued on, but the archduke's car took a wrong turn. Realizing the mistake, the driver stopped in order to turn around. Only a few feet away, a member of the Black Hand, Gavrilo Princip, stepping out of a sandwich shop, saw his chance and, walking up to the car, shot both the archduke and his wife. As the car sped away, Franz Ferdinand saw Sophie collapse and cried out, "*Sopherl! Sopherl! Sterbe nicht! Bleibe am Leben für unsere Kinder!*" ("Dear Sophie! Dear Sophie! Do not die! Remain alive for our children!") Sophie died before reaching the governor's palace, and Franz Ferdinand did not long survive her.

The shot that killed the archduke was the first in a long war that in a mere four years would claim millions of human lives. The government of

Archduke Franz Ferdinand, his wife, Sophie, and their family, 1910

Europe in 1914

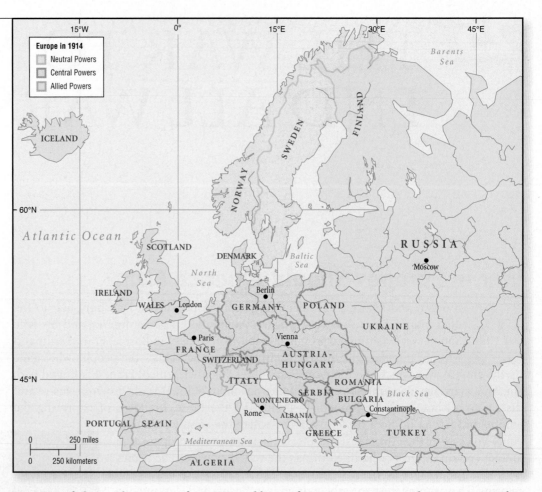

Europe in 1914
- Neutral Powers
- Central Powers
- Allied Powers

Franz Josef, the aged emperor of Austria and king of Hungary, acting on the assumption that the government of Serbia was responsible for the assassination of the emperor's nephew and heir, made harsh demands of Serbia. If the demands were not honored, Austria-Hungary threatened war on the small nation. When Serbia refused to accede to all of the demands and began a partial mobilization of its army, Austria-Hungary, on July 28, declared war. Russia, which, under the rule of Tsar Nikolai II wanted a wider union of Slavic peoples, backed Serbia, and began a partial mobilization of Russian armies—at the time considered a belligerent act, tantamount to a declaration of war. Austria's ally, the German Empire, then declared war on Russia.

The nations of Europe at the time were divided into two alliances. Germany was the leader of one alliance that included Austria-Hungary and Italy. The high command of the German army and the *kaiser*, Wilhelm II (Teddy Roosevelt's old friend), had promised to back the tottering Habsburg empire if it went to war with Serbia. This was a gamble, for Germany realized that war with Serbia would entail war with Russia as well as France, for France had formed an alliance with Russia as a check on Germany's power. Such a war would involve Germany in a two-front war, on the east and the west. Yet, the German high command was confident that they could prevail in such a war. On August 3, Germany declared war on France.

German war plans for attacking France entailed crossing the level plains of Belgium. The problem was that Belgium was a nation whose neutrality was guaranteed by Great Britain, the foremost sea power of the world. On August 4, the day after declaring war on France, Germany invaded Belgium; and at midnight of the same day, Great Britain declared war on Germany. The "Great War," as it would be called, had begun.

America Shall Not Fight

On August 19, 1914, in his message to Congress, President Woodrow Wilson declared that, in the face of the war raging in Europe, "the United States must be neutral in fact as well as in name. . . . We must be impartial in thought as well as in action, must put a curb upon our sentiments." He need not have given this counsel; for, as of August 1914, American opinion was largely for staying out of the war. The policy of George Washington and of Thomas Jefferson, that the United States should remain free of foreign entanglements, was a deep-seated conviction in the hearts and minds of most Americans. Too, almost everyone, both in Europe and America, thought the war would be over in a matter of months; there was no point in intervening in a short-lived conflict overseas. Teddy Roosevelt, in the *Outlook* of August 22, said of the war, "I am not now taking sides"; and a month later he called Germany a "stern, virile and masterful people" against whom it would be "folly" to fight.

Yet, American opinion about the war was not entirely neutral. On the east and west coasts of the nation, college-educated and prosperous Americans favored intervention on the side of the Entente, as the British, Russian, and French alliance was called; and in the South, where there was strong pro-English sentiment, many were in favor of aiding Great Britain. With Canada entering the war as a British dominion, some American college graduates tried to land commissions in the British army. Others joined the French foreign legion and formed a division of the French air force called the Lafayette Escadrille (named for the French Marquis de Lafayette who fought for America in the revolution), or organized an American ambulance service for the Entente.

The greatest anti-war sentiment was found in the Midwest, where were many settlements of Germans, whose sympathies naturally lay with the Fatherland. There, too, Populist sentiment, still strong, saw the war as the work of commercial interests vying for foreign markets. Bankers and munitions makers, too, who stood to profit from the conflict, were at the root of the war, in Populist minds. Even the great Detroit automobile manufacturer, Henry Ford, did his part for peace; he chartered a steamship to carry preachers and pacifists to the belligerent European nations to persuade them to "get the boys out of the trenches by Christmas."

In Europe, the initial German push had looked impressive. In the east, Generals Hindenburg and Ludendorff had defeated Russian armies at Tannenberg and the Masurian lakes (August 26–September 15, 1914). In the West, the German offensive had pushed within a few miles of Paris. In early September, French and British forces attacked the Germans in five separate battles, which the French later combined into one "Battle of the Marne." After each battle, the Allies retreated. But the German high command, deciding that its army was holding insecure positions, commanded it to retreat about 31 miles to a strong defensive position on the River Aisne. The Allies could thus claim that they had forced the enemy to abandon the field. Through the remainder of the year, neither side gained any significant advantage, and by year's end the war developed into a bloody slugging match between two armies ensconced in trenches.

Britain's superiority at sea became decisive early on. The Royal Navy formed a tight blockade of German ports and bottled up the German fleet in its harbors. British naval ships stopped all neutral ships bound for Europe and confiscated all cargo marked for Germany. Though the British were doing the same thing that the union did in her blockade of southern ports in the Civil War, President Wilson and his secretary of state, William Jennings Bryan, protested Britain's "highhanded" policy. Feeling against Great Britain intensified and was only allayed when the Entente began placing large orders for food and munitions in the United States. The United States had been suffering from an economic recession in 1914, which this increased buying relieved. The Entente nations also took out direct loans from American banks.

But in the end, Germany's response to the British blockade did more to irritate America than the blockade itself. Since the German surface navy was powerless against British sea

A German U-Boat with crew

A British military recruiting poster, ca. 1915, depicting the sinking of the *Lusitania*

might, Germany began to dive under sea to attack British ships. This submarine, or "U-boat" (for *Unterseeboot*) warfare was at first directed only against British warships; but in order to cripple British trade like the British had crippled Germany's, the German high command decided to direct U-boat warfare against commercial shipping. Since the U-boats were slow and were ineffective at stopping ships, they simply sank merchant ships instead of boarding and searching them.

On February 4, 1915, Kaiser Wilhelm announced that all waters around the British Isles were a war zone and that all merchant ships bound for Allied ports within those waters would be sunk. On February 10, Wilson told the German government that the United States would hold them "to a strict accountability" for any American "property damaged or lives lost." At this early period of U-boat warfare, German policy was to grant sufficient time for crews to disembark onto lifeboats before their ship was destroyed. But on May 1, 1915, a U-boat sank an American tanker, the *Gulflight,* without warning. The United States accepted Germany's offer of an apology and reparations for what the German government called an "unfortunate accident."

The same day the *Gulflight* was sunk, the British liner *R.M.S. Lusitania* set sail from New York, bound for England. Though a passenger ship, the *Lusitania* had been outfitted with 12 six-inch guns in 1913 (in case of war with Germany.) On this voyage, among other cargo, the ship carried munitions—shrapnel shells and rifle shells. On April 22 the Imperial German Embassy in the United States had issued the following notice:

> Travelers intending to embark on the Atlantic voyage are reminded that a state of war exists between Germany and her allies and Great Britain and her allies; that the zone of war includes the waters adjacent to the British Isles; that, in accordance with formal notice given by the Imperial German Government, vessels flying the flag of Great Britain, or any of her allies, are liable to destruction in those waters and that travelers sailing in the war zone on ships of Great Britain or her allies do so at their own risk—

Despite this warning, only one passenger on the *Lusitania* changed his travel arrangements.

On May 7, near Queenstown, Ireland, the *Lusitania* met a German U-boat that had been patrolling the waters off the coast of Iceland. The U-boat commander, without warning, fired his last torpedo at the liner—not thinking it would sink the ship, it was said, but out of curiosity to see what damage it would do. A great explosion from the hold of the *Lusitania* followed the smaller detonation of the torpedo. In the sinking of the *Lusitania,* more than 1,100 civilian passengers lost their lives; 128 of them were American.

The sinking of the *Lusitania* aroused American opinion against Germany. Still, many Americans preferred that the United States not join the war against Germany. Some of these were German-Americans, with ties to the old country. Others were Irish-Americans who, while not exactly loving the Germans, hated the English. Theodore Roosevelt, who had grown quite anti-German, spoke with contempt of these "hyphenated Americans." "Our citizens," he said, "must act as Americans; not as Americans with a prefix and qualifications; not as Irish-Americans, German-Americans, native Americans—but as Americans pure and simple." Roosevelt spoke the language of the melting pot—the boiling down of all national groups until they were indistinguishable in a common cultural soup. "We are making a new race, a new type, in the country," Roosevelt declared; and the language this people should speak is "the language of the Declaration of Independence and the Constitution, of Lincoln's Gettysburg speech and Second Inaugural, and of Washington's farewell address."

"If I were President now," said Theodore Roosevelt, "I would take the most emphatic action about the German conduct in sinking the *Lusitania*. I regard this as sheer murder, and the German attitude in this war has been a return . . . toward the attitude of the Huns. There is only one way to meet people who adopt such an attitude, and that is to make them suffer for maintaining it."

In speaking of the attitude of the Hun, Roosevelt referred not only to the *Lusitania* but to Allied reports of German atrocities against civilians in Belgium. Whatever truth there was to these reports, they were vastly exaggerated by the Allies; and since Great Britain had cut Germany's transcontinental cable, the "Huns" had no way of telling their side of the story to Americans. Thus, the sinking of the *Lusitania*, coupled with French and English propaganda, embittered Americans against the German *Reich*.

If Roosevelt had been president, he, perhaps, would have used public sentiment to wring out of Congress a declaration of war against Germany. As events proceeded, he became more and more critical of Wilson and his neutrality. "In a really tremendous world struggle, with a great moral issue involved," Roosevelt said, "neutrality does not serve righteousness, for to be neutral between right and wrong is to serve wrong." Roosevelt thought Wilson himself was a "scholarly, acrid pacifist of much ability and few scruples"; and though Teddy's father had bought his way out of serving in the Civil War, Roosevelt could criticize Wilson for coming "of a family none of whose members fought on either side in the Civil War."

Yet, Roosevelt was not president, and the man who was, was not eager for war. Almost a week after the sinking of the *Lusitania*, Wilson, through Secretary of State Bryan, demanded that the German government take responsibility for the sinking and make reparations in order to "prevent the recurrence of anything so obviously subversive of the principles of warfare." Wilson said that, though Germany undertook her submarine warfare as retaliation for the British blockade, still the "Imperial German Government" must accept—as Wilson was sure it did—that "the lives of non-combatants, whether they be of neutral citizenship or citizens of one of the nations at war, can not lawfully or rightfully be put in jeopardy by the capture or destruction of an unarmed merchantman." Germany, said Wilson, must, like other nations, "take the usual precaution of visit and search to ascertain whether a suspected merchantman is in fact of belligerent nationality or is in fact carrying contraband of war under a neutral flag."

Wilson's message recognized the fact that "it is practically impossible for the officers of a submarine to visit a merchantman at sea and examine her papers," and so, "manifestly submarines cannot be used against merchantmen." Since, the president, in effect, was telling Germany she must forgo her only means of blockading England, it is not surprising that the

The cover of the weekly French journal for soldiers, *La Baïonnette*, depicting the German *kaiser* as a death's head. The caption below the pictures reads, *Bas les masques? . . . Voila!*—"Off with the masks? There it is!"

German government delayed returning a reply. On June 9, Wilson composed another note to the German government in which he denied the legality of forming a war zone around an enemy country. Secretary Bryan, who was strongly in favor of the U.S remaining neutral, so opposed the second note that he resigned rather than sign it. "Germany has a right to prevent contraband from going to the Allies," said Bryan, "and a ship carrying contraband should not rely upon passengers to protect her from attack—it would be like putting women and children in front of an army."

The sinking of the *Lusitania* was a crisis moment. While it didn't bring the United States into the European war, it certainly led to significant policy changes in Wilson's administration. Wilson had never been strong at foreign policy; rather, he had focused on domestic problems. Now, forced to attend to the international arena he began to think that war, though undesirable, was a real possibility. He began to believe that America's army and navy must be made ready just in case war proved to be the country's lot.

Preparedness

Wilson did nothing immediately to prepare the country for the event of war. Instead, civilians provided the catalyst for military preparedness. General Leonard Wood had, in 1913, established a military training camp at Plattsburg, New York, to train civilians in the techniques of modern warfare. With the outbreak of war in Europe, these camps spread throughout the country and, in 1915, included two of Roosevelt's sons, Theodore, Jr., and Quentin. The elder Roosevelt went about the country promoting the camps and military preparedness in general. The "military tent, where boys sleep side by side," he said, "will rank next to the public school among the great agents of democracy."

The sinking of the passenger liner *Arabic* on which three Americans were killed on August 19 added fuel to the military preparedness movement. On August 30, Wilson demanded that Germany abandon warfare of this sort; the German government agreed and forbade the sinking of passenger liners. On September 19, the Germans took the further step of withdrawing all U-boats from the English Channel. Wilson, it seemed, had scored a diplomatic victory.

In the fall of 1915, Wilson himself took up the cry of preparedness. In a speech before Congress on November 4, he referenced Ezekial 33:6 as proof-text for military preparedness:

Trench warfare in World War I

"But if the watchman see the sword come, and blow not the trumpet, and the people be not warned . . . his blood will I require at the watchman's hands." Wilson faced stiff opposition. William Jennings Bryan and Senator La Follette declared that Wilson was the dupe of men who wanted to profit off the production of armaments; preparedness they said would lead ultimately to war. Farm and labor groups joined Bryan and La Follette in denouncing the president. To drum up support for preparedness, Wilson toured the country, stumping for his policies.

German war policies in the winter and spring of 1916 helped Wilson and others make their case for military preparedness. On March 13, when the Allies began arming merchant ships, the German high command again loosened restrictions on sinking non-military vessels. U-boat commanders could now fire on British ships in British waters as long as the ships were not passenger vessels. Nonetheless, on March 24, a German U-boat sank the French passenger liner *Sussex*, injuring two American passengers. U.S. Secretary of State Robert Lansing told the German government that its submarine warfare was "utterly incompatible with the principles of humanity" and with international law and threatened to break off diplomatic relations. About three weeks later, the German high command again instructed U-boat commanders not to sink passenger ships without warning.

Allied actions in the war, however, soured some Americans against the Entente. Britain's crushing of the Sinn Féin rebellion in Dublin, Ireland on Easter Monday, April 24, 1916 increased anti-British feelings, especially amongst Irish Americans. Americans resented the publication by Britain of a blacklist of 87 American and 350 Latin American business firms that were dealing directly with Germany.

News of battle losses in Europe bolstered the desire of Americans to remain neutral. In halting the German advance at the Battle of Verdun in February 1916, the French lost about 350,000 men. At the Battle of the Somme, July 1, 1916, combined French and British forces suffered 600,000 casualties. The losses in Galicia, where the Germans and Austrians stopped a Russian offensive, mounted to about one million. The Great War had become a brutal bloodletting in which most Americans wanted no part.

Nevertheless, the efforts of Wilson and his new secretary of war, Newton D. Baker, to push preparedness were successful. On August 29, 1916, Congress passed the "Big Navy Act," a ten-year plan to make the United States navy the equal to any other in the world. The United States Shipping Board Act, passed September 7, allocated $50 million for the purchase or construction of merchant ships that would form a national merchant marine.

Peace Without Victory

Woodrow Wilson's desire to remain neutral in the European war was probably no less sincere than that of the average American. In fact, Wilson hoped to be a peacemaker. In early 1916 he had sent his confidant, Colonel Edward Mandell House, on a secret mission to England, France, and Germany to feel out whether the warring powers would accept Wilson's mediation to help end the war. None of the powers were interested: the Allies hoped to break the German lines in a big spring drive, while the German chancellor said his government would not accept peace without large indemnities and German control of Belgium and Poland.

Louis Brandeis

Soon Wilson had his own struggles to attend to at home—he had to win an election in November. To do this, he had to enlist the support of those progressives who were estranged from him on account of Bryan, La Follette, and Roosevelt. The summer of 1916, thus, saw a flurry of progressive activity on the part of Wilson and congressional Democrats. In June, against stern opposition on the part of conservative Republicans and the business interests, the Senate approved Wilson's appointment of Louis Dembitz Brandeis to the Supreme Court. Brandeis, a pro-labor and social justice lawyer, was the darling of progressives. On July 17, Congress passed the Rural Credits Act, which created 12 federal farm loan banks that would offer low interest mortgages to farmers. In August, Congress passed a Workmen's Compensation Act that assured pay to federal employees in the event of injury or sickness. In September, Congress won for railroad workers the eight-hour workday and other benefits.

At their convention in June, the Democrats adopted a platform built from the planks of the Bull Moose platform of 1912. (At the Progressive Party convention of 1916, Theodore Roosevelt refused an offered candidacy and advised party members to return to the Republican fold.) In his keynote speech at the Democratic convention, Governor Martin H. Glynn of New York recited a list of Wilson policies that had kept America out of the European war. Glynn's recurring assertion—"We didn't go to war!"—was transformed into the battle cry of the Democratic campaign: "He kept us out of war!"

The Republicans nominated Charles Evans Hughes, an associate justice of the Supreme Court. Hughes was as progressive as Wilson, though he accused the president of giving into pressure from railroad "brotherhoods" in supporting legislation for an eight-hour day for railroad workers. Teddy Roosevelt campaigned for Hughes; both of them accused Wilson of failing to take sufficient precautions to ensure the protection of American lives and honor on the seas.

The election of 1916 was the closest election since 1876. The Republicans took all the northeastern states (in large part because they secured the Irish vote in the cities). Hughes went to bed on election night with the assurance that he had won the presidency. But the next morning, when his son answered the telephone saying the "president" could not be disturbed, he was told to tell his father he was not the president. Hughes had lost California and its electoral vote by 4,000 votes—enough to put Wilson over the top, 277 electoral votes to Hughes' 254.

With the election behind him, Wilson could pursue his peace initiatives. Confident from a series of victories in 1916, but frustrated by British control of the sea, the Germans seemed ready to negotiate with the Allies. On December 18, 1916, Wilson sent a note to all the belligerent countries, asking them to state "the precise objects which would . . . satisfy them and their people that the war had been fought out." Lloyd George, prime minister of England, replied that Great Britain sought "complete restitution, full reparation, and effectual guarantees" that in the future Germany would maintain peace with her neighbors. Germany's Chancellor Bethmann-Hollweg, however, did not reply, and Wilson's peace effort came to nothing.

On January 22, 1917, Wilson addressed Congress, laying out his ideas on how peace could be achieved in Europe without any side being the victor. He wanted, in his words, a "peace without victory." Wilson claimed he spoke for the "silent mass of mankind everywhere" when he said that peace should be attained through compromise. But the attainment of peace, he said, required a guarantee of peace, which could only come through a recognition of the equality of nations. In the future, no nation should seek to dominate

President Wilson throws the first ball of the baseball season, 1916

another nation, no one power should rule the seas or the lands, and all nations should agree on limiting their armaments.

In the future, said Wilson, nations should avoid "entangling alliances" but should join together in a "concert of power." "Is the present war a struggle for a new balance of power?" Wilson asked. If so, "who will guarantee, who can guarantee the stable equilibrium of the new arrangement? . . . There must be, not a balance of power, but a community of power, not organized rivalries, but an organized common peace." Wilson proposed that "a force be created . . . so much greater than the force of any nation now engaged or any alliance hitherto formed or projected that no nation, no probable combination of nations could face or withstand it."

Wilson insisted that the principles expressed in his speech were "American principles, American policies . . . And they are also the principles and policies of forward looking men and women everywhere, of every modern nation, of every enlightened community. They are the principles of mankind and must prevail."

"The World Must be Made Safe for Democracy"

By early 1917, the British blockade of Germany was beginning to have dire consequences on German civilians. Plagued by food shortages, the German people's morale suffered and their enthusiasm to continue the war flagged. To counter the British blockade effectively, the German government decided it must resume its own blockade of Great Britain. In late January, the German government communicated, along with its minimum terms for peace, an announcement that on February 1 it would commence unrestricted submarine warfare against Allied and neutral ships sailing into the restricted "war zone." On February 3, President Wilson broke off diplomatic relations with Germany.

Germany knew it was gambling—unrestricted submarine warfare could bring the United States into the war on the side of the Entente. Still, the German government hoped that it could break the Entente's power before America could assemble her war power. On his side, Wilson still was unwilling to push Germany into any hasty action that would force the United States to enter the war. The president even ordered a slow down on military preparedness measures. But events would not wait on the president's desires.

On February 17, the Cunard passenger liner *Laconia* set sail from New York harbor, bound for England. Eight days later, it was sunk by a German U-boat off the coast of Ireland. Then, on February 26, the British Naval Intelligence Service presented the United States Department of State with a note, a decoded message from the German foreign secretary Zimmerman to the German minister in Mexico. If the United States should enter the war on the Allied side, said the note, the German government proposed "an alliance on the following basis with Mexico: That we shall make war together and together make peace. We shall give general financial support, and it is understood that Mexico is to reconquer the lost territory in New Mexico, Texas, and Arizona."

The sinking of the *Laconia* and the Zimmerman telegram jolted many Americans from their neutrality. Public meetings were held, petitions were signed, manifestos were issued—all in favor of a declaration of war against Germany. On February 26, Wilson asked Congress' permission to arm merchant ships and to "employ any other instrumentalities or methods to protect them on their lawful occasions." This was the 64th Congress' last session, and Senator La Follette's filibuster defeated the legislation. A disgusted Wilson declared that "a little group of willful men have rendered the great government of the United States helpless and contemptible." The president ignored Congress and ordered the arming of merchant ships.

Then, on March 15, revolution in Russia; Tsar Nikolai II abdicates; a "republican" government is established in Moscow. Now every Allied government is a "government of the people," at least in Wilson's mind. Germany and her allies remain monarchies. The war now appears to be a war between democracy and autocracy, between freedom and tyranny.

This is a fight the idealist Wilson could enter, and the sinking of three unarmed American merchantmen, without warning, by U-boats on March 18 gave him further reason to enter it.

Wilson had called the new 65th Congress into special session for April 2. That day, before the assembled legislators, Wilson laid out the country's grievances against Germany, calling the "warfare against commerce"—a warfare in which innocents died—"a warfare against mankind." Armed neutrality, he said, "now appears . . . impracticable" because it was impossible for ships to protect themselves against submarine attack. "With a profound sense of the solemn and even tragical character of the step I am taking," continued Wilson, "and of the grave responsibilities which it involves, but in unhesitating obedience to what I deem my constitutional duty, I advise that the Congress declare the recent course of the Imperial German Government to be in fact nothing less than war against the government and people of the United States; that it formally accept the status of belligerent, which has thus been thrust upon it; and that it take immediate steps not only to put the country in a more thorough state of defense but also to exert all its power and employ all its resources to bring the Government of the German Empire to terms and end the war."

Wilson declared that the United States would continue to follow the same object in war as she had in peace—"to vindicate the principles of peace and justice in the life of the world as against selfish and autocratic power and to set up amongst the really free and self-governed peoples of the world such a concert of purpose and of action as will henceforth insure the observance of those principles." Then, alluding to the ideal, expressed in the "Peace without Victory Speech," of the establishment of a "concert of power" among all nations, Wilson said, "we are at the beginning of an age in which it will be insisted that the same standards of conduct and of responsibility for wrong done shall be observed among nations and their governments that are observed among the individual citizens of civilized states."

Always the idealist, Wilson asserted that the United States was "about to accept gauge of battle" with Germany, "this natural foe to liberty," for "the ultimate peace of the world and

President Wilson asks Congress for a declaration of war against Germany (a color halftone photomechanical print)

for the liberation of its peoples, the German peoples included: for the rights of nations great and small and the privilege of men everywhere to choose their way of life and of obedience. *The world must be made safe for democracy,*" proclaimed Wilson. "Its peace must be planted upon the tested foundations of political liberty. We have no selfish ends to serve. We desire no conquest, no dominion. We seek no indemnities for ourselves, no material compensation for the sacrifices we shall freely make. We are but one of the champions of the rights of mankind. We shall be satisfied when those rights have been made as secure as the faith and the freedom of nations can make them."

It was Holy Week. The Senate, on April 4, 1917, voted 82–6 to declare war on Germany. The House followed suit, 373 to 50, on Friday, April 6: Good Friday. The country, it seemed, was not so much about to enter a war, but a crusade for democracy, freedom, and, maybe, permanent peace. The war to make the world "safe for democracy" would become, for many, the war to end all wars. The defeat of Germany was to usher in an era of peace.

But not everyone had such high-flown notions. "We did not go to war to make democracy safe," Theodore Roosevelt would later write, "and we did not go to war because we had a special grievance. We went to war, because, after two years, with utter contempt of our protests, [Germany] had habitually and continually murdered our noncombatant men, women and children on the high seas, Germany formally announced that she intended to pursue this course more ruthlessly and vigorously than ever. This was the special grievance because of which we went to war, and it was far more than an empty justification for going to war . . . my own belief is that we should have acted immediately after the sinking of the *Lusitania*."

America Goes to War

Though publicly critical of Wilson's policies, Roosevelt was quick to ask him a favor after war was declared. Though 59 years old, blind in one eye, his body weakened by tropical fever, Roosevelt wanted to fight. He wrote Wilson, "In view of the fact that Germany is now actually engaged in war with us, I again earnestly ask permission to be allowed to raise a division for immediate service at the front."

Roosevelt told the French ambassador that, though he was too old to survive the circumstances of war, and though he should "crack" under its strain, still, he could "arouse the belief that America was coming." That was what he was "good for now, and what difference would it make if I cracked or not!" But though he paid Wilson a personal visit, the president refused to give Roosevelt a commission. "There is a sweetness about him that is very compelling, you can't resist the man," said Wilson. Yet, Wilson would deal only one way with his old rival. "I really think the best way to treat Mr. Roosevelt," he said, "is to take no notice of him. That breaks his heart and is the best punishment that can be administered."

Though he repulsed Roosevelt, Wilson was not remiss in war preparations. The president had an efficient assistant secretary of the navy, one Franklin Delano Roosevelt (Teddy's distant cousin), and an able commander of the Atlantic fleet, Admiral Henry Thomas Mayo. In the early days after America's declaration of war, when the United States army was as yet unprepared, the navy was of great importance. U-boat warfare had reduced Great Britain to the state where it had a food supply of only three weeks. American Rear Admiral William S. Sims helped Britain's prime minster Lloyd George set up naval convoys across the Atlantic to guard merchant ships traveling from America to England.

Upon the appeal of Admiral Sims, the United States secretary of the Navy sent destroyers to Queenstown, Ireland, as an anti-submarine patrol. The patrol arrived at Queenstown on May 4 and was placed under the command of British Vice Admiral Sir Lewis Bayly. On November 17, an American destroyer sank its first U-boat. The destroyer patrol and the convoy would dramatically cut down on shipping losses to U-boats: from 850,000 tons in April, to 293,000 tons in November.

As things stood in the spring of 1917, the United States Army had only 200,000 officers and men, 67,000 of whom were not regular military. General Hugh L. Scott, the army's chief of staff, persuaded Wilson and Congress to beef up the army by conscription. On May 18, 1917, Congress passed, and Wilson signed, the Selective Service Act requiring all men between the ages of 21 and 30 to register for service. By June 5, 1917, 9.6 million men had registered for the draft; in 1918, when registration was extended between the limits of 18 and 45 years of age, this number increased to 24.2 million men. The number of men actually inducted into service from the two registrations, however, only amounted to 2.2 million.

In waging war, Wilson advocated centralization policies that increased federal presence in the life of Americans. Taxes, of course, including the new income tax, were raised to meet war expenditures. In August 1917, Congress, at the urging of the president, passed the Lever Act, which gave the federal government the power to create a food and a fuel administration that would regulate industry in the United States. Wilson contemplated, but could not carry out, a federal takeover of the railroads.

On the home front, the federal government waged a war of propaganda against Germany. The congressional committee on public information issued printed material, sent out 75,000 "four minute men" to deliver anti-German oratory at movie houses, and commissioned movies to portray for citizens the barbarity of the "Huns." Though Wilson had asserted that the United States' quarrel was with the German government, not the German people ("we have no feeling towards them but one of sympathy and friendship," he had said), government-sponsored propaganda, purportedly written by "experts," argued that the German race itself had always been depraved.

American propaganda poster

SOMEBODY'S LITTLE GIRL
Suppose She Were Yours
Buy Liberty Bonds To Save Her

Propaganda of that sort could not fail to stir up public sentiment against Americans of German ancestry. In some places in the United States, laws were passed forbidding the teaching of the German language in schools and colleges. German books were thrown out of public libraries; the playing of German music was forbidden. Even the vast majority of German-Americans who supported the Allied side in the war were held suspect.

Acting on the belief that secret agents of the *kaiser* were infiltrating all sectors of American society, Congress, on June 15, 1917, passed the Espionage Act, which punished with a $10,000 fine and 20 years in prison anyone who interfered with the draft or who spread information to the enemy. In May of the following year, reacting to rumors that anarchists, communists, and other radicals were subverting the war effort, Congress passed the Sedition Act, which punished anyone who criticized, in writing, speech or action, "the conduct or actions of the United States government or its military forces, including disparaging remarks about the flag, military uniforms, similar badges or symbols."

The fear of communists and other leftists—called the "Red Scare"—was occasioned by events in Russia. In November 1917, under the leadership of Lev Davidovich ("Leon") Trotsky and Vladimir Ilyich Lenin, Bolsheviks—particularly brutal adherents of Marxist communism—overthrew the weak Russian provisional government and organized a Communist All-Russian government. On March 3, 1918, the new Russian government made a separate treaty with Germany at Brest-Litovsk and withdrew from the war.

Over 1,500 persons were arrested under the Espionage and Sedition Acts. Most of these were peace advocates, among whom were numbered many anarchists and socialists. Perhaps the most famous man to suffer under the Sedition Act was Eugene V. Debs, who had been arrested for a ringing anti-war speech he delivered in Canton, Ohio, on June 16, 1918. During his trial in Cleveland, Debs, acting as his own defense, admitted he had uttered the "treasonable" words, but argued that the Constitution assured him of the right to freedom of speech. He also told the court, "I am doing what little I can to do away with the rule of the great body of people by a relatively small class and establish in this country industrial and social democracy"—but this statement failed to move the jury in his favor. He was convicted and sentenced to ten years in prison.

Except for the navy, the United States' contribution to the war effort in 1917 was small. The U.S. First Infantry Division arrived in France in the summer and paraded down the Champs Élysées in Paris on July 4. Its numbers were promptly divided among Allied units along the front. By the end of 1917, only 180,000 American soldiers had arrived in France.

Army Medical Examiner: "At last a perfect soldier!"

An army medical examiner says, "At last a perfect soldier!" An anti-war illustration from the radical leftist magazine, *The Masses*, June 1916

The Pope and the President

The war had been raging a month when Pope Benedict XV ascended the throne of Peter. His predecessor was the saintly Pius X, who had ruled the Church ably since the death of Leo XIII in 1903. Pius' final days had been shadowed by war. He had exhorted the leaders of Europe to abandon their "murderous struggle" and seek peace. It fell to his successor, Benedict, to take up the call. The new pope chose November 1, 1914, the feast of All Saints, to issue an encyclical letter, *Ad Beatissimi*—a declaration that war violates the mystical union of men in the Communion of Saints.

In *Ad Beatissimi*, Pope Benedict insisted that the war came about because of a lack of mutual love among men. "Paradoxically," wrote the pope, "human brotherhood has never been preached more than it is preached today"; yet, without the Gospel, all such preaching is vain. Men's disregard for divinely established authority in state and church—particularly, the divorce of public authority from the religion of Christ, as well as strife among classes—said Benedict, have fostered the war. But, ultimately, greed for money (which, the pope noted, St. Paul had called "the root of all evils") was the ultimate cause of war:

> When godless schools, molding as wax the tender hearts of the young, when an unscrupulous press, continually playing upon the inexperienced minds of the multitude, when those other agencies that form public opinion, have succeeded in propagating the deadly error that man ought not to look for a happy eternity; that it is only here that happiness is to be found, in the riches, the honors, the pleasures of this life, it is not surprising that men, with their inextinguishable desire for happiness should attack what stands in the way of that happiness with all the impelling force of their desire.

Pope Benedict never ceased calling for peace. Criticized for not condemning Germany, Benedict replied that men on both sides of the conflict were his children. Besides, he had received news of alleged German atrocities only from the mouths and pens of Germany's enemies and thus would hold his peace until better evidence was

Pope Benedict XV

Archbishop Pacelli at Bamberg, Germany, 1924

proffered him. The pope did not want to jeopardize the possibility of bringing Germany to the peace table by any undue and hasty condemnation.

To secure Germany's consent to a truce and peace negotiations, in April 1917, Benedict appointed Archbishop Eugenio Pacelli as apostolic nuncio to the court of Ludwig III, king of Bavaria (a state in the German empire). Pacelli, a consummate diplomat, in June visited German Chancellor Theobald von Bethmann-Hollweg and won from him an oral agreement on these four points: a general limitation of armaments on both sides; the establishment of international courts to judge grievances between the warring sides; the restoration of the independence of Belgium; and a peaceful settlement with France of the possession of Alsace-Lorraine (a territory Germany had taken during the Franco-Prussian War in 1870–71).

The *kaiser* himself met with Pacelli on June 29. About two weeks later, Wilhelm II indicated his pleasure with a draft peace proposal including the four points Bethmann-Hollweg was to present to the *Reichstag*. But when the German high command heard that the *kaiser* and his chancellor were resolved to secure peace, they made their displeasure known. Bethmann-Hollweg, understanding the influence of the military, resigned and was replaced as chancellor by Georg Michaelis, the choice of the general staff.

Still, despite his ties to the military, Chancellor Michaelis told Pacelli in July that he was willing to discuss peace proposals based on the four points. With this happy news, Pope Benedict received Count John Francis Charles de Salis, Great Britain's minister to the Holy See, and gave him several sealed envelopes to be delivered to Allied leaders. The envelopes contained copies of the pope's peace proposal, laid out in seven points.

In his seven points, Benedict called on nations to replace the "material force of arms" with the "moral force of right" and, on all sides, simultaneously to reduce armaments "in accordance with rules and guarantees to be established hereafter." Instead of relying on armies and war to settle international disputes, said Benedict, nations should establish an "institution of arbitration" to decide international questions. This institution should have the power, said Benedict, to level sanctions against a state that refused to submit international questions to it for arbitration, or which refused to accept its decision.

The pope's seven points called for the elimination of "all obstacles to the free intercourse of people" by assuring "true liberty and common rights over the sea." The warring nations, he said, should reciprocally renounce war indemnities for the damages and cost of the war, as "the continuation of such carnage solely for economic reasons would be inconceivable." All occupied territories, said Benedict, should be evacuated and restored to their nations. Germany should evacuate Belgian and French territory, and, in return, the Allies should restore to Germany her foreign colonies. As for rival claims of territory—between Austria and Italy and between France and Germany—the pope urged the concerned nations to consider each other's claims "in a conciliatory spirit," giving "due weight, within the limits of justice and feasibility . . . to the aspirations of the populations, and, on occasion, bringing their particular interests into harmony with the general welfare of the great community of mankind."

The response from the Allied leaders was not encouraging. They were in a tight spot—in order to win Italy over to the Allied side, Great Britain and France had secretly promised the Italian government in Rome large chunks of Austrian territory. The allies had also pledged to give Japan German colonies in Asia after the war was over. The British government instructed De Salis to inform the Holy See that the king's government put no stock in the German assurances communicated by Pacelli, because they were oral. When the papal secretary of state reminded De Salis that the German *Reichstag* had voted on a resolution of peace without the annexation of territory, the British minister replied that that the *Reichstag* had no power in Germany and that the British had received no authentic text of the resolution. France, which had no delegation at the Vatican, asked Britain "to discourage any further attempt on the part of the papal secretary of state in the direction of an official intervention between the belligerents."

When Wilson received the pope's note with the seven points, it is said he remarked testily, "What does he want to butt in for?" The president's reply to Benedict, signed by Secretary of State Lansing, was long and preachy. It began, condescendingly, "every heart that has not been blinded and hardened by this terrible war must be touched by this moving appeal of His Holiness the Pope, must feel the dignity and force of the humane and generous motives which prompted it, and must fervently wish that we might take the path of peace he so persuasively points out." Yet, wrote Wilson, the pope's proposal to return to the state of things before the war, was not possible unless there could be established a "firm and satisfactory basis for it." The object of the war, Wilson reminded Benedict, "is to deliver the free peoples of the world from the menace and the actual power of a vast military establishment controlled by an irresponsible government which . . . secretly planned to dominate the world."

Having expressed his doubts that the pope's plan could secure the desired peace, Wilson lessoned Benedict in the ideals of the American people. "They believe," said Wilson, "that peace should rest upon the rights of the people, not the rights of governments—the rights of peoples great and small, weak or powerful—their equal right to freedom and security and self-government and to a participation upon fair terms in the economic opportunities of the world." The test, therefore, of any peace proposal, said Wilson, should be whether "it is based upon the faith of all the peoples involved or merely upon the word of an ambitious and intriguing government on the one hand and of a group of free peoples on the other." Since the United States could not "take the word of the present rulers of Germany as a guaranty of anything that is to endure" unless the "will and purpose of the German people" supported it, Wilson said he could not accept the pope's peace plan.

Though the *kaiser*, it seems, was enthusiastic about the pope's proposals for peace, the official reply, sent by Chancellor Michaelis, did not convey Wilhelm's full intentions. Michaelis wrote that "His Highness" embraced all the proposals offered by His Holiness; but the chancellor failed to mention Belgium, though Wilhelm was favorable to abandoning plans for annexing that land. On September 22, Archbishop Pacelli reminded the German government that, without Belgium, "the whole peace action of His Holiness may definitely be regarded as defeated." Two days later, Pacelli received a letter from Michaelis that the German government was in accord with the Holy See's peace efforts, that all countries should openly state their war aims, and that all questions connected with Belgium should be the first items of negotiation. The peace negotiations, however, went no further.

So ended Pope Benedict's efforts to end the war.

Kaiser Wilhelm II

Wilson's Peace Points

A little over four months after he rejected Pope Benedict's peace proposal, Woodrow Wilson offered one of his own. In a speech he delivered to Congress, January 8, 1918, on war aims and peace terms, Wilson reminded Congress that what "we demand in this war . . . is nothing peculiar to ourselves. It is that the world be made fit and safer to live in; and particularly that it be made safe for every peace-loving nation which, like our own, wishes to live its own life, determine its own institutions, be assured of justice and fair dealing by other peoples of the world as against force and selfish aggression."

The "Fourteen Points" for peace Wilson delivered to Congress were very similar to Pope Benedict's seven points, which the president had dismissed as unrealistic. Benedict's second point, calling for reciprocal decrease of armaments, was essentially Wilson's fourth point. The pope's third point was Wilson's 14th point, where the president called for "a general association of nations . . . formed under specific covenants for the purpose of affording mutual guarantees of political independence and territorial integrity to great and small states alike"—a "league of nations," in other words. Wilson's second point was Benedict's fourth, calling for freedom and community of the seas. Wilson's points five, eight and, in part, 11, were more detailed versions of Benedict's point six, while Benedict's seventh point (in which the pope proposed an examination of territorial claims), was, in substance, found in Wilson's points nine, ten, part of 11, and in points 12 and 13.

Emperor Karl I and Zita, by Carl Pietzner

Benedict, however, did not call for breaking up existing political units or for forming new states along national lines. For his part, Wilson declared that, in the Balkans, "the relations of the several . . . states to one another" should be "determined by friendly counsel along historically established lines of allegiance and nationality." Point ten dealt with the multicultural, multinational Austro-Hungarian Empire. "The peoples of Austria-Hungary," said Wilson, "whose place among the nations we wish to see safeguarded and assured, should be accorded the freest opportunity of autonomous development."

This point worried Karl I, who, in 1916, had succeeded his uncle, Franz Josef, as emperor of Austria and king of Hungary. A devout Catholic, Karl thought the war inhuman and in violation of the Gospel of Christ. In the spring of 1917 he had sent a secret note to his brothers-in-law, Prince Sixtus and Prince Xavier of Bourbon-Parma, who fought on the Allied side. The princes shared the note's contents with the king of Belgium and the president of France. Emperor Karl wrote that he was willing to support not only the restoration of Serbia and German withdrawal from Belgium, but that he favored the return of Alsace-Lorraine to France. Karl was willing, too, to part with some Austrian territory by ceding Austria's Italian-speaking Trentino region to Italy. Though Karl's letter was sent under the strictest secrecy, the French government later publicized it, creating a rift between Germany and Austria-Hungary.

Karl saw that Wilson was implying the dismemberment of Austria-Hungary in the tenth of the Fourteen Points. In February 1918, the emperor sent a direct appeal to Wilson requesting talks between representatives of the two governments. Karl reiterated his pledges that he would relinquish territory, though he insisted that not all of Italy's territorial claims were just, since some of the regions in question were German-speaking. Karl asked Wilson to clarify what he meant by "self-determination for the peoples of Austria-Hungary," but the American president was unmovable. On March 6, Wilson replied to Karl that he would not accede to any of the emperor's requests.

"Lafayette, We Are Here!"

In the Spring of 1918, the Germans opened their last great series of offensives on the Western Front, pitting 207 divisions against 173 Allied and nine American divisions. The first assault slammed into the British lines from Arras to La Fére. In one week, the Germans pushed the British back 25–40 miles. On April 9, another German offensive pushed the British back

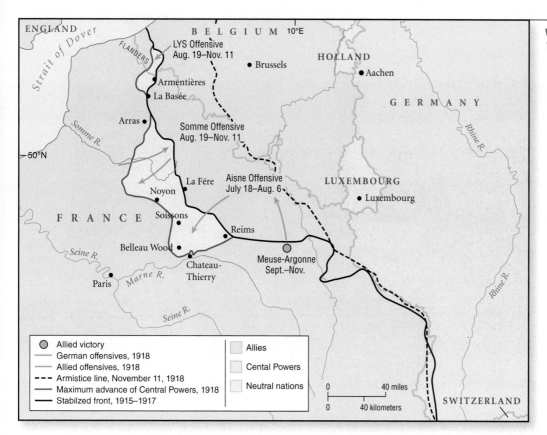

from Ypres to Armentières, and in May a German assault against the French between Noyon and Rheims forced them back behind the Marne. The Germans, now only 56 miles from Paris, shelled the city with their gun, *Dicke Berte* ("Fat Bertha").

In desperation, the Allies, in early June, sent an urgent request to President Wilson for 313,000 additional American troops. Wilson agreed to send the troops, who would arrive in July. Meanwhile, American Marines had dug in along the line just north of the village of Lucy-le-Bocage, near Chateau-Thierry. When the French, under whose command the Americans fought, advised the Marines to withdraw, Marine Captain Lloyd Williams replied, "Retreat! Hell, we just got here!" On June 2 and 3, German units, advancing against the French, British, and American line, occupied Belleau Wood. On June 4, the Germans attacked the center of the Allied lines at Les Mares farm; but they were driven back.

Two days later a bloody fight ensued when U.S. Marines assailed the Germans, firmly ensconced in Belleau Wood. The assault on the west of Belleau Wood was successful, and the marines captured a hill commanding the German position. The frontal assault on the wood from the south and east, however, was disastrous. Crying, "Come on, ya sons of bitches! Ya want to live forever?" Marine gunnery sergeant Dan Daly urged his men across a wheat field in which they were exposed to murderous machine gun fire. The marines suffered heavy casualties in their assault on the wood; one battalion was nearly annihilated. Marines took the village of Bouresches, but the struggle to maintain it was desperate. The Americans were exposed on all sides to machine gun fire. That day, the marines lost 1,087 men.

Combined forces of French and American marines and army took Belleau Wood after a week of bitter fighting. Then the Battle of Chateau-Thierry (July 1–10), where Americans and French took the village of Vaux, began a series of Allied victories. On July 15, the Second Battle of the Marne opened. At Soissons, two American divisions—the First French Colonial Division and the Gordon Highlanders—struck the German lines in a battle that, American General Pershing said, "turned the tide of war." The German chancellor agreed. On July 15, he believed the defeated Allies would sue for peace; three days later he saw the

A U.S. Signal Corps photograph showing victorious American soldiers renaming the street Hindenburgstrasse to Wilson U.S.A. in Vigneulles, France—a town they had captured from the Germans, 1918

bald reality. "On the eighteenth," he wrote, "even the most optimistic among us knew that all was lost. The history of the world was played out in three days."

The chancellor's words were not mere hyperbole. Following the Meuse-Argonne offensive in late September, in which the 896,000 Americans (out of a combined Allied force of 1,031,000) participated, the cause of Germany was lost. But not only Germany's cause died but the cause of monarchy as well. Kaiser Wilhelm had wanted peace all throughout the war, and in August a Crown Council, over which he presided, called for peace negotiations. Nothing was done, however, until October. By then it was clear that the Allied powers, particularly President Wilson, would not consider peace without Wilhelm's abdication. Prince Max of Baden, whom Wilhelm appointed chancellor in October, with a majority in the *Reichstag*, called for Wilhelm's abdication. Wilhelm, on the front lines with the army, hesitated; but the outbreak of socialist-inspired revolutions in Germany in November made an immediate response most necessary. On November 9, Prince Max took matters into his own hands, declared that the *kaiser* would abdicate, and formed a Liberal government.

Wilson's objection to Wilhelm—that he was not an elected official—applied as well to Karl von Habsburg. In October, Karl sought to reform Austria-Hungary along the lines of a federation of equal states—a plan he favored even before he had become emperor. But this was not enough to satisfy more radical elements in his kingdoms and throughout the world, for under Karl's plan, the emperor would remain head of state in a reformed Austria-Hungary. It was all too late. On November 11, Austrian officials arrived at Schönbrunn Palace and demanded Karl's abdication. Karl refused to abdicate, saying that to give up his imperial authority would be an affront to God who had entrusted it to him. The emperor agreed, however, to withdraw from power at least for a time in order to spare his people from Allied vengeance. Two days later, he made the same proclamation for Hungary.

On November 11, 1918, representatives of Germany met Allied leaders in a dining car on a rail siding in the forest of Compiègne in France. At 11 a.m. both sides signed an armistice. The guns fell silent all along the Western Front. The bloodiest war the world had then known had ended.

Peace and The League of Nations

The armistice was to last only 60 days, time enough, it was thought, for peace negotiations to reconcile the belligerent nations. German leaders had been assured that any peace treaty would be drawn up along the line of Wilson's Fourteen Points, and with that assurance they had signed the armistice. But the 60 days' armistice turned into a six-month waiting period in which the British maintained their blockade of German shipping and the Allies prepared their strategy of revenge against Germany and her allies. When the warring nations finally met around the negotiating table at the French palace of Versailles in January 1919, it was clear that the Fourteen Points had been scrapped and that Germany would be made to pay.

President Wilson wanted to cool the Allies' burning thirst for vengeance with the milk of his idealism. He hoped to convince the Allied nations of his dream of a League of Nations in which international disputes could be solved peacefully. Though in London, in Paris, and in Rome, enthusiastic crowds had greeted the American president, Wilson came to Versailles with diminished prestige. The congressional elections of 1918 had been a disappointment to him; he had appealed to voters to elect only Democrats to assure his aims, but the American people ignored him. The Senate, which approves all treaties, went Republican. Despite this political setback, in January 1919, when peace negotiations began, Wilson was able to convince Allied leaders to accept the principle of a league of nations. On February 14, the peace conference approved the preliminary draft for the covenant of the League of Nations.

The actual peace negotiations, however, did not go entirely as Wilson wanted. Wilson's fellow negotiators—Georges Clemenceau of France and Lloyd George of Great Britain—wanted vengeance, and they wanted to keep Germany weak. Italy, too, and Japan wanted territorial concessions; the first wanted a large chunk of Austrian territory and the latter the German colony in Shantung, China. Wilson was able to lessen the severity of some Allied demands: Germany would not be burdened with the whole cost of the war ($120 billion) nor would she lose the entire industrial Rhineland region. Poland would not receive the whole of East Prussia. Still, the Allies enacted stern measures against their defeated enemy.

Germany and Austria-Hungary had no say in the peace negotiations. With the blockade unlifted, the population of Germany suffered from hunger and want. Thus, the representatives of the German and Austrian governments could say or do little when it became clear that the terms of peace were nothing like the Fourteen Points. According to the Treaty of Versailles, Germany was required to admit war guilt, was to be stripped of all her foreign colonies and lose Alsace-Lorraine to France. The military and naval disarmament forced on Germany rendered the nation incapable of defending itself, and the immediate **indemnity** of $5 billion, plus future indemnities of undetermined amounts, placed a tremendous financial burden on Germany. Another great burden—and indignity—was the placing of the German economic system under Allied control.

Wilson directed the redrawing of the boundaries of eastern Europe in order to assure the "self-determination" of various racial groups.

indemnity: a sum of money paid as compensation for some loss, especially a sum demanded by a victor in war as one condition of peace.

A photograph of Woodrow Wilson and Raymond Poincare, then president of France, taken during Wilson's European tour to attend the Versailles Peace Conference, 1919

His ideal was that peoples of like language and nationality should be grouped in nations together. Thus, Austria-Hungary was divided into two republics, Austria and Hungary, and the Southern Slav portions (including Bosnia and Herzegovina) of the Habsburg domain were joined to Serbia to form the kingdom of Yugoslavia.

While the union of Slavic speaking peoples might have made sense on the basis of an abstract theory of nationalism, it did not make sense in the concrete historical circumstances. The peoples who made up Yugoslavia were divided by religion (the Serbs were Orthodox, the Croats, Catholic, and the Bosnians, Moslem). These peoples had experienced centuries of tension and warfare, and so their union created a weak and unstable state.

The same was true of another Wilsonian creation, carved out of Austria-Hungary—the Republic of Czechoslovakia. The largely Protestant Czechs (with a large number of Austrian Germans detached from Austria) dominated the Catholic Slovaks. The new republic contained a large number of Hungarians and Ukrainians. Divided by race and religion, with no commonly recognized authority (such as the Habsburg emperor) to adjudicate disputes, Czechoslovakia, like Yugoslavia, became torn by internal dissent.

Since nations were being formed along the lines of common race and language, it seemed reasonable that Austria should be united to Germany. Wilson acknowledged this, but one scruple kept him from agreeing to the union. If Austria joined Germany, then Germany would have a Catholic majority and that, said Wilson, "would mean the establishment of a great Roman Catholic nation which would be under the control of the Papacy."

Developments in Russia shook the confidence of the victors and the Versailles Peace Conference. The Bolsheviks, under Lenin, had established a "dictatorship of the proletariat" in Russia, which threatened worldwide Communist revolution. Russia, of course, at the time was not powerful enough to bring about such a revolution, but the establishment of a short-lived communist dictatorship under Bela Kun in Hungary disturbed the peace of the peace negotiators. What's more, the Russian Bolsheviks were cruel beyond measure, and France and Great Britain secretly supported counter-revolutionary Russian armies; even Wilson

The scene at the Trianon Palace at Versailles when French premier, Georges Clemenceau (standing, far right), announced the Entente' terms to the Germans

himself sent a small contingent of American soldiers to the Russian port of Arkhangelsk in support of counter-revolution. But the Russian Red Army under Trotsky drove all invaders from Russian soil and crushed the counter-revolution. By the time the Treaty of Versailles was signed by Germany on June 28, 1919, the Bolsheviks were in undisputed control of Russia. An ominous development for the future.

The End of Progressivism?

"I promised myself," Theodore Roosevelt told his sister, Corinne, "that I would work up to the hilt until I was sixty, and I have done it. I have kept my promise, and now, even if I should be an invalid, or if I should die"—and here he snapped his fingers—"what difference would it make?"

Roosevelt had been hospitalized since November 1918 with a swollen foot. Doctors told him he would have to be confined to a wheel chair, but even this news did not dampen his spirits. "All right," he told the doctors, "I can live and work that way, too!" By Christmas, Roosevelt was home. Twelve days later, on January 6, 1919, he died, quickly and painlessly, of heart failure.

The death of Roosevelt seemed to symbolize the eclipse of progressivism that followed the war. The first evidence that the American pendulum was swinging away from the progressive legacy was the congressional elections of 1918, when voters gave the Republicans control of the Senate. The second was President Wilson's failure to push through the Senate the ratification of the Versailles treaty and the League of Nations covenant.

Part of Wilson's failure can be attributed to his refusal to compromise with the Republican-dominated Senate. The Republicans had become the party of isolationism, the old American belief that the United States should avoid foreign entanglements. The League of Nations seemed to promise no end of foreign entanglements. Founded "to promote international co-operation to achieve international peace and security," the League was to include every nation of the world in what was called the "Assembly." Every member nation would have one vote. Besides the Assembly, the League would have a "Council" of the five great powers (including the United States) along with four other nations, appointed by the five great powers. The League was to have a permanent secretariat at Geneva, Switzerland, as well as a court of international justice at The Hague. All member nations were to submit their disputes to the League for settlement. They were to pledge their participation in any military and economic sanctions the League declared against nations that disregarded its mandates.

Theodore Roosevelt in 1918

Though many in his own party (and such Republicans as William Howard Taft) supported the Versailles treaty and the League covenant, Wilson faced stiff opposition from both conservative and progressive Republicans. Theodore Roosevelt had said the League, lacking its own military force, could never successfully impose sanctions. La Follette and others pushed the isolationist card. The majority of both Republicans and Democrats in the Senate had reservations about parts of the treaty and wanted the president to negotiate with them on those points. Wilson refused to negotiate except on the most minor matters.

Instead, the president thought he would appeal directly to the American people. After all, he thought, they and God were on his side! On September 4, 1919, Wilson embarked on a speaking tour of the Mid- and Far West. "I can predict with absolute certainty," he told crowds, "that within another generation there will be another world war if the nations of the world do not concert the method by which to prevent it." But the strain of his fight with the Senate, combined with the pressure of his whirlwind trip, was too much for Wilson's constitution. At Pueblo, Colorado, on September 25, the president collapsed from a stroke. He returned to Washington, paralyzed in his left arm and leg.

For two months, Wilson lay near death. No one, not even members of his cabinet, were allowed in to see the president; only Edith Wilson, his wife, and the president's personal physician, Dr. Grayson, entered the president's chamber. Since her husband was not fully conscious, Mrs. Wilson acted in his stead, submitting anything to be signed to his shaking hand, refusing to entertain any suggestion that Vice President Thomas R. Marshall assume the duties of president. (Marshall, it is said, did not inspire confidence, his most memorable utterance being, "What this country needs is a good five cent cigar!") After November 1, 1919, however, Wilson had regained the use of his mental faculties and could dictate letters and talk for short periods at a time with cabinet members and other dignitaries.

A photograph of Wilson in 1923, showing the effects of his stroke

On November 6, 1919, the president received bad news. Senator Gilbert M. Hitchcock informed him that the Democrats could not carry the ratification of the Versailles treaty and the League covenant through the Senate. When Hitchcock suggested that, perhaps, the president might compromise on a few points, Wilson retorted: "Better a thousand times to go down fighting than to dip your colors to dishonorable compromise." On November 19, the Senate failed to muster the necessary two-thirds majority to ratify the treaty and the covenant. Four months later, in March 1920, at the beginning of the next legislative session, the Senate sent formal notice to Wilson that they were unable to ratify the Treaty of Versailles and the Covenant of the League of Nations.

The failure to pass the Treaty of Versailles and the League of Nations covenant was not the final sign that the people had had it with the Wilson legacy (and progressivism); but the election of 1920 was. Wilson, because of ill-health, could not run again, and the Democrats chose Governor James M. Cox of Ohio as their candidate, a relatively unknown man, and Franklin Delano Roosevelt of New York, as his running-mate. The Republican candidate, Senator Warren Gamaliel Harding of Ohio, was not much better known, but his running-mate, Calvin Coolidge, had captured the public's admiration. As governor of Massachusetts, Coolidge had halted a police strike in Boston, declaring there existed "no right to strike against the public safety by anybody, anytime, anywhere." That was the sort of conservative message post-war America, seemingly, wanted to hear.

Warren G. Harding

Harding won the presidential election with an enormous landslide: a popular vote of 16,152,200 and an electoral vote of 404. Cox's totals were depressingly low: a popular vote of 9,147,353 and an electoral vote of 127. The results seemed a repudiation of Wilsonian progressivism, of Wilsonian high-mindedness and idealism. Americans wanted to settle down, it seems, and that's perhaps why they voted in such great numbers for Harding. "America's present need," Harding had declared during the campaign, "is not heroics but healing; not nostrums but normalcy; not revolution but restoration . . . not surgery but security." In other words, the country had to withdraw from idealism abroad and social reconstruction at home. The American people needed a rest.

Yet, perhaps, progressivism was not so dead as some might have thought, given the results of the election of 1920. Still in prison on account of his anti-war activities, Eugene V. Debs ran for president on the Socialist ticket and garnered 920,000 votes. This was a respectable return for a third party whose candidate was a convict. It reflected that, maybe, the sun of progressivism had not set but had only been eclipsed for a time; that, in time, it would again shine as brightly (or, some would say, as witheringly) as before.

English cartoon showing Debs, the imprisoned presidential candidate. Debs refers to Harding's "front porch campaign."

Red Scare

Dread of the German "Hun" conquering the world gave way, after the World War, to fear of Russian Bolshevism and its stated aim to spark a worldwide proletarian revolution. Some, like A. Mitchell Palmer, whom Wilson appointed attorney general in June 1919, thought Bolshevism threatened the United States with unrest and revolution. In 1920, Palmer described the state of things as he saw them in 1919:

> Like a prairie-fire, the blaze of revolution was sweeping over every American institution of law and order a year ago. It was eating its way into the homes of the American workmen, its sharp tongues of revolutionary heat were licking the altars of the churches, leaping into the belfry of the school bell, crawling into the sacred corners of American homes, seeking to replace mar-riage vows with libertine laws, burning up the foundations of society.

This account perhaps did not seem so exaggerated to men whose imaginations had been stirred up by war and war propaganda and who, in the summer of 1919, had experienced a good deal of social conflict. The movement of blacks from the South to the factories and cities of the North during the war had already caused a good deal of social unrest. White workers feared that black competition would affect their wages. A riot between blacks and whites in East St. Louis in 1917 left 47 dead and hundreds wounded. Another race riot in Washington, D.C. in July of 1919 was so violent that thousands of troops had to be called in to quell it. The same month, 36 died in a three-day riot in Chicago. The same year, racial tensions made themselves felt in New York, Omaha, and in the South.

In Seattle, a strike of 35,000 shipyard workers in January 1919

A. Mitchell Palmer (right) with the President Wilson

(continued)

turned into a general strike a month later when 60,000 workers in other trades joined the shipyard workers. Since the strike was falsely laid to the charge of the Industrial Workers of the World, the peaceful strikers were accused of being Reds and of fomenting revolution. When Seattle mayor Ole Hanson threatened to call out police and federal troops to battle the "revolutionary" strikers, union leaders on February 10 called off the strike. Because of Seattle, subsequent strikes would be ascribed to revolutionary "Reds."

But it was probably the bombings in June 1919 that spurred the anti-Red campaign. On June 2, bombs went off in eight U.S cities, including Washington, D.C. This last bombing destroyed part of Attorney General Palmer's

house and gave him a cause. No one was certain who planted the bombs, but since anarchists received the blame, Palmer commenced a campaign against them, and communists and radicals in general. His agents raided communist, socialist, IWW, and other leftist headquarters, and broke into union halls, arresting suspected Red revolutionaries. Palmer's primary targets were foreigners, who, since they were not American citizens, could be deported. Alexander Berkman and "The Girl," Emma Goldman, both Russian émigrés, were deported to the Soviet Union for their "Red" activism.

The Red Scare spread across the country. Congress in 1919 had refused to sit the duly-elected Socialist Party representative from Wisconsin. New York state expelled five Socialist members from the state legislature. A clothes salesman, Joseph Yenowsky, was sentenced to six months in jail because he was accused of calling the Bolshevik revolutionary, Vladimir Lenin, "the most brainiest man in the world."

The Red Scare influenced the court trial of two Italian anarchists, Nicola Sacco and Bartolomeo Vanzetti. Sacco and Vanzetti were arrested for the murder of Alessandro Berardelli in Braintree, Massachusetts, a suburb of Boston, on April 15, 1920. The evidence against Sacco rested on the testimony of ballistics experts that the bullet found in Berardelli's body was "consistent with being fired from [Sacco's] pistol," but the evidence against Vanzetti was purely circumstantial. Despite this, the jury found both men guilty of murder, and the judge sentenced them to death.

A series of appeals on the part of Sacco and Vanzetti's lawyers to spare them from the electric chair were

A 1919 resolution of the Benevolent and Protective Order of Elks, pleading its adherence to American principles and forbidding membership to anyone who "openly, or covertly, directly or individually, gives aid, comfort or support to the doctrines, practices or purposes of the Bolsheviki, Anarchists, the I.W.W., or kindred organizations or who does not give undivided allegiance to our Flag, and the great principles of constitutional free government of which it is the emblem."

Sacco and Vanzetti

(continued)

unsuccessful, and both were executed at midnight of August 23, 1927. As the guard secured him to the electric chair, Nicola Sacco cried out in Italian, "long live anarchy!" Then, more quietly, and in English, "Farewell my wife and child and all my friends." Bartolomeo Vanzetti, having entered the death chamber, said: "I wish to say to you that I am innocent. I have never done a crime, some sins, but never any crime. I thank you for everything you have done for me. I am innocent of all crime, not only this one, but of all, all. I am an innocent man." As the guards prepared him for execution, Vanzetti said, "I now wish to forgive some people for what they are doing to me."

By the time Sacco and Vanzetti were executed, Attorney General Palmer was a distant memory. Under Secretary William Wilson and his assistant, Louis Post, the United States Labor Department began to grant fair hearings to aliens arrested by Palmer. Almost one-half of those seized by Palmer's men in a great raid in January 1920 were released. When Palmer demanded that Post be fired, the latter defended himself before Congress. Even his greatest critics could not accuse Post of any impropriety.

Palmer finally did himself in by issuing a series of warnings that the Reds would launch a revolution to overthrow the United States government on May 1, 1920. The National Guard was called out, the New York Police Department was put on special 24-hour duty to meet the Red threat. But May 1 came and went, and no revolution materialized. Palmer's reputation was ruined and the Red Scare dissipated with the coming of the Harding administration in 1921.

Chapter 25 Review

Summary

- In Sarajevo in Bosnia, a member of the Black Hand, a Serbian terrorist group, assassinated Archduke Franz Ferdinand of Austria and his wife. Austria-Hungary made harsh demands of Serbia in reparation for the assassination of the archduke. When Serbia refused to accede to the demands and began a partial mobilization of its army, Austria-Hungary declared war on July 28, 1914. Russia backed Serbia and was allied to France. Germany, which was allied with Austria-Hungary and Italy, declared war on Russia as well as France. When Germany invaded Belgium on August 4, Great Britain entered the war. President Wilson declared that the United States must remain neutral in the conflict.

- German forces were doing well at the beginning of the war; in the east, the German army defeated Russian armies, and in the west, the German offensive had pushed within a few miles of Paris. Throughout the rest of the year, however, the war on the Western Front developed into a bloody slugging match, with neither side gaining any significant advantage.

- Britain gained a superiority at sea, and British naval ships stopped all neutral ships bound for Europe. This intensified feeling against Great Britain in the United States, which was allayed when Britain began placing large orders for food and munitions with America, thus relieving an economic recession.

- Germany began to dive undersea in U-boats as a response to Britain's blockade of German ports. At first these attacks were only directed against British warships, but in order to cripple British trade, the Germans began to direct U-boat warfare against all commercial shipping. Kaiser Wilhelm announced that the waters around the British Isles were a war zone and that all merchant ships bound for Allied ports within these waters would be sunk. The first American ship to be sunk was the *Gulflight*. On May 7, 1915, a British liner, *R.M.S. Lusitania*, with Americans on board, was sunk by a German U-boat. This incident, coupled with anti-German propaganda, aroused American opinion against Germany.

- While President Wilson did nothing to prepare the country for war, civilians made their own preparations. Following the sinking of the passenger liner, *Arabic*, carrying three Americans, Wilson demanded that Germany abandon warfare of this sort. The German government agreed, and on September 19 withdrew all U-boats from the English Channel.

Chapter 25 Review (continued)

- Wilson took up the cry for preparedness in the Fall of 1915, facing stiff opposition. Wilson's case was furthered by German war policies. On March 13, Allies began arming merchant ships, and Germany loosened restrictions on sinking non-military vessels. Allied actions, however, soured some Americans against the Entente, while news of battle losses in Europe bolstered the desire to remain neutral. After the Battle of the Somme in 1916, Americans wanted no part in the war. Despite that, Congress passed the "Big Navy Act" on August 29.

- Wilson was re-elected in 1916 and began to pursue peace initiatives. He sent a note to all the belligerent countries asking them to state what they required for peace. Wilson's peace efforts came to nothing when Germany would not reply, though Wilson still continued to press his peace initiative.

- In late January of 1917, the German government communicated its minimum terms for peace as well as an announcement that it would commence unrestricted submarine warfare against Allied and neutral ships sailing in restricted war zones. This caused Wilson to break off diplomatic relations with Germany.

- When German U-boats sunk the passenger liner *Laconia*, many Americans were jolted from their neutrality. Wilson tried, and failed, to get Congress to arm merchant ships. Then a revolution took place in Russia, changing the face of the war for Wilson. The sinking of three unarmed American merchant ships on March 18 gave Wilson further reason to enter the war. On April 4, 1917, the Senate voted to declare war on Germany. The House followed on April 6.

- On May 18, 1917, Congress passed the Selective Service Act in order to increase army enlistment. Anti-German propaganda increased in the United States, and rumors that anarchists, communists, and other radicals were subverting the war effort caused Congress to pass the Espionage and Sedition Acts.

- After the Bolsheviks in November of 1917 overthrew the Russian government, the new Communist government made a separate treaty with Germany on March 3, 1918, and withdrew from the war.

- Pope Benedict XV had been exhorting leaders of Europe to abandon the war since 1914, when he issued his encyclical letter, *Ad Beatissimi*. He refused to take sides and continued to call for peace. Benedict drew up four points for peace that he sent to Germany. Kaiser Wilhelm II indicated his pleasure, and the pope laid out his peace proposal in seven points. President Wilson would not accept the pope's peace plan. Though the German government was in accord with the pope's peace efforts, the peace negotiations went no further.

- Soon after rejecting the pope's proposals, Wilson offered peace proposals of his own that were very similar to Pope Benedict's. Benedict's plans, however, did not call for breaking up existing political units or forming new states as Wilson's did.

- Emperor Karl I of Austria-Hungary, a devout Catholic, was against the war and sent a secret note to his brothers-in-law, the princes of Bourbon-Parma, who fought on the Allied side, expressing his willingness to support the restoration of Serbia and German withdrawal from Belgium as well as the return of Alsace-Lorraine to France. Despite the note's secrecy, the French government publicized it, creating a rift between Germany and Austria-Hungary. Emperor Karl tried to negotiate with President Wilson, but Wilson would not accede to any of the emperor's requests.

- The Germans opened their last great series of offensives on the Western Front in the Spring of 1918. In desperation the Allies requested additional troops from President Wilson, and these arrived in July. At Soissons, two American divisions struck the German lines in a battle that turned the tide of war. Following the Meuse-Argonne offensive in September, the cause of Germany was lost. On November 9, Prince Max of Baden, Wilhelm's chancellor, declared that the *kaiser* would abdicate, and formed a Liberal government. On November 11, 1918, representatives of Germany and Allied leaders met to sign an armistice.

- The armistice was to last only 60 days, but those 60 days turned into six months during which the British maintained their blockade of German ports and the Allies prepared their strategy of revenge against Germany and her allies. When the warring nations finally met in December 1919, it was clear that the Fourteen Points had been scrapped and Germany had to pay.

- To cool the thirst for vengeance, President Wilson presented the Allied nations with his dream of a League of Nations. He was able to convince Allied leaders to accept the principle of the league, and on February 14 the peace conference approved the preliminary draft for the Covenant of the League of Nations.

- Wilson directed the redrawing of the boundaries of Eastern Europe. Meanwhile, developments in Russian shook the confidence of the victors and the Versailles Peace Conference. The Bolsheviks had established a "dictatorship of the proletariat," threatening worldwide Communist revolution. By the time the Treaty of Versailles was signed by Germany on June 28, 1919, the Bolsheviks were in undisputed control of Russia.

- Theodore Roosevelt died on January 6, 1919, symbolizing the eclipse of progressivism. In 1918, voters gave the Republicans control of the Senate, and President Wilson failed to push through the Senate the ratification of the Versailles treaty and the League of Nations covenant. Wilson tried to appeal to the American people by going on a speaking tour. In the fall of 1920, Warren G. Harding was elected president.

Key Concepts

Entente: a name for the British, Russian, and French alliance in World War I

Seven Points: Pope Benedict XV's proposal to end the First World War and to provide for a future peace

Fourteen Points: President Woodrow Wilson's proposal to end of the First World War and to provide for a future peace. The Fourteen Points were to be the basis of the Treaty of Versailles but were abandoned by the Allies.

League of Nations: an organization composed of representatives of the world's nations for the peaceful solution of international disputes

Communism: a revolutionary socialist movement that aims at creating a classless social order based on common ownership of productive property

Dates to Remember

1914: assassination of Archduke Franz Ferdinand of Austria-Hungary (June 28)

Austria-Hungary declares war on Serbia (July 28).

Germany invades Belgium, and Great Britain declares war on Germany (August 4).

President Wilson declares U.S. neutrality (August 4).

Pope Benedict XV issues the encyclical, *Ad Beatissimi* (November 1).

1915: a German U-boat sinks the *Lusitania* (May 7).

1916: Congress passes the "Big Navy Act" (August 29).

1917: the United States enters the war on the side of the Allies.

Pope Benedict XV issues his Seven Points for peace.

1918: President Wilson offers his Fourteen Points.

Germany and the Allies meet to sign the armistice ending the First World War (November 11).

Central Characters

Archduke Franz Ferdinand (1863–1914): archduke of Austria whose assassination sparked World War I

Woodrow Wilson (1856–1924): 28th president of the United States, who led the country in World War I

Benedict XV (1854–1922): pope from 1914 to 1922, who attempted to make peace between the warring nations in World War I

Blessed Karl I (1887–1922): the last emperor of Austria and king of Hungary who attempted to make peace during World War I

Questions for Review

1. How did the assassination of Archduke Franz Ferdinand spark the Great War?

2. What were President Wilson's reasons for remaining neutral at the beginning of the war?

3. Explain the significance of the sinking of the *Lusitania*.

Chapter 25 Review (continued)

4. How did Theodore Roosevelt view the war, and how did his opinion compare with those of the American people?

5. What did Wilson think was the United States' duty in the war?

6. Why, according to Wilson, was the United States going to war?

7. What did Pope Benedict XV think was the cause of the war?

8. Describe Pope Benedict's Seven Points. How were they similar to, and how different from, Woodrow Wilson's Fourteen Points?

9. Explain Wilson's concept of a League of Nations.

10. What American liberties were curtailed during the war?

11. What were the signs that Americans had rejected Progressivism after World War I?

Ideas in Action

1. Study and discuss the poetry of the Great War. (A good source is *The Penguin Book of First World War Poetry*, Jon Silkin, ed.)

2. Listen to the songs of the Great War, and discuss how they embodied the spirit of the time.

3. Consider President Lincoln and President Wilson's curtailment of cherished American liberties during wartime and their reasons for doing so. Is such a curtailment of these liberties ever justified? Stage a debate on the question.

4. As we have seen in this chapter, both President Wilson and Pope Benedict XV supported the formation of a world authority to curtail war. This world authority would exercise powers that we normally associate with national governments. Popes since Benedict XV have continued to favor the existence of such a world authority. Research the question of why they have supported it and discuss why or why not such an authority is desirable. And if it is desirable, what should be the extent of its powers. Should it concern itself only with war or with other matters as well?

Highways and Byways

Poetry of a New Era

War has never been a pleasant thing, and in every war there has been bloodshed and horrors. The Great War, however, ushered in a new form of warfare, which is described in the writings of poets who lived through it. Many war-time poets wrote of the horrors of the war, including Siegfried Sassoon and Wilfred Owen, two of the most famous of the World War I poets.

Before 1916, war poetry (as Rupert Brooke's "The Soldier" and Siegfried Sassoon's "To Victory") tended to be very positive about the war; the poets evinced intense patriotism, a sense that their struggle was righteous, and that military service is chivalric and heroic. After the Battle of the Somme, however, a sense of disillusionment sets in. The poetry from 1916 on portrays the disillusionment brought on by involvement in a senseless war, the shattering cost of modern warfare, and the desolation and emptiness of the modern battlefield. Sassoon was probably the most bitter of the war poets, and this bitterness comes out in his poems, such as "Glory of Women" and "The Dug-Out."

The world changed during the "Great War," and not only poets but prose authors of the time noted it. In Erich Maria Remarque's novel, *All Quiet on the Western Front*, the main character, Paul, notes how the world is changing: "We are forlorn like children, and experienced like old men, we are crude and sorrowful and superficial—I believe we are lost."

26

THE ROARING TWENTIES AND THE GREAT CRASH

Revolutionary Forces

Folks in Norfolk, Virginia had gathered to witness an unusual funeral on January 16, 1920. The flamboyant evangelist, Billy Sunday, commended to hell one John Barleycorn, the "body" drawn off from a cheering crowd in a 20-foot horse drawn coffin. This was a large coffin made for one whom Billy Sunday thought a big enemy—perhaps man's biggest enemy. "Good-bye, John," cried Sunday. "You were God's worst enemy. You were Hell's best friend . . . the reign of terror is over."

John Barleycorn was, of course, no man. He was a symbol of the "demon liquor"—"barley" and "corn" being the two crops from which whiskey is distilled. The 18th Amendment to the Constitution and the Volstead Act that enforced it had done Barleycorn to death—and temperance crusaders, like Billy Sunday, rejoiced in his damnation.

As we have seen, the temperance movement went back a long way in American history. Though somewhat eclipsed by abolitionism and the Civil War, the temperance movement revived with a vengeance in the 1870s. Frances Willard organized women into the Women's Christian Temperance Union, which she founded in 1874. Twenty years later, temperance activists formed another organization, the Anti-Saloon League of America. Both organizations were filled with zealous women and men who believed the consumption of alcohol led to innumerable social ills, such as poverty, disease, crime, and insanity.

Members of the Women's Christian Temperance Union used moral persuasion to convince folks to abandon drink. Armed with Bibles, women marched on saloons to shame owners into abandoning their "wicked" trade. Sometimes the anti-drink crusaders were successful, and saloon keepers poured their booze out on the thirsty ground. One Union member, however, employed more than moral persuasion in fighting the demon rum. Calling herself a "bulldog running along at the feet of Jesus, barking at what he doesn't like," Carrie Nation of Medicine Lodge, Kansas, had a bark with a hefty bite. In 1900, this six-foot tall, 180-pound woman, wielding an axe, destroyed bottles, kegs and furniture in a saloon in the town of Kiowa, Kansas. For the next ten years, Carrie Nation and her women crusaders committed "hatchetation" (as they called it) on one saloon after another. "Smash, ladies, smash!" cried Nation, and even strong saloon keepers quailed at her approach.

With wide support from evangelical Protestant churches and preachers (such as Billy Sunday), temperance activists made great headway in the first two decades of the 20th century. (Except for Archbishop Ireland and a few priests, Catholics generally opposed the

Billy Sunday

Carrie Nation, with her hatchet

temperance movement; mainline Protestants, too, were generally not enthusiastic.) They received the support of women who were tired of their husbands wasting their paycheck at the local bar and from business leaders who wanted productive employees on Monday morning. By 1917, 27 states had passed laws making the production, sale, and consumption of alcoholic beverages illegal. Other states passed "local option" legislation that allowed towns and counties to "go dry" if they chose. (In some states such legislation continues to this day.) But states complained that unless all states went dry, state and local prohibition laws were useless—folks could purchase booze by simply crossing state lines. Thus the stage was set for temperance's greatest victory.

One year from the ratification of this article, the manufacture, sale, or transportation of intoxicating liquors within, the importation thereof into, or the exportation thereof from the United States and all territory subject to the jurisdiction thereof for beverage purposes is hereby prohibited.

So ran the 18th Amendment to the Constitution, approved by Congress on December 18, 1917. A little over a year would pass before the required three-fourths of the states ratified the amendment. In the meantime, Republican House member, Andrew Volstead of Minnesota, introduced a prohibition bill, passed by Congress on October 28, 1919. This "Volstead Act" prohibited the production, sale, and manufacture of all liquors that contained over one-half of one percent of alcohol. The Volstead Act went into effect January 16, 1920, one year after the ratification of the 18th Amendment.

With characteristic intemperance, Billy Sunday haled January 16, 1920 as the dawn of a golden age. Now that America was "dry," cried Sunday, "the slums will be only a memory. We will turn our prisons into factories and our jails into storehouses and corncribs. Men will walk upright now, women will smile, and the children will laugh. Hell will be forever for rent." The years ahead would amply prove how nonsensical this prediction was. Prohibition, if anything, would have quite other effects than those Billy Sunday and other temperance advocates foresaw.

Votes for Women

The day before Wilson's first presidential inauguration in 1913, thousands of women marched in parade down Pennsylvania Avenue in Washington, D.C. They had come to demand what, to them, was a basic right—the suffrage. Called "suffragettes," these women had become a powerful political force to be reckoned with, despite their lack of the vote.

The two movements, women's suffrage and temperance, overlapped with one another. So identified were these movements that liquor companies opposed women's suffrage, in part it seems because they feared votes for women equaled votes for prohibition. The two most prominent leaders of the women's suffrage movement, Susan B. Anthony and Elizabeth Cady Stanton, were prominent in the temperance movement. Before the Civil War they had also been active in the abolitionist movement.

Susan B. Anthony

From its earliest days, the suffragette movement had been demanding the vote as the key and guarantee of other natural rights that the movement believed belonged to women. Some

Women's suffrage supporters demonstrating with signs reading, "Wilson Against Women," in Chicago on October 20, 1916.

suffragettes rejected traditional notions of male authority, both in the state and the family. They held that all professions, including law, political office, and the ministry, should be open to women. "The speedy success of our cause," wrote Elizabeth Cady Stanton, "depends upon the zealous and untiring efforts of both men and women for the overthrow of the monopoly of the pulpit, and for the securing to woman an equal participation with men in the various trades, professions, and commerce."

As it did with temperance, the Civil War overshadowed the issue of women's suffrage. After the war, the movement split over support for the 14th and 15th Amendments. The more radical wing, led by Anthony and Stanton, had argued that the rights of blacks were already theirs by nature; they didn't need amendments to guarantee them. In the words of the social contract, Anthony wrote:

> We throw to the winds the old dogma that governments can give rights. Before governments were organized, no one denies that each individual possessed the right to protect his own life, liberty and property. And when 100 or 1,000,000 people enter into a free government, they do not barter away their natural rights; they simply pledge themselves to protect each other in the enjoyment of them, through prescribed judicial and legislative tribunals. They agree to abandon the methods of brute force in the adjustment of their differences, and adopt those of civilization.

Anthony applied these arguments to women. She held that the suffrage is a woman's inalienable right and so to deprive women of the right to vote is an act of tyranny. Anthony acted on her convictions in 1872 when she attempted to vote for President Grant. She was arrested and tried in court for the attempt. Sojourner Truth also attempted to vote in the '72 election.

Not all suffragettes went as far as Anthony and Stanton. In 1895, more conservative elements in the women's suffrage movement distanced themselves from Stanton when she published *The Women's Bible*. In this work, Stanton argued that one had to look at God in a

Political cartoon, "The Sky is Now Her Limit," depicting women's progress from "Slavery and House drudgery" through "Equal Suffrage" to "Presidency." Published October 1920

new light—not as masculine only, but as feminine; not only as Heavenly Father, but as Heavenly Mother. This was too revolutionary, and Stanton lost her voice in the movement she had helped to found.

Many opposed the suffragette movement because they thought that giving woman the right to vote would remove her from her proper sphere, the home. The notion of equality espoused by proponents of women's suffrage was in opposition to the traditional notion that the father represented his family in society. To give women the suffrage assumed that wives had interests opposed to their husbands'. Those opposed to the implications of women's suffrage formed, in 1911, the National Association Opposed to Woman Suffrage, led by Mrs. Arthur Dodge. A prominent member of the National Association was Cardinal Gibbons. "When I deprecate female suffrage I am pleading for the dignity of woman," wrote Cardinal Gibbons. "I am contending for her honor, I am striving to perpetuate those peerless prerogatives inherent in her sex, those charms and graces which exalt womanhood and make her the ornament and coveted companion of man. Woman is queen indeed, but her empire is the domestic kingdom." Another critic of the women's suffrage movement—and of feminism in general—was that relentless labor leader, Mother Mary Jones. Speaking of feminism, she said, "I don't belong to the women's club. I belong to the fighting army of the working class." As for suffrage, she said she was "in no sense of the word . . . in sympathy with" it:

> In a long life of study of these questions I have learned that women are out of place in political work. There already is a great responsibility upon women's shoulders—that of rearing rising generations. It has been in part their sad neglect of motherhood which has filled reform schools and which keeps the juvenile courts busy. If women had been really industrious in their natural field they might have warded off some horrors of the time. They can begin now to be more useful than they have been by studying these economic problems and helping toward industrial peace.
>
> The average working woman is unfitted for the ballot. She will rarely join in an organization of the industry she works in. Give her the vote and she'll neglect it. Home training of the child should be her task, and it is the most beautiful of tasks. Solve the industrial problem and the men will earn enough so that women can remain at home and not leave it.

"I have never had a vote and I have raised hell all over this country!" Mother Jones said. "You don't need a vote to raise hell! You need convictions and a voice!"

But no opposition could slow the momentum of the women's suffrage movement. In 1917, the state of New York gave women the suffrage, with the endorsement of the powerful state Democratic machine, Tammany Hall. Two years later, the United States Congress approved the 19th Amendment: "The right of citizens of the United States to vote shall not be denied or abridged by the United States or by any State on account of sex." By August 26, 1920, the requisite 36 states had approved the amendment, and it became part of the Constitution.

The adoption of the 19th Amendment did not end agitation for women's rights. In 1923, the National Woman's Party (NWP) introduced into Congress the Equal Rights Amendment

(ERA), which would forbid all discrimination on the basis of sex. In line with their devotion to women's equality, the NWP opposed legislation directed at protecting women workers because such legislation treated them as a special class, not as equals to men. Indeed, critics of the ERA charged that it would overthrow all legislation directed to protecting women in industry. In this case, at least, the NWP was allying itself with the *laissez-faire* National Association of Manufacturers, which endorsed the ERA.

Women's activists would prove unsuccessful in obtaining passage of the ERA, both in the 1920s and in the decades to come. But in the decade of the '20s, they would succeed in fomenting a sexual revolution the effects of which influence our world today.

Automobiles and Planes

Henry Ford didn't particularly like farm life. The son of William Ford, an English Protestant from Cork, Ireland, was far more interested in mechanics than in manure and crop rotation. This was a help to his father, whose machinery Henry kept in working order; but it was also a trial, for William wanted his son to become a farmer. The fact that Henry repaired watches and clocks for the neighbors without charge displeased William—the boy, he thought, should accept payment for his work—and, besides, fixing time pieces was no way to learn farming.

Henry Ford

In 1879, when he was 16 years old, Henry left his father's farm near Dearborn, Michigan, for the nearby city of Detroit, where he worked long days in machine shops and engine works. In 1885, he made his acquaintance with an invention that would become the central passion of his life—the internal combustion engine. Nine years before, in Germany, Nikolaus August Otto had invented this noisy, smelly contraption that ran on gasoline. Henry Ford had, doubtless, known for a long time about Otto's invention; now, as an employee of the Westinghouse Engine Company, Ford was actually repairing one! He did not lose the opportunity of intently studying the mechanical marvel.

Love brought Henry Ford back to the farm. In 1886, in preparation for his marriage, he moved onto a farm his father bought him near Dearborn. There for two years he labored at a sawmill, sold lumber, and fixed his neighbors' machines. But the lure of engineering proved too strong, and in 1888 Ford returned to Detroit. Employed by day as an engineer and machinist for the Edison Illuminating Company, he worked for seven years on a model car in a shed behind his house. He completed this "horseless carriage" in 1896 and by 1899 had built three more. His first attempt to form an automobile company failed in 1900, and for the next three years he built racers; one of these, the "999," won many a race for the famous race car driver, Barney Oldfield. The fame of the "999" attracted the interest of several investors, with whom Henry formed the Ford Motor Company in 1903.

Ford was not the first to make automobiles. Though Germany had led the way with the Otto engine and with the Diesel engine (invented by Rudolf Diesel in 1892), it was France that became the leader in automobile manufacture. By 1900, motor cars were causing numerous traffic problems in Paris. Only the well-to-do, however, could afford these motor cars. Ford wanted to produce cars that the typical working man could afford. In 1908 he came up with a simple design for a car that would require low maintenance and would be easy to fix—the "Model T." In 1909, Ford announced that his company would only manufacture Model Ts. "Any customer," said Ford, "can have a car painted any color that he wants, so long as it is black." The Model T, also called the "Tin Lizzie" and the "Flivver," was a success. By 1916, Ford Motor Company had sold over 500,000 cars and, by 1923, about 2,500,00. In 1927, the company reached the 15 million mark in cars sold worldwide.

If the sole production of Model Ts greatly simplified the manufacturing process, Ford's institution of the assembly line in 1914 greatly accelerated it. The assembly line allowed

A Ford assembly line

for continuous production, making it possible for one car to be built in just 93 minutes. While the assembly line greatly increased production, it had the mind numbing effect of reducing each worker to a mere cog in a wheel. Before, an individual worker was involved in the manufacturing process from beginning to end and so would do a number of different tasks and be able to see the fruits of his labor; on the assembly line, however, he performed one simple task over and over and over again. Little skill was, therefore, required of the worker; he became merely one easily replaceable part of a great manufacturing machine. In the coming years, other industries would adopt the assembly line model, significantly reducing the cost of manufactured goods, but at the high price of further demeaning the workman in his dignity as craftsman.

In order to attract better workers (and to increase their buying power) Ford raised wages in his industries from $2.40 for a nine-hour day to $5 for an eight-hour day. Workers that increased in skill and speed could see their wages raised to $6 or $7 a day. Such wages assured for the auto tycoon a steady and loyal workforce and increased his factory output. It also allowed (through greater efficiency) for a gradual decrease in the price of the Tin Lizzie. The Model T, which sold for $950 in 1909, fell to $295 in 1922. By 1925, Ford's assembly lines were producing a new car every 15 seconds.

A Ford motor car

Oil wells, Venice Beach, California

Ford was not the only automobile manufacturer in the United States. Others included: Dodge, Maxell, Willys-Overland, Buick, Oldsmobile, Cadillac, Parkland, Pierce-Arrow, and numerous small-time carmakers. Though New England was, at first, the center of the auto industry in the United States, the success of Ford brought more and more auto manufacturers to the Detroit area, making that city the center of the auto industry. Gradually, larger manufacturers absorbed the smaller ones (for instance, Cadillac became an arm of General Motors.)

The automobile transformed American life perhaps more than any other single invention. Since the Ford car was so inexpensive, a common worker could buy one and live farther from his place of employment. This led, eventually, to the building of suburban communities outside of large cities and to a gradually spreading urbanization of the countryside. Farmers benefited by having trucks that could haul produce to market; and they could remove the wheels of their trucks, hook up chains to the rear wheel hubs, and use auto power to operate pumps and other equipment. State governments began funding the construction of roads, since automobiles bogged down easily on rain-soaked dirt roads. By 1925, states began paying for hardtop roads, and the following year the federal government offered funds to match whatever the states raised themselves. Thus, increasingly, distant parts of the country began to be connected by a network of highways.

Automobile production had an adverse effect on other forms of transportation and the industries that supported them. In time, the bus would replace the rural trolley car. Coastal steamboat and freight traffic would give way to truck transportation. With the increasing use of oil and petroleum, coal mining regions languished while oil producing areas increased in population and prosperity. The population of California, the leading oil producing state in 1925, increased dramatically during the 1920s, as did that of Texas, which would eventually surpass California as the chief oil producer in the nation.

Orville Wright in flight at Huffman Prairie, Dayton, Ohio, November 16 1904

With the expansion of good roads and the growing abundance of gasoline, Americans began taking road trips. Before the hard mid-western winter hit the plains and prairies, farmers could pack up their belongings in their cars and drive to warmer climates. Other Americans, too, began vacationing, and along the routes they traveled sprouted filling stations, restaurants, tourist camps, and motor hotels. This growing ease of transportation exacerbated what had long been a peculiarly American characteristic—a lack of rootedness and of fidelity to one's native soil. Indeed, the automobile would become the symbol of individual freedom and would take its place as a constituent part of the "American dream" of individual autonomy and material prosperity.

While many Americans began motoring about on roads and highways across the nation, some had taken to the air. In the 1890s, two brothers, Orville and Wilbur Wright of Dayton, Ohio, had been trying to find ways to fulfill an ancient human dream—the dream of flight. By 1900, the two brothers had developed a glider plane design and were testing a model plane at Kitty Hawk on the coast of North Carolina. By 1902, they had flown hundreds of successful glider flights and could now focus their minds on a new problem: how to make a glider that was self-propelled.

In December 1903, the brothers were again at Kitty Hawk with a glider to which they had fixed a four-cylinder, 200-pound, 12-horsepower engine that they had designed. On the morning of December 17, the Wrights made four powered flights on the beach at Kitty Hawk. The flights covered 120 to 582 feet of ground, the plane remaining in the air from 12 seconds to one minute, all the while fighting a strong wind. The Wright brothers had conquered the problem of flight, and the age of air transportation was born.

The Wrights continued to perfect their airplane design. Two years after Kitty Hawk, Wilbur flew a Wright plane 24 miles in 38 minutes. Wilbur took a 35 horsepower plane he and Orville had designed to France in 1908 and flew it 62 miles, 361 feet above the ground, in one hour and 54 minutes.

Though airplanes were not a significant factor during World War I, the war accelerated their design and manufacture. Instead of sticks and canvass, airplane makers began using light, strong steel for the bodies of their planes. In 1919, Lieut. Commander Albert C. Read of the United States Navy made the first transatlantic flight from Newfoundland to Portugal in a seaplane, with only one stop in the Azores. Only a few weeks later, two Englishmen, John Alcock and Arthur W. Brown, made the first non-stop trans-Atlantic flight from Newfoundland to Ireland in only 16 hours and 12 minutes. Four years later, two army lieutenants made the first non-stop transcontinental flight from New York to San Diego in a German Fokker monoplane in 26 hours and 50 minutes. A Wright engine powered the plane of Lieut. Commander Richard E. Byrd in the first flight over the North Pole on May 9, 1926. A Wright engine powered the Ryan monoplane, the "Spirit of St. Louis," in which the young Charles Augustus Lindbergh made his non-stop flight from Roosevelt Field on Long Island to the Le Bourget airdrome in Paris on May 20–21, 1927. Lindbergh had flown the longest distance yet: 3,735 miles in 33 hours and 39 minutes.

The development of passenger airlines would eventually end the reign of the railroad and of passenger ships in long-distance passenger transportation. The first passenger air service began in 1927, between New York and Boston. In the early 1930s, Trans World Airlines would initiate the age of modern airline transportation.

"Give Me Your Tired and Your Poor"—No More

Since 1892, thousands of immigrants had come into the United States through the portal of Ellis Island in New York harbor. The immigration station on Ellis Island lay in the shadow of the Statue of Liberty, that colossal symbol of freedom for many a weary wanderer from his native land. "Lady Liberty," a gift of the French people to the United States, had, since 1886, stood, not only for liberty, but for America's unrestricted immigration policy, summed up in the words of the poetess, Emma Lazarus:

> Give me your tired, your poor,
> Your huddled masses yearning to breathe free,
> The wretched refuse of your teeming shore.
> Send these, the homeless, tempest-tossed to me.
> I lift my lamp beside the golden door.

By the 1920s, however, many Americans had become convinced that the United States had received more than its share of "huddled masses" and "wretched refuse." Labor leaders had made significant gains for workers in higher wages and shorter work days during the war—they didn't want these lost by an influx of laborers who would work for much lower wages. Some intellectuals argued that, since most of the immigrants now were coming from southern and eastern Europe, their traditions of subservience to "tyrannical" leaders would corrupt American freedom. In this spirit, New England novelist Kenneth Roberts wrote in the *Saturday Evening Post* of these immigrants as "human parasites," a "hybrid race of good-for-nothing mongrels."

Congress had earlier passed a bill that would limit immigration, but President Wilson had vetoed it. Congress passed a similar bill, the Johnson Act, in 1921, and the new president, Warren Harding, signed it. The Johnson Act limited the number of aliens coming into the country to 385,000, "three percent of the number of foreign-born persons of such nationality resident in the U.S." according to the 1910 census. The Johnson Act also set quotas according to the immigrants' countries of origin: the majority, 200,000, from Northern Europe; the remainder, from southern and eastern Europe.

Subsequent Congressional acts further lowered immigration quotas. Another Johnson Act in 1924 decreased the quotas to two percent of each racial group (Germans, Irish, English, French, etc.) that entered the country in 1890. This was clearly an attempt to cut off southern and eastern European immigration, for the great wave of immigrants from those regions had begun only after 1890. Also, in 1924, Congress approved the visa system, which

Immigrants at Ellis Island in 1921

required immigrants to prove that they would not end up on the public dole and that they were not communists, anarchists, or polygamists. The immigration laws did not apply to Canadians, Mexicans, or immigrants from the West Indies.

Limiting immigration led to a decline in foreign ghettos in the cities and of foreign language publications and journals. Formerly European ethnic ghettos became increasingly black and Puerto Rican, as these peoples moved north to take advantage of industrial jobs in the cities.

Urbanization

The United States Census of 1920 reported a surprising statistic. For the first time in American history, city dwellers outnumbered those who lived on farms and in small towns. Since 1880, when the census reported that rural dwellers constituted 71 percent of the population, the farm population had been decreasing. By 1910, the rural population had shrunk to only 54.2 percent of the population. In 1920, it had decreased to 48.6 percent of a population numbering 117.8 million.

What caused the decline of the farm population—the people whom Thomas Jefferson had thought the only sure foundation of republican liberty? Of course, there was the lure of the excitement of city life and the hope of striking it big that drew farm boys to the big city. Yet, many rural workers who came to the cities would probably have remained in the country had not the forces of industrialism compelled them to move. The mechanization of farming, along with the rest of life, while easing the farmer's lot, was undermining the viability of farming society.

Improved farming technology was not new to the 20th century. From Thomas Jefferson's improved moldboard plow to Cyrus McCormick's mechanical reaper to mechanical threshing machines, technology had for well over a century been transforming agricultural life in the United States and Europe. Far into the 19th century, farms had been self-sufficient enterprises. Farm families grew not only all their own food but made even their own clothes and shoes. Farmers processed the foods they grew, bringing their own crops to market, turning fruits and berries they grew into jams and jellies; and, when they couldn't get their corn to market, they distilled it into moonshine whiskey. As industrialization increased, tasks once performed by farmers or others in their immediate neighborhood—slaughtering cattle, packaging meat, flour milling, manufacture of butter and cheese, the preserving of fruits—were taken over by factories in city centers. The manufacture of clothing and shoes passed to factories as well, and homespun no longer covered the backs of the proud tillers of the soil.

In the late 19th century, more farmers began to specialize in growing one or a few crops, which they sold for the cash with which they would buy what they formerly had produced for themselves. A man would be a wheat farmer or a corn farmer or a cotton grower, simply; in a certain sense, farming had become merely an industry, not a means of subsistence or a way of life. Mechanical harvesters and reapers made this industry more efficient. Steam tractors and, by 1905, gasoline-driven tractors enhanced productivity even more, decreasing the number of laborers needed in the fields. Unemployed farm laborers, naturally, left the country for the city, swelling the population of urban areas.

Farms grew larger as lands formerly reserved for growing feed for draft animals could now be tilled for cash crops. Mechanization made it easier to work more and more land. The increased productivity resulted in the overproduction of farm products; and since the supply of food exceeded the demand for food, the price of crops fell. Soon, only farmers who could afford the machinery to work the ever-growing farmsteads could compete on the market. Those who could not afford the machinery were forced out of business and moved to the cities.

The move from the country to the city had tremendous social significance. Farming communities tend to be conservative, are slow to change, and so preserve traditions. Moving to the city, country folk were thrown into the maelstrom of an ever-changing American culture where old values were being questioned and new ones were being created to replace the old. With the dwindling of the country population, America lost an important bastion of conservatism needed to withstand an ever-swelling tide of new-fangledness, not only in mechanical inventions, but in the social and moral life of the people as well.

The Wild Decade

The writer Sinclair Lewis saw little good in the American middle class. In his 1920 novel, *Main Street*, Lewis describes the plight of a young woman, Carol Kennicott, when she finds herself the inhabitant of the small Minnesota town of Gopher Prairie. Married to a prominent doctor of the town, Carol tries to bring "cultural uplift" to Gopher Prairie; but the smugness of the townsfolk on "Main Street," their devotion to material prosperity, their rejection of anyone who fails to live up to their narrow standards, in the end thwart Carol's every attempt to "enlighten" them. Still, at the end of the book, she confides to her husband that though she is beaten, she is not bowed:

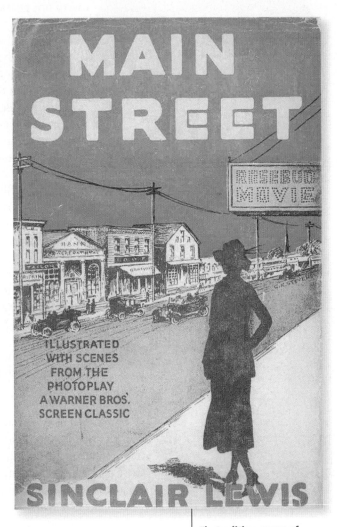

First edition cover of
Main Street

> But I have won in this: I've never excused my failures by sneering at my aspirations, by pretending to have gone beyond them. I do not admit that Main Street is as beautiful as it should be! I do not admit that Gopher Prairie is greater or more generous than Europe! I do not admit that dish-washing is enough to satisfy all women! I may not have fought the good fight, but I have kept the faith.

To which Kennicott replies, dully: "'Sure. You bet you have . . . Well, good night. Sort of feels to me like it might snow tomorrow. Have to be thinking about putting up the storm windows pretty soon. Say, did you notice whether the girl put that screw-driver back?'"

Gopher Prairie Everywhere

On visiting America in 1921, the English author, G.K. Chesterton (who would convert to the Catholic Church in the early '30s) noted that he had heard a lot about *Main Street* and the screw-driver line. But Chesterton did not share Lewis' disdain for towns like Gopher Prairie. The men in these towns, Chesterton wrote in *What I Saw in America*, "may be provincials . . .

> . . . but they are certainly citizens; they consult on a common basis. And I repeat that in this, after all, they do achieve what many prophets and righteous men have died to achieve. This plain village, fairly prosperous, fairly equal, untaxed by tyrants and untroubled by wars, is, after all the place which reformers have regarded as their aim; whenever reformers have used their wits sufficiently to have any aim. The march to Utopia, the march to the Earthly Paradise, the march to the New Jerusalem, has been very largely the march to Main Street. And the latest modern sensation is a book written to show how wretched it is to live there.

Still, Chesterton saw a point to Carol's angst. "There is a case," he wrote, "for the lady and a case against the gentleman and the screw-driver. And when we have noted what it really is we have noted the real disadvantage in a situation like that of modern America, and especially the Middle West. And with that we come back to the truth . . . that industrialism is spreading because it is decaying; that only the dust and ashes of its dissolution are choking up the growth of natural things everywhere and turning the green world grey."

Chesterton said that the problem with rural Americans was that they were not peasants:

> In this relative agricultural equality, the Americans of the Middle West are far in advance of the English of the twentieth century. It is not their fault if they are still some centuries behind the English of the twelfth century. But the defect by which they fall short of being a true peasantry is that they do not produce their own spiritual food, in the same sense as their own material food. They do not, like some peasantries, create other kinds of culture besides the kind called agriculture. Their culture comes from the big cities; and that is where all the evil comes from.

G.K. Chesterton

Indeed, the millions of Americans living and working in Gopher Prairies all across the great heartland of America looked to the great cities for their culture. City dress was the standard for country dress; city manners determined country manners; country folk were listening to city music, being entertained by city "moving picture shows," decorating their homes according to the latest city fads, eating the same bland food that folks ate in cities. The Carol Kennicotts of America were no better—all their standards were the standards of the citified intelligentsia and arts crowd. In *Main Street,* Carol comes off looking more ridiculous than the townsfolk at whom both she and Sinclair Lewis sneer with such affected superiority. Neither she nor her fellow townsmen were the makers of their own culture.

What might such a homemade culture look like? "If a man had gone across England in the Middle Ages," wrote Chesterton, "or even across Europe in more recent times . . .

> . . . he would have found a culture which showed its vitality by its variety. We know the adventures of the three brothers in the old fairy tales who passed across the endless plain from city to city, and found one kingdom ruled by a wizard and another wasted by a dragon, one people living in castles of crystal and another sitting by fountains of wine. These are but legendary enlargements of the real adventures of a traveler passing from one patch of peasantry to another and finding women wearing strange head-dresses and men singing new songs.

People in the 1920s were singing new songs, but the same new songs everywhere. Just as Ford was mass-producing cars, music publishers on "Tin Pan Alley" (West 28th Street between Broadway and Sixth Avenue in New York City) were mass-producing music. Beginning in the 1890s, Tin Pan Alley had been hiring songwriters to compose music for the mass market. Hearing these songs performed in Vaudeville stage shows or in Broadway performances, people wanted to sing and play them themselves; so the Alley's publishers produced sheet music with voice and piano accompaniment, and so papered the country with show music.

Such popular music was nothing new in the United States. In the first half of 19th century, minstrel show music, including that of the composer Stephen Foster, was widely distributed throughout the country. Folks gathered around their pianos and sang "Old Folks at Home," "I Dream of Jeannie With The Light Brown Hair," and "Dixie," just as in the 1920s they would sing "I'm Just Wild About Harry," "Toot, Toot, Tootsie," and "I Wanna Be Loved

By You (Boop Boop-a-Doop)." Yet the older popular music had the sound of American folk music—that music whose origins lay far back in the history of the Scots, Irish, English and French peoples who had settled America. Though to a lesser extent than in Europe, different varieties of folk music and songs could be found in the various regions of America. Tin Pan Alley helped destroy all that variety. From the seacoasts of Maine, south, to the Gulf, and westward to California, everyone was listening to the same music and singing the same songs.

The record industry, which produced those flat black disks played on the Gramophone, spread Tin Pan Alley everywhere. So did that new invention, the radio. Not only did American composers—George and Ira Gershwin, Jerome Kern, Irving Berlin—become famous, but so did singers, such as Rudy Valley, Bessie Smith, and Al Jolson. Recordings of popular singers made certain pieces "hits" with the public.

Recordings also helped spread another sort of music: Jazz. Born among black musicians in the South, it was not long before Jazz had captivated whites. The African rhythms, extemporaneous style, and sensual tone of Jazz were alluring. Some said Jazz was dangerous music, that it awakened impure passions in the young, but such criticisms meant nothing to its enthusiasts. People loved the unrestrained, "cut loose" feeling of the music. They danced new dances devoid of all the staidness, dignity, and decorum of many of the older traditional dances. Instead of the waltz, the polka, and other old ballroom styles, young people danced the Charleston, the Varsity Drag, the Black Bottom, and the Shimmy, which combined wild abandon with suggestive movements of the body.

Tin Pan Alley sheet music from 1919

Equally influential in forming the mass-produced culture of the '20s were motion pictures. The film mecca of Hollywood, California, where producers such as D.W. Griffith had been making motion pictures since before the war, was producing swashbuckling adventure films, romances, dramas, and comedies. Though these "moving pictures" were soundless, they drew ever-growing audiences to cinemas across the country. Movie goers thrilled to see their favorite "stars" on the screen; such names as Douglas Fairbanks, Mary Pickford, Rudolf Valentino, and Charlie Chaplin became household words. Americans became so captivated by movie stars they began patterning their habits and dress after what they saw on the screen.

The 1920s were a prosperous time. The stock market continued to rise to unprecedented heights throughout the decade. It seemed as if everyone was entering the middle class and could enjoy the comforts of life. The American dream was more and more defined as the possession of "things"—of cars, radios, factory-made furniture, and clothing of the latest fashion. Such possessions defined the middle-class family (or so advertisements told people), and everywhere salesmen peddled big city standards of "respectable" and comfortable living.

Salesmanship and advertising were more aggressive in the '20s than in any previous decade of American history. The mass production of automobiles and other products required a vigorous sales effort to convince people to buy, and this contributed to

Mary Pickford

mass culture. Men like Henry Ford tried to convince people that they needed their products; they sent out their sales forces, they created printed advertisements, they used radio broadcasts to tantalize the public to purchase products that they had never before dreamed they wanted, much less needed. Movie stars and popular singers were enlisted to tell Americans to buy everything from cars to cosmetics. It was touted as un-American not to want a modern kitchen with a gas stove, refrigerator, and pop-up toaster; or an automobile; or a radio. Advertising convinced Americans to define their lives by material standards—to keep up with their neighbors in the race toward prosperity and comfort. Companies convinced people to "buy on time"—that is, to go into debt—to purchase items that they could well do without. Most Americans purchased their Fords by paying them off over time.

Mass production and advertising influenced even American cuisine, making it everywhere the same. Manufacturers produced foods that required a minimum of preparation. Clarence Birdseye perfected the freeze-drying of vegetables, and soon his product and his name became American institutions. Americans consumed pre-processed foods, such as the goo-like Velveeta processed cheese, breakfast cereals, ice treats (Good Humor Bars, Eskimo Pies, and Popsicles), candy bars (Mounds, Milky Way, and Baby Ruth), and washed it all down with soft drinks like Coca-Cola, 7 Up, and Kool-Aid.

Commerce and the passion to "get-ahead" had long been American preoccupations, but they had been modified and sometimes eclipsed by causes that called for sacrifice and heroism. Abolition had been such a cause; the Southern fight for independence, another. The labor struggle had moved men to lay down their lives for their brothers. Except for a few isolated souls, the men of the 1920s wanted no causes, desired no struggles; they wanted "normalcy," they longed only for a comfortable, prosperous life. They could well ignore the hand wringing and sneers of the Carol Kennicotts and Sinclair Lewises of the world; they would not understand the reservations of a G.K. Chesterton on their mode of life. Comfortable houses, automobiles, modern kitchens, convenience foods, gramophones, nights out at the cinema, stylish living—what more could anyone want? The bland prosperity of a Gopher Prairie suited most Americans of the '20s just fine.

Speakeasies and Gangsters

"The reign of terror is over," Billy Sunday had cried upon the passage of Prohibition. How wrong he was. If anything, the reign of terror had only just begun. It was not enough simply to forbid the sale and consumption of whiskey, wine or beer; if people wanted to drink, they would drink. The government had not enough agents to inspect every house and cellar in America for barrels of fermenting hops and barley or grapes, nor every backwoods shack for a distillery. Nor could they stop lawbreakers who would capitalize on the thirst of Americans for even the worst rot-gut booze.

So, in the years following the passage of the Volstead Act, bootleggers stoked their distilleries and smugglers criss-crossed the Mexican and Canadian borders to bring in foreign liquor, for which they charged high prices. Ships from foreign countries, anchored off the three-mile limit of the American coastline, awaited motor launches that would carry smuggled alcohol to shore.

Those who could not afford the smuggled alcohol made their own. Many a household brewed its own beer

MODEL N-12
(WALNUT CABINET)
MODEL N-14
(MAHOGANY CABINET)
ALL-ELECTRIC
with Peerless Dynamic Speaker, using
UX20 Power Tube.
$195.00 (less tubes)
All prices slightly higher west of Denver

FRESHMAN
YOUR ULTIMATE RADIO

Advertisement from 1928

"Masked criminal at the grave of John Barleycorn," an illustration for Walt Mason's satirical poem "So Runs the World Away," published in *Judge*, October 29, 1921

Dumping of liquor during Prohibition

and hard cider. People took industrial alcohol and converted it into "bathtub gin" and whiskey. Such wretched stuff—"hooch," it was called—was not reserved for private use but was sold to clandestine drinking holes called "speakeasies." These bars were found in basement apartments and other out-of-the-way places in towns and cities throughout the country. Speakeasies served soft drinks, which the bartenders spiked with gin or whiskey; but they also served the stuff straight. Not only was much of this booze bad, it was downright dangerous. Hooch, especially when made from badly converted wood alcohol, caused thousands of deaths. Ironically, Prohibition didn't decrease the drinking of hard liquor; with the closing of breweries and wineries, drinkers turned instead to hard beverages like gin and whiskey.

Many a speakeasy was raided by government agents, its liquor destroyed, and its owners carted away to jail. Yet speakeasies benefited from the patronage of large crime syndicates in the cities that bribed police and government officials to turn a blind eye to speakeasy traffic or to deal gently with speakeasy operators. After the passage of Prohibition, crime syndicates arose in big cities such as New York and Chicago to coordinate the illegal trade in alcohol and bootlegging. The money that formerly went to big alcohol producers, to brewers and to vineyards, was now going to the black market. Gangsters and the mafia grew rich and powerful off the illegal traffic in alcohol.

The most famous gangster of the period was Al Capone, nicknamed "Scarface." Though he came from a respectable Italian working-class family in New York, Capone as a young man fell under the influence of the genteel New York racketeer, Johnny Torrio, who ran a series of brothels and gambling houses throughout the city. Torrio liked Capone, and after moving to Chicago to build up a new gambling and prostitution empire in that unruly city, he asked Capone to join him. Capone moved to Chicago in 1921 and soon became Torrio's partner.

The illegal liquor trade brought Capone and Torrio enormous profits but also increased tensions among the various gangs in Chicago. Gangland murders increased. In 1924, Torrio was shot several times in front of his home by members of the rival George "Bugs" Moran gang. Torrio survived; but weakened and tired of the crime racket, he left Chicago for retirement abroad. Al Capone then became undisputed head of the crime syndicate. As his profits increased, so did the violence between his and rival gangs. Gangsters armed with machine guns shot down rival gang members or their own double-crossing members. Between 1925 and 1929, Chicago had 215 unsolved murders—unsolved because of Capone's power and influence.

Al Capone

The most spectacular of these murders occurred on St. Valentine's Day, 1929. Capone wanted to be rid of Bugs Moran's competition. While vacationing in Miami, Florida, Capone sent "Machine Gun" McGurn to Chicago to handle the execution. McGurn's plan was clever. He lured Moran and his men to a parking garage, supposedly to sell them a shipment of whiskey. McGurn then had his henchmen, dressed up as policemen, meet Moran and his men at the garage, while McGurn himself rented a hotel room far from the scene of the crime. The "policemen" burst in on Moran's men at the garage, pretending to make a raid; they lined the gangsters against the wall and then shot them down. It was a successful plan, except for one thing: Bugs Moran was not there. Seeing what he thought were policemen making a raid, he drove off to safety.

The St. Valentine's Day Massacre made newspaper headlines across the country. Capone and McGurn were both arrested; but since the police had no evidence against them, they were released. Neither the police nor federal agents could get at Capone for his real crimes. Not until 1931—and only by convicting him for income tax evasion—were federal officials able to put Capone behind bars.

The Lost Generation

Suffrage was not the only new "freedom" women enjoyed in the 1920s. The decade witnessed a loosening of age-old standards of feminine decorum that, in turn, had its effects on the relationship between the sexes. Young people, especially, of the 1920s, rejected what they thought was the over rigid morality of the late 19th century (called the "Victorian Age" for Queen Victoria of England, who ruled during that period). Instead, they reveled in a culture of sexual promiscuity that expressed itself in dress, music, courtship, and conversation.

In reaction to Victorian Age styles of women's dress with their layers of clothing, ankle-length skirts, long sleeves, and neckline collars, girls adopted a freer, more suggestive style of clothing. They wore loose fitting dresses, often sleeveless, with skirts descending no farther than the knees. While this might not seem shocking to people of our time, it was considered scandalous in the early 20th century. Girls dressed the way they did because it *was* scandalous. They cut their hair short like a man's—"bobbed" it—in reaction to the Victorian era's long-flowing tresses.

Girls called "flappers" set the style for women's dress and behavior. Theirs was the most revealing clothing; theirs, the most saucy habits. Flappers drank hard liquor, smoked cigarettes (then thought unbecoming of women), and were notoriously promiscuous. Of course, not all women who dressed like flappers were promiscuous or particularly bad; they simply followed the fads peddled by advertisements and movies. Still, flapper morality (or the lack of it) had its effect in breaking down standards of behavior in society.

Actress and dancer Violet Romer in flapper dress

The young people of the post-war era called themselves the "lost generation." They just didn't fit into or sympathize with the world that had died in the trenches of France. Old standards of courtship were collapsing; instead of chaperoned meetings of young men and women, dating (where a boy and girl would go out alone to dance halls, speakeasies, cinemas and other rendezvous) became the norm. Cheap, hard liquor, the sensuous tones of Jazz music, unrestrained dances like the Argentine Tango, the Bunny-Hug, the Fox Trot, and the Turkey Trot, broke down the resistance of many young people to immoral behavior.

Various new ideas that were floating about aided in the decline of morality during the decade of the '20s. John Dewey's educational theories attacked all forms of "authoritarianism," including in that term parental authority and the authority of religion. For Dewey, there was no absolute right or wrong, but, he said, ethics must be adjusted to the peculiar conditions of each time and place. Knowledge, too, according to Dewey, was not about truth but about dealing with practical difficulties in the here and now. Closely allied with Dewey's Pragmatism was Permissiveness. Influencing first the schools, these doctrines eventually influenced parents who were told by various "authorities" that they should not restrict their children's behavior but allow them to follow the thrust of their desires as much as possible.

Popularized and distorted versions of Psychoanalysis, developed by the Austrians Sigmund Freud and Carl Jung, and introduced to the English speaking world by Havelock

Havelock Ellis

Ellis, justified all manner of behavior. American youth were told that it was psychologically "unhealthy" to "repress" their sexual desires; that by doing so, they would develop unpleasant psychological conditions called "neuroses." It became faddish for groups of young men and women to talk freely about sexual matters and to throw around such Freudian terms as "ego," "id," "super-ego," and "libido."

The effect of such philosophies was to weaken further the hold religious belief had on Americans. Religious belief had been declining in America before the 1920s and, with it, the institution of the family. For decades, the family had suffered various strains that, according to a 1919 pastoral letter written by the American Catholic bishops, had tended to weaken its influence in society. These strains, said the bishops, were "the demands of industry, of business, and of social intercourse." The industrial world had reduced many families to grinding poverty. It had divorced economic activity from the home and so separated fathers for long periods of time from their families. (Previously, on farms, families labored together to produce their daily bread, and even in cities the father, his wife and children had worked together in small shops and stores.) These strains, together with the new permissive philosophies, wreaked havoc on family life. If, as the bishops wrote, "the esteem in which marriage is held furnishes an index of people's morality," then America was in a poor state. Between 1910 and 1928, the divorce rate in the United States doubled.

Along with the burdens placed on the traditional family, the 1920s witnessed a campaign waged against the large family. Margaret Sanger and her American Birth Control League (later renamed Planned Parenthood) led the charge in this war. Sanger, whose mother was Catholic and whose father was a "free-thinker," came from a family of 11 children. As a nurse to poor families in New York City, Sanger became involved with the Industrial Workers of the World and came to know Emma Goldman. Goldman's views on free love and her anarchist espousal of women's rights led Sanger to think that issues of reproduction and women's health had political significance. After Sanger published a pamphlet with instructions on how to use contraceptives, a warrant was issued for her arrest. She avoided imprisonment by fleeing to Europe.

Margaret Sanger (center) on court house steps in Brooklyn, New York, 1917. Sanger had been accused of opening a birth control clinic in New York City. She was found guilty.

Sanger later returned to the United States. She founded the American Birth Control League to disseminate the idea that women could only be free if they were able to control their reproductive faculties. In 1920, Sanger argued that statistics detailing the high infant mortality rate among the families of coal miners (who lived in extraordinarily poor and unhealthy conditions) demonstrated "the immorality of large families." Perhaps somewhat ironically, she declared, "The most merciful thing that the large family does to one of its infant members is to kill it."

Sanger saw birth control as an instrument for eugenics—producing a race free of "defectives," as she called those with mental physical disabilities. "Birth control," she wrote, "often denounced as a violation of natural law, is nothing more or less than the facilitation of the process of weeding out the unfit, of preening the birth of defectives or of those who will become defectives."

The process will be realized, she said, when, "in compliance with nature's working plan, we must permit womanhood its full development before we can expect of it efficient motherhood. If we are to make racial progress, this development of womanhood must precede motherhood in every individual women." Elsewhere she declared that "we must . . . not permit an increase in population that we are not prepared to care for to the best advantage, that we are not prepared to do justice to, educationally and economically. We must popularize birth control thinking."

Sanger's thought would in time make more and more parents think that they had a moral duty not to have too many children. Many would come to think that the way to stop poverty and other social ills was to limit the increase of the population.

The Catholic bishops of the United States took a different position than Sanger on the ills of society, their causes and their remedies. Not mechanical contrivances to insure a "superior race," said the bishops, not more freedom which is really more license, but moral reform was the key to problems besetting the country. In their 1919 pastoral letter the bishops declared that society's reform must be based on an acknowledgment of the position of Christ and his Church and must recognize what Pope Benedict XV called the sources of evil: "lack of mutual good will, contempt for authority, conflict of class with class, and absorption in the pursuit of the perishable goods of this world, with utter disregard of things that are nobler and worthier of human endeavor." Men, said the bishops, had become "absorbed in worldly pursuits" and had neglected "those which belong to our eternal welfare."

Ultimately, people must practice charity, said the bishops, if they wanted a better life for all. Charity, said the bishops, is not a merely private virtue but one that touches on every human endeavor. "As commonly understood," they wrote, "charity is manifested in deeds that tend to the relief of suffering in any of its various forms, or that provide opportunities of advancement for those who have none, or that add somewhat to the scant pleasures of many laborious lives. . . . By its very nature, charity is also social virtue."

Boom Years

Warren G. Harding had won the presidency in 1920 by calling for a return to "normalcy" in government and business. In choosing his cabinet, the new president did the normal thing—he appointed a few outstanding men and a larger number of mostly mediocre men. Charles Evans Hughes, the new secretary of state, was one of the outstanding ones; so was the new secretary of commerce, Herbert Hoover (who had ably handled government's food distribution during the war). The Pennsylvania industrialist, Andrew W. Mellon, the new secretary of the treasury, was a third. But many of Harding's cabinet and other appointments to federal posts were just members of the "Ohio Gang," the political circle to which Harding had belonged in Ohio.

Still, there was something *abnormal* about Harding's circle of intimates. Poker parties, complete with illegal booze, were common in the White House. The Harding administration was rife with political corruption. Though certainly present at the drinking bouts and poker parties, the president himself was not involved in the corruption of his cabinet, though he may have known of it and turned a blind eye to much of it. When it became clear that his friend "Colonel" Charlie Forbes, whom Harding had appointed director of the new Veteran's Bureau, had been embezzling money earmarked for the construction of veterans hospitals, Harding made him resign. Yet, his administration was filled with far more corruption than what the Colonel himself generated.

Warren G. Harding

On the other hand, Harding was a genial and kind man. He let Eugene Debs out early from prison (where he had gone for violating the Sedition Act during the war), so he could

Ku Klux Klan parade in Washington, D.C., 1926

spend Christmas with his family. He favored a reduction of the 12-hour workday still in place in most industries. In the South, he spoke out against the segregation of blacks and for their full voting rights. He publicly attacked what he called "factions of hatred and prejudice and violence" that challenged civil and religious liberty.

These "factions" included a new Ku Klux Klan. This Klan was not the same organization that terrorized blacks after the Civil War; the new Klan had on its hate list not only blacks, but Catholics and Jews. Swathed in the white robes and hoods of the older Klan, the new Klan had added another symbol—the burning cross—which it ignited before the houses of its intended victims.

The new Ku Klux was not just a Southern phenomenon; the organization throve in the northern Midwest, where blacks were moving in great numbers for work, and in the Far West. The Klan was able to get sympathetic governors elected in Oklahoma and Oregon and nearly took control of the government of Indiana.

Anti-semitism was on the rise in the 1920s, and one of its chief proponents was none other than Henry Ford. The Ford-controlled Dearborn, Michigan newspaper published the spurious "Protocols of the Elders of Zion," which purported to be a document written by Jews in which they planned a subversion of Christian civilization. In 1920, Ford published a book, *The International Jew,* in which he argued that Jews were at the bottom of war and all its ills.

Harding did not share Ford's prejudice or the Klan's bigotry; he appointed Jews to public offices and sent a Catholic priest, Father Joseph Denning, to Tangiers as United States agent and consul general.

In domestic policy, Harding worked to curtail government expenditures and to cut taxes. With Secretary Mellon, Harding dramatically slashed income tax rates, which Wilson had drastically raised during the war. The president was in favor of tariffs with rates flexible enough to rise and fall according circumstances.

Harding opposed joining the League of Nations because he thought it would form a super-state that would rob member states of their sovereignty. In rejecting the League, he said "we make no surrender of our hope and aim for an association to promote peace, in which we would most heartily join." Harding signed separate treaties of peace with Germany, Austria, and Hungary; these treaties kept to the main provisions of the Treaty of Versailles but did not mention the League of Nations.

Harding's great foreign policy triumph was the National Disarmament Conference, held in Washington, D.C. in 1921–22. Delegates from the United States, Britain, Japan, France, Italy, Belgium, Holland, Portugal, and China met to reach an agreement on naval disarmament. In the treaty that resulted, the three major naval powers, Great Britain, the United States, and Japan, agreed to limit their naval tonnage. In particular, the United States agreed not to strengthen its naval bases west of Pearl Harbor (excepting Guam and Manila); and Great Britain made the same guarantee for its bases east of Singapore and north of Australia. Still, Japan benefited most from the treaty because, though her navy was to be smaller than the navies of either the United States or Great Britain, she had only one ocean to cruise, while the United States had to divide her fleets over two seas, and Great Britain over three.

Though firmly in favor of avoiding "foreign entanglements," the Harding administration answered the plea of the Soviet Union for food relief. Lenin's abolition of private property and his government's forced contributions of food from the Russian peasants had created widespread hunger. Headed by Secretary Herbert Hoover, the American Relief Association in 1922 began directing 18,000 relief stations in the Soviet Union, which fed four million children and six million adults. Medical aid was also given. The Harding administration oversaw similar relief efforts in other countries.

The year 1921 was the high water mark of Harding's popularity; after that, criticism of the incompetence of his appointments increased and rumors spread of the corruption in his administration. Farmers, who were suffering the effects of low prices for their crops, were not happy with Harding because he opposed giving them government relief. In 1923, Harding made a tour of the western United States and Alaska to reassure farmers about his policies and to bolster flagging enthusiasm for his administration. Already tired from the trials of being president, Harding succumbed to pneumonia and died in San Francisco on August 2, 1923.

The shadow of a lynching darkens a crowd of white people, gathered to watch it.

With the death of Harding, news of the scandals in his administration became public. It became known that Albert B. Fall, Harding's secretary of the interior, and Edwin M. Denby, the secretary of the navy, had received the president's permission to transfer naval petroleum deposits from the naval to the interior department. It turned out that Fall (Denby, it seems, was duped) was in league with the oil magnates, Edward Doheny and Harry Sinclair. Fall illegally leased the public oil reserve, Elk Hill, to Doheny, and to Sinclair, the Teapot Dome reserve in Wyoming, in return for some oil storage tanks the oil men agreed to build at the naval base at Pearl Harbor. On top of that, Fall received $300,000 from Sinclair and $100,000 from Doheny.

The "Teapot Dome Scandal" was but the tip of the iceberg of scandal. Among other uncovered scandals was one involving Attorney General Henry Daugherty, who had used his office as the chief law enforcement agent in the country to sell liquor permits. There were other scandals, which, though Harding was not implicated in them, besmirched the reputation of his administration. Because of these scandals, Warren G. Harding has won the reputation as the worst president the United States has had—a distinction, given his accomplishments, that he, perhaps, did not entirely deserve.

Albert B. Fall

Cool Cal

Harding's 51-year old vice-president, Calvin Coolidge, was visiting his home in Plymouth, Vermont when news reached him of the president's death. On August 3, Coolidge took the oath of office before his own father, a justice of the peace in Plymouth.

A taciturn New Englander (the first president from that region since Franklin Pierce), Coolidge quickly earned the epithet, "Silent Cal." "I have never been hurt by what I have not said," was one of his pithy aphorisms. For the first four months he was in office, Coolidge gave no presidential message concerning his policies or what the nation could expect from him.

He was not idle, though. Entirely uninvolved with the scandalous goings-on in the Harding administration, Coolidge, as president, had to deal with their aftermath. He

Calvin Coolidge (right) with Harding

appointed a special counsel to investigate the scandals and stood ramrod straight against public opinion, which thirsted for vengeance. Coolidge made it clear he would move methodically and justly, even if his political future were at stake. "I do not propose," he said, "to sacrifice any innocent man for my own welfare, nor do I propose to maintain in office any unfit man for my own welfare."

When Coolidge finally gave his first presidential address in December of 1923, the nation, itching to find out what they could expect from him, listened attentively. Coolidge's talk had no rhetorical flair; it was a simple and clear explication of the policies he favored and those he opposed. He favored maintaining the tariff, but without frequent revisions. He was for tax reduction through tax reform. He disapproved of government aid to relieve farmers as well as any bonuses to war veterans. He opposed joining the League of Nations but agreed to U.S. participation in the World Court. Though not eloquent, Coolidge's clear and conservative speech was a reassurance to many Americans that nothing unusual would happen under the new president.

One of the chief difficulties Coolidge faced as president was opposition from within his own Republican party. Some Republicans would have preferred another candidate in the election of 1924, but they dared not oppose the public which had come to like Silent Cal. The Republicans nominated Coolidge, while the Democrats, divided between the "dry" (pro-Prohibition) William McAdoo and the "wet" Al Smith of New York, settled on a corporate lawyer named John W. Davis. Former Bull Moose party members and assorted Liberals and socialists formed the Conference for Political Action and nominated Robert La Follette.

Voters, who were told to "Keep Cool with Coolidge," gave the president a firm majority in the election. Coolidge won 15,700,000 votes in the popular vote and secured 382 electoral votes, while Davis boasted only 8.4 million in the popular vote and 136 electoral votes. Robert La Follette polled 4.8 million votes and took the state of Wisconsin, while the communist Workers Party's William Z. Foster garnered only 33,000 votes.

Secretary Kellogg opening international talks

In domestic affairs, Coolidge, like the frugal New Englander he was, stressed strict "economy" in government. "Economy," he said, "is idealism in its most practical form." Economy to "Cool Cal" meant, in part, a reduction and, even, elimination of the national debt. In 1924 and 1926, he supported cutting taxes. He opposed the Veterans Bonus Bill, but the Republican Congress overrode his veto. His veto, though, of the McNary-Haugen Farm Relief Bill, stood. Coolidge opposed the bill, partly because he thought it unconstitutional but mostly because he was against schemes to fix prices. He thought the farmers could help themselves by forming cooperatives to market their crops. But in 1928, he signed the Jones-White Act, which doubled the amount of money the federal government gave to the builders of merchant ships.

The Coolidge administration furthered the peace-making policies of Harding. Secretary of State Kellogg and Aristide Briand of France in 1928 drew up the Kellogg-Briand Peace Pact, to which 62 nations, including Italy, Japan, and Germany signed on. In the pact, the signing powers pledged that they would "renounce war as an instrument of national policy," and that they would solve "all disputes or conflicts of whatever nature or of whatever origin" by peaceful means.

"We Must Think the Thoughts the Founders Thought"

Despite his straight-lipped, unsmiling demeanor, Coolidge was a popular speaker. He addressed the American people on his favorite theme of the importance of "economy," on the need for improved local government, and on the importance of being law-abiding and tolerant of different religions. Coolidge, too, told the American people that government must have a "spiritual" element. In a speech he gave on the 150th anniversary of the Declaration of Independence in 1926, Coolidge, in the tradition of Daniel Webster and Abraham Lincoln, spoke of America's founding as of something almost religious. "It is little wonder, said Coolidge, "that people at home and abroad consider Independence Hall as hallowed ground and revere the Liberty Bell as a sacred relic . . . They have long been identified with a great cause. They are the framework of a spiritual event. The world looks upon them, because of their associations of one hundred and fifty years ago, as it looks upon the Holy Land because of what took place there nineteen hundred years ago. Through use for a righteous purpose they have become sanctified."

Coolidge could speak of the founding of the United States as a spiritual event because he believed that the founding arose from ideals rooted in "religious" conviction. "In its main features the Declaration of Independence is a great spiritual document," declared the president. "It is a declaration not of material but of spiritual conceptions. Equality, liberty, popular sovereignty, the rights of man—these are not elements which we can see and touch. They are ideals. They have their source and their roots in the religious convictions. They belong to the unseen world. Unless the faith of the American people in these religious convictions is to endure, the principles of our Declaration will perish. We can not continue to enjoy the result if we neglect and abandon the cause."

Since the principles of the Declaration, said Coolidge, are spiritual and true ideals, they cannot be questioned. Though, on account of human progress since 1776, "we have had new thoughts and new experiences which have given us a great advance over the people of that day," we cannot, he said, "very well discard their conclusions for something more modern . . .

> If all men are created equal, that is final. If they are endowed with inalienable rights, that is final. If governments derive their just powers from the consent of the governed, that is final. No advance, no progress can be made beyond these propositions. If anyone wishes to deny their truth or their soundness, the only direction in which he can proceed historically is not forward, but backward toward the time when there was no equality, no rights of the individual, no rule of the people. Those who wish to proceed in that direction can not lay claim to progress. They are reactionary. Their ideas are not more modern, but more ancient, than those of the Revolutionary fathers.

The Declaration of Independence set a certain limit on progress, said Coolidge, "there is far more danger of harm than there is hope of good in any radical changes." The country does not need change, but a "better understanding and comprehension" of Declaration principles "and a better knowledge of the foundations of government in general." Before Americans can understand the conclusions the founding fathers came to about government, they "must go back and review the course which [the founders] followed. We must think the thoughts which they thought," declared Coolidge:

> Their intellectual life centered around the meeting-house. They were intent upon religious worship. While there were always among them men of deep learning, and later those who had comparatively large possessions, the mind of the people was not so much

engrossed in how much they knew, or how much they had, as in how they were going to live. While scantily provided with other literature, there was a wide acquaintance with the Scriptures. Over a period as great as that which measures the existence of our independence they were subject to this discipline not only in their religious life and educational training, but also in their political thought. They were a people who came under the influence of a great spiritual development and acquired a great moral power.

While "we live in an age of science and of abounding accumulation of material things," perorated Coolidge, "these did not create our Declaration. Our Declaration created them. The things of the spirit come first. Unless we cling to that, all our material prosperity, overwhelming though it may appear, will turn to a barren scepter in our grasp. If we are to maintain the great heritage which has been bequeathed to us, we must be like-minded as the fathers who created it. We must not sink into a pagan materialism. We must cultivate the reverence which they had for the things that are holy. We must follow the spiritual and moral leadership which they showed. We must keep replenished, that they may glow with a more compelling flame, the altar fires before which they worshiped."

Rise and Fall of Wall Street

"I do not choose to run for president in 1928," announced Coolidge on August 2, 1927. He could easily have won the Republican nomination, but he insisted he did not want it. Despite all the attempts to "draft Calvin" for the Republican ticket, Coolidge refused to budge. The nomination went, instead, to his efficient secretary of commerce, Herbert Hoover.

Al Smith

Franklin Delano Roosevelt promoted the nomination of Alfred Emanuel Smith in the Democratic Party. As four-term governor of New York, Al Smith was an efficient administrator and a progressive. He was also "wet" (that is, he favored the repeal of Prohibition). Smith, a native of Brooklyn, New York, was a tough, frank campaigner. When the press attacked him, saying he was a "creature" of Tammany Hall, Smith responded that this was not so; he was not a "creature" of Tammany Hall, he said—he was Tammany Hall! The press, and the Republicans, assailed Smith for being a Catholic (a Republican button, for Protestant Democrats, read, "A Christian in the White House"—referring, of course, to Hoover, not Smith); and the cocky Smith answered the charge by admitting that, not only was he Catholic, but he prayed the rosary as well.

In the election, Smith took the big cities but lost in the rural areas—he was the first presidential candidate to have no farming origins. Hoover even was able to break the Democratic party's hold on the Solid South, where Smith's Catholicism was especially distasteful. Hoover took 58 percent of the popular vote and a whopping electoral vote of 444.

Perhaps the biggest reason for Hoover's victory in 1928 was the booming economy. Since 1923, when Coolidge assumed the presidency, the American economy had been growing and expanding. While campaigning, Hoover had declared, "We shall soon with the help of God be in sight of the day when poverty shall be banished from this nation." Millions of Americans believed this rhetoric—the stock market was rising to unprecedented heights; common people could buy such "luxuries" as an automobile, a radio, and the accoutrements for the "modern kitchen." Widespread optimism assured the nation that, soon, every American could achieve the "American dream" of middle class comfort—so, why switch from the party under whose administration all this prosperity had come?

Coolidge could well claim, in 1928, that prosperity had come to America precisely because government had taken a hands-off policy toward business. Of course, this was not entirely true, but it was mostly so; Coolidge had intervened in favor of business by maintaining a high tariff wall on foreign imports, but he had refused to intervene when a wild fit of speculation sent the stock market soaring.

Yet, all was not as good as it looked on the surface. For one thing, not all sectors of the economy had been doing well. The biggest industries were those that produced automobiles and radios, along with those industries tied to automobiles and radios (for instance, the rubber and tire-making industries). Other industries, though, were not so fortunate. Agriculture, for instance, had taken huge hits after the war. During the war, the government had encouraged farmers to expand their fields and to buy machinery to produce surpluses for the army and the war-devastated peoples of Europe. The government even artificially hiked the prices of wheat and other grains to $2 a bushel. By 1920, however, the price of wheat had fallen to 67 cents a bushel, and farmers fell deep into debt. Under Harding and Coolidge, the federal government refused to do anything to help remedy a situation for which it was, in large part, responsible; and, though by 1925, the price of wheat had risen to almost $1.50 a bushel, the next year it dropped again to $1.03 a bushel. It continued to fall over the next two years.

The farmers' problem was overproduction. There was just too much wheat, corn, and other crops for the demand; and when supply exceeds demand, prices fall. Overproduction would have plagued even the auto industry and its related industries, but for several factors. For one, these industries allowed consumers to buy cars, radios, toasters, and other items "on time"; that is, they extended credit to buyers. So, if a family did not have the money to buy a Ford, a dealership would allow them to pay a portion of the sale price while, in effect, lending the rest of the money to be paid over time, with interest. The problem was that this could only go on so long before families became so indebted that they could not afford to purchase more products, even "on time." If that happened, orders to factories for new products would fall, factories would have more products than they could sell, production would slow or grind to a halt, and companies would lay off workers.

Wall Street in New York

The European market was another source of growth for American industries in the 1920s. Europe had been devastated by the war; much of its industry lay prostrate. After the war, the United States had made many large loans to Europe, a large percentage of which returned to the United States in the form of purchases for manufactured goods. High U.S. tariffs, though, kept reviving European industries from competing in the American market, and European industry languished. Though Europe experienced an economic boom in the mid '20s, the good times could not continue. With an insufficient economic base of its own, Europe could not pay off debts to America; loans from the United States thereafter decreased as did European purchases of American goods.

Perhaps the biggest boom in American business resulted from widespread speculation in stocks. It seemed like everyone was playing the stock market. Much like automobile dealerships with their time-buying schemes, stock brokers allowed investors to buy stocks "on margin." That is, for, say, a $10 down payment on a stock costing $75 a share, a broker would loan the remaining $65 at interest. If the investor cashed in his stock when it reached, say, $400 a share, he would repay the $65 he owed the broker, plus any interest that had accrued on the loan, and keep the remainder. The broker, in turn, would repay the bank whatever he owed when he borrowed the money to loan to the investor. This all worked well, as long as stocks continued to rise; but what if they fell, and fell dramatically? Such an event might occur if, for instance, a business downturn, arising from slackened consumer spending, decreased investors' confidence in the market. Enough investors selling their stocks could quickly depreciate the value of the stocks.

Speculation schemes brought instability to the market. Stock pools, for instance, were formed in which a group of investors traded stocks in a particular industry back and forth between themselves. This prearranged buying and selling artificially increased the price of the stocks, which made them tantalizing to new investors. The original investors lured new investors in to buy the stock, and when enough outsiders had "gotten in on the action," the original group of investors sold the stock they held. The original investors, then, realized a large profit, while the suckers they had drawn in were left with valueless stock.

Another scheme was the "bear raid." Operators of a company spread rumors that their company was in trouble. The rumors led investors to sell their stock, thus seriously decreasing its value. The operators then bought up the stock at a low price and waited for it to rise in value. Similar to the bear raid was the scheme by which larger companies drove smaller competitors out of business. Members of a holding company approached shareholders in a smaller company that had been doing a steady, profitable business and offered them high prices for their stocks. When the holding company, by this method, came to control 51 percent of the stocks in the smaller company, it closed that company and took whatever money reserves the company possessed. This underhanded practice devastated some communities for whom a company might be the sole economic anchor.

Another source of instability for the economy of the booming '20s was the ill distribution of wealth. In 1929, only 0.1 percent of the people had income that equaled the combined income of the lowest 42 percent of the people; this same 0.1 percent controlled one-third of the savings, while 80 percent of the people had no savings at all. This was a serious problem, since 0.1 percent of the population could not make up for the combined buying arising from the needs and wants of 42 percent of the people. If the spending of so large a percentage of the population declined, the whole structure of the economy could come crashing down.

The Black Days of October

A few voices had warned that America's boom could not continue, but they were not heeded. These prophets of disaster were criticized as naysayers and vilified as "scaremongers." Optimism and the confidence of investors was too high. They expected continued, limitless economic expansion.

Investors' confidence was still high even when, on September 3, 1929, stock prices began to fall. Confidence was shaken, however, on Monday, October 21, when stock prices plummeted. Panicky investors began selling. Though over the next two days prices stabilized, on "Black Thursday," October 24, prices took another dive. Prices stabilized again on Friday and Saturday, when major bankers intervened to shore up the market; but on Monday, prices again plummeted, and the market fell by 13 percent. The next day, Tuesday, October 29, 1929, terrified investors frantically sold off their stocks. Over 16 million stocks changed hands that "Black Tuesday." Sometimes stocks had no buyers.

Like circular waves emanating from a stone toss, the lost confidence and panic of Wall Street spread across the nation. Consumers, both rich and middle class, stopped buying on credit, and industrial production fell by nine percent between October and December 1929. Industrial downturn led to worker layoffs, and those laid off could not afford to

Investors attempt to withdraw their deposits from a bank, 1933

make further payments on the items they had bought on credit. Instead, they returned such items to manufacturers, only exacerbating the glut of manufactured goods and leading to yet further layoffs. By 1930, unemployment reached five million; by 1932, it had climbed to 12 million—25 percent of the normal working force. Fearful of the security of their savings, investors formed long lines outside of banks to withdraw their deposits, and many banks folded.

The "Crash of '29" was a stern blow to a country that, only a short time before, had been basking in unparalleled prosperity. Millions, jobless, wandered the countryside. Shantytowns began springing up to house those who had been turned out of their houses. Farmers resorted to arms to resist the repossession of their farms by banks. While many of the rich could weather the hard times, a large number of the middle class and the poor were caught between the hammer and the anvil. They felt they had no place to turn to find protection from the forces that threatened to overwhelm them.

"We Have Now Passed the Worst"

Herbert Hoover, whose ill-fortune it was to be president during the crash and through the worst years of the Great Depression that followed, maintained his confidence in the Liberal economic system he had espoused in more prosperous times. In his mind, the president must give encouragement to the country; he should promote policies to help business revive, but he must never support measures that give direct relief to the suffering nor suffer the government to interfere in the economy beyond what is necessary to maintain equal opportunity and the freedom of individual enterprise—what Hoover praised as "rugged individualism." Thus, Hoover was behind the formation of a charity drive that raised $15 million for the needy in 1929/30, but he opposed policies supported by progressives like La Follette, who suggested that the federal government initiate a program of public works to employ the jobless. Private and local charity, said men like La Follette, could not care for all the needy; the government must step in to help.

Despite the deepening crisis, Hoover continued to speak as if all would soon be well. On January 21, 1930 he declared, "business and industry have turned the corner." On May 1, he said, "We have now passed the corner." Yet, despite these optimistic prognostications, the depression grew worse and worse.

In the congressional election of 1932, Democrats took control of the House of Representatives while a coalition of Republicans and Democrats controlled the Senate. The new Congress, meeting in March 1932, approved a conservative measure to turn the country toward recovery. This was the Reconstruction Finance Corporation (RFC), which could lend money to railroads, banks, and industrial and commercial companies. The RFC was expanded in July with the Emergency Relief Act to include agricultural agencies and state and local government public works projects. The philosophy behind the RFC was that aid given to corporations would eventually trickle down to everyone else. Such a philosophy was Hoover's own, and he signed the legislation. During the remainder of the year, the RFC was instrumental in saving many banks from going bust.

Herbert Hoover and his dog, Tut

A New Deal

The election of 1932 was one of the most pivotal in the history of the country. It would determine whether the United States would continue to be dominated by 19th century *laissez-faire* policies or follow the path of such countries as Great Britain and adopt a more active role for the central government in the economy. The latter course was the path of progressivism—of Wilson, La Follette, and the Bull Moose party. Americans had rejected progressivism in 1920, but now, with the specter of a long depression ahead of them, would they again embrace it?

Al Smith with Franklin
Delano Roosevelt (left)

A number of candidates vied for their party's presidential nomination at the Democratic Party convention of 1932. Al Smith again sought the nomination, but his poor showing at the polls in 1928 dissuaded Democratic politicos from supporting him. The two main contenders for the nomination were Democratic speaker of the House, "Cactus Jack" Garner of Texas, and the governor of New York, Franklin Delano Roosevelt. Roosevelt was fortunate to have the support of the wealthy financier, Joseph P. Kennedy of Massachusetts, who raised funds for him. Kennedy did Roosevelt another good turn; he convinced the wealthy newspaper mogul, William Randolph Hearst, to turn his support to Roosevelt. Hearst controlled the California delegates to the convention, and his support meant their support. With California's 44 votes in the bag, Roosevelt secured the Democratic nomination for president.

The 50-year old Roosevelt had had all the advantages of a wealthy upbringing. He had attended Harvard and Columbia Law School; he had traveled widely through Europe. A distant cousin to Theodore Roosevelt (whom Franklin greatly admired), he cemented closer relations with the former president by marrying Eleanor Roosevelt, Teddy's niece. Franklin Roosevelt had served as Assistant Secretary of the Navy under Wilson and was later elected to a seat in the New York Senate. Struck by polio in 1921, Franklin by determination regained his health, though he remained unable to walk without braces. In 1928, Al Smith encouraged him to run for governor of New York, to which office he was elected. So popular a governor was Roosevelt that he was reelected governor in 1930 by a majority of 700,000 votes.

The Republican nominee was, again, Herbert Hoover. The president had to contend against an aggressive campaign in which Roosevelt stumped the country, visiting nearly every state, detailing how he planned to turn the country around. Roosevelt proposed active government intervention in the economy. He called for federal unemployment relief, for legislation directly to aid agriculture and railroads and to protect consumers and investors. He wanted to lower tariffs and to repeal Prohibition. All this he called the "New Deal"—which was really not all that new, being an extension of Teddy Roosevelt's "Square Deal," Wilson's "New Freedom," and the policies promoted by the Progressive Bull Moosers. Roosevelt was but the heir to the progressive policies that had been in abeyance during the Republican-dominated 1920s.

Hoover warned of the dangers of the New Deal. "Any change of policies will bring disaster to every fireside in America," he warned. Hoover was not alone; other conservatives opposed Roosevelt's New Deal, warning that it would visit disaster on the country. Even Al Smith grew alarmed when Roosevelt began talking about how the New Deal was for "the forgotten man at the bottom of the pyramid." "This is no time for demagogues!" declared Smith.

Yet, in spite of conservative warnings, 22.8 million voters cast their ballots for "F.D.R." in November. Roosevelt not only took 57.3 percent of the popular vote but won with a landslide of 472 votes in the electoral college. Poor Hoover took only 39.6 percent of the vote (15.8 million) and won only 59 electoral votes. Despite the hard times, Socialists and Communists together won less than one million votes. The Democrats took the presidency and won substantial majorities in the House and the Senate.

Nothing, But Fear Itself

The months between November and March, 1933, when Roosevelt would be sworn in as president, must have seemed long indeed to those who hoped for great things from the New

Deal. Ever faithful to his *laissez-faire* policies, President Hoover tried to get Roosevelt to make statements repudiating the New Deal, but to no avail. F.D.R. was committed to the policies that had won him the election.

"This nation asks for action, and action now!" declared Roosevelt in his inaugural address on March 4, 1933. Though the stock market had begun an upswing, the country was still beset by disaster. Roosevelt knew this, and in this his first of many addresses, he sought to lift the peoples' spirits. "Let me assert," he declared, "my firm belief that the only thing we have to fear is fear itself—nameless, unreasoning, unjustified terror which paralyzes needed efforts to convert retreat into advance. In every dark hour of our national life a leadership of frankness and vigor has met with that understanding and support of the people themselves which is essential to victory. I am convinced that you will again give that support for leadership in these critical days."

The country's "distress," said Roosevelt, "comes from no failure of substance . . . Nature still offers her bounty and human efforts have multiplied it. Plenty is at our doorstep, but a generous use of it languishes in the very sight of the supply." Why is this? Because, said Roosevelt, "the rulers of the exchange of mankind's goods have failed, through their own stubbornness and their own incompetence, have admitted their failure, and abdicated. Practices of the unscrupulous money changers stand indicted in the court of public opinion, rejected by the hearts and minds of men." These "rulers," "cast in the pattern of outworn tradition . . . know only the rules of a generation of self-seekers. They have no vision, and when there is no vision the people perish."

Roosevelt with Hoover on election day, 1933

What is the vision by which the people will be preserved? "Happiness," declared Roosevelt, "lies not in the mere possession of money; it lies in the joy of achievement, in the thrill of creative effort. The joy and moral stimulation of work no longer must be forgotten in the mad chase of evanescent profits. These dark days will be worth all they cost us if they teach us that our true destiny is not to be ministered unto but to minister to ourselves and to our fellow men."

Emergency measures were needed, said Roosevelt, to meet the current crisis. And then followed these words, of ill-omen or hope, depending upon who was listening: "It is to be hoped that the normal balance of executive and legislative authority may be wholly adequate to meet the unprecedented task before us," said Roosevelt. "But it may be that an unprecedented demand and need for undelayed action may call for temporary departure from that normal balance of public procedure." If, said Roosevelt, "the normal balance of executive and legislative authority" should be inadequate to meet the crisis, he as president would ask Congress for "broad executive power to wage a war against the emergency as great as the power that would be given to me if we were in fact invaded by a foreign foe." Thus, Roosevelt indicated that he might seek presidential powers unprecedented in the history of the United States. The powers that Lincoln wielded during the crisis of the Civil War Roosevelt might claim to counter an economic threat.

How did all this square with the Constitution? "Our Constitution is so simple and practical that it is possible always to meet extraordinary needs by changes in emphasis and arrangement without loss of essential form," said Roosevelt. "That is why our constitutional system has proved itself the most superbly enduring political mechanism the modern world has produced. It has met every stress of vast expansion of territory, of foreign wars, of bitter internal strife, of world relations." This statement, vague as it was, seemed to point to only one result. The centralization of government in the federal government, dreamed of by Hamilton, begun under Abraham Lincoln, furthered by the Radical Republicans and Reconstruction, perfected by Teddy Roosevelt and Woodrow Wilson, was about to reach its logical practical expression under F.D.R.

Chapter 26 Review

Summary

- The temperance movement, led by people such as Billy Sunday, Frances Willard, Carrie Nation, and others, took on new life in the early 20th century. On December 18, 1917, Congress approved the 18th Amendment, forbidding the manufacture, sale, and transportation of alcohol in the United States. Andrew Volstead introduced a prohibition bill that Congress approved in 1919; it went into effect on January 16, 1920, with the 18th Amendment.

- Women, led by Susan B. Anthony and Elizabeth Cady Stanton, began to demand the suffrage. Despite opposition on all sides, in 1917 New York gave women the suffrage, and two years later Congress approved the 19th Amendment, giving women the right to vote. The amendment became part of the Constitution on August 26, 1920.

- The National Woman's Party introduced into Congress the Equal Rights Amendment, forbidding all discrimination on the basis of sex.

- Henry Ford made his first automobile in 1896 and formed the Ford Motor Company in 1903. In 1908 he came up with a simple, affordable design, the "Model T." His production was greatly increased by his institution of the assembly line in 1914.

- The automobile transformed American society and increased the tendency to urbanization. It had adverse effects on other forms of transportation and exacerbated the American tendency to rootlessness.

- Orville and Wilbur Wright developed their first glider plane design in 1900 and their first self-propelled plane in 1903. By 1919, the first transatlantic flight was made.

- By the 1920s many Americans were convinced that the United States had received more than its share of immigrants. Congress passed the Johnson Act in 1921, limiting immigration. Another Johnson Act in 1924 further limited immigration.

- A census in 1920 showed that for the first time there were more city dwellers than rural dwellers in the United States.

- During the '20s, Americans looked to the great cities for their culture. Tin Pan Alley in New York City began to market music on a mass scale, and soon all of American was singing the same music. This tendency was propelled by the Gramophone and the radio. Jazz became popular, and motion pictures were influential in forming the mass-produced culture of the '20s.

- The '20s were a prosperous time in which the American dream was more and more defined as the possession of "things." Salesmanship and advertising became more aggressive, and people began to buy things they didn't know they needed or even wanted.

- Following the Volstead Act, the government began to send agents to inspect every house and cellar in America for alcohol. Bootleggers took industrial alcohol and converted it into gin and whiskey, selling it to clandestine drinking holes called "speakeasies." Crime syndicates arose in big cities to coordinate illegal trade in alcohol and bootlegging. The most famous gangster of this period was Al Capone.

- The '20s ushered in new "freedoms," and young people reveled in a culture of sexual promiscuity expressed through dress, music, courtship, and conversation. These young people called themselves the "lost generation" because they didn't fit into or sympathize with the world that had died in the trenches of France.

- New educational ideas came to the fore in '20s. John Dewey's educational theories attacked all forms of authoritarianism, including parental and religious authority.

- Distorted versions of Psychoanalysis in the United States justified all manner of behavior. Such philosophies weakened further the hold religious belief had on Americans.

- Margaret Sanger founded the American Birth Control League, later renamed Planned Parenthood, and encouraged the use of contraceptives. She saw birth control as an instrument to produce a race free of "defectives"and to perfect womanhood. Her thought began to make more parents believe it their moral duty not to bear too many children.

- Warren G. Harding's administration was fraught with political corruption. The president himself was not involved in the corruption of his cabinet, though he may have known of it and turned a blind eye to much of it.

- President Harding attacked "factions of hatred and prejudice and violence," including a new Ku Klux Klan that terrorized not only blacks but Catholics and Jews, as well. Harding showed himself a foe to a rising anti-Semitism in the United States.

- Harding held the National Disarmament Conference in 1921–22 in which delegates from different countries met to reach an agreement on naval disarmament. The conference resulted in a treaty in which the three major naval powers, Great Britain, the United States, and Japan, agreed to limit their naval tonnage.

- Harding died on August 2, 1923, and his vice-president, Calvin Coolidge, took office. A year later Coolidge won the presidential election. In his term, Coolidge stressed strict economy.

- In the late 1920s, the economy boomed. Things were not so good under the surface, however. Agriculture had taken a big hit, and speculation schemes brought instability to the market. Operators of companies led "bear raids" on smaller companies, driving them out of business. The wealth in America was not well distributed.

- In October of 1929, stock prices began to fall, and investors began frantically to sell off their stock. People stopped buying on credit, industrial production fell, and workers were laid off. By 1932 unemployment had reached 12 million. Investors withdrew their deposits from banks, which caused many of them to fold.

- In 1932 Franklin Delano Roosevelt became president by promoting what he called his "New Deal"—an attempt to turn the country towards recovery.

Key Concepts

suffragette: an advocate for women's suffrage

Pragmatism: a school of thought that holds that knowledge is not about truth but is to be directed toward dealing with practical difficulties

Permissiveness: an opinion in psychology that says parents should not restrict their children's behavior but allow them to follow the thrust of their desires as much as possible

Dates to Remember

1917: Congress approves the 18th Amendment.

1920: the Volstead Act goes into effect along with the 18th Amendment (January 16).

Ratification of the 19th Amendment permitting woman's suffrage

1921: Congress passes the first Johnson Act limiting immigration.

1929: beginning of the Great Depression

1933: Franklin Delano Roosevelt becomes president and institutes his "New Deal."

Central Characters

Billy Sunday (1862–1935): an American evangelist influential in promoting the temperance movement

Carrie Nation (1846–1911): American temperance leader famous for demolishing barrooms

Susan B. Anthony (1820–1906): crusader for the woman's suffrage movement in the United States

Elizabeth Cady Stanton (1815–1902): a radical proponent of woman's suffrage and a leader in the suffrage movement

Henry Ford (1863–1947): American industrialist who introduced an affordable automobile to America as well as the assembly-line method of production

Al Capone (1899–1947): famous American gangster who headed a crime syndicate in Chicago from 1925–1931

John Dewey (1859–1952): American philosopher and educator who founded Pragmatism

Margaret Sanger (1879–1966): founder of the birth-control movement in the United States and the American Birth Control League (Planned Parenthood)

Warren G. Harding (1865–1923): 29th president of the United States, whose administration has been remembered chiefly for its corruption scandals

Calvin Coolidge (1872–1933): 30th president of the United States, who restored integrity to the federal

Chapter 26 Review (continued)

government after the scandals of Warren G. Harding's administration

Herbert Hoover (1874–1964): 31st president of the United States, under whose watch the Great Depression began

Questions for Review

1. Why did people such as Cardinal Gibbons and Mother Jones oppose woman's suffrage?

2. How did the assembly line affect the worker as a craftsman?

3. What effects did the automobile have on American life?

4. What American traits did the automobile exacerbate?

5. Why did Americans became so opposed to immigration by the 1920s?

6. What social forces led to the decline of the farm population and the growth of cities?

7. How did increased urbanization influence and change American society?

8. Explain Chesterton's claim that "the problem with rural Americans was that they were not peasants."

9. What were some of the "freedoms" enjoyed by the Lost Generation?

10. How did Pragmatism, Permissiveness, and Psychoanalysis affect religion and family in America?

11. Briefly lay out the causes of the economic crash of 1929.

Ideas in Action

1. Read Chesterton's *What I Saw in America*. Discuss whether his description of America in the 1920s remains true today.

2. Read more about Henry Ford and the Wilbur brothers and how they made their inventions.

3. Obtain a copy of the American bishops' 1919 pastoral letter. Discuss whether their diagnosis of American culture remains true today.

4. Read Franklin Delano Roosevelt's first inaugural address. Would a modern politician speak as he did? Why or why not?

Highways and Byways

Isle of Tears

Ellis island lies in upper New York Bay. The island has an area of about 27 acres, consisting mostly of landfill, since ship's ballast was dumped on the island for a time. The name of the island comes from a Manhattan merchant, Samuel Ellis, who owned it in the late 18th century. The state of New York sold the island to the federal government in 1808, and after that it was used as a fort.

From 1892 to 1924 the island was used as the major station for immigration into the U.S., and during that time about 17 million immigrants passed through the island. When immigrants, who sailed often in crowded and unsanitary conditions, arrived in New York City, they were transported by ferry to Ellis Island where they had to undergo a medical and legal inspection. In the Registry Room, or Great Hall, doctors would briefly examine each immigrant. Because they had so many people to examine, doctors at Ellis Island became very efficient, and could identify a great number of diseases and conditions in only a few seconds. Those who were physically fit and could legally work were allowed to go on, while those who had diseases were sent home or held in the island's hospital. About two percent of the immigrants who came over to Ellis island were not admitted, and many of these died in the hospital. For this reason, the island became known as the "Island of Tears." Today the island is part of the Statue of Liberty National Monument, and the immigration station is a museum. Many songs, movies, and stories have been made about the island where immigrants experienced both hope and sorrow.

DEPRESSION AND WAR

The One Hundred Days

The day after his inauguration, President Franklin Delano Roosevelt met with advisers long into the night to decide what to do about the country's economic crisis. Since November, the federal government had done nothing about the depression. Hoover did not want to initiate any new policies to which Roosevelt would be opposed, and Roosevelt (fearful that he would be hamstrung by agreeing to policies not fully his own) refused to collaborate with Hoover in working up new policies. Facing government inaction, people took matters into their own hands and withdrew their savings from banks. Bank failures proliferated until some state governors began proclaiming "bank holidays"—days on which no transactions could occur.

It was doubtful whether the course Roosevelt finally decided to take was constitutional or not, but people were too desperate to ask any questions. On March 6, the president ordered the closing of all banks for four days. Roosevelt followed this up with more decisive action. On March 9, the first day of Congress' session, he submitted an emergency bank bill to Congress. In the record time of eight hours, Congress passed this bill, which allowed the banks to reopen with a new license system and under the direction of conservators. This was decisive action, indeed! It caught everyone's attention and filled them with a confidence that they had not known for three years. When the banks reopened on March 13, there was no run on savings. On March 15, the stock market began its slow upward trend.

Roosevelt again surprised the country on March 12 by addressing them on the banking crisis over the radio. This was the first of his "Fireside Chats," as he called them, with which, over the next several years, he explained and promoted his policies to the public. Roosevelt had a resonant voice that he used to effect to instill confidence in his policies.

The first 100 days of Roosevelt's administration were a dizzying whirlwind of activity. The men he had gathered around him as advisers (called the "brain trust" because most were from college and universities) with the president worked out the policies that formed the first onslaught of the New Deal. Between March 9 and June 16, 1933, the president presented Congress with 13 bills, each

Roosevelt giving a Fireside Chat, 1935

of which the Senate and House passed in record time. Bills normally took months to pass through Congress; but these bills, many of which were revolutionary in character, took only hours to pass.

The bills of the first 100 days were either emergency measures to take care of immediate problems or were meant to be permanent. The emergency measures included the Federal Emergency Relief Act (passed May 12, 1933), which dedicated $500 million in federal funds for the relief of states, cities, and counties. Later, this figure would rise to $5 billion. With the Agricultural Adjustment Act (AAA, passed May 12), the federal government could appoint county agents to oversee a reduction in the planting of grains, tobacco, sugarcane, and other crops to increase their price. Under the AAA, fields were left fallow, and farmers plowed crops under and slaughtered livestock. In the fall of 1933, farmers slaughtered 6 million piglets and the government froze 100 million pounds of pork, which was sent to families on government relief. The federal government paid $200 million in subsidies to farmers who cooperated with the AAA. The Emergency Farm Mortgage Act (also passed May 12) stopped bank foreclosures on farms, while the Home Owners Loan Corporation was established to refinance small mortgages on houses.

Roosevelt did not believe that it was good for a man's sense of self-dignity to receive handouts, so he pushed through Congress measures that would provide work for the unemployed. On March 31, Congress created the Civilian Conservation Corps (CCC). Established under army control, the CCC employed young men to help conserve natural resources, the care of which had been neglected since the days of Teddy Roosevelt. By August, the CCC had employed over 300,000 men. The National Industrial Recovery Act (passed June 16) in 1935 established the Works Projects Administration (WPA), which employed men in reforestation and flood control projects, in building schools and in clearing slums. The WPA also employed "white collar" workers and college graduates to write guides for regions and

Dry No More

The Democratic victory in 1932 meant not only the end of Republican economic policies; it spelled the end of Prohibition.

It was not that the Republicans necessarily favored maintaining the 18th Amendment; their platform for 1932 said "the people should have an opportunity to pass upon a proposed amendment" that would overturn Prohibition, whole or in part, but stopped short of endorsing a repeal of Prohibition. The Democratic platform was more direct. It called on Congress to "immediately propose a Constitutional Amendment" to repeal the 18th Amendment and present it to state conventions for their ratification or refusal.

And in February 1933, the new, Democratic-dominated Congress did just that. It adopted a resolution calling for a repeal of the 18th Amendment—the 21st Amendment to the U.S. Constitution. By December 5, 1933, the amendment had received the requisite number of states (then 36) for ratification and so became part of the Constitution. Prohibition had been repealed.

Men in Bangor, Maine, enjoying beer on the first July 4 following the repeal of Prohibition

states and hired out-of-work librarians to staff government-run libraries. Artists were employed to create public art. Similar to the WPA was the CWA, Civil Works Administration, which had been set up under the Federal Emergency Relief Act. By 1934, the CWA had employed over 4 million workers in building roads, schoolhouses, parks, airports, as well as in other projects.

The National Industrial Recovery Act established as well the National Recovery Administration (NRA). The purpose of the NRA was to apply to industry codes that governed relations between labor and management. These codes set maximum hours of work and, in some cases, maximum prices for goods. The codes determined minimum wages and forbade child labor. Industries that volunteered could negotiate their own codes with representatives of government and labor, while those that refused were governed by blanket codes imposed by the government. NRA volunteers were allowed to post a blue eagle in their windows and on their products as a sign of their good faith; if they violated the codes they could lose this distinctive symbol.

Though the NRA only governed businesses engaged in interstate commerce, it went far beyond the commerce clause in the Constitution that allowed the federal government to regulate commerce between states. Relations between labor and management had, before, been a state concern. By forbidding child labor, the federal government was entering into the realm of the family by making decisions regarding child welfare. Such decisions had, traditionally, been reserved to parents. On the other hand, among the poor, parental freedom to direct family life had already been curtailed by the wage system that had prevailed in the United States. The poverty suffered by industrial and rural workers alike often compelled poorer parents to send their children into the workplace.

Among the chief concerns of the architects of the New Deal (many of whom were women, including the secretary of labor, Frances Perkins, and the first lady, Eleanor Roosevelt) was to provide heads of families with a living wage so that, not only children, but even mothers of families need not leave the home in search of gainful employment. Roosevelt himself said the NRA codes would "guarantee living wages." "By living wages, I mean," said Roosevelt, "more than a bare subsistence living—I mean the wages of decent living." That these were living wages for head of families (because the family breadwinner was presumed to be a man) is shown by the fact that New Deal programs tended to discourage female employment and assured men a higher wage structure than women.

The 100 days also produced more permanent legislation. On May 18, Congress passed an act establishing the Tennessee Valley Authority (TVA). The TVA governed the 652-mile valley of the Tennessee River, that ran through Tennessee, Alabama, Mississippi, and Kentucky. The TVA, an independent public

IF WE WOULD GUIDE BY THE LIGHT OF REASON WE MUST LET OUR MINDS BE BOLD

A mural created by an artist working for the WPA

A woman placing the NRA blue eagle emblem in a restaurant window, 1934

body, built dams for flood control and for production of electricity; it erected power plants and nitrate plants for fertilizer. A total of six dams were built by the TVA between 1933 and 1936. The damns and power plants brought electrical power to most of Tennessee and to portions of Georgia, Alabama, Mississippi, and Kentucky.

One of the most significant acts of the hundred days was Roosevelt's decision, on April 19, to abandon the gold standard. (Congressional ratification followed on June 5.) This, and the subsequent Thomas amendment to the Agricultural Adjustment Act, would allow the president to determine at will the value of the dollar up to fifty percent of the current value it had in 1933. Abandoning the gold standard meant the government would no longer redeem greenbacks with their equivalent value in gold. This broke an implicit understanding with the people that paper money could be redeemed with gold. Later, Roosevelt would set the value of the dollar at roughly 60 cents gold, thus devaluing the savings of Americans by nearly half. Though men like Al Smith criticized going off the gold standard (Smith said he was "for gold dollars as against baloney dollars"), Wall Street praised it because, they said, it would make American industries more competitive in the world market.

Another important act contained a provision that even Roosevelt thought too radical, though he signed it anyway. This was the Glass-Steagall Banking Act of June 16. Besides ruling that commercial banks (which took in deposits from savers and made loans) might no longer use investors' funds to speculate on the stock market, Glass-Steagall established the Federal Deposit Insurance Corporation (FDIC) which guaranteed all bank deposits up to $5,000. Only the most elastic constructionist could find justification for this act in the Constitution.

AAA, WPA, CCC, FDIC, NRA, CWA—this alphabet soup of laws represented a prodigious effort on the part of Roosevelt, his "brain trust," and Congress. By June 16, when a tired Congress went into recess, it left not only a ton of legislation as the token of all its sweat, but a new nation. The federal government had embarked on a new course; it would become what Alexander Hamilton, over 150 years earlier, had hoped for when he proposed the abolition of the states. The federal government, henceforth, would be sole sovereign in the nation.

More New Deals

Eleanor Roosevelt in 1932

The New Deal did not end with the adjournment of Congress on June 16, 1933. In fireside chats, in addresses to Congress, Roosevelt continued to promote more programs that he said would restore prosperity "by reestablishing the purchasing power of half the people," would bring about a better balance between agriculture, manufacturing and commerce, and would eliminate abuses and excesses in the economy.

The first lady, Eleanor Roosevelt, ardently supported her husband's crusade. Breaking tradition, Eleanor (as everyone began to call her) addressed audiences across the country, and, though herself a patrician, met and conversed easily with common folk. Other first ladies had taken active roles in their husbands' presidency—Wilson's wife ran the country during her husband's sickness; still, none of these were ever *public* in their involvement. Eleanor Roosevelt, in contrast, not only spoke publicly in person and over the radio, but gave press conferences.

A program that Eleanor particularly favored was the Subsistence Homestead Program. Inspired by a "back-to-the-land" movement in the 1920s, the program sought to draw Americans away from the city and back to the country. The NIRA provided $25 million to establish subsistence farming homesteads. Under the program, the government built villages with houses on three to ten acre lots that would be rented to families, who could buy them in time if they wanted to. The homestead would have gardens, chicken coops, and maybe pigs or cows for the use of the family alone, not for commercial sale. The homestead villages, it was hoped, would renew family and community life by restoring (said a project staff member, Clarence Pickett), the "yearnings for a home, for a good life for children, [and] for community."

Roosevelt intended his New Deal to benefit not only whites. Like his cousin, Theodore, F.D.R. awarded blacks with public office posts and abolished segregation in federal offices. While trying to push integration in the military, Roosevelt made equal opportunity for employment part and parcel of New Deal industry measures. Such policies, together with Eleanor's very apparent concern for the plight of blacks, affected the balance of political power. Blacks began moving from the Republican party into the Democratic party in ever increasing numbers.

The New Deal even included Indians in its reach. Native Americans had not fared well since the Dawes Act in the 1880s tried to turn them into individual proprietors by breaking up tribal lands. A study conducted under Calvin Coolidge culminated in the Meriam Report in 1928 that detailed the failure of the Dawes Act to integrate Indians into white American society. "An overwhelming majority of the Indians are poor, even extremely poor," said the report, "and they are not adjusted to the . . . system of the dominant white civilization." The report recommended that Indian children be educated in schools in their own communities, rather than sent away from the parents, as had been the practice. By the end of Hoover's administration, such boarding schools had been abolished.

Under Roosevelt, the Commission of Indian Affairs adopted policies that encouraged the strengthening of tribal government and the preservation of native culture. The Indian Reorganization Act, passed June 18, 1934, repealed the Dawes Act and allowed reservations to purchase more land if they needed to.

The strengthening of the Democratic majority in Congress in the election of 1934 encouraged Roosevelt to continue with his policies. In January 1935, the new Congress gave Roosevelt $4.88 billion to spend pretty much as he saw fit. In June 1934, Congress had approved the formation of the Securities and Exchange Commission, which established federal oversight of the stock market. This commission was placed under Joseph P. Kennedy, who had made his fortune in the unregulated market. On August 14, 1935, Congress passed perhaps the most significant and far-reaching of New Deal measures—the Social Security Act. The act established a payroll tax of one percent (since risen to 12.4 percent)—that is, the self-employed would pay the government one percent. The monies collected went as a bonus to boost state old-age pensions and as grants to states for children's health and welfare, to the blind, and to expand the state public health systems.

The Social Security Act was an important turning point in American history. For one, it established the federal government—not local communities, not the states—as the primary guardian of public welfare. Secondly, it undermined the importance of the family by removing one of its important functions. The Committee on Economic Security's 1935 report to

MORE SECURITY FOR THE AMERICAN FAMILY

THE SOCIAL SECURITY ACT AS AMENDED OFFERS GREATER OLD-AGE INSURANCE PROTECTION TO PEOPLE NOW NEARING RETIREMENT AGE.

FOR INFORMATION WRITE OR CALL AT THE NEAREST FIELD OFFICE OF THE **SOCIAL SECURITY BOARD**

Poster from the 1930s detailing the benefits of Social Security the president, detailing the economic plight of many of the aged, admitted that "children, friends, and relatives have borne and still carry the major cost of supporting the aged. Several of the State surveys have disclosed that from 30 percent to 50 percent of the people over 65 years of age were being supported in this way." However, because, "during the present depression, this burden has become unbearable for many of the children, with the result that the number of old people dependent upon public or private charity has greatly increased," the federal government, said the report, must provide economic security to the old.

New Deal legislation racked up huge amounts of debt. By June of 1934, expenditures on emergency relief had risen above $5 billion; by the autumn of 1935, the public debt of the United States government exceeded $30 billion, far surpassing the $4 billion public debt Wilson had racked up during the World War I. All this might have been tolerable if the New Deal had shown that it was helping matters; but, despite Roosevelt's repeated emphasis on a slow, but steady business recovery, the number of unemployed was still extremely high. In 1936, three years after the inception of the New Deal, unemployment was still between 10 and 12 million—down from 15 million in 1933.

This seeming failure of his policies emboldened Roosevelt's political opponents. They thought they might be able to beat the Democrats in the presidential election of 1936. And for a time, it seemed that they were right.

The Opposition

It is somewhat inaccurate to class the Supreme Court amongst Roosevelt's opposition in his first term, though it did figure as such. Of the nine justices, four were certainly "liberals," four were "conservative." The liberals followed the judicial philosophy laid down by the late associate Supreme Court justice, Oliver Wendell Holmes, Jr. Holmes, whom Theodore Roosevelt had appointed to the court in 1901, held that the interpretation of the Constitution should be flexible enough to allow government to respond to current needs and circumstances. Law, he said, "corresponds at any given time with what is understood to be convenient. That involves continual change, and there can be no eternal order." While strict constructionists among the founding fathers insisted that only a legislative amendment process could alter the Constitution, liberals like Holmes saw the courts as another avenue of Constitutional change.

The four "conservative" justices of the Supreme Court were essentially proponents of *laissez-faire*—the federal government, they believed, had no place in regulating business activities. The swing vote was Chief Justice Charles Evans Hughes. Because Hughes sided at times with the conservatives and at times with the liberals, Supreme Court decisions on the constitutionality of New Deal legislation were confusing and inconsistent.

Legal challenges to New Deal policies were not long in coming. In the May 1935 case, *Schechter Poultry v. the United States*, the A.L.A. Schechter Poultry Company contended that poultry codes imposed by the NRA were in violation of the 10th Amendment of the Constitution. Chief Justice Hughes wrote the unanimous opinion of the justices that the National Industrial Recovery Act was unconstitutional because it went beyond the powers vested in the federal government by the commerce clause of the Constitution. If the Recovery Act were allowed to stand, wrote the chief justice, then "federal authority would embrace practically all the activities of the people and the authority of the state over its domestic concerns would exist only by sufferance." On January 6, 1936, Chief Justice Hughes joined the conservative justices in a six to three decision declaring the Agricultural Adjustment Act (AAA) unconstitutional. It invaded, said the majority, the reserved rights of states.

Charles Evans Hughes, by Thomas C. Corner

But in other cases, Chief Justice Hughes sided with the liberal justices. Perhaps the most important of these cases was *Steward Machine Co. v. Davis*, challenging the Social Security Act as a violation of the 10th Amendment. Justice Benjamin Nathan Cardozo, writing for the five to four majority, said that the Social Security Act did not violate state sovereignty since states did not have to comply with the act. Cardozo then noted that the Depression had necessitated the Social Security Act. The unemployment "problem had become national in area and dimensions," wrote Cardozo:

> There was need of help from the nation if the people were not to starve. It is too late today for the argument to be heard with tolerance that, in a crisis so extreme, the use of the moneys of the nation to relieve the unemployed and their dependents is a use for any purpose narrower than the promotion of the general welfare . . . The *parens patriae* has many reasons—fiscal and economic as well as social and moral—for planning to mitigate disasters that bring these burdens in their train."

Justice Cardozo's argument cited the preamble to the Constitution— "We the people of the United States of America in order . . . to promote the general welfare"—as granting the federal government a specific power, rather than as merely declaring the purpose for which the Constitution was written. A more conservative justice might argue that the purpose enunciated in the Constitution is distinct from the powers the Constitution grants the federal government; the powers delineate how the federal government will contribute to the general purpose. That the federal government is not alone responsible for the general welfare is implied by the Tenth Amendment, which states, "The powers not delegated to the United States by the Constitution, nor prohibited by it to the States, are reserved to the States respectively, or to the people." To a conservative, the federal government may promote the general welfare only in constitutionally specified ways. The problem was, then as ever, to define the extent of the federal government's powers according to the Constitution.

Benjamin Cardozo

In *Stewart Machine Co. v. Davis*, Cardozo cited the principle of *parens patriae* (the "parenthood of the state") to justify the new extension of federal power. *Parens patriae* is a principle derived from common law; it allows the public authority to provide for orphaned minor children. In 1839, the Pennsylvania Supreme Court stretched the meaning of *parens patriae* to include state power over children raised by what were deemed unfit parents. "May not the natural parents, when unequal to the task of education or unworthy of it be supplanted by the *parens patriae*, or common guardianship of the community?" the court asked. The principle of *parens patriae* was later used to justify compulsory education laws. Now, the Supreme Court of the United States was applying the principle to the federal government as if it were the common guardian of all citizens.

In 1936, Roosevelt still had a year to wait before receiving Cardozo's favorable ruling. In the meantime, he was growing more and more impatient with those "nine old men," as he derisively called the justices. Unfortunately for the president, none of the justices showed any signs of leaving the bench. Without retirements, Roosevelt was unable to appoint any new justices favorable to his views. More radical expedients could be tried, but in an election year it was not safe to do anything too rash. He would have to wait to see if, and by how much, he won the next presidential election, before taking any action.

Opponents to Left and Right

Aside from business leaders and the wealthy, the president's opposition was composed of sundry groups who widely disagreed among themselves. Some were "conservative" and *laissez faire*; some were just more conservative than Roosevelt, though progressive. Some groups were more liberal, while others were just downright radical. If anything united these disparate groups, it was this—opposition to Franklin Delano Roosevelt.

Opposition to Roosevelt came even from within his own party, the Democrats. Though he originally backed Roosevelt for the governorship of New York and for the presidential nomination, Al Smith now opposed what he called Roosevelt's demagoguery. Smith and others, including the wealthy industrial Du Pont family, formed the American Liberty League in 1934 to counteract what they saw as the New Deal's erosion of personal and property rights. The league disseminated its views through pamphlets and radio broadcasts.

One of the most powerful voices against Roosevelt was a Catholic priest, the pastor of the Shrine of the Little Flower in Detroit, Father Charles Coughlin. Coughlin, a popular homilist, began broadcasting over the radio in the late 1920s. After a time he turned from religious themes to political and social themes. He organized the Radio League of the Little Flower (membership one dollar) to finance wider radio exposure for his views. In 1929, he bought airtime on the CBS radio network and thus could spread his message of anti-communism and opposition to international banking nationwide.

Father Charles Coughlin in 1933

Blaming the Depression on President Hoover's policies, Coughlin had supported the candidacy of Roosevelt. Coughlin had believed Roosevelt shared his conviction that greed and profit-mongering lay at the root of the Depression; that the country must adopt principles of "social justice," of a Christian economy, to restore prosperity. But it was not long before the priest turned on the president. "If there is plenty for all in this country," said Coughlin in 1934, "plenty of fields of wheat and of cotton, plenty of factories, mechanics and scientists—the only reason why this plenitude of God's blessing is not shared by all is because our Government has not, as yet, faced the problem of distribution. In other words, it may boast that it has driven the money changers from the temple but it permits industry to cling tenaciously to the cast-off philosophy of the money changers. Our Government still upholds one of the worst evils of decadent capitalism, namely, that production must be only at a profit for the owners, for the capitalist, and not for the laborer. This philosophy of finance, or of distribution of profits, based on the theory of *'pay-while-you-work'* for the laborer can only be identified with destruction of the entire system of capitalism."

Father Coughlin thought that in order to assure a living wage to the worker, the government needed to restrain the greed of money-lenders and revalue the dollar so that workers could have a living annual salary, even when not working. When it became clear that Roosevelt would not follow his policies, Coughlin, in 1934, organized the National Union for Social Justice to promote his ideas. Besides a living wage, the National Union for Social Justice called for the nationalization of resources "too important to be held in the control of private individuals"; for the private ownership of other property while admitting its control "for the public good"; for the abolition of the Federal Reserve system and its replacement with a government-controlled national bank, among other issues. Finally, declared Coughlin, "I believe in preferring the sanctity of human rights to the sanctity of property rights; for the chief concern of government shall be for the poor because, as it is witnessed, the rich have ample means of their own to care for themselves."

Father Coughlin's final break with Roosevelt came in 1935 when the president agreed to join the World Court, which the "Radio Priest" thought was controlled by international bankers. The National Union for Social Justice now began to converge with another grassroots movement initiated by the bombastic senator from Louisiana, Huey Pierce Long.

Born poor in the piney woods of northern Louisiana, Huey Long worked his way up into prominence. By the age of 22 he had passed the Louisiana bar after attending only two law classes and spending one year reading law books. Three years later, in 1928, he campaigned for governor of Louisiana and won by appealing to the poor and downcast (his campaign motto was "Every Man a King.") As governor, Long secured his dominance of Louisiana through bribery, violence, and blackmail, but also by projects he instituted for the poor. Under Long, schools were built, the state university was enlarged, and new hard-top roads were laid, connecting rural areas with the cities. Long also abolished the poll-tax which had kept blacks from voting. Through these means, some fair, some foul, Long became virtual dictator of Louisiana.

In 1930, Louisianans elected Long to the United States Senate; and with a puppet governor in place at Baton Rouge, Long went to Washington. In the Senate he dubbed himself the "Kingfish" because, he said, "I'm a small fish here in Washington. But I'm the Kingfish to the folks down in Louisiana." Kingfish offended Senators, even those from his own Democratic party. He supported Roosevelt's bid for the presidency in 1932 but later turned against him. In the Senate, Long came up with his "Share-Our-Wealth" program. The government, he said, should tax fortunes and inheritances in order to assure to every American family a $5,000 house and an annual income of $2,000 a year. His fellow senators, of course, gave him no heed, but that didn't bother the Kingfish. He used his position as a pulpit to trumpet his program to the American people.

Huey Long

In the first years of the Depression, the membership of the American Communist Party doubled, reaching perhaps as high 90,000 to 100,000 members by 1939. The leader of the party, Earl Browder, took his orders from Moscow and, in accord with the current policy of the Soviet premier, Josif Stalin, told party members to infiltrate various political movements and political parties. Some members obtained federal posts and passed on any government information they could to Moscow. The Communist *Daily Worker* in New York attacked Roosevelt as a tool of the capitalist powers.

Dust Bowl

Among the states hardest hit by the Great Depression was California. California's industries—the growing of fruit (thought more of a luxury than a staple by most Americans), motion pictures, and vacation spots—were of the sort to suffer most hurt during an economic downturn. Moreover, with its regions of mellifluous climate, California attracted the out-of-work from across the nation; they thought it would easier to bear poverty in a pleasant clime than in the regions where harsh winters prevailed. They also increased the number of poor unemployed in the state.

The poverty of the Depression received little effective response from California's state government. The governor, James "Sunny Jim" Rolph ignored

A young woman in a California migrant farm worker camp, by Dorothea Lange, 1936

New Deal solutions to the crisis and continued the policies of the Hoover administration. When Rolph died after a heart attack on June 2, 1934, the lieutenant governor, Frank Merriam, assumed the governorship and perpetuated Rolph's policies.

For the November 1934 election, the Democratic Party nominated a surprising gubernatorial candidate—the author and former Socialist Party member, Upton Sinclair. In a self-authored pamphlet, *I, Governor of California, and How I Ended Poverty: A True Story of the Future*, Sinclair promoted a plan that, he said, would end poverty in California. EPIC (End Poverty In California) he called the plan that proposed a series of state land colonies or communes where the unemployed could be put to work on farming projects

(continued)

under the direction of agricultural experts. The state, too, could set idle factories running, said Sinclair, and employ even more workers. Sinclair called for the abolition of the sales tax and the removal of all property taxes on houses and ranches valued at $3,000 or under, while he favored a steeply graduated income tax (targeted at wealthier citizens) and increased inheritance, public utility, and corporation taxes. Though his policies were considered radical by New Deal Democratic standards (and opposed by the Republican candidate, Governor Merriam, and the third-party candidate, Raymond Haight of the Commonwealth-Progressive Party), it appeared for a time that Sinclair might pull off an electoral win in the Golden State. He received the endorsement of such famous American writers and intellectuals as Theodore Dreiser, Archibald MacLeish, and Clarence Darrow. The radio priest, Father Coughlin, came out in support of Sinclair's program.

But Sinclair faced an unlikely opponent—the weather. Not the weather in California, but a drought in the Great Plains. With profits to be made in farming following the Great War, the grasslands of the Plains (in the region west of the 100th meridian) had been turned from cattle raising to wheat growing. These regions, however, enjoyed little rainfall (about 20 inches a year) and relied on the native grasses growing there to anchor the soil against erosion. Concerned more for profits than for proper cultivation, and encouraged by extraordinary rainfalls in the 1920s, farmers engaged in poor soil management and overcultivation. But already in the 1920s, overcultivation had so eroded soils in 100 counties in Colorado, Kansas, New Mexico, Texas, and Oklahoma, that they were declared "dust bowls"—unfit for further cultivation.

But the worst was yet to come—and it came on November 11, 1933. Strong wind storms hit drought stricken fields in South Dakota, driving before them the exposed soil. By noon, the sky was darker than night, and in a matter of hours fields were turned to drifting sand while soil dunes covered roads, trees, buildings, and farming machines. From South Dakota, the winds continued into the south, toward Texas, spreading similar destruction. By 1934, storms had spread the "Dust Bowl," as it was called, into the Texas Panhandle and Oklahoma and included 756 counties in 19 states. The devastation was apocalyptic. According to statistics from the National Resources Board, by 1934, 35 million acres of arable land had been completely obliterated, 125 million acres were nearly gone, and 100 million more acres faced similar destruction.

Farmers in the Dust Bowl regions had already been suffering from falling prices, foreclosures, and unemployment. Larger farms, run with farm machinery, had displaced thousands of workers. Now, drought and destructive winds forced a vast migration of the poverty-stricken from the region stretching from the Dakotas to Texas—and it was the lure of California's rich agricultural lands that drew them. Families, utterly wretched, piled all their earthly belongings in ramshackle

Two scenes from the Dust Bowl

(continued)

cars and headed west. Arriving in California, these migrants (derisively called "Okies" because some many came from Oklahoma) glutted the migrant farm labor market. Paid low wages and suffering violence from organized police resistance in support of California growers, the migrants discovered that they had not left poverty, suffering, and injustice behind them.

Californians, already suffering from the Depression, regarded the Okies as a rapacious and potentially revolutionary horde. During the state election of 1934, Upton Sinclair's political opponents capitalized on this fear. Even chicanery was brought into play to promote Governor Merriam and to paint Sinclair as the harbinger of a socialist revolution, such as had transformed Russia in 1917. Metro-Goldwyn-Mayer film studios in Hollywood stepped into the political fray, requiring its employees to support the anti-Sinclair campaign with money and to act in fake newsreels. One such newsreel depicted criminals and prostitutes pouring from freight trains (they were really extras from Hollywood movie sets) and described them as the dreaded Okie invaders. Some rowdy "migrants," wearing fake beards and speaking with "Russian" accents, declared that they warmly supported Sinclair's policies. "Vell, his system vorked vell in Russia, vy can't it vork here?" they declaimed.

Fear that Sinclair's EPIC plan was more radical than it appeared was one element, it seems, that won the election for Governor Merriam, who beat the author-candidate by a margin of 250,000 votes. Merriam returned to Sacramento, while Sinclair again took up his pen. His next offering to the reading public of America was the book, *I, Candidate for Governor: And How I Got Licked.*

A farmer from Missouri seeking work as a migratory laborer in California, by Dorothea Lange, 1936

Landslide

The Republicans thought they could take the presidency from Roosevelt in 1936—his New Deal, they declared, had hardly decreased unemployment, and was, further, destroying "free-enterprise, private competition, and equality of opportunity." They ran Governor Alfred M. Landon of Kansas, an old Bull-Moose associate of Theodore Roosevelt. The Progressive Landon's policies would not be far removed from Roosevelt's.

Senator Huey Long had said in 1935 that he would run for president in '36. When the Senate adjourned in August 1935, the Kingfish returned to Louisiana. On September 8, a doctor whose family Long had ruined, killed him in front of the state capitol. With Long dead, the Rev. Gerald L.K. Smith took over leadership of the Share-Our-Wealth campaign. Smith joined forces with Father Coughlin's National Union for Social Justice in running William Lemke for president on the Union Party ticket. At the Union Party's nominating convention, Coughlin called Roosevelt "the great betrayer and liar . . . who promised to drive the money changers from the temple." Roosevelt, said Coughlin, "had succeeded in driving the farmers from their homesteads and the citizens from their homes in the cities . . . I ask you to purge the man who claims to be a Democrat, from the Democratic Party, and I mean Franklin Double-Crossing Roosevelt."

Polls taken before the election seemed to predict a Landon victory. How disappointed the Republicans were, then, when on election day Roosevelt not only beat Landon, but soundly whipped him. Roosevelt, with 60.7 percent of the popular vote, took every state in the union, except Maine and Vermont, which went for Landon. Lemke received about 900,000 votes.

Roosevelt had received a greater plurality in '36 than he had in '32. The majority of Americans had, it seemed, approved his policies, and he could continue on with his reforms.

Even More Is Needed

In his address to Congress in January 1937, Roosevelt assured the representatives that it had been the "definite intent and expectation" of those who drew up the Constitution "that a liberal interpretation in the years to come would give the Congress the same relative powers over new national problems as they themselves gave Congress over the national problems of their day." The "vital need" of the day, said Roosevelt "is not an alteration of our fundamental law but an increasingly enlightened view with reference to it. Difficulties have grown out of its interpretation; but rightly considered, it can be used as an instrument of progress and not as a device for the prevention of action."

Roosevelt delivered this address on January 6, 1937. In accordance with the recently ratified the 20th Amendment to the Constitution, Congress opened its first session on that day while, in just two weeks, on January 20, Roosevelt would begin his second term as president. He wanted his second administration to tackle more problems besetting the nation—the regulation of hours and wages; relief to help farm tenants buy their own land; the elimination of slums and bettering of housing for the poor, among other items. Unless further action was taken, he warned, democracy itself might be threatened. The people might conclude that democracy was too inflexible to handle crises of the complex modern world and so would opt for more totalitarian forms of government. "The process of our democracy must not be imperiled by the denial of essential powers of free government," he warned Congress.

Roosevelt also had a veiled warning for the Supreme Court: "The judicial branch also is asked by the people to do its part in making democracy successful. We do not ask the courts to call nonexistent powers into being, but we have a right to expect that conceded powers or those legitimately implied shall be made effective instruments for the common good."

Roosevelt did not wait to see if the court would heed the voice of democracy, for in February he made a surprising request of Congress. Roosevelt asked Congress to authorize him to appoint one new justice to the Supreme Court for every Supreme Court justice over 70 who would not retire. Since six justices were over 70, Roosevelt wanted to increase the size of the Supreme Court to 15. His intent was clear. Since the Supreme Court had declared so many New Deal acts unconstitutional, Roosevelt would pack the court with six new justices who were amenable to his policies. Perhaps too overconfident from the election, Roosevelt here went too far. The public was angry with the justices, but they opposed presidential tampering with the august institution of the court. Bolstered by strong public opposition, Congress refused the president's request.

Roosevelt, however, ultimately triumphed. After his attempt to pack the court, the Supreme Court justices began rubber-stamping all New Deal legislation brought before them. Moreover, over the next four years, on account of justices dying or resigning, Roosevelt could appoint men to the court who shared

A political cartoon depicting Roosevelt as hungry for power, by Joseph L. Parrish, *Chicago Tribune*

his progressive and "broad construction" reading of the Constitution. By 1941, Roosevelt had created a new, progressive court.

The president could say, with some satisfaction that during 1937 the economy seemed to be gaining steam. Production had reached its highest mark since the crash in 1929, and the national income stood at $70 billion—$50 billion higher than it had been in 1932. True, conditions were still bad, as the president had admitted in his inaugural address. "In this nation," he had said, "I see tens of millions of its citizens—a substantial part of its whole population—who at this very moment are denied the greater part of what the very lowest standards of today call the necessities of life." Still, the growing prosperity witnessed to the possibilities that lay ahead if "effective government," heeding the voice of the people, guided the destinies of the nation. "I see a United States," Roosevelt had said, "which can demonstrate that, under democratic methods of government, national wealth can be translated into a spreading volume of human comforts hitherto unknown, and the lowest standard of living can be raised far above the level of mere subsistence."

But then in the fall, recession hit. Production fell, as did the price of stocks. Unemployment rose again to the 10 million mark and the rolls of relief agencies swelled. On November 15, Roosevelt called a special session of Congress. He urged the passage of measures, such as the extension of Social Security to more groups; but the mostly Democratic Congress was not responsive. Roosevelt could not command the energies of Congress as he did in the first 100 days of his presidency.

Congress did pass one important measure in June 1938. This Fair Labor Standards Act established a 44-hour work week, which was gradually reduced to 40 hours, as well as a federal minimum wage of 25–40 cents per hour. Roosevelt called this act "the most far-reaching, far-sighted program for the benefit of workers ever adopted in this or any other country." In a case challenging the constitutionality of the new act, the Supreme Court, now thoroughly docile, wrote it off as constitutional.

Catholics and the New Deal

Father Coughlin's was not the only Catholic voice addressing the economic and social ills of the 1930s, though it was perhaps the loudest. Though he said he drew his ideas from papal teaching, Coughlin made it clear that he did not speak as a priest or representative of the Church when he addressed political and economic issues, but as a citizen of the United States. His principles, he said, were obvious to all Americans, regardless of whether they were Catholic, Protestant, or Jewish.

Not all Catholics agreed with Coughlin's analysis of, or solutions to, the social questions. One prominent authority on Catholic social teaching, Father John Augustine Ryan of the Catholic University of America in Washington, D.C., disagreed vehemently with Father Coughlin. Since the publication of his book, *A Living Wage*, in 1906, Father Ryan had written, taught, and spoken on social justice themes in light of Catholic doctrine. With Father Raymond A. McGowan, Ryan headed the Social Action Department of the National Catholic Welfare Conference, a body formed by the bishops in the 1920s to coordinate national Catholic life. The Social Action Department had distributed thousands of pamphlets detailing social programs based on papal encyclicals. Ryan was disturbed that so many Americans, both Catholic and Protestant, considered Father Coughlin's ideas to be authoritative Catholic teaching. On October 8, 1936, Ryan criticized Coughlin over the radio. In a letter to the American Catholic journal *Commonweal* the same month, Ryan explained that the purpose of his broadcast was "to shout that [Father Coughlin's] 'condemnation of the New Deal as communistic was false and absurd,' but more earnestly than that I desired to offset, insofar as I could, the evil effect of Father Coughlin's speeches upon Catholic interests and upon the peace of mind . . . of Catholics." Ryan said Father Coughlin's "explanation of our economic maladies is at least 50 per cent wrong and his monetary theories and proposals at least 90 per cent wrong, even though the overwhelming majority of the economists would put down these estimates as understatements."

Because of Leo XIII's *Rerum Novarum* and the work of Father Ryan and other American Catholics in explaining it, Catholics were able to make their first clear contribution to the public life of the United States. The social teaching was not something dreamed up by Rome to answer the crisis of the Depression, but rooted in Christian tradition; thus, as summarized in such a profound way by Pope Leo 30 years before the Great Depression, it carried the conviction of an ancient truth. For the first time in the history of Anglo-America, the Catholic voice was heard with some respect.

Unlike the nostrums of the progressives, socialists, and communists, the Catholic social teaching rooted itself in a spiritual order while not losing itself in mere individual piety. In a 1930 letter addressing the problem of unemployment, the American bishops praised those engaged in relieving the immediate needs of the poor but declared that more than the corporal acts of mercy were needed to meet the crisis. "The failure" leading to the current crisis, wrote the bishops, "is not due to lack of intelligence nor any more to ignorance. It is due to lack of good will. It is due to neglect of Christ." The solution lay, said the bishops, in almsgiving but also in trying "to remold the institutions that surround work, ownership and trade to the image of the Savior of the world." One such "institution" the bishops cited was the wage system. It is not enough, said the bishops, merely to assure workers a minimum wage; morality and economic security demanded a living wage—a wage sufficient enough to allow a laborer becomingly to support a family.

Pope Pius XI

Catholic social teaching received a further boost in 1931 when Pope Pius XI (who had succeeded Benedict XV in 1922) published an encyclical commemorating the 40th anniversary of *Rerum Novaurm*. In *Quadragesimo Anno*, Pope Pius reiterated the doctrines of Pope Leo's encyclical and sought to apply them to the changed world conditions. Pius reaffirmed that men have a right to private property but emphasized that the possession of property carried with it certain social obligations. In order that property might meet those social obligations, the state had a role in regulating its use. "Provided that the natural and divine law be observed," wrote Pius, "the public authority, in view of the common good, may specify more accurately what is licit and what is illicit for property owners in the use of their possessions."

Though in *Quadragesimo Anno*, Pope Pius asserted that "no one can be at the same time a good Catholic and a true socialist," he made it clear he would have no truck with *laissez-faire* capitalism. He wrote:

> Just as the unity of human society cannot be founded on an opposition of classes, so also the right ordering of economic life cannot be left to a free competition of forces. For from this source, as from a poisoned spring, have originated and spread all the errors of individualist economic teaching. Destroying through forgetfulness or ignorance the social and moral character of economic life, it held that economic life must be considered and treated as altogether free from and independent of public authority, because in the market, i.e., in the free struggle of competitors, it would have a principle of self direction which governs it much more perfectly than would the intervention of any created intellect. But free competition, while justified and certainly useful provided it is kept within certain limits, clearly cannot direct economic life—a truth which the outcome of the application in practice of the tenets of this evil individualistic spirit has more than sufficiently demonstrated. Therefore, it is most necessary that economic life be again subjected to and governed by a true and effective directing principle.

While reasserting the right of workers to organize unions, Pius emphasized that workers must respect the rights of owners. Thus, in the struggle for a living wage, workers must consider how much an employer can actually pay. Like Leo XIII, however, Pius XI saw the living or just wage as a means for workers to acquire "by skill and thrift" a "certain moderate ownership." But Pius went further than Leo and called for industries to provide workers a participation in the ownership, management, and profits of business. "In the present state of human society," wrote the pope, "We deem it advisable that the wage-contract should, when possible, be modified somewhat by a contract of partnership . . . In this way wage-earners are made sharers in some sort in the ownership, or the management, or the profits."

Like the American bishops, Pope Pius called for a "reform of the social order"—"principally the state." His alternative vision was of a society made up not mostly of large businesses (though these were not excluded), but more characteristically of small farmers, craftsmen, shopkeepers, and merchants. Each group would be organized in a guild or corporation that negotiated disputes between employers and employed (the state only stepping in when the corporation hit an impasse) and looked out for members and their families, made sure they received a just wage or charged a just price for their goods, and protected their interests. Such corporations would not be arms of the government; and though they would receive recognition from the government, they would serve as effective intermediary bodies between the government and the people.

Because of "individualism," said Pius, institutions and associations (similar to his proposed corporations) that once stood between the state and the individual had been damaged and destroyed, "leaving thus virtually only individuals and the state." The government, said the pope, must respect such bodies; for, says *Quadragesimo Anno*, "just as it is wrong to withdraw from the individual and commit to the community at large what private enterprise and industry can accomplish, so, too, it is an injustice, a grave evil and a disturbance of right order for a larger and higher organization to arrogate to itself functions which can be performed efficiently by smaller and lower bodies." Leaders of nations must heed this notion of social order, called the principle of *subsidiarity*; they must "be convinced," said the pope, "that the more faithfully this principle be followed, and a graded hierarchical order exist between the various subsidiary organizations, the more excellent will be both the authority and the efficiency of the social organization as a whole and the happier and more prosperous the condition of the state."

Some Catholics thought that New Deal policies accorded well with the means and aims of *Rerum Novarum* and *Quadragesimo Anno*. Father Coughlin, at first, seemed to think so. Other Catholic social justice leaders, such as Father Ryan, did not categorically condemn Roosevelt's program but praised some or much of it. But most rank and file Catholics probably didn't even think about how or whether the New Deal or even capitalism accorded with the social teachings of the Church. They were of peasant stock or of the working class and not usually well-educated. The Democratic Party had for many years been their party, and Roosevelt had effectively worked them into his coalition. Catholics were a minority in the United States, many of them were poor, and they were trying to find their place in the prevailing culture and achieve a bit of the American dream for themselves. Most Catholics were, perhaps, unsuited to present a social vision that challenged the prevailing ideas of most of their neighbors.

Catholic Anarchists

It is ironic that a communist and free-love radical was among those who understood the sense of the Catholic bishops' 1919 message that "charity is also social virtue." Dorothy Day, the daughter of a journalist father in Chicago, had from her teen years felt a deep concern for the lot of the poor. She had read such books as Victor Hugo's *Les Miserables* and Charles Dickens' *Bleak House* and *Little Dorritt*, which had inspired her with a keen sense of the injustice of the world. But it was Upton Sinclair's *The Jungle,* which detailed the filth and degradation of the meat-packing industry in her own Chicago, that stirred her to her depths.

Walking the streets in working class neighborhoods, she learned to see beauty in the lives of the poor. "From that time on," she later wrote, "my life was to be linked to theirs, their interests would be mine: I had received a call, a vocation, a direction in life."

At the University of Illinois in Urbana, Dorothy became a political radical. She began to believe that charity towards the poor is not enough. She questioned the good religion did for the poor and oppressed. "Where," she asked, "were the saints to try to change the social order, not just to minister to slaves but to do away with slavery?" In 1915, at the age of 18, she moved to New York City, where she began working as a journalist for a socialist paper, *The Call.*

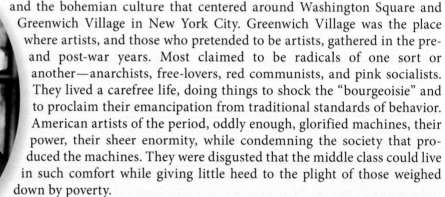

Dorothy Day became involved with groups of radical artists and writers and the bohemian culture that centered around Washington Square and Greenwich Village in New York City. Greenwich Village was the place where artists, and those who pretended to be artists, gathered in the pre- and post-war years. Most claimed to be radicals of one sort or another—anarchists, free-lovers, red communists, and pink socialists. They lived a carefree life, doing things to shock the "bourgeoisie" and to proclaim their emancipation from traditional standards of behavior. American artists of the period, oddly enough, glorified machines, their power, their sheer enormity, while condemning the society that produced the machines. They were disgusted that the middle class could live in such comfort while giving little heed to the plight of those weighed down by poverty.

Dorothy Day at least shared her friends' disdain for the smug attitudes of the American middle class. Casting aside middle class morality, she had a love affair with a man in her circle of acquaintances. When he discovered that, despite all precautions, Dorothy had become pregnant, he insisted that she get an abortion. She agreed to the abortion so he would not leave her; but afterward she found he had abandoned her. Dorothy felt deep shame over what she had done and feared that she would never bear another child.

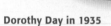

Dorothy Day in 1935

Several years later Dorothy was living on Staten Island with her common-law husband, Forster Battenham—himself an anarchist. There she made a discovery that would change her life. Far from being another bourgeois instrument of oppression, the Catholic Church, she found, was really the church of the poor. Attending daily Mass she saw washerwomen, maids, poor workers coming into the church to pray and hear Mass. Her interest piqued, she began to receive instruction in the Faith from a nun who lived on Staten Island.

Forster was not happy with Dorothy's interest in the Church, which he thought had aided the powerful in oppressing the poor. He opposed Dorothy's desire to have their daughter, Tamar (born in 1927), baptized. After Tamar's baptism, the rift between the couple grew wider until Forster, unable to accept Dorothy's faith, left her. The break with Forster complete, Dorothy herself was baptized on December 8, 1927.

For the next few years, Dorothy wondered how she could as a Catholic fulfill her longing to work for the poor and for social justice. She wrote articles for the Catholic journal, *Commonweal,* and for the Jesuit journal, *America,* but felt that her activities were inadequate. In 1932, she covered a "Hunger March" that had begun in New York and ended in Washington, D.C. Though the march was organized by Communists, Dorothy was inspired by the "joy and pride in the courage of this band of men and women" who suffered the abuse of the newspapers and police brutality to advertise to the government the plight of the poor. Feeling that her efforts, since becoming Catholic, had been "self-centered and lacking in a sense of community," Dorothy went to the unfinished Shrine of the Immaculate Conception in Washington to pray for guidance. It was December 8, the feast of the Immaculate Conception, the fifth anniversary of her baptism.

God sometimes answers prayers in strange ways. In Dorothy's case, he answered it in the form of a short, graying Frenchman with a dirty shirt-collar, and dressed in a suit that, she was to discover, he slept in. *Commonweal's* editor, George Shuster, had sent this fellow, Peter Maurin, to Dorothy because he thought they had similar ideas. The very night Dorothy had returned from Washington, Peter visited her apartment. "What struck me first about him," she later wrote, "was that he was one of those people who talked you deaf, dumb and blind, who each time he saw you began his conversation just where he had left off at the previous meeting, and never stopped unless you begged for rest, and that was not for long. He was irrepressible and he was incapable of taking offense. . . . I was thirty-five years old and I had met plenty of radicals in my time and plenty of crackpots, too; people who had blueprints to change the social order were a dime a dozen around Union Square."

Peter had a "blueprint" to change the social order, but it was one based on Catholic tradition and the social teachings of the popes. Peter, 55-years old when he met Dorothy Day, had come from a French peasant family. At the age of 16 he had entered the Christian Brothers, a teaching order, but was forced to join the French military in 1892. (France had obligatory military service, even for religious.) In 1900, he returned to the Christian Brothers but left the order in 1902. Because of France's obligatory military service, Peter in 1909 emigrated to Canada where, for a time, he was a homesteader in Saskatchewan. Failing at that, he supported himself doing manual labor and, at times, by teaching French both in Canada and the United States. By 1932, Peter was working in a boys' camp in upstate New York and spending what time he could in the city, living in Bowery flop houses and holding forth on his ideas in Union Square and anywhere else he could get an audience.

Peter Maurin taught Dorothy that the key to social change was not agitation, not class warfare (which he despised), but sanctity. Any change without sanctity, he said, is like a "clean shirt on a dirty back." A new social order, he declared, must be built up within the shell of the old. In private, Peter would call himself an "anarchist," but not of the bomb-throwing variety; he was an anarchist because he was a "personalist"—he believed men and women should take responsibility, not only for themselves, but for others. Each person,

A shanty town— housing for the poor in Depression-era New York City

himself, must feed the poor, clothe the naked, teach the ignorant. "His whole message was that everything began with one's self," Dorothy Day would later write. "He termed his message a personalist one, and was much averse to the word socialist, since it had always been associated with the idea of political action, the action of the city or the state. He wanted us all to be what we wanted the other fellow to be. If every man became poor there would not be any destitute, he said. If everyone became better, everyone would be better off. He wanted us all 'to quit passing the buck,' and trying to pass on the work to George to do."

Peter Maurin was not opposed to government but to the modern state because it sought to control the whole of life. He would continually propose the principle of subsidiarity as the model of government. Dorothy Day wrote that Peter Maurin thought "everything needs to be broken down into smaller units to be workable and according to man's nature, whether it is States, cities, factories. A union, a cooperative, is no better than the men in it, than the locals or cells which make it up."

Peter's program was simple. He wanted a social order where it was easy for men and women to be good. To achieve this, he wanted "round table discussions" where men and women could discuss the principles of a just social order. Next, would come "houses of hospitality" where the poor and needy could come to find help in their material needs and where they would learn to work cooperatively. He hoped bishops would establish such houses in their dioceses. The next step would be "agronomic universities" or farming colonies. "People will have to go back to the land," said Maurin. "The machine has displaced labor, the cities are overcrowded. The land will have to take care of them."

Peter Maurin provided the ideas, Dorothy Day, the practical leadership, for what became a new Catholic movement. Peter suggested Dorothy start a newspaper, and when she objected that they had no money, he replied: "In the history of the saints capital is raised by prayer. God sends you what you need when you need it. You will be able to pay the printer. Just read the lives of the saints." Peter was right. They raised the $57 needed for the first printing, and the first number of the paper, *The Catholic Worker,* came out in 1933.

The paper became the nucleus of the Catholic Worker movement. Soon, Peter, Dorothy, and others who had joined them were serving soup, bread, and coffee to poor men on the streets. In time, they rented two buildings through whose doors long lines of men and women passed to receive food and clothing, and shelter. News of what they were doing spread, and new Catholic Worker houses sprang up in cities across the United States. Like the first house, these new houses of hospitality fed the hungry, clothed the naked, and propagated personalism through round table discussions and, in some cases, new papers. Each house was autonomous and organized on "anarchist" principles of personal freedom and voluntary consent. There were no official leaders, though Dorothy Day exercised a moral sway over the members.

The Catholic Worker was remarkable because it was a purely lay movement within the structure and obedience of the Catholic Church. Both Dorothy Day and Peter Maurin held tenaciously to Catholic orthodoxy and were obedient to the bishops and the pope. Still, the movement followed its own initiatives and never became an official Church movement in the way religious orders of priests, brothers, and nuns have been.

Some Catholic Worker ideas were held suspect by rank and file Catholics, most especially the movement's position on non-violence. Dorothy Day and, it seems, Peter Maurin held that, because of the destructiveness of modern weaponry, no modern war could be just. War making, especially modern war making, they believed, violated the Christian's call to be a peacemaker. Thus, many Catholic Workers refused to serve in the military and, in the Second World War, became conscientious objectors. Yet, Catholic Workers went farther than this. They rejected all forms of violence, even in self-defense.

Day and Maurin were critical of the capitalist system and trumpeted a wider distribution of private, productive property as an alternative. They were equally critical of such governmental welfare schemes as the New Deal. "We believe," wrote Dorothy Day in 1945, "that

Men in a bread line, East 25th Street, New York City, 1930

social security legislation, now billed as a great victory for the poor and for the worker, is a great defeat for Christianity. It is an acceptance of the Idea of force and compulsion. It is an acceptance of Cain's statement, on the part of the employer. 'Am I my brother's keeper?'. . . . Certainly we all should know that it is not the province of the government to practice the works of mercy, or go in for Insurance. Smaller bodies, decentralized groups, should be caring for all such needs. . . . The first unit of society is the family. The family should look after

What the Catholic Worker Believes

Peter Maurin never wrote anything except his "Easy Essays." These free-form, quasi poems, he hoped, would appeal to the poor who had no time, or patience, for long, drawn-out dissertations. What follows is, perhaps, Maurin's most famous Easy Essay, "What the Catholic Worker Believes."

1. The Catholic Worker believes in the gentle personalism of traditional Catholicism.

2. The Catholic Worker believes in the personal obligation of looking after the needs of our brother.

3. The Catholic Worker believes in the daily practice of the Works of Mercy.

4. The Catholic Worker believes in Houses of Hospitality for the immediate relief of those who are in need.

5. The Catholic Worker believes in the establishment of Farming Communes

where each one works according to his ability and gets according to his need.

6. The Catholic Worker believes in creating a new society within the shell of the old with the philosophy of the new, which is not a new philosophy but a very old philosophy, a philosophy so old that it looks like new.

its own and, in addition, as the early fathers said, 'every home should have a Christ room in it, so that hospitality may be practiced.' 'The coat that hangs in your closet belongs to the poor.' 'If your brother is hungry, it is your responsibility.'"

In many ways, the Catholic Worker was a thoroughly American expression of Catholic tradition in its embrace of individual responsibility, in its radical style of lay communitarianism and espousal of Jefferson's dictum that the less government there is, the better. Yet, because it was Catholic, the Worker tempered individualism with the doctrine of the mystical body of Christ; it qualified the claims of personal conscience and freedom by obedience to the hierarchy of the Church; and it understood radicalism, not as rebellion, but as adherence to a philosophy so very old it seems forever new.

TROUBLES ABROAD

Totalitarian Regimes

The Great Depression had dispelled the optimism of the 1920s. Americans no longer embraced the illusion of uninterrupted prosperity; they knew, from bitter experience, that good times end. One attitude they did not lose—they still believed that the United States could, and should, isolate itself from the rest of the world. The nation's foray into world affairs in the Great War had been enough. Many believed that America, surrounded as she was by great oceans like moats about a castle, had nothing to fear from the disturbances of Europe or Asia. America had her own problems—the Depression, after five years of the New Deal, still held the economy in its icy grip. The rest of the world could take care of its own problems.

The problem was that the United States *was* involved in the world. She had colonies and military bases in the Pacific. She was a creditor to European nations. Her policy of maintaining a high tariff on imports had caused other nations to follow suit, though it only retarded their industrial development since they had become dependent on American loans and exports. The abandonment of the gold standard by Great Britain in 1931 and, subsequently, by Roosevelt in 1933, to inflate the currency (and so artificially raise prices) lessened the value of currency and disrupted international exchange.

The world was, indeed, racked by problems. Though Woodrow Wilson had hoped the Great War would make the "world safe for democracy," the state of Europe after the war belied this fond dream. Though Great Britain and France would remain democratic, other states embraced regimes that gave the government absolute control over all aspects of life. Such totalitarian regimes brought great instability to Europe and led that continent into a war as destructive in its effects than the one that everyone in that time still called the Great War.

Despite the attempts of the Allies to oust him in 1917, Vladimir Ilyich Lenin, who had established his Bolshevist Communist regime in Russia during the Great War, remained firmly in power. In 1922, he organized Russia, Ukraine, White Russia, and Georgia into a confederation of four Soviet Socialist Republics, called the Union of Soviet Socialist Republics. The regime was nominally democratic but in reality was controlled by the Communist Party, and, ultimately by Lenin, the head of the party. Though under the Soviet constitution the party and the state were formally separate, in practice the All Union Congress of Soviets merely rubber-stamped party decisions.

Lenin's paralysis in 1922 initiated a power struggle between two party leaders—the war hero Lev Trotsky and Josif Stalin, the president of the Communist Party's Central Committee. Because of his important position, Stalin succeeded Lenin as dictator upon the latter's death in 1924. To assure his power base, Stalin purged the Communist party of Trotskyites, forcing Trotsky himself into exile in 1929. Stalin then instituted a "Five Year Plan" to turn Russia into a great industrial power. In the decade following 1928, Russia's industrial production multiplied almost five times. By 1938, Russia was the fourth greatest industrial power in the world, after the United States, Germany, and Great Britain. In the production of iron, steel, and some other manufactures, Russia had moved ahead of Great Britain.

Russia's industrialization came at a heavy price. Stalin pushed heavy industry at the expense of consumer goods, a move that led to widespread popular discontent. To increase industrial production, Stalin forced 25 million peasants from the countryside to the cities to work in factories. To increase food production for the rapidly growing urban population, Stalin collectivized farming. Stalin brutally broke peasant resistance to collectivization by sending over five million peasants into exile or to concentration camps on the frigid Siberian frontier. The collectivization of agriculture resulted in mass starvation in which some say 5–6 million died in the Ukraine. Others say that number reached as high as 11 million.

Though, in the mid '30s, Stalin adopted certain capitalistic measures to spur industrial production, he actively promoted Communist revolution throughout the world. Centered in Moscow, the Third International (called *Komintern*) coordinated Communist Party action in Europe, the United States, Mexico, and in China. In theory, Communism was anti-nationalistic, for it sought the worldwide union of all workers, regardless of race or nationality. Yet, despite the Soviet threat, Great Britain and Italy both recognized the Soviet Union in 1924. The United States, under Harding, Coolidge, and Hoover continued to recognize the Russian government in exile; but under Roosevelt, in 1934, the United States recognized the Soviet Union.

Vladimir Lenin (left) and Josif Stalin

Communist agitation shook the uncertain stability of Italy. In the early '20s, old-line Liberals still controlled the Italian government, while newer parties, like the Social Democrats and the Catholic Popular Party led by Don Luigi Sturzo, were growing more influential. Economic woes in the 1920s led to widespread discontent, and Soviet-inspired socialists instigated a number of paralyzing strikes. Militarists, upset that Italy had not secured territories in Africa and the Near East after the war, also stirred up discontent. Against such forces the liberal government, under the nominal leadership of King Vittorio Emanuele III, was powerless.

Into this uncertainty came Benito Mussolini. Before the war, Mussolini had been a Socialist, an anti-Catholic, an anti-imperialist, and a pacifist; during the course of the war, he became a nationalist, an imperialist, pro-war, and an anti-communist. He remained anti-Catholic. In 1919, he formed in Milan a club centered around what became known as Fascism (so named from its symbol, the ancient Roman *fasces,* a bundle of rods, tied together to a bronze ax head). Mussolini's Fascism was like Stalinism in that it espoused state control of all commercial and social life. It was the opposite of Communism in that it was nationalistic, glorying in and seeking to glorify the Italian nation, at the expense of other nations and peoples, when expedient. In 1921, Mussolini organized his and allied clubs (called *fasci*) throughout Italy into a political party. His followers, decked out in black shirts, adopted elaborate ceremonies to evoke the ancient glories of the Roman Empire. They carried the Roman *fasces* as their emblem, and saluted each other, Roman-fashion, with their right arms outstretched.

Mussolini, called *Il Duce* (the Leader) by his followers, used violence and intimidation to achieve his ends. In 1922, he and his Fascists took control of the Italian government and

Benito Mussolini in the "March on Rome" that won him governmental power

drove out the Socialists. Mussolini became dictator and instituted a number of public works program to relieve unemployment. Abolishing labor unions, he set-up 13 syndicates to handle disputes between management and labor. In 1929, Mussolini concluded the Lateran Treaty with Pope Pius XI in which the Italian government recognized the independence of Vatican City in Rome and made the Catholic Church the official religion of Italy in return for the Church's recognition of Mussolini's government. It was a tenuous agreement; it would not be long before the Church would find herself again in conflict with the Fascist state.

Socialists, Liberals and Soviet-inspired Communists disturbed the unstable German republic established at Weimar in 1919. Germany had suffered a serious economic collapse after the war. Unreasonable war reparation payments weighed heavily on the country. The value of the German *Mark* became so inflated that a loaf of bread sold for a bucketful of *Mark* notes, and the middle class suffered the loss of their savings accounts and investments. Though prosperity returned in 1924, aided, in large part, by substantial loans from the United States, the stability of the middle class had been destroyed. When the worldwide depression hit in 1929, U.S. loans to Germany ceased, and German prosperity came to a crashing halt. In 1928, unemployment had stood at 1,350,000; in 1930, it reached 3,150,000. In 1932, it stood at 5,600,000.

Poverty in Germany was exacerbated in the minds of her people by humiliation. The memory of Versailles rankled with many Germans. The treaty had placed the whole blame for the Great War on Germany. Versailles had so demilitarized Germany that she had not sufficient forces to defend her borders if attacked. The glory of the second German *Reich* or "empire" (the first being the Holy Roman Empire of the Middle Ages) had been humbled to the dust. Germany was ripe for any demagogue who would promise to revive her prosperity and restore her power.

Like Italy, Germany throughout the '20s was torn between left-wing socialist and right-wing nationalist factions. The nationalists included many of the Prussian *Junkers* (landed gentry) who spread the tale that the German army had not been defeated in the war but had been betrayed by socialists, internationalist Jews, and Catholics. The *Junkers* and other groups formed the Nationalist Party. Their candidate, the old General Paul von Hindenburg, won the presidency in 1925. More extremist than the Nationalists was the National Socialist Party founded by Adolf Hitler in 1920. Committed to nationalist principles similar to those of Mussolini's Fascists and promoting the superiority of the German "Aryan" race over all others, Hitler and the "Nazis" promised to restore Germany to her glory. Though failing to pull off two coups to overthrow the government, Hitler's party grew, especially after 1929, by gaining new allies among the lower middle class and among members of the Nationalist Party. In 1932, Hitler ran for president against Hindenburg, but lost. But fearing the growth of the Communist Party, Hindenburg formed a coalition with the Nazis. In 1933, he appointed Hitler chancellor of Germany.

Adolf Hitler did not have the support of the majority of the German people; still he knew how to wield power. Using the Nazi Party guards (called *Schutzstaffeln*, or SS, for short) and regular police, he terrorized his opposition during the March 1933 elections. Though the Nazi party gained only 17 million votes out of the 39 million cast, the *Reichstag* on March

23 voted to delegate all power to Hitler's government. Hitler hailed this as the beginning of what he called the Third *Reich*.

When Hindenburg died in 1934, Hitler became president as well as chancellor of Germany. Like Stalin and Mussolini, he crushed all political opposition, promoted his doctrine of German racial superiority, instigated a persecution against Jews, and imprisoned any Protestant or Catholic clergy who opposed his policies. Politically, Hitler centralized the government at Berlin; the *Reichstag* transferred all the powers held by the individual German states to the central government. To end the Depression and to put men to work, Hitler instituted government programs of public works. But nothing was more effective in reviving German prosperity than Hitler's program of rebuilding the German military, with which, in a few years, he would shatter the peace of Europe and the world.

International Conflicts

In 1928, the government of Japan had signed the Kellogg-Briand Pact to renounce war as a means of solving international problems; three years later, Japan was engaged in an undeclared war with China in the latter's province of Manchuria. Though the Japanese emperor, Hirohito, was peaceful, his government had fallen to militarists who wanted to seize Manchuria from China and establish Japanese hegemony over east Asia: India, Burma, Indonesia, Indochina, and the Philippines.

Japanese policy, of course, could spell war with France, Great Britain, and the United States, all of whom had East Asian colonies and dependencies; but that did not dissuade Japanese militarists. Already, in 1932, Japanese planes had been bombing American and European churches, hospitals, schools, and colleges in China, in an effort to drive out all Western influence from the Orient. The League of Nations was powerless to do anything about Japanese aggression, and the governments of France, the United States, and Great Britain, absorbed by domestic problems, issued only protests. The Hoover administration's Stimson Doctrine in 1932 merely stated that the United States would recognize no territorial changes in violation of international treaties.

By 1932, Japan had set-up a puppet government in Manchuria (which it renamed Manchukuo), and the following year forced a truce from the Chinese government of Chiang Kai-shek. More ominously, in 1934, Japan renounced the Washington naval disarmament agreements of 1921–22 and began to build up her navy. And the nations that had signed the agreements with Japan did nothing to stop her. In 1935, Japan invaded the Chinese provinces of Chakar and Hopei, forcing the Chinese government to place officials acceptable to Japan in those provinces. This bald aggression united the Chinese people (then engaged in civil war) against the invader. In 1937, Chiang Kai-shek made peace with Communist rebels in the northwest, and an actual, if undeclared, war erupted between Japan and China. Again, throughout all these incidents, the governments of the United States, Great Britain, and France did nothing.

A terrified infant in Shangai's South Station after the Japanese bombing of Shanghai, August 28, 1937

Of course, Great Britain and France were facing their own problems in Europe. Adolf Hitler, in 1934, secretly backed a *coup d'etat* in Austria staged to bring that country into union with Germany. The *coup* failed, and Hitler backed down from any conquest of Austria when Italy and France threatened war. In 1935, Hitler denounced the disarmament clauses in the Treaty of Versailles and initiated his program of rearmament. The following year, Hitler commenced the military occupation of the Rhineland—the region in western Germany which, according to the Treaty of Versailles, was to remain a demilitarized buffer between France and Germany.

Germany's actions brought France, Great Britain, and Italy, briefly, into an alliance. France also concluded an alliance with Russia and Czechoslovakia. The alliance of these nations might have been sufficient to check any further German aggression, but other tensions dissolved it. Because of her alliance with Italy, France had agreed to Mussolini's designs on Ethiopia. By May 1936, superior Italian forces defeated the primitive Ethiopian military, drove Ethiopian emperor, Haile Selassie, from his throne in Addis Ababa, and occupied the country. Popular reaction to the conquest in England and France, however, forced their gov-

Haile Selassie (center) and his court, 1930

ernments to back League of Nations' sanctions against Italy. Hitler saw his chance and courted Mussolini by giving him military aid. In October 1936, Italy and Germany entered into an accord, forming the "Rome-Berlin Axis."

The major ideological divide in Europe between Communists and Fascists led to violence in Spain. In the '20s, Spain's King Alphonso XIII had established a dictatorship under the control of General Primo de Rivera. In 1931, after Primo de Rivera's resignation, a revolution overthrew the king and made Spain a republic. In 1936, the "Popular Front" (a union of republicans, socialists, anarchists, and Communists) secured a majority in the *Cortés* (the Spanish parliament) and announced radical measures—the break-up of large landed estates, the secularization of Church property along with other restrictions on the Church, and a drastic reduction in the army. When it became clear that the Popular Front was coming increasingly under the control of Communists, a group of high military officers attempted a *coup d'etat*.

A Republican soldier passing a dead horse on the Plaza de Toros during the Battle for Teruel, Spain, about 1938

The *coup* failed but brought on civil war. The "Nationalists," as the rebels called themselves, soon united themselves under the leadership of General Francisco Franco. They represented the interests of the large landowners, the monarchists, industry, the Church, as well as the people in the south and west of the country. The government forces, called "Loyalists," held the center of the country at Madrid, the northern Basque regions, and the east. The struggle represented a microcosm of the ideological conflicts of Communism and Fascism. Germany and Italy sent arms, airplanes and personnel to Franco, while Russia supplied and aided the Nationalists. The bitterness of civil war was exacerbated by the ideological conflict. Franco, not a fascist, represented the forces of Spanish tradition and of quasi-fascist, authoritarian thought, while the Loyalists were radical liberals and thoroughgoing Communists. No peace could prevail between such contrary visions of society.

The Road to War

Most Americans were not eager for war. Between 1935 and 1939, Congress echoed popular American sentiment by passing a series of neutrality acts that forbade the sale or transport of arms or munitions and private lending of money to warring nations. Another act forbade the entry of Americans into war zones.

Though he signed all these neutrality acts, President Roosevelt's sentiments were far from neutral. In a speech he gave in Chicago in 1937, he called for a quarantine of aid to aggressor nations—meaning Germany, Italy, and Japan. If such nations, he said, continued their aggressions, "let no one imagine that America will escape, that America may expect mercy, that this Western Hemisphere will not be attacked." Yet, Roosevelt, even if he wanted to, could not suggest a more active engagement in efforts to restrain the aggressor nations. Popular opinion was still strong against it.

Still, Roosevelt intervened in European affairs to the degree he could. On November 5, 1937, Adolf Hitler informed foreign powers that he would seek new territories for Germany. Great Britain's prime minister, Neville Chamberlain, took the path of appeasement with Germany—he would not oppose Hitler if he pursued only the limited objective of annexing German-speaking regions. When in January of 1938, Roosevelt proposed holding a conference of leading powers in Washington, D.C., to discuss European problems and Japan's presence in China, Chamberlain demurred.

And still Chamberlain and the French premier, Daladier, did nothing when, in March 1938, Hitler invaded Austria and annexed the old Habsburg domain to Germany. Though Roosevelt, in September 1938, reminded the signatory nations that they had agreed, in the Kellogg-Briand Pact, to outlaw war, Hitler convinced Chamberlain, Mussolini, and Daladier to look the other way while German troops invaded Czechoslovakia. Hitler assured European leaders that he merely wanted the Sudetenland, a German-speaking region of Bohemia, and the leaders chose to believe him. Hitler soon showed his bad faith. In March 1939, a few months after occupying the Sudetenland, Hitler took Prague, the capital of Czechoslovakia. Bohemia and Slovakia became satellite states of the Third *Reich*.

Noting Great Britain's and France's unwillingness to oppose conquest, Mussolini tore a page from Hitler's book and invaded and occupied Albania, Italy's neighbor across the Adriatic. These last acts of aggression awakened Great Britain and France from their torpor. On March 31, they guaranteed that they wold protect Poland and Romania against German aggression. Hitler, however, knew the impotence of Germany's World War I enemies. Both he and Mussolini ignored Roosevelt when, on April 14, 1939, he tried to exact from them a promise not to attack 20 small nations. Hitler returned an insulting reply to Roosevelt, while Mussolini called the message "a result of infantile paralysis."

Meanwhile, in the Far East, Japan continued its aggression against China and against the Americans and Europeans who lived there. On December 12, 1937, Japanese planes bombed and sank the U.S.S. *Panay*, a Navy gunboat on the Yangtze river. This act could have precipitated into war with the United States had Japan not called the attack an accident, offered a formal apology, and paid an indemnity. Despite the attack, American opinion in 1938 was still strong against intervention in the Far East and favored a complete American withdrawal from China. But when, in 1939, Japan conquered Shanghai and intensified her ill-treatment of Americans overseas, opinion in the U.S. changed somewhat. Even isolationists supported Roosevelt's renunciation, on July 26, of the United States' treaty of commerce with Japan.

From "Phony" to Actual War

The news that the rival tyrants, Adolf Hitler and Josif Stalin, had signed a non-aggression pact on August 23 stunned the world. How much greater would world dismay have been if it were known that the dictators had secretly agreed to divide up Poland among themselves? Hitler knew that an invasion of Poland would bring on war with Great Britain and France; but with Russia pulled from an alliance with those powers, he was assured of peace on his eastern front. In the west Hitler was secure behind the defenses of his "Siegfried Line."

On September 1, 1939, Adolf Hitler unleashed his *Blitzkrieg* ("lightning war") against Poland, while Russia invaded that land from the east. Two days later, Great Britain and France declared war on Germany; but as far as Poland was concerned, it was an impotent gesture. By the end of September, Russia and Germany had mowed down Poland's feeble but brave resistance and parceled out the prostrate land between themselves.

Months of inaction on the part of the belligerents followed the conquest of Poland, leading U.S. Senator Borah to call what was happening in Europe a "phony war." But the omens pointed to real war. Then, in March 1940, Russia forced Finland to cede territory to her, invaded the neighboring countries, Estonia, Latvia and Lithuania, and recovered Bessarabia and Bukovina from Romania. In April, Germany invaded and conquered Denmark and Norway. With equal resolution and speed, Hitler then turned his sights southward. On May 10, German armies and air force invaded neutral Belgium and Holland, leaving Rotterdam a pile of rubble in their wake. Within five days, German armies had conquered Holland. Hitler now turned his sights on hated France.

The German invasion of France would not bog down as it had in World War I. German forces pushed northward toward the Channel ports and, on May 21, cut off the British

Polish cavalry during the invasion of Poland, 1939

expeditionary force that had come to the aid of France. The British sea withdrawal from Dunkerque was impressive but a sign of weakness in the face of Hitler's onslaught. Hitler's armies then turned south, and the French army melted before them. On June 14, 1940, Paris fell. Hitler had occupied one-half of France; he left the south in the control of a French puppet president at Vichy, Marshal Henri Philippe Pétain. Autumn brought more bad news to Hitler's enemies. On September 27, Japan entered into a mutual defensive alliance with Germany and Italy. The now "Triple Axis" had a power base in the Pacific.

The American Response

In one of his Fireside Chats on September 3, 1939, the day Great Britain and France had declared war on Germany, Roosevelt promised that "this nation will remain a neutral nation." Yet, said the president, "I cannot ask that every American remain neutral in thought as well."

Roosevelt was certainly not "neutral in thought"; neither were most members of Congress. With the fall of Paris, Roosevelt came up with the "Short of War" policy. This policy's main points were to help Great Britain, to gain time for American rearmament, and to restrain Japan in the Far East by diplomatic measures and naval deterrence. In accord with this policy, Congress, on June 14, 1940, passed a bill (which Roosevelt signed) to build up and expand the navy and three days later granted Admiral Stark, Chief of Naval Operations, $4 million to commence the building of a two-ocean navy. In September, the Burke-Wadsworth bill, establishing the first peace-time draft in the history of the United States, passed Congress. All men between the ages of 21 and 35 were required to register for the draft, and a total of 800,000 of these were inducted into the armed forces. The United States also signed an agreement whereby Great Britain received 50 naval destroyers in return for a 99-year lease on naval and air bases in the British West Indies, Newfoundland, and Bermuda.

Roosevelt could do little more than this. Nineteen-forty was an election year, and he was planning to break a 150-year tradition by which presidents, in honor of George Washington, limited themselves to two terms. If Roosevelt triumphed in November, he could claim the mandate of the people to continue his policies. Though many Americans were in favor of aiding the "Allies," as Great Britain and France were called, many others opposed any intervention in Europe. The America First Committee, under the leadership of aviator Charles Lindbergh, led the opposition to war. Though newspapers, such as the *New York Times* and the New York *Herald-Tribune,* supported Roosevelt, the Chicago *Times* and the Hearst papers opposed him.

The isolationists, however, could claim no organized party support in the election. The Republicans, meeting in Philadelphia in June, nominated Wendell Willkie, president of the Commonwealth and Southern Utilities Corporation, who supported aiding the Allies and thought the only problem with the New Deal was that it had been inefficiently executed. Roosevelt thus entered the election from a position of strength. Increased war spending was succeeding where the New Deal had failed—men were put to work, and America was coming out of the Depression. Too, the American people were unlikely to change helmsmen when the ship of state was heading into troubled waters. Nevertheless, though Roosevelt captured 449 electoral votes in November and Willkie only 82, the popular vote was closer than it had been since 1932, with Willkie's vote total standing at 45 percent.

Riding on what seemed an overwhelming popular mandate for his policies, Roosevelt addressed Congress on January 6, 1941. The United States, declared Roosevelt, should come to the aid of the nations fighting for what he called the "Four Freedoms": Freedom of Speech, Freedom of Religion, Freedom from Want, Freedom from Fear. Four days later, he submitted to Congress the Lend-Lease Act, which they passed on March 11 after much bitter debate. Lend-Lease authorized the president to "sell, transfer, lease, lend" war materials to any nation the president deemed "vital to the defense of the United States." Because of Lend-Lease, $50 billion in army foodstuffs and other services went to the Allies, and American industry turned to the production of war material.

When Germany invaded Greece and Yugoslavia, and German tanks under General Rommel rolled across North Africa, Roosevelt took a more warlike stance. Though the United States was still officially neutral, the president ordered the seizure of all Axis ships in American ports. In May, when a German U-boat sank an American freighter, Roosevelt proclaimed an "unlimited national emergency." In June, he ordered the freezing of all Axis assets in America and closed Axis consulates. On June 22, when Hitler broke his pact with Stalin in order to commence a conquest of Russia, Roosevelt wasted no time and declared, on June 24, that Russia could take advantage of the Lend-Lease program. Tensions between the United States and Germany increased in September when a German U-boat closed in battle with the U.S.S. *Greer*; thenceforth, Roosevelt ordered American ships to "shoot on sight" any German submarine they encountered.

About a month before the *Greer* incident, Roosevelt had met with Great Britain's new fighting prime minister, Winston Churchill, in Newfoundland to discuss the common defense. On August 14, 1941, Roosevelt and Churchill signed the Atlantic Charter—a set of "common principles in the national policies of their respective countries on which they base their hopes for a better future for the world." In the Atlantic Charter, Roosevelt and Churchill pledged that their countries sought "no aggrandizement, territorial or other." They declared that they wanted no territorial changes that do not accord with the freely expressed wishes of the peoples concerned; that they respected "the right of all peoples to choose the form of government under which they will live"; and that they wished "to see sovereign rights and self-government restored to those who have been forcibly deprived of them."

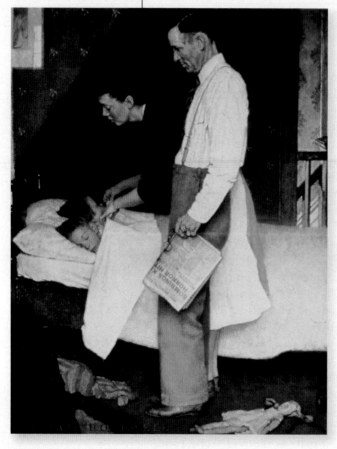

Norman Rockwell's illustration of "Freedom from Fear"—one of his illustrations of Roosevelt's "Four Freedoms"

For the future, the Atlantic Charter declared that all states, whether "great or small, victor or vanquished," shall have equal access to trade in the world's raw materials; that the "fullest collaboration" shall be established between all nations to secure "improved labor standards, economic adjustment and social security." Roosevelt and Churchill declared that, "after the final destruction of the Nazi tyranny," they hoped for a peace "which will afford to all nations the means of dwelling in safety within their own boundaries, and which will afford assurance that all the men in all the lands may live out their lives in freedom from fear and want." To achieve this goal, the leaders said the world must abandon "the use of force," that, "pending the establishment of a wider and permanent system of general security" (something like the League of Nations), "the general disarmament" of "nations is essential."

Beginning with Lend-Lease and culminating with the Atlantic Charter, Roosevelt had moved the officially neutral United States into an undeclared war with Germany. Popular American sentiment, however, was still so strongly against war that Roosevelt could not call on Congress actually to declare war. He needed a catalyst. The Axis powers must do something so significant that Americans would throw aside their love of peace and security and rush headlong into war. That catalyst would come, but not from Germany.

Japan's desperation would draw the United States, once again, into world war.

The Day of Infamy

When Germany was crushing all resistance on the continent of Europe, Japan was extending her power over the Far East. Her target was now not China alone, but the Philippines, Malaysia, and Indonesia, over which, she said, she would form the "Greater East Asia Co-Prosperity Sphere." On July 25, 1941, Japan announced that she was establishing a "protectorate" over French Indochina.

Congress sought to meet the threat to the Philippines (where the United States maintained a military base) by authorizing the president to establish a partial embargo against Japan and to restrict the shipment of war materials to that country. When the Japanese seized French Indochina, Roosevelt received the armed forces of the Philippines into the United States army and appointed General Douglas MacArthur to command the U.S. and Filipino troops in the Far East. Roosevelt took the further step of freezing all of Japan's financial assets in the United States. Great Britain and the Netherlands joined the United States in cutting off Japan's source of financial credit (so she could not borrow money) as well as all imports of rubber, scrap iron, and fuel oil to the island country.

After the bombing of Pearl Harbor, the *U.S.S. Arizona* rests on the harbor's bottom

Cutting off credit and exports of oil could only provoke Japan to some desperate act. Japan was in dire need of oil if she were to continue her conquest of China. The Japanese generals, who stood to lose face if they evacuated China, decided that, unless the United States, Great Britain, and the Netherlands restored the flow of credit and oil, they would go to war with them.

On November 20, 1941, Japan's prime minister, General Tojo, sent an ultimatum to the United States. Japan, said Tojo, would occupy no more Asian territory if, in turn, the United States evacuated Southern Indochina, cut off all aid to Chiang-Kai-shek, unfroze Japanese assets, and ceased reinforcing the Philippines. Roosevelt refused even to consider these conditions.

Six days later, a Japanese force of six big cruisers with 423 airplanes, two battleships, two heavy cruisers, and eleven destroyers set out across the Pacific from Kurile Island in Japan. Their destination was the U.S. naval base in the Hawai'ian Islands, Pearl Harbor.

The next day, November 27, 1941, Washington sent a warning to Pearl Harbor and to Manila in the Philippines to be on the alert; Japanese troop transports were seen steaming south from Formosa (Taiwan). Their possible destinations—Thailand, Malay Peninsula, or the Philippines.

Despite Washington's warning, the American fleet at Pearl Harbor felt no fear of attack. After all, they were thousands of miles from Formosa; the Japanese transports could do them no harm. Yet, on December 7, the Japanese fleet from Kurile Island had reached a point 275 miles north of Pearl Harbor. At 6 a.m., the Japanese launched their squadron of bombers and winged fighters. An hour and 40 minutes later, the first Japanese attack group sighted the island of Oahu and the ships of the U.S. Pacific Fleet strung out, two by two, in Pearl Harbor. Fifteen minutes later, bombs and torpedoes fell on the sleeping harbor. In confusion, American sailors and marines rushed to their anti-aircraft guns, but the Japanese held the advantage of surprise. By the end of the day, the Japanese had sunk the U.S.S. *Arizona*, capsized the U.S.S. *Oklahoma*, sank or run aground four other battleships,

An American poster calling for revenge for Pearl Harbor

damaged three destroyers and destroyed 149 planes. Among American casualties were 2,403 soldiers, sailors, and civilians, killed; 1,178, wounded. The Japanese had lost only 29 planes with their pilots.

Roosevelt called December 7, 1941 the "day that shall live in infamy." But there was more. The same day, at about 12 noon (3 p.m. in Hawai'i), Japanese bombers from Formosa attacked the U.S. at Manila, destroying most of the B-17 American bombers parked there. Before dawn, the Japanese had landed on the Malay Peninsula and, at 8:30 a.m., were bombing Guam from Saipan.

The Pearl Harbor attack kindled anger in American hearts; the desire for revenge and for justice banished all devotion to neutrality. On December 8, 1941, the Congress followed the president's urging and voted to declare war on Japan. Three days later, in fidelity to their pact with Japan, Germany and Italy declared war on the United States.

In asking Congress for a declaration of war against Germany and Italy, Roosevelt declared, "the long-known and the long-expected has thus taken place. The forces endeavoring to enslave the entire world now are moving toward this hemisphere. Never before has there been a greater challenge to life, liberty and civilization. Delay invites greater danger. Rapid and united effort by all the peoples of the world who are determined to remain free will ensure a world victory of the forces of justice and of righteousness over the forces of savagery and of barbarism . . .

"I therefore request Congress to recognize a state of war between the United States and Germany, and between the United States and Italy."

Chapter 27 Review

Summary

- With government inaction regarding the Depression under Hoover, people took matters into their own hands and withdrew their savings from banks, causing bank failures to proliferate. When he became president, Roosevelt ordered the closing of all banks for four days. He submitted an emergency bank bill to Congress, and when the banks reopened on March 13, there was no run on savings. Two days later, the stock market began to climb slowly.

- During the first 100 days of his administration, Roosevelt and his advisers worked out the policies that formed the first onslaught of the New Deal. Congress passed 13 bills between March 9 and June 16, 1933. These bills were either emergency measures to take care of immediate problems or were meant to be permanent.

- One of the emergency measures passed was the National Recovery Administration, which applied to industry codes that governed relations between labor and management.

- One of the most significant acts of legislation was Roosevelt's decision, on April 19, 1933, to abandon the gold standard. Some criticized this policy, but Wall Street praised it because, they said, it would make American industries more competitive in the world market.

- After the adjournment of Congress on June 16, 1933, Roosevelt continued to promote programs that he said would restore prosperity. The first lady, Eleanor Roosevelt, ardently supported her husband's crusade, and breaking tradition, addressed audiences across the country.

- Roosevelt intended his New Deal not only for whites. It included blacks and Indians in its reach. Roosevelt awarded blacks with public office posts and abolished segregation in federal offices. The Commission of Indian Affairs adopted policies that encouraged the strengthening of tribal government and the preservation of native culture. The Indian Reorganization Act repealed the Dawes Act.

- On August 14, 1935, Congress passed the Social Security Act, perhaps the most significant and far-reaching of the New Deal measures.

Chapter 27 Review (continued)

- New Deal legislation racked up huge amounts of debt, and the number of unemployed was still between 10 and 12 million. These failures emboldened Roosevelt's political opponents. Opposition came sometimes from the Supreme Court, and even from his own party, the Democrats. Another Roosevelt opponent, a Catholic priest, Father Charles Coughlin, organized the National Union for Social Justice to promote his ideas and gave talks over the radio. The National Union for Social Justice converged with the "Share-Our-Wealth" program of Senator Huey P. Long. Despite opposition, however, Roosevelt was re-elected in 1936.

- Although the economy seemed to be gaining steam in 1937, a recession hit in the fall of that year. Roosevelt tried to push through more New Deal measures, but Congress was not responsive, though it did approve the Fair Labor Standards Act in 1938.

- Catholics, including Father John Augustine Ryan, addressed the economic and social ills of the 1930s. The New Deal era saw Catholics making their first clear contribution to the public life of the United States; and for the first time in American history, the Catholic voice was heard with some respect.

- Dorothy Day, who had been a communist and free-love radical, became Catholic in 1927. Over the following years she worked with Peter Maurin to create the Catholic Worker Movement.

- Even after the optimism of the '20s was dispelled, Americans still thought the United States should and could isolate itself from the rest of the world. Such isolation was becoming more difficult, since the United States was in fact involved in the world. The world in which it was involved was racked with problems. Totalitarian regimes brought great instability to Europe. In Russia, Vladimir Ilyich Lenin organized the Union of Soviet Socialist Republics. When Lenin died, Josef Stalin became dictator and instituted a "Five Year Plan" which made Russia the fourth greatest industrial power in the world.

- Communist agitation shook Italy. In 1919 Benito Mussolini formed the Fascist Party and in 1922 took over the government. In Germany, Adolf Hitler founded the National Socialist party in 1920. In 1934, Hitler became president of Germany, initiating what he called the Third *Reich*. Meanwhile, Japan was engaged in a war with China

- In 1934, Japan renounced the Washington naval disarmament agreements and began to build up her navy. The following year Hitler renounced Germany's post war agreement and initiated his program of rearmament. Hitler then commenced the military occupation of the Rhineland, the demilitarized buffer between France and Germany. In October 1936, German and Italy entered into an accord, forming the "Rome-Berlin Axis."

- Americans were not eager for war, and Congress passed a series of neutrality acts forbidding the sale or transport of arms or munitions to warring nations. In 1937, Hitler informed foreign powers that he would seek new territories for Germany. Great Britain and France did nothing while Germany invaded several countries. When Mussolini invaded and occupied Albania, Great Britain and France guaranteed they would protect Poland and Romania against German aggression.

- On August 23, 1939, Adolf Hitler and Josif Stalin signed a non-aggression pact. On September 1, 1939, Hitler and Stalin invaded Poland. Two days later Great Britain and France declared war on Germany. On September 27, 1940, Japan entered into alliance with Germany, forming the "Triple Axis."

- When Paris fell to the Axis, Roosevelt declared a "Short of War" policy, and Congress passed a bill to build up and expand the navy. On December 7, 1941, a Japanese fleet attacked Pearl Harbor in Hawai'i. On December 8, Congress declared war on Japan. Three days later, Germany and Italy declared war on the United States.

Key Concepts

parens patriae: a principle derived from common law that allows the public authority to provide for orphaned minor children. It has been extended to include state power over children raised by what are deemed unfit parents, as well as government care over all citizens.

subsidiarity: the organizing principle that political and social matters should be handled by the smallest competent authority and higher authorities should only perform tasks which cannot be performed at a local level

Fascism: a nationalistic regime which espouses state control of all commercial and social life

Nazism: (from the German *Nationalsozialismus*) a form of Fascism that incorporates racism and anti-Semitism

Dates to Remember

1933: President Roosevelt begins instituting his New Deal.

1935: Congress passes the Social Security Act.

1936: Italy and Germany enter into the "Rome-Berlin Axis."

1939: Adolf Hitler unleashes his *Blitzkrieg* against Poland (September 1).

1941: Japan attacks Pearl Harbor (December 7).

The United States declares war on Japan (December 8).

Germany and Italy declare war on the United States (December 11).

Central Characters

Franklin Delano Roosevelt (1882–1945): 32nd president of the United States. He instituted the "New Deal" during the Great Depression and led the U.S. into the Second World War.

Charles Coughlin (1891–1979): American Catholic priest who, over the radio, opposed Roosevelt's New Deal programs

John Augustine Ryan (1869–1945): American Catholic priest and noted scholar on the social teaching of the Catholic Church

Dorothy Day (1897–1980): American journalist who co-founded the *Catholic Worker* newspaper and Catholic Worker Movement with Peter Maurin

Peter Maurin (1877–1949): Catholic social activist who helped Dorothy Day found the Catholic Worker Movement in 1933

Josif Stalin (1878–1953): dictator of the U.S.S.R. who made Russia the fourth greatest industrial power in the world

Benito Mussolini (1883–1945): Italian dictator who founded the Fascist Party

Adolf Hitler (1889–1945): leader of the National Socialist (or Nazi) Party and president/chancellor of Germany

Questions for Review

1. Why might some Americans have doubted that Roosevelt's New Deal measures were constitutional? Why, according to Roosevelt, were they constitutional?

2. What were the goals of the National Recovery Administration (NRA)? How was the NRA geared to helping the family?

3. What were the benefits of the Social Security Act, and what were its problems?

4. Explain the views of Roosevelt's opponents (both conservative and progressive) to the the New Deal.

5. What did Catholics think about the New Deal?

6. What did the American bishops think the solution to the crisis of the Depression necessarily involved?

7. Lay out the main points of Pope Pius XI's encyclical, *Quadragesimo Anno,* and what it called for.

8. Explain Dorothy Day and Peter Maurin's ideas about how best to bring reform to society.

9. Explain the course of events that led the United States to declare war against the Axis powers.

Ideas in Action

1. Listen to Roosevelt's Fireside Chats and discuss them. (These can be found on the Internet.)

2. Discover what projects sponsored by the NRA (such as murals) or the WPA (such school buildings, libraries, parks, and airports) can be found in your own region, town, or city.

3. Read and discuss some of the writings of Dorothy Day and Peter Maurin. Day and Maurin's writings are archived at www.catholicworker.org.

4. Read and discuss Pope Pius XI's encyclical, *Quadragesimo Anno.* It may be found on the website of the Holy See.

Chapter 27 Review (continued)

5. What would Thomas Jefferson have said about Franklin Delano Roosevelt's flexible interpretation of the Constitution? Did Roosevelt capture the intention of the authors of the Constitution? Why or why not?

6. If there is a Catholic Worker House of Hospitality near your home, visit it and learn more about it.

Highways and Byways

Barnyard Fashion

During the Great Depression, few farming families had the money to buy new shoes or clothing. "Repair, reuse, make do, and don't throw anything away," became the motto of the time. Socks were mended, patches were sewn over holes in clothing, and when you outgrew your dress or trousers, they were handed down to a younger sibling. Nothing was thrown away.

So what were you to do if you didn't have any older siblings and you needed a new dress? Fortunately, a farmer had to buy feed for his livestock, and that feed came in a cloth feed sack. In the early 19th century, manufacturers found that they could sell more sacks of feed if they printed patterns on the cloth sack; in other words, decorate them so they would be desirable to the farmer's wife. Feed sacks began to be made in a variety of colors and patterns with a paper label so that the fabric could be more easily reused. Such cloth was often made into dish towels or linens; but, during the Depression, women would use the cloth from the feed sacks to make dresses for themselves and clothing for their children. A typical woman's dress took three feed sacks. By the end of the Second World War, cloth sacks were replaced by paper and plastic. Now, in the 21st century, feed sack patterns have made a come-back and are used widely by quilters.

28 WORLD WAR II AND THE COLD WAR

War at Sea

In quick succession they fell before the Japanese onslaught—the Island of Guam, December 10, 1941; Wake Island, 13 days later; British Hong Kong, on Christmas day. General Douglas MacArthur, commanding an American and Filipino army on the island of Luzon in the Philippines, retreated to the Bataan Peninsula where he was besieged by a larger Japanese force. MacArthur himself took refuge in the underground fortress of Corregidor. After two months, Roosevelt moved MacArthur to Australia to prepare for an American counterattack.

Confident in their strength, the Japanese extended their empire over the Netherlands East Indies and Malaya and Indonesia. In April 1942, the Japanese navy destroyed a fleet of American, British and Dutch ships. On April 9, Bataan fell and, a month later, Corregidor, surrounded by Japanese land and sea forces, surrendered its 11,500 men. So hard was the march to the Japanese prison camps the captured soldiers underwent, so numerous were its casualties, that it is remembered as the "Bataan Death March."

Only one event served to relieve the gloom of defeat during the first months of the Pacific war. Roosevelt ordered General James H. Doolittle to stage an air raid over Tokyo, the capital and chief industrial and port city of Japan. The American carrier *Hornet*, having come within 750 miles of Tokyo, launched 16 B-25 bombers. The planes had enough fuel to reach Tokyo and, from there, to fly to the coast of China, but not enough to return to their ship. The Japanese did not expect an attack on their capital from the air; and though the planes did little damage, the raid shook Japanese morale.

By May 1, 1942, Japan had conquered the Philippines and almost all

Japanese photograph of the surrender of American troops at Corregidor

795

The explosion of depth charges from U.S.S. *Hammann* as she sank alongside U.S.S *Yorktown* during the Battle of Midway. Both ships were torpedoed by a Japanese submarine while the *Hammann* was assisting with the salvage of *Yorktown*.

atoll: a coral island made up of a reef surrounding a lagoon

of East Asia. Japanese warlords now set their sights on New Guinea. To guard the approaches to Australia, Admiral Chester Nimitz, in command of U.S. sea forces, sent an American fleet to contest the advance of the Japanese fleet against Port Moresby, on the Australian side of New Guinea. On May 7–8, the two fleets engaged in battle. Aircraft battled with aircraft, and aircraft with ships, but ship never closed on ship. The fleets never saw each other. The battle of the Coral Sea was indecisive, but afterwards, the Japanese gave up their attempt to conquer New Guinea. For a time, Australia was safe.

Admiral Isoroku Yamamoto, over-all commander of the Japanese fleet, knew that if he did not destroy the American Pacific fleet in 1942, American industrial production of ships and planes would, even as early as the following year, outstrip Japanese production. Yamamoto needed to destroy the U.S. fleet, and soon, to assure Japanese victory in the Pacific.

Yamamoto chose Midway Island as his target. An **atoll**, 1,134 miles northwest of Pearl Harbor, Midway was an American air base; its capture would pose a dire threat to the American fleet at Pearl Harbor. Yamamoto hoped that by attacking Midway, he could lure the American Pacific fleet into a battle in which he could destroy it. It was a good plan but, unfortunately for Yamamoto, the United States, by breaking the Japanese code, got wind of it. When, on June 4, Japanese planes had destroyed half of the American planes grounded on Midway, three American ships—the *Hornet, Enterprise* and *Yorktown*—were ready to counterattack.

At 9:25 a.m., while the Japanese planes were refueling on their carriers in preparation for another attack, 15 old American torpedo planes struck the unsuspecting Japanese ships. These planes, armed with one torpedo each, were slow, easy targets. The first strike force

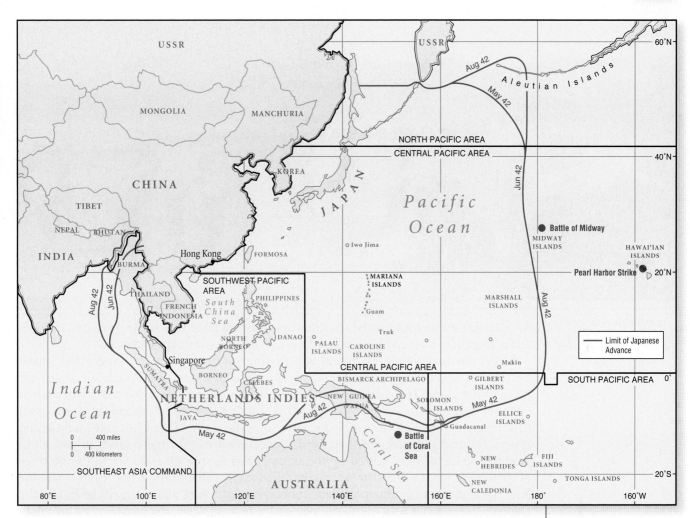

The Pacific Theater in 1942

was followed by another of 26 torpedo planes, and out of the two assaults, only six planes returned to their ships. Still, the surprise attack forced the Japanese so to maneuver their ships that they became easy targets for the onslaught to come. American dive bombers followed in the wake of the torpedo planes, striking deadly blows to the Japanese fleet. That day, the dive bombers sank three of the four Japanese ships, and on the following day, June 5, destroyed the fourth.

Midway was an important victory for the United States. Yamamoto lost four of the best carriers in his fleet, as well as 3,500 men and 332 aircraft. The Americans had paid back Japan for the strike on Pearl Harbor, for it was Yamamoto who had made December 7, 1941 what Roosevelt had called a day of infamy.

War Off the Atlantic Coast

The first six months of 1942 were a time of preparation for war against Germany and Italy. Because of preparations before the war, the United States military was in better shape than it had been at its entry into the First World War, but still much needed to be done. Conscription of men into the army, navy, and coast guard began in earnest (the Marines, 600,000 strong, were all volunteers). The typical draftee, called a "G.I." (for "General Issue"), was not always willing to fight and was even less prepared to fight. He had to be trained, and that took time. Though the United States refused to conscript women, as many as 250,000 women served the war effort as nurses or as female auxiliaries of the army and navy (called "Waves," "Wacs," and "Spars"). Women would also serve on the home front; they went to

American troops land on a beach near Algiers during Operation Torch

work in factories, replacing the workingmen who had gone to war. By war's end in 1945, about 15 million men and women had served in the American armed forces.

Under the direction of the federal War Production Board, American industrial output for the war would be phenomenal; it would soon supply, not only American needs, but those of her allies. The chief shortages faced by the United States and her allies were in oil, steel, and rubber. To supply the first, the United States and Venezuela stepped up oil drilling and refinement. To supply the latter two, the United States instituted a rationing system for steel and rubber. Citizens held collection drives for these sorely needed commodities while industry geared up to increase their supply. One answer to the shortage of rubber (due to the fact that Japan controlled many rubber producing regions) was the building of plants to produce synthetic rubber. Production of war commodities buried the Depression for good; with 6 million men and women at work, the problem of unemployment was solved.

The American government paid for all this war preparation by raising taxes but also by going into deep debt. Taxes financed only 40 percent of the cost of war; the remaining 60 percent was paid for by bonds, borrowed from banks at one to one and a half percent interest, and sold to American citizens. The war would cost the United States government $40 billion a year. By its end, the total cost of the war would reach $350 billion.

Meanwhile, the Germans did not hold back from attacking the United States. Admiral Karl Doenitz, who commanded the German navy, sent U-boats into the Atlantic to cut-off sea communications between America and Europe. Beginning in January, 1942, German U-boats prowled the waters off the coast of North America sinking any merchant ships they found. Sinkings occurred off the coast of Cape Cod in Massachusetts, 30 miles outside of New York City, and within sight of Virginia Beach, Virginia. Between January and April 1942, U-boats sank about 200 ships from as far north as Maine to as far south as the waters of the Gulf of Mexico, the Caribbean, and around Bermuda. In May and June, about 182 ships were torpedoed in the straits of Florida, the Gulf of Mexico, and in the Caribbean. In these southern waters over half of the ships sunk were oil tankers, thus exacerbating the American shortage of oil. U-boat depredations threatened to cut off shipping between the United States and her allies. Admiral Ernest J. King, commander-in-chief of the U.S. fleet, met the emergency by ordering the building of small, armed escort vessels and by establishing inshore and offshore patrols and convoy systems for merchant ships. King's system went a long way to meet the U-boat threat, though it would be another year or more before U-boats ceased to be a grave threat.

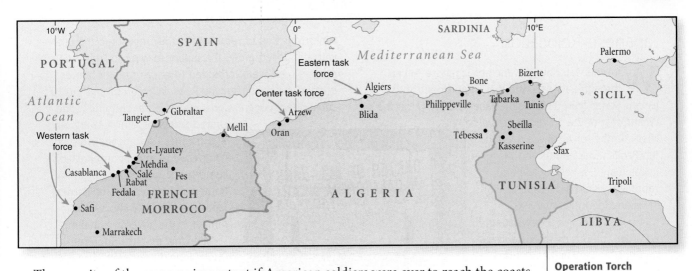

The security of the seas was important if American soldiers were ever to reach the coasts of Europe. Throughout the first half of 1942, Great Britain's prime minister, Winston Churchill, and President Roosevelt discussed where Allied forces should initiate their strike into Europe, but they could not agree. That they needed to strike soon was clear, if for no other reason than that their third ally, Russia, was suffering the brunt of the war. Hitler had invaded Russia in 1940, and though his forces had been pushed back the following year, by the spring of 1942 they were again advancing toward Moscow. Stalin called on his allies to open a second front in Europe to draw part of Hitler's strength from Russia.

Roosevelt and Churchill agreed on what became known as "Operation Torch." A combined American and British force would seize the North African port cities of Oran and Algiers on the Mediterranean coast and Morocco on the Atlantic coast. After securing North Africa (by defeating the German *Nord Afrika* Corps under General Erwin Rommel), the allies would invade Italy. Under American General Dwight David Eisenhower (commander-in-chief of the ground forces) and British admiral Sir Andrew Cunningham (commander of naval operations), Operation Torch was set to commence in the fall of 1942.

The Tide Turns in the Pacific

The Japanese held strong positions along the probable route the American navy would take in its push toward Japan. The route lay along a ribbon of islands that began in the South Pacific and included the Philippines, Formosa (Taiwan), and the Ryukyus. At the very gate of this route, however, the Japanese held Tulagi Island in the Solomon Islands, Rabaul on the island of New Britain, off the north coast of New Guinea, and two positions on the north coast of New Guinea itself. From these bases, land-based Japanese planes commanded all approaches to the coveted invasion route.

The American forces needed to break through this Japanese "wall" of islands. On August 7, 1942, U.S. Marines landed at Guadalcanal in the Solomons where the Japanese were building an air base. The landing was uncontested but the possession of Guadalcanal, as events would prove, would be hotly contested. Over the next several months, so many naval battles were fought in the waters about Guadalcanal that soldiers named them Ironbottom Sound, for all the ships that sank there.

In the first major naval battle, that of Savo Island, the United States lost four cruisers. For the next three months, control of the seas around Guadalcanal changed every 12 hours. During the day, because of superior air power, the American navy held sway; but at night the Japanese dominated. Every night, Japanese transports dropped soldiers into the waters off Guadalcanal, and these, swimming to shore, fought desperate battles with American Marines and army. So brutal was the fighting that American soldiers thought Guadalcanal a foretaste of Hell.

Japanese Relocation

With the victorious advance of Japanese forces through East Asia, the War Department of the United States feared a possible Japanese attack on the West Coast of the United States. A large number of Japanese lived in the Pacific Coast states and these, it was feared, by espionage and sabotage, would aid a Japanese invasion. So, on February 19, 1942, President Roosevelt issued an order authorizing the establishment of "military areas . . . from which any or all persons may be excluded" and where their right to enter or remain could be restricted. Though the order did not specify the "persons" whom this order affected, it applied to 112,000 Japanese (two-thirds of whom were U.S. citizens) who lived in Washington, Oregon, and California.

The government established Civil Control Stations along the West Coast, to which Japanese

Newspapers announcing the impending Japanese relocation policy

Americans had to report. After they registered themselves with the government, the Japanese went to "relocation centers" and were forbidden to return to their homes. In court cases challenging Roosevelt's order and the subsequent congressional resolution supporting it, the United States government argued that Japanese Americans were not compelled to remain at relocation centers; still, separated from their homes and places of employment, Japanese had little choice but to remain at the government camps.

The United States Supreme Court upheld Roosevelt's order, arguing that it fell under the power of the "national government . . . to wage war successfully." Though in *Hirabayashi v. United States*, the court conceded that "distinctions between citizens solely because of their ancestry are by their very nature odious to a free people whose institutions are founded upon the doctrine of equality," it argued that the emergency of war allows the government to take precautions it could not take in peacetime.

After three months of futile fighting, the Japanese planned an all out bombardment of the American airfield at Guadalcanal. On the night of Friday, November 13, the American fleet steamed out to surprise the incoming Japanese fleet. A confusing battle ensued, with American ships firing on American ships as well as on the Japanese. That night, though five American and three Japanese ships had been severely damaged, the Japanese failed to destroy the American airfield.

For three more months the Japanese tried to dislodge the Americans from Guadalcanal but failed in every attempt. Finally, the Japanese gave up and, on February 9, 1943, evacuated their troops from Guadalcanal. By capturing Guadalcanal, the Americans had punched an opening in the Japanese wall of defense. By the end of January, 1943, American and Australian soldiers had driven the Japanese from the coast of New Guinea, from Papua to Huon Gulf. The tide had turned. The United States could now take the offensive in the Pacific war.

Invasion of Europe and Advance into The Pacific

The invasion of North Africa was a complex operation. Three amphibious task forces had to coordinate their movements so that they arrived undetected on the coast of North Africa at roughly the same time. By midnight of November 7–8, 1942, the task forces had landed: two forces, under British command, at Oran in Algiers, and one under American command, at Casablanca. The Germans and Italians were completely surprised. The troops from Vichy France, which held North Africa, gave only a weak resistance, and General Eisenhower was able to persuade Admiral J.L. Darlan, the Vichy commander of the French in Algiers, to issue a cease-fire. This sparing of the Vichy French army angered many Communists and other leftists in the United States, who accused Roosevelt of compromising with Fascists. The "Darlan Deal," however, probably spared the lives of many Allied soldiers.

With North Africa in their possession, Roosevelt and Churchill met in Casablanca in January 1943 to discuss the further conduct of the war. Stalin, occupied with the German invasion of Russia, could not attend the conference. The news from the war fronts was good. The Russians had stopped the Germans at Stalingrad and captured an army of 91,000 men; the British had saved Egypt from Rommel's advance at Alamein; Allied forces in Morocco and Algiers were gathering strength. In order draw at least some German forces from Russia, Churchill, Roosevelt and the their combined military chiefs-of-staff decided, once they had fully secured Tunisia, to invade Sicily and, from there, to advance into Italy.

At Casablanca, the Allied leaders agreed on policies that would have profound effects on the war effort. Hearkening back to the example of General Ulysses S. Grant at Fort Donelson, Roosevelt proposed that the Allies accept nothing short of "unconditional surrender" from the Axis powers. "In an attempt to ward off the inevitable disaster" of defeat, Roosevelt told the American people after the Casablanca Conference in a February Fireside Chat, "the Axis propagandists are trying all of their old tricks in order to divide the United Nations. . . .

> This is their final effort to turn one nation against another, in the vain hope that they may settle with one or two [nations] at a time—that any of us may be so gullible and so forgetful as to be duped into making "deals" at the expense of our Allies. To these panicky attempts to escape the consequences of their crimes, we say . . . that the only terms on which we shall deal with an Axis government or any Axis factions are the terms proclaimed at Casablanca: "Unconditional Surrender." In our uncompromising policy we mean no harm to the common people of the Axis nations. But we do mean to impose punishment and retribution in full upon their guilty, barbaric leaders. . . .

Roosevelt and Churchill at Casablanca

But the "common people of the Axis nations" would be affected by another policy adopted at Casablanca—the "Combined Bomber Offensive," which included strategic bombing. Before the American entry into the war, the British Royal Air Force (RAF) had been engaged in night air raids on strategic cities of Germany—cities with war industries, oil refineries, synthetic rubber factories, etc. Because the raids were carried out at night, civilian centers in cities, as well as the strategic targets, suffered destruction. The Combined Bomber Offensive (CBO) would continue and expand this war policy: the RAF would bomb strategic cities by night, while the United States Army Air Force carried on more precise strikes during the day. The CBO's objective, according to a general directive issued from Casablanca, was "the progressive destruction and dislocation of the German military, industrial and economic system, and the undermining of the morale of the German people to the point where their capacity for armed defense is fatally weakened." Thus, the targets would not be purely military, but civilian, as well.

The Germans did not long delay in meeting the Allied threat in North Africa. No sooner had the Allies invaded than the Germans flew 20,000 men to North Africa and established fighter and bomber bases in Tunisia. In February, General Rommel (called "Desert Fox" for his wiliness) maneuvered his *Nord Afrika* Corps to cut the Allied forces in two. At the battle of the Kasserine Pass, February 14, 1943, Rommel defeated the inexperienced American troops. Five days later, however, American General George Patton, with two armored divisions, the Allied air force, and British forces forced Rommel to retreat into Tunisia. Pursuing Rommel, the Allied force of 500,000 men attacked Rommel at two points—the British at Tunis and the Americans at Bizerbe. Both cities fell to the Allies on May 7. Six days later, the cornered German army of 275,000 men surrendered. Tunisia had been secured for the allies. They could now advance into Italy.

Allied Bombing and The Invasion of Italy

While Allied armies fought Rommel in the North African desert, Allied bombing raids wreaked destruction on Germany's industrial cities. Beginning in March 1943, the RAF began bombing cities in the industrial Ruhr region of Germany. Because it was difficult to spot industrial complexes at night, British planes dropped their bombs on city centers, which burned more quickly than outlying areas. Bombing laid waste old, beautiful works of art and architecture in Düsseldorf, Essen, and Köln (Cologne). In late May, 2,000 tons of bombs were dropped on Dortmund. In July, the RAF began firebombing cities. In Hamburg the bombing created a firestorm that destroyed one-half of the houses in the city and killed 50,000 inhabitants. In November, the RAF and the United States Army Air Force began round-the-clock bombing of the German capital, Berlin, destroying three and one-half square miles of the city.

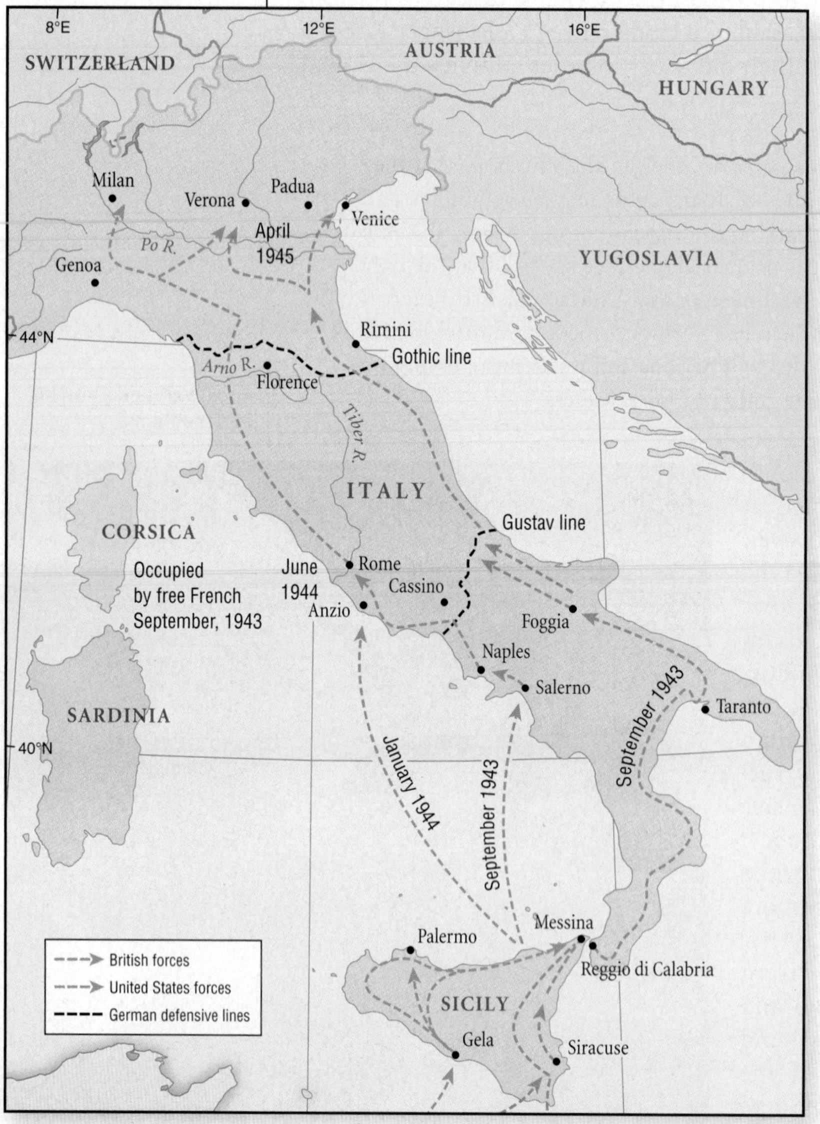

In July 1943, an Allied force of 250,000, commanded by General Dwight David Eisenhower, landed on Sicily, surprising the island's German and Italian defenders. Breaking through stiff German resistance at the Gela beachhead, the Seventh Army under General Patton swept across Sicily. On July 22, Patton entered Palermo on the north coast of Sicily. By August 17, the Allies had taken the entire island. The stage was now set for the invasion of the Italian peninsula.

The Italians, sick of the war, were on the verge of complete capitulation. On July 25, six days after 560 Allied planes bombed Rome, Italy's King Vittorio Emanuele III forced Benito Mussolini to resign as pre-

Invasion of Italy, 1943

Map labels: SWITZERLAND, AUSTRIA, HUNGARY, YUGOSLAVIA, ITALY, CORSICA, SARDINIA, SICILY. Cities: Milan, Verona, Padua, Venice, Genoa, Po R., Arno R., Florence, Tiber R., Rimini, Gothic line, Rome, Cassino, Anzio, Gustav line, Foggia, Naples, Salerno, Taranto, Palermo, Messina, Reggio di Calabria, Gela, Siracuse. Dates: April 1945, June 1944, January 1944, September 1943. Occupied by free French September, 1943.

Legend:
- British forces
- United States forces
- German defensive lines

The U.S.S. *Rowan* explodes after being hit by a German bomb, near Gela, Sicily, during the invasion of Sicily

mier and appointed Marshal Pietro Badoglio in his place. Badoglio immediately began to seek peace terms with the Allies; but because of the Allies' policy of unconditional surrender, negotiations dragged out to early September—enough time for the Germans to move reinforcements into Italy. Thus, though Italy formally surrendered on September 3, 1943, German forces held key positions in Italy, including Rome.

German forces bitterly contested the Allied landing at Salerno on September 9, but by September 16, the Allies had established a beach head there. The Germans made an orderly retirement northward. On October 1, Allied forces seized Naples, a city the Germans had attempted to destroy. Only 100 miles lay between Naples and Rome, but stiff German resistance bogged down the Allied advance for eight months. Though outnumbered, the Germans held a stout defensive line whose anchor was the monastery of Monte Cassino, founded by St. Benedict of Nursia in the sixth century. Unable to break the Gustav line, the Allies, on January 22, 1944, attempted another landing at Anzio, to the north of Naples, to draw off some of the German forces. Another German force, unknown to the Allies, met them at Anzio, and the attempt to break the German line failed.

In February 1944, the Allies assaulted the Gustav line and bombed the historic monastery. As it turned out, the bombing of Monte Cassino had no strategic significance; the Germans had used it neither as a headquarters nor as a depot for arms or soldiers. In May, 1944, the Allies finally pushed the Germans from the Gustav line. Retiring, the Germans formed another line (the "Gothic line") to the north of the Arno River, while the victorious Allies marched into and liberated Rome on June 4, 1944.

A priest leads soldiers through the ruins of Monte Cassino

Playing Leap Frog in the Pacific

For five months after Guadalcanal, the Pacific witnessed no major battles between the Allies and Japan. General MacArthur used this period of relative calm to work out his war strategy. Instead of attacking heavily fortified Japanese positions, MacArthur decided to seize less strongly fortified islands between Japanese positions and the home island. By "leap-frogging" (as MacArthur termed it) from island to island, the United States forces it was hoped could sever the limbs of the Japanese military from their trunk and so neutralize them. MacArthur himself would move by way of the Bismarck Islands, and Admiral Nimitz, through the Gilberts, Marshalls, and Carolines. Their forces would meet and together make a drive into the Philippines, China, or Japan itself.

Beginning in mid 1943, the U.S. Navy began the campaign by which it would wrest control of the waters around the Solomon Islands. Having secured a passage through the Coral Sea and the Bismarcks into the western Pacific, MacArthur leap-frogged around the Japanese position at Rabaul, neutralizing 100,000 Japanese troops in March 1944. Admiral Nimitz, further north, took Makin and Tarawa islands, and by August 1, 1944 occupied Saipan, Tinian, and Guam in the Marianas.

On June 16, the Japanese received a foretaste of what defeat held in store for them. U.S. B-29 bombers brought death to the Japanese homeland, bombing not only military and industrial targets, but civilian centers as well. Three days later, Japan's Admiral Jisaburo Ozawa engaged the American fleet in the Philippine Sea. Wave after wave of Japanese fighter planes were downed by American aircraft. The next day, June 20, Ozawa ordered another attack but was soundly repulsed. Out of 420 planes, only 35 remained to Ozawa at the end of the day. The Japanese admiral had been decisively defeated.

Teheran

The surrender of Rommel's *Nord Afrika* Corps in May 1943 had given the Allies control of the Mediterranean. The British and Americans could now directly aid and supply the Russians by way of the Suez Canal, the Red Sea, and the Persian Gulf. The Allied victory gave the three central Allied leaders the opportunity to meet face-to-face. From November 28 to December 1, 1943, Roosevelt, Churchill, and Stalin met at Teheran in Iran to discuss the progress of the war and, after victory had been won, how to rebuild Europe.

Neither Roosevelt nor Churchill thought Stalin a champion of freedom and democracy, yet Roosevelt expressed the fond hope that he could accomplish much by appeasing the Communist dictator. "I think that if I give him [Stalin] everything I possibly can and ask nothing from him in return . . . ," said Roosevelt, "he won't try to annex anything and will work with me for a world of democracy and peace." And Stalin did agree to some of Roosevelt's desires: the establishment, after the war, of a United Nations organization and Russian entrance into the war against Japan. But Stalin demanded much in return.

Stalin, Roosevelt, and Churchill at Teheran

Stalin claimed he needed a "security belt" (that would include the Baltic states, and eastern Poland) to protect Russia from future invasion. In private talks, Roosevelt agreed to Stalin's demands and said he was willing to give Stalin German East Prussia; he only asked the Soviet dictator to keep their deal under raps until after the 1944 election. Roosevelt further agreed to a new eastern border for Germany, at the Oder River, and to the deportation, "on a voluntary basis," of Poles from eastern Poland.

Among Roosevelt's proposals at Teheran was the post-war division of Germany into five small zones—a proposal that surprised even Churchill, who was no lover of Germany. When, at dinner, Stalin suggested that, after the war, the Allies would have to execute 50,000 German officers, Churchill strongly objected. Such an act would be "barbaric," he said. Roosevelt, however, laughed off Stalin's suggestion. Perhaps they would need execute only 49,500 officers, he joked.

The Catholic Response to the War

American Catholics were initially no more willing to rush to war than were other Americans. Indeed, many Catholics of German ancestry were loathe to fight against Germany, and Irish Catholics wished to give no aid to embattled Britain. In the election of 1940, many German and Irish Catholics opposed Roosevelt on account of his obvious support for Great Britain against Germany.

Even after the German invasion of Catholic Poland, the American bishops gave little support for a U.S. role in the European war. In a 1939 statement, the bishops warned Americans "neither to be carried away by intemperate emotion, nor to become victims of hate mongers who set loose the evils of cupidity, anger, envy and revenge . . . Our primary duty is that of preserving the strength, stability, and security of our own nation, not, indeed, in a spirit of selfish isolation, but rather in a spirit of justice and charity to those people whose welfare is our first and chief responsibility."

Prior to the outbreak of the war, the American bishops had voiced their strong opposition to atheistic Communism. When Catholics of Jewish ancestry, members of the German Catholic Center Party, and others opposed to Nazism fled Germany for the United States, the bishops, besides establishing an aid committee for these refugees, turned their thoughts to the evils of Nazism. In 1937, the American bishops spoke out publicly against the Nazi government of Germany. In April 1939, the Administrative Board of the National Catholic Welfare Conference (NCWC), as the body representing the nation's bishops was called, condemned anti-Semitism. The condemnation was repeated in a bishops' pastoral letter of November 1941: "We cannot too strongly condemn the inhuman treatment to which the Jewish people have been subjected in many countries."

After the bombing of Pearl Harbor, Archbishop Edmund Mooney of Detroit, who sat on the NCWC's Administrative Board, declared in a letter to Roosevelt the bishops' support for the war. Most Catholics agreed. In their minds, Japan and Germany were unjust aggressors and stopping their predations was obviously a just cause. The American bishops, however, warned against excesses. In a November 1942 pastoral letter they declared that the war must maintain the high moral purpose enunciated by Roosevelt in his war aims. That young men, merely teenagers, were being drafted and that women left their homes to work in factories was a matter of concern for the bishops. Then, the lack of a religious dimension to the struggle disturbed the bishops. "Secularism," they wrote, "cannot write a real and lasting peace."

In November 1943, the bishops issued another statement outlining the conditions for a lasting peace. The recognition of the sovereignty of God and of the primacy of the moral law, the bishops wrote, were the necessary foundations for peace. All men, regardless of race, said the bishops, have natural rights that cannot be violated. The sovereignty of all nations, the bishops said, must also be respected.

The Second World War saw the first stirrings of a pacifist movement among Catholics. Some Catholics, including a few priests, had come to the conclusion that, because of its destructive power, modern war could not possibly be justified by just war criteria. In 1944, a popular retreat priest, Father John J. Hugo, published a book, *The Gospel of Peace*, which argued this point. Though some who took this stand changed their minds after Pearl Harbor, others remained steadfast in their conviction and refused to enlist in the military or submit to the draft. At the center of the Catholic pacifist movement was Dorothy Day and the Catholic Worker Movement. In the late '30s, Day's neutral stance over the Spanish Civil War angered some of her readers; but her espousal of pacifism in the face of Hitler and the Japanese further alienated many Catholics. Some Catholic Worker houses closed over the issue, and the *Catholic Worker* lost a large number of subscribers. Still, the Catholic Workers would not back down over their pacifism. (Peter Maurin, because of a debilitating stroke, did not engage in the war controversy.) In explanation of her pacifist stance, Dorothy Day wrote in 1940:

> Many Catholics oppose the use of the word pacifism. But Father Stratmann, O.P., writes: "The triumph of Pacifism, the condemnation of war, and the declaration of passive resistance, is just as little opposed to tradition as was the attitude of the Church towards slavery or serfdom, or the dogma of the Immaculate Conception, or the Infallibility of the Pope. Only he who does not realize the wonder of the Church and her life in Christ, can be disturbed that her progress is impeded—not he who believes in Christ and His Church." Theologians have laid down conditions for a just war . . . and many modern writers, clerical and lay, hold that these conditions are impossible of fulfillment in these present times of bombardment of civilians, open cities, the use of poison gas, etc. Fr. Stratmann, in his book, *The Church and War*, speaks of how "many fervent Catholics are awaiting a moral definition about war, for a decisive word as to its immorality . . . That the Church should forbid war belongs to those things of which our Lord says: 'I have many things to say unto you but you cannot hear them now.'" And how agonizingly true is it when we consider the millions in Europe and China defending with their lives and at untold suffering, believing it the only way for their country, their families, their institution and their Faith.

Pope Pius XII at his coronation, seated in the *Sedes Gestatoria*

Though Dorothy Day and other Catholic pacifists appealed to the writings of Popes Pius XI and Pius XII for a justification of their pacifism, the popes never went so far as to condemn modern war absolutely. Still, Pope Pius XII could use strong language in speaking of the instruments of modern war. In his 1940 Easter Message, the pope acknowledged "the valor and loyalty of all those who with a deep sense of duty are fighting for the defense and prosperity of their homeland" and "the many generous and praiseworthy gestures of magnanimity which have been made towards the enemy." Still, Pius said:

> We feel obliged nonetheless to state that the ruthless struggle has at times assumed forms which can be described only as atrocious. May all belligerents, who also have human hearts molded by mothers' love, show some feeling of charity for the sufferings of civilian populations, for defenseless women and children, for the sick and aged, all of whom are often exposed to greater and more widespread perils of war than those faced by soldiers at the front!
>
> We beseech the belligerent powers to abstain until the very end from the use of still more homicidal instruments of warfare; for the introduction of such weapons inevitably results in their retaliatory use, often with greater violence by the enemy. If already We must lament the fact that the limits of legitimate warfare have been repeatedly exceeded, would not the more widespread use of increasingly barbarous offensive weapons soon transform war into unspeakable horror?

In his 1942 Christmas message, broadcast by radio to the world, the pope said the sorrows of war came from the world's rejection of God and truth. The "earthly city," he said, had been separated from the "City of God." Mankind had embraced false ideas about God and man. The pope condemned "Marxist socialism," but he spoke out against the Liberal economic system that oppressed workers, depriving them of a just wage for their labor and robbing them of their dignity. Liberal ideas about the state, said Pius, had destroyed a true idea of the state and led finally to the belief that the state has complete power over everyone and everything in society.

The Last Years

The Allied air war on Germany had been harsh but it had not seriously affected Germany's war production. Nor had it weakened German civilian morale. The rising civilian death tolls only convinced Germans that the Allies were brutal enemies and steeled German resolve to resist the Allies to the last extremity.

The air war, though, had this effect; it so weakened the German *Luftwaffe* (air force) that control of the air passed to the Allies. By April 1944, the Allies held a 30-to-one ratio of air superiority over the Germans, though this came at the heavy loss of 158,000 aviators. Still, control of the airways would be crucial in the next stage of the war: the invasion of France.

The allies had been building up their forces in southern England in preparation for an invasion of Normandy. Allied troops, 2.8 million strong, awaited only the command of General Eisenhower to fall upon the enemy, who lay behind stout defenses—mines, bristling artillery, tank, artillery "pill boxes"—across the English Channel. The Allies had fooled the German high command, which expected General Patton to cross the Straits of Dover from southeast England to Pas-de-Calais; instead, the invasion would come from farther west against the less stoutly defended coastline of Normandy.

Before dawn on June 6, 1944, code named "D-Day," 600 warships, 4,000 support craft, carrying 176,000 men, crossed the channel. At dawn, three Allied paratroop divisions were dropped behind the beachheads, and the Battle for Normandy began. Following the naval bombardment, which commenced at first light, American divisions landed on the westward beaches, while British forces assailed the enemy to the east. Within the first week, the Allies landed

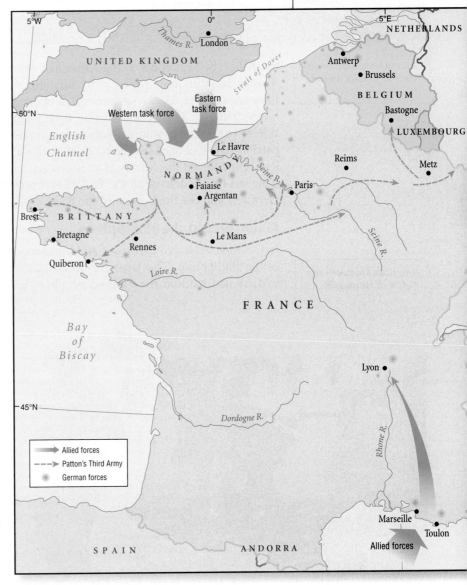

D-Day landings and Patton's Third Army attacks

American troops disembark at Omaha Beach, Normandy

326,000 men, 50,000 vehicles, and 100,000 tons of supplies on the beachhead at Normandy. German opposition was fierce but ineffective at stopping the Allied advance. Though the unleashing of Hitler's secret weapons on London—the V-1 "buzz bombs"—wrought much destruction, they could not halt the Allies.

By July 24, the Allies occupied Normandy. On July 25 began the Battle for France. Over the next two weeks, General Patton's army swept through Brittany to the Loire and Le Mans and destroyed the German VII Army at Falaise Gap. On August 15, the Allied VII Army invaded southern France from the ports of Toulon and Marseilles, and pushed, by way of the Rhone Valley to Lyons. On August 25, General Patton's army liberated Paris, and Charles de Gaulle took up the presidency of restored France.

The German army melted away before the Allies. By September 4, the Allies had entered Belgium, taking Brussels and Antwerp. A week later, another Allied army liberated Luxembourg and crossed into Germany. In the east, on June 23, Soviet forces had opened an 800 mile front, from Leningrad to the Carpathians. In five weeks, Russian forces had crossed Ukraine and Poland, parking outside of the Polish capital of Warsaw long enough to allow Nazis in the city to kill Polish patriots who had opposed the Nazis and would oppose Communist rule. Further south, the Red Army forced the surrender of Romania. In Italy, the Allies had driven the Germans to their last line of defense in the Po Valley. Everything was now prepared for the invasion of Germany and the final defeat of the Axis.

MacArthur in the Philippines

In October 1944, two thrusts of American forces in the Pacific coalesced in the Leyte Gulf in the Philippines. The Japanese occupation of the Philippines had been cruel. Japanese soldiers had reduced the Filipino people to poverty. At times, Japanese soldiers marched groups of Filipino men into the jungles and murdered them. Thus, MacArthur's proclamation upon landing on Leyte Island on October 23—"People of the Philippines, I have returned"—filled that oppressed people with hope.

American troops in the Battle of Normandy

But the winning of the Philippines would not be easy. The Japanese high command, staking all to drive MacArthur and Nimitz from the Philippine islands, sent the entire Japanese fleet south. The Battle of Leyte Gulf, October 25, 1944, proved to be the largest sea battle history has seen. The American navy and air force were able to defeat a formidable foe and drive the Japanese navy from Philippine waters. Never again would the Japanese navy prove

Douglas MacArthur (center) and troops alight at Leyte

a significant threat to U.S. ships, though in this battle Americans experienced the force of a new weapon, the *kamikaze* (meaning "Divine Wind")—aviators who flew their planes in suicide missions to destroy American ships. Winning a sea battle, too, did not fully liberate the Philippines. Months of ground fighting against the dogged Japanese opposition awaited the American army.

The victories in the Pacific and in Europe, perhaps, helped Roosevelt to victory in the 1944 election. The Republicans had wanted to run Douglas MacArthur as their candidate, but the general, though eager to be president, declined the honor; he had first, he said, to liberate the Philippines. The pro-war, pro-internationalist Wendell Willkie also shied from seeking the candidacy after losing a primary in Wisconsin where isolationist sentiment was still strong. The Republicans finally chose Thomas E. Dewey, the governor of New York, as their presidential candidate.

The Republicans took heart from the results of the 1942 congressional elections, where they had gained a 30 percent increase in the House of Representatives. Pro-war as they were, the Republicans had to resort to a platform that said it was a dangerous thing for one party (not to mention one man) to remain in power for 12 years. There was, too, some question about Roosevelt's health, though his doctors insisted that he was fit to continue in office. But none of this was enough to convince the people to throw over a president in the middle of a war. Roosevelt and his running mate, Harry S. Truman of Missouri, took 36 states, winning 432 electoral votes to Dewey's total of 12 states and 99 electoral votes.

The Invasion of Germany

The Allied onslaught in Europe bogged down along the fortifications that guarded the German fatherland. Though by mid-October, Aachen, the ancient capital of Charlemagne, had fallen and the Allies had taken Metz and Strasbourg, the Allied advance into the Saar region in November was halted by fierce German opposition in early December. Dreading the dishonor of unconditional surrender (a policy that Pope Pius XII had asked the Allies to abandon) and fearing the vengeful violence of the invading armies, the Germans put up the stubborn defense of despair.

In mid-December, the German army made one last desperate gamble to break the Allied lines. In the Battle of the Bulge, the German army assaulted the Allied lines around Bastogne. Though by December 22, the Allied situation looked desperate, by December 26 Allied reinforcements saved Bastogne. German losses were heavy—1,000 planes and 120,000 men. By January 15, the lines had returned to what they had been before mid-December.

In late January, the Allies resumed their advance to the Rhine while the Russians, in the east, were directing an invasion along a 1,000-mile front. To hamper German troop movements, the Allies decided to bomb eastern German cities. B-29s assaulted Dresden, a city with no military significance, no anti-aircraft defenses, but filled with hundreds of thousands of war refugees. On February 13, 1945, Allied planes dropped incendiary bombs that ignited firestorms that laid waste the city. Three hours later came more B-29s and more incendiary bombs. The fires that consumed Dresden claimed an estimated 135,000 lives.

Yalta and the Fall of Germany

Though the Red Army had reached Berlin, Stalin, on February 3, ordered his general to delay his assault on the German capital. The Russian dictator had first to meet with Churchill and Roosevelt to discuss the disposition of Europe after the defeat of Hitler. Stalin had become indispensable to the Allied war effort. His was the largest army in Europe—12 million men in 300 divisions, three times the size of Eisenhower's army. The Red Army engaged 125 to 200 German divisions on the Eastern Front, keeping them from the Western Front. Stalin could negotiate with Great Britain and the United States from a position of strength.

Stalin had already won concessions from Churchill. In 1944, the two leaders had met to divide up their respective "spheres of influence" in Eastern Europe. To Great Britain would go Greece and to Russia, Romania. The two powers would split Yugoslavia and Hungary between them. Churchill, perhaps, thought that Yugoslavia and Greece would have enough democrats to keep them from falling under Communist domination. Though Roosevelt objected to this deal, he did nothing to hinder it. Stalin was too important an ally to alienate.

Thus, when Churchill and Roosevelt met with Stalin at Yalta on the Black Sea on February 4, 1945, the stage was well set for further concessions and capitulations to the Soviet Union.

Dresden after the bombing, as seen from the *Ratshaus* (city hall). The statue is an allegory of goodness.

Churchill, Roosevelt, and Stalin at the Yalta Conference

Stalin, like Hitler, could be very pleasant one on one; Roosevelt gave him the homely nickname, "Uncle Joe." Roosevelt wanted assurance from Stalin that Russia would support the formation of an international organization called the United Nations. In return, F.D.R. was willing to grant Stalin's demands—three votes in the United Nations, the right to regulate the formation of the government of Poland (Stalin promised democratic elections there), and the right to the use of forced German labor for a period of ten years. In return for his promise to enter the war against Japan, Churchill and Roosevelt gave Stalin control of the Manchuria railroad, of the port of Darien, and of naval bases at Port Arthur, the Kurile Islands, and South Sakhalin. When the Yalta conference ended on February 12, 1945, Roosevelt, in answer to criticisms of these concessions, said, "I didn't say the result was good. I said it was the best I could do."

Meanwhile, on the western front, the Allies were finally able to break through the German defensive lines. Beginning in late March 1945, Allied armies began crossing the Rhine and advanced to the Ruhr River. After April 14, all effective German opposition ended. Allied armies marched through Bavaria in the South, discovering the concentration camps where Nazis had imprisoned Jews and Gypsies, along with Germans, including Catholic and Protestant clergy, who had opposed the Nazi regime. From the west, Allied armies pierced to the Elbe while the Russians attacked Berlin. On April 30, Adolf Hitler and his longtime mistress, Eva Braun, committed suicide in a bunker in Berlin and, soon after, the Russians captured the German capital. Admiral Doenitz, the new head of the German government, approached Eisenhower to discuss surrender, but the American general insisted, in the spirit of Yalta, that Doenitz instead surrender to the Russians. On May 4, the Allies crushed all German resistance in Italy, and three days later, the German government signed an agreement of unconditional surrender with the Allies. The war in Europe had ended.

Roosevelt did not live to see the end of his efforts. Returning to the United States after the Yalta Conference, the president retired to his winter home in Warm Springs, Georgia. There, he prepared for the opening of the United Nations Organization in San Francisco, California. On April 12, 1945, as he sat writing his address for the upcoming Jefferson Day, he died suddenly from a cerebral hemorrhage. The last words he had written before his death succinctly expressed the progressivism he had always championed: "The only limit to our realization of tomorrow will be our doubts of today. Let us move forward with strong and active faith."

Victory in the Pacific

The American army and navy in the Pacific were making steady advances against the Japanese while German resistance crumbled in Europe. From the island of Saipan, American bombing raids pounded Japanese cities to dust, progressively destroying Japan's industrial capability to make war, as well as killing tens of thousands of Japanese civilians—men, women and children. The U.S. firebombing of Tokyo laid waste to 56 square miles of the city, killing upwards to 135,000. On February 19, 1945, American forces landed on the island of Iwo Jima, commencing a bloody battle that would continue until March 14. On February 23, American Marines took Mount Suribachi on Iwo Jima, placing the American flag on its height. In taking Iwo Jima, the army and Marines lost 6,855 men as well as suffering 21,000 additional casualties.

On Easter Sunday, April 1, the Americans landed on Okinawa island in the Ryukyus. Japanese *kamikaze* raids took a heavy toll of American ships, sinking 32 of them and badly damaging 61 others. Japanese resistance resulted in the death of over 12,500 American sailors, soldiers, and aviators. Not until late June was Japanese resistance on the island at last overwhelmed.

The fall of Hitler's Germany allowed British forces to join the American effort in the Pacific. Though some sectors of the Japanese government were sending out feelers for peace negotiations (they were, it seems, willing to agree to all Allied demands, but wanted assurance that the Emperor Hirohito would remain head of government), the Allies insisted on complete surrender, without any conditions. This policy of unconditional surrender meant that the Allies faced the prospect of a land invasion of Japan that would likely result in the deaths of tens of thousands of Allied soldiers, as well as of countless civilians. If they did not abandon their policy of unconditional surrender, the Allies had either to accept the grim prospects of an invasion or use other means to end the war.

When Harry Truman became president following Roosevelt's death, he learned for the first time that the United States had been working on a new, secret weapon. Among the refugees from Europe were a number of physicists, including the German Jew Albert Einstein, the Italian Enrico Fermi, and the Hungarian Leó Szilárd. These physicists had warned President Roosevelt that German scientists were working on the concept of uranium

The theater of war around Japan, 1945

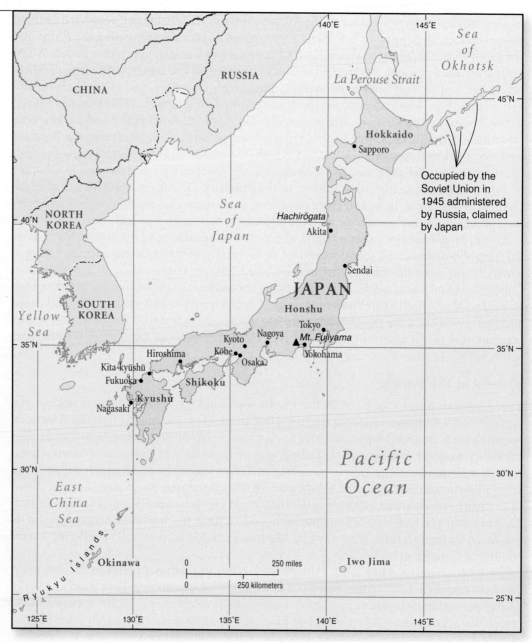

fission to produce a bomb that could wipe out large sections of cities. To beat the Germans, the United States commenced the Manhattan Project. In centers throughout the country, this top-secret project worked to master the splitting of the atom. On December 2, 1942, Fermi and other physicists had produced the first self-sustaining nuclear chain reaction. By 1944, J. Robert Oppenheimer, at the laboratories at Los Alamos, New Mexico, had developed the first atomic bomb. On July 16, 1945, this atomic bomb was successfully exploded at Los Alamos. The United States now possessed a weapon that the broken but desperate might of Japan could not withstand. In a message to Churchill, Truman declared, "this is the Second Coming in wrath."

A committee of high officials and atomic scientists recommended to Truman that, if Japan did not agree to an unconditional surrender, an atomic bomb should be exploded without warning, and as soon as possible, over Japan. Meeting at Potsdam, Germany, with Allied leaders, Truman, on July 25, sent an order to the Army Air Force division on Saipan:

if Japan does not surrender by August 3, drop two atomic bombs on the Japanese mainland as soon as practicable.

On July 26, Truman, Churchill, and the Combined Chiefs of Staff at Potsdam gave Japan an ultimatum. "We call upon the government of Japan to proclaim now the unconditional surrender of Japanese armed forces, and to provide proper and adequate assurances of their good faith in such action." Japan must surrender all lands she had conquered since 1895 and must allow Allied occupation of Japan until "a peacefully inclined and responsible government" be established. If this ultimatum is refused, said the Allies, "the alternative for Japan is prompt and utter destruction." No assurance was given to the fulfillment of Japan's one remaining demand—that the Emperor Hirohito (whom the Japanese considered divine) remain on the throne.

Japan's reply to the Potsdam ultimatum was the laconic, "no comment." The Japanese government had no inkling of the new power the United States held to fulfill the Allied threat.

On the morning of August 6, 1945, Colonel Paul W. Tibbets and his crew boarded the B-29 bomber, the *Enola Gay,* for an expedition over the Japanese city of Hiroshima. Tibbets knew his plane carried a new sort of bomb but of its nature be knew nothing. He and his men knew it as "The Gimmick." Just before 9:15 a.m., Captain Robert Lewis, on board the *Enola Gay,* wrote in his log, "There will be a short intermission while we bomb our target." Then they dropped the bomb. A tremendous shock followed. The sky was suffused with the light of many suns, the blinding dawn of a new and terrible day. Lewis' next entry was merely, "My God."

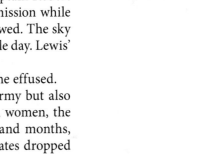

J. Robert Oppenheimer

Truman, hearing the news, rejoiced. "This is the greatest thing in history," he effused.

The atomic bomb that struck Hiroshima destroyed the second Japanese army but also leveled four square miles of the city and killed 60,175 people—soldiers, men, women, the old, and children; the innocent with the guilty. In subsequent days, weeks and months, many more would die of radiation poisoning. Three days later, the United States dropped the second atomic bomb, this time on nearby Nagasaki, a city with no military significance. Nagasaki was the Catholic center of Japan; ground zero was near the Catholic cathedral. Thirty-six thousand civilians died in this terror bombing.

The bombings had their desired effect. On August 14, the Emperor Hirohito, long an advocate of peace, surrendered. The formal act of unconditional surrender was signed aboard the *U.S.S Missouri* on September 2, 1945. The Second World War was finished.

The mushroom cloud from the atomic bomb dropped on Nagasaki

The American people, for the most part, greeted the bombings of Hiroshima and Nagasaki with enthusiasm; the terrible ordeal of war was over, no more sacrifice of our men was required. But some voices protested. Hanson Baldwin, writing in the *New York Times,* declared, "We are the inheritors of Genghis Khan and of all those in history who have justified the use of utter ruthlessness in war." On August 29, the influential Protestant journal, the *Christian Century* declared:

Ruins of a Buddhist temple in Nagasaki, after the bombing (left). The Catholic cathedral of Nagasaki rises in the background (right).

The atomic bomb was used at a time when Japan's navy was sunk, her air force virtually destroyed, her homeland surrounded, her supplies cut off, and our forces poised for the final stroke . . . Our leaders seem not to have weighed the moral considerations involved. No sooner was the bomb ready than it was rushed to the front and dropped on two helpless cities . . . The atomic bomb can fairly be said to have struck Christianity itself . . . The churches of America must dissociate themselves and their faith from this inhuman and reckless act of the American Government.

Like their countrymen American Catholics, for the most part, approved of the bombings, but some Catholics vociferously condemned them. Hiroshima and Nagasaki, said *Commonweal*, "are names for American guilt and shame." In the *Catholic Worker*, Dorothy Day made a play on the president's name: "Mr. Truman was jubilant," she wrote:

President Truman. True man; what a strange name, come to think of it. We refer to Jesus Christ as true God and true Man. Truman is a true man of his time in that he was jubilant. He was not a son of God, brother of Christ, brother of the Japanese, jubilating as he did. He went from table to table on the cruiser which was bringing him home from the Big Three conference, telling the great news; "jubilant" the newspapers said. *Jubilate Deo*. We have killed 318,000 Japanese. That is, we hope we have killed them, the Associated Press, on page one, column one of the *Herald Tribune*, says: "the effect is hoped for, not known." It is to be hoped they are vaporized, our Japanese brothers—scattered, men, women and babies, to the four winds, over the seven seas. Perhaps we will breathe their dust into our nostrils, feel them in the fog of New York on our faces, feel them in the rain on the hills of Easton. *Jubilate Deo*. President Truman was jubilant. We have created. We have created destruction.

And, far away, in Rome, Pope Pius XII, as we have noted, had contemplated such terror bombings and condemned them. "More than once, to our great distress," he had said in the course of the war, "the laws which bind civilized people together have been violated; most lamentably, undefended cities, country towns and villages have been terrorized by bombing, destroyed by fire, and reduced to ruins; unarmed citizens, even the sick, helpless, old people and innocent children have been turned out of their homes, and often killed." On August 7, the Vatican's newspaper, *L'Osservatore Romano*, summed up the war and made a dire prediction. "This war," it said, "provides a catastrophic conclusion. Incredibly this destructive weapon remains a temptation for posterity, which, we know by bitter experience, learns so little from history."

Cold War and The Iron Curtain

From 1941 to the close of the war, Josif Stalin had shown the West a kindly demeanor. His policy, which trickled down the chain of command, from the highest echelons of Soviet government to the lowliest Communist operatives worldwide, was to make the Soviet Union seem the friend of the western democracies. Thus he fooled leaders like Roosevelt and Churchill (or gave them the opportunity to fool themselves), who believed that the Soviets would help them promote freedom and democracy in post-war Europe.

Thus at Potsdam, in July 1945, Stalin was able to win important concessions from Truman and Britain's new prime minister Clement Attlee. (British voters had voted out Churchill's party and voted in Attlee's Labour Party.) The Allies divided Germany into four occupation zones: one each for the United States, Great Britain, Russia, and reconstituted France. The cities of Berlin and Vienna were likewise parceled out to the victorious powers. Truman and Attlee agreed that Russia should establish interim governments, to be "broadly representative of all democratic elements," in Austria, Hungary, Czechoslovakia, Bulgaria, and Romania. Stalin pledged that these interim governments would eventually allow for free elections. The British and the Americans agreed to Russian annexation of eastern Poland and to Stalin's request that the Soviet-established government of Poland be given East Prussia and a large swath of German territory from the Oder River eastward. Though Russia's contribution in the Pacific theater amounted to only five days of fighting, Truman and Attlee agreed to Russia's control of Manchuria. Stalin's demeanor during the Potsdam conference must have been friendly enough, for President Truman was heard to say afterwards, "I like Uncle Joe!"

But it soon became clear that "Uncle Joe" was not so benevolent as he had appeared. With the exception of Austria and Czechoslovakia, which set up democratic governments, Russia imposed Communist governments over all the countries in her "sphere of influence." Any elections held were only pretenses to give the Communist governments a semblance of legitimacy. It soon became apparent to everyone that the "Western" democratic nations had a new and formidable enemy; that the Soviet Union had succeeded Nazi Germany as the new threat to "freedom," not only in Europe, but, indeed, the world over. War with the Soviets was, in 1945, unthinkable; indeed, some in the United States thought the only way to ensure world peace was continually to appease Stalin. Truman, soon disabused of the illusion that Stalin was a benign Uncle Joe, decided that the way to deal with him was to make it clear that the Soviets would gain nothing by any act of war.

So, began a new age, not only for the United States, but for the entire world; a period men would call the "Cold War," for never was there actual war between the U.S. and her allies and the Soviet Communist powers. Instead, two opposing political blocs stared death at each other along a line that divided Europe and, soon, the whole world. Winston Churchill described the state of things well in March 1946 in a speech he gave in the presence of President Truman at Westminster College in Fulton, Missouri. "From Stettin in the Baltic," said Churchill, "to Trieste in the Adriatic an iron curtain has descended across the Continent."

Harry Truman (center), Clement Atlee (left), and Josif Stalin at Potsdam

The United Nations and the Atomic Bomb

One of Roosevelt's dreams became reality shortly after his death in April 1945—the United Nations Organization. It had been his secretary of state, Cordell Hull, who had initiated the course of events that led to the formation of this international body. In 1944, representatives of Great Britain, the United States, the Soviet Union, and China had met in Washington, D.C. to draft a preliminary sketch of what a new world organization, a successor to the League of Nations, would look like. In April 1945, shortly after Roosevelt's death, representatives of 50 nations met in San Francisco, California and drafted a charter for the United Nations. The United States Senate ratified the charter on July 28, 1945.

Atomic bomb tests at Bikini Atoll in the Pacific, 1946

The United Nations Charter established a world organization, divided into two bodies: the Security Council and the Assembly. Five nations sat on the Security Council: the United States, Great Britain, the Soviet Union, China, and France. Each Security Council member had veto power over any resolution approved by the other council members—a provision that the United States and Great Britain insisted on. Though the Soviet Union did not propose this policy, it later turned to its advantage; in the coming decades Russia (and later, China) would use the veto to hamper policies promoted by the other council members. Alongside the Security Council, the charter established an Assembly in which member nations each had one vote and unlimited time for discussion and debate. The charter gave the United Nations powers that the League of Nations never possessed. The organization could approve the use of force against nations that defied its decrees; it could establish economic sanctions and even call for war measures against the recalcitrant. The United Nations could establish its own permanent armed forces.

The United Nations General Assembly gathered for its first session in London on January 10, 1946. There it took up the important question of the future use of atomic energy. The destruction of Hiroshima and Nagasaki had made it clear that atomic energy, used for war purposes, had the potential to destroy civilization. The General Assembly voted to establish the United Nations Atomic Energy Commission to look for ways to control atomic energy throughout the world.

The Lilienthal-Acheson Report, published in the United States in March 1946, presented a plan by which the world's nations could channel atomic research in the ways of peace instead of war. The report, authored by David Lilienthal, the director of the Tennessee Valley Authority, called for the establishment of an international authority that would own the raw materials (plutonium and uranium) used in the production of atomic energy, as well as all the reactors and facilities connected to the production and use of atomic energy. This atomic authority would be under the control of the nations of the world and thus, it was hoped, would assure that nuclear materials would not fall under the control of any one nation.

President Truman sent Bernard Baruch to present a modified version of the Lilienthal-Achison plan to the first meeting of the UN Atomic Energy Commission in June 1946. In Baruch's proposal, the international authority would not own the world's plutonium and uranium but simply have oversight of them. It specified that oversight must extend to every country of the world before the United States would divest itself of its atomic arsenal and raw materials. The international authority, according to the Baruch plan, would have the power to levy sanctions against nations that refused to participate in the inspection. The veto power of members of the Security Council, said Baruch, would not apply to the international authority.

The Soviets and Poland, however, balked at the Baruch plan. It seemed to give the United States control of the international authority. Furthermore, instead of dismantling atomic weapons, the plan called for their "elimination from national arsenals"—meaning that, undestroyed, they might remain in the hands of the international authority as a threat against recalcitrant nations. The Soviets offered their own plan, which called for the immediate dismantling of all atomic arsenals (at that time, only the United States possessed atomic weapons) and the establishment of an international authority with only limited powers of inspection. The United States rejected this proposal.

The true reason the Soviets rejected the Baruch proposal was that Stalin was moving ahead on his own atomic program. Whether Truman was fully committed to atomic disarmament is unclear. It was the United States that suggested an Atomic Energy Commission at the first session of the UN General Assembly; but, at the very same time, the U.S. military was making plans for more atomic testing. Two weeks after Baruch made his proposal, declaring that the United States "stands ready to proscribe and destroy this instrument—to lift its use from death to life—if the world will join in a pact to that end," the United States military was conducting atomic tests on Bikini Atoll in the Pacific.

Post-War Occupation of Europe and Japan

The four nations that formed the Allied Control Council that governed occupied Germany after the war had a tremendous task before them. Germany had been devastated by the war; her cities had been laid waste by bombings; her people had been demoralized. In the best of circumstances the task of governing under such conditions would have been hard; but when the Allies who held joint custody of the government disagreed among themselves, the task was made far more difficult.

Initially, after the war, the Allies had determined to leave Germany to her own devices, to keep her weak for a good time to come. But when it was clear that such a policy would result only in mass starvation and in epidemics, the United States and Great Britain began shipping food into the war-torn land. France, however, was uncooperative in this and in other measures proposed by the United States and Great Britain to revive Germany economically and politically. France intended to annex the industrial Saar region and the Rhineland and wanted to shackle Germany so she would never be powerful again. The Soviets, with the excuse of France's intransigence, began gutting factories in the east German sector, sending parts and machinery into Russia. The Soviets justified their actions by claiming a right to war reparations from Germany.

The Allied occupation of Germany and Austria introduced tribunals to try and convict men accused of "war crimes" and other atrocities. Trials held at Nürnberg in Bavaria convicted 12 leading Nazis for the bloody and depraved crimes they committed in the course of the war. The Allies also worked to stamp out any remaining vestiges of Nazism from Germany, to prepare, at least, the western sectors of the country to adopt a republican form of government.

The United States did a great deal to help all of post-war Europe rebuild itself amid the rubble of war, funding 68 percent of relief efforts to bring food to Europe, helping resettle displaced persons and transporting Jews from Europe to their new homeland (established by Great Britain) in Palestine. Trade restrictions were eased between the United States and European countries. The United Nations, with U.S. aid, established two financial institutions to help with recovery: the International Monetary Fund (IMF) and the International Bank for Reconstruction and Development.

A parade in Greece in honor of the Marshall Plan's millionth ton of food for Greece, 1947

Then, in 1947, Great Britain, France, Italy and other countries suffered a severe financial collapse. The situation was especially perilous for France and Italy, both of which had strong, well-organized Communist parties that might use this "failure of capitalism" to launch themselves into power. To forestall such a catastrophe, the United States proposed what became known as the Marshall Plan. The Marshall Plan proposed to European countries that if they came up with economic reconstruction plans that would "permit the emergence of political and social conditions in which free institutions can exist," the United States would give them the money to institute these plans. Sixteen countries, which sent representatives to a conference on the Marshall Plan in Paris, approved it. Those countries under Communist governments, however, turned to Russia, which offered the same benefits.

President Truman wanted the United States to provide $17 billion out of the $22 billion budget for the Marshall Plan. Opposition in Congress was stiff and debate continued for well over a year. Then, in February 1948, a Communist *coup d'etat* that overthrew the democratic government of Czechoslovakia convinced many Congressmen that the same could happen elsewhere if nothing were done to ease the economic plight of European countries. On April 3, 1948, with large majorities in both houses, Congress approved the Marshall Plan. Over the next ten years, American money combined with European skill and invention helped make Western Europe, once again, one of the most prosperous regions in the world.

Since Russia had not entered the Pacific war until late, the occupation of Japan fell to the United States alone. Truman appointed General Douglas MacArthur Supreme Commander of Allied Powers with the authority to oversee the occupation of Japan. MacArthur entered into his duties with religious fervor; he wanted his government to be a shining example of

Douglas MacArthur with Emperor Hirohito

justice and of Christian charity. "If the historian of the future," he later wrote, "should deem my service worthy of some slight reference, it would be my hope that he mention me not as a commander engaged in campaigns and battles, even though victorious to American arms, but rather as that one whose sacred duty it became, once the guns were silenced, to carry to the land of our vanquished foe the solace and hope and faith of Christian morals."

MacArthur worked assiduously to inculcate Japanese society with American political and social principles. He ended the secret police. He instituted land reform, breaking up large estates and distributing over 4.5 million acres to Japanese peasants. Under his aegis, Japan adopted a democratic and representative government (with a prime minister and a parliament called the Diet) and allowed women to vote in the first general election, held in 1946. Under MacArthur, Japan disestablished its state religion; the Emperor cast off all the divine attributes that, for over 2000 years, had been associated with his office. Because of American occupation, Japan would eventually take her place among the most secular and prosperous nations of the world.

Yet, though he wanted Japan to enjoy "the solace and hope and faith of Christian morals," it was during MacArthur's command of the American Occupational Force that the Japanese Diet legalized abortion. Like Europe, post-war Japan was laboring under economic and social collapse; and this, coupled with a sharp increase in the birth rate, induced many Japanese women to seek illegal abortions. Moreover, Japan's post-war prime minister, Shigeru Yoshida, thought a rapid increase in the population would retard Japan's economic recovery. Thus it was that in May 1948 he backed the passage of the Eugenic Protection Law in the Diet. Proposing "to prevent the birth of eugenically inferior offspring, and to protect maternal health and life," the law allowed abortion in cases of fetal abnormality and where a pregnancy resulted from rape or could gravely harm a woman's health. The bill received MacArthur's approval (without which it could not have become law); he agreed with Yoshida's analysis of the dangers population growth posed to the Japanese economy. Following the passage of the Eugenic Protection Law, the abortion rate in Japan climbed dramatically, while the birthrate began the steady decline from which Japan has never recovered.

A U.S. plane drops candy to children as it flies supplies into Berlin.

Containment

In a message to Congress on March 12, 1947, President Truman outlined the objectives of his foreign policy. Truman said the United States should seek the "creation of conditions in which we and other nations will be able to work out a way of life free from coercion . . . I believe that it must be the policy of the United States to support freed peoples who are resisting attempted subjugation by armed minorities or by outside pressures."

With this policy, which became known as "containment," Truman sought to prevent more countries falling prey to Communist groups from within or to Soviet pressures from without. Truman received Congressional approval on March 12 to test his containment policy with Greece and Turkey, which were fighting Communist uprisings within their borders. American aid sent to these countries helped their legitimate governments overcome the Communist threat. Stalin's experience with these two countries convinced him to pull back the pressure he was exerting on the Middle East.

In Germany, conditions were reaching a critical point when Stalin announced a blockade of the non-Communist western zones of Berlin. Surrounded as it was by the Soviet occupation zone, Berlin was easy to isolate. Shipments of food, medicines, and fuel were cut off. If nothing were done, Stalin would starve West Berlin into submission. In response to this challenge, Truman and the British organized an airlift to fly supplies into the beleaguered city. For 321 days, British and American planes flew in supplies, and flew out products of the city. Seeing himself beat, Stalin finally backed down. On May 12, 1949, he lifted the blockade of West Berlin.

To protect the nations of Western Europe from Soviet aggression, the United States, Canada, and ten nations of Western Europe signed a treaty of mutual protection to form the North Atlantic Treaty Organization, on April 4, 1949. Under NATO, the United States pursued its policy of containment by shipping arms to Western Europe and by organizing the armed forces under the single command of Dwight Eisenhower, who became supreme commander of NATO. In 1954, West Germany (those non-Russian sectors organized in 1949 as the Federal Republic of Germany) was allowed to join NATO.

Though a success in Europe, containment failed in the Far East. Throughout the war, Mao Zedong's Communist government in the north of China had remained independent of Chiang Kai-shek's nationalist government in the south. Though at first he supported

Chiang, Stalin later began sending supplies to Mao. In November 1945, Truman had sent General George Marshall as his special representative to China to convince Chiang to agree to a coalition government with Mao. When Chiang refused, Marshall ordered an arms embargo against China. In April 1948, Congress approved an arms shipment to Chiang, but the state department sent the Chinese leader defective guns and planes without fuel. By the end of 1949, Chiang's government was forced to flee to the island of Taiwan, where it established its government. On mainland China, Mao set up a Communist regime, expelling all western missionaries and persecuting all who, for their religion, opposed his atheistic order.

In the three years following its founding in the 1946, the United Nations Atomic Energy Commission continued to hold meetings to discuss the Baruch and Soviet plans for future atomic policy. New proposals were debated, time-lines worked out and scrapped, details haggled over, but all to no use. All along, the Soviets were secretly working to develop their own atomic bomb, while the United States continued to develop its atomic weaponry. The three years of discussions over how to use atomic energy closed on July 29, 1949, no closer to an agreement than before. A month later, the event that the world dreaded occurred. The Soviet Union successfully tested its first atomic bomb.

The nuclear arms race had begun.

Chapter 28 Review

Summary

- With preparations for the war, the Depression in the United States was buried for good. By 1942, Japan had conquered the Philippines and almost all of East Asia. The Japanese set their sights on New Guinea but abandoned attempts to conquer it when they met the U.S. Navy in the Coral Sea. The U.S. then won an important victory against the Japanese at Midway Island.

- Throughout the first half of 1942, Great Britain's prime minister, Winston Churchill, and President Roosevelt discussed where Allied forces should initiate their strike into Europe. They agreed on "Operation Torch," a strike into North Africa.

- In February 1943 the Americans took Guadalcanal in the Solomon Islands, punching an opening in the Japanese wall of defense.

- Once Roosevelt and Churchill had North Africa in their possession, they met in January 1943 to discuss the further conduct of the war. The Allied leaders agreed on demanding nothing short of "unconditional surrender" from the Axis powers. They adopted the "Combined Bomber Offensive," which wreaked destruction on Germany's civilian population.

- By August 17, 1943, Allies had taken the entire island of Sicily and got set to invade Italy. The Italians were sick of war, however, and under the new premier, Marshal Badaglio, Italy sought peace with the Allies. Italy formally surrendered on September 3, 1943. The Germans still occupied Italy, however, and after a long fight, the Allies liberated Rome on June 4, 1944.

- In the United States, many Catholics were opposed to the war before the bombing of Pearl Harbor. Afterward, many Catholics supported the war, although the bishops warned against excesses and outlined the conditions for lasting peace. The war saw the stirrings of a pacifist movement among Catholics, among them Dorothy Day and the Catholic Workers.

- The air war weakened the German *Luftwaffe* so much that control of the air passed to the Allies. Gradually the Allies began to beat back the weakening German army, beginning with "D-Day" on June 6, 1944. On August 25, the Americans liberated Paris, and the German army began melting away before the Allies. In the Pacific, in October, the Americans began the liberation of the Philippines.

- In late January of 1945, the Allies advanced to the Rhine. On February 13, Allied planes dropped incendiary bombs on Dresden, laying waste to the city. After April 14, when the Allies broke through German defensive lines, all effective German opposition ended. Adolf Hitler and his mistress, Eva

Chapter 28 Review (continued)

Braun, committed suicide on April 30. The Allies crushed German resistance in Italy on May 4, and three days later the German government signed an agreement of unconditional surrender with the Allies, ending the war in Europe.

- On April 12, 1945, President Roosevelt died, leaving the presidency to his vice-president, Harry Truman. It still remained to defeat the Japanese. On March 14, 1945, the American army took Iwo Jima. Now the Allies faced the prospect of a land invasion of Japan to secure Japan's unconditional surrender. The United States, however, had a new secret weapon. On July 26, Allied leaders gave the Japanese an ultimatum: they were to surrender unconditionally or face destruction. When Japan refused to comment, the U.S. on August 6, 1945 dropped the atomic bomb on Hiroshima, and three days later on nearby Nagasaki. On August 14, 1945, the Emperor Hirohito surrendered.

- The Allies divided Germany and Austria into four occupation zones. Josef Stalin imposed Communist governments over nearly all the countries in Russia's sphere of influence. The division of Europe and the world between the Communist bloc of nations and the "free world" led to a state of undeclared conflict, called the "Cold War."

- The United Nations General Assembly, founded in 1945, assembled in 1946 for its first session to discuss the future use of atomic energy. The Lilienthal-Acheson Report presented a plan to channel atomic research in the ways of peace. The United States endorsed a modified version of this report, which the Soviets rejected. Meanwhile, Stalin was moving ahead on his own atomic program.

- During the post-war occupation of Europe and Japan, the United States did a great deal to help Europe restore its prosperity. When Great Britain, France, and Italy suffered a severe economic collapse, the United States proposed the Marshall Plan, which gave European countries economic help. With the help of the United States, Western Europe once again became one of the most prosperous regions in the world.

- On March 12, 1947, President Truman outlined the objectives of his foreign policy in what became known as the "containment" policy to support freed

peoples who were resisting attempted subjugation by Communists. To protect the nations of Western Europe from Soviet aggression, the United States, Canada, and ten nations of Western Europe formed the North Atlantic Treaty Organization, NATO, on April 4, 1949.

- In August 1949, the Soviet Union successfully tested its first atomic bomb, thus beginning the nuclear arms race.

Key Concepts

containment: the American policy announced under President Truman to check the advancement of Communism

Cold War: the period of open rivalry waged diplomatically, politically, and culturally, but not in full scale war, between the United States and its allies and the Soviet Union and its allies

Dates to Remember

1943: the Allies begin the Combined Bomber Offensive.

Italy surrenders to the Allies (September 3).

1944: the Allies liberate Rome (June 4).

"D Day" campaign opens (June 6).

The Allies liberate Paris (August 25).

1945: the Allies bomb and lay waste to Dresden (February 13).

Germany surrenders to the Allies (May 7).

The United States Senate ratifies the United Nations charter (July 28).

The Americans drop the first atomic bomb on Hiroshima (August 6).

Japan surrenders to the Allies (August 14).

1946: first session of the United Nations Organization

1949: the formation of the North Atlantic Treaty Organization (April 4)

Central Characters

Douglas MacArthur (1880–1964): American general who commanded the U.S. war effort in the Pacific

Chapter 28 Review (continued)

during World War II and who served as Supreme Commander of Allied Powers in Japan during post-war occupation

Josif Stalin (1878–1953): dictator of the U.S.S.R. who led Russia in World War II and at the beginning of the "Cold War"

Winston Churchill (1874–1965): British prime minister who led Great Britain during World War II

J. Robert Oppenheimer (1904–1967): American physicist who developed the atomic bomb

Harry Truman (1884–1972): 33rd president of the United States, who led the country through the final stages of World War II and into the early years of the Cold War

Questions for Review

1. How did the decisions made by the Allies at Casablanca in 1943 affect the war effort?

2. What was the objective of the Combined Bomber Offense? Did it achieve this objective?

3. Why were American Catholics hesitant to support the war before the Japanese attack on Pearl Harbor? What was their attitude to the war after the attack?

4. Describe the American Catholic bishops' conditions for lasting peace in 1943.

5. What was Dorothy Day's defense of pacifism?

6. What effect did the Allied war on Germany have on its civilians?

7. What important decisions were made by the Allies at Teheran in 1943?

8. Describe the course of events that led to the atomic bombings of Hiroshima and Nagasaki.

9. How did the American public opinion greet the atomic bombings of Hiroshima and Nagasaki?

10. Explain how the United Nations sought to deal with the threat of the atomic bomb.

11. Describe Truman's containment policy. What events led to the institution of this policy?

Ideas in Action

1. Discuss how the decisions made by world leaders during World War II have affected our world and the nature of warfare today.

2. Learn about the splitting of the atom and atomic power. To what uses is this technology put today? What controversies surround its use?

3. Read news accounts of the activities and policies of the United Nations Organization. Discuss whether the UN has been or is an effective force for world peace.

4. Discuss the morality of the warfare policies of both the Axis and Allied powers in World War II in light of the discussion on the Fifth Commandment in the *Catechism of the Catholic Church*, paragraphs 2258–2317.

Highways and Byways

The Holy Hill

Monte Cassino is a hill southeast of Rome, where St. Benedict of Nursia founded his first monastery around the year 529. In his *Life of Saint Benedict of Nursia*, Pope St. Gregory the Great says that the monastery was constructed on the site of a former pagan temple to Apollo. When Benedict came to Monte Cassino, he smashed the statue of Apollo, destroyed the god's altar, and then dedicated the temple to St. Martin. On the site of the pagan altar, Benedict built a chapel, which he dedicated to St. John the Baptist. At Monte Cassino, Benedict wrote his *Rule* for monastic life, which became the principle inspiration for western monasticism. Benedict was buried in the monastery, as were many other saints, including his own sister, St. Scholastica.

The site of Monte Cassino has always been of strategic importance, and throughout history it has been sacked and destroyed a number of times. During the dissolution of the Italian monasteries in 1866, Monte Cassino was made a national monument—though Benedictine monks continued to use it. After its destruction in World War II, it was rebuilt, and Pope Paul VI reconsecrated it in 1964.

29 THE ATOMIC AGE

War, Cold and Hot

The Soviet Union's first successful testing of an atomic bomb took the world by surprise. That the Soviets were looking to make an atomic bomb was not the surprise, but the fact that they did it so quickly. Many thought that the Soviets could not have progressed so quickly if U.S. atomic secrets had not been leaked to them. Fear of Communist espionage and infiltration moved the congressional House Un-American Activities Committee to conduct investigations in the hopes of flushing out secret Communist influences in the United States.

The House Un-American Activities Committee had been founded in 1938 to investigate "subversive groups," particularly Nazis, in the United States. After the war, the committee turned its attention to Communists. In 1947, the committee investigated alleged Communist infiltration in the Hollywood film industry. In the course of hearings, a group of witnesses (who included Walt Disney, Jack Warner of Warner Brothers, and the president of the Screen Actors Guild, Ronald Reagan) declared that they believed a small group of Communist actors, directors, and writers were, indeed, active in Hollywood. The committee finally narrowed their suspects down to ten. When these suspects were brought to trial the committee asked them, "Are you now or have you ever been a member of the Communist party?" The ten, by prior arrangement, were silent. All, indeed, were, or had been Communists. The "Hollywood Ten," as they became known, were cited with contempt of Congress and sentenced to short terms in prison. But of more lasting effect in dealing with Communists in Hollywood was the blacklist of suspected persons that the studios voluntarily adopted. Those whose names were blacklisted could find no work in the movie capital.

In August 1948, the House Un-American Activities Committee subpoenaed a known former-Communist to appear before them. Whittaker Chambers, an editor of *Time* magazine, had once been a leading American Communist but, after converting to Christianity, had abandoned the party. At a hearing on August 3, Chambers surprised his listeners by including the name of Alger Hiss in a list of those he said he knew to be Communists. Hiss had been one of Roosevelt's chief advisers at Yalta; he had been one of the chief architects of the United Nations, and was, then, president of the Carnegie Endowment for World Peace! That such a prominent man would be a secret Communist was not only surprising, but frightening, as well.

Chambers said that in the 1930s, he and Hiss had been members of the same Communist group and that Hiss had passed secret state documents to Moscow. In December, a grand

Whittaker Chambers

Julius and Ethel Rosenberg, shortly after their conviction, by Roger Higgins, *New York World Telegram and the Sun*

jury tried to convict Hiss of perjury (the statue of limitations for treason had passed), but failed. At a second trial, the jury found him guilty of perjury and sentenced him to five years in prison. Though lauded by conservatives and anti-Communists, Chambers would find himself vilified in the press for his testimony. For his part, Hiss never ceased to deny Chambers' allegations and maintained that he had never been a Communist or worked as a secret agent for the Soviet government.

A closely watched case was that of Julius and Ethel Rosenberg, who were convicted of giving nuclear secrets to the Soviets. Though neither were convicted of treason but of conspiracy to commit espionage (a lesser charge that normally only carried a penalty of imprisonment), the Rosenbergs were condemned to death. When they had exhausted all attempts for appeal and had been refused pardon by President Truman (among others, Pope Pius XII had, without commenting on the merits of the case, directly appealed to the president for clemency), the couple were executed by electric chair on April 5, 1951.

The Rosenberg's trial occurred during a time when Communists could expect little mercy. On June 25, 1950, faraway Korea erupted in a war instigated by Communists. At the end of the Second World War, Korea had been divided along the 38th parallel into two nations. The north was Communist, while the south, called the Republic of Korea, was governed by the aged patriot, Syngman Rhee. The government of South Korea was highly unstable and its army melted before the advance of North Korean troops (supported by Communist China), who crossed the 38th parallel on June 25, 1950.

The United States had not expected anything like the war in Korea. It had been assumed that, with the dawn of the nuclear age, the next war would be worldwide and atomic. But here were Communists conducting a conventional war to spread Communism. President Truman was intent on stopping the Communist forces and gave his full support to the United Nations Security Council's declaration of war on North Korea on June 27. (This was the first war the United States entered without a formal declaration of war by Congress.) Ten nations responded to the U.N.'s appeal for what it called a "police action" against North Korea. On July 8, the Security Council made General Douglas MacArthur Commander-in-Chief of U.N. forces.

The Korean War

During the first months of the war, as United Nations forces were gathering, the North Koreans were able to push South Korean and what U.N. forces there were in Korea into the southeastern corner of the country. Meanwhile, U.N. navy bombarded the coasts of Korea, while air force carried on round-the-clock bombing strikes in support of U.N. forces. On September 1, 1950, the North Koreans opened a general offensive along the line of the Naktong River and were initially able to penetrate U.N. lines; but after much bitter fighting, U.N. troops pushed the North Koreans back across the Naktong.

General MacArthur conceived of a counteroffensive to strike the North Koreans from behind. On September 15, U.N. troops made an amphibious landing behind enemy lines at Inchon on the west coast of Korea and marched on Seoul, the capital of South Korea. Ten days later, Seoul fell to U.N. forces. By the end of the month, U.N. forces had encircled more than half the North Korean army and forced it to surrender. On October 1, South Korean forces invaded North Korea, capturing the port of Wonsan while U.N. troops remained below the 38th parallel to hunt down the last remaining North Korean divisions there.

A combat photograph showing United States Marines, fighting Chinese Communists in Korea, moving forward with close air support of F4U-5 Corsairs

The United Nations General Assembly on October 7 approved an invasion of North Korea in order to reunite the country. U.N. forces now penetrated into North Korea and, on October 19, captured Pyongyang, the capital of North Korea. From Pyongyang, they continued north, pushing North Korean troops to the Yalu River, Korea's border with Communist China. By the end of October 1950, North Korean resistance had been broken.

To complete the conquest of North Korea, MacArthur divided his army, landing half of it at Wonsan. According to his plan, the two prongs of his army would envelop what remained of the North Korean opposition. The problem was, however, that the two prongs of his army were separated by a rugged mountain range that cut off effective communication between them. On November 24, the two prongs commenced an offensive to the north; but after two days, strong opposition from Communist Chinese forces that had crossed the Yalu into Korea forced U.N. forces to take the defensive. The Chinese pushed the western prong of the U.N. forces south of the 38th parallel until, by mid-December, they had formed a defensive line north and east of Seoul. Chinese forces pushed the eastern prong of the U.N. forces to the port of Hungnam. There, in mid December, under cover of naval guns, U.N. forces withdrew from North Korea.

Before this reversal, MacArthur's plan had been not only to take North Korea but to invade Communist China in concert with Chiang Kai-shek's Chinese Republican army, which U.N. ships would transport from Taiwan. The United Nations Security Council, however, opposed such grand plans. The one uncertain factor was Russia—would the Soviet Union declare war if China were invaded? Would the world have to suffer a destructive atomic world war? France and Great Britain were not in favor of taking any chances. In December Great Britain even suggested the admission of Red China into the United Nations to appease the Communists.

The events of January 1951, too, gave little encouragement to MacArthur's plan. On January 4, Communist forces took Seoul, pushing U.N. forces south of the Han River.

North and South Korea, 1950–195

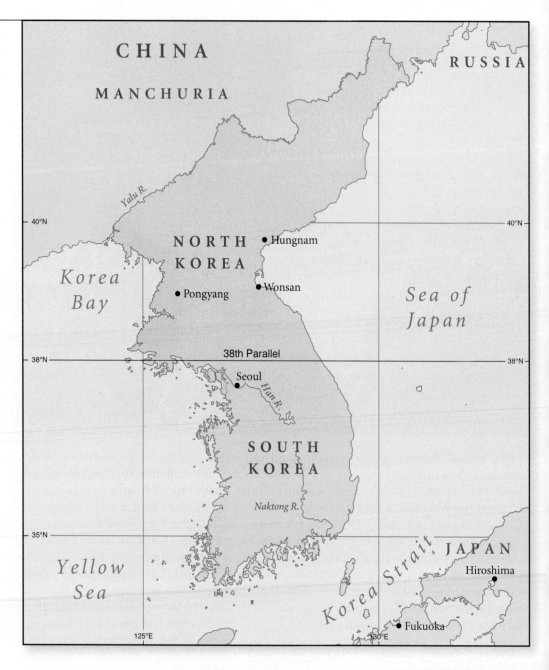

U.N. forces continued to give ground until late January when they were able to stabilize their lines.

In March, U.N. troops began a new counter-offensive. By March 14, U.N. forces retook Seoul and on April 3, pushed across the 38th parallel. With a new offensive underway, MacArthur insisted on bombing Manchuria, blockading the Chinese coast, and supporting a Chinese Republican invasion of the mainland from Taiwan. President Truman opposed MacArthur's plans. An angry MacArthur tried to stir up popular support for his proposed invasion and on March 24 took the unprecedented step of releasing the plans to the press. On April 6, MacArthur sent a letter critical of Truman's war policy to the Republican leader of the House of Representatives, who released it to the public. In the letter, MacArthur complained "that we have to fight Europe's war with arms while the diplomats there still fight it with words." Referring to his plan to invade China, MacArthur declared, "There is no substitute for victory." Angry that his general would publicly disagree with his war policy, Truman dismissed MacArthur on April 11, replacing him with General Matthew B. Ridgeway.

In the spring, and into early July 1951, U.N. forces pushed back several Communist offensives. By the end of May, the battle lines once again lay along the 38th parallel. They would change little for the remainder of the war.

Peace negotiations between the warring sides began in July of 1951 and continued for nearly two years. At issue was whether to restore the boundary of North and South Korea at the 38th parallel and what to do with prisoners. The Communists wanted the return of all North Korean and Chinese prisoners; the United Nations were reluctant to return any of these, without their consent, to the Communists. The Communists eventually dropped their demands for prisoners for certain other concessions, and the United Nations agreed to the 38th parallel as the boundary between North and South Korea. But the guns did not fall silent until July 27, 1953 when both sides signed a cease-fire.

Political Sea Change

The invasion of South Korea heightened American fears of a world-wide spread of Communism and of Communist infiltration of the United States government, the media, and university intelligentsia. Joseph McCarthy, a German-Irish Catholic elected to the U.S. Senate from Wisconsin in 1946, led a crusade to weed out Communists who, he said, were infiltrating the United States government—particularly the highly sensitive state department, which dealt with international affairs.

Senator Joseph McCarthy

McCarthy splashed onto the political scene in February 1950 when he told the Ohio County Women's Republican Club in Wheeling, West Virginia that he knew the names of a number of Communists in the state department. On February 20, he repeated these charges before the Senate, waving above his head a document that, he said, contained those names. (No one besides McCarthy, however, was allowed to see the document.) Because the security threat such Communist infiltrators posed, the Senate established a special committee to investigate McCarthy's charges, placing it under the leadership of Democratic Senator Millard Tydings of Maryland. When the Tydings Committee report came out, it condemned McCarthy rather than those he had accused. (Tydings and other Democrats who sided with him would pay dearly for their opposition to McCarthy; all lost in their re-election bids in 1952.)

By July 1950 McCarthy had become one of the most powerful men in the Senate. He was popular, especially, among Irish Catholics—Massachusetts' Catholic U.S. Senator, John Fitzgerald Kennedy, gave McCarthy his tentative support; John's younger brother, Robert, joined McCarthy's staff in 1953. Still, McCarthy made many enemies. His charges were often exaggerated and, at times, untrue. That Communists had infiltrated government and were security threats was certainly true; whether their threat was as great as McCarthy claimed, is uncertain. On June 14, 1951, McCarthy attacked the Truman administration, declaring that the president was the dupe of men in his cabinet. McCarthy made Secretary of Defense George Marshall his special target, accusing him of serving Soviet interests in World War II and of handing North Korea over to the Communists. Marshall, McCarthy said, was one of the chief reasons that, since the Second World War, the United States had grown weaker than Russia.

The election of 1952 in large part focused on Truman's foreign policy. The Republicans nominated General Dwight David Eisenhower for president and California U.S. Senator Richard Milhous Nixon as his running mate (Nixon had been instrumental in Alger Hiss' conviction.) The Republicans attacked Truman's betrayal of Chiang Kai-shek, his "losing" the Korean War, and his policy of containment. The Republicans also played up

An Adlai Stevenson poster implying that Eisenhower would return the country to the policies of Herbert Hoover while Stevenson followed in the tradition of the New Deal

administration scandals—presidential pardons for convicted criminals who had supported Democrats, bribery of office holders, and fraud. Though Truman himself was not corrupt, the dishonesty of his underlings was grist for the Republican mill.

Since the 21st Amendment limiting the president and vice-president to two terms had not yet been ratified, Truman could have run for a third term, but he declined. The Democratic nomination went to Governor Adlai Ewing Stevenson of Illinois. Stevenson was the choice of "intellectuals," but "Ike" Eisenhower, as a war hero, had the popular appeal. The slogan, "I Like Ike," won the day, with the largest majority of any candidate since Roosevelt's great victory in 1936. Eisenhower won 55.2 percent of the popular vote and 442 electoral votes; Stevenson secured only 89 electoral votes, mostly in the South. After 20 years, the Republicans again controlled the presidency.

"Dynamic Conservatism"

In contrast to Roosevelt, who had chosen intellectuals to fill his cabinet, President Eisenhower picked leaders of big business to occupy the chief posts in his administration. Ike's secretary of defense, for instance, was Charles E. Wilson of Detroit, president of General Motors; his treasury secretary was the chairman of the boards of several important steel and coal companies. Only Martin Durkin, the secretary of labor, was from the working class, having served as president of the Journeyman Plumbers and Steelfitters union. But Durkin soon resigned. (While he remained, the cabinet, as one newspaper quipped, consisted of "eight millionaires and a plumber.")

Eisenhower's cabinet appointments reflected a new brand of conservatism. No longer were business leaders calling for the old days of *laissez-faire* competition but were willing to accept the government as their referee. But big business profited from its cooperation with government. By 1956, 135 corporations had come to own 45 percent of all industrial assets in the United States. In such industries as oil refining, meat packing, iron and steel, a few companies, banded together, controlled the pricing of raw materials and of manufactured goods, and so set the pace for smaller competitors. Indeed, most competition was not within industries but between competing products: oil competed with coal; synthetic textiles (like nylon and dacron), with cotton; plastics and aluminum, with iron and steel. Talented, ambitious young men were less likely to open new businesses but were content with the fat paychecks they received from working for corporations.

The arms race between the United States and the Soviet Union helped unite government and big business more firmly than ever before. Though military spending declined in the first years after World War II, beginning in 1949, with Russia's development of the atomic bomb, military spending climbed dramatically. Large companies benefited tremendously from government contracts. Eisenhower, in his farewell address in 1961, would say that, during the post-war period, the government had been "compelled to create a permanent armaments industry of vast proportions"—an industry, he admitted, which had never existed before. In his address, Eisenhower would warn against the "unwarranted influence" that this "military-industrial complex" could wield in the future—an influence he helped create and sustain.

Eisenhower characterized his policies as "dynamic conservatism." This "dynamic conservatism" did not abandon the big government model of Roosevelt; it was more openly favorable to private big business, while still maintaining and even expanding federal social programs. On the one hand, the Eisenhower administration canceled price and rent controls, abolished the Reconstruction Finance Corporation (begun by Hoover and continued under Roosevelt), and opened up public reserves to the exploitation of private capital. On the other hand, the administration extended Social Security to 10 million more recipients, included another 4 million in unemployment compensation, raised the national minimum wage to one dollar an hour, established a federal housing program, and promoted a bill that promised $50 billion towards the construction of new schools. Eisenhower furthered federal regulation of unions by supporting laws to curb corruption and racketeering in workers' organizations.

Dwight David Eisenhower

Ike's response to Communist threats on the domestic front was neither specifically "conservative" nor "liberal," since both sides supported a strong anti-Communist campaign. Eisenhower extended security checks to all government agencies and, in 17 months time, dismissed 6,900 government employees who were deemed security risks. Secretary of State John Foster Dulles carried out a similar "purge" of the foreign service. The House Un-American Activities Committee continued to function, spreading the message that Communists could be found in every sector of society. (One government pamphlet noted, "Where Can Communists be found? Everywhere.")

Despite the campaign against Communist infiltration, Senator Joseph McCarthy was disliked, both by his colleagues in Congress and the president. McCarthy spared no one, liberal or conservative, in his hunt for Communists. Eisenhower, he said, was soft on Communism. In the spring of 1953, McCarthy investigated Voice of America, the government-sponsored radio network that beamed pro-American broadcasts around the world but especially into Communist countries. That summer, he purged from the state department's overseas information libraries 30,000 allegedly pro-Communist books.

The year 1953 proved to be the pinnacle of McCarthy's power. In March 1954, he attacked the Protestant clergy and the United States Army, which led to the two-month long "Army-McCarthy" hearings that resulted in a tightening of security on army bases. But in July, Senator Ralph Flanders introduced a resolution in Congress, accusing McCarthy of conduct "unbecoming a member of the United States Senate." In November 1954, the Senate formally censured McCarthy. The press used the censure against McCarthy, and he gradually lost whatever influence he had had. He eventually took to heavy drinking and died on May 2, 1957 from acute hepatitis.

Thus ended what was called the "McCarthy Era," but the movement called Anti-Communism would continue for several years to come.

Interventions Abroad

It was under Eisenhower that the cease-fire that ended the Korean War was signed. Though the United States engaged in no other wars in the Eisenhower years, the administration did conduct covert operations in other countries. The chief instrument in these operations was the Central Intelligence Agency, or CIA, founded during the Roosevelt years. Though no war was declared, nor U.N. police action voted on, the United States, through the CIA, helped topple and establish governments as far away as Asia and as close to home as Central America.

One such intervention centered on Mohammed Mosaddegh. Mosaddegh was a flamboyant political leader in Iran. He would address the Iranian parliament in his pajamas or from his bed, which he had carried into chambers. Besides being somewhat odd in his behavior

Mohammed Mosaddegh (right) with Truman

(which he used to political purpose), Mosaddegh was an ardent nationalist who prevented the Soviet Union from establishing oil drilling rights in northern Iran. He also wanted to nationalize, with compensation to its owners, the British-owned Anglo-Iranian Oil Company—a measure that the Iranian parliament approved in March 1951. This kind of nationalism only alienated Mosaddegh from many of the elite class in Iran and from the Iranian head of state, the Shah (who had been compelled to make Mosaddegh premier); but, more importantly it set British Petroleum, which controlled the Anglo-Iranian Oil Company, against him. British Petroleum appealed to the United States for aid. In August 1953, the Shah, backed by the CIA, demanded Mosaddegh's resignation. A popular leader, Mosaddegh refused to step down as premier, and the Shah was forced to flee the country. A few days later, with CIA support and after a nine-hour tank battle in the streets of Teheran, the Shah was restored to power, and Mosaddegh forced out of office.

The CIA was involved in training insurgent troops to overthrow the government of Jacobo Árbenz, the president of Guatemala. Árbenz was a socialist and a nationalist; his influential wife, a communist. Árbenz had come to power with the support of communists who admired his nationalist plans, which included strong support for labor unions and a program of agrarian reform in which the government would expropriate, with compensation to owners, unused land that exceeded a specified acreage and redistribute it to the landless poor of Guatemala. (About 2.2 percent of the population owned 70 percent of Guatemalan land, most of which went unused.) Árbenz ran into trouble when his government took 234,000 acres of unused land that belonged to the powerful United Fruit Company, which owned plantations throughout Central America.

United Fruit could pride itself on many accomplishments in Central America. It had built roads, houses, and schools for its workers. Its permanent employees were paid better than those who worked for other industries in Central America. But the lot of the seasonal workers, who picked fruit, was not good; their pay was insufficient to carry them throughout the year, and they were continually exposed to dangerous pesticides. United Fruit suppressed any attempts made by workers to form unions; the company destroyed the schools and housing in the districts where unionization had been attempted.

United Fruit had powerful friends in the Eisenhower administration. Though the Guatemalan government had compensated the company for expropriated lands with government bonds, United Fruit claimed the compensation was not sufficient. Moreover, United Fruit claimed that the Árbenz government was Communist and supported by Communists. In June 1954, a force of Guatemalan exiles and foreign recruits under Colonel Carlos Castillo Armas, in a coup orchestrated by the CIA, overthrew Árbenz and established a new government more friendly to United Fruit and the United States.

From Arms Race to Space Race

In the Congressional elections of 1954, the Republicans lost the control of Congress they had won in 1952. But if Democrats hoped this presaged a Democratic victory in the presidential election of 1956, they were wrong. In 1956, the Democratic candidate, Adlai Stevenson, again lost badly to Eisenhower and Nixon. But Democrats could, at least, take this comfort: the Congress, both Senate and House, remained in their control.

A Democratic Congress meant an uphill battle for Eisenhower for passage of any of his policies that required spending cuts. Yet, president and Congress agreed on extending certain social programs and on increasing funding for national defense. That national defense should rest, as Secretary Dulles said in 1954, on "the deterrent of massive retaliatory power" was the creed of both liberals and conservatives. And with government air-raid drills that kept citizens ever aware of the Soviet threat, and reports that the United States lagged behind Russia in its nuclear capability, the American public did not object to massive military expenditures.

Even after the death of Stalin in 1953, the United States' power of military retaliation remained massive. By 1955, the U.S. nuclear stockpile was about 40 times that of Russia; by 1960, the United States had about 30,000 nuclear warheads to the Soviets' 2,000. Throughout this period, too, the United States produced more Intercontinental Ballistic Missiles (ICBMs) than the Soviet Union and had more submarines and bombers for nuclear attack. It appeared that it was the Soviet Union, not the United States, that had to do the catching up.

This period saw, too, the development of more powerful and deadly weapons. There was the ICBM, a guided missile with intercontinental range that could deliver an atomic warhead over long distances—a capability that Russia also had developed. Then came the successor to the atomic bomb—the hydrogen or thermonuclear bomb. The United States tested the first hydrogen bomb at Enewetak in the Pacific Marshall Islands in 1952. A year later, the Soviet Union tested its first hydrogen bomb.

The Soviets struck fear into many American hearts in October 1957 when they launched *Sputnik*, the world's first earth-orbiting satellite. The 183-pound, basketball-sized satellite orbited the earth in about 98 minutes. A month later, the Soviets launched *Sputnik II*, a heavier satellite that carried in its payload a dog named Likita. If the Soviets could launch such wonders, could they not easily bomb any place in the United States? An angry and fearful American public demanded to know why the government was allowing itself to be so outstripped by Communist Russia.

The United States answered the Russian challenge in January 1958 by launching a satellite, *Explorer I.* This lightweight craft, later instrumental in discovering the earth's magnetic belt, was the first of a series of other space craft. The Soviet challenge also led to a beefing up of scientific education in the United States and to passage by Congress of the National Aeronautic and Space Act in July 1958, which led to the founding, three months later, of the National Aeronautics and Space Administration (NASA).

The explosion of the first hydrogen bomb, 1952

Civil Rights

One of Eisenhower's acts that would have long-lasting effects was his appointment of Earl Warren of California as Chief Justice of the Supreme Court. Warren would, in the coming years, preside over cases that would change the complexion of American society. The first of these, *Brown v. Board of Education of Topeka,* overthrew one of the institutions of post-Reconstruction America: racial segregation in schools.

The case arose when Oliver Brown, a black man residing in Topeka, Kansas, brought the Topeka Board of Education to trial for refusing to allow his third-grade daughter to attend a white school. Assisted by the National Association for the Advancement of Colored Persons (NAACP), Brown's attorneys brought forward witnesses that argued that segregation gave blacks the message that they were inferior to whites. Though the United States District Court agreed that "segregation of white and colored children in public schools has a detrimental effect upon the colored children . . . A sense of inferiority affects the motivation of a child to learn," they found in favor of the defendants. The court said it was bound by the 1896 Supreme Court decision, *Plessy v. Ferguson*, which decided that racially "separate but equal" accommodations on public transportation did not contradict the equal protection clause of the 14th Amendment to the Constitution.

Brown and the NAACP appealed *Brown* to the Supreme Court in 1951. At first, the court investigated whether the authors of the 14th Amendment had desegregation of schools in mind when they wrote that no state shall "deny to any person within its jurisdiction the equal protection of the laws." But in the decision he wrote for the court in 1954, Chief Justice Warren said what the authors of the amendment, members of Congress and of state legislatures "had in mind cannot be determined with any degree of certainty." Since this was so, the court's decision, wrote Warren, must consider "public education in the light of its full development and its present place in American life throughout the Nation." Whether or not the 14th Amendment was intended to apply to schools was unimportant. The question for Warren was: did segregation, in 1954, deprive students of equal protection?

Warren admitted that black and white schools had been or were becoming equal in buildings, in curricula, in qualifications and salaries for teachers—what he called "tangible factors." However, because segregation gave blacks a sense of inferiority, Warren concluded that "in the field of public education the doctrine of 'separate but equal' has no place. Separate educational facilities are inherently unequal. Therefore, we hold that the plaintiffs and oth-

A sign directing blacks to a separate waiting room (left), a segregated theater (right)

ers similarly situated . . . are, by reason of the segregation complained of, deprived of the equal protection of the laws guaranteed by the Fourteenth Amendment."

The Warren court, in May 1955, followed up its *Brown* ruling with another that demanded that desegregation must proceed with "all deliberate speed" and gave lower courts the responsibility of applying this ruling. Still, the court gave no timetable for desegregation, and some states ignored the issue.

In March 1956, 96 southern congressmen issued a declaration denouncing *Brown* as a violation of the Constitution and called upon states to, in effect, nullify it. In *Brown*, declared the congressmen, the judicial branch was exercising the powers of the legislature and encroached "upon the reserved rights of the states and the people." The debates that preceded the submission of the 14th Amendment in the 1860s, wrote the congressmen, "clearly show that there was no intent that it should affect the systems of education maintained by the states." The "separate but equal" doctrine, they said, was an "established legal principle almost a century old"; thus, "the Supreme Court of the United States, with no legal basis for such action, undertook to exercise their naked judicial power and substituted their personal political and social ideas for the established law of the land."

Rosa Parks

In Montgomery, Alabama, a black woman, Rosa Parks, met segregation head on. In December 1955, she refused to give up her seat on a bus to a white man—a "crime" for which she was arrested. Under the leadership of a black Baptist minister, Martin Luther King, Jr., blacks in Montgomery formed carpools and began a boycott of public transportation. The boycott continued for about a year; then, in November 1956, the Supreme Court ruled that that segregation in local transportation was unconstitutional.

Eisenhower became involved in the segregation issue in the fall of 1957 when nine black children tried to enter a white public high school in Little Rock, Arkansas. The governor of Arkansas stirred up Arkansans over the issue and called out the national guard to prevent the black children from entering the school. The threat of mob violence loomed on the horizon. Though the Constitution allows the president to protect a state "against domestic violence" only "on application of the legislature, or of the executive," Eisenhower did not await the governor's plea for aid (which, of course, would not have come). Instead, the president sent national guard units into Little Rock to maintain order. "When a state refuses," declared Eisenhower, "to utilize its police powers to protect persons who are peacefully exercising their rights under the Constitution as defined in such [federal] court orders, the oath of office of the President requires that he take action to give that protection. Failure to act in such a case would be tantamount to acquiescence in anarchy and the dissolution of the Union."

Eisenhower, and Truman before him, had requested legislation from Congress to provide for federal enforcement of civil rights guarantees. On September 9, 1957, Congress passed the first civil rights act since 1870. This, the Civil Rights Act of 1957, created a federal Civil Rights Commission and a civil rights division in the office of the United States attorney general. The latter would have the power to prosecute those who placed any obstacles to any citizen's exercise of his or her constitutional rights. Offenders, even if they were state officials, could be fined or imprisoned if they ignored the orders of federal judges in these matters.

Suburbanization

A period of prosperity dawned on the United States following the Second World War. Foreign aid through the Marshall Plan helped bring prosperity to Western European nations and thus opened up markets for American goods. A post-war upsurge in population called the "Baby Boom" (U.S. population climbed by 29 million in just 20 years) meant the necessity for increased production. This produced more jobs. But among the chief causes of the

A new suburban development in Richfield, a suburb of Minneapolis, Minnesota, ca. 1950

post-war prosperity was the dramatic rise in government military spending, especially after Korea. When an economic recession hit in 1957–58, Eisenhower and Congress did not institute New Deal-style public works projects to help the country weather the slump; they increased military spending.

In the post-war period, unions insisted that companies pay working men a wage sufficient to support a family; this helped raise the real weekly earnings of factory workers by 50 percent. A GI bill, passed by Congress, allowed more men to go to college and so increased the number of "white collar" workers who benefited from the high salaries paid by prosperous corporations. The rise in wages brought many more people into the middle class. Despite the large pockets of poverty that remained in the United States in the '50s, being "middle class" was becoming the leading characteristic of American life.

Both blue and white collar workers took advantage of federal aid for housing to achieve the "American dream" of home ownership. Of all the available housing in the 1950s, about one-quarter was new housing. Because of federal policy that favored the purchase of new houses over existing houses in cities, much of this housing went up on the outskirts of cities and led to a new phenomenon of American life—suburbanization.

Prime examples of suburbanization were the Levittowns of New York, Pennsylvania, and New Jersey, built from the late '40s to the mid '50s. Levitt and Sons, Inc., had learned how to mass produce housing by constructing houses for the navy during World War II. The company applied the same methods to civilian housing after the war, laying out vast neighborhood tracts upon a general plan that included spaces for shopping centers and for schools. The houses, built after a very limited number of models, though comfortable, made for architecturally monotonous neighborhoods. Still, they fit the bill for many lower and upper middle class families who wanted to flee the crowded conditions of the cities. Just as their parents had fled the country for the cities in the first two decades of the 20th century, so their children fled the cities for the suburbs.

Suburban culture was characterized by the automobile—it was, in fact, automobiles and federal and state-improved highways that made suburbs possible, since workers now had to commute longer distances to their jobs. In the five years from 1945 to 1950, automobile registrations rose from 26 million to 40 million. Indeed, more than ever, automobile ownership became a hallmark of American life. In Los Angeles and other cities, highways became the primary means of transportation, replacing public transit. Highways allowed suburbs to be built ever farther from city centers, creating, in time, large, sprawling urban areas.

In part because of suburban development, from New York to San Francisco, from Maine to Florida, American culture grew ever more homogenous. Everywhere, suburbs shared common characteristics: neighborhoods full of mass produced houses, the red brick public school complexes, shopping centers more and more given to "chain" stores that sold brand name, ready-made foods and products. Television, which by 1953 had invaded two-thirds of American households, destroyed much of what remained of homespun entertainment and spread mass fads that influenced dress, speech, and and social mores nationwide.

Industrialism had already undermined home-based industries and so separated the father from his family for long periods throughout the day. Suburbanization exacerbated this development by increasing the distances between home and work, thus adding long commutes to the breadwinner's day. Wives, separated from husband and children (who went to school) for long hours, found their lives increasingly occupied in house cleaning, shopping, and socializing. Unlike the farm wives of earlier times, and even the women of the working poor, who were integral to the family economy, the "modern" wife began to seem increasingly ornamental. Many women began to suffer from boredom and dissatisfaction.

The wealth of the 1950s allowed even youth to become consumers, and an entire youth industry arose to meet (and create) the demand. Popular music, particularly Rock 'n' Roll, jeans, hula hoops, surfboards, frisbees characterized youth culture. By 1960, American teenagers were spending $22 billion a year on consumer goods.

The culture of the 1950s was, at least externally, religious, conservative, and family-centered. Most Americans attended religious services and upheld a morality that valued family cohesiveness, self-reliance, honesty, hard work, and patriotism. Compared to our own day, family life was stable and divorce was relatively rare because it was socially unacceptable. Children were raised to respect their parents and other adults and to trust government authorities. On the surface, at least, all seemed well with America.

But other signs indicated impending troubles. The media and advertising spread the notion that happiness lay in the possession of material goods. Indeed, the "American dream" was increasingly defined in material terms—home ownership, the possession of consumer goods, the freedom to better one's condition. The mass-produced culture was not only shallow, it could be sexually suggestive. This was especially true of Rock 'n' Roll "stars" like Elvis Presley whose stage antics were more than suggestive. Adults, however, were little better than their children in this regard, as the popularity of the actress and "sex symbol" Marilyn Monroe attests. Thus, while, on the one hand, marital fidelity was honored in the '50s, public lust was condoned.

In the end, the morality of the Eisenhower era would be seen as a morality of respectability. American youth would come to conclude that their parents' ethics were a mere veneer to make them appear "upstanding" in the eyes of their neighbors. The charge of "hypocrisy," leveled against the middle-class society of the 1950s, would, in a few short years, shake American culture to its foundations.

"Camelot"

It has been said that television lost the Republicans the presidential election in 1960. Their candidate, Vice-President Richard Nixon, could not compete well, visually, with the handsome, young (43-year old) Democratic candidate, John Fitzgerald Kennedy. Though only a year older than Kennedy, Nixon didn't exude youthfulness. Still, the election was the closest in American history to

A family watching television, 1958

Advertisement from 1953

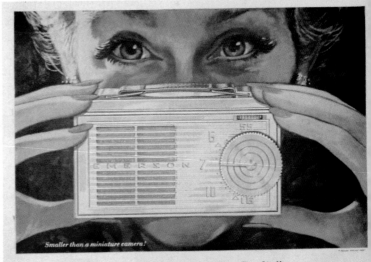

Smaller than a miniature camera!

New! Emerson "Pocket Radio"

WORLD'S SMALLEST PERSONAL PORTABLE
A Miracle of Precision Engineering!

There's never been anything like it! The usual personal radio is a *giant* compared to it. It plays anywhere you go. It's the kind of thing that makes you gasp, that makes you wonder how anyone can create a jewel so small...yet so perfect in every part!

It's a Modern Engineering Marvel made with miraculous subminiature parts. And only Emerson, world's greatest specialist in small radios, has the know-how to create it.

Weighs Less Than a Pound! it's only six inches wide...yet has such crystal-clear tone and such power that you can hear it in a crowd or across a large room. The Emerson "Pocket Radio" is a gem of design with its smart coloring and gilt accents. It's a thrilling, personal gift! Only **$40.00** including batteries.

So small—tucks into a small purse!
So small—fits a man's breast pocket!

A thrilling gift!
Model 747

Emerson
America's Best Buy! Over 14,000,000 Satisfied Owners!

Kennedy campaigning in Florida, 1960

that time: "JFK" secured 303 electoral votes, with a popular vote of 34.2 million; Nixon garnered 219 electoral votes and 34.1 million in the popular vote.

The Democrats had been somewhat leery of Kennedy. After all, he was a Catholic, and that had been an issue in the Al Smith campaign 32 years earlier. But in a campaign, liberally funded by his wealthy father, Joseph P. Kennedy, JFK was put on the Democratic presidential ticket, along with Lyndon Baynes Johnson of Texas. As for his Catholicism, Kennedy assured voters that it would not influence his decisions as president. On September 12, the candidate told the Greater Houston Ministerial Alliance: "whatever issue may come before me as president, if I should be elected—on birth control, divorce, censorship, gambling, or any other subject—I will make my decision . . . in accord with what my conscience tells me to be in the national interest, and without regard to outside religious pressure or dictation, and no power or threat of punishment could cause me to decide otherwise."

In his stirring inaugural address, Kennedy told Americans that "the torch has been passed to a new generation of Americans, born in this century, tempered by war, disciplined by a hard and bitter peace, proud of our ancient heritage, and unwilling to witness or permit the slow undoing of those human rights to which this nation has always been committed, and to which we are committed today at home and around the world." In his peroration he told citizens, "ask not what your country can do for you, ask what you can do for your country."

Kennedy came into office with his own federal aid program, called the "New Frontier," and it seems he wanted to open his presidency with a dramatic "100 days" flurry of legislation. During its first session, Kennedy delivered 25 messages to Congress calling for legislation for economic recovery, expansion of national defense, foreign aid, conservation of natural resources, federal aid for housing and schools. JFK, however, did not have Roosevelt's political clout; conservative Democrats joined with Republicans to block most New Frontier legislation.

Congress did approve increased military spending and eventually passed such New Frontier measures as an increase in the minimum wage from one dollar to $1.25 an hour (something over $10 an hour in today's dollars) and a housing act that gave grants to towns and cities for local transportation systems and middle-income housing. Congress approved the formation of the Peace Corps, which would send American college students and other youth to impoverished countries around the world to teach, build houses and schools, and otherwise help poor people improve their condition

From left to right: John F. Kennedy, Jacqueline Kennedy, and Senator Patrick McNamara

Kennedy came under fire from his political opposition for making his brother, Robert, his attorney general, as well as his brother-in-law, Sargent Shriver, director of the Peace Corps. Indeed, with the arrival of Kennedy's youngest brother, Edward, as U.S. Senator from Massachusetts in 1962, Washington, it seemed, was becoming a Kennedy town. Still, John Kennedy and his attractive wife, Jacqueline, lent an air of youthful romance to the White House. After eight years of a staid, elderly president like Eisenhower, many Americans found the Kennedy vitality and idealism invigorating. So it is that the

Kennedy years have taken on the aura of a fairy tale and have been likened to another court of legend: King Arthur's Camelot.

Kennedy vs. Communism

Throughout the 1950s, in Africa and Asia, former European colonies became independent states. Sometimes this was done peacefully; other times, violently. In 1954, Communist Vietnamese rebels defeated French forces at Dien Bien Phu in French Indochina, and the now independent Vietnam was divided between a Communist state under rebel leader Ho Chi Minh and a southern republic under the autocratic Ngo Dinh Diem. When North Vietnam began a guerrilla war against the south, Eisenhower in 1955 sent military advisers and supplies to South Vietnam. By the time Kennedy took office, the number of American military personnel in Vietnam had grown to 3,000. Kennedy continued Eisenhower's policy and expanded it, sending "Green Berets" as a special counter-insurgency force to South Vietnam.

Kennedy found that he had to deal with another crisis closer to home. In 1956, in Cuba, Fidel Castro and Ernesto "Che" Guevara initiated a revolution against the regime of the brutal Cuban dictator, Fulgencio Batista. Though the revolution began with only a handful of men, it soon swelled with peasant recruits wishing to overthrow Batista's oppressive regime. On New Year's Day, 1959, Batista fled Havana and, soon after, Castro became dictator. While, in the beginning, Castro's objectives called for an end to political imprisonment, the restoration of popular elections, a congress, and a free press, under the influence of Che and his own brother, Raúl, Castro gravitated towards Communism. After the revolutionary government began confiscating sugar planta-

Fidel Castro in 1959

tions and major industries (many owned by Americans), President Eishenhower broke off diplomatic relations with Cuba and forbade Americans to trade with the island. In 1961, Castro proclaimed himself a Marxist-Leninist, and his closure of Catholic churches earned him excommunication. Nikita Khruschev, the Soviet premier, extended credit to Cuba and agreed to buy the island's sugar crop, thus cementing an alliance between Cuba and the Communist block of nations.

Like Eisenhower, Kennedy wanted Castro overthrown. In April 1961, a force of anti-Castro Cubans who had been trained by the CIA landed at the Bay of Pigs on the southwestern coast of Cuba, hoping to foment a revolution; but Castro was still popular, and the insurgents were routed. This failure reflected badly on Kennedy, and he publicly apologized for the armed fiasco.

But in the late summer, early fall of 1962, the U.S. government learned that the Russians were building missile sites on the island of Cuba, thus placing major American cities in the range of atomic missile attack. Though the Russian minister said the missile sites were "purely defensive," Kennedy demanded their removal, hinting that if the Soviets didn't comply, the U.S. would launch a missile strike on Cuba. On October 23, the Organization of American States voted to approve a blockade of Cuba suggested by Kennedy, while U.S. nuclear armed B-52s, submarines armed with polaris missiles, and ICBMs were made ready, and the army, navy and marines were mobilized in Florida and in the Gulf ports. For a few tense days the world waited, wondering if it stood on the brink of the long-dreaded nuclear war; but on October 26, Khrushchev offered to evacuate the missiles if Kennedy agreed not to invade Cuba. The crisis had been averted.

Kennedy signs the order for the blockade of Cuba, October 23, 1962

Though the United States had given Russia $50 million in wheat, the Cuban missile crisis was not the first indication of declining relations between the two world powers. On August

13, 1961, the Soviets began the construction of the Berlin Wall, to cut East Berlin off from all contact with free West Berlin. The wall would remain a poignant symbol of Communist oppression until it was torn down 28 years later.

Rivalry between the superpowers continued in the space race. In April 1961, the Soviets became the first to send a manned spacecraft around the earth. A month later, the United States rocketed its first "astronaut," Alan Shephard, into space. On February 20, 1962, American astronaut John Glenn orbited the earth thrice in five hours. After a Russian satellite photographed the dark backside of the moon, Congress, with President Kennedy's blessing, voted more money for what was dubbed "Project Apollo." Kennedy promised that the United States would be the first to land a man on the moon.

The nuclear race remained a serious threat during the Kennedy years. In August 1961, Khrushchev broke a verbal agreement he made with Eisenhower and resumed nuclear open-air testing, exploding 50 nuclear devices. On April 25, 1962, Kennedy followed suit, and ordered the resumption of nuclear testing. Fear over the long-term health effects of nuclear radiation fall-out in the atmosphere finally brought the Americans and the Soviets to the negotiating board. On August 5, 1963, the United States, the Soviet Union, and Great Britain met in Moscow and signed the Nuclear Test Ban Treaty, agreeing that both sides would end open-air nuclear testing. Approved by the Senate, the treaty went into effect on October 10.

Sit-Ins and Freedom Riders

Meanwhile, the fight for black civil rights continued. Following Dr. Martin Luther King, Jr.'s call for non-violent resistance, on February 1, 1960, four black college students from the Agricultural and Technical College of North Carolina in Greensboro peacefully challenged segregation. They sat themselves at a "whites only" lunch counter at Woolworth's variety store in Greensboro and requested service. When refused, they continued sitting. News of the students' defiance of segregation spread, and soon students and others throughout the South staged similar "sit-ins," as well as "read-ins" in segregated libraries and "wade-ins" on segregated beaches. The sit-ins were effective. By 1961, many eating establishments had removed segregated seating.

In May 1961, groups of blacks tested federal laws against segregation in public transportation. These "Freedom Riders," as they were called, set out by bus from Washington, D.C., headed toward New Orleans. Mobs attacked the Freedom Riders at several stops, but violence could not deter them. In the wake of the Freedom Rides, the Interstate Commerce Commission in September 1961 prohibited racial segregation on buses and in terminals used in interstate commerce.

A Wall of Separation?

In 1963, the Warren Supreme Court heard a case, *Abington School District v. Schempp*, challenging the right of public schools to carry on religious exercises. Madeline Murray of Maryland, an atheist, had challenged the reading of the Bible in Baltimore public schools, and a Unitarian, Edward Schempp, of Pennsylvania, was challenging a Pennsylvania law that required the reading, without comment, of ten Bible verses at the beginning of the school day, followed by the Lord's Prayer. The Pennsylvania law specified that parents, upon request, could remove their children from such exercises. Murray and Schempp challenged the laws on the grounds that they violated the First Amendment to the Constitution.

The Warren court agreed with Murray and Schempp. Though the First Amendment only binds Congress from erecting an "establishment of religion" (that is, a state-sponsored church), the court decided it did more—it erected (in the words of Thomas Jefferson) a "wall of separation" between church and state. Prayer and other religious exercises in public schools, argued the court, violated the First Amendment. "The test," said the court, as to whether an act of a state legislature violates or does not violate the "establishment clause" is whether it has a "secular legislative purpose and a primary effect that neither advances nor inhibits religion." That is, all state acts, said the court, must be religiously neutral.

Despite a federal court order allowing him to attend the University of Mississippi, James Meredith, a black man, found the entrance to the institution physically barred against him when he tried to enroll in September 1962. Riots erupted after Meredith, accompanied by hundreds of armed federal marshals, enrolled at the university. After rioting students and townsmen killed two persons and injured many more, President Kennedy ordered federal troops onto the scene. Troops remained to protect Meredith until his graduation in the spring.

In June 1963, Kennedy sent in the national guard to the University of Alabama when Governor George Wallace prohibited the enrollment of two black students. Confronted with such force, the governor backed down, and the blacks enrolled. In the spring of 1963, mass demonstrations for racial equality were held, not only in the South, but in the North as well; for racial injustice was present in all parts of the nation. Though peaceful in intent, the demonstrations sometimes grew violent, as in Birmingham, Alabama, where police used high-pressure fire hoses, electric cattle prods, and dogs against demonstrators. Though the city and the protestors finally reached an agreement on desegregation, another tragedy alerted the nation to the ills of racial injustice. In September 1963, a bomb, thrown into a black church in Birmingham, killed four girls attending a Sunday school class.

Governor Wallace (standing between two guards) blocks the entrance to the University of Alabama. Deputy U.S. Attorney General Nicholas Katzenbach confronts him.

In Congress, representatives from southern states had successfully blocked a civil rights bill that Kennedy had introduced in June 1963. To draw attention to the bill, Martin Luther King, Jr., organized a massive march on Washington, D.C. In August 1963, 200,000 demonstrators (60,000 of them white) marched into Washington, D.C., processing from the Washington to the Lincoln memorials. There they heard King declare that, despite the issuance of the Emancipation Proclamation 100 years before, "we must face the tragic fact that the Negro is still not free . . . the life of the Negro is still sadly crippled by the manacles of segregation and the chains of discrimination. One hundred years later, the Negro lives on a lonely island of poverty in the midst of a vast ocean of material prosperity. One hundred years later, the Negro is still languishing in the corners of American society and finds himself an exile in his own land.

Civil Rights March on Washington, D.C., 1963

"In a sense," continued King, "we have come to our nation's capital to cash a check. When the architects of our republic wrote the magnificent words of the Constitution and the Declaration of Independence, they were signing a promissory note to which every American was to fall heir . . . It is obvious today that America has defaulted on this promissory note insofar as her citizens of color are concerned."

King declared that the demonstrators had come "to this hallowed spot to remind America of the fierce urgency of now. This is no time to engage in the luxury of cooling off or to take the tranquilizing drug of gradualism. Now is the time to rise from the dark and desolate valley of segregation to the sunlit path of racial justice. Now is the time to open the doors of opportunity to all of God's children. Now is the time to lift our nation from the quicksands of racial injustice to the solid rock of brotherhood." King

Martin Luther King, Jr., in 1964

declared that the Negro would not rest until he achieved justice; but in "gaining our rightful place," King told his listeners, "we must not be guilty of wrongful deeds. Let us not seek to satisfy our thirst for freedom by drinking from the cup of bitterness and hatred . . . Again and again we must rise to the majestic heights of meeting physical force with soul force. The marvelous new militancy which has engulfed the Negro community must not lead us to distrust of all white people, for many of our white brothers, as evidenced by their presence here today, have come to realize that their destiny is tied up with our destiny and their freedom is inextricably bound to our freedom. We cannot walk alone.

"I am not unmindful," continued King, "that some of you have come here out of great trials and tribulations . . . You have been the veterans of creative suffering. Continue to work with the faith that unearned suffering is redemptive. Go back to Mississippi, go back to Alabama, go back to Georgia, go back to Louisiana, go back to the slums and ghettos of our northern cities, knowing that somehow this situation can and will be changed. Let us not wallow in the valley of despair."

King declared he had "a dream," one "deeply rooted in the American dream":

I say to you today, my friends, that in spite of the difficulties and frustrations of the moment . . . I have a dream that one day this nation will rise up and live out the true meaning of its creed: "We hold these truths to be self-evident: that all men are created equal" . . . I have a dream that my four children will one day live in a nation where they will not be judged by the color of their skin but by the content of their character.

Assassination

Lyndon B. Johnson takes the presidential oath of office not long after Kennedy's assassination. Jacqueline Kennedy stands at Johnson's left.

In November 1963, Kennedy went on a speaking trip to Texas that was, partly, a political junket in view of the national election of 1964. On November 22, the president spoke at a breakfast in Forth Worth, after which he was to address a luncheon crowd in Dallas. With Texas governor John B. Connolly and Mrs. Connolly, with his wife, Jacqueline, Kennedy rode in an open car in a motorcade through the streets of Dallas.

As the president greeted cheering crowds, a bullet struck him in the back of the neck. Another bullet hit Governor Connolly. A third bullet struck Kennedy in the back of the head. He fell into his wife's lap, staining her dress with his blood. A few minutes later, the president was dead.

Vice-President Lyndon Johnson, who rode in a car behind the Kennedy car, was sworn in as president on the plane that carried Kennedy's body back to Washington. Beside Johnson stood Mrs. Kennedy, still wearing the dress stained with her husband's blood. On November 25, Kennedy was buried in Arlington Cemetery, outside Washington.

"All I have I would have given gladly not to be standing here today," President Johnson told a joint session of Congress two days later. "The greatest leader of our time has been struck down by the foulest deed of our time.

Today John Fitzgerald Kennedy lives on in the immortal words and works that he left behind. He lives on in the mind and memories of mankind. He lives on in the hearts of his countrymen."

Then Johnson listed Kennedy's "dreams"—of international partnership, of education for all American children and of jobs for all American workers, of care for the elderly, "and above all, the dream of equal rights for all Americans, whatever their race or color." These "ideas and ideals," said Johnson, which Kennedy "so nobly represented must and will be translated into effective action. . . ."

Revolutionary Years

"Let us here highly resolve that John Fitzgerald Kennedy did not live—or die—in vain." Thus President Johnson addressed Congress and the American people, on January 8, 1964, in his first state of the union address. Johnson called on Congress to carry out Kennedy's "plans and programs" and so wage a relentless "war on poverty." He urged Congress to pass Kennedy's civil rights legislation and to approve the "most far-reaching tax cut of our

time." As part of an "all-out war on human poverty and unemployment," Congress, said Johnson, should provide health care for the elderly and should approve federal aid for the building of houses, schools, libraries and hospitals. With these measures, the president asked Congress and the country to join him "in expressing and fulfilling that faith in working for a nation, a nation that is free from want and a world that is free from hate; a world of peace and justice, and freedom and abundance, for our time and for all time to come."

Senator Barry Goldwater (left) meets with Lyndon B. Johnson, January 1964

Congress followed the president's urging and in July passed the Civil Rights Act of 1964. Besides strengthening voting rights protection, the act prohibited segregation in places of "public accommodation"—restaurants, hotels, terminals, etc.; required the federal government to withhold assistance to state or county programs that favored racial discrimination; gave the attorney general authority to institute lawsuits against segregation in schools; and established the Equal Employment Opportunity Commission (EEOC) to fight racial preferences in employment.

Nineteen-Sixty-Four was an election year. The Republicans, for the first time in many years, nominated a thoroughgoing conservative, Senator Barry Goldwater of Arizona. Goldwater had voted against the Civil Rights Act in the Senate and was opposed to the New Frontier social programs. "Extremism in the defense of liberty is no vice," declared the Arizona senator. "Moderation in the pursuit of justice is not virtue." The election was a landslide victory for Johnson and his vice-presidential running mate, Senator Hubert Humphrey of Minnesota. They won by the largest popular margin ever—61 percent of the popular vote—and trounced Goldwater in the electoral college (486 votes to 52). The Republican had taken only the Gulf states and Arizona.

With even greater Democratic majorities in Congress, Johnson entered his second term triumphant. The country, he declared in his first inaugural address, was in the midst of a "time of change—rapid and fantastic change, baring the secrets of nature, multiplying the nations, placing in uncertain hands new weapons for mastery and destruction, shaking old values and uprooting old ways." With echoes of the Rev. John Winthrop, Johnson continued: "Our destiny in the midst of change will rest on the unchanged character of our people—and on their faith. They came here—the exile and the stranger, brave but frightened—to find a place where a man could be his own man. They made a covenant with this land. Conceived in justice, written in liberty, bound in union, it was meant one day to inspire the hopes of all mankind."

In his state of the union address, given January 4, 1965, Johnson had already laid out his program for what he called his "Great Society." The new Congress was amenable to Johnson's programs—the greatest extension of federal power in American history. Congress approved a multi-billion dollar federal aid to schools and libraries bill; expanded Social Security to include "Medicare," medical care for people over age 65; and added anti-poverty programs. After a black civil rights worker and a white minister from the North were killed in Selma, Alabama for helping blacks to register to vote, Congress passed the Voting Rights Act. This act abolished most literacy tests for voting and authorized the sending of federal examiners to register voters in any county that practiced racial discrimination.

Sunk in A Morass

"In Asia, communism wears a more aggressive face.

"We see that in Viet Nam.

"Why are we there?"

Thus, President Johnson, in his second state of the union address, posed a question many would ask in the next eight years. Johnson answered his own question. "We are there," he said, "first, because a friendly nation has asked us for help against the Communist aggression. . . . What is at stake is the cause of freedom and in that cause America will never be found wanting."

As we have noted, since Eisenhower, U.S advisers and army personnel had aided South Vietnam in her war against Communist North Vietnam and South Vietnamese Communist guerrillas called the Viet Cong. In early August 1964, the American public learned that North Vietnamese torpedo boats had, within a two-day period, attacked U.S. destroyers in the Gulf of Tonkin. (They did not learn of the covert U.S. attacks in North Korea that prompted the violent exchange, nor did they know that, at the second of these Tonkin incidents, no North Vietnamese sea craft had been present.) In response, Johnson pushed the "Tonkin Resolution" through Congress, which gave him authority to halt further aggression. Johnson then launched retaliatory air attacks on North Vietnam and increased military aid to South Vietnam. A month after the president asked, "Why are we there?" Communist guerrillas attacked U.S. bases in South Vietnam. Johnson then ordered an all-out bombing of North Vietnam, south of the 20th parallel.

It soon became clear that air power alone could not overcome guerrilla forces. Though Congress had made no formal declaration of war, Johnson, on June 28, 1965, ordered more U.S. ground troops into Vietnam. The numbers of U.S. military sent to Vietnam would continue to increase, so that by 1968, about a half a million Americans were fighting in a war that, to many Americans, would seem a hopeless morass from which the country would not be able to extricate itself.

U.S. Marines evacuate an injured soldier from the battlefield in Vietnam

The Rise of the Counter Culture

The election of Kennedy, his youth, his seeming idealism had inspired the rising, post-war baby boom generation who, in the early '60s, had reached high school and college age. Many youth, it seems, had become disillusioned with

In a defoliation mission, a UH-1D helicopter from the 336th Aviation Company sprays Agent Orange on a dense jungle area in the Mekong Delta, Vietnam

an American dream that seemed to promise only more material prosperity, ease, and comfort; they had grown impatient with a society that proclaimed freedom and equality but denied them to some simply because they were not white. The civil rights movement had given these eager and idealistic youth a cause for which to fight, and many of them took up the cause with fervor.

Beginning in 1960, with the formation of Students for a Democratic Society at the University of Michigan in Ann Arbor, student groups fighting for civil rights and other causes began to form throughout the country. After eight students were suspended from the University of California at Berkeley for handing out leaflets and raising money for a civil rights group, the Free Speech Movement (FSM) sprang up. The FSM organized a student sit-in in Sproul Hall on the Berkeley campus, for which 800 students were arrested on December 3, 1964.

The Vietnam War further radicalized many American youth. In bombing North Vietnam, the United States used a chemical agent called napalm, a petroleum-based gelatinous substance that burned jungles where guerrilla forces lay in hiding. But Napalm also burned and destroyed villages and the civilian population. The military used Agent Orange, a highly toxic defoliant, to expose Viet Cong hideouts. Students groups protested the bombing and demanded that Johnson end it immediately. They were joined by prominent public figures, including Robert Kennedy and U Thant, Secretary General of the United Nations.

The television media throughout the war brought into American living rooms horrific film footage of the war; of bodies burnt by napalm, of refugee children, of American soldiers killed. Media coverage, coupled with the rising American death count (by 1969, 14,350 Americans would be killed, 323,600 wounded), made the war highly unpopular. Military conscription was in place. Young men, between the ages of 18 and 35, could be called for service, unless they were college students. Thousands of young men, some for conscience sake, others because they feared to be maimed and wounded in a war they despised, evaded the draft; some fled to Canada and even Europe. Protest rallies were held in which men publicly burned their draft cards.

The war became an occasion for unrest among blacks in the ghettos of American cities. By the mid '60s, nearly 70 percent of American blacks lived in cities, particularly in the North. Though northern cities had no segregation laws, the fact that blacks earned much less than whites meant that they lived separated from whites in the poorest and most run-down sections of the cities. Many blacks began to think that the government was diverting promised funds from them to the war effort. Dissatisfaction among blacks was, in some cases, fanned

Malcolm X (right) with Martin Luther King, Jr.

by radical black groups, such as the Nation of Islam. Founded in 1930 by Elijah Muhammad, the Nation of Islam favored the complete separation of the races in their own geographical regions. By the 1960s, Elijah Muhammad's disciple, Malcolm X, became the spokesman for the movement. Malcolm X rejected Martin Luther King, Jr.'s call for non-violence as naïve and advocated that blacks meet white violence with violence.

In the summers of 1966 and 1967, dissatisfaction in the ghettos boiled over in rioting. Riots and looting rocked Newark, New Jersey and Los Angeles, California. In the Detroit riots, which stretched from July 23–30, 1967, 43 were killed and over 2,000 were injured. Federal troops and the national guard were called in to quell the violence.

The decade of the '50s had already created a youth culture; the '60s gave rise to a youth counterculture. In January 1964, a British rock group called the Beatles had made its appearance on the American music scene and became a wild success. Their mushroom-like hairstyle inspired youth to abandon the short hair and crew cuts of the '50s and grow their hair long. Singers like Joan Baez and Bob Dylan helped popularize both traditional folk music and newer songs of social protest.

The war in Vietnam was splitting America down generational lines, with parents by and large supporting the war, their children opposing it. Soon, youth were not merely questioning the war but the entire adult world they had inherited. Their parents, they declared, were materialistic; they were hypocrites, espousing a code of conduct they violated in their daily lives. Unfortunately, their criticisms were often right on the mark; the older generation had given these youth many comforts, but few high, spiritual ideals. After a time many youth began to question, not only government but all the institutions of society—the church, marriage, and the family. What they wanted was freedom from what they thought were false and oppressive restraints on freedom. One did not need a marriage certificate to love another person, they argued—in fact, in the words of the Beatles song, "All you need is love," and then you can do what you wish.

The Haight-Ashbury neighborhood in San Francisco became, by early 1966, the center of the "hippie" culture. There young people gathered to live according to their ideals of

Joan Baez (left) and Bob Dylan at the Civil Rights March in Washington, D.C., 1963

peace, anarchic freedom, and free love. Men let their hair and beards grow long; both sexes dressed in colorful, outlandish clothing. Inspired sometimes by popular songs, hippies smoked pot and indulged in dangerous chemical "psychedelic" drugs, such as LSD, or "acid." In what was called the "Summer of Love," hippie culture spread across the United States. Soon nearly every major American city had its hippie center where middle class youth did drugs, indulged in sexual license, and, generally, escaped from an unpleasant, bland, and threatening world.

The hippie movement, with its disdain for marriage and embrace of free love, was but one facet of what became known as the "sexual revolution." Feminism revealed another aspect. In 1963, a book, *The Feminine Mystique* by Betty Friedan, claimed that society had reduced women to mere servants of men and so questioned what many considered the middle class achievement of the post-war world: the middle-class family. Under the leadership of writers like Friedan and Gloria Steinem, and of Bella Abzug and Shirley Chisholm (both U.S. representatives from New York), feminism, muted since the days of women's suffrage, returned with a vengeance. In 1966, Friedan and others formed the National Organization for Women (NOW) to fight, both socially and politically, for women's rights.

Feminists demanded full legal, economic and social equality with men. Just as earlier feminists had championed contraception to "free" women from "biological slavery" to men, so the feminists of the '60s trumpeted the cause of inexpensive, readily available abortion. Ironically, feminism tended to demean women further in men's eyes. The more women became like men in other areas, the more pronounced became their merely sexual differences. All the customs and traditions, the "chivalry," that had taught men not to treat women merely as objects of pleasure, were swept away as "demeaning" to women. Men were no longer to open doors for women, to stand when they sat down at table, to treat them with deference and respect. All that remained were the strong desires that civilization had always tried to temper and channel into marriage and family life.

The late '60s, in many ways, revived and magnified all the strange radical movements of the 1840s and the post-Civil War period. Feminism had returned, but with an added emphasis on abortion. Free love was reborn, far wilder than Moses Harmon's wildest dreams. Henry David Thoreau's radical individualism, which despised the wisdom of the past, inspired a mass movement whose members read (or talked about reading) *Walden* and *Civil Disobedience*. In sum, American progressivism and individualism had come to full flower—and many thought it a noxious weed, indeed.

Year of Unrest

On January 30, 1968, on the day of Tet, a great Vietnamese festival, the North Vietnamese launched their largest offensive against South Vietnam and her American ally. The North Vietnamese and the Viet Cong attacked 30 South Vietnamese cities and drove American troops from 100 major positions, inflicting heavy casualties. President Johnson had promised victory to the American people, but the Tet offensive led many to believe Vietnam a costly and hopeless war.

Amid the chants of protestors gathered around the White House—"LBJ, LBJ, how many kids have you killed today?"—Johnson weighed the political fallout of the Tet offensive. Since, in his first term, he had served as president for less than two years, Johnson could run again in November; the plummeting approval rating for him in the polls, however, convinced the president that, if he ran again, he would lose. On March 31, 1968, Johnson, in a television address to the American people, announced that he was calling a partial halt to the bombing of North Vietnam and that he would pursue peace negotiations with the North Vietnamese. Then came the surprising revelation: Johnson declared he would neither seek, nor accept, his party's nomination for the election in November.

Only a few days later, another event stunned the nation and sent it reeling. In March, Martin Luther King, Jr., had come to Memphis, Tennessee to lead a peaceful rally in support of the city's striking garbage workers. When the rally began to turn violent, King left Memphis but returned about a week later to address his followers. On April 4, while standing on the balcony of his hotel room, King was assassinated. As news of the assassination spread, black riots erupted in many American cities. In Washington, D.C. rioters came within two blocks of the White House before army units turned them back.

With Johnson's withdrawal from the race, new contenders arose to claim the Democratic nomination. Senator Eugene McCarthy of Wisconsin ran as a peace candidate, calling for immediate withdrawal from Vietnam. Robert Kennedy, who had become a United States Senator from New York, also threw his hat into the ring, calling for an end to the Vietnam

Robert Kennedy as attorney general speaking to blacks gathered outside the Justice Department, Washington, D.C., June 1963

War and for more federal aid to blacks and the poor. While campaigning in Los Angeles, California on June 5, Kennedy was shot by a Palestinian gunman, Sirhan Sirhan. Robert fell, clutching his rosary beads. He died the following day.

Violence seethed around the Democratic National Convention, which met in Chicago that year. Chicago's mayor, Richard Daley, had denied permits to protestors and called out 12,000 police, 5,000 national guard, and 7,500 federal troops to guard the convention site. On August 28, 3,000 anti-war demonstrators gathered outside and then tried to enter the convention hall. Police and national guardsmen attacked the protestors with clubs. Television cameras caught the entire scene, beaming images of the violence across the country. Hopes for victory for the Democratic candidate, Vice President Hubert Humphrey (President Johnson's choice), looked dim.

Though he had lost to Kennedy in 1960 and in his bid for California governor two years later, Richard Nixon secured the Republican Party presidential nomination in 1968. Nixon, with his vice presidential running mate, Spiro T. Agnew of Maryland, ran a relaxed campaign against Humphrey, refusing even to debate the Democratic candidate on television. Governor George C. Wallace and Air Force General Curtis LeMay ran on the American Independent Party ticket, calling for a conservative agenda and for a swift end of the war—which LeMay thought could be accomplished by dropping an atomic bomb on North Vietnam.

Meanwhile, Vietnam peace talks in Paris had yielded no results. North Vietnam insisted on a complete cessation of American bombing. On October 31, just days before the election, Johnson announced that he had ordered an end to all bombing of North Vietnam and had decided to include representatives of South Vietnam and the Viet Cong in the negotiations. This announcement, and Humphrey's endorsement of it, secured him the votes of those who wanted peace; but it was too little, too late. On November 3, Nixon and Agnew took 32 states (301 electoral votes), mostly in the Midwest, the West, and the South, while Humphrey won only 13 states and 191 electoral votes. Wallace followed with five states, yielding 46 electoral votes.

The year 1968 ended, however, on what many thought a positive note. Almost a year before, the spacecraft Apollo 1 had exploded on the launching pad at Cape Kennedy in Florida, killing its three astronauts. But in December 1968, Apollo 8 was launched successfully, carrying three men 240,000 miles into space. In 147 hours the astronauts orbited the moon ten times and then returned safely to Earth.

Post-War Catholics: Into the Mainstream

Richard Nixon campaigning in Philadelphia in 1968

Besides the peculiarly religious differences—obedience to pope and bishops, abstaining from meat on Fridays, confession of sins to a priest, etc.—American Catholics, after World War II, became hardly distinguishable from their fellow citizens. Like other Americans, Catholics were entering the middle class, moving to the suburbs, buying and enjoying consumer goods. Even the birthrate among Catholics, though higher than the average, was not remarkable, since the national birthrate, on the whole, had risen. Besides embracing a more pronounced anti-Communism, Catholics had no common set of political goals on which they all agreed. Like other Americans, poorer Catholics favored more progressive policies, while the upwardly mobile grew ever more conservative. Catholics, thus, after a long wade in the shallows, had entered the American mainstream.

On the whole, the post-war Catholic Church in America seemed to be thriving. Dioceses built new churches, schools, and hospitals. Sixty-five percent of Catholics attended Mass weekly. About 60,000 priests served the Catholic population, while 25,000 men attended the country's seminaries. A number of Americans, attracted to the Church, converted. New contemplative monasteries were springing up around the country. A few Catholic books had even reached the best-seller list, and Bishop Fulton Sheen's weekly television broadcast rivaled the popular Ed Sullivan Show in ratings. Though slow in coming, Catholic lay movements like Catholic Action were gaining momentum, and the Catholic Worker still held its own; Catholic journals such as *Commonweal, America,* and *Integrity* lent a sometimes radical Catholic perspective to the issues of the time. On the whole, educated Catholics seemed to have a good grasp of their faith and were trying to apply it to the conditions of the world in which they lived.

Archbishop Fulton Sheen

Among the topics that engaged the interest of Catholic laymen as well as clergy were the role of the laity in the Church and the world and the question whether there should be a reform of rules in seminaries and in the life of religious sisters. The reform of the liturgy, instituted under Pope Pius X and continued under the reigning pontiff, Pius XII, held significant interest, with the magazine *Orate Fratres* (later *Worship*), published by the Benedictine monks of St. John's Collegeville in Minnesota, in the forefront of liturgical debate. Catholics explored the question whether the Church could ever allow the use of artificial contraception and, if the United States became Catholic, where Church and state should remain separate. Father John A. Ryan argued that in a Catholic United States, the state would have to accord public acknowledgment to the Catholic Church as the true religion and accept Catholic teaching as its moral guide. But Father John Courtney Murray, a Jesuit, argued that even a Catholic United States should maintain the Church/state separation and that the Church had no power over the state, not even indirectly (as an acknowledged moral guide.) For his nontraditional views, Murray's superiors silenced him.

In the 1950s, the conversion of the United States to the Church did not seem an unreal possibility. English convert and writer Evelyn Waugh (who generally had little good to say about Americans), perhaps, expressed the sentiment of many when he wrote in *Life* magazine in 1949 that the Catholic faith "is not something alien and opposed to the American spirit, but an essential part of it." Waugh spoke of a "purely American 'way of life' led by every good American Christian"—a life, he said, "that is point-for-point opposed to the publicized and largely fictitious 'way of life' dreaded in Europe and Asia. And that, by the Grace of God, is the 'way of life' that will prevail."

Opening Windows

Pope Pius XII died on October 9, 1958. Many thought his successor, the 76-year-old John XXIII, had been chosen by "liberal" and "conservative" factions in the curia as a compromise candidate. But if any thought that a compromise pope's pontificate would be uneventful, they were wrong. On January 25, 1959, John XXIII announced that he would call an ecumenical council. The announcement surprised the Church and the world, for ecumenical councils were usually called to clarify some doctrinal point that has been in question, or in times of crisis. Pope Pius IX had called the last ecumenical council in 1870 (called simply *the* Vatican Council) during the crisis of 19th century Liberalism. What was Pope John's purpose in calling a new council?

At the opening of the council on October 11, 1962, Pope John declared he had called the gathering of the world's bishops to take "into account the errors, the requirements, and the opportunities of our time" so that the eternal truths of the Church "might be presented in exceptional form to all men throughout the world." The pope said he disagreed "with those prophets of gloom, who are always forecasting disaster, as though the end of the world was at hand." And he insisted that "in the present order of things, Divine Providence is leading us to a new order of human relations which, by men's own efforts and even beyond their very expectations, are directed toward the fulfillment of God's superior and inscrutable designs."

In the early '60s such optimism resonated with people, especially in the United States. American Catholics felt that they had "arrived" and that the world could be changed for the better. In Rome, they had Pope John XXIII, beloved for his kindness by all the world; in the United States, John Fitzgerald Kennedy was president, a man brimming with optimistic idealism. Pope John's call for *aggiornamento,* or the "updating" of the Church, ended, it seemed, the state of war that had existed between the Church and the modern world since before the days of Pius IX. All in all, it seemed that a new day was dawning for the Church, both in the world and in the United States.

Catholics eager to know what the council was up to gleaned little from the official reports of the American bishops. But when the *New York Times* published an account of the council that revealed deep divisions between "liberal" and "conservative" council fathers, more than just Catholics became interested. The *Times* began running daily accounts of council happenings, and American Catholics began to think that the Church was doing something more than updating herself. Revolutionary changes, it seemed, were afoot.

Pope John XXIII

"The Church Here is in Crisis"

In 1963, Cardinal Spellman, the archbishop of New York City, did a surprising thing. He brought the long-silenced John Courtney Murray to Rome as a *peritus* ("expert"), thus seeming to bless Murray's non-traditional views on the mutual roles of Church and state. What's more, John Courtney Murray became a chief architect of what was to become a most important conciliar document, *Dignitatis Humanae,* the *Declaration on Religious Liberty.* The first drafts of this document presented to the council fathers seemed in direct contradiction to traditional papal teaching on the relationship of Church and state. The traditional teaching held that the state must acknowledge the truth of the Catholic faith, protect the Church as the institution founded by Christ for the salvation of men, and accept the Church as the moral guide of society. As for personal freedom of religion, the Church taught that no one had the right to adhere to a false religion, since error has no rights. Nor should the state acknowledge freedom of religion or freedom of conscience, except where prudence dictates it must. Catholic theologians had argued that a society constituted this way was in accord with natural and divine law. They acknowledged, however, that such a society was not always possible: that Catholic governments could not always suppress false ideas or all immorality but had, instead, to tolerate them. But if a government had to tolerate a false religion and grant its adherents religious liberty, it was not to acknowledge the religion's inherent right to exist or, worse yet, place it on an equal footing with the Catholic Church. The early drafts of *Dignitatis Humanae* seemed to alter this traditional doctrine.

In defense of the declaration, Murray published a paper for the council fathers called "The Problem of Religious Freedom." In this paper, Murray argued that the Church's traditional teachings on Church-state relations were conditioned by the historical consciousness of the times in which they were enunciated. In the 20th century, the historical consciousness demanded complete religious liberty; thus, said Murray, the Church must seek how she can authoritatively give her approval to religious liberty. He said the only right the Church could demand from the state in the modern world was the freedom to carry out her own proper duties. He approved of the situation where the state treated the Catholic Church no differently than it treats other religious bodies; the state, he said, should acknowledge freedom of religion and freedom of conscience, except where they came into conflict with the "public order," as the common opinion of the people defined it. Murray did not entirely dismiss the possibility of a modern state recognizing by law the Catholic Church as "the common religion of the people." But there could be no tolerance, he said, for religious intolerance in the modern world:

> [N]o argument can be made today that would validate the legal institution of religious intolerance, much less canonize it as a Catholic ideal. The institution cannot even be tolerated today as a harmless archaism. Nor is it even permissible to raise the question, whether legal intolerance may be useful to the people—either to the people of God or to the civil people. The fact is that legal intolerance stands condemned today by the common consciousness of the peoples of the world. The condemnation is binding today on all civilized states . . . Today, religious freedom, as a human and civil right, personal and corporate, which requires the protection of a legal institution, has emerged as an exigence of the personal and political reason. As such, it claims the sanction of Catholic doctrine.

Cardinal Spellman in 1946

The final draft of *Dignitatis Humanae,* though including much of Murray's thought, did not go as far a Murray wanted. In fact, the declaration stated that the council "leaves intact the traditional Catholic doctrine on the moral duty of men and societies towards the true religion and the one Church of Christ"—thus signifying that that the declaration had to be interpreted in light of the traditional Catholic teaching on Church-state relations. Still, the declaration insisted that since, in order to discover truth, men need a certain degree of liberty, the state should grant citizens the widest possible freedom of religion and conscience. Such freedoms, however, were in no way absolute, but had to be adjusted to the good of

Pope Paul VI presides at the Second Vatican Council, by Lothar Wolleh

the "common welfare" or "public order." Public order is safeguarded, said the council, where the rights of all citizens are protected, where public peace is preserved, and where public morality is duly given due protection.

Though the Church did not change any teaching with *Dignitatis Humanae* (or, indeed in any of the council documents), many authors gave the impression that she had. American Catholics were told that the Church had altered her teaching on religious liberty, on the relationship between the Catholic Church and other churches and religions, and in other areas as well. What's more, Catholics were told that the Church was about to lift the "ban" on artificial contraception. At the opening of the council, Pope John XXIII had removed the subject of contraception from the discussions of the council fathers and had, instead, appointed a commission to look into the question. When Pope John died on June 3, 1963, the new pope, Paul VI, continued the commission and expanded it. The majority of the commission concluded that the Church should change her teaching on artificial contraception.

Given the commission's conclusion, many Catholic theologians and priests began saying that it was permissible for Catholic married couples to use artificial contraceptives to limit the size of their families. But the problem was, the commission had spoken, the pope hadn't. When, on July 25, 1968, the pope finally spoke, in the encyclical letter *Humanae Vitae* ("Of Human Life"), he reiterated traditional Church teaching that artificial contraception violated the natural ends of marriage and of sexual intercourse.

The storm of protest was swift and furious. Priests, prominent theologians, and journalists publicly criticized *Humanae Vitae* and Pope Paul. A standard tactic was to deny that *Humanae Vitae* delivered infallible teaching, but some theologians went even further and questioned the very doctrine of papal infallibility. Father Charles Curran, a professor at the Catholic University of America and vice-president of the Catholic Theological Society of America, issued a statement, signed by 200 theologians, denying the authority of *Humanae Vitae*.

The theologians' statement, published in the July 30, 1968 *New York Times*, was profoundly revolutionary. Theologians denied the unique authority of pope, asserting that "Christian Tradition assigns theologians the special responsibility of evaluating and interpreting pronouncements of the Magisterium." Indeed, the theologians claimed, one cannot accept what the pope and bishops say without taking into account "the witness of the life of the Church in its totality," which includes (in the case of contraception) the witness of Catholic couples and the "witness of the separated Christian churches." The encyclical, furthermore, wrote the theologians, is "insensitive to the witness of many men of good will" and pays "insufficient attention to the ethical import of modern science."

Though on July 31, the U.S. bishops spoke out in support of *Humanae Vitae,* they could not offset the rebellion of Curran and the theologians. In seminaries, in theologates, in books, in the pages of the national weekly, *The National Catholic Reporter,* voices were calling for a new, democratic Church. The "Spirit," they said, speaks through the laity as well as the clergy, and the hierarchy must listen to their witness. If Catholics disagreed with a teaching of the magisterium, they could reject it.

As the revolution of the late '60s progressed, thousands of men left the priesthood, and many women religious abandoned their orders. The once teeming population of the seminaries dwindled dramatically. Millions of Catholic faithful, too, dropped out of the Church, and regular Mass attendance declined by 30 percent. The lay movements languished or openly promoted heresy. The once flourishing American Catholic Church was undergoing what Paul VI (speaking of the entire Church) called "autodestruction."

In the November 1971 issue of the *Homiletic and Pastoral Review,* Father Kenneth Baker described the state of the Church in America in the years after the Second Vatican Council:

> With each year it seems that we get closer to an "American Church" separate from Rome. For millions of Catholics it already exists in fact, though not yet officially . . . Even though the entrenched bureaucracy will not admit it, the Church here is in bad shape. There has been a loss of morale and élan. But what should one expect when most Catholic children do not know the basics of the faith, when heresy is openly taught and defended in "Catholic" universities, when seminarians have declined from 48,000 to about 5,000, and when only 14 million out of 55 million Catholics go to Church regularly on Sunday? It is not an exaggeration to say that the Church here is in a crisis.

A Nation Divided Again

Richard Nixon summed up the state of the country well in his inaugural address on January 20, 1969. "We find ourselves rich in goods," said the new president, "but ragged in spirit; reaching with magnificent precision for the moon, but falling into ravenous discord on earth." America, indeed, was divided over the war in Vietnam, over issues of race and, even, over what constitutes fundamental morality. In 1968, the country had seemed to totter on the brink of chaos; could America stand another such year and survive as a nation?

Within the first month of his administration, the new president and South Vietnam resumed peace talks with North Vietnam and the Viet Cong. In June, however, Nixon announced that the talks were going nowhere. He would begin withdrawal of American troops, he said, from the war zone as long as the South Vietnamese enhanced their ability to defend their country and the North Vietnamese did not increase their attacks on remaining American forces. But despite troop withdrawals, the war continued into Nixon's second term, which began in 1973.

Nixon's policy towards peace protests was to ignore them. He took a similar tack in race relations; unlike Kennedy and Johnson, Nixon treated the race question with "benign neglect." Yet, though he vetoed a number of health and education bills the Democratic-dominated Congress sent him, Nixon did not try to whittle down the size and scope of the federal government. In his state of the union address in January 1970, he called for the appropriation of $10 million to clean the nation's rivers and lakes. It seems he hoped the environment would be an issue that would unite Americans. "Restoring nature to its natural state," said Nixon, "is a cause beyond party and beyond factions. It has become a common cause of all the people of this country."

Most Americans could agree on the significance and importance of America's—and mankind's—first landing on the moon on July 20, 1969. People all over the world watched televised footage of astronaut Neal Armstrong descending from his spacecraft to tread the moon's surface. "That's one small step for man, one giant leap for mankind," he said. To the three astronauts, across 200,000 miles of space, Nixon said "for one priceless moment in the whole history of men all the people on this earth are truly one—one in their pride in what you have done and one in our prayers that you will return safely to earth." Between July 1969 and December 1972, the United States would conduct five more moon landings.

Nixon's landslide presidential victory in 1972 (with 60.7 of the popular vote) indicated the public's approval of his administration. The end of the Vietnam War the following year could have begun what would probably be a long period of national healing. Yet it would not be so. Revelations of scandals in the Nixon administration surrounding the break-in and bugging of the Democratic national headquarters at the Watergate building in Washington, D.C. during the 1972 campaign would force Richard Nixon to resign the presidency (August 1974) and reopen wounds that, it seemed, had just begun to heal.

Apollo 11 moon print, 1969

A Thaw in the Cold War

The moon landings showed to the world that the United States had won the space race. They indicated, too, that the United States was also winning in the race for world dominance against the Soviet Union. It was, perhaps, with confidence in America's superiority that President Nixon in 1972 began making friendly overtures to both Communist China and the Soviet Union. In February 1972, Nixon became the first U.S. president to visit China. There, for eight days, he met with, and was entertained by, Red China's leaders. Nixon called his visit "the week that changed the world."

The United States and China agreed to expand their cultural, educational, and journalistic contacts and to broaden trade between their two nations. Though the United States still formally recognized Taiwan's government as the government for all China, the Nixon administration, in October 1972, agreed to remove its objections to Red Chinese membership in the United Nations. Subsequently, the United Nations admitted Red China and expelled Taiwan.

Nixon traveled to Moscow to meet with Soviet premier Leonid Ilyich Brezhnev in May 1972. They met to discuss progress in the Strategic Arms Limitation Treaty (SALT) talks between the two countries, but they forged other agreements as well: on limiting atomic weapons; protecting the natural environment; on sharing medical, space and technological knowledge; on forming a joint trade commission. Nixon was even allowed to address the Russian people by television. To reciprocate the good will, the United States government entertained Brezhnev in Washington in June of the following year.

A New Fight for Justice

As we have seen, under Chief Justice Earl Warren, the Supreme Court of the United States invoked progressive interpretations of the Constitution, particularly of the 14th Amendment, to end segregation in and to remove religion from public schools. The court would soon use similar interpretations to destroy the right of states to protect public morality and unborn human life.

In 1965, the Supreme Court struck down a Connecticut law that penalized the use of contraceptives. The state court had convicted the medical director of the Planned Parenthood League of Connecticut for prescribing a contraceptive device to a married couple. The Supreme Court heard this case, *Griswold v. Connecticut,* on appeal, and on June 7 laid down its controversial decision that the Connecticut law was unconstitutional because it violated a married couple's constitutional right to privacy.

Chief Justice Earl Warren

The justices knew that "privacy" was not among the enumerated Constitutional rights; Justice Douglas, however, argued that the enumerated rights have "penumbras"—non-enunciated rights—"that help give [enumerated rights] life and substance." For instance, the First Amendment's right to freedom of speech doesn't just protect speaking one's thoughts; it also protects other rights, which are penumbras of the right to speak freely: the rights to distribute, receive and read literature, for instance. Likewise, wrote Douglas, the enunciated right to freedom of association implies a penumbral right to privacy in one's associations.

The problem with the Connecticut law, wrote Douglas, was that it forbade the *use* of contraceptives, not their sale and manufacture. By forbidding the use of contraceptives, the law violated a married couple's *constitutional* right to privacy. Justice Arthur Goldberg, who concurred in the decision, went further. In a separate opinion, Goldberg said that the 9th Amendment (which states that "the enumeration in the Constitution of certain rights, shall not be construed to deny or disparage others retained by the people") gave the Supreme Court the power to protect "fundamental rights." The justices, wrote Goldberg, would not make up such rights based on their own personal beliefs but would consult the "'tradition and [collective] conscience of our people' as to whether a principle is 'so rooted [there] . . . as to be ranked as fundamental.'" Thus, Supreme Court justices were not simply supposed to decide whether a law was in accord with the Constitution but whether it was in accord with the "collective conscience" of the people.

Justice Hugo Black wrote in his dissenting opinion that Goldberg's interpretation of the 9th Amendment gave the federal courts the power "to invalidate any legislative act which the judges find irrational, unreasonable, or offensive." Indeed, far from granting the federal courts more power, the Ninth Amendment, said Black, limits federal power by forbidding the government to violate unenumerated rights simply because they are not mentioned in the Constitution. It does not give the federal courts the right to declare what those rights are. "The adoption of such a loose, flexible, uncontrolled standard for holding laws unconstitutional," wrote Black, "if ever it is finally achieved, will amount to a great unconstitutional shift of power to the courts which I believe and am constrained to say will be bad for the courts and worse for the country." Justice Potter Stewart, who concurred with Black, wrote in a separate opinion that "the idea that a federal court could ever use the Ninth Amendment to annul a law passed by the elected representatives of the State of Connecticut would have caused James Madison [the architect of the Bill of Rights] no little wonder."

Justice Black protested against what he called the court's attempt to update the Constitution. The Fathers who drafted the Constitution, wrote Black, had already provided a means to update that instrument—the amendment process. "That method of change was good for our Fathers," wrote Black, "and being somewhat old-fashioned, it is good enough for me."

Eight years later, the Supreme Court invoked the "right to privacy" in one of the most controversial judicial decisions in American history—*Roe v. Wade.* A single woman, "Jane Roe" (a pseudonym) who wanted to have an abortion challenged a Texas law that banned abortions except to save the life of the mother. Justice Harry A. Blackmun (appointed by Nixon in 1970) argued for the court that the Texas law was unconstitutional because it violated Jane Roe's right to privacy. "State criminal abortion laws," wrote Blackmun, "like those involved here, that except from criminality only a life-saving procedure on the mother's behalf without regard to the stage of her pregnancy and other interests involved violate the Due Process Clause of the Fourteenth Amendment, which protects against state action the right to privacy, including a woman's qualified right to terminate her pregnancy." (The 14th Amendment states that a state shall not "deprive any person of life, liberty or property without due process of law . . .")

Though the 14th Amendment declares a state shall not "deprive any *person* of life, liberty, or property," Blackmun declared that, since society is not agreed as to whether the definition of "person" includes unborn human life, the life of unborn children is not protected by the Constitution. Refusing to define when life begins, Blackmun drew the line for a legal definition of *person* at "viability"—the point where an unborn child is able to survive on its own, independent of the mother.

Blackmun, however, declared that the right to privacy is not absolute; that the state, at some point, may have an interest in protecting the unborn before viability. This interest "in protecting both the pregnant woman's health and the potentiality of human life . . . grows and reaches a 'compelling' point at various stages of the woman's approach to term," wrote Blackmun. In the first three months (the first trimester) of pregnancy, the state has no compelling interest in protecting the woman's health and the unborn life, so the abortion decision "must be left to the medical judgment of the pregnant woman's attending physician." After the first trimester, the state may regulate the abortion procedure but only in ways that "are reasonably related to maternal health." After viability, the state, "in promoting its interest in the potentiality of human life, may, if it chooses, regulate, and even proscribe, abortion except where necessary, in appropriate medical judgment, for the preservation of the life or health of the mother."

Justice William Rehnquist (another Nixon appointee) disagreed with the majority decision. Rehnquist wrote that the right to privacy has nothing to do with abortion. The 14th Amendment, he said, doesn't protect citizens against being deprived of their liberty simply but only if they are so deprived without due process of law. In other words, the amendment says that one cannot be deprived of liberty unless he be convicted of a crime in a court of law; it says nothing about state laws which, inevitably, limit some freedom. (Traffic laws, for instance, limit one's freedom to drive the wrong way on a one-way street.)

William Rehnquist in 1972

Rehnquist argued that when the court decides to do things, such as "break pregnancy into three distinct terms," it is not acting like a court but like a legislature. The role of the Supreme Court, said Rehnquist, is not to decide when and where a state has a compelling interest in restricting abortion but simply to determine the intent of the men who drew up the 14th Amendment. Did they, indeed, intend to restrict the state's right to determine what are the best laws for their people?

The decision in *Roe v. Wade* effectively struck down, not only the Texas statutes restricting abortion, but all such statutes nationwide. Already, in the late '60s, California and Colorado had become the first states to liberalize their abortion laws; but after 1973, all the states had to follow the same path, by command of the Supreme Court. Organizations such as NOW and Planned Parenthood, thus, haled the court's decision as a great victory for women's rights; others praised the decision as a further guarantee of individual liberty. But there were others who saw it for what it was: not only a further erosion of state sovereignty but a blow to the respect and protection owed to the dignity of human life.

Indeed, critics of *Roe v. Wade* were not lacking. They coalesced in a new movement for justice, the "right-to-life" or "pro-life" movement. Though many of the early leaders of the movement were Catholic, it would soon embrace a wide coalition of faiths and of those, even, who embraced no religion. Though present worldwide, the pro-life movement would be strongest in the United States. The movement would assail the corridors of political power, both on the state and national levels, but would also turn to direct action, reminiscent of the anti-war protests of the '60s and early '70s. Though a very few pro-life activists embraced violence, the vast majority engaged in prayer vigils, acts of peaceful civil disobedience, sidewalk counseling of women seeking abortions, and public education. These actions would inspire disgust, hatred and even, at times, violence, for they had that characteristic present in all movements for social justice—they challenged the conscience of the people.

Chapter 29 Review

Summary

- Before, during, and after the Second World War, the congressional House Un-American Activities Committee investigated "subversive groups," especially Nazis and Communists.

- On June 25, 1950, Korea erupted in a war instigated by Communists in North Korea. On June 27, President Truman gave his support to the United Nations Security Council's declaration of war on North Korea. The United Nations sent in troops, and soon U.N. forces compelled more than half of the North Korean army to surrender. On October 7 the United Nations General Assembly approved an invasion of North Korea, and by the end of the month North Korean resistance had been broken. When Chinese forces came into the fight, U.N. Forces withdrew from North Korea until they were able to stabilize their lines, and began a new counter-offensive. Peace negotiations began in July 1951 and continued for two years.

- The invasion of South Korea heightened American fears of Communism, and Senator Joseph McCarthy led a crusade to weed out Communists, who, he said, were infiltrating the United States government. In 1954, McCarthy was accused of conduct "unbecoming a member of the United States Senate" and formally censured.

- In the presidential election of 1952, Dwight D. Eisenhower became president, giving the Republicans control of the executive branch again after 20 years. Eisenhower chose big businessmen to fill the chief posts in his administration. Eisenhower's "dynamic conservatism" was more openly in favor of private big business while still maintaining and even expanding federal social programs.

- During Eisenhower's administration, covert operations were conducted in other countries, under the auspices of the Central Intelligence Agency (CIA). The CIA helped topple and establish foreign governments. When the Democrats regained control of Congress in the elections of 1954, Eisenhower had a hard time getting his policies approved. Even after the death of Stalin, U.S. military spending remained massive, and more powerful and deadly weapons were developed.

Chapter 29 Review (continued)

- In October 1957, the Soviets launched the world's first earth-orbiting satellite, *Sputnik*. In January 1958, the United States launched a satellite, *Explorer I.* This led to the passage of the National Aeronautic and Space Act in July 1958 and the founding of the National Aeronautics and Space Administration (NASA).

- President Eisenhower appointed Earl Warren as Chief Justice of the Supreme Court, an act that would have long-lasting effects. During Warren's term, the Supreme Court overthrew racial segregation in schools. A black woman, Rosa Parks, fought segregation by refusing to give up her seat on a bus to a white man. In November 1956, the Supreme Court ruled segregation in local transport unconstitutional. Eisenhower became involved in the segregation issue in 1957, and on September 9, Congress passed the first civil rights act since 1870, creating a federal Civil Rights Commission.

- After the Second World War, prosperity dawned on the United States, including an upsurge in population called the "Baby Boom," increased production, and more jobs. The working man's wage rose, and a GI bill allowing more men to go to college led to an increase in the number of "white collar" workers. The rise in wages brought more people into the middle class. An increase in housing led to suburbanization, which in turn led to an increase in private transportation and highways. American culture grew even more homogenous through the proliferation of "chain" stores and popular entertainment, such as television. In the 1950s youth became consumers, and an entire youth culture arose.

- In 1960, John Fitzgerald Kennedy became president and introduced his federal aid program called the "New Frontier." Kennedy was unable to get Congress to approve most of his New Frontier legislation, however. Many Americans found the Kennedy vitality and idealism invigorating.

- In 1961, the Soviets sent a manned spacecraft around the earth. The United States sent its first astronaut, Alan Shepard, into space a month later. The arms race continued when the Soviets broke the verbal agreement to stop nuclear testing. Kennedy followed suit on April 25, 1962 and ordered the resumption of nuclear testing. Fearing

the long-term health effects of nuclear radiation, the United States, the Soviet Union, and Great Britain signed the Nuclear Test Ban Treaty on August 5, 1963.

- Following Martin King Luther, Jr.'s call for non-violent resistance, students began to challenge racial segregation through "sit-ins." Consequently, many eating establishments removed segregated seating, and the Interstate Commerce Commission prohibited racial segregation on buses and in terminals used in interstate commerce. In the spring of 1963, mass demonstrations for racial equality were held in the North as well as the South.

- On November 22, 1963, President Kennedy was shot while on a speaking trip in Texas. His vice president, Lyndon Johnson, was sworn in as president on the plane on the way back to Washington. Johnson called on Congress to carry out Kennedy's plans and programs, and at his urging Congress passed the Civil Rights Act of 1964.

- When in August 1964 North Vietnamese torpedo boats attacked U.S. destroyers, President Johnson pushed the "Tonkin Resolution," which gave him authority to halt further aggression. He then launched retaliatory air strikes on North Vietnam and increased military aid to South Vietnam. When Communist guerrillas attacked U.S. bases in South Vietnam, Johnson ordered an all-out bombing of North Vietnam and sent more troops into Vietnam.

- During the 1960s, the youth of the baby boom generation became disillusioned with the American dream and what they deemed the hypocrisy of society. The civil rights movement gave them a cause to fight for. The Vietnam war further radicalized American youth, and they began protesting the bombings and atrocities of the war. The youth began questioning not only government but all the institutions of society.

- The Vietnam War affected other groups. Media coverage of the war and the rising death count of American soldiers made the war highly unpopular and caused unrest amongst blacks in the ghettos of American cities. Malcolm X, a spokesman for the Nation of Islam movement, encouraged violence against segregation.

Chapter 29 Review (continued)

- Feminism arose as a facet of the "sexual revolution." Feminists formed the National Organization for Women to fight for women's rights. They promoted contraception and abortion and full legal, economic, and social equality with men.

- After the Tet Offensive in Vietnam in January 1968, President Johnson called a partial halt to the bombing of North Vietnam and said he would pursue peace negotiations. On October 31, Johnson ordered an end to all bombing in North Vietnam.

- On October 11, 1962, Pope John XXIII called an ecumenical council in order to "update" the Church. When the media started covering the council, it seemed as if revolutionary changes were afoot. In 1963 Cardinal Spellman of New York brought the long-silenced John Courtney Murray to Rome as a *peritus*, and Murray became a chief architect of the conciliar document, *Dignitatis Humanae*, the *Declaration on Religious Liberty*. In defense of the declaration, Murray published a paper for the council fathers called, "The Problem of Religious Freedom."

- Though the Church did not change any teaching in Vatican II, many authors gave the impression that she had, especially in regards to artificial contraception. Thousands of priests and women religious abandoned their vocations. John XXIII's successor, Paul VI, addressed the question of contraception in the encyclical letter, *Humane Vitae*. Following this, American Catholic theologians criticized the pope and his encyclical. Some Catholic theologians denied the authority of the pope.

- Richard Nixon, who had become president in 1968, resumed peace talks with North Vietnam, but they were going nowhere. To unite Americans around a common issue, he addressed environmental problems. Then on July 20, 1969, Neal Armstrong landed on the moon. Nixon began making friendly overtures to both Communist China and Russia.

- In 1965, the Supreme Court struck down a Connecticut law that penalized the use of contraceptives, based on a constitutional "right to privacy." Eight years later, the Supreme Court invoked the "right to privacy" in *Roe v. Wade* that struck down not only Texas statutes restricting abortion, but all such statutes nationwide. Critics of the deci-

sion coalesced in a new movement for justice, the right-to-life or "pro-life" movement.

Key Concepts

dynamic conservatism: the program of the Eisenhower administration that openly favored private big business while maintaining and even expanding federal social programs.

suburbanization: the growth of residential and business areas on the edges of cities

Dates to Remember

1950: the United States enters the war in Korea.

1955: Rosa Parks refuses to give up her seat on a public bus to a white man.

The Rev. Martin Luther King, Jr. begins his fight against segregation.

1957: the Soviets launch the world's first earth-orbiting satellite.

1958: the United States launches its first satellite.

1960: black students begin "sit-ins" against segregation.

1961: the Soviets first and then the Americans send manned spacecraft into Earth's orbit.

1962: the Second Vatican Ecumenical Council begins (October 11).

1964: Congress approves the Tonkin Resolution.

1966: feminists form the National Organization for Women.

1968: President Johnson calls an end to all bombing in North Vietnam (October 31).

1968: Pope Paul VI promulgates the encyclical, *Humanae Vitae*.

1969: Neal Armstrong lands on the moon (July 20).

1973: the Supreme Court lays down its *Roe v. Wade* decision.

Central Characters

Joseph McCarthy (1908–1957): U.S. senator who led a campaign against Communist subversion in government

Dwight D. Eisenhower (1890–1969): 34th president of the United States, who instituted "dynamic conservative" policies

Rosa Parks (1913–2005): black civil rights activist who refused to give up her seat to a white man on a bus, thus sparking the civil rights movement

Martin Luther King, Jr. (1929–1968): social activist who led the civil rights movement until his assassination in 1968

John F. Kennedy (1917–1963): 35th president of the United States and the first and only Catholic president of the United States. He was assassinated during a speaking tour in Texas.

Lyndon Johnson (1908–1973): 36th president of the United States, who signed into law the Civil Rights Act of 1964, promoted "Great Society" social programs, and expanded involvement in the Vietnam War

Earl Warren (1891–1974): chief justice of the U.S. Supreme Court under whose leadership the court made rulings dismantling racial segregation and overturning laws protecting public morality and banning abortion

Saint John XXIII (1881–1963): the pope who called the Second Vatican Council

Blessed Paul VI (1897–1978): the pope who presided over the conclusion of the Second Vatican Council and who wrote *Humanae Vitae* in response to the question of contraception

Questions for Review

1. Why did the United States participate in the Korean War?

2. What effects did the policies of the Eisenhower Administration have on society?

3. What was the role of the CIA in U.S. foreign interventions in the 1950s?

4. Lay out Chief Justice Earl Warren's reasoning in his decision in *Brown v. Board of Education of Topeka*. On what grounds did 96 southern congressman criticize the decision in March 1956?

5. Explain the effects the phenomenon of suburbanization had on the culture of the United States in the 1940s–1960s.

6. Describe the "middle class" culture of the United States in the 1950s and early 1960s.

7. What "dream" did Martin Luther King, Jr. have?

8. Why, according the President Johnson, was the United States in Vietnam?

9. How did the culture of the 1960s and the Vietnam War serve to radicalize the American youth and bring about the hippie movement?

10. What were the goals of the feminist movement of the 1960s?

11. What was the character of the post-World War II Catholic Church in the United States?

12. Explain the reasons Pope John XXIII gave for calling the Second Vatican Ecumenical Council.

13. What led to the upheavals in the Catholic Church in the United States after the Council?

14. How did the Supreme Court in *Abington School District v. Schempp* interpret the First Amendment in regards to religion?

15. What is the "right to privacy"? Where did Justice William O. Douglas in the *Griswold* decision say he found this right in the Constitution? How was the "right to privacy" used in the Supreme Court decision, *Roe v. Wade*?

Ideas in Action

1. Read about and watch videos of the first moon landing.

2. Interview someone who lived during the cultural revolution of the 1960s. Ask his or her opinion of the changes and how they have affected our society today.

3. Discuss Justice William O. Douglas' understanding of penumbral rights in the Constitution. Does, for instance, the right to freedom of association imply a right to privacy? If it does, is it the business of courts to define such a penumbral right? And if penumbral rights exist, how do we determine which rights are more fundamental?

4. We have seen in our study that the conviction that the United States has a special mission to the world as a sort of City on a Hill was common in American history. How was this conviction appar-

Chapter 29 Review (continued)

ent in the post-World War II world? Who upheld it? Did anyone question it?

5. Read documents of the Second Vatican Council (*Lumen Gentium* and *Gaudium et Spes* recommended) and compare what the council fathers said to what is happening in the Church now.

Highways and Byways

The Cloth of Immortality

The 1960s were a time of great change, not only socially, but in fashion as well. Bell-bottom jeans, tie-dye, and psychedelic colors became very popular. Some interesting costumes of the period were made out of a new kind of cloth: polyester. Polyester is a man-made material, scientifically classified as a polymer, a substance made up of very large molecules called macromolecules. There are many kinds of polyesters, but the term most often refers to polyethylene terephthalate. Polyesters include both natural chemicals and synthetics. Most synthetic polyesters are not biodegradable.

Polyester has many uses in the modern world, including in cushioning and insulating material, in making plastic materials, as a finish on wood instruments, and in vehicle interiors. During the 1960s, clothing, even whole suits, was often made out of polyester. Today, fabrics woven or knitted from polyester thread are used to make anything from shirts and pants to blankets and computer mouse mats. While synthetic clothing has a less natural feel than natural fiber fabrics such as cotton and wool, polyester fabrics have some advantages over natural fabrics. Polyester is wrinkle resistant, durable, and retains its color very well. Polyester fabric is resistant to wind and water, and can be heat resistant.

Without polyester we would not have some of the classic suits of the 1960s. And, thanks to polyester, we will have them for many years to come. It is the fabric that lasts forever.

EPILOGUE

Into a New Century

We have ended our story in 1973. But the story is not over—what of the 40 some years that have passed since then? What of the events and persons of this epoch? What of the ideas? Is this period of history—our period of history—insignificant? Or, if it is not insignificant, why do we pass over it in silence?

It is not for its insignificance that we do not discuss the history of the past 40 years, for it is not at all insignificant. Rather, it is because we lack the perspective to judge it aright. The history of this period is our history. All of us—the author of this history text and its readers—are actors in the drama of contemporary history. Though if only in seemingly unimportant ways, each of us is helping to make this history. We are caught up in the events we would wish to understand. They are too close to us.

History is like a parade. Those marching in the parade may see their companions to right and left, to the immediate front and rear. They may view, part by part, the sections of the street along which they pass. But they cannot see all the parade's participants, nor the entire parade route. They may not know where they are going, their destination, even though they discern the general direction. However, those who view the parade from above, from say an

Pope John Paul II at Yankee Stadium, 1979, by Thomas J. O'Halloran

airplane or helicopter, can see the whole parade, all the participants, from whence they come, and to where they are going. Those who thus view the parade cannot discern all the details that those marching in the parade can see. But what they lose in detail they gain in perspective. They see, at least, the parts in relation to the whole.

The historian is like our example of a person flying over a parade route. From the perspective of the present, the historian can better discern the course of past history, for he stands in some ways apart from it. He can know what people living in an epoch could not see—the direction in which history has been tending, what persons, events, and ideas have proven the most significant, and which (though seemingly important at the time) have failed to be of consequence. Of course, an historian may err

President Ronald Reagan and First Lady Nancy Reagan, inauguration parade, 1981

in judgment, and this sometimes because he fails to discern important details of the epoch he is studying. The historian may be blinded by his own prejudices and enthusiasms. He may be obtuse. Nevertheless, he holds a privileged place, the only place from which he can justly comprehend his subject.

This is not to say that contemporaries cannot at all understand the era in which they live and act. They can distinguish vice from virtue; they can discriminate between wisdom and folly and truth and error. They can exercise prudence—the virtue by which we choose the best means to achieve a purpose or goal. Yet, if they want to understand all the myriad events, issues, movements, and ideas swirling around them; if they seek to penetrate the very character of the time in which they live, they need to view it in the perspective of history. For our time is the product of the times that have preceded it. We have been formed by the choices and ideas of those who have gone before us.

Homeless man in New York City

Let us, then, try to look at the present in light of the past. The past 40 years have witnessed many changes, but these changes have not sprung from nothing; they are rooted in the deep loam of decades and centuries. They cannot be understood apart from the events of past times. To understand them, it is necessary to consult history.

The events of the past 40 years can be arranged according to topics. We offer here a partial list of such topics that we encourage our readers to discuss in small groups or in the classroom in light of the history they have learned in *Lands of Hope and Promise*. How can we explain the events included in these topics by what has happened in history? What ideas lie behind these events? What in history has made it possible that the modern world has developed in the way it has? Could things have been different? If so, how? If not, why?

Here are some topics for discussion:

- Modern expressions of American patriotism: do Americans today still see the United States as a "city on a hill"?
- The relationship today between secular society and religion
- The status of religious freedom in the U.S. and Latin America (and the Catholic Church's response to modern developments in religious liberty)
- How, according to U.S. law, freedom of worship differs from freedom of religion

- The state of the Catholic Church, and religion in general, in Anglo- and Latin America
- The influence of the pontificates of John Paul II, Benedict XVI, and Francis on the Church in Anglo and Latin America
- The current state of marriage and family life in the United States and Latin America
- Sexual morality and current attitudes toward marriage
- Abortion and the pro-life movement (developments in the U.S. and Latin America)
- The rise in illegal drug use and the trade in illegal drugs
- Race relations in modern America
- Modern expressions of "progressivism" and "conservatism" in the U.S. and Latin America (and their relation to classical American and Latin American Liberalism and republicanism)
- The current status of the separation of powers between the branches of the U.S. federal government, and between federal, state, and local governments
- How freedom of speech is understood today (what it includes and what it excludes)
- The condition of modern education (at the elementary, secondary, and collegiate levels)
- Economic changes (the effect of "Reaganomics," free trade and deregulation policies; the status of the social assistance or "welfare" state; changes in capitalism and socialism; the eclipse of organized labor; the status of family income)
- What the Catholic Church (in the United States and Latin America as well as in papal teaching) has been saying about economic justice since 1973
- Illegal immigration (its causes and effects on society)
- Poverty (including homelessness) in the United States and Latin America
- The presidencies of Ronald Reagan and George H.W. Bush
- The fall of the Soviet Union and the end of the Cold War
- The rise of the United States as the world's sole super power
- U.S. interventions in Latin America
- U.S. relations with post-Soviet Russia and Communist China
- The presidency of William Jefferson Clinton
- The presidency of George W. Bush
- The presidency of Barack Obama
- The United States' relationship with Israel and the Arab nations of the Middle East
- Conflicts in the Middle East (the Gulf War, the Afghanistan invasion, the Iraq War)
- Terrorism and the "War on Terrorism"

People stand atop the Berlin Wall near the Brandenburg Gate, November 9, 1989, the day the East German government announced that citizens of East Germany could pass into West Germany. That day, both East and West Germans, drinking beer and champagne, began chanting, "Open the Gate!" At midnight, they began pushing their way through the wall's checkpoints. The text on the sign reads *Achtung! Sie verlassen jetzt West-Berlin.* ("Attention! You are now leaving West Berlin"), but it has been modified with the words, *Wie denn?* ("How?")

President William Jefferson Clinton at Norfolk (Virginia) Naval Station, by Brandon T. Nelson

The topics above refer to events that have provided people today with opportunities, but also challenges. Moreover, they suggest another question that we can ask concerning history—what it teaches us about how we

The 3rd Stryker Brigade on patrol in Dora, Iraq, May 2007

may properly use the opportunities provided us and how we can meet the challenges that face us? History gives us examples of how men and women have acted (both well and badly) in relation to the opportunities and challenges presented them; these can serve as examples of how to deal with the events and issues of our own time. What lessons can history teach us about how we ought to play our part as protagonists in the story of the modern world?

As Catholics, believers in Christ, the Lord of History, we are called to participate in the story of the world, to help realize in whatever way we can the great purpose of God in the incarnation of his Son—the restoration of all things in Christ. We have called this volume *Lands of Hope and Promise* because North America—and not just North America, but all the world—has been purchased by the blood of Christ in the hope that it might be renewed with him in his resurrection. He who commanded the apostles to preach the Gospel to all nations (Matt. 28:19–20) beckons his modern disciples to apply the teachings of Christ and his Church to the struggles and sufferings, hopes and aspirations, of the peoples and societies in which they live. And though all may seem quite dark, we have the assurance that the light of Christ shines in the darkness. And where the light of Christ shines, there is hope. There, indeed, is promise.

Credits continued from page iv

Shutterstock; (b) Everett Historical/Shutterstock; **p. 151** © Philip Dawe/ Public Domain; **p. 153** © Everett Historical/Shutterstock; **p. 154** © Joshua Reynolds/Public Domain; **p. 155** © Marco Rubino/Shutterstock; **p. 157** © John Singleton Copley/Public Domain; **p. 158** © Everett Historical/ Shutterstock; **p. 159** © Everett Historical/Shutterstock; **p. 160** © Everett Historical/Shutterstock; **p. 162** (t) © Everett Historical/Shutterstock; (b) Everett Historical/Shutterstock; **p. 163** © Charles Wilson Peale/Public Domain; **p. 164** © Thomas Millière/Public Domain; **p. 165** © Susan Law Cain/Shutterstock; **p. 167** © Richard Wilson/Public Domain; **p. 170** © John Trumbull/Public Domain; **p. 171** © Nagel Photography/Shutterstock; **p. 173** © Everett Historical/Shutterstock; **p. 174** © Everett Historical/Shutterstock; **p. 176** © Everett Historical/Shutterstock; **p. 177** © Everett Historical/ Shutterstock; **p. 181** John Trumbull/Public Domain; **p. 183** © Everett Historical/Shutterstock; **p. 184** © Everett Historical/Shutterstock; **p. 187** © Orhan Cam/Shutterstock; **p. 189** © Everett Historical/Shutterstock; **p. 191** © National Picture Gallery, Smithsonian Institution/Public Domain; **p. 192** © Everett Historical/Shutterstock; **p. 193** © Everett Historical/Shutterstock; **p. 195** (t) © Everett Historical/Shutterstock; (b) © Everett Historical/ Shutterstock; **p. 197** © Rich Koele/Shutterstock; **p. 198** © Billy Hathorn/ Public Domain; **p. 199** (t) © Everett Historical/Shutterstock; (b) © Gilbert Stuart/Public Domain; **p. 201** © Everett Historical/Shutterstock; **p. 204** © Andrew Ellicott/Public Domain; **p. 205** © Everett Historical/Shutterstock; **p. 207** © Everett Historical/Shutterstock; **p. 213** © Everett Historical/ Shutterstock; **p. 214** © Everett Historical/Shutterstock; **p. 215** © Everett Historical/Shutterstock; **p. 216** © Everett Historical/Shutterstock; **p. 218** © Everett Historical/Shutterstock; Everett Historical/Shutterstock; **p. 221** © Everett Historical/Shutterstock; **p. 222** (t) and (b) © Everett Historical/ Shutterstock; **p. 224** © James Herring/Public Domain; **p. 225** © Rembrandt Peale/Public Domain; **p. 226** © Everett Historical/Shutterstock; **p. 227** © Dennis Malone Carter/Public Domain; **p. 229** © Everett Historical/ Shutterstock; **p. 230** © Everett Historical/Shutterstock; **p. 231** © Everett Historical/Shutterstock; **p. 232** © Karl Bodmer/Public Domain; **p. 233** (tl) and (tr) © Karl Bodmer/Public Domain; **p. 233** (br) © Everett Historical/ Shutterstock; **p. 234** © Everett Historical/Shutterstock; **p. 235** © Everett Historical/Shutterstock; **p. 236** © Gilbert Stuart/Public Domain; **p. 237** © Matthew Harris Jouett/Public Domain; **p. 238** © Everett Historical/ Shutterstock; **p. 239** © Everett Historical/Shutterstock; **p. 240** © Everett Historical/Shutterstock; **p. 241** © Everett Historical/Shutterstock; **p. 243** © Everett Historical/Shutterstock; **p. 244** © Everett Historical/Shutterstock; **p. 245** © Everett Historical/Shutterstock; **p. 246** © Public Domain; **p. 247** © Everett Historical/Shutterstock; **p. 248** © Everett Historical/Shutterstock; **p. 253** © Louis Choris/Public Domain; **p. 255** (t) © Everett Historical/ Shutterstock; (b) © Louis Choris/Public Domain; **p. 256** © Ilya Gavrilovich Voznesenskii/Public Domain; **p. 257** © Carleton Watkins/Public Domain; **p. 258** © Alfred Robinson/Public Domain; **p. 259** (t) © Alfred Robinson/ Public Domain; (b) © Roger Sturtevant/Public Domain; **p. 260** © David Rumsey Map Collection—Cartography Associates/Public Domain; **p. 262** © C. Malte-Brun/Public Domain; **p. 263** © Luis de la Cruz/Public Domain; **p. 264** © José Guadalupe Posada/Public Domain; **p. 265** (t) © Luis de la Cruz/Public Domain; (b) © Alberto Loyo/Shutterstock; **p. 268** © age fotostock/Alamy; **p. 271** © Everett Historical/Shutterstock; **p. 272** © Roman Sagredo/Public Domain; **p. 273** © Joanna Zaleska/Shutterstock; **p. 275** © Jaontiveros/Public Domain; **p. 276** (t) © Public Domain; (b) © Everett Historical/Shutterstock; **p. 281** © Everett Historical/Shutterstock; **p. 282** © The Baltimore Basilica, **p. 284** © Villanova University; **p. 285** © Public Domain; **p. 286** © Smallbones/Public Domain; **p. 287** © Elyabe/Public Domain; **p. 288** © Samuel F. B. Morse/Public Domain; **p. 289** © Everett

Historical/Shutterstock; **p. 290** © Everett Historical/Shutterstock; **p. 292** © Gilbert Stuart/Public Domain; **p. 293** © Everett Historical/Shutterstock; **p. 294** (t) and (b) © Everett Historical/Shutterstock; **p. 295** © Everett Historical/Shutterstock; **p. 297** © Everett Historical/Shutterstock; **p. 298** © Everett Historical/Shutterstock; **p. 300** © Everett Historical/Shutterstock; **p. 301** © C. B. King/Public Domain; **p. 302** © Chatanooga Public Library; **p. 303** © Everett Historical/Shutterstock; **p. 307** © Richard Evans/Public Domain; **p. 308** © Public Domain; **p. 309** © (t) Anacleto Escutia/Public Domain; (b) Public Domain; **p. 311** © Public Domain; **p. 312** © Public Domain; **p. 313** © Thomas Flintoff/Public Domain; **p. 314** © Chester Harding/Public Domain; **p. 315** © Public Domain; **p. 316** © Public Domain; **p. 317** © Everett Historical/Shutterstock; **p. 318** © Public Domain; **p. 319** © Public Domain; **p. 320** © Public Domain; **p. 321** (t) © Bancroft Library (m) © Bancroft Library (b) © Bancroft Library; **p. 322** © Public Domain; **p. 323** (t) © Public Domain (b) © Public Domain; **p. 325** (t) © Public Domain; (b) © Public Domain; **p. 326** © Public Domain; **p. 327** (t) © Public Domain; (b) © Bancroft Library; **p. 329** © Emanuel Leutze/Public Domain; **p. 330** © Everett Historical/Shutterstock; **p. 331** (t) © Everett Historical/Shutterstock; (b) © Everett Historical/Shutterstock; **p. 333** © Everett Historical/ Shutterstock; **p. 334** © George Gibbs/Public Domain; **p. 335** © Public Domain; **p. 336** (t) © Everett Historical/Shutterstock; (m) © Public Domain; (b) © Public Domain; **p. 337** © Major Eaton/Public Domain; **p. 338** © J. Cameron/Public Domain; **p. 339** © Public Domain; **p. 345** © Everett Historical/Shutterstock; **p. 347** (t) © Everett Historical/Shutterstock; (b) © Everett Historical/Shutterstock; **p. 349** (t) © Everett Historical/Shutterstock; (b) © Everett Historical/Shutterstock; **p. 350** © Public Domain; **p. 351** (t) © Public Domain; (b) © Everett Historical/Shutterstock; **p. 352** (t) © Everett Historical/Shutterstock; (b) © Public Domain; **p. 353** © Public Domain; **p. 354** © Library of Congress; **p. 355** (tl) © Everett Historical/Shutterstock; (tr) © Harper's Monthly; (mr) © Everett Historical/Shutterstock; (br) © Public Domain; **p. 356** © Everett Historical/Shutterstock; © Everett Historical/Shutterstock; **p. 357** (t) © Everett Historical/Shutterstock; (m) © Everett Historical/Shutterstock; (b) © Punch Magazine/Public Domain; **p. 358** © The Metropolitan Museum of Art; **p. 359** (t) © Matthew Brady/ Public Domain; (b) © William Henry Brook/Public Domain; **p. 360** © Public Domain; **p. 361** (t) © Everett Historical/Shutterstock; (b) © Everett Historical/Shutterstock; **p. 363** © Public Domain; **p. 366** © Everett Historical/Shutterstock; **p. 367** © John James Audubon/Public Domain; **p. 368** © Everett Historical/Shutterstock; **p. 369** © Public Domain; **p. 370** © Everett Historical/Shutterstock; **p. 371** © Library of Congress; **p. 372** (t) (b) © Public Domain; **p. 373** © Public Domain; **p. 374** © Everett Historical/ Shutterstock; **p. 375** © Everett Historical/Shutterstock; **p. 376** © Public Domain; **p. 381** © Public Domain/Quadell; **p. 382** (t) (b) © Public Domain; **p. 383** (t) (b) © Public Domain; **p. 384** © Everett Historical/Shutterstock; **p. 385** © Public Domain; **p. 386** © Public Domain; **p. 387** © Everett Historical/Shutterstock; **p. 388** © Public Domain; **p. 390** (t) © Everett Historical/Shutterstock (b) © Public Domain; **p. 391** (t) © Everett Historical/ Shutterstock; (b) Matthew Brady/Public Domain; **p. 392** © Matthew Brady/ Public Domain; **p. 393** © Everett Historical/Shutterstock; **p. 394** © Everett Historical/Shutterstock; **p. 395** (t)(b) © Everett Historical/Shutterstock; **p. 396** © Everett Historical/Shutterstock; **p. 397** © Everett Historical/ Shutterstock; **p. 398** © Public Domain; **p. 399** © Everett Historical/ Shutterstock; **p. 400** © Everett Historical/Shutterstock; **p. 401** © Public Domain; **p. 402** © Public Domain; **p. 403** (t) © Public Domain; (b) © Everett Historical/Shutterstock; **p. 404** © Everett Historical/Shutterstock; **p. 406** © Everett Historical/Shutterstock; **p. 407** © Everett Historical/Shutterstock; **p. 408** © Everett Historical/Shutterstock; **p. 409** © Everett Historical/

Domain; **p. 688** © Public Domain; **p. 689** © Public Domain; **p. 691** © Public Domain; **p. 692** (t) (b) © Public Domain; **p. 693** © Aurelio Escobar Castellanos Archive; **p. 694** © Public Domain; **p. 695** © Everett Historical/ Shutterstock; **p. 701** © Public Domain; **p. 704** (t) © Public Domain; (b) © Everett Historical/Shutterstock; **p. 705** © Everett Historical/Shutterstock; **p. 706** © Everett Historical/Shutterstock; **p. 707** © Everett Historical/ Shutterstock; **p. 708** © Everett Historical/Shutterstock; **p. 710** © Public Domain; **p. 712** © Everett Historical/Shutterstock; **p. 713** (t) (b) © Public Domain; **p. 714** © Public Domain; **p. 715** © Everett Historical/Shutterstock; **p. 716** © Carl Pietzner/Public Domain; **p. 718** © Everett Historical/ Shutterstock; **p. 719** © Everett Historical/Shutterstock; **p. 720** © Public Domain; **p. 721** © Public Domain; **p. 722** (t) (b) © Everett Historical/ Shutterstock; **p. 723** (t) © Library of Congress; (b) © Public Domain; **p. 724** (t) © Public Domain; (b) © Boston Public Library; **p. 729** © Public Domain; **p. 730** (t) © Public Domain; (b) © Everett Historical/Shutterstock; **p. 731** © Everett Historical/Shutterstock; **p. 732** © Everett Historical/Shutterstock; **p. 733** © Public Domain; **p. 734** (t) © Public Domain; (b) © Everett Historical/Shutterstock; **p. 735** © Everett Historical/Shutterstock; **p. 736** © Everett Historical/Shutterstock; **p. 737** © Everett Historical/Shutterstock; **p. 739** © Public Domain; **p. 740** © Public Domain; **p. 741** (t) (b) © Public Domain; **p. 742** (l) (r) © Public Domain; **p. 743** (t) (b) © Public Domain; **p. 744** (t) (b) © Public Domain; **p. 745** © Public Domain; **p. 746** (t) (b) © Public Domain; **p. 747** © Everett Historical/Shutterstock; **p. 748** © Everett Historical/Shutterstock; **p. 749** (t) © Everett Historical/Shutterstock; (b) © Public Domain; **p. 750** (t) (b) © Everett Historical/Shutterstock; **p. 752** © Everett Historical/Shutterstock; **p. 753** © Everett Historical/Shutterstock; **p. 754** © Everett Historical/Shutterstock; **p. 755** © Public Domain; **p. 756** © Public Domain; **p. 757** © Public Domain; **p. 791** © Public Domain; **p. 762** © Everett Historical/Shutterstock; **p. 763** (t) © Everett Historical/Shutterstock; (b) © Public Domain; **p. 764** © Public Domain; **p. 765** © Everett Historical/ Shutterstock; **p. 766** © Thomas C. Corner/Public Domain; **p. 767** © Public Domain; **p. 768** © Public Domain; **p. 769** (t) © Public Domain; (b) © Everett Historical/Shutterstock; **p. 770** (t) (b)© Everett Historical/Shutterstock; **p. 771** © Everett Historical/Shutterstock; **p. 772** © Public Domain; **p. 774** © Public Domain; **p. 776** © Bettmann Archives; **p. 777** © Everett Historical/ Shutterstock; **p. 779** © Everett Historical/Shutterstock; **p. 781** © Public Domain; **p. 782** © Public Domain; **p. 783** © Everett Historical/Shutterstock; **p. 784** (t) © Everett Historical/Shutterstock; (b) © Public Domain; **p. 785** © Everett Historical/Shutterstock; **p. 787** © Public Domain; **p. 788** © Norman Rockwell/Public Domain; **p. 789** © Everett Historical/Shutterstock; **p. 790** © Public Domain; **p. 795** © Public Domain; **p. 796** © Public Domain; **p. 798** © Public Domain; **p. 800** © Public Domain; **p. 801** © Public Domain; **p. 803** (t) © Everett Historical/Shutterstock; (b) © Public Domain; **p. 804** © Public Domain; **p. 806** © Public Domain; **p. 808** (t) (b) © Everett Historical/ Shutterstock; **p. 809** © Public Domain; **p. 810** (t) (b) © Public Domain; **p. 813** (t) © Public Domain; (b) © Everett Historical/Shutterstock; **p. 814** © Public Domain; **p. 815** © Public Domain; **p. 816** © Public Domain; **p. 818** (t) © Everett Historical/Shutterstock; (b) © Public Domain; **p. 819** © Public Domain; **p. 823** © Public Domain; **p. 824** © Roger Higgins/Public Domain; **p. 825** © Public Domain; **p. 827** © Public Domain; **p. 828** © Public Domain; **p. 829** © Public Domain; **p. 830** © Public Domain; **p. 831** © Everett Historical/Shutterstock; **p. 832** (l) (r) © Everett Historical/Shutterstock; **p. 833** © United States Information Agency; **p. 834** © Public Domain; **p. 835** (t) (b) © Public Domain; **p. 836** (t) (b) © Public Domain; **p. 837** (t) (b) © Public Domain; **p. 839** (t) © Public Domain; (b) © Everett Historical/ Shutterstock; **p. 840** (t) (b) © Public Domain; **p. 841** © Public Domain; **p. 842** © Public Domain; **p. 843** © Everett Historical/Shutterstock; **p. 844** (t) (b) © Public Domain; **p. 846** (t) (b) © Public Domain; **p. 847** © Public Domain; **p. 848** © Public Domain; **p. 849** (t) © Dutch National Archives; (b) © Lothar Wolleh/Public Domain; **p. 851** © Everett Historical/Shutterstock; **p. 852** © Public Domain; **p. 853** © Public Domain; **p. 859** © Thomas J. O'Halloran/Public Domain; **p. 860** (t) (b) © Public Domain; **p. 861** (t) (b) © Public Domain; **p. 862** © Public Domain.

INDEX